EVERYWOMAN'S GUIDE TO
COLLEGES AND UNIVERSITIES

An Educational Project of
The Feminist Press

Sponsoring Organizations

American Alliance of Health, Physical Education, Recreation and Dance
Representative: Carol Thompson, Executive Director, National Association for Girls and Women
in Sport

American Association of Community and Junior Colleges
Representatives: Carol Eliason, Director, Center for Women's Opportunities
Jackie Woods, Consultant

American Association of University Women
Representatives: Peg Downey, Assistant Director for Program Development
Sarah Harder, Assistant to the Chancellor, University of Wisconsin-Eau Claire

American Council on Education's Office of Women in Higher Education
Representatives: Donna Shavlik, Director
Judith G. Touchton, Associate Director

American Personnel and Guidance Association
Representative: Olivia A. Brown, Assistant Director of Cooperative Education, The Career
Development Center, University of the District of Columbia

Association of American Colleges' Project on the Status and Education of Women
Representative: Bernice Resnick Sandler, Director

Federation of Organizations for Professional Women
Representatives: Margaret C. Dunkle, former President
Nancy Felipe Russo, President

National Association for Women Deans, Administrators and Counselors
Representatives: Laurine E. Fitzgerald, Dean, University of Wisconsin-Oshkosh
Gail Short Hanson, Dean of Students, The George Washington University

National Women Students Coalition
Representative: Maribeth Oakes

National Women's Studies Association
Representatives: Elaine Reuben, Education Policy Fellow, Department of Education; former
Coordinator, NWSA
Jan Meriwether, former Program Associate, NWSA
Susan Gore, former Coordinator, NWSA

Project Staff

Florence Howe, Director
Maxine McCants, Administrator
Suzanne Howard, Associate Director
Mary Jo Boehm Strauss, Associate Director
William Zeisel, Text Editor
Nancy M. Porter, Senior Writer
Lea Smith, Production Manager
Denyse Brabham, Administrative Assistant and Production Assistant
Sheila Dugan, Typist

Writers: Lois Fenichell, Walteen Grady Truly, Alice Hemenway, Nancy Hoffman, Ellen Jacobs, Esther Katz, Nora Licht, Patti Lowery, Alice Miller, Eleanor Riemer, Adria Steinberg

Proofreaders: Jane Clancy, Ruth Danon, Abe Fogle, Shirley Frank, Ann J. Gumbinner, Paul Lauter, Vernon Liang, Thalia Loomis, Jill L. Newmark, Marianne Paskowski, Marian Robinson, Arlene Winnick, Susan Wrench, Carol Wreszin

Typists: Victoria Moskowitz, Gerrie Nuccio, Evelyn Triantafillou

EVERYWOMAN'S GUIDE TO COLLEGES AND UNIVERSITIES

An Educational Project of The Feminist Press

Edited by Florence Howe, Suzanne Howard
and Mary Jo Boehm Strauss
Introduction by Florence Howe
Text Editor: William Zeisel
Senior Writer: Nancy M. Porter

THE FEMINIST PRESS
Old Westbury, New York

Library of Congress Cataloging in Publication Data:
Main entry under title:

EVERYWOMAN'S guide to colleges and universities.

Includes index.
1. Women's colleges United States Directories
I. Howe, Florence. II. Howard, Suzanne. III. Strauss, Mary Jo Boehm. IV. Porter, Nancy M.

LC1756.E93 1982   376′.8′02573 82-15402

ISBN 0-9-35312-09-9

First Edition
Manufactured in the USA

EVERYWOMAN'S GUIDE TO COLLEGES AND UNIVERSITIES was developed by The Feminist Press with partial support from the Fund for the Improvement of Post-Secondary Education, and was published with the help of a recoverable grant from The Carnegie Corporation of New York. The statements made and the views expressed do not necessarily reflect the position or policy of the Fund or the Corporation.

Text and symbol design: Lea Smith
Artwork: Pat Murphy (drawings of states); Publications, Illustrations, Presentations, Inc. (mechanicals of symbols)
Typesetting: Times Roman and Tiffany Heavy by Precision Typographers, Inc.
Printing: R. R. Donnelley & Sons

TO TITLE IX, ON ITS TENTH BIRTHDAY

CONTENTS

Acknowledgments

This book was born in September 1979 during a conference held at Wellesley College's Center for Research on Women, in conjunction with the New England Higher Education Resources Services (HERS, New England), to consider aspects of a research agenda focused on educational environments, particularly though not exclusively as they relate to women. Several themes emerged, and several major questions. While there were few institutional barriers to women's access to higher education, it was far from clear what happened to women once they entered either coeducational or single-sex institutions. Researchers present at the conference reported that women were entering graduate or professional schools in increasing numbers; they reported on the employment rates and fields of women leaving colleges after the B.A., and on the numbers marrying and bearing children. But the four college years were still almost entirely a mystery; did it matter which colleges women attended? Could a research agenda address this question? And, if so, what were women to do in the meantime? What information might they draw on to decide whether the choice of college or university might make a difference to their futures?

Sitting on Wellesley's campus, I heard one speaker bemoan the fact that female college-goers must make choices with very little information specific to women. What if, I wrote in a small notebook, we could produce "The Intelligent Woman's Guide to Colleges and Universities"? Would that meet the needs of women?

I passed the notebook to two persons who happened to be seated beside me, Carol Stoel and Alison Bernstein, program officers at the Fund for the Improvement of Post-Secondary Education (FIPSE). They wrote encouraging scribbles in return—"a good idea"; "why not?"

Like all ideas, however, this one had several informal antecedents. For some years through the 1970s, Women's Studies pioneers had talked of a "guide to women's studies." Indeed, The Feminist Press (with Ford Foundation support prompted by Mariam Chamberlain) had produced *Who's Who and Where in Women's Studies* in 1974. At a Barnard College conference held at Arden House in the spring of 1979, on the subject of new women-centered institutions and their achievements through the 1970s, one of a series of concluding resolutions called on the "National Women's Studies Association to undertake . . . publication of a women's guide to higher education . . . which evaluates the adequacy of support for women on campus. . . ." Prepared by Elizabeth Minnich and others, the resolution was introduced by Joan Kelly, while Elaine Reuben, then National Coordinator of NWSA, and I reacted with pleasure to the expression of an idea we had already talked about. In addition, the American Association of University Women had produced, in 1978, under the direction of Suzanne Howard, a monograph called *But We Will Persist: A Comparative Research Report on the Status of Women in Academe.* A study of 600 colleges, this monograph reported on some elements of the educational environment that **EVERYWOMAN'S GUIDE** features.

EVERYWOMAN'S GUIDE was funded in the summer of 1980. While I appreciate, in general, the care with which the Fund for the Improvement of Post-Secondary Education reviewed the proposal, I want to express special thanks to Alison Bernstein for suggesting that I ask Suzanne Howard to work with me; for Nancy Hoffman's and Carol Stoel's encouragement; and, most of all, for Russell Garth's fidelity, intelligence, and resourcefulness as the program officer responsible for this project during the past two years.

The project staff spent much of the first year designing a questionnaire and a strategy for bringing in completed questionnaires from as many campuses as possible; we spent most of the second year still receiving questionnaires, planning and writing the entries, and then editing and producing this volume.

To help us, we invited a group of distinguished scholars, teachers, students, administrators, and writers to join an Advisory Board and a team of Research Consultants; and we invited another group of important national associations to join us as Sponsoring Organizations and to name as delegates individuals with particular expertise for this project. We held two Working Conferences, the first in the fall of 1980, the second a year later. On the first occasion, the topic was the questionnaire; on the second, the translation of that questionnaire into a readable entry. We want to express our appreciation here to those who attended the Working Conferences, critiqued the questionnaire, field-tested early versions of the questionnaire, and distributed hundreds of brochures.

For a most difficult task—bringing in the questionnnaires—we want to thank our Sponsoring Organizations, listed earlier in the book. The American Association of University Women and the National Women's Studies Association were especially helpful to this process. To hundreds of individuals we cannot name here—students, faculty, administrators—we also owe a special debt of gratitude. Without their concern for the success of this project, we would not have had as many completed questionnaires. We will name only a few individuals, symbolic of the rest: Sue Armitage, NWSA liaison in the Pacific Northwest region, and Betty Schmitz, in Montana; Patrick Callan, Suzanne Ness, Jeanine Stevens, and Linda Barton White, of the California Postsecondary Education Commission, and Donne Brounsey of the California State Student Association; Frances Dodson Rhome, University Director of Affirmative Action for Indiana University, who assembled all the materials for the seven campuses in the IU system; Jon Fuller, President of the Great Lakes Colleges Association; Jean Walton, Emerita Dean at Pomona College, for special work with the Claremont Colleges; Susan Arpad, who walked the questionnaire around Bowling Green State University, and then wrote an article for the *Women's Studies Quarterly* about its effect on the campus; Nancy Schniedewind, Nancy Cott, Deborah Rosenfelt, and Blanche Hersch, for their efforts on their own campuses—SUNY/New Paltz, Yale University, San Francisco State University, and Northeastern Illinois University, respectively.

At the project's second Working Conference, participants agreed that it would be useful to rate specific aspects of institutions rather than whole institutions. Mary Ann Millsap of the National Institute of Education deserves the credit for encouraging me to attempt a rating scale, even in the original proposal. We are grateful to Jessie Bernard, Theodore J. Marchese, and Mariam Chamberlain for helping the staff formulate the assumptions for rating the three items under **Women in Leadership.** Similarly, we want to express our appreciation to Joanne S. Hult of the Department of Physical Education of the University of Maryland for advising us about rating **Women and Athletics;** and to Mariam Chamberlain and Nancy M. Porter for advice about rating **Women and the Curriculum.**

With the generous and skillful assistance of Victoria Albright, analyst at Econometric Research, Inc., in Washington, D.C., project staff turned questionnaires into aggregate data and began to plan how to translate this information into readable entries. As entries began to come in from the writers, we organized a validation process to judge whether the entries were both accurate and honest to the information we had collected. We are grateful to validators Jessie Bernard, Louis Brakeman, Maria Chacon, and Mariam Chamberlain. To Peg Downey of the American Association of University Women and Mary Ann Millsap, who read and critiqued entries a bit later on in the process, we are also grateful.

In addition, we are grateful for other kinds of criticisms from readers unfamiliar with the project. Helene Goldfarb, a guidance counselor in the White Plains, New York, school system, read early entries for us, as did several students: at SUNY/Purchase, Marietta Hedges; and at the Teaneck, New Jersey, Alternative High School—Heidi Friedman, Suzanne Lightman, and Amanda McGibney.

Without an especially talented and committed staff, this project could not have been completed. I owe a special debt to Suzanne Howard and Mary Jo Boehm Strauss: together, we designed the questionnaire, planned the collection of aggregate data, and designed the format of entries. Together, we also trained the writers, checked and edited each institution entry for accuracy and tone, and shared responsibility for the ratings. In addition, Mary Jo Boehm Strauss directed the computer operations and analysis.

No project is functional without at least one key administrator: we had two—Maxine McCants and William Zeisel. Maxine McCants served in this capacity for the entire life of the project, organizing meetings, mailings, the production and dissemination of the questionnaire; managing the communications with the network designed to bring completed questionnaires to us; and maintaining fiscal control.

If the first most difficult task was bringing in the questionnaires, the second was producing readable and accurate entries. In December 1981, Maxine McCants was joined by William Zeisel, who took on the administrative and other tasks associated with editing the text of **EVERYWOMAN'S GUIDE**. Without his patient, calm intelligence, we could not have had this book so quickly. He recruited and trained additional writers and editors, as well as proofreaders. To the twelve writers, Lois Fenichell, Walteen Grady Truly, Alice Hemenway, Nancy Hoffman, Ellen Jacobs, Esther Katz, Nora Licht, Patti Lowery, Alice Miller, Nancy M. Porter, Eleanor Riemer, and Adria Steinberg, we wish to express our appreciation, for without their work, we would not have the text. Senior Writer Nancy M. Porter wrote more than one-fifth of the text, and, in addition, edited almost as much again. Similarly, Esther Katz devoted several weeks to the onerous details of final editing, proofreading, and verifying ratings and other details. In these tasks, she was joined by Sheila Dugan, who also probably typed most of the entries in the volume at least once; and Jill L. Newmark, who spent the first third of a summer internship proofreading **EVERYWOMANS GUIDE**. We appreciate also the work of assistant editors William Bischoff and Vernon Liang.

Many Feminist Press staff members worked on **EVERYWOMAN'S GUIDE**. Typists included Gerrie Nuccio, Victoria Moskowitz, and Evelyn Triantafillou. Arlene Winnick and Shirley Frank, along with Denyse Brabham, assisted Lea Smith in production. Proofreaders included some of those already mentioned, as well as Jo Baird, Shirley Frank, Paul Lauter, Marian Robinson, and Carol Wreszin. We are especially grateful to Marilee Talman, our former Marketing Director, for urging us to complete the book this year, not next; and to Lea Smith, whose talent for design is matched only by her ability to manage an impossible production schedule.

Finally, as we thanked FIPSE for helping us to begin this project, we want to thank The Carnegie Corporation for helping us to see the project into a bound book. We are grateful to Sarah Engelhardt's inventiveness in a difficult fiscal period.

With regard to the Introduction to this volume, I wish to thank Paul Lauter for editing, William Zeisel for copyediting, and Marilee Talman and Mary Jo Boehm Strauss for making useful suggestions and corrections. I could not have made my own deadlines without the special editorial assistance of Nancy M. Porter and Mary Jo Boehm Strauss. In general, though I shared decision-making with many staff members throughout the development of this project, and though many others deserve credit for the book, its shortcomings and remaining errors are my responsibility.

Florence Howe

Everywoman's Educational Health

Florence Howe

We began this book less than two years ago with a set of questions in our minds. These questions were not ours. They came from thousands of women who had asked where they and their daughters should go to college. The questions began in the same way: Where would a woman get the best education? What kind of an education is *healthy* for women? What kind of campus really welcomes women students? What campuses want to prepare women for the real world of work? On which campuses can women expect to take charge of their own lives?

Other questions were more specific. Where could I major in marine biology, co-major in Women's Studies, play soccer, and edit the campus newspaper? Or where will I find childcare on campus and counseling so that I can complete the college education interrupted ten years ago and find the career that will help me to rear my children and provide them with an education?

An earlier student generation—even 15 years ago—would not have included the "older," "reentry" woman asking about childcare. The young woman going to college in the 1950s and 1960s would have asked where she could get a good education, probably for a teaching career before marriage, play some sports, and have a fair chance at student leadership experience. The single answer—before 1970—was a women's college. A woman could have had a good education at a coeducational college or university, but she would not have had opportunities there for campus-wide student leadership or for sports—and she may not have considered them important to her life. In all cases, Women's Studies would have been absent from her experience, as soccer would have been absent, and, in virtually all cases, such fields of study as marine biology or engineering.

But all of that has changed. By now, most people know that some significant shift has occurred on campuses, though no one has known the details, nor how to find them. This book responds to those changes, charts and measures them, and presents information essential to women for making more discriminating choices about higher education.

The Need for
EVERYWOMAN'S GUIDE

We began this book, we said, with a set of questions not our own. To these we added another set, not about individual institutions, but about collegiate education as a whole. Beyond the 300–400 Women's Studies Programs we knew about, how far had Women's Studies touched most other campuses? What were colleges doing about the health and safety of women students? Did colleges all have policies to deal with sexual harassment? Did any colleges consider childcare a campus responsibility?

When we began this book in 1980, we knew the history of the period, and we had some conception of the changes in progress on many campuses. But there was no way to draw a portrait of these changes. And most of them were not reflected in the college guides still being produced. Nor were they reflected in college catalogs,

unless one looked specifically for Women's Studies courses and programs. We wanted to know how far along the path to equity most colleges and universities had travelled in the decade of the 1970s.

Further, we began to consider *types* of collegiate institutions: Could one begin to generalize about which kinds of institutions offered which kinds of services and benefits to women students? Were public universities doing more for women students than two-year community colleges? Were women's colleges still the only institutions that offered women opportunities for student leadership experience and for competitive athletics? In short, our new set of questions were general institutional ones. What had changed and on which kinds of campuses?

We also thought that such information collected and distributed to a very broad audience might make a difference to the future of women's higher education. We assumed, even before beginning, that the process of answering questions—some of which had not been asked before—could stimulate campuses to consider their attitudes toward women students and to reevaluate the services they offer. Thus, this volume was designed to serve multiple purposes.

Even before we began, the need was multiple. We wanted to supply college-going women, their families, their counselors, and their teachers with information unavailable through any other source. We wanted to assess the achievements of a decade of work toward educational equity. And we expected that the process would remind collegiate institutions of the need to continue the effort to offer women an educational environment as "healthy" as that ordinarily offered to men.

The Concept of Educational "Health" for Women

We used the word "healthy" early in the conception of this book. It came from an appreciation for the peculiarly Western idea that the university educates the "whole man," "his" body and mind. "He" is offered not only intellectual stimulation and encouragement, but a world of peers with whom to associate both in clubs and on the athletic field. The catalog of a prestigious university, for example, announces as its purpose "to develop the whole man, the sensitive, cultured, open-minded citizen who grounds his thinking in facts, who is intellectually and spiritually aware, who believes that life is significant, and who is concerned with society and the role he will play in it." This "man" studies the history of the nation's fathers and lawmakers; he finds his social and moral identity both in the experiences recorded by writers like Melville and Hemingway, and in the philosophical constructs of male thinkers; and he learns appropriate leadership and group behavior through participating in team sports and in other student activities.

If this is normal and "healthy" for the "whole" college *man*, then what might be "health" for the *woman* sitting beside him? Is the coeducational collegiate environment "healthy" for women? Is it "healthy" for minority women as well as white women? What would this concept of educational "health" prescribe for women?

The answers to these questions provide the frame for this book *and for choosing a college.* They are, like most answers to questions raised during periods of social change, tentative. But they are useful enough to act on.

Title IX and the Whole Woman

First, there is the concept of "wholeness." The "whole" woman, like the "whole" man, is both a physical and intellectual being. She is also a social creature, and—in the late 20th century—one who needs and wants paid employment. Indeed, Title IX, passed by the Congress in 1972, helped to define this aspect of "health" for women, since its framers assumed that women need and are entitled to whatever men already have.[1] In practice, this has often meant that facilities traditionally available to male students should also become available to females—access to sports, for example, including athletic scholarships, to student activities, and to all academic programs and opportunities on campus.

Sex equity also meant fair employment practices on campus: policies should be designed to ensure fair representation of minority and white women, and minority men, in all positions, and also in connection with affirmative action programs designed to make up for past inequities. Hence, indirectly, equity came to mean that students have a right to "role models"—to teachers and mentors of their own sex and race. This is a much-debated idea: that the presence of adults who are male or female and of a particular race matters to students' self-concept, since the adults serve as "models" of students' future attainments. For white male students, the presence of a majority of white male professors and administrators on campuses across the country teaches a silent lesson: you too can achieve in this manner. For members of minority groups of both sexes and for white women, there is no comparable lesson, except on campuses where they are the majority: the historically black campus, the two black women's colleges, the other women's colleges. Thus we defined as "healthy" for women a campus that allows them to see women in action as professors and administrators, and also as campus student leaders.

Women's Studies and the Whole Woman

In addition, we added what Title IX omitted: that the "whole" woman, like the "whole" man, requires for educational health access to the history and culture of women, and to a full understanding of the achievements and potential of women, individually and as a group, in relation to race, nationality, and other social realities. In brief, we believe that an educationally healthy environment should provide a *coeducational,* rather than a male-centered, curriculum for all its students. Further, during the long process of constructing that coeducational curriculum, which has only just begun in the decade of the 1970s, women (and men) need an ample measure of a female-centered curriculum—Women's Studies—at least to balance the male-centered one still in place on most campuses.

The concept of educational "health" for women assumes that women, like men, need to feel they are "whole" human beings, needing intellectual and spiritual sustenance, as well as opportunities for athletics, leadership, and the vision and accessibility of teachers and other mentors of their own sex. At the same time, since we live in a world only beginning to recognize that women are, indeed, men's equals, women also need several additional services or facilities, at least to compensate for the current social inequities. Hence, we added also a lengthy list of items untouched by Title IX, items generally not useful for male students, but essential for women. These include the presence of childcare facilities on or near the campus; policies on sexual harassment; the presence of rape crisis centers, of programs for displaced homemakers, and for reentry women students; and the presence of other new institutional services and facilities aimed at women.

Most of these items—as well as Title IX itself, and Women's Studies—were fought for by women students, faculty, and staff on campuses across the land during the past decade and a half. Such battles are still in progress, still part of the second century of struggle for women's rights, in education as in political life.

Some Recent History: The New Women's Movement

In the early 1960s, the second women's movement began, mainly because groups of college-educated women in their thirties and forties noticed that their lives were very different from those of the male friends, brothers, and husbands they had once sat beside in coeducational classrooms on coeducational campuses. The men were employed, often in well-paying jobs, sometimes in high places, including the political leadership of city, state, and nation. The women were, in the main, housewives and mothers, isolated in suburban homes or urban apartments, only partly using the intelligence and the creativity that had won them high grades in college or graduate school. Those employed were under-employed or underpaid, their salaries were 60 percent of their male peers', and they were not to be found in high places. Even most of the presidents of women's colleges, by 1970, were men.

The energy of these women organized NOW—the National Organization for Women—focused initially on the bread-and-butter issues of equal employment and fair wages.

Civil Rights and Women's Rights

In the 1960s also, groups of somewhat younger, college-educated women engaged in the civil rights and anti-war movements of the period made similar discoveries about the working relationships between women and men. The sexual division of labor in these political movements suddenly surfaced—at least for the women in them. Women served coffee, answered phones, stuffed envelopes, swept up offices; men made the political decisions. These men and these women had both been to college at the same time, sometimes on the same campuses. Why were the women making coffee, the men making decisions? Just as white women in the nineteenth century had connected their own social status and the struggle to abolish slavery, white and black female civil rights workers in the 1960s began to consider their own position in relation to men in political leadership.

These younger women, most of whom left the deep South after the summers of 1964 and 1965 for their northern urban homes, became, in various cities along the east and west coasts, and in Chicago, nuclei of change. Joined by others, they formed women's liberation organizations and initiated consciousness-raising groups for hundreds, eventually thousands, of participants. By the late 1960s, when the media had taken hold of this new women's movement, the single most famous event of those exciting years became the alleged "bra-burning" of "women's libbers" in Atlantic City, New Jersey, during a demonstration against the Miss America contest.

Given the U.S. male's fixation about women's breasts, it is understandable that freedom from the brassiere rather than the right to employment and a fair wage should have become the media's symbol of what women wanted. Perhaps it is useless to report that the bra-burning never took place. What took place was the beginning of a change in consciousness, the kind of change that occurs only once in a century.

We are living during this shift of consciousness, brought about not by the media, but by more than a decade of organized work by thousands of feminists, in national and local organizations, as well as in women's liberation groups.

The contemporary women's movement emerged from the civil rights movement of the 1950s and 1960s in another respect. Many of the leaders of the civil rights movement were minority women. Some of them were willing, from the first, to be identified with feminism; at the very least, many saw themselves as advocates for and organizers of women, including women on welfare, for example. Not surprisingly, most minority women expressed an urgency about their connections to racial communities; to "join" the women's movement meant to join with white women, who, however "liberal," were part of the history of racial oppression. Nevertheless, it is important to an understanding of the changes that have taken place on college campuses to see the multiracial composition of feminism; and to realize, as well, the ground-breaking force of the efforts in the late 1960s to establish Black studies and other ethnic studies programs. These, together with the other elements of the women's movement we have described, were among the critical components in producing the change in consciousness of which this book is one expression.

A Teaching Movement

By the early 1970s, in towns and cities across the land, women talked intimately of their lives in consciousness-raising groups, shared bitterness and joy, and planned for the future. In larger groups and organizations, some of national scope, women began to plan agendas for social action and reform—in political life, in health, sexuality, and reproduction, as well as in economic and educational rights. Individually, and in large and small groups, through talking or in manifesto, pamphlet, and book, they were demonstrating that the women's movement was a *teaching* movement, that its future strength rested on that shift of consciousness. Women had to apprehend their position in a male-controlled world they were beginning to call "patriarchy." Women had to understand all the forms of patriarchy before they could begin to change it.

Counting on Campuses

Although some school and college teachers were in consciousness-raising groups in the 1960s, the women's movement did not reach the campus until the end of that decade. And then it appeared in its characteristic form: the research called "counting." We began by counting the numbers of women employed on teaching faculties, the numbers of men, and in what positions. As we then went on to count the numbers of female and male students who entered as undergraduates and the number who graduated and went on to graduate school, we couldn't help noticing the high grades women had achieved, and the smaller numbers of women who went on to M.A. programs, Ph.D. programs, or, smallest still, medical, law, and other professional schools. We wondered why women—and not men—*seemed to choose not* to go on to graduate school, *not* to apply to medical school, even when their grades were as good as, or better than, those of the men who did so choose. The statistics *galvanized* hundreds of women—first to ask questions, then to try to answer them.

Why were women 80 percent of undergraduate English majors and 20 percent of students earning doctorates in English? Why were women 60 percent of undergraduate sociology majors and only 17 percent of students earning doctorates in sociology? How did the 20 percent of male undergraduates who had majored in English become the 80 percent of doctorates in English? Were they more capable than the women students? Or were they more encouraged; and if so, by what or by whom were they encouraged? What told male students that they might go on to become professors or doctors or lawyers or political leaders? What told women to take temporary jobs, marry, and drop out of the workforce altogether?

Even before 1970, some of us on campuses had gone on to count the faces of women in textbooks, and to note women's absence from history as it was taught, from political science and economics, from psychology, even from studies of inequality in sociology courses. We noticed that art history textbooks were filled with portraits of women, sometimes in the nude, but there was not a sign of a woman painter.

When men wrote about women in the poems or novels we read in college textbooks, women were objects of sexual desire, or they were wives and mothers. They were not working women, they were not heads of households, they did not share the burdens of responsibility for the maintenance of life, they were not political creatures conscious of human rights and working for a peaceful world. In short, women in fiction did not resemble the women who had lived through history and had helped make history. The few women writers to be found in the curriculum as it then existed were regarded as "unique" (Jane Austen or George Eliot) or "queer" (Emily Dickinson or Emily Bronte). Black women writers were entirely absent, as were female members of other minority groups.

What were we to make of the message of this curriculum? Women were invisible or distorted into caricature. The message was clear: men worked and achieved; women married. If women achieved, they did so at the expense of being "true" women. They were "unique" or "queer," and only very few of them could be that.

The Change of Consciousness on Campuses

The shift in consciousness we have been describing occurred only a little over a decade ago. Thousands of people in organizations and on campuses began to count the numbers of women in every feature of collegiate life. They analyzed expenditures for women's and men's athletics, they reviewed employment practices, they compared salary schedules, ranks, and promotions of males and females in various jobs; they concluded that patterns of discrimination were both open and subtle. When one major result of these efforts, Title IX, passed the Congress in 1972, such discrimination became illegal.

Title IX was designed to protect students, faculty, staff, and administrators in educational institutions from discrimination in many different areas, including employment, admissions, and financial aid, as well as to ensure equal access to sports, engineering, or other programs in which women had not traditionally participated. One key area, textbooks and the curriculum, was declared excluded from Title IX.

During the same period that Title IX was conceived, adopted by the Congress, and assigned for campus implementation to affirmative action officers, Women's Studies courses and programs began to appear. Women's Studies was designed to bring into texts and into the curriculum—and hence into public view—the hitherto invisible female half of the population. The history of women, the psychology and sociology of gender, the politics of relationships between the sexes, the status of women before the law, the treatment of women by women and men in the arts—all of these topics and more became newly significant subjects both for research and for teaching.

The conception of Women's Studies emerged from the same statistical pattern as had Title IX: that is, the higher in the educational system one looked, the fewer women one saw there—as students, as faculty, or as administrators. Women's Studies emerged also from a review of the sex-segregation of academic fields, which followed quite predictably the patterns of segregation of male and female students in campus departments. Women's colleges and men's colleges were, to state the idea in another way, not the only sex-segregated institutions of higher education. The large state university, for example, coeducational in its liberal arts program, became a sex-segregated institution as soon as one considered each of its graduate and professional schools, or even most of its pre-professional programs. Before 1970, for example, less than one percent of all students enrolled in engineering were women and approximately six percent of those enrolled in medical or law schools were women; on the other hand, almost all students in teaching, social work, nursing, and home economics were women. Most students in library science were women, and most in agriculture, forestry, mining, and metallurgy, as well as in physics and chemistry, were men. Indeed, most students in programs above the B.A. were male. Collegiate education seemed to send women either to sex-segregated occupations or to domesticity.

Why? What controlled this phenomenon? Why were women apparently content with the fact that, though they were 42 percent of the undergraduate population, they were 13 percent of those earning Ph.D.'s, six percent of those earning law or medical degrees, and one percent or less of those earning advanced degrees in engineering?

Pioneers of Women's Studies assumed that, while discrimination could account for the fact that women who did complete the Ph.D. did not often find jobs in high places, discrimination could not account for the millions who chose, all too often unhappily, not to seek work or pursue careers, not even to follow the traditional female tracks into low-paying, low-status professions. It was precisely in the area excluded from Title IX—curriculum and textbooks—that the pioneers of Women's Studies located a root cause of why women selected themselves out of the stream of academic achievers. The treatment of women—largely their omission—in the curriculum and in texts provided the best explanation of why decreasing numbers of women went on to graduate school, into research or teaching at the university level, or into the traditionally male professions of medicine, law, engineering, and politics. Women didn't have to be discriminated against in the admissions policies of medical schools; they learned early and late that doctors were male, nurses female. Everything in the culture embodied in the curriculum from kindergarten to graduate school signalled young women and men that they were to envision very different futures, though they might sit side by side in Advanced Organic Chemistry. Her future led to the kitchen, his to the clinic.

The curriculum was, of course, set in a sex-segregated social context. Male and female students were bombarded by textbooks portraying male achievement in a male-made world. They saw men teaching in the university classroom, directing the labs, administering the campuses. Most women who taught at the college level were to be found in women's colleges, in two-year community colleges, or in some of the least prestigious four-year or state or city universities. It was possible to graduate from any of the Ivy League institutions, or from a Big Ten campus, or from such smaller coeducational colleges as Oberlin, Reed, or Swarthmore, without having had even one female professor, without having set eyes on a single female administrator. It was also possible to graduate from any college or university in the country without having studied the history of one woman, read one woman writer, seen one painting by a woman, or considered the inequities of women before the law, or the history of the long struggle of black and white women for the suffrage, and for the opportunity to attend colleges at all.

And while it is still possible for women and men to graduate from college ignorant about women and the subject of gender, it is less possible than it was a decade ago.

We cannot overemphasize the importance of the shift in consciousness between the beginning of the 1970s and the beginning of the 1980s. It is not only that Women's Studies exists as a legitimate academic program in more than 400 colleges and universities; that there are more than 30,000 Women's Studies courses, thousands of new scholarly books and articles about women, new bibliographies, journals, and professional associations. The intellectual ferment of the past decade has begun to affect the rest of the curriculum and traditional scholarship as we have known it in this century. No respectable scholar in the social sciences, for example, can generalize about "human nature" solely on the basis of experiments or statistics gathered from male subjects. Statements about "what women want or think" cannot be made without asking women; or, if they were women in history, without searching for their perspective, even in the mute statistics of birth, employment, marriage, childbirth, and death.

The 1970s Change Collegiate Life

Between 1972 and 1982, both the implementation of Title IX and the growth of Women's Studies changed campus life, not only for women but also for men. Athletics is one of those areas most affected by the changes. On a few campuses women now receive half of the athletic scholarships awarded; on many more, 30 percent. Most colleges provide some opportunities for intercollegiate as well as intramural sports for women. Does this mean that men have *less?* Yes; it may mean that sports facilities have to be shared, as well as scholarship funds. It may also mean that only the very best athletes of *both* sexes can compete, perhaps excluding some men from some intercollegiate sports. But it may also mean the broadening of athletic programs to provide new opportunities for all students.

A similar phenomenon may be observed in relation to academic programs that are now trying to attract female students. Again, if the size of the engineering or medical school remains constant, there will be fewer male students if there are increasing numbers of female students gaining admission competitively. Many of these shifts in the gender of student populations are beginning to be visible in such

technically focused institutions as Carnegie-Mellon, Purdue, or M.I.T. While the numbers of female students entering traditionally male areas of study in technical institutions are still small, the proportions have leaped in a single decade from one percent to more than 15 percent, in some cases to more than 30 percent.

In other areas of campus life, there have also been significant changes, in keeping with Title IX's focus on equity. For example, special housing rules for female residents on campus have been abolished. In general, campuses have identical rules for both sexes, or they have no restrictive visiting rules at all.[2]

But equity for women is more complex than Title IX. In the past decade, campuses have taken "affirmative actions" to add services for women students because women in a sexist society need them. Childcare is one of those services. While it can be argued that childcare serves both parents, in reality the daily care of children is still mainly the responsibility of female parents. Hence, the presence of childcare facilities on campus or near campuses is an attraction for women with children. Women of all ages need certain kinds of medical treatment and counseling that men may never require, and some campuses have begun to provide these services. Similarly, women need physical protection from sexual abuse and sexual harassment that men generally do not need.

New institutions for women help them to feel welcome on coeducational campuses that are arranged, consciously or unconsciously, with male students in mind. Hundreds of Women's Centers now provide a place for women to meet other women socially, even as the men's clubhouse, the male-controlled student leadership activities, or the fraternities or drinking clubs have always provided places for men to meet. Sometimes Women's Centers also house special services for women—mathematics-confidence clinics, assertiveness-training sessions, a hotline or a warmline for referrals, counseling, job training programs. It is hard to imagine that only a decade ago these did not exist, nor did the additional programs and services especially designed for "reentry" women.

New student organizations reflect the changes on campus. Not only are there racially centered campus organizations, but there are some specifically for black women, for example, or for Chicanas. Many campuses have at least one lesbian organization that serves both white women and women of color. Campuses with large populations of "older" students have special organizations for them as well. Most campuses also have at least one major advocacy organization for all women students, in addition to the separate interest groups. Sometimes, that major organization is the formal Commission on the Status of Women, including students as voting participants. Some campuses also have a Commission on Minority Affairs. Obviously, both groups should, and often do, include women of color in their mandate.

Institutionally, most colleges and universities have adopted new policies on such problems as sexual harassment, and have appointed administrators to implement them as well as Title IX. In addition, most campuses have similar policies, procedures, and administrators to treat the new legislation regarding the handicapped.

By now, Title IX and Women's Studies have become part of the language and consciousness of most members of the campus community. Now also women have become the majority of the undergraduate population, despite the fact that the number of high school graduates has begun to shrink. Women are now the majority of undergraduates because of "returning" women students—women who dropped out of the educational pipeline to get married, have babies, join the population of housewives. They have returned to campuses, both to complete their education and, through that process, to change their lives. As a group, they understand that college is one essential route to independence—of mind and spirit—as well as of income.

Both older and younger female students in the 1980s know that, like their male peers, they will have to earn a living the rest of their days, and they see college as the route to paid employment. Many women are learning fast that the traditionally male fields and professions pay more than the traditionally female ones. Many women also understand what their mothers and grandmothers before them did not: that mathematics is one of the critical "filters"—or entry gates—to a large group of professions. Without mathematics, professional futures are restricted to the humanities and the arts, to social work, the library, and some aspects of home economics and the social sciences.

Thus, there are two curricular directions, both new for women. First, more women than ever before in history are choosing to study in formerly nontraditional fields. (We will have more to say about this question in a later section of the Introduction.) Second, more women—and men—than ever before are studying about women, and not only in Women's Studies Courses. On more than fifty campuses—including Wheaton College, the University of Arizona, the University of Southern California, Montana State University, the University of Maine, Orono—there are "mainstreaming" projects in progress aimed at reforming the male bias of the traditional curriculum. At the center of these projects is the new scholarship on women, usually in the form of Women's Studies courses. Women's Studies faculty who create that scholarship are key to the process of reform. Often, it is part of their job to teach other faculty in college-sponsored workshops about the new scholarship on women. Thus, undergraduates are beginning to hear—even in such courses as Introduction to Sociology and Survey of U.S. History—about "patriarchy" and "sexism," about "feminist movements" and "antisuffrage campaigns."

EVERYWOMAN'S GUIDE:
What Does It Tell You

EVERYWOMAN'S GUIDE contains information not available in other college guides. It also offers several judgments in the form of "stars" (★) about items we consider of special importance. They are not the only items of special importance, we must note at the outset, but they are the only ones we could measure. Yes, we are still counting!

EVERYWOMAN'S GUIDE tells you what the campuses have told us, through a complex questionnaire that we have printed at the back of this book. In addition to the answers to questions, institutions sometimes sent us additional information; most of the time, they accepted our offer and wrote a 50-word description which we print at the conclusion of each entry.

EVERYWOMAN'S GUIDE also tells you three kinds of statistical information we gathered from governmental sources: enrollments by gender and race; the full-time faculty by gender; the degrees awarded to students by gender. From these statistics, we extrapolated certain others that may serve as useful *indicators of progress toward equity.* They include the percentage of female students on each campus; the faculty-student gender ratios; and the percentage of female students in nontraditional fields of study.

Indicator One: The Percentage of Female Students on Each Campus

Though undergraduate women are the majority of students on all campuses combined, the variation on individual campuses is both interesting and significant. Clearly, women are more numerous at two-year colleges and on less prestigious campuses in general; and less in evidence on the campuses of technical institutes and the Ivy League universities.

Indicator Two: The Faculty/Student Gender Ratio

Faculty-student ratios are one of the normal gauges of excellence on campus and even in schools: the higher the ratio of faculty to students, the higher the quality of education hypothesized, because the teacher has more time to spend with each student as class-size shrinks. The ratio of 4 faculty for every 100 students, for example, is not as "good" as the ratio of 8 faculty for every 100 students, since in the latter instance, each student would have twice as many opportunities to encounter faculty.

We owe the faculty-student *gender* ratio to the inventiveness of Princeton women students and faculty attempting in the 1970s to highlight the special inequities on their campus, even when compared with other Ivy League campuses. They were measuring not the theoretical excellence of academic instruction on a campus, but rather the accessibility of faculty of each sex to students of each sex. Thus, they printed a flyer that listed, for each of a dozen campuses, comparable faculty-student ratios—by gender—with Princeton near the bottom.

We had a somewhat different purpose: to establish a national norm, and then to consider the statistical variants from campus to campus. Because we were including all kinds of campuses—from the Ivy League through the two-year community college—we chose to use full-time faculty and full-time students. The ratio excludes the part-time student-going population, as well as the part-time faculty, both of which are significantly female in proportion. At the same time, it includes all full-time faculty, even on research university campuses where the full-time (mostly male) faculty does not do much teaching. The statistic, therefore, probably heightens the differences between the (theoretical) availability of male faculty for male students and female faculty for female students. On the other hand, if we are interested in the perceptions of students about adults of their own sex in significant teaching positions on campuses, then the statistics provide a fair portrait.

On average, the ratio for all institutions in **EVERYWOMAN'S GUIDE** is between 3 and 4 full-time female faculty for every 100 full-time female students; and 10 full-time male faculty for every 100 full-time male students. In other words, on average, men have two and one-half times to three times the opportunity to encounter faculty of their own sex as female students have to encounter faculty of theirs. For women's colleges, the average ratio for women moves to 5 full-time faculty for every 100 full-time students. For private research universities, the ratio is also 5 for women but 15 for men. For public research universities, the average ratio drops to between 2 and 3 full-time female faculty for every 100 female students, and 10 full-time male faculty for every 100 male students. At public two-year community colleges, the average ratio for females is 5 full-time faculty for every 100 full-time students, and for males 8 full-time faculty for every 100 students. As with the percentage of female students, this statistic also tells you that the opportunities for women students to encounter female faculty vary according to the type of institution: the more prestigious the institution, the fewer opportunities for women students to encounter women faculty. This ratio, therefore, may become an especially useful indicator for judging the seriousness with which an institution has attempted to achieve educational equity.

Indicator Three: The Percentage of Female Students in Nontraditional Fields of Study

Because of the way in which this information is collected by federal agencies, we can report on it only for four-year institutions. (At two-year colleges, for example, a major or potential major in mathematics or chemistry would be reported as in "liberal arts.") For four-year institutions, we included the following areas of study as nontraditional for females: agriculture, architecture, computer science, engineering, mathematics, military science, physical sciences, and theology. Possibly, we should have omitted mathematics, since women earn 42 percent of the degrees in that field. But the field itself is a small one, in which relatively few women or men earn degrees in any one year. In 1980, for example, 11,480 bachelor's degrees were conferred in mathematics, 69,000 in engineering, and 189,000 in business.[3]

At four-year colleges, the average proportion of men earning nontraditional degrees is approximately 18 percent; at universities, 30 percent. On some two dozen campuses in **EVERYWOMAN'S GUIDE**, more than 15 percent of women earn degrees in these fields. We consider this an important indicator for the future, though we would temper its significance with close attention to the percentage of female students on each campus. One may have to balance, for example, the fact that 15 percent of women students graduate in nontraditional fields from large universities like Berkeley or Rutgers—where women are approximately half the student body—with the fact that more than 50 percent of women students may graduate in nontraditional fields from small technical institutes where they are less than 15 percent of the student body.

EVERYWOMAN'S Ratings

Our primary intention has been to *report* on the progress that institutions have made toward establishing a "healthy" educational environment for women. Each entry, in intentionally *flat* language, reports on the information that the questionnaire contained. Each questionnaire was filled out by a person or persons responsible to the president or chief executive officer of each institution—to whom the questionnaire had been addressed. We have not written "PR" for any institution; we have not *imagined* what students might or might not enjoy; we have not asked students to describe their pleasures for us. Nor have we invited anyone to complain about a particular institution or its practices.

On the other hand, we make some evaluative statements. We decided to judge, not the value of whole institutions, but the progress made in the areas we have described as "changing in the 1970s." To rank whole institutions, we believed, would be premature. But we had both the conception and the tools with which to *rate* several institutional *features*. They are not the only important items women need to consider in choosing a college, but they are in and of themselves important. They are also items for which we had sufficient detailed information that could be rated for all institutions.

At a glance, a reader will be able to see campuses with from one to three stars: ratings for three items under **Women in Leadership Positions** (*students, faculty, administrators*), and then **Women and the Curriculum**, and **Women and Athletics**. The stars indicate that opportunities for student leadership experience are outstanding at "Everywoman's University," but not as good, or non-existent, at other institutions. The patterns of stars throughout **EVERYWOMAN'S GUIDE** indicate that, for some items, some types of institutions are, in general, better than others. If a woman wants student leadership experience, for example, the huge university—with certain rare exceptions—is not the place to go.

Where *will* women find the greatest leadership opportunities—in terms both of opportunities for themselves as students seeking experience, and as observers of "role models"—women on the faculty and in the administrative leadership of the institution? Ratings here are based on a finite expectation: women are half the general population, and little over half the undergraduate population. They ought to hold half the leadership positions; they ought to be half the faculty and half the administrators. Thus, a rating of three stars (★★★) became perfection at equity—or 50 percent.

Student Leadership

The rating of three stars is based on the percentage of women students in each campus's undergraduate population. Thus, if 100 percent of the student body is female—as at the slightly more than 100 women's college campuses still in existence, then the institution receives a rating of three stars for student leadership—since all such positions are held by women. If, on the other hand, 30 percent of the institution's undergraduates are women, perfection (★★★) for student leadership is 30 percent of leadership positions. In all cases, we asked campuses for information about the gender of students holding leadership posts during a recent three-year period (1978–1981), and we used that information plus enrollment statistics to rate the item.

Since the *average* proportion of women in student leadership positions for coeducational institutions in **EVERYWOMAN'S GUIDE** is 33 percent, we use that figure for one star (★); and award two stars (★★) when the proportion is more than 42 percent; three stars (★★★) at 50 percent—when women are 50 percent of the student body. When the enrollment for women varies from 50 percent, the proportions used for rating also vary accordingly.

Women on the Faculty

Here, we began with a national statistic: women are 25 percent of the full-time teaching faculty, if one averages information from all institutions. Historically, women have been employed mainly at women's colleges, at the least prestigious four-year colleges and state universities, and at the two-year public community colleges whose history usually goes back no further than the 1960s. At some of these institutions, women are more than 50 percent of the faculty, whereas on Ivy League campuses and among the Big Ten universities, they are far fewer than 20 percent.

We use the national norm as the base line at which institutions get one star (★); we award two stars (★★) if the percentage of full-time women faculty falls between 35 and 49 percent; over 50 percent, the rating is three stars (★★★).

Women Among the Top Administrators

Our ratings are similar with regard to administrators. The questionnaire inquires about the ten top positions—ranging from the chief executive officer to the heads of the library and athletics; and including the persons responsible for the academic program and for the lives of students (on university or large community college campuses, these might be vice presidents; on smaller college campuses, these would be deans). We omit other deans and directors. And we use the same scale as for the faculty: 25 percent to 34 percent rates one star (★); 35 percent to 49 percent, two stars (★★); and 50 percent, three stars (★★★).

For the nearly 600 institutions in **EVERYWOMAN'S GUIDE,** the average proportion for all women among these top administrators is 21 percent. For white women, the figure is 19 percent; for minority women, 2 percent. Omitting women's colleges, for coeducational institutions alone, the statistic drops to 16 percent (again, 2 percent minority women; 14 percent white women).

The Ratings for Curriculum and Sports

With regard to curriculum and athletics, we had different problems to solve. We could not assign three stars to "perfection," since no institution—even including women's colleges—has developed a curriculum which provides a fully equitable view of women and which provides women with full access to all fields of study. Nor is there any institution in which women have opportunities for experiences in athletics fully comparable to men's. "Perfection" had to be measured, therefore, along a continuum that would be understood as a measure of progress. One star (★) therefore says that a campus is "good"—it has made a start at progress; two stars (★★) say that a campus is "better than good"—it has moved beyond the star; and three stars (★★★) say that a campus is, at this moment, "best" among those beginning to establish equity for women. In fact, the campuses judged "best" provide the outer boundaries of the ratings.

Women and the Curriculum

Two elements form the basis for these ratings, though they are also influenced by two additional matters. The central matters are access to nontraditional fields of study, and access to the new scholarship on women—through courses on women or through Women's Studies Programs. Even if institutions have no courses on women, they rate one star (★) if women constitute more than 15 percent of the students *and* more than 15 percent of these women students are taking degrees in agriculture, architecture, computer science, engineering, mathematics, military science, physical sciences, and theology.

Institutions rate one star (★) if they have a Women's Studies Program that offers courses through Women's Studies or through other academic units. Similarly, institutions rate one star (★) if 12 or more courses on women are offered, even without the coordination of a Women's Studies Program and an organized progression of courses. Institutions rate two stars (★★) if the Women's Studies Program offers a structured or autonomous B.A. program and an annual roster of more than 30 courses through Women's Studies and other academic units. Institutions rate three stars (★★★) if the Women's Studies Program offers a minor, a B.A., and a roster of 50 or more courses annually through Women's Studies and other academic units.

In some cases, ratings are based on a combination of factors: the presence of a Women's Studies Program or courses on women *and* the percentage of women taking degrees in nontraditional fields. In other cases, two additional items, still rare among institutions nationally and in **EVERYWOMAN'S GUIDE**, are worth additional stars. These items do not occur without Women's Studies Programs, or, at the very least, without the presence of some courses on women.

The first item is the presence of a college-wide requirement that all students, regardless of major field, take at least one course focused on discrimination against women and/or minority group members of both sexes. Within **EVERYWOMAN'S GUIDE**, five institutions get this particular star—Denison University in Ohio, Stephens College in Missouri, Eastern Washington University in Washington, West Chester College in Pennsylvania, and Indian Valley College in California.

The second item is the presence on campus of a Center for Research on Women (CROW). There are more than two dozen of these nationally, not all of them on campuses, but all of them responses to the burgeoning field of Women's Studies. Within **EVERYWOMAN'S GUIDE**, there are eleven centers: the University of California at Berkeley, the University of California at Los Angeles, Harvard University in Massachusetts, Wellesley College in Massachusetts, Duke University in North Carolina, Brown University in Rhode Island, Memphis State University in Tennessee, the University of Arizona, the University of Michigan, Rutgers University in New Jersey, and the George Washington University in Washington, D.C.

Women and Athletics

We rated athletics on a complex scale that awarded "points" for certain features. Included, for example, was the presence of both an intramural program and an intercollegiate program, as well as club sports—all of which would be normal for male students in most institutions. We awarded points for the number of sports, and for the presence of a variety of individual and team sports. We gave points to institutions awarding athletic scholarships in proportion to the participation of women in intercollegiate sports. The total points awarded ranged from nine for one star (★) to 13 for three stars (★★★). An institution that was awarded 13 points, for example, might offer more than 10 intramural sports and as many as 12 intercollegiate sports, including three team sports—basketball, volleyball, or field hockey—and two individual sports—tennis and track. In this three-starred athletic program, women might be more than 30 percent of intramural and intercollegiate athletes, and hold that proportion or more of the athletic scholarships.

Clearly, the largest campuses usually offer the greatest variety of sports, and perhaps also the highest proportion of scholarships. But it may be useful to mention that, since intercollegiate teams have a finite number of athletes on them, students on smaller campuses—where there is less competition for those team places—may actually have more opportunity to play.

EVERYWOMAN'S GUIDE
Summarized

EVERYWOMAN'S GUIDE says what is reasonably obvious, that different kinds of institutions offer different kinds of opportunities. If educational health for women means that they must have opportunities for leadership, significant presence in and access to the full curriculum, and opportunities for athletics, then, for the most part in the 1980s, women will have to attend more than one institution if they are to have all of these. The ratings in **EVERYWOMAN'S GUIDE** make palpable the fact that during the 1970s different kinds of institutions poured their resources into different areas of the campuses—in order to respond to women. Some increased their affirmative action efforts, and hired more women onto the faculty and more female administrators; some added budgets to athletics for women, some to Women's Studies Programs. Other institutions put their energies and their budgets into areas we have discussed but not rated:

those services specific to women like gynecological care, special safety features, childcare, the Women's Center, the reentry program.

If you are a woman interested in leadership opportunities, you must still consider those women's colleges important that, because of their historical mission, are filled with women faculty and administrators. In a world that now understands the importance of "role models," as well as opportunities for students' leadership experience, women's colleges have something special to offer women. Similarly, the two-year community college and certain state institutions also provide good opportunities for leadership.

If you are interested in Women's Studies or in a substantial athletic program, however, with rare exceptions—Wellesley College, for example—you will be interested in the largest universities, perhaps even those in which women have the fewest opportunities for leadership. There is hardly an institution today in which full educational health for women—in all that that concept includes—can be found. In short, there is still much room for progress during the decades to come.

The Future for EVERYWOMAN'S GUIDE

It is hard to consider futures when one has come to an initial conclusion. But if **EVERYWOMAN'S GUIDE** is to be useful, it will have to be comparative. This volume is an index to the progress that campuses have made through a decade and a half of significant social action. It is an image of movement caught in pages of statistics. Of change captured in cool phrases. It is a compilation long overdue, though it probably could not have been done sooner. It tells us where we are, not where we are going.

The success of **EVERYWOMAN'S GUIDE** will be measured by the number of people who use it. We hope that women across the land will respond to this book both by reading it and by taking a close—and organized—look at the campuses of their choice. We are going to assume that this book—dedicated as it is to Title IX on its tenth birthday—will help to strengthen campuses. And we are going to assume that there will be a second **EVERYWOMAN'S GUIDE**.

And so we invite you to write to us with your comments and suggestions. We will listen, and we will add your name to a special list of people to whom we will send news every now and then about **EVERYWOMAN'S GUIDE**.

Notes
[1] Title IX, a federal law passed by Congress in 1972, says: "No person shall, on the basis of sex, be excluded from participation in, be denied the benefits of, or be subjected to discrimination under any education program or activity receiving federal financial assistance." Since most colleges and universities in the country receive some federal financial assistance, at least through the student aid program, most institutions of higher education are affected by this law, as are all public schools, and some private ones. The law covers all employees of educational institutions, as well as all students. The law guarantees equality of treatment to all employees, regardless of gender—which means that faculty, staff, and administrators are to be hired through an equitable process, and that they are to be paid an equal wage for equal work, whether they are males or females. For students, the law addresses five areas in which both females and males are to be treated fairly.

First, all students are guaranteed access to all courses of study: females should be as welcome as males to those areas called "nontraditional" for women—agriculture, architecture, computer science, engineering, mathematics, military science, physical sciences, and theology. Second, all students are guaranteed access to coeducational classes. Only a few exceptions are allowed to this rule—separate classes may be held for girls and boys during the teaching of human sexuality, and during physical education involving bodily contact. Third, all students have a right to receive nonsexist advice, counseling, and other forms of information essential to students' lives—ranging from the descriptions of courses and careers, to the portrayal of appropriately clothed persons in career manuals. Fourth, all students must be treated equally in terms of institutional rules, including those that affect personal behavior, extra-curricular life, and such matters as health and insurance benefits. Separate toilet facilities in dormitories, gymnasiums, and other public places are guaranteed. Fifth, all students have a right to athletics: institutions may choose to arrange the athletic program so that all teams are coeducational; or so that all teams are separate for males and females; or so that there are some teams of each kind, coeducational and separate for each sex. But however this is arranged by campus, both male and female students must be treated equitably.

A useful brief guide for students, called *Title IX for Beginners,* is available for 50 cents per copy from the Bismarck Commission on the Status of Women, 207 Arbor Avenue, #105D, Bismarck, ND 58501.

[2] In **EVERYWOMAN'S GUIDE**, there is one exception: Piedmont College reports that "we close the women's residence hall at 11 p.m. with all women in."

[3] *Earned Degrees Conferred, 1979–1980,* published by the National Center for Education Statistics, U.S. Department of Education, Washington, DC 20202.

The entries in **EVERYWOMAN'S GUIDE** were written mainly from two sources: 1) the **Questionnaire** filled out by each institution (see sample at back of book), and 2) statistical information obtained from the National Center for Education Statistics (NCES).

1 Ratings indicate whether an institution's progress is good (★), excellent (★★), or outstanding (★★★). Ratings refer to these two areas only.

2 Ratings indicate whether an institution is better than average (★), much better than average (★★), or close to perfection (★★★). Ratings refer to these three areas only.

3 Total of full- and part-time students who are registered in programs leading to degrees or certificates (NCES data).

4 The racial/ethnic/gender information is for full- and part-time undergraduates (NCES data).

5 Symbols emphasize information also contained in the text.

🏠	On-campus evening and/or weekend classes	[M A]	Commission on minority affairs
🏛	Off-campus classes	📖	Women's Studies program
🚐	Accessible by public transportation	👤	Women's center
👫	On-campus childcare facilities	AAUW	Member, American Association of University Women
✎	Publicly communicated sexual harassment policy, includes students	NWSA	Member, National Women's Studies Association
[S W]	Commission on status of women	CROW	On-campus Center for Research on Women

6 Total of all students—graduate and undergraduate—who take courses. Some are registered in programs leading to degrees or certificates, some are not.

7 Half the undergraduates are this age or older; half are younger.

8 Childcare, when available, is always mentioned in a separate paragraph, here.

9 See **Everywoman's Questionnaire** (p. 499) for kinds of positions surveyed.

10 Faculty-student gender ratios are of *full-time* faculty and *full-time* undergraduates only (NCES data).

11 See **Everywomen's Questionnaire** (p. 499) for kinds of positions surveyed.

12 Information about degrees awarded is from NCES.

13 These are the intercollegiate sports in which women participate.

14 These are the institution's own words, describing those features that would be important to prospective women students.

15 These sections appear only when there was sufficient information for them.

SAMPLE

Everywoman's University
5050 Equity Road
New Era, KS 67000
Telephone: (913) 666-6666 — ①

② **Women in Leadership**
★★★ students   ★★★ **Women and the Curriculum**
★★★ faculty
★★★ administrators   ★★★ **Women and Athletics**

③ 8,000 undergraduates

④
	Amer. Ind.	Asian Amer.	Blacks	Hispanics	Whites
F	58	50	832	100	3,020
M	52	40	768	100	2,880
%	1.4	1.1	26.3	2.5	74.7

⑤ 🏠 🏛 🚐 👫 ✎ [S W] [M A] 📖 👤 AAUW NWSA
CROW

⑥⑦ Founded as a men's academy in 1827, Everywoman's is now a publicly supported, four-year comprehensive university. It has 9,500 students, including 8,000 undergraduates. Fifty-two percent of the undergraduates are women, and 20 percent of the women attend part-time. The median age of undergraduates is 22.

The university offers bachelor's degrees in a wide variety of liberal arts and pre-professional fields, as well as master's degrees in some areas. On- and off-campus evening classes, a Saturday College, and self-paced/contract learning facilitate flexible scheduling. The suburban campus is accessible by public transportation, and free on-campus parking is provided. Sixty percent of students commute.

⑧ University-sponsored childcare facilities give priority to students. Open from 7 a.m. to 10 p.m., the facilities charge a fixed daily rate. Private childcare is available near campus.

⑮ **Policies to Ensure Fairness to Women.** The Affirmative Action Officer is responsible full-time for making policy and enforcing compliance concerning equal-employment-opportunity, educational-sex-equity, and handicapped-access legislation. A publicized written policy prohibits sexual harassment of students, faculty, and staff. The Commission on the Status of Women meets frequently and issues reports of interest to women, including minority women. The Commission on Minority Affairs also addresses the concerns of minority women.

⑨ **Women in Leadership Positions.** *Students.* During a recent three-year period, women held half the available campus-wide student leadership positions. Women head six of 12 honorary societies.

Faculty. Fifty-two percent of the 300 full-time faculty are women, a proportion considerably above the national
⑩ average. There are 6 female faculty for every 100 female

ENTRY

students; for males, the ratio is the same.

(11) *Administrators.* Women hold 4 of the 8 top positions: chief executive officer, chief business officer, head librarian, and director of athletics. Of 32 academic departments, women chair 16, including business, chemistry, English, and mathematics. Half the members of the faculty senate and the Board of Trustees are women. A woman was the 1981 commencement speaker; 3 of 8 honorary degrees were awarded to women.

(12) **Women and the Curriculum.** Most bachelor's degrees earned by women are in social sciences (23 percent), education (20 percent), psychology (20 percent), and fine arts (9 percent). Twenty percent of women graduate in the nontraditional fields of architecture, engineering, mathematics, and physical sciences. Innovative programs encourage women to major in computer design and aeronautical engineering.

The Women's Studies Program awards an undergraduate minor, the B.A. in Women's Studies, and the M.A. through various departments. Seventy-six undergraduate courses on women are offered by Women's Studies and through 30 departments, including anthropology, biology, history, English, political science, French, Afro-American studies, and Mexican-American studies. Core courses offered by Women's Studies include Introduction to Women's Studies, History and Function of Women's Education, Women and the Law, and Women and Reproduction. Recent courses offered through departments include Women and Politics after Suffrage, the Biochemistry of Women, Women and the Economy of Third World Countries, Women in Latin American Literature, Women as Social Workers, The History of Women in the Progressive Era, and Women in Classical Rome.

The Center for Research on Women, newly established with a grant from the Stanley Foundation, will focus its attention on the relationship between women and educational institutions in the U.S. and in developing countries. Its aim is to develop models of educational processes that encourage the establishment of equity for women.

(15) **Minority Women.** Twenty-five percent of undergraduate women are members of minority groups, mainly black and Hispanic. Among the 156 full-time faculty women are 30 black women, 8 Hispanic, 1 American Indian, and 2 Asian American women. The chief business officer of the university is an Hispanic woman; the head librarian is an American Indian woman. Two black women chair academic departments. A black woman and an Asian American woman received honorary degrees at the 1981 commencement.

The Black Students Alliance and MECHA are among the advocacy groups for minority women on campus.

Women and Athletics. The athletic program for women is outstanding, offering a wide variety of organized, competitive, individual and team sports. Women are approximately half the participants in intramural, intercollegiate,

(13) and club sports; women receive half of the athletic scholarships. Nine of the 17 paid intercollegiate coaches are women. Intercollegiate sports offered are basketball, fencing, field hockey, golf, gymnastics, ice hockey, lacrosse, riflery, soccer, softball, swimming and diving, tennis, track, and volleyball.

(15) **Housing and Student Organizations.** Single-sex and coeducational dormitories that have no restrictive hours for visitors of the opposite sex are available to the 40 percent of undergraduates who live on campus. Housing is also available for students with children. A woman student whose spouse is not enrolled may live in married students' housing. Seven of 14 residence-hall directors are women; directors receive in-service training on sexism and racism.

In addition to the minority-group student organizations mentioned earlier, there are four other advocacy groups for women: the local NOW chapter, Reproductive Choice, Lesbian Matrix, and Women Working.

Special Services and Programs for Women. *Health and Counseling.* Student Health, staffed by 4 female and 4 male physicians and 12 health-care providers (6 of whom are female), offers treatment for gynecological problems, birth control, and abortion. The 8-member counseling staff, which includes 4 women, offers counseling on birth control, abortion, and anorexia nervosa.

Safety and Security. Measures include campus police who have arrest authority, high-intensity lighting, emergency alarms and telephones, and instruction sessions on campus safety for students. Two rapes and 18 assaults (nine on women) were reported for 1980–81.

(15) *Career.* Services include nonsexist/nonracist printed information on nontraditional careers for women and men, lectures and panels for students by women employed in nontraditional fields, and networking between students and alumnae employed in nontraditional fields.

(15) *Other.* The Women's Center, directed by a full-time administrator on a budget of $74,000, serves about 3,000 women each year. It offers counseling and workshops for a wide variety of students, sponsors a program for displaced homemakers, and runs a telephone warmline for referrals and information. In conjunction with the drama department, it sponsors theater and other arts events for women.

(15) **Returning Women Students.** A Continuing Education for Women Program, operated under Adult Continuing Education, serves 1,500 women each year. Women in the program have their own lounge and are offered special orientation and tutorial sessions.

(15) **Special Features.** The Everywoman's campus houses the Museum of Women's Art.

(14) **Institutional Self-Description.** "Here women will find full equality with men in their pursuit of higher education. Here also women will find other women (and men) who regard equality as a woman's birthright, not a privilege."

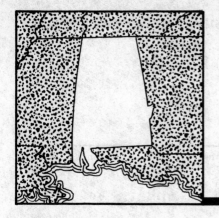

ALABAMA

Alabama State University

915 Jackson St., Montgomery, AL 36195
Telephone: (205) 832-6072

Women in Leadership
- ★ students
- ★★ faculty

3,971 undergraduates

	Amer. Ind.	Asian Amer.	Blacks	Hispanics	Whites
F	0	1	2,268	5	5
M	0	1	1,655	3	3
%	0.0	0.1	99.5	0.2	0.2

 AAUW

Established in 1874 as a school "for education of the Colored Teachers and Students," today Alabama State University offers bachelor's and master's programs in the liberal arts, fine arts, business, sciences, teacher education, and other pre-professional areas. In addition to a summer session, alternative scheduling is available through the Evening and Weekend College, which also sponsors an adult continuing education program. Alabama State has a total enrollment of 4,794 students, of whom 3,971 are undergraduates, whose average age is 22. Fifty-eight percent of the undergraduates are women; 6 percent of the women attend part-time. Over 99 percent of the student body is black.

The campus, located in the city of Montgomery, is accessible by public transportation. On-campus parking at a fee is also available for the 60 percent of students who commute.

Private childcare facilities are available near campus.

Policies to Ensure Fairness to Women. The Director of Personnel Services, on a part-time basis, reviews policies and monitors compliance with legislation on equal employment opportunity, sex equity for students, and handicapped access. A written campus policy prohibits sexual harassment of students; complaints are resolved both informally and confidentially and through a formal campus grievance procedure. A university committee addresses the concerns of women.

Women in Leadership Positions. *Students.* Women have good opportunities to gain leadership experience. In three recent years, two of the five campus-wide student posts have been held consistently by women: president of the student body and editor-in-chief of the campus newspaper.

Faculty. Forty-four percent of the full-time faculty of 168 are women, a proportion higher than average for colleges in this guide. There are 3 female faculty for every 100 female students and 6 male faculty for every 100 male students. The largely black faculty includes 2 Asian American and 10 white women.

Administrators. All top-level administrators are men, with the exception of the director of institutional research, who is a black woman. The Dean of the College of Arts and Sciences is also a black woman. Eight of the 29-member faculty senate are women,

7 of them black and 1 white. One of the 10 trustees is a white woman. Two black women and 2 white women chair four of 21 departments: social sciences, business education and career development, personnel services, and basic studies.

Women and the Curriculum. Most women earn degrees in education (58 percent), with fewer numbers in business (12 percent), public affairs (9 percent), and biology (6 percent). Over 2 percent of women graduates major in such nontraditional fields as computer sciences and physical sciences.

There are no courses on women. The division of education provides instruction on the development and use of sex-fair curricula and the division of physical education provides instruction on the teaching of coeducational classes.

Women and Athletics. The athletic program for women is adequate. Women participate in five intramural sports. Twenty-seven percent of the intercollegiate athletes are women, as are two of the seven paid intercollegiate coaches. The university awards approximately 20 percent of athletic scholarships to women. The intercollegiate sports offered are basketball, cross-country, tennis, track, and volleyball.

Housing and Student Organizations. Approximately half of all undergraduates live in residence halls. Single-sex dormitories with restrictive hours for visitors of the opposite sex are available, along with housing for married students with or without children. A married woman student whose husband is not enrolled is permitted to live with her husband in married students' housing.

Seven percent of students join social sororities and fraternities, which do not provide housing for members.

Special Services and Programs for Women. *Health and Counseling.* The student health service has 3 male physicians on call and employs 1 female nurse. Two of the 3 counseling center staff members are women, 1 white and 1 black. Medical treatment and counseling for gynecological problems and rape and assault are available, along with birth control counseling.

Safety and Security. Measures consist of local police, campus police with arrest authority, night-time escort for women students, high-intensity lighting in all areas, information sessions on campus safety and rape and assault prevention, and a rape crisis center. No rapes or assaults on women were reported on campus during 1980–81.

Career. The Career Placement office provides nonsexist/nonracist printed information on nontraditional fields of study for women, as well as information on job discrimination.

Other. The office of the Dean of Students and the City of Montgomery provide programs for battered women, assertiveness/leadership training, as well as a women's lecture series.

Institutional Self-Description. "Alabama State University seeks 'to provide students. . . with affordable programs of high quality. . . designed for their intellectual and personal growth in pursuit of meaningful employment and responsible citizenship; and to provide cultural enrichment, continuing education, research, and public services for individuals who desire to better themselves and the world in which they live.' "

Alexander City State Junior College
699 Cherokee Road
Alexander City, AL 35010
Telephone: (205) 234-6346

Women in Leadership
★★ faculty

1,200 undergraduates

	Amer. Ind.	Asian Amer.	Blacks	Hispanics	Whites
F	1	0	204	0	384
M	0	0	203	1	407
%	0.1	0.0	34.0	0.1	66.0

This two-year, public commuter college is located on an urban campus in central Alabama. Of the 1,210 students, half are women and one-third are black students. The median age of all students is 21. Students with jobs or childcare responsibilities may take advantage of a wide range of alternative full-time and part-time schedules, including evening classes, summer and weekend sessions, and contract learning. Free parking is provided. Private childcare facilities are available near campus.

Women in Leadership Positions. *Students.* The only leadership position, president of the student body, has been held by men during a recent three-year period. A woman presides over the one honorary society.

Faculty. Forty-six percent of the 39 faculty members are women, higher than average for public two-year colleges in this guide. There are 5 female faculty for every 100 female students, about the same as the ratio of male faculty to male students.

Administrators. Of 10 chief administrators, the head librarian is a woman. Women chair 6 of the 8 academic departments, including those in nontraditional fields such as mathematics and science/pre-engineering, as well as in language arts, social sciences, fine arts, and continuing education and community services. The 5-member faculty senate includes 3 women, 1 of whom is black.

Women and the Curriculum. Most of the degrees and certificates awarded to women are in arts and sciences, and business and commerce.

There are no courses on women. The business department provides instruction about job discrimination, sexual harassment in the workplace, and women in management.

Women and Athletics. Few women participate in the two intramural sports, basketball and softball.

Special Services and Programs for Women. *Health and Counseling.* There is no student health service. Counseling is available, but not treatment, concerning matters of birth control, gynecology, abortion, and rape and assault. The counseling center is staffed by one man and two white women.

Safety and Security. Security measures include campus police, high-intensity lighting, and a rape crisis center. No assaults on women were reported for 1980–82.

Institutional Self-Description. None provided.

![] On-campus evening and/or weekend classes		![] Commission on minority affairs	
![] Off-campus classes		![] Women's Studies program	
![] Accessible by public transportation		![] Women's center	
![] On-campus childcare facilities		AAUW Member, American Association of University Women	
![] Publicly communicated sexual harassment policy, includes students		NWSA Member, National Women's Studies Association	
![] Commission on status of women		CROW On-campus Center for Research on Women	

Auburn University, Montgomery
Montgomery, AL 36193
Telephone: (205) 279-9110

Women in Leadership
★ students
★ faculty

2,710 undergraduates

	Amer. Ind.	Asian Amer.	Blacks	Hispanics	Whites
F	0	12	220	0	1,186
M	0	13	118	0	1,161
%	0.0	1.0	12.5	0.0	86.7

 AAUW

The branch campus of a public, land-grant university, Auburn at Montgomery provides both undergraduate and selected graduate programs. The university offers a variety of alternative schedules, including summer sessions and a weekend college, to its 4,399 students. Of 2,710 undergraduates, 52 percent are women, and 15 percent of the women attend part-time. The median age of all undergraduates is 24. Free on-campus parking, but no public transportation, is available for the 92 percent of the student body who commute.

On-campus childcare facilities can accommodate nearly all requests, with faculty and staff having the highest priority. Private childcare facilities are available off-campus.

Policies to Ensure Fairness to Women. The director of personnel, on a part-time basis, reviews policies and practices generated by councils and committees regarding equal opportunity, sex equity, and accessibility for the handicapped. A written campus policy prohibits sexual harassment of faculty and staff but not of students. In addition, a formal campus grievance procedure which ensures due process resolves complaints of sexual harassment.

Women in Leadership Positions. *Students.* Women have good opportunities to exercise campus leadership. A woman has held the position of editor of the student newspaper for the past three years. During the same period, except for a year when a woman served as presiding officer of the student court, all other student leadership positions were held by men. Women head three of the four honor societies.

Faculty. Women are a third of the full-time faculty of 157, a proportion that is above the national average. There are 9 male faculty for every 100 male students and 4 female faculty for every 100 female students.

Administrators. All top administrators, except the chief academic officer, are male. The Dean of Nursing is a white woman. One department—English—is chaired by a woman.

Women and the Curriculum. Education is the most popular area of study for women; 4 percent graduate in nontraditional fields.

Several courses on women are offered by the departments of English and history. The department of physical education and the schools of education and social work provide some instruction on matters specific to women. Faculty workshops are held on nontraditional occupations for women and the needs of reentry women.

Women and Athletics. Women do not compete in intercollegiate or club sports; over 300 women participate in team and individual intramural sports.

Housing and Student Organizations. For the 8 percent of undergraduates who live on campus, coed dormitories are available, with no restrictive hours for visitors of the opposite sex. A married woman student whose husband is not enrolled is permitted to live in married students' housing.

Sororities and fraternities do not provide housing for their members. Ten percent of undergraduate women belong to sororities; 20 minority women belong to all-minority sororities.

Special Services and Programs for Women. *Health and Counseling.* There is no student health service or counseling center.

Safety and Security. Measures taken include armed campus police with the authority to make arrests, local police whose jurisdiction includes the campus, high-intensity lighting in all areas, an emergency alarm system at isolated locations, and a rape crisis center. No information was provided about the incidence of rapes and assaults on women.

Career. Career workshops focus on nontraditional occupations and job discrimination.

Institutional Self-Description. None provided.

Huntingdon College
1500 East Fairview Avenue
Montgomery, AL 36106
Telephone: (205) 265-0511

Women in Leadership
★ faculty

620 undergraduates

	Amer. Ind.	Asian Amer.	Blacks	Hispanics	Whites
F	0	0	37	1	311
M	1	0	33	1	221
%	0.2	0.0	11.6	0.3	88.0

Huntingdon is a four-year, liberal arts college affiliated with the United Methodist Church. Chartered in 1854 as Tuskegee Female College, it officially became coeducational in 1946. The campus, in a black residential area of the state capital, serves 575 full-time undergraduates. The median age of all students is 19. On-campus parking is available for a fee to the 52 percent of students who commute. There is a summer session.

Private childcare facilities are available off campus.

Policies to Ensure Fairness to Women. The business manager is responsible for compliance with equal-opportunity laws. Although there is no formal policy on sexual harassment, there is a formal grievance procedure for handling complaints.

Women in Leadership Positions. *Students.* Women have held less than a quarter of the leadership positions in recent years.

Faculty. Women constitute 26 percent of the full-time faculty and 28 percent of the permanent faculty. Three women are found among the 18 members of key faculty committees. There are 3 female faculty for every 100 female students and 12 male faculty for every 100 male students.

Administrators. The sole woman among the nine chief administrators is the director of institutional research. Two of the ten chairs of academic departments are women: biology and visual arts. In 1980–81, women received all four alumni awards.

Women and the Curriculum. Twenty-three percent of degrees awarded to women are in education. In a recent year, three women (but no men) received degrees in theology. Most students in cooperative education and internship practicums are women. Half the students in science field service are women.

No individual courses on women are offered. The departments of education, physical education, and social work provide instruction on some matters specific to women.

Women and Athletics. Huntingdon gives 40 percent of its athletic scholarships to women. Women's participation in intra-

mural team sports is good. Intercollegiate sports available are tennis and volleyball.

Housing and Student Organizations. Single-sex dormitories are available; they have restrictive hours for visitors of the opposite sex. Twenty percent of full-time women students are members of sororities. Sororities do not provide housing.

Special Services and Programs for Women. *Health and Counseling.* There is no student health center. The counseling center provides no counseling specific to women.

Safety and Security. The campus police have no authority to make arrests. Information sessions on rape-assault prevention are available, along with a rape crisis center. One assault on a woman was reported for 1980–81.

Other. A Domestic Abuse Center in the community serves battered women. Assertiveness/leadership training is co-sponsored by the department of behavioral sciences and the Human Resources Center.

Returning Women Students. Approximately 200 women, including 50 reentry women, take courses in the division of continuing education. The division offers instruction in mathematics confidence. A Women's Center and a Continuing Education for Women Program are being developed.

Institutional Self-Description. None provided.

Livingston University
Livingston, AL 35470
Telephone: (205) 652–9661

Women in Leadership
★★★ students
★★ faculty

1,034 undergraduates

	Amer. Ind.	Asian Amer.	Blacks	Hispanics	Whites
F	1	1	135	0	338
M	0	1	116	1	430
%	0.1	0.2	24.5	0.1	75.1

Livingston University occupies a campus near the Mississippi border, one hour from Tuscaloosa, Alabama. Although it now offers graduate courses as well as several undergraduate degrees, it began, in 1835, as a teacher-training school for women. In 1929 it became a state teachers' college, and not until 1957 did it become a university. A total of 1,247 students attend, 1,034 of them undergraduates. Forty-six percent of undergraduates are women, and 14 percent of women attend part-time. The median age of all undergraduates is 21. The 40 percent of students who commute use private transportation; free parking is available on campus.

Private childcare facilities are available near campus.

Policies to Ensure Fairness to Women. Responsibilities for equal employment opportunity, sex equity, and access for the handicapped are shared by three administrators.

Women in Leadership Positions. *Students.* Women have been prominent in all-campus student leadership positions, holding 56 percent of the available offices, including editor-in-chief of the campus newspaper for two consecutive years and presiding officer of the residence-hall council for three consecutive years. A woman heads one of the three campus honorary societies.

Faculty. Women constitute 38 percent of the 67-member faculty. There are 6 female faculty for every 100 female students and 8 male faculty for every 100 male students.

Administrators. Men hold all top-level positions. Women chair three of the nine departments (physical education, nursing, and English). Women are poorly represented on other governing and policymaking bodies. A woman was among the four recipients of honorary degrees at the 1981 commencement.

Women and the Curriculum. Most women take degrees in education; about one-fifth graduate in business and 1 percent in nontraditional areas of study. There are no courses on women.

Women and Athletics. Ten percent of athletic scholarships are awarded to women, who are 21 percent of the intercollegiate athletes. Thirty-four percent of the students who compete in intramural sports are women. Intercollegiate basketball, softball, and volleyball are open to women.

Housing and Student Organizations. Single-sex dormitories are available for the 60 percent of undergraduates who live on campus. Visitors of the opposite sex are not admitted. A married woman student whose husband is not enrolled is permitted to live in married students' housing.

Fourteen percent of the full-time undergraduate women belong to sororities. Twenty-five minority women belong to all-minority sororities.

Special Services and Programs for Women. *Health and Counseling.* A student health service, staffed by one male physician and a female health-care provider, is located on campus, but provides no services specific to women. The counseling service, staffed by a woman and a man, likewise offers no services specific to women.

Safety and Security. Campus and local police patrol the campus, which has high-intensity lighting. One assault against a woman was reported for 1980–81.

Institutional Self-Description. ''Athletics are exceptional here for women interested in sports. Campus organizations concerning university policy, such as S.G.A., are other successful opportunities in which women may participate. These opportunities, along with participation in fraternal organizations, create a good environment for all women.''

Spring Hill College
Mobile, AL 36608
Telephone: (205) 460-2121

Women in Leadership
- ★★ students
- ★ faculty
- ★★ administrators

841 undergraduates

	Amer. Ind.	Asian Amer.	Blacks	Hispanics	Whites
F	0	1	10	2	360
M	0	0	11	14	433
%	0.0	0.1	2.5	1.9	95.4

 AAUW

Spring Hill is a four-year, Roman Catholic, liberal arts college run by the Jesuits. Founded in 1830 as a men's school, it became coeducational in 1952. The wooded campus, located in a white residential area six miles from downtown Mobile, serves 375 female and 466 male full- and part-time students. The median age of all students is 19. Seventy-four percent of students live on campus, and there is free parking for commuters.

Private childcare facilities are available off campus.

Policies to Ensure Fairness to Women. The Director of Institutional Planning reviews policies and practices relating to equal opportunity laws. There is no written policy prohibiting sexual harassment, and an informal mechanism resolves complaints.

Women in Leadership Positions. *Students.* Women students have often exercised campus leadership. In three recent years, 38 percent of the leadership positions have been held by women, including president of the student body once and editor-in-chief

of the campus newspaper three times. Two of the five honorary societies are headed by women.

Faculty. Thirty-one percent of the 48 full-time faculty are women, higher than the national average. There are 4 female faculty for every 100 female students and 7 male faculty for every 100 male students.

Administrators. Women hold the positions of Executive Vice President, director of Institutional Research, chief planning officer, and head librarian. Three of 15 department chairs are women: teacher education, psychology, and communication arts. A woman heads the division of the social sciences.

Women and the Curriculum. Seven percent of degrees awarded to women are in the nontraditional fields of mathematics and physical sciences, although the most popular fields are psychology (16 percent), education (14 percent), and business (14 percent). No courses on women are offered. Faculty workshops are available on relationships among sex, race, and the selection of a major field.

Women and Athletics. For a college of its size, the intramural sports program is good. One-third of athletic scholarships go to women. Twenty-nine percent of intercollegiate athletes are women. The intercollegiate sports offered are basketball and tennis.

Housing and Student Organizations. Over 70 percent of women students live in single-sex residence halls, which have restrictive hours for male visitors. Residence-hall staff receive awareness-training about sex education, birth control, and rape crisis.

The sororities have a total of 88 members, all white, about a quarter of the full-time women students. Other women's organizations include the Spring Hill Women's Association, Alpha Lambda Tau (''to promote honor and academic excellence among women''), and Gavel, a service and fellowship organization.

Special Services and Programs for Women. *Health and Counseling.* The student health service has one male physician available on call and does not provide treatment on problems specific to women. The counseling center employs two men and one woman and offers counseling for rape and assault.

Safety and Security. Measures include local and campus police, information sessions on campus safety, and a night-time escort service for women. No rapes or assaults on women were reported for 1980–81.

Returning Women Students. The adult education program, entitled the Lifelong Learning Division, includes 34 black and 22 white women aged 25 to 40, and 31 black and 24 white women over age 40, almost all of whom attend part-time. The college provides faculty workshops on the needs of reentry women.

Institutional Self-Description. ''Spring Hill College believes in providing opportunities for women to develop self-realization and self-reliance. There are many role models here: women have high profiles in administration (a vice president, admissions director, and two assistants); in the faculty (counselors, department chairwomen). More of our business graduates this year were women than men. Senior seminar programs provide opportunities for women to design courses relating specifically to women.''

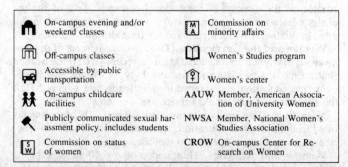

Icon	Description	Icon	Description
	On-campus evening and/or weekend classes	MA	Commission on minority affairs
	Off-campus classes		Women's Studies program
	Accessible by public transportation		Women's center
	On-campus childcare facilities	AAUW	Member, American Association of University Women
	Publicly communicated sexual harassment policy, includes students	NWSA	Member, National Women's Studies Association
SW	Commission on status of women	CROW	On-campus Center for Research on Women

Tuskegee Institute
Tuskegee, AL 36088
Telephone: (205) 727-8011

Women in Leadership
- ★ **faculty**
- ★ **administrators**

2,936 undergraduates

	Amer. Ind.	Asian Amer.	Blacks	Hispanics	Whites
F	0	12	1,471	7	7
M	0	47	1,128	25	6
%	0.0	2.2	96.2	1.2	0.5

 AAUW

Tuskegee Institute's campus is located in a rural setting one hour from the city of Montgomery. Established as a preparatory school for black teachers, Tuskegee Institute's services now range from basic continuing education programs through master's level instruction, with an emphasis on career-oriented undergraduate professional training. Summer session classes are available.

The Institute has a total enrollment of 3,298 students, of whom 2,936 are undergraduates. Fifty-three percent of the undergraduates are women; 2 percent of women attend part-time. The median age of undergraduates is 20. Free on-campus parking is available to the 46 percent of students who commute.

Private childcare facilities are located near the campus.

Policies to Ensure Fairness to Women. The Affirmative Action Officer serves part-time as a compliance administrator with no policymaking responsibility. Campus policy and procedures on sexual harassment are communicated in writing to students, faculty, and staff; complaints are resolved through a formal campus grievance procedure.

Women in Leadership Positions. *Students.* Women have some opportunities for leadership experience. In three recent years, women served once as president of the student body and president of the senior class, twice as editor-in-chief of the campus newspaper, and three times as presiding officer of the student union board. Women head eight of 14 campus honorary societies.

Faculty. Thirty-four percent of the full-time faculty of 269 are women, a proportion far above the national average. There are 6 female faculty for every 100 female students and 13 male faculty for every 100 male students. Recent data indicate that the 113 full-time female faculty include 97 black and 16 white women.

Administrators. The chief development officer and head librarian are black women; men hold the other administrative positions on campus. Black women chair the departments of art, political science, home economics and food administration, counseling, psychology and student development, and vocational and adult education. The Dean of Nursing is a black woman. Nineteen of the 43-member faculty senate are women, one a white woman, the others black women. Three of 24 trustees are women, all of them black. Of 4 recent honorary degree recipients, 1 was a black woman, as was 1 of 3 alumni award recipients.

Women and the Curriculum. The health professions (16 percent) and education (21 percent) are the most popular areas of study for women. A higher proportion of women earn degrees in business than in similar institutions nationwide. A significant number (12 percent) of Tuskegee's women graduates earn degrees in such nontraditional areas as agriculture, architecture, engineering, and mathematics. Such areas as accounting, computer science, and veterinary medicine also enroll significant numbers of women. Tuskegee attributes the high enrollments in nontraditional areas for black women to "an informal guidance system that operates among the faculty, which promotes women students'

aspirations, encourages their entry, and supports their progress."

Thirty percent of students in cooperative education programs are women, as are 40 percent of students in pre-college summer engineering programs and 35 percent of students in the summer veterinary medicine program. Fifty percent of the undergraduates holding "Reach-Out" apprenticeships in biomedical research are women.

There are no courses on women. Courses in the departments of business, nursing, physical education, and social work provide instruction on some matters specific to women. The Humanities Learning Resources Center, funded by the National Endowment for the Humanities, contains an extensive collection of books and other materials (films, slides) on the role of women in the arts and literature.

Women and Athletics. Tuskegee offers a wide variety of intramural sports. Thirty-seven percent of intramural and 33 percent of intercollegiate athletes are women, as are three of ten paid intercollegiate sports coaches. Women receive 20 percent of athletic scholarship aid. The intercollegiate sports offered are basketball, softball, tennis, track and volleyball.

Housing and Student Organizations. Tuskegee Institute provides single-sex dormitories, as well as housing for married students, for the 54 percent of students who live on campus. Restrictive hours are in effect for visitors of the opposite sex in all dormitories. A married student whose husband is not enrolled may live with her husband in married students' housing. Ten of the 14 residence-hall directors are women. Residence-hall staff receive awareness-training on sexism, sex education, and birth control.

Twelve percent of full-time female undergraduates belong to social sororities. Neither sororities or fraternities provide housing for members.

Special Services and Programs for Women. *Health and Counseling.* The student health service has 2 male physicians and 1 woman health-care provider. The student counseling center is staffed by 8 people, 5 of them minority women. In addition to general medical/surgical care, such services specific to women as treatment and counseling in gynecology, birth control, abortion, and rape and assault are available.

Safety and Security. Measures consist of campus police with weapons training, high-intensity lighting in all areas, a highly conspicuous campus-wide emergency telephone system, and information sessions on campus safety and rape and assault prevention for women. Out of 22 total assaults reported for 1980–81, six involved women; there was one rape.

Career. Services include workshops focused on nontraditional occupations, and lectures and panels for students by women employed in these fields. Nonsexist/nonracist printed information on nontraditional fields of study for women, job discrimination information, and programs to establish contacts and networks between alumnae and female students are also available.

Other. The Human Resources Development Center is responsible for operating an adult continuing education program. Some 340 reentry women, 98 percent of them black women, are enrolled in these courses. The Comprehensive Counseling Center (CCC) offers a program for battered women and assertiveness/ leadership training for women. The CCC also provides support to handicapped women and rape and assault victims.

Institutional Self-Description. "Tuskegee Institute, a national and international resource institution, provides educational services through master's level instruction, with special attention to career-oriented undergraduate professional training. A caring academic environment that encourages the fullest development of the individual produces high numbers of women majoring in science, engineering, agriculture, computer science, mathematics, architecture, and veterinary medicine. Tuskegee students develop leadership qualities and build satisfying personal lives as well as successful careers."

University of Alabama
University, AL 35486
Telephone: (205) 348-5666

★ **Women and the Curriculum**

★★ **Women and Athletics**

13,130 undergraduates

	Amer. Ind.	Asian Amer.	Blacks	Hispanics	Whites
F	0	0	872	46	5,315
M	0	0	540	63	6,180
%	0.0	0.0	10.9	0.9	88.3

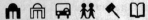

Founded in 1831 for the purposes of teaching, research, and service, the University of Alabama in Tuscaloosa is a state-supported school with a total student population of around 16,900, of whom 13,130 are undergraduates. Forty-eight percent of the undergraduates are women; 9 percent of women attend part-time. The median age of undergraduates is 22.

The university provides a range of undergraduate, graduate, and professional programs. The division of continuing education and the External Degree Program serve the needs of the adult continuing education student. Alternative schedules, which include weekend college, self-paced learning formats, and off-campus locations, are available.

Seventy-six percent of undergraduates live off campus or commute. The campus is accessible by public transportation. Parking on campus is free, with shuttle service to classroom buildings and residence halls.

The four campus childcare centers accommodate 150 children. Private childcare facilities are available close to the university.

Policies to Ensure Fairness to Women. Administrative personnel share responsibility for affirmative action. The university compliance officer and assistant handle policy related to equal employment opportunity, sex equity for students, and handicapped accessibility. A published policy prohibits sexual harassment. Complaints are handled both informally and through a formal grievance procedure.

Women in Leadership Positions. *Students.* Opportunities for women students to exercise campus-wide leadership are considerably below the average for public research institutions in this guide. In recent years the sole position held by a woman was presiding officer of the student union board.

Faculty. Women are 24 percent of faculty. Among part-and full-time faculty are 10 black, 1 Hispanic, and 3 Asian American women. The ratio of full-time female faculty to full-time female students is 3 to 100; for males, the ratio is 8 to 100.

Administrators. The director of institutional research is a woman. The other high administrative posts are filled by men. Women chair the departments of English; clothing; textiles; interior design; and food, nutrition, and institutional management. The Dean of Home Economics and the Dean of Nursing are female.

Women and the Curriculum. The majority of women graduate with majors in education (21 percent), business (14 percent), communications (11 percent), and home economics (10 percent). Four percent major in such nontraditional areas as computer science, engineering, mathematics, and the physical sciences. The university reports that women make up 30 percent of students in programs that combine academic with related work experience, 50 percent in internships and practicums.

The Women's Studies Program, under a director who is a full-time faculty member, offers a 21-credit minor for undergraduates and a graduate minor through American Studies. Among recent courses available through the College of Arts and Sciences are Introduction to Women's Studies, Culture of Southern Black Women, Women in the Visual Arts, Women in Contemporary Society, and Mothers and Daughters.

Such issues as mathematics confidence among females, sex-fair curricular materials, services for abused spouses, and discrimination in the workplace are part of the instruction in the preparation of teachers, social workers, and business students. Faculty are offered workshops in affirmative action and equal opportunity.

Minority Women. Black women are 14 percent of undergraduate women, Hispanic women less than 1 percent. Approximately 8 percent of the reentry students in the continuing education and external degree programs are black women. The African-American Student Association is active on campus. The university reports a concern for black culture that includes the Archive of American Minority Cultures and its collection of such resource materials on women as audio-visual tapes and oral histories, as well as the federally sponsored project to develop curriculum in the culture of southern black women.

Women and Athletics. Intramural and intercollegiate programs provide women with excellent opportunities for organized, competitive individual and team sports. Thirty-four percent of intramural and 53 percent of intercollegiate athletes are women. Women receive half of the athletic scholarships. Women are a third of participants in club sports. Only 14 percent of coaches are assigned to women's sports, and 7 of the 50 paid coaches are women. All teams, including gymnastics, played tournament competition in 1980. The intercollegiate sports offered are basketball, cross-country, golf, gymnastics, swimming and diving, tennis, track and field, volleyball.

Housing and Student Organizations. Twenty-four percent of students live on campus. Residential accommodations include single-sex and coeducational dormitories and housing for married students and single parents. A married woman whose spouse is not enrolled may live in married students' housing. Dormitories for men and women restrict hours for visitors of the opposite sex. Residence-hall staff are offered awareness-training on sex education, alcohol abuse, and racism.

Sororities and fraternities provide housing for their members. Among student organizations which serve as advocates for women on campus are the Anderson Society, Phi Chi Theta, and the Women's A Club.

Special Services and Programs for Women. *Health and Counseling.* The student health service provides some medical attention specific to women, including gynecological, birth control, and rape and assault treatment. Half of the 6 physicians are female, as are 37 of the other 40 health-care providers. The 3 counselors in the counseling service include a minority woman and a white woman. Gynecological, birth control, and rape trauma counseling are available.

Safety and Security. Measures include campus and local police, night-time escort and shuttle service, emergency alarm and telephone systems, self-defense courses for women, and a rape crisis center. Sixteen assaults (5 on women) and no rapes were reported for 1980–81.

Returning Women Students. The External Degree Program, under a full-time female administrator, enrolls 75 women. About 10,000 women are involved in credit and noncredit courses offered through the Division of Continuing Education.

Special Features. In addition to the collection of women's resource materials in the Archive of American Minority Cultures, the Women's Studies Program has begun to compile books, journals, slides, and tapes of oral interviews on women artists, both national and regional.

Institutional Self-Description. "Our institution has a keen sense of contemporary regional consciousness, with special focus on rural and black cultures. The environment is semi-urban with space, land, trees, and easy access to rural, open areas. With only 17,000 students, we have kept the best aspects of a small school. Grant successes keep things moving and changing."

University of North Alabama

Florence, AL 35632
Telephone: (205) 766-4100

Women in Leadership
★ faculty

4,185 undergraduates

	Amer. Ind.	Asian Amer.	Blacks	Hispanics	Whites
F	2	4	216	0	2,011
M	0	2	147	4	1,785
%	0.1	0.1	8.7	0.1	91.0

 NWSA

Founded in 1872 as a teachers' preparatory school, North Alabama has now expanded its program to include many bachelor's and master's degrees and pre-professional programs. Ninety percent of the 5,146 students are enrolled full-time. Women compose 54 percent of the 4,185 undergraduates. There is an adult continuing education program. On-campus parking is free to those students who pay a one-time registration fee.

Policies to Ensure Fairness to Women. Issues of sex equity and access for the handicapped are handled separately for employees and students by two full-time administrators, described as "Coordinators on nondiscrimination policies [who] may participate in policy formulation and review."

Although the university reports having no policy on sexual harassment, a grievance procedure for handling such complaints is in place.

Women in Leadership Positions. *Students.* Of five student positions, a woman has held one, co-editor of the campus newspaper, for a single year.

Faculty. Women account for 30 percent of the 181 full-time faculty, a proportion somewhat above the national average. They hold 28 percent of all permanent appointments. There are 3 female faculty for every 100 female students and 7 male faculty for every 100 male students.

Administrators. Women hold none of the top-level administrative positions. One of the 24 department chairs is a woman, and 1 of 4 deanships is held by a woman—the school of nursing. Women are better represented on the faculty senate (30 percent) at North Alabama than at most other four-year institutions.

Women and the Curriculum. Most women take degrees in education (30 percent) and business (22 percent); and 5 percent graduate in nontraditional fields. In a recent year six women (but no men) took degrees in architecture, and seven women (and 12 men) in mathematics.

The university reports no courses on women in the curriculum. The school of nursing provides training on health-care information important to minority women, and the school of social work provides instruction on services for battered spouses, displaced homemakers, and childcare.

Women and Athletics. Twenty percent of the athletic scholarships are awarded to women, who are 16 percent of the intercollegiate athletes. No information on intramural or club sports is available. Two of the 12 paid coaches for intercollegiate sports are women. Intercollegiate sports are basketball, tennis, and volleyball.

Housing and Student Organizations. Single-sex dormitories with restrictive hours for members of the opposite sex house about 18 percent of all undergraduates. Apartments for married students (with or without children) are also available. Fraternities provide some housing; sororities do not.

Special Services and Programs for Women. *Health and Counseling.* Four female health-care providers staff the student health service; three women and one man staff the counseling service. Neither unit offers services specific to women.

Safety and Security. Measures include campus police empowered to make arrests, local police (upon request), high-intensity lighting, and information sessions on safety and rape/assault prevention. Information on the incidence of rape and assault for 1980–81 was not provided.

Career. The university provides workshops about nontraditional occupations and lectures by women employed in such fields.

Institutional Self-Description. "With a very long history of coeducation (since 1874), the university believes it truly offers equal opportunities, and that where vestiges remain of typical male dominance, arrogance, and stereotyping, they are very much tempered by traditional Southern respect and courtesy."

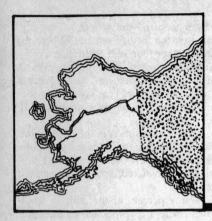

ALASKA

Kenai Peninsula Community College
Box 848, Soldotna, AK 99669
Telephone: (907) 262-5801

Women in Leadership
- ★ **faculty**
- ★★ **administrators**

1,419 undergraduates

	Amer. Ind.	Asian Amer.	Blacks	Hispanics	Whites
F	39	3	1	4	768
M	33	4	4	4	550
%	5.1	0.5	0.4	0.6	93.5

Established under a cooperative agreement between the University of Alaska and the local school district, Kenai Peninsula Community College serves 135 full-time and 1,284 part-time commuter students. The college is located on a rural campus near Anchorage. Fifty-eight percent of the students are women, most of whom attend part-time. The median age of all students is 27.

The college offers the first two years of liberal arts as well as vocational and technical programs. Evening classes on and off campus are available, as well as selfpaced/contract learning.

Private childcare facilities are available near campus.

Women in Leadership Positions. *Students.* During a recent three-year period, men have held the only leadership position, student body president.

Faculty. Five of the 20 full-time faculty are women. There are 8 female faculty for every 100 female students and 20 male faculty for every 100 male students.

Administrators. Of five top positions, women hold two—chief academia office and head of the library. Women chair three of the six departments: math/natural science, social and behavioral science/art, and office occupations; 44 percent of trustees are women.

Women and the Curriculum. About three-fourths of degrees awarded to women are in arts and sciences and the rest in business. Women are encouraged to enter such nontraditional programs as petroleum technology and forest technology. The humanities department offers a course on women in literature; the social and behavioral science department offers Psychology of Women; and the division of community services offers Money Management for Women. Affirmative action and equal opportunity have been topics of workshops offered to the faculty.

Women and Athletics. There is no opportunity for structured competitive sports.

Special Services and Programs for Women. *Health and Counseling.* There is no student health service. The counseling center is staffed by one man and one woman.

Safety and Security. There were no assaults reported on campus for 1980–81. There is a community-based rape crisis center.

Institutional Self-Description. "The Petroleum Technology programs and Forest Technology programs lead to exceptionally well paying jobs. More and more women are entering these training programs."

Sheldon Jackson College
Box 479, Sitka, AK 99835
Telephone: (907) 747-5220

Women in Leadership
- ★ **faculty**
- ★ **students**

297 undergraduates

	Amer. Ind.	Asian Amer.	Blacks	Hispanics	Whites
F	104	0	0	1	69
M	63	0	0	0	57
%	56.8	0.0	0.0	0.3	42.9

Sheldon Jackson, the oldest educational institution in Alaska, is a private, four-year college affiliated with the United Presbyterian Church. Located in a small city about 100 miles from Juneau, the college has a special interest in serving the needs of native Alaskans. In 1878 it was founded as a two-year training school for Tlingit Indians. Now it offers associate and bachelor's degrees to its 297 students. Sixty percent of the students are women, and over half the women attend part-time. Ninety-three percent of the students reside on campus; there is free on-campus parking for commuters.

Childcare facilities are available off campus.

Women in Leadership Positions. *Students.* The only campus-wide leadership post, president of the student body, was held by a woman once during the past three years.

Faculty. Three of the 11 full-time faculty are women.

Administrators. One of the seven chief administrative positions is held by a black woman—the head librarian. The directors of Cooperative Education and the Learning Center are white women.

Women and the Curriculum. In 1980–81, 7 bachelor's degrees were awarded in education, 4 of them to women; 14 women and 5 men received associate degrees in public-service technologies, and 2 women and 2 men earned degrees in natural-science technologies. Sixty-one percent of the students participating in the Cooperative Education program are women.

Women and Athletics. No intercollegiate or club sports are offered. Intramural sports are limited to basketball and volleyball.

Housing and Student Organizations. Single-sex and coeducational residences are available; all have restrictive hours for visitors of the opposite sex. Housing is also available for married students with and without children and single parents with children.

Special Services and Programs for Women. None were reported.

Institutional Self-Description. "Sheldon Jackson College provides a learning environment that is culturally sensitive. It is especially sensitive to minority needs. Its career counseling program is especially relevant for women. Housing accommodations for single parents also serve women returning to college."

University of Alaska, Fairbanks
Fairbanks, AK 99701
Telephone: (907) 479-7821

2,089 undergraduates

	Amer. Ind.	Asian Amer.	Blacks	Hispanics	Whites
F	152	11	22	4	747
M	102	26	26	6	978
%	12.3	1.8	2.3	0.5	83.2

 AAUW

Established in 1917 as an agricultural and mining college for the Alaskan Territory, the University of Alaska, now enrolls some 4,300 students in a variety of undergraduate, graduate, and professional programs. Adult education and extension units provide credit and noncredit studies for nontraditional students. Alternative class schedules, off-campus locations, and a summer session are available.

Women are 45 percent of the 2,089 undergraduates; 29 percent of women attend part-time. The median age of all students is 26. For the 60 percent of students who commute, the university is accessible by public transportation. On-campus parking is provided for a fee, with free transportation from distant parking lots.

Private childcare arrangements may be made close to campus.

Policies to Ensure Fairness to Women. A full-time affirmative action officer reviews policies and practices related to equal employment opportunities. A formal campus grievance procedure resolves complaints of sexual harassment.

Women in Leadership Positions. *Students.* Opportunities for women students to exercise leadership are slightly below average. In recent years women have presided over the student court and the residence-hall council, managed the campus radio, and been editor-in-chief of the newspaper.

Faculty. Over 20 percent of the full-time faculty are female, including 1 Hispanic, 2 Asian American, and 3 American Indian women. There are 6 female faculty for every 100 female students and 18 male faculty for every 100 male students.

Administrators. Men hold all the higher administrative posts. Women chair four of 38 departments, including humanities, and anthropology. The College of Arts and Sciences and the Institute of Marine Science are headed by women.

Women and the Curriculum. More women graduate with bachelor's degrees in education, social science, and business than in other fields. Twelve percent graduate in such nontraditional fields as agriculture, engineering, and the physical sciences. Women hold 40 percent of the science field-service positions in experiential learning programs.

There are no courses on women. Consideration of such current issues as services for battered spouses, displaced homemakers, and childcare is part of the instruction of social-work students.

Minority Women. Sixteen percent of undergraduate women are American Indian, 2 percent black, 1 percent Asian American, and less than 1 percent Hispanic. One-fifth of women taking continuing education courses are members of minorities, with Amer-

ican Indian women forming the largest group. One residence-hall director is a minority woman.

Women and Athletics. Intramural and intercollegiate programs provide opportunities for women to engage in organized competitive sports. Riflery is available on both an intramural and an intercollegiate basis. Women receive 30 percent of athletic scholarships. The intercollegiate sports offered are basketball, field hockey, riflery, volleyball.

Housing and Student Organizations. Forty percent of the undergraduates live on campus. Residential accommodations include single-sex and coeducational dormitories, and housing for married students. A married woman student whose husband is not an enrolled student may live in married students' housing. Seven of 12 residence-hall directors are women.

Special Services and Programs for Women. *Health and Counseling.* Medical attention specific to women provided by the student health service includes gynecological, birth control, abortion, and rape and assault treatment. The health service physician is female, as are three other health-care providers. Birth control, abortion, and rape and assault counseling is available. Counselors receive in-service training on avoidance of sex-role stereotyping.

Safety and Security. Measures consist of police without arrest authority, a night-time escort service for women students, night-time bus service to residential areas, and an emergency telephone system. A rape crisis center is available. One assault on a woman and no rapes were reported for 1980–81.

Institutional Self-Description. None provided.

University of Alaska, Juneau
11120 Glacier Highway,
Juneau, AK 99801
Telephone: (907) 789-2101

Women in Leadership
★ faculty

140 undergraduates

	Amer. Ind.	Asian Amer.	Blacks	Hispanics	Whites
F	7	1	1	1	72
M	3	1	3	0	51
%	7.1	1.4	2.9	0.7	87.9

The University of Alaska, Juneau occupies ten acres on the shores of Lake Auke and Auke Bay, in an area populated by Eskimos and Asian Americans. This very small university (total students: 564) offers associate and bachelor's degrees; master's programs can be arranged in business, education, and agriculture (biology and fisheries). Almost all students commute, either by car (parking is available on campus) or public transportation. Of the 140 undergraduates, 59 percent are women, and, like men, most are part-time. According to recent information, 59 percent of women are 25-40 years old and 24 percent are over 40; the median age of undergraduates is 32. An adult continuing education program is available, as well as off-campus day and evening classes.

Private childcare facilities are available near campus.

Policies to Ensure Fairness to Women. A woman administrator has part-time responsibility for developing policies and monitoring practices relating to equal employment opportunity, sex equity for students, and handicapped access. Although there is no policy on sexual harassment, a formal grievance procedure is used to resolve complaints.

Women in Leadership Positions. *Students.* The only student leadership position, president of the student body, was held by a woman once in a recent three-year period.

Faculty. One-quarter of the 47 full-time faculty members are women, but both permanently appointed faculty are men. Recent data record one Asian American woman on the full-time faculty.

Administrators. No woman holds a top-level administrative position. Two of the six departments (business and continuing education and public service) are chaired by women. An American Indian woman was awarded one of the two honorary degrees at the spring 1981 commencement.

Women and the Curriculum. All degrees awarded to women are in education. Three undergraduate courses on women are offered: Preparing Women for Management; Women: Sex and Identity; and Women in the Economy.

Women and Athletics. There is no sports program.

Housing and Student Organizations. Two old homes have been remodelled to accommodate unmarried students who need to live on campus. The residence-hall director is a man.

Special Services and Programs for Women. *Health and Counseling.* There is no health service. The minority woman who constitutes the counseling center staff provides counseling on matters specific to women.

Safety and Security. No services or facilities are provided. No rapes or assaults were reported for 1980–81.

Career. Information is available about nontraditional careers for women and about job discrimination.

Institutional Self-Description. "UAJ's small classes provide for individual attention to women students. The college is located in a beautiful, peaceful environment conducive to study and introspection. The local community offers a variety of services for women and a wide selection of cultural activities."

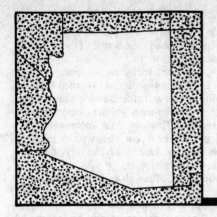

ARIZONA

Arizona State University
Tempe, AZ 85287
Telephone: (602) 965-9000

★★ Women and the Curriculum

★ Women and Athletics

25,901 undergraduates

	Amer. Ind.	Asian Amer.	Blacks	Hispanics	Whites
F	172	1361	307	540	10,485
M	119	157	371	716	12,537
%	1.1	1.2	2.7	5.0	90.1

🏠 🏛 🚌 🔦 ⛹ 📖 ⚧ AAUW NWSA

Established in 1885 and located in the culturally diverse city of Tempe, Arizona State University is a state-supported institution that serves some 37,000 students, including 25,901 undergraduates. Forty-five percent of undergraduates are women; 18 percent of women attend part-time. The median age of undergraduates is 22. The university provides a variety of undergraduate, graduate, and professional programs. A division of continuing education serves the needs of the adult student. Recent information indicates that about 5,000 women over age 25 enroll part-time, and that a quarter of these women are over age 40. Alternative class schedules, off-campus locations, and a summer session are available.

Eighty-nine percent of undergraduates commute or live off campus. Public transportation is reportedly sparse, but the fee for on-campus parking is reasonable, and there is free transportation from distant parking lots.

Private arrangements for childcare may be made close by.

Policies to Ensure Fairness to Women. A full-time director of affirmative action and two full-time assistants are responsible for policy on such matters as equal employment opportunity, sex equity for students, and handicapped accessibility. A published policy prohibits sexual harassment. Complaints are handled both informally and confidentially and through a formal grievance procedure. The Committee on the Status of Women makes recommendations to the university president and hears grievances. The Committee on Minority Affairs addresses the concerns of minority women.

Women in Leadership Positions. *Students.* In recent years women have been president of the student body, twice editor-in-chief of the newspaper, and presiding officer of the student senate.

Faculty. Twenty-one percent of a full-time faculty of 1,268 are female. According to a recent report, 5 black, 2 American Indian, 8 Asian American, and 7 Hispanic women are on the faculty. There are 3 female faculty for every 100 female students and 9 male faculty for every 100 male students.

Administrators. Men occupy all higher administrative positions.

Women chair four of 60 departments, including educational psychology, elementary education, and home economics. The Dean of the School of Nursing is a woman.

Women and the Curriculum. Women graduating with bachelor's degrees major in education (30 percent) and business (15 percent), with significant numbers in health professions, social sciences, and the fine arts. Five percent major in such nontraditional fields as agriculture, architecture, computer science, engineering, mathematics, and the physical sciences. The university reports that innovative programs to encourage women to prepare for nontraditional careers in science, engineering, agriculture, computer science, electronics, and management have been made possible by contracts and grants.

A 21-credit certificaten Women's Studies is available within several B.S. and B.A. undergraduate majors. The Women's Studies Program, coordinated by a half-time administrator who also teaches in the program offers 40 courses each year through Women's Studies and academic departments. An official committee advocates the teaching of women's materials and perspectives across the curriculum and monitors accessibility of curriculum and activities to women students.

Such issues as sex-role stereotyping in sports and curriculum, mathematics confidence among women, innovative health-care delivery and health information important to minority women, services for abused spouses, and workplace discrimination are part of the instruction offered in the preparation of teachers, health-care workers, social workers, and business students.

Minority Women. Among undergraduate women, 3 percent are black, over 1 percent American Indian, 1 percent Asian American, and 5 percent Hispanic. There are 50 women in all-minority sororities. Such student organizations as the Student Alliance of Black Social Workers and Feminists United for Action meet on campus. Minority women would also find support from MECHA, the Black Student Union, the Native American Association, and Oriental Clubs. Awareness training on racism is offered to residence-hall staff.

Women and Athletics. Intramural and intercollegiate programs offer good opportunities for organized, competitive individual and team sports. Club sports are also available. The university reports special fields for flag football and softball.

Twenty-six percent of intramural and 35 percent of intercollegiate athletes are women; athletic scholarships are awarded. Seven of the 19 paid coaches in intercollegiate sports are women. Two teams, archery and badminton, are coeducational, and most played tournament competition during 1980. The intercollegiate sports offered are archery, badminton, basketball, golf, gymnastics, softball, swimming and diving, track and field, tennis, volleyball.

Housing and Student Organizations. Twelve percent of undergraduates live on campus in single-sex and coeducational dormitories. Men's and women's dormitories restrict visiting hours for members of the opposite sex. Three of seven residence-hall directors are female; awareness training is offered residence-hall staff on such issues as sexism, birth control, stress management, and depression.

Approximately 12 percent of full-time undergraduate women are members of social sororities, which provide housing for their members. Such student organizations as Patrol Against Sexual Assault, Arizona Right to Choose, the Older Students Club, and the Gay Academic Union serve women on campus, in addition to the organizations mentioned above.

Special Services and Programs for Women. *Health and Counseling.* The student health service provides some medical attention specific to women, including gynecological and birth control treatment. The regular student health insurance policy covers abortion. One of 8 physicians is female, as are 20 other health-care providers. Four of 7 professional staff in the counseling center are women. Gynecological, birth control, and rape/assault counseling are available.

Safety and Security. Measures include campus police with arrest authority, night-time escort service for women, emergency alarm and telephone systems, self-defense courses for women, and sessions on safety and crime prevention. A rape crisis center is available. No rapes or assaults on women were reported in 1980–81.

Career. Job discrimination information, career workshops, and lectures featuring women employed in nontraditional occupations are among materials and activities available through Career Services.

Other. A Women's Center is attached to the Women's Studies Program. Organizations sensitive to the needs of older women and handicapped women include AWARE and Disabled Student Services.

Special Features. The school of education faculty are associated with the *Journal of Educational Equity and Leadership,* which focuses on research on white women and members of minority groups of both sexes.

Institutional Self-Description. "ASU offers a wide range of support services for women; the comprehensive Women's Studies offerings of an interdisciplinary nature are a very positive and integral part of the curriculum. The Faculty Women's Association has provided excellent leadership for female faculty. ASU received an American Association of University Women award in 1979 for assisting the academic women to achieve equity."

Prescott College
220 Grove Ave., Prescott, AZ 86301
Telephone: (602) 778-2090

67 undergraduates

	Amer. Ind.	Asian Amer.	Blacks	Hispanics	Whites
F	0	0	0	0	38
M	0	0	0	1	28
%	0.0	0.0	0.0	1.5	98.5

Prescott is an experimental, private college in the mountain town of Prescott. It stresses experiential and student-directed learning, physical endurance, and outdoor activities. Its one-building campus, located north of Phoenix, attracts 72 students, 67 of whom are undergraduates. Fifty-seven percent of the students are women, and 13 percent of women attend part-time. The median age of all undergraduates is 22. Prescott offers four-year degrees in a variety of traditional areas. There is also an adult degree program. The students, all of whom commute, design their own academic programs. There is free parking on campus.

Local, private childcare facilities serve the needs of students who are parents.

Women in Leadership Positions. *Students.* There are no campus-wide student leadership positions.

Faculty. Two of the ten full-time faculty are women.

Administrators. Men hold most key positions. Women hold the positions of chief student-life officer and chief development officer. A woman chairs one of five departments—human development. Among the 22-member Board of Trustees, four are women.

Women and the Curriculum. In a recent year, women received 12 of the 16 degrees granted; they were in psychology, biology, education, social sciences, and letters.

No courses on women are given, although some students design independent courses in the area of Women's Studies. All programs offer students opportunities in experiential learning.

Women and Athletics. There is no opportunity for organized competitive sports, but all students participate to some extent in an Outdoor Action Program that offers rock-climbing, white-water rafting, kayaking, cross-country skiing, winter mountaineering, and backpacking.

Special Services and Programs for Women. *Health and Counseling.* There are no health or counseling services.

Safety and Security. Local police provide protection. No rapes or assaults on women were reported for 1980–81.

Institutional Self-Description. "Prescott College offers an alternative to traditional forms of education. A woman might choose to study here because of the unique philosophy of the college, because of the emphasis the college places on incorporating physical stress and challenge into every student's academic program, because of the responsibility the college expects each student to take for the design of her/his own course of study, because the college encourages every student to grow personally as well as academically, because such a program and process exists nowhere else."

University of Arizona
Tucson, AZ 85721
Telephone: (602)626-0111

★★★ Women and the Curriculum

★★ Women and Athletics

18,455 undergraduates

	Amer. Ind.	Asian Amer.	Blacks	Hispanics	Whites
F	59	70	99	330	7,679
M	59	83	122	440	8,939
%	0.7	0.9	1.2	4.3	93.0

 AAUW NWSA CROW

Established in 1885 as a land-grant college, the University of Arizona, located in a bicultural city of 500,000, enrolls some 26,900 students in a diversity of undergraduate, graduate, and professional programs. The division of continuing education serves the adult student. Alternative class schedules, which include self-paced learning contracts, off-campus locations, and a summer session, are available. The Traveling Scholars Program permits enrollment in classes at Arizona State University and Northern Arizona University.

Women are 45 percent of the 18,455 undergraduates; 14 percent of the women attend part-time. The median age of all students is 22. Seventy-two percent of undergraduates live off campus or commute. The university is accessible through public transportation, and on-campus parking is available.

University-run childcare facilities accommodate 27 children, on a first-come, first-served basis. Private facilities are located near campus.

Policies to Ensure Fairness to Women. Responsibility for such matters as equal employment opportunity, sex equity for students, and handicapped access resides with two full-time officers. Complaints of sexual harassment are handled both informally and confidentially and through a formal grievance procedure. The ad hoc Committee on the Status of Women, which includes students as voting members, takes public stands on issues of concern to students and advises other interested groups.

Women in Leadership Positions. *Students.* Opportunities for women students to exercise campus-wide leadership are below average for public research universities in this guide. In recent years women have headed the student senate and been editor-in-chief of the campus newspaper.

Faculty. Women are 17 percent of a full-time faculty of 1,382. According to recent information, 3 black, 5 American Indian, 4 Asian American, and 6 Hispanic women are on the faculty. The ratio of female faculty to female students is 3 to 100; for males, it is 13 to 100.

Administrators. Men fill all higher administrative posts. The Dean of the College of Nursing is female.

Women and the Curriculum. Most degrees earned by women are in the fields of education (26 percent), the health professions (10 percent), social sciences (10 percent), and business and management (8 percent). Eleven percent are in such nontraditional majors as agriculture, architecture, computer science, engineering, mathematics, and the physical sciences. Innovative programs to encourage women to prepare for careers in science, engineering, and architecture are available. Women in Science and Engineering sponsors a program to build confidence in mathematics. Opportunities for Women, a university continuing-education program, and other units provide activities, information, and support for women in nontraditional careers.

Under the leadership of a full-time director, the Women's Studies Program spearheads a variety of activities across the campus and in the community. The program offers a 21-credit minor and a graduate minor through the English department. Some 40 individual undergraduate or graduate courses on women are available annually. They are offered through the departments of history, sociology, English, home economics, oriental studies, nursing, political science, management, romance languages, anthropology, education, guidance and counseling, as well as through Women's Studies. A three-year federal grant aims to introduce the new scholarship on women into many of the introductory and basic courses in the social sciences and humanities.

Under a grant from the Ford Foundation, and with more than $1 million in federal and other grants, the Women's Studies Program has established the Southwest Institute for Research on Women (SIROW) to serve as a regional resource. The Women's Studies Program and SIROW also sponsor professional development and training in the community—especially to school teachers—through the Institute for Equality in Education.

The Women's Studies Committee sponsors pre-service training for future teachers on mathematics confidence among women and sex-fair curricula in the schools. The school of nursing provides instruction on innovative health-care delivery and health-care information of special concern to minority women. Such issues as discrimination in the workplace and sexual harassment are part of the curriculum in the school of business.

Women and Athletics. Intramural and intercollegiate programs offer a wide variety of organized, competitive individual and team sports. Twenty-five percent of intramural and 33 percent of intercollegiate athletes are women; women receive an impressive 40 percent of athletic scholarships. Women's intercollegiate teams played tournament competition in 1980. The intercollegiate sports offered are basketball, cross-country, field hockey, golf, gymnastics, softball, swimming and diving, synchronized swimming, tennis, track and field, and volleyball.

Housing and Student Organizations. Twenty-eight percent of undergraduates live on campus. Single-sex and coeducational dormitories and housing for married students and single parents with children are available. A married woman student whose spouse is not enrolled may live in married students' housing. Residence halls restrict hours for visitors of the opposite sex. Staff are offered awareness training on birth control and alcoholism.

Seventeen percent of undergraduate women belong to sororities. Fifty-four minority women belong to racially integrated and 20 to all-minority sororities. Sororities and fraternities provide housing for their members.

Special Services and Programs for Women. *Health and Counseling.* The student health service provides some medical attention specific to women, including gynecological, birth control, and rape and assault treatment. Three of 11 physicians are female, as are 12 other health-care providers. Three of 5 professional staff in the counseling center are female. Gynecological, birth control, abortion, and rape and assault counseling are available. Staff receive in-service training on the avoidance of sex-role stereotyping.

Safety and Security. Measures consist of campus police with arrest authority, night-time escort service for women students, self-defense courses for women, information sessions on safety and crime prevention, and a rape crisis center. Six assaults on women and three rapes were reported for 1980–81.

Other. The Associated Students of the University of Arizona houses a Women's Center staffed part-time by a student. Sponsored activities include an annual women's week and theater and other arts programs.

Returning Women Students. Opportunities for Women is a program for returning women students within the division of continuing education. Career-placement services include a special program to assist reentry women who hold degrees. Assertiveness training, lecture series, and a telephone line of information, referral, and support are among the program's services. A displaced homemaker program is associated with Opportunities for Women.

Institutional Self-Description. "Tucson and the University of Arizona support a sophisticated network of services, programs, and opportunities for women. On campus, the Women's Studies Program and the returning students program, Opportunities for Women, are strong and receive the support of administrators, faculty, and students. An active and effective Tucson Women's Commission provides a wide range of community programs."

University of Phoenix
1427 N. Third Street
Phoenix, AZ 85004
Telephone: (602) 258-3666

Enrollment Data Not Available.

The University of Phoenix is a private, four-year, coeducational institution that serves students "whose access to higher education may be restricted or non-existent." Bachelor's degree programs include business administration and health-services administration. All students attend full-time, and their median age is 36. Evening classes are offered.

Policies to Ensure Fairness to Women. The Vice-President for Administration and Personnel serves as part-time equal-opportunity officer. A formal grievance procedure resolves complaints of sexual harassment.

Women in Leadership Positions. The university reports that there are no student leadership positions.

Faculty. The 7 full-time faculty are men. According to recent data, 26 percent of the 173 part-time faculty are women.

Administrators. Men hold all top positions, except for the chief business officer and the head librarian. Two of the 4 division managers are women, as are 2 of 10 members of the board of directors. The speaker at the 1981 commencement was a woman.

Women and the Curriculum. Information was not provided.

Women and Athletics. There is no athletics program.

Special Services and Programs for Women. *Health and Counseling.* There is no student health service and no counseling center.

Safety and Security. No information was provided.

Institutional Self-Description. None provided.

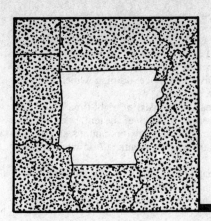

ARKANSAS

Phillips County Community College
Box 785, Helena, AR 72342
Telephone: (501) 338-6474

Women in Leadership
★★★ faculty

1,498 undergraduates

	Amer. Ind.	Asian Amer.	Blacks	Hispanics	Whites
F	25	1	359	2	437
M	31	5	211	2	425
%	3.7	0.4	38.1	0.3	57.6

Located in eastern Arkansas, within commuting distance of Memphis, Tennessee, this two-year commuter college serves 1,500 students, just over half of whom are women. Forty-seven percent of women students attend part-time. Almost half of all women students are over age 26; the median age of all students is 26.

The college offers the first two years of liberal arts as well as nursing and other two-year vocational and experiential learning programs. Women are three-fourths of those participating in co-operative education, internships, and practicums. Public transportation, free on-campus parking, and evening as well as daytime classes both on and off campus are available.

Private childcare facilities are available nearby.

Women in Leadership Positions. *Students.* Information on student leadership positions is not available.

Faculty. Women constitute half the 54 full-time faculty. According to recent data, 4 of the full-time women faculty are black. There are 6 female faculty for every 100 female students; for males, the ratio is 8 to 100.

Administrators. A woman serves as head librarian; men hold the other top administrative positions. Women chair the departments of English, fine arts, developmental skills, and nursing.

Women and the Curriculum. Of the 57 women graduating in a recent year, 25 received certificates in nursing and other health technologies; the next most popular degrees were arts and sciences and business. The business and nursing programs offer instruction on some matters specific to women. There are no courses on women.

Women and Athletics. Women have an intercollegiate basketball team, coached by a man. A small number of women also participate in a range of intramural sports, including volleyball, softball, basketball, archery, and tennis. In 1980, half of the athletic scholarship aid went to women.

Special Services and Programs for Women. *Health and Counseling.* There is no student health service. Five counselors are available at the student counseling center, including one white woman and one black woman.

Safety and Security. Campus police, with no authority to make arrests, are augmented by local police. There is high-intensity lighting in all areas. No rapes or assaults on women were reported in 1980–82.

Career. The college sponsors career workshops focused on non-traditional occupations.

Institutional Self-Description. "Phillips County Community College is pledged to the idea that all persons should have the opportunity to develop to the limits of their abilities. The Board of Trustees, administration, and faculty recognize the dignity and worth of the individual and endeavor to provide higher education to all who wish to take advantage of it."

University of Arkansas, Fayetteville
Fayetteville, AR 72701
Telephone: (501) 575-2000

Women in Leadership
★ students

11,393 undergraduates

	Amer. Ind.	Asian Amer.	Blacks	Hispanics	Whites
F	34	25	253	16	4,292
M	64	57	272	31	6,083
%	0.9	0.7	4.7	0.4	93.2

AAUW

Established in 1871 as a land-grant institution, the University of Arkansas at Fayetteville offers a variety of undergraduate, graduate, and professional studies to some 15,700 students. There is a division of adult continuing education. A summer session, correspondence courses, and off-campus classes are available.

Women are 41 percent of the 11,393 undergraduates; 7 percent of women attend part-time. The median age of undergraduates is 19. For the 53 percent of undergraduates who commute, the university is accessible by public transportation. On-campus parking is provided for a fee, but transportation from distant parking lots is free.

Campus childcare facilities can accommodate an estimated 25 percent of student requests, with single parents having the highest priority. Private childcare arrangements may be made near the campus.

Policies to Ensure Fairness to Women. One full-time and one part-time equal opportunity officer are responsible for policy on such matters as employment, sex equity for students, and handicapped accessibility. A policy on sexual harassment is being developed; complaints are currently handled informally and confidentially. There is an active Committee on the Status of Women which takes public stands on issues and includes students as voting members. The Committee on Minority Affairs addresses the concerns of minority women.

Women in Leadership Positions. *Students.* Opportunities for women students to exercise campus-wide leadership are slightly above the average for public research institutions in this guide. In recent years women have presided over the student court, headed the student union board three times, presided over the residence hall council, and been editor-in-chief of the campus newspaper.

Faculty. Women are 16 percent of a full-time faculty of 693. According to recent report, 6 black and 2 Asian American women are on the faculty. There are 2 female faculty for every 100 female students and 9 male faculty for every 100 male students.

Administrators. Men fill all higher administrative posts. Women chair 4 of 51 departments: home economics, nursing, philosophy, and secretarial studies.

Women and the Curriculum. Education is the major field for close to one-third of women earning bachelor's degrees. Ten percent earn bachelor's degrees in such nontraditional areas as agriculture, architecture, computer science, engineering, mathematics, and the physical sciences. Departmental organizations and some programming designed to encourage women students to prepare for those nontraditional careers are available. The mathematics department sponsors a program to build mathematics confidence.

Courses on women are offered by the departments of English, sociology, history, and humanities. Recent titles include Introduction to Women's Studies and Regional Women's Literature.

Such current issues as sex-role stereotyping in curriculum and sports, mathematics confidence among females, reproductive choice, health-care information of importance to minority women, services for abused spouses, and workplace discrimination are part of the instruction offered in the preparation of teachers, health-care workers, social workers, and business students.

Minority Women. Of 4,620 undergraduate women, 5 percent are black and less than 1 percent each American Indian, Asian American, and Hispanic. A minority woman is a residence hall director; two minority women are on the staff of the counseling service. Training in awareness of racism and racial bias is available to residence hall and counseling staffs.

Five minority women belong to integrated sororities. Sixty women are in all-black sororities. Black women are represented in the membership of such campus groups as the Alliance for Women's Concerns, the Northwest Arkansas Rape Crisis Center, and the Panhellenic Council.

Women and Athletics. Intramural and intercollegiate programs give women adequate opportunities for organized, competitive individual and team sports. Club sports are also available. The university reports special facilities for frisbee and golf.

Twenty-two percent of intramural and 30 percent of intercollegiate athletes are women. One-fifth of the paid coaches for intercollegiate sports are women. Women receive more than 20 percent of athletic scholarshps. All women's intercollegiate teams played tournament competition in 1980. The intercollegiate sports offered are basketball, cross-country, swimming and diving, track and field, tennis.

Housing and Student Organizations. Forty-seven percent of undergraduates live on campus in residential accommodations that include single-sex and coeducational dormitories and housing for married students, single parents with children, and disabled students. A married woman student whose spouse is not enrolled may live in married students' housing. Residence halls restrict hours for visitors of the opposite sex. Staff are offered awareness-training on such issues as sexism, sex education, and birth control.

Twenty-six percent of undergraduate women belong to social sororities, which offer housing for their members. Among advocacy groups for women are the Associated Women Students and Lifeline Pregnancy Service.

Special Services and Programs for Women. *Health and Counseling.* The student health service provides medical attention specific to women, including gynecological, birth control, rape

and assault, and follow-up abortion treatment. The chief of staff of the health service is a female, as are 14 other health-care providers. Four of 7 professional staff in the counseling center are women. Counseling specific to women's concerns is available. Staff receive comprehensive in-service training which includes avoidance of sex-role stereotyping.

Safety and Security. Measures consist of night-time escorts for women students, emergency telephone system, self-defense courses for women, information sessions on campus safety, and a rape crisis center. One rape and 18 assaults (7 on women) were reported for 1980–81.

Career. Workshops about women in nontraditional careers, lectures, and printed information on nontraditional fields of study and work are among the resources for career-planning available in the university.

Other. A Women's Center is a part of Student Services. An annual women's week, assertiveness training, and a women's film festival are among Student Services' offerings. Additional programs include a women's lecture series sponsored by the English department, and theater and other arts activities for women sponsored by the drama and music departments. The Union Information Desk operates several crisis lines for telephone information, referral, and support. A displaced homemaker program is run by the department of vocational education, and a project for victims of family violence is operated by the community.

Special Features. The Clara Trio plays music by women composers. Women artists are frequently featured in exhibits.

Institutional Self-Description. "The women's community in and around Fayetteville is extensive and diverse; any woman is likely to find others who share her interests and needs. The institution offers the most comprehensive curriculum in the state and in the surrounding area. Tuition and living expenses are reasonable."

University of Arkansas at Pine Bluff
14 North Cedar St., Pine Bluff, AR 71601
Telephone: (501) 541-6500

Women in Leadership
★★ faculty

2,927 undergraduates

	Amer. Ind.	Asian Amer.	Blacks	Hispanics	Whites
F	3	3	1,474	23	170
M	2	3	1,030	24	156
%	0.2	0.2	86.7	1.6	11.3

The University of Arkansas at Pine Bluff (formerly Arkansas Agricultural, Mechanical and Normal College), a public, four-year institution, is one of two land-grant institutions in the state and the original predominantly black institution within the University of Arkansas system. The university offers bachelor's degrees in a range of fields, including liberal arts and sciences, education, business, and agriculture. A few two-year degrees are awarded. Evening classes are held both on and off campus and there is a summer session.

Some 3,000 students are enrolled, 87 percent of them black. Fifty-seven percent of the 2,927 undergraduates are women; 12 percent of women attend part-time. The campus, located on the north edge of Pine Bluff, is accessible by public transportation, and on-campus parking is provided.

Private childcare facilities are available near campus.

Policies to Ensure Fairness to Women. The Coordinator of Affirmative Action is responsible part-time for reviewing policies and practices and monitoring compliance with laws concerning equity for students, faculty, and the disabled. Complaints of sexual harassment are resolved through a formal grievance procedure.

Women in Leadership Positions. *Students.* In three recent years, no campus leadership positions were held by women students. Women preside over the five campus honorary societies.

Faculty. Thirty-nine percent of the 172 full-time faculty are women, a proportion far above the national average. There are 5 female faculty for every 100 female students and 10 male faculty for every 100 male students. Recent data indicate that the full-time female faculty includes 1 Asian American and 53 black women.

Administrators. All top positions are held by men. Two of 10 trustees are white women. Six of 30 deans/directors of academic units are black women, as are 6 of the 19 department chairs: English, music, home economics, nursing, elementary and early childhood education, and vocational teacher education. In a recent year, the sole recipient of an honorary degree was a black woman.

Women and the Curriculum. Most women earn degrees in education (53 percent), with fewer numbers majoring in business and public affairs. In business programs, the proportion of women is above the national average. Four percent of women earn degrees in nontraditional fields, including agriculture and mathe-matics. Fifty-eight percent of students in cooperative education programs and 14 percent of student interns are women.

There are no courses on women.

Women and Athletics. Opportunities for participation in athletics are extremely limited. Three intramural team sports are offered. The women's basketball team participated in recent intercollegiate competition. The only intercollegiate sport offered is basketball.

Housing and Student Organizations. Single-sex dormitories are available. Eight percent of full-time female undergraduates belong to social sororities; neither sororities nor fraternities provide housing for members.

Special Services and Programs for Women. *Health and Counseling.* The student health service has two male physicians and five female health-care providers. One male and two minority-female therapists staff the counseling center. Counseling and medical treatment for rape and assault and counseling on birth control are available.

Safety and Security. Measures consist of campus police with weapons training, self-defense courses for women, and a rape crisis center. No information on rapes and assaults was reported by the university.

Institutional Self-Description. None provided.

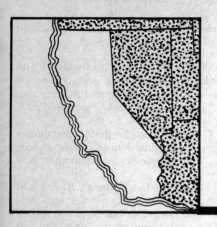

CALIFORNIA

Armstrong College
2222 Harold Way, Berkeley, CA 94704
Telephone: (415) 848-2500

Women in Leadership
★★★ students
★★★ faculty
★★★ administrators

184 undergraduates

	Amer. Ind.	Asian Amer.	Blacks	Hispanics	Whites
F	0	8	22	2	33
M	0	6	13	2	28
%	0.0	12.3	31.0	3.5	53.5

A private, commuter college, Armstrong was founded in 1918 as a school to train secretaries. Today it is a coeducational institution offering bachelor's and associate degrees in business. The college has two locations—a four-acre campus in El Cerrito and a building in downtown Berkeley—which attract 582 students. Women are 43 percent of the 184 undergraduates, and 13 percent of women attend part-time. The median age of degree students is 26. On-campus parking is provided for a fee, and the college is accessible by public transportation.

Childcare facilities are available near campus.

Women in Leadership Positions. *Students.* During the past three years, women have held most of the few student leadership positions available, including president of the student body for three consecutive terms and editor of the newspaper.

Faculty. Women are more than half the full-time faculty.

Administrators. Five of the nine principal administrators are women, although the chief executive officer and chief academic officer are men. Women head two of the four departments: the American English Center, and the School of Secretarial Administration.

Women and the Curriculum. All degrees are in business. In 1978-79 women received 7 of the 10 associate degrees and 6 of 15 four-year degrees. Half the students in internships and practicums are women. There are no courses on women.

Women and Athletics. The sports program offers intramural basketball and volleyball, and intercollegiate volleyball.

Special Services and Programs for Women. *Health and Counseling.* There is no student health service, but the student counseling center, staffed by two men and two women, provides gynecological, birth control, abortion, and rape and assault counseling.

Safety and Security. Security precautions include high-intensity lights, a night-time escort service for women, and safety information sessions. No rapes or assaults were reported on campus for 1980-81.

Other. A Women's Association has 42 members, half of whom are minority women.

Institutional Self-Description. "Armstrong College has been a pioneer in the education of women for careers in business. Since its founding in 1918, women have held key positions of responsibility in the administration and on the faculty. Women have always comprised a substantial portion of the student body and many women graduates have moved into managerial positions in the business world. The college has an extensive scholarship program designed to encourage women to seek careers in business."

California Maritime Academy
Vallejo, CA 94590
Telephone: (707) 644-5601

484 undergraduates

	Amer. Ind.	Asian Amer.	Blacks	Hispanics	Whites
F	0	1	0	0	16
M	0	16	8	16	427
%	0.0	3.5	1.7	3.3	91.5

Founded in 1929 as a training school for officers in the Merchant Marine, California Maritime Academy now attracts 484 women and men to its state-supported, four-year college program in engineering. The school is located in the small city of Vallejo, north of San Francisco. About 4 percent of the student body is female. The median age of all students is 20.

The institution offers an undergraduate degree program in addition to continuing education courses. All undergraduates reside on campus.

Policies to Ensure Fairness to Women. A sexual harassment policy protects all members of the school community. The policy has not been publicly communicated in writing to students; complaints are handled through a formal procedure.

Women in Leadership Positions. *Students.* All student offices have been occupied by men during a recent three-year period.

Faculty. There are no women among the 30 faculty.

Administrators. Men hold all top positions and chair all departments, although two of eight trustees are women.

Women and the Curriculum. All degrees awarded are in engineering. There are no courses on women.

Women and Athletics. Information was not provided on the nature of the intercollegiate and intramural sports program.

Housing and Student Organizations. All students live on campus in coeducational dormitories that have restrictive visiting hours for members of the opposite sex.

Special Services and Programs for Women. *Health and Counseling.* A student counseling center has one counselor, but there is no student health center. Information was not provided on the nature of counseling services specific to women.

Safety and Security. Measures include local police protection and high-intensity lighting. No rapes or assaults on women were reported for 1980-81.

Institutional Self-Description. "The Academy offers a career-oriented program with opportunities for women interested in responsibility and outstanding fringe benefits at graduation. The maritime industry assigns licensed personnel to ships regardless of sex, race, etc."

California State Polytechnic University, Pomona

Pomona, CA 91768
Telephone: (714) 598-4249

★ **Women and the Curriculum**

12,885 undergraduates

	Amer. Ind.	Asian Amer.	Blacks	Hispanics	Whites
F	84	192	201	426	3,689
M	126	506	284	843	5,633
%	1.8	5.8	4.1	10.6	77.8

Established in 1938 as an agricultural college for men, the institution's mission changed in 1961, when it became a polytechnic college to emphasize preparation in the fields of agriculture, engineering, science, and business. In the 1970s its scope broadened to include teaching and environmental design, with supplemental preparation in the arts and humanities. The university offers alternative schedules including both on- and off-campus evening classes, summer sessions, and limited extension-external degree programs.

Of 12,885 undergraduates, 37 percent are women, 26 percent of whom attend part-time. The median age of all undergraduate students is 23. Ninety-two percent of the students commute to campus. Public transportation, on-campus parking for a fee, and free transportation from remote parking lots to classroom buildings are available.

Childcare facilities are available on campus for students who are parents. Additional, private childcare facilities are available nearby.

Policies to Ensure Fairness to Women. The Director of Affirmative Action, and the Coordinator of Disabled Students each serve full-time to ensure compliance with equal-opportunity laws. The Director of Affirmative Action Services is a voting member on policymaking councils or committees and reviews policies and practices generated by councils and committees.

A written campus policy prohibits sexual harassment of students, faculty, and staff, and both formal and informal confidential campus mechanisms exist to resolve complaints of sexual harassment. Although there is no Committee on Minority Affairs, a student-commissioner position has been approved for 1981-82.

Women in Leadership Positions. *Students.* During the past three years, 10 percent of the leadership positions have been occupied by women, including editorship of the student newspaper for one year.

Faculty. Fifteen percent of the 566 full-time faculty members are women, a proportion lower than the national average. There are 2 female faculty for every 100 female students and 8 male faculty for every 100 male students.

Administrators. None of the top administrative positions is occupied by a woman. Women chair the departments of urban plan-

ning, social services, ethnic studies, foods and nutrition/home economics.

Women and the Curriculum. A high proportion of all degrees earned by women (18 percent) is in nontraditional fields, particularly agriculture, engineering, and architecture. Business, interdisciplinary studies, and agriculture are the most popular fields for women, while engineering is most popular for men.

An official committee is developing a Women's Studies Program under the direction of a black woman. The school of social work provides instruction on services for battered spouses, displaced homemakers, and childcare, and the school of business provides instruction about job discrimination in the workplace and women in management.

Women and Athletics. Women participate in intramural sports as well as in intercollegiate basketball, gymnastics, softball, tennis, track and field, volleyball. Twenty percent of athletic scholarships are awarded to women.

Housing and Student Organizations. Coeducational dormitories as well as single-sex dormitories, with no restrictive hours for visitors of the opposite sex, are available to the 8 percent of students who live on campus. Social sororities and fraternities provide housing for members.

Special Services and Programs for Women. *Health and Counseling.* The student health service includes 1 woman on its staff of 6 doctors, and 13 women among 15 other health-care providers. The counseling center has 1 white and 1 minority woman on its staff of 10 counselors/therapists. Counseling and medical treatment are available for gynecological problems, birth control, rape, and assault. Abortion and pre-marital counseling, along with pregnancy testing, are also available.

Safety and Security. Measures include a campus police force with the authority to make arrests, night-time escort service for women students, night-time campus-wide bus service to residence halls, high-intensity lighting in all areas, a highly conspicuous campus-wide emergency telephone system at isolated locations, periodic self-defense courses for women, information sessions on campus security and rape and assault prevention, and a rape crisis center. No rapes and three assaults (one on a woman) were reported for 1980-81.

Other. The campus Women's Center, serving approximately 2,500 people, 15 percent of them black and Mexican American women, is run by a full-time salaried administrator. The Women's Center sponsors a telephone service for information, referrals, and support, and maintains a library/resource file, and annually hosts a career conference, Women at Work: Moving Ahead.

Institutional Self-Description. "Cal Poly, Pomona has numerous technical fields of study which are typically considered nontraditional areas for women. Through sensitive faculty, our Women's Center, and the Reentry Services program, incoming students will find a very supportive atmosphere for their educational/personal lives. We have a 'buddy' system in which we couple incoming/transfer students with currently attending reentry-age students."

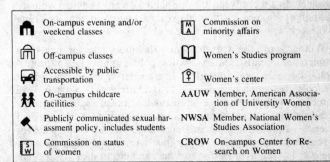

🏠	On-campus evening and/or weekend classes	[M A]	Commission on minority affairs
🏛	Off-campus classes	📖	Women's Studies program
🚐	Accessible by public transportation	🏠	Women's center
👫	On-campus childcare facilities	AAUW	Member, American Association of University Women
✎	Publicly communicated sexual harassment policy, includes students	NWSA	Member, National Women's Studies Association
[S W]	Commission on status of women	CROW	On-campus Center for Research on Women

California State University, Chico

Chico, CA 95929
Telephone: (916) 895-6116

★★ Women and the
Curriculum

★★ Women and Athletics

11,441 undergraduates

	Amer. Ind.	Asian Amer.	Blacks	Hispanics	Whites
F	38	108	108	18	5,185
M	40	127	157	271	4,925
%	0.7	2.1	2.4	4.1	90.7

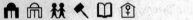

Founded in 1887 as a teacher-training school, California State University, Chico is now a liberal arts institution. Since 1972 it has been part of the state university system. Its rural campus, 90 miles north of Sacramento, draws 13,135 students. Half of the 11,441 undergraduates are women, and 13 percent of the women attend part-time. The median age of all students is 21.

The university offers a wide range of bachelor's and master's degrees, as well as continuing education and external-degree programs. Classes meet on and off campus, during the day and evening, and also on weekends; there is a summer session. Parking is provided at a fee, on campus.

A campus childcare facility gives priority to low-income families in the community and full-time students. It accommodates 52 children, at an average daily fee of $.50 per child. Additional, private childcare facilities are available near campus.

Policies to Ensure Fairness to Women. A full-time affirmative action officer is responsible for examining policies and practices pertaining to legal requirements for sex-fair employment, sex equity for students, and handicapped access. A published policy prohibits sexual harassment; complaints are resolved informally.

Women in Leadership Positions. *Students.* Women have limited opportunities to exercise student leadership. In the last three years, women have held two leadership posts (for two years each): student body president and student senate president. One of the five honorary societies has a female head.

Faculty. Twenty-two percent of the 587 full-time faculty are women, a proportion which is slightly below average for similar colleges in this guide. Recent data show that among the 133 full-time faculty women there are 2 blacks, 1 American Indian, 2 Asian Americans, and 1 Hispanic. There are 3 female faculty for every 100 female students, compared with 9 male faculty for every 100 male students.

Administrators. Men hold all top positions, except for the chief student-life officer. The Dean of the School of Humanities and Fine Arts is a woman. Women chair seven departments out of 46, including home economics, American studies, art, Latin American studies, nursing, political science, and women's athletics. Women occupy one-third of the seats on the Board of Trustees. In a recent year, the one alumni award went to a woman, and half of the speakers invited to campus were women, including two black women.

Women and the Curriculum. The most popular fields for women are interdisciplinary studies, public affairs, health professions, business, and education. In a recent year, one-quarter of students graduating with degrees in agriculture were women. Five percent of women graduate in the nontraditional areas of agriculture, computer science, engineering, mathematics, and physical sciences. Innovative programs encourage women to prepare for careers in science, engineering, agriculture, accounting, computer science, law enforcement/corrections, and electronics. Thirty-five

percent of the students in cooperative education and approximately 45 percent in internships/practicums are women. Students in education, social work, and business are introduced to women's issues that they will encounter in their respective places of work.

A Women's Studies Program—a full decade old—is run under the auspices of the combined Department of Ethnic and Women's Studies. Twenty credits are required for a minor in the field. Ten Women's Studies courses are available as well as 13 courses on women through other departments. Among the courses offered are Women's Nontraditional Literature, Women in the Working World, and Women in Politics. An official committee oversees the Women's Studies Program and collects and develops new teaching materials on women.

A course on racial and sex discrimination is required of all undergraduates.

Minority Women. Minority women are 4 percent of all undergraduates. An Asian American woman chairs an academic department; a black woman sits on the faculty senate, another on the tenure, reappointment, and promotions committee; one black and one Hispanic woman sit on the Board of Trustees. Two minority women are counselors at the student counseling center. Counselors and residence hall staff attend awareness training sessions on the avoidance of racism.

Women and Athletics. The excellent women's sports program offers a variety of activities on a high level of participation. Forty percent of the intercollegiate and 37 percent of the intramural athletes are women. Intercollegiate sports offered are basketball, cross-country, field hockey, gymnastics, softball, swimming, tennis, track and field, and volleyball.

Housing and Student Organizations. Eight percent of the undergraduates live on campus in coeducational dormitories that have no restrictive hours for visitors.

About 10 percent of the undergraduates belong to social sororities and fraternities, which provide housing for members. Phi Chi Theta and the Women's Center serve as advocates for women.

Special Services and Programs for Women. *Health and Counseling.* The student health center is staffed by 5 physicians, 1 of whom is female, and 7 female health-care providers. Seven of the 15 counselors at the student counseling center are women. Counseling and treatment for rape and assault and birth control are offered, as well as treatment for gynecological problems.

Safety and Security. Measures consist of campus police protection, night-time escort for women, and instruction on self-defense and campus safety for women. There is a rape crisis center in the community. One assault on a woman and one rape were reported for 1980–81.

Career. The career placement services for women include workshops, lectures, and information on nontraditional occupations, assistance in forming networks with alumnae, and files on alumnae careers.

Other. A small Women's Center, run by student volunteers, is under the direction of a Coordinator of Women's Programs in the Office of Student Affairs. On $4,000 annually, it serves 5,400 women, mainly undergraduates over age 25 and community women. Additional programs for women include a community-based battered women's shelter, an annual women's week, a women's lecture series, assertiveness training, and a warmline. Disabled Student Services extends support to 54 handicapped women students.

Returning Women Students. The Center for Regional and Continuing Education, which enrolls 2,250 women, sponsors a displaced homemakers' program.

Institutional Self-Description. "Chico State University has increased its commitment to affirmative action, thus providing more opportunities for women to affect changes and impact the university's academic, social, and supportive environments."

California State University, Dominguez Hills

1000 East Victoria Street,
Carson, CA 90747
Telephone: (213) 516-3300

Women in Leadership
★ faculty

5,117 undergraduates

	Amer. Ind.	Asian Amer.	Blacks	Hispanics	Whites
F	32	220	1,193	166	1,047
M	21	238	862	191	1,040
%	1.1	9.1	41.0	7.1	41.7

Founded in 1960 as a liberal-arts state college, California State University, Dominguez Hills is one of the newest additions to the California State University system. Its campus, located in a racially mixed community in a Los Angeles suburb, attracts 8,464 students, of whom 5,117 are undergraduates. Fewer than 40 percent of students are white. Fifty-three percent of the undergraduates are female, about a third of whom attend part-time. The median age of all undergraduates is 25.

The institution offers a range of undergraduate and graduate degree programs, in addition to adult education courses given by the extended education department. To serve the sizable number of part-time and older students, classes are scheduled in the evening, on and off campus, as well as in the daytime. Self-paced/contract learning is available. All students commute, either by car or public transportation; parking on campus is provided for a fee.

There are childcare facilities on and near campus. The campus daycare program gives priority to low-income students and charges a daily fee of $8. The center can meet most student parents' requests and accommodates 44 children.

Policies to Ensure Fairness to Women. The Dean of University College has the part-time responsibility for matters relating to sex equity, and has policymaking power as well. The Dean of Faculty and Student Affairs assumes the part-time responsibility for implementing sex-fair-employment and handicapped-access laws, and may also make policy in these areas.

A sexual harassment policy is being developed. Complaints are now resolved through a formal campus grievance procedure.

Women in Leadership Positions. *Students.* Women do not often hold either of the two campus-wide student leadership positions. During recent three years, a woman served one term as editor-in-chief of the campus newspaper.

Faculty. Twenty-eight percent of the full-time faculty are women, a proportion which is slightly above the national average. There are 4 female faculty for every 100 female students and 10 male faculty for every 100 male students.

Administrators. Men hold all top positions, except for the chief student-life officer. Of the departments chaired by women, two are biology and energy studies. The Deans of University College, School of Social and Behavioral Sciences, and of the School of Humanities and Fine Arts are women.

Women and the Curriculum. Most degrees are earned by women in interdisciplinary studies, public affairs, social sciences, and business.

Women are the focus of eleven courses, including one graduate course, offered by the departments of Mexican-American studies, English, sociology, and psychology, and by University College and Small College. One of the courses is Aging Woman: Emerging Issues. The physical education department instructs on methods for teaching coeducational classes in its courses for prospective teachers.

Women and Athletics. The small intercollegiate sports program draws 45 female athletes; women receive 30 percent of athletic scholarship aid. Five intramural sports are offered. An Olympic-sized velodrome is being built for cycling. Intercollegiate sports offered are badminton, basketball, cross-country, softball, tennis, and volleyball.

Special Services and Programs for Women. *Health and Counseling.* The student health center is staffed by 1 full-time male physician and 3 female health-care providers, in addition to 1 female and 3 male physicians who work part-time. The student counseling center employs 3 women and 2 men. Medical treatment and counseling are available for birth control and gynecological matters. Abortion and rape and assault counseling services are also offered.

Safety and Security. Measures consist of campus police protection, night-time escort for women, high-intensity lighting, emergency telephone and alarm systems, self-defense courses for women, and general information sessions about women's safety. For 1980-81, no rapes and five assaults on women were reported.

Career. The university maintains career files on alumnae, disseminates information about nontraditional careers, and invites women employed in these fields to speak on campus.

Other. A Women's Center reaches 1,500 persons, mainly undergraduates and university staff. Directed by a salaried student who works part-time, the center sponsors a women's lecture series and assertiveness training sessions.

Institutional Self-Description. "CSUDH's mission is to provide a comprehensive public university which meets the needs of its urban population. The student body is diverse in terms of ethnicity, cultural backgrounds, socio-economic circumstance and age (average 30), providing a rich learning environment for nontraditional students."

California State University, Fresno

Shaw and Cedar Aves., Fresno, CA 93740
Telephone: (209) 487-9011

★ Women and the Curriculum

11,858 undergraduates

	Amer. Ind.	Asian Amer.	Blacks	Hispanics	Whites
F	48	352	259	625	4,352
M	58	371	204	798	4,238
%	0.9	6.4	4.1	12.6	76.0

California State University at Fresno was founded in 1911 as a teachers' preparatory school. Today, it awards bachelor's degrees in business, education, agriculture, health professions, and arts and sciences. Master's degrees are available in certain fields. Of its 14,995 students, 11,858 are undergraduates. Forty-nine percent of undergraduates are women, 19 percent of whom attend part-time. The median age of undergraduates is 21. Evening and summer classes are available. The Extension/Summer Session Office administers adult continuing education. Ninety percent of students commute, using public transportation or on-campus parking that is available for a fee.

On-campus childcare, accommodating 80 children, charges fees on a sliding scale. Private childcare services are available off campus.

Policies to Ensure Fairness to Women. The full-time Affirmative Action Officer participates in policy decisions regarding equal employment opportunity. The Executive Vice President is responsible part-time for sex equity. A written campus policy prohibits sexual harassment of students, faculty, and staff.

Women in Leadership Positions. *Students.* Information on opportunities for student leadership was not provided.

Faculty. Twenty-two percent of 632 full-time faculty are women, 64 percent of whom hold permanent appointments. The ratio of female faculty to female students is 3 to 100; the corresponding ratio for males is 10 to 100.

Administrators. Except for the Dean of Graduate Studies and the head librarian, the top administrators are men. Women chair four of 37 departments: home economics, chemistry, nursing, and art.

Women and the Curriculum. Most bachelor's degrees earned by women are in health professions (16 percent), business (13 percent), interdisciplinary studies (12 percent), education (10 percent), and public affairs (10 percent). Six percent are in nontraditional areas, especially agriculture (5 percent), with smaller numbers in mathematics, physical sciences, and engineering.

The Women's Studies Program offers a 20-unit minor. Besides the required Women's Studies courses—Introduction to Changing Women and Seminar in Women's Studies—23 courses on women are offered in 13 departments, including drama, music, and foreign languages, as well as criminology, social welfare, history, La Raza, and Black Studies. Courses include Feminist Art, Legal Rights of Women, Women in Science, Female Sexuality, Educational and Sex-Role Stereotyping, and Jung and the Consciousness of Women.

Women and Athletics. No information on intramural or club sports was provided. Twenty-three percent of 480 intercollegiate athletes are women, who receive 20 percent of athletic scholarships. Six of the 29 paid varsity coaches are women. Women's intercollegiate sports include badminton, basketball, gymnastics, softball, swimming, tennis, and volleyball.

Housing and Student Organizations. Single-sex and coeducational dormitories, managed by 31 residence-hall directors, accommodate 10 percent of students. Eight percent of full-time undergraduate women join social sororities, which provide housing for their members.

Special Services and Programs for Women. *Health and Counseling.* The Health service provides treatment for gynecological problems, birth control, and rape and assault. Two white women, two minority women, and eight men counsel on gynecological problems, birth control, abortion, rape and assault.

Safety and Security. Measures include campus police with arrest authority, emergency telephones, and safety courses. Information on the incidence of rapes and assaults was not provided.

Other. A small Women's Center is part of Women's Studies. The Fresno Commission on the Status of Women sponsors an annual women's week. Women's Studies offers assertiveness/leadership training.

Institutional Self-Description. None provided.

California State University, Long Beach
Bellflower Blvd., Long Beach, CA 90840
Telephone: (213) 498-4111

★★ Women and the
Curriculum
★★ Women and Athletics

24,141 undergraduates

	Amer. Ind.	Asian Amer.	Blacks	Hispanics	Whites
F	141	1,305	1,340	914	8,530
M	129	1,241	960	1,121	7,854
%	1.1	10.8	9.8	8.6	69.6

Founded in 1949, Long Beach is one of the largest of the 14 California state universities, attracting 32,898 students to its campus on the periphery of the city of Long Beach. About half of the 24,141 undergraduates are women, and 32 percent of women attend part-time. The median age of all undergraduates is 23.

A wide variety of undergraduate, professional, pre-professional, and graduate degrees is available. The extended education and summer sessions division is responsible for adult continuing education. Classes meet during the daytime and evenings; a winter intersession is offered.

For the 97 percent of undergraduates who commute, public transportation and on-campus parking at a fee are available.

The university-sponsored childcare facility fills all students' requests and charges an average of $1 per hour. Private childcare centers are available off campus.

Policies to Ensure Fairness to Women. A full-time coordinator of affirmative action is responsible for monitoring compliance with laws pertaining to equal opportunity, sex equity for students, and handicapped accessibility. A written sexual harassment policy protects faculty and staff.

Women in Leadership Positions. *Students.* The incomplete information provided suggests that women have some opportunities to participate in campus-wide student leadership positions. In recent years, women have twice been student body president and student senate president.

Faculty. Twenty-three percent of the 891 full-time faculty are women. There are 3 female faculty for every 100 female students, and 9 male faculty for every 100 male students.

Administrators. The chief academic officer and the chief business officer are women. Women chair 17 of 63 departments.

Women and the Curriculum. Most women graduating with bachelor's degrees major in business (16 percent), health professions (12 percent), fine arts (10 percent), and interdisciplinary studies (9 percent). Three percent pursue such nontraditional fields as engineering, mathematics, or physical sciences. Eleven percent of the engineering graduates are women; a special Women in Engineering Program encourages women to study in this male-dominated field. Women in Law and Women in Business are two additional programs designed to encourage women to major in these fields. The mathematics department and Women's Studies sponsor workshops to help women gain skills in mathematics. Fewer than half of the cooperative education appointments and more than half of the student internships are awarded to women.

The Women's Studies Program offers a 21-credit minor and the B.A. as a special major. Some 17 courses are available through the program, including such courses as Women and their Bodies, Women in Contemporary Society, and Women's Oral History. Additional courses are cross-listed with over 12 departments and include such titles as Economics of Women, History of American Women, and Women Artmakers. Steering Advisory committees oversee the program.

Courses in social work, business, nursing, and education address some women's issues.

Minority Women. Among the 12,433 undergraduate women, 11 percent are black, 10 percent Asian American, 7 percent Hispanic and 1 percent American Indian. Courses on minority women, offered by Women's Studies and various ethnic studies programs, include Racism and Sexism, Asian Man/Woman, Black Male/Female Relations, Images of Black Women, La Chicana, and History of Women in a Cross-Cultural Perspective. According to recent information, the women on the permanently appointed faculty include 1 American Indian, 3 Hispanic, 6 Asian American, and 8 black women. Mexican American Studies is chaired by a woman. Several residence-hall advisors and one member of the student counseling center staff are minority women; all staff are offered training in the avoidance of racial bias.

Thirty-eight percent of those who belong to social sororities are minority women; 50 are in racially integrated sororities and 100 are in all-minority sororities.

Women and Athletics. An excellent intercollegiate program offers 13 individual and team sports. Thirty-eight percent of the intercollegiate athletes are women; women receive 30 percent of the athletic scholarships. Ten of the 34 paid varsity coaches are women. Twenty-nine percent of intramural athletes are women. An active coeducational intramural program supplements such women's sports as volleyball and racquetball. Intercollegiate sports offered are archery, badminton, basketball, cross-country, fencing, field hockey, golf, gymnastics, softball, swimming and diving, tennis, track and field, and volleyball.

Housing and Student Organizations. Three percent of the undergraduates live on campus in single-sex or coeducational dormitories that have no restrictions on visiting hours for members of the opposite sex.

Three percent of the female undergraduates belong to social sororities, some of which provide off-campus housing for members. The Associated Students Women's Committee, Women's Coalition Against Violence, and the Women's Studies Association are advocacy groups for women.

Special Services and Programs for Women. *Health and Counseling.* The student health center is staffed by 10 physicians, 2 of whom are female, and 28 health-care providers, 21 of whom are female. The 12-member staff of the student counseling center includes 3 women. Counseling and treatment are available for gynecological problems, birth control, and rape and assault, in addition to abortion counseling. Counselors receive training in the avoidance of sex-role stereotyping and racial bias.

Safety and Security. Measures consist of campus police protection, night-time escort for women, emergency telephone system, and instruction on self-defense and campus safety for women. Two rapes and eight assaults on women were reported for 1980–81.

Career. Workshops and lectures by women working in nontraditional occupations are available, along with networking between students and alumnae.

Other. The Women's Center, with a budget of $60,000 and a full-time director, draws over 6,000 women annually to its programs and services. The center sponsors a battered women's program, annual women's week, a women's lecture series, theater and women's arts performances, assertiveness training, telephone referral and information, a newsletter, and its own reference library on women. The Adult Reentry Program provides assistance to approximately 5,000 reentry women.

Institutional Self-Description. "Our Women's Studies Program is active and growing, and offers a wide variety of courses in all academic areas. The University Women's Center is the most politically active center in the California system. It is non-hierarchical in structure, offers a well-rounded and diverse program to all campus and community women, as well as a wide range of services. The sports program is excellent and has experienced healthy growth in student participation and in funding in the past five years."

Cogswell College
600 Stockton Street
San Francisco, CA 94108
Telephone: (415) 433-5550

Women in Leadership
★ administrators

410 undergraduates

	Amer. Ind.	Asian Amer.	Blacks	Hispanics	Whites
F	1	4	1	2	16
M	1	61	20	21	114
%	0.8	27.0	8.7	9.5	54.0

Cogswell is a private, four-year college offering associate and bachelor's degrees in engineering technology and architecture. Among the 410 undergraduates are 30 women, a third of whom attend part-time. More recent information indicates that 51 women are enrolled. Although all students commute, there is no on-campus parking.

Private childcare facilities are available off campus.

Policies to Ensure Fairness to Women. No formal policy on sexual harassment exists, but a formal grievance procedure resolves complaints.

Women in Leadership Positions. *Students.* Men have held the sole leadership position for the past three years.

Faculty. Two of the 21 full-time faculty are women.

Administrators. Two of the six chief administrative officers are women: the chief academic officer and the chief business officer. The chair of the department of general studies is a woman.

Women and the Curriculum. All students major in either engineering technology or architecture. An innovative program is offered to encourage women to enter the field of construction. A program to build mathematics confidence is also offered. There are no courses on women. Programs on nontraditional occupations for women and the needs of reentry women are offered to faculty.

Women and Athletics. No information was provided about opportunities for organized competitive sports.

Special Services and Programs for Women. *Health and Counseling.* There is no student health service. The counseling center, staffed by a white man and a minority woman, provides no services specific to women.

Safety and Security. Measures consist of student security guards. Information was not provided concerning the incidence of rapes and assaults.

Career. Information on nontraditional fields for women is provided, as is job-discrimination information about nontraditional fields. Updated files of alumnae by specific careers are maintained. There is a student society of Women Engineers, nine of whose 15 members are black women.

Institutional Self-Description. None provided.

Claremont Colleges:
see Pitzer College, Pomona College, and Scripps College.

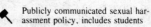
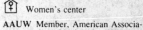

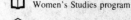
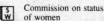
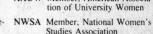
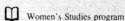

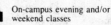
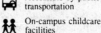

On-campus evening and/or weekend classes

Off-campus classes

Accessible by public transportation

On-campus childcare facilities

Publicly communicated sexual harassment policy, includes students

Commission on status of women

Commission on minority affairs

Women's Studies program

Women's center

AAUW Member, American Association of University Women

NWSA Member, National Women's Studies Association

CROW On-campus Center for Research on Women

College of Marin
Kentfield, CA 94904
Telephone: (415) 457-8811

Women in Leadership
★ faculty

4,840 undergraduates

	Amer. Ind.	Asian Amer.	Blacks	Hispanics	Whites
F	20	61	47	78	2,386
M	39	54	138	74	1,855
%	1.2	2.4	3.9	3.2	89.3

Located on a suburban campus, the College of Marin enrolls 6,400 students. Educational services consist of two years of a comprehensive college program in liberal arts, business, and pre-professional training, as well as a wide range of one- and two-year programs in business and technical areas, and continuing education for adults. Women are 54 percent of the 4,840 students enrolled in degree programs; 55 percent of women attend part-time. The median age of all degree students is 28. The college offers evening and weekend classes both on and off campus, as well as arrangements for contract learning. Of 250 handicapped students, more than half are women.

The college provides daytime childcare, at $1.10 per hour (free to recipients of Aid to Families with Dependent Children), for up to 37 children.

Policies to Ensure Fairness to Women. The Women's Program plays an active role in ensuring fairness to women. Students and faculty meet together to prepare reports regarding sex equity and to take public stands on issues of concern to students. In addition to a written policy prohibiting sexual harassment of students, faculty, and staff, the College of Marin has a formal grievance procedure to resolve complaints of sexual harassment. Policy procedures on sexual harassment have been publicly communicated in writing to students, faculty, and staff.

Women in Leadership Positions. *Students.* In recent years, women have not held the two leadership positions for which information was provided—president of the student government and chief editor of the newspaper.

Faculty. Twenty-nine percent of the 132 full-time faculty are women, a proportion slightly below average for public two-year colleges in this guide but above the average for all colleges nationwide. There are 4 female faculty for every 100 female students and 9 male faculty for every 100 male students.

Administrators. The chief development officer and the director of institutional research are women. Three of the four trustees are women. Women chair two departments—business and behavioral sciences.

Women and the Curriculum. Two-thirds of all degrees to women are in arts and sciences; other popular fields are health-care technologies (20 percent) and business and commerce (7 percent). There are two specially funded, short-term, innovative programs—Women in Electronics and Engineering Technologies, and Women and Apprenticeships. Five courses on women are offered through the departments of social science, history, English, and behavioral science. They include Aspects of Womanhood, Futures Perspective, History of Women, Women in Literature, and Human Sexuality.

Women and Athletics. No information was provided.

Special Services and Programs for Women. *Health and Counseling.* The student health service is staffed by 1 woman health-care provider; it provides no services specific to women. Student counseling employs 14 counselors, 7 of whom are women (4 white, 3 minority). Counselors receive in-service training on the avoidance of sex-role stereotyping and racial bias. Counseling

is available for gynecological problems, birth control, and abortion.

Safety and Security. Measures include campus police with arrest authority, high-intensity lighting in all areas, and self-defense courses for women. There is a community-based rape crisis center. No information was provided on the incidence of rapes and assaults.

Career. The college offers career workshops, lectures, and information on nontraditional occupations. It maintains files on alumnae careers and encourages networking between alumnae and students.

Other. The Women's Center at Marin, now called the Reentry Center, coordinated by a faculty member, with a budget of approximately $60,000, offers a wide variety of programs and services, including an annual women's week, a women's lecture series, and mathematics confidence workshops.

Institutional Self-Description. "The College of Marin's Women's Program (now in its eighth year) has been continually touted as a model program for services and programs offered. The college is presently focusing on offering expanded services to a reentry population and to supporting students interested in pursuing careers nontraditional to their sex."

College of Notre Dame
1500 Ralston Avenue, Belmont, CA 94002
Telephone: (415) 593-1601

Women in Leadership
★★ faculty
★★★ administrators

833 undergraduates

	Amer. Ind.	Asian Amer.	Blacks	Hispanics	Whites
F	0	25	43	20	376
M	0	10	26	10	161
%	0.0	5.2	10.3	4.5	80.0

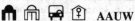 AAUW

The College of Notre Dame is an independent, four-year liberal arts college affiliated with the Roman Catholic Church and run by the Sisters of Notre Dame of Namur. Originally a women's college, Notre Dame became coeducational in 1968. The campus, located approximately 25 miles south of San Francisco, serves 833 students, 65 percent of whom are women. Thirty-nine percent of the women (210) and 39 percent of men (116) attend part-time. The median age of all students is 28; 45 percent of undergraduate women are over age 25. The division of continuing education enrolls about 200 reentry women. Four handicapped men and one handicapped woman are enrolled. Seventy percent of students commute and pay for parking on campus.

Private childcare facilities are available off campus.

Women in Leadership Positions. *Students.* Although they are 65 percent of the student body, women have held one-third of the campus-wide student leadership positions during the past three years. The president of one of the two student honorary societies is a woman.

Faculty. Forty-nine percent of the 43 full-time and 50 percent of the 12 permanent faculty are women. There are 6 female faculty for every 100 female students and 12 male faculty for every 100 male students.

Administrators. Half the chief administrators are women, including the president and vice president. Five of the 20 heads of departments are women (the chairs of music, English, biology, French, and education).

Women and the Curriculum. Most women major in interdisciplinary studies (22 percent), the social sciences (19 percent), arts and letters (18 percent), and psychology (18 percent). Seventeen percent of women take degrees in business. Most of the students in cooperative education and internships are women.

No courses on women are offered.

Women and Athletics. There are limited opportunities for organized competitive sports. Three intramural and two intercollegiate sports are offered. Twenty-five women participate in intercollegiate sports; two of the five intercollegiate coaches (one of them a woman) coach the women's teams. Intercollegiate sport are basketball and volleyball.

Housing and Student Organizations. Thirty percent of th students live on-campus in single-sex and coeducational residenc halls, all of which have restrictive hours for visitors of the op posite sex. A white woman and a minority woman are among the four residence-hall directors; they receive awareness training on sex education.

Special Services and Programs for Women. *Health and Counseling.* The student health service does not employ physicians, but there is one female health-care provider. Two male and two female counselors provide gynecological, birth control, abortion, and rape and assault counseling.

Safety and Security. There is a campus police force, and a nighttime escort service is provided for women. No rapes or assaults were reported on campus for 1980–81.

Career. The career placement office offers information and workshops on nontraditional occupations for women, and programs to establish contacts between alumnae and female students.

Other. The Women's Center, which has 600 square feet of office space and a budget of $1,500, serves about 200 women annually, most of them undergraduates over age 25 and community women. The center is directed by a part-time, salaried administrator.

Institutional Self-Description. "College of Notre Dame, the only four-year liberal arts college in San Mateo County, has the small-college environment which is conducive to class size that encourages interaction between students and faculty. The institutional aims of the college, faculty, staff, and administration, which convey attitudes that are positive and supportive, provide academic and student service activities so that the needs of the whole person are addressed."

Columbia College
PO Box 1849, Columbia, CA 95310
Telephone: (209) 532-3141

Women in Leadership
★ administrators

1,979 undergraduates

	Amer. Ind.	Asian Amer.	Blacks	Hispanics	Whites
F	18	6	1	27	1,118
M	12	5	5	10	767
%	1.5	0.6	0.3	1.9	95.7

Located in the Sierra foothills near Yosemite National Park, this public, two-year commuter college, founded in 1968, serves 2,263 students. Fifty-nine percent of students are women, and 76 percent of women are enrolled part-time. The median age of all students is 29.

Columbia offers a variety of liberal arts transfer programs as well as degrees and certificates in such specialties as ecology, health, and business. Fifty-five percent of students transfer to four-year institutions. There is an adult continuing education program as well as a special college-involvement program for high-

school seniors. A summer session is offered. The campus is accessible by public transportation. On-campus parking is available. Private childcare facilities are available near campus.

Policies to Ensure Fairness to Women. A written campus policy prohibits sexual harassment of students. An administrator is responsible part-time for monitoring compliance with sex-equity laws for students.

Women in Leadership Positions. *Students.* In the past three years, men have held the two campus leadership positions.

Faculty. Of 39 full-time faculty, 23 percent are women. There are 3 female faculty for every 100 female students and 10 male faculty for every 100 male students. According to recent information, there are also 90 part-time faculty, among whom are 28 women.

Administrators. The chief business officer and student-life officer are women. Men hold the other five top administrative positions.

Women and the Curriculum. Most degrees to women are in arts and sciences. The division of social science offers a course called Women in Society. Courses in the departments of social work and business provide some instruction on matters specific to women. Faculty workshops treat such topics as sexism, the relationships among gender, race, and the curriculum, nontraditional careers, the needs of reentry women, and affirmative action.

Women and Athletics. Eighteen of the 40 intercollegiate athletes are women; women play intramural tennis and volleyball. Among the three paid varsity coaches, one is a woman. The college fields intercollegiate women's teams in tennis and volleyball.

Special Services and Programs for Women. *Health and Counseling.* The student health service, staffed by a woman health-care provider, offers medical treatment for gynecological problems, birth control, and rape and assault. The student counseling center has a staff of two men and one white woman. No counseling specific to women is available.

Safety and Security. Local police patrol the campus, and the community has a rape crisis center. One rape and one assault on a woman were reported for 1980–81.

Career. A Gender Equity Program encourages women students to prepare for nontraditional careers. The center provides information on nontraditional occupations and on job discrimination.

Other. The adult continuing education and evening programs serve senior citizens as well as reentry women (among whom are Hispanic women). Each year the college hosts a weekend women's symposium organized by the community.

Institutional Self-Description. "Columbia College surrounds a lake in a rural, wooded area of the Gold Country adjacent to Columbia State Historic Park. Our small faculty and student body lend themselves to a personalized and individualized learning environment, where respect for each student's worth and dignity is primary in the pursuit of basic, general, vocational, recreational, transfer, and continuing education."

Cosumnes River College
8401 Center Parkway
Sacramento, CA 95823
Telephone: (916) 421-1000

4,221 undergraduates

	Amer. Ind.	Asian Amer.	Blacks	Hispanics	Whites
F	33	145	314	184	1,820
M	29	161	303	136	1,073
%	1.5	7.3	14.7	7.6	68.9

This two-year commuter college serves 4,708 students with a wide variety of liberal arts transfer, vocational, and technical programs. Fifty-nine percent of students are women, and 76 percent of women attend part-time. Fifty-seven percent of the undergraduate women are over age 26. The average age of all students is 25.

Among the specialties offered are agricultural technology, animal science, construction, business, landscape, plant science, secretarial science, small engine repair, and farm machinery. The campus is accessible by public transportation; on-campus parking is free. There is a summer session.

An on-campus childcare facility can accommodate one-third of requests; first choice is given to mothers receiving Aid to Families with Dependent Children.

Policies to Ensure Fairness to Women. Two staff members, on a part-time basis, monitor compliance with affirmative-action and sex-equity legislation. A full-time enabler/counselor is responsible for programs for the 138 handicapped students on campus. An active Committee on the Status of Women, appointed by the president, reports regularly to the campus community; student members have voting rights. This committee also addresses the concerns of minority women. A written campus policy prohibiting sexual harassment has been communicated to students and staff. Complaints are resolved informally.

Women in Leadership Positions. *Students.* In three recent years, of the five campus leadership positions, women have held three for one year each: as president of the student body; president of the student senate, and editor-in-chief of the campus newspaper.

Faculty. Twenty-three percent of the 74 full-time faculty are women. There are 3 female faculty for every 100 female students and 9 male faculty for every 100 male students.

Administrators. A woman directs the athletics program; the other key administrative positions are held by men. Women chair two departments: humanities and social science, and physical education. The eight trustees include a white woman and an Hispanic woman.

Women and the Curriculum. Most degrees awarded to women are in arts and sciences, health technologies, and business and commerce. The departments of agriculture, architecture, and accounting offer programs to encourage women to major in these subjects, and the office of occupational education runs a sex-equity project. There are no courses on women. Faculty workshops are available on nontraditional careers, affirmative action, and sexual harassment in the workplace.

Women and Athletics. Women participate in a variety of individual and team intramural sports. Women are 25 percent of intercollegiate athletes. Five of 16 paid coaches for the intercollegiate program are women. Intercollegiate sports include cross-country, track, softball, tennis, and volleyball.

Special Services and Programs for Women. *Health and Counseling.* The student health service is staffed by one female health-care provider. No medical treatment or counseling specific to women is available.

Safety and Security. Measures consist of campus police and high-intensity lighting. Information was not provided on the incidence of rapes and assaults.

Career. An active career placement office informs students about nontraditional occupations through lectures, workshops, and printed material. The office also establishes contacts between alumnae and students. There is a reentry program for older students returning to college

Institutional Self-Description. "Cosumnes River College commits itself to the concept of the inherent worth and dignity of individual human beings, without regard to race, age, sex, creed, or national origin. The varied offerings of the college provide both general educational background and specialized concentration and training in occupations nontraditional to women."

Diablo Valley College
Pleasant Hill, CA 94523
Telephone: (415) 685-1230

Women in Leadership	★ Women and the
★ students	Curriculum
★ administrators	

14,705 undergraduates

	Amer. Ind.	Asian Amer.	Blacks	Hispanics	Whites
F	56	193	151	241	6,714
M	102	239	252	280	6,398
%	1.1	3.0	2.8	3.6	89.7

Diablo Valley College provides 19,000 students with two-year degree programs, one- and two-year career and technical training certificates, and adult continuing education. Women are half of the 14,705 degree students and nearly half the 215 handicapped students. About 68 percent of women attend part-time; evening and weekend classes are offered both on and off campus. The median age of all students is 23. All students commute. The college is accessible by public transportation, and there is free campus parking.

Low-cost, on-campus childcare facilities can accommodate half the requests of students.

Women in Leadership Positions. *Students.* The only student leadership position, that of student body president, was held by a woman during one of the last three years.

Faculty. Women are 20 percent of the full-time faculty. There are 2 female faculty for every 100 female students and 7 male faculty for every 100 male students.

Administrators. Six of the eight top administrative positions are held by men. The director of institutional research is a black woman; the head librarian is a white woman. The director of cooperative education and the chairs of the counseling and business departments are white women.

Women and the Curriculum. Three-quarters of women major in arts and sciences. The Women's Studies Program, headed by a part-time director who is a black woman, offers 12 courses leading to an associate degree. The Women's Studies courses are in counseling and career development, as well as in economics, psychology, sociology, and the humanities.

Women and Athletics. A third of the participants in intercollegiate sports are women. The 115 women athletes compete in basketball, cross-country, gymnastics, softball, swimming and diving, tennis, track, and volleyball. Three of the 40 paid intercollegiate coaches are women. There are no intramural or club sports.

Special Services and Programs for Women. *Health and Counseling.* Student health service is staffed by 1 female health-care provider. On the 16-member staff of the counseling center are 2 white women and 1 minority woman. No medical treatment or counseling specific to women is available. Counselors receive in-service training on sex-role stereotyping.

Safety and Security. Measures include campus police and local police, high-intensity lighting in all areas, a night-time escort for women students, information sessions on campus safety and rape and assault prevention, and a rape crisis center. No rapes or assaults on women were reported for 1980–81.

Career. The college offers career workshops and panels on women in nontraditional occupations.

Other. The Women's Center, which serves approximately 2,000 women annually, operates a telephone service for information, referrals, and support.

Returning Women Students. The Women's Program, which is the reentry women's program, is a single administrative unit that contains three components: Women's Studies, the Re-entry

Program, and the Women's Center. The Women's Program also sponsors a lecture series, assertiveness/leadership training, and training in mathematics confidence.

Institutional Self-Description. "Diablo Valley College was among the first post-secondary institutions to develop a program specifically for mature women interested in returning to college. This, coupled with the myriad of ancillary services—childcare, financial aid, tutorial service center, job placement, special non-traditional occupational programs, and comradeship—make the college especially inviting for reentry women."

East Los Angeles College
Monterey Park, CA 91754
Telephone: (213) 265-8650

Women in Leadership
★★ faculty

12,401 undergraduates

	Amer. Ind.	Asian Amer.	Blacks	Hispanics	Whites
F	77	677	392	4,551	853
M	90	645	298	4,200	575
%	1.4	10.7	5.6	70.8	11.6

Located on an urban campus in East Los Angeles, this public, two-year commuter college serves close to 15,000 students in a variety of full- and part-time, day and evening programs. The median age of the 12,401 degree students is 23. Women are slightly more than half the students, and 70 percent of the women attend part-time.

The college offers the first two years of liberal arts and a wide range of one- and two-year vocational and technical programs. Off-campus courses, offered at such diverse locations as the Los Angeles County Sheriff's Academy, Fire Communications Center of Los Angeles County, White Memorial Medical Center, and Los Angeles Airport, make the college accessible to working students and provide first-hand experience at potential job sites. Free and paid parking are available on campus.

There are private childcare facilities near campus.

Policies to Ensure Fairness to Women. A Commission on the Status of Women, including student members with voting rights, takes public stands on issues of concern to women students; it especially addresses the concerns of minority women. The commission is appointed by the president of the college.

Women in Leadership Positions. *Students.* In one of the three most recent years women held three top positions—president of the student body, presiding officer of the student senate, and presiding officer of the student court.

Faculty. Of 215 full-time faculty, 39 percent are women. There are 4 female faculty for every 100 female students and 6 male faculty for every 100 male students.

Administrators. Nine of the 11 chief administrative positions are held by men. A woman serves as one of two directors of athletics. Nine of the 28 major departments and divisions are chaired by women, including cooperative education, advanced-studies institute, art, chemistry, family and consumer studies, journalism, mathematics, nursing, office administration, women's physical education, and social sciences.

Women and the Curriculum. Most women take degrees in arts and sciences (57 percent), public service (20 percent), and health technologies (17 percent). The Chicano Studies Program includes a course on the Mexican American Woman in Society, and the Psychology of Women's and Men's Changing Roles is offered by the psychology department. The college offers faculty workshops on nontraditional occupations for women and men, the

needs of reentry women, and affirmative action. Students in physical education classes receive instruction in how to teach coeducational classes.

Minority Women. In keeping with the ethnic composition of its student body, East Los Angeles College has a number of programs and support services directed to Chicana women. In addition to the Chicano Studies Program there is a Chicano Service Action Center. The Women's Center, with a budget of almost $30,000, serves 5,000 women yearly, 80 percent of whom are Chicanas. The full-time coordinator of the center is a Chicana.

Women and Athletics. Slightly more than 100 women participate in a wide variety of intercollegiate sports, including coeducational archery, coeducational badminton, basketball, cross-country, soccer, softball, swimming, tennis, track and field, and volleyball. There are no intramural or club sports.

Special Services and Programs for Women. *Health and Counseling.* Student health services are provided by 1 female health-care worker. The student counseling center is staffed by 15 counselors, including 4 white women and 4 minority women. Rape and assault counseling is provided.

Safety and Security. Measures include campus police with authority to make arrests and a conspicuous campus-wide emergency phone system. Information was not provided about the incidence of rapes and assaults on women.

Career. The career placement office offers workshops about nontraditional careers, and lectures and panels by women employed in nontraditional occupations.

Other. The Office of Student Services sponsors programs for battered women and displaced homemakers, as well as an annual women's week, women's lecture series, assertiveness/leadership training, and a telephone warmline.

Institutional Self-Description. "East Los Angeles College provides instructional and student support programs which will contribute to the students' ability to successfully achieve their personal, intellectual, and vocational goals. Additionally, the college assures equal academic access to all programs with supportive programs to eliminate sex bias and sex-role stereotyping."

Gavilan Community College
Gilroy, CA 95020
Telephone: (408) 847-1406

Women in Leadership
★ faculty
★ administrators

2,024 undergraduates

	Amer. Ind.	Asian Amer.	Blacks	Hispanics	Whites
F	13	31	10	283	687
M	12	34	28	273	540
%	1.3	3.4	2.0	29.1	64.2

Gavilan is a two-year college, located south of San Jose. Women are 54 percent of the 2,024 matriculated students; 69 percent of women attend part-time. The median age of all students is 28. Gavilan offers a special reentry program and a Continuing Education for Women Program, as well as evening classes both on and off campus. All students commute.

Low-cost, on-campus childcare is available for about 30 children. Full and part-time students who are single parents are eligible.

Policies to Ensure Fairness to Women. A written campus policy prohibiting sexual harassment of students, faculty, and staff has been publicly communicated to all three groups. There is a formal campus grievance procedure to resolve complaints of sexual harassment.

Women in Leadership Positions. *Students.* No information was provided on opportunities for student leadership.

Faculty. Of 64 full-time faculty, 30 percent are women. There are 6 female faculty for every 100 female students and 10 male faculty for every 100 male students.

Administrators. Four of the six top positions are held by men. The head librarian and the director of athletics are women.

Women and the Curriculum. Most women take degrees in arts and sciences (55 percent) and business and commerce (22 percent). Programs for women in law enforcement/corrections and women in electronics are offered to encourage entry into nontraditional careers. Special efforts are made both to recruit women for pre-electronics and to help women build their skills through a program in mathematics confidence.

The college offers several courses on women, including Contemporary American Women, the Sociology of Women, and Women in American History. Courses in education, nursing, and sociology offer instruction on subjects specific to women.

Women and Athletics. There are no intramural or club sports. Women participate in five intercollegiate sports: basketball, cross-country, softball, track, volleyball.

Special Services and Programs for Women. *Health and Counseling.* Student health service is provided by one female health-care worker. There is no centralized student counseling service, but seven counselors, including one woman, are available to students. No medical care or counseling specific to women is available.

Safety and Security. Information sessions are provided on campus safety and rape and assault prevention. There is a community-based rape crisis center. No information was provided on the incidence of rapes and assaults.

Other. A woman's network composed of faculty, staff, and students meets monthly to discuss selected topics of interest to the group. The reentry program, staffed by a full-time coordinator, and with an annual budget of $19,000, operates a center providing services to about 400 women, 35 percent of whom are Chicanas.

Institutional Self-Description. None provided.

Indian Valley Colleges
Novato, CA 94947
Telephone: (415) 883-2211

Women in Leadership
★★ faculty
★★ administrators

★ **Women and the Curriculum**

2,206 undergraduates

	Amer. Ind.	Asian Amer.	Blacks	Hispanics	Whites
F	19	28	26	46	1,261
M	16	23	25	26	713
%	1.6	2.3	2.3	3.3	90.4

Founded in 1971, this public, two-year college is located in Marin County near San Francisco. The total student body numbers 3,003, with 2,206 enrolled as undergraduates. Women are 63 percent of the student body. Three-quarters of the women attend part-time;

58 percent of the undergraduate women are over 25. The median age of all students is 28.

Indian Valley offers a college transfer program in the liberal arts and sciences, adult continuing education, and degrees and certificates in a range of occupational areas. Day and evening classes both on and off campus are available, as well as a summer session. The college is accessible by public transportation; on-campus parking is provided for a fee.

The on-campus childcare facility can accommodate 90 percent of students' requests. Open from 7:45 a.m. to 5:15 p.m., the center charges fees on a sliding scale.

Women in Leadership Positions. *Students.* There are two student leadership positions. During a recent three-year period, a woman has been editor of the newspaper twice. A woman heads the sole honorary society.

Faculty. Sixteen of the 43 full-time faculty are women, a proportion slightly above average for public, two-year colleges in this guide. There are 5 female faculty for every 100 female students and 10 male faculty for every 100 male students.

Administrators. Women hold two of the five top positions, including President and head librarian. Indian Valley is the only community college in this guide that is headed by a black woman. Two of three deans are women: Arts, and the Science College.

Women and the Curriculum. Most degrees awarded to women are in arts and sciences (51 percent) and business and commerce (27 percent). The Women's Studies Program offers 21 courses through the departments of anthropology, English, history, psychology, political science, health education, and management. Students can earn a minor or an associate degree in Women's Studies. A committee oversees the development of the Women's Studies Program.

This college is one of the few in the guide that requires students to take at least one course on discrimination against women and/or minorities. Issues of job discrimination, sexual harassment in the workplace, and women in management are addresssed in business courses. Nontraditional careers is a topic offered to faculty in workshops.

Women and Athletics. There are no organized, competitive sports programs.

Special Services and Programs for Women. *Health and Counseling.* The student health service is staffed by one female health-care provider. No medical treatment specific to women is available. The student counseling center employs six counselors, including two white women and a black woman. Counseling is provided for gynecological problems, birth control, abortion, and rape and assault.

Safety and Security. Measures consist of campus police with authority to make arrests, a night-time escort service for women, self-defense courses for women, and a rape crisis center. For 1980–81, one assault (on a man) was reported on campus.

Career. Services include workshops and lectures on women in nontraditional fields, as well as networking with alumnae.

Other. The Women's Center serves approximately 3,000 women, with the most frequent participants being undergraduates over age 25. Twenty percent of the users are minority group women, predominantly Hispanic women. Coordinated by a faculty member, the center has a budget of $15,000. Many of its programs and services are co-sponsored with other groups and include a displaced homemaker program, a mathematics/science conference, an annual women's week, a program to build mathematics confidence, and a telephone referral service.

Institutional Self-Description. "Women students get particular encouragement because of the predominance of female administrators and faculty who are feminists. Some of the most active feminists are members of national boards, commissions on women, and regularly initiate and plan special workshops, conferences, and programs encouraging women to enter fields nontraditional to their gender. For a community college, Indian Valley has the most feminist orientation of any in California."

Los Angeles Valley College

Van Nuys, CA 91401

Telephone: (213) 781-1200

Women in Leadership

★ **faculty**

★★★ **administrators**

17,097 undergraduates

	Amer. Ind.	Asian Amer.	Blacks	Hispanics	Whites
F	292	589	550	1,127	7,261
M	221	593	529	1,096	4,777
%	3.0	6.9	6.3	13.	70.7

Located within commuting distance of Los Angeles, on a suburban campus of 106 acres, this public community college offers 21,159 students the first two years of liberal arts and a variety of career-oriented programs. Fifty-eight percent of the 17,097 students in degree programs are women, three-quarters of whom attend part-time. Women are 1,200 of the 2,000 handicapped students. The median age of all students is 30.

Self-paced/contract learning and day and evening classes both on and off campus are available.

Low-cost day and evening childcare is available on campus for 186 children—about 60 percent of students' requests.

Policies to Ensure Fairness to Women. A formal grievance procedure resolves complaints of sexual harassment; an Affirmative Action Committee reports to the president.

Women in Leadership Positions. *Students.* In a recent three-year period, women have held one-third of student leadership positions: for two years a woman edited the campus newspaper, and for one year a woman presided over the student court.

Faculty. Of 277 full-time and part-time faculty, 34 percent are women. Recent information specifies that the faculty includes 4 black women, 4 Asian American women and 6 Hispanic women.

Administrators. Both the chief executive officer and the chief business officer are white women; black women hold the positions of development officer, head librarian, and director of athletics. Ten of the 25 department and division chairs are women, including art, cooperative education, earth science, English, family and consumer studies, health science, history, library science, music, and office administration.

Women and the Curriculum. Most women take degrees in arts and sciences (42 percent), health technologies (36 percent), and business and commerce (16 percent).

Several courses on women are offered each year, including the Mexican-American Woman in Society and The Role of Women in the History of the U.S.

Women and Athletics. Almost half of the participants in intramural sports are women. A smaller number of women participate in intercollegiate basketball, softball, swimming, and volleyball.

Special Services and Programs for Women. *Health and Counseling.* Student health services are provided by 1 physician and 1 public-health nurse on call. The 17-member staff of the counseling center includes 6 white women and 3 minority women. No medical treatment specific to women is provided.

Safety and Security. Measures include campus police with weapons training and arrest authority, high-intensity lighting in all areas, an emergency telephone system in the parking lots, night-time escort for women students, self-defense courses, information sessions on campus safety and rape and assault prevention, and a rape crisis center. For 1980-81, three rapes and four assaults (two on women) were reported on campus.

Other. The S/He Center, coordinated by a minority woman who holds a full-time faculty appointment, has an annual budget of $1,600. About 20 percent of the 5,000 women served annually are members of minority groups, chiefly Hispanic women. The center sponsors an annual women's awareness week, women's groups, and women's classes.

Institutional Self-Description. "Over 51 percent [of students] are women, older returning students. Los Angeles Valley College is located in an area where many women want to go to college. As a result, Los Angeles Valley College has many special programs geared to women."

Menlo College

Menlo Park, CA 94025

Telephone: (415) 323-6141

624 undergraduates

	Amer. Ind.	Asian Amer.	Blacks	Hispanics	Whites
F	1	4	1	1	145
M	0	6	3	2	316
%	0.2	2.1	0.8	0.6	96.2

Menlo College is a private, four-year, coeducational institution located in a suburban area about 30 miles from San Francisco. Originally a two-year college offering a letters and science program, it added a school of business administration in 1950 and now grants a four-year bachelor's degree in business as well. Self-paced/contract learning, summer sessions, and an interim (intensive four-week) program are available.

Undergraduate enrollment includes 190 women and 434 men, virtually all of whom attend full-time. The median age of all undergraduates is 20. Free on-campus parking is available for commuting students.

Private childcare facilities are available off campus.

Policies to Ensure Fairness to Women. An affirmative action-Title IX officer is responsible part-time for compliance with federal sex-equity laws. An educational program on affirmative action and equal opportunity is offered to department heads and college administrators.

Women in Leadership Positions. *Students.* During a recent three-year period, women have held 11 percent of student leadership positions.

Faculty. Four of the 33 full-time faculty are women. The ratio of female faculty to female students is 2 for every 100; the ratio for males is 7 for every 100.

Administrators. Men hold all top positions.

Women and the Curriculum. Menlo offers only an associate degree in arts and science and a bachelor's degree in business. Twenty-nine percent of students earning business degrees are women; women are 32 percent of those earning two-year arts and science degrees. Thirty percent of students participating in internships are women. No courses on women are offered.

Women and Athletics. For a school of its size, Menlo offers women good opportunities to participate in organized competitive sports. Four intramural and four intercollegiate women's sports are offered. Eleven percent of the athletic scholarships went to women in 1980-81. Twenty-seven women participate in four intercollegiate sports: cross-country, tennis, track, and volleyball.

Housing and Student Organizations. Single-sex and coeducational dormitories are available. The five male and five female residence-hall directors receive awareness training on gay issues and rape.

The Women's Collective of Menlo College, which has 25 members, sponsors a women's lecture series and assertiveness/awareness training.

Special Services and Programs for Women. *Health and Counseling.* The student health program is run in conjunction with a local clinic that has 25 male physicians and one female physician. There is no counseling specific to women.

Safety and Security. Measures include a campus security staff, information on campus safety and rape and assault prevention for women. Four rapes and 14 assaults (13 on women) were reported on campus for 1980-81.

Career. The college keeps records of alumnae by specific fields and has information on job discrimination in nontraditional fields for women.

Institutional Self-Description. "With few women on campus, we get to know each other well. We're concerned about each other. Our group is small but activist, composed of women faculty, administrators, students, alums, and support staff."

Mills College
Oakland, CA 94613
Telephone: (415) 430-2255

Women in Leadership   ★ **Women and the Curriculum**
★★★ students
★★★ faculty
★★★ adminstrators

851 undergraduates

	Amer. Ind.	Asian Amer.	Blacks	Hispanics	Whites
F	5	63	85	26	610
M	0	0	0	0	0
%	0.6	8.0	10.8	3.3	77.3

Mills College, established in 1852, is one of two independent women's liberal arts colleges on the West Coast. All but 4 percent of the 851 undergraduates, who include a sizable number of reentry women, attend full-time. A variety of undergraduate and graduate degree programs are available. Classes meet during the day and evening. For the 28 percent of undergraduates who commute, public transportation, free parking on campus, and free transportation from remote parking lots to classroom buildings are available.

The campus childcare facility serves all members of the Mills community as well as local residents. It accommodates 55 children (an estimated 90 percent of students' requests) for a daily fee of $1.25 to $1.60. Private childcare facilities are available nearby.

Policies to Ensure Fairness to Women. The Director of Personnel assumes full-time responsibility for administering sex-equity, equal-employment-opportunity and handicapped-access laws, and makes policy in these areas. Complaints of sexual harassment are resolved informally.

Women in Leadership Positions. *Students.* Women hold all student leadership positions.

Faculty. Fifty-seven percent of the 56 full-time faculty are women, a figure which is about average for women's colleges in this guide. There are 4 women faculty for every 100 women students.

Administrators. Most key administrators are women, including the chief executive officer, the chief student-life officer, chief development officer, and director of institutional research. Women direct the division of fine arts and the division of educational services, and chair eight of 14 departments: dance, music, English, foreign languages, psychology, education, health and movement studies, and mathematics. Half of the members of the Board of Trustees are women. In a recent year the spring commencement speaker and all three speakers at campus-wide lectures series were women.

Women and the Curriculum. Most degrees awarded to women are in social sciences (19 percent) and fine arts (18 percent). Nine percent are in nontraditional areas such as computer science, physical sciences, and mathematics. Mills reports special programs to encourage women to prepare for careers in science, engineering, and computer science, as well as in administration and legal processes. A program that builds mathematics skills is available.

A Women's Studies Program offers the B.A. Some nine courses are available through Women's Studies and the departments of sociology, social sciences, history, and Ethnic Studies. Recent titles include Sociology of Sexism, Women and Work, and Women and the Law. The education department offers instruction on some matters relevant to the nonsexist training of prospective teachers. An official committee oversees the Women's Studies Program and collects and creates new teaching materials on women. Faculty are offered workshops on sexism and the curriculum.

Minority Women. Minority women are almost one-fourth of the student body, mostly black and Asian American women. Thirty percent of the returning women students are from minority groups. Ethnic Studies offers three courses on minority women: Asian American Women, History of Black Women through Literature, and Bay Area Ethnic Women Writers. One black and one Hispanic woman sit on the Board of Trustees. The student counseling center and the residence halls each have a minority woman on their staffs. Residence-hall staff are offered awareness-training on racism.

Minority women's support and advocacy groups include the Black Women's Collective, Asian Students Association, and the International Students Association. An Asian American student coordinates the Women's Center as a part-time volunteer.

Women and Athletics. The organized sports program is small but varied. There are eight intramural teams. The four paid varsity coaches are women. Intercollegiate sports offered are basketball, crew, tennis, and volleyball.

Housing and Student Organizations. Seventy-two percent of the undergraduate women live on campus in either women's or coeducational dormitories. Housing is provided for married students with or without children and for single parents. Dormitories have no restrictions on visiting hours for members of the opposite sex. The 150-member Associated Students of Mills College as well as the minority women's organizations previously mentioned serve as advocates for women, as does the Gay People's Union.

Special Services and Programs for Women. *Health and Counseling.* The student health center is staffed by one physician and three health-care providers—all women. The student counseling center's staff consists of five women. Counseling and treatment are available for gynecological problems, birth control, abortion, and rape and assault. Student health insurance covers abortion and maternity expenses.

Safety and Security. Measures consist of campus and local police protection, night-time bus service to residence areas, an emergency telephone system, and instruction on self-defense and campus safety. One rape and assault on a woman were reported for 1980–81.

Career. Mills offers career workshops, lectures, and information on nontraditional occupations, maintains files on the careers of its alumnae, and encourages networking between students and alumnae. The office of the Dean of Students offers assertiveness training.

Other. The Women's Center serves 500 women annually. The English department sponsors a women's lecture series and programs about women writers. The drama department, with the English department, produces theater programs for women. The Mary Atkins Association operates a federally-funded program for displaced homemakers and serves older women in general.

Institutional Self-Description. "The mission of Mills is to help able, aspiring women develop their potential to the full. The college does so by offering a liberal arts education of the highest quality, within an environment that provides special reinforcement for women."

Monterey Peninsula College
Monterey, CA 93940
Telephone: (408) 646-4000

Women in Leadership
★ **faculty**

5,057 undergraduates

	Amer. Ind.	Asian Amer.	Blacks	Hispanics	Whites
F	24	247	281	117	2,028
M	24	190	378	119	1,649
%	1.0	8.7	13.0	4.7	72.7

This public community college, located on a suburban campus, offers the first two years of liberal arts and a wide range of one- and two-year career programs, including data processing, dental assisting, drafting, electronics, engineering, hotel-restaurant operation, manufacturing processes, police science, and secretarial. All of its 6,929 students commute. Women are 53 percent of the 5,057 degree students; 69 percent of the women attend part-time. The college offers evening classes, off-campus locations, free on-campus parking. It is accessible by public transportation.

Childcare facilities are available both on and off campus. The on-campus facilities, open during the day, charge according to a sliding scale, ranging from free to $13 per day.

Policies to Ensure Fairness to Women. The college has both a Commission on the Status of Women and a Commission on Minority Affairs. The Commission on the Status of Women is appointed by and reports to the president. A full-time affirmative action officer is responsible for compliance with all equal-opportunity laws.

Women in Leadership Positions. *Students.* A woman held the position of student body president for one of the last three years; the only other campus position, the presiding officer of the student court, has been held by men.

Faculty. Twenty-five percent of the full-time faculty are women. There are 3 female faculty for every 100 female students and 7 male faculty for every 100 male students.

Administrators. Six of the seven chief administrators are men; the head librarian is a woman. Of 10 division/department chairpersons 2 are women, life science, and humanities and English. Two of the 5 trustees are women.

Women and the Curriculum. Sixty percent of women major in arts and sciences. Courses on women offered include Women in American History, Women in History, Images of Women, Self Defense, and Sex Roles. An official committee is responsible for developing courses on women as well as developing a Women's Studies Program.

Women and Athletics. No information was provided on intramural sports. The intercollegiate sports in which women compete are basketball, cross-country, softball, swimming, tennis, track, and volleyball.

Special Services and Programs for Women. *Health and Counseling.* One woman health worker provides limited services to students; no treatment specific to women is available. A student counseling center has 8 counselors, among whom are 2 white women and 2 minority women. Counseling is available for gynecological, birth control, abortion, and rape and assault issues.

Safety and Security. Campus police with no arrest authority and local police patrol the campus. Self-defense courses for women are available, as is a rape crisis center. In 1980-81, two assaults on women were reported on campus.

Other. The Office of Continuing Education, with the psychology department, sponsors assertiveness training.

Institutional Self-Description. None provided.

Orange Coast College
Costa Mesa, CA 92626
Telephone: (714) 556-5542

Women in Leadership
★★★ **students**
★ **faculty**
★ **administrators**

15,608 undergraduates

	Amer. Ind.	Asian Amer.	Blacks	Hispanics	Whites
F	236	365	65	376	6,623
M	236	629	106	491	6,391
%	3.0	6.4	1.1	5.6	83.9

This public, two-year commuter college serves a student body of 26,334. The college offers a transfer program and training in 98 semi-professional fields. Half of the 15,608 degree students are women, and 69 percent of the women attend part-time. The median age of all students is 23.

An on-campus childcare facility, which charges on a sliding scale from free to $12 per day, can accommodate about a third of requests for care. Private facilities are available off campus.

Policies to Ensure Fairness to Women. A written campus policy prohibiting sexual harassment of students, faculty, and staff has been publicly communicated to all of those groups. Complaints of sexual harassment are resolved by a formal campus grievance procedure. The Affirmative Action and Gender Equity officer is responsible part-time for equal opportunity, sex equity for students and handicapped access. The Handicapped Liaison Officer monitors compliance with handicapped access.

Women in Leadership Positions. *Students.* The two student leadership positions are president of the student body and editor-in-chief of the campus newspaper. In a recent three-year period, a woman has been president of the student body once and editor of the newspaper three times.

Faculty. About a third of the 334 full-time faculty members are women. There are 4 female faculty for every 100 female students and 7 male faculty for every 100 male students.

Administrators. Two of the six chief administrative officers are women: the head librarian and the director of institutional research. Women chair two of ten divisions: consumer and health sciences, and health and physical education.

Women and the Curriculum. About half of women graduate in arts and sciences and about a quarter in business and commercial programs. In a recent year, five women and 109 men graduated in mechanical and engineering programs.

The psychology department offers several Women's Studies courses. The English department offers a course on women writers and one on the images of women in literature and film.

Women and Athletics. Intramurals are not popular on this campus, but women participate in a wide range of intercollegiate sports, including badminton, basketball, cross-country, field hockey, gymnastics, sailing, skiing, softball, swimming/diving, tennis, track and field, and volleyball.

Special Services and Programs for Women. *Health and Counseling.* The student health service is staffed by 11 physicians (3 women and 8 men), all of whom work part-time, and 10 additional, female health-care providers. The health service provides gynecological and birth control assistance. The counseling center has a staff of 7, 4 of whom are women. They provide counseling on gynecological, birth control, abortion, and rape and assault issues. Counselors are provided with in-service training on the avoidance of sex-role stereotyping and racial bias.

Safety and Security. The campus, patrolled by local police, has high-intensity lighting in all areas. Additional services include self-defense courses, information sessions on campus safety and rape and assault prevention, and a rape crisis center. For 1980-81, six rapes and six assaults on women were reported on campus.

Career. The Gender Equity Committee sponsors a conference week on nontraditional careers for women, as well as a math-anxiety workshop. Workshops for the faculty and a "shadowing" program whereby students are introduced to women who work in nontraditional jobs are available.

Other. The Women's Center offers a women's perspective support group, facilitated by professional counselors, focusing on self-identity, goals clarification, and life planning. The center also schedules lectures on sexual harassment, nutrition, and establishing financial credit. Staffed by a part-time coordinator, with a budget of $10,663, the center serves nearly 7,000 women annually, with the largest groups being students over age 25 and community women. There is an advocacy group for Chicano students and one for Vietnamese students; both groups are 40 percent female.

Institutional Self-Description. "Orange Coast College is aware of the special needs of women. Through the Women's Center and special programs there is a focus upon personal information, stimulating experiences, promotion of nontraditional career potentials, and the development of reentry women into higher education and the world of work."

Oxnard College
Oxnard, CA 93033
Telephone: (805) 488-0911

Women in Leadership
★★ students
★ faculty
★ administrators

3,372 undergraduates

	Amer. Ind.	Asian Amer.	Blacks	Hispanics	Whites
F	22	86	166	473	997
M	13	141	158	536	758
%	1.0	6.8	9.7	30.1	52.4

This public, two-year community college is located on a suburban campus north of Los Angeles. The student body of 4,295 includes 3,372 undergraduates, just over half of whom are women. Slightly more than half the students are white; 30 percent are Hispanic students. Eighty percent of the female students attend part-time. More than half of the students are over age 32.

Oxnard offers the first two years of liberal arts and sciences, as well as a variety of occupational programs. Evening classes both on and off campus, self-paced/contract learning, and a summer session are available. There is also an adult continuing education program. A commuter college, Oxnard is accessible by public transportation and offers on-campus parking for a fee.

A small childcare facility that can accommodate 24 children fills approximately 40 percent of students' requests. Open from 7:45 a.m. to 4:30 p.m., the center charges $.75 per hour.

Policies to Ensure Fairness to Women. The college has a full-time Affirmative Action Officer who reviews campus policy and compliance regarding equal-employment-opportunity, sex-equity-in-education, and handicapped-accesibility laws. Campus policies and procedures on sexual harassment have been communicated in writing to students, faculty, and staff. Complaints of sexual harassment are resolved through a formal campus grievance procedure.

Women in Leadership Positions. *Students.* Women have excellent opportunities to exercise campus-wide leadership. In two of the past three years women have been president of the student body and presiding officer of the student governing body — the two student leadership positions. A woman is president of the only honorary society.

Faculty. One-third of the 42 full-time and 57 percent of the 215 part-time faculty members are women, proportions average for public two-year colleges in this guide. Virtually all full-time male faculty, but none of the female faculty, hold permanent appointments. There are 4 female faculty for every 100 female students and 6 male faculty for every 100 male students.

Administrators. Women hold two of the six top positions—chief business officer and director of athletics. Of five divisions, a woman heads business/public services.

Women and the Curriculum. Three-fourths of the women major in arts and sciences and 18 percent in business and commercial subjects. The college offers innovative programs to encourage women to prepare for nontraditional careers in such areas as agriculture, auto mechanics, ornamental landscape maintenance, truck driving, welding and fabrication, industrial mechanics, and diesel mechanics.

Courses on women include Women in Fiction, Women in Modern Theater, and Alcoholism and Women.

Minority Women. Of women enrolled in degree programs, almost half are members of minority groups: 27 percent are Hispanic, 10 percent are black, 5 percent are Asian American, and 1 percent are American Indian. Ninety-eight percent of those using the Women's Center are minority women. One black woman and two Hispanic women serve on the faculty senate.

Women and Athletics. No intramural sports are offered, but some women participate in intercollegiate sports. All varsity teams played in tournament competition in a recent year. One of the five paid varsity coaches is a woman. Intercollegiate sports offered are basketball, cross-country, track and field, and volleyball.

Special Services and Programs for Women. *Health and Counseling.* Two male physicians and one female health-care worker provide health services, which include gynecological and birth control treatment. A student counseling center counsels on gynecological problems and birth control.

Safety and Security. Measures include campus police with arrest authority, self-defense courses, and a rape crisis center. Two assaults (none on women) were reported for 1980–81.

Career. Workshops on nontraditional occupations and printed information on nontraditional fields of study for women are available. Faculty members are offered workshops on nontraditional occupations for women and men.

Other. The Women's Center is staffed part-time by a student volunteer. Handicapped students receive support from the Disabled Students' Organization; one-third of the 200 identified handicapped students are women. The Career Center sponsors a women's lecture series, and the humanities division sponsors theater and other arts programs for women.

Returning Women Students. Approximately 30 percent of returning women students take courses in the Continuing Education Program; about 15 percent of these are minority women. The program is headed by a full-time, female faculty member. An annual women's week is co-sponsored by the Career Center and by Re-entry, a support group having 40 percent minority women among its members.

Institutional Self-Description. "Community colleges offer tuition-free, local, comprehensive education in both occupational and transfer-preparation areas. These obvious advantages, coupled with convenience and a supportive environment for women, make Oxnard College an obvious choice for residents of its service area."

Patten College

2433 Coolidge Avenue
Oakland, CA 94601
Telephone: (415) 533-8300

Women in Leadership   ★ Women and the
  ★★ students   Curriculum
 ★★★ faculty
 ★★★ administrators

81 undergraduates

	Amer. Ind.	Asian Amer.	Blacks	Hispanics	Whites
F	1	0	17	0	23
M	0	3	13	3	15
%	1.3	4.0	40.0	4.0	50.7

Formerly Patten Bible College, Patten College is a coeducational Christian Evangelical institution that is located in a racially mixed community in Oakland. The school attracts 186 students. Fifty-seven percent of the 81 undergraduates are women; about a third of women attend part-time. In one recent year, two-thirds of women were over age 25. The median age of all students is 30.

Patten offers associate and bachelor's degree programs. Classes are scheduled during the evening, as well as the daytime, to accommodate part-time and adult students. The 80 percent of the undergraduates who commute may reach the campus by public transportation. Free parking is also available for commuters. The college provides single-sex and coeducational dormitories for the few students who reside on campus, including housing for married students with or without children and for single parents.

Private childcare facilities are available near campus.

Women in Leadership Positions. *Students.* Women have excellent opportunity to exercise student leadership. In a recent three year period, women have been manager of the campus radio station and senior-class president.

Faculty. Three of the five full-time faculty are Hispanic women.

Administrators. Seven of nine key posts, including chief executive officer and Academic Dean, are held by women. Women chair two of the three departments—biblical studies and professional studies.

Women and the Curriculum. The major field of study for bachelor's degree candidates is theology. In a recent year, women received six of the ten bachelor's degrees awarded. A program encourages women to prepare for the ministry. There are no courses on women.

Women and Athletics. There is no opportunity for organized competitive sports.

Special Services and Programs for Women. *Health and Counseling.* The student health service employs two female health-care providers. The student counseling center has one counselor, a woman. No services specific to women are available.

Safety and Security. Measures consist of city-police protection and high-intensity lighting. No information was provided on the incidence of rapes and assaults on women.

Institutional Self-Description. "Although we do not have any specific programs in Women's Studies, we offer an atmosphere of equality and freedom for women. Since the president and several key administrators are women, women are free to excel to the ultimate of their abilities. Women are encouraged to aim for excellence, not only academically but in whatever field they choose. In short, women can be assured of equal opportunities and advantages at Patten."

Pitzer College

1050 N. Mills Avenue,
Claremont, CA 91711
Telephone: (714) 621-8000

Women in Leadership   ★ Women and the
   ★ students   Curriculum
   ★ faculty
 ★★★ administrators

790 undergraduates

	Amer. Ind.	Asian Amer.	Blacks	Hispanics	Whites
F	0	19	36	34	395
M	0	9	17	22	241
%	0.0	3.6	6.9	7.2	82.3

AAUW NWSA

Pitzer, a member of the Claremont Colleges, was founded in 1963 as a women's college emphasizing the social and behavioral sciences. Located 35 miles south of Los Angeles, Pitzer shares the resources of the other colleges in the Claremont group. Pitzer became coeducational in 1970, although its undergraduate student body is still predominantly female: 494 women and 296 men. Twelve percent of the women and 6 percent of the men attend part-time. The median age of all undergraduates is 19. Free on-campus parking is available for students who commute.

Private childcare is available off campus.

Policies to Ensure Fairness to Women. The Treasurer, Director of Administrative Services, and Dean of Faculty have part-time responsibility for monitoring compliance with legislation concerning equal employment opportunity, sex equity for students, and handicapped access. The Office of Black Student Affairs and the Chicano Studies Center—jointly shared with the other Claremont Colleges—address the concerns of minority women.

Women in Leadership Positions. *Students.* Women make up 61 percent of the full-time students and have held slightly fewer than half the student leadership positions during the past three years.

Faculty. Women constitute a third of full-time faculty and an unusually high 32 percent of permanent faculty. There are 3 female faculty for every 100 female students and 11 male faculty for every 100 male students.

Administrators. Women hold five of the ten top administrative positions. Women are one-third of the faculty senate members.

Women and the Curriculum. Forty-five percent of degrees awarded to women are in social sciences, 27 percent in psychology, 19 percent in arts and letters, and virtually all the rest in biological sciences and foreign languages.

The Women's Studies Program, which is directed by a woman who holds a permanent, full-time faculty appointment, offers an undergraduate major and minor. Pitzer's courses on women include Introduction to Women's Studies; Women at Work; Women in Asia; Inequality: Cross-National View; Changing Roles of Men and Women in the Chicano Community; and Images of Women in Film. An official Claremont Colleges committee is responsible for developing the Women's Studies Program. (See also Scripps College and Pomona College.)

Women and Athletics. Women are 10 percent of intramural and 27 percent of intercollegiate athletes. Six of the 17 paid coaches for intercollegiate sports are women. Intercollegiate sports are basketball, cross-country, golf, swimming, tennis, track, and volleyball.

Housing and Student Organizations. The 76 percent of students who live on campus reside in coeducatonal dormitories with male and female units. The residence-hall directors, two men and one woman, receive awareness training on sexism, sex education, racism, and self-defense. The Gay Student Union of the Claremont Colleges is another student organization.

Pitzer students may join the women's groups of other Claremont Colleges. There is also a black women's organization, The Black Women of Pitzer and Pomona.

Special Services and Programs for Women. *Health and Counseling.* The Claremont Colleges share common health and counseling facilities. The health center is staffed by 3 physicians, 1 of whom is female, and 1 female health-care provider. The counseling center employs 2 female and 3 male counselors. Counseling and treatment are provided for gynecological problems, birth control, and rape and assault. Abortion counseling is also available. Counselors receive awareness training on the avoidance of sex-role stereotyping and racial bias. Partial maternity coverage is included in the student health insurance policy at no extra charge.

Safety and Security. Measures include a night-time escort service for women, high-intensity lighting, an emergency telephone system, self-defense courses for women, and information sessions on safety and rape and assault prevention. A community-based rape crisis center is available. No rapes or assaults were reported on campus in 1980–81.

Other. The Women's Center, sponsored by the Intercollegiate Deans of Students of the Five Claremont Colleges, occupies 200 square feet of space, has a budget of $685, and is run part-time by a student volunteer. Open to members of all the Claremont Colleges, the center holds theater and other women's arts programs and provides assertiveness/leadership training. It serves 350 women.

Returning Women Students. Pitzer offers a "New Resources" program for students over age 25. Eighty-one students, 66 of them women, are enrolled on either a full- or part-time basis. New Resources students are matriculated and participate in campus life, as do other undergraduates, and have access to their own New Resources Lounge.

Institutional Self-Description. "The Women's Center of the Claremont Colleges is located on the Pitzer campus, with its activities open to all members of the Claremont Colleges. Located four blocks from the campus is the Women's Center of the city of Claremont, which offers a variety of activities annually. In addition, Pitzer offers a concentration in the Study of Women that explores such issues as the changing roles and conception of women; women in cross-cultural perspective; and the participation of women in the major constructions of society."

Pomona College
Claremont, CA 91711
Telephone: (741) 621-8000

Women in Leadership ★★★ students			★★ Women and the Curriculum	

1,341 undergraduates

	Amer. Ind.	Asian Amer.	Blacks	Hispanics	Whites
F	0	62	25	47	496
M	2	51	21	40	560
%	0.2	8.7	3.5	6.7	81.0

 AAUW NWSA

Established in 1887, Pomona is an independent, coeducational college and the largest in the cluster of five Claremont Colleges. The campus, situated in a small town an hour from downtown Los Angeles, attracts 1,341 students, nearly half of whom are women. The median age of all undergraduates is 20. Pomona

offers degrees in a variety of liberal arts and pre-professional areas. Students can cross-register for most courses and majors at other Claremont Colleges. Most classes meet during the day.

For the less than 10 percent of undergraduates who commute or live off campus, public transportation is available, as is free parking on campus.

Private childcare facilities are located close to campus.

Policies to Ensure Fairness to Women. The Dean of Women assumes the part-time responsibility for handling matters pertaining to equal-employment-opportunity and sex-equity laws, and has policymaking power as well. The Treasurer oversees handicapped-accessibility policies and practices. A written and publicized sexual harassment policy covers all members of the campus community. Complaints are resolved through formal means.

The Commission on the Status of Women, on which students have voting rights, reports to the president, sponsors campus speakers, meets regularly, and publicizes its views on issues of concern to all women students, including minority women.

Women in Leadership Positions. *Students.* During three recent years, women have held the major leadership posts for at least one year each.

Faculty. Seventeen percent of the 124 full-time faculty are women, a figure below average for coeducational colleges in this guide. There are 3 female faculty for every 100 female students, and 15 male faculty for every 100 male students.

Administrators. Men hold all top positions. One of 21 departments—physical education—is chaired by a woman. Five of 34 trustees are women. In one recent year, two of the four commencement speakers were women, as were half of the speakers in major campus-wide lecture series.

Women and the Curriculum. The most popular fields among women graduates are social sciences (30 percent), biology (15 percent), letters (14 percent), and fine arts (13 percent). The proportion of degrees earned in biology by women is above the national average for private institutions. Ten percent of women major in such nontraditional areas as physical sciences and mathematics, a figure which is above average for similar schools in this guide. Pomona actively encourages women to prepare for careers in science and has a special exchange program with the California Institute of Technology. Women in Sciences provides additional support for students.

As a member of the Claremont Consortium, Pomona's Women's Studies Program offers the B.A. as a special concentration. Of the approximately 25 Women's Studies courses offered at all Claremont Colleges combined, Pomona's include Women and Work, Psychology of Women, and Men and Women in Politics. Representatives from each of the Claremont Colleges belong to the Women's Studies Coordinating Committee, which oversees the administration of the program and promotes the further integration of women into the existing curriculum. (See also Scripps College.)

Minority Women. Minority women constitute about 10 percent of the undergraduates. The residence-hall staff, which includes a minority woman, receives awareness training on the avoidance of racism. The Office of Black Student Affairs and the Chicano Studies Center serve minority women.

Women and Athletics. One-third of participants in intercollegiate sports are women. An estimated 8 percent of intramural athletes are women; sports clubs are available. Six of the 27 paid intercollegiate coaches are women. Intercollegiate sports offered are basketball, cross-country, golf, swimming, tennis, track, and volleyball.

Housing and Student Organizations. More than 90 percent of the students live on campus in coeducational dormitories that have no restrictions on visiting hours for members of the opposite sex. Residence-hall staff, half of whom are women, receive awareness training on sex education and birth control. Coeducational fraternities provide housing for members; 5 percent of the full-time undergraduate women belong. Feminists Against

Repression (FAR), and the Gay Students Union and Claremont's Women's Center on the Pitzer campus serve as advocates for women.

Special Services and Programs for Women. *Health and Counseling.* The Claremont Colleges share common health and counseling facilities. The health center is staffed by 3 physicians, 1 of whom is female, and 1 female health-care provider. The counseling center employs 2 female and 3 male counselors. Counseling and treatment are provided for gynecological problems, birth control, and rape and assault. Abortion counseling is also available. Counselors receive awareness training on the avoidance of sex-role stereotyping and racial bias. Partial maternity coverage is included in the student health insurance policy at no extra charge.

Safety and Security. Measures consist of campus and local police protection, night-time escort service for women, high-intensity lighting in most areas, instruction on self-defense and campus safety for women, and a rape crisis center. No rapes and seven assaults (four on women) were reported for 1980–81.

Career. The college offers career workshops, lectures and information on nontraditional occupations, encourages students to consult files on the careers of alumnae, and promotes networking between alumnae and female students.

Other. The Claremont Colleges' Women's Studies Coordinating Committee and Women's Studies Program organize lecture series. Assertiveness training workshops are conducted by the counseling center. Feminists Against Repression sponsors women's art shows.

Institutional Self-Description. None provided.

Rio Hondo College
Whittier, CA 90608
Telephone: (213) 692-0921

Women in Leadership
★★ faculty

11,533 undergraduates

	Amer. Ind.	Asian Amer.	Blacks	Hispanics	Whites
F	105	157	52	2,188	2,690
M	124	189	62	2,265	3,587
%	2.0	3.0	1.0	39.0	55.0

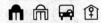

Rio Hondo College enrolled its first students in the fall of 1963, using local high-school classrooms. Now located on a suburban campus near Los Angeles, this public, two-year, commuter college serves 12,993 students, of whom 11,533 are enrolled in degree programs. Forty-five percent of the undergraduates are women, three-fourths of whom attend part-time. The median age of students is 30.

The college offers the first two years of liberal arts as well as a variety of vocational programs. Serving a district that includes five small cities, the college offers day and evening classes, in on- and off-campus locations. There is an adult continuing education program, a weekend college, and a summer session. The college is accessible by public transportation, and on-campus parking is available for a fee. There is also free transportation from remote parking lots to classroom buildings.

An off-campus facility, which provides childcare from 8 a.m. to 6 p.m., charges fees on a sliding scale.

Policies to Ensure Fairness to Women. There are three part-time equal-opportunity officers. One is responsible for compliance with handicapped-access legislation and two for sex equity for students. One of the officers has policymaking responsibilities. A written campus policy prohibiting sexual harassment of students, faculty, and staff has been communicated in writing to faculty and staff. Complaints of sexual harassment are resolved through a formal campus grievance procedure.

Women in Leadership Positions. *Students.* The three campus leadership positions—president of the student body, editor-in-chief of the campus newspaper, and manager of the campus radio station—have all been held by men in recent years. A woman presides over the sole honorary society.

Faculty. Women are 39 percent of a full-time faculty of 205; this proportion is somewhat above the average for public two-year colleges in this guide and is significantly above the average nationwide. There are 6 female faculty for every 100 female students and 8 male faculty for every 100 male students.

Administrators. All three of the chief administrative positions are held by men; a woman is head librarian. Four of the eleven departments are chaired by women, including business, biology, humanities, and women's physical education. Two of the five trustees are women.

Women and the Curriculum. Thirty-seven percent of women earning two-year degrees major in arts and sciences, 35 percent major in health, 17 percent in business, and 9 percent in public-service technologies. Fewer than 3 percent of students majoring in mechanical and engineering technologies are women. Half of the students enrolled in cooperative education programs are women. The humanities department offers a course entitled Women in Films, and the physical education department offers Women's Personal Health.

Minority Women. Of 5,192 matriculated women students, 42 percent are Hispanic, 3 percent Asian American, 2 percent American Indian, and 1 percent black. One minority woman is employed as a counselor. Counselors are offered training to avoid racial bias. About 40 percent of the women using the Women's Center are of Hispanic origin. A Hispanic woman chairs an academic department.

Women and Athletics. No information was provided.

Special Services and Programs for Women. *Health and Counseling.* The student health service has a staff of 4 male and one female physicians, and 2 female health-care providers. The health facility offers gynecological and birth control services. Counseling on gynecological problems, birth control, abortion, and rape or assault is available through the student counseling center. The 8-member staff includes 2 white women and 1 minority woman. Counselors are provided with in-service training on avoidance of sex-role stereotyping and racial bias.

Safety and Security. The campus is patrolled both by campus police and local police. Other security services include a night-time escort for women students, information sessions on campus safety and rape and assault prevention, and a rape crisis center. For 1980–81, one assault on a woman was reported.

Career. The college provides workshops, lectures, and printed information on nontraditional occupations for women. Faculty are offered workshops on nontraditional occupations for women and men and on affirmative action and equal opportunity.

Other. The Women's Center is operated by the occupational education division, under the direction of a full-time coordinator. Activities include discussion groups and individual counseling, workshops on mathematics confidence, assertiveness/leadership training, and a women's lecture series. The center coordinates a telephone service for information and referrals. A Handicapped Center provides services for the 150 female and 75 male handicapped students.

Institutional Self-Description. "A fine vocational education can be obtained at Rio Hondo College, or a good academic basis for transfer to a four-year college may be sought. All classes are open to women, who are especially encouraged to participate in courses nontraditional to their gender. The Women's Center on campus is always available to lend extra support to students on a daily basis."

San Diego Miramar College
San Diego, CA 92126
Telephone: (714) 271-7300

Women in Leadership
★★★ students
★★★ administrators

844 undergraduates

	Amer. Ind.	Asian Amer.	Blacks	Hispanics	Whites
F	5	17	22	27	320
M	2	14	34	32	367
%	0.8	3.7	6.7	7.0	81.8

Originally established to provide vocational training in specific areas, since 1977 this public, two-year college has offered a fully comprehensive educational program. With such a recent change in mission, the college has an expanding student body. Although official statistics for 1978–79 reveal 484 female students out of a total student population of 1,032, more recent data provided by the college indicate that there are now twice as many students on campus. The median age of undergraduates is 26. Forty percent of women students are over age 40, and three-fourths of these students attend part-time.

The college offers two-year degrees and certificates in the arts and sciences, mechanics and engineering, business and commerce, and public services. Two percent of students transfer to four-year colleges. Evening classes both on and off campus, a weekend college, and a summer session are available. Located on a suburban campus near San Diego, the college serves commuter students only. Public transportation and free on-campus parking are available.

An on-campus childcare facility, which accommodates all students' requests for care, is open from 8 a.m. to 4 p.m. and charges fees on a sliding scale.

Policies to Ensure Fairness to Women. The college has one equal-opportunity officer who, on a part-time basis, oversees compliance with equal-employment-opportunity, educational-sex-equity, and handicapped-accessibility legislation. Sexual harassment of students, faculty, and staff is prohibited by a written campus policy that has been publicly communicated to all three groups. A formal campus grievance procedure which ensures due process is used to resolve complaints of sexual harassment. Sex equity and sexual harassment have been the topics of faculty workshops.

Women in Leadership Positions. *Students.* Women students play a major role in campus leadership. In two of three recent years, women have held the positions of president of the student body and editor-in-chief of the campus newspaper, the only two campus-wide leadership positions. A woman heads the one student honorary society.

Faculty. Three of the 27 full-time faculty are women, a proportion far below average for public, two-year colleges in this guide. More recent data from the college indicate that an additional 3 male and 2 female faculty have been hired. Twenty percent of 266 part-time faculty are women, including 2 Hispanics, 1 Asian American, and 1 American Indian. There are 4 female faculty members for every 100 female students and 25 male faculty members for every 100 male students.

Administrators. Women hold four of six top-level administrative positions: chief business officer, chief development officer, director of institutional research, and head librarian. The proportion of women administrators is unusually high for public, two-year colleges in this guide. One of three deans (arts and sciences) is a woman.

Women and the Curriculum. Women earn 18 percent of the two-year degrees, primarily in public service (62 percent) and in

arts and sciences (36 percent). Women hold all of the student internships. There are no courses on women.

Women and Athletics. There are no intercollegiate or intramural sports.

Special Services and Programs for Women. *Health and Counseling.* The college has a student counseling center, but no student health service. There are three male counselors; in-service training in the avoidance of sex-role stereotyping is available to them.

Safety and Security. Measures consist of campus police with authority to make arrests, and self-defense courses for women. The campus, which houses an academy for police and sheriffs, is frequented by many law-enforcement personnel. No assaults on women or rapes were reported for 1980–81.

Institutional Self-Description. "We do offer training in several nontraditional occupations—i.e. fire-fighting, administration of justice, aviation mechanics, diesel mechanics. We encourage women to enroll, and more support is being provided for women as we go along."

San Diego State University
San Diego, CA 92182
Telephone: (714) 265-5200

★★ **Women and the Curriculum**

23,758 undergraduates

	Amer. Ind.	Asian Amer.	Blacks	Hispanics	Whites
F	224	489	645	1,033	9,149
M	230	574	559	1,012	9,347
%	2.0	4.6	5.2	8.8	79.5

 NWSA

Founded in 1897 as a two-year preparatory college for teachers, San Diego State University has become one of the largest campuses in the California State University system, drawing 32,625 students, 23,758 of whom are undergraduates. Almost half of the undergraduates are women, 28 percent of whom attend part-time. The median age of all undergraduates is 22.

This public university offers a wide range of undergraduate, pre-professional, professional, and graduate degree programs, in addition to an adult education program run by the College of Extended Studies. Students may choose from courses given during the day and evening, on and off campus, and may pursue independent study.

The university, located in the city of San Diego, is within easy reach by public transportation. For the 95 percent of undergraduates who commute or live off campus, parking on campus is provided at a fee.

A childcare facility on campus, serving mainly student parents, accommodates 130 children, ranging from infants to pre-schoolers. Fees are based on ability to pay, the age of the child, and the length of stay, on a sliding scale from no charge to $12 per day. There are other, private childcare facilities near the campus.

Policies to Ensure Fairness to Women. An Affirmative Action Coordinator has the part-time responsibility for examining policies and practices relating to sex-equity and handicapped-access laws. Legal matters involving the handicapped are the full-time responsibility of the Dean of Student Affairs. Both officers have policy-making powers. A formal and well-publicized sexual harassment policy protects all members of the university community. Complaints are handled in accordance with a formal grievance procedure.

Women in Leadership Positions. *Students*. Men have held all student offices during three recent years. Women head four of 14 honorary societies.

Faculty. Twenty-two percent of the 1,023 full-time faculty are women, a proportion slightly below the national average. There are 3 female faculty for every 100 female students and 10 male faculty for every 100 male students.

Administrators. Men hold all top positions. Women chair 20 of 100 departments, including religious studies, Women's Studies, special education, social work, and recreation. The deans of Undergraduate Studies, the Imperial Valley campus, and the College of Human Services are women. The proportion of women on the Board of Trustees (27 percent) is about average for comparable institutions.

Women and the Curriculum. Nearly half of the female graduates major in either business, health professions, interdisciplinary studies, or public affairs; 2 percent specialize in nontraditional areas. Special programs encourage women to pursue careers in business and engineering.

The Women's Studies department, the first of its kind in the country, is directed by a full-time, permanently appointed faculty member. A faculty of ten offers 25 courses, including New Views on Women, Introduction to Women's Studies, Sexism and the Social Sciences, Socialization of Women, Women and the Law, The Black Woman, and Chicana/Chicano Issues. The program offers an 18-unit minor and an opportunity to construct a major through the Liberal Studies Program. In recent years, approximately 200 students have been minors and 30 have been majors. Selected courses in Women's Studies may be used to fulfill general education requirements.

Minority Women. Minority women are 20 percent of all students. The Affirmative Action Advisory Council is an administrative organ that responds to the concerns of minority women. Minority student organizations include the North American Indian Student Alliance and Minority Business Students Association; minority women are active in the Women's Resource Center. Chicana women are in the process of forming their own organization.

One black and 2 Hispanic women head departments; an Hispanic woman is a dean; and 1 black and 1 Hispanic woman are members of the Board of Trustees. The student counseling staff and the residence-hall staff are offered awareness-training on racism. Three minority women are employed as counselors at the student counseling center.

Women and Athletics. There is an adequate intercollegiate sports program, in which 30 percent of the participants are women. Women receive 20 percent of athletic scholarship aid. The intercollegiate sports offered are basketball, cross-country, golf, gymnastics, softball, swimming, tennis, track and field, and volleyball.

Housing and Student Organizations. Five percent of the undergraduates live in campus on either single-sex or coeducational dormitories. Some women's dormitories restrict visiting hours for members of the opposite sex.

Nine percent of the full-time female undergraduates belong to sororities, which furnish housing for their members. Advocacy groups include Women in Business, Women in Advertising, and the Society for Women Engineers. There are two Women's Studies groups: the Student Chapter of the Center for Women's Studies and the Women's Studies Student Association.

Special Services and Programs for Women. *Health and Counseling*. A student health service offers treatment for gynecological problems and birth control. The student counseling center is staffed by six female and eight male counselors. Additional medical services specific to women are birth control, abortion, and rape and assault counseling. Counselors are offered in-service training on sex-role stereotyping.

Safety and Security. Measures consist of campus and local police protection, night-time escort for women, emergency telephone system, and a rape crisis center. No information was provided on the incidence of rapes and assaults on women.

Career. The placement office disseminates information about nontraditional careers, encourages networking between students and alumnae, and organizes support groups and conferences for women contemplating nontraditional careers.

Other. The Women's Resource Center operates on a limited budget under the direction of a student volunteer. Each year about 900 people use the center, which serves all women, including displaced homemakers, handicapped women, older women, welfare women, and lesbians. Minority women are part of the core of 20 active members. Handicapped women may join a support group called RENEWD.

Among the special programs for women are occasional concerts sponsored by the Women's Resource Center and Women's Studies; creative arts performances by the Annual Arts Festival; a conference on women, technology, and the future; a women's lecture series; and assertiveness training workshops.

Institutional Self-Description. None provided.

San Francisco State University
1600 Holloway Ave.
San Francisco, CA 94132
Telephone: (415) 469-2141

★★★ Women and the Curriculum

17,794 undergraduates

	Amer. Ind.	Asian Amer.	Blacks	Hispanics	Whites
F	69	1,881	1,063	588	5,692
M	72	1,510	839	572	4,889
%	0.8	19.7	11.1	6.8	61.6

A publicly supported institution, San Francisco State offers its 26,298 students bachelor's degrees in arts, sciences, business, education, and pre-professional areas, as well as master's degrees in some fields. Women are 54 percent of the 17,794 undergraduates; 31 percent of women attend part-time. The Continuing Education Program serves the adult student.

Most students commute. Public transportation to the campus is readily available, and on-campus parking is provided at a fee. Coeducational dormitories house a small proportion of undergraduates who live on campus.

On-campus daycare facilities can accommodate 75 percent of requests by students. Fees, charged on a sliding scale, range from $10 to $20 for three half-days of care.

Policies to Ensure Fairness to Women. The Affirmative Action Officer is responsible full-time for policies and practices relating to equal employment, sex equity for students, and handicapped access. The university has adopted the California State University and College system's policy that prohibits sexual harassment, and is now formulating an additional policy of its own.

Women in Leadership Positions. *Students*. No information was provided on student leadership. Women head ten of 25 honorary societies.

Faculty. Women are 24 percent of the 768 full-time faculty. There are 3 female faculty for every 100 female students and 11 male faculty for every 100 male students.

Administrators. Women are chief business officer, head librarian, and Dean of the School of Humanities. Men hold all other key administrative positions. Women chair 13 of 65 departments, including American Indian studies, broadcast communication arts, economics, and Women's Studies.

Women and the Curriculum. Most degrees awarded to women are in business (14 percent), health professions (13 percent), interdisciplinary studies (11 percent), social sciences (11 percent), and psychology (10 percent). A very low proportion (1 percent) of women take degrees in the nontraditional fields of engineering, mathematics, and physical sciences. The mathematics department offers courses to build skills, including Math without Fear, Statistics without Fear, and Computers without Fear. The engineering department has a program on women in engineering.

The Women's Studies Program is one of the largest and oldest in the U.S., and the first in California to award the B.A. in Women's Studies. SFSU's program offers some 20 interdisciplinary courses each term, in addition to coordinating more than 40 courses on women offered by disciplinary departments ranging from English to engineering, and including Asian American studies, American Indian studies, and ethnic studies. Unique to Women's Studies Programs are the series of "core" courses especially designed for majors: these include Women in Groups, Women as Creative Agents, and Critical Thinking and Research in Women's Studies. A strong emphasis of the major in Women's Studies focuses on the intersections of gender, race, and class. Undergraduates at San Francisco State are required to take at least one course which examines discrimination against members of minority groups. During the past five years, the program has had approximately 100 majors. In the fall of 1982, a new minor in Women's Studies will also be available.

Women's Studies is directed by a tenured faculty member; an official commitee supervises the program. Women's Studies offers workshops that encourage faculty to include materials on women and minorities of both sexes in introductory and general education courses.

Minority Women. Forty percent of the female undergraduates are members of minority groups. About 10 percent of the full-time faculty are minority women: 42 are Asian American women and 27 black women. Two black women are members of the faculty senate; one American Indian women heads a department.

Women and Athletics. Thirty-four percent of the intercollegiate and 10 percent of the intramural athletes are women. Seven of 26 paid varsity coaches are women. Intercollegiate sports are badminton, basketball, cross-country, gymnastics, soccer, softball, swimming, and track and field.

Special Services and Programs for Women. *Health and Counseling.* The student health service provides some medical treatment specific to women. The staff consists of 14 physicians, five of whom are women. The counseling center offers assertiveness training, and counseling on birth control and rape. Half of the counseling staff are female; staff receive awareness training on avoiding racism and sexism.

Safety and Security. Measures consist of a night-time escort for women students and workshops on rape and assault prevention. No information was provided on the incidence of rapes and assaults on women.

Career. Services include career workshops, information about nontraditional occupations, networking between students and alumnae, and files on alumnae careers.

Other. The Women's Center, run by salaried student administrators, provides a drop-in center, literature for and about women, and self-help and consciousness-raising groups. Associated Students sponsors an annual women's week and a warmline of information, referral, and support. Disabled Student Services and a Re-entry Students Program are available.

Institutional Self-Description. "San Francisco State University, an urban university, has a multi-ethnic student body, and over half is female. The Women's Studies Program was one of the first to offer a B.A.; about 40 courses on women are offered throughout the university each semester. The Women's Center offers excellent programs. The administration generally supports women's issues and programs."

San Jose State University
San Jose, CA 95192
Telephone: (408) 277-2000

Women in Leadership	★ Women and the
★ students	Curriculum
★ administrators	

20,638 undergraduates

	Amer. Ind.	Asian Amer.	Blacks	Hispanics	Whites
F	206	1,114	1,053	937	6,488
M	149	1,253	840	1,038	6,821
%	1.8	11.9	9.5	9.9	66.9

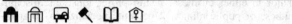

Founded in 1857 as a preparatory school for teachers, San Jose State has been a university in the state system since 1972. Located in a large, multi-cultural city south of San Francisco, it attracts some 29,400 students to a range of undergraduate and graduate programs. Continuing education is available. Alternative class schedules include a summer session; some evening classes are held in off-campus locations.

Women make up 48 percent of the 20,638 undergraduates; 30 percent of the women attend part-time. The estimated median age of undergraduates is 27. For the 91 percent of undergraduates who commute, the university is accessible by public transportation. On-campus parking is available at a fee.

Private childcare facilities near campus, which charge fees on a sliding scale, accommodate 54 percent of students' requests.

Policies to Ensure Fairness to Women. The Affirmative Action Officer, on a full-time basis, reviews policies and practices related to equal employment opportunity and handicapped accessibility. Compliance with sex equity for women students is monitored part-time by a Vice-Presidential Assistant. A campus policy prohibits sexual harassment. Complaints are handled informally or through a formal grievance procedure.

Women in Leadership Positions. *Students.* Opportunities for women students to exercise campus-wide leadership are above average for four-year institutions in this guide. In a recent three years, women have presided over the student body and twice been editor-in-chief of the campus newspaper. Women head two of the six honorary societies.

Faculty. Women are 22 percent of a full-time faculty of 845. According to a recent report, 7 black, 6 Asian American, and 10 Hispanic women are on the full-time faculty. The ratio of full-time female faculty to full-time female students is 3 to 100. The ratio of full-time male faculty to full-time male students is 9 to 100.

Administrators. The President of the university, the head librarian, and the Director of Women's Athletics are female. Women, including 1 black and 1 Hispanic woman, head 11 of 63 departments. The Dean of Humanities and Arts is female. One-third of members of the Board of Trustees are women, including 1 black and 1 Hispanic woman.

Women and the Curriculum. The majority of women graduating with bachelor's degrees major in business and management (21 percent), the health professions (15 percent), interdisciplinary studies (10 percent), fine arts (9 percent), and the social sciences (9 percent). Five percent major in such nontraditional areas as architecture, engineering, mathematics, and the physical sciences. The university hosts a mathematics and science conference for high school women.

The Women's Studies Program offers an undergraduate minor and a master's degree. Three Women's Studies courses are offered through the social sciences department and 15 courses on women through the departments of religious studies, African American studies, Asian American studies, Mexican American graduate studies, psychology, English, history, anthropology, business, political science, and sociology. Recent offerings include Women's Cultural Visions, Mothers and Daughters, Gods and Goddesses, Women and Work, History of Women in the U.S., Women in Cross-Cultural Perspectives, Women as Managers, and Women's Health Issues. A official committee works to further the Women's Studies Program.

Such current issues as mathematics confidence among women, sex-fair curricula, coeducational physical education classes, health-care information important to minority women, services for abused spouses, and discrimination in the workplace are part of the course work offered future teachers, health-care providers, social workers, and business students.

Minority Women. Of 9,983 undergraduate women, 11 percent are black, 2 percent American Indian, 11 percent Asian American, and 9 percent Hispanic. Among courses which reflect concern for minority experiences are The Black Woman, Afro-American Women in History, Asian American Women, and La Chicana. One minority woman is a residence-hall director, 3 are on the staff of the counseling service, and 2 of the 3 co-directors of the Women's Center are Hispanic. Residence-hall and counseling staff are offered awareness-training on racial bias. The Chicana Alliance serves as an advocacy group for women.

Women and Athletics. Intramural and intercollegiate programs are somewhat limited. Fencing and water polo are among the seven intramural sports offered. One-quarter of the varsity athletes are female; women receive one-fifth of the athletic scholarships. Intercollegiate teams played in tournaments during 1980. The intercollegiate sports offered are basketball, fencing, field hockey, golf, gymnastics, swimming, tennis, and volleyball.

Housing and Student Organizations. For the 9 percent of undergraduates who live on campus, coeducational dormitories and housing for married students and single parents with children are available. A married student whose spouse is not enrolled may live in married students' housing. Dormitories do not restrict hours for visitors of the opposite sex. Two of eight residence-hall directors are women. Awareness-training on sexism, sex education, racism, birth control, assertiveness, and health are offered to residence-hall staff.

Social sororities and fraternities provide housing for their members. Among groups which promote women's interests are the Gay and Lesbian Student Union, Society of Women Engineers, and California Women in Higher Education.

Special Services and Programs for Women. *Health and Counseling.* The student health service provides some medical attention specific to women; gynecological and birth control treatment are available and abortion by referral. Two of 9 physicians are female, as are 18 other health-care providers. The regular student health insurance covers maternity as an elective. The counseling service, staffed by 5 women and 7 men, offers some counseling of particular concern to women. Staff receive in-service training on avoiding sex-role stereotyping and racial bias.

Safety and Security. Measures include campus police with arrest authority, high-intensity lighting, emergency alarm and telephone systems, self-defense courses for women, information sessions on safety and crime prevention, foot patrols and canine units, and a rape crisis center. No information was provided about the incidence of rapes and assaults on women.

Career. Services includes career workshops, guest speakers, and nonsexist/nonracist printed materials on women in nontraditional occupations, as well as assertiveness training and networking between students and alumnae.

Other. The Women's Center—with a budget of $7,000—is staffed by three student coordinators. It co-sponsors an annual women's week and a telephone service of information, referral, and support. The Re-Entry Advisory Program serves older and reentry students.

Institutional Self-Description. "Women are visible on the sunny urban/suburban campus. The university has a strong Women's Studies Program, which offers a M.A. Twenty percent of the faculty and administrators are women, and there is a woman president. Students may be 18 or 69 (many are 25 to 45), Asian, Hispanic, white or black; most work and go to school."

Santa Ana College
17th at Bristol, Santa Ana, CA 92706
Telephone: (714) 667-3000

Women in Leadership	★ Women and the
★★ students	Curriculum
★★ faculty	

11,227 undergraduates

	Amer. Ind.	Asian Amer.	Blacks	Hispanics	Whites
F	91	116	257	700	4,117
M	101	148	317	806	4,087
%	1.8	2.5	5.3	14.0	76.4

Located on an urban campus near Los Angeles, this public, two-year college serves 14,040 students. Of the 11,227 degree students, 48 percent are women, and 77 percent of women attend part-time. Sixteen percent of women are over age 40; the median age of students is 31.

The college offers a transfer program, as well as continuing adult education and occupational terminal curricula. Degree and certificate programs include liberal arts, data processing, health technologies, business, mechanics and engineering, communications and media, natural science, and public services. The college offers evening and weekend classes, at off-campus centers as well as on-campus, a summer session, self-paced/contract learning, and opportunities for the assessment of prior learning. All students commute. The college is accessible by public transportation, and on-campus parking is available.

Childcare is available on campus from 7 a.m. to 10 p.m., in a facility that can accommodate 150 children. It is open to full-time and part-time students, and charges fees on a sliding scale. Childcare is also available at some of the continuing education centers.

Policies to Ensure Fairness to Women. A full-time equal-employment-opportunity officer reviews policies and practices generated by campus committees. The college has a Committee on Affirmative Action, and an active Committee for Women's Programs and Services that includes student members with voting rights.

A written campus policy prohibiting sexual harassment of students has been communicated in writing to students. Complaints of sexual harassment are handled informally and confidentially.

Women in Leadership Positions. *Students.* There is excellent opportunity for women undergraduates to exercise campus leadership. During recent years, women have been president of the student body for one year, presiding officer of the student governing body for two years, and presiding officer of the student judiciary and of the student union board for one year.

Faculty. The full-time faculty of 262 is 38 percent female, a proportion higher than average for public two-year colleges in this guide. Women are 30 percent of the part-time faculty of 352. The ratio of women faculty to women students is 8 to 100. The ratio of men faculty to men students is 10 to 100.

Administrators. Eight of the ten chief administrative positions are held by men. The chief development officer and the director of institutional research are women. Women chair the departments of nursing and child development and serve as deans of Applied Arts and Sciences, Instructional Services, Fine Arts and Humanities, the director of Media Services, and the Dean of Occupations.

Women and the Curriculum. The majority of women (56 percent) earn associate degrees in arts and sciences; fewer graduate from two-year vocational programs in health (15 percent), business (15 percent), and public-service technologies (10 percent). Three percent earn degrees in science-engineering and data-processing technologies. The college offers innovative programs on women in architecture and women in drafting.

A Women's Studies Program, operated under the direction of the Dean of Humanities, offers an associate degree and a minor. Eleven courses on women are offered through various departments, including Women: A Kaleidoscope View; Women in Transition; Women's Health; Women in U.S. History; and Sociology of Women. Faculty workshops include a course on sexism in the curriculum.

Minority Women. Among 5,281 women students, 5 percent are black, 2 percent American Indian, 2 percent Asian American, and 13 percent Hispanic. Four minority women serve on the counseling staff, who receive training on avoiding racial bias. About 20 percent of participants in the New Horizons Program sponsored by the counseling division are minority women. The sociology division offers a course called The Black Family in America.

Women and Athletics. Women participate in several intercollegiate sports. During one recent year, all teams entered tournament competition. The intercollegiate sports offered are basketball, cross-country, softball, tennis, track and field, and volleyball.

Special Services and Programs for Women. *Health and Counseling.* The student health service is staffed by 7 male physicians and 7 female health-care providers. Gynecological treatment is available, as are services for birth control and rape and assault. The 14-member student counseling staff includes 9 women, 4 of whom are members of minority groups. Counseling is available on gynecological problems, birth control, and rape and assault. In-service training for counselors includes workshops on sex-role stereotyping, racial bias, careers for women, and suicide/depression. The counseling division offers assertiveness/leadership training.

Safety and Security. Services include campus police with authority to make arrests, city police, night-time escort for women students, high-intensity lighting, emergency alarm system, self-defense courses, information sessions on campus safety, and a rape crisis center. For 1980–81, six assaults were reported, one of them on a woman.

Career. Career workshops and lectures by women employed in nontraditional occupations, networking between alumnae and female students, and a career shadowing program encourage women to enter nontraditional fields.

Other. The Women's Center is part of the New Horizons Program and draws from the $250,000 New Horizons budget. Coordinated by a full-time, salaried staff member, the center sponsors an annual women's week, a women's lecture series, and a telephone referral service. The most frequent participants in Women's Center activities are students over 25 years of age. About 20 percent of those using the center are minority women, predominantly Hispanic and Vietnamese.

Older women and displaced homemakers receive support from the New Horizons program; handicapped women find support at the Disabled Students' Center.

Institutional Self-Description. None provided.

Santa Rosa Junior College
Santa Rosa, CA 95401
Telephone: (707) 527-4375

Women in Leadership
★★ students
★ faculty

10,473 undergraduates

	Amer. Ind.	Asian Amer.	Blacks	Hispanics	Whites
F	80	83		215	5,555
M	45	97	115	225	3,876
%	1.2	1.7	1.8	4.3	91.0

Originally established to prepare students for transfer to the University of California, this public, two-year college changed its mission in 1952 to include terminal occupational education programs and non-transfer general education courses. The total enrollment in all college programs is 13,228. Women are 58 percent of the 10,473 degree students, and two-thirds of women attend part-time. The median age is 27. Of 417 students indentified as handicapped, approximately 40 percent are women.

Serving a large number of reentry students, the college offers day and evening classes (both on and off campus), a summer session, and adult continuing education. Located north of San Francisco, Santa Rosa is largely a commuter college, with only 1 percent of undergraduates residing on campus. The sole dormitory on campus, which is coeducational, houses 44 women. The college is accessible by public transportation and offers on-campus parking for a fee.

A childcare facility, within two blocks of the campus, can accommodate 78 children of full- and part-time students—three-quarters of all requests. The facility, which charges fees on a sliding scale, is open from 7:45 a.m. to 4:30 p.m.

Policies to Ensure Fairness to Women. The Associate Dean of Administrative Services and the Gender Equity Coordinator serve as full-time equal opportunity officers. Both are voting members of policymaking councils, and review policies and practices generated by councils and committees.

Sexual harassment of students, faculty, and staff is prohibited in a written campus policy that has been publicly communicated to all three groups. Both an informal, confidential mechanism and a formal grievance procedure exist for resolving complaints of sexual harassment. An Affirmative Action Committee and a Third World Faculty Committee review the status and the concerns of women and minorities on campus.

Women in Leadership Positions. *Students.* The two campus leadership positions—president of the student body and editor-in-chief of the campus newspaper—have been held by women half the time in the three recent years.

Faculty. Of 174 full-time faculty members, 47 are female, including 2 Hispanics, 1 Asian American, and 1 black. The proportion of full-time female faculty (27 percent) is below average, for public, two-year colleges in this guide, but above the national average for all institutions. Data supplied by the college cite an additional 545 part-time faculty, 40 percent of whom are female. There are 2 female faculty for every 100 female students and 7 male faculty for every 100 male students.

Administrators. All of the chief administrative positions in the college are held by men. Of 28 department chairs, 6 are women: business-office technology, consumer and family studies, foreign languages, guidance, health occupations, and child development. Ten of 22 faculty senate members are women (including an Asian American woman).

Women and the Curriculum. Approximately 90 percent of women earn associate degrees in arts and sciences, while the remainder graduate from vocational programs in health, engineering, or public service technology.

Six courses on women are offered in the departments of health education, guidance, psychology, sociology, and social science. They include Women, Work, and Survival; History of Women and Social Change in the U.S.; and Psychology Looks at Women. An official committee collects curricular material on women and reports on curricular development relating to women in the curriculum.

Women and Athletics. Approximately one-fourth of those participating in both intercollegiate and intramural sports are women. All intramurals are coeducational and include a wide range of team and individual sports. There are 17 paid intercollegiate coaches, five of whom are women. The intercollegiate program also offers a wide variety of team and individual sports, including basketball, cross-country, gymnastics, softball, swimming and diving, tennis, track and field, and volleyball.

Special Services and Programs for Women. *Health and Counseling.* No student health services specific to women are available. The student counseling center is staffed by nine counselors, three of whom are women. Counselors receive in-service training on sex-role stereotyping, racial bias, depression, stress reduction, and values clarification.

Safety and Security. The campus is patrolled by campus police and local police. Additional security services and training include a night-time escort for women students, high-intensity lighting in all areas, self-defense courses for women, information sessions on campus safety and rape and assault prevention, and a rape crisis center. In 1980–81, fewer than ten assaults were reported on campus, fewer than five of which involved women.

Career. The Gender Equity Program provides workshops and information that encourage women students to prepare for nontraditional careers. Students can attend career workshops and lecture panels about women in nontraditional fields of study and use updated files of alumnae by specific careers. There is also a program that establishes contacts between female students and alumnae.

Other. Handicapped women find support from Enabling Services; lesbians from the Gay Student Union; battered women and displaced homemakers through Student Services Reentry Program and a local YWCA shelter.

Returning Women Students. The reentry program, operating under Student Services, is oriented to the needs of women students. This program revolves around a Women's Center, which serves community women as well as students. An annual women's week, assertiveness/leadership training, personal counseling and support groups, library and resource materials, weekly workshops, conferences, academic advising, and telephone information and referrals are all conducted by the Student Services Reentry Program. A faculty member serves as full-time administrator of the program.

Institutional Self-Description. "This institution provides excellent preparation for a university or college education at little cost, and complete training for an occupation. The Reentry Program offers support and guidance for women returning to school. The Gender Equity Program is also extremely helpful for women interested in nontraditional areas of study."

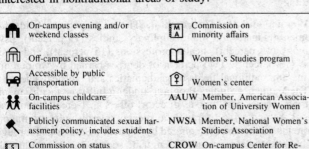

🏛	On-campus evening and/or weekend classes	Ⓜ️Ⓐ	Commission on minority affairs
🏛	Off-campus classes	📖	Women's Studies program
🚐	Accessible by public transportation	🏠	Women's center
👫	On-campus childcare facilities	AAUW	Member, American Association of University Women
✒	Publicly communicated sexual harassment policy, includes students	NWSA	Member, National Women's Studies Association
Ⓢ Ⓦ	Commission on status of women	CROW	On-campus Center for Research on Women

Scripps College

Claremont, CA 91711
Telephone: (714) 621-8000

Women in Leadership	★ **Women and the Curriculum**
★★★ students	
★★ faculty	
★★★ administators	

559 undergraduates

	Amer. Ind.	Asian Amer.	Blacks	Hispanics	Whites
F	1	25	18	35	457
M	0	0	0	0	0
%	0.2	4.7	3.4	6.5	85.3

🏛 🚐 📖 🏠 AAUW NWSA

Founded in 1926, Scripps is the only single-sex and women's college in the cluster of six institutions that comprise the Claremont Colleges. Located near Los Angeles, the college draws 559 students, all of whom are registered in degree programs. About 2 percent attend part-time. The median age of students is 20.

A variety of undergraduate degrees is available, in addition to a small continuing education program. Students can also cross-register for most courses and majors at the other Claremont Colleges. Most courses are conducted during the day. For the less than 10 percent of the undergraduates who commute or live off-campus, public transportation and on-campus parking are available.

The nearest childcare facility is located off campus.

Policies to Ensure Fairness to Women. The Dean of Faculty has part-time responsibility for handling equal employment opportunity for faculty. The Director of Financial and Business Affairs has the same responsibility for staff other than faculty, and works with the Dean of Students on handicapped accessibility. All three administrators have policymaking powers. Complaints of sexual harassment are resolved informally and confidentially.

Women in Leadership Positions. *Students.* Women hold all student leadership positions.

Faculty. Forty-four percent of the 48 full-time faculty are women. There are 4 female faculty for every 100 female students.

Administrators. Although the President is a man, five of seven other key administrators are women, including the chief academic officer. Women chair seven of 15 departments: Hispanic studies, German, Italian, comparative literature, psychology, music, and religion. Half of the members of the Board of Trustees are female, as well as its chair.

Women and the Curriculum. The most popular fields for women graduates are fine arts (21 percent), social sciences (20 percent), letters (17 percent), and psychology (15 percent). Three percent of women pursue such nontraditional fields of study as mathematics and physical science.

While the Women's Studies Program is a cooperative effort of all the Claremont Colleges, it is located on the Scripps campus. An individualized major may be arranged by Scripps students. Approximately 25 Women's Studies courses are offered on all Claremont College campuses combined. Recently, on the Scripps campus, courses included American Women Poets, Women in the Renaissance, and Self Defense. At least 20 other courses throughout the Claremont Colleges give substantial attention to women's issues.

Representatives from each of the Claremont Colleges belong to the Women's Studies Coordinating Committee, which is responsible for the development of the Women's Studies Program. Recently, the committee organized a series of faculty workshops on Women and Achievement.

Minority Women. Fifteen percent of the students are minority women. Members of the staffs of the residence halls and student counseling center participate in awareness-training on racism. MECHA, an Hispanic student group, serves Chicana women at all the Claremont College campuses. At Scripps black students have their own support and advocacy group, Wannawake Weisi.

The Claremont College departments of black studies and Chicano studies serve as additional resources for minority women. Courses on minority women include Women and Men in The Chicano Community and Women in Native North America.

Women and Athletics. While the athletic program is shared with two coeducational colleges, most of the female athletes are from Scripps. Thirty-one percent of the intercollegiate athletes and 17 percent of the intramural athletes are women. Sports clubs are also popular. Intercollegiate sports offered are basketball, cross-country, swimming, tennis, track and field, and volleyball.

Housing and Student Organizations. More than 90 percent of the women live on campus in dormitories that have no restrictions on men's visiting hours. Residence-hall staff are offered awareness-training on sexism, sex education, racism, and birth control, among other matters.

Special Services and Programs for Women. *Health and Counseling.* The Claremont Colleges share common health and counseling facilities. The health center is staffed by 3 physicians, 1 of whom is female, and 1 female health-care provider. The counseling center employs 2 female and 3 male counselors. Counseling and treatment are provided for gynecological problems, birth control, and rape and assault. Abortion counseling is also available. Counselors are offered awareness-training on sex-role stereotyping and racial bias. Partial maternity coverage is included in the student health insurance policy at no extra charge.

Safety and Security. Measures consist of campus and local police protection, night-time escort service for women, emergency alarm system, a course on self-defense, and a booklet on campus safety for women. No rapes or assaults on women were reported for 1980–81.

Career. The college has a special Corporate Training for Liberal Arts Women program that offers summer work experience for women interested in business careers. Career days bring alumnae and other women in nontraditional occupations together with students. Additional support comes from the Association of Women in Science and the student chapter for the Society for Advancement of Management.

Other. The Scripps feminist group, Vita Nova, has its own meeting room and reference library. The Women's Studies Program organizes a women's lecture series. The Gay and Lesbian Students of the Claremont Colleges serve lesbians at Scripps. A small Continuing Education for Women Program admits about ten returning women students, who attend class on a full-time basis with traditional-aged students.

Special Features. The Macpherson Collection in the Ella Strong Denison Library houses more than 2,500 books by and about significant women—including primary sources (manuscripts and rare books) unavailable elsewhere.

Institutional Self-Description. "Scripps offers an ideal blend of small college lifestyle with university facilities. Thus Scripps students may study and major in subjects not offered on the home campus, while enjoying the special strengths of a college whose sole mission is the education of women, organized around a distinctive interdisciplinary Humanities Core Curriculum. Scripps students are voting members of most faculty/administration/trustee committees, and have close rapport with a talented faculty, half of whom are women."

Sonoma State University
Rohnert Park, CA 94928
Telephone: (707) 664-2880

Women in Leadership ★ faculty	★ Women and the Curriculum

4,135 undergraduates

	Amer. Ind.	Asian Amer.	Blacks	Hispanics	Whites
F	28	49	74	86	2,074
M	31	40	81	95	1,544
%	1.4	2.2	3.8	4.4	88.2

Founded in 1960, Sonoma State is one of the newer and smaller campuses in the California State University and College system. Its campus, located in a rural setting an hour from San Francisco, has a total enrollment of 5,851 students, of whom 4,135 are undergraduates. Women are 56 percent of the undergraduates and 32 percent attend part-time. The median age of all undergraduates is 28.

Sonoma awards bachelor's and master's degrees in a wide variety of fields. It also offers extended education and adult continuing education programs. Classes meet day and evening and during the summer. For the 91 percent of undergraduates who live off campus or commute, on-campus parking at a fee and public transportation are available.

The university-sponsored childcare center serves 100 children of primarily low-income families and accommodates only 15 percent of students' requests. The hourly fee for non-subsidized childcare is $2.15. Additional, private childcare facilities are available nearby.

Policies to Ensure Fairness to Women. The full-time Director of Affirmative Action is responsible for examining policies and practices pertaining to equal employment opportunity, sex equity for students, and handicapped access. A published sexual harassment policy protects all members of the Sonoma State community.

Women in Leadership Positions. *Students.* Women students have little opportunity to exercise student leadership. In three recent years, a woman held one of five campus offices—for one year.

Faculty. Twenty-seven percent of the full-time faculty are women, a figure which is above the national average. There are 4 female faculty for every 100 female students and 14 male faculty for every 100 male students. Recent data show that among the 74 full-time female faculty there are 1 black, 1 American Indian, 1 Asian American, and 8 Hispanic women.

Administrators. Except for the head librarian and the Dean of Graduate Studies and Research, the chief administrators are male. An American Indian woman and a black woman are among 10 women who chair departments, including art, English, foreign languages, theater arts, nursing, environmental studies, and gerontology.

Women and the Curriculum. The most popular fields for women graduates are interdisciplinary studies (19 percent), psychology (15 percent), health professions (15 percent), and business (13 percent). Two percent of degrees earned by women are in the nontraditional fields of mathematics and physical sciences.

The Women's Studies Program, under a full-time faculty member who serves part-time as director, offers a 21-credit minor and the B.A. and M.A. through a special interdisciplinary major. More than 20 courses are offered by Women's Studies and through eight departments, including English, sociology, and multi-cultural studies. Recent titles include History of Women in the U.S.,

Lesbians in Literature, Racism and Sexism, The Contemporary Black Woman, and Men/Women and Power.

Undergraduates, regardless of major or field, are required to take a course which examines discrimination against minorities. An official committee is responsible for developing the Women's Studies Program. The departments of education, management, nursing, and physical education provide instruction on some matters specific to women.

Women and Athletics. The organized athletic program for women consists of eight intercollegiate teams: basketball, cross-country, fencing, gymnastics, softball, tennis, track and field, and volleyball.

Housing and Student Organizations. Single-sex and coeducational dormitories that have no restrictions on visiting hours for members of the opposite sex house nine percent of the undergraduates. The residence-hall staff are offered awareness-training on sexism, sex education, racism, and birth control. The Women's Union, an advocacy group, meets on campus.

Special Services and Programs for Women. *Health and Counseling.* The student health center is staffed by three male physicians. Two of the five professionals at the student counseling center are women. Counseling and treatment for birth control and gynecological problems as well as abortion and rape and assault counseling are available.

Safety and Security. Measures consist of campus police with authority to make arrests, emergency telephone systems, self-defense courses for women, and a rape crisis center. No rapes and one assault on a woman were reported for 1980–81.

Career. The university offers career workshops, lectures and information on nontraditional occupations, in addition to maintaining files on the careers of alumnae.

Other. Women's Studies helps program the annual women's week, a women's lecture series, assertiveness training, a telephone information and referral service, films, and other special events. The local Santa Rosa YWCA operates a battered women's shelter. The Disability Office serves the 132 handicapped students, most of whom are women.

The Reentry Program and the Reentry Students Association serve adult women. Faculty are offered workshops on the needs of reentry women.

Institutional Self-Description. "Sonoma State is an excellent college for adult and returning women students. It has active and excellent Women's Studies and reentry programs; an outstanding liberal arts facility which is placing increasing emphasis on career-oriented programs; a number of excellent women faculty, who work well together. Sonoma County has an active women's community and many women's cultural events."

University of California, Berkeley

Berkeley, CA 94720
Telephone: (415) 642-7609

| Women in Leadership | ★★★ Women and the |
| ★★★ students | Curriculum |

★★ Women and Athletics

19,999 undergraduates

	Amer. Ind.	Asian Amer.	Blacks	Hispanics	Whites
F	53	1,709	357	264	6,068
M	47	2,145	338	435	8,127
%	0.5	19.7	3.6	3.6	72.6

🏠 🚌 👫 S/W M/A 📖 CROW

Founded in 1855 across the bay from San Francisco, the University of California at Berkeley is a state-supported institution that serves some 30,000 students with a comprehensive range of undergraduate, graduate, and professional studies. University extension programs are responsible for adult continuing education. Evening classes and a summer session are available.

Women are 43 percent of the 19,999 undergraduates; 10 percent of women attend part-time. The median age of undergraduates is 21. For the 72 percent of undergraduates who live off campus or commute, the university is accessible by public transportation. On-campus parking is limited to the disabled.

University-sponsored childcare facilities accommodate an estimated 70 percent of student requests, with fees on a sliding scale. Private childcare arrangements may be made close to campus.

Policies to Ensure Fairness to Women. Three equal-opportunity officers monitor equity in employment, sex equity for students, and handicapped accessibility. A campus policy prohibits sexual harassment, and a formal grievance procedure to handle complaints is approaching final form. An active faculty Committee on the Status of Women takes public stands on issues of concern to students. The Committee on Minority Affairs addresses the concerns of minority women.

Women in Leadership Positions. *Students.* Women have outstanding opportunities to exercise campus-wide leadership. In recent years they have been student body president, presided over the student senate, student court, student union board, and residence-hall council, and three times managed the campus radio station. Women head six of eight honorary societies.

Faculty. Women are 13 percent of a full-time faculty of 1,434. There are 2 female faculty for every 100 female students and 12 male faculty for every 100 male students.

Administrators. Men hold all top positions. Women chair four of 85 departments: education, African-American studies, physiology-anatomy, and physical education. The university Provost is a woman, as is the head of the Center for East European and Slavic Studies. In 1980–81, women received three-fourths of alumni awards.

Women and the Curriculum. Most women graduating with bachelor's degrees major in social sciences (22 percent), general letters (11 percent), and biological sciences (9 percent). Around 16 percent major in nontraditional fields, with the percentage of women earning degrees in agriculture and architecture above the national average. The university reports innovative programs to encourage women to prepare for careers in science, engineering, computer science, architecture, and agriculture. Women make up 28 percent of students in cooperative education programs that combine academic with related work experience. The majority of students in science field service, individual field study, and course-related internships are women.

The Women's Studies Program offers a B.A. and a graduate minor. Some 50 students have declared majors in recent years. Sixty courses on women are available. The Women's Studies Program reports developing a series of core courses. Recent offerings include a two-quarter sequence called Humanities Methodology and a course called Language and Gender. Other courses offered through departments include Psychology of Sex Roles, Women and Politics, Women in Russia, The Chicano Family, and Sex Roles and Children.

The School of Education offers a course on educating males and females for the 1980s, and faculty provide instruction on mathematics confidence among females.

The Center for the Study, Education and Advancement of Women, formerly the Women's Center for Continuing Education, offers research fellowships to scholars for study focused on women and the work force, with special attention to minority women. In addition, the center provides counseling and other services to a broad spectrum of women, including returning women students.

Minority Women. Of 8,451 undergraduate women, 20 percent are Asian American, 4 percent black, 3 percent Hispanic, and less than 1 percent American Indian. Five minority women work in the centers for counseling and psychological service, and three direct residence halls. The Director of the Center for the Study, Education and Advancement of Women is a black woman.

Sixteen women are in all-minority sororities. Such student organizations as the Chinese Student Association, La Raza Business Association, and MECHA serve the interests of minority women on campus. Additional services for minority women may be found in the Educational Opportunity Program and the Student Learning Center.

Women and Athletics. The intramural and intercollegiate programs are excellent, with a high number and variety of individual and team sports. A woman directs intercollegiate athletics for women. Club sports are also available and women constitute 38 percent of participants. Sixty-three percent of intercollegiate athletes are women; women receive 30 percent of athletic scholarships. All women's intercollegiate teams played tournament competition in 1980. The intercollegiate sports offered are basketball, crew, cross-country, field hockey, gymnastics, softball, swimming and diving, tennis, track and field and volleyball.

Housing and Student Organizations. Twenty-eight percent of undergraduates reside on campus in residential accommodations that include single-sex and coeducational dormitories and housing for married students and single parents with children. A married woman whose spouse is not enrolled as a student may live in married students' housing. The 16 residence-hall directors, seven of whom are women, are offered awareness-training on issues of sex education and birth control.

Eighteen percent of undergraduate women belong to social sororities, which provide housing for some of their members. The Boalt Hall Women's Association, the Berkeley Feminists Alliance and the Physically Disabled Students Union are student organizations that serve as advocates for women on campus.

Special Services and Programs for Women. *Health and Counseling.* Limited medical attention specific to women is provided by the student health service. Regular student health insurance covers pregnancy care. Over one-fourth of the physicians, and half the professional staff in the counseling centers, are women. Gynecological, birth control, rape/assault, and pregnancy counseling are available as needed, as is assertiveness training.

Safety and Security. Measures include night-time escort for women students, limited night-time bus service to residence areas, high-intensity lighting, an automated 911 emergency telephone system, an emergency alarm system, self-defense courses for women, rape prevention education, and two full-time police employees assigned to all aspects of crime prevention. A rape crisis center is available. A total of 87 assaults and two rapes were reported for 1980–81.

Career. The Counseling Center sponsors workshops and other activities, and provides materials, relating to nontraditional careers for women.

Special Features. The Berkeley campus has a number of caucuses for graduate women, as well as feminist research groups and a feminist pedagogy group sponsored by the Women's Studies Program. The campus thrives on its involvement with the women's community in the Bay Area—poetry readings, coalitions, battered wives' shelters, bookstores, and the like.

Institutional Self-Description. "A degree from a 'prestige' institution is an advantage for women. Berkeley is big; but the moment she arrives on campus a woman can find support groups and resources through the Women's Studies Program, the Women's Center, and many student organizatons. The campus and the Bay Area provide unlimited opportunities for creative and intellectual growth and for feminist work."

University of California, Davis
Davis, CA 95616
Telephone: (916) 752-2222

★★ Women and the Curriculum

★★★ Women and Athletics

12,606 undergraduates

	Amer. Ind.	Asian Amer.	Blacks	Hispanics	Whites
F	36	578	190	199	5,167
M	35	586	181	244	5,166
%	0.5	9.4	3.0	3.6	83.5

Founded in 1906 as an agricultural test site and school, the University of California at Davis, located northeast of San Francisco, now attracts over 17,500 students to a variety of undergraduate, graduate, and professional degree programs. The University Extension serves the adult student. A summer session and evening classes are available.

Women are half of the 12,606 undergraduates; 8 percent of women attend part-time. For the students who live off campus or commute, the university is accessible by public transportation. There is on-campus parking.

A half-day laboratory nursery school can accommodate approximately 31 percent of students' requests for childcare. Private arrangements for childcare may be made near the university.

Policies to Ensure Fairness to Women. The Vice Chancellor for Academic Affairs is responsible for policy related to equal employment opportunity, sex equity for students, and handicapped accessibility. A campus policy prohibits sexual harassment. Complaints are handled informally and confidentially and through a formal grievance procedure. The Committee on the Status of Women, which includes students as voting members, is active on behalf of women in the university and also takes public stands on issues of concern to students. A Committee on Minority Affairs addresses the needs of minority women.

Women in Leadership Positions. *Students.* Opportunities for women students to assume positions of campus-wide leadership are considerably below average for public research universities in this guide. In a recent three-year period, a woman served one year as presiding officer of the student senate; men held the other five positions.

Faculty. Women are 16 percent of a full-time faculty of 775. There are 2 female faculty for every 100 students and 11 male faculty for every 100 male students.

Administrators. Men hold all top-level positions. Women, including one black woman, chair four of 87 departments: Chicano studies, animal physiology, avian science, and French and Italian. One of 27 directors of other academic units is an Hispanic woman.

Women and the Curriculum. The most popular majors for undergraduate women are the biological sciences (20 percent), agriculture (13 percent), the social sciences (12 percent), and interdisciplinary studies (11 percent). Twenty-one percent of the women major in such nontraditional areas as agriculture, architecture, engineering, mathematics, and the physical sciences, a proportion which is considerably above the national average. Programs encourage women to prepare for careers in science, engineering, and agriculture. Half of the students in cooperative education programs that combine academic with related work experience are female.

The Women's Studies Program offers a 24-credit minor and the B.A. in Women's Studies. The major brings together courses from 15 different departments including Afro-American studies, American studies, anthropology, English, history, Mexican American studies, political science, sociology, Asian American studies, and Native American studies. Among recent offerings are The Popular Image of Women in America, Women Writers, Women in 19th-Century Russian Literature, Sexual Stratification and Politics, and Women in Africa. The program is housed in the Women's Resources and Research Center which has a good Women's Studies library. A committee is responsible for the program; a tenured faculty member administers it. Such topics as mathematics confidence among females, sex-fair teaching materials, and coeducational physical education classes are included in the preparation of future teachers. Courses in the business school include information about discrimination against women in the workplace.

Minority Women. Of 6,170 undergraduate women, 3 percent are black, less than 1 percent American Indian, 9 percent Asian American, and 3 percent Hispanic. The curriculum offers such courses as Afro-American Women, La Chicana in Contemporary Society, Asian American Women, and Native American Women.

Thirty-three women are in all-minority sororities. Two of the residence-hall directors and two of the staff in the counseling service are minority women. The faculty administrator of the Women's Center is an Hispanic woman.

Women and Athletics. The intramural and intercollegiate programs are outstanding, both for high participation and variety in offerings. Club sports are also available. Thirty-one percent of intramural and 77 percent of varsity athletes are women. Varsity teams played tournament competition in 1980; three of 18 paid varsity coaches are women. The intercollegiate sports available are basketball, cross-country, field hockey, gymnastics, softball, swimming, tennis, track and field, and volleyball.

Housing and Student Organizations. For the 16 percent of undergraduates who live on campus, residential accommodations include coeducational dormitories and housing for married students and single parents with children. Dormitories do not restrict hours for visitors of the opposite sex. Five of eight residence-hall directors are women. Awareness-training on sexism, sex education, racism, and birth control, among other issues, is offered residence-hall staff.

Twelve percent of full-time undergraduate women belong to social sororities. Sororities and fraternities provide housing for some of their members. Among organizations which serve as advocates for women on campus are the Women's Studies Student Community, Gay Student Union, Women's Leadership Network, Davis Pro-Choice, Women's Alliance for Change, and Women in Medicine.

Special Services and Programs for Women. *Health and Counseling.* The student health center provides medical attention specific to women; gynecological, birth control, abortion, and rape and assault treatment are available. Four of 14 physicians and 7 of 26 health-care providers are female. The regular student health insurance covers abortion and maternity after primary insurance is used. In the counseling service, staffed by 9 women and 5 men, students have access to counseling of particular concern to women.

Safety and Security. Measures include campus police with arrest authority, limited night-time bus service to residence areas, high-intensity lighting, self-defense courses for women, information sessions on safety and crime prevention, a rape prevention education program, and a rape crisis center. No rapes or attempted rapes were reported for 1980–81.

Career. Career workshops, guest speakers, and nonsexist/nonracist printed information focused on nontraditional occupations and fields of study for women are available.

Other. The well-funded ($112,000) Women's Center sponsors various cultural events and information and support services. Women of varying ages and life circumstances would find support from the Academic Reentry Program and the Women's Resources and Research Center.

Institutional Self-Description. "Our university has a very active Women's Center which has as one of its goals the academic success of women students. Additionally, we have a strong reentry program and a Women's Studies major and minor. There are numerous groups for women in athletics, agriculture, politics, and law. Our local community is small, and we therefore have a relatively low crime rate. We are two hours from the snow (Tahoe), and one and one-half hours from San Francisco, and one hour from UC Berkeley."

University of California, Los Angeles
Los Angeles, CA 90024
Telephone: (213) 825-4321

★★★ Women and the Curriculum

★★★ Women and Athletics

20,167 undergraduates

	Amer. Ind.	Asian Amer.	Blacks	Hispanics	Whites
F	33	1,431	613	608	7,188
M	50	1,429	421	687	7,157
%	0.4	14.6	5.3	6.6	73.1

🚌 👥 🔦 🆂🆆 📖 🏠 **AAUW CROW**

Founded in 1919 as a two-year institution, the University of California, Los Angeles occupies a campus at the foot of the Santa Monica Mountains. It offers its 31,700 students a comprehensive range of undergraduate, graduate, and professional degree programs. The UCLA Extension Division is responsible for adult continuing education.

Women are half of the 20,167 undergraduates; 6 percent of the women attend part-time. The median age of undergraduates is 19. For the 81 percent of undergraduates who live off campus or commute, public transportation is available. Limited on-campus parking is available for a fee; there is free transportation from distant parking lots.

Fees for childcare in university-sponsored facilities are based on a sliding scale. On-campus facilities accommodate 11 percent of student requests.

Policies to Ensure Fairness to Women. One full- and two part-time affirmative action officers are responsible for, or review, policy relating to equal employment opportunities, sex equity for students, and handicapped accessibility. A published campus policy prohibits sexual harassment; complaints are handled through a formal grievance procedure. The Chancellor's Advisory Committee on the Status of Women, which includes students as voting members, identifies and analyzes problems and makes recommendations on matters of concern to women, including minority women.

Women in Leadership Positions. *Students.* Opportunities for women students to exercise campus-wide leadership are below average for public research universities in this guide. In recent years, women have presided over the student senate and the student court.

Faculty. Eighteen percent of a full-time faculty of 1,462 are women. There are 3 female faculty for every 100 female students and 13 male faculty for every 100 male students.

Administrators. Men hold all higher administrative positions. Women chair five of 66 departments: bio-mathematics, dance, Italian, kinesiology, and nursing. The Dean of the Graduate Division is a woman.

Women and the Curriculum. Women graduating with bachelor's degrees major in social sciences (34 percent), psychology (14 percent), fine arts (12 percent), and general letters (11 percent). Five percent major in such nontraditional fields as engineering, mathematics, and the physical sciences, a proportion below the average for public research universities in this guide. UCLA reports innovative programs to encourage women to prepare for careers in science, engineering, management, law, and public health. Additional support comes from such organizations as the Society of Women Engineers, Women in Management, Women in Public Health, and the Women's Law Union. A program to build mathematics skills is available.

The Women's Studies Program offers a 32-credit undergraduate specialization (the equivalent of a minor). The director of Women's Studies is also the editor of *The Psychology of Women Quarterly*. Thirty undergraduate or graduate courses on such subjects as Women in Literature, Women in Antiquity, Sexuality and Women's Health in Victorian America, Women and the Law, and Middle Eastern Women are available through Women's Studies and ten other departments or divisions. Students who specialize are required to take the introductory Women's Studies course, which emphasizes minority women.

UCLA houses the Higher Education Research Institute, which conducts institutional research, with an emphasis on the relationship of women in postsecondary education to the labor market.

The division of education provides future teachers with instruction in sex-fair curricula. The division of nursing provides training in innovative health-care delivery, including nurse practitioner training. An official committee oversees Women's Studies governance and policy and collects curricular materials for the development of courses. The relations among sex, race, and choice of major and the needs of reentry women are among topics for faculty workshops or institutional research.

Minority Women. Two courses on minority women are offered: Asian American Women, and The Insurgent Black Woman in the U.S. Fifteen percent of continuing-education-for-women students are minority women, Asian American being the largest group. Three minority women are on the professional staff of the counseling service. Staff receive in-service training on avoiding racial bias.

A variety of minority student organizations meet on campus, including the Asian Coalition, American Indian Student Association, MECHA, International Women's Solidarity Coalition, as well as minority-student associations for those in public health, and planning and architecture. An estimated 25 percent of the users of the Women's Center are members of minority groups, with black women the largest group.

Women and Athletics. UCLA has outstanding intramural and intercollegiate programs, with a high number and variety of individual and team sports in both. Club sports and coeducational sports are also available. All women's intercollegiate teams played tournament competition in 1980. Thirty-three percent of intercollegiate athletes are women; women receive 30 percent of athletic scholarships. Twelve of 60 paid coaches in varsity sports are women. The intercollegiate sports offered are badminton, basketball, crew, cross-country, fencing, golf, gymnastics, track and field, softball, swimming and diving, tennis, and volleyball.

Housing and Student Organizations. Nineteen percent of undergraduates live on campus; coeducational dormitories are available. There is housing for married students off campus. Dormitories restrict hours for visitors of the opposite sex.

Twenty-two percent of undergraduate women belong to social sororities, which provide housing for their members. All sororities are integrated. Many of the wide spectrum of student organizations serve as advocates for women including the Lesbian Support Group.

Special Services and Programs for Women. *Health and Counseling.* Student health services specific to women include gynecological, birth control, abortion, and rape and assault treatment. Five of 12 physicians are female, as are 21 other health-care providers. The regular student health insurance covers abortion and some maternity expenses at no extra cost. The counseling center, staffed by 7 women and 15 men, offers counseling of particular concern to women.

Safety and Security. Measures consist of campus police with arrest authority, night-time escort service for women students, night-time bus service to residence areas, self-defense courses for women, information sessions on safety and crime prevention, and a rape crisis center. Sixteen assaults (four on women) and two rapes were reported for 1980-81.

Other. The Women's Resource Center, under a full-time director, provides an environment and programs that encourage and support the personal and academic growth of women. The center sponsors speakers, workshops, support groups, and conferences, as well as provides referral information on topics of concern to women. Special features are Women in Science Mentor Project, services for battered women and displaced homemakers, and a rape prevention and education project. Women of varying ages, lifestyles, and life circumstances use the center.

Returning Women Students. The Chancellor's Advisory Committee on the Status of Women has a task force on women returning to education. The Extension Division, which is responsible for continuing education for women, enrolls 1,800 reentry women in its courses. Counseling services include assertiveness training.

Institutional Self-Description. "In fulfilling its mission to serve society as a center of higher learning, UCLA is committed to providing women with the supportive environment necessary to ensure educational equity. Support services are available to both traditional and nontraditional students."

University of California, Riverside
Riverside, CA 92521
Telephone: (714) 787-5604

★ Women and the Curriculum

3,247 undergraduates

	Amer. Ind.	Asian Amer.	Blacks	Hispanics	Whites
F	13	96	134	131	1,172
M	18	108	95	166	1,285
%	1.0	6.3	7.1	9.2	76.4

On a large campus located an hour from Los Angeles, this branch of the University of California system serves some 4,610 students. Forty-eight percent of the 3,297 undergraduates are women; 9 percent of women attend part-time. Seventeen percent of women are over age 25; the median age of all undergraduates is 20. Known for its environmental and agricultural research facilities, the university offers a variety of undergraduate and graduate degree programs. All classes meet during the day; there is a summer session. For the 58 percent of undergraduates who commute or live off campus, public transportation is available. On-campus parking is available for a fee.

A university-sponsored childcare center, which accommodates 90 percent of students' requests, charges on a sliding scale for those receiving financial assistance and at $.70 per hour for others. Private childcare facilities are available near campus.

Policies to Ensure Fairness to Women. The Affirmative Action Office reviews policies and practices related to equal educational opportunities. Complaints of sexual harassment are resolved by a formal grievance procedure; policies and procedures have not yet been communicated in writing to students, faculty, and staff. An Affirmative Action Advisory Committee, appointed by the Chancellor, concerns itself with the status of women on campus, including the concerns of minority women.

Women in Leadership Positions. *Students.* Women have some opportunities to exercise student leadership. In recent years, women have held two of five student leadership posts: residence-hall council president for two years and student-senate president for one year.

Faculty. Thirteen percent of the 299 full-time faculty are women, a proportion which is far below average for similar schools in this guide. There are 3 female faculty for every 100 female students and 17 male faculty for every 100 male students.

Administrators. With the exception of the chief business officer, men hold the top-level positions. Women chair two of 31 departments—dance and black studies.

Women and the Curriculum. Most degrees awarded to women are in interdisciplinary studies (23 percent), biology (21 percent), and social sciences (17 percent). Four percent are in such non-traditional fields as physical sciences or mathematics, a figure that is about average for public, four-year colleges. Approximately half of the appointments in cooperative education and intern programs go to women.

The Women's Studies Program offers an 18-credit minor. Fifteen courses are available, including The Politics of Women's Liberation, Women in Theater, Psychology of Women, Black Women in America, La Chicana, and Women in Cross-Cultural Perspective. A tenured faculty member serves part-time as coordinator of Women's Studies. An official committee oversees the operation of the Women's Studies Program and devises and collects teaching materials about women. The department of education instructs prospective teachers on the use of non-sexist curricula.

Minority Women. About one-fourth of undergraduate women are members of minority groups, mainly Hispanic and black. Twenty minority women belong to all-minority social sororities and ten are in racially-integrated sororities. Advocacy groups for minority women include Las Chicanas, MECHA, Black Women's Union Study Group, and the Women's Resource Center.

Women and Athletics. No information was provided on intramural sports, nor on the proportion of athletic scholarship aid that is awarded to women. Forty-three percent of intercollegiate athletes are female. Three of 12 paid coaches are women. Intercollegiate sports offered are basketball, cross-country, softball, swimming, tennis, track and field, and volleyball.

Housing and Student Organizations. Forty-two percent of the undergraduates live in coeducational dormitories that have no restrictions on visiting hours for members of the opposite sex. Housing is available for married students with or without children and for single parents. Residence-hall staff receive awareness-training on homosexuality, sex education, racism, and sexism.

Social sororities provide housing for members; 7 percent of full-time undergraduate women are members.

Special Services and Programs for Women. *Health and Counseling.* The student health center employs 2 full-time female physicians and 13 part-time male physicians, as well as 8 female and 2 male health-care providers. Counseling and treatment are available for gynecological problems, abortion, and rape and assault, in addition to birth control counseling. Student health insurance covers $150 of the cost of an elective abortion or normal pregnancy.

Safety and Security. Measures consist of campus police protection (with dogs), night-time escort for women, instruction on self-defense and campus safety, and a rape crisis center. No rapes and five assaults on women were reported for 1980–81.

Other. The Women's Resource Center, with a budget of $43,000, operated by Student Affairs and administered by a full-time director, reports that it serves 1,500 persons, primarily undergraduates, each year. In cooperation with women's organizations in the surrounding community, the center sponsors an annual women's week and a telephone information and referral service. California State College at San Bernardino and the center jointly operate assertiveness-training workshops. The center also organizes a women's lecture series.

The Reentry Program and the local YMCA sponsor a program for displaced homemakers. The Gay and Lesbian Students Organization is a campus group. There is a Disabled Students Union active on campus.

Institutional Self-Description. None provided.

University of California, Santa Barbara
Santa Barbara, CA 93106
Telephone: (805) 961-3273

★ **Women and the Curriculum**

12,612 undergraduates

	Amer. Ind.	Asian Amer.	Blacks	Hispanics	Whites
F	48	294	117	369	5,619
M	57	320	135	417	5,076
%	0.8	4.9	2.0	6.3	85.9

Established in 1891 as a training school in home economics, industrial arts, and education, UCSB is now one of the fourth largest universities in the University of California system. Its campus, located just outside of the city of Santa Barbara, overlooks the Pacific Ocean. The institution serves 14,512 students, 12,612 of whom are undergraduates. Women are about half of the undergraduate student body, and 4 percent of women attend part-time. The median age of all students is 20.

A wide range of undergraduate, pre-professional, professional, and graduate degree programs is available. Classes are held during the day and evening, on and off campus, and students may pursue independent study. Alternative scheduling and locations are available, through the Adult Reentry Program and the College of Letters and Science. Three-fourths of all undergraduates live off campus and enjoy easy access to public transportation. There is on-campus parking, with transportation from distant parking lots.

The campus childcare facility accommodates 120 children for a flat fee of $7.50 per day. Additional, private childcare facilities are located close to campus.

Policies to Ensure Fairness to Women. The Assistant to the Vice Chancellor for Students and Community Affairs monitors compliance with educational sex equity. The Affirmative Action Coordinator oversees equal employment and handicapped access and monitors compliance.

A policy prohibiting sexual harassment protects all members of the academic community; formal procedures for handling complaints are currently being developed. Currently, complaints are handled with informally. A Commission on the Status of Women, which includes students with voting rights among its members, meets regularly and publicizes its views.

Women in Leadership Positions. *Students.* Women have had few opportunities to exercise student leadership. In recent years women have served single terms as president of the student body, student judiciary, and student union board, and manager of the campus radio station.

Faculty. Women constitute 15 percent of the 631 full-time faculty, a proportion below the average for similar institutions in this guide. There are 2 female faculty for every 100 female students and 9 male faculty for every 100 male students.

Administrators. Men hold all top positions, except for the chief student-life officer. Women chair the departments of music, psychology, dramatic art, physical activities, and Germanic and Slavic languages.

Women and the Curriculum. Most degrees awarded to women are in the social sciences, psychology, and interdisciplinary studies. Four percent of women graduate in nontraditional fields.

The College of Engineering encourages women to specialize in computer science and engineering.

Some fifteen courses on women are listed in a brochure distributed by the WCSB Women's Center. They are offered in the departments of anthropology, Chicano studies, classics, film studies, history, linguistics, and sociology. They include Women and Work; Sex Roles and Language; and three courses on The Evolving Chicana Historical, Contemporary, and Emphasis on Research. The departments of education and physical activities instruct prospective teachers about non-sexist teaching methods.

Minority Women. Minority women constitute 7 percent of all students. Minority women's organizations include two Chicano groups—M.U.J.E.R. and Mujeres en Cambio—a Native American Women's support group, and Daughters of the Rainbow, an Asian/Pacific women's group. Thirty-three women belong to all-minority sororities. The Chicano studies department gives three courses on Chicana women. A Chicano woman serves on the Board of Regents

Women and Athletics. An adequate and varied intercollegiate sports program is offered. Thirty-seven percent of all intercollegiate athletes are women, and they receive 35 percent of athletic scholarship aid. There is no information available on the number of participants in intramural sports; nearly half of all club participants are female. Intercollegiate sports offered are basketball, cross-country, gymnastics, softball, swimming, tennis, track and field, and volleyball.

Housing and Student Organizations. Coeducational dormitories on campus house nearly a quarter of all undergraduates, including married students with or without children and single parents. Isla Vista, a residential student community adjacent to campus, is home for 46 percent of undergraduates.

Sororities and fraternities have 1,152 members. Eleven percent of the full-time women undergraduates join sororities, which provide some housing for members.

In addition to the organizations mentioned above, women's advocacy groups include the Associated Students Commission on the Status of Women, the Women's Writing Project, and People Against Violence in Pornography.

Special Services and Programs for Women. *Health and Counseling.* The student health center employs 6 female and 17 male physicians, in addition to 22 female and 11 male health-care providers (full and part-time). The student counseling center is staffed by 8 female and 6 male full- and part-time counselors. Health services specific to women include counseling and treatment for gynecological problems, birth control, and rape and assault. Abortion counseling is also available. The voluntary student health insurance plan covers part of abortion and maternity expenses.

Safety and Security. Measures consist of campus and county police protection, night-time escort for women, night-time bus service to residential areas, an emergency telephone system, and self-defense courses for women. There is a rape crisis center on campus, and a hotline. For 1980–81, 26 assaults on women and two rapes were reported.

Other. The Women's Center at UCSB, administered by a salaried, full-time director, serves 7,000 women annually, mostly undergraduates and community residents. Some of the center's programs (co-sponsored with other campus offices) are an annual international women's week, a women's lecture series, creative arts performances, assertiveness training workshops, a mathematics confidence clinic, and, with the cooperation of the local police, a rape education prevention program.

Special Features. The Social Progress Research Institute is working on such issues as family violence, dual-career couples, and women workers. The Hutchins Center sponsors lectures by prominent feminists.

Institutional Self-Description. "UCSB is a medium-sized university (14,000) situated in a beautiful location. The university is striving to make programs, services and policies more equitable—

dealing with sexual harassment, rape education, affirmative action, including hiring more women faculty and promoting women in administration. The Women's Center acts on behalf of all the women on campus."

University of Southern California
Los Angeles, CA 90007
Telephone: (213) 743-5371

Women in Leadership ★★★ students	★★ Women and the Curriculum
	★Women and Athletics

14,946 undergraduates

	Amer. Ind.	Asian Amer.	Blacks	Hispanics	Whites
F	26	737	627	459	3,612
M	42	961	454	597	5,442
%	0.5	13.1	8.3	8.2	69.9

 AAUW

Established in 1880, the University of Southern California, a private non-sectarian institution of some 27,500 students, is located in Los Angeles. USC provides a variety of undergraduate, graduate, and professional programs. There is a College of Continuing Education. Off-campus day and evening classes and a summer session are available.

Women are 41 percent of 14,946 undergraduates; 15 percent of women attend part-time. The median age of undergraduates is 20. For the 40 percent of undergraduates who commute, there is public transportation. On-campus parking is available for a fee, with free transportation from distant parking lots.

University-sponsored childcare facilities accommodate an estimated 90 percent of requests. Private childcare arrangements may be made close to campus.

Policies to Ensure Fairness to Women. A full-time affirmative action officer is responsible for policy on equal employment opportunities, accessibility of curriculum and activities to students, and handicapped access. A formal policy prohibiting sexual harassment and a grievance procedure are in the process of development. The Committee on the Status of Women, which includes students as voting members, takes public stands on issues, addresses the concerns of minority women, and sponsors campus programs and speakers.

Women in Leadership Positions. *Students.* Opportunities for women students to exercise leadership on campus are outstanding for private research institutions in this guide. In a recent three-year period, women have twice presided over the student senate and the student union board, have presided over the student court and residence-hall council, and have twice been editor-in-chief of the newspaper.

Faculty. Fifteen percent of a full-time faculty of 966 are female. There are 3 female faculty for every 100 female students and 11 male faculty for every 100 male students.

Administrators. Men occupy all higher administrative posts. Women chair eleven of 77 departments; a woman is Dean of the College of Continuing Education.

Women and the Curriculum. Most women graduating with bachelor's degrees major in business and management (21 percent), education (11 percent), psychology (9 percent), and social sciences (9 percent). Seven percent major in such nontraditional areas as architecture, computer science, engineering, mathematics, and the physical sciences. USC reports innovative programs or associations that encourage women to prepare for careers in engineering, computer science, and law.

The Program for the Study of Women and Men in Society, under a full-time director, coordinates some 26 courses on women and offers a B.A. and a certificate. The program has an endowed professorship in Women's Studies—the first in the nation—and maintains its own library and film collection.

Recent Women's Studies courses include Changing Images of Women, Men, and Family in American Culture; Introduction to Feminist Theory and the Women's Movement; and Women and Ethnicity. Courses on women are available in the departments of English, anthropology, ethnic studies, international relations, organizational behavior, sociology, comparative literature, French, gerontology, history, physical education, political science, communication arts and sciences, psychology, and philosophy. An official committee advocates and monitors the integration of women's scholarship and perspectives into the curriculum.

A new federal grant will enable the Program for the Study of Women and Men in Society and USC to move more rapidly toward a curriculum that includes women in all courses.

Instruction on sex-role stereotyping in sports and curricular materials, mathematics confidence among women, innovative health-care delivery and health information of particular concern to minority women, services for abused spouses, and workplace discrimination is part of the preparation of future teachers, health-care workers, social workers, and business students.

Minority Women. Of 5,461 undergraduate women, 11 percent are black, less than 1 percent American Indian, 13 percent Asian American, and 8 percent Hispanic. Two residence-hall directors are minority women. Residence-hall staff are offered awareness training on racism. Four of the professional staff in the counseling service are minority women.

One hundred minority women are in racially integrated and 50 in all-minority sororities. Organizations on campus supportive of minority women's concerns include the Women's Center, the Black Women's Caucus, and the Asian-Pacific Student Organization. The Program for the Study of Women and Men in Society sponsors a conference on Ethnic American Women.

Women and Athletics. Intramural and intercollegiate programs offer women good opportunities for organized, competitive individual and team sports. Club sports are also available. USC will be the site of the 1984 Olympic swimming events.

Twenty-eight percent of intercollegiate athletes are female. Athletic scholarships are awarded. Women constitute over a third of paid coaches for intercollegiate teams. All teams, including gymnastics and crew, played tournament competition in 1980. The intercollegiate sports offered are basketball, crew, cross-country, golf, gymnastics, swimming and diving, tennis, track and field, and volleyball.

Housing and Student Organizations. Thirty-four percent of undergraduates live on campus. Single-sex and coeducational dormitories and housing for married students and single parents with children are available. A married woman student whose spouse is not enrolled may live in married students' housing. With a few exceptions, residence halls do not restrict hours for visitors of the opposite sex. Residence hall staff are offered awareness training on sex education, birth control, and rape prevention among other issues.

Twenty-three percent of undergraduate women belong to social sororities, which provide housing for their members. The YWCA Women's Center, the Gay and Lesbian Student Union, and the Women's Coordinating Council are some of the student organizations which serve as advocates for white and minority women on campus.

Special Services and Programs for Women. *Health and Counseling.* Medical attention specific to women provided by the student health service includes gynecological, birth control, and rape and assault treatment. Five of the 14 physicians are women, as are 16 other health-care providers. Five of nine counselors in the counseling service are female. Counseling for rape victims is available.

Safety and Security. Intensive security measures prevail. Campus and city police, night-time escort and bus services, high-intensity lighting, emergency telephone and alarm systems, self-defense courses for women, and safety and crime prevention information sessions are available. There is a rape crisis center and hot line. A total of 51 assaults and three rapes were reported for 1980-81.

Career. Materials and activities concentrating on women and work are available through career placement or other units; they include nonsexist/nonracist printed information, lectures by women employed in nontraditional careers, interview workshops, and a student-alumnae networking program.

Other. A small Women's Center is operated by the Office of Student Affairs. The campus YWCA Women's Center offers assertiveness training.

Institutional Self-Description. "Since its beginning, USC has been dedicated to equal educational opportunities. USC enjoys the many benefits of a major cultural center with a large women's art movement. On campus, women receive approximately 40 percent of the degrees in pharmacy, 30 percent of the degrees in public administration, urban and regional planning, and business administration. USC's excellent women's athletic program is among the top five in the country."

University of West Los Angeles
10811 Washington Boulevard
Culver City, CA 90230
Telephone: (213) 204-0000

136 undergraduates

	Amer. Ind.	Asian Amer.	Blacks	Hispanics	Whites
F	2	6	20	6	90
M	1	0	3	0	8
%	2.2	4.4	16.9	4.4	72.1

The University of West Los Angeles, located in the racially mixed community of Culver City, prepares its 897 students for careers as lawyers, paralegals, and legal secretaries. The only bachelor's degree granted is in general law. Ninety-one percent of the 136 undergraduates are women, and most of the women attend part-time. The median age of all undergraduates is 28. Most students attend evening classes, but some day classes are offered. A summer session and adult continuing education classes are available. A commuter school, the University of West Los Angeles can be reached by public transportation; free parking is provided on campus.

Private childcare facilities are available near campus.

Women in Leadership Positions. *Students.* Women students have very limited opportunities to gain leadership experience. In a recent three-year period, a woman held one of three major campus offices, and that for one term.

Faculty. Information is not available.

Administrators. Except for the head librarian, all chief administrators are men. Two departments—paralegal studies and secretaries training—are chaired by women.

Women and the Curriculum. In a recent year, women earned 12 of the 16 general law degrees awarded. No courses on women are offered.

Women and Athletics. There is no opportunity for organized competitive sports.

Special Services and Programs for Women. *Health and Counseling.* The student counseling service has four professionals, two of whom are women. No counseling services specific to women are available. There is no student health center.

Safety and Security. Measures consist of local police protection and high-intensity lighting. No rapes or assaults on women were reported for 1980–81.

Career. The university offers career workshops and lectures by employed women; it also maintains files on the careers of alumnae and promotes networking between alumnae and students.

Institutional Self-Description. "The University of West Los Angeles has a large female student population in both law and paralegal schools, a supportive environment, and the scheduling of classes and modified programs to accommodate both working women and women with children at home."

West Hills Community College
300 Cherry Lane, Coalinga, CA 93210
Telephone: (209) 935-0801

Women in Leadership
★ ★ ★ students

1,530 undergraduates

	Amer. Ind.	Asian Amer.	Blacks	Hispanics	Whites
F	12	19	34	103	547
M	19	34	59	105	583
%	2.1	3.6	6.1	13.7	74.6

Located in the mountains, southwest of Fresno, this public two-year community college serves a diverse group of students, most of whom live in the surrounding rural areas. Of 1,530 students, just under half are women. West Hills offers college transfer programs in agriculture, liberal arts, business administration, engineering, and physical sciences, and pre-professional programs in secretarial studies, auto mechanics, diesel mechanics, vocational agriculture, and laboratory technology. Day and evening classes on and off campus are available. The median age of students is 24. One-quarter of the 1,530 undergraduates live on campus in single-sex dormitories with restricted hours for visitors of the opposite sex. Free on-campus parking is available for commuters.

Childcare may be arranged off campus.

Policies to Ensure Fairness to Women. The college is currently drafting a sexual harassment policy, which will be publicly communicated to students, faculty, and staff. Two staff persons are responsible part-time for reviewing and enforcing policies pertaining to equal employment opportunity and sex equity for students.

Women in Leadership Positions. *Students.* Women have held most of the campus-wide student leadership positions during the past three years, including president of the student body and presiding officer of the student governing body. A woman presides over the sole honorary society.

Faculty. Six of the 49 full-time faculty are women. There are 3 female faculty for every 100 female students and 11 male faculty for every 100 male students.

Administrators. Men hold all top positions. A woman chairs the department of physical education. The 1981 commencement speaker was a woman.

Women and the Curriculum. Of degrees awarded to women, most are in arts and sciences (75 percent) and business and commercial programs (19 percent). There are no courses on women.

Women and Athletics. Although no intramural or club sports are offered, West Hills offers an adequate intercollegiate program, including softball, tennis, track and field, and volleyball.

Special Services and Programs for Women. *Health and Counseling.* Three men and one woman staff the student counseling center. There are no health services available. No medical treatment or counseling specific to women is provided.

Safety and Security. Local town police patrol the campus, along

with campus police and a student patrol on weekend nights. The campus is equipped with high-intensity lighting. There were no rapes or assaults reported for 1980–81.

Institutional Self-Description. "West Hills College has small classes which afford more individual instruction. WHC has a residence hall on campus and a dining hall. The campus is very small (about 700 full-time, day students) in a small community with less crime. West Hills offers academic transfer courses as well as vocational courses."

West Kern Community College District, Taft College
29 Emmons Park Drive, Taft, CA 93268
Telephone: (805) 763-4282

Women in Leadership
★ faculty

747 undergraduates

	Amer. Ind.	Asian Amer.	Blacks	Hispanics	Whites
F	7	1	0	12	391
M	10	2	28	8	264
%	2.4	0.4	3.9	2.8	90.6

This public two-year college is located on a rural campus, 40 miles from Bakersfield. The total enrollment of 903 includes 747 matriculated students. Women constitute 56 percent of the enrollment; 79 percent of women attend part-time. The median age of undergraduates is 24.

The college offers two-year pre-professional college or university training and terminal programs in business education and industrial arts. Taft provides day and evening classes both on and off campus, as well as a program of self-paced/contract learning and a summer session. There is a Continuing Education for Women Program. Just over half of the undergraduates commute to the campus; there is free on-campus parking.

A childcare facility, located near campus, can accommodate 50 children—enough to satisfy all students' requests. Open from 7:45 a.m. to 4:15 p.m., the facility charges fees on a sliding scale.

Policies to Ensure Fairness to Women. A part-time affirmative action officer serves as a voting member of policymaking councils, reviews policies and practices, and monitors compliance concerning equal-opportunity legislation. Sexual harassment of students, faculty, and staff is prohibited by a written campus policy that has been publicly communicated to all three groups. A formal campus grievance procedure resolves complaints of sexual harassment.

Women in Leadership Positions. *Students.* The information supplied does not allow an assessment of student leadership opportunities for women.

Faculty. Six of the 23 full-time faculty are women. There are 7 female faculty for every 100 female students and 11 male faculty for every 100 male students.

Administrators. Men hold all top positions. The department of business is chaired by an Asian American woman; four of 17 members of the faculty senate are women.

Women and the Curriculum. Women receive 52 percent of the degrees awarded, all of them in arts and sciences. There are no courses on women.

Women and Athletics. There are no intramural or club sports, and only limited opportunities exist for women to participate in intercollegiate sports. All teams enter post-season tournaments. The single paid coach is a woman. Intercollegiate sports include softball, track and field, and volleyball.

Housing and Student Organizations. Forty-seven percent of undergraduates reside on campus in single-sex dormitories that have restrictive hours for members of the opposite sex. Residence-hall staff receive awareness training on sexism, sex education, and racism.

Special Services and Programs for Women. *Health and Counseling.* The student health service is staffed by one female health-care provider. Referrals are made for women seeking gynecological and birth control treatment. The student counseling center is staffed by four counselors, two of whom are women.

Safety and Security. No information was provided. There were no rapes or assaults reported for 1980-81.

Other. A displaced homemakers' program is offered through the Dean of Students' Office; an annual women's week and women's arts programs, sponsored by Community Services; and assertiveness and leadership training offered by the Dean of Instruction.

Institutional Self-Description. ''The college is strongly student-centered, and there are few barriers to full participation by women in all aspects of student life. Classes are small and there are excellent resources for student learning.''

Whittier College
13416 E. Philadelphia
Whittier, CA 90608
Telephone: (213) 693-0771

Women in Leadership
★ faculty

1,066 undergraduates

	Amer. Ind.	Asian Amer.	Blacks	Hispanics	Whites
F	1	32	45	106	307
M	3	29	44	94	301
%	0.4	6.3	9.3	20.8	63.2

Whittier College is an independent, four-year, liberal arts institution founded by the Quakers. Its campus, located in a suburban area near Los Angeles, serves 1,712 students. Women are 50 percent of the 1,066 students in degree programs, and 94 percent of women attend full-time. The median age of all undergraduates is 20. On-campus parking is available to the 49 percent of students who commute. There is a summer session.

Private childcare facilities are available off campus.

Policies to Ensure Fairness to Women. There is no formal policy on sexual harassment, but an informal campus mechanism resolves complaints.

Women in Leadership Positions. *Students.* During a recent three-year period, women have held few student offices: president of the entering class twice and of the student body once.

Faculty. Twenty-five percent of the 97 full-time faculty are women. There are 5 female faculty for every 100 female students and 15 male faculty members for every 100 male students.

Administrators. There is 1 woman among the 8 chief administrators. Two of 21 departments are chaired by women—music and home economics.

Women and the Curriculum. Most degrees awarded to women are in home economics (20 percent), arts and letters (17 percent), social sciences (15 percent) and biological sciences (13 percent). Two percent of women and of men take degrees in mathematics. Women are 58 percent of students in internships and practicums, and 49 percent of science field-service participants. The department of social work provides instruction on services for battered spouses, displaced homemakers, and childcare. There are no courses on women.

Women and Athletics. Some opportunities for organized com-

petitive sports are available. Four intramural (two coeducational) sports are offered. Intercollegiate sports are basketball, cross-country, tennis, track, swimming, and volleyball.

Housing and Student Organizations. Single-sex and coeducational dormitories are provided. The three male and two female residence-hall directors receive awareness training on the avoidance of sexism, racism, and on birth control.

Twenty-eight percent of full-time undergraduate women belong to sororities.

Special Services and Programs for Women. *Health and Counseling.* The student health service employs one male physician. Gynecological and birth control treatment are provided and abortion counseling is available.

Safety and Security. Measures consist of campus police, a nighttime escort service for women, and information on safety and rape/assault prevention. No rapes and one assault (none on women) were reported for 1980–81.

Institutional Self-Description. ''Whittier is a high-quality liberal arts institution. It is a small, friendly environment where each person is respected and treated as an individual. Women assume leadership roles in a number of situations. This year the student body president, the chairperson of the faculty, and the Dean of Students are all women.''

Yuba Community College
Marysville, CA 95901
Telephone: (916) 742-7351

Women in Leadership
★ faculty

★ **Women and the Curriculum**

5,306 undergraduates

	Amer. Ind.	Asian Amer.	Blacks	Hispanics	Whites
F	90	80	94	248	2,258
M	73	55	133	219	2,005
%	3.1	2.6	4.3	8.9	81.1

Operated by the Yuba Community College District, this two-year college is located in Marysville, 50 miles from Sacramento. The student body of 5,574 includes those attending courses on campus and at educational centers at Beale Air Force Base, Lake County, and Woodland. The undergraduate enrollment of 5,306 is just over half female; 63 percent of the women attend part-time. The median age of undergraduates is 29. Of the 252 handicapped students, half are women.

The college offers comprehensive educational services, including a college transfer program and terminal programs in vocational fields. Day and evening classes both on and off campus are offered. A summer session and self-paced/contract learning program are also available. On-campus parking for a fee and limited public transportation are available to the 98 percent of students who commute.

A childcare facility on campus can accommodate 26 children, just over half of requests for childcare. Open from 8 a.m. to 5 p.m., the center charges $.70 an hour for part-time and $.50 an hour for full-day care. Private childcare facilities are available off campus.

Policies to Ensure Fairness to Women. Two part-time affirmative action officers have responsibility for policy on equal employment opportunity, sex equity for students, and handicapped accessibility. In addition, the college has a Commission on Minority Affairs, which addresses the concerns of minority women. Sexual harassment of students, faculty, and staff is prohibited by a written campus policy, which has been publicly communicated to all three groups.

Women in Leadership Positions. *Students.* The only campus leadership position, president of the student body, was held by a man for three recent years.

Faculty. Of the full-time faculty of 106, 28 percent are women, a proportion that is above the national average. Additional data from the college indicate that approximately one-fourth of the part-time faculty are women, including 5 Hispanic, 3 black, and 2 Asian American women. There are 3 female faculty for every 100 female students and 7 male faculty for every 100 male students.

Administrators. All seven of the chief administrative positions are held by men. The division of art, humanities, and languages is chaired by a woman, and a woman serves as Assistant Dean of Instruction. A third of the faculty senate members are women.

Women and the Curriculum. The most popular degree for women is in arts and sciences (60 percent). Twenty percent of women students major in business and commerce and 10 percent major in health technologies. A few women major in data processing, mechanical engineering, natural sciences, and public services.

A Women's Studies Program, coordinated by a full-time, permanently appointed faculty member, offers a certificate and an associate of arts degree. Courses offered include Women in Art, Women in American History, Psychology of Women, and Women in Management. Faculty workshops focus on sexism and the curriculum, nontraditional occupations for women and men, and affirmative action and equal opportunity.

Women and Athletics. There are no intramural or club sports. Almost a third of participants in intercollegiate sports are women. Of the seven paid coaches for intercollegiate sports, three are women. Intercollegiate sports include cross-country, field hockey, track and field, softball, tennis, and volleyball.

Housing and Student Organizations. The college has single-sex and coeducational dormitories for the 2 percent of students who reside on campus. There are no restrictive hours for visitors of the opposite sex. The two residence-hall directors (one man and one woman) receive awareness-training on the avoidance of sexism and racism. United Students for Women serves as an advocacy group.

Special Services and Programs for Women. *Health and Counseling.* One male physician and 1 female health-care provider staff the student health service. The 9-member staff of the student counseling center includes 1 white woman and 2 minority women. Counseling is available on issues related to gynecology, birth control, abortion, rape, and assault. Counselors receive in-service training on sex-role stereotyping and racial bias.

Safety and Security. The campus is patrolled by campus police and local police. Additional facilities and services include high-intensity lighting in all areas, self-defense courses for women, and a rape crisis center. In 1980-81 one assault was reported on campus, and this did not involve a woman.

Career. Career workshops, printed information, and other programs on women in nontraditional occupations are provided.

Other. The Women's Center, with a part-time faculty coordinator, offers a variety of programs and services. These include an annual women's week, a women's lecture series, theater and other arts programs, and assertiveness/leadership training. Approximately 300 women take part in these programs.

Institutional Self-Description. "Yuba College is located in a rural community north of Sacramento, with the advantage of small-town friendliness and a low crime rate, yet within three hours of Reno, Lake Tahoe, and the San Francisco Bay Area. The weather is mild, with average temperatures ranging from 35 in winter to 95 in summer."

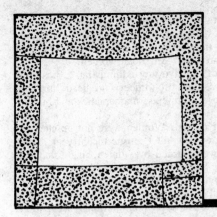

COLORADO

Colorado State University
Ft. Collins, CO 80523
Telephone: (303) 491-6064

★ Women and the Curriculum

★ Women and Athletics

15,346 undergraduates

	Amer. Ind.	Asian Amer.	Blacks	Hispanics	Whites
F	16	94	73	120	7,027
M	30	82	78	183	7,561
%	0.3	1.2	1.0	2.0	96.1

🏠 🏛 🔨 ⬛ 📖 ⚲ AAUW

Established in 1870 as the agricultural college for the Territory of Colorado, Colorado State University, located in Fort Collins, now provides diverse studies for undergraduate, graduate, and professional degree students. Over 18,000 students enroll. The division of continuing education is responsible for adult continuing education programs. Evening classes are available on and off campus; a summer session is offered.

Women make up 48 percent of the 15,346 undergraduates; 9 percent of women attend part-time. The median age of undergraduates is 20. For the two-thirds of the undergraduates who commute, the university is accessible by public transportation. On-campus parking is available at a fee.

Private childcare arrangements may be made nearby.

Policies to Ensure Fairness to Women. Two full-time Equal Opportunity Officers review policy and practices in such areas as employment, accessibility of curriculum and activities to all students, and handicapped access. A published policy prohibits sexual harassment of students, faculty, and staff. Complaints are handled through a formal grievance procedure. An active ad hoc Committee on the Status of Women takes public stands on issues of concern to students and serves as an advocate for faculty women. The Equal Opportunity Council addresses the concerns of minority women, among other matters.

Women in Leadership Positions. *Students.* In recent years, women have managed the radio station three times, twice presided over the student senate, and been editor-in-chief of the newspaper. Women head half of campus honorary societies.

Faculty. Ten percent of a full-time faculty of 1,102 are women. There are 2 female faculty for every 100 female students and 14 male faculty for every 100 male students.

Administrators. Men hold all higher administrative positions. Women chair four of 56 departments: anthropology, English, computer science, and housing and occupational therapy. A woman is Dean of the College of Home Economics.

Women and the Curriculum. Women graduating with bachelor's degrees major in home economics (18 percent), business and management (11 percent), agriculture (11 percent), and public affairs (10 percent). Sixteen percent major in fields nontraditional for women.

There is no Women's Studies Program as such. A student may earn a certificate in Women's Studies upon completion of 21 credits in courses approved by the Women's Studies Advisory Board. A Seminar in Women's Studies is offered. The departments of physical education, social work, and business provide instruction on some matters specific to women.

Minority Women. Of 7,330 undergraduate women, 1 percent are black, less than 1 percent American Indian, 1 percent Asian American, and about 2 percent Hispanic. A minority woman is a residence-hall director. Two of the permanent staff in the counseling service are minority women. Residence-hall and counseling staffs are offered training on the avoidance of racial bias. The university reports that minority women would find support from Women's Programs, Black Student Services, Centro Chicano, Native American Student Services, and MECHA, among other groups.

Women and Athletics. Intramural and intercollegiate programs provide good opportunities for organized, competitive individual and team sports. Club sports are also available. Athletic scholarships are awarded. Four of the 23 paid varsity coaches are women. All teams played tournament competition in 1980. The intercollegiate sports offered are basketball, field hockey, golf, softball, swimming and diving, tennis, track and field, and volleyball.

Housing and Student Organizations. Thirty-four percent of undergraduates live on campus. Coeducational dormitories and housing for married students and single parents with children are available. A married woman whose spouse is not enrolled may live in married students' housing. Residence halls do not restrict hours for visitors of the opposite sex. Six of ten residence-hall directors are female. Staff are offered awareness-training on sexism, sex education, and birth control.

Eleven percent of undergraduate women belong to social sororities. Sororities and fraternities provide housing for their members. Student organizations which serve as advocates for campus women include Feminist Group and Students Against Sexual Harassment and the Gay Alliance.

Special Services and Programs for Women. *Health and Counseling.* The student health service provides medical attention specific to women, including gynecological, birth control, abortion, and rape and assault treatment. The regular student health insurance covers abortion and maternity at no extra charge for students only. One of 7 physicians in the health center is female as are 4 other health-care providers. Five of 9 professional staff in the counseling service are women. Psychological, birth control, abortion, rape and assault, and sexuality counseling is available, along with regular educational and vocational services. Staff receive in-service training on sex-role stereotyping, among other issues. The counseling service also sponsors assertiveness training and programs to improve mathematics confidence.

Safety and Security. Measures include campus police, emergency alarm and telephone systems, self-defense courses for women, and lectures on all aspects of crime prevention. A rape crisis center is available. Thirteen assaults on women and three attempted rapes were reported for 1980–81.

Career. Workshops focused on nontraditional occupations, lectures, and printed information on nontraditional fields of study are available.

Other. Student Affairs houses a Women's Center with an annual budget of $47,500 and a full-time faculty director. Services for battered women, conferences, and various cultural activities are sponsored by the center.

The Women's Resource Center has books, files, films, tapes, periodicals, and other materials of interest to women. There is a new organization for those interested in women in international development.

Returning Women Students. Approximately 1,000 women take courses in the division of continuing education. The Adult Student Advisory Committee has a strong focus on returning and reentry women. There are brown-bag lunch programs for new and returning "older" women students.

Institutional Self-Description. "Colorado State University recognizes and respects people as individuals and as members of social groups. It has an active commitment to cultural diversity in its community membership, and provides an environment that contributes to interpersonal, intercultural, and international understanding. By accommodating individual differences, the university seeks to maximize personal growth and development."

men have held the only two student offices—student government president and campus newspaper editor.

Faculty. Of the 20 full-time faculty, four are women. One full-time faculty member is an Asian American woman.

Administrators. Two of the five key administrative posts are held by women—chief student-life officer and head librarian. Women chair two of five departments, mathematics and humanities.

Women and the Curriculum. Women were not granted any of the 31 bachelor's degrees awarded in one recent year. Three of 84 two-year degrees were earned by women, in mechanical/engineering technologies. Special programs encourage women to pursue careers in electronics and engineering. An official committee reports on curricular development that includes women. There is also a faculty workshop on nontraditional occupations for women and men. There are no courses on women.

Women and Athletics. There is no opportunity for organized competitive sports.

Special Services and Programs for Women. *Health and Counseling.* There is no student health service. A student counseling center employs three women and one male counselor.

Safety and Security. No counseling specific to women is available. High-intensity lighting has been installed. No rapes or assaults on women were reported for 1980–81.

Career. Career workshops, lectures by women employed in nontraditional occupations, and printed information are available. The college maintains an updated file on alumnae by specific career.

Institutional Self-Description. "Today's job market for women in technology is totally open. CTC actively encourages women to enter this lucrative technical market."

Colorado Technical College

655 Elkton Drive
Colorado Springs CO 80907
Telephone: (303) 598-0200

Women in Leadership
　★★ administrators

360 undergraduates

	Amer. Ind.	Asian Amer.	Blacks	Hispanics	Whites
F	0	0	1	1	26
M	2	2	11	16	290
%	0.6	0.6	3.4	4.9	91.0

Colorado Technical College is a private, non-denominational institution that prepares men and women for engineering careers and jobs as technicians in industry. The college has 360 students, 8 percent of whom are women. About a third of the women attend part-time. The median age of all students is 27.

Classes are available on and off campus; a summer session is also offered. No student housing is provided. The campus is accessible by public transportation. Free on-campus parking is available.

Private childcare facilities are located near campus.

Policies to Ensure Fairness to Women. A member of the administration oversees policies and practices regarding compliance with equal-employment-opportunity, sex-equity, and handicapped-access legislation. A published sexual harassment policy protects students.

Women in Leadership Positions. *Students.* Opportunities for women to exercise student leadership are limited. In recent years,

Community College of Denver, North Campus

3645 West 112th Avenue
Westminister, CO 80030
Telephone: (303) 466-8811

Women in Leadership
　★ students
　★★ faculty

4,084 undergraduates

	Amer. Ind.	Asian Amer.	Blacks	Hispanics	Whites
F	23	36	54	175	1,846
M	20	33	58	221	1,569
%	1.1	1.7	2.8	9.8	84.6

One of three branches of the Community College of Denver, this public, two-year, commuter college, founded in 1969, serves 4,630 students. Fifty-two percent of the students are women, and 65 percent of the women are enrolled part-time. The median age of all students is 28.

The college offers a comprehensive range of programs, including liberal arts transfer, certificate, and degree programs in such areas as agriculture, business, health, and technology. The continuing education program serves 7,000 students, 65 percent of whom are women. Accessible by public transportation, the campus provides free parking.

Childcare is available on campus from 7:45 a.m. to 9 p.m., Monday through Thursday, and until 4 p.m. on Friday.

Women in Leadership Positions. *Students.* Of the two leadership positions, president of the student body and editor of the newspaper, the first has been held by men in recent years and the second has been held by women for two of three recent years.

Faculty. Of 119 full-time faculty, 41 percent are women. According to the most recent information, 5 of the full-time faculty are black women and 2 are Hispanic women. There are 7 female faculty for every 100 female students; for males, the ratio is the same.

Administrators. Women hold none of the top positions, nor are they deans or department chairs.

Women and the Curriculum. Most of the two-year degrees awarded to women are in health technologies and arts and sciences. One course on women—Biology of Women—is offered by the Science and Health Program.

Women and Athletics. No intercollegiate or club sports are offered. No information was provided about intramural sports.

Special Services and Programs for Women. *Health and Counseling.* The student health center, staffed by two male physicians and three female health-care providers, offers birth control. One male counselor staffs the student counseling center. Services include counseling for birth control, abortion, rape, and assault.

Safety and Security. There is a campus police force and an emergency alarm system. A night-time escort is available for women students. No information was provided about the incidence of rapes and assaults.

Other. The division of community services and continuing education sponsors a Women's Center that is staffed by a part-time, salaried administrator. The center, with a budget of $10,321, serves 1,500 community women and college students each year, about 5 percent of whom are Hispanic. The Women's Center sponsors a program for displaced homemakers, and assertiveness training is offered by the division of community services and continuing education. Women are 41 percent of the 513 handicapped students, and find support at the Center for the Physically Disadvantaged.

Institutional Self-Description. None provided.

Pikes Peak Community College
5675 South Academy.
Colorado Springs, CO 80906
Telephone: (303) 576-7711

Women in Leadership
★★★ students
★★ faculty

4,082 undergraduates

	Amer. Ind.	Asian Amer.	Blacks	Hispanics	Whites
F	15	25	136	94	1,285
M	27	34	252	183	1,942
%	1.1	1.5	9.7	6.9	80.8

Established in 1969, this public, two-year commuter college in Colorado Springs serves about 5,000 students. Of the 4,082 degree students, 39 percent are women; 41 percent of the women attend part-time. The college offers vocational, technical, and on-the-job training, as well as college transfer programs. Day and evening classes both on and off campus, short-term job training, and an active counseling center assist reentry women. The median age of all students is 25. On-campus parking is available.

On-campus childcare facilities, charging fees on a sliding scale, are available during the day to virtually all students who request

them. Private facilities are available off campus.

Policies to Ensure Fairness to Women. A written policy prohibiting the sexual harassment of students, faculty, and staff has been communicated to all three groups; a formal procedure resolves complaints.

Women in Leadership Positions. *Students.* Opportunities for women students to exercise campus leadership are excellent. During recent years, women have been president of the student body and presiding officer of the student government for three consecutive terms, and edited the campus newspaper for two consecutive terms.

Faculty. Thirty-six percent of the 143 full-time faculty are women, a proportion slightly above the average for similar institutions. Recent information indicates that among the full- and part-time faculty are 35 black, 9 American Indian, 10 Asian American, and 22 Hispanic women. There are 5 female faculty for every 100 female students and 7 male faculty for every 100 male students.

Administrators. Men hold all major administrative positions. Women chair three of ten departments: counseling, developmental studies, and health occupations. A woman is Dean of Arts and Sciences.

Women and the Curriculum. Most women take degrees in arts and sciences (32 percent), business and public service (23 percent), and health technologies (18 percent).

Psychology of Women is the sole course offered on women. Faculty workshops are offered on nontraditional occupations for women and men, the needs of reentry women, and affirmative action and equal opportunity.

Women and Athletics. No information was provided.

Minority Women. Seventeen percent of undergraduate women are members of minority groups. Their interests are addressed by the Committee on Minority Affairs. The Black Student Union, International Student Club, Minority Affairs Association, and Los Companeros meet on campus. A black woman sits on the 15-member Board of Trustees.

Special Services and Programs for Women. *Health and Counseling.* For gynecological and other health services, students are referred to local agencies. There are five counselors, one of whom is a woman.

Safety and Security. Measures include campus police with authority to make arrests, night-time escort service, high-intensity lighting, and self-defense courses for students. For 1980–81, two assaults (none on a woman) were reported.

Career. The counseling center, in conjunction with the Women's Center, sponsors workshops and programs to train women in assertiveness, to build mathematics skills, and to help clarify career goals and values.

Other. Eight hundred students, 10 percent of them minority (largely black) women, use the Women's Center annually. The center, which does not have a separate budget and shares its office with the counseling center, co-sponsors courses and support groups and provides assistance to reentry women. It also sponsors a warmline and programs for battered women and displaced homemakers. Three times a year there is an "All-Campus Women's Coffee." The Women's Center sends a representative to the Colorado Network of Women's Centers and to the Women's Education Consortium for Women Students.

Institutional Self-Description. "Reentry women enroll at PPCC in great numbers and with great enthusiasm because 1) they know that the college offers short-term job skill programs as well as the first two years of a baccalaureate degree, and 2) they have heard that the faculty, staff, and administrators have a very special commitment to help them through the reentry transition; to be there to counsel with them and give extra help; and to provide an exciting, personalized, stimulating environment for learning. In addition, opportunities are available throughout the year for them to get together in formal and informal groups to become acquainted and to provide mutual support."

University of Colorado, Boulder
Boulder, CO 80309
Telephone: (303) 492-6294

★★★ **Women and the Curriculum**

17,424 undergraduates

	Amer. Ind.	Asian Amer.	Blacks	Hispanics	Whites
F	59	173	197	276	7,043
M	29	225	204	350	8,621
%	0.5	2.3	2.3	3.6	91.2

🏠 🚌 👫 ⛏ 📖 ⚲ **AAUW NWSA**

Established in 1876, the University of Colorado at Boulder, a state-supported institution set in the front range of the Rockies, attracts some 21,300 students to a variety of undergraduate, graduate, and professional studies. Summer session, weekend college, and vacation college (December-January) are available.

Women are 45 percent of the 17,424 undergraduates; 8 percent of women attend part-time. The most recent enrollment figures show that 9 percent of women students are over age 25, and that 31 women over age 40 attend full-time. The median age of all undergraduates is 20. The university is accessible by public transportation, and it provides on-campus parking at a fee for the 75 percent of undergraduates who live off campus or commute.

University-sponsored childcare facilities, giving priority to students who are residents of family housing, can accommodate 60 children. Private childcare arrangements may be made close to campus.

Policies to Ensure Fairness to Women. A full-time affirmative action officer is responsible for policy on equal employment opportunities, sex equity, and handicapped accessibility. A published policy prohibits sexual harassment of students, faculty, and staff, and complaints are handled through a formal grievance procedure. An active faculty Committee on the Status of Women takes public stands on issues of concern to all women, including minority women.

Women in Leadership Positions. *Students.* Opportunities for women students to exercise all-campus leadership are considerably below average for public research universities in this guide. In recent years, no woman has held student office.

Faculty. Women make up 12 percent of a full-time faculty of 860. The most recent data show 7 black women, 7 Asian American women, and 7 Hispanic women on the total faculty. The ratio of female faculty to female students is 1 to 100; of male faculty to male students, 8 to 100.

Administrators. The chief student-life officer and the director of institutional research are women. Women chair four of 50 departments: comparative literature; the Center for Interdisciplinary Studies; French and Italian; and physical education and recreation. A woman is Dean of the Law School.

Women and the Curriculum. Most women take undergraduate degrees in social sciences (15 percent), business and management (12 percent), arts and letters (11 percent), education (10 percent), and psychology (9 percent). Slightly under 10 percent major in such nontraditional fields as architecture, computer science, engineering, mathematics, and the physical sciences. The university reports innovative programs to encourage women to prepare for careers in engineering and computer science. Professional organizations support women in nontraditional careers.

The Women's Studies Program offers a 24-credit certificate, and an individualized major. The Women's History field is available to history Ph.D. candidates. Recent course offerings in Women's Studies include Asian Women in Development and Women and Ethnicity. Courses on women available through Chicano Studies and the department of history include La Chicana and Women and Society in Industrial Europe.

The Women's Studies Program has been instrumental in developing and sustaining state and regional associations and a local network of personal and professional support for women. It sponsors a women's lecture series and publishes *Frontiers*, a Women's Studies journal.

Minority Women. Of 7,748 undergraduate women, 3 percent are black, less than 1 percent American Indian, 2 percent Asian American, and 4 percent Hispanic. Two residence-hall counselors are minority women. Residence-hall staff are offered awareness-training on racism. Approximately 40 minority women are members of integrated sororities.

Women and Athletics. Intercollegiate sports provide limited opportunities for women to compete. Twenty-five percent of intercollegiate athletes are women; women receive 20 percent of athletic scholarships. Two of 19 paid coaches in intercollegiate athletics are women. Three of four women's intercollegiate teams, including skiing, played in tournaments in 1980. The intercollegiate sports offered are basketball, track and field, skiing, tennis.

Housing and Student Organizations. A quarter of the undergraduates live on campus in accommodations that include single-sex and coeducational dormitories and housing for married students. A married woman student whose spouse is not enrolled may live in married students' housing. One women's dormitory restricts male visiting hours if requested by the residents. The 13 residence counselors, seven of them women, are offered awareness-training on sexism, sex education, and birth control.

Approximately 15 percent of undergraduate women belong to social sororities, which provide housing for their members. Feminist Alliance, Women Engineers, Women in Business, the Lesbian Caucus, and Single Parents on Campus are among organizations that serve women.

Special Services and Programs for Women. *Health and Counseling.* The student health service provides some medical attention specific to women, including gynecological, birth control, and rape and assault treatment. Six of 14 physicians are female as are 38 other health-care providers. Regular student health insurance covers abortion and maternity (delivery only) at no extra cost. The 12 counselors in the counseling service, 5 of whom are women, provide gynecological, birth control, rape and assault, and sexuality counseling.

Safety and Security. Measures consist of campus police with arrest authority, night-time escort service for women students, night-time bus service to residence areas, high-intensity lighting in most areas, emergency alarm and telephone systems, occasional self-defense seminars for women, information sessions on safety and crime prevention, and a rape crisis center. Seventy assaults (31 on women) and two rapes were reported for 1980-81.

Career. Services include lectures by women employed in nontraditional careers, printed information on nontraditional fields of study, a program of contacts between alumnae and students, job search strategies, resume writing, and interviewing techniques.

Other. Counseling Services, which includes a small Women's Center, offers assertiveness training and a program to build confidence in mathematics. Women of varying ages and life circumstances find support at the Women's Center. The University of Colorado Student Union sponsors an annual women's week and a telephone service of information, referral, and support.

Institutional Self-Description. "The Boulder Campus of the University of Colorado has made significant advances on behalf of hiring women administrators. The Women's Studies Program provides academic support. The Women's Center and Career Counseling are active in personal support programming for women."

University of Colorado, Colorado Springs

Austin Bluffs Pky., Colorado Springs, CO 80907

Telephone: (303) 593-3000

Women in Leadership ★ students	★ Women and the Curriculum

2,559 undergraduates

	Amer. Ind.	Asian Amer.	Blacks	Hispanics	Whites
F	1	26	45	59	1,125
M	5	40	52	54	1,142
%	0.2	2.6	3.8	4.4	88.9

Established in 1963 to meet the educational and urban needs of the Pikes Peak region, the University of Colorado at Colorado Springs enrolls 4,390 students, of whom 2,559 are undergraduates. Half of the undergraduates are women; 36 percent of women attend part-time. The median age of all students is 27.

The university offers bachelor's and master's programs in business, education, liberal arts, and pre-professional areas. Flexible scheduling includes evening classes, summer sessions, vacation college, and self-paced/contract learning. The division of continuing education serves the adult student and offers several classes geared to the needs of reentry women. All students commute. The campus is accessible by public transportation. The university provides on-campus parking at a fee.

University-sponsored childcare facilities can accommodate all students' requests for service. Additonal, private facilities are located near the campus.

Policies to Ensure Fairness to Women. The Equal Opportunity Officer is responsible for policy on equity in education and employment. A policy prohibiting sexual harassment of students, faculty, and staff has been formulated, but not yet published; complaints are resolved through a formal grievance procedure.

A Committee on the Status of Women, appointed by the faculty senate, takes stands on issues of concern to women, including minority women.

Women in Leadership Positions. *Students.* There are four student leadership positions. Women have been student body president and editor-in-chief of the campus newspaper for two of three recent years.

Faculty. Sixteen percent of the 114 full-time faculty are women, a proportion well below the national average. There are 2 female faculty for every 100 female students and 11 male faculty for every 100 male students. The full-time faculty includes 1 American Indian, 2 black, and 5 Hispanic women.

Administrators. The chief administrators are men. Women chair 3 of 20 departments: English, fine arts, and communications. One woman sits on the 6 member committee on tenure and promotions. The sole female regent is a black woman. Twenty-seven percent of the faculty senate are women, including 2 black and 2 Hispanic women. One of the 2 recent honorary degree recipients was an Asian American woman.

Women and the Curriculum. The majority of women graduates major in social sciences (23 percent), business (22 percent), and education (17 percent). Three percent earn degrees in the nontraditional fields of mathematics, engineering, and computer science. Programs encourage women to prepare for careers in engineering and computer science. Women hold 80 percent of the practicums and internship appointments.

Eighteen courses on women are offered through nine departments; sociology, for example, offers six courses on women. Recent offerings include Women in Cross-Cultural Perspective; Economics of Discrimination; and Women's Space, Women's Place: Women's Role in Changing the Face of the Earth. A faculty committee is responsible for developing a Women's Studies Program. The divisions of business and education provide instruction on some matters specific to women.

Women and Athletics. There is no women's sports program.

Special Services and Programs for Women. *Health and Counseling.* There is no health service. The regular student health insurance policy covers maternity, at extra cost. A woman and a man staff the counseling center, which provides counseling for rape and assault. Both counselors are offered in-service training in the avoidance of sex-role sterotyping and racial bias.

Safety and Security. Measures consist of local police, campus police with weapons training and arrest authority, night escort service for women students, high-intensity lighting in all areas, campus-wide emergency telephone system, self-defense courses, and a rape crisis center. No rapes and 14 assaults on women were reported for 1980–81.

Career. Lectures, workshops, and literature on nontraditional occupations are available to students. Career counseling is provided by the student counseling center.

Other. The Office of Counseling and Special Programs operates a Women's Resource Center that serves about 600 campus and community women each semester. It sponsors an annual women's week and provides assertiveness training. University of Colorado Women, founded in 1980, is a four-campus, university-wide organization with chapters on each campus. Composed of staff, faculty, administration, and students, UCCS Women is a political network that cuts across the university hierarchy in an attempt to address campus problems and develop solutions to improve the conditions of women at UCCS.

The College of Liberal Arts and Sciences sponsors a women's lecture series and women's art programs. The division of continuing education offers several courses geared to reentry women. About 400 women, including about 100 minority women, mostly Hispanic, are enrolled in these courses.

Institutional Self-Description. "UCCS is a commuter campus of the University of Colorado system, serving students primarily from the Pike's Peak region. The campus itself is relatively new and its faculty young (average age 42). There is a sense of excitement on this growing campus, which is located on a bluff overlooking Colorado Springs and facing Pike's Peak and the front range of the Rocky Mountains."

University of Northern Colorado

Greeley, CO 80639

Telephone: (303) 351-2121

Women in Leadership ★ faculty	★ Women and the Curriculum

9,005 undergraduates

	Amer. Ind.	Asian Amer.	Blacks	Hispanics	Whites
F	14	49	144	174	4,908
M	15	28	108	126	3,394
%	0.3	0.9	2.8	3.4	92.7

NWSA

The University of Northern Colorado is a public institution founded to provide programs in teacher training, nursing, business, music, and recreation. The total number of students enrolled is 10,794. Of 9,005 undergraduates, women make up 59 percent, and almost all women attend full-time. Handicapped women make up 36 percent of the 210 handicapped students. The median age of all undergraduates is 22.

Private childcare facilities are available off campus.

Policies to Ensure Fairness to Women. An affirmative action

58 COLORADO

officer, on a part-time basis, reviews policies and practices generated by councils and committees. A written campus policy, which has been communicated in writing to students, faculty, and staff, prohibits sexual harassment. The Women's Caucus elects the Commission on the Status of Women, which reports to the administration. This commission, which includes student members with voting rights, takes public stands on issues of concern to women and prepares, at least annually, a report that is distributed to the campus community. Both this commission and the Commission on Minority Affairs address the concerns of minority women.

Women in Leadership Positions. *Students.* During a recent three-year period, women served single terms as president of the student body and presiding officer of the student senate, student union board, and residence-hall council. A woman was editor-in-chief of the student newspaper for two consecutive years.

Faculty. Women are 30 percent of the 455 full-time faculty, a proportion above the national average. There are 3 female faculty for every 100 female students and 9 male faculty for every 100 male students.

Administrators. Men hold all top positions. Women hold 3 of 58 department chairs (home economics, foreign language, mathematics). Women are Deans of the School of Nursing and the Division of Health, Physical Education and Recreation. Women are 3 of 7 trustees, including 1 black woman. Of 5 alumni awards in 1980–81, 1 went to a black woman and 1 to a white woman; of 8 speakers at campus-wide lecture series 3 were women, including 1 black woman and 1 Hispanic woman.

Women and the Curriculum. Over half of women graduate in education, about 10 percent in business, and another 10 percent in health professions. The university offers innovative programs for women in science, accounting, computer science, and business management, and is developing a program for women in law enforcement; 1 percent of women major in nontraditional fields. The School of Education provides instruction on the development and use of sex-fair curricula. The School of Business provides instruction about problems of women in the workplace.

The Women's Studies Program, directed by a woman who holds a permanent faculty appointment, offers an undergraduate minor and a bachelor's degree. It is also possible to earn graduate degrees in Women's Studies through the School of Educational Change and Development. Courses include a Senior Seminar in Women's Studies, Women and Sex in Science Fiction, and Women and Men in Perspective. An official committee, composed equally of students and faculty, is responsible for encouraging the development of courses on women. An annual Women's Studies conference attracts 400-500 participants each year.

Women and Athletics. Women are 42 percent of all intercollegiate and 50 percent of all intramural athletes. They receive 30 percent of athletic scholarships. The intramural program includes sports for the handicapped. Intercollegiate sports for women include basketball, cross-country, field hockey, golf, gymnastics, swimming and diving, softball, track, tennis, and volleyball.

Housing and Student Organizations. The 25 percent of undergraduates who live on campus have a variety of housing to choose from: single-sex and coeducational dormitories, as well as housing for married students and single parents. There is special housing for disabled students.

Social sororities, which claim 8 percent of full-time undergraduate women as members, also provide housing. Four minority women belong to racially integrated sororities and 50 to all-minority sororities.

Special Services and Programs for Women. *Health and Counseling.* The university has both a student health service and a counseling center. Women are 2 of the 13 physicians on staff and 3 of 5 counselor/therapists (1 of whom is a minority woman). Counseling and medical treatment are available for gynecological problems, birth control, abortion, and rape and assault. Abortion and maternity coverage is part of the student health insurance policy at no extra charge. The university provides in-service training for professional counselors/therapists on the avoidance of both sex-role stereotyping and racial bias.

Safety and Security. Measures include a campus police force with weapons training and the authority to make arrests, nighttime escort and bus service, high-intensity lighting, an emergency telephone system, self-defense courses, information sessions on safety and assault prevention, and a rape crisis center. Four rapes and ten assaults (four on women) were reported for 1980–81.

Other. A Women's Center, run by the counseling center, is headed part-time by a woman administrator. It sponsors an annual women's week and lecture series. The counseling center offers programs for battered women and displaced homemakers, assertiveness/leadership training, mathematics confidence, and a warmline.

The Center for Human Enrichment operates to meet the needs of displaced homemakers, minority women, and older women. Handicapped women are served by the Disabled Student Center.

Institutional Self-Description. None provided.

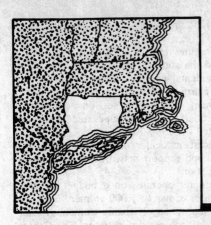

CONNECTICUT

Asnuntuck Community College
111 Phoenix Avenue, Enfield, CT 06082
Telephone: (203) 745-1603

Women in Leadership
★★ faculty

959 undergraduates

	Amer. Ind.	Asian Amer.	Blacks	Hispanics	Whites
F	2	3	5	2	521
M	0	1	6	5	363
%	0.2	0.4	6.4	0.7	92.3

A public, two-year commuter college, Asnuntuck serves 1,631 students, of whom 959 are degree students. Fifty-six percent of the undergraduates are women; 80 percent of women attend part-time. Recent information indicates that 40 percent of women on campus are over age 40. The median age of all undergraduates is 29. The college offers liberal arts, business, communications and media, and public-service programs. There is also a continuing education program. Evening classes, both on and off campus, as well as a weekend college, make the programs accessible to part-time students who have work and childcare responsibilities. Although there is no public transportation, free on-campus parking is available.

Childcare for 30 children is available daily from 9:00 a.m. to 4:00 p.m. at no charge. Private childcare facilities are also available near campus.

Policies to Ensure Fairness to Women. The Assistant to the President for Affirmative Action serves as a compliance administrator for equal-employment-opportunity, educational-sex-equity, and handicapped-accessibility policies. Sexual harassment is prohibited by a written campus policy that has been publicly communicated to students, faculty, and staff.

Women in Leadership Positions. *Students.* The editorship of the campus newspaper, the only campus leadership position, has been held by a woman once in a three-year period.

Faculty. Of 16 full-time faculty, 6 are women, 1 of whom is Hispanic. The ratio of female faculty to female students is 6 to 100; for males, the ratio is 19 to 100.

Administrators. Of the 6 chief administrators, the chief academic officer is a woman. Four of the 16 trustees are white women; 2 are black women.

Women and the Curriculum. Women earn 45 percent of two-year awards. The largest number of women receive degrees or certificates in business and commerce. The next largest group are those in the arts and sciences; a few women graduate in data processing. The mathematics department sponsors a program to build mathematics confidence. There are no courses on women.

Women and Athletics. There are no opportunities for organized competitive sports.

Special Services and Programs for Women. *Health and Counseling.* The college has a student counseling center, but no student health service. The counseling center has a staff of three, two of whom are women. Services include counseling on gynecological concerns, birth control, abortion, and rape and assault. Pregnancy testing is also available.

Safety and Security. Measures consist of patrols by local police, and high-intensity lighting in all areas. There were no rapes or assaults reported on campus for 1980–81.

Other. An active Women's Center is operated by Student Services. With a full-time, salaried administrative coordinator, the center sponsors a variety of programs and services that are used primarily by community women and undergraduates over the age of 25. The services include a displaced homemakers program, an annual women's week, a women's lecture series, assertiveness/leadership training, a telephone service for information, referrals, and support, and a reading room for pre-school children of students. Handicapped women are serviced by the Stewardship Program for the Physically Handicapped.

Institutional Self-Description. "We will share with others a past and a present, preparing for a future that is unsure. We look upon life as an opportunity to both develop self and to assist others. We shall strive to create patterns in self that make a person an individual without forgetting their part in the human race. We shall try to develop appreciation of beauty and seek to create beauty through work, caring, and life."

Central Connecticut State College
1615 Stanley Street
New Britain, CT 06050
Telephone: (203) 827-7000

Women in Leadership
★★★ students

9,337 undergraduates

	Amer. Ind.	Asian Amer.	Blacks	Hispanics	Whites
F	8	17	101	45	3,992
M	7	31	93	35	5,008
%	0.2	0.5	2.1	0.9	96.4

 AAUW

Founded in 1849 as a preparatory school for teachers, in 1959 Central Connecticut State College became a multi-purpose, comprehensive state college with programs in teacher education, business, arts and sciences, and technology. Of a total 11,433 students, 9,337 are undergraduates, 45 percent of them women. Thirty percent of the women attend part-time. The median age of all undergraduate students is 21. On-campus parking is available at a fee for the 58 percent of students who commute; public transportation is available but not convenient. Handicapped women make up about one-quarter of the 83 disabled students enrolled.

Childcare facilities accommodate 40 percent of requests by students. Private facilities are available off campus.

Policies to Ensure Fairness to Women. The Compliance and Non-Discrimination Officer, on a part-time basis, reviews policies and practices generated by councils and committees for equal-employment, sex-equity, and handicapped-access. Campus policy and procedures forbidding the sexual harassment of students, faculty, and staff have been publicly communicated to all three groups.

The appointed Commission on the Status of Women reports directly to the President of the college. The commission, which includes students among its voting members, meets regularly to prepare and distribute an annual report, takes stands on issues of concern to students, and does research on topics related to the concerns of women. Both it and the Commission on Minority Affairs address the concerns of minority women.

Women in Leadership Positions. *Students.* Women students have outstanding opportunities to gain leadership experience. They have held a majority of the campus-wide positions during recent years, including presiding officer of the student body, student union board, sophomore, junior, and senior classes, and editor-in-chief of the student newspaper. Women head at least three of the eleven campus honorary societies.

Faculty. Twenty-three percent of the 414 full-time faculty are women. There are 3 female faculty for every 100 female students and 9 male faculty for every 100 male students.

Administrators. Men hold all top positions; women chair the departments of business education and psychology.

Women and the Curriculum. Most women take degrees in education and business, with significant numbers also in social sciences and psychology. Three percent of women graduate in nontraditional areas. Innovative programs include Women in Industrial Technology and Cooperative Education.

The college offers one course on women, Psychology of Women. The department of physical education and the Schools of Nursing and Business provide some instruction on matters specific to women. An official committee is responsible for collecting and developing curricular materials on women. Faculty workshops address sexism and the curriculum, the needs of reentry women, affirmative action, and equal opportunity.

Women and Athletics. Women are 27 percent of the intercollegiate and 46 percent of the intramural athletes. The university offers an adequate variety of intramural and intercollegiate sports, for a school of its size. Ten percent of all athletic scholarships are awarded to women, and three of the 13 paid varsity coaches are women. Intercollegiate sports for women include basketball, cross-country, field hockey, swimming and diving, softball, track and field, tennis, and volleyball.

Housing and Student Organizations. Single-sex and coeducational dormitories are available for the 27 percent of undergraduates who live on campus; they have restrictive hours for visitors of the opposite sex. A married student whose husband is not enrolled is not permitted to live in married students' housing. Fifteen percent of undergraduates live in private housing near campus. Of the 859 women who live on campus, 86 percent are white, 7 percent are black, 5 percent Asian American, and 2 percent Hispanic. Two of the eight residence-hall directors are white women. Awareness-training is offered to residence-hall staff on sexism, sex education, and birth control.

Social sororities and fraternities do not provide housing for members.

Special Services and Programs for Women. *Health and Counseling.* The student health service is staffed by 1 male physician and 11 female nurses. The 4 counselor-therapists include 1 woman. Counseling and medical treatment are provided for gynecological needs and rape and assault, counseling alone for birth control and abortion.

Safety and Security. Measures include a campus police force with weapons training and the authority to make arrests, night-time escort for women students, campus-wide emergency telephone system, emergency alarm system at isolated locations, self-defense courses for women, information sessions on campus safety, and a campus rape crisis center. No rapes and 27 assaults (3 on women) were reported for 1980–81.

Career. The career placement center offers workshops, lectures, printed information, and support networks for women entering nontraditional occupations.

Other. The Women's Center operates on a budget of about $15,000 a year. It serves approximately 1,000 women, 5 percent of whom are minority women, mostly Hispanic women. A salaried white woman serves part-time as administrator. The Center, which provides programs for battered women and displaced homemakers, offers a women's lecture series and assertiveness/leadership training. Along with the mathematics department it sponsors a program to build mathematics confidence, and with the Health Center it provides a warmline.

The Extension College serves 1,455 reentry women, 11 percent of whom are minority women, mostly black women.

Institutional Self-Description. "The availability of a professionally staffed Women's Center which focuses upon issues of direct concern to women (with different needs) through programs, supportive services, research files, and crisis counseling, increases the potential successful participation in college life on the part of the women. The close working relationships between the Women's Center staff and the teaching faculty aid women in the successful completion of their academic programs."

Charter Oak College
c/o Board for State Academic Awards
340 Capitol Ave., Hartford, CT. 06115
Telephone: (203) 566-7230

Women in Leadership
★★★ faculty
★★★ administrators

Enrollment Data Not Available

Charter Oak is the external degree program of the State of Connecticut. It was established in 1973 to "assist the adult undergraduate earn a college degree outside the traditional college classroom." Of the 440 undergraduate women, half are aged 26–40, and one-quarter are over age 40. All undergraduates attend part-time. There is no campus.

Women in Leadership Positions. *Students.* There are no student leadership positions.

Faculty. The faculty members are consultants appointed from both public and private institutions of higher learning in Connecticut. Twenty-five of the 40 faculty are women, a proportion above the national average.

Administrators. Seven of the 8 administrative staff are women, as are 2 of the 5-member Governing Board.

Women and the Curriculum. No information is available.

Women and Athletics. There is no organized athletic program.

Special Services and Programs for Women. There are no health services or counseling center and no security measures.

Institutional Self-Description. "An external degree program offers women who may be working full-time or who have family or financial responsibilities an opportunity to earn a college degree outside the traditional classroom by combining previously earned college credits with standardized proficiency examinations. Low costs and flexibility of program are especially attractive."

Connecticut College
New London, CT 06320
Telephone: (203) 447-1911

Women in Leadership
★ **faculty**
★ **administrators**

★ **Women and the Curriculum**

1,746 undergraduates

	Amer. Ind.	Asian Amer.	Blacks	Hispanics	Whites
F	2	3	34	9	987
M	0	2	20	5	646
%	0.1	0.3	3.2	0.8	95.6

 AAUW

Although now a coeducational, private, four-year, liberal arts college, Connecticut was founded as a women's college in 1911, when Wesleyan University, the only institution in the state open to women, closed its doors to them. Connecticut College enrolls 1,746 undergraduates. Women are 61 percent of students; 8 percent of the women attend part-time. The median age of all undergraduates is 21. Alternative schedules include evening classes and a summer session. Free on-campus parking is available for the 8 percent of students who commute.

Policies to Ensure Fairness to Women. The Director of Administrative Services and Personnel is responsible, on a full-time basis, for reviewing policies and monitoring compliance concerning equal employment opportunity, sex equity for students, and handicapped-access legislation. A formal campus procedure resolves complaints of sexual harassment. The Committee on Minority Affairs addresses the concerns of minority women.

Women in Leadership Positions. *Students.* Opportunities for women to exercise campus-wide student leadership are about average for similar institutions in this guide. In recent years, women have been editor of the campus newspaper, president of the student body, and head of the junior class—each for three terms. They have served for one term as head of the student court and of the senior, sophomore, and entering classes.

Faculty. Women are 33 percent of the 125 full-time faculty, a proportion that is above the national average. The ratio of female faculty to female students is 4 to 100; that for males is 13 to 100.

Administrators. Two of 8 top administrators are women: the academic dean and the chief-student life officer. Of the 28 academic departments, women chair 10. Women are 4 of the 6 deans, including the Dean of the College, and over half of the trustees (1 of them a black woman). In 1981 a woman received the sole alumni award.

Women and the Curriculum. Most degrees awarded to women are in the social sciences (27 percent), letters and fine arts (28 percent), home economics (10 percent), and psychology (10 percent). Eighty-five percent of student internships are held by women.

Twelve courses on women are available through various departments. Courses include Introduction to Women's Studies, team taught, as well as Women in Greek Literature, Twentieth-Century Women in Literature, and Gender Roles in Modern Society. A committee of faculty and students is developing a Women's Studies program.

Women and Athletics. There is good variety in the intramural and intercollegiate programs. Coeducational team sports are popular in intramurals. Club sports are also available. A skating rink and a river suitable for crew are special features. Five of 15 paid varsity coaches are women. Intercollegiate sports are basketball, crew, cross-country, field hockey, gymnastics, lacrosse, swimming, tennis, volleyball.

Housing and Student Organizations. Ninety-two percent of undergraduates live on campus in coeducational dormitories that have no restrictive hours for visitors of the opposite sex. The 8

female and 12 male residence-hall directors are offered awareness training on sexism, sex education, racism, birth control, and health and safety.

The Women's Group, Unity, an advocacy group for blacks on campus, and the Connecticut College Gay Community meet on campus.

Special Services and Programs for Women. *Health and Counseling.* The student health service employs a male physician; the counseling center has a staff of two women and a man. Medical treatment and counseling are available for matters of gynecology, birth control, abortion, and rape and assault. The student health insurance covers abortion at no extra charge. Counselors receive in-service training on sexuality.

Safety and Security. Measures include a campus police force, local police, a night-time escort service, and information sessions on safety. A community-based rape crisis center is available. No rapes and four assaults (none on women) were reported for 1980-81.

Career. Services include the maintenance of files on alumnae by specific careers and programs to establish contacts between alumnae and female students.

Other. The Women's Center of Southeastern Connecticut, a community-based organization, operates a women's program, a displaced homemakers' program, and a telephone information and referral service; and provides assertiveness training.

Institutional Self-Description. "One third of the faculty are women, many of them interested in Women's Studies, as attested by the increasing number of such courses offered over the past ten years. Although there is as yet no formal program, a student may design her own major in Women's Studies from courses in eleven different departments as well as from survey courses in Women's Studies."

Greater New Haven State Technical College
North Haven, CT 06473
Telephone: (203) 789-7225

Women in Leadership
★ **faculty**

1,200 undergraduates
Complete enrollment data unavailable.

Operated by the state of Connecticut since 1977, this two-year technical college serves 1,200 students, 30 percent of whom are women. Eighty percent of the women attend part-time. According to information supplied by the college, the undergraduate enrollment includes 220 women: 6 Asian Americans, 18 blacks, 2 Hispanics, and 194 whites. The median age of all undergraduates is 23.

Designed to prepare men and women for immediate employment as technicians in business and industry, Greater New Haven offers programs in such fields as the technologies of automotive management, biomedical engineering, data processing, graphic communications, industrial management, manufacturing, and mechanical engineering. The suburban campus, near New Haven, is accessible by public transportation. On-campus parking is available.

Policies to Ensure Fairness to Women. An affirmative action officer is responsible part-time for monitoring compliance with policies on equal employment opportunity, sex equity for students, and handicapped accessibility.

Women in Leadership Positions. *Students.* The president of the student body, the only campus leadership position, has been a male in recent years.

Faculty. The 13 full-time faculty include 4 women, 1 of whom is a black woman. Three women are among the 43 part-time faculty.

Administrators. The four chief administrative officers are men, as are all the deans and department chairs.

Women and the Curriculum. Information on major fields of study and degrees granted to women is not available. The college reports innovative programs to prepare women for careers in engineering, computer science, and electronics. Faculty workshops are offered on nontraditional occupations for women and men, and on the needs of reentry women. There are no courses on women.

Women and Athletics. The college does not offer intercollegiate or intramural sports.

Special Services and Programs for Women. *Health and Counseling.* There is no student health service on campus. A counseling center provides no services specific to women.

Safety and Security. The jurisdiction of local police includes the campus. The college provides information sessions on campus safety and rape and assault prevention for women. No assaults on women were reported for 1980–81.

Career. The college provides career workshops, lectures, and printed information on nontraditional occupations for women and on job discrimination. There is also a program to establish contacts between female students and alumnae.

Institutional Self-Description. ''The college is committed to providing its graduates with the skills necessary for employment in our highly technological state. It is also working diligently on encouraging the enrollment of women and minority students. Currently, women comprise 30 percent of the student population.''

Norwalk Community College
333 Wilson Avenue, Norwalk, CT 06854
Telephone: (203) 853-2040

Women in Leadership
★★ faculty

2,135 undergraduates

	Amer. Ind.	Asian Amer.	Blacks	Hispanics	Whites
F	1	11	176	43	988
M	1	8	98	24	761
%	0.1	0.9	13.0	3.2	82.9

Since 1966 a part of the state system of regional two-year colleges, Norwalk Community College serves 3,207 students, two-thirds of whom are enrolled in degree or certificate programs. Fifty-eight percent of the students are women; 58 percent of women attend part-time. The median age of all students is 25. The college offers two-year degrees and certificates in liberal arts and a variety of business-related and vocational fields.

Alternative schedules include evening classes on campus, day and evening classes off campus, weekend classes, a summer session, and a community-service continuing education program. The college is accessible by public transportation, and free parking is provided on campus.

Policies to Ensure Fairness to Women. The Executive Dean of the college is the compliance administrator for equal-employment-opportunity, sex-equity, and handicapped-accessibility laws. A Commission on Minority Affairs addresses the concerns of minority women. Sexual harassment of students, faculty, and staff is prohibited by a policy publicly communicated to the faculty and staff. A formal campus grievance procedure which ensures due process resolves complaints of sexual harassment.

Women in Leadership Positions. *Students.* Women have some opportunities to exercise campus leadership. A woman was presiding officer of the student governing body for one of three recent years. Women were editor-in-chief of the campus newspaper twice during that time.

Faculty. Of 59 full-time faculty members, 28 (or 47 percent) are women, which is above the national average. There are 2 Hispanic women on the faculty. There are 5 female faculty for every 100 female students, and 7 male faculty for every 100 male students.

Administrators. Seven of the eight key administrative positions are held by men. The chief academic officer is a woman. Women chair three of 12 academic divisions: humanities, human services, and early-childhood education. Sixty percent of the members of an important faculty committee are women.

Women and the Curriculum. Most women earn vocational degrees in business (33 percent), health (28 percent), and public-service technologies (20 percent). One-fifth of women earn associate degrees in arts and sciences. Eighty-five percent of available student internships are held by women.

There are no courses on women. The nursing school and the division of social work provide instruction on some matters specific to women. Faculty are offered workshops on the needs of reentry women, on affirmative action and equal opportunity.

Women and Athletics. One-fourth of intercollegiate athletes are women; there are no intramural sports. Three of nine paid varsity coaches are women. The three varsity teams (basketball, softball, and volleyball) participated in tournament competition in one recent year.

Special Services and Programs for Women. *Health and Counseling.* There is no health service for students. The student counseling center staff of one woman and three men provides crisis counseling and referrals related to gynecological, birth control, abortion, rape and assault issues.

Safety and Security. The campus is patrolled by campus police with no authority to make arrests. Additional measures include high-intensity lighting in all areas and a night-time escort service for women students. Two assaults on women were reported for 1980-81.

Career. The college offers career workshops and lectures about women in nontraditional occupations.

Other. A female counselor works part-time with reentry women. Minority women have organized The Coalition of Minority Students.

Institutional Self-Description. None provided.

Saint Joseph College
1678 Asylum Avenue
West Hartford, CT 06117
Telephone: (203) 232-4571

Women in Leadership
★★★ students
★★★ faculty
★★★ administrators

★ **Women and the Curriculum**

764 undergraduates

	Amer. Ind.	Asian Amer.	Blacks	Hispanics	Whites
F	0	2	15	7	735
M	0	0	0	0	4
%	0.0	0.3	2.0	1.0	96.9

 AAUW

Founded in 1932 by the Sisters of Mercy, Saint Joseph College is a four-year, Roman Catholic, liberal arts college for women.

Located in suburban West Hartford, the college enrolls 1,273 students in undergraduate, graduate, and professional degree programs. An adult continuing education program is also available. There are 764 undergraduates, 14 percent of whom attend part-time.

Day and evening classes on and off campus, weekend and summer session classes are available. The campus is accessible by public transportation. For the 42 percent of the undergraduates who commute, there is also free on-campus parking.

Private childcare facilities are available close to campus.

Policies to Ensure Fairness to Women. The Director of Personnel is responsible for policies and practices relating to equal employment opportunity, sex equity in education, and handicapped accessibility. A sexual harassment policy is near completion and will stipulate formal complaint procedures. Currently, complaints are handled on an informal and confidential basis. A Committee on Minority Affairs addresses the concerns of minority women.

Women in Leadership Positions. *Students.* Women hold all student leadership positions.

Faculty. Fifty-eight percent of the full-time faculty of 59 are women. There are 5 female faculty for every 100 students.

Administrators. Three-fourths of all key administrators are women. Woman chair 13 of 21 departments, including mathematics, economics/business, sociology, and history. Women also head the divisions of natural science, social science, humanities, nursing, and continuing education. A woman serves as Dean of the Graduate Studies Program.

Women and the Curriculum. The most popular majors are education (37 percent) and health professions (25 percent). Special programs encourage women to pursue careers in such nontraditional fields as science, accounting, computer science, and engineering. The college offers a dual degree program with George Washington University that allows students to combine liberal studies and engineering.

The Women's Studies Program offers an undergraduate minor. Fifteen courses available through various departments include Women in Classical Literature, Women in European History, and The Psychology of Women. The departments of business/economics and nursing and the division of social work provide some instruction on matters specific to women.

A Task Force on general education requirements helps integrate new scholarship on women into the curriculum. Faculty are offered workshops on sexism in the curriculum, nontraditional occupations, and affirmative action and equal opportunity.

Women and Athletics. Information was not provided on the size of the organized sports program. Clubs and intramural teams compete in softball, track and field, and volleyball. Intercollegiate sports offered are basketball, softball, tennis, and volleyball.

Housing and Student Organizations. Fifty-eight percent of women live on campus in dormitories that have restrictive visiting hours for men. The residence-hall staff receive awareness-training on sex education and birth control.

Special Services and Programs for Women. *Health and Counseling.* The student health service is staffed by three male physicians and three female health-care providers. The student counseling center employs one female counselor. Services specific to women are counseling and medical treatment for gynecological problems, birth control, and rape and assault.

Safety and Security. Measures include campus and local police protection, night-time escort, high-intensity lighting, information on safety precautions, and instruction on self-defense. No rapes or assaults were reported for 1980–81.

Career. Services include networking between students and alumnae, and workshops, lectures, and job discrimination information on nontraditional occupations. Updated files on alumnae by specific career are also maintained.

Other. The Office of Continuing Education sponsors a variety of programs for women, such as an assertiveness-training clinic, a women's lecture series, an annual women's week, and a displaced-homemakers' program. The art department sponsors theater-arts events. An Annual Women's Forum draws participants to discuss issues of importance to women.

Returning Women Students. Reentry women receive special attention from a program on Continuing Education for Women, directed by a full-time, female administrator. In addition, AWARE (Adults Who Are Returning to Education), a large advocacy group of reentry women, meets on campus. Faculty are offered workshops on the needs of reentry women.

Institutional Self-Description. "Founded by the Sisters of Mercy, Saint Joseph College seeks to educate women of all ages to assume responsible positions and face confidently the challenges of equal opportunity in society. The college accomplishes this by a creative curriculum combining liberal arts and career preparation, and a supportive atmosphere free of sexism."

Southern Connecticut State College
501 Crescent St., New Haven, CT 06515
Telephone: (203) 397-4000

Women in Leadership   ★ **Women and Athletics**
   ★★ **faculty**

6,619 undergraduates

	Amer. Ind.	Asian Amer.	Blacks	Hispanics	Whites
F	4	4	109	25	4,049
M	1	13	56	20	2,325
%	0.1	0.3	2.5	0.7	96.5

AAUW

Founded as a teachers' preparatory school in 1893, Southern Connecticut State College became a multi-purpose institution for liberal arts and professional studies in 1959. In addition to bachelor's and graduate degrees, some two-year degrees are offered. Both evening and summer sessions are available. The Office of Continuing Education serves the adult student. The college enrolls 11,800 students, of whom 6,619 are undergraduates. Sixty-three percent of the undergraduates are women; 5 percent attend part-time. The median age of all undergraduates is 23.

Both public transportation and free on-campus parking are available to the 75 percent of students who commute.

Childcare facilities are available on campus for children over three years old.

Policies to Ensure Fairness to Women. A full-time Equal Opportunity and Affirmative Action officer reviews policies and practices related to equal employment opportunity and sex equity for students. The Coordinator of Disabled Students acts as a part-time compliance administrator monitoring accessibility for disabled students. A written campus policy prohibits sexual harassment of students; procedures for handling complaints are being written.

A self-designated Commission on the Status of Women reports to the President, includes student members with voting rights, and meets at regular intervals. This commission as well as the Commission on Minority Affairs address the concerns of minority women.

Women in Leadership Positions. *Students.* In three recent years, women occupied 27 percent of the available student leadership positions, including one-year terms as president of the student body, editor-in-chief of the campus newspaper, and presidents of the junior and sophmore classes; and two-year terms as presidents of the student union and the residence-hall council. One of the two campus honorary societies is headed by a woman.

Faculty. Thirty-six percent of the 424 full-time faculty are women, a proportion higher than the national average. There are 4 female faculty for every 100 female students and 12 male faculty for every 100 male students. The college reports 1 Asian American, 2 black, and 3 Hispanic women among the full-time female faculty.

Administrators. All chief administrative positions are held by men. Women chair seven of 33 departments: art, education, foreign languages, library science, nursing, physical education for women, and social work. Thirty-four percent of the faculty senate, 60 percent of the tenure and promotions committee, and 38 percent of the trustees are women.

Women and the Curriculum. Nearly half of the women who earn bachelor's degrees major in education, with significant numbers graduating in public affairs. Less than 2 percent of women earn degrees in the nontraditional fields of mathematics and physical sciences. Sixty percent of student interns are women.

While the college reports the existence of no formal Women's Studies Program, "The Minor in Women's Studies" is a curricular feature. It consists of 18 credits taken in a variety of fields, beginning with a sociology course called Women's Changing Roles, and concluding with another called Twentieth-Century Feminist Theory. A total of 12 courses are available, some of them not offered every semester. An official committee is responsible for developing a Women's Studies Program, additional courses on women in departments, and curricular materials on women. The departments of economics, mathematics, nursing, physical education, and social work provide instruction on some matters specific to women.

Women and Athletics. For a college of its size, SCSC provides a wide array of intramural and intercollegiate sports. Ten intramural sports are offered, including water polo, floor hockey, and gymnastics. Intercollegiate sports offered are basketball, cross-country, field hockey, gymnastics, softball, swimming, tennis, track and field, and volleyball.

Housing and Student Organizations. Coeducational and single-sex dormitories are available to the 24 percent of students who reside on campus. Though the single-sex dormitories restrict hours for visitors of the opposite sex, coeducational dormitories do not. Three of the six residence-hall directors are women, including one minority woman.

Social fraternities and sororities do not provide housing for members.

Special Services and Programs for Women. *Health and Counseling.* The student health center employs 1 female and 1 male physician, as well as a part-time, male health-care provider. The counseling center's staff of 4 includes 3 women, 1 of them a minority woman. Birth control, abortion, and rape and assault counseling are available, along with medical treatment for gynecological problems.

Safety and Security. Measures consist of local police, campus police with arrest authority, a night-time escort for women, night-time bus service to residence areas, self-defense courses for women, information sessions on campus safety, and a rape crisis center. Eight assaults, two on women, were reported for 1980–81.

Career. The college provides nonsexist/nonracist printed materials and job discrimination information on nontraditional occupations for women.

Other. The student health center operates the college's Women's Center, which serves faculty, staff, and community women, as well as students. The center sponsors an annual women's week and a telephone hotline for information, referrals, and support.

The Organization of Afro/American Students and the Organization for Latin/American Students are active organizations on campus.

Institutional Self-Description. None provided.

University of Connecticut at Storrs
Storrs, CT 06268
Telephone: (203) 486-2000

Women in Leadership ★ students			★★ Women and the Curriculum	

14,547 undergraduates

	Amer. Ind.	Asian Amer.	Blacks	Hispanics	Whites
F	4	52	267	70	6,467
M	11	54	242	86	7,273
%	0.1	0.7	3.5	1.1	94.6

 NWSA

Founded in 1881 as a land-grant, agricultural college, the University of Connecticut has been a state university since 1939. The main campus at Storrs attracts over 21,000 students to a wide range of undergraduate, graduate, and professional programs. Extended and continuing adult education are available.

Women are 47 percent of the 14,547 undergraduates: 6 percent of the women attend part-time. For the 34 percent of undergraduates who commute, there is limited public transportation. On-campus parking is available at a fee, with free transportation from distant lots.

Policies to Ensure Fairness to Women. The full-time Director of Affirmative Action Programs reviews and monitors compliance with sex-equity policies. The Assistant Vice-President for Student Affairs chairs a committee on handicapped accessibility. A published campus policy prohibits sexual harassment.

Women in Leadership Positions. *Students.* Opportunities for women students to exercise campus-wide leadership are above average for public research universities in this guide. In recent years, women have presided twice over the student senate and once over the student union board, in addition to being editor-in-chief of the campus newspaper.

Faculty. Women are 19 percent of a full-time faculty of 1,149. There are 3 female faculty for every 100 female students and 13 male faculty for every 100 male students.

Administrators. Men hold nearly all key positions; a woman is director of institutional research. No women currently chair any of the 50 departments. Women head the School of Nursing and the School of Allied Health Professions.

Women and the Curriculum. Twenty percent of women take bachelor's degrees in agriculture, and 11 percent major in such additional nontraditional fields as mathematics, engineering, and physical sciences. Other popular fields are the health professions (16 percent), home economics (11 percent), business and management (12 percent), and social sciences (10 percent).

The Women's Studies Program, under a director who holds a full-time faculty appointment, offers a bachelor's degree as an individualized major. Thirty courses on women are available through Women's Studies and cooperating departments. The University of Connecticut at Storrs was host to the Third Annual Convention of the National Women's Studies Association in 1981.

Women and Athletics. Intercollegiate athletics, including many teams that play in tournaments, provide some opportunities for women to compete. Women constitute 36 percent of intercollegiate athletes and receive 20-25 percent of athletic scholarships. No intramural or club sports are offered. The women's intercollegiate sports offered are basketball, cross-country, gymnastics, field hockey, soccer, softball, swimming and diving, tennis, track and field, volleyball.

Housing and Student Organizations. Two-thirds of the undergraduates live on campus. Residential accommodations include single-sex and coeducational dormitories. Single-sex dormitories restrict hours for visitors of the opposite sex. Seventeen of 45 residence-hall staff are female, including one minority woman.

Social fraternities and sororities provide some housing for their members.

Special Services and Programs for Women. *Health and Counseling.* The student health service provides medical attention specific to women, including gynecological and rape and assault treatment. One of 6 physicians is female, as are 29 of 30 health-care providers. Six of 10 counselors in the counseling service are women. Birth control counseling is available.

Safety and Security. Measures consist of campus and local police, a night-time escort service for women students, and a rape crisis center. Sixteen assaults (12 on women) and one rape were reported for 1980-81.

Other. The Women's Center, under the direction of a full-time administrator, is housed in its own building.

Institutional Self-Description. None provided.

Waterbury State Technical College
Waterbury, CT 06708
Telephone: (203) 756-7035

1,300 undergraduates

	Amer. Ind.	Asian Amer.	Blacks	Hispanics	Whites
F	0	1	7	0	251
M	1	7	15	13	1,002
%	0.1	0.6	1.7	1.0	96.6

Waterbury State is a public, two-year technical college that serves 1,585 students. Twenty percent of the 1,300 matriculated students are women; 61 percent of women attend part-time. The median age of all undergraduates is 24.

The college offers associate degrees in the technology of data processing, as well as in chemical, manufacturing, mechanical, and electrical-engineering technologies. The college offers day and evening classes, a summer session, and independent study programs. All students commute; both public transportation and on-campus parking are available.

Policies to Ensure Fairness to Women. Policy review and compliance with laws on equal employment opportunity, handicapped accessibility, and sex equity is the part-time responsibility of the Dean of Instruction. A published campus policy, communicated to students, faculty, and staff, prohibits sexual harassment; complaints are resolved through a formal grievance procedure.

Women in Leadership Positions. *Students.* Of the six campus-wide student leadership positions held during a recent three-year period, a woman held the presidency of the senior class for one year.

Faculty. Two of 39 full-time faculty are women. The ratio of female faculty to female students is 2 to 100; the ratio for men is 9 to 100.

Administrators. The chief administrators are men. Eight of the 15 trustees are women, 2 of these minority women. The department of physics is chaired by an Hispanic woman.

Women and the Curriculum. Women earn 16 percent of the two-year degrees and certificates awarded. Most women major in data processing (79 percent) and engineering technology (21 percent). There are no courses on women.

Women and Athletics. No information was provided.

Special Services and Programs for Women. *Health and Counseling.* There are no student health service and counseling center.

Safety and Security. Measures include campus police with no authority to make arrests, high-intensity lighting, an emergency alarm system at isolated locations. No rapes or assaults were reported for 1980–81

Institutional Self-Description. None provided.

Yale University
New Haven, CT 06520
Telephone: (203) 436-8330

| Women in Leadership | ★★ Women and the |
| ★ students | Curriculum |

★ Women and Athletics

5,231 undergraduates

	Amer. Ind.	Asian Amer.	Blacks	Hispanics	Whites
F	2	131	134	61	1,626
M	6	141	149	118	2,614
%	0.1	5.5	5.7	3.6	85.1

NWSA

Yale University is one of the oldest private institutions of higher education in the country. It provides undergraduate, graduate, and professional studies for over 9,700 students. Founded as a men's college in 1701, Yale began admitting women to its undergraduate program —Yale College — in 1969. Women are 39 percent of the 5,231 undergraduates; the estimated age of all undergraduates is 20. A summer session is offered. The university is accessible by public transportation for the 10 percent of students who commute. There is on-campus parking, with free transportation from distant parking lots.

On-campus childcare is available; private arrangements may be made off campus.

Policies to Ensure Fairness to Women. Three administrative officers are responsible for policy relating to equal employment, sex equity for students, and handicapped accessibility. A published policy prohibits sexual harassment; complaints are resolved through a formal grievance procedure. An active Committee on the Status of Women, which includes students as voting members, identifies and examines problems of importance to women. The Committee on Minority Affairs addresses the concerns of minority women.

Women in Leadership Positions. *Students.* Opportunities for women students to exercise all-campus leadership are good for private research universities in this guide. In recent years, women were editor-in-chief of the newspaper, manager of the radio station, and members of the executive committee of Yale College.

Faculty. Women are 18 percent of a full-time faculty of 830. According to a recent report 3 black, 9 Asian American, and 4 Hispanic women are on the total faculty. The ratio of female faculty to female students is 7 to 100; the ratio for men is 21 to 100.

Administrators. The top-level administrative positions are held by men. A woman chairs the German department. The Dean of the School of Nursing, the Director for Physical Education and Recreation, and the Director of Women's Studies are female.

Women and the Curriculum. Most of the bachelor's degrees earned by women are in the social sciences (25 percent), letters (20 percent), biological sciences (11 percent), fine arts (11 percent), and area studies (9 percent). Nine percent are earned in such nontraditional areas as architecture, computer science, engineering, mathematics, and the physical sciences. Yale reports an innovative program encourages women to prepare for careers in science.

The Women's Studies Program, under a full-time faculty member who directs the program part-time, offers the B.A. in Women's Studies. Eight courses are offered by the Women's Studies Program, and 17 courses on women are offered through ten departments, including Afro-American studies, English, history, French, political science, and psychology. Women's Studies offers Women's History: Methodological and Comparative Inquiry; Contemporary Women Writers: Cross Cultural; as well as Introduction to Women's Studies, Interdisciplinary Research, and an

Advanced Seminar. Courses offered through departments include Images of Women in the Middle Ages; Image of Women in African Art; Gender and Politics: Cross-Cultural Perspectives on Women; Research in the Psychology of Women—with a Laboratory Course.

The Women's Studies Council and the 26 women and three men associated with the program are responsible for developing Women's Studies courses and encouraging the development of courses on women in departments. Women's Studies sponsors a Faculty Seminar responsible for integrating the study of women into the traditional curriculum. The program reports that 19 courses in such departments as history, sociology, Afro-American studies, and anthropology include substantial material on women. The Bieneke Library houses the manuscripts of many well-known women writers, including Gertrude Stein, Edith Wharton, George Eliot, the poet H.D., Zora Neale Hurston, and the artist Georgia O'Keefe.

Minority Women. Of 1,820 undergraduate women, over 6 percent each are black or Asian American, 3 percent Hispanic, and less than 1 percent American Indian. Courses offered on minority women include Black Women and Their Fictions, Images of Women in African Art, Topics in Contemporary Chinese Society, and Women Writers in Spanish America. Such organizations as Latina Perspectives, Black Undergraduate Women's Group, and Asian American Women's Group serve as advocates for minority women on campus.

Women and Athletics. Yale has good intramural and intercollegiate programs; some intramural teams are coeducational. Twenty-six percent of the varsity and 27 percent of the intramural athletes are women, as are 5 of 28 professional coaches. Some intercollegiate teams played tournament competition in 1980. The intercollegiate sports offered are basketball, crew, cross-country, fencing, field hockey, golf, gymnastics, ice hockey, lacrosse, soccer, swimming and diving, tennis, and track and field. Yale reports the "world's largest indoor gym for the use of intramural and intercollegiate sports."

Housing and Student Organizations. For the 90 percent of the undergraduates who live on campus, coeducational dormitories and housing for married students are available. Residence halls do not restrict hours for visitors of the opposite sex. A married woman student whose spouse is not enrolled may live in married students' housing. Four of 12 residence-hall directors are female.

Women-focused groups that meet on campus, in addition to the minority-women's groups mentioned above, include Yalesbians, Undergraduate Women's Caucus, and Graduate Women's Group.

Special Services and Programs for Women. *Health and Counseling.* The student health service provides medical treatment specific to women. Five of 29 physicians are female. The regular student health insurance covers abortion and maternity at no extra cost. Half of the staff in the counseling center is female. Students have access to human sexuality counseling, as well as counseling of particular concern to women.

Safety and Security. Measures consist of campus and city police, night-time escorts for women, night-time bus service to residence areas, emergency alarm and telephone systems, self-defense courses, information sessions on safety and crime prevention, and a rape crisis center. No information was provided about the incidence of rapes and assaults an women.

Career. Workshops, guest speakers, and printed materials concentrated on women in nontraditional occupations and fields of study, as well as a program of contacts between alumnae and students are provided.

Other. The Yale Women's Center, under the direction of a salaried student, sponsors speakers, an annual women's week, arts programs, and a telephone service of information, referral, and support. Women of varying ages, lifestyles, and life circumstances are welcomed at the Women's Center. Handicapped women would find additional support from the Committee on Handicapped.

Institutional Self-Description. None provided.

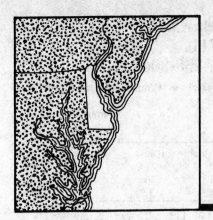

Brandywine College
P. O. Box 7139, Wilmington, DE 19803
Telephone: (302) 478-3000

Women in Leadership
★★★ faculty

1,120 undergraduates

	Amer. Ind.	Asian Amer.	Blacks	Hispanics	Whites
F	0	0	60	0	613
M	0	0	18	1	424
%	0.0	0.0	7.0	0.1	93.0

This private, two-year college, founded in 1965, offers degrees and certificates in liberal arts, secretarial science, business administration, travel and tourism, law enforcement administration, and general studies. Sixty percent of the students are women; nearly a third of the women attend part-time. The median age of all students is 19. There are evening as well as daytime classes. Sixty-six percent of the student body live on campus. Public transportation and on-campus parking are available for commuting students.

Women in Leadership Positions. *Students.* In three recent years women have served in several campus leadership positions, including president of the student body, the student governing body, and the sophomore class; women have also been editor-in-chief of the newspaper twice during this time.

Faculty. Two-thirds of the full-time faculty of 33 are women. There are 5 female faculty for every 100 female students and 4 male faculty for every 100 male students.

Administrators. Of 9 chief administrators, 2 are women: the chief student-life officer and the head librarian. Women chair two of five departments—secretarial science and fashion merchandising. Of the 15 faculty senate members, 6 are women, and women are 3 of the 4-member campus-wide tenure committee.

Women and the Curriculum. Eighty-six percent of all degrees and certificates awarded to women are in business and commerce, the rest in arts and sciences. There are no courses on women.

Women and Athletics. Just over half of those participating in intercollegiate sports at Brandywine are women. The intercollegiate program is adequate but there are no intramural or club sports. Of the 14 paid coaches for intercollegiate sports, seven are women. The intercollegiate sports offered are basketball, field hockey, golf, softball, tennis, and volleyball.

Housing and Student Organizations. Coeducational dormitories house the 66 percent of students who live on campus. The four residence-hall directors include a white woman and a minority woman. Residence staff are offered awareness-training on sex education, racism, birth control, and communication skills.

The dormitories post restrictive hours for visitors of the opposite sex.

Nineteen percent of the full-time undergraduate women belong to sororities. There are three minority women in racially integrated sororities.

Special Services and Programs for Women. *Health and Counseling.* The student health service is staffed by a male physician and two female health-care providers. The student counseling center has a staff of five, four of whom are women. Medical treatment and counseling are available for gynecological problems, birth control, abortion, and rape and assault.

Safety and Security. Measures include campus police and local police. There is high-intensity lighting in all areas, a highly conspicuous campus-wide emergency telephone system, and a rape crisis center. No rapes or assaults on women were reported for 1980-81.

Career. Services include updated files of alumnae by specific careers, and printed information on nontraditional fields of study for women and on job discrimination in nontraditional occupations.

Institutional Self-Description. "The majority of students at Brandywine College are women, and women play a pre-eminent role in almost every curricular and extracurricular program at the college."

Delaware State College
Dover, DE 19901
Telephone: (302) 736-4901

Women in Leadership
★★ faculty

1,628 undergraduates

	Amer. Ind.	Asian Amer.	Blacks	Hispanics	Whites
F	0	0	602	0	192
M	0	0	575	0	229
%	0.0	0.0	73.7	0.0	26.3

 AAUW

Founded in 1891, Delaware State is a public, four-year, coeducational college offering bachelor's degrees in a range of liberal arts and sciences and pre-professional fields. Seventy-four percent of the undergraduates are black students. Some 2,100 students are enrolled, 1,628 of whom are registered in degree programs. Half of the degree students are women. All students attend full-time. Evening classes are held both on and off campus, and there is a summer session. The suburban campus, located an hour from

Wilmington, is not accessible by public transportation. Free on-campus parking, along with some parking at a fee, is provided for those students who commute.

Private childcare facilities are available nearby, off-campus.

Policies to Ensure Fairness to Women. The Affirmative Action Officer, who has part-time responsibility for equal employment opportunity, sits on policymaking councils and reviews policies and practices.

Women in Leadership Positions. *Students.* In three recent years, women held 26 percent of the student leadership positions. They served twice as editor-in-chief of the campus newspaper and president of both the junior and senior classes, and once as president of the entering class.

Faculty. Forty-five percent of the 130 full-time faculty are women, a proportion higher than the national average. There are 7 female faculty for every 100 female students and 9 male faculty for every 100 male students.

Administrators. Men occupy the top-level administrative positions. Women chair the departments of art, chemistry, foreign languages, health, physical education and recreation, home economics, nursing, physics and astronomy. The Director of Continuing Education is female. Three of the 7-member tenure and promotions committee are women—1 black and 2 white women. The 13 trustees include 2 black women and 1 white woman.

Women and the Curriculum. Most women earn degrees in education (31 percent), business (24 percent), and health (13 percent). Eleven percent of women major in the nontraditional fields of agriculture, mathematics, and physical sciences. Eight percent of students in cooperative education programs and 40 percent of the student interns are women.

There are no courses on women.

Women and Athletics. Opportunities for women to participate in intramural and intercollegiate sports are limited. Ten percent of all athletic scholarship aid is awarded to women. One of eleven paid varsity coaches is female. Both women's varsity teams competed in recent tournaments. The intercollegiate sports offered are basketball and track.

Housing and Student Organizations. Single-sex dormitories have restrictive hours for visitors of the opposite sex. Ninety-eight percent of all residents of the women's dormitories are black women, 2 percent are white. Residence-hall staff are offered awareness-training on the avoidance of sexism.

Social fraternities and sororities do not provide housing for members.

Special Services and Programs for Women. *Health and Counseling.* The student health service has two male physicians on staff. Half of the counseling center's eight-member staff is female, including one minority woman. In-service training in the avoidance of sex-role stereotyping is available to counselors. The college did not provide information on the health and counseling services specific to women.

Safety and Security. Measures consist of campus police with no authority to make arrests, local police whose jurisdiction includes the campus, and high-intensity lighting in all areas. No information was provided on the incidence of rapes and assaults.

Career. Workshops focused on nontraditional occupations, and lectures and panels for students by women employed in these fields are available.

Institutional Self-Description. "Delaware State College considers as a priority the changing needs of its students. Hence it is our promise that: all students must be given the background required for employment and upward mobility; students of low socio-economic status and female enrollees must be prepared for graduate and professional education, especially in areas in which they are traditionally underrepresented; and students should be exposed to new configurations of currently existing curricula. To this end, the college acknowledges the traditional teaching, research, and public service function of higher education. At Delaware State College, the major emphasis is on teaching."

University of Delaware
Newark, DE 19711
Telephone: (302) 738-8063

★ **Women and the Curriculum**

★ **Women and Athletics**

13,554 undergraduates

	Amer. Ind.	Asian Amer.	Blacks	Hispanics	Whites
F	6	30	253	22	6,806
M	10	21	186	26	5,988
%	0.1	0.4	3.3	0.4	96.1

AAUW NWSA

Delaware College, a liberal arts college for men, and Women's College (founded in 1914) were combined in 1945 to become the University of Delaware, a publicly supported private institution located in a community of 25,000 between Philadelphia and Baltimore. Some 18,700 students enroll in a variety of undergraduate, graduate, and professional degree programs. The division of continuing education enrolls over 2,800 women in credit and non-credit courses. Alternative class schedules include a between-semester winter session and a summer session. Off-campus class locations are available.

Women are 53 percent of the 13,554 undergraduates; 8 percent of women attend part-time. The median age of undergraduates is 20. For the 40 percent of undergraduates who live off campus or commute, the university is accessible by public transportation. On-campus parking is available for a fee, with free transportation from distant parking lots.

Private childcare arrangements may be made close to campus.

Policies to Ensure Fairness to Women. The full-time Affirmative Action Coordinator monitors compliance with equal employment opportunity, educational sex equity, and handicapped accessibility. A published policy prohibits sexual harassment; complaints are handled both informally and confidentially or through a formal grievance procedure. An active Committee on the Status of Women, which includes students as voting members, identifies problems, makes recommendations, and works closely with the Office of Women's Affairs for implementation. A Committee on Minority Affairs addresses the concerns of minority women.

Women in Leadership Positions. *Students.* Opportunities for women students to exercise campus-wide leadership are poor. In recent years, a woman has been editor-in-chief of the newspaper. Women head seven of 12 honorary societies.

Faculty. Women are 23 percent of a full-time faculty of 813. According to a recent report, 5 black, 3 Asian American, and 3 Hispanic women are on the faculty. The ratio of female faculty to female students is 3 to 100; the ratio of male faculty to male students is 11 to 100.

Administrators. The head librarian is a woman. All other higher administrative posts are held by men. Women chair three of 42 departments: political science, individual and family studies, and textile design and consumer economics. The Dean of the College of Arts and Sciences and the Dean of the College of Nursing are female.

Women and the Curriculum. The majority of women graduating with bachelor's degrees major in education (16 percent), health professions (13 percent), the social sciences (13 percent), and business (12 percent). The percentage of women earning degrees in communications is above the national average. Twelve percent of women major in such nontraditional areas as agriculture, computer science, engineering, mathematics, and the physical sciences.

The Women's Studies Program offers an 18-credit minor. Recent courses offered Women's Studies include Biography and

Women's Lives; Feminism and White Racism; and Castles, Queens, and Troubadors: The Medieval Woman. Courses on women offered through departments include Black Women Writers, Women's Status and Clothing, History of Women in America, Women and Health, and Philosophical Issues of Feminism. Among Women's Studies-sponsored activities is a series of speakers on women and research. The College of Nursing and the department of physical education offer instruction on some matters specific to women.

Minority Women. Four percent of undergraduate women are members of minority groups. Four residence-hall directors are minority women. A minority woman is on the professional staff of the counseling service. Residence-hall staff are offered awareness-training on the avoidance of racism. The Minority Center sponsors lecture series, women's theater, other arts programs, and an annual women's week.

Women and Athletics. Intramural and intercollegiate programs offer good opportunities for organized, competitive, individual and team sports. Twenty percent of intramural and 33 percent of intercollegiate athletes are women. Twelve of 33 paid varsity coaches are women. Most teams played in tournaments in 1980. The intercollegiate sports offered are basketball, field hockey, lacrosse, softball, swimming and diving, tennis, track and field, and volleyball.

Housing and Student Organizations. Sixty percent of undergraduates live on campus. Residential accommodations include single-sex and coeducational dormitories and married students' housing. A married woman student whose husband is not enrolled may live in married students' housing. Awareness-training is offered residence-hall staff on sexism, sex education, and birth control.

Two percent of undergraduate women belong to social sorori-ties. Sororities and fraternities provide some housing for their members. Groups supportive of women include Women For Working For Change, the Gay Student Union, the Returning Adult Student Association, the Handicapped Student Association, the Society of Women Engineers.

Special Services and Programs for Women. *Health and Counseling.* The student health service provides some medical attention specific to women. Half of the physicians are women. The regular student health insurance covers abortion and maternity at no extra charge. Five of ten professional staff in the counseling service are female. Students have access to gynecological, birth control, abortion, and rape and assault counseling.

Safety and Security. Measures include campus and local police, night-time bus service to residence areas and escorts for women after bus service stops, an emergency telephone system, and information sessions on safety and crime prevention. A rape crisis center is available. Sixty-six assaults (28 on women) and one rape were reported for 1980–81.

Career. Workshops, lectures, and nonsexist/racist printed materials about women in nontraditional occupations and fields of study are available through the Women's Studies Program.

Other. The Office of Women's Affairs houses a well-used and well-funded ($60,000 annually) Women's Center, under a full-time director. Among services offered are assertiveness training, a program to build confidence in mathematics, and a telephone line of information, referral, and support.

Institutional Self-Description. "A medium-sized university located in a small town, Delaware has the advantage of proximity to the cultural resources of major Eastern cities. The large residence-life staff provides support to the students. A core of outstanding and committed faculty women is available to encourage the full intellectual development of women students."

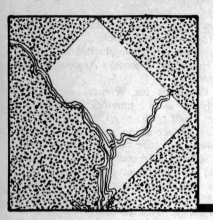

DISTRICT OF COLUMBIA

American University
4400 Massachusetts Ave., N.W.
Washington, DC 20016
Telephone: (202) 686-2211

5,475 undergraduates

	Amer. Ind.	Asian Amer.	Blacks	Hispanics	Whites
F	3	30	425	44	2,095
M	3	37	307	22	1,955
%	14.9	0.1	1.4	1.3	82.3

Some 12,200 students attend this private research university affiliated with the United Methodist Church. Founded in 1893, American University offers graduate and undergraduate programs through colleges of arts and sciences, public affairs, business administration and schools of law and nursing. Evening classes are available both on and off campus, and there is a summer session. The university also offers cooperative education and study abroad programs.

Fifty-one percent of the 5,475 undergraduates are women, 22 percent of whom attend part-time. The median age of undergraduates is 20. The university reports that 8 percent of the women students are over age 25.

Fifty-two percent of undergraduates commute. Public transportation to the university is available, and on-campus parking is provided for a fee.

On-campus childcare facilities can accommodate 30 children. Full-time students and faculty are given priority for the service; charges are based on a fixed, daily fee. Private childcare facilities are available near the campus.

Policies to Ensure Fairness to Women. Six Equal-Opportunity Officers share part-time responsibility for overseeing compliance with equal-employment-opportunity, sex-equity, and handicapped-access legislation. A written campus policy prohibiting sexual harassment has been publicly communicated to students, faculty, and staff. Complaints are resolved informally and confidentially; a formal campus grievance procedure is currently being established for faculty and staff.

Women in Leadership Positions. *Students.* There are five campus-wide student offices. During a recent three-year period women served once as president of the student body and twice as editor-in-chief of the campus newspaper. Women head six of the 14 honorary societies.

Faculty. Twenty-four percent of the 373 full-time faculty are women. According to a recent report, 2 black and 6 Asian American women are on the female faculty. There are 4 female faculty for every 100 female students and 15 male faculty for every 100 male students.

Administrators. All top-level administrative positions are held by men. Women chair four of 19 departments: American studies, biology, chemistry, and public relations. Women also serve as deans of the schools of government and public administration, education, and nursing. Women constitute 35 percent of the faculty senate and 22 percent of the trustees.

Women and the Curriculum. Over half of the women earning bachelor's degrees major in social science (27 percent), communications (14 percent), or business (19 percent). Four percent major in such nontraditional fields as mathematics, physical sciences, and computer sciences. Thirty percent of the two-year degrees awarded are earned by women, who major in arts and sciences and public service. A program encourages women to prepare for careers in science. There is a Center for Research and Development of Women Executives.

A Women's Studies Program will be instituted in 1982–83. Currently, there are six courses on women offered through the departments of government and public administration, Jewish studies, American studies, anthropology, and the School of Justice. Recent offerings include Women in Crime, The Jewish Woman in America, and Women in Popular Media. Workshops for faculty are offered on the topics of sexism and racism in the curriculum. Courses in the schools of business, education, and nursing provide instruction on some matters specific to women.

Minority Women. Eighteen percent of female undergraduates are minority women, largely black women. One of the 10 female trustees, 1 recent recipient of an alumni award, and 1 recent commencement speaker were black women. Of the 2 female residence-hall directors, 1 is a minority woman, as is 1 of the 4 female counselors in the counseling service. Approximately 35 percent of women in adult education courses are minority, mainly black, women. Thirty-five minority women belong to all-minority sororities.

Women and Athletics. Intramural sports draw some 400 women participants. Club sports are also available. Thirteen percent of the 2,300 intramural athletes and 33 percent of intercollegiate athletes are women. Five of the 18 paid coaches for intercollegiate sports are female, and women receive between 30 and 40 percent of athletic scholarship aid. The intercollegiate sports in which women take part are basketball, hockey, swimming, tennis, track, and volleyball.

Housing and Student Organizations. Coeducational dormitories having restricted hours for visitors of the opposite sex are available for the 48 percent of undergraduates who reside on campus. Two of the five residence-hall directors are women and all residence-hall staff are offered awareness-training on sexism, sex education, racism, birth control, crisis intervention, peer counseling, and other issues.

Four percent of full-time undergraduate women belong to sororities. While fraternities provide on-campus housing for members, sororities do not. Among the groups that function as advocacy organizations for women students are the Mortar Board Senior National Honor Society, American University for E.R.A., Women in Communications, and the Aerobics Club.

Special Services and Programs for Women. *Health and*

Counseling. The student health service employs 1 male physician and 5 health-care providers (4 women and 1 man). The student counseling center has a staff of 8 counselors, half of them women. Counseling and medical treatment for gynecological problems, birth control, abortion, rape and assault, and sexually transmitted disease are available. The regular student health insurance covers abortion and maternity expenses up to $150.00, at no extra cost.

Safety and Security. Measures include local police, campus police with arrest authority, night-time escort for women students, night-time campus-wide bus service, high-intensity lighting, an emergency alarm system, information sessions on safety and crime prevention, and a rape crisis center. No rapes and 34 assaults (one on a woman) were reported for 1980–81.

Career. Services include workshops, job discrimination information, and printed materials on nontraditional occupations for women. The university also maintains updated files of alumnae by specific careers.

Special Features. The Women's Institute (TWI), affiliated with American University, provides an educational and political forum for a wide variety of women's issues. It offers non-credit, issue-oriented seminars on personal development. The university's Washington College of Law was founded by women in 1896 as the first law school in the District of Columbia where women were admitted. Women constituted 40 percent of the recent entering class. The School of Education operates the Mid-Atlantic Center for Sex Equity, located on campus. This federally funded center provides technical assistance and sex-equity training for teachers and school personnel in the District of Columbia and five states: Delaware, Maryland, Pennsylvania, Virginia, and West Virginia.

Institutional Self-Description. None provided.

Catholic University of America
Washington, DC 20064
Telephone: (202) 635-5247

Women in Leadership
★ students
★ faculty

2,636 undergraduates

	Amer. Ind.	Asian Amer.	Blacks	Hispanics	Whites
F	1	12	83	21	1,122
M	3	22	63	24	1,064
%	0.2	1.4	6.1	1.9	90.5

🏠 🏛 🚐 👫 🔲 🔲 AAUW

Founded in 1887, the Catholic University of America, located in the nation's capital, has admitted women to undergraduate programs since the 1950s. Although its emphasis is on graduate studies and research, the university offers a range of undergraduate and professional programs. Some 7,700 students enroll. University College is responsible for adult continuing education. Alternative class schedules, including weekend college, a summer session, evening classes, and off-campus locations are available.

Women are half of the 2,636 undergraduates; 7 percent of the women attend part-time. For the 30 percent of the undergraduates who commute, the university is accessible by public transportation. On-campus parking is available at a fee.

University-sponsored childcare facilities can accommodate 20 children per hour. Private childcare arrangements may be made close to campus.

Policies to Ensure Fairness to Women. The full-time Equal Opportunity Office monitors compliance with equal-employment-opportunity, sex-equity, and handicapped-access legislation. A policy on sexual harassment is being developed; a formal grievance procedure handles complaints. An active Committee on the Status of Women reports to the President. The Committee on Minority Affairs addresses the concerns of minority women.

Women in Leadership Positions. *Students.* Women students exercise campus-wide leadership to a degree above average for private research institutions in this guide. In recent years, women have been president of the student body; presiding officers of the student senate, the student court, the student union board (three times), and the residence-hall council; editor-in-chief of the newspaper (two times); and president of the junior, sophomore, and entering classes. Women head eight of 17 honorary societies.

Faculty. Women are 33 percent of a full-time faculty of 332. There are 9 female faculty for every 100 female undergraduates and 18 male faculty for every 100 male undergraduates. The ratio of female faculty to female students is significantly above the average for other private research universities in this guide. However, the proportion of women faculty who receive permanent appointments is 14 percent below the average for private research universities.

Administrators. Men fill all top administrative positions. Three of 26 departments are chaired by women: anthropology, psychology, and history. Women head the School of Nursing, the School of Library and Information Services, and the National Catholic School of Social Work. In 1980–81, women received 3 of 13 alumni awards.

Women and the Curriculum. The majority of women graduating with bachelor's degrees major in the health professions and fine arts. Ten percent of women earn degrees in nontraditional fields, the largest number being in architecture and engineering.

Courses on women, offered by the departments of theology and sociology, include Women in the Early Church, and Sex-Role Stereotyping.

Women and Athletics. Intramural and intercollegiate programs offer some opportunities for organized, competitive, individual and team sports. Thirty-three percent of intramural and 38 percent of intercollegiate athletes are women; women receive 30 percent of athletic scholarships. Five of 18 paid varsity coaches are female. The intercollegiate sports offered are basketball, cross-country, field hockey, softball, tennis, track and field, and volleyball.

Housing and Student Organizations. Seventy percent of undergraduate students live on campus in women's and men's dormitories. Residence halls restrict hours for visitors of the opposite sex. Five of six residence-hall directors are female, including one minority female. Staff are offered awareness-training on sexism, sex education, racism, and birth control.

Seven percent of undergraduate women belong to social sororities. Approximately 30 women are in all-minority sororities. Sororities and fraternities do not provide housing for their members.

Special Services and Programs for Women. *Health and Counseling.* The student health service does not provide medical treatment specific to women. The 2 physicians are male; 2 health-care providers are female. Fourteen of 25 counselors in the counseling service are women, including 2 minority women. Students have access to gynecological, birth control, and rape and assault counseling.

Safety and Security. Measures include campus and city police, night-time escorts for women, night-time bus service to residential areas, an emergency alarm system, and information sessions on safety and crime prevention. One assault on a woman and no rapes were reported for 1980–81.

Career. Nonsexist nonracist printed information on nontraditional fields of study for women is available.

Institutional Self-Description. "As a church-related institution, the university is committed, even apart from legal requirements, to the eradication of 'every type of discrimination, whether social or cultural, whether based on sex, race, color, social condition, language, or religion' (Second Vatican Council). It has a long-standing policy and record of faculty promotions of women to the highest academic rank and to continuous tenure."

George Washington University
Washington, DC 20052
Telephone: (202) 676-6000

★★ **Women and the Curriculum**

★ **Women and Athletics**

6,457 undergraduates

	Amer. Ind.	Asian Amer.	Blacks	Hispanics	Whites
F	10	77	330	78	2,259
M	9	88	162	90	2,422
%	0.3	3.0	8.9	3.0	84.7

AAUW NWSA CROW

Established in 1821 as a liberal arts college for men, George Washington University became coeducational in 1890. Some 19,600 students enroll in a comprehensive range of undergraduate, graduate, and professional studies. Two-year degrees are awarded in health technologies and arts and sciences. The division of continuing education houses a Continuing Education for Women Program. Daytime and evening off-campus classes and a summer session are available.

Women are 47 percent of 6,457 undergraduates; 28 percent of women attend part-time. The median age of undergraduates is 25. Sixty-five percent of undergraduates commute. The university is accessible by public transportation; on-campus parking is provided at a fee, with free transportation from distant parking lots.

Private childcare arrangements may be made close to campus.

Policies to Ensure Fairness to Women. The full-time Assistant Provost for Affirmative Action generates policy on equal employment opportunity, sex equity for students, and handicapped accessibility. A full-time Director of Equal Employment Opportunity Activities proposes policy on employment and the handicapped. The university is developing a formal written policy on sexual harassment which will include procedures for resolving complaints. Complaints are currently handled informally and confidentially.

Women in Leadership Positions. *Students.* Opportunities for women students to exercise campus-wide leadership are about average for private research institutions in this guide. In recent years, women have presided once over the student senate, the student court, the student union board, and been editor-in-chief of the newspaper; they have presided over the residence-hall council twice. Women head six of the 22 campus honorary societies.

Faculty. Women are 20 percent of a full-time faculty of 513. According to a recent report, 16 black, 17 Asian American, and 9 Hispanic women are on the total faculty. The ratio of female faculty to female students is 5 to 100; the ratio of male faculty to male students is 15 to 100.

Administrators. Men hold all top positions, except for the director of women's athletics. Women chair four of 68 departments: art, history, sociology, and special education. The Dean of the School of Government and Business Administration is a woman. In a recent year, a third of speakers in campus-wide lecture series were women.

Women and the Curriculum. The majority of women graduating with bachelor's degrees major in social sciences (24 percent), business (12 percent), the health professions (11 percent), and psychology (11 percent). Around 4 percent major in such nontraditional areas as engineering, mathematics, and the physical sciences. Innovative programs to encourage women to prepare for careers in landscape architecture and fund-raising administration are available. Seventeen percent of the students in cooperative education programs are women. Women hold half of the internships and 70 percent of the science field-study positions. A fifth

of the students in the Engineering Honors Research Program are female.

The Women's Studies Program, under a director who holds a full-time faculty position, offers a master's degree through Special Studies. Undergraduate courses on women are available in the departments of sociology, American civilization, history, political science, psychology, religion, English, and economics. Recent titles include Women and Social Change, Sex and Race in America, Women in European History, Psychology of Sex Differences, Women in Western Religion, and Women in the Labor Market.

The Women's Studies Program and Policy Center sponsors research and such educational projects as the Congressional Fellowships on Women and Public Policy Program which allows graduate students to combine course work with direct legislative experiences.

Such current topics as mathematics confidence among females, sex-fair curricula, coeducational physical education classes, and discrimination in the workplace are included in courses offered by the School of Education and Human Development and the School of Government and Business Administration.

Minority Women. Of 2,754 undergraduate women, 12 percent are black, less than 1 percent American Indian, 3 percent Asian American, and 3 percent Hispanic. An estimated 10 percent of women in continuing education courses are from minority groups, with black women the largest group. Eighteen women are in all-minority sororities.

Women and Athletics. Intramural and intercollegiate programs provide good opportunities for organized competitive athletics. The intramural program offers largely individual sports activities. A special feature of the institution is a rowing clinic on the Potomac River. Forty-nine percent of intramural and 40 percent of intercollegiate athletes are women. Nearly half the participants in club sports are female. Women receive 40 percent of athletic scholarships. Nine of the 31 paid varsity coaches are women. The intercollegiate sports offered are badminton, basketball, crew, gymnastics, soccer, squash, swimming and diving, tennis, and volleyball.

Housing and Student Organizations. Thirty-five percent of students live on campus. Single-sex and coeducational dormitories are available. Hours for visitors of the opposite sex are not restricted. Five of eight residence-hall directors are women. Staff are offered awareness-training on the avoidance of racism and sexism and on sex education, birth control, and rape among issues.

Two percent of undergraduate women belong to social sororities. Sororities do not provide housing for their members. Among groups that serve as advocates for white and minority women on campus are Womanspace, Women's Athletic Advisory Council, the Gay People's Alliance, The Association of Students with Handicaps, and Law Association for Women.

Special Services and Programs for Women. *Health and Counseling.* The student health service provides medical attention specific to women, including gynecological, birth control and rape and assault treatment, and abortion on referral. Five of 11 physicians are female, as are 5 other health-care providers. Regular student health insurance covers abortion and maternity at no extra charge. Six of 9 professional staff in the counseling service are women. Gynecological, birth control, abortion, and rape and assault counseling is available. Staff receive in-service training on avoiding sex-role stereotyping and racial bias. A program for battered women is available through the counseling center.

Safety and Security. Measures consist of campus and city police, night-time escort service for women, high-intensity lighting, emergency telephone and alarm systems, self-defense courses for women, information sessions on safety and crime prevention, special security for parking garages, and a rape crisis center. Four assaults (two on women) and no rapes were reported for 1980–81.

Career. There is a special section on women and careers in the career library; the university sponsors monthly a workshop on career planning for women.

Returning Women Students. George Washington University's Continuing Education for Women Program enrolls an estimated 1,500 reentry women. Among special interest programs offered under its auspices are a displaced homemakers' program, assertiveness training, and a program to build skills in mathematics. The university plans to open a separate CEW Women's Center in 1982.

Institutional Self-Description. "Students interested in participating in activities unique to the Washington area might choose to study at George Washington University. The university has formal programs, such as internships, which utilize the resources of the government and the city. Many students are also involved through part-time employment or volunteer work."

Mount Vernon College
2100 Foxhall Road, N.W.
Washington, DC 20007
Telephone: (202) 331-0400

Women in Leadership
★★★ students
★★★ faculty
★★★ administrators

478 undergraduates

	Amer. Ind.	Asian Amer.	Blacks	Hispanics	Whites
F	0	2	37	19	375
M	0	0	0	0	0
%	0.0	0.5	8.6	4.4	86.6

This private, liberal arts women's college serves 517 students. Of the 478 undergraduates, 5 percent attend part-time. Mount Vernon was founded in 1875 as a four-year preparatory school and two-year college for women. It continues to offer two-year degrees and, since 1973, has awarded four-year degrees as well. Because Mount Vernon is a member of the Consortium of Universities of the Washington Metropolitan Area, its students may specialize in fields not taught at Mount Vernon, including languages, philosophy, mathematics, and science. Continuing education courses are also available. Classes are held during the day and at night; there is a summer session. The college is accessible by public transportation and there is on-campus parking for the one-quarter of students who commute.

Private childcare facilities are located near campus.

Policies to Ensure Fairness to Women. An affirmative action officer is responsible part-time for reviewing policies and monitoring compliance with educational-sex-equity, equal-employment-opportunity, and handicapped-accessibility legislation. A written policy prohibits sexual harassment of students; complaints are handled through a formal grievance procedure.

Women in Leadership Positions. *Students.* Women hold all campus-wide leadership positions.

Faculty. Half of the 22 full-time faculty are women. There are 3 female faculty for every 100 female students.

Administrators. All top-ranking administrators are women, except for the chief business officer. Of six departments, four are chaired by women: communications, public affairs/government, interior design, and human development.

Women and the Curriculum. All associate degrees granted are earned in arts and sciences. Among the women receiving bachelor's degrees, the most popular fields are interior design, business, communications, and social sciences. Almost one-third

of graduates take bachelor's degrees in interior design. A program encourages women to pursue accounting careers. Business students are informed about problems of discrimination and sexual harassment in the workplace. There are no courses on women.

Minority Women. Black women have organized Black Alliance, which has 20 active members. One minority woman serves on the residence-hall staff. One of five women speakers in a recent lecture series was a black woman.

Women and Athletics. An intercollegiate sports program attracts 67 women; two of the three paid intercollegiate coaches are women. The intramural sports program offers golf, bowling, badminton, tennis, field hockey, and soccer. Intercollegiate sports offered are basketball, field hockey, tennis, and volleyball.

Housing and Student Organizations. Three-fourths of all students live on campus in dormitories that have no restrictions on visiting hours for men. Residence-hall staff receive awareness-training on sex education and birth control.

Special Services and Programs for Women. *Health and Counseling.* The student health service employs one female and one male physician, in addition to one female health-care provider. Medical treatment for gynecological problems, abortion, and rape and assault is available. There are no counseling services specific to women.

Safety and Security. Measures consist of campus police, gatecheck for guests, alarms on doors, and instruction on self-defense and safety. No rapes or assaults on women were reported for 1980-81.

Career. The college provides workshops and panel discussions on nontraditional occupations and promotes networking with alumnae.

Returning Women Students. Continuing Education for Women enrolls 300 students, of whom a small number are minority women. The program is directed full-time by a female administrator.

Institutional Self-Description. "Mount Vernon College, especially for women, offers an academic program that provides a foundation for lifelong learning, combining a liberal arts core with professional career preparation. The college emphasizes individual attention in a congenial interpersonal environment. It uses the distinctive resources of its Washington location to enhance academic programs and student life."

Washington International College
814 20th Street, N.W.
Washington, DC 20006
Telephone: (202) 466-7220

Women in Leadership
★ faculty

262 undergraduates

	Amer. Ind.	Asian Amer.	Blacks	Hispanics	Whites
F	0	0	95	4	19
M	0	3	75	3	51
%	0.0	1.2	68.0	2.8	28.0

Founded in 1970, Washington International is a private, nonsectarian liberal arts college. More than 70 percent of its students are members of minority groups. The campus consists of one administration building in Washington D.C.; students use the cultural and educational resources of Washington for learning rather than the traditional classroom. Forty-five percent of the 262 students enrolled are women, and nearly half of the women attend part-time. The median age of students is 24.

The college offers a variety of associate and bachelor's degrees as well as a television extension program. Independent study is available. Day and evening classes meet on and off campus and during the summer. All students commute to the campus, which is easily reached by public transportation.

Policies to Ensure Fairness to Women. There is no written policy on sexual harassment; complaints are handled informally and formally.

Women in Leadership Positions. *Students.* There are no student leadership offices.

Faculty. Four of the 12 full-time faculty are women.

Administrators. Men hold all top positions except that of the chief academic officer. Women chair three of eleven departments: bilingual education, computer science, and office administration and management.

Women and the Curriculum. In a recent year, men earned all eleven associate degrees. Women received three of the ten bachelor's degrees granted in education, fine arts, and social sciences. Experiential learning is stressed, and 70 percent of the student interns are women.

A Women's Studies Program now in planning will offer a Women's Studies concentration as part of the B.A. in social sciences.

Minority Women. Thirty-eight percent of the students are minority women, largely black women. Hispanic women serve as chief academic officer, head of an academic department, director of an academic division, and hold two positions on the 12-member full-time faculty. Of the three women on the Board of Trustees, two are Hispanic women.

Women and Athletics. There is no opportunity for women's organized sports.

Special Services and Programs for Women. *Health and Counseling.* There is no student health service, nor counseling service.

Safety and Security. The sole measure is high-intensity lighting. No information was provided about the incidence of rapes and assaults.

Institutional Self-Description. "The goal of Washington International College is to become a multilingual, interdisciplinary, transcultural institution of higher learning that meets the learning needs of its community and prepares students to feel at home in a rapidly changing, increasingly transnational world. This learning environment is especially conducive to the personal professional growth of women."

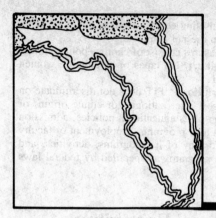

FLORIDA

Broward Community College

3501 Davie Road
Ft. Lauderdale, FL 33314
Telephone: (305) 475-6601

Women in Leadership
  ★students
  ★★ faculty

14,988 undergraduates

	Amer. Ind.	Asian Amer.	Blacks	Hispanics	Whites
F	27	8	632	157	7,175
M	19	14	324	154	5,878
%	0.3	0.2	6.6	2.2	90.7

Founded in 1959, this public, two-year college serves 15,385 students at three urban campuses in Fort Lauderdale, Hollywood, and Pompano Beach. Of 14,988 degree students, 55 percent are women, more than half of whom attend part-time. Nine percent of the students are members of minority groups. The median age of undergraduates is 29.

Broward offers a university-parallel program, in addition to one- and two-year technical, health, and semi-professional programs. Continuing education is available through Community Services Open College. Alternative schedules and locations, including a summer session and evening and off-campus classes are available. All students commute. The campuses are accessible by public transportation, and on-campus parking is available.

There are private childcare facilities nearby.

Policies to Ensure Fairness to Women. A full-time equal-opportunity officer, a presidential assistant who works part-time on women's affairs, and a coordinator with part-time responsibility for sex equity monitor college policies and practices dealing with equal employment opportunity, educational sex equity, and access for the handicapped. Sexual harassment of students, faculty, and staff is prohibited by a policy publicly communicated in writing to all three groups. Complaints of sexual harassment are resolved informally or through a formal grievance procedure.

A Commission on the Status of Women is appointed by the Executive Vice President and the president of the faculty senate. The commission, which reports to the presidential assistant on women's affairs, includes student members with voting rights. It meets at least six times annually, takes public stands on issues of concern to students, prepares an annual report for the campus community, and addresses the concerns of minority women.

Women in Leadership Positions. *Students.* Women have good opportunities to exercise leadership on campus. In three recent years, women were elected president of the student body twice, presiding officer of the student senate once, and presiding officer of the student court once. A woman served for one year as editor-in-chief of the campus newspaper. A woman heads one of the two honorary societies.

Faculty. Forty-one percent of the 310 full-time faculty are women, a proportion above average for two-year public institutions. The female faculty include 11 blacks, 1 Hispanic, and 1 Asian American. There are 4 female faculty for every 100 female students and 5 male faculty for every 100 male students. Data from the college indicate that of a part-time faculty of 484, 42 percent are female.

Administrators. Of the eight chief administrative positions, the director of institutional research is a woman. Departments chaired by women include English, nursing, medical technology programs, insurance, secretarial science, modern languages, reading, community services, business administration, communications, and cooperative education. Two of six deans—Academic Affairs and Student Development—are women. A black woman and a white woman sit on the five-member Board of Trustees.

Women and the Curriculum. Most of the degrees and certificates awarded to women are in arts and sciences (63 percent), health and paramedical technologies (24 percent), and business and commerce (6 percent). Women constitute half the students in cooperative education programs.

There are no courses on women. The business program includes instruction about the problems of job discrimination, sexual harassment in the workplace, and women in management. Faculty are offered workshops on nontraditional occupations for women and men, the needs of reentry women, and affirmative action and equal opportunity.

Women and Athletics. For a community college, Broward offers a large number and good variety of intramural and intercollegiate sports for women. Approximately 1,500 women participate in intramural sports, ranging from team sports like basketball, volleyball, bowling, and softball, to individual sports like rollerskating, ice skating, sailing, and golf. The campus has unique facilities for both sailing and weight-lifting. One hundred and ten women participate in intercollegiate sports. Over 50 percent of the athletic scholarship aid goes to women. Intercollegiate sports for women include basketball, golf, softball, swimming and diving, tennis, and volleyball.

Special Services and Programs for Women. *Health and Counseling.* The student health service is staffed by three female health-care providers. The student counseling center staff of seven includes four women. No services specific to women are provided.

Safety and Security. Campuses are patrolled by campus police with no arrest authority. Security measures include high-intensity lighting in all areas, self-defense courses for women, and information sessions on campus safety and rape and assault prevention. For 1980-81, no assaults on women were reported.

Career. The college offers career workshops and lectures and panels by women employed in nontraditional occupations. Printed information on nontraditional fields of study for women and on job discrimination in nontraditional occupations is also available.

Other. Each of Broward's three campuses has a Women's Center that is operated under the direction of Community Services and staffed by a full-time, salaried coordinator. Their services include programs for displaced homemakers, annual women's weeks, lecture series, arts programs, assertiveness/leadership training, programs to build mathematics confidence, and telephone referral. Most participants in the programs are community women, staff, and students over the age of 25. Approximately 2,000 women participate in programs or visit the Women's Centers annually.

Over one-third of handicapped students at Broward are women; they receive support from Handicapped Services.

Institutional Self-Description. "Broward Community College is committed to helping women explore and follow realistic career and educational options. Services include: Women's Centers, counseling, placement, assessment, and a Math and Science Remediation Program. The Offices of Women's Affairs, Counseling, Community Services, and the Women's Centers furnish a cooperative and supportive network for women who are 'on their way.' "

Florida Institute of Technology
Box 1150, Melbourne, FL 32901
Telephone: (305) 723-3701

★ **Women and the Curriculum**

3,016 undergraduates

	Amer. Ind.	Asian Amer.	Blacks	Hispanics	Whites
F	0	1	13	3	467
M	1	3	50	46	2,060
%	0.0	0.2	2.4	1.9	95.6

Florida Institute of Technology, founded in 1958, is a private, non-sectarian, coeducational institution located one hour south of Cape Canaveral. Its institutional mission is, in part, to "provide educational and research programs in the physical sciences, the life sciences including psychology, engineering and the engineering sciences, management and technology." The institute offers both two- and four-year undergraduate degrees and master's and doctoral programs. Almost 5,000 students attend classes, and 3,016 of the students are enrolled in undergraduate degree programs. Women are 17 percent of the undergraduates; 18 percent of women attend part-time. Alternative schedules evening classes, off-campus classes, and a summer session. Continuing education courses are available.

Three-fourths of undergraduates live on campus in single sex dormitories. Students who live off campus or commute can reach the campus by public transportation; parking is available for those who drive.

Women in Leadership Positions. *Students.* No information was supplied.

Faculty. Ten percent of the faculty are women. There are 3 female faculty for every 100 female students and 6 male faculty for every 100 male students.

Administrators. Men hold all top positions.

Women and the Curriculum. Most bachelor's degrees awarded to women are in physical sciences (41 percent), biological sciences (18 percent), business (13 percent), and engineering (12 percent). Eighty percent of degrees to women are in nontraditional fields. Women receive 10 percent of the two-year degrees awarded in health, science, and engineering technologies. There are no courses on women.

Women and Athletics. No information was supplied.

Special Services and Programs for Women. *Health and Counseling.* The student health service has one male physician;

there is also a student counseling center. Medical and counseling services specific to women are not available.

Safety and Security. Measures consist of campus police protection and high-intensity lighting. No rapes or assaults on women were reported for 1980–81.

Institutional Self-Description. "FIT does not discriminate on the basis of race, color, sex, age, national, or ethnic origin, or handicap, in administration of its educational policies, admission policies, scholarships, and loan programs, employment of faculty and staff, and athletics, for any of its programs, activities, and other school administered programs as specified by federal laws and regulations."

Florida International University
Tamiami Trail, Miami, FL 33199
Telephone: (305) 552-2000

Women in Leadership
★★★ students
★ faculty
★ administrators

6,654 undergraduates

	Amer. Ind.	Asian Amer.	Blacks	Hispanics	Whites
F	2	42	340	939	1,735
M	3	108	278	1,013	1,955
%	0.1	2.3	9.6	30.4	57.5

AAUW

Florida International University is a public, coeducational institution that serves 11,824 students, 6,654 of them undergraduates in their junior and senior years. Forty-seven percent of undergraduates are women, and 54 percent of women attend part-time. The median age of undergraduates is 28. Degrees are awarded in arts and sciences and five technical areas—business, education, hospitality, technology, and public affairs and service. On- and off-campus day and evening classes, a summer session, and self-paced/contract learning are available. The division of continuing education administers adult education. All student commute, using public transportation or free on-campus parking.

An on-campus daycare facility accommodates one-third of students' requests, charging fees on a sliding scale whose maximum is $33 per week. Private childcare is available off campus.

Policies to Ensure Fairness to Women. The full-time Director of Minority Affairs and Women's Concerns is a voting member on policymaking committees and is responsible for policy on equal employment opportunity, affirmative action, and handicapped access. A published policy forbids sexual harassment of students, faculty, and staff; complaints are resolved either informally or through a formal grievance procedure. A Commission on Minority Affairs addresses the concerns of minority women.

Women in Leadership Positions. *Students.* In a recent three-year period, women have held four of five possible leadership positions: twice they have been president of the student body, president of the student senate, and editor of the newspaper; and once, president of the student union. Women chair two of five honorary societies.

Faculty. Twenty-five percent of 337 faculty members are women, of whom 41 percent hold permanent appointments. According to recent information, the female faculty includes 6 black, 1 American Indian, 2 Asian, and 9 Hispanic women. There are 6 female faculty for every 100 female students and 17 male faculty for every 100 male students.

Administrators. Of nine top administrators, the chief development officer, director of institutional research, and director of athletics are women. The Director of Academic Computer Services is a woman. Of 42 departments, women chair seven: dietetics and nutrition, home economics, social work, vocational and adult education, medical records, medical technology, and occupational therapy. Eight of 46 trustees and 1 of 10 regents are women. In 1981, the commencement speaker and 4 of 13 speakers at campus-wide lecture series were women.

Women and the Curriculum. Most degrees awarded to women are in health professions (19 percent), education (19 percent), and public affairs (12 percent). Six percent are in the nontraditional fields of computer science, engineering, physical sciences, architecture, and mathematics. Forty percent of interns and 49 percent of participants in cooperative education programs are women.

Courses on women are available through the departments of English, psychology, public adminstration, sociology, industrial systems, and criminal justice. They include Women in Literature; Psychology of Women; Administration and the Role of Women; Role of Women in Contemporary Society; Women in Industry; and Women, Crime, and the Criminal Justice System. An official committee is developing a Women's Studies Program.

Women and Athletics. Forty-six percent of intercollegiate, 33 percent of intramural, and 45 percent of club athletes are women. Women receive 30 percent of athletic scholarships. Nine of 29 paid intercollegiate coaches are women. The limited intramural program is composed primarily of individual sports. The intercollegiate program offers basketball, cross-country, golf, softball, tennis, and volleyball. In 1980–81, the FIU women's cross-country team finished third in regional competition. The women's volleyball team finished second in the national championships.

Special Services and Programs for Women. *Health and Counseling.* One male physician and 5 female health-care providers offer treatment for gynecological problems and birth control. The counseling center staff consists of 1 women and 1 man, who counsel on gynecological problems, birth control, abortion, and the avoidance of rape and assault. Counselors are offered training on sex-role stereotyping.

Safety and Security. Measures include campus police, high-intensity lighting, emergency alarms, information on safety, and a rape crisis center. For 1980–81, eight assaults (three on women), including two rapes, were reported.

Career. Services include programs by women in nontraditional occupations, literature on nontraditional fields, and updated files of alumnae by career.

Institutional Self-Description. "Florida International University is located in an urban and international community which is emerging as a flourishing center for world trade, international banking, international tourism, communications, and apparel manufacturing. This setting provides a vibrant 'laboratory' for students studying in the College of Arts and Sciences and the five professional schools of FIU."

Jacksonville University
Jacksonville, FL 32211
Telephone: (904) 744-3950

Women in Leadership
★ students

1,905 undergraduates

	Amer. Ind.	Asian Amer.	Blacks	Hispanics	Whites
F	2	6	54	35	652
M	2	9	48	52	954
%	0.2	0.8	5.6	4.8	88.5

 **AAUW**

Founded in 1934 as a two-year community college, in 1956 Jacksonville became a private, coeducational, four-year institution offering a range of liberal arts programs. Located on a riverfront campus in a suburban area of Jacksonville, the university serves 2,121 students. Women are 40 percent of the 1,905 students enrolled in undergraduate degree programs. Twelve percent of female undergraduates attend part-time; 177 of all women attending are over age 25. The median age of all students is 23. A continuing education program is available. Forty-three percent of the students reside on campus; there is free on-campus parking for those who commute.

Private childcare facilities are available off campus.

Policies to Ensure Fairness to Women. No written policy on sexual harassment exists; a formal grievance procedure resolves complaints. Two administrators work part-time on monitoring compliance with equal-opportunity laws; one of the administrators is a voting member of policymaking councils.

Women in Leadership Positions. *Students.* Women have had good opportunities to exercise campus leadership. In recent years, women have been editor of the campus newspaper and presiding officer of the student senate, and for two consecutive years have presided over the student court. Women head two of eight honorary societies.

Faculty. Twenty-two percent of the 95 full-time faculty are women. There are 3 female faculty members for every 100 female students, and 7 male faculty members for every 100 male students.

Administrators. With the exception of the chief executive officer, the chief administrators are men. The department chairs are men, as are the three deans. Four of the 61 trustees are women.

Women and the Curriculum. The most popular fields for women are education (28 percent) and social sciences (18 percent). Four percent of women graduates earn degrees in nontraditional areas; 14 percent of men graduate in these fields.

No courses on women are offered. The departments of education and business offered instruction on some matters specific to women.

Women and Athletics. Twenty-six percent of athletic scholarships go to women. Ten intramural and four intercollegiate sports are offered. Intercollegiate sports are crew, softball, tennis, and volleyball.

Housing and Student Organizations. Single-sex dormitories have restrictive hours for visitors of the opposite sex. The residence-hall directors, one man and one woman, receive awareness-training on sex education and birth control.

Twenty-two percent of the full-time undergraduate women (none of them minority women) belong to sororities. The Association of Women Students has 200 members, 10 percent of whom are black women. The United Minority Alliance, with 12 female and 13 male members, acts as an advocate for minority women on campus.

Special Services and Programs for Women. *Health and Counseling.* The health service, which employs one male physician, provides gynecological counseling and treatment, and counseling on birth control, abortion, and rape and assault.

Safety and Security. Measures consist of campus police with no arrest authority, local police, night-time escort service for women students, and self-defense courses and information on campus safety. No rapes and two assaults on women were reported for 1980–81.

Other. The office of the Dean of Women sponsors assertiveness training; the mathematics department offers a program to build confidence in mathematics; older women are served by the DAWN program and by Continuing Education.

Institutional Self-Description. "Despite being outnumbered, women students at Jacksonville University have a strong history of leadership and frequently hold many of the top student offices. The NROTC unit was one of the first in the country to enroll women; a woman has held the position of cadet commander. Women have excelled in all academic disciplines."

Lake-Sumter Community College
Leesburg, FL 32748
Telephone: (904) 787-3747

Women in Leadership
★★★ students
★★ faculty

1,325 undergraduates

	Amer. Ind.	Asian Amer.	Blacks	Hispanics	Whites
F	2	3	80	4	520
M	4	0	129	9	573
%	0.5	0.2	15.8	1.0	82.6

Established in 1962 as a public, two-year college, Lake-Sumter Community College is located on a rural campus in central Florida. The college enrolls 1,926 students, including 1,325 undergraduates. Forty-six percent of the undergraduates are women, 44 percent of whom attend part-time. The median age of undergraduates is 29, and 44 percent of female students are over age 25.

The college offers a university-parallel curriculum for transfer to four-year colleges, as well as degrees and certificates in business, secretarial science, banking, and law enforcement and corrections. The division of continuing education serves about 500 reentry women students, 9 percent of them black women. The college offers day and evening classes, both on and off campus, and a summer session. Self-paced/contract learning is also available. Lake-Sumter is a commuter college. Free parking is available on campus.

Private childcare is available near campus.

Policies to Ensure Fairness to Women. An equal-opportunity officer has the responsibility, on a part-time basis, for review of policy and practices relating to equal employment opportunity, access for the handicapped, and sex equity. A Committee on Minority Affairs addresses the concerns of minority women.

Women in Leadership Positions. *Students.* Opportunities for women to exercise leadership are outstanding. In three recent years, women held both of the student campus leadership positions, serving twice as presiding officer of the student governing body and once as editor-in-chief of the newspaper. A woman heads the sole honorary society.

Faculty. The full-time faculty of 36 include 13 women, 1 of whom is black. There are 4 female faculty for every 100 female students and 7 male faculty for every 100 male students.

Administrators. Of 7 chief administrators, the chief student-life officer is a woman. Women chair two of three major divisions: technology/business/health, and humanities and social sciences. Four of the 9 trustees are women, 1 of them a black woman.

Women and the Curriculum. Eighty-six percent of the degrees awarded to women are in arts and sciences. The remaining degrees are in business and commerce. The college offers one course on women, the Psychology of Women.

Women and Athletics. Opportunities for women to participate in intercollegiate and intramural sports are limited. Sixty-three women participate in three intramural sports. Eight of the 21 intercollegiate athletes are women, and women receive 30 percent of athletic scholarship aid. The intercollegiate sports in which women compete are golf and tennis.

Special Services and Programs for Women. *Health and Counseling.* The student counseling center has three counselors, one of whom is a woman. It provides special support for displaced homemakers and older women. There is no student health service.

Safety and Security. Measures include campus police with no arrest authority, high-intensity lighting in all areas, and an emergency alarm system in isolated locations. No assaults on women were reported for 1980–81.

Career. Nonsexist and nonracist printed material on nontraditional fields of study for women is available, along with information on job discrimination in nontraditional occupations.

Institutional Self-Description. "This is an open-door institution which provides individualized admissions counseling and career advisement to women who are facing a mid-life career change, who need to upgrade job skills, or who are preparing for initial entry into the workforce."

University of South Florida
4202 Fowler Ave.
Tampa, FL 33620
Telephone: (813) 974-2011

★★ **Women and the Curriculum**

17,041 undergraduates

	Amer. Ind.	Asian Amer.	Blacks	Hispanics	Whites
F	8	31	519	322	7,249
M	12	30	304	378	8,093
%	0.1	0.4	4.9	4.1	90.5

A state-supported institution founded in 1956 as Florida's first urban university, the University of South Florida enrolls 22,682 students, of whom 17,041 are undergraduates. Forty-eight percent of undergraduates are women; about 27 percent of the women attend part-time. One-quarter of the female undergraduates are between the ages of 25 and 40, and 4 percent are over age 40.

The median age of all students is 23. The university offers a wide range of degree programs and choice of schedules, including self-paced learning, a weekend college, a summer session, radio and TV courses, off-campus sessions, and an external degree program. Junior, senior, and graduate courses are given at the St. Petersburg campus. The School of Continuing Education serves the adult student. For the 83 percent of students who commute, on-campus parking and limited public transportation are available.

On-campus childcare facilities accommodate 50 percent of requests by students. Additional facilities are available off campus.

Policies to Ensure Fairness to Women. A full-time equal opportunity officer reviews policies relating to equal-opportunity laws. A presidential memorandum against sexual harassment has been issued and a written policy is being formulated. The Commission on the Status of Women, which includes student members, prepares an annual agenda for the President and takes stands on issues of student concern. The university also has Committees on Black Affairs and Equal Opportunity Affairs.

Women in Leadership Positions. *Students.* Information was not provided on the gender of students holding campus-wide leadership positions. Eighteen of the 21 presidents of honorary societies are women.

Faculty. Seventeen percent of the 808 full-time faculty are women. According to recent information, among the 158 full-time faculty women are 7 black, 2 Asian American, and 4 Hispanic women. There are 2 female faculty for every 100 female students and 11 male faculty for every 100 male students.

Administrators. Of the chief administrators, the head librarian is a woman. One of the university's 69 departments is chaired by a woman.

Women and the Curriculum. Most degrees awarded to women are in education (27 percent), business (16 percent), social sciences (9 percent), and health professions (8 percent). Three percent of women graduates earn degrees in the nontraditional fields of engineering, mathematics, and physical sciences. All women who graduate with two-year degrees major in arts and sciences.

The Women's Studies Program offers an undergraduate minor and a major within the interdisciplinary social studies program. The program offers a two-semester introductory course, a two-semester survey of Women in Western Civilization, and 26 other courses, including Women in Cross-Cultural Perspective, Feminism in America, Human Sexual Behavior, Psychology of Women, and Women and Work. The Director of Women's Studies holds a full-time, permanent faculty appointment. In the past five years, 30 students have been majors, nine minors, in the program. Appropriate departments provide instruction on mathematics confidence, sex-fair curricula, services for battered women and displaced homemakers, and health issues of particular concern to minority women.

Women and Athletics. The university offers limited intercollegiate and more extensive intramural sports opportunities for women. Intercollegiate sports for women include basketball, golf, softball, swimming, tennis and volleyball. Women are 22 percent of the intramural and 38 percent of the intercollegiate athletes.

Housing and Student Organizations. Seventeen percent of undergraduate students live on campus in single-sex dormitories. Three of the seven dormitory directors are women. Dormitory staff are offered awareness-training on racism, sexism, sex education, and birth control.

About 7 percent of the full-time undergraduate women and men belong to sororities or fraternities. Fifty-five women belong to all-minority sororities. Student organizations serving as advocacy groups for women include the Women's Center, the Society of Women Engineers, and Women's Peer Counseling.

Special Services and Programs for Women. *Health and Counseling.* A women is director of the student health service, which has 2 female and 5 male physicians. Of the 20 other healthcare providers, 19 are women. Counseling and medical treatment are provided for gynecological problems, birth control, and rape.

Safety and Security. Measures consist of campus police with weapons training and arrest authority (supplemented by local police), student safety teams that provide night escort service and other assistance, self-defense courses, and a rape crisis center. Four rapes and 47 assaults on men and women were reported for the 1980 calendar year.

Other. The School of Continuing Education provides assertiveness training. In 1980, the College of Social and Behavioral Sciences, along with several other divisions of the university, sponsored a ''Women in History'' conference. It is now developing one on ''Women and the Law.''

Institutional Self-Description. ''The University of South Florida's institutional mission is geared to its urban environment. Consequently, in addition to its traditional structure, it has a strong Program for Emphasis in Human Services in Social Sciences, within which the Women's Studies Program is securely housed. Administrative support for Women's Studies/women's issues is firm.''

University of West Florida
Pensacola, FL 32504
Telephone: (904) 476-9500

Women in Leadership
★ students

3,522 undergraduates

	Amer. Ind.	Asian Amer.	Blacks	Hispanics	Whites
F	8	13	153	21	1,577
M	3	11	82	36	1,606
%	0.3	0.7	6.7	1.6	90.7

 AAUW

This public, coeducational upper-division college was founded in 1963. Its suburban campus has a total enrollment of 5,190. Women are half of an undergraduate population of 3,522; 38 percent of women attend part-time. Forty percent of women students are between ages 26 and 40, and 15 percent are over age 40. The median age of all students is 28.

West Florida offers only the last two years of bachelor of arts programs, as well as graduate education. Alternative scheduling includes off-campus evening classes and summer sessions. Free on-campus parking is available for the 87 percent of students who commute.

Childcare facilities, at $.75 an hour, accommodating 70 children of students, faculty, and staff, are available daily from 7 a.m. to 5 p.m. All requests from students for this service have been met. Private childcare facilities are also available nearby.

Policies to Ensure Fairness to Women. The Assistant to the President is assigned part-time responsibility for monitoring compliance with legislation mandating equal employment opportunity, sex equity, and access for the handicapped. A campus policy prohibiting sexual harassment of students has been communicated in writing to members of the faculty and administrative staff. A self-designated Committee on the Status of Women, which includes student representatives with voting rights and meets at least six times during the year, reports to the vice presidents of the areas involved and takes public stands on issues of concern to female students. Both this commission and the Commission on Minority Affairs address the concerns of minority women.

Women in Leadership Positions. *Students.* Of the four positions available in three recent years, women have served once each as president of the student body, president of the student union board, editor-in-chief of the campus newspaper, and manager of the campus radio station. Women head two of the five honorary societies.

Faculty. Women are one-fifth of a full-time faculty of 245. There are 4 female faculty members for every 100 female students, and 18 male faculty members for every 100 male students.

Administrators. One of the ten major administrative positions, that of chief planning officer, is held by a woman. Women chair three of 25 departments: nursing, history, and sociology. One of 10 regents is a woman. The commencement speaker in 1981 and 1 of 2 honorary degree recipients were women. During a recent year, 3 of 12 speakers in campus-wide lecture series were women.

Women and the Curriculum. Most women take degrees in education (42 percent) and business (15 percent), with significant numbers in public affairs, health, and psychology. Four percent of women earn degrees in the nontraditional field of physical sciences. Women make up 45 percent of students in cooperative education programs, 53 percent in internship programs, and 36 percent in the marine biology field-service program. Innovative programs in nontraditional fields include Women in Accounting, and Women in Computer Science.

There are no courses on women. Courses in the schools of education and social work, the department of physical education, and the division of business, provide some instruction on matters

---

�House On-campus evening and/or weekend classes	ⓂⒶ Commission on minority affairs
🏛 Off-campus classes	📖 Women's Studies program
🚌 Accessible by public transportation	⚲ Women's center
👫 On-campus childcare facilities	AAUW Member, American Association of University Women
✎ Publicly communicated sexual harassment policy, includes students	NWSA Member, National Women's Studies Association
�Ⓢ︎Ⓦ Commission on status of women	CROW On-campus Center for Research on Women

specific to women. Faculty are offered workshops on nontraditional careers for women, the needs of returning women, and affirmative-action/equal-employment-opportunity regulations.

Women and Athletics. Women are 36 percent of intercollegiate, 30 percent of intramural, and 38 percent of club-sports athletes. One of the three paid varsity coaches is a woman. Women are awarded 20 percent of athletic scholarships. Team sports predominate in the ten intramural programs, and facilities include an Olympic-sized swimming pool. Intercollegiate sports offered are basketball and tennis.

Housing and Student Organizations. Coeducational dormitories and housing for married students and single parents with children are available for the 13 percent of students who reside on campus. The residence-hall director is offered awareness-training on racism.

Seven percent of full-time undergraduate women belong to sororities. Forty minority women belong to all-minority sororities.

Special Services and Programs for Women. *Health and Counseling.* A student health service, staffed by 1 woman physician and 3 women health-care providers, and a student counseling center of 4, including 1 white and 1 minority woman and 2 men, provide counseling and treatment for gynecological matters, birth control, and rape and assault. Counseling only is available on abortion.

Safety and Security. Measures include campus police with authority to make arrests, night-time escort service for women students, high-intensity lighting, information on campus safety, and a rape crisis center. No rapes or other assaults were reported for 1980–81.

Career. The Career Placement Officer sponsors career workshops, lectures on nontraditional occupations, and programs to establish contacts between alumnae and women students.

Institutional Self-Description. ''Located in a low-cost area, University of West Florida offers: small classes; one-to-one faculty curriculum advising; exceptional (thus far, all needs met) financial aid; instruction by faculty, not graduate assistants; nationally renowned accounting, biology, and computer programs; outstanding library; cooperative education opportunities; model childcare program; unbelievably beautiful campus; and diverse regional recreation.''

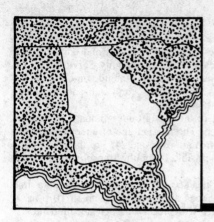

GEORGIA

Agnes Scott College
Decatur, GA 30030
Telephone: (404) 373-2571

Women in Leadership
★★★ **students**
★★ **faculty**
★★★ **administators**

525 undergraduates

	Amer. Ind.	Asian Amer.	Blacks	Hispanics	Whites
F	0	4	12	9	481
M	0	0	0	0	0
%	0.0	0.8	2.4	1.8	95.1

 AAUW

A liberal arts college for women, Agnes Scott was founded in 1889 by Presbyterians. Although it is now independent and non-sectarian, it retains some ties to the Presbyterian Church. Of the 525 undergraduate women, 2 percent attend part-time. The median age of all students is 20. The campus, located near downtown Atlanta, lies within easy reach of public transportation and also provides parking space for the 15 percent of students who commute.

Private childcare facilities are available off campus.

Policies to Ensure Fairness to Women. The Vice President for Business has the part-time responsibility for making policy and handling matters pertaining to sex-fair-employment and handicapped-access laws. A new, ad hoc Committee on the Status of Women, appointed by the President, reports on women's issues.

Women in Leadership Positions. *Students.* Women hold all student leadership positions.

Faculty. Forty-nine percent of the 68 full-time faculty are women, a proportion about average for women's colleges in this guide. There are 6 female faculty for every 100 female students.

Administrators. Women hold half of the key administrative positions. Women are chief academic officer, head librarian, and chief student-life officer. According to recent information, the new president of Agnes Scott is a woman, the first to have held this office since the college was founded. Women chair eleven of the 21 academic departments, including mathematics, biology, and chemistry. The representation of women on the Board of Trustees is below average for women's colleges in this guide.

Women and the Curriculum. About half of the graduates earn degrees in social sciences and psychology. In a recent year, two women majored in mathematics and one in physical sciences. Women can prepare for nontraditional careers in engineering science, and computer science through a special five year-degree program with Georgia Institute of Technology.

Agnes Scott offers six courses on women, including Contem-

porary Women Artists, Women in Hebrew Scripture, and Philosophy and Feminism. An official committee is responsible for encouraging the interpretation of scholarship on women into the curriculum.

Women and Athletics. The intramural program consists of five team and individual sports; club sports are also available. The two paid intercollegiate coaches are women. The intercollegiate sports are field hockey and tennis.

Housing and Student Organizations. Eighty-five percent of the students live on campus in dormitories that have restrictive hours for male visitors.

Students for Black Awareness and Chimo, composed largely of foreign students of color, meet on campus. Working for Awareness is also a student advocacy group.

Special Services and Programs for Women. *Health and Counseling.* A student health service is staffed by one male physician and two female health-care providers. Gynecological and birth control counseling and treatment are available, as well as abortion and rape and assault counseling.

Safety and Security. Measures consist of campus police, nighttime escort, instruction on self-defense and campus safety, and a rape crisis center. No rapes and two assaults on women were reported for 1980–81.

Career. Services include information workshops, panel discussions on nontraditional careers, and networking between students and alumnae.

Returning Women Students. A Return-to-College program serves older women whose educations have been interrupted. They attend classes with other undergraduate women and fulfill the usual requirements for a degree. The sociology department offers a course entitled Reentry Women.

Institutional Self-Description. "Women choose to study at Agnes Scott because of the strong academic program and close student-faculty relationships. The positive environment of a women's college encourages women to define themselves and outline their life goals in an atmosphere free from traditionally imposed sex-related expectations and limitations."

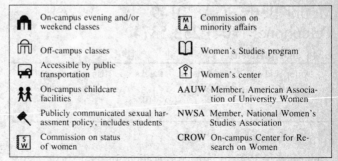

🏛 On-campus evening and/or weekend classes	Ⓜ Commission on minority affairs
🏛 Off-campus classes	📖 Women's Studies program
🚌 Accessible by public transportation	🏠 Women's center
🚶 On-campus childcare facilities	AAUW Member, American Association of University Women
⬦ Publicly communicated sexual harassment policy, includes students	NWSA Member, National Women's Studies Association
S/W Commission on status of women	CROW On-campus Center for Research on Women

Atlanta College of Art
1280 Peachtree St. N.E.,
Atlanta, GA 30309
Telephone: (404) 898-1159

Women in Leadership
 ★ faculty
 ★★★ administrators

257 undergraduates

	Amer. Ind.	Asian Amer.	Blacks	Hispanics	Whites
F	0	3	11	0	121
M	1	2	28	1	88
%	0.4	2.0	15.3	0.4	82.0

Atlanta College of Art is an independent, professional college of art located in the Atlanta Memorial Art Center. It enrolls 257 students, 53 percent of whom are women. Thirteen women attend part-time. The median age of all undergraduates is 21. Parking for a fee is available for the 66 percent of students who commute.

Women in Leadership Positions. *Students.* Information provided by the college does not permit an assessment of women in student leadership.

Faculty. Twenty-six percent of the full-time faculty members are women—a proportion just above the national average. All the permanently appointed faculty are male. There are 4 female faculty for every 100 female students, and 13 male faculty for every 100 male students.

Administrators. Four of the six chief administrative positions are held by women. Two of the eight chairs of departments are women: foundation studio and liberal arts. The president and vice-president of the faculty are women.

Women and the Curriculum. All degrees are in fine arts. There are no courses on women.

Women and Athletics. There are no opportunities for organized competitive sports.

Housing and Student Organizations. On-campus housing consists of coeducational residences that have no restrictions on hours for visitors of the opposite sex. A married woman whose husband is not a student may live in student housing.

Special Services and Programs for Women. *Health and Counseling.* The college employs a nurse. Medical or counseling services specific to women are not provided.

Safety and Security. Measures consist of high-intensity lighting and a campus police force. No information on the incidence of rapes or assaults for 1980–81 was provided.

Other. Career workshops on nontraditional occupations and lectures by women employed in nontraditional fields are available.

Institutional Self-Description. None provided.

Berry College
Mount Berry, GA 30149
Telephone: (404) 232-5374

1,344 undergraduates

	Amer. Ind.	Asian Amer.	Blacks	Hispanics	Whites
F	0	5	26	4	743
M	0	0	10	5	541
%	0.0	0.4	2.7	0.7	96.3

Established in 1902 to provide education for rural youth, Berry College now attracts a diverse student body to its campus, which is located an hour from Atlanta. Some 1,500 students enroll. Bachelor's degrees in the liberal arts, sciences, and pre-professional areas and graduate degrees in business and education are offered. Continuing Education and Community Service sponsors non-credit courses. Alternative schedules include on-campus evening classes, off-campus day classes, and self-paced/contract learning. There is a summer session.

Women are 58 percent of the 1,344 undergraduates; 2 percent of women attend part-time. The median age of undergraduates is 20. Three percent of women are over age 24. For the commuting student, the college is accessible by public transportation. There is on-campus parking.

Campus childcare facilities accommodate 36 children on a first-come, first-served basis. Fees are fixed. Care up to 10 p.m. is available if enough requests are received. Private childcare arrangements can be made near the campus.

Policies to Ensure Fairness to Women. A member of the administration is responsible for policy on equal employment opportunity, sex equity for students, and handicapped access.

Women in Leadership Positions. *Students.* In a recent three-year period, women held 11 percent of the student leadership positions, including presiding officer of the student union (twice) and president of the senior class (once). Women head two of 11 honorary societies.

Faculty. Women are 24 percent of the 85 full-time faculty, a proportion close to the national average. There are 3 female faculty for every 100 female students and 12 male faculty for every 100 male students.

Administrators. The head librarian is a woman; all other top administrative positions are held by men. Women chair two of 16 departments: home economics and English. The director of Evening Programs is a woman; half of the campus-wide personnel commitee and two of 16 trustees are women.

Women and the Curriculum. Most women earn four-year degrees in education (36 percent), business (17 percent), psychology (12 percent), and social sciences (8 percent). Ten percent of the women graduates major in agriculture, mathematics, and the physical sciences. The college reports that the number of women in industrial technology programs is increasing. One-quarter of the cooperative education, 65 percent of the internship, and 40 percent of the marine biology field-study positions go to women.

One course on women is offered: Psychology of Women. Such current issues as sex-fair curricula, coeducational physical education classes, and women in the workplace are part of the preparation of future teachers and business students.

Women and Athletics. The intramural program offers ten sports, including basketball, softball, volleyball, and tennis. Club sports are available. The college reports special facilities for canoeing and horseback riding. Forty-six percent of intramural and 35 percent of intercollegiate athletes are women; women receive 30 percent of athletic scholarships. Two of six paid coaches are women. Varsity teams play in tournaments. The intercollegiate sports are basketball, cross-country, tennis, and track.

Housing and Student Organizations. For the 67 percent of undergraduates who live on campus, single-sex dormitories are available. Residence halls restrict hours for visitors of the opposite sex. Two of three directors are women.

The Berry College Student Home Economics Association and Sigma Alpha Iota serve as advocates for women on campus. The Black Student Association meets on campus.

Special Services and Programs for Women. *Health and Counseling.* The student health service, staffed by a male physician and four female health-care workers, does not provide medical treatment specific to women. One of two staff in the counseling center is a woman. Gynecological, birth control, abortion, and rape and assault counseling is available.

Safety and Security. Measures consist of campus police with weapons training and arrest authority, night-time escorts to and from the library, high-intensity lighting, emergency telephones, and information on campus safety and crime prevention. No assaults and no rapes were reported for 1980-81.

Career. Services include workshops, speakers, and printed information on women in nontraditional careers and fields of study.

Other. Some 20 percent of students who enroll in continuing education courses are black women.

Institutional Self-Description. "Berry was founded by a woman—Martha Berry—in 1902. Its original, threefold purpose, appealing to both sexes, was to provide a quality academic program with work opportunity and religious-faith emphasis to deserving students. This purpose later expanded into four dimensions with the addition of student participation in governance. The environment for education and living, created by Berry's unique campus and community (with many faculty living in the campus), is particularly beneficial to women students."

Crandall College

1283 Adams Street, Macon, GA 31201
Telephone: (912) 745-6593

Women in Leadership
★★★ faculty
★★★ administrators

354 undergraduates

Complete enrollment information unavailable.

Established in 1951 as a women's secretarial school, Crandall College is now a private, coeducational, two-year business college. There are 278 female degree students attending full-time. The median age of undergraduates is 23. Black women are 61 percent of the enrollment. Evening as well as daytime classes are available. Crandall is a commuter college that is accessible by public transportation; free on-campus parking is available.

Private childcare facilities are available near campus.

Women in Leadership Positions. *Students.* No information was provided on student leadership.

Faculty. Four of the five full-time faculty members are women.

Administrators. Of the four top administrators, three are white women, including the chief executive officer, chief academic officer, and head librarian. The director of the word-processing division is female.

Women and the Curriculum. Information is not available concerning degrees awarded. The business curriculum includes instruction about the problems of job discrimination, sexual harassment in the workplace, and women in management. There are no courses on women.

Women and Athletics. There are no intercollegiate or club sports. Approximately 50 women participate in intramurals, including softball, volleyball, and rollerskating.

Special Services and Programs for Women. *Health and Counseling.* There is no student health service. A counseling center is staffed by one male counselor. No services specific to women are available.

Safety and Security. The campus, patrolled by local police, has high-intensity lighting in all areas. For 1980–81, no rapes or assaults were reported on campus.

Institutional Self-Description. "Crandall College is dedicated to preparing its students to join the progressive workforce in tomorrow's business world, today. The business marketplace is in a constant state of technological change and advancement. At Crandall, we maintain an up-to-date, practical business curriculum, so that our graduates might meet those needs."

Emory University

Atlanta, GA 30322
Telephone: (404) 329-6123

Women in Leadership
★★★ students

4,033 undergraduates

	Amer. Ind.	Asian Amer.	Blacks	Hispanics	Whites
F	0	13	73	19	1,741
M	0	9	31	23	2,059
%	0.0	0.6	2.6	1.1	958

 AAUW

Founded in 1836 by the Methodist Episcopal Church, Emory University is a private, denominational institution in Atlanta. Some 7,800 students enroll in a range of undergraduate, graduate, and professional programs. Community Education Services is responsible for adult continuing education. A summer session and an overseas-study program are available.

Women are 46 percent of the 4,033 undergraduates; 1 percent of women attend part-time. The median age of undergraduates is 20. For the 33 percent of undergraduates who commute or live off campus, the university is accessible by public transportation. On-campus parking is available for a fee.

Private childcare arrangements may be made close to campus.

Policies to Ensure Fairness to Women. A full-time Coordinator of Equal Opportunity Programs reviews policies and practices related to employment, sex equity, and handicapped access. A full-time assistant monitors compliance. A published policy prohibits sexual harassment; complaints are handled informally and confidentially or through a formal grievance procedure. The Committee on the Status of Women, which includes students as voting members, takes public stands on issues of concern to students. The Committee on Minority Affairs addresses the concerns of minority women.

Women in Leadership Positions. *Students.* Women students have had outstanding opportunities for student leadership in recent years. They have twice been president of the student body and the student senate, presided once over the student court, presided three times over the residence-hall council, and been editor-in-chief of the newspaper once.

Faculty. Women constitute 23 percent of a full-time faculty of 420. There are 5 female faculty for every 100 female students and 15 male faculty for every 100 male students.

Administrators. Men fill all top administrative positions. Two of 43 departments are chaired by women: modern languages and classics, and the medical school library. The Dean of the Graduate School of Arts and Sciences and the Dean of the Nursing School are women.

Women and the Curriculum. Most women earning bachelor's degrees major in the health professions (31 percent), psychology (16 percent), and social sciences (15 percent). The percentage of women majoring in business and management is above the national average. Five percent major in the nontraditional fields of physical sciences and mathematics. Half of the internship and science field-service positions in experiential learning programs are held by women.

While there is no Women's Studies Program, a graduate minor and a Ph.D. in Women's Studies are available through the Institute of Liberal Arts. Courses on women, several for undergraduates, are available through the departments of English, history, and classics. These include British Women Writers, Women in Latin American Society, and Women in Antiquity. An official committee reports on the inclusion of women in the curriculum. Faculty workshops are available on the relationships among sex, race, and choice of major field, and on affirmative action.

Minority Women. Of 1,846 undergraduate women, 6 percent

are members of minority groups, with black women the largest group. An estimated 4 percent of women living in residence halls are black women, 1 percent each Asian American and Hispanic. Seven women are in all-minority sororities. A minority woman is on the professional staff of the counseling center. Counseling staff receive in-service training in the avoidance of racial bias.

Women and Athletics. The intramural program provides some opportunities for organized, competitive individual and team sports. The intercollegiate program is limited to individual sports. Club sports are also available. Thirty percent of intramural and 43 percent of intercollegiate athletes are women. Athletic scholarships are not awarded. Two of five paid intercollegiate coaches are female. The intercollegiate sports offered are: cross-country, swimming and diving, tennis, and track and field.

Housing and Student Organizations. Over two-thirds of the undergraduates live on campus. Single-sex and coeducational dormitories and housing for married students and single parents with children are available. A married woman student whose spouse is not enrolled may live in married students' housing. Dormitories do not restrict hours for visitors of the opposite sex. Two of 12 residence-hall directors are women. Staff are offered awareness-training on sex education and birth control.

Twenty-nine percent of undergraduate women belong to social sororities. Sororities do not provide housing for their members. Among groups which serve as advocates for women on campus are the Legal Association of Women, the Medical Women's Association, Mortarboard, and the Women's Assembly.

Special Services and Programs for Women. *Health and Counseling.* The student health service provides some medical attention specific to women, including gynecological, birth control, and rape and assault treatment. Three of five physicians are female, as are 12 other health-care providers. Half of the counseling service staff are women. Students have access to gynecological, birth control, abortion, rape and assault, sexuality, and family planning counseling. Staff are offered in-service training on the avoidance of sex-role stereotyping.

Safety and Security. Measures include campus police with arrest authority, high-intensity lighting, emergency alarm and telephone systems, self-defense courses for women, information sessions on safety and crime prevention, and a rape crisis center. Twelve assaults (nine on women) and one rape were reported for 1980–81.

Career. The Office of Career Planning and Placement offers lecture series, workshops, printed information, and other materials on women in nontraditional occupations and fields of study, as well as a network of contacts between alumnae and students. The office also sponsors assertiveness training.

Other. The Center for Women's Interest Law provides a telephone service for information, referral, and support.

Institutional Self-Description. "Emory is vigorously committed to academic excellence and broadening the range of professional opportunities for graduates. Women, comprising half the student body, are actively involved in top campus leadership. Diverse faculty in arts, sciences, professions; strong support services for women; active commissions, caucuses, and workshops; and a rich blend of campus activities are features of the university."

Georgia State University
University Plaza, Atlanta, GA 30303
Telephone: (404) 658-2000

Women in Leadership
★ faculty

13,098 undergraduates

	Amer. Ind.	Asian Amer.	Blacks	Hispanics	Whites
F	15	36	1,452	26	5,368
M	14	39	843	31	4,992
%	0.2	0.6	18.0	0.4	80.8

Founded as an evening business school, Georgia State became a university in 1969. It offers its 20,021 students associate, bachelor's, master's, and doctoral degrees. The division of continuing education serves the adult student. Alternative schedules include evening classes both on and off campus, a summer session, and a weekend college.

Of the 13,098 undergraduates enrolled, 54 percent are women; 54 percent of women attend part-time. The median age of undergraduates is 26. All undergraduates commute to the campus, which is accessible by public transportation. On-campus parking is provided for a fee.

Both on-campus and private, off-campus childcare facilities are available.

Policies to Ensure Fairness to Women. The Vice President for Academic Services reviews policies and practices in educational sex equity and handicapped access. A written, published campus policy prohibits sexual harassment of students, faculty, and staff; complaints are resolved through a formal grievance procedure.

The University Women's Committee, which includes student members with voting rights, recognizes achievements of women on campus and sponsors educational and self-development programs. This Committee reports to the Vice President of Academic Services and addresses some concerns of minority women.

Women in Leadership Positions. *Students.* Women have limited opportunities to exercise campus leadership. In a recent three-year period, women served one-year terms as president of the student body and editor-in-chief of the campus newspaper.

Faculty. Twenty-five percent of the full-time faculty of 683 are female. There are 5 female faculty for every 100 female students, and 17 male faculty for every 100 male students. According to a recent report, the full-time female faculty includes 11 black and 3 Asian American women.

Administrators. A woman serves as director of institutional research; the other chief adminstrative positions are held by men. Women chair the departments of foreign languages, early childhood education, and physical therapy. The School of Nursing is directed by a woman. The university's Honors Program, the Instructional Resources Center, and Developmental Studies are also directed by women. One of the 15 university regents is a white woman.

Women and the Curriculum. Most bachelor's degrees earned by women are in business (24 percent), education (17 percent), health professions (15 percent), and social sciences (9 percent). One percent of women graduates major in mathematics and physical sciences. The department of mathematics offers a program to build skills in mathematics. Approximately 70 percent of all two-year degrees are awarded to women, two-thirds in health technologies. About half the internship and science field-service assignments are held by women.

Courses on women are offered in five departments. Recent offering include Women's History, Cross-Cultural Perspectives on Woman, Philosophical Reflections on Woman, Sex Roles, and

⋔	On-campus evening and/or weekend classes	M̄A̲	Commission on minority affairs
⋒	Off-campus classes	📖	Women's Studies program
🚍	Accessible by public transportation	🏠	Women's center
👫	On-campus childcare facilities	AAUW	Member, American Association of University Women
✎	Publicly communicated sexual harassment policy, includes students	NWSA	Member, National Women's Studies Association
S̲W̲	Commission on status of women	CROW	On-campus Center for Research on Women

the Politics of Gender. Faculty workshops are offered on affirmative action and equal opportunity.

Women and Athletics. Women students have good opportunities to participate in individual and team sports through the large intramural program, but limited opportunities in the small intercollegiate program. Thirty percent of athletic scholarship aid is awarded to women. One of the three paid varsity coaches is a woman. The intercollegiate sports offered are basketball, cross-country, softball (slow pitch), swimming, and tennis.

Special Services and Programs for Women. *Health and Counseling.* The student health service employs 2 male physicians and 1 female health-care provider; the student counseling center has a staff of 15, including 6 white and 1 minority women. No medical treatment on problems specific to women is provided Counseling on gynecological matters, birth control, abortion, and rape and assault is available. Counselors receive in-service training on avoiding sex-role stereotyping and racial bias.

Safety and Security. Measures consist of local police, armed campus police with arrest authority, a night-time escort service for women students, high-intensity lighting, emergency alarm system, self-defense courses for women, information sessions on campus safety and crime prevention, and a rape crisis center. No rapes and 12 assaults (10 on women) were reported for 1980–81.

Career. Resources include career workshops, lectures, nonsexist/nonracist printed materials, and job discrimination information on women in nontraditional occupations. Also available are updated files of alumnae by specific careers and networking between alumnae and female students.

Institutional Self-Description. "Georgia State University considers its urban setting to provide a wide variety of learning opportunities on and off campus. The institution fosters a belief in the potential and worth of each student while attempting to be appreciative of individual and cultural differences."

ulty. There are 4 female faculty for every 100 female students and 11 male faculty for every 100 male students.

Administrators. Two of the five chief administrators, including the chief academic officer and the business officer, are women. Women chair three of 16 departments: foreign languages, art, and education.

Women and the Curriculum. Most degrees awarded to women are in education (52 percent), public affairs (16 percent), and business (12 percent). There are no courses on women.

Women and Athletics. For a college of its size, Piedmont offers an adequate women's athletic program. Women receive 10 percent of the athletic scholarship aid. The three intercollegiate sports are basketball, tennis, and track and field.

Housing and Student Organizations. Single-sex and married students' residences are available. No female visitors are permitted in men's dormitories, and male visitors are permitted only during specified hours in the lobby of the women's residence.

Twenty-five women, five of them minority women, belong to social sororities.

Special Services and Programs for Women. *Health and Counseling.* There are no health or counseling services specific to women on campus. Students can obtain gynecological, birth control, abortion, and rape and assault treatment from an off-campus physician.

Safety and Security. Measures consist of campus police protection. No rapes or assaults were reported for 1980–81.

Institutional Self-Description. "From the beginning, Piedmont College has offered education without discrimination as to race, creed, or sex. In a rural setting, we do not have the problems faced by many colleges—our residence halls are strictly separated by sex and we close the women's residence hall at 11 p.m. with all women in. We offer a Christian approach to sex and marriage and do not condone premarital or extramarital sex, alcohol, or drugs."

Piedmont College
Demorest, GA 30535
Telephone: (404) 778-8009

Women in Leadership
★★★ students
★★ administrators

376 undergraduates

	Amer. Ind.	Asian Amer.	Blacks	Hispanics	Whites
F	0	0	9	1	146
M	0	1	12	0	194
%	0.0	0.3	5.8	0.3	93.7

Piedmont College is a liberal arts college affiliated with the Congregational Churches of America. Founded in 1978 to provide men and women with an opportunity for earning an education in a Christian environment, the college is located in a rural setting two hours from Atlanta. Forty-two percent of the 376 undergraduates are women. Twenty women attend part-time. The median age of all undergraduates is 21.

On-campus parking is available for a fee to the 72 percent of students who commute.

Private childcare facilities are available off campus.

Women in Leadership Positions. *Students.* Opportunities for women to exercise all campus leadership are outstanding. About half the campus-wide student leadership positions have been held by women in recent years. A woman heads one of the two honorary societies.

Faculty. There are 6 women on the 22-member full-time fac-

Spelman College
350 Spelman Lane S.W., Atlanta, GA 30314
Telephone: (404) 681-3643

Women in Leadership
★★★ students
★★★ faculty
★★ administrators

★ **Women and the Curriculum**

1,258 undergraduates

	Amer. Ind.	Asian Amer.	Blacks	Hispanics	Whites
F	0	1	1,243	0	0
M	0	0	0	0	0
%	0.0	0.1	99.9	0.0	0.0

 AAUW

Some 1,260 students attend Spelman, the first college established for black women. Founded in 1881 to provide a basic religious and practical education for women not long out of slavery, and now one of two colleges principally serving black women, Spelman offers bachelor's degrees in a range of liberal arts and pre-professional fields. Virtually all of the 1,258 women enrolled in degree programs attend full-time. The median age of students is 19. Free on-campus parking is provided for the 38 percent of students who commute. The campus is accessible by public transportation.

There is a nursery-kindergarten on campus.

Women in Leadership Positions. *Students.* Women hold all student leadership positions.

Faculty. Two-thirds of the full-time faculty of 94 are women. There are 5 female faculty for every 100 female students. The college reports that the full-time female faculty includes 44 black and 12 white women.

Administrators. Four of the nine top-level administrative positions are held by black women, including Dean of the College, chief student-life officer, head librarian, and director of athletics. Nine black and 2 white women chair 11 of 17 departments, including biology, chemistry, economics, English, mathematics, music, psychology, and political science. Six of 8 members of the tenure and promotions committee are black women. Six black and 5 white women sit on the 24-member Board of Trustees.

Women and the Curriculum. The majority of graduates earn degrees in social sciences (34 percent), psychology (18 percent), and letters (14 percent), with significant numbers in biology, education, and fine arts. Eight percent of degrees are awarded in mathematics and physical sciences. The department of mathematics offers a program to build mathematics confidence.

Fourteen courses on women are offered in the departments of drama, history, political science, sociology, psychology, drama, economics, English, and religion. Recent offerings include Human Worth and Women; Black Women Developing Public Leadership; Women, Values, and the Law; Black Women, Status and Achievement; and Women in the Economy.

Women and Athletics. Spelman offers opportunities for participation in eight team and individual intramural sports, and a limited intercollegiate program. Facilities include a pool and a bowling alley. Almost 400 women participate in the intramural program: 25 women participate in the two intercollegiate sports offered, tennis and volleyball.

Housing and Student Organizations. Sixty-two percent of students live on campus in dormitories with restricted hours for male visitors. All of the residence-hall directors are black women.

Campus sororities do not provide housing for members.

Special Services and Programs for Women. *Health and Counseling.* Three male physicians serve the student health service part-time, along with 6 health-care providers and 3 relief nurses. The student counseling center employs 4 minority women. Counseling and medical treatment for gynecological matters, birth control, and family planning are among the available services specific to women, along with rape and assault and abortion counseling.

Safety and Security. Measures consist of armed campus police with arrest authority, and high-intensity lighting in most areas. Information was not provided about the incidence of rapes and assaults.

Career. Lectures and panels are available for students by women employed in nontraditional occupations.

Institutional Self-Description. "Spelman, an outstanding, historically black college for women, offers students a comprehensive liberal arts background through studies in the fine arts, humanities, social sciences, and natural sciences. Students are encouraged to think critically, logically, and creatively; to develop competence in decision-making and problem-solving; and to improve their use of communicative and quantitative skills. Spelman seeks to develop the total person. Spelman promotes excellence by reinforcing a sense of pride and hope, developing character, and inspiring the love of learning."

Wesleyan College
4760 Forsyth Road, Macon, GA 31297
Telephone: (912) 477-1110

Women in Leadership
★★★ students
★★ faculty
★★★ administrators

482 undergraduates

	Amer. Ind.	Asian Amer.	Blacks	Hispanics	Whites
F	0	0	50	3	411
M	0	0	0	0	0
%	0.0	0.0	10.8	0.7	88.6

🏛 🚐 👫 AAUW

Founded in 1836 by the United Methodist Church to provide a liberal arts and fine arts education for women, Wesleyan is now a four-year, non-sectarian college for women; it remains church-affiliated. A range of undergraduate, pre-professional, and professional degree programs is offered, as well as an adult education program. Evening classes and a summer session are available.

Located in a suburban setting near Atlanta, the college enrolls 498 students. Of the 450 students registered in degree programs, 7 percent attend part-time. The median age of students is 20. For the 25 percent of students who commute, the campus can be reached by public transportation, and there is free parking.

A childcare facility on campus serves 16 children—virtually all students' requests. Priority is given to full-time students, and service is based on a fixed hourly fee. Additional, private childcare facilities are located near campus.

Policies to Ensure Fairness to Women. The Vice President has part-time responsibility for policies and practices relating to laws concerning equal employment opportunity, sex equity, and handicapped access. Sexual harassment complaints are resolved through a formal grievance procedure.

Women in Leadership Positions. *Students.* Women hold all student leadership positions.

Faculty. Thirty-six percent of the 45 full-time faculty members are women. There are 4 female faculty for every 100 female students.

Administrators. Women are three-fourths of the key administrators. Six of 14 departments are chaired by women: English, communications, American studies, political science, history, and health and physical education. Thirty percent of the trustees are women. In a recent year, two of the four honorary degree recipients were women and all three alumni awards went to women.

Women and the Curriculum. Nearly one-half of the women earn degrees in education and fine arts; 8 percent major in the nontraditional fields of mathematics and physical sciences.

There are no courses on women. Information on battered spouses, displaced homemakers, and childcare is included in the social-work curriculum; information on discrimination in the workplace, in the business curriculum.

Women and Athletics. The sports program is limited. Forty women participate in intercollegiate competition, and 100 participate in intramural basketball, soccer, tennis, and volleyball. Intercollegiate sports are tennis and volleyball.

Housing and Student Organizations. Three-fourths of all students live on campus in dormitories that have restrictive hours for visiting males. An advocacy and support group for minority women, the Black Students Alliance, has 25 active members.

Special Services and Programs for Women. *Health and Counseling.* The student health service staff, consisting of one male physician and one female health-care provider, offers birth control and gynecological treatment. The student counseling center, which employs one female counselor, provides birth control and abortion counseling.

🏛 On-campus evening and/or weekend classes	MA Commission on minority affairs
🏛 Off-campus classes	📖 Women's Studies program
🚐 Accessible by public transportation	🚻 Women's center
👫 On-campus childcare facilities	AAUW Member, American Association of University Women
⚡ Publicly communicated sexual harassment policy, includes students	NWSA Member, National Women's Studies Association
SW Commission on status of women	CROW On-campus Center for Research on Women

Safety and Security. Measures consist of campus police, nighttime escort, emergency telephone and alarm systems, and information on safety precautions. No rapes or assaults on women were reported for 1980–81.

Career. Wesleyan maintains files on the careers of alumnae and encourages networking between students and alumnae. Career workshops, panel discussions, and job discrimination information. on nontraditional occupations are available. The Student Services Office sponsors assertiveness-training sessions.

Returning Women Students. One hundred and fifteen reentry women are enrolled in credit and non-credit courses in the adult education program. Eight percent are minority women with black women predominant. The Entry/Reentry program's staff serves displaced homemakers and welfare women, as well as other returning women students.

Institutional Self-Description. "Wesleyan College holds the distinction of being the first college in the world chartered to grant degrees to women. All of Wesleyan's programs, resources, and activities are designed to meet the unique needs of women so as to foster leadership and achievement in the professions, the family and society."

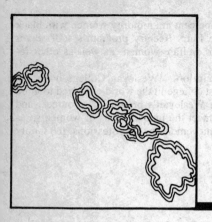

HAWAII

University of Hawaii, Manoa
Honolulu, HI 96822
Telephone: (808) 948-7837

★ **Women and the Curriculum**

15,305 undergraduates

	Amer. Ind.	Asian Amer.	Blacks	Hispanics	Whites
F	9	5,752	28	89	1,672
M	12	5,435	38	107	1,445
%	0.1	76.69	0.5	1.3	21.4

Established in 1907 in the Manoa Valley of Honolulu, the University of Hawaii at Manoa offers its multi-ethnic student body of over 21,000 a variety of undergraduate and graduate programs. The College of Continuing Education and Community Services offers programs to the adult student. A summer session and evening classes at locations on and off campus are available.

Women are 51 percent of the 15,305 undergraduates; 17 percent of women attend part-time. The median age of undergraduates is 21. For the 85 percent of undergraduates who commute, the university is accessible by public transportation. There is on-campus parking.

Private childcare arrangements may be made close to campus.

Policies to Ensure Fairness to Women. An Equal Opportunity Officer is responsible part-time for compliance with equal employment opportunity, sex equity, and handicapped-access. A published policy prohibits sexual harassment; complaints are handled informally and confidentially.

Women in Leadership Positions. *Students.* In recent years, women have been president of the student body, presiding officer of the residence-hall council, manager of the campus radio station, and editor-in-chief of the newspaper.

Faculty. Women are 21 percent of a full-time faculty of 994. According to a recent report, 1 black, 1 American Indian, 104 Asian American, and 3 Hispanic women are on the full-time faculty. The ratio of female faculty to female students is 3 to 100; of male faculty to male students, 13 to 100.

Administrators. The director of institutional research is a woman; all other top posts are held by men. Women chair 13 of 111 departments; five department heads are Asian American women. The acting Dean of the Graduate Division is female.

Women and the Curriculum. The majority of women graduating with bachelor's degrees major in business (17 percent), home economics (16 percent), psychology (10 percent), the social sciences (10 percent), and fine arts (7 percent). Six percent major in such nontraditional areas as agriculture, architecture, computer science, engineering, mathematics, and the physical sciences.

The Women's Studies Program, under a faculty member who serves part-time as director, offers a B. A. in Interdisciplinary and Women's Studies. Twenty-three courses are available, several cross-listed with the departments of religion, general science, sociology, and educational foundations. Recent titles include Social Policy and Women, Literature by Women, History and Education of American Women, Asian-Pacific Women and Modernization, and Women in Therapy. Additional courses are offered in the School of Nursing, including Health Assessment of Women. During the past five years, 36 students have majored in Women's Studies.

Such current issues as mathematics confidence among females, coeducational physical education classes, trans-cultural health information, services for battered spouses, and discrimination in the workplace are part of the preparation of teachers, health-care workers, social workers, and business students.

Minority Women. Of 7,550 undergraduate women, 76 percent are Asian American, 1 percent Hispanic, and less than 1 percent each black and American Indian. Five of the staff in the counseling service are minority women; they receive in-service training on cross-cultural counseling. The director of the Continuing Education for Women Program is Asian American. Approximately 37 percent of Continuing Education for Women students are minority women, with Asian American the largest group.

Women and Athletics. The intramural program offers opportunities for organized, competitive individual and team sports. Individual sports predominate in the intercollegiate program. Sixteen percent of intramural and 35 percent of intercollegiate athletes are women; women receive 20 percent of athletic scholarships. Ten of 21 paid varsity coaches are female. All women's intercollegiate teams played in tournaments during 1980. The intercollegiate sports offered are basketball, cross-country, golf, swimming and diving, tennis, track and field, and volleyball.

Housing and Student Organizations. Fifteen percent of undergraduates live on campus. Residential accommodations include single-sex and coeducational dormitories and housing for married students without children. Residence halls do not restrict hours for visitors of the opposite sex. Half of the residence-hall directors are female. Awareness-training is offered staff on sex education, equal rights, and rape prevention.

Two percent of undergraduate women belong to social sororities, which do not provide housing for their members. The university chapter of the YWCA is active on behalf of campus women.

Special Services and Programs for Women. *Health and Counseling.* The student health service provides some medical attention specific to women, including gynecological, birth control, and rape and assault treatment. One of the 5 physicians is female, as are 9 other health-care providers. One of the student health plan options covers abortion at no extra charge. Nine of 17 professional staff in the counseling service are women. Students have access to gynecological, birth control, abortion, and rape and assault counseling. There is also counseling for women in transition.

Safety and Security. Measures include campus and local police, night-time escorts for women, high-intensity lighting, information sessions on safety and crime prevention, and a rape crisis center. Fourteen assaults (ten on women) and no rapes were reported for 1980–81.

Career. Printed information on nontraditional careers for women and on job discrimination is available.

Other. The university YWCA sponsors a program for displaced homemakers.

Returning Women Students. The College of Continuing Education and Community Services houses a Continuing Education for Women Program. In 1980–82, over 500 women enrolled in continuing education courses. A program to build confidence in mathematics is one of the CEW services.

Institutional Self-Description. ''The university offers pursuit of higher education in a multi-ethnic setting.''

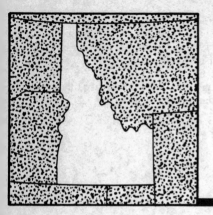

IDAHO

Boise State University
1910 University Drive, Boise, ID 83725
Telephone: (208) 385-1011

Women in Leadership
★ students

8,083 undergraduates

	Amer. Ind.	Asian Amer.	Blacks	Hispanics	Whites
F	28	63	16	55	3,809
M	17	49	51	50	3,929
%	0.6	1.4	0.8	1.3	95.9

Nearly 10,000 students attend this public university, located in a residential section of central Boise. Established as a junior college in 1932, the university joined the state system in 1974, after having expanded to four-year status in 1965. Some 8,000 undergraduates now enroll in a variety of programs. Half of all undergraduates are women, and 43 percent of all women attend part-time (about one-third of all male students attend part-time). Twenty-seven percent of the undergraduate women are between 26 and 40 years old; 7 percent are over age 40. The median age of all undergraduates is 26.

The university offers a summer session, a weekend college, and evening and off-campus classes. Almost all students commute. On-campus parking is available for a fee, as is public transportation.

Childcare is available on campus; full-time students have priority for the 28 places. About 60 percent of all students' requests for this service, offered at a fee on a sliding scale, can be met.

Policies to Ensure Fairness to Women. The Director of Affirmative Action, on a part-time basis, is responsible for monitoring compliance with legislation on sex equity and access for the handicapped. A formal campus grievance procedure is available for complaints of sexual harassment.

Women in Leadrship Positions. *Students.* There are five student leadership positions on campus. In a recent three year period, women have served once as president of the student body, once as editor-in-chief of the campus newspaper, twice as president of the student governing body, and once as head of the student court.

Faculty. Women are 22 percent of the 312 full-time faculty, a proportion below the national average. There are 3 female faculty for every 100 female students and 9 male faculty for every 100 male students.

Administrators. Men hold the top-level administrative positions. Women chair four of 33 departments: home economics, health occupations, service occupations, and adult basic education.

Women and the Curriculum. Women earn 43 percent of degrees awarded, about 3 percent of them in nontraditional areas. The most popular majors for women are business (22 percent),

education (29 percent), public affairs (11 percent), and social sciences (9 percent). Most two-year degrees awarded to women are in health technologies. No courses on women are offered.

Women and Athletics. Women make up 35 percent of intercollegiate athletes and receive 20 percent of athletic scholarships. There are a few coeducational sports among the eight intramural sports. Women are 20 percent of the 250 participants in club sports. Seven of 18 paid varsity coaches are women. Women compete in intercollegiate basketball, cross-country, field hockey, gymnastics, tennis, track, and volleyball.

Housing and Student Organizations. Coeducational and single-sex dormitories house the eight percent of undergraduates who live on campus. Housing for married students and single students with children is also available. Sororities and fraternities provide housing for their members.

Special Services and Programs for Women. *Health and Counseling.* Two male physicians and 3 female health-care providers staff the health service. The counseling service is operated by a staff of 5, 2 of whom are women.

Safety and Security. Measures include campus patrol by town police, high-intensity lighting in all areas, and a self-defense course for women. No information was provided on the incidence of rapes and assaults.

Other. Student Advisory Special Services is the locus for women with special needs. Minority women are served by the Black Students' Union, MECHA, and Dan Soghop. Women's Alliance serves lesbians. Several religious clubs on campus offer support to women. Off campus, the Boise YWCA provides a program for battered women and offers training in assertiveness/leadership.

Institutional Self-Description. None provided.

College of Idaho
Caldwell, ID 83605
Telephone: (208) 459-5011

Women in Leadership
★ students

534 undergraduates

	Amer. Ind.	Asian Amer.	Blacks	Hispanics	Whites
F	2	14	1	5	204
M	0	22	4	4	272
%	0.4	6.8	1.0	1.7	90.2

This private, coeducational, liberal arts college, located near Boise, serves 911 students. Of the 534 students enrolled in degree programs, 43 percent are women, almost all of whom attend full-time. Alternative schedules include evening classes both on and off campus, and a summer session. Free parking is provided on campus for the 24 percent of students who commute.

Private childcare is available off campus.

Women in Leadership Positions. *Students.* Opportunities for women students to exercise campus-wide leadership are good. In recent years, women have presided over the student senate twice, served one-year terms as head of the student court and student union board, and been editor-in-chief of the campus newspaper for one year.

Faculty. Seven of the 34 full-time faculty are women. There are 3 female faculty for every 100 female students, and 11 male faculty for every 100 male students.

Administrators. Men hold all top positions except chief student-life officer. Women chair 4 of 18 departments: modern languages, health and physical education, biology, and psychology. Six of the 30 trustees are women. A woman was one of three honorary degree recipients at the 1981 commencement.

Women and the Curriculum. Six percent of women graduates major in mathematics and physical sciences. The most popular fields of study are education (24 percent) and social sciences (20 percent). The college offers no courses on women.

Women and Athletics. For a school of its size, the college provides a good intercollegiate and intramural women's athletic program. A fifth of all athletic scholarships go to women. The six intramural and three intercollegiate women's sports offered are coached by two men and a woman. Intercollegiate sports are skiing, tennis, and volleyball.

Housing and Student Organizations. Single-sex and coeducational residence halls have restrictive hours for visitors of the opposite sex. The three female and two male residence-hall directors receive awareness training on the avoidance of sexism.

The racially integrated sororities have 90 members, representing 41 percent of full-time female students, including four minority women.

Special Services and Programs for Women. *Health and Counseling.* A woman health provider staffs the health service. No medical treatment specific to women is available. A staff of three women and a man provide counseling on matters of birth control, abortion, and rape and assault. Counselors receive training on the avoidance of sex-role stereotyping.

Safety and Security. Measures include a campus police force, high-intensity lighting, and self-defense and campus safety courses for women. No rapes or assaults on women were reported on campus for 1980-81.

Career. Workshops focused on nontraditional careers for women are provided. The department of student affairs offers assertiveness/leadership training.

Institutional Self-Description. "All programs at the College of Idaho are open to both men and women with no discrimination with regard to any criteria. The community and student body make-up provide for a generally safe environment with little necessity for concern about harassment or danger."

Idaho State University

Pocatello, ID 83209
Telephone: (208) 236-3193

4,299 undergraduates

	Amer. Ind.	Asian Amer.	Blacks	Hispanics	Whites
F	13	16	16	19	2,065
M	7	39	15	22	2,086
%	0.5	1.3	0.7	1.0	96.6

🏠 🏛 🚌 👫 🔨 AAUW

This state-supported institution, established in 1901, offers undergraduate and graduate programs, vocational and extension courses, as well as adult education programs, to 6,470 students. Women are half the 4,299 undergraduates, and about a quarter of the women attend part-time. The university estimates the median age for undergraduates at 25.

Women account for 41 percent of 185 handicapped students; housing for the handicapped and visually impaired is provided in a centrally located building. About 30 percent of all undergraduates commute to the campus, located in Idaho's second largest city. On-campus parking is available, as is public transportation.

Childcare facilities on the campus can accommodate 35 children, or about 35 percent of all requests by students, for a flat daily fee of $6. Students have priority for available space, although children of faculty and staff are also served.

Policies to Ensure Fairness to Women. The full-time Affirmative Action Officer, who is a voting member of policymaking bodies, is responsible for ensuring educational equity and compliance with provisions relating to access for the handicapped. Sexual harassment of students, faculty, and staff is prohibited, and this policy has been publicly communicated in writing to all three groups.

Women in Leadership Positions. *Students.* Although women constitute nearly one-half of all full-time undergraduates, in a recent three-year period they held one-fourth of the available student leadership positions: presiding officer of the student union for one year and, for two consecutive years, editor of the student newspaper. Women head four of the eight honorary societies.

Faculty. Of 367 full-time faculty, 23 percent are women, slightly below the national average. Women constitute just under 15 percent of all permanently appointed faculty. The ratio of female faculty to female students is 5 to 100, the ratio for males, 16 to 100.

Administrators. The chief academic officer is a woman; all other top administrators are men. Women chair five academic departments, including dental hygiene.

Women and the Curriculum. Health care and education are the most popular majors for women. Of the 273 women who earned degrees in a recent year, 2 percent graduated in such nontraditional fields as agriculture, architecture, and physical sciences. There are no courses on women.

Women and Athletics. Women are 30 percent of the intramural and 41 percent of the intercollegiate athletes. No information is available on athletic scholarships awarded to women. The university boasts a playing field covered by a mini-dome. Facilities are also available for water polo, skiing, bowling, golf, racquetball, and other indoor and outdoor sports. Women compete in intercollegiate basketball, softball, tennis, track, and volleyball.

Housing and Student Organizations. On-campus housing is available in single-sex dormitories with restrictive hours for visitors of the opposite sex. Married students, with and without children, and single parents may also use on-campus housing. Two of four residence-hall directors are women.

Sororities, whose members represent 7 percent of full-time undergraduate women, provide no housing, though fraternities do. Five minority women belong to racially integrated sororities. Organizations that serve as advocates for women include Associated Black Students, Native American Student Association, Mexican American Student Association, Student Association for Female Quality, Non-Traditional Student Caucus, and Idaho State Professional Women.

Special Services and Programs for Women. *Health and Counseling.* Two male physicians and 5 health-care providers (1 of them a man) staff the health service, which offers treatment for gynecological problems and birth control. The counseling service, staffed by 3 white women and 1 man, offers gynecological, birth control, and abortion counseling. The student health insurance policy covers both abortion and maternity costs.

Safety and Security. Measures consist of a rape crisis center and information on rape and assault prevention for women. One assault against a woman was reported on campus for 1980–81.

Other. The local YWCA and the Pocatello Women Advocates offer a women's lecture series, a program for battered women, a warmline, and other events and services of special interest to women.

Institutional Self-Description. "Regarding women's programs at ISU, there is lots of room for growth. ISU reflects a conservative attitude in this area. However, the potential exists for growth and it is relative to the energy of the people to develop. The growth is in the area of nontraditional populations. As support systems can be found or established, such programs may be formed."

University of Idaho
Moscow, ID 83843
Telephone: (208) 885-6111

★ **Women and the Curriculum**

6,210 undergraduates

	Amer. Ind.	Asian Amer.	Blacks	Hispanics	Whites
F	20	24	5	5	2,239
M	16	43	30	9	3,731
%	0.6	1.1	0.6	0.2	97.5

🏠 🏛 👫 ⚒ 🅼🅰 ⚲ **AAUW**

A land-grant institution established in 1889, the University of Idaho, located in a small community close to the Idaho-Washington border, attracts some 8,100 students to a variety of undergraduate and graduate programs. There is an adult continuing education unit. Alternative class schedules, including self-paced learning contracts, evening classes, and off-campus locations, are available.

Women are 37 percent of the 6,210 undergraduates; 12 percent of the women attend part-time. One-fifth of women students are over age 25, and the median age of all undergraduates is 21. For the 30 percent of undergraduates who commute, on-campus parking is available at a fee.

University-sponsored childcare facilities can accommodate 42 children. Private childcare arrangements may be made close to campus.

Policies to Ensure Fairness to Women. A full-time affirmative action officer is responsible for policy on equal employment opportunity, educational sex equity, and handicapped accessibility. A published policy prohibits sexual harassment of students, faculty, and staff. The Committee on Minority Affairs addresses the concerns of minority women.

Women in Leadership Positions. *Students.* Opportunities for women students to exercise all-campus leadership are about average for public research universities in this guide. In recent years women have presided over the student court and residence-hall council, managed the campus radio station, and been editor-in-chief of the newspaper.

Faculty. Women are 13 percent of a full-time faculty of 371. According to a recent report, 1 black, 2 American Indian, and 3 Asian American women are on the faculty. The ratio of female faculty to female students is 2 to 100; of male faculty to male students, 9 to 100.

Administrators. All top administrative posts are filled by men. Of 45 departments, women chair chemistry; home economics; and health, physical education and recreation. Two of eight regents are women.

Women and the Curriculum. The majority of women graduating with bachelor's degrees major in education (25 percent), business (12 percent), agriculture (8 percent), and social sciences (7 percent). Fifteen percent major in nontraditional areas. An innovative program encourages women to prepare for careers in engineering. Fifteen percent of the students in cooperative education programs which combine academic with related work experience are women. Thirty-five percent of internships and at least one-fifth of Forestry and Geology Summer Camp positions go to women.

Courses on women, offered in the departments of English, communications, and psychology, include Women in Literature, Communication of the Feminist Movement, and Human Sexuality.

Women and Athletics. Intramural and intercollegiate programs offer opportunities for organized, competitive, individual and team sports. Club sports are also available. The university reports special facilities for Forestry Club Woodsman Competition. Thirty-seven percent of intercollegiate athletes are women; women receive 30 percent of athletic scholarships. There are six women among the 20 paid intercollegiate coaches. All teams played tournament competition in 1980. The intercollegiate sports offered are basketball, cross-country, field hockey, gymnastics, swimming and diving, tennis, track and field, and volleyball.

Housing and Student Organizations. Seventy percent of undergraduates live on campus. Residential accommodations include single-sex and coeducational dormitories and housing for married students and single parents with children. Men's and coeducational dormitories do not restrict hours for visitors of the opposite sex. In women's dormitories restricted hours are optional. A married woman student whose spouse is not enrolled may live in married students' housing.

Approximately 23 percent of undergraduate women belong to social sororities. Sororities and fraternities provide housing for their members.

Special Services and Programs for Women. *Health and Counseling.* The student health service provides some medical attention specific to women, including gynecological, birth control, and rape and assault treatment. The 3 physicians are men; 3 other health-care providers are women. Regular student health insurance covers maternity at no extra charge. Two of 7 counselors in the counseling service are women. Students have access to gynecological, birth control, abortion, and rape and assault counseling.

Safety and Security. Campus security is a division of the Moscow city police. The campus has a dispatcher, and other university employees act as support personnel. Security measures include an emergency alarm system, self-defense courses for women, information sessions on safety and crime prevention, and a rape crisis center. Two assaults (one on a woman) and one rape were reported for 1980–81.

Other. Student Advisory Services operates a Women's Center, with a full-time director. The Women's Center provides lectures by women employed in nontraditional occupations and nonsexist/

racist printed information on nontraditional fields of study and employment. A battered women's program, assertiveness training, and a telephone line of information, referral, and support are sponsored by the center. The school of home economics sponsors a displaced homemakers' program. The Northwest Gay People's Alliance meets on campus.

Special Features. The Rural Women's History Project collects oral history interviews with women throughout northern Idaho. The New Dimensions Project delivers continuing education workshops and courses on personal growth, communication skills, and mathematics and money to rural women in their communities.

Institutional Self-Description. "The University of Idaho is located in a clean, safe, beautiful small town in northern Idaho; everything is accessible on foot or bicycle. Colleges of Forestry, Engineering, and Agriculture are experiencing dramatic increases in women's enrollments. The university has a creative, supportive, and unique women's community which encourages tolerance, diversity, and growth for women."

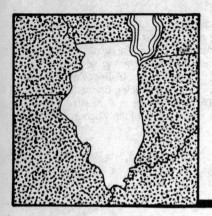

ILLINOIS

Barat College
700 E. Westleigh Road
Lake Forest, IL 60045
Telephone: (312) 234-3000

Women in Leadership	★ Women and the
★★★ students	Curriculum
★★★ faculty	
★★★ administrators	

595 undergraduates

	Amer. Ind.	Asian Amer.	Blacks	Hispanics	Whites
F	0	7	20	9	530
M	0	0	0	0	0
%	0.0	1.2	3.5	1.6	93.6

Founded in 1858, Barat is a non-sectarian, liberal arts college for women that is affiliated with the Roman Catholic Church. The college's suburban campus, located near Lake Michigan, one hour from Chicago, attracts 702 students, of whom 595 are undergraduates. Thirty-six percent of the women attend part-time. The median age of all students is 24. Nearly one-fifth of the students are over age 40.

The college offers a variety of undergraduate degree programs, as well as an adult continuing education program. Classes are offered in the evening and on Saturday. Summer session classes are also available. For the three-fourths of the undergraduates who commute, the campus is accessible by public transportation. On-campus parking is provided at a fee.

Barat's on-campus childcare facility is open to all members of the college community and accommodates 26 children at a fixed hourly fee. Additional, private childcare facilities are available nearby.

Policies to Ensure Fairness to Women. Three officers share the responsibility, on a part-time basis, of monitoring compliance with equal-opportunity legislation. The Title IX Coordinator oversees sex-equity policies and practices; the Director of Health Services oversees handicapped-access provisions; and the Personnel Director handles sex-fair-employment matters and handicapped-access cases for employees. A sexual harassment policy is being developed.

Women in Leadership Positions. *Students.* Women hold all campus-wide student leadership positions.

Faculty. Sixty-four percent of the 33 full-time faculty are women. There are 5 female faculty for every 100 female students.

Administrators. Six of the eight top administrators are women, including the President, chief academic officer, chief development officer, head librarian, and director of institutional research. Women chair eleven of the 18 departments, including economics,

chemistry, biology, mathematics, history, and political science. Nearly all the members of the faculty senate and the tenure, reappointments, and promotions committee are women. Forty-one percent of the lay Board of Trustees are women.

Women and the Curriculum. Most degrees earned by women are in fine arts (20 percent), social sciences (18 percent), business (13 percent), and psychology (13 percent).

All academic departments offer courses which focus on topics of specific interest to women as well as other courses which incorporate material related to women. Students may design an interdisciplinary major in Women's Studies by selecting from these courses. Possibilities include, for example, The Legacy of Eve (humanities), Women in the American Economy (economics), Psychology of Sexual Behavior, Pregnancy and Childbearing (psychology), and Female Image in Western Art (art). The department of mathematics offers a special program to build mathematics confidence in women. Business students receive instruction about the problems of job discrimination, sexual harassment in the workplace, and women in management. The division of education provides instruction on the development and use of sex-fair curricula.

Minority Women. Minority women are 6 percent of all undergraduates. The advocacy group for black women is Black Sisters United. The residence-hall directors and the counseling staff are offered awareness training on the avoidance of racism. The chief student-life officer is a black woman.

Women and Athletics. There are very limited opportunities for women to compete in organized sports. The one paid coach is male. Neither intercollegiate sports nor club sports are available. Forty women participate in intramural basketball and volleyball.

Housing and Student Organizations. Twenty-seven percent of undergraduates live on campus, in dormitories with restrictive hours for male visitors. The two residence-hall directors, one a white woman, are offered awareness-training on racism, sexism, sex education, and birth control. The Barat College chapter of NOW, Black Sisters United, and the Come Back Club for adult students function as advocacy groups for students.

Special Services and Programs for Women. *Health and Counseling.* The student health service employs three female health-care providers and refers students to physicians as needed. Three female counselors, who make up the staff of the counseling center, are offered in-service training on the avoidance of sex-role stereotyping, and on sexuality, divorce, and grief therapy. Counseling is available for gynecological problems, birth control, abortion, and rape and assault.

Safety and Security. Measures include campus police patrols, high-intensity lighting, self-defense courses for women, and information sessions on safety and rape prevention. One assault against a woman and no rapes were reported for 1980–81.

Career. Women are aided in career planning through individual advisement, workshops, and panel discussions by women employed in nontraditional occupations. The college also maintains files on alumnae by specific careers and sponsors programs to help form networks between women students and alumnae.

Other. Special arts programs for women are sponsored by the departments of art, theater, and dance. The Student Affairs Office organizes assertiveness-training programs.

Returning Women Students. Returning women attend the same classes and meet the same requirements as other students. One admissions counselor is responsible solely for advising older women. The Come Back Club organizes special orientation events for reentry women, and the Student Affairs Office sponsors programs for adult returning students, including a support program for displaced homemakers.

Special Features. A Professional Development Program, organized for working women who seek a college degree, will emphasize preparation for public and professional life in addition to a liberal arts education.

Institutional Self-Description. "As a liberal arts college, Barat fosters in students intellectual, professional, and human competence. As a woman's college, its environment and curriculum respond to women's needs and new opportunities. As a small college, its faculty give particular attention to the development of each student."

Bradley University
Peoria, IL 61625
Telephone: (309) 676-7611

Women in Leadership   ★ **Women and Athletics**
★★ students
★ faculty

4,644 undergraduates

	Amer. Ind.	Asian Amer.	Blacks	Hispanics	Whites
F	1	5	194	10	1,747
M	1	14	130	9	2,462
%	0.0	0.4	7.1	0.4	92.0

 AAUW

Founded in 1897 as a polytechnic institute to provide men and women with a practical knowledge of the useful arts and sciences, Bradley, a private nonsectarian institution in Peoria, has been a university since 1947. A variety of undergraduate and graduate programs attracts some 5,200 students. Continuing education offers non-credit courses for adults. Alternative class schedules include audio-visual tape tutorials, a January interim, and a summer session.

Women make up 43 percent of the 4,644 undergraduates; 8 percent of women attend part-time. The median age of undergraduates is 20. For the 48 percent of undergraduates who commute, the university is accessible by public transportation, and there is on-campus parking.

Private childcare arrangements may be made near the university.

Policies to Ensure Fairness to Women. Two part-time equal-opportunity officers review policies and practices related to employment, accessibility of curriculum and activities to all students, and handicapped access. Policy and procedures on the sexual harassment of students have been communicated in writing to faculty and staff. Complaints are handled both informally and confidentially and through a formal grievance procedure.

Women in Leadership Positions. *Students.* In recent years women have been president of the student body, presiding officer of the student senate (twice), editor-in-chief of the newspaper, and presiding officers of the student union board and the residence-hall council. Women head nine of the 20 honorary societies.

Faculty. Women are one-quarter of a full-time faculty of 270.

There is one black woman on the full-time faculty. The ratio of female faculty to female students is 4 to 100; of male faculty to male students, 8 to 100.

Administrators. The director of institutional research is a woman. Women chair nine of 43 departments or divisions: accounting, clinical experiences and field services, home economics, counseling and human development, secondary education, special education, nursing, physical education, and sociology.

Women and the Curriculum. Over half of the women graduating with bachelor's degrees major in the health professions, business, and education. Eight percent major in such nontraditional areas as computer science, engineering, mathematics, and physical sciences. The university reports innovative programs to encourage women to prepare for careers in business and engineering. Women hold over a quarter of the cooperative education and half of the internship positions in experiential learning programs.

An official committee is working to develop a Women's Studies Program. A new course, Introduction to Women's Studies, was taught for the first time in 1981–82. Seven courses on women are available in the departments of English, history, psychology, and sociology. Such current issues as sex-fair curricula, coeducational physical education classes, and innovative health-care delivery are part of the preparation of future teachers and health-care workers.

Minority Women. Eleven percent of the 1,957 undergraduate women are from minority groups, black women being the largest group. Eleven percent of women living in residence halls are black women, 3 percent each are Asian American and Hispanic. There are 75 women in all-minority sororities. Thirteen residence-hall staff are black women. One of the professional staff in the counseling service is a minority woman. Residence-hall and counseling staff are offered training in the avoidance of racial bias.

Women and Athletics. The intramural and intercollegiate programs provide good opportunities for organized, competitive individual and team sports. Club sports are also available. Forty-three percent of intramural and 38 percent of intercollegiate athletes are women; women receive 30 percent of athletic scholarships. Two of the eleven paid intercollegiate coaches are women. The intercollegiate sports offered are basketball, cross-country, softball, tennis, track and field, and volleyball.

Housing and Student Organizations. Fifty-two percent of undergraduates live on campus. Residential accommodations include single-sex and coeducational dormitories. A married woman student whose spouse is not enrolled may live in university housing. Residence halls do not restrict hours for visitors of the opposite sex. Residence-hall staff are offered awareness-training on sexism and other issues.

One-fourth of undergraduate women belong to social sororities. Sororities and fraternities provide housing for their members. Among student groups that serve as advocates for women are the Council on Women's Awareness, which sponsors an annual women's week and lecture series, and the Nontraditional (Reentry) Women's Organization.

Special Services and Programs for Women. *Health and Counseling.* The student health service provides some medical attention specific to women: gynecological and rape and assault treatment is available. The health service physician is male; the three nurses are female. Two of five professional staff in the counseling center are women. Students have access to gynecological, birth control, abortion, and rape and assault counseling. Staff receive in-service training on sex-role stereotyping. The counseling center sponsors assertiveness training and a telephone service of information, referral, and support.

Safety and Security. Measures consist of campus police with arrest authority, night-time escort for women students, high-intensity lighting, information sessions on safety and crime prevention conducted by campus security officers, and a rape crisis center. Ten assaults (six on women) and no rapes were reported for 1980-81.

Career. The university provides materials and activities focused on women in nontraditional occupations and fields of study. The career library has a special section on women and minorities.

Institutional Self-Description. "For a university of its size, Bradley has a wide range of extracurricular and sports activities for women. Women's enrollments have grown substantially in both the College of Business and Engineering and Technology."

City Colleges of Chicago, Loop College

64 East Lake Street, Chicago, IL 60601
Telephone: (312) 269-8000

Women in Leadership
★★ faculty

6,814 undergraduates

	Amer. Ind.	Asian Amer.	Blacks	Hispanics	Whites
F	0	111	3,252	272	542
M	0	64	1,386	175	306
%	0.0	2.9	75.9	7.3	13.9

Loop College provides programs that parallel the first two years of traditional institutions. It also provides occupational and adult education programs, as well as remedial and special services. Alternative schedules include evening classes (on and off campus) and a summer session; a weekend college is being planned. Some 7,800 students attend the college, 6,814 of whom are registered in degree programs. Sixty-four percent of degree students are women; 76 percent of the women attend part-time. The median age of all undergraduates is 28. All students commute. Public transportation is available; there is no on-campus parking.

Private childcare facilities are located near the campus.

Policies to Ensure Fairness to Women. The Vice-Chancellor is responsible for equal employment opportunity and sex equity for students.

Women in Leadership Positions. *Students.* In a recent three-year period, no woman held a campus-wide office.

Faculty. Thirty-seven percent of the 182 full-time faculty are women, a proportion above the average for public two-year colleges in this guide. There are 6 female faculty for every 100 female students and 17 male faculty for every 100 male students.

Administrators. The chief student-life officer is a black woman. Other top administrators are men. Women chair the departments of counseling, speech, and social studies.

Women and the Curriculum. Women earn two-thirds of the two-year degrees and certificates awarded, mostly in arts and sciences (60 percent) and business (28 percent). The college sponsors programs to encourage women to prepare for careers in engineering, architecture, accounting, computer science, and law enforcement. Eighty percent of students in cooperative education programs are women.

Two courses on women are offered in the English and social science departments: Women in Literature, and Women in History. The division of social work includes issues of concern to women in its courses. Faculty workshops are offered on affirmative action and equal opportunity.

Women and Athletics. The college does not have an organized athletics program.

Special Services and Programs for Women. *Health and Counseling.* The student health service is staffed by two female health-care providers; the counseling center employs five women, three of them minority women. No medical services specific to women are provided; but counseling on gynecological matters, birth control, and abortion is available.

Safety and Security. Measures consist of local police, armed campus police with arrest authority, night-time escort for women

students, and information sessions on campus safety security. No rapes or assaults on women were reported for 1980–81.

Career. Services include workshops, nonsexist/nonracist printed materials, and job discrimination information on nontraditional occupations. The Office of Career Programs sponsors an annual women's week. Women's success seminars are offered each year.

Institutional Self-Description. "Loop College is located in Chicago's business district, making it an ideal location for working women and women returning to the work-world. Returning women students feel comfortable at Loop College; the median age of students is 28, and a returning women students' support group is being established. In addition, our female faculty serve as competent and supportive role models."

City Colleges of Chicago, Wilbur Wright College

3400 N. Austin Avenue, Chicago, IL 60634
Telephone: (312) 777-7900

Women in Leadership
★ students
★ faculty

2,893 undergraduates

	Amer. Ind.	Asian Amer.	Blacks	Hispanics	Whites
F	4	15	208	80	761
M	6	26	299	118	1,163
%	0.4	1.5	18.9	7.4	71.8

Founded in 1935, this two-year municipal college serves 7,126 students, 40 percent of whom are women. Two-thirds of women attend part-time; one-third are over age 25. The median age of undergraduates is 22. Twenty-eight percent of women students are from minority groups.

Wright offers the first two years of liberal arts and a variety of pre-professional programs for transfer to four-year colleges. It also offers 15 career-oriented technical-occupation programs, a general studies program, and an adult continuing education program. The adult reentry program is responsible for continuing education for women. A summer session is available.

All students commute to the campus, which is accessible by public transportation. On-campus parking is also available.

Policies to Ensure Fairness to Women. The business manager has full-time responsibility for monitoring compliance with laws regulating equal employment opportunity, sex equity for students, and handicapped access. An informal and confidential mechanism resolves complaints of sexual harassment.

Women in Leadership Positions. *Students.* Opportunities are good for women students to exercise campus leadership. In three recent years, a woman served as presiding officer of the student governing body once, and editor-in-chief of the campus newspaper twice. One of the two presidents of honorary societies is a woman.

Faculty. One-fourth of the 192 full-time faculty are women. Of the 46 female faculty, 3 are black women. There are 4 female faculty for every 100 female students and 8 male faculty for every 100 male students.

Administrators. All seven of the chief administrators are men. Women serve as the Director of Adult Education and the Dean of Career Programs and General Studies. The departments of mathematics, foreign languages, home economics, and business are chaired by women. One of the trustees is a black woman.

Women and the Curriculum. The most popular two-year degree area for women is arts and sciences, followed by business and commerce, data processing, and health technologies.

Three departments—humanities, biology, English—offer three courses on women: Women in the Performing Arts, Biology of Women, and Women's Literature.

Women and Athletics. Seven percent of intramural athletes and 21 percent of intercollegiate athletes are women. Of eleven paid coaches for intercollegiate sports, three are women. The intercollegiate sports that women participate in include basketball, cross-country, track and field, softball, tennis, and volleyball.

Special Services and Programs for Women. *Health and Counseling.* Limited student health services are provided by 1 male physician and 2 female health-care providers. The student counseling center has a staff of 9, 2 of whom are women. Counseling, but not treatment, is provided on issues related to gynecology, birth control, abortion, and rape and assault.

Safety and Security. Measures consist of campus police with authority to make arrests, and high-intensity lighting in all areas. There were no rapes or assaults reported for 1980-81.

Career. Women are encouraged to consider nontraditional occupations through career workshops, lectures and panels by women employed in nontraditional occupations, contact with alumnae, and printed information on nontraditional occupations and fields of study for women. Faculty are offered workshops on nontraditional occupations for women and men and on the special needs of reentry women.

Other. The Black Student Union is 80 percent female and led by a female president.

Returning Women Students. The 30 active members of Wright Women offer a peer counseling session each week to provide friendship and encouragement to reentry women. The alumnae of the group return to Wright each year to meet with older women students and displaced homemakers.

Coordinated by a full-time, minority female administrator, the Adult Reentry Program provides continuing education for women. Special services, such as a women's lecture series, assertiveness/leadership training, and a telephone line for information and referrals, are provided through the division of adult education.

Institutional Self-Description. "Wright College and the Adult Reentry Program provide assistance to help adults, primarily women, return to college. Women who seek to enlarge their horizons, who seek job training, or who seek changes in their lives are equally welcome at Wright. Special programs are set up to enable women to plan classes around their children's school hours or around job hours. Our job placement program helps women find suitable positions."

Concordia College
7400 Augusta, River Forest, IL 60305
Telephone: (312) 771-8300

★ **Women and Athletics**

871 undergraduates

	Amer. Ind.	Asian Amer.	Blacks	Hispanics	Whites
F	0	4	13	3	525
M	0	0	10	1	312
%	0.0	0.5	2.7	0.5	96.4

Concordia College is a private, four-year college affiliated with the Lutheran Church. Founded to educate parochial-school teachers, its mission was broadened in 1972 to that of a liberal arts college and to education for other church professions. The campus, in a multi-racial area near Chicago, serves 1,182 students. Women are 63 percent of the 871 undergraduates; all but a few of the women attend full-time. The median age of all students is 20, but about 8 percent of the women students are over age 25.

Ninety-five percent of the students live on campus. On-campus parking for a fee is available for commuters.

Private childcare facilities are available near campus at $5.40 per day. The highest priority is given to community children, then to faculty, staff, and part-time and non-credit students.

Policies to Ensure Fairness to Women. Three officers are responsible part-time for different aspects of affirmative action. There is no written policy on sexual harassment, but a formal procedure resolves complaints. The Multicultural Committee addresses the concerns of minority women.

Women in Leadership Positions. *Students.* One woman held a campus-wide leadership position during a recent three-year period.

Faculty. Twenty-one percent of the 75 full-time faculty are women, a proportion lower than the national average. Half of the 16 faculty women hold permanent appointments. There are 3 female faculty for every 100 female students, and 19 male faculty for every 100 male students.

Administrators. All top administrators are male. Of the 14 department heads, 2 are female: the chairs of speech and drama, and natural sciences. Two of the 5 honorary degree recipients in spring 1981 were female.

Women and the Curriculum. The majority of degrees for women and men are earned in education.

One course on women, The Psychology of Women, is offered by the department of psychology. The physical education department provides instruction in how to teach coeducational classes in physical education.

Women and Athletics. Concordia offers good opportunities for women to participate in organized competitive sports. Ten intramural and seven intercollegiate sports are offered. Five of the eleven paid varsity coaches are women. Intercollegiate sports are basketball, gymnastics, field hockey, softball, tennis, track and field, and volleyball.

Housing and Student Organizations. Single-sex dormitories restrict hours for visitors of the opposite sex. The residence-hall directors, two men, two white women, and one minority woman, are offered awareness-training on the avoidance of sexism, and on sex education and rape.

Special Services and Programs for Women. *Health and Counseling.* The student health service employs one male physician; the counseling center has one male and one female counselor. Gynecological, birth control, abortion, and rape and assault counseling but not medical treatment is provided.

Safety and Security. Measures include a campus police force, high-intensity lights, and self-defense and safety and rape prevention instruction for women. No rapes or assaults were reported for 1980-81.

Institutional Self-Description. None provided.

De Lourdes College
353 North River Rd., Des Plaines, IL 60016
Telephone: (312) 208-6942

Women in Leadership
★★★ **faculty**
★★★ **administrators**

103 undergraduates

	Amer. Ind.	Asian Amer.	Blacks	Hispanics	Whites
F	0	1	0	0	102
M	0	0	0	0	0
%	0.0	1.0	0.0	0.0	99.0

De Lourdes, a private, four-year teachers' college for Roman Catholic women, is located in the small city of Des Plaines. Of 294 students enrolled, 103 are undergraduates; 27 percent of them attend part-time. The median age of all students is 38. Classes are held on and off campus, during the day and evening; there is also a summer session. All students commute. Parking on campus is available.

Private childcare facilities are available near the campus

Women in Leadership Positions. *Students.* There are no campus-wide student leadership positions.

Faculty. The seven full-time faculty are women.

Administrators. Women hold all key administrative positions. Of six departments, five are chaired by women: education, theology, music, science, and mathematics. All nine trustees are women.

Women and the Curriculum. With a few exceptions, most students specialize in education. There are no courses on women.

Women and Athletics. There are no opportunities for organized competitive sports.

Special Services and Programs for Women. *Health and Counseling.* There is no student health service or student counseling center.

Safety and Security. Measures consist of local police and high-intensity lighting. No rapes or assaults on women were reported for 1980–81.

Other. The college sponsors assertiveness-training sessions for students.

Institutional Self-Description. "De Lourdes is a women's college with a program primarily designed to prepare teachers for elementary schools. Special efforts are made to accommodate the needs of mature women who wish to complete an interrupted college education. Convenient hours provide opportunity for part-time study for women who because of family responsibilities cannot undertake full-time study."

Felician College
3800 W. Peterson Avenue
Chicago, IL 60659
Telephone: (312) 539-1919

Women in Leadership
★★★ students
★★★ faculty
★★★ administrators

197 undergraduates

	Amer. Ind.	Asian Amer.	Blacks	Hispanics	Whites
F	0	3	7	17	117
M	0	4	0	0	17
%	0.0	4.2	4.2	10.3	81.2

Established in 1953 to educate members of the Felician Order, this private, Roman Catholic, two-year college now serves 431 students, 197 of whom are in degree programs. Eighty percent of students are women, just over half of whom attend part-time. The median age of undergraduates is 23.

The college offers transfer and terminal programs in liberal arts and pre-professional education. Evening classes are offered, both on and off campus; a summer session is available. The college is accessible by public transportation. On-campus parking and free transportation from remote lots are available.

Women in Leadership Positions. *Students.* Both student lead-

ership positions—the president of the student body, and the presiding officer of the student governing body—have been held by women in recent years.

Faculty. All full-time faculty are women. There are 16 female faculty for every 100 female students.

Administrators. All top administrative positions are held by women. Most of the trustees are women. In 1981, a woman received the sole honorary degree awarded.

Women and the Curriculum. All degrees awarded are in arts and sciences. Women are encouraged to enter nontraditional careers through programs in science, accounting, and computer science. There are no courses on women.

Women and Athletics. There are no intercollegiate or club sports at the college. Two-thirds of intramural athletes are women, who have opportunities to participate in team and individual sports.

Special Services and Programs for Women. *Health and Counseling.* There is no student health service. Counseling is available on rape and assault.

Safety and Security. No information was provided.

Career. Career workshops on nontraditional occupations, as well as lectures and panels by women employed in such occupations, are available. Faculty are offered workshops on nontraditional occupations for women and men and the needs of reentry women.

Institutional Self-Description. "The environment at Felician is conducive to study. Counseling and guidance services assist students in self-evaluation; financial aid is available in the form of scholarships, grants, and work-study programs. The tuition note is reasonable; library facilities are extensive; and the location is easily accessible."

Governors State University
Rt. 54 at Stunkel Rd.
Park Forest South, IL 60466
Telephone: (312) 534-5000

Women in Leadership	**★ Women and the**
★★★ students	**Curriculum**
★ faculty	

1,238 undergraduates

	Amer. Ind.	Asian Amer.	Blacks	Hispanics	Whites
F	2	3	257	16	377
M	1	1	140	11	421
%	0.2	0.3	32.3	2.2	64.9

This public, commuter university, located near Chicago, offers bachelor's and master's programs. Some 3,900 students enroll. Women make up 53 percent of the 1,238 undergraduates, 60 percent of women attend part-time. The median age of undergraduate students is 35.

The college offers alternative part-time and full-time schedules, based on a 12-month trimester calendar which includes evening classes, summer session, weekend college, and contract learning. The Board of Governors and the University Without Walls offer two special degree programs. A continuing education program is available. On-campus parking for a fee and public transportation are available.

An on-campus childcare facility, open from 8:30 a.m. to 7:30 p.m. charges an hourly rate plus lunch fee; it can accommodate 95 percent of requests. Full-time students receive priority.

Policies to Ensure Fairness to Women. An assistant to the president is assigned part-time responsibility for policy on equal employment opportunity, educational sex-equity, and handicapped access. A published campus policy prohibits sexual harassment of students, faculty, and staff. Complaints are resolved informally and confidentially or through a formal grievance procedure. A Commission on Minority Affairs addresses the concerns of minority women.

Women in Leadership Positions. *Students.* Opportunities for women to exercise leadership on campus are outstanding. Of the two campus-wide leadership positions available in recent years, a woman has been editor-in-chief of the newspaper for three terms and president of the student senate for one term.

Faculty. Women are 34 percent of the 158 full-time faculty members, significantly above average for public four-year colleges. There are 21 female faculty for every 100 female students and 62 male faculty for every 100 male students. The high proportion of part-time students contributes to making the faculty-to-student ratios much higher than for other institutions in this guide.

Administrators. The head librarian is a woman. The rest of the top administrative posts are held by men. A black woman and a white woman chair 2 of 16 departments: health, sciences, and nursing. Five of 14 members of the Board of Governors program are women, 2 of whom are black women. One of 2 commencement speakers at the 1981 commencement was a woman.

Women and the Curriculum. Most women take degrees in education (29 percent), public affairs (21 percent), and interdisciplinary studies (22 percent). Three-fourths of students in the internship program and 60 percent of students in the cooperative education program are women. Forty-six percent of students in the Board of Governors program and 44 percent of the participants in the University Without Walls program are women.

The Women's Studies Program offers the B.A. and M.A. degrees through the social sciences division of the College of Arts and Sciences. The program is administered part-time by a permanent faculty member. An official committee is responsible for developing the program, as well as for encouraging the development of courses in traditional departments. Faculty workshops focus on the needs of reentry women and on issues related to affirmative action.

Women and Athletics. The university reports that it does not offer in intercollegiate or intramural sports. All recreational activities are run by the adjacent YMCA.

Special Services and Programs for Women. *Health and Counseling.* A student health service with one woman health-care provider and a student counseling service staffed by four women and three men provide counseling but not treatment for gynecological problems, birth control, abortion, rape and assault.

Safety and Security. Measures consist of campus police with authority to make arrests and high-intensity lighting in all areas. Three assaults against women and no rapes were reported for 1980–81.

Other. The Women's Resource Center, administered by a salaried faculty member under the auspices of the Office of Student Activities, serves 200 members of the college and neighboring community each year; one-fourth of the women who use the center are black women. Monthly "Brown Bag Lunches," sponsored by the Women's Center, feature "women of national acclaim" speaking on a wide range of subjects.

The Office of Special Programs administers the adult continuing education program which attracts 866 reentry women students each year, 15 percent of whom are black women.

Institutional Self-Description. "Governors State Univesity is a future-oriented, service-directed, experimenting institution for commuter students. It has been planned to be open, flexible, humane, efficient, utilitarian, and academically excellent. Its unusual programs encourage innovative search for solutions to many of humanity's most profound problems."

Illinois State University
Normal, IL 61761
Telephone: (309) 436-7657

Women in Leadership	★ Women and the
★ faculty	Curriculum
	★★ Women and Athletics

16,648 undergraduates

	Amer. Ind.	Asian Amer.	Blacks	Hispanics	Whites
F	32	49	1,011	54	8,232
M	19	36	629	39	6,426
%	0.3	0.5	10.9	0.6	88.0

 AAUW NWSA

Founded in 1857 as a state-supported teachers' college, the institution changed its name to Illinois State University when it became multi-purpose in 1966. Eighty percent of the 20,158 students are undergraduates, of whom 54 percent are women. Six percent of the female undergraduates are part-time students.

The university offers a wide range of liberal arts and professional/vocational programs. Alternative schedules are available through self-paced learning and off-campus classes. Students have the option of fulfilling general education requirements through completely individualized programs. Adult students are served by the College of Continuing Education. The university is accessible by public transportation. On-campus parking is available at a fee for the 54 percent of students who commute.

University-sponsored on-campus childcare facilities can accommodate 70 percent of requests by students. Private facilities are available off campus.

Policies to Ensure Fairness to Women. The institution employs two full-time affirmative action officers, one for white women and one for members of minority groups. A written policy prohibiting sexual harassment of students, faculty, and staff has been publicly communicated to the university community. Complaints may be resolved informally or through a formal grievance procedure. The Committee on the Status of Women, which includes student representatives, advises the affirmative action officer for women, takes public stands on issues of student concern, and addresses the concerns of minority women. The Commission on Minority Affairs also addresses the interests of minority women.

Women in Leadership Positions. *Students.* Opportunities for women to exercise student leadership are not proportional to their representation in the student body, since men hold the top student offices three-fourths of the time. Women head ten of the 20 honorary societies.

Faculty. Twenty-six percent of the 826 full-time faculty are women. There are 2 female faculty for every 100 female students and 9 male faculty for every 100 male students.

Administrators. One of the top administrators, the head of women's athletics, is a woman. Women chair three departments: economics; home economics; and sociology, anthropology, and social work. A woman received 1 of the 2 honorary degrees awarded at the 1981 commencement. Two of the 15 alumni awards for 1980–81 went to women.

Women and the Curriculum. One-third of degrees awarded to women are in education, with significant numbers also in business and public affairs. The proportion of women who major in public affairs is 25 percent above the national average. Four percent of degrees to women are in the nontraditional fields of agriculture, computer science, engineering, mathematics, and physical sciences.

The Women's Studies Program offers 19 Women's Studies courses through the program and 13 departments, including Research in Women's Studies, Minority Relations, Philosophy of Feminism, Studies in Women and Literature, and Women in Management. A full-time, permanent faculty member directs the program part-time. The program offers an undergraduate minor, an individualized "contract" major, and a graduate minor. In addition, graduate students may choose Women's Studies as their area of emphasis.

Women and Athletics. Illinois State offers a good program of intramural and intercollegiate sports for women. Women account for 41 percent of the intercollegiate athletes and receive 37 percent of athletic scholarship funds. Thirteen of the 37 paid varsity coaches are women. Intercollegiate sports for women are badminton, basketball, cross-country, field hockey, golf, gymnastics, softball, swimming, tennis, track, and volleyball.

Housing and Student Organizations. Forty-six percent of undergraduates live on campus in single sex or coeducational dormitories, or in fraternity or sorority houses. All single students who attend full-time are required to live in dormitories their first four semesters. University housing is available for single students with children and married students with or without children. Seven of the 15 dormitory directors are women, including two minority women. Awareness-training on racism, sexism, and sex education is offered to dormitory staff.

Women are almost half of the 1,250 members of Greek organizations. Eighty minority women belong to all-minority sororities. Most of the members of the two student advocacy organizations, the Peace and Justice Coalition and the Worker-Student Alliance, are women.

Special Services and Programs for Women. *Health and Counseling.* The health service has 3 male physicians, 1 female physician, and 34 other health-care providers, of whom all but 3 are women. Seven of the 23-member staff of the student counseling staff are women, including 3 minority women. Counseling is available for gynecological problems, birth control, abortion, and rape, and medical care for all items except abortion. The regular student health insurance policy covers maternity and abortion at no extra cost. Counselors receive in-service training on sex-role stereotyping and racial bias.

Safety and Security. Campus police with weapons training and arrest authority are supplemented by local police. Security measures include night escort for women students, emergency alarm and telephone systems, self-defense courses, and a rape crisis center. Five rapes and 61 assaults on men and women were reported for 1980–81.

Career. Women students have access to information about non-traditional careers, job discrimination, and student-alumnae networks.

Other. The counseling center provides information about services for battered women and displaced homemakers, as well as training in assertiveness and leadership. The Women Faculty Association and the Women's Student Association sponsor an annual women's week and women's lecture series. The mathematics department offers a mathematics-confidence training course.

Special Features. With funding from national and state arts and humanities councils, the university has sponsored a widely-shown art exhibit of "African-American Women, 1862–1980" and a concert tour of music by women composers.

Institutional Self-Description. "Illinois State University is committed to quality teaching at all levels, offers more than 100 academic degree programs, and awards scholarships and graduate assistantships equitably. Fifty-four percent of those enrolled are women and there is overall campus respect for women students. The undergraduate program is complemented by strong graduate programs."

Kaskaskia College,
Shattuc Road, Centralia, IL 62801
Telephone: (618) 532-1981

Women in Leadership
★ faculty

2,789 undergraduates

	Amer. Ind.	Asian Amer.	Blacks	Hispanics	Whites
F	7	6	45	3	1,670
M	6	5	32	4	1,009
%	0.5	0.4	2.8	0.3	96.1

Kaskaskia College, formerly Centralia Junior College, is a public, two-year institution serving 2,789 students, 62 percent of whom are women. Seventy percent of women are enrolled part-time, and 45 percent of women are over age 25. The median age of students is 28.

The college offers transfer degrees in liberal arts and a variety of pre-professional, as well as one- and two-year occupational programs in a range of business, mechanical, and health technologies. Kaskaskia offers day and evening classes both on and off campus, self-paced/contract learning, and a summer session. Located on a rural campus in southern Illinois, the college is accessible only by car; free on-campus parking is available.

On-campus childcare is provided from 8 a.m. to 4:30 p.m at a flat rate of $4.50 a day.

Women in Leadership Positions. *Students.* Women have few opportunities to exercise student leadership. Of the two positions available during a recent three-year period, a woman has co-edited the campus newspaper one semester.

Faculty. The full-time faculty of 57 are 30 percent female, a proportion slightly lower than average for public community colleges, but higher than the national average. There are 3 female faculty for every 100 female students and 9 male faculty for every 100 male students.

Administrators. One of the eight chief administrators, the head librarian is a woman. The sole department chaired by a woman is health occupations. One of the eight trustees is a woman.

Women and the Curriculum. Most two-year degrees and certificates awarded to women are in the arts and sciences, health technologies, and business and commerce. A few women graduate in the fields of data processing and public service. Over two-thirds of students enrolled in internships and practicums—forms of experiential learning—are women. Courses in the schools of nursing, social work, and business provide instruction on some matters specific to women. Faculty are offered workshops on sexism and the curriculum, nontraditional occupations for women and men, and affirmative action and equal opportunity. No courses on women are offered.

Women and Athletics. Women have limited opportunities to participate in athletics. Fifteen women play intramural volleyball. Intercollegiate sports for women include basketball, softball, tennis, and volleyball.

Special Services and Programs for Women. *Health and Counseling.* There is no student health service. The student counseling center has a staff of four, two of whom are women. No services specific to women are available.

Safety and Security. Measures consist of campus police without authority to make arrests, night-time escort for women students, and high-intensity lighting in all areas. For 1980–81 one assault on a woman was reported on campus.

Career. The college provides career workshops and printed material on nontraditional occupations, as well as an updated file of alumnae by specific careers.

Institutional Self-Description. "Women students at Kaskaskia College of all ages, occupations, and interests seem to be relatively comfortable with the college and its programs. Kaskaskia affirms that education is a life-long process and accepts the responsibility of making it possible for students to participate in learning activities to the maximum of their potentialities."

Loyola University of Chicago
Chicago, IL 60611
Telephone: (312) 670-2910

| Women in Leadership | ★ Women and the |
| ★ faculty | Curriculum |

7,451 undergraduates

	Amer. Ind.	Asian Amer.	Blacks	Hispanics	Whites
F	5	92	473	177	3,104
M	6	76	234	141	3,060
%	0.2	2.3	9.6	4.3	83.7

 AAUW NWSA

Founded in 1869 as a private, Jesuit institution, Loyola University of Chicago offers a wide range of undergraduate, graduate, and professional programs. Some 13,100 students enroll. The division of continuing education and University College are responsible for adult continuing education programs. Alternative schedules, including Saturday and evening classes, and a summer session, are available.

Women are 52 percent of the 7,451 undergraduates; 22 percent of women attend part-time. About one-fifth of women are over age 25. The median age of undergraduates is 22. Seventy percent of undergraduates live off campus or commute. The university is accessible by public transportation. On-campus parking is available for a fee.

Private childcare arrangements can be made near the university.

Policies to Ensure Fairness to Women. The Vice President for Administration is responsible for policy on equal employment opportunity, accessibility of curriculum and activities to all students, and handicapped access. A campus policy that prohibits sexual harassment is in the process of being communicated to students; complaints are handled through a formal grievance procedure. A Committee on Minority Affairs addresses the concerns of minority women.

Women in Leadership Positions. *Students.* Women twice presided over the student union board and were editor-in-chief of the newspaper, manager of the campus radio station, and presiding officer of the residence-hall council. Three honorary societies are headed by women.

Faculty. Women are 28 percent of a full-time faculty of 553, a proportion which is above the average for comparable institutions in this guide. There are 5 female faculty for every 100 female students and 14 male faculty for every 100 male students.

Administrators. The chief student-life officer is a woman. Other top administrative positions are occupied by men. Women chair 13 of 39 departments. One black and one Hispanic woman are department heads. The Dean of the School of Nursing is female.

Women and the Curriculum. Most women graduating with bachelor's degrees major in the health professions (36 percent),

business, psychology, and social sciences (10 percent each), and the biological sciences (9 percent). Two percent major in computer science, mathematics, and the physical sciences. The College of Arts and Sciences offers a program to build mathematics and science skills among women.

The Women's Studies Program, under a director who holds a full-time faculty position, offers a 15-credit undergraduate minor. In addition to three Women's Studies courses, 12 courses on women are available in the departments of anthropology classical studies, communication arts, English, German, history, physical education, and sociology. Recent offerings include Sex Discrimination and the Law, Women in Cross-Cultural Perspectives, Women in Contemporary Drama, and American Women Black and White.

Minority Women. Of 3,851 undergraduate women, 12 percent are black, less than 1 percent American Indian, 2 percent Asian American, and 5 percent Hispanic. Two minority women are on the professional staff of the counseling service; a minority woman directs a residence hall. Residence-hall and counseling staffs are offered training on the avoidance of racial bias. Among student groups which address minority women's interests are the African-American Student Association, the Oriental Student Association, the Latin American Student Organization, and the Black Cultural Center.

Women and Athletics. Intramural and intercollegiate programs provide limited opportunities for organized competitive sports. Twenty-nine percent of intercollegiate athletes are female. Athletic scholarships are awarded. One of the seven paid varsity coaches is a woman. The intercollegiate sports offered are basketball, swimming and diving, track and field, and volleyball.

Housing and Student Organizations. Thirty percent of undergraduates live in single-sex and coeducational residence halls. Community floors are run cooperatively with the University Ministry. Residence halls restrict hours for visitors of the opposite sex. Awareness-training is offered to staff on sexism and rape prevention.

Five percent of undergraduate women belong to social sororities. Sororities and fraternities provide housing for members.

Special Services and Programs for Women. *Health and Counseling.* The student health service provides some medical attention specific to women, including gynecological and rape and assault treatment. One of the four physicians is female, as are six other health-care providers. Half of the professional staff in the counseling service are women. Gynecological, birth control, abortion, and rape and assault counseling is available. Staff receive in-service training on the avoidance of sex-role stereotyping.

Safety and Security. Measures consist of campus police with arrest authority, night-time escorts for women students, high-intensity lighting, an emergency alarm system, self-defense courses for women, information sessions on safety and crime prevention, and a rape crisis center. No assaults on women or rapes were reported for 1980–81.

Career. Information and activities which concentrate on women in nontraditional occupations and fields of study are provided.

Other. The Women's Studies Program sponsors lecture series, an annual women's week, and, in conjunction with theater and fine arts departments, women's cultural programs. Assertiveness training is offered by the division of continuing education.

Institutional Self-Description. "Over 7,000 women chose to study at Loyola this year because of: 1) Loyola's commitment to ethics, values, and the dignity of individuals; 2) excellent undergraduate, graduate, and professional academic programs; 3) academic support programs in reading, writing, and mathematics; and 4) extensive student services and counseling programs."

Midstate College
244 S.W. Jefferson, Peoria, IL 61602
Telephone: (309) 673-6365

Women in Leadership
★★★ faculty
★★★ administrators

321 undergraduates

	Amer. Ind.	Asian Amer.	Blacks	Hispanics	Whites
F	0	3	22	0	178
M	0	0	16	0	101
%	0.0	0.9	11.9	0.0	87.2

A public, two-year college, Midstate offers liberal arts courses as well as career and vocational programs in such fields as court reporting, fashion, data processing, and accounting. Of 321 students, 63 percent are women. The median age of all students is 19. Public transportation, but not on-campus parking, is available to students who commute. Eighteen percent of female students live on campus in single-sex dormitories that have restrictive hours for male visitors.

Private childcare is available off campus.

Women in Leadership Positions. *Students.* Men held the only campus leadership position, that of student body president, during a recent three-year period.

Faculty. Of eight full-time faculty, five are women. For both women and men, the ratio of faculty to students is 3 to 100.

Administrators. Women hold five positions, including vice president, chief academic officer, business officer, development officer, and head librarian. Women also chair the secretarial, court-reporter, fashion, airlines, and English departments. An Hispanic woman is Dean of the College.

Women and the Curriculum. Seventy-three percent of degrees awarded to women are in business programs. The college offers no courses on women.

Women and Athletics. Women have no opportunity for organized competitive sports.

Special Services and Programs for Women. *Health and Counseling.* Midstate provides no services.

Safety and Security. Local police patrol the campus, which is equipped with high-intensity lighting. No rapes or assaults on women were reported for 1980-81.

Institutional Self-Description. ''Eighty to 85 percent of students are women. Most programs are oriented to women.''

Monmouth College
Monmouth, IL 61462
Telephone: (309) 457-2311

Women in Leadership
★ students

659 undergraduates

	Amer. Ind.	Asian Amer.	Blacks	Hispanics	Whites
F	0	1	12	3	292
M	0	1	15	3	309
%	0.0	0.3	4.3	0.9	94.5

AAUW

Monmouth College, a four-year, coeducational institution affiliated with the United Presbyterian Church, is located on a 30-acre campus in a residential area nine miles southwest of Chicago. Enrollment is 659 students, of whom 48 percent are women. All students attend full-time. Ninety-five percent of the students reside on campus. For commuters there is free parking on campus.

Policies to Ensure Fairness to Women. An informal mechanism resolves complaints of sexual harassment.

Women in Leadership Positions. *Students.* Women have good opportunities to exercise campus-wide student leadership.

Faculty. Of the 52 full-time faculty, 6 are women, 4 of them holding permanent appointments. There are 2 female faculty for every 100 female students, and 13 male faculty for every 100 male students.

Administrators. Men hold all key positions. Women chair two of 21 academic departments—classics and sociology.

Women and the Curriculum. Most degrees awarded to women are in education (30 percent), social sciences (16 percent), and letters (13 percent). All two-year degrees awarded to women are in arts and sciences. There are no courses on women.

Women and Athletics. For a college of its size, Monmouth's intramural program offers a wide variety of sports. Two of the 10 paid varsity coaches are women. Intercollegiate sports in which women participate are basketball, softball, tennis, and volleyball.

Housing and Student Organizations. Single-sex and coeducational dormitories have restrictive hours for visitors of the opposite sex. The residence-hall directors, three women and three men, are offered awareness training on sexism, sex education, racism, birth control, and alcohol abuse.

Almost half of all undergraduates belong to social fraternities and sororities. An Association of Women Students serves as an advocate for women, and a coeducational Black Action and Affairs Council addresses the concerns of black women.

Special Services and Programs for Women. *Health and Counseling.* The campus health service employs one female health-care provider. The counseling center has one male and one female counselor. No information was provided about counseling or medical treatment for matters specific to women.

Safety and Security. Measures consist of campus police and high-intensity lighting. No assaults or rapes were reported on campus in 1980–81.

Institutional Self-Description. ''In the classroom and in a broad range of extracurricular opportunities, Monmouth College stresses that personal interests are fully cultivated and personal values examined only through participation. Our smallness affords all our students the opportunity to take part, not just the stars, and to know themselves through knowing others.''

Mundelein College
6363 N. Sheridan Road Chicago, IL 60660
Telephone: (312) 262-8100

Women in Leadership
★★★ students
★★★ faculty
★★★ administrators

★ Women and the
Curriculum

1,471 undergraduates

	Amer. Ind.	Asian Amer.	Blacks	Hispanics	Whites
F	2	23	223	69	1,023
M	0	1	19	6	74
%	0.1	1.7	16.8	5.2	76.2

AAUW

Founded in 1929 as a liberal arts college for women, Mundelein is affiliated with the Roman Catholic Church. The campus, situated in a racially mixed community in Chicago, along Lake

Michigan's shoreline, draws 1,563 students. Of the 1,471 undergraduates, 93 percent are women, and 44 percent of women attend part-time. Seventeen percent of undergraduates are age 40 or older, which is reflected in the high median age of the student body—27.

Mundelein offers a range of undergraduate, pre-professional, and professional degrees as well as a master's degree in religious studies and a large continuing education program. Adult students may pursue independent study or enroll in the Weekend College in Residence, which is coeducational. Fifty-three percent of undergraduates commute, by public transportation or car, and there is parking on campus for a fee.

Private childcare facilities are located both on and near the campus. The campus facility, a pre-school and kindergarten, accommodates 40 children on a first-come, first-served basis. The fee is $11 for a full day and $7 for a half day.

Policies to Ensure Fairness to Women. An Affirmative Action Officer is responsible part-time for monitoring compliance with sex-equity, sex-fair-employment, and handicapped-access laws. A Committee for Women reports to the Academic Dean and President on matters of concern to women; it also addresses the concerns of minority women. The committee, which includes students as voting members, plans special programs such as the women's history week.

Women in Leadership Positions. *Students.* Women have outstanding opportunities to exercise leadership, and in recent years have presided over the student body, the student judiciary, four honorary societies, and managed the campus radio station.

Faculty. Seventy-four percent of the 73 full-time faculty are women, a proportion far above the average for women's colleges. There are 7 female faculty for every 100 female students.

Administrators. Except for two positions, women hold all the top posts, including that of President. Three-fourths of all department heads are female, a proportion above the average for women's colleges. Among the 15 departments chaired by women are chemistry, mathematics, economics, and management. Forty percent of trustees are women.

Women and the Curriculum. Most women earn degrees in business, home economics, and social sciences; less than 3 percent specialize in mathematics or physical sciences. Special programs in science, management, computer science, accounting, and engineering (in cooperation with Georgia Institute of Technology) are designed to prepare women for these nontraditional fields.

Students may design a Women's Studies major and select courses that focus on women from those offered by the departments of religious studies, English, communications, history, psychology, and philosophy. At least eight courses are offered every year. An official committee oversees the development of a Women's Studies Program and the inclusion of women in the curriculum.

Prospective teachers learn about mathematics avoidance and are trained to develop and use nonsexist curricula. The social work division provides instruction on the concerns of women and the family; the Business School offers instruction on women in the workplace.

Women and Athletics. The small athletic program offers intercollegiate, intramural, and club sports. Thirteen women participate in intercollegiate sports, 33 in intramural (including table tennis, badminton, volleyball, and basketball); and 42 in club sports. There are three paid female coaches for the intercollegiate sports, which are basketball and volleyball.

Housing and Student Organizations. Forty-seven percent of all undergraduates reside in women's dormitories that have restrictive hours for male visitors. About a third of dormitory residents are minority women. Housing is also provided for male and female students who attend the weekend college. The staff of the residence-halls are offered awareness-training on the avoidance of racism.

Special Services and Programs for Women. *Health and Counseling.* The student health service is staffed by two female health-care providers. The student counseling center staff of four women provide counseling on rape and assault. For all other medical services that are specific to women, students are referred to private physicians. Student health insurance covers abortion and maternity expenses. Counselors are trained to avoid sex-role stereotyping.

Safety and Security. Measures consist of campus and local police protection, emergency telephone and alarm systems, nighttime escorts for women (upon request), and instruction on self-defense and safety for women. No rapes or assaults on women were reported for 1980–81.

Career. Services include workshops, lectures and printed materials on nontraditional occupations, networking between alumnae and students and updated alumnae files organized by career.

Other. A variety of special programs includes an annual women's week, a women's lecture series, assertiveness-training, workshops to build mathematics confidence, and sessions on financial matters for women.

Returning Women Students. Of 225 reentry women, 10 percent are members of minority groups, enrolled in the Adult Degree Program. In addition to having their own support groups, returning women students are served by the career center and the Committee for Women. Faculty are offered workshops on the needs of reentry women.

Institutional Self-Description. "Mundelein College attracts women of all ages and expectations to its innovative and flexible programming. The college was the first in the Midwest to initiate both a Continuing Education Program and a Weekend College in Residence. Its personal atmosphere and individualized approach to instruction make Mundelein a leader in women's education."

National College of Education
2840 N. Sheridan Rd., Evanston, IL 60201
Telephone: (312) 256-5150

Women in Leadership
★★ **students**
★★★ **faculty**

386 undergraduates

	Amer. Ind.	Asian Amer.	Blacks	Hispanics	Whites
F	1	9	49	9	285
M	0	0	7	0	24
%	0.3	2.3	14.6	2.3	80.5

The National College of Education, a private, four-year college founded in 1886, offers bachelor's and master's programs in liberal arts and teacher education. It has since 1975 also offered programs in allied health and human services. The main campus is located north of Chicago. A smaller, second campus, located in downtown Chicago, emphasizes education in city schools. The college has a total enrollment of 3,252. Undergraduate enrollment at the main campus is 386 students, 92 percent of whom are women; virtually all women attend full-time. The median age of undergraduates is 21; 23 percent of women are over age 25 and 8 percent are over age 40.

Alternative scheduling includes evening classes, held both on and off campus, and a summer session. Adult education is available through the School of Continuing Education. Forty-five percent of undergraduates reside on campus in coeducational dormitories with restrictive hours for visitors of the opposite sex. For those students who commute, the campus is easily reached by public transportation. On-campus parking for a fee is available.

Private childcare facilities are located near the campus.

Policies to Ensure Fairness to Women. The college reports that issues of sex equity in education and employment and sexual harassment "have not surfaced" in this small, "female-oriented" institution.

Women in Leadership Positions. *Students.* Most of the campus-wide student leadership positions are held by women. The three campus honorary societies are headed by women.

Faculty. Twelve of the 20 full-time faculty are women. The ratio of female faculty to female students at the main campus is 4 for every 100; the ratio of male faculty to male students is 27 for every 100.

Administrators. Among the top administrators, the student-life officer is a woman. Women head four departments: behavioral science, music, art, and student teaching. Eight of the 12 members of the faculty senate are women, as are 6 of 32 trustees.

Women and the Curriculum. Eighty-four percent of women graduates earn degrees in education, also the most popular field for men graduates. Ninety-five percent of students participating in internship programs are women.

The college offers no courses on women. Pre-service training for mathematics and elementary school teachers includes information about mathematics avoidance by girls and instruction in the development and use of sex-fair curricula. Social-work students are informed about services for battered spouses, displaced homemakers, and childcare.

Women and Athletics. Ninety-three percent of the 75 intramural athletes and all 30 intercollegiate athletes are women. One of the three paid intercollegiate coaches is a woman. Six intramural sports are offered. The two intercollegiate sports offered are basketball and volleyball.

Special Services and Programs for Women. *Health and Counseling.* The student health service employs 1 male physician and 1 female health-care provider. The counseling center is staffed by 2 men and 1 woman. Medical treatment for gynecological problems and birth control is available; as is counseling on these matters and on abortion and rape and assault.

Safety and Security. Measures consist of local police and high-intensity lighting in all areas. No rapes or assaults were reported for 1980–81.

Career. Workshops, printed materials, and job discrimination information, as well as panels by women employed in these fields are available. The college also maintains updated files of alumnae. Faculty workshops are held on nontraditional occupations for women and men.

Institutional Self-Description. "Founded by a woman in 1886, National College is the oldest private college for the preparation of elementary school teachers. Our founding was based on meeting the needs of mothers, in working with their pre-school children. This kind of dedication has continued through our history, expanding into related areas of early childhood, human services, education, and allied health."

Northeastern Illinois University

5500 N. St. Louis Avenue
Chicago, IL 60625
Telephone: (312) 583-4050

Women in Leadership ★ faculty			★★ Women and the Curriculum	

7,335 undergraduates

	Amer. Ind.	Asian Amer.	Blacks	Hispanics	Whites
F	12	110	537	494	2,822
M	14	142	379	344	2,348
%	0.4	3.5	12.7	11.6	71.8

🏠 🏛 👫 🔨 📖 ⛺ NWSA

Some 10,000 students are enrolled in this urban, state university. Founded in 1867 as Chicago Teachers College, the university now offers a comprehensive range of bachelor's and master's level programs in the liberal arts and education. An adult continuing education program is also available. In addition to summer session and evening classes both on and off campus, there is a program for self-paced, independent study.

Women are 55 percent of the 7,335 undergraduates; 35 percent of women attend part-time. The median age of undergraduates is 22. Eighty undergraduates belong to social sororities and fraternities. All students commute, and both public transportation and on-campus parking for a fee are available.

A university-sponsored childcare facility, accommodating 104 children, is located approximately six blocks from the main campus. The service is self-supporting, meets most students' requests, and charges a fixed daily rate. Additional private facilities are available nearby.

Policies to Ensure Fairness to Women. Review of policy relating to equal-employment opportunity, accessibility for the handicapped, and sex-equity is the part-time responsibility of the Assistant to the President. A written campus policy prohibiting sexual harassment will be disseminated to students, faculty, and staff, pending board approval. Complaints are currently resolved informally and confidentially. There is also a formal campus grievance procedure.

Women in Leadership Positions. *Students.* Although more than half of the undergraduate student body is female, women hold few campus-wide leadership positions. In a recent three-year period, women were presiding officer of the student union board three times and presiding officer of the student governing body. Women head two of the three campus honorary societies.

Faculty. Thirty-four percent of the 352 full-time faculty are women, an above-average proportion for public four-year institutions in the guide. The ratio of female faculty to female students is 4 to 100; that of male faculty to male students is 12 to 100.

Administrators. Men hold all of the top administrative posts.

Women chair eight of the 32 departments: anthropology, early childhood education, educational foundations, geography and environmental studies, human services, political science, secondary education, and sociology. A woman also serves as the Director of the Division of Business and Management. Sixty-eight percent of the faculty senate and 55 percent of the tenure committee are female.

Women and the Curriculum. Most undergraduate degrees earned by women are in the fields of education (25 percent), social sciences (14 percent), and business (11 percent). Five percent are in such nontraditional fields as architecture, computer science, mathematics, and physical sciences. Women constitute 60 percent of the participants in the university's extensive field-experience programs, and 65 percent of the students in the Board of Governors/B.A. Program, an experiential learning program for mature adults. In addition, 58 percent of students enrolled in the University Without Walls are women.

The Women's Studies Program offers a bachelor's and a master's degree, as well as an undergraduate minor. More than 30 courses on women are available in such departments as criminal justice, philosophy, and sociology. Recent offerings include Feminist Philosophy; Sociology of Working Women; Women and Film; and Women, Money and Power. The Women's Studies Board is responsible for continued efforts to develop the curriculum. The Resource Center of the Women's Studies Program houses a collection of books, periodicals, and other material on women, for classroom use and for research by students and faculty.

Minority Women. Of the 4,014 undergraduate women, 13 percent are black, 13 percent are Hispanic, 3 percent are Asian American, and less than 1 percent are American Indian. A black woman on the Board of Trustees. The institution provides in-service training for professional counselors in the avoidance of racial bias. Thirty-five percent of the 900 women served by the Office of Continuing Education are drawn from minority groups, the largest of which is black.

Women and Athletics. A variety of organized, competitive, individual and team sports is available in the intramural and intercollegiate programs. Fifty-four percent of intramural and 34 percent of intercollegiate athletes are women; women receive 30 percent of athletic scholarships. Of the 19 paid intercollegiate coaches, eight are female. Intercollegiate sports in which women compete are basketball, cross-country, gymnastics, softball, tennis, and volleyball.

Special Services and Programs for Women. *Health and Counseling.* The student health service has a staff of three female health-care providers. The counseling center offers gynecological, birth control, abortion and rape and assault counseling. Three of the six member staff are female; all counselors receive in-service training on avoiding sex-role stereotyping.

Safety and Security. Measures include campus police with arrest authority, night-time escort for women students, and self-defense courses and crime prevention lectures for women. No rapes or assaults were reported for 1980–81.

Other. The campus Women's Center, headed by a full-time, salaried administrator, serves over 800 women. A 20-member Feminist Club serves as an advocacy group for women.

Institutional Self-Description. "Women, especially older, minority, and international women, will find a relatively comfortable environment at Northeastern Illinois University, an urban commuter school where diversity and informality are the rule. The university supports a vigorous Affirmative Action Program, an active undergraduate Women's Studies Program offering a strong minor, and an Office of Women's Services. Off-campus centers provide educational services to the black and Hispanic communities."

Northern Illinois University
DeKalb, IL 60115
Telephone: (815) 753-1000

| Women in Leadership | ★ Women and the |
| ★ Faculty | Curriculum |

★★ **Women and Athletics**

16,741 undergraduates

	Amer. Ind.	Asian Amer.	Blacks	Hispanics	Whites
F	8	74	700	107	7,842
M	16	70	422	99	7,147
%	0.2	0.9	6.8	1.3	91.0

Established in 1895 as a teacher-training school and since 1957 a state university, Northern Illinois enrolls some 24,800 students in a range of undergraduate, graduate, and professional programs. The College of Continuing Education serves the needs of the adult student. Alternative class schedules include a weekend college, self-paced learning contracts, off-campus evening classes, and a summer session.

Women are 53 percent of the 16,741 undergraduates; 9 percent of women attend part-time. The median age of undergraduates is 21. For the 15 percent of undergraduates who commute, there is on-campus parking, with free transportation from distant parking lots.

University-sponsored childcare facilities accommodate an estimated 95 percent of students requests. Private childcare arrangements may be made close to campus.

Policies to Ensure Fairness to Women. A full-time Director of Affirmative Action for Women reviews policies and practices related to equal-employment opportunity, sex equity for students, and handicapped accessibility. A full-time Officer for Minorities reviews equal employment practices. An official committee is developing a sexual harassment policy and implementation procedures for students; complaints are handled informally and confidentially. The Commission on the Status of Women, which includes students as voting members, takes public stands on issues of concern to students, and addresses the concerns of minority women.

Women in Leadership Positions. *Students.* In recent years, women have held 20 percent of student leadership positions. Women have presided over the student union board twice, been editor-in-chief of the newspaper three times, and manager of the campus radio station once. Women head 12 of 32 honorary societies.

Faculty. One-quarter of the 1,012 full-time faculty are women. According to a recent report, 10 black, 1 American Indian, 11 Asian American, and 5 Hispanic women are on the faculty. The ratio of female faculty to female students is 3 to 100; of male faculty to male students, 11 to 100.

Administrators. The head librarian and the co-director of athletics are women. Women chair five of 36 departments: curriculum and instruction, library science, allied health, nursing, and home economics. The Dean of the College of Professional Studies is female. Two of the nine regents with voting rights are women.

Women and the Curriculum. Most women graduating with bachelor's degrees major in education (26 percent), business and management (16 percent), the health professions (12 percent), and home economics (12 percent). Four percent major in nontraditional fields, with the larger number in computer science, mathematics, and physical sciences. A National Science Foundation "Women in Science Career Day" encourages women to consider careers in science. Over one-quarter of the science field-service positions go to women students.

The Women's Studies Program offers a 15-credit undergraduate

🏠	On-campus evening and/or weekend classes	Ⓜ︎Ⓐ	Commission on minority affairs
🏛	Off-campus classes	📖	Women's Studies program
🚐	Accessible by public transportation	⚲	Women's center
👫	On-campus childcare facilities	AAUW	Member, American Association of University Women
✎	Publicly communicated sexual harassment policy, includes students	NWSA	Member, National Women's Studies Association
Ⓢ︎Ⓦ	Commission on status of women	CROW	On-campus Center for Research on Women

minor. Some 13 Women's Studies courses and courses on women are available through the departments of English, history, sociology, anthropology, physical education, psychology, management, and allied health professions. Recent titles include Women Across Cultures and Centuries, Women and Mental Health, Psychology of Human Sexuality, and Feminist Perspectives in Education. An official committee advocates and monitors the integration of women's materials and perspectives across the curriculum.

Such current issues as mathmatics confidence among females, sex-fair curricula, coeducational physical education classes, health-care information important to minority women, services for battered spouses, and discrimination in the workplace are part of the instruction provided future teachers, health-care providers, professional-service workers, and business students.

Minority Women. Ten percent of undergraduate women are members of minority groups, mainly black women. Nine percent of female dormitory residents are black, 2 percent Asian American, and 2 percent Hispanic. Residence-hall staff are offered awareness-training on the avoidance of racism. Two minority women are on the professional staff of the counseling center. Counseling center staff receive in-service training on avoiding racial bias.

There are four all-minority sororities. A number of student organizations serve as advocates for minority women on campus: The Angels, SISTERS (black), FLORES, the Minority Organization of Nursing Students, Minorities for Professional and Creative Communications, Black Theatre Workshop, Organization of Black Business Students, Black Greek Council, Chinese Students Club, and the Black Student Union. A black woman is a member of the Board of Regents.

Women and Athletics. Intercollegiate and intramural programs offer excellent opportunities for organized competitive sports. Some intramural sports are coeducational, most are team. The university reports special facilities for racquetball. Of 28 paid varsity coaches, 10 are women. Forty percent of intramural and intercollegiate athletes and 35 percent of club-sports participants are women. Women receive 30 percent of athletic scholarships. The intercollegiate sports offered are badminton, basketball, cross-country, field hockey, golf, gymnastics, softball, swimming and diving, tennis, track and field, and volleyball.

Housing and Student Organizations. Forty-four percent of undergraduates live on campus. Single-sex and coeducational dormitories and housing for married students and single parents with children are available. A married student whose spouse is not enrolled may live in married students' housing. Some parts of residence halls restrict hours for visitors of the opposite sex. Five of eight residence-hall directors are female. Staff are offered awareness-training on sexism, sex education, racism, birth control, and crisis intervention.

There are 12 sororities on campus. Sororities and fraternities provide housing for their members. In addition to the groups mentioned above, student groups that serve as advocates for women are the Women's Center, Women in Communications, Hillel Jewish Students' Organization, and the International Relations Club, and the Gay/Lesbian Student Association.

Special Services and Programs for Women. *Health and Counseling.* The student health service provides medical attention specific to women, including gynecological, birth control, abortion, and rape and assault treatment. Two of 12 physicians are female, as are 24 other health-care providers. Regular student health insurance covers abortion and maternity at no extra charge. Two-thirds of the professional staff in the counseling service are women. Students have access to counseling specific to women. Staff receive in-service training on avoiding sex-role stereotyping and racial bias. Assertiveness training is available through the center.

Safety and Security. Measures consist of campus police with arrest authority, night-time bus service to residence areas, self-

defense courses for women, information sessions on safety and crime prevention, and a rape crisis center. Forty-one assaults and 2 rapes were reported for 1980-81.

Career. Career workshops which concentrate on nontraditional occupations for women, lectures, and printed information on non-traditional jobs are available.

Other. There are both a Women's Center, staffed by student volunteers, and an Office of Resources for Women, under a full-time director. Among activities sponsored by the Women's Center are an annual women's week and a telephone line of information, referral, and support. The Organization for Academic Women's Equality sponsors a lecture series. Grants from the Illinois Arts Council support women's theater and arts programs. There are programs for battered women and displaced homemakers.

Special Features. The Rhoten Smith Assistantship Fund provides graduate assistantships to women and minority students in nontraditional disciplines. Annual Women's Leadership Awards go to 75 high-achieving students.

Institutional Self-Description. "Seeking to provide a quality education to women students, Northern Illinois University places a high priority on eliminating sex bias from academic programs, support services, and extracurricular activities; incorporating Women's Studies courses and other gender-related topics into the curriculum; and increasing the number of women administrators and full-time women faculty."

Northwestern University
Evanston, IL 60201
Telephone: (312) 492-5680

Women in Leadership ★ Women and the
★ students   Curriculum

7,711 undergraduates

	Amer. Ind.	Asian Amer.	Blacks	Hispanics	Whites
F	4	62	392	41	3,061
M	2	95	279	51	3,547
%	0.1	2.1	8.9	1.2	87.7

 AAUW

Established in 1851 as a private college for men, Northwestern has been coeducational since 1869. Located in a large urban area, the university provides undergraduate, graduate, and professional studies for some 15,100 students. The division of continuing education serves the adult student. Evening classes amd a summer session are available.

Women are 47 percent of 7,711 undergraduates; 13 percent of women attend part-time. For the 24 percent of undergraduates who commute, the university is accessible by public transportation. On-campus parking is available for a fee.

Private childcare arrangements can be made close to campus.

Policies to Ensure Fairness to Women. The Equal Opportunity Officer and Handicapped Services Coordinator work with policy and practices in the areas of employment, sex equity for students, and handicapped accessibility. University administrators and department heads have been advised of the policy which prohibits sexual harassment; complaints are resolved informally and confidentially.

Women in Leadership Positions. *Students.* Women have good opportunities to exercise campus-wide student leadership. In recent years, women have twice presided over the student senate and three times been president of the student court. They have been editor-in-chief of the campus newspaper, manager of the campus radio station, and head of the residence-hall council. Women head two of the ten honorary societies.

Faculty. Women are 13 percent of a full-time faculty of 793. According to a recent report, 6 black, 1 American Indian, and 3 Hispanic women are on the total faculty. The ratio of female faculty to female students is 3 to 100; the ratio of male faculty to male students is 18 to 100.

Administrators. Men occupy all higher administrative positions. Women chair two of 25 departments. The Dean of Continuing Education is female. In 1980-81, women received one-quarter of alumni awards.

Women and the Curriculum. Most bachelor's degrees earned by women are in communications and the social sciences; over 9 percent are in nontraditional fields. Roughly one-third of the positions in cooperative education programs go to women. Most two-year degrees in health technology and business are awarded to women.

The Women's Studies Program, called the Program on Women, offers a 12-credit undergraduate certificate, comparable to a minor. Introductory courses, research seminars, and internships in women's services are available through the program. Seventeen courses on women are given in nine departments. Recent titles include Courtship and Marriage: Puritans to the Present; Women Artists in the Twentieth Century; Women in Science Fiction; American Women: A Multi-Ethnic Approach; and Feminist Film Criticism. The School of Education and the division of nursing offer some instruction on matters specific to women.

Minority Women. Of 3,560 undergraduate women, 11 percent are black, 2 percent Asian American, 1 percent Hispanic, and less than 1 percent American Indian. There are an estimated three minority women in racially integrated, and 42 in all-minority, sororities. One of the therapists in the counseling section of the student health service is a minority woman. Minority women are represented on the Women's Coalition. Black women would find support from African-American Student Affairs. In 1980-81, a black woman received an alumni award.

Women and Athletics. Intramural and intercollegiate programs provide adequate opportunities for organized, competitive athletics. Club sports are also available. Most of the intramural sports are team, some are coeducational. Twenty-three percent of intramural and 31 percent of intercollegiate athletes are women; women receive 22 percent of athletic scholarships. About 40 percent of paid coaches for intercollegiate teams are women. All teams played tournament competition in 1980. The intercollegiate sports are basketball, cross-country, field hockey, softball, swimming and diving, tennis, track and field, and volleyball.

Housing and Student Organizations. Three-quarters of the undergraduates live on campus in single-sex and coeducational dormitories. Three of eleven directors of residence halls are female. Staff are offered awareness-training on sex education.

Social sororities include 30 percent of undergraduate women; some sororities provide housing for their members. Among student groups which serve as advocates for women on campus are the Women's Coalition, Graduate Women United, the Women's Caucus of the Progressive Student Coalition, Women in Communications, Women in Management, and the Gay and Lesbian Alliance.

Special Services and Programs for Women. *Health and Counseling.* Medical attention specific to women provided by the student health service includes gynecological and birth control treatment; abortion and rape and assault treatment are provided by referral. Both female and male physicians are available. Regular student health insurance covers abortion and maternity at no extra charge. Eight of 13 professionals in the mental health department are women. Students have access to counseling specific to women. Staff receive in-service training on homophobia and female sexuality.

Safety and Security. Measures include university police with arrest authority who patrol the campus on foot, limited night-time shuttle service, emergency telephones, and information sessions and literature on safety and crime prevention. There is a rape crisis center at Evanston Hospital. A total of eight assaults and two rapes were reported for 1980-81.

Other. The Program on Women sponsors a women's lecture series, a program to build mathematics among women, and a telephone service of information, referral, and support. Additional events directed to women include an annual women's week and theater arts programs.

Returning Women Students. The Program on Women sponsors programs and conferences for the community. With the co-operation of Continuing Education and Summer Sessions, the program offers credit and non-credit continuing education courses for non-matriculated adult women. Some 230 women, 11 percent of them black women, registered for courses in a recent year. The program also provides informal counseling and maintains a library resource center.

Special Features. The Women's Collection in Special Collections of the library is the most comprehensive archival collection on the women's movement in America from 1963 to the present. The Women's Studies Residential College provides undergraduates with the housing option of a supportive women's community.

Institutional Self-Description. "Northwestern University offers a fine undergraduate curriculum in Women's Studies, leading to an interdisciplinary certificate. Also available are research opportunities and continuing education for women through the Program on Women, a nationally known women's collection in the university library, and a Women's Studies Residential College."

Quincy College
1831 College Avenue, Quincy, IL 62301
Telephone: (217) 222-8020

889 undergraduates

	Amer. Ind.	Asian Amer.	Blacks	Hispanics	Whites
F	1	3	13	3	450
M	2	0	11	9	385
%	0.3	0.3	2.7	1.4	95.2

 AAUW

Quincy College is a coeducational, four-year, Roman Catholic college operated by the Franciscan Fathers. Its total enrollment is 990. Of 889 undergraduates, 53 percent are women; 10 percent of the women attend part-time. The median age of all undergraduates is 20. Free on-campus parking is available to the 20 percent of students who commute. A summer session is offered.

Policies to Ensure Fairness to Women. The Director of Equal Opportunity has part-time responsibility for the enforcement of sex-equity and equal-employment-opportunity laws and regulations.

Women in Leadership Positions. *Students.* Opportunities for women students are rare: one woman held a campus-wide leadership position during a recent three-year period.

Faculty. Ten of the 69 full-time faculty are women. There are 2 female faculty for every 100 female students and 15 male faculty for every 100 male students.

Administrators. Men hold all top positions. Of 18 academic departments a woman chairs modern languages. The director of continuing education is a woman.

Women and the Curriculum. Most degrees awarded to women are in education (39 percent) and business (22 percent); 2 percent are in physical sciences. Five percent of men, but no women, receive degrees in theology.

There are no courses on women. Instruction in the use of sex-fair curricula is offered by the department of education. Instruction on services for battered spouses, displaced homemakers, and childcare is offered in the department of social work.

Women and Athletics. Information was provided only on the intercollegiate sports offered: basketball, softball, tennis, and volleyball.

Housing and Student Organizations. The 80 percent of undergraduates who live on campus are accommodated in single-sex dormitories and in housing for married students (with and without children) and single parents with children. A married woman student whose husband is not enrolled is permitted to live in married students' housing. Single-sex dormitories have restrictive hours for visitors of the opposite sex. The three female and one male residence-hall directors are offered awareness-training on sexism, sex education, racism, and birth control.

Social sororities and fraternities provide housing for their members.

Special Services and Programs for Women. *Health and Counseling.* No information was provided on student health services. A counseling service is staffed by a woman and a man; no services specific to women are provided.

Safety and Security. Measures include campus police, high-intensity lights, and a campus-wide emergency telephone system. No information was provided on the incidence of rapes and assaults.

Career. Information and services on nontraditional careers for women are offered, along with the maintenance of updated files of alumnae by specific careers.

Institutional Self-Description. None provided.

Rock Valley College
3301 W. Mulford Road
Rockford, IL 61101
Telephone: (815) 654-4250

Women in Leadership
★★★ students
★ faculty

6,925 undergraduates

	Amer. Ind.	Asian Amer.	Blacks	Hispanics	Whites
F	5	10	191	31	3,383
M	8	21	139	55	2,970
%	0.2	0.5	4.8	1.3	93.3

Established in 1965 as a public, two-year community college, Rock Valley serves 6,955 students, just over half of whom are women. Seventy-eight percent of the women attend part-time. The median age of students is 27.

The college offers a comprehensive educational program, including associate degrees in arts, sciences, and applied science, and a variety of vocational-technical certificates. Evening classes both on and off campus are available, as well as an adult continuing education program. All students commute. The suburban campus in northern Illinois is accessible by public transportation, and free on-campus parking is provided.

Private childcare facilities are available nearby.

Policies to Ensure Fairness to Women. The Vice President of the college has part-time responsibility for reviewing policies and practices relating to equal employment opportunity, sex equity for students, and handicapped access. A written campus policy prohibiting sexual harassment of students, faculty, and staff has been publicly communicated in writing to all three groups.

Women in Leadership Positions. *Students.* Women hold most of the few available campus-wide student leadership positions. A woman was president of the student body once in three recent

years, and women were editor-in-chief of the campus newspaper during that time.

Faculty. The full-time faculty is 26 percent female. There are 4 female faculty for every 100 female students and 9 male faculty for every 100 male students.

Administrators. Of 7 chief administrative positions, the director of athletics is a woman. Women chair 2 of the 8 departments: communications, and personal and public services. Two of the 7 trustees are women. In one recent year, women received 5 of the 9 alumni awards. Two of the 4 speakers in major campus-wide lecture series were women, including 1 black woman.

Women and the Curriculum. Most of the two-year degrees and certificates earned by women are in the arts and sciences, health technologies, and business and commerce.

There are no courses on women. The departments of nursing, social work, and business address some issues specific to women in their courses. The college provides faculty workshops on nontraditional occupations for women and men, the needs of reentry women, and affirmative action and equal opportunity.

Women and Athletics. There are no intramural or club sports. Of seven paid intercollegiate coaches, two are women. Forty-six women athletes participate in four intercollegiate sports—basketball, softball, tennis, and volleyball.

Special Services and Programs for Women. *Health and Counseling.* There is no student health service. The seven-member student counseling center staff, who include two women, provide rape and assault counseling.

Safety and Security. Measures consist of campus police with arrest authority, high-intensity lighting in all areas, and information sessions on campus safety and rape and assault prevention for women. There were no rapes or assaults reported for 1980-81.

Career. Services include career workshops, lectures and panels by women employed in nontraditional occupations, and printed information on nontraditional careers and fields of study for women.

Other. A small Women's Center is headed by a full-time faculty member and funded through the counseling budget. Approximately 300 women make use of the center annually, the most frequent participants being students over 25.

Institutional Self-Description. "Rock Valley College is a comprehensive community college established to serve the educational, occupational, cultural, and social needs of its citizens, within the limits of its various resources and consistent with its legal mandate. The typical student is a 27-year-old female."

Rosary College
7900 W. Division, River Forest, IL 60305
Telephone: (312) 366-2490

Women in Leadership   ★ **Women and the Curriculum**
   ★ students
  ★★ faculty
★★★ administrators

881 undergraduates

	Amer. Ind.	Asian Amer.	Blacks	Hispanics	Whites
F	0	5	60	15	608
M	0	2	18	7	156
%	0.0	0.8	9.0	2.5	87.7

Rosary College is a Roman Catholic, liberal arts college operated by the Dominican Sisters of Sinsinawa, Wisconsin. Originally a women's college, it became coeducational in 1970. Located in a small town 30 minutes from downtown Chicago, the campus enrolls 1,529 students. Seventy-nine percent of the 881 undergraduates are women. Fifteen percent of women undergraduates attend part-time. On-campus parking is available for the 73 percent of students who commute.

Childcare facilities are provided on campus between the hours of 7:30 a.m. and 5:30 p.m., at a cost of $10-15 per week for 20-30 hours of childcare. The center can accommodate all students' requests. Childcare can also be arranged near campus.

Policies to Ensure Fairness to Women. An Affirmative Action Officer is responsible part-time for compliance with laws concerning equal employment opportunity and sex equity. There is no formal policy on sexual harassment; an informal campus mechanism resolves complaints.

Women in Leadership Positions. *Students.* Leadership opportunities for women students are good: women have held 52 percent of the campus-wide student leadership positions in recent years. Women head five of the six honorary societies.

Faculty. Twenty of the 45 full-time faculty are women. There are 3 female faculty for every 100 female students, and 16 male faculty for every 100 male students.

Administrators. Women hold nearly two-thirds of the top positions, including President of the college. Women head eleven of the 14 departments. Twelve women, including a black woman, sit on the 23-member Board of Trustees, and 2 of 4 honorary degree recipients in 1981 were women, including 1 black woman.

Women and the Curriculum. Nineteen percent of women graduate in business, 15 percent in psychology, 13 percent in fine arts, 12 percent in social sciences, 11 percent in letters, and 11 percent in home economics. Two percent of women earn degrees in mathematics and physical sciences.

The Women's Studies Program, whose director holds a full-time faculty appointment, offers a bachelor's degree. Women's Studies courses, offered through departments include Feminism and Film, Images of Women in Drama, Novels by Women, Woman as Force in History, Feminist Roots and Branches, Images of Women in Religion, and Psychology of Women. Educational programs on sexism and racism in the curriculum are offered to faculty. The department of business provides instruction about the problems of job discrimination and sexual harassment in the workplace.

Women and Athletics. Rosary offers intramural and intercollegiate women's athletic programs. Athletic scholarships will be provided, beginning in 1981-82. Intercollegiate sports are basketball, tennis, and volleyball.

Housing and Student Organizations. The 27 percent of undergraduates living on campus are housed in single-sex dormitories that have restrictive hours for visitors of the opposite sex. The residence-hall directors, one man and one woman, are offered awareness-training on sexism, racism, communication leadership, and suicide prevention.

Special Services and Programs for Women. *Health and Counseling.* The student health service employs two male physicians and the counseling center, two women counselors. No medical services specific to women are available. Gynecological, birth control, abortion, and rape and assault counseling is provided. Counselors are offered in-service training on the avoidance of sex-role stereotyping and racial bias.

Safety and Security. Measures consist of a campus police force, high-intensity lighting, and self-defense and campus safety courses for women. No rapes or assaults were reported for 1980-81.

Institutional Self-Description. "Rosary College has a tradition of education and leadership training for women. A Women's Studies Program, an inexpensive childcare facility, a sensitivity on the part of faculty and administration to the position of reentry women, and numerous female role models create an environment for women that is at once comfortable and challenging."

Sangamon State University
Shepherd Road, Springfield, IL 62708
Telephone: (217) 786-6600

★ **Women and the Curriculum**

1,456 undergraduates

	Amer. Ind.	Asian Amer.	Blacks	Hispanics	Whites
F	0	5	42	2	611
M	0	8	36	2	733
%	0.0	0.9	5.4	0.3	93.4

 AAUW

Sangamon State is an innovative institution founded in 1970 to provide the last two years of undergraduate education. Its programs are designed to explore the relationship between higher education and social responsibilities and to emphasize the study and understanding of public affairs. About half of the regular courses are offered in the evening. Additional alternative schedules include independent study opportunities, a weekend college, a summer session, and media courses through newspaper, wideband radio, and cable television programs. The Office of Continuing Education offers noncredit courses and is a vehicle for community services and outreach programs. All undergraduates must complete one semester of applied study.

The university enrolls 3,469 juniors, seniors, and graduate students. There are 1,456 undergraduates of whom 46 percent are women; 55 percent of the women attend part-time. The median age of undergraduates is 30; two-thirds of undergraduate women are over age 25 and 15 percent are over age 40. The campus is accessible by public transportation for the 95 percent of students who commute. On-campus parking is available at a fee.

A university-run childcare center can accommodate 40 children. Students receive priority for the services and all students' requests for childcare can be met. Charges are based on a fixed hourly rate, with a reduction for students. Additional facilities are available at a nearby community college.

Policies to Ensure Fairness to Women. The full-time Affirmative Action Officer reviews policies and monitors compliance with equal employment opportunity, sex equity, and handicapped access legislation. A published policy forbids sexual harassment; complaints are resolved through a formal grievance procedure. A Committee on the Status of Women, appointed by the President, includes faculty, staff, and student representatives, all with voting rights. That committee and a Commission on Minority Affairs consider issues of concern to minority women.

Women in Leadership Positions. *Students.* In recent years, opportunities for women students to acquire leadership experience have been limited. The two campus-wide student offices have been held by men.

Faculty. Seventeen percent of the 168 full-time faculty are women, including three black women. There are 4 female faculty for every 100 female students and 18 male faculty for every 100 male students.

Administrators. Two of 7 top administrators are women—the vice president for academic affairs and the head librarian. Women chair 13 of the 38 academic programs, including biology, communications, mathematical systems, management, gerontology, and creative arts.

Women and the Curriculum. Most women earn bachelor's degrees in public affairs (30 percent), business (18 percent), and health (17 percent). Seventy percent of graduates in public affairs, an area of special emphasis at this institution, are women; this proportion is well above the national average. The fields of computer science, engineering, and physical sciences are not emphasized by men or women on this campus. One percent of women graduate in mathematics. The mathematics program and Academic Affairs sponsor a program to help students gain confidence in mathematics. Women hold about half of the undergraduate practicums.

The Women's Studies Program offers an undergraduate minor and a self-designed B.A. or M.A. degree in Women's Studies through an Individual Option Program. Six interdisciplinary courses are offered in Women's Studies, along with several courses on women offered through the departments of psychology, law, and sociology/anthropology. Recent offerings include Feminist History: Then and Now; Implications of Feminism and Racial Justice; Women and the Law; and Women's Horizons and Visions. Faculty workshops have been offered on affirmative action, equal opportunity, and the needs of reentry women.

Women and Athletics. Sangamon State offers a varied intramural program for women, including bowling, exercise, softball, table tennis, and indoor tennis. Forty percent of intramural, 25 percent of intercollegiate, and 25 percent of club athletes are women. One of the two paid varsity coaches is a woman; women receive about 20 percent of athletic scholarship funds. The intercollegiate sport offered for women is tennis.

Housing and Student Organizations. Five percent of the students live on campus in apartment-style housing, which is available for single students as well as married students with or without children.

Special Services and Programs for Women. *Health and Counseling.* The student health service has a part-time, male physician and a full-time female nurse. One of the two women on staff of the student counseling center is a minority woman. Counseling is available for gynecological problems, birth control, abortion, and rape and assault. Medical treatment is available for birth control.

Safety and Security. Measures consist of campus police with weapons training and arrest authority, and a rape crisis center. No rapes or assaults on women were reported for 1980–81.

Career. Lectures and literature on nontraditional and other careers are available.

Other. The Office of Academic Affairs sponsors a women's lecture series, a program on women in the arts, and assertiveness training for women. The Black Student Caucus, Women Artists Gathering are two campus groups.

Special Features. The Center for Policy Studies, in cooperation with the Illinois Department of Commerce and Community Affairs, sponsors a state-wide network for displaced homemakers. The university has an oral history project and a library collection which focus on women in Springfield and Illinois.

Institutional Self-Description. "Given its public-affairs and innovative-teaching missions, SSU *must* serve the interests of women. Open admissions and the age range of students are plusses for reentry women. Our location in a state capital with many activist women's organizations, and SSU's public-affairs focus and experiential learning programs, can provide experience in state government, community and political action, and service to women."

Southern Illinois University, Carbondale
Carbondale, IL 62901
Telephone: (618) 453-2121

| Women in Leadership | ★ Women and the |
| ★★★ students | Curriculum |

★★ **Women and Athletics**

18,697 undergraduates

	Amer. Ind.	Asian Amer.	Blacks	Hispanics	Whites
F	27	171	684	22	5,932
M	77	174	693	78	10,181
%	0.6	1.9	7.6	0.6	89.3

Established in 1868 as a teachers' preparatory school, Southern Illinois University at Carbondale, located in a predominantly rural part of the state, now enrolls 22,500 students in a comprehensive range of undergraduate, graduate, and professional programs. The division of continuing education serves the adult student. Alternative schedules, including weekend college, summer session, evening classes, and off-campus locations, are available. Two-year degrees are awarded in five vocational fields.

Women are 38 percent of the 18,697 undergraduates; 7 percent of women attend part-time. Among the 11 percent of undergraduate women who are over age 25, about 40 percent attend part-time. The median age of undergraduates is 21. On-campus parking is available, at a fee, to the one-quarter of undergraduates who commute.

The university sponsors three childcare programs, which accommodate from 65 to 90 percent of students' requests. Private childcare arrangements may be made close to campus.

Policies to Ensure Fairness to Women. An affirmative action officer on full-time assignment is responsible for policy relating to equal employment opportunity, sex equity for students, and handicapped accessibility. A published policy prohibits sexual harassment. Complaints are handled through a formal grievance procedure. An active Committee on the Status of Women, which includes students as voting members, advises the President. The Committee on Minority Affairs addresses the concerns of minority women.

Women in Leadership Positions. *Students.* Women students have exercised a high degree of leadership. In recent years they have held a higher proportion of student offices than their representation among undergraduates. They have presided over the student court three times, the student union board three times, been editor-in-chief of the newspaper three times, and managed the campus radio station. Women head 22 of the 51 honorary societies.

Faculty. Women constitute 17 percent of a full-time faculty of 1,085. According to a recent report, 6 black and 7 Asian American women are on the faculty. There are 3 female faculty for every 100 female students and 8 male faculty for every 100 male students.

Administrators. Men hold all top positions. Women chair three of 78 departments. One department head is a black woman. The Dean of General Academic Programs is female.

Women and the Curriculum. Roughly half of the women graduating with bachelor's degrees major in education, home economics, public affairs, and interdisciplinary studies. Ten percent major in nontraditional areas, with the greater number in agriculture and architecture. The percentage of women taking degrees in architecture is significantly above the national average. The university reports innovative programs to encourage women to prepare for careers in engineering, agriculture, law, psychology, journalism, sociology, and mathematics. One-third of the students

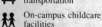

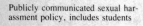

in cooperative education programs that combine study with related work experience are female. Five percent of science field-service positions are held by women.

The Women's Studies Program offers an undergraduate minor. Seven recent Women's Studies courses are cross-listed with the departments of sociology, human development, psychology, history, art, philosophy, and English. They include such titles as Sexes in the Modern World, Psychology of Women, Women in Visual Arts, and Philosophical Perspectives on Women. An official committee promotes and monitors the teaching of women across the curriculum.

Such current issues as mathematics confidence among females, sex-fair teaching materials, coeducational physical education classes, services for battered spouses, and discrimination in the workplace are part of the curriculum for the preparation of teachers, social workers, and business students.

Minority Women. Of 6,836 undergraduate women, 10 percent are black, 3 percent Asian American, and less than 1 percent each American Indian and Hispanic. There are 52 women in all-minority sororities. Awareness-training on the avoidance of racism is offered residence-hall staff. Professional staff in the counseling service receive in-service training on the avoidance of racial bias. One counselor is a minority woman. The Woman's Caucus and the Black Affairs Council are supportive of minority women.

Women and Athletics. Intramural and intercollegiate programs offer excellent opportunities for organized, competitive, individual and team sports. A woman is co-director of athletics. Forty percent of intramural and 22 percent of intercollegiate athletes are women. Nearly half the participants in club sports are women. Women receive 20 percent of athletic scholarships. The university reports that special sports facilities include an Olympic pool, campus lake, computerized golf room, and climbing wall. Eleven of the 33 paid intercollegiate coaches are women. All teams played in tournaments in 1980. The intercollegiate sports offered are badminton, basketball, cross-country, field hockey, golf, gymnastics, softball, swimming and diving, tennis, track and field, and volleyball.

Housing and Student Organizations. Twenty-five percent of undergraduates live on campus. Single-sex and coeducational dormitories and housing for married students and single parents with children are available. A married woman student whose spouse is not enrolled may live in married students' housing. Residence halls do not restrict hours for visitors of the opposite sex. Staff are offered awareness-training on sexism, sex education, racism, and birth control.

Three percent of undergraduate women belong to social sororities. Sororities and fraternities provide housing for their members. Among student groups that serve as advocates for women on campus are the Student Chapter of the Society of Women Engineers, Women in Communications, Women in Agriculture, the Women's Caucus, National Women's Self-Defense Council, and the Women's Club.

Special Services and Programs for Women. *Health and Counseling.* The student health service provides medical attention specific to women: gynecological, birth control, and rape and assault treatment are available. The health service physicians are male. Six of 14 professional staff in the counseling center are women. Gynecological, birth control, abortion, and rape and assault counseling are offered. Staff receive in-service training on sex-role stereotyping, racial bias, and a range of general psychological and educational diagnostics and therapy.

Safety and Security. Measures consist of campus police with arrest authority, night-time escorts for women, night-time bus service to residence areas, high-intensity lighting, emergency telephone system, self-defense courses for women, information sessions on safety and crime prevention, and a rape crisis center. One rape and 68 assaults (24 on women) were reported for 1980-81.

Career. The university provides workshops and other activities and information that include women in nontraditional careers and fields of study.

Institutional Self-Description. "SIU-C believes that merely providing a nonsexist environment is not enough; therefore, we attempt to provide an environment that overtly encourages women students to pursue their goals. 'Women's concerns' are not just the concerns of areas that primarily work with women, but are shared throughout the university community."

Southern Illinois University, Edwardsville
Edwardsville, IL 62026
Telephone: (618) 692-2512

Women in Leadership	★★ Women and the
★ students	Curriculum
★ administrators	
	★ Women and Athletics

8373 undergraduates

	Amer. Ind.	Asian Amer.	Blacks	Hispanics	Whites
F	11	18	1230	13	3144
M	4	20	527	23	3185
%	0.2	0.5	21.5	0.4	77.4

 AAUW NWSA

This public, four-year university, near St. Louis, provides a variety of undergraduate, graduate, and pre-professional programs to some 11,000 students. Alternative schedules include weekend classes, evening classes both on and off campus, and a summer session. The Office of Continuing Education offers a program for the adult student. Women are 53 percent of the 8,373 undergraduates; 22 percent of the women attend part-time. One-fourth of the women are over age 25, and half of these older women attend part-time. Ten percent of the undergraduates commute to the campus, which is accessible by public transportation. On-campus parking is also available. During the winter, shuttle buses run between remote parking lots and classroom buildings.

A university-run childcare facility can accommodate 28 children. There are two sessions daily and fees are based on a fixed rate per session. Nearby, private facilities are also available.

Policies to Ensure Fairness to Women. Review of policies and practices relating to equal employment opportunity, handicapped access, and sex equity is the responsibility of University Central Affirmative Action. A published campus policy prohibits sexual harassment of students, faculty, and staff. Complaints are handled through a formal campus grievance procedure that has been communicated to faculty and staff but not to students.

Women in Leadership Positions. *Students.* During a recent three-year period, of the three chief campus leadership positions, for three terms, the presiding officer of the student union board has been a woman. Women head three of the eleven campus honorary societies.

Faculty. Women are 21 percent of a full-time faculty of 557. The ratio of female faculty to female students is 3 to 100; for males, it is 15 to 100.

Administrators. Two of the seven key administrative positions are held by women—executive vice president and chief academic officer. Women head four of the 42 departments, including that of business education. The deans of the social science division, humanities division, Graduate School, and School of Nursing are women. One of nine trustees is a woman.

Women and the Curriculum. Most degrees earned by women are in education (21 percent), health (21 percent), and business (15 percent). Four percent are in such nontraditional majors as computer science, mathematics, physical sciences, and engineering.

The Women's Studies Program offers a 28-credit minor. Approximately 30 courses are available through Women's Studies and cooperating departments. Recent offerings include Issues in Feminism, The Literature of Feminist Rebellion, Women in Cross-Cultural Perspectives, Sexism in American Education, and Practicum in Women's Studies.

Minority Women. Twenty-nine percent of female undergraduates are minority women, with black women the largest group. There are 14 black and 3 Asian American women on the full-time faculty. One of the department chairpersons is a black woman. The Coordinator of Minority Affairs addresses the concerns of minority women. Black women are also served by the Black Student Association. The English department and Women's Studies offer Black Women in American Literature.

Women and Athletics. Intramural and intercollegiate programs offer good opportunities for participation in competitive individual and team sports. Forty percent of intramural athletes and 35 percent of intercollegiate athletes are women. Forty percent of athletic scholarships are awarded to women. Five of the 12 paid intercollegiate coaches are women. Intercollegiate sports offered are basketball, cross-country, field hockey, softball, tennis, and track and field.

Housing and Student Organizations. Apartment-style housing is available for the 10 percent of undergraduates who live on campus. There is also housing for married students with and without children. Four of the five residence-hall directors are women, three of them minority women.

Social sororities and fraternities are present on campus, but they do not provide housing for members. Women for Women serves as an advocacy group for women students.

Special Services and Programs for Women. *Health and Counseling.* The student health service provides medical treatment for gynecology and birth control. The staff consists of two male physicans and seven other health-care providers, five of them female. The student counseling center offers counseling on gynecology, birth control, abortion, and rape and assault.

Safety and Security. Measures include campus police with weapons training and arrest authority, night-time escort for women students, night-time, campus-wide bus service, an emergency alarm system at isolated locations, information sessions on safety and crime prevention for women, and a rape and sexual abuse center in the community. Six assaults (three on women) and one rape were reported for 1980–81.

Career. Services include workshops and lectures by woman employed in nontraditional fields and updated files on alumnae.

Other. Handicapped women are served by the Coordinator for Handicapped Services, while older women are served by the Coordinator of Women's Affairs.

Returning Women Students. The Office of Continuing Education, in conjunction with the Women's Studies Program and the Center for Management Studies, sponsors a Continuing Education for Women Program, under the direction of a full-time administrator. Fifty percent of students in these courses are minority women, with black women the largest group.

Institutional Self-Description. None provided.

Springfield College
1500 N. Fifth Street, Springfield, IL 62702
Telephone: (217) 525-1420

Women in Leadership
★★★ **faculty**
★★★ **administrators**

489 undergraduates

	Amer. Ind.	Asian Amer.	Blacks	Hispanics	Whites
F	3	2	10	1	315
M	0	1	11	3	128
%	0.6	0.6	4.4	0.8	93.5

This private, two-year, Roman Catholic college was founded in 1929 and is operated by the Ursuline Sisters. Its campus in the suburbs of Springfield attracts 524 students. Women are 68 percent of all undergraduates, and half of the women attend part-time. Fifteen percent of women are over age 25. The median age of all undergraduates is 19.

Springfield offers the first two years of liberal arts, fine arts, pre-professional fields, and music. The college offers evening as well as day classes; a summer session is available. Continuing Education serves the adult student. The college is accessible by public transportation, and parking is available on campus.

Private childcare can be arranged off campus.

Women in Leadership Positions. *Students.* The sole campus leadership position, president of the student body, has been held by a woman once in recent years. A woman heads the one honorary society.

Faculty. Thirteen of the 20 full-time faculty are women. There are 8 female faculty for every 100 female students and 5 male faculty for every 100 male students. Women are more than half of the part-time faculty.

Administrators. Women hold 6 of the 9 chief administrative positions, including President of the college. Women chair 5 of the 10 major departments, including art, biological sciences, physical sciences, and social studies. More than half the trustees are women.

Women and the Curriculum. All two-year degrees awarded to women are in arts and sciences. There are no courses on women.

Women and Athletics. There are no intercollegiate sports. The 50 intramural athletes, about half of whom are women, bowl and play volleyball. Exercise classes are also offered.

Special Services and Programs for Women. *Health and Counseling.* There is no student health service. The student counseling center is staffed by a woman. No services specific to women are available.

Safety and Security. Measures consist of campus and local police, a night-time escort for women, information sessions on campus safety and rape and assault prevention, and a rape crisis center. There were no assaults or rapes reported for 1980-81.

Career. Information on nontraditional fields of study for women is available.

Institutional Self-Description. ''For over 50 years, Springfield College has provided equal employment and educational opportunities for women. Being small has provided the necessary flexibility to the development of curricular choices for women of all races and creeds.''

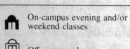

🛏 On-campus evening and/or weekend classes	📖 Commission on minority affairs
🏛 Off-campus classes	📖 Women's Studies program
🚍 Accessible by public transportation	👤 Women's center
👫 On-campus childcare facilities	AAUW Member, American Association of University Women
✎ Publicly communicated sexual harassment policy, includes students	NWSA Member, National Women's Studies Association
⬛ Commission on status of women	CROW On-campus Center for Research on Women

Triton College
2000 Fifth Avenue, River Grove, IL 60171
Telephone: (312) 456-0300

Women in Leadership
★ **faculty**

19,444 undergraduates

	Amer. Ind.	Asian Amer.	Blacks	Hispanics	Whites
F	18	136	689	186	9,949
M	15	146	502	269	7,458
%	0.2	1.5	6.1	2.4	89.9

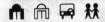

Triton is a public, two-year college, most of whose 19,444 students are reentry students who attend part-time. Women account for 57 percent of students, and 79 percent of the women attend part-time. Sixty percent of women are over age 25, and one-quarter are over age 40. The median age of all students is 30.

Triton offers a college transfer program in liberal arts and pre-professions, a variety of occupational and technical programs, and an extensive adult-education program. Alternative scheduling includes day and evening classes both on and off campus, self-paced/contract learning, a weekend college, and a three-year Tuesday-Thursday college for students completing the associate degree in data processing, accounting, or business administration.

The campus, near Chicago, is accessible by public transportation. All students commute and free on-campus parking is available.

Campus childcare facilities are open from 7 a.m. to 5 p.m., at the rate of $9 a day. The facilities accommodate just under a third of students' requests. Private childcare facilities are available off campus.

Women in Leadership Positions. *Students.* There are few opportunities for women to exercise campus-wide student leadership. A woman served as editor-in-chief of the newspaper once in a recent three-year period.

Faculty. The full-time faculty is 31 percent female. There are 3 female faculty for every 100 female students and 6 male faculty for every 100 male students.

Administrators. Men hold all top positions. Of the 14 departments, three white women and one black woman chair four: English, associate-degree nursing, licensed practical nursing, and secretarial science.

Women and the Curriculum. Most women receive degrees or certificates in the arts and sciences, health technologies, and business and commerce.

There are no courses on women. Courses offered by the departments of nursing, business, and physical education provide some instruction on matters specific to women. Faculty are offered workshops on the needs of reentry women.

Women and Athletics. Women participate in a wide variety of individual and team intercollegiate and intramural sports. Of 23 paid intercollegiate coaches, seven are women. The large, modern gymnasium has an indoor running track. Intercollegiate sports for women include basketball, cross-country, gymnastics, softball, tennis, track and field, and volleyball.

Special Services and Programs for Women. *Health and Counseling.* The student health service is staffed by 2 male physicians and 4 female health-care providers. The student counseling center has a staff of 10, including 3 white women and 1 minority woman. No medical treatment specific to women is available. Birth control counseling is available.

Safety and Security. Measures consist of police with arrest authority, night-time escort service for women, campus-wide emergency telephone system, emergency alarm system, and information sessions on campus safety and rape and assault prevention.

No information was provided about the incidence of rapes and assaults.

Career. Services include workshops on nontraditional occupations, lectures by women employed in nontraditional occupations, printed information on nontraditional fields of study for women, and networking between alumnae and female students. The Employee Development Institute regularly holds seminars and workshops for women in business.

Other. The Adult Reentry Program offers educational and vocational counseling, testing, preview seminars, and workshops on women's programs and skills. The School of Continuing Education sponsors an annual women's week, assertiveness/leadership training, and a program to build mathematics confidence.

Institutional Self-Description. "Triton College is a broad-based community institution which offers a vast array of high-quality educational options at reasonable cost, including easily transferable college credit courses, 84 different career education offerings, a Job Training Institute in which one can develop a marketable skill in three to eight weeks, and hundreds of adult education courses and seminars."

University of Illinois, Chicago Circle
Chicago, IL 60680
Telephone: (312) 996-3000

★★ **Women and the Curriculum**

★★ **Women and Athletics**

16,688 undergraduates

	Amer. Ind.	Asian Amer.	Blacks	Hispanics	Whites
F	37	397	1,945	684	3,966
M	42	566	1,279	793	6,476
%	0.5	5.9	19.9	9.1	64.5

NWSA

Established in 1946 as a state college, the University of Illinois at Chicago Circle became a university for commuting students in 1965. Over 20,300 individuals enroll in a range of undergraduate and graduate programs. There is an extension division. Evening classes and a summer session are available

Women are 43 percent of the 16,688 undergraduates; 17 percent of the women attend part-time. The median age of undergraduates is 21. The university is accessible by public transportation and there is on-campus parking.

Campus childcare facilities charge on a sliding scale and can accommodate half of students' requests. Private arrangements for childcare can be made nearby.

Policies to Ensure Fairness to Women. On a part-time basis, the Assistant Vice-Chancellor for Academic Affairs monitors compliance with equal-employment-opportunity, sex-equity, and handicapped-accessibility legislation. A published campus policy prohibits sexual harassment; complaints are resolved through a formal grievance procedure.

Women in Leadership Positions. *Students.* Information on opportunities for women students to exercise campus leadership is incomplete. A woman served as president of the student body in 1980–81.

Faculty. Women are one-fifth of the full-time faculty of 829. According to a recent report, 9 black, 10 Asian American, and 7 Hispanic women are on the full-time faculty. The ratio of female faculty to female students is 3 to 100; for males, the ratio is 8 to 100.

Administrators. The Director of Libraries is a woman; all other higher administrative posts are held by men. Women chair five of 31 departments, including anthropology, mathematics, Slavic languages, and Latin American studies.

Women and the Curriculum. The most popular majors for undergraduate women are business and management (21 percent), social sciences (16 percent). education (14 percent), and psychology (11 percent). Nine percent of women major in such non-traditional areas as architecture, computer science, engineering, mathematics, and the physical sciences.

The Women's Studies Program, under a full-time director, offers an undergraduate minor and an individually designed major. Twenty-two Women's Studies or courses on women are offered through the departments of Slavic languages, black studies, philosophy, anthropology, sociology, English, classics, linguistics, Latin American studies, nursing, history, and political science. Recent titles include The American Woman Today; Women in Art, History, and Literature; Women in Comparative Cultures; Women in Russian Literature; Sex Roles in Non-Western Cultures; Women in Antiquity; Language and Sex; Women and Mental Health; and Topics in the History of Women. An official committee works to develop the Women's Studies offerings and courses on women across the curriculum.

A new three-year federal grant will enable the Women's Studies Program to offer a summer institute aimed at improving the teaching about minority women by Women's Studies faculty.

Such current issues as mathematics confidence among females, sex-fair curricula, coeducational physical education classes, innovative health-care delivery, health-care information of particular concern to minority women, services for abused spouses, and women in management are part of the coursework for future teachers, health-care workers, social workers, and business students. The needs of reentry women and affirmative action are topics of faculty workshops.

Minority Women. Of 7,121 undergraduate women, 27 percent are black, less than 1 percent American Indian, 6 percent Asian American, and 10 percent Hispanic. Among courses of interest to minority women are The Black Woman as Writer, Topics in the Black Female Experience, Latin American Women in Latin America, and Latin American Women in the U.S.A. Fifteen percent of the users of the Women's Center are black and Hispanic women. Minority Women can find other supportive women through some sororities, Circle Women's Alliance, the black, Latin American, and Women's Studies programs, and the Native American Support Program.

Women and Athletics. Excellent intramural and intercollegiate programs provide a mix of individual and team sports. Softball and volleyball teams in the intramural program are coeducational. One-third of the varsity and 44 percent of the intramural players are female. Varsity teams played tournament competition during 1980. Intercollegiate sports offered are basketball, cross-country, gymnastics, track and field, softball, swimming, tennis, and volleyball.

Special Services and Programs for Women. *Health and Counseling.* The student health service provides some medical attention specific to women. Gynecological and birth control treatment is available on campus; for treatment of abortion and rape and assault, students are referred to the university hospital. Four of seven physicians are women. The regular student health insurance covers abortion and maternity at no extra cost. Five women therapists work at the counseling center. They offer counseling specific to women.

Safety and Security. Measures include campus police with arrest authority, night-time escorts for women, bus service at night to public transportation, emergency alarm and telephone systems, self-defense courses for women, information sessions on safety and crime prevention, and a rape crisis center. Forty assaults were reported for 1980–81.

Career. Services include workshops, speakers, and nonsexist/nonracist published materials which concentrate on nontraditional careers and fields of study for women, as well as updated alumnae files by specific careers.

Other. Student Organizations and Activities funds a small Women's Center staffed by a student volunteer. Among the center's activities are assertiveness training and a telephone service of information, referral, and support. The Women's Studies Program sponsors a lecture series and helps organize a program to build mathematics confidence, which is available as a course. The Circle Women's Alliance serves as an advocate for women.

Special Features. The Midwest Women's Historical Collection is part of the university's manuscript archives.

Institutional Self-Description. None provided.

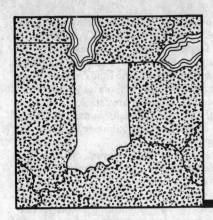

INDIANA

Ball State University

2000 University Avenue
Muncie, IN 47306
Telephone: (317) 285-1420

Women in Leadership	★ Women and the
★ faculty	Curriculum
	★★★ Women and Athletics

14,462 undergraduates

	Amer. Ind.	Asian Amer.	Blacks	Hispanics	Whites
F	18	9	395	30	7,553
M	9	13	281	28	6,083
%	0.2	0.2	4.7	0.4	94.6

🏠 🏛 ⚑ 📖 **AAUW**

Established as a teacher-training school in 1918 and a university since 1965, Ball State University in Muncie attracts over 16,900 students to a variety of undergraduate, graduate, and professional studies. A summer session, evening, and off-campus classes are available.

Women are 55 percent of the 14,462 undergraduates; 12 percent of the women attend part-time. The average age of undergraduates is 20. Forty-five percent of undergraduates commute. Public transportation operates within the city. There is on-campus parking, with free transportation from distant parking lots.

Policies to Ensure Fairness to Women. A full-time Director of Equal Opportunity and Affirmative Action is responsible for policy and compliance related to employment, sex equity for students, and handicapped accessibility. A published policy prohibits sexual harassment. Complaints are handled through a formal grievance procedure. The university has an appointed Advisory Committee on Affirmative Action.

Women in Leadership Positions. *Students.* In recent years, women have twice presided over the student senate, the student union board, the student court, and the residence hall council, and been editor-in-chief of the campus newspaper once. Women head 16 of the 37 honorary societies.

Faculty. Women are 29 percent of a full-time faculty of 881. There are 4 female faculty for every 100 female students and 11 male faculty for every 100 male students.

Administrators. Men occupy all top administrative posts. Women chair six of 50 departments. Forty percent of the faculty senate, half of the campus-wide personnel committee, and a quarter of the trustees are female.

Women and the Curriculum. Most women graduating with bachelor's degrees major in education (30 percent), the health professions (14 percent), and business and management (13 percent). Less than 4 percent major in nontraditional areas. A program in the department of mathematics helps women build math-ematics confidence. Women receive three-fourths of two-year degrees awarded, most of them in business and arts and sciences.

The Women's Studies Committee sponsors a 36-credit interdisciplinary minor in Women's Studies. The program offers a course called General Studies Colloquium: Women's Studies, along with courses on women through the departments of history, classical culture, English, anthropology, sociology, psychology, political science, and health, science, physiology. Courses include Women and Health, Culture and Women, Women and Politics, and Women in Ancient Greece and Rome.

Minority Women. Of 8,005 undergraduate women, 5 percent are black and less than 1 percent each are American Indian, Asian American, and Hispanic. There are 31 women in all-minority sororities. Two residence-hall directors are minority women. Residence-hall staff are offered awareness-training on the avoidance of racism.

Women and Athletics. Outstanding intramural and intercollegiate programs provide a high number and variety of individual and team sports. Club sports are also available. Fourteen percent of intramural and 32 percent of intercollegiate athletes are women. Women receive half of the athletic scholarships. Twelve of the 37 paid varsity coaches are women. Most of the women's teams played in tournaments in 1980. The intercollegiate sports offered are badminton, basketball, cross-country, field hockey, golf, gymnastics, lacrosse, softball, swimming and diving, tennis, track and field, and volleyball.

Housing and Student Organizations. Fifty-five percent of undergraduates live on campus. Single-sex and coeducational dormitories and housing for married students and single parents with children are available. A married woman whose husband is not enrolled may live in married students' housing. Dormitories restrict hours for visitors of the opposite sex. Over half of the residence-hall staff are female; staff are offered awareness-training on sex education and on the avoidance of sexism and racism.

Fourteen percent of full-time undergraduate women belong to social sororities. Sororities do not furnish housing for their members. The National Organization for Women (NOW) serves as an advocate for women on campus.

Special Services and Programs for Women. *Health and Counseling.* The student health service provides gynecological treatment. Two of seven physicians are female, as are 17 other health-care providers. The counseling service provides birth control, abortion, and rape and assault counseling. No information was provided on the number and gender of counselors.

Safety and Security. Measures consist of campus police with the authority to make arrests, night-time campus-wide bus service, high-intensity lighting, emergency telephones, courses on self-defense and safety for women, and a rape crisis center. For 1980-81, 47 assaults (ten on women) and two rapes were reported.

Other. Special services, including a telephone line of information, referral, and support, are available through community organizations. A women's lecture series and assertiveness training are sponsored by departments.

Institutional Self-Description. ''General education, liberal and applied arts, pre-professional and professional study lead to various degrees. Cultural opportunities include literary, artistic, or avocational areas. Undergraduate interdepartmental Women's Studies is among new programs available.''

Butler University
Indianapolis, IN 46208
Telephone: (317) 283-9350

Women in Leadership
★★ students

2,230 undergraduates

	Amer. Ind.	Asian Amer.	Blacks	Hispanics	Whites
F	0	12	23	3	1,208
M	4	6	15	8	942
%	0.2	0.8	1.7	0.5	96.8

Established in the mid-19th century, Butler University is an independent, non-sectarian, urban institution of 3,800 students. Undergraduate, graduate, and professional programs of study are offered. Evening classes and a summer session are available.

Women make up 56 percent of the 2,230 undergraduates; 11 percent of women attend part-time. For the one-quarter of undergraduates who live off campus or commute, the university is accessible by public transportation. On-campus parking is free.

Private childcare arrangements can be made close to campus.

Policies to Ensure Fairness to Women. University officers monitor practices related to equal employment opportunity, educational equity for women and men, and handicapped access. The equity concerns of women and minorities are handled by Presidential Cabinet or appropriate governance committees.

Women in Leadership Positions. *Students.* Opportunities for women to assume all-campus leadership are excellent. In recent years, women have been president of the student body, presiding officers of the student senate, court, union board, and residence hall council (three times), manager of the campus radio (twice), and editor-in-chief of the newspaper. Women preside over ten of 19 honorary societies.

Faculty. Women are 24 percent of a full-time faculty of 152. There are 3 female faculty for every 100 female students and 13 male faculty for every 100 male students.

Administrators. Men hold most key positions. The chief student-life officer is an American Indian woman. Women chair the departments of home economics and dance.

Women and the Curriculum. Over one-third of the bachelor's degrees awarded to women are in the fields of education and the health professions, with significant numbers in business and management, communications, and fine arts. Five percent are in the nontraditional fields of computer science, mathematics, and physical sciences. Half of the science field-service positions go to women.

Recent courses on women offered in the departments of home economics, English, and history include Contemporary Living for Singles, Women in Changing Perspective, and Women in American History. Such current issues as sex-fair curricula and coeducational physical education classes are part of the preparation of future teachers.

Women and Athletics. Intramural and intercollegiate programs provide limited opportunities for organized, competitive, individual and team sports. Eighteen percent of intercollegiate athletes are women; women receive 20 percent of athletic scholarships. Half of the paid intercollegiate coaches are female. All women's varsity teams played in tournaments in 1980. The intercollegiate sports offered are basketball, softball, tennis, and volleyball.

Housing and Student Organizations. Three-quarters of the undergraduates live on campus. Residential accommodations include single-sex and coeducational dormitories and Greek housing units. Residence halls restrict hours for visitors of the opposite sex. Two of three residence-hall directors are female.

Twenty-seven percent of the undergraduate women belong to social sororities. Butler Women's Organization serves as an advocate for women on campus.

Special Services and Programs for Women. *Health and Counseling.* The student health and counseling services provide rape and assault treatment and counseling.

Safety and Security. Measures include campus police who have arrest authority and weapons training, night-time escort service for women, and information sessions on safety and crime prevention. Three assaults (one on a woman) and no rapes were reported for 1980-81.

Career. Nonsexist/nonracist printed information on nontraditional fields of study for women is available.

Institutional Self-Description. ''Butler was founded as the first college or university in Indiana—and the third in the nation—to admit women on an equal basis with men. In 1858, Butler appointed a woman to the faculty. The Demia Butler chair, established over 100 years ago, was the first endowed professorship in English literature and also the first created for a woman faculty member in an American college or university.''

Depauw University
Greencastle, IN 46135
Telephone: (317) 658-4800

2,196 undergraduates

	Amer. Ind.	Asian Amer.	Blacks	Hispanics	Whites
F	2	3	19	5	1,143
M	2	4	22	10	979
%	0.2	0.3	1.9	0.7	96.9

A residential university located an hour from Indianapolis, Depauw is a private, non-sectarian institution affiliated with the United Methodist Church. Founded in 1834, it now enrolls some 2,300 students, of whom 2,196 are registered in degree programs. Fifty-four percent of the undergraduates are women; virtually all women attend full-time. Bachelor's and master's degrees are offered through the Asbury College of Liberal Arts and the Schools of Music and Nursing.

Policies to Ensure Fairness to Women. The Director of Personnel has part-time responsibility for review of policies and practices related to equal employment opportunity.

Women in Leadership Positions. *Students.* Women have limited opportunities to exercise campus-wide leadership. In recent years, women have served as editor-in-chief of the campus newspaper for three terms. Women head three of the five campus honorary societies.

Faculty. Fifteen percent of the 131 full-time faculty are women, a proportion below average for comparable institutions in this guide. There are 2 female faculty for every 100 female students and 11 male faculty for every 100 male students. The full-time faculty includes 1 black woman.

Administrators. Except for the chief student-life officer, all major administrative positions are held by men. Women chair two of the 22 departments: education and nursing. Of the 52 trustees, 3 are women.

Women and the Curriculum. In a recent year, most women

earned degrees in letters (19 percent), social sciences (17 percent), health professions (14 percent), and education (12 percent); 6 percent majored in such nontraditional fields as mathematics and physical sciences. There are no courses on women.

Women and Athletics. Women have some opportunities to participate in organized team and individual sports. There are six paid female coaches for intercollegiate sports, and all seven women's varsity teams participated in recent tournament competition. Intercollegiate sports available to women are basketball, field hockey, golf, softball, swimming, tennis and volleyball.

Housing and Student Organizations. Single-sex and coeducational dormitories are available to those students who live on campus. Two of the four residence-hall directors are women.

Eighty-three percent of full-time undergraduate women belong to sororities, including four minority women in racially integrated sororities. Both sororities and fraternities provide housing for members. Associated Women Students and The Panhellenic Council serve as advocacy groups for women students.

Special Services and Programs for Women. *Health and Counseling.* One male physician staffs the student health service; the counseling center employs one woman and one man. Services specific to women include treatment and counseling for gynecological problems, birth control, abortion, and rape and assault.

Safety and Security. Measures consist of campus and local police and a night-time escort service for women students. No rapes and 19 assaults (11 on women) were reported for 1980–81.

Career. The university sponsors lectures and panels for students by women employed in nontraditional occupations.

Institutional Self-Description. "Depauw is a traditional liberal arts university with small schools of music and nursing, located in a small town. Most of the problems emphasized in the *Everywoman's Guide* Questionnaire, such as sexual harassment, assaults and rapes, and the need for security which goes with them, are fortunately absent. There is strong support for women students in both the faculty and staff. Most of our women graduates enter either graduate school or the workforce, and they tend to enter the same occupations that men do."

Goshen College
Goshen, IN 46526
Telephone: (219) 533-3161

Women in Leadership
- ★ **faculty**
- ★ **administrators**

1,179 undergraduates

	Amer. Ind.	Asian Amer.	Blacks	Hispanics	Whites
F	1	4	18	13	632
M	0	1	14	12	416
%	0.1	0.5	2.9	2.3	94.3

 AAUW

Goshen College, founded in 1894, is a four-year coeducational college affiliated with the Mennonite Church. Some 1,200 students attend the campus, located one hour from South Bend. Women are 60 percent of the 1,179 undergraduates; 8 percent of women attend part-time. The median age of all undergraduates is 21. Goshen offers bachelor's degrees in a variety of fields, including nursing. Schedules include evening classes, summer sessions, and a continuing education program. Thirty-one percent of the undergraduates commute to campus; free on-campus parking is available.

Private childcare facilities are available within one mile of the campus.

Women in Leadership Positions. *Students.* In a recent three-year period, women have held slightly less than one-third of student leadership positions. They have been head of the student union board twice, editor-in-chief of the campus newspaper, manager of the radio station, and head of senior, junior, and sophomore classes.

Faculty. Women are 33 percent of the 76-member full-time faculty, a figure above the national average. They are 26 percent of the permanently appointed faculty, a higher proportion than at most four-year colleges in this guide. There are 4 female faculty for every 100 female undergraduates and 12 male faculty for every 100 male undergraduates.

Administrators. Two of eight top administrators are women; the chief development officer and the director of athletics. Four of the 20 departments are chaired by women: nursing, physical education, home economics, and social work. All but one of the seven deans and directors of academic units are men.

Women and the Curriculum. The majority of women graduates earn degrees in the health professions (35 percent) and education (23 percent). Less than 1 percent earn degrees in mathematics. Women are 60 percent of the students participating in internships and 24 percent of students in science field service.

Courses on women, offered in several departments, include Womanhood in America, Bible and Sexuality, and Contemporary Women's Issues. The departments of nursing and social work provide instruction on some matters specific to women.

Women and Athletics. Women participate in four intramural team sports and five intercollegiate sports. Seven of 16 paid varsity coaches are women. Intercollegiate sports offered are basketball, field hockey, tennis, track and field, and volleyball.

Housing and Student Organizations. Sixty-nine percent of the students reside on campus in single-sex and coeducational residences that have restrictive hours for visitors of the opposite sex. A woman student whose husband is not enrolled may live in married students' housing. The two female and two male residence-hall directors are offered awareness-training on sexism and sex education.

Special Services and Programs for Women. *Health and Counseling.* The health service, staffed by a male physician, provides treatment for gynecological problems, birth control, and rape and assault. The student counseling service offers counseling on gynecological problems, birth control, rape and assault, and abortion. Professional counselors are offered in-service training on the avoidance of sex-role stereotyping, racial bias, and in feminist counseling.

Safety and Security. Local police have jurisdiction over the campus, and the college provides information sessions on campus safety and rape and assault prevention. The college reports one rape on campus for 1980-81 and states that "we know through Local Operations Support [a YWCA community group] that some assault/rapes have occurred."

Other. Community groups sponsor a battered women's program, a warmline referral service, and a women's lecture series. Residence Life sponsors assertiveness/leadership training for women.

Returning Women Students. The Continuing Education for Women Program enrolls 269 reentry women in non-credit courses. Approximately 500 reentry women attend courses offered by other adult and continuing education programs.

Institutional Self-Description. "Efforts are underway to encourage more women to enroll in business, pre-medical (natural science), pre-law, pre-dental, and graduate programs in the arts and humanities. A small but committed group of feminist professors and administrators seeks to support women's search for self-understanding and social fulfillment. A required trimester in a developing country provides opportunity to students to observe women's roles in other cultural settings."

Indiana State University, Evansville

8600 University Boulevard
Evansville, IN 47712
Telephone: (812) 464-1761

2,868 undergraduates

	Amer. Ind.	Asian Amer.	Blacks	Hispanics	Whites
F	1	4	60	3	1,349
M	4	9	39	4	1,371
%	0.2	0.5	3.5	0.3	95.6

 AAUW

The Evansville campus of Indiana State University offers bachelor's degrees in business, education, and the arts and sciences. Continuing education is available. Alternative schedules include on- and off-campus evening classes, off-campus day classes, and a summer session.

ISU at Evansville enrolls some 2,800 undergraduates; half are women. Forty-three percent of women attend part-time; one-fourth are over age 25. All students commute. The campus is accessible by public transportation. On-campus parking is available at a fee.

A college-operated childcare facility, which can accommodate 30 children and is open from 7:45 a.m. to 9:00 p.m., gives priority to students. Fees are charged at a fixed daily rate.

Policies to Ensure Fairness to Women. The Personnel Director has part-time responsibility for review of policies and practices related to equal employment opportunity, educational sex equity, and handicapped accessibility. A campus policy prohibits sexual harassment; complaints are handled through a formal grievance procedure. Policy and procedure have not been communicated to students in writing.

Women in Leadership Positions. *Students.* Two of four campus honorary societies are headed by women. No information was supplied regarding other campus-wide student leadership positions.

Faculty. Twenty-one percent of the 94 full-time faculty are women, a proportion slightly below the average for similar colleges in this guide. There are 2 female faculty for every 100 female students and 8 male faculty for every 100 male students.

Administrators. Among the seven top administrators, the head librarian is a woman. Women chair five administrative units: media services, personnel, publications, the computer center, and health services. Two of nine members of the Board of Trustees are women.

Women and the Curriculum. Most women earn bachelor's degrees in education (31 percent), business (22 percent), and social sciences (14 percent). Three percent of women graduate in the nontraditional fields of mathematics and engineering. Women earn almost three-fourths of the two-year degrees, and 77 percent of the two-year women major in health technologies. Half of student internship and cooperative education positions go to women.

The university offers one course on women, Women in America, through the department of social science. The departments of education and physical education include instruction on some matters specific to women in their curricula.

Women and Athletics. Thirty-nine percent of intercollegiate and 23 percent of intramural athletes are women. Women receive 30 percent of athletic scholarships. The intramural sports program offers a variety of individual and team activities, including bowling, basketball, swimming, track and field, football, softball, and volleyball. Three of ten paid varsity coaches are women. Intercollegiate sports offered are basketball, softball, tennis, and volleyball.

Special Services and Programs for Women. *Health and Counseling.* The student health service employs one female health-care provider; the counseling center is staffed by one male counselor. Birth control and abortion counseling are available. There is no medical treatment specific to women.

Safety and Security. Measures consist of campus police without arrest authority and a night-time escort service for women. No rapes or assaults were reported for 1980–81.

Career. Files on the careers of alumnae are accessible to students.

Other. The coordinator of programs for women organizes a series of non-credit programs several times during the year. The university also offers a special orientation program for reentry women.

Institutional Self-Description. "The university's mission is to serve the educational needs of the people of southwestern Indiana. In our 16 years of existence, the number of women students enrolled has gradually increased and is not limited only to traditional-age students. A substantial percentage of students are women over the age of 25, and appropriate support services are extended to them. These women generally achieve very well in the classroom and in the job market after graduation."

Indiana State University, Terre Haute

Terre Haute, IN 47809
Telephone: (812) 232-6311

Women in Leadership	★ Women and the
★★ students	Curriculum
★ faculty	
	★★ Women and Athletics

9,651 undergraduates

	Amer. Ind.	Asian Amer.	Blacks	Hispanics	Whites
F	8	20	448	16	4,228
M	11	12	352	21	4,335
%	0.1	0.1	8.0	0.1	90.1

 AAUW NWSA

Founded in 1865 as a teacher-training school, Indiana State at Terre Haute became a teachers' college in 1929, a state college in 1961, and part of the Indiana State University system in 1965. Now a public research university, it offers some 11,500 students undergraduate and graduate programs in a variety of liberal arts, pre-professional, and professional programs. Adult education is provided through Continuing Education, Academic Services, and Special Programs. Evening classes both on and off campus and a summer session are available.

Women constitute half of the 9,651 undergraduates; 17 percent of women attend part-time. The university reports that 14 percent of women undergraduates are over age 25. Located southwest of Indianapolis, the campus is accessible by public transportation; on-campus parking for a fee is available for the 53 percent of students who commute.

A university-operated childcare center accommodates 40 pre-schoolers; fees are based on a sliding scale. Additional, private childcare facilities are located nearby.

Policies to Ensure Fairness to Women. The Director of Affirmative Action has full-time responsibility for policy and compliance with equal-employment-opportunity, sex-equity, and handicapped-access regulations. The Affirmative Action Committee, appointed by the President, is concerned with the status of women, minority affairs, and all aspects of equal opportunity. A published policy prohibits sexual harassment; complaints are handled either informally and confidentially or through a formal grievance procedure.

Women in Leadership Positions. *Students*. Women have excellent leadership opportunities. In a recent three-year period, women held 6 of 8 campus-wide offices for one or more terms. Women preside over 10 of 21 honorary societies.

Faculty. Twenty-five percent of the 668 full-time faculty are women, a proportion which is average for institutions nationwide. There are 4 female faculty for every 100 female students and 12 male faculty for every 100 male students.

Administrators. Most top-level administrators are men; a woman serves as Dean of the School of Graduate Studies. Women also serve as Deans of the College of Arts and Sciences, the School of Nursing, and Academic Services and Special Programs. Women chair three of 41 departments: home economics, business (distributive education and office administration), and women's physical education. Women hold two seats on the nine-member Board of Trustees. Thirty-five percent of the faculty senate are women.

Women and the Curriculum. Most women earn bachelor's degrees in education (39 percent), health professions (13 percent), business (12 percent), social sciences (9 percent), and home economics (9 percent)., Three percent of women graduate in the nontraditional fields of engineering, mathematics, and physical sciences. Of the two-year degrees awarded to women, 45 percent are in health professions, 38 percent in business, and 12 percent in public service technologies. About half of the students in cooperative education and internship programs are women, as are 30 percent of students in science field-service programs.

The Women's Studies Program, which offers an undergraduate minor, is headed by a full-time, permanent faculty member who is Asian American. Sixteen undergraduate or graduate courses on women are offered through the Women's Studies Center and eleven departments: economics, history, home economics, psychology, English, humanities, foreign language, sociology, political science, physical education, and graduate education. Recent offerings include Images of Women; The Education of Girls and Women; Women in Contemporary Society; Women Writers of Great Britain; Women and the Law; Women in Sports. The School of Education and the department of physical education offer instruction on some issues specific to women. An official committee is responsible for the development of additional courses on women.

Women and Athletics. The organized athletic program for women is excellent, with a high number and variety of team and individual sports. Women compete in 13 intercollegiate and ten intramural sports. Women receive 30 percent of the athletic scholarships. Nine of eleven paid intercollegiate coaches are women. Intercollegiate sports offered are archery, badminton, basketball, bowling, cross-country, field hockey, golf, gymnastics, softball, swimming, tennis, track, and volleyball.

Housing and Student Organizations. Single-sex and coeducational dormitories and housing for married students are available for the 47 percent of undergraduates who live on campus. While single-sex dormitories restrict hours for visitors of the opposite sex, coeducational dormitories do not. Six of the 12 residence-hall directors are women. Residence-hall staff are offered awareness-training on the avoidance of sexism and racism, and on birth control and sex education.

Fifteen percent of undergraduate women belong to social sororities. Sorority members are assigned suites in residence halls. Gays, Lesbians and Friends is a student advocacy group.

Special Services and Programs for Women. *Health and Counseling*. The student health service is staffed by 4 male physicians, along with 1 male and 18 female health-care providers. One of 4 professionals at the student counseling center is a woman. Counseling and medical treatment are available for rape and assault. Medical treatment for birth control is also available.

Safety and Security. No information was supplied.

Career. Information on nontraditional occupations for women and files on alumnae careers are available. A career program and women's opportunity workshops are sponsored by the Dean of Academic Services and Special Programs.

Other. A Women's Center, operated by Student Affairs on a budget of $9,981, attracts 1,450 primarily undergraduate and community women. The Dean of Academic Services and Special Programs sponsors a Financial Forum for Women.

Institutional Self-Description. None provided.

Indiana University, Bloomington
Bloomington, IN 47405
Telephone: (812) 337-0661

★★ **Women and the Curriculum**

★★★ **Women and Athletics**

22,811 undergraduates

	Amer. Ind.	Asian Amer.	Blacks	Hispanics	Whites
F	24	96	645	84	10,327
M	19	57	538	100	10,558
%	0.2	0.7	5.3	0.8	93.0

Founded in 1820, Indiana University at Bloomington is the oldest of eight campuses in the Indiana University system. It is also the main residential campus in the system. The campus serves 31,500 students, of whom 22,811 are undergraduates. Women are half of the undergraduates; 8 percent of women attend part-time. The median age of all undergraduates is 22. A broad range of associate, bachelor's, and graduate degree programs is available, in addition to a continuing education program. Alternative scheduling includes a summer session, evening classes, and self-paced/contract learning.

Bloomington's campus, located mostly within the town, is accessible by public transportation. Forty percent of the undergraduates commute to the campus; on-campus parking is available at a fee.

Campus childcare facilities, serving all members of the academic community, can accommodate all students' request for service. Charges are based on a fixed monthly fee of $40. Private childcare facilities are located near the campus.

Policies to Ensure Fairness to Women. An Affirmative Action Officer and an Administrative Assistant are responsible full-time for policy and monitoring compliance concerning equal employment opportunity, sex equity, and handicapped access. The Affirmative Action Officer is a voting member of a policymaking body. A sexual harassment policy, in the process of being conveyed in writing to students, faculty, and staff, protects all members of the college community. Complaints of sexual harassment are resolved either informally and confidentially, or through a formal campus grievance procedure.

The Office for Women's Affairs assumes the functions of a Committee on the Status of Women, in addition to providing programming and support. The office has a full-time dean and an associate director, who report to the Vice President of the university. The dean is assisted by an advisory panel. An Academic Women's Coalition responds to the concerns of faculty and other female academic employees. Two additional Affirmative Action Committees, one for faculty and one for staff, also address the employment-related concerns of women.

In place of a Committee on Minority Affairs, Bloomington has an Office for Afro-American Affairs and an Office for Latino Affairs. The Office for Women's Affairs, the Office for Afro-

American Affairs, and The Office for Latino Affairs address the concerns of minority women.

Women in Leadership Positions. *Students.* Women have few opportunities to gain campus-wide leadership experience. In a recent three-year period, women served one-year terms as president of the student union board and editor-in-chief of the campus newspaper. Six of the 15 honorary societies are led by women.

Faculty. Seventeen percent of the 1,271 faculty members are women. There are 2 female faculty for every 100 female students and 10 male faculty for every 100 male students.

Administrators. All key administrators except the head librarian are male; all 11 academic deans are male. Six of 65 departments are chaired by women: forensics, political science, classical archeology, classics, home economics, and nursing. Ten of 40 members of the faculty senate are women, as are 4 of 25 members of an important faculty committee.

Women and the Curriculum. Over one-third of women graduate in education (18 percent) and business (17 percent). Other popular fields for women are public affairs (11 percent), fine arts (10 percent), and social sciences (8 percent). Four percent of women major in such nontraditional fields as mathematics and physical sciences. Programs encourage women to study science, accounting, and law enforcement/corrections. Half of the students in experiential learning programs offered by the Living Learning Center are women.

The Women's Studies Program offers a 24-credit certificate, a B.A. through an independent major, and a 12-credit graduate minor. More than 40 courses focus on women, through Women's Studies and at least 13 departments, including Afro-American studies, anthropology, biology, comparative literature, forensic studies, folklore, history, West European studies, and sociology. Recent offerings include Biological Sex Roles; Women in Sports: A Historical Perspective; Sex and Society in America; Folklore and Women; Women in Russia and the Soviet Union; Women and the Criminal Justice System; and Women in the Economy. The program is headed by a full-time faculty member. During the past five years, 20 undergraduates have majored in Women's Studies; 16 have begun the graduate minor in Women's Studies. An official committee supervises the development of the Women's Studies Program and encourages the integration of the new scholarship on women across the curriculum. Nursing, social work, and business offer instruction on some matters specific to women.

Minority Women. Eight percent of undergraduate women are members of minority groups. Two deans and three directors, appointed by the Vice President, staff the Office for Latino Affairs and the Office for Afro-American Affairs. Women's Studies and the Spanish and Portuguese department offer Women in Hispanic Culture. Three all-minority sororities have 44 members. Residence-hall staff are offered awareness-training on the avoidance of racism.

Women and Athletics. Women students have outstanding opportunities to participate in organized competitive sports. Both the intramural and intercollegiate programs offer a variety of team and individual sports. Forty-three percent of the intercollegiate athletes are women; women receive 30 percent of the athletic scholarships; 28 percent of the paid intercollegiate coaches are women. Many of the varsity teams participate in tournament competition. Intercollegiate sports offered are basketball, cross-country, field hockey, golf, gymnastics, softball, swimming, tennis, track and field, and volleyball.

Housing and Student Organizations. Sixty percent of the undergraduates reside on campus in single-sex or coeducational dormitories, and in housing for married students and single parents. A married student whose husband is not enrolled is permitted to live in married students' housing. Residence-hall staff are offered awareness-training on sexism, racism, human sexuality, birth control, and sexual preference.

Fourteen percent of women students join sororities, some of which provide housing for members.

Campus advocacy groups for women include the Task Force on Women's Concerns, IU-Student Affairs/Women's Affairs Group, the Student Affirmative Action Committee, the Feminist Academic Women's Coalition, the Women's Law Caucus, Graduate Women in Business, and Graduate Women.

Special Services and Programs for Women. *Health and Counseling.* No information was provided about the staffs of the student health and student counseling centers. Counseling and medical treatment are offered for birth control, gynecological problems, and rape and assault. Student health insurance covers maternity expenses.

Safety and Security. Measures consist of campus and local police, night-time escorts, night-time bus service to residence areas, instruction on self-defense, and a rape crisis center. For 1980–81, six rapes and 26 assaults (on men and women) were reported.

Career. Services include workshops, printed materials, and job discrimination information on nontraditional occupations for women, panels by women employed in these fields, files on alumnae careers, and networking with alumnae. Faculty workshops are held on nontraditional occupations for women and men. Programs to help women gain confidence in mathematics are offered through Student Services and the School of Continuing Studies.

Other. The Office for Women's Affairs operates a telephone information and referral service and offers assertiveness training (in conjunction with Student Services). An annual women's week, a women's lecture series, and theater and other women's arts performances are sponsored by various campus groups.

Returning Women Students. The School of Continuing Studies runs a Continuing Education for Women Center, under the direction of a full-time administrator. Workshops instruct faculty on the needs of reentry women.

Institutional Self-Description. "The Bloomington campus has a strong Women's Studies Program at the graduate and undergraduate levels; opportunities for research and financial support; an active and involved feminist community exists both on campus and in town. A large, long-standing Returning Women's Student Program provides support to nontraditional women students. An active Office for Women's Affairs serves as an advocate for all women on campus; a sympathetic administration has implemented significant legal and social changes."

Indiana University, East
Richmond, IN 47374
Telephone: (317) 996-8261

Women in Leadership
★★★ students
★★ faculty

1,176 undergraduates

	Amer. Ind.	Asian Amer.	Blacks	Hispanics	Whites
F	1	0	33	1	602
M	1	1	9	1	525
%	0.2	0.1	3.6	0.2	96.0

A regional campus of Indiana University, this public, two-year college provides educational services to 1,381 students. Women constitute 54 percent of the 1,176 degree students; 70 percent of women attend part-time. The median age of all undergraduates is 26. IU East offers a university-parallel curriculum, associate degrees, and continuing education. Flexible scheduling and locations include off-campus and evening classes, self-paced/contract learning, a weekend college and a summer session. The suburban campus, located in Richmond, is accessible by public transportation; on-campus parking is available for a fee. All students commute.

Private childcare facilities are available near campus.

Policies to Ensure Fairness to Women. On a part-time basis, an affirmative action officer reviews policies and practices relating to equal-employment, sex-equity-for-students, and handicapped-accessibility legislation. A written policy prohibiting sexual harassment of students, faculty, and staff will be communicated to all by fall 1982. Complaints of sexual harassment are resolved informally and confidentially or through a formal procedure.

Women in Leadership Positions. *Students.* In a recent three-year period, women held the two campus-wide leadership positions five-sixths of the time; women were presiding officer of the student governing body for two years and editor-in-chief of the newspaper for three years.

Faculty. Eleven of 23 full-time faculty are women. There are 6 female faculty for every 100 female students and 10 male faculty for every 100 male students.

Administrators. Of the seven chief administrators, the student-life officer is a woman. Two of the eight departments are chaired by women: nursing and human services. About one-quarter of the members of the faculty senate are women.

Women and the Curriculum. Most degrees are awarded to women in the arts and sciences or business and commerce. Eighty percent of students in the internships and practicums offered by the college are women. There are no courses on women.

Women and Athletics. Club sports are offered, in which 12 of 20 participants are women.

Special Services and Programs for Women. *Health and Counseling.* There is no student health service. The student counseling center is staffed by four counselors, one of whom is a minority woman. No counseling specific to women is available.

Safety and Security. Measures consist of campus police and local police, a night-time escort service for women students, and a rape crisis center. No information was provided on the incidence of rapes and assaults.

Career. Services include workshops about nontraditional occupations, lectures and panels by women employed in nontraditional occupations, and printed information on nontraditional fields of study for women. The Office of Continuing Studies provides assertiveness training.

Institutional Self-Description. "Indiana University East is a commuter campus which serves primarily adults and nontraditional students. It emphasizes flexibility and responsiveness to student needs in course scheduling and teaching methods. As a result, many women discover that they can continue their education while managing other personal responsibilities."

Indiana University, Kokomo
2300 S. Washington, Kokomo, IN 46901
Telephone: (317) 453-2000

Women in Leadership
- ★★ students
- ★ faculty
- ★ administrators

1,645 undergraduates

	Amer. Ind.	Asian Amer.	Blacks	Hispanics	Whites
F	1	0	20	4	931
M	2	2	13	2	668
%	0.2	0.1	2.0	0.4	97.3

Indiana University at Kokomo is a state-supported institution that offers both two-year and four-year degrees. Its 2,313 students include 1,645 undergraduates. Fifty-eight percent of the under-

graduates are women; 65 percent of women attend part-time. The median age of all undergraduates is 24. Evening classes meet on and off campus. A summer session and continuing education are available. All students commute, and pay for parking on campus.

A campus daycare facility, which accommodates 25 children, gives priority to students. The facility is open until 8 p.m. and charges $.60 per hour plus $5 per month. Additional, private childcare facilities are located off campus.

Policies to Ensure Fairness to Women. The Affirmative Action Officer has part-time responsibility for examining policies and practices and monitoring compliance with laws on sex equity for students, equal employment opportunity, and handicapped access. A sexual harassment policy is being developed. The Affirmative Action Committee, appointed by and responsible to the Chancellor, addresses issues of concern to women, particularly minority women.

Women in Leadership Positions. *Students.* Opportunites for campus leadership are excellent. In a recent three-year period, women twice were president of the student body and the student senate, presided over the student union board, and were editor-in-chief of the campus newspaper.

Faculty. Thirty-two percent of the 50 full-time faculty are women, a proportion above the national average. There are 5 female faculty for every 100 female students and 15 male faculty for every 100 male students.

Administrators. Women hold 2 of the 6 top-level positions: head librarian and chief development officer. Women chair the departments of nursing and general technical studies. One of 2 deans is a black woman. The 60-member faculty senate includes 19 women, among them 1 black woman and 1 Asian American woman. Two of the 5 members of the campus-wide personnel committee are women.

Women and the Curriculum. Women earn two-thirds of the bachelor's degrees; 60 percent are in education, the rest in interdisciplinary studies and health professions. All but a few of the two-year degrees awarded to women are in health technologies.

The continuing education department offers two courses on women: Leadership Training, and Women—Working It Out. Faculty are offered workshops on nontraditional occupations for men and women, affirmative action and equal opportunity, and the needs of reentry women.

Women and Athletics. No intercollegiate sports or club sports are offered. For women, the intramural program is limited to swimming and volleyball.

Special Services and Programs for Women. *Health and Counseling.* There is no student health service. The student counseling center is staffed by one male counselor. Counseling is available for gynecological problems, birth control, abortion, and rape and assault.

Safety and Security. Measures include local police protection, night-time escort for women, high-intensity lighting, self-defense courses, and information on safety and crime prevention. No rapes or assaults on women were reported for 1980–81.

Career. Services include information and career workshops on nontraditional occupations, networking between students and alumnae, and alumnae files organized by careers.

Other. The Affirmative Action Committee functions as a center of support for all women. The continuing education department presents a women's lecture series.

Institutional Self-Description. "IU Kokomo is a full, degree-granting partner in the statewide Indiana University system. A 24-acre commuter campus with over 2,500 students, the campus provides four-year degree programs in the arts, sciences, education, business, medical technology, and general studies. Two-year associate degrees are available in a range of disciplines. Because the campus focus is on the nontraditional student, support for women is strong. There are many non-credit opportunities for the development of skills, the enhancement of knowledge, and personal enrichment."

Indiana University, Northwest
3400 Broadway, Gary, IN 46408
Telephone: (219) 980-6500

Women in Leadership
★ faculty

3,266 undergraduates

	Amer. Ind.	Asian Amer.	Blacks	Hispanics	Whites
F	3	5	676	112	1,276
M	1	2	235	62	869
%	0.1	0.2	28.1	5.4	66.2

🏠 🚐 👫 ⬚ AAUW

Indiana University Northwest, founded in 1948, is one of six state-supported commuter institutions in the university system. Located in the city of Gary, it attracts 4,204 students, of whom 3,266 are undergraduates. Sixty-four percent of the undergraduates are women, and about half of the women attend part-time. The university awards associate, bachelor's, and master's degrees in education, business, liberal arts, and pre-professional fields. The division of continuing education, an external degree program, a summer session, and evening classes are available. The campus can be reached by public transportation, and on-campus parking is available for a fee.

Childcare facilities are available both on and off campus.

Policies to Ensure Fairness to Women. An affirmative action officer, with the authority to make policy, has the responsibility part-time for policy pertaining to educational sex equity, handicapped access, and equal employment opportunity. A written policy prohibiting sexual harassment of all members of the campus community exists but has not yet been officially communicated; complaints are resolved informally and confidentially or through a formal grievance procedure. A Committee on the Status of Women and an Affirmative Action Committee address issues relating to minority women.

Women in Leadership Positions. *Students.* No information was supplied regarding opportunities for women to exercise campus-wide leadership.

Faculty. Twenty-six percent of the 113 full-time faculty members are women, a proportion slightly above the national average. There are 3 female faculty for every 100 female students and 15 male faculty for every 100 male students.

Administrators. No information was supplied.

Women and the Curriculum. Most four-year degrees awarded to women are in business (33 percent), education (19 percent), and the social sciences (17 percent). Three percent graduate in the nontraditional fields of mathematics and physical sciences. Women earn 82 percent of all two-year degrees, most of them in health technologies (79 percent) and business programs (20 percent).

There are no courses on women. Courses offered by the schools of education, nursing, and business provide instruction on some matters specific to women.

Women and Athletics. No information was provided.

Special Services and Programs for Women. *Health and Counseling.* No information was supplied on health-related personnel or services specific to women. Counselors are offered training in the avoidance of sex-role stereotyping and racism.

Safety and Security. No information was supplied.

Career. Recently, the Women's Studies Steering Committee organized a conference on how to develop skill for specific careers, and the division of continuing studies conducted a two-day seminar on improving women's effectiveness as workers and overcoming barriers to male/female communication.

Institutional Self-Description. "Indiana University Northwest serves a diverse demographic and economic area. The campus offers a wide range of degree programs at the associate, baccalaureate, and master's levels as well as certificate and post-baccalaureate certification programs. Services provided for nontraditional students and a strong division of continuing studies enhance the educational opportunities of women."

Indiana University, South Bend
1700 Mishawaka Avenue
South Bend, IN 46615
Telephone: (219) 237-4111

★ **Women and the Curriculum**

3,928 undergraduates

	Amer. Ind.	Asian Amer.	Blacks	Hispanics	Whites
F	3	7	139	14	2,030
M	7	6	82	8	1,611
%	0.3	0.3	5.7	0.6	93.2

🏠 🏛 🚐 👫 🔑 📖 🏺 AAUW NWSA

Founded in 1940 as a two-year extension center, the South Bend campus became Indiana University at South Bend in 1965. It offers associate, bachelor's and master's degree programs in a broad range of fields. Adult students are served by the division of continuing education. Fifty-seven hundred students attend IU at South Bend, of whom 3,928 are undergraduates. Women are 56 percent of all undergraduates; 61 percent of women attend part-time. The median age of all undergraduates is 27.

All students commute. Alternative scheduling includes off-campus evening classes, a weekend college, and a summer session. The campus is accessible by public transportation; parking on campus is available at a fee.

A college-operated childcare facility, located off campus, can accommodate 100 children (54 at a time). Charges are based on fixed weekly or hourly rates. Ninety-five percent of students' requests for this service can be met. Additional, private childcare facilities are located nearby.

Policies to Ensure Fairness to Women. An Affirmative Action Officer has responsibility full-time for policy pertaining to equal employment opportunity, sex equity for students, and handicapped access. A written and publicized sexual harassment policy protects students, faculty, and staff; complaints are resolved through a formal campus grievance procedure.

Women in Leadership Positions. *Students.* Women students have limited opportunities to gain leadership experience. In a recent three-year period, women held two of the six leadership posts: president of the student senate for one year and campus newspaper editor for two years.

Faculty. Twenty percent of the 132 full-time faculty are women, a proportion below average for comparable institutions in this guide. There are 3 female faculty for every 100 female students and 15 male faculty for every 100 male students. According to recent data from the college, the full-time female faculty includes 2 black, 2 Hispanic, and 3 Asian American women.

Administrators. There are no women among the top-ranking administrators. Four of the 23 departments are chaired by women: modern languages, nursing, psychology, and extended programs. Two women sit on an important 7-member faculty committee. One of the 7 members of the academic senate, the faculty governing body, is a woman.

Women and the Curriculum. Most women earn bachelor's degrees in business (25 percent), education (24 percent), social sciences (16 percent), and psychology (8 percent). Three percent of women graduate in such nontraditional fields as mathematics or physical sciences. Women earn 60 percent of the two-year degrees awarded: 42 percent in health technologies and 38 percent in business, with the balance in public service or arts and sciences. Seventy-seven percent of student interns are women.

The Women's Studies Program, directed part-time by a permanent faculty member, offers a 15-credit minor. Courses on women are available through such departments as psychology, English, sociology, and communicative arts. Recent offerings include Women in Contemporary Society; Women: A Psychological Perspective; and Interdisciplinary Analysis of Women's Role. The departments of education, nursing, physical education, and business include instruction on some matters specific to women. The continued development of the Women's Studies Program is supervised by an official committee. Faculty workshops are offered on the needs of reentry women.

Women and Athletics. No information was provided on the intercollegiate sports program. The intramural sports program has limited opportunities for women athletes. Small numbers of women participate in tennis, volleyball, table tennis, golf, and racquetball. Thirty percent of the participants in intramural sports are women.

Special Services and Programs for Women. *Health and Counseling.* The university does not have a student health service. A counseling center, staffed by two men and eight women, including one minority woman, does not offer counseling on matters specific to women.

Safety and Security. Measures consist of campus police without arrest authority. No rapes or assaults on women were reported for 1980–81.

Career. Services include workshops, lectures, job discrimination information, and printed materials on nontraditional occupations for women. Career Placement Services sponsors a Women in the Workplace Program, as well as Women Leadership Skill Training.

Other. The division of arts and sciences operates the Women's Center. Under the direction of a faculty member, the center serves about 300 women annually. The Women's Studies Program sponsors a women's lecture series. Forty-eight handicapped undergraduate women are served by the Office of Services for the Handicapped. The division of continuing education, in cooperation with the Greater Elkhart Chamber of Commerce Women, recently held a series of seminars for women who want to become more self-reliant in the home, in a profession or job, or in work as volunteers. Workshops on sexual harassment are held for women students, faculty, and staff. Twenty-six percent of the Student Government Budget was allocated for childcare.

Institutional Self-Description. "As the largest regional campus of the IU system, South Bend offers women students the advantages of a traditional university and the flexibility of a commuter campus. IUSB provides associate degree programs, 56 baccalaureate degree programs in business, education, and public service. Childcare facilities, continuing education and career counseling, special services, and student services develop the environment women need to pursue an education."

Indiana University, Southeast
4201 Grantline Road
New Albany, IN 47150
Telephone: (812) 945-2731

Women in Leadership　　　　★ **Women and the**
　★★★ **students**　　　　　　　　**Curriculum**
　★★ **faculty**

3,103 undergraduates

	Amer. Ind.	Asian Amer.	Blacks	Hispanics	Whites
F	4	2	42	3	1,623
M	9	4	26	4	1,380
%	0.4	0.2	2.2	0.2	97.0

🏠 🏛 👫 ⬛ Ⓜ 📖 NWSA

Founded in 1941, Indiana University, Southeast, is a state-supported institution that attracts 3,998 students. Of the 3,103 undergraduates, 54 percent are women; half of the women attend part-time. The median age of all students is 25.

The university offers bachelor's degrees in business, education, arts, and sciences; associate and master's degrees are also available. A continuing education program serves the adult student. Classes are held on and off campus during the day and evening; a weekend college and a summer session are available. All students commute to the campus, located near Louisville, Kentucky. On-campus parking is available at a fee. Nine percent of full-time undergraduate women belong to social sororities.

A campus childcare facility operates as a drop-in center and accommodates 30 to 40 children daily. Open until 10 p.m., the center charges a fixed hourly fee. All students' requests for this service can be met. Additional, private childcare facilities are located close to campus.

Policies to Ensure Fairness to Women. An affirmative action officer has responsibility part-time for review of policies and practices related to sex equity for students, equal employment opportunity, and handicapped access. A sexual harassment policy protects students, faculty, and staff; complaints are resolved through a formal grievance procedure which is newly formulated and currently being publicized.

A Committee on the Status of Women, appointed by and responsible to the Chancellor, meets regularly and publicizes its findings and views on issues of importance to students. The committee includes student members with voting rights who are appointed by the student government president. Both this committee and the Committee on Minority Affairs address the concerns of minority women.

Women in Leadership Positions. *Students.* Women have outstanding opportunities to gain leadership experience. Though they constitute 54 percent of the total student body, during a recent three-year period, women held 73 percent of campus-wide leadership positions. They served three times as president of the student court and editor-in-chief of the campus newspaper; twice as president of the student body and president of the student senate; and once as president of the senior class. Three of six honorary societies have women presidents.

Faculty. Thirty-five percent of the 82 full-time faculty are women, a proportion above the average for similar colleges in this guide. There are 4 female faculty for every 100 female students and 7 male faculty for every 100 male students.

Administrators. Women hold 2 of the 9 top administrative posts: head librarian and director of institutional research. Thirty percent of the faculty senate are women. Women chair 2 of 7 departments: natural sciences and nursing.

Women and the Curriculum. Most women earn bachelor's degrees in education (53 percent), business (11 percent), and social sciences (11 percent). Eight percent of women major in such nontraditional fields as mathematics and physical sciences. About three-fourths of two-year degrees are earned by women: 68 percent in health technologies, 14 percent in business, 10 percent in public service, and 7 percent in arts and sciences.

The Women's Studies Program, directed by a permanent faculty member part-time, awards a certificate. Recent offerings include Women in Literature; French Literature: Male and Female Roles; Women in Politics; Women in Economy; and Women in History. Continued development of the program is the responsibility of an official committee. The departments of education and business offer instruction on some matters specific to women.

Women and Athletics. The university provides a good intramural sports program and a limited intercollegiate program. About one-fourth of the intercollegiate athletes are women. Women are 30 percent of the intramural athletes. The intramural program includes such team sports as badminton, basketball, flag football, tennis, bowling, cross-country, and volleyball. Intercollegiate sports offered are basketball and tennis.

Special Services and Programs for Women. *Health and Counseling.* There is no student health service. A student counseling center, staffed by three women and three men, offers no counseling for medical problems specific to women.

Safety and Security. Measures consist of campus police protection, an emergency alarm system, and instruction on self-defense and campus safety for women. Information on the incidence of rapes and assaults was not reported.

Career. Services include workshops, lectures, and information on nontraditional occupations for women, files on alumnae careers for students' use, and networking between female students and alumnae.

Other. A series of brown-bag lectures entitled "Especially for Women" addresses such issues as female/male relationships, careers, women's health, and aging. The Student Development Center provides support for returning students. Free tutoring for students with mathematics difficulties is provided.

Institutional Self-Description. "IU Southeast is a commuter campus situated in the metropolitan Louisville area, where students benefit from the many cultural, recreational, and employment opportunities. Continuing Studies provides courses in personal and career growth which are especially valuable to women. A strong Women's Studies Program and active women faculty members provide the support and role models women students need. Childcare facilities and special degree programs enhance the educational opportunities of nontraditonal students."

Indiana University-Purdue University, Fort Wayne

2101 Coliseum Boulevard East
Fort Wayne, IN 46805
Telephone: (219) 482-5121

Women in Leadership
★★★ students
★ faculty

★ Women and the
Curriculum

6,121 undergraduates

	Amer. Ind.	Asian Amer.	Blacks	Hispanics	Whites
F	3	10	130	16	2,878
M	3	17	93	13	2,905
%	0.1	0.4	3.7	0.5	95.3

🏠 🚌 👫 📖 **AAUW NWSA**

Indiana University at Fort Wayne was founded in 1917 and merged with Purdue University at Fort Wayne in 1964. The combined, state-supported institution attracts 8,992 students, 6,121 of whom

are undergraduates. Women are half of the undergraduate student body; 53 percent of women attend part-time. The median age of all undergraduates is 26.

The university offers a range of associate and bachelor's degrees. Adult students are served through the division of continuing education. Evening, weekend, and summer session classes are available. All students commute to the suburban campus, accessible by public transportation. Free on-campus parking is available, along with some parking at a fee.

A college-run childcare facility serves students, faculty, and staff, and accommodates 54 children, or 95 percent of all requests. Childcare is available from early morning until 9 p.m. Fees are based on fixed hourly rates, with reduced charges for each additional child from the same family.

Policies to Ensure Fairness to Women. An Equal Employment Officer is responsible part-time for policy and monitoring compliance concerning sex-equity, equal-employment-opportunity, and handicapped-access legislation. A written policy prohibiting sexual harassment is being developed.

Women in Leadership Positions. *Students.* In a recent three-year period, half of the campus-wide student offices were held by women, including president of the student body, student senate, student union, and senior class.

Faculty. Women hold 26 percent of the 226 full-time faculty positions, a proportion which is slightly above the national average. There are 5 female faculty for every 100 female students and 12 male faculty for every 100 male students.

Administrators. All top administrators and all four deans are men. Women chair two of 29 departments—nursing and audiology/speech sciences. Twenty-one percent of the faculty senate are women.

Women and the Curriculum. Most women earn bachelor's degrees in education (25 percent), health professions (14 percent), business (13 percent), and social sciences (11 percent). Four percent of women graduate in the nontraditional fields of mathematics and physical sciences. Among women who earn two-year degrees, most major in health technologies (60 percent) and business and commerce (28 percent).

Headed by a permanent faculty member, the Women's Studies Program offers an undergraduate minor and the bachelor's degree through an individualized-major program. Recent courses on women include Women in World Literature, Women Artists, Women in Hispanic Literature, Interdisciplinary Perspectives on Women and Men, and Women in Supervision. An official committee develops the Women's Studies Program and encourages the development of new courses on women.

Women and Athletics. A small intramural and intercollegiate sports program is available. Thirty-eight percent of the intercollegiate and 30 percent of the intramural athletes are women. Three of the five paid intercollegiate coaches are women. Intercollegiate sports offered are basketball, tennis, track and field, and volleyball.

Special Services and Programs for Women. *Health and Counseling.* The student health service employs two female healthcare providers. For medical treatment specific to women, students are referred to other agencies. The counseling center, staffed by three male and three female counselors, offers counseling for gynecological problems, birth control, abortion, and rape and assault. Student health insurance covers abortion and maternity expenses.

Safety and Security. Measures consist of campus police with arrest authority, night-time escorts, high-intensity lighting, and a community rape crisis center. No rapes or assaults were reported for 1980–81.

Career. Services include information, lectures, and career workshops on nontraditional occupations for women.

Other. The Women's Studies Program sponsors a women's lecture series.

The Office of Counseling and Testing conducts assertiveness-training sessions for women. The departments of transitional studies and mathematics offer a skills clinic in mathematics. An annual women's week and a telephone service for information and referrals are projects sponsored by the Community Women's Bureau. A battered women's program is run by the local YWCA women's shelter. The Student Gay Rights Organization and the Black Student Assembly meet on campus.

Institutional Self-Description. "IPFW's urban location, flexible scheduling, childcare facilities, community involvement, development and support programs, and wide range of Indiana and Purdue undergraduate and graduate degree programs make it a quality institution, easily accessible to women of all ages and backgrounds, and particularly to those with responsibilities at home or outside the home."

Indiana University-Purdue University, Indianapolis

355 N. Lansing,
Indianapolis, IN 46202
Telephone: (317) 624-4417

Women in Leadership
★★ **faculty**

★ **Women and the Curriculum**

12,431 undergraduates

	Amer. Ind.	Asian Amer.	Blacks	Hispanics	Whites
F	9	44	903	27	5,526
M	13	32	477	24	5,248
%	0.2	0.6	11.2	0.4	87.6

Founded in 1946, Indiana University at Indianapolis has shared its campus with Purdue University since 1969. The combined institution now offers more than 20,000 students a full range of undergraduate, graduate, and professional degree programs. Evening classes are available both on and off campus, as well as a weekend college and a summer session. An adult education program is offered through the division of continuing studies.

Fifty-three percent of the 12,431 undergraduates are women, 57 percent of whom attend part-time. The median age of undergraduates is 22. Ninety-six percent of undergraduates commute; the campus is accessible by public transportation; on-campus parking is also available to students for a fee.

University-run childcare facilities, which can accommodate 30 children at a time, give priority to students. Fees are based on a fixed hourly rate. For students with more than one child in the facility, the fee is halved for each additional child.

Policies to Ensure Fairness to Women. A full-time administrator is responsible for reviewing policies and practices regarding equal employment opportunity, sex equity for students, and handicapped accessibility. A campus policy prohibiting sexual harassment of students will be publicly communicated in writing to students, faculty, and staff by fall 1982. Complaints are resolved through a formal campus grievance procedure and through informal methods depending upon the severity of the case. An appointed Committee on the Status of Women and a Committee on Minority Affairs address the concerns of minority women.

Women in Leadership Positions. *Students.* Female representation among student campus leaders is limited. In recent years, a woman was editor-in-chief of the campus newspaper.

Faculty. Women are 38 percent of the full-time faculty. There are 8 female faculty for every 100 female faculty for every 100 female students and 18 male faculty for every 100 male students.

Administrators. Men fill all top administrative positions. The university reports that 13 of 72 heads of academic units are women, including the Dean of the School of Nursing and the

Dean of the School of Liberal Arts. Of the 61 departments, nursing administration and psychiatric/mental health nursing are chaired by women.

Women and the Curriculum. Health professions account for almost half of the four-year degrees earned by women; another 15 percent are in education and 12 percent in business. Less than one percent are in nontraditional fields. Of the two-year degrees awarded to women, 70 percent are in health technologies.

The Women's Studies Program offers a 15-credit undergraduate minor and an interdisciplinary liberal arts major. In addition to Women in Contemporary American Society, and Readings and Research in Women's Studies offered by The Women's Studies program, ten courses on women are available through departments, including Women in the Hebrew Bible; Seminar in Criminal Justice; The Female Offender; Biology of Women; Recent Writing: Women's Autobiographies; and Women in Modern French Literature. Courses in the departments of education and business and the School of Nursing provide instruction on some matters specific to women.

Women and Athletics. Women have limited opportunities to participate in intramural and varsity sports although women receive 50 percent of athletic scholarships. Nine percent of intramural atheletes are women, who participate in such sports as tennis, basketball, volleyball, and running. Club sports are also available. Forty-nine percent of the 85 intercollegiate athletes are women as are 3 of the 11 paid varsity coaches. All three women's teams played in recent tournament competitions. The intercollegiate sports offered are basketball, softball, and volleyball.

Housing and Student Organizations. Four percent of undergraduates live on campus in single-sex and coeducational dormitories. All residence halls restrict hours for visitors of the opposite sex. Housing for married students, with and without children, is also available and is open to married women whose spouses are not enrolled.

Special Services and Programs for Women. *Health and Counseling.* The student health service provides birth control and gynecological treatment. Two of the 3 physicians are female, as are the 4 health-care providers. One male provides gynecological, birth control, abortion, and rape and assault counseling.

Safety and Security. Measures include campus police with arrest authority, night-time escort for women students, night-time bus service to residence areas, high-intensity lighting, an emergency alarm system at isolated locations, information sessions for women on safety and crime prevention, and a rape crisis center. No rapes and 17 assaults (10 on women) were reported for 1980–81.

Career. Career workshops, job discrimination information and printed material on nontraditional occupations for women are available, as well as lectures and panels by women employed in these fields.

Other. The Women's Center, under the direction of a full-time, salaried administrator, sponsors a variety of services for approximately 2,500 women annually, including counseling, testing, and a Job Club. The Student Gay Rights Organization and the Black Student Assembly meet on campus. Women with special needs (such as handicapped women and welfare women) would find additional support from the Student Affairs Administration, which also runs a displaced homemaker program. The Office of Women's Studies sponsors a number of services and programs, among them a women's lecture series.

An assertiveness-training program is available through the Office of Counseling and Testing, while the department of mathematics sponsors a program to build confidence in mathematics.

Returning Women Students. The division of continuing studies operates a Continuing Education for Women Program headed by a full-time administrator. There are 1,200 returning women currently enrolled in these courses, while another 3,780 reentry women are enrolled in other adult and continuing education courses. The needs of reentry women are also addressed by RAP (Returning Adult Place), an organization for older students. Continuing Education for Women maintains a career library; in conjunction with television station WTTV it sponsors a "Women's Forum."

Special Features. Students may attend a series of free Women's Studies Seminars held both in the day and evening. The university also hosts a research project on obesity that focuses on women.

Institutional Self-Description. "Because IUPUI is a commuter, urban university, women are able to study at nontraditional hours and in convenient locations while maintaining residence at home. The CECW offers counseling, vocational testing, Job Club and non-credit courses; and a career library and referral service. The warm, home-like atmosphere provides an environment for the returning woman student which undergirds her decision to continue her education."

Purdue University, Calumet

Hammond, IN 46323
Telephone: (219) 844-0520

Women in Leadership ★ faculty		★ Women and the Curriculum

4,671 undergraduates

	Amer. Ind.	Asian Amer.	Blacks	Hispanics	Whites
F	4	17	243	104	1,714
M	1	21	178	142	2,245
%	0.1	0.8	9.0	5.3	84.8

Founded as a land-grant institution and extension center for northwest Indiana, the Calumet campus is now a branch of Purdue University. Located in a suburb of Hammond, the university attracts a total of 6,676 students, half of whom attend part-time. Women are 45 percent of the 4,671 undergraduates. The median age of all undergraduates is 25.

Undergraduate, professional, and pre-professional degree programs are available, as well as an adult education program. Classes are held on and off campus, during the day and evening, in addition to a weekend college. All students commute, and campus parking is provided at a fee.

A small childcare facility on campus, open to all members of the school community, has room for 30 children. The fee is $1.10 per hour.

Policies to Ensure Fairness to Women. Matters pertaining to sex equity and handicapped access are part of the responsibilities of the Executive Assistant to the Chancellor. A memorandum issued by the main Purdue campus prohibits sexual harassment of students, faculty, and staff.

Women in Leadership Positions. *Students.* Women have had few opportunities to exercise student leadership. In recent years women have served single terms as student body president and editor of the campus newspaper.

Faculty. Thirty-one percent of the full-time faculty are female, a proportion which is above the national norm. There are 6 female faculty for every 100 female students and 12 male faculty for every 100 male students.

Administrators. Men hold all top positions. Women chair the departments of modern languages, nursing, and biology. There is one woman on the Board of Trustees.

Women and the Curriculum. Nearly half the degrees awarded to women are in the health professions and education. Ten percent of women graduate in the nontraditional areas of mathematics, physical sciences, computer science, and engineering. Most two-year degrees awarded to women are in health technologies.

The Women's Studies Program offers a 12-credit minor. Seven courses on women are offered by Women's Studies and the departments of biology, psychology, communications, English, and history. Courses include Rhetoric of Women's Rights, Sociology of Sex Roles, Gender and Genre, and Women in American History. A faculty member serves part-time as coordinator of the program, which operates under the general direction of an official Women's Studies Committee.

Women's Studies sponsors a rich variety of programs, including brown-bag lunch discussions on topics of interest to women and a biannual all-day conference, "Wide World of Women," that enlists prominent feminist speakers. It also sponsors a feminist film series, a monthly discussion group on women's books, and a lecture series that focuses on the concerns of minority women.

Women and Athletics. A limited intercollegiate sports program attracts 45 participants, of whom 16 are women. The large intramural program offers a variety of individual and team sports. Athletic scholarship aid is available to women. Intercollegiate sports offered are basketball and volleyball.

Special Services and Programs for Women. *Health and Counseling.* There is no student health service. The student counseling center employs three women counselors, one of whom is a minority woman. No medical services specific to women are available.

Safety and Security. Measures consist of campus police protection, a night-time escort for women, high-intensity lighting, an emergency telephone system, a self-defense course for women in the continuing education department, and a rape crisis center. For 1980-81 no rapes or assaults on women were reported.

Other. A Women's Center, operating out of a tiny space and with a shoestring budget, draws about 50 people—predominantly older undergraduates, staff, and faculty—to its activities each year. A faculty member serves as part-time coordinator. Women's Coalition, the only women's advocacy group on campus, runs support groups for returning women.

Institutional Self-Description. "Purdue University at Calumet provides good preparation in nursing, engineering, science, and management for women. Many returning women come to Calumet—our average age is about 25 years—so older women feel comfortable. Since Purdue stresses technology over humanities, women can prepare for nontraditional careers here, if they're tough and use the support systems that Women's Studies and allied groups try to provide. The community is working-class, Hispanic, black, and multi-racial—very much a part of the real world that women need to engage and produce in if we are to effect change."

Purdue University, West Lafayette

West Lafayette, IN 47907
Telephone: (317) 749-2681

	★★ Women and the Curriculum
	★ Women and Athletics

24,658 undergraduates

	Amer. Ind.	Asian Amer.	Blacks	Hispanics	Whites
F	9	60	401	69	9,301
M	10	98	455	109	13,829
%	0.1	0.7	3.5	0.7	95.0

 AAUW NWSA

Established in 1869 as a land-grant college primarily for providing training in science, agriculture, and engineering, Purdue University now offers 31,000 students a comprehensive range of undergraduate, graduate, and professional programs. There is a division of continuing education; the Span Plan Office provides special assistance to the older student. Alternative class schedules, which include a summer session, contract learning, and off-campus class locations, are available.

Women are 40 percent of the 24,658 undergraduates; 6 percent of the women attend part-time. The median undergraduate age is 19. For the 45 percent of undergraduates who commute, the university is accessible by public transportation. Parking on campus is available for a fee.

Some cooperative childcare is available through married students' housing and other student or community groups. Private arrangements for childcare can be made nearby.

Policies to Ensure Fairness to Women. An Equal-Opportunity Officer is responsible part-time for policy on employment, accessibility of programs and facilities to students, and handicapped access. Five other university officers review policies and monitor practices. General campus guidelines for conduct cover cases of sexual harassment. Complaints are handled either informally and confidentially or through a formal grievance procedure.

Women in Leadership Positions. *Students.* The participation of women students in campus-wide leadership is below the average for public research institutions in this guide. In recent years, women have twice presided over the student senate.

Faculty. Women make up 14 percent of a full-time faculty of 1,359. According to a recent report, 5 black, 15 Asian American, and 5 Hispanic women are on the full-time faculty. The ratio of female faculty to female students is 2 to 100. The ratio of male faculty to male students is 8 to 100.

Administrators. The Dean of Students is a woman. Other top administrative posts are held by men. Women chair three of 64 departments: foreign languages and literature, nursing, and retailing. The Dean of the School of Consumer and Family Sciences is female.

Women and the Curriculum. Most bachelor's degrees awarded to women are in home economics (17 percent), business and administration (14 percent), education (12 percent), and the health professions (10 percent). One-quarter are in such nontraditional areas as agriculture, architecture, computer science, engineering, mathematics, and the physical sciences. The proportion of women taking nontraditional degrees is far above the national average, making Purdue's record in this repect one of the best in the nation. Most women earning two-year degrees and certificates major in health technologies. Almost 9 percent major in mechanical/engineering technologies, a proportion which is above the national average. The university reports programs to encourage women to prepare for careers in science, computer science, engineering, and communication. Thirty percent of the students in the engineering cooperative education program, which combines academic work with practical experience, are female. A majority of the experiential learning positions in the pharmacy program go to women.

The Women's Studies Program offers an undergraduate minor. In addition to the introductory Women's Studies course, 16 other courses on women are available through the departments of history, English, psychology, French, philosophy, sociology, political science, and communications. Recent offerings include Rhetoric of Women on the Public Platform; Theories of Feminist Discourse; From Literature to Film: The Impact of French Women; Philosophy of Women; History of Women in America; Women, Politics and Public Policy; Women: A Psychological Perspective; and Sex Roles in Modern Society. An official committee promotes the teaching of scholarship on women and the acquisition of library materials pertaining to women.

Such topics as building mathematics confidence among females and instruction on coeducational sports are part of the preparation of future teachers. The division of nursing provides training on health-care information important to minority women.

Minority Women. Of 9,930 undergraduate women, 4 percent are black, less than 1 percent American Indian, 1 percent Asian American, and 1 percent Hispanic. Thirty-seven women are members of all-minority sororities; some minority women are in in-

tegrated sororities. A graduate course on the History of Black Women is offered through the history department. The Society of Black Engineers and the Society of Black Science Students have chapters on campus. The university reports that minority women would find other supportive women through the Dean of Students' Office, Horizon Programs, Affirmative Action, and the Assistant Provost (who is a black woman).

Women and Athletics. Purdue has good intramural and intercollegiate programs, with a variety of individual and team sports in both. Nineteen different activities are offered to women in the intramural program. Club sports are also available. Sixteen percent of intramural and 31 percent of intercollegiate athletes are women; women receive 20 percent of the athletic scholarships. Six of 27 paid coaches in varsity sports are women. All women's intercollegiate teams played in tournament competition in 1980. The intercollegiate sports offered are basketball, cross-country, field hockey, golf, swimming, tennis, track and field, and volleyball.

Housing and Student Organizations. Forty-three percent of the undergraduates live on campus. Residential accommodations include single-sex and coeducational dormitories, cooperative housing, and housing for married students and single parents with children. A married woman student whose husband is not enrolled may live in married students' housing. Dormitories restrict hours for visitors of the opposite sex. Six of 18 residence-hall directors are female.

Twelve percent of full-time undergraduate women belong to social sororities. Sororities and fraternities provide housing for their members. The Associated Women Students, ERA Campus Action Team, Feminist Union, the Gay Alliance, and Neighborhood Anti-Rape Coalition are among campus groups which serve as advocates for women.

Special Services and Programs for Women. *Health and Counseling.* The student health service provides some medical attention specific to women, including gynecological, birth control, and rape and assault treatment. One of seven physicians is female. Half of the counseling staff of four are women. Students have access to counseling of particular concern to women. Additional services are available through the Psychological Counseling Center and the Dean of Students' Assessment Center.

Safety and Security. Measures consist of campus and local police, limited night-time escort service for women, limited night-time bus service to residence areas, high-intensity lighting, emergency telephones, self-defense courses for women available at the St. Thomas Aquinas Center, information sessions on safety and crime prevention, and a community rape crisis center. Nine assaults on women and three rapes were reported for 1980–81.

Career. The university offers workshops concentrated on nontraditional occupations, lectures featuring role models, nonsexist/nonracist printed information on women in nontraditional fields of study, and a network of contacts between alumnae and students.

Other. An off-campus Women's Center serves the university and larger community. An annual women's week, women's lecture series, and a program to build confidence in mathematics are sponsored on campus. A telephone line of information, referral, and support, and services for battered women and displaced homemakers are available in the community. A wide range of other programs, including assertiveness training, is sponsored by various campus and community groups.

Returning Women Students. The Span Plan Office serves reentry, first-time, and non-degree students. Luncheon meetings for older students, counseling on an informal basis, and student-spouse grants are sponsored through the Dean of Students' Office.

Institutional Self-Description. ''The institution offers outstanding degree programs in many nontraditional fields for women, such as science, engineering, agriculture, and computer science. Purdue enrolls more women in veterinary medicine, engineering, and pharmacy than any other institution in the country.''

St. Mary-of-the-Woods College

St. Mary-of-the-Woods, IN 47876

Telephone: (812) 535-4141

Women in Leadership
- ★★★ students
- ★★★ faculty
- ★★★ administrators

553 undergraduates

	Amer. Ind.	Asian Amer.	Blacks	Hispanics	Whites
F	0	1	17	6	497
M	0	0	0	0	0
%	0.0	0.2	3.3	1.2	95.4

 AAUW

St Mary-of-the-Woods, a Roman Catholic, liberal arts college for women, is operated by the Sisters of Providence. Founded in 1840 and located in a rural setting just outside of Terre Haute, the college attracts 564 women, 23 percent of whom attend part-time. The average age of all undergraduates is 20.

A variety of undergraduate degree programs is available, in addition to a Women's External Degree Program. A summer session is available. For the 7 percent of undergraduates who commute, there is free parking on campus.

Private childcare facilities are available off campus.

Policies to Ensure Fairness to Women. An Equal Opportunity Coordinator is responsible part-time for monitoring compliance and examining policies and practices pertaining to handicapped-access, sex-fair-employment, and sex-equity laws. Complaints of sexual harassment are resolved through a formal campus grievance procedure.

Women in Leadership Positions. *Students.* Women hold all student leadership positions.

Faculty. Three-fourths of the 49 full-time faculty members are women. There are 9 female faculty for every 100 female students.

Administrators. Women hold every major administrative post and head two of the three divisions: science, mathematics, and home economics; and social and behavioral sciences. Nineteen of 24 departments are chaired by women, including biology, mathematics, and physics. The majority of campus-wide speakers, members of the Board of Trustees, and honorary degree recipients are female.

Women and the Curriculum. One-third of the degrees awarded to women are in interdisciplinary studies and another third in business, fine arts, and education. Programs in science, accounting, and computer science encourage women to prepare for non-traditional careers.

One course on women—Women in Business—is offered by the business administration department. An official committee works on the development of new courses on women and collects new resource material about women. The education department provides pre-service training on mathematics avoidance and on the development and use of sex-fair curricula. The department of social work provides instruction on some issues specific to women.

Women and Athletics. For a college of this size, the athletic program is adequate. There are 50 intercollegiate and 70 intramural athletes. Only team sports are offered in the intramural program; intercollegiate sports offered are basketball, softball, swimming, tennis, and volleyball.

Housing and Student Organizations. Ninety-three percent of students live in campus dormitories that restrict visiting hours for men. Residence-hall staff receive awareness-training on birth control, sex education, and the avoidance of sexism and racism.

Special Services and Programs for Women. *Health and Counseling.* The student health service employs one male physician and one female health-care provider. The student counseling center is staffed by two female counselors. Counseling and treatment for gynecological problems are available, in addition to counseling for birth control, abortion, and rape and assault.

Safety and Security. Measures consist of campus and local police, high-intensity lighting, and instruction on self-defense and campus safety. There is a rape crisis center. No rapes or assaults on women were reported for 1980–81.

Career. Information, workshops, and lectures about nontraditional careers are available, in addition to networking with alumnae.

Other. Special programs are organized by the theater and mathematics departments. Assertiveness-training sessions are sponsored by the Student Affairs Office.

Returning Women Students. The Women's External Degree Program, housed in its own quarters and with a budget of $294,982, attracts 146 women, of whom 7 percent are minority, predominantly black, women. Women enrolled may reside on campus for as few as two or three days every six months. The director of the program holds a full-time faculty appointment. Faculty are offered special workshops on the needs of reentry women.

Institutional Self-Description. "St. Mary-of-the-Woods College has been an institution dedicated to serving women for 140 years. The mission of SMWC is 'to prepare women personally and professionally for responsible roles in contemporary society.' Three major programs are the resident, undergraduate program; the Women's External Degreee program; and the English Language Institute for International Women."

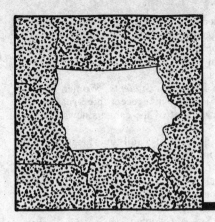

Clarke College
1550 Clarke Drive, Dubuque, IA 52001
Telephone: (319) 588-6300

Women in Leadership
- ★★★ students
- ★★★ faculty
- ★★★ administrators

403 undergraduates

	Amer. Ind.	Asian Amer.	Blacks	Hispanics	Whites
F	0	0	2	2	395
M	0	0	0	0	0
%	0.0	0.0	0.5	0.5	99.0

Clarke College is a private, liberal arts institution affiliated with the Roman Catholic Church. Founded in 1843 as a women's college, it became coeducational in 1979. The most recent enrollment statistics, however, show only female students in attendance. The total enrollment of 643 includes 403 undergraduates. The median age of undergraduates is 22.

The college offers bachelor's and master's degrees. Schedules include evening classes, summer sessions, and a continuing education program. Sixty-five percent of the undergraduates live on campus in single-sex and coeducational dormitories that have restrictive hours for visitors of the opposite sex. Commuting students may take advantage of free on-campus parking and public transportation.

Childcare facilities are available near campus.

Policies to Ensure Fairness to Women. A female administrator has part-time responsibility for policy review and compliance concerning legislation on equal employment opportunity, sex equity, and handicapped accessibility.

Women in Leadership Positions. *Students.* Almost all positions in a recent three-year period were held by women.

Faculty. Three-quarters of the 47 full-time faculty are women. There are 9 female faculty for every 100 female students.

Administrators. Most of the top administrators, including the President, are women. Women chair 10 of the 15 academic departments, including chemistry, computer science, and mathematics. Women constitute a majority of the faculty senate (30 of 45 members) and hold 3 of 6 positions on a major faculty committee. In 1981, the commencement speaker was a woman, as was 1 of the 2 honorary degree recipients..

Women and the Curriculum. One-quarter of the bachelor's degrees awarded to women are in fine and performing arts; 7 percent are in mathematics and physical sciences. Clarke offers a major in computer science. The department of mathematics sponsors a clinic to build skills in mathematics.

Three courses on women are offered in the psychology, English, and philosophy departments: Feminist Thought, Women Writers, and Female Sexuality. The departments of business and social work provide instruction on some matters specific to women.

Women and Athletics. The athletic program is limited. Women participate in intramural and intercollegiate sports. Intercollegiate sports offered are basketball, softball, and volleyball.

Special Services and Programs for Women. *Health and Counseling.* The student health service, staffed by one female health-care provider, refers students to private physicians. The counseling center employs two women. No counseling specific to women is provided.

Safety and Security. Measures consist of a campus police force, high-intensity lighting, and information sessions on campus safety. No rapes or assaults were reported for 1980–81.

Career. The college offers workshops on nontraditional occupations, lectures by women employed in nontraditional fields, and job discrimination information.

Other. Continuing education courses attract 220 women; the continuing education division provides support for older women. The office of the Dean of Students sponsors an Institute for Student Leadership.

Institutional Self-Description. None provided.

Des Moines Area Community College
2006 S. Ankeny Blvd., Ankeny, IA 50021
Telephone: (515) 964-6200

Women in Leadership
- ★★ faculty

5,081 undergraduates

	Amer. Ind.	Asian Amer.	Blacks	Hispanics	Whites
F	18	11	40	13	2,774
M	11	26	37	19	2,016
%	0.6	0.8	1.6	0.6	96.5

A public, two-year community college located in a suburb just north of Des Moines, the Ankeny campus is part of a statewide system offering liberal arts transfer programs, high school completion, and vocational and technical studies. About 60 percent of students transfer to four-year institutions. Of 5,081 students, 57 percent are women (almost a third of them over age 25). All students commute. The campus is accessible by public transportation, and on-campus parking is provided for a fee. Evening and daytime classes are available at off—campus location.

Low-cost childcare facilities capable of accommodating a third of requests are available on campus; private facilities are located nearby.

Women in Leadership Positions. *Students.* No information was provided.

Faculty. Forty-two percent of the full-time faculty are women, including 2 black women. There are 6 female faculty for every 100 female students and 9 male faculty for every 100 male students.

Administrators. Men hold all top positions. Of 35 departments, women chair 15, including nursing, operating-room technician, childcare, adult education, commercial art, human services, dental hygiene, and data processing. Women also direct the divisions of communications and humanities, financial aid, health sciences, and the Career Development Center.

Women and the Curriculum. Among women graduates the most popular fields are health technologies (43 percent), arts and sciences (23 percent), business (16 percent), and public services (14 percent). The college offers no courses on women.

Women and Athletics. There are limited opportunities for organized competitive sports.

Special Services and Programs for Women. *Health and Counseling.* The student health service is staffed by one woman health-care provider. No treatment specific to women is available. One woman and one man provide counseling on gynecological problems, birth control, abortion, and rape and assault.

Safety and Security. Both campus and town police patrol the campus, which is lighted in all areas. No rapes or assaults were reported for 1980-81.

Career. The career placement office provides nonsexist/non-racist printed information on nontraditional fields of study and keeps a file of alumnae by specific careers.

Other. Reentering students are represented in a club called Re-zoomers.

Institutional Self-Description. "The college offers the opportunity for women to become independent through high-school completion and vocational and college transfer programs. The student body is older than the 'typical' four-year college student, with the average age being 23.3."

Drake University
Des Moines, IA 50311
Telephone: (515) 271-3751

4,392 undergraduates

	Amer. Ind.	Asian Amer.	Blacks	Hispanics	Whites
F	1	27	144	10	1,913
M	4	28	122	18	2,078
%	0.1	1.3	6.1	0.6	91.9

 AAUW

Founded in 1881, Drake University, a private nondenominational institution in Des Moines, enrolls some 6,200 students in a variety of undergraduate, graduate, and professional studies. The College of Continuing Education serves the adult student. A summer session and alternative class schedules, including a weekend college, evening classes, and off-campus classes, are available.

Women are 48 percent of the 4,392 undergraduates; 11 percent of the women attend part-time. About a third of the full-time women undergraduates are more than 25 years old. The median age of undergraduates is 22. For the 60 percent of undergraduates who commute or live off campus, the university is accessible by public transportation. On-campus parking is available both free and at a fee.

Private childcare arrangements can be made close to campus.

Policies to Ensure Fairness to Women. The director of personnel and the assistant academic vice president review policies and practices related to equal employment opportunity, sex equity for students, and handicapped accessibility. Complaints of sexual harassment are resolved informally and confidentially, or through a formal grievance procedure.

Women in Leadership Positions. *Students.* Women students have not been active in leadership in a recent three-year period. A woman has been editor-in-chief of the campus newspaper for one year.

Faculty. Women are 17 percent of a full-time faculty of 250. One Asian American and one Hispanic woman are on the faculty, according to a recent report. The ratio of female faculty to female students is 2 to 100; of male faculty to male students, 10 to 100.

Administrators. Men occupy all higher administrative positions. A woman chairs the department of foreign languages. The Dean of the College of Liberal Arts is a woman.

Women and the Curriculum. Most women taking bachelor's degrees major in education, with significant numbers also in the social sciences, business and management, the fine arts, and the health professions; 3 percent major in nontraditional areas, with the largest number in architecture. Fifty-five percent of the positions in cooperative education programs go to females.

Several courses on women are offered through the division of social sciences—Women in America, an interdisciplinary course, and Social Organization and Sex Roles, a course offered by the sociology department. Such current issues as sex-fair curricula and coeducational physical education classes are a part of the preparation of future teachers. The School of Business provides instruction on discrimination in the workplace.

Women and Athletics. Intramural and intercollegiate programs provide adequate opportunities for organized competitive individual and team sports. Eighteen percent of intramural and 42 percent of intercollegiate athletes are women. Women receive 30 percent of athletic scholarships. Four of 23 paid intercollegiate coaches are female. All women's teams played tournament competition in 1980. The intercollegiate sports offered are basketball, cross-country, track and field, softball, tennis, volleyball.

Housing and Student Organizations. Forty percent of undergraduates live on campus. Single-sex and coeducational dormitories and housing for married students are available. A married woman student whose spouse is not enrolled may live in married students' housing. Dormitories restrict hours for visitors of the opposite sex. Three of eight residence-hall directors are female. Awareness training is offered staff on sex education and birth control, and on the avoidance of sexism and racism.

Eighteen percent of undergraduate women belong to social sororities. Five minority women are in integrated, 25 in all-minority, sororities. Sororities and fraternities provide housing for their members.

Special Services and Programs for Women. *Health and Counseling.* The student health service provides some medical attention specific to women, including gynecological and birth control treatment and abortion and treatment for rape and assault by hospital on referral. One of 3 counselors in the counseling service is a woman. Students have access to gynecological, birth control, abortion, and rape and assault counseling.

Safety and Security. Measures consist of campus and city police, night-time escorts for women students, an emergency telephone system, self-defense courses for women, information sessions on safety and crime prevention, volunteer student patrols during late night hours, and a rape crisis center. Five assaults (four on women) and one rape were reported for 1980–81.

Other. The Division of Women's Programs in the College of Continuing Education functions as a multi-purpose Women's Center on campus. The Drake Gay Community, a student organization, meets on campus.

Returning Women Students. The Division of Women's Programs operates out of the College for Continuing Education. Components include a Community Career Planning Center for

Women; two displaced-homemaker programs; a non-credit Women/School offering 17 courses per semester; and a research project on alternative working arrangements. Assertiveness training is also available.

Special Features. The Association for Women Students, funded through the Student Fees Allocations Committee, sponsors and supports a number of cultural and political activities which center around issues of special concern to women.

Institutional Self-Description. "Drake University houses an extensive Division of Women's Programming. Through a combination of national and local sources, the Division's 15-person staff serves 3,000 women per year."

Grand View College
1200 Grandview Avenue
Des Moines, IA 50316
Telephone: (515) 266-2651

Women in Leadership
★★ faculty

1,186 undergraduates

	Amer. Ind.	Asian Amer.	Blacks	Hispanics	Whites
F	0	3	32	2	702
M	0	1	27	2	328
%	0.0	0.4	5.4	0.4	93.9

A four-year, coeducational institution affiliated with the Lutheran Church in America, Grand View College is located in the city of Des Moines. Founded in 1896 as a Danish folk school and theological seminary, it was a junior college from 1924 to 1975, when it began offering bachelor of science degrees in nursing. Today it is a fully accredited liberal arts college.

Women are 63 percent of the 1,186 students; 28 percent of the women attend part-time. The college estimates that 20 percent of the undergraduate women are between 25 and 40 years old and 1 to 3 percent are over age 40. Self-paced learning and summer sessions are offered in addition to regular day and evening classes. For the 85 percent of the students who commute, there is free on-campus parking.

Private childcare facilities are available near campus.

Women in Leadership Positions. *Students.* Two major campus-wide student leadership positions exist, the president of the student body and the editor of the campus newspaper; women have been editors of the newspaper twice in a recent three-year period.

Faculty. Women are almost half of the 54 full-time faculty, a very high figure for a private coeducational college in this guide. There are 5 female faculty for every 100 female undergraduates and 8 male faculty for every 100 male students.

Administrators. The head librarian is a woman; and the other chief administrative positions are held by men. Five of the 21 academic departments are chaired by women, including business and mathematics. Half the campus-wide speakers during a recent year were women.

Women and the Curriculum. No information on degrees awarded is available. No courses on women are offered. The departments of nursing and business provide instruction on some matters specific to women. An official committee is responsible for collecting and developing curricular materials on women.

Women and Athletics. The intramural and intercollegiate women's athletics programs emphasize team sports. Women are 32 percent of the intercollegiate participants and receive 40 percent of athletic scholarships. Two of the six paid intercollegiate

coaches are women. Intercollegiate sports offered are basketball, softball, and volleyball.

Housing and Student Organizations. Fifteen percent of the undergraduates reside on campus in single-sex dormitories that have restrictive hours for visitors of the opposite sex. The two male and two white female residence-hall directors are offered awareness-training on sexism and racism.

Special Services and Programs for Women. *Health and Counseling.* For treatment specific to women, students are referred to private physicians. The counseling center employs two men and one minority women. Gynecological, birth control, abortion, and rape and assault counseling are provided.

Safety and Security. The local police have jurisdiction for the campus; there are high-intensity lights, and self-defense courses are provided for women. A rape crisis center is available. Information was not provided on the incidence of rapes and assaults on women.

Career. Services include programs focused on nontraditional careers for women. Updated files of alumnae by specific careers are maintained.

Other. The Women's Concerns Committee sponsors a women's week and a women's lecture series.

Special Features. The college reports an excellent women's collection in the library.

Institutional Self-Description. "The faculty teach 'students,' not males and females. The emphasis is on developing every individual's potential. Competition with a much larger university in the same city has created an emphasis on personal support for all students in order to develop our institution's uniqueness."

Iowa State University of Science and Technology
Ames, IA 50011
Telephone: (515) 294-4111

★★ **Women and the Curriculum**

★ **Women and Athletics**

19,045 undergraduates

	Amer. Ind.	Asian Amer.	Blacks	Hispanics	Whites
F	6	36	72	16	7,452
M	7	64	137	26	10,767
%	0.1	0.5	1.1	0.2	98.0

Founded in 1858 as a land-grant institution emphasizing agriculture and mechanic arts, Iowa State is a broad-based university offering a range of undergraduate and graduate programs. Adult continuing education is available through a University Extension Program. Evening classes, both on and off campus, and a summer session are available.

Of the 23,507 students, 19,045 are undergraduates, 40 percent of them women. Seven percent of women undergraduates are part-time students. The median age of all students is 21; 8 percent of female students are older than 25. Parking for a fee, but no public transportation, is available for the 6 percent of students who commute.

Childcare facilities are available near campus.

Policies to Ensure Fairness to Women. Two full-time Affirmative Action Officers are responsible for policy on equal employment opportunity, sex equity for students, and handicapped accessibility. A published policy prohibits sexual harassment of students, faculty, and staff. Complaints are resolved informally and confidentially or through a formal grievance procedure.

The Committee on the Status of Women, appointed by and responsible to the Assistant Vice President for Academic Affairs, includes student members with voting rights, takes stands on issues of importance to students, and develops relevant programs. Both this committee and the Committee on Minority Affairs address the concerns of minority women.

Women in Leadership Positions. *Students.* Opportunities for women students to exercise campus-wide leadership are limited. In a recent three-year period, women presided over the student senate and were editor-in-chief of the newspaper.

Faculty. Twenty percent of the 1,253 full-time faculty are women, a proportion above the average for research universities in this guide, but below the national average. There are 3 female faculty for every 100 female students and 9 male faculty for every 100 male students.

Administrators. The chief administrative posts are held by men. A woman is Dean of the Home Economics Division, and women chair seven of 62 departments: speech, physical education, food and nutrition, home economics, institution management, textiles and clothing, and veterinary anatomy. Three of the nine university regents and almost a third of the faculty council are women.

Women and the Curriculum. Most degrees awarded to women are in home economics (17 percent), education (17 percent), and business (10 percent). Twenty-three percent of women earn degrees in agriculture, computer science, engineering, mathematics, and physical sciences. The university maintains programs to encourage women to prepare for careers in science, engineering, agriculture, and communications. Sixty-three percent of student interns, 30 percent of science field-service participants, and 20 percent of cooperative-education participants are women.

The Women's Studies Program, directed part-time by a permanent faculty member, offers an undergraduate minor, as well as a major through the honors or individualized major program. Twelve courses on women are offered through Women's Studies and various departments, including English, foreign languages, history, political science, and economics. Courses include Economics of Discrimination, and Status of Women in the Arab World. A Committee on Women's Studies helps to develop the program as well as individual courses, and monitors the inclusion of women's issues in traditional courses. Faculty workshops include the topics of sexism and racism in the curriculum, nontraditional occupations, and affirmative action.

Women and Athletics. Iowa State offers women good opportunities to participate in organized, competitive, team and individual sports. Women account for 25 percent of intramural, 29 percent of intercollegiate, and 45 percent of club athletes, and receive over half the athletic scholarships. Nine of the 31 paid intercollegiate coaches are women. The intercollegiate sports offered are basketball, cross-country, golf, gymnastics, softball, swimming, tennis, track, and volleyball.

Housing and Student Organizations. Single-sex and coeducational dormitories are provided for the 45 percent of students who live on campus. University housing is also available for single students with children and married students with or without children. Twelve of the 20 dormitory directors are women, including two minority women. Awareness training on sexism and racism, sex education, and birth control is available for the dormitory staff.

Fifteen percent of women belong to sororities. Both sororities and fraternities provide housing for members.

The Student Women's Advisory Board serves as an advocacy group for women on campus. There is a Black Students' Cultural Center.

Special Services and Programs for Women. *Health and Counseling.* The university health service has 3 female and 6 male physicians and 14 female nurses. Eight of the 17-member staff of the student counseling center are women, 1 a minority woman.

Counselors receive in-service training on avoiding sex-role stereotyping and racial bias. Counseling and medical care are available for gynecological problems and birth control. The regular student health insurance policy covers maternity and abortion at no extra cost.

Safety and Security. Measures consist of unarmed campus police with arrest authority, high-intensity lighting, self-defense courses for women, information sessions on campus safety and crime prevention, and a rape crisis center, No rapes and 29 assaults were reported for 1980–81.

Other. The university's newly opened Women's Center provides central housing, coordination, and visibility for a variety of programs such as *Womenews*, a women's publication, and the Committee on Women's Projects. The Office of Student Life sponsors an annual women's week, a women's lecture series and, in cooperation with the local YWCA, assertiveness training. The city of Ames maintains a women's theater.

Institutional Self-Description. "The university grew from a land grant college. Its past enrollment has been primarily male, because of the technological emphasis of the curricula. Efforts have been made to recruit women and establish or facilitate an equitable learning and working environment for all minority populations. The university's humanities and arts programs have grown with its scientific and research programs. Women's Studies and programs have not been neglected. Space and funds for a campus Women's Center were approved and allocated, and a campus (landmark) building restored to house the centralized activity, in spite of overall budget cuts in all university offices and programs this year."

Loras College
1450 Alta Vista, Dubuque, IA 52001
Telephone: (319) 588-7106

1,659 undergraduates

	Amer. Ind.	Asian Amer.	Blacks	Hispanics	Whites
F	0	1	1	1	653
M	0	0	2	1	997
%	0.0	0.1	0.2	0.1	99.6

  AAUW

Loras College, a private, liberal arts institution, was founded in 1839 as a college for men. It became coeducational in 1971. Located on a campus accessible to downtown Dubuque, the college offers both bachelor's and master's degrees to its more than 1,700 students, 1,659 of them undergraduates. Women are 40 percent of the undergraduates, and 16 percent of women attend part-time. The median age of all undergraduates is 19.

Alternative schedules include evening and summer classes; cooperative programs are maintained with Clarke College and the University of Dubuque. Public transportation and on-campus parking are available to the 47 percent of the undergraduates who commute. Free transportation is provided to classes at Clarke and Dubuque.

Women in Leadership Positions. *Students.* Of seven student leadership positions, women have held two during a recent three-year period, president of the junior class and of the senior class.

Faculty. Ten percent of the 79 full-time faculty are women, a figure well below the national average. There is 1 female faculty member for every 100 female students and 9 male faculty for every 100 male students.

Administrators. All the chief administrators are men; the departments of history and English are chaired by women.

Women and the Curriculum. The most popular degrees for women are social sciences (27 percent), education (18 percent), and business (15 percent).

No courses on women are offered. The departments of physical education, social work, and business provide some instruction on matters specific to women.

Women and Athletics. Loras offers an adequate number and variety of intercollegiate women's sports. No information was supplied on intramurals. Twenty-nine percent of the participants in intercollegiate sports are women. Five of 13 paid varsity coaches are women. Intercollegiate sports are basketball, cross-country, softball, swimming, tennis, track, and volleyball.

Housing and Student Organizations. Fifty-three percent of the undergraduates reside on campus in single-sex or coeducational residence halls, all of which have restrictive hours for visitors of the opposite sex.

Twenty-two percent of the full-time undergraduate women belong to sororities, which do not provide housing.

Special Services and Programs for Women. *Health and Counseling.* The health service employs one woman health-care provider, but no physicians. No health services specific to women are available.

Safety and Security. Measures consist of campus police without arrest authority. No rapes or assaults were reported for 1980-81.

Career. Information and workshops focusing on nontraditional occupations are provided, and there are programs to establish contacts and networks between alumnae and female students. The counseling center has two male and two female counselors, who provide assertiveness training and programs on mathematics avoidance by women.

Institutional Self-Description. None provided.

Scott Community College
Belmont Rd., Betterdorf, IA 52722
Telephone: (319) 359-7531

Women in Leadership
★★ **faculty**
★★ **administrators**

1,354 undergraduates

	Amer. Ind.	Asian Amer.	Blacks	Hispanics	Whites
F	21	9	25	16	699
M	16	5	20	12	528
%	2.7	1.0	3.3	2.1	90.8

Founded in 1966 as a two-year, vocational/technical institution, Scott added a liberal arts curriculum in 1979, making it a comprehensive community college. The college is located on the Iowa-Illinois border in the Davenport-Moline area. Of 1,354 students, 57 percent are women; 43 percent of women attend part-time.

Among associate degree programs are applied arts, business, trade, and technology. Alternative schedules include evening, summer, and weekend classes and on- and off-campus locations. There are opportunities for self-paced/contract learning. The college also has a continuing education program. All students commute to the campus, which is accessible by public transportation; on-campus parking is available.

Policies to Ensure Fairness to Women. A full-time equal-opportunity officer is responsible for making policy as well as monitoring compliance with affirmative-action and equal-employment-opportunity regulations. A formal grievance procedure resolves complaints of sexual harassment.

Women in Leadership Positions. *Students.* The six campus leadership positions available have all been held by men during a recent three-year period.

Faculty. Of 61 full-time faculty, 36 percent are women, a proportion which is above the national average. There are 5 female faculty for every 100 female students and 10 male faculty for every 100 male students.

Administrators. The chief student-life officer, the head librarian, and the development officer are women. Men hold the other four key administrative positions. Women chair the departments of health and business, and a woman directs Community Education.

Women and the Curriculum. Women are awarded three-quarters of the associate degrees, 98 percent of them in health technologies. There are no courses on women.

Women and Athletics. Two team sports are offered in the intramural program: basketball and volleyball. There are no intercollegiate athletics.

Special Services and Programs for Women. *Health and Counseling.* There is no student health service. The counseling center, staffed by two women and one man, offers counseling on abortion, rape and assault, and sexual harassment. Staff receive in-service training on the avoidance of sex-role stereotyping and racial bias.

Safety and Security. Local police patrol the campus, which is equipped with high-intensity lighting. There are self-defense courses for women and a rape crisis center. No rapes or assaults were reported for 1980-81.

Career. The career placement office provides counseling, lectures and workshops on nontraditional careers, as well as non-sexist/nonracist information on nontraditional fields of study and on job discrimination. There is also networking between alumnae and female students.

Other. The division of continuing education offers a program for displaced homemakers, as well as a women's lecture series.

Institutional Self-Description. "We are a comprehensive community college. We offer classes in the day and evening. We have a comprehensive program of career-counseling assistance for women. Because Scott is a commuter college, women may live at home and still attend college."

University of Dubuque
2050 University Avenue
Dubuque, IA 52001
Telephone: (319) 589-3223

Women in Leadership
★ **students**
★ **faculty**

889 undergraduates

	Amer. Ind.	Asian Amer.	Blacks	Hispanics	Whites
F	0	1	15	6	414
M	1	0	19	7	404
%	0.1	0.1	3.9	1.5	94.4

 AAUW

The University of Dubuque is a private, four-year coeducational college affiliated with the United Presbyterian Church. Founded in 1852 as a seminary for German Presbyterian ministers, it became an undergraduate college in 1911. Today the total enrollment is just over 1,000, with 889 undergraduates. Forty-nine percent of undergraduates are women; nearly 39 percent of the women attend part-time. The median age of all students is 23.

The college offers bachelor's and terminal two-year pre-professional/vocational programs. Schedules include on- and off-campus evening classes, summer sessions, tutorials, continuing education classes, and cross-registration with Loras and Clarke Colleges. Forty-five percent of the students commute to campus; public transportation and free on-campus parking are available.

Campus childcare facilities, open from 8 a.m. to 5 p.m., cost $7.50 per day, and can accommodate a third of all requests for childcare. Private childcare facilities are available off campus.

Policies to Ensure Fairness to Women. The Committee on the Status of Women is appointed by the President and reports to the Assistant to the Academic Dean.

Women in Leadership Positions. *Students.* Women undergraduates have good opportunities to obtain leadership experience. During a recent three-year period, women held over one-third of the student leadership positions (the editor-in-chief of the student newspaper was a woman three years in a row). A woman heads one of the two honorary societies on campus.

Faculty. Women are 27 percent of the 52-member full-time faculty, a proportion slightly above the national average. There are 5 female faculty members for every 100 female students; the ratio for males is 9 for every 100.

Administrators. All the chief administrators are men. Women chair three academic departments: English, drama and speech, and nursing. A woman received the sole honorary degree awarded at the 1981 commencement.

Women and the Curriculum. About one-third of the women earning bachelor's degrees major in the health professions, the next most popular field being education (15 percent). The majority of men receive degrees in business (51 percent), compared to 11 percent of women.

Two courses on women are offered, Women in Business and Women Writers. Courses in the departments of education, physical education, social work, and business provide some instruction on matters specific to women.

Women and Athletics. About one-quarter of the intercollegiate and intramural athletes are women; women receive over 50 percent of the athletic scholarships, an unusually high share. Three intramural and four intercollegiate sports are offered. One of the seven paid varsity coaches is a woman. Intercollegiate sports offered are basketball, softball, track, and volleyball.

Housing and Student Organizations. Fifty-five percent of the undergraduates live on campus. Single-sex and coeducational dormitories and married students' and single-parents' housing are provided. Dormitories have restrictive hours for visitors of the opposite sex.

One hundred men and 70 women (including three black women) belong to fraternities and sororities.

Special Services and Programs for Women. *Health and Counseling.* The student health service employs two female healthcare providers; the counseling center employs one woman and three men. No medical treatment or counseling specific to women is provided.

Safety and Security. Measures consist of a campus police force. Two assaults, both on women, were reported for 1980-81.

Career. The career placement office, which is directed by a woman, offers workshops on nontraditional careers, provides information on nontraditional fields of study for women, and keeps updated files of alumnae by specific careers.

Other. Twenty returning women take courses in the continuing education department, which also offers a women's lecture series and assertiveness/leadership training.

Institutional Self-Description. "The woman of the '80s can find herself at the University of Dubuque. Our programs in business, the sciences, teaching, and the humanities prepare you for your career. Extracurricular activities (publications, athletics, student government) develop your leadership skills."

University of Iowa
Iowa City, IA 52242
Telephone: (319) 353-3361

| Women in Leadership | ★★ Women and the |
| ★★ administrators | Curriculum |

14,465 undergraduates

	Amer. Ind.	Asian Amer.	Blacks	Hispanics	Whites
F	30	37	190	37	6,875
M	20	38	177	49	6,772
%	0.4	0.5	2.6	0.6	95.9

 AAUW NWSA

The University of Iowa, founded in 1847 as a school for residents of the state, first admitted women in 1860. Located in a medium-sized community, it attracts over 24,000 students to a comprehensive range of undergraduate, graduate, and professional studies. A continuing education program serves the adult student. Alternative schedules include Saturday classes and a summer session; off-campus locations are available, as is credit by correspondence.

Women make up half of the 14,465 undergraduates; 12 percent of the women attend part-time. The median age of undergraduates is 21. For students who live off campus or commute, the university is accessible by public transportation. Parking is available on campus, with free transportation from distant parking lots.

University-sponsored childcare facilities charge on a sliding scale. Private arrangements may be made close to campus.

Policies to Ensure Fairness to Women. A full-time affirmative action officer reviews policies and practices related to equal employment opportunity, sex equity for students, and access for the handicapped. A published campus policy prohibits sexual harassment; complaints are handled either informally or through a formal grievance procedure. The Committee on the Status of Women, which includes students as voting members, takes stands on issues of concern to students, and addresses the concerns of minority women.

Women in Leadership Positions. *Students.* In recent years, no woman has held student office.

Faculty. Women constitute one-fifth of a full-time faculty of 1,022. There are 3 female faculty for every 100 female students and 13 male faculty for every 100 male students.

Administrators. Of seven top administrators, the chief academic officer, the director of institutional research, and the director of women's athletics are women. Women chair eight of 87 departments. The Dean of the College of Nursing and the Director of the School of Music are women. A third of the nine regents are women.

Women and the Curriculum. A majority of the women who graduate with bachelor's degrees major in the health professions (22 percent), business and management (16 percent), and education (14 percent). Four percent major in such nontraditional areas as computer science, engineering, mathematics, and the physical sciences. The proportion (one-fifth of those awarded) of degrees earned by women in engineering is significantly above the national average.

The Women's Studies Program offers both a 30-credit undergraduate minor and a graduate minor through the Graduate College Interdisciplinary Program. Thirty-four courses on women are available through the departments of American studies, anthropology, area studies, communication and theater arts, counseling, English, history, home economics, physical education and dance, psychology, sociology, and social work. Recent offerings include Women and Work; Women's Roles: Cross-Cultural Perspectives; Sexes and Film; Coaching Women's Sports; Gender and Genre in Shakespeare; American Women in the 20th Century; Feminist Theory; and Women and Society: Introduction to Women's Studies. Women's Studies courses are also available through guided correspondence.

Minority Women. Five percent of the undergraduate women are members of minority groups, with black women the largest group. Residence-hall and counseling staff are offered awareness-training on avoiding racial bias. The Afro-American Cultural Center offers services and cultural events.

Women and Athletics. The intercollegiate program offers good variety in individual and team sports. Information on intramural and club sports was not reported. One-quarter of the intercollegiate athletes are women; women receive 30 percent of the athletic scholarships. The intercollegiate sports offered are basketball, field hockey, golf, gymnastics, softball, swimming, tennis, track and field, and volleyball.

Housing and Student Organizations. For the 35 percent of undergraduates who live on campus, women's and coeducational dormitories and housing for married students and single parents with children are available. Coeducational dormitories do not restrict hours for visitors of the opposite sex. Three of ten residence hall directors are women. Awareness-training on sex education and racism is offered to residence-hall staff.

Sixteen percent of the full-time undergraduate women belong to social sororities; sororities and fraternities provide housing for their members. Among groups which serve as advocates for women are the Women's Resource and Action Center, the Association of Student Women, and the Women's Medical Student Association.

Special Services and Programs for Women. *Health and Counseling.* The student health service provides some medical attention specific to women, including gynecological, birth control, and abortion treatment. Five of 11 physicians are female. The regular student health insurance covers abortion and maternity services at no extra cost. Eight of 14 professional staff in the counseling service are women; staff are offered in-service training on avoiding sex-role stereotyping and racial bias. Students have access to counseling of particular concern to women.

Safety and Security. Measures consist of campus and local police with arrest authority, night-time bus service to residence areas, self-defense courses for women, information sessions on safety and crime prevention, and a rape crisis center. No information was supplied on the incidence of rapes and assaults.

Career. Workshops, speakers, and nonsexist/nonracist printed materials on nontraditional occupations and fields of study for women, as well as a network of contacts between alumnae and female students, are available.

Other. The Women's Center, under a full-time administrator, sponsors assertiveness training, a program to build confidence in mathematics administered through the Math Test Lab, an annual women's week, lecture series, and a telephone line of information, referral, and support.

Institutional Self-Description. None provided.

Westmar College
LeMars, IA 51031
Telephone: (712) 546-7081

614 undergraduates

	Amer. Ind.	Asian Amer.	Blacks	Hispanics	Whites
F	0	0	13	0	272
M	2	1	38	1	280
%	0.3	0.2	8.4	0.2	90.9

 AAUW

Westmar College is a private, liberal arts college affiliated with the United Methodist Church. Founded in 1890, it now enrolls 642 students. Its campus is located near Sioux City. Women are 47 percent of the undergraduate student body; 11 percent of the women attend part-time. The median age of all undergraduates is 21; 18 percent of the women students are over age 25.

The college offers professional and pre-professional programs and has a continuing education division. Off-campus courses are offered during day and evening hours and there is a summer session. No public transportation or on-campus parking facilities are available to the 2 percent of students who commute.

Women in Leadership Positions. *Students.* Insufficient information was provided to evaluate the opportunities for women in student leadership positions. A woman was head of the student body in one recent year.

Faculty. The 40 full-time faculty members include 8 women, a lower proportion than the national average. There are 3 female faculty for every 100 female students and 10 male faculty for every 100 male students.

Administrators. The head librarian is an Asian American woman. Other top administrative positions, department chairs, and deanships are held by men. The Director of Continuing Education is a woman.

Women and the Curriculum. The most popular degrees for women are education (24 percent) and business (15 percent). No courses on woman are offered.

Women and Athletics. No information was supplied.

Housing and Student Organizations. Ninety-eight percent of the undergraduates reside on campus in single-sex and coeducational dormitories. All dormitories have restrictive hours for visitors of the opposite sex.

Special Services and Programs for Women. *Health and Counseling.* The student health service employs one female health-care provider and no physicians. No health or counseling services specific to women are reported. The counseling center employs one male counselor.

Safety and Security. Local police have jurisdiction over the campus. Information was not provided on the incidence of rapes or assaults on campus.

Institutional Self-Description. "Westmar is a small religious college in a small Midwestern town where traditional values are for the most part adhered to by students and staff. Women at our college tend to be skeptical toward the Equal Rights Amendment, which reflects the state's population in general during the last election, in which an Equal Rights Amendment was voted down."

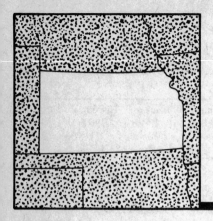

KANSAS

Bethel College

North Newton, KS 67117
Telephone: (316) 283-2500

Women in Leadership
★ ★ ★ students

574 undergraduates

	Amer. Ind.	Asian Amer.	Blacks	Hispanics	Whites
F	2	4	10	0	234
M	0	0	25	3	265
%	0.4	0.7	6.5	0.6	91.9

Bethel is a liberal arts college affiliated with the Mennonite Church. Founded in 1877, the college is located in a village north of Wichita, Kansas. The total enrollment is 629, of whom 574 are undergraduates. Forty-six percent of the undergraduates are women; 5 percent of women attend part-time. The median age of all undergraduates is 20.

The college offers bachelor's and associate degree programs, taught in day and evening classes, summer sessions, and self-paced learning. Continuing education classes are offered. For the 21 percent of the students who commute, free parking on campus is provided.

Childcare facilities are available near campus.

Women in Leadership Positions. *Students.* Opportunities for women students are outstanding: 75 percent of the campus-wide student leadership positions were held by women during three recent years, an unusually high proportion for coeducational colleges in this guide.

Faculty. Six women (15 percent) are among the 41 full-time faculty members, a proportion far below average for four-year colleges in this guide. There are 2 female faculty for every 100 female students; the ratio for males is 12 for every 100.

Administrators. With one exception (the head librarian), the chief administrators are men, as are the seven heads of divisions. Women head five academic departments: health, home economics, nursing, physical education and recreation, and secretarial studies. Ten of the 36 trustees are women.

Women and the Curriculum. Most bachelor's degrees are earned by women in education (41 percent) and social sciences (17 percent); 2 percent major in mathematics. Most two-year degrees are earned by women in business communications. Half of the students in internships and cooperative education are women, as are 35 percent of the students in science field service.

One course on women, Women and Society, is offered by the home economics department. Courses in the departments of phys-

ical education, social work, and business provide some instruction on matters specific to women.

Women and Athletics. Bethel provides an adequate number of intramural and intercollegiate women's sports; team sports dominate in intramurals. One of the 13 paid varsity coaches is a woman. Twenty percent of the athletic scholarships go to women, who are 24 percent of the intercollegiate athletes. Intercollegiate sports offered are basketball, cross-country, tennis, track, and volleyball.

Housing and Student Organizations. Single-sex and coeducational dormitories, and married students' and single parents' housing are provided. All dormitories have restrictive hours for visitors of the opposite sex. Residence-hall counselors (three men, one woman) are offered awareness training on sexism and sex-role stereotyping.

Women's Consciousness Raising has ten white women members.

Special Services and Programs for Women. *Health and Counseling.* The student health service employs one female health-care provider. The counseling center has one male and two female counselors. Gynecological, birth control, abortion, and rape and assault counseling, but not medical treatment, is provided. The regular student health policy covers maternity expenses at no extra charge.

Safety and Security. Measures consist of local police who have jurisdiction over the campus, high-intensity lighting, and a rape crisis center. No rapes or assaults on women were reported on-campus for 1980-81.

Returning Women Students. The continuing education program enrolls 45 returning women, 15 of them minority women. The College Women's Association, an auxiliary group, sponsors a women's day during which women in the area may attend classes and "taste" a day at college. The continuing education program offers a course entitled Women and Finance.

Institutional Self-Description. "The location of Bethel in a community of 1,700 provides our women with a great deal of personal freedom and safety, as does our commitment to being a Christian, church-related college and community. Interpersonal

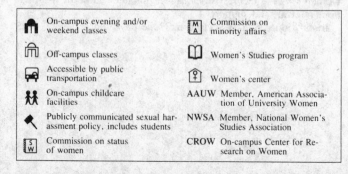

	On-campus evening and/or weekend classes		Commission on minority affairs
	Off-campus classes		Women's Studies program
	Accessible by public transportation		Women's center
	On-campus childcare facilities	AAUW	Member, American Association of University Women
	Publicly communicated sexual harassment policy, includes students	NWSA	Member, National Women's Studies Association
	Commission on status of women	CROW	On-campus Center for Research on Women

relationships among students, faculty, and staff are important, cherished, and cultivated."

Emporia State University
1200 Commercial Street
Emporia, KS 66801
Telephone: (316) 343-1200

★ **Women and Athletics**

4,096 undergraduates

	Amer. Ind.	Asian Amer.	Blacks	Hispanics	Whites
F	9	3	90	30	2,121
M	8	9	87	43	1,631
%	0.4	0.3	4.4	1.8	93.1

Founded in 1863 as Kansas State Normal School, Emporia State University is a public, four-year coeducational institution. Its campus, located southwest of Topeka, draws a total of 5,850 students. Women are 55 percent of an undergraduate population of 4,096; 11 percent of women attend part-time. The median age of all students is 26.

The university offers a wide range of undergraduate and graduate degree programs, including liberal arts, business, education, music, and fine arts. It provides alternative full-time and part-time scheduling, including off-campus evening classes and a summer session. On-campus parking is available at a fee for the 5 percent of undergraduates who commute.

The university reports that a proposal to establish childcare facilities on-campus is in process. Private childcare facilities are available nearby.

Policies to Ensure Fairness to Women. The full-time Affirmative Action Officer reviews policies and monitors compliance concerning legislation on equal employment opportunity, sex equity, and access for the handicapped. A Commission on the Status of Women, appointed by and responsible to the President of the university, has met at least six times in the past year. A formal campus grievance procedure resolves complaints of sexual harassment.

Women in Leadership Positions. *Students.* Of seven campus-wide leadership positions available at Emporia during a recent three-year period, less than 25 percent have been held by women. For one year each, women have been president of the student body, president of the student senate, editor-in-chief of the campus newspaper, president of the student union board, and presiding officer of the residence-hall council. Women preside over ten of 24 campus honorary societies.

Faculty. Women make up 21 percent of the 242 full-time faculty, slightly below average for public four-year colleges. Slightly more than one-fourth of the faculty senate members are women, including one black and one Hispanic. There are 3 female faculty for every 100 female students and 12 male faculty for every 100 male student.

Administrators. Of 8 major administrators, the chief academic officer is a woman. Of 18 departments, the department of home economics is chaired by a woman. Two of 9 regents are women. In 1980–81, 1 of 4 alumni awards was awarded to a woman, and 1 of 2 speakers in the spring 1981 commencement ceremony was a woman.

Women and the Curriculum. Most women take degrees in education (42 percent), business (16 percent), psychology (10 percent), and fine arts (7 percent). Three percent of women earn degrees in the nontraditional fields of mathematics, physical sciences, and computer science. Fifty-five percent of students in internship programs are women, as are 60 percent of those participating in the student teaching program.

Courses on Women in Management, Women in Literature, Women in European Life and Thought, and Rules and Mechanics of Officiating Women's Sports are offered in the departments of business, English, social science and health, physical education and recreation, respectively. The physical education department provides instruction on teaching coeducational classes in physical education and the business department provides instruction on the problems of job discrimination and sexual harassment.

Women and Athletics. Women can choose from a good range of intercollegiate and intramural sports. Many students participate in an extensive program of intramural and club sports, including coeducational water polo and weight lifting. Thirty-eight percent of intercollegiate athletes are women, as are three of 11 paid varsity coaches. Women receive 30 percent of athletic scholarship awards. Intercollegiate sports for women are basketball, cross-country, gymnastics, softball, swimming and diving, tennis, track, and volleyball.

Housing and Student Organizations. Fifty-one percent of undergraduates reside on campus in either single-sex or coeducational dormitories, or in housing provided for married students or single parents with children. Six of ten residence-hall directors are women; directors are offered awareness-training on racism, sexism, and sexual assault.

Some fraternities and sororities provide housing for members. Fourteen percent of the full-time undergraduates belong to fraternities and sororities. There are five minority women in racially-integrated sororities and 40 in all-minority sororities. Advocacy groups for women include the Association of Women Students, Black Student Union, MECHA, and Students for Responsible Free Speech.

Special Services and Programs for Women. *Health and Counseling.* The student health service is staffed by 2 male physicians and 5 female health-care providers. The 5-member counseling center staff includes 2 white women and 1 minority woman. Counseling and medical treatment are available for gynecological problems, birth control, and rape and assault; counseling on abortion is also available.

Safety and Security. Measures include campus police with authority to make arrests, high-intensity lighting, and a rape crisis center. No rapes and five assaults—two against women—were reported for 1980–81.

Other. A small Women's Center, administered under the division of student affairs by a salaried part-time staff person, serves 1,700 women and 500 men annually; it also publishes a newsletter. In conjunction with the Emporia SOS it sponsors a program for battered women and a program for rape prevention and assisting rape victims. In conjunction with the Association of Women Students it sponsors an annual women's week that includes theater arts programming. Leadership training is offered in conjunction with Residence Halls Counseling Center. There is a Minority Resource Center.

"Kansas Women: Past & Perspectives," a conference held on campus in October 1980, explored the contributions of Kansas women to politics, economics, and social organization.

Institutional Self-Description. "Emporia State University is large enough to offer women a broad spectrum of graduate and undergraduate programs in liberal and practical arts and sciences, yet small enough to afford them the personal support of administrators, faculty and student groups. We cordially invite women to enroll at our university."

Hutchinson Community College
1300 N. Plum, Hutchinson, KS 67501
Telephone: (316) 665-3500

Women in Leadership
★★★ **students**
★ **faculty**

2,018 undergraduates

	Amer. Ind.	Asian Amer.	Blacks	Hispanics	Whites
F	1	4	22	20	779
M	10	5	99	29	1,041
%	0.6	0.5	6.0	2.4	90.6

Founded in 1928 as a public junior college offering liberal-arts transfer and general education, Hutchinson Community College expanded its mission in 1950 to include two-year vocational-technical and community-service programs. The college serves a total of 2,326 students, 2,018 of whom are registered for degrees. Women account for 41 percent of the undergraduates; one-third of women attend part-time. The median age of all students is 22. The most recent data show that 45 percent of all women students are over age 25.

The college offers associate degrees, technical awards and certificates, and adult continuing education. Flexible scheduling includes both on- and off-campus classes and a summer session.

Hutchinson has two campuses: a north campus, within the city limits, and a south campus, a few miles from the city. Most students commute, and parking is available on campus for a fee.

Private childcare facilities are available near campus.

Policies to Ensure Fairness to Women. On a part-time basis, an affirmative action officer serves as a voting member of policy-making councils and is responsible for equal-opportunity laws. Sexual harassment of students, faculty, and staff is prohibited by a written campus policy that has been communicated to all three groups. Complaints of sexual harassment are resolved by a formal campus grievance procedure that ensures due process.

Women in Leadership Positions. *Students.* Women have outstanding opportunities to exercise leadership on campus. In three recent years, women served for one year as presiding officer of the student governing body and of the student court, and for two years as editor-in-chief of the campus newspaper. The one honorary society is headed by a woman.

Faculty. Woman are 27 percent of the full-time faculty, a proportion that is above the national average, but below the average for two-year colleges in this guide. There are 5 female faculty for every 100 female students and 10 male faculty for every 100 male students.

Administrators. The presence of women among the top administrators cannot be determined from the information provided. The Director of Records, the Director of Admissions, and the Director of Special Services are women. Of eleven academic departments, a woman chairs one—health, physical education, and recreation. One of the 4 faculty senate members and 3 of 6 trustees are women.

Women and the Curriculum. Most undergraduate women receive two-year degrees or certificates in the arts and sciences, health technologies, and business and commerce. Eighty percent of those participating in the cooperative education program are women.

The social sciences division offers a course called The Changing Roles of Women and Men. The departments of nursing and business provide instruction on some issues specific to women. Faculty workshops consider the concerns and needs of reentry women.

Women and Athletics. The intramural and intercollegiate programs are adequate. One-fourth of intercollegiate athletes are women; women receive 30 percent of all athletic scholarship aid. Intercollegiate sports available to women include basketball, track and field, tennis, and volleyball.

Housing and Student Organizations. Sixteen percent of undergraduates reside on campus in single-sex dormitories that have restrictive hours for visitors of the opposite sex. Of 24 residence-hall directors, eleven are white women and one is a minority woman. All are offered awareness–training on sex education.

Special Services and Programs for Women. *Health and Counseling.* Two health-care providers, a woman and a man, staff the student health service. Eleven counselors, including 5 white females and 1 minority female, provide counseling on gynecological problems, birth control, abortion, and rape and assault.

Safety and Security. Measures consist of local police and a rape-crisis center. For 1980-81, one assault on a woman was reported on campus.

Career. Services include career workshops, lectures on nontraditional occupations, and printed information on nontraditional fields of study for women.

Institutional Self-Description. "Hutchinson Community College has a long record of stability—quality instruction, constructive student lifestyle, and diverse activities. The college works closely with elements in the local community to be knowledgeable and responsive to known needs."

Saint Mary College
4100 South 4th Street Trafficway, Leavenworth, KS 66048
Telephone: (913) 682-5151

Women in Leadership
★★★ **students**
★★★ **faculty**
★★★ **administrators**

432 undergraduates

	Amer. Ind.	Asian Amer.	Blacks	Hispanics	Whites
F	2	8	28	12	302
M	1	2	15	1	36
%	0.7	2.5	10.6	3.2	83.1

 AAUW

Saint Mary, a liberal arts women's college founded in 1923, is affiliated with the Roman Catholic Church and operated by the Sisters of Charity of Leavenworth. Some 690 students are enrolled, 432 of whom are registered in degree programs. The median age of all students is 26. A handful of male students are registered as special students. Nine percent of women attend part-time.

The college offers bachelor's degrees in a range of liberal arts and pre-professional fields; some two-year degrees are also awarded. Continuing education programs are offered for adult students. Alternative schedules include evening, summer session, and weekend classes; off-campus class locations are also available. About three-fourths of students commute to the rural campus. Free on-campus parking is provided for commuters.

College-run daytime childcare facilities accommodate 90 percent of students' requests. Charges vary according to income. Private childcare facilities are located near the campus.

Policies to Ensure Fairness to Women. A Coordinator for Title IX serves part-time to monitor compliance with legislation on equal employment opportunity and educational sex equity. Complaints of sexual harassment are handled through a formal grievance procedure.

Women in Leadership Positions. *Students.* Women hold all student leadership positions

Faculty. Nine of the 17 full-time lay faculty are female. There are 3 female faculty for every 100 female students.

Administrators. With the exception of the chief business officer, all top administrators are female. Women chair 14 of 18 departments, including chemistry, education, history, mathematics, nursing, and theology. The seven trustees are women; the 1981 commencement speaker was a woman.

Women and the Curriculum. Most of the bachelor's degrees awarded to women are in business (24 percent), education (19 percent), and home economics (10 percent); 7 percent are in mathematics and physical sciences. Special programs include Women as Managers, and Training for the Ministry.

The departments of sociology and English offer two courses on women: I Am A Woman, and Women in Literature. The departments of business and education provide some instruction on matters specific to women. Topics for faculty workshops include nontraditional occupations for men and women, the needs of reentry women, and education in leadership for women.

Minority Women. Among the 352 women enrolled in degree programs, 8 percent are black, 3 percent are Hispanic, 2 percent are Asian American, and less than 1 percent are American Indian. The residence-hall staff are offered awareness training on the avoidance of racism. The college reports 1 Asian American, 2 Hispanic, and 3 black women among the full-time faculty. One Hispanic woman chairs a department.

Women and Athletics. The college emphasizes recreational rather than competitive team sports. The intramural sports program attracts 25 women. The sole intercollegiate team—tennis—includes 9 women. Sports clubs draw 17 female participants. The paid intercollegiate coach is male. The campus has a fitness trail and jogging course.

Housing and Student Organizations. About one-fourth of the students reside in on-campus dormitories, which have restrictive hours for male visitors. Residence-hall staff are offered awareness-training on sexism, sex education, birth control, and women and leadership. Three advocacy groups include Student Government Association, International Club, and the Intercollegiate Association of Women Students.

Special Services and Programs for Women. *Health and Counseling.* The student health service employs one female healthcare provider and refers students to either a nearby hospital or a medical clinic. The student counseling center, staffed by one male and two female counselors, offers counseling on gynecological problems, birth control, abortion, and rape and assault.

Safety and Security. Measures consist of local and campus police, night-time escorts, self-defense courses, information sessions on campus safety, a rape crisis center, and a resident-assistants' alert plan. No rapes or assaults were reported for 1980–81.

Career. Services include workshops, lectures, printed materials, and job discrimination information on nontraditional occupations, as well as networking with alumnae, updated files on alumnae careers, and information and training for careers in the ministry.

Other. A battered women's program is sponsored by the college childcare facility and the Dean of Students Office. The fine arts department sponsors women's arts programs. Leadership-training sessions are coordinated by the Dean of Students Office and the Life Planning Center. The Dean of Students Office maintains a telephone warmline of information and referral. The Campus Ministry sponsors retreats for women.

Institutional Self-Description. "Saint Mary is a college for women. The core program, designed for women students, is taught and administered chiefly by women. The campus is beautiful and so are the buildings—because we think beauty is important. The growth and development of each student is central to all we do—we think of growth as spiritual as well as intellectual, as aesthetic as well as academic. We are a college founded by women for women."

Wichita State University
1845 Fairmount, Whicita, KS 67208
Telephone: (316) 689-3456

★★ **Women and the Curriculum**

10,146 undergraduates

	Amer. Ind.	Asian Amer.	Blacks	Hispanics	Whites
F	54	35	361	78	4,121
M	45	69	266	87	4,853
%	1.0	1.0	6.3	1.7	90.0

 AAUW

Founded in 1895 as a liberal arts college for women and continued in 1926 as a coeducational, municipal institution, Wichita State University attracts some 16,000 students to a variety of undergraduate, graduate, and pre-professional programs. Alternative class schedules including a summer session, a weekend college, and off-campus day and evening locations are available.

Women are 46 percent of the 10,146 undergraduates; 39 percent of women attend part-time. The median age of undergraduates is 25. For the 89 percent of undergraduates who commute, the university is accessible by public transportation. On-campus parking is available for a fee.

University childcare facilities operate both day and evening hours, which is rare among public research universities in this guide. The facilities accommodate an estimated three-quarters of students' requests. Private childcare facilities are located near the campus.

Policies to Ensure Fairness to Women. The Vice President for Student Affairs is responsible for policy on student employment, educational sex equity, and handicapped accessibility. Other officers review practices and monitor compliance with equal employment opportunity for faculty and staff. Students' complaints of sexual harassment are handled informally and confidentially.

Women in Leadership Positions. *Students.* In recent years, no woman has held a student office.

Faculty. Women constitute 24 percent of a full-time faculty of 508. According to recent reports, 10 black, 2 Asian American, and 2 Hispanic women are on the faculty. The ratio of female faculty to female students is 4 to 100; of male faculty to male students, 12 to 100.

Administrators. Men occupy all key administrative positions. Women chair ten of 57 departments.

Women and the Curriculum. Most women graduating with bachelor's degrees major in health professions and education. Around 3 percent graduate in such nontraditional fields as computer science, engineering, mathematics, and physical sciences. Most students in cooperative education programs are female. The mathematics department and Learning Resource Center sponsor a program to build mathematics skills.

The Women's Studies Program offers a 15-credit undergraduate minor and a B.A. More than 25 courses on women are available through Women's Studies and the departments of philosophy, sociology, religion, social work, administration of justice, and minority studies. Recent titles include Philosophy of Feminism, Minority Women in America, American Male, Human Sexuality, and Women in Administration of Justice.

The Center for Women's Studies promotes research on women and works to enhance the overall awareness of the campus and community regarding the current needs of women. The center maintains a small resource library of books, periodicals, films, records, and cassette tapes.

Such issues as sex-fair curricula and coeducational physical education classes, health-care information important to minority women, and services for abused spouses are part of the preparation of future teachers, health-care workers, and social workers.

Faculty workshops cover sexism and the curriculum and the needs of reentry women.

Women and Athletics. The intercollegiate program provides adequate opportunities for organized, competitive, individual and team sports. The intramural program is limited. Club sports are also available. Thirty-two percent of intercollegiate athletes are women; women receive 10 percent of athletic scholarships. One-fourth of the paid varsity coaches are women. All teams played in tournaments in 1980. The intercollegiate sports offered are basketball, cross-country, golf, softball, tennis, and track and field.

Housing and Student Organizations. Six percent of undergraduates live on campus. Women's and coeducational dormitories are available. A married woman whose spouse is not enrolled may live in campus housing. Dormitories do not restrict hours for visitors of the opposite sex. One of three residence-hall directors is female. Residence-hall staff are offered awareness-training on rape prevention.

Eleven percent of undergraduate women belong to social sororities. Two of eight sorority houses provide accommodations for their members.

Special Services and Programs for Women. *Health and Counseling.* The student health service provides some medical attention specific to women, including gynecological, birth control, and rape and assault treatment. One of 12 physicians is female, as are 5 other health-care providers. Eight of 12 professional staff in the counseling service are women including one minority woman. Students have access to gynecological, birth control, abortion, and rape and assault counseling. Staff receive in-service training on avoidance of sex-role stereotyping and racial bias.

Safety and Security. Measures include campus and city police, night-time escorts for women students, night-time bus service to residence areas, high-intensity lighting, self-defense courses for women, information sessions on safety and crime prevention, and a rape crisis center. Five assaults (four on women) and no rapes were reported for 1980–81.

Other. There is a Women's Center on campus. Wichita community groups sponsor a variety of services including a telephone line of information, referral, and support. The Women's Studies Program runs a women's lecture series.

Institutional Self-Description. "WSU considers itself an 'urban university.' More than half of the population attends part-time, utilizing an extensive system of night courses. The Women's Studies Program is ten years old. A further commitment to higher education for women continues to be supported through such facilities as the on-campus pre-school and the counseling center which offer a variety of workshops for women."

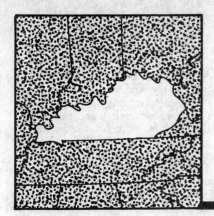

KENTUCKY

Eastern Kentucky University
Richmond, KY 40475
Telephone: (606) 622-2101

Women in Leadership
- ★ **students**
- ★ **faculty**

11,399 undergraduates

	Amer. Ind.	Asian Amer.	Blacks	Hispanics	Whites
F	2	2	430	8	5,598
M	4	6	393	6	4,822
%	0.1	0.1	7.3	0.1	92.5

Eastern Kentucky, established as a teachers' preparatory school in 1906, became a public university in 1966. Among its 13,736 students are 11,399 undergraduates, 53 percent of whom are women; 15 percent of women attend part-time. The average age of undergraduates is 20. Associate, bachelor's, and master's degrees are awarded in a range of career-oriented and pre-professional fields, as well as in liberal arts. Continuing education is available.

Scheduling includes on- and off-campus evening classes and a summer session. The campus is accessible by public transportation for the 30 percent of students who commute. On-campus parking and free transportation from remote parking lots are provided.

A college-run childcare facility operates during morning hours and is part of a child-development training program. The facility can accommodate 16 children and charges a fixed rate. Private childcare facilities are located near the campus.

Policies to Ensure Fairness to Women. The Personnel Director and the Affirmative Action Officer review university policies regarding equal employment opportunity and sex equity for students. Student Special Services oversees accessibility for the handicapped. A written campus policy prohibits sexual harassment of students, faculty, and staff; complaints are resolved informally or through formal grievance procedures.

Women in Leadership Positions. *Students.* Of the 5 campus-wide leadership positions available in recent years, women have served three times as editor-in-chief of the campus newspaper and presiding officer of the women's residence-hall council. Women chair 15 of 22 honorary societies.

Faculty. Of 602 faculty members, 34 percent are women. There are 4 female faculty for every 100 female students and 9 male faculty for every 100 male students.

Administrators. All top positions are held by men. One of the ten regents is a woman. Women chair the departments of mathematics, home economics, curriculum and instruction, social science, nursing, medical records, and medical technology.

Women and the Curriculum. Most women earn bachelor's degrees in education (33 percent), health professions (19 percent), public affairs (12 percent), and business (9 percent). Seven percent of women earn degrees in the nontraditional fields of architecture, agriculture, computer science, engineering, mathematics, and physical sciences. Two-thirds of the two-year degrees are earned by women: half are in health, 20 percent in business, 15 percent in public service, and 15 percent in science-related technologies. Forty-five percent of participants in cooperative education programs are women, as are 31 percent of student interns.

There are no courses on women. The departments of education, nursing, physical education, and social work provide some instruction on matters specific to women. Faculty receive training on the needs of reentry women.

Women and Athletics. Eastern Kentucky provides some opportunities for women to participate in a variety of team and individual sports. Facilities for indoor tennis are available. Women, who are 32 percent of intercollegiate athletes and 20 percent of intramural athletes, receive 35 percent of athletic scholarships. Six of 12 paid varsity coaches are women; 1 of 2 paid intramural coordinators is a woman. Intercollegiate sports are basketball, field hockey, gymnastics, riflery, swimming, tennis, and track and field.

Housing and Student Organizations. Single-sex dormitories with restrictive hours for visitors of the opposite sex, along with student family housing, accommodate 70 percent of undergraduates; 54 percent of the residents are women. Ten of the 27 residence-hall directors are women, two of them minority women.

Eleven percent of women join non-residential sororities. Fifty-two minority women join all-minority groups.

Special Services and Programs for Women. *Health and Counseling.* One female and 2 male physicians, aided by 4 other women, operate the student health service, which offers gynecological treatment. Three women, 1 a minority woman, and 2 men offer counseling on birth control, abortion, and rape and assault. All counselors are trained in the avoidance of sex-role stereotyping and racial bias.

Safety and Security. Measures consist of campus police, nighttime escorts for women students, high-intensity lighting, emergency telephones, self-defense courses, and a rape crisis center. No rapes and 30 assaults (11 on women) were reported for 1980–81.

Career. Career workshops include information on nontraditional occupations. Faculty workshops on nontraditional occupations for women and men are also provided.

Institutional Self-Description. "While Eastern Kentucky University has no programs exclusively designed for women, all of its programs are operated on a non-discriminatory basis. The results of this are reflected in the fact that women have constituted more than half of the institution's enrollment since the early 1970s."

Jefferson Community College
Louisville, KY 40202
Telephone: (502) 584-0181

Women in Leadership
★★ **faculty**

Enrollment data unavailable.

One of 13 two-year colleges operated by the University of Kentucky, Jefferson Community serves 3,580 female students, who account for approximately 60 percent of the enrollment. Just over half the women attend part-time. The median age of all undergraduates is 28, and 14 percent of female students are over age 40. One quarter of the female students are black women.

The college offers the first two years of liberal arts and a range of pre-professional programs. Students can transfer their credits to the University of Kentucky to complete the baccalaureate degree. Alternative scheduling includes evening classes and a summer session. The college also operates a continuing education/community service program. A commuter college, Jefferson has two urban campuses, one in downtown and one in southwest Louisville. Both are accessible by public transportation; on-campus parking is available for a fee.

A childcare facility, open from 7:45 a.m. to 5:00 p.m. is available at the Downtown Campus for students who are parents; priority is given to full-time students and faculty. Private childcare facilities are available off campus.

Policies to Ensure Fairness to Women. The administration of equal-opportunity policies is handled through the University of Kentucky.

Women in Leadership Positions. *Students.* Women have few opportunities to exercise student leadership on campus. The two positions, president of the student body and editor-in-chief of the newspaper, have been held by men in recent years.

Faculty. Thirty-five percent of the full-time faculty of 98 are women, which is above average for institutions of higher education nationwide. According to a recent report, there are nine black women and one Asian American woman on the full-time faculty. The part-time faculty is 34 percent female.

Administrators. At the Downtown Campus men hold 6 of the 7 chief administrative positions; at the Southwest Campus they hold 5 of the 7. The head librarian on both campuses and the student-life officer on the Southwest Campus are women. Women chair 2 of the 4 major divisions: allied health, and humanities. Six of eight faculty on the tenure and reappointments committee are women.

Women and the Curriculum. Information on degrees awarded is not available. Courses on women include Women in American History; Women in Literature, Education, and Society. The library on the Southwest Campus has an extensive collection of materials on women. Workshops on the needs of reentry women are provided to the faculty.

Women and Athletics. There is no athletic program.

Special Services and Programs for Women. *Health and Counseling.* The Downtown Campus has a student health service, but the Southwest Campus does not. Downtown also offers a larger student counseling center, with a total of 10 counselors, including 3 white women and 3 minority women. Southwest has 3 counselors, including a white woman and a minority woman. No information was supplied concerning health or counseling services.

Safety and Security. Measures consist of campus police with arrest authority, information sessions on campus safety and rape and assault prevention for women, and a rape crisis center. No assaults or rapes were reported for 1980–81.

Career. Services include counseling and printed information on nontraditional occupations and on job discrimination. In addition, the college is part of the Catalyst National Network of Career Resource Centers, which provides career resources for women. The division of continuing education offers workshops on women in management.

Other. The College Adult-Re-Entry Services (CARES) program, which is open to all adults, serves primarily reentry women age 25 and older. It offers them complete and coordinated information on the reentry process, support services and special programs, and referrals to off-campus agencies such as Spouse Abuse, Displaced Homemakers, and Creative Employment.

Institutional Self-Description. "Jefferson Community College is an open-door institution offering low-cost educational opportunities to all segments of the community without regard for prior qualifications. We have traditionally served large numbers of minority and first-generation college students with a commitment to individualizing the learning process for all students."

Morehead State University
University Blvd., Morehead, KY 40351
Telephone: (606) 783-2221

Women in Leadership   ★ **Women and Athletics**
★ **faculty**

4,974 undergraduates

	Amer. Ind.	Asian Amer.	Blacks	Hispanics	Whites
F	10	4	102	6	2,547
M	10	6	130	6	2,129
%	0.4	0.2	4.7	0.2	94.5

Some 750 students attend Morehead State, a public university founded as a teacher-training school in 1922. The university now enrolls 4,974 undergraduates, 54 percent of whom are women; 16 percent of women attend part-time. The median age of undergraduates is 20.

Scheduling alternatives include on- and off-campus evening classes and a summer session. The division of continuing education administers adult education. Forty-seven percent of undergraduates commute; on-campus parking is available for a fee.

Private childcare facilities are available near the campus.

Women in Leadership Positions. *Students.* In recent years, men have held the only two campus-wide student positions available. Women chair five of the nine honorary societies.

Faculty. Twenty-eight percent of the 302 faculty are women. There are 4 female faculty for every 100 female students and 11 male faculty for every 100 male students. Recent data from the university indicate that the full-time faculty includes 2 Asian American women.

Administrators. Except for the director of institutional research, all top posts are held by men. Nine of 30 faculty on the university senate and 3 of 12 members of an important faculty committee are white women. One of 10 regents is a black women. Women chair the departments of home economics, allied health sciences, and information sciences.

Women and the Curriculum. Most women earn bachelor's degrees in education (35 percent), home economics (11 percent), and public affairs (8 percent). Seven percent graduate in nontraditional fields. Of the women who earn two-year degrees, 69 percent major in health technologies.

There are no courses on women. The departments of physical education, social work, and business include instruction on some matters specific to women.

Women and Athletics. Morehead offers a good selection of intercollegiate and intramural sports. Thirty percent of intramural athletes are women, who participate in a large variety of individual and smaller selection of team sports. Four of 16 varsity coaches are women. The intercollegiate sports offered are basketball, bowling, cross-country, golf, soccer, softball, swimming, tennis, and volleyball.

Housing and Student Organizations. Single-sex dormitories with restrictions on visiting hours for members of the opposite sex are available for the 53 percent of students who live on campus. Housing for married students with and without children, as well as for single parents, is also available. Nine of the 17 residence-hall directors are women.

Fourteen percent of full-time undergraduate women join social sororities. Twenty-one minority women belong to all-minority sororities. Neither sororities nor fraternities provide housing for members.

Special Services and Programs for Women. *Students.* Health services, including gynecological care, are provided by contract with a local clinic. Two men staff the counseling center but do not offer counseling on issues specific to women.

Safety and Security. Measures consist of campus police with arrest authority, and information sessions on campus safety and crime prevention. No assaults on women and one rape were reported for 1980–81.

Career. Career placement services include nonsexist/nonracist literature on nontraditional fields of study and job discrimination. Students also have access to files of alumnae by careers.

Institutional Self-Description. None provided.

Northern Kentucky University
University Drive
Highland Heights, KY 41076
Telephone: (606) 572-5338

Women in Leadership   ★ **Women and the Curriculum**
   ★ **faculty**

5,673 undergraduates

	Amer. Ind.	Asian Amer.	Blacks	Hispanics	Whites
F	1	7	31	0	2,829
M	1	5	34	1	2,736
%	0.1	0.2	1.2	0.1	98.6

🏠 🏛 🚐 👫 ⚓ Ⓜ 📖 AAUW NWSA

A public, coeducational institution located near Cincinnati, Ohio, Northern Kentucky University enrolls some 6,800 students, including 5,673 undergraduates. Fifty-one percent of the undergraduates are women, and 45 percent of women attend part-time. Forty percent of the female students are over age 25; 13 percent are over age 40.

Northern Kentucky offers a range of bachelor's and master's programs in liberal arts and sciences, education, and pre-professional studies. Classes are available in the evenings, both on and off campus, as well as during the summer. Opportunities for self-paced/contract learning are also available. All students commute to the urban campus, which is accessible by public transportation. On-campus parking is available at a fee.

University-run childcare can accommodate 40 children, with full-time students given priority for the service. Charges are based on a fixed, hourly rate. Private childcare facilities are available near campus.

Policies to Ensure Fairness to Women. The Affirmative Action Coordinator has full-time responsibility for policy and monitors compliance with matters relating to equal-employment-opportunity, access-for-the-handicapped, and sex-equity legislation. A campus policy prohibiting sexual harassment of students, faculty, and staff has been communicated in writing to the faculty

and staff. A Committee on Minority Affairs addresses the concerns of minority women.

Women in Leadership Positions. *Students.* Women have limited opportunities to exercise campus-wide leadership. In recent years, women have held two campus leadership positions for one year each—presiding officer of the student court and editor-in-chief of the campus newspaper. The president of the one campus honorary society is female.

Faculty. Women are 30 percent of the full-time faculty. According to recent information, among the 78 full-time female faculty are 1 Asian American and 2 black women. There are 5 female faculty for every 100 female students and 11 male faculty for every 100 male students.

Administrators. Men hold all key positions. A woman chairs one of the 18 academic departments: political science. Among the nine deans, the Director of Educational Services is a woman. Ten of the 35-member faculty senate are women. Of the 63 alumni awards in 1980–81, 47 went to women, including 2 black women.

Women and the Curriculum. Most four-year degrees awarded to women are in administration (36 percent), business (11 percent), and psychology (11 percent). About 4 percent of degrees to women are in the nontraditional areas of mathematics and physical sciences. Most two-year degrees to women are in health technologies (68 percent) and business and commerce (23 percent). Forty-seven percent of students in cooperative education programs are women.

The Women's Studies Program, headed by a director who holds a full-time faculty appointment, offers a 21-credit minor. Courses on women are offered through six departments. Courses include Women in Business, History of Feminism in the U.S., Women's Autobiographical Writings, and Philosophy and Human Sexuality. An official committee is charged with developing the Women's Studies Program, reporting on developments that include women in the curriculum, and collecting curricular materials on women.

Faculty workshops are available on sexism and racism in the curriculum, the needs of reentry women, and affirmative action and equal employment opportunity. Courses in the schools of education, nursing, social work, and business, and in the department of physical education, provide some instruction on matters specific to women.

Women and Athletics. Women participate in a variety of team and individual intramural sports. Women are 41 percent of intercollegiate athletes and receive 50 percent of athletic scholarship aid. Two of the eight paid varsity coaches are women. Intercollegiate sports are basketball, softball, tennis, and volleyball.

Special Services and Programs for Women. *Health and Counseling.* One female health-care provider staffs the health service; the counseling center is staffed by one man. Counseling but not treatment is available for gynecological problems, birth control, abortion, and rape and assault. The student health insurance policy covers both abortion and maternity expenses at no additional charge.

Safety and Security. Measures consist of campus police with weapons training and the authority to make arrests, high-intensity lighting, and a rape crisis center. No rapes or assaults on women were reported for 1980–81.

Career. Services include lectures by women employed in nontraditional occupations, and printed materials on nontraditional fields of study. Faculty are offered workshops on nontraditional careers for women and men.

Other. The continuing education program serves about 1,450 women annually. A peer support program is directed toward women students, especially those over age 25. The Women's Law Caucus and the Black United Students are advocacy groups for women on campus. A college-sponsored program serves displaced homemakers.

Six percent of undergraduate women belong to sororities, which do not provide housing for members.

Institutional Self-Description. "Unique features of Northern Kentucky University include its emphasis on preprofessional training balanced against a sound liberal arts education and its young, excellently prepared faculty. Convenient course times and offerings allow flexibility in class scheduling."

St. Catharine College
St. Catharine, KY 40061
Telephone: (606) 336-9304

Women in Leadership
★★★ faculty
★★★ administrators

159 undergraduates

	Amer. Ind.	Asian Amer.	Blacks	Hispanics	Whites
F	0	0	4	0	80
M	0	0	6	0	66
%	0.0	0.0	6.4	0.0	93.6

Established by the Sisters of St. Dominic in 1931 as a women's college, this private, Roman Catholic two-year college now offers associate degrees and professional programs to a coeducational student body. Of the 161 students, 54 percent are female; three-fourths of women attend full-time. The median age of all undergraduates is 21.

St. Catharine's offers the first two years of arts and sciences and professional courses in business, social work, agriculture, and education. The college operates an adult continuing education program. The campus is located near a small town, about an hour's drive from Louisville. On-campus parking is available to the 82 percent of students who commute.

Policies to Ensure Fairness to Women. An equal opportunity officer, on a part-time basis, is a voting member of policymaking councils and assumes responsibility for equal-employment, sex-equity-for-students, and handicapped-accessibility legislation. Complaints of sexual harassment are resolved through a formal grievance procedure.

Women in Leadership Positions. *Students.* In a recent three-year period, women held nearly one-third of leadership positions, including president of the student body for three consecutive years and head of the student government and of the student court for one-year terms. The one honorary society is headed by a woman.

Faculty. Two of the four full-time faculty members are women.

Administrators. Women hold all seven key positions except director of athletics. Women chair two of the three college divisions—mathematics and science, and humanities.

Women and the Curriculum. Women students receive their two-year degrees and certificates in the arts and sciences and in business and commerce.

There are no courses on women. The physical education department provides instruction on how to teach coeducational classes.

Women and Athletics. About half of athletes in the two intramural team sports (coeducational basketball and volleyball) are women. Several coeducational varsity sports are available.

Housing and Student Organizations. The 18 percent of students who reside on campus live in single-sex dormitories that do not allow visitors of the opposite sex.

Special Services and Programs for Women. *Health and Counseling.* One female nurse provides limited health-care to students. The student counseling service is staffed by one woman. Services of particular interest to women are available upon request.

Safety and Security. The campus is patrolled by local police and is lighted in all areas. No assaults or rapes were reported for 1980–81.

Career. The division of continuing education offers assertiveness/leadership training, and the mathematics division offers mathematics confidence workshops. Career services include workshops about nontraditional occupations and about reentering work or school.

Institutional Self-Description. "The religious congregation of women who founded this institution still retain all administrative positions and some faculty positions. Role models for women in top positions are readily available, but the atmosphere on campus (we hope) is equal opportunity for men and women."

University of Louisville
Louisville, KY 40292
Telephone: (502) 588-5555

★ **Women and the Curriculum**

★ **Women and Athletics**

12,465 undergraduates

	Amer. Ind.	Asian Amer.	Blacks	Hispanics	Whites
F	12	27	600	29	5,038
M	15	57	493	31	5,924
%	0.2	0.7	8.9	0.5	89.7

 NWSA

Established in 1798 as a liberal arts seminary, the University of Louisville entered the Kentucky state system in 1970 as a comprehensive university with a special urban mission. Some 18,300 students enroll. The Council for Continuing Education serves the adult student. Evening classes and a summer session as well as off-campus class locations are available.

Women are 46 percent of 12,465 undergraduates; 41 percent of women attend part-time. The median age of undergraduates is 25. For the 93 percent of undergraduates who live off campus or commute, the university is accessible by public transportation. On-campus parking is provided for a fee.

Recently-opened university childcare facilities charge on a sliding scale and can accommodate 80 children. Private childcare arrangements may be made close to campus.

Policies to Ensure Fairness to Women. A full-time Affirmative Action Officer reviews policy on equal employment opportunity, accessibility of curriculum and activities to students, and handicapped access. Complaints of sexual harassment are handled informally and confidentially. The Office of Minority Affairs addresses the concerns of minority women.

Women in Leadership Positions. *Students.* Opportunities for women students to exercise campus-wide leadership are below the average for public research universities in this guide. In recent years, a woman was president of the student body for one term. Women head five of the 21 honorary societies.

Faculty. Women are 22 percent of a full-time faculty of 614. According to a recent report, 6 black, 6 Asian American, and 2 Hispanic women are on the full-time faculty. There are 4 female faculty for every 100 female students and 11 male faculty for every 100 male students.

Administrators. Men hold all key positions. Women chair ten of 89 departments. One of the female department heads is Asian American. The Dean of the College of Arts and Sciences and the Dean of the School of Nursing are female.

Women and the Curriculum. Most women graduating with bachelor's degrees major in education, business and management, and the health professions. Three percent major in such nontraditional areas as engineering, mathematics, and the physical sciences. Significant numbers receive two-year degrees in health and business technologies. Women are encouraged to prepare for careers in law by a special program in the political science department. The Speed Scientific School, a program that combines study with practical work experience, reports increasing enrollments of women students. Thirty-nine percent of science field service positions go to women.

Seventeen courses on women are offered through academic departments and coordinated by the director of the Women's Studies Program. Recent titles include Finding, Evaluating, and Editing Women's Manuscripts; Feminism in Western Civilization; Eastern Religions and Sexism; The Black Woman; and Sex and Values. The Women's Studies Program is developing an undergraduate minor for approval in 1982.

Such current issues as mathematics confidence among females, sex-fair curricula, and coeducational physical education classes are part of the preparation of future teachers. The division of nursing includes reproductive-choice and health-care information important to minority women. Child abuse is touched on in the division of social work.

Minority Women. Twelve percent of undergraduate women are members of minority groups. In residence halls, 40 percent of the women are black, 2 percent Asian American, and 1 percent Hispanic. There are 43 women in all-minority sororities. Awareness-training on racism is offered staff of residence halls. The Office of Minority Affairs is supportive of minority women's concerns.

Women and Athletics. Intramural and intercollegiate programs provide good opportunities for organized, competitive, individual and team sports. Twenty-three percent of intramural and 30 percent of intercollegiate athletes are women. Women receive 30 percent of athletic scholarships. Ten of 32 paid coaches of intercollegiate sports are female. All women's intercollegiate teams played in tournaments in 1980. The intercollegiate sports offered are basketball, cross-country, field hockey, gymnastics, softball, tennis, track and field, and volleyball.

Housing and Student Organizations. Seven percent of undergraduates live on campus. Coeducational dormitories, including a Panhellenic dormitory, are available. A married woman student whose spouse is not enrolled may live in university housing. Dormitory residents determine any restrictions on hours for visitors of the opposite sex. One of three residence-hall directors is female. Staff are offered awareness-training on sexism, sex education, and racism.

Six percent of full-time undergraduate women belong to social sororities.

Special Services and Programs for Women. *Health and Counseling.* The student health service provides some medical attention specific to women, including gynecological, birth control, and rape and assault treatment. The 2 health service physicians are female, as are 3 other health-care providers. One of 5 counselors in the counseling service is female. Students have access to gynecological, birth control, abortion, and rape and assault counseling.

Safety and Security. Measures include campus police with arrest authority, night-time escorts for women students, an emergency alarm system, and information sessions on campus safety and crime prevention. A rape crisis center is available. Twenty-six assaults (nine on women) and no rapes were reported for 1980-1981.

Career. Activities and materials that concentrate on women in nontraditional occupations and fields of study and a program to establish contacts between alumnae and students are available through career placement, the Women's Resource Library, and women's career exploration workshops.

Other. Transitions is a cooperative effort to inform students about campus and community resources, to answer questions about returning to school, and to offer supportive educational programs.

Women's Studies sponsors an annual women's week. Assertiveness training and a program to build confidence in mathematics are available through the counseling center. Special Student Services operates a telephone line for information, referral, and support.

Returning Women Students. Several units are involved in programming for the adult entry or reentry student (recent data show that almost half of undergraduate women are over age 25). Over 200 women, including minority women, enroll in continuing education courses. The Life Planning Center sponsors a women's lecture series. The Women's Resource Library provides information and research materials useful to reentry women.

Institutional Self-Description. "Forty-six percent of our students are women. Accordingly, the university provides, through the Life Planning Center, Special Student Services, and the counseling center, special workshops, direction finders, and transitional assistance, creating thereby an atmosphere for the pursuit of traditional and innovative academic programs which will contribute to fuller, more satisfying lives."

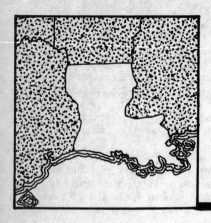

LOUISIANA

Tulane University
New Orleans, LA 70118
Telephone: (504) 865-4011

★ Women and the Curriculum

6,033 undergraduates

	Amer. Ind.	Asian Amer.	Blacks	Hispanics	Whites
F	4	25	102	96	1,953
M	29	38	153	190	3,078
%	0.6	1.1	4.5	5.1	88.8

 AAUW

Founded in 1834 as a state medical school and established in 1884 as a private university, Tulane University, located in the multi-cultural city of New Orleans, enrolls some 9,600 students in a range of undergraduate, graduate, and professional programs. Newcomb College is the liberal arts division for women. University College serves the continuing education needs of the adult student. Alternative class schedules include evening classes, a summer session, and off-campus daytime classes.

Women are 39 percent of the 6,033 undergraduates; 20 percent of the women attend part-time. For the 67 percent of undergraduates who live off campus or commute, the university is accessible by public transportation. On-campus parking is available for a fee.

University childcare facilities, accommodating 20 children, charge on a sliding scale. Private childcare arrangements may be made close to campus.

Policies to Ensure Fairness to Women. A full-time equal opportunity officer is responsible for reviewing policy on employment, sex equity for students, and handicapped accessibility. A published campus policy prohibits sexual harassment. Complaints are handled informally and confidentially. The Affirmative Action Office addresses the concerns of minority women.

Women in Leadership Positions. *Students.* Opportunities for women students to exercise all-campus leadership are considerably below the average for private research universities in this guide. In recent years a woman has twice presided over the student union board. Newcomb College has a separate, student senate which provides additional opportunities for leadership. A woman heads one of the 27 honorary societies.

Faculty. Women are 17 percent of a full-time faculty of 419. There are 4 female faculty for every 100 female students and 11 male faculty for every 100 male students.

Administrators. The director of institutional research is a woman. All other key administrative posts are held by men. Women chair three of 22 departments: anthropology, education, and earth sciences. The Dean of Newcomb College is female, as is the acting Dean of the School of Social Work.

Women and the Curriculum. A majority of women graduating with bachelor's degrees major in the social sciences, fine arts, psychology, general letters, and business and management. Thirteen percent major in nontraditional fields, a proportion significantly above the national average for private research universities.

Students interested in Women's Studies have the option of a self-designed major. Nine courses on women are offered in the departments of history, sociology, English, psychology, anthropology, classics, and biology, or through colloquia. An official committee is responsible for preparing materials on women and for developing a Women's Studies Program.

Such current issues as sex-role stereotyping in materials and instruction, services for abused spouses, and discrimination in the workplace are part of the preparation of future teachers, social workers, and business professionals.

Minority Women. Of 2,180 undergraduate women, 5 percent are black, 4 percent Hispanic, 1 percent Asian American, and less than 1 percent American Indian. Forty minority women are in integrated sororities. An American Indian woman sits on the faculty senate. Women of color are the subject of two courses, Women in Latin American History and, in the department of anthropology, African Worlds.

Women and Athletics. The intramural program of Newcomb College offers a variety of individual and team sports. The women's intercollegiate program is limited. Twenty-six percent of intramural, 21 percent of intercollegiate, and 16 percent of club athletes are women. Women receive 40 percent of the athletic scholarships awarded, a high proportion for institutions in this guide. Four of the 18 paid varsity coaches are women. All teams played tournament competition in 1980. The intercollegiate sports offered are basketball, swimming and diving, and tennis.

Housing and Student Organizations. One-third of the undergraduates live on campus. Single-sex and coeducational dormitories and housing for married students and single parents with children are available. A married woman student whose spouse is not enrolled may live in married students' housing. Dormitories do not restrict hours for visitors of the opposite sex. Five of 13 residence-hall directors are female. Staff are offered awareness-training on birth control, crime prevention, rape, and gay issues.

One-quarter of undergraduate women belong to social sororities, which provide housing for their members.

Special Services and Programs for Women. *Health and Counseling.* The student health service provides some medical attention specific to women; gynecological and birth control treatment is available. One of 4 full-time physicians is female, as are 10 of 18 other health-care providers. Four of 6 professional staff in the counseling center are women. Students have access to gynecological, birth control, abortion, and rape and assault counseling.

Safety and Security. Measures consist of campus police with arrest authority, emergency telephone and alarm systems, information sessions on campus safety and crime prevention, and a rape crisis center. Twenty-three assaults (seven on women) and no rapes were reported for 1980-81.

Career. Newcomb College houses a Women's Center, which is directed by a full-time, salaried administrator. Career workshops, lectures, and printed materials concentrated on women in nontraditional occupations and fields of study, as well as a program of contacts between alumnae and students, are available through the center. The office of the Dean of Students sponsors assertiveness training and a program to build confidence in mathematics.

Institutional Self-Description. "Tulane University offers women the choice of a small women's liberal arts and science college or a professional program in business, architecture, or engineering. The Graduate School and professional schools of law, medicine, public health, and social work combine with these programs to provide a high quality and complete educational experience."

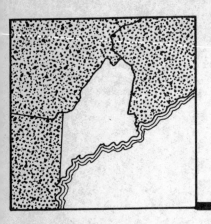

MAINE

Bangor Theological Seminary

300 Union Street, Bangor, ME 04401
Telephone: (207) 942-6781

Women in Leadership
★ administrators

23 undergraduates

	Amer. Ind.	Asian Amer.	Blacks	Hispanics	Whites
F	0	0	0	0	13
M	0	0	0	0	10
%	0.0	0.0	0.0	0.0	100.0

Bangor Theological Seminary is affiliated with the United Church of Christ and trains women and men for the ministry. Among a total enrollment of 110 are 23 undergraduates, 13 of whom are women. Two of the women attend part-time. Public transportation and free on-campus parking are available.

Private childcare facilities are located close to the campus.

Policies to Ensure Fairness to Women. A Committee on the Status of Women reports to the President. Elected by the Women's Group, it includes students with voting rights, but does not meet frequently or take public stands on issues of concern to students.

Women in Leadership Positions. *Students.* In recent years, a woman held one of the seven campus-wide leadership positions—presiding officer of the residence-hall council—for one year.

Faculty. One of the six full-time faculty members is a woman.

Administrators. One administrator, the executive vice president, who also acts as chief development officer, is a woman; the other three are men. A woman was among the three speakers in major lecture series held recently.

Women and the Curriculum. No information is available on degrees granted to women. The seminary has a program to encourage women to enter the ministry.

Women and Athletics. Thre is no opportunity for organized competitive sports.

Housing and Student Organizations. Fourteen of the undergraduates live on campus in coeducational dormitories that have no restrictions on visitors of the opposite sex. Housing for married students and single parents is available. A married woman whose husband is not enrolled may live in married students' housing.

Special Services and Programs for Women. *Health and Counseling.* There is no student health or counseling center. The student health insurance policy covers maternity at no extra cost.

Safety and Security. No information was provided. There were no rapes or assaults reported on campus for 1980–81.

Institutional Self-Description. "Bangor Seminary is ecumenical in spirit and includes representatives of most of the major denominations in its faculty and student body. It offers equal opportunity in its admissions and employment practices regardless of race, sex, religious affiliation, national or ethnic background."

Beal College

629 Main Street, Bangor, ME 04401
Telephone: (207) 947-4591

Women in Leadership
★★★ faculty
★ administrators

421 undergraduates

	Amer. Ind.	Asian Amer.	Blacks	Hispanics	Whites
F	5	1	0	1	256
M	0	0	0	0	157
%	1.2	0.2	0.0	0.2	98.3

A private, two-year business college chartered in 1891, Beal prepares men and women in such fields as accounting, data processing, health-care management, and airline careers. The total enrollment of 592 includes 421 students registered for degrees. Women are 63 percent of the degree students and 34 percent of women attend part-time. The median age of all undergraduates is 25. A summer session is available, as well as a continuing education program. For the 88 percent of students who commute, there is free on-campus parking but no public transportation. Students who reside on campus live in coeducational dormitories that have restrictive hours for visitors of the opposite sex.

Women in Leadership Positions. *Students.* During three recent years, women have held all three campus leadership positions for one year each: presiding officer of the student senate, and head of the entering class and the sophomore class.

Faculty. Of eleven full-time faculty, eight are women. The ratio of both female faculty to female students and male faculty to male students is 5 to 100.

Administrators. Women hold a third of the top positions, including chief business officer and head librarian. Of seven department chairs, four are women, including secretarial sciences, medical assisting, business management, and liberal studies.

Women and the Curriculum. Nearly all the degrees awarded to women are in business and commercial technologies. There are no courses on women.

Women and Athletics. There is no opportunity for organized competitive sports.

Special Services and Programs for Women. *Health and Counseling.* Beal offers neither health services, health insurance, nor counseling.

Safety and Security. City police patrol the campus, and high-intensity lighting has been installed. A rape crisis center is available. No rapes or assaults on women were reported in 1980–81.

Institutional Self-Description. "Beal College provides a small-college environment for women preparing for careers in business."

Casco Bay College
477 Congress Street, Portland, ME 04101
Telephone: (207) 772-0196

Women in Leadership
★★★ faculty
★★★ administrators

241 undergraduates

	Amer. Ind.	Asian Aer.	Blacks	Hispanics	Whites
F	0	0	0	0	184
M	0	1	2	0	54
%	0.0	0.4	0.8	0.0	98.8

Established in 1863 to teach business mathematics, typing, and bookkeeping, Casco Bay became an accredited coeducational junior college of business in 1973. It is wholly owned and operated by women, and over three-quarters of the students are women. The campus is accessible through public transportation, and on-campus parking is available for a fee. All students commute.

Private childcare can be arranged off campus.

Women in Leadership Positions. *Students.* The single campus leadership position, president of the student government, was held by a woman once in the past three years.

Faculty. Of six full-time faculty, three are women. There are 2 female faculty for every 100 female students and 13 male faculty for every 100 male students.

Administrators. Women hold all key positions. All of the trustees are women; the spring 1981 commencement speaker was a man.

Women and the Curriculum. Of the two-year degrees awarded to women, almost all are in business and commercial programs, the remainder in data processing. There are no courses on women.

Women and Athletics. Although there are no opportunities for organized competitive sports, the college rents the Portland YMCA for rollerskating, swimming, volleyball, and jogging.

Special Services and Programs for Women. *Health and Counseling.* There are no health or counseling services.

Safety and Security. No information was provided about services or facilities. There were no rapes or assaults reported for 1980-81.

Career. A course on assertiveness-training is offered, as well as programs to encourage women to choose careers in accounting, computer science, and management. The business program and the career placement office provide information on such issues as job discrimination, affirmative action, and nontraditional careers. The college offers workshops to faculty on such issues.

Institutional Self-Description. "The college is owned and operated by women. It is coeducational. Women study in the accounting, computer science, and management fields. All areas of secretarial sciences are offered. There is no discrimination as to sex, race, physical disability, color, national origin."

College of the Atlantic
Bar Harbor, ME 04609
Telephone: (207) 288-5015

Women in Leadership
★ students
★ administrators

125 undergraduates

	Amer. Ind.	Asian Amer.	Blacks	Hispanics	Whites
F	0	1	0	0	74
M	0	0	0	0	50
%	0.0	0.8	0.0	0.0	99.2

College of the Atlantic defines itself as an institution of "human ecology" that focuses on "the study of relationships between people and their natural and social environments." It was founded in 1969 in response to increasing ecological and social consciousness and to student dissatisfaction with large universities. This private college enrolls 130 students, 60 percent of whom are women. Fifteen percent of the women attend part-time. The median age of students is 22.

Students may earn bachelor's degrees in human ecology through self-designed programs. Independent study opportunities, a summer session, and evening classes are available. Area residents may audit academic programs and courses for a special fee.

Located on the Maine shore, near Acadia National Park, the campus is a renovated estate that accommodates the one-fourth of students who live on campus. Parking is available for those who commute.

Private childcare facilities are available near campus.

Policies to Ensure Fairness to Women. An Affirmative Action Officer, with the advice of an affirmative action committee, makes policy and examines practices pertaining to equal-employment-opportunity, sex-equity, and handicapped-access laws. A self-designated Committee on the Status of Women, which includes student members with voting rights, reports to the President of the college, publicizes its positions on women's issues, and takes stands on issues of importance to students. It also addresses the concerns of minority women.

Women in Leadership Positions. *Students.* The college has two campus-wide leadership posts: presiding officer of the "All-College Meeting" and editor-in-chief of the campus newspaper. Women have held both of these positions for at least one semester during each of the past three years.

Faculty. One of the 12 full-time faculty is a woman. The ratio of female faculty to female students is 2 to 100; the ratio of male faculty to male students is 25 to 100.

Administrators. Except for the business officer and head librarian, the five other chief administrators are men. Five of the 23 trustees are women.

Women and the Curriculum. All bachelor's degrees are in interdisciplinary studies of human ecology. According to the college, an equal number of women and men participate in its programs in environmental design and environmental sciences. Recently, women have held internships in architecture, urban planning, solar energy, and genetic laboratory research, among other fields. Boatbuilding, carpentry, and science field-service projects are also available.

The college offers three courses on women: Women in Transition, Women's History and Literature, and a student-initiated, credit workshop on the E.R.A. An official committee reports on and collects new Women's Studies curricula. The topics of sexism and the curriculum and affirmative action and equal opportunity have been raised at all-faculty workshops.

Women and Athletics. The college does not offer organized competitive sports.

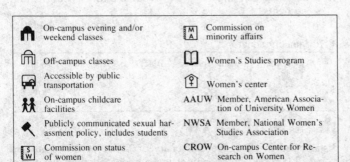

🏠 On-campus evening and/or weekend classes	🄼🄰 Commission on minority affairs	
🏛 Off-campus classes	📖 Women's Studies program	
🚌 Accessible by public transportation	👤 Women's center	
👫 On-campus childcare facilities	AAUW Member, American Association of University Women	
🔨 Publicly communicated sexual harassment policy, includes students	NWSA Member, National Women's Studies Association	
🆂🆆 Commission on status of women	CROW On-campus Center for Research on Women	

Special Services and Programs for Women. *Health and Counseling.* Students are referred to the Bar Harbor Medical Association, local counselors, and the local counseling center. Student health insurance covers maternity and abortion expenses at no extra cost.

Safety and Security. The only measure is local police protection. No rapes or assaults on women were reported for 1980–81.

Career. The college provides information on nontraditional occupations for women, maintains updated files on alumnae careers, and sponsors networking between alumnae and female students. Career planning services are also made available to the community, especially to displaced homemakers and to women returning to careers outside the home.

Institutional Self-Description. "An interdisciplinary, problem-solving approach to an innovative curriculum in human ecology (including environmental studies and social change) promotes exploration of nontraditional fields. Emphasis on community participation and self-governance provides constant training in decision-making and assertiveness skills. Over half of our students are women; the environment is physically safe, academically self-directed, and non-competitive in evaluation."

Unity College
Unity, ME 04988
Telephone: (207) 948-3131

Women in Leadership
★★★ students
★ administrators

428 undergraduates

	Amer. Ind.	Asian Amer.	Blacks	Hispanics	Whites
F	0	0	1	3	82
M	0	0	1	2	339
%	0.0	0.0	0.5	1.2	98.4

Unity College, established in 1966, is a private, non-sectarian institution located in rural, central Maine. Its campus has a total enrollment of 726 students, of whom 428 are enrolled in degree programs. Women are one-fifth of the undergraduates; 5 percent of women attend part-time. The median age of all students is 20. Unity offers associate and bachelor's degrees. On-campus day and evening classes are supplemented by off-campus day classes. A summer session is available. On-campus parking is available to the 50 percent of students who commute.

The college-operated childcare center accommodates 12 children on a first-come, first-served basis, and charges a $5 daily fee. Private childcare facilities are available nearby.

Policies to Ensure Fairness to Women. A Commission on the Status of Women, appointed by and responsible to the Director of Career Planning and Placement, responds to the concerns of women, including minority women, and publicizes its views and findings. A published sexual harassment policy protects students, faculty, and staff. Complaints are resolved through a formal grievance procedure or informally and confidentially.

Women in Leadership Positions. *Students.* Women students have outstanding opportunities to gain leadership experience. In recent years, they have held the three campus-wide offices most of the time: student body president, editor of the campus newspaper, and student judiciary president.

Faculty. Four of the 26 full-time faculty are women. There are 5 female faculty for every 100 female students and 7 male faculty for every 100 male students.

Administrators. Two-thirds of the chief administrators are men. Women hold the posts of chief student-life officer, chief devel-

opment officer, and head librarian. Men chair the five academic departments.

Women and the Curriculum. In a recent year, women received 13 of 125 bachelor's degrees: 6 in health, 4 in agriculture, 2 in interdisciplinary studies, and 1 in business; women received 17 of 63 associate degrees, including 8 in natural sciences and 7 in arts and sciences. The Career Planning and Placement Service encourages women to enter the nontraditional fields of science, agriculture and outdoor recreation. Faculty are offered workshops on nontraditional careers.

The Center of Motivational Resources offers a course on women entitled Women in Society. An official committee is responsible for developing a Women's Studies Program as well as collecting and reporting on new curricular materials on women.

Women and Athletics. The organized sports program for women is limited. One fifth of the intercollegiate and intramural athletes are women. There are two intramural team sports, and club sports. One of the two paid varsity coaches is a woman. The intercollegiate sport offered is volleyball.

Housing and Student Organizations. Half of the undergraduates live on campus in single-sex and coeducational dormitories that have no restrictions on visiting hours for members of the opposite sex. Housing is also available for married students with and without children and for single parents. A married woman student whose husband is not enrolled is permitted to live in married students' housing. Residence-hall staff are offered awareness training on sexism, sex education, racism, and birth control.

Special Services and Programs for Women. *Health and Counseling.* The student health service is staffed by one female health-care provider. There are no health services specific to women. One male professional works at the student counseling service. Counseling is available for gynecological problems, birth control, abortion, and rape and assault. Student health insurance covers abortion and maternity expenses.

Safety and Security. The only measure is local police protection. No rapes or assaults on women were reported for 1980–81.

Career. The Career Planning and Placement Service offers career workshops and information on nontraditional occupations, and keeps files on the careers of alumnae.

Other. The Center for Motivational Resources, which operates a mathematics confidence clinic for women, serves as a general resource for all women students.

Institutional Self-Description. "Although a minority, women at Unity are encouraged by faculty and male students in nontraditional roles and programs: forestry, environmental sciences, outdoor recreation. Women head some of the major clubs and organizations. Even with the 3 to 1 ratio, we have no history of assaults against women."

University of Maine, Orono
Orono, ME 04469
Telephone: (207) 581-2638

Women in Leadership   ★ **Women and the Curriculum**
★ students

                             ★ **Women and Athletics**

8,724 undergraduates

	Amer. Ind.	Asian Amer.	Blacks	Hispanics	Whites
F	37	7	6	3	3,707
M	32	19	8	7	4,877
%	0.8	0.3	0.2	0.1	98.6

 AAUW

Established in 1865, the University of Maine at Orono attracts some 12,000 students to various undergraduate and graduate programs. Classes are available evenings, on and off campus, and during the summer.

Women make up 43 percent of the 8,724 undergraduates; 9 percent of women attend part-time. In one recent year about 20 percent of women students were older than 25, and two-thirds of these older women attended part-time. The median age of all undergraduates is 20. For the 48 percent of undergraduates who commute to campus, public transportation is available. On-campus parking is provided at a fee.

Low-cost, university-sponsored childcare facilities accommodate an estimated 40 percent of students' requests in all-day and after-school sessions. Private childcare arrangements may be made close to campus.

Policies to Ensure Fairness to Women. A full-time Equal-Opportunity Officer reports to the president and reviews policies and practices in employment, sex equity for students, and handicapped accessibility. The Equal Opportunity Program provides for, and coordinates, student and employee services, including complaint investigation and resolution. A formal policy prohibiting sexual harassment and a grievance procedure are being developed. Policy and procedures will be communicated to students.

Women in Leadership Positions. *Students.* Opportunities for women to exercise campus-wide leadership are good. In recent years women have been presiding officer of the student senate, the student court (twice), the student union board, and residence-hall council, editor-in-chief of the newspaper (twice), and president of the senior class. Women head seven of the nine honorary societies.

Faculty. Women are 15 percent of a full-time faculty of 462. One American Indian, 2 Asian American, and 2 Hispanic women are on the faculty, according to recent report. The ratio of female faculty to female students is 2 to 100; the ratio of male faculty to male students is 8 to 100.

Administrators. The director of institutional research is a woman. All other higher administrative positions are occupied by men. Women chair 3 of 42 departments: English, human development, and food science. The Director of the School of Human Development and the acting Dean of the Graduate School are women, 1 of whom is a black woman. The 4-member tenure committee consists of 1 black woman and 3 men; one-fifth of the university trustees are women.

Women and the Curriculum. Forty percent of women graduating with bachelor's degrees major in education or home economics. Over 13 percent of women major in such nontraditional areas as agriculture, engineering, mathematics, and the physical sciences, which is a significantly higher proportion than at most public research universities. Over one-fifth of the positions in cooperative education programs go to women. Thirty-eight percent of the science field-service students and three-fourths of undergraduate intern students are women. Most two-year degrees earned by women are in health technologies (44 percent), public service (19 percent), and business (19 percent).

While there is no formal Women's Studies Program, a special project for faculty, called Women and Curriculum, has encouraged the development of several courses on women, including Images of Women in Literature, Sociology of Sex Roles, Sex Role Stereotypes in the American Classroom, and Women in Political and Governmental Careers. The divisions of social work and business offer instruction on some matters specific to women.

Women and Athletics. Intramural and intercollegiate programs offer good opportunities for organized, competitive, individual and team sports. Some intercollegiate teams are coeducational. Club sports are also available. Twenty percent of intramural, 28 percent of intercollegiate, and 36 percent of club athletes are women; women receive 20 percent of athletic scholarships. Ten of the 28 paid varsity coaches are women. The intercollegiate sports offered are basketball, cross-country, field hockey, gymnastics, riflery (coeducational), sailing (coeducational), skiing, softball, swimming and diving, tennis, track and field, and volleyball.

Housing and Student Organizations. Fifty-two percent of undergraduates live on campus. Single-sex and coeducational dormitories and housing for married students and single parents with children are available. A married woman student whose spouse is not enrolled may live in married students' housing. Twelve of 27 residence-hall staff are female. Staff are offered awareness-training on sexism, sex education, birth control, and alcoholism.

Twelve percent of undergraduate women belong to social sororities, which do not provide housing for their members. The Women's Center serves as an advocate for women on campus, as does the Wilde-Stein Club.

Special Services and Programs for Women. *Health and Counseling.* The student health service provides medical attention specific to women, including gynecological, birth control, abortion, and rape and assault treatment. The regular student health insurance covers 80 percent of abortion and maternity expenses at no extra charge. One of 5 physicians is female, as are 17 of 25 other health-care providers. Five of 11 professional staff in the counseling center are women. Counseling specific to women is available. Staff receive in-service training on sex-role stereotyping, child abuse, and incest.

Safety and Security. Measures include campus police with arrest authority, information sessions on safety and crime prevention, and a rape crisis center. Two assaults on women and two rapes were reported for 1980–81.

Career. Information offered to students includes materials on women in nontraditional occupations and fields of study.

Other. A Women's Center operates under auspices of the student senate. The Office of Nontraditional Students sponsors a displaced homemakers program and provides support to women of varying ages and life circumstances. The Women and Curriculum Project sponsors a women's lecture series.

Institutional Self-Description. "The University of Maine at Orono is a land-grant university committed to high quality in instruction, research, and public service. The university is small enough to be responsive to individual students' needs and concerns, but large enough to offer diverse undergraduate and graduate programs, including science, engineering, and business programs, of high quality. The president of our university, both publicly and privately, supports the mainstreaming of women's studies into academic and professional curricula.

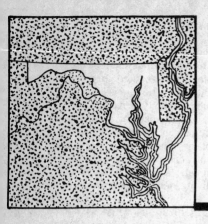

MARYLAND

Anne Arundel Community College
101 College Parkway, Arnold, MD 21012
Telephone: (301) 269-7201

Women in Leadership
★ students
★★ faculty

6,502 undergraduates

	Amer. Ind.	Asian Amer.	Blacks	Hispanics	Whites
F	16	32	230	33	3,254
M	22	41	214	34	2,618
%	0.6	1.0	6.8	1.0	90.4

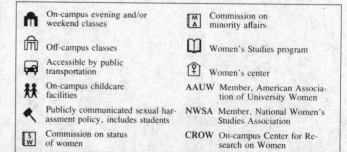

This public two-year college was founded in 1961. Women are 55 percent of a student population of 6,502; almost three-fourths of women attend part-time. The median age of all students is 27.

Anne Arundel offers a wide range of programs in arts and sciences, business, communications/media, health, public service and data processing. Alternative full-time and part-time scheduling includes off-campus day and evening classes, television courses, a 13-week summer session, a weekend college, and limited contract learning arrangements. Adult education courses are provided by the Community and Extension Services Division. All students commute to campus which is accessible by public transportation. Free, on-campus parking is available.

College-run childcare facilities are available daily from 7:45 a.m. to 10 p.m. Ninety-six percent of student requests for the service can be met, and charges are based on a fixed hourly rate.

Policies to Ensure Fairness to Women. Four administrators and an Affirmative Action Committee are assigned part-time to make policy or monitor compliance with equal-employment-opportunity, sex-equity-for-students, and handicapped-access legislation.

Women in Leadership Positions. *Students.* Women have held 44 percent of the available positions in the past three years, including president of the student body, manager of the campus radio station, and a two-year tenure as editor-in-chief of the campus newspaper.

Faculty. Women are 35 percent of a full-time faculty of 173, a proportion significantly above average for colleges nationwide. There are 6 female faculty for every 100 female students and 10 male faculty for every 100 male students. The full-time female faculty include 1 Asian American and 2 black women.

Administrators. The eight major administrative positions are held by men. The Dean of Instructional Systems is a woman. Two of nine departments are chaired by women: public service and nursing. Three of 8 trustees are women.

Women and the Curriculum. Women earn 55 percent of the two-year degrees awarded, most in arts and sciences (44 percent), health (26 percent), business (20 percent), and data processing (7

percent). More than half of the students in cooperative education and internship programs are women, as are 20 percent of students involved in science field service and 47 percent of those in retail management.

One course on women, Women in Literature, is offered through the department of English. Faculty workshops are held on non-traditional occupations for women and men, the needs of reentry women, and affirmative action and equal opportunity.

Women and Athletics. Women account for 39 percent of intercollegiate and 22 percent of intramural athletes. There are 11 coaches for women's varsity sports programs; no coaches are paid. Intramural sports include team and individual sports; water polo facilities are available. Intercollegiate sports for women are badminton, basketball, cross-country, field hockey, lacrosse, sailing, softball, swimming, tennis, track, and volleyball.

Special Services and Programs for Women. *Health and Counseling.* A student health service staffed by a woman health-care provider and a student counseling center staffed by one woman and one man provide counseling but not medical treatment for gynecological matters, birth control, abortion, and assault. Two annual health fairs provide opportunities for women to obtain gynecological and basic laboratory blood tests. The regular student health insurance covers abortion and maternity expenses.

Safety and Security. Measures consist of local and campus police, night-time escort service for women students, high-intensity lighting in all areas, self-defense courses for women, information sessions on campus safety, a community-sponsored Sexual Offense Crisis Center, and lectures on rape and assault prevention. No rapes or assaults on women were reported on campus for 1980–81

Career. Arundel offers workshops, printed materials, and job discrimination information on nontraditional occupations for women. Career issues are also addressed by a coffee-hour lecture series and conference workshops sponsored by the Community and Extension Services Division. Topics for workshops include How to Start Your Business, Working at Home, and Where the Jobs Are. Alumnae are invited to address female students at conference workshops.

Other. The small campus Women's Center, staffed by professional counselors and some female paraprofessionals, but with no

Icon	Description	Icon	Description
🏛	On-campus evening and/or weekend classes	MA	Commission on minority affairs
	Off-campus classes		Women's Studies program
	Accessible by public transportation		Women's center
	On-campus childcare facilities	AAUW	Member, American Association of University Women
	Publicly communicated sexual harassment policy, includes students	NWSA	Member, National Women's Studies Association
SW	Commission on status of women	CROW	On-campus Center for Research on Women

separate budget, offers academic counseling and career planning services. In 1981 it co-sponsored a Rape Crisis Seminar.

Institutional Self-Description. None provided.

Bowie State College
Jericho Park Road, Bowie, MD 20715
Telephone: (301) 464-3200

Women in Leadership
★ students
★★ faculty

1,519 undergraduates

	Amer. Ind.	Asian Amer.	Blacks	Hispanics	Whites
F	2	0	606	2	117
M	1	2	589	2	116
%	0.2	0.1	83.2	0.3	16.2

Located in a suburb of Washington, D.C., Bowie State was founded in 1865 as a college for black students, and it is still a predominantly black college. Forty-nine percent of the 1,519 undergraduates are women; 18 percent of women attend part-time. The median age of undergraduates is 20. According to recent information from the college, 43 percent of women students are over age 25, and 11 percent are over 40.

The college offers bachelor's degrees in a wide range of liberal arts and pre-professional areas. A master's degree program is also available. Evening, weekend, and summer session classes are offered, and off-campus locations are available. Adult education courses are provided by the division of continuing education. The campus is accessible by public transportation. Free on-campus parking is available for the 80 percent of students who commute.

A college-operated childcare center, which accommodates 25 children, charges a fixed daily fee and offers its services first to full-time students. The center meets 90 percent of students' requests. Private childcare facilities are also available close to the college.

Policies to Ensure Fairness to Women. A Committee on Minority Affairs addresses the concerns of minority women.

Women in Leadership Positions. *Students.* In recent years, women have held one-third of campus-wide leadership posts, mainly one- or two-year terms as class presidents. Women also preside over five of the seven honorary societies.

Faculty. Forty-three percent of the 106 full-time faculty are women, a proportion well above average for colleges nationwide. Fifteen of the full-time female faculty are white; most of the rest are black women. There are 7 female faculty for every 100 female students and 9 male faculty for every 100 male students.

Administrators. The top-ranking administrators are men, except for the head librarian who is a black woman. One white and 3 black women chair four of seven departments, including business administration, communications, and public administration. Three white women and 1 black woman sit on the 12-member Board of Trustees. Thirty percent of the faculty senate are black women. Two of 3 recent honorary degree recipients were black women.

Women and the Curriculum. The most popular fields for women graduates are education (43 percent), business (22 percent), and public affairs (10 percent). The department of mathematics sponsors a program to build confidence in mathematics. Thirty percent of the students in cooperative education are women. There are no courses on women. The education department trains teachers to recognize and treat mathematics avoidance in female students.

Women and Athletics. The college provides no intramural competition for women and only two intercollegiate sports. Eighteen percent of the varsity athletes are women, as are two of eleven

paid varsity coaches. Intercollegiate sports offered are basketball and volleyball.

Housing and Student Organizations. One-fifth of the undergraduates live in women's or coeducational dormitories, including a dormitory for honor students. All residence halls restrict hours for visitors of the opposite sex. The residence-hall staff—one man and six minority women—are offered awareness-training on sex education and on the avoidance of sexism and racism.

Ten percent of women belong to social sororities. Neither sororities nor fraternities provide housing for members. A campus chapter of the National Association for the Advancement of Colored People and Ladies of Distinction are two advocacy groups for women.

Special Services and Programs for Women. *Health and Counseling.* The student health service employs 2 male and 2 female physicians, in addition to 4 female health-care providers. One of 3 professional counselors is a woman. Available services specific to women include medical treatment and counseling for gynecological problems and birth control, as well as counseling for abortion, and rape and assault.

Safety and Security. Measures consist of campus police protection, high-intensity lighting, and information on campus safety for women. One rape and 22 assaults, 18 on women, were reported for 1980–81.

Career. Career Planning and Placement sponsors a women's lecture series.

Other. The counseling center runs leadership-training sessions, and serves as a center of support for all women students. The Respond Center's Peer Counseling is a resource for women.

Institutional Self-Description. "The following objectives are conducive to women studying at Bowie State College: (1) a curriculum which integrates a liberal arts education with development in professional knowledge and skills; (2) educational programs and services to meet the capacities of all students; (3) assistance in defining educational aspirations and career objectives; (4) programs to foster positive human relations, integrate understanding and appreciation of cultural differences; (5) to strengthen and maintain a well educated and productive faculty."

Chesapeake College
Wye Mills, MD 21679
Telephone: (301) 758-1537

Women in Leadership
★★★ students
★★ faculty

1,016 undergraduates

	Amer. Ind.	Asian Amer.	Blacks	Hispanics	Whites
F	1	0	74	2	526
M	0	2	47	1	363
%	0.1	0.2	12.0	0.3	87.5

Chesapeake is a two-year college that offers a wide range of college transfer, associate degree, and certificate programs in such fields as ecology, agriculture, law enforcement, and marine maintenance. Its rural campus attracts 1,468 students, 61 percent of whom are women. The median age of all students is 30. Flexible scheduling includes evening classes on and off campus, day classes off campus, a summer session, and self-paced/contract learning. All students commute, and on-campus parking is free.

An on-campus childcare facility can accommodate all students' requests.

Policies to Ensure Fairness to Women. The Affirmative Action Officer, who is a voting member of policymaking councils, is responsible for monitoring compliance with legislation concerning equal employment opportunity, sex equity for students, and access for the handicapped. A written campus policy prohibits sexual harassment of students, faculty, and staff. Policy and procedure have been communicated in writing to the Student Advisory Board. Complaints of harassment are resolved through a formal grievance procedure.

Women in Leadership Positions. *Students.* Of the two leadership positions, women served once as head of the student senate and three times as editor-in-chief of the campus newspaper during a recent three-year period.

Faculty. Fourteen of the 29 full-time faculty are women. There are 6 female faculty for every 100 female students and 8 male faculty for every 100 male students.

Administrators. Men hold all key positions. A woman chairs the humanities department; another chairs the Cluster of Human Understanding and Expression. The director of Continuing Education and Community Services is a woman. The 12-member Board of Trustees includes a black woman and an Hispanic woman.

Women and the Curriculum. Most two-year degrees and certificates awarded to women are in business and commercial programs (41 percent) and arts and sciences (34 percent). There are no courses on women.

Women and Athletics. Two of four paid varsity coaches are women. Intercollegiate sports in which women compete are softball, tennis, and volleyball.

Special Services and Programs for Women. *Health and Counseling.* The student counseling center, staffed by one man, offers no services specific to women. There are no health services.

Safety and Security. Measures include campus police and high-intensity lighting. A night-time escort service is also available. There were no rapes or assaults reported for 1980–81.

Career. The career placement office provides information and workshops on nontraditional fields of study.

Other. Theta Chi, whose 15 members are women, functions as an advocacy group for women. The Dean of Students, in cooperation with the local community's Department of Human Resources, offers a special program for displaced homemakers. An adult continuing education unit enrolls 30 reentry women.

Institutional Self-Description. None provided.

Community College of Baltimore
2901 Liberty Heights Avenue
Baltimore, MD 21215
Telephone: (301) 396-0996

Women in Leadership
★★ faculty

8,253 undergraduates

	Amer. Ind.	Asian Amer.	Blacks	Hispanics	Whites
F	8	13	4,359	12	935
M	8	14	2,077	7	584
%	0.2	0.3	80.3	0.2	19.0

The Community College of Baltimore awards two-year degrees in a range of fields. Alternative schedules include evening, summer session, and weekend classes. Some classes meet off campus. Sixty-six percent of the 8,253 students are women; 57 percent of women attend part-time. Eighty percent of the students are black, 19 percent white. The median age of all students is 24. All students commute; both public transportation and on-campus parking are available.

On-campus daytime childcare facilities can accommodate 75

children and meet approximately half of all students' requests for service.

Policies to Ensure Fairness to Women. The Dean of the College serves part-time to ensure equity for racial minorities, women, and the disabled. The self-designated Committee on the Status of Women reports to the executive committee of the faculty senate and includes student members with voting rights. The committee prepares reports, sponsors a seminar series, promotes the enrollment of women in the college, and addresses the concerns of minority women.

Women in Leadership Positions. *Students.* Information was not supplied by the college.

Faculty. Of the 162 full-time faculty, 45 percent are women, a proportion far above the national average. There are 3 female faculty for every 100 female students and 7 male faculty for every 100 male students. The college reports that 22 of the 45 full-time female faculty members are black women.

Administrators. No information was provided.

Women and the Curriculum. Most women major in health technology (27 percent), arts and sciences (27 percent), and public service (23 percent), with a subtantial proportion (18 percent) in business and commercial programs. Two percent of women graduate in the nontraditional fields of mechanical and engineering technologies and natural science. The college offers programs to encourage women to prepare for careers in science and in technologies. About three-quarters of students in internship and cooperative education programs are women.

Two courses on women are offered in the departments of English and social science: Women in Literature, and Women in History. The departments of education, nursing, social work, and business address issues specific to women in their curricula. Faculty workshops are held on such topics as sexism and racism in the curriculum, nontraditional occupations for women and men, the needs of reentry women, and affirmative action and equal opportunity.

Women and Athletics. No information was provided.

Special Services and Programs for Women. *Health and Counseling.* The student health service employs two female health-care providers and provides counseling and medical treatment for gynecological problems, birth control, and rape and assault.

Safety and Security. Measures consist of campus police without arrest authority. No rapes or assaults on women were reported for 1980–81.

Other. The Office of Displaced Women offers a program to build confidence in mathematics; it also provides general support for older women on campus. The Office of Staff Development sponsors a women's lecture series. Student Life and Student Services sponsor theater and other women's arts programs, as well as assertiveness/leadership training.

Institutional Self-Description. "CCB is the only public, lower-division college in the city of Baltimore offering both transfer and occupational programs at reasonable cost and accessible by public transportation. The college supports women seeking to further their education with daycare facilities, a displaced homemakers' center, and extensive tutorial programs for the educationally disadvantaged."

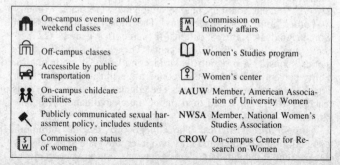

Symbol	Description	Symbol	Description
	On-campus evening and/or weekend classes	Ɱ	Commission on minority affairs
	Off-campus classes		Women's Studies program
	Accessible by public transportation		Women's center
	On-campus childcare facilities	AAUW	Member, American Association of University Women
	Publicly communicated sexual harassment policy, includes students	NWSA	Member, National Women's Studies Association
	Commission on status of women	CROW	On-campus Center for Research on Women

Dundalk Community College
7200 Sollers Point Road
Dundalk, MD 21222
Telephone: (301) 282-6700

Women in Leadership
★★★ students
★★ faculty

2,033 undergraduates

	Amer. Ind.	Asian Amer.	Blacks	Hispanics	Whites
F	5	7	90	4	1,034
M	4	8	79	4	798
%	0.4	0.7	8.3	0.4	90.1

This public, two-year commuter college, founded in 1971, occupies a suburban campus near Baltimore. Women are 56 percent of the 2,033 undergraduates; 75 percent of women attend part-time. The median age of all students is 29.

The college offers associate degree and certificate programs in liberal arts, engineering/technology, business, public service, communications/media, and agriculture. There is a continuing education program for adult students. Alternative scheduling includes off-campus day and evening classes, a weekend college, contract learning, and a summer session. Public transportation as well as on-campus parking are available.

Childcare facilities accommodate 40 children of students, faculty, and staff and are available on campus daily from 7 a.m. to 5:30 p.m. Private childcare facilities are available nearby.

Policies to Ensure Fairness to Women. Two members of the administrative staff have part-time responsibility for policy regarding equal-employment-opportunity, sex-equity, and handicapped-access legislation.

Women in Leadership Positions. *Students.* Women have excellent opportunities to exercise student leadership. Of two available positions, women have served as editor of the campus newspaper during a recent three-year period, and as president of the student body for one of those years.

Faculty. Women are 45 percent of the 42 full-time faculty, a proportion above average for public two-year colleges in this guide. There are 7 female faculty for every 100 female students and 8 male faculty for every 100 male students.

Administrators. Women hold two of ten major administrative positions, including director of student-life programs and chief librarian. The Director of Continuing Education and Student Services is a woman. One of six departmental chairs, in humanites and arts, is a woman.

Women and the Curriculum. Most women earn two-year degrees and certificates in the liberal arts (38 percent), natural science (27 percent), public service (21 percent), and business and commerce (14 percent). Approximately half of the students in the cooperative education program are women.

Woman to Woman is a course offered by Continuing Education. The division of education provides instruction on some issues specific to women. Faculty are offered workshops on nontraditional occupations for women and men and the needs of reentry women.

Women and Athletics. Insufficient information was provided to assess the intercollegiate program. Four intramural sports are offered. Women receive 20 percent of the athletic scholarships awarded.

Special Services and Programs for Women. *Health and Counseling.* There is no student health service on campus. A student counseling center, staffed by four women and three men, provides counseling for gynecological problems, birth·control, and abortion.

Safety and Security. Measures consist of campus police with weapons training, night-time escorts, high-intensity lighting, an emergency alarm system at isolated locations, and self-defense courses. No rapes or assaults were reported for 1980–81.

Career. Workshops and printed information on nontraditional occupations, lectures and panels by women employed in these fields, and updated files concerning the career choices of alumnae are available.

Institutional Self-Description. None provided.

Frostburg State College
Frostburg, MD 21532
Telephone: (301) 689-4000

2,932 undergraduates

	Amer. Ind.	Asian Amer.	Blacks	Hispanics	Whites
F	1	1	83	9	1,411
M	3	0	107	9	1,293
%	0.1	0.0	6.5	0.6	92.7

 AAUW

Frostburg State College, founded as a preparatory school for teachers in 1935, became a four-year state college in 1963. It awards bachelor's and master's degrees. The total student population is 3,651, almost all of whom attend full-time. Of the 2,932 undergraduates, 52 percent are women. The median age of undergraduate students is 20. Although Frostburg still emphasizes teacher training, it also offers programs in liberal arts and sciences. All classes are held on campus, and both evening and summer sessions are offered. Frostburg's office of admissions, along with the evening and extension programs, administers the continuing education program. Both public transportation and free, on-campus parking are provided for the one-third of students who commute.

Private childcare is available near campus.

Policies to Ensure Fairness to Women. One of the duties of the Assistant to the President is compliance with equal employment opportunity. The State of Maryland's grievance mechanism is used to resolve complaints of sexual harassment; an Affirmative Action Coordinator and Committee are appointed by the President of the college. The Office on Minority Affairs addresses concerns of minority women.

Women in Leadership Positions. *Students.* In a recent three-year period, women held one-fifth of campus-wide leadership positions: student body president, newspaper editor (for two years), and president of the residence-hall council.

Faculty. Frostburg has 175 full-time faculty members, of whom 23 percent are women. There are 3 female faculty for every 100 women students and 10 male faculty for every 100 male students.

Administrators. Men hold all top positions, except for the vice president for student affairs. A woman co-chairs the department of physical education and men chair 24 other departments. Four of 6 deans are women, including 1 black woman. Two of 11 trustees are women and 1 is a black woman.

Women and the Curriculum. Most women take degrees in education (41 percent), social sciences (19 percent), business (13 percent), and psychology (9 percent).

A committee is charged with developing courses on women. The department of history offers Women in Western Civilization, History of American Women, and Spanish-Speaking Minorities; the department of English offers Women and Literature. Faculty are offered workshops that address matters of affirmative action and equal opportunity.

Women and Athletics. For a school of this size, Frostburg offers women good opportunities to participate in organized competitive sports. Thirty-six percent of intercollegiate athletes are women. A good variety of individual and team intramural sports is available. The campus has squash courts and an Olympic-sized pool. The intercollegiate sports offered are basketball, field hockey, lacrosse, swimming, tennis, and track.

Housing and Student Organizations. Two-thirds of undergraduates live on campus in single-sex or coeducational housing that has no restrictions on visitation. Of six residence-hall directors, two are women, including one minority woman.

Some 20 percent of undergraduates join social sororities and fraternities, which provide no housing.

Special Services and Programs for Women. *Health and Counseling.* The student health service is staffed by 1 male physician and 4 female nurses, who provide gynecological and birth control services. Four counselors, 2 of them women, provide counseling on abortion, rape, and assault.

Safety and Security. Measures consist of campus and municipal police, information sessions on rape and assault prevention and campus safety, and a rape crisis center. Information on the incidence of rapes and assaults on women was not provided.

Career. Career workshops on nontraditional occupations, programs for students by women in nontraditional occupations, and alumnae files organized by career are provided.

Other. The counseling center provides assertiveness/leadership training for women.

Institutional Self-Description. "Frostburg State College is a comprehensive college offering high-quality arts and science, business, and education programs at baccalaureate and master's levels. It has a beautiful setting in the Allegany Mountains within 150 miles of Washington, Baltimore, and Pittsburgh."

Garrett Community College
McHenry, MD 21541
Telephone: (301) 387-6666

Women in Leadership
★★★ students

549 undergraduates

	Amer. Ind.	Asian Amer.	Blacks	Hispanics	Whites
F	0	0	1	0	233
M	0	0	6	0	309
%	0.0	0.0	1.3	0.0	98.7

Garrett, a public community college, offers two-year arts and sciences and pre-professional programs, as well as one- and two-year terminal programs in environmental and renewable resources technology, business occupations, and secretarial science. The college operates an adult continuing education program. Alternative schedules include summer session, evening, and off-campus classes.

Forty-three percent of the 549 students are women; 60 percent of women attend part-time. The median age of all undergraduates is 26. Located on a rural campus in western Maryland, Garrett is accessible by public transportation; on-campus parking is provided.

College-run daytime childcare facilities are available on campus for students who are parents. Fees are based on a fixed daily rate. The facilities can accommodate 20 percent of students requests for childcare.

Policies to Ensure Fairness to Women. A part-time equal opportunity officer develops policies for review and monitors compliance with federal regulations on equal employment opportunity, educational sex equity, and access for handicapped students. Sexual harassment of students, faculty, and staff is prohibited by a written campus policy that has been publicly communicated to all three groups. Complaints are handled informally and confidentially. The Commission on the Status of Women, which includes students with voting rights, is appointed by the President of the college. The commission recommends development in curricula and student services and addresses the concerns of minority women.

Women in Leadership Positions. *Students.* There are two student leadership positions. In a recent three-year period, women served as president of the student body for three consecutive terms and as editor-in-chief of the campus newspaper for two terms.

Faculty. Five of the 21 full-time faculty are women, a proportion below average for public two-year colleges nationwide. The ratio of female faculty to female students is 5 to 100; the ratio of male faculty to male students is 9 to 100

Administrators. The six chief administrative officers are men. Women chair two of the four departments: humanities and social services. Two of seven trustees are women.

Women and the Curriculum. Most women earn degrees in arts and sciences, with small numbers graduating in health, natural science, business and commerce, and public service technologies. The curriculum in physical education includes instruction in how to teach coeducational classes. Workshops that focus on nontraditional occupations for women and men, the needs of reentry women, and affirmative action and equal opportunity are offered faculty. There are no courses on women.

Women and Athletics. Garrett offers some opportunity for women to participate in organized competitive sports. Approximately one-third of the intramural, club, and intercollegiate athletes are women. Forty percent of athletic scholarships are awarded to women. One of the two paid coaches for intercollegiate sports is a woman. Women's intercollegiate sports include basketball and volleyball.

Special Services and Programs for Women. *Health and Counseling.* There is no student health service. The student counseling center is staffed by one male counselor.

Safety and Security. Measures consist of local town police who patrol the campus, and a rape crisis center. For 1980–81, there were no rapes or assaults reported on campus.

Career. The college reports that the entry of women into nontraditional occupations receives college-wide emphasis. Career workshops and job discrimination information focused on nontraditional occupations, as well as lectures and panels by women employed in these areas, are offered. Career counseling for women is also available.

Other. An all-female student organization, The Women's Recreational Committee, serves as an advocacy group for women students.

Institutional Self-Description. None provided.

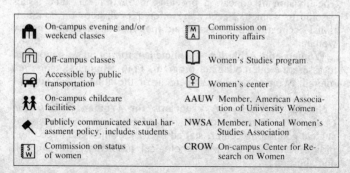

On-campus evening and/or weekend classes		Commission on minority affairs	
Off-campus classes		Women's Studies program	
Accessible by public transportation		Women's center	
On-campus childcare facilities		AAUW Member, American Association of University Women	
Publicly communicated sexual harassment policy, includes students		NWSA Member, National Women's Studies Association	
Commission on status of women		CROW On-campus Center for Research on Women	

Goucher College
Towson, MD 21204
Telephone: (301) 825-3300

Women in Leadership
★★★ students
★★ faculty
★★★ administrators

★ **Women and the Curriculum**

905 undergraduates

	Amer. Ind.	Asian Amer.	Blacks	Hispanics	Whites
F	2	24	59	14	795
M	0	0	0	0	0
%	0.2	2.7	6.6	1.6	88.9

Founded in 1885, Goucher is an independent, liberal arts college for women. Its campus, located in a northern suburb of Baltimore, attracts 976 students, of whom 905 are undergraduates; 3 percent of undergraduates attend part-time.

A range of undergraduate degree programs is available, in addition to a master's degree program in dance-movement therapy. Classes are conducted on and off campus during the day and evening hours. There is also a continuing education program. The 37 percent of undergraduates who commute can take advantage of public transportation and on-campus parking.

Private childcare facilities are available near campus.

Policies to Ensure Fairness to Women. The Vice President of the college assumes the part-time responsibility for handling matters relating to affirmative-action, sex-equity, and handicapped-access laws, and can make policy in these areas. A publicized, written sexual harassment policy protects students. Complaints are resolved through a formal campus grievance procedure.

Women in Leadership Positions. *Students.* Women hold all campus-wide student leadership positions.

Faculty. Forty nine percent of the 74 full-time faculty members are women, a proportion that is average for women's colleges. There are 4 female faculty for every 100 female students.

Administrators. The President and four of the other six administrators are female. The chief academic and business officers are men. Departments chaired by women are: dance, economics, education, history, mathematics, physical education, and psychology. Women are 55 percent of the Board of Trustees.

Women and the Curriculum. Fifty-four percent of graduates earn degrees in social sciences, fine arts, and letters. Eight percent of women specialize in mathematics or physical sciences and about 10 percent in biology.

The Women's Studies Program offers the bachelor's degree. Courses include Women and the Economy, Women as Heroes, and Women and the Law. The director of the program holds a full-time faculty appointment. An official committee oversees the development of the program. Courses in the departments of education, social work, and business provide some instruction on matters specific to women.

Minority Women. Minority women are 11 percent of students. Residence-hall and student counseling staff receive awareness-training on racism. An Asian American woman is a department head; black women are represented on the Board of Trustees. The 1981 commencement speaker was a black woman.

Women and Athletics. An intercollegiate program attracts 218 women to a variety of individual and team sports. More than 400 students participate in six intramural sports. The campus has special facilities for horseback riding. Intercollegiate sports offered are basketball, cross-country, fencing, field hockey, horseback riding, lacrosse, softball, swimming, tennis, and volleyball.

Housing and Student Organizations. Sixty-three percent of undergraduates live on campus in dormitories that have no restrictions on hours for male visitors.

All student organizations are, in varying degrees, women's advocacy groups, including an ERA club that has 20 active members, the Black Students Association, and the Blue Jean Collective.

Special Services and Programs for Women. *Health and Counseling.* The student health service employs 1 male physician, 2 female physician's assistants, and 3 female health-care providers. The student counseling center is staffed by 7 women. Counseling and treatment for gynecological problems are available, in addition to counseling for birth control, abortion, rape and assault. Student health insurance covers maternity expenses. The counseling staff receive training in the areas of sex-role stereotyping, racism, and anorexia nervosa.

Safety and Security. Measures consist of campus police, nighttime escort, night-time bus service to dormitories, high-intensity lighting, and information on self-defense and campus safety. There is a rape crisis center. One rape was reported for 1980-81.

Career. The college offers workshops on nontraditional careers, panel discussions and information about nontraditional careers, and encourages in networking between students and alumnae.

Returning Women Students. The Center for Educational Resources operates a Continuing Education for Women Program that has an enrollment of 40. A full-time, permanently appointed female faculty member directs the program. An all-day program, is held once a week, for returning women.

Institutional Self-Description. "Goucher aims to provide a demanding liberal arts education which will prepare women for responsible and active places in society. Fostering literacy and competence is a particular concern of the academic program, but all activities of the college are intended to provide settings in which students develop social consciousness and commitment."

Hood College
Rosemont Avenue, Frederick, MD 21701
Telephone: (301) 663-3131

Women in Leadership
★★★ students
★★★ faculty
★★★ administrators

★★ **Women and the Curriculum**

1,052 undergraduates

	Amer. Ind.	Asian Amer.	Blacks	Hispanics	Whites
F	0	6	27	4	964
M	0	1	2	0	41
%	0.0	0.7	2.8	0.4	96.2

 AAUW

When founded in 1893, Hood College was affiliated with the United Church of Christ. Now it is an independent, non-sectarian liberal arts and career-oriented college for women, although since 1971 it has admitted a few men, mainly to graduate programs. The campus, located west of Baltimore and northwest of Washington, D.C., enrolls 1,791 students. Of the 1,052 undergraduates, 96 percent are women; 6 percent of women attend part-time. One-fifth of the women are over age 25. The median age of all undergraduates is 20.

A wide range of undergraduate and graduate programs is available, in addition to continuing education. Classes are scheduled during the day, evening and, occasionally, the weekend. For the 37 percent of undergraduates who commute, on-campus parking is available for a fee.

Private childcare facilities are available near campus.

Policies to Ensure Fairness to Women. The Executive Assistant to the President, who is the Equal Opportunity Officer, has the part-time responsibility for policies and practices relating to sex-fair-employment, sex-equity, and handicapped-access laws. Complaints of sexual harassment are resolved informally and confidentially. A statement by the college President condemning ''sexual harassment of any type'' has been communicated in writing to students, faculty, and staff.

Women in Leadership Positions. *Students.* Women hold all campus-wide leadership positions.

Faculty. Two-thirds of the 88 full-time faculty are women, a proportion above the average for women's colleges in this guide, and well above the national average. There are 6 full-time female faculty for every 100 female students.

Administrators. Five of the 8 top-level administrators are women, including the President, academic dean, and chief student-life officer, Women chair 6 of 15 departments: economics and management, English, foreign languages and literature, home economics, physical education, recreation and leisure studies, and sociology and social work. Women are 3 of 5 members of the faculty tenure and promotions committee and 15 of the 30 trustees. The 1981 commencement speaker was a woman, and women received 2 alumnae awards and 2 honorary degrees.

Women and the Curriculum. Of degrees awarded, 19 percent are in home economics, 18 percent in interdisciplenary studies, 14 percent in education, and 10 percent in biology. Three percent are in mathematics and physical sciences. Special programs are available on women in science, engineering, management, computer science, and law and society. The Learning Assistance and Resource Center helps women build confidence in mathematics.

Women are the focus of eleven courses, taught by the departments of art, English/communications, foreign languages/literature, history/political science, psychology, and sociology/social work. Students may design a Women's Studies major. The departments of business, education, and sociology/social work provide some instruction on matters specific to women. Through a new core curriculum all students ''are exposed to the issue of inequality.'' A Women's Studies committee monitors the integration of scholarship on women into traditional courses and collects new curricular materials on women. Faculty are offered workshops on sexism and racism, the concerns of reentry women, and nontraditional occupations.

Minority Women. About 4 percent of the undergraduate women are from minority groups. A federal grant allows for increased enrollment of Hispanic students and improved services for them: for example, one new course called Women in the Hispanic World. Faculty and residence-hall counselors are offered awareness-training on racism. The Black Student Union meets on campus.

Women and Athletics. Hood provides a varied sports program. The intramural program excels in individual sports, including orseback riding (the college has its own riding stables), racquetball, rollerskating, badminton, table tennis, and swimming. There are also several sports and recreational clubs. The director of intramural sports is a woman, and five of the six paid coaches for intercollegiate teams are women. Intercollegiate sports offered are badminton, basketball, field hockey, lacrosse, swimming, tennis, and volleyball.

Housing and Student Organizations. Sixty-three percent of all undergraduates live on campus in dormitories. Hours for male visitors are determined by the residents of each dormitory. Student residence-hall counselors are offered workshops on sex education, birth control, sexism, and racism.

Special Services and Programs for Women. *Health and Counseling.* The part-time student health service staff consists of 1 female gynecologist, 3 male physicians, and 3 female health-care providers. The student counseling center employs 2 female counselors, who are offered workshops on sex-role stereotyping. Counseling and treatment for gynecological problems and birth control are provided, in addition to abortion and rape and assault counseling. Student health insurance covers abortion and maternity expenses.

Safety and Security. Measures consist of campus police, nighttime escort for women, high-intensity lighting, emergency telephone system, and instruction on self-defense and campus safety. There is a rape crisis center. No rapes and one assault on a woman were reported for 1980–81.

Career. The college offers career workshops, lectures, information on nontraditional occupations, and encouragement to students in networking with alumnae. Faculty are offered workshops about job opportunities for women in nontraditional fields.

Returning Women Students. Continuing Education, in cooperation with community groups, government agencies, and student organizations, sponsors programs for battered women and displaced homemakers, an annual women's week, theater and arts performances and displays, and assertiveness-training sessions.

The Continuing Education Office is a multi-purpose center for reentry women. In addition to counseling, it provides special programs, such as ''learning lunches'' and career workshops, designed to meet the needs of returning women. Faculty are sensitized to the concerns of reentry women. The office is under the direction of a full-time, female administrator.

Special Features. The college library has a designated Women's Room that houses its collection on women. Individual departments also have their own women's resource centers.

Institutional Self-Description. ''Hood has always been and has chosen to remain a college for women. The college's purpose is to educate women of all ages for the challenges of equal participation in society. Hood believes that this is best accomplished through an innovative curriculum of liberal arts and career programs offered in an environment free of sexism and stereotyping.''

Johns Hopkins University
Charles and 34th Streets
Baltimore, MD 21218
Telephone: (301) 338-8020

2,317 undergraduates

	Amer. Ind.	Asian Amer.	Blacks	Hispanics	Whites
F	1	32	64	4	626
M	2	69	53	24	1,409
%	0.1	4.4	5.1	1.2	89.1

🏠 🚐 👫 🔨 ⚲ AAUW

Founded in 1876 as a private research university, John Hopkins University began admitting women as undergraduates in 1970. Some 9,500 students enroll in a range of undergraduate, graduate, and professional degree programs. Evening and summer classes are offered for part-time students in the Evening College, which is responsible for continuing adult education.

Women are 32 percent of the 2,317 undergraduates; 11 percent of the women attend part-time. The median age of undergraduates is 20. One-tenth of the undergraduates commute to campus. The university is accessible by public transportation. On-campus parking is free but limited.

On-campus childcare operates on a cooperative basis during morning hours. Private childcare arrangements may be made close to the university.

Policies to Ensure Fairness to Women. A full-time equal-opportunity officer reviews policies and practices related to employment, educational sex equity, and handicapped access. A published policy prohibits sexual harassment. An Affirmative Action Committee has overview responsibilities for women and minorities. Two committees oversee program and facility accessibility for the handicapped.

Women in Leadership Positions. *Students.* Opportunities for women students to exercise campus leadership are well below the average for private research institutions in this guide.

Faculty. Women are 20 percent of a full-time faculty of 541. There are 17 female faculty for every 100 female students and 28 male faculty for every 100 male students.

Administrators. The head librarian is a woman. All other higher administrative posts are filled by men. One of 28 department heads in the School of Arts and Sciences is a woman.

Women and the Curriculum. A majority of the women earning bachelor's degrees major in interdisciplinary studies, the health professions, and the social sciences. Eleven percent major in engineering, mathematics, and the physical sciences. Only ten percent of science field-service positions are held by women.

Three courses on women are available, one each in the departments of anthropology, Romance languages, and social relations.

Minority Women. Of 727 undergraduate women, 9 percent are black, 4 percent Asian American, and less than 1 percent each Hispanic and American Indian. Two of four residence-hall directors are minority women, as are four of the counselors in the counseling service. Awareness-training on racism is offered residence-hall staff. There is a Black Student Union. Black women are involved in the Women's Center.

Women and Athletics. The intramural program is limited. The number and variety of individual and team sports available in the intercollegiate program offer good opportunities for organized competition. Club sports are also available. Thirty-two percent of intercollegiate athletes and four of the seven paid varsity coaches are women. The institution does not offer athletic scholarships. The intercollegiate sports offered are basketball, cross-country, fencing, field hockey, lacrosse, squash, swimming and diving, and tennis.

Housing and Student Organizations. Forty-seven percent of undergraduates live on campus. Single-sex and coeducational dormitories and housing for married students and single parents with children are available. A married woman student whose spouse is not enrolled may live in married students' housing. Dormitories do not restrict hours for visitors of the opposite sex. Half of the residence-hall directors are women. Awareness-training on sexism, sex education, and racism is offered residence-hall staff.

Eight percent of undergraduate women belong to social sororities, which do not provide housing for their members.

Special Services and Programs for Women. *Health and Counseling.* The student health service provides medical attention specific to women, including gynecological, birth control, abortion, and rape and assault treatment. Two of 6 physicians are women, as are 5 other health-care providers. Thirty-eight of 45 professional staff in the counseling service are women. Counseling specific to women is available.

Safety and Security. Measures consist of campus police with weapons training, city police, night-time escort service for women students, night-time bus service to residence areas, an emergency alarm system, information sessions on safety and crime prevention, and a rape crisis center. Five assaults on women and no rapes were reported for 1980-81.

Career. Panels by women employed in nontraditional careers, updated alumnae files by specific careers, and a program of contacts between alumnae and students are offered through the career placement office or other units.

Other. The small Women's Center, staffed by a student, serves as an advocate for women on campus. An annual women's week and assertiveness training are sponsored by Academic Services and Health Services.

Special Features. During 1980-81, the Graduate Student Organization sponsored a ''Week for Women,'' which included a symposium on feminism and capitalism. The members of the Intellectually Gifted Child Study Group have been leaders in research on women and cognitive achievement in mathematics.

Institutional Self-Description. ''Women should choose to study here at Hopkins for the excellence of the university's educational offerings in arts and sciences and engineering at the graduate and undergraduate levels. We offer students a very exciting and creative academic atmosphere, and the chance to learn with and from outstanding individuals of both sexes.''

Loyola College
4501 N. Charles St., Baltimore, MD 21210
Telephone: (301) 323-5473

2,306 undergraduates

	Amer. Ind.	Asian Amer.	Blacks	Hispanics	Whites
F	4	7	66	7	876
M	11	12	36	6	1,240
%	0.7	0.8	4.5	0.6	93.4

🏠 🚌 [M̄A] AAUW

Some 4,774 students attend Loyola, an independent, Roman Catholic liberal arts college. Founded in 1852 as a Jesuit college for men, it merged in 1971 with Mount Saint Agnes, a women's college operated by the Sisters of Mercy. Forty-two percent of the 2,306 undergraduates are women; 17 percent of the women attend part-time. The median age of undergraduates is 21.

Loyola offers undergraduate degrees in liberal arts and pre-professional areas and also awards master's degrees. Adult students are served by Professional Development and Programs and the Evening Program. Evening and summer session classes are available. Located in a residential section of Baltimore, the 53-acre campus is accessible by public transportation. Free on-campus parking is available for the 66 percent of full-time undergraduates who commute.

Private childcare facilities are available near campus.

Policies to Ensure Fairness to Women. The full-time Affirmative Action Officer monitors compliance and recommends policy with regard to sex-equity and equal-employment-opportunity laws. The Assistant Dean for Student Development oversees accessibility for the handicapped. There is no formal policy on sexual harassment, but formal procedures exist to resolve complaints. Affirmative action and equal opportunity are discussed in faculty workshops. The Committee on Minority Affairs addresses the concerns of minority women.

Women in Leadership Positions. *Students.* The proportion of women in campus-wide leadership positions is considerably below the average for private, four-year colleges. In a three-year period, women have served once as president of the student court, once as president of the senior class, and twice as president of the junior class. One of four honorary societies is headed by a woman.

Faculty. Women are 21 percent of the full-time faculty of 126, a proportion below the national average. The ratio of female faculty to female students is 3 for every 100; for males, it is 9 for every 100.

Administrators. The head librarian is a woman, and all other chief administrators are men. Two of the 16 department chairs are women, one of whom heads the department of theology. Twenty-five percent of the trustees are women, including one black woman. In a recent year, one of the three recipients of honorary degrees was a black woman.

Women and the Curriculum. Thirty-one percent of women graduates major in business, 19 percent in health professions; 6 percent of women earn degrees in the nontraditional fields of mathematics and engineering. One-third of the graduates in engineering are women. The college offers programs to encourage women to prepare for careers in engineering, science, accounting, and computer science. About half of the student interns are women, as are 95 percent of students participating in science field service.

Loyola does not offer courses on women. The department of business provides some instruction on the problems of job discrimination, sexual harassment in the workplace, and women in management.

Women and Athletics. Women receive 10 percent of the athletic scholarships. Six of 23 paid intercollegiate coaches are women. Intercollegiate sports offered are basketball, field hockey, lacrosse, swimming, tennis, and volleyball.

Housing and Student Organizations. Single-sex dormitories and apartment complexes are available for the 34 percent of full-time undergraduates who reside on campus. All dormitories restrict hours for visitors of the opposite sex. Two of the four residence-hall directors are women.

Special Services and Programs for Women. *Health and Counseling.* The student health service employs one male physician and two female health-care providers. The counseling center is staffed by one woman and two men counselors. Medical treatment and counseling for gynecological problems and rape and assault are provided.

Safety and Security. Measures consist of local police, a campus police force with arrest authority, a night-time escort service for women, high-intensity lighting, information sessions for women on campus safety, and a community-based rape crisis center. No rapes or assaults on women, but three assaults on men, were reported for 1980–81.

Career. The college offers programs and printed information on nontraditional occupations for women, maintains updated files of alumnae by specific careers, and establishes contacts between alumnae and women students. The career planning office provides support for older women and displaced homemakers.

Other. The Office of Student Development sponsors an annual women's week and provides support to handicapped women.

Institutional Self-Description. "New programs and activities, notably in the area of women's athletics, have been developed in Loyola's first decade as a coeducational institution, and women have entered and have excelled in every academic discipline at Loyola."

St. Mary's College of Maryland
St. Mary's City, MD 20686
Telephone: (301) 863-7100

Women in Leadership
★ students
★ faculty

1,161 undergraduates

	Amer. Ind.	Asian Amer.	Blacks	Hispanics	Whites
F	0	2	37	4	568
M	0	5	39	5	494
%	0.0	0.6	6.6	0.8	92.0

Some 1,300 students attend this four-year, state-supported college located in rural St. Mary's City, near Washington, D.C. Established as a female seminary in 1859, it now offers a full range of bachelor's programs in the liberal arts and sciences. There are opportunities for self-paced/contract learning at the college, as well as a program in adult continuing education. Evening and summer session classes are also available.

More than half (53 percent) of the 1,161 undergraduates are women, 6 percent of whom attend part-time. The median age of undergraduates is 22. On-campus parking is available at a fee for the 30 percent of undergraduate students who commute.

Private childcare facilities are available near the campus.

Policies to Ensure Fairness to Women. The Assistant to the President serves as a part-time compliance administrator for policy relating to equal-employment-opportunity legislation. A written campus policy prohibiting sexual harassment has been publicly communicated to students, faculty, and staff. Complaints of sexual harassment can be handled informally and confidentially, but there is also a formal campus grievance procedure to ensure due process.

Women in Leadership Positions. *Students.* Women have good opportunities to exercise campus-wide leadership. In recent years, women have served as president of the student body and of the senior, junior, and sophomore classes.

Faculty. Twenty-six percent of the 62 full-time faculty are women. There are 3 female faculty for every 100 female students and 9 male faculty for every 100 male students.

Administrators. With the exception of director of institutional research, all top-level administrative positions are held by men. Of the four divisions, women chair those of arts and letters and natural science and mathematics. Women make up 33 percent of the faculty senate, 50 percent of campus-wide tenure and promotions committees, and 42 percent of the trustees.

Women and the Curriculum. Most women earn degrees in social sciences (27 percent), fine arts (23 percent), letters (16 percent), and interdisciplinary fields (15 percent). Eleven percent of the women major in the nontraditional fields of mathematics and physical sciences. Sixty-four percent of the students participating in internship programs are women.

The college offers one course on women, Women and the Law, through the department of social science and history.

Women and Athletics. For a college of its size, St. Mary's has excellent intramural and intercollegiate sports programs, with a high level of participation in competitive individual and team sports. Among the intramural sports offered are water polo, lacrosse, softball, and racquetball. The college also has special facilities for sailing. Club sports are also available. Sixty percent of intramural athletes and 46 percent of intercollegiate athletes are women, as are three of the 17 paid intercollegiate coaches. All five of the women's intercollegiate teams played in recent tournament competition. The intercollegiate sports offered are basketball, lacrosse, sailing, tennis, and volleyball.

Housing and Student Organizations. Single-sex and coeducational dormitories house the 70 percent of undergraduates who live on campus. None of the residence halls restrict hours for visitors of the opposite sex. Of the four residence-hall directors, two are women.

Special Services and Programs for Women. *Health and Counseling.* The student health service, staffed by 3 physicians (1 female and 2 male) and 6 other health-care providers (all female), offers medical treatment specific to women, including birth control and gynecological care. The student counseling center has 2 female and 2 male counselors and offers abortion referrals and rape and assault counseling.

Safety and Security. Measures consist of campus police with arrest authority, self-defense courses for women, information sessions for women on safety and crime prevention, and a rape crisis center. No assaults were reported for 1980–81.

Career. The college provides career workshops, printed material, and job discrimination information on women in nontraditional occupations. The Counseling Office sponsors an assertiveness training program.

Other. Programs for battered women and displaced homemakers, as well as a telephone service for information, referrals, and support are available. Displaced homemakers would find additional support from the Part-Time Studies Program. The Continuing Education and Part-Time Studies Programs serve older women students.

Institutional Self-Description. "The mission of the college is very clear and stated elsewhere: 'The primary task is to encourage students to realize their full human potentialities and responsibilities.' All programs are open equally to men and women, and many women have strong leadership roles. A liberal arts curriculum encourages all students to explore options and think creatively about careers and non-academic goals.''

Salisbury State College
Salisbury, Maryland 21801
Telephone: (301) 546-3261

Women in Leadership
★ faculty
★ administrators

3,156 undergraduates

	Amer. Ind.	Asian Amer.	Blacks	Hispanics	Whites
F	5	7	134	6	1,570
M	3	4	99	7	1,303
%	0.3	0.4	7.4	0.4	91.6

 AAUW

Some 4,300 students are enrolled in this state-supported college near Baltimore. Founded in 1925 as a two-year teacher-training college, Salisbury State now offers a wide range of bachelor's and master's level liberal arts, education, and pre-professional programs. Women are 55 percent of the 3,156 undergraduates, whose median age is 22. According to recent information from the college, 36 percent of the undergraduate women are over age 25, and about three-fourths of these women attend part-time.

Day and evening classes are offered both on and off campus; a summer session is also available. Adult students are served by the continuing education division. On-campus parking is available at a fee for the 69 percent of undergraduates who commute.

Policies to Ensure Fairness to Women. A full-time affirmative action officer is responsible for policy relating to equal employment opportunities, handicapped accessibility, and sex-equity issues. A self-designated Women's Caucus, which includes student members, prepares annual reports for the campus community on the status of women. The caucus and a Committee on Minority Affairs address the concerns of minority women.

Women in Leadership Positions. *Students.* During a recent three-years period, women have held one-third of the available positions.

Faculty. Thirty percent of the full-time faculty of 184 are women, a proportion above the average for similar institutions in this guide. Two of the full-time faculty are black women. There are 4 female faculty for every 100 female students and 10 male faculty for every 100 male students.

Administrators. Of the eight chief administrative positions, women serve as Dean of Student Affairs and Director of institutional Research. Women chair two of the 21 departments: English and nursing. Two of the 10 trustees are female, 1 of them a black woman.

Women and the Curriculum. Most degrees earned by women are in education (23 percent), interdisciplinary studies (19 percent), business (13 percent), and public affairs (13 percent). Less than 2 percent of women (and men) earn degrees in science or mathematics. Salisbury reports an innovative program designed to encourage women to enter the field of accounting. Women hold half of the student internships.

The college offers two courses on women: Psychology of Women and Women in Literature. Courses in the divisions of education and physical education, the business department, and the nursing program provide some instruction specific to women.

Women and Athletics. Salisbury State has a rather limited intramural sports program, though its intercollegiate program is marked by a variety of sports and a relatively high level of female participation. Thirty-two percent of intramural athletes and 32

percent of intercollegiate athletes are women. Seven of the 14 paid varsity coaches are women. The intercollegiate sports offered are basketball, field hockey, lacrosse, softball, swimming, tennis, track and field, and volleyball.

Housing and Student Organizations. Sngle-sex and coeducational dormitories house the 31 percent of undergraduates who live on campus. Dormitories do not have restricted hours for visitors of the opposite sex. Nine percent of undergraduate women living in residence halls are black and 1 percent Asian American women. The residence-hall staff of five women and two men are offered awareness-training on sexism, sex education, racism, and birth control.

Seven percent of the full-time undergraduate women belong to social sororities, which do not provide housing for members.

Special Services and Programs for Women. *Health and Counseling.* One male physician and 4 female health-care providers staff the student health center, which provides medical treatment for gynecological problems, birth control, abortion, and rape and assault. The counseling center staff of 1 woman and 2 men offer counseling for rape and assault, abortion, and other matters specific to women.

Safety and Security. Measures consist of local police, campus police with arrest authority, night-time escort for women students, an emergency alarm system, high-intensity lighting, self-defense courses for women, information sessions on safety and crime prevention, and a rape crisis center. Twelve assaults (four on women) were reported for 1980–81.

Career. Salisbury State offers career workshops, printed material and information on job discrimination in nontraditional occupations for women, along with lectures by women employed in these fields.

Other. The Student Affairs office operates the small campus Women's Center. Run on a part-time basis by a student volunteer, the center has a telephone information and referral service and offers support to a variety of women, including displaced homemakers and older students. Genesis sponsors a telephone referral and support service. The Sexual Minority Alliance and the Black Student Union are two advocacy groups that meet on campus. The Student Affairs office sponsors a women's lecture series and the counseling center offers assertiveness training.

Institutional Self-Description. None provided.

Towson State University
Baltimore, MD 21204
Telephone: (301) 321-2000

Women in Leadership
★ students
★★ faculty
★ administrators

★★ **Women and the Curriculum**
★★ **Women and Athletics**

10,469 undergraduates

	Amer. Ind.	Asian Amer.	Blacks	Hispanics	Whites
F	7	35	781	20	5,011
M	4	19	401	19	4,080
%	0.1	0.5	11.4	0.4	87.6

AAUW NWSA

Towson State University, founded in 1866 as a teacher-training school, became a public liberal arts college in 1963, and a comprehensive university in 1976. Its student body totals 15,292, including 10,469 undergraduates, 56 percent of whom are women. Sixteen percent of women attend part-time. The median age of undergraduates is 23; about 4 percent of all undergraduate women are over 40.

The university offers bachelor's degrees in a range of fields, including business, education, health professions, arts and sciences, and the social sciences. Master's degrees are offered in some fields. Evening, summer, and weekend classes, as well as off-campus evening classes, are offered. Continuing Education administers an adult education program. Ninety-two percent of undergraduates commute to the campus, located five miles north of downtown Baltimore. Public transportation is available, though described by the university as inadequate. On-campus parking at a fee and fringe parking are available.

Day and evening childcare for children aged two to five is available on a sliding-fee basis for 70 percent of students requesting it. Additional private facilities are located near the campus.

Policies to Ensure Fairness to Women. The Special Assistant to the President/Affirmative Action Officer is responsible for equal employment opportunity, sex equity for students, and handicapped accessibility. The Special Assistant develops policies for approval by officials and committees and is a non-voting member of some policymaking committees. A policy prohibiting the sexual harassment of students, faculty, and staff has been formally communicated to all members of the Towson State community. Complaints are resolved either through an informal, confidential campus mechanism or through a formal grievance procedure. A Commission on the Status of Women addresses the concerns of minority women, among other issues.

Women in Leadership Positions. *Students.* Women have good opportunities to gain leadership experience. In a recent three-year period, women have served as student body president, student union president (three times), campus newspaper editor, campus radio station manager, president of the residence-hall council, and president of the junior class. Of seven honorary societies, five are chaired by women.

Faculty. Of the 464 full-time faculty, 35 percent are women, a proportion significantly above the average for public, four-year institutions. There are 3 female faculty for every 100 female students and 8 male faculty for every 100 male students.

Administrators. The Vice President for Student Services and the Vice President for Institutional Development are women; the other top administrators are men. The Dean of Continuing Studies and the Dean of Social, Humanistic, and Managerial Studies are women. Eight of 30 departments are chaired by women: mass communications, secondary education, early childhood education, history, biology, physical education, nursing, and occupational therapy. Of eleven trustees, 3 are women; of 11 regents, 4 are women.

Women and the Curriculum. Most women earn degrees in education (28 percent), business (18 percent), social sciences (11 percent), health professions (9 percent), and psychology (9 percent). Two percent of women major in the nontraditional fields of mathematics and physical sciences. The mathematics department provides programs to build confidence in mathematics.

Established in 1972, the Women's Studies Program, under the direction of a full-time, permanent faculty member, offers an 18-credit minor and the B.A. through General Studies. Five courses on women are offered through the Women's Studies Program and more than 20 others through departments. Women's Studies courses include Women's Perspective, Changing Sex Roles, Directed Readings in Women's Studies, Practicum in Women's Studies, and Feminist Ideology for Change. An official committee is responsible for the development of the Women's Studies Program. The university library has an extensive Women's Studies collection.

Faculty workshops address such topics as sexism and racism in the curriculum, nontraditional occupations, needs of reentry women, and affirmative action and equal opportunity. Courses in the departments of business, health science, and nursing, and the division of education provide some instruction on matters specific to women.

Minority Women. Thirteen percent of undergraduate women are black women; 1 percent are American Indian, Asian American, or Hispanic. Eleven percent of the reentering women students are black women. The college reports that the full-time faculty includes 1 American Indian, 1 Hispanic, 5 Asian American, and 12 black women. One department is chaired by a black woman. Faculty, counseling staff, and residence-hall staff are offered training on racism. The Black Student Union and the African-American Cultural Center are available to minority women.

Women and Athletics. Women students have excellent opportunities to participate in organized competitive sports. A wide variety of both individual and team sports is available. Thirty percent of intercollegiate, 40 percent of intramural, and 44 percent of club athletes are women. Women receive 14 percent of athletic scholarships. One-third of the paid coaches for intercollegiate sports are women. Women's intercollegiate sports are basketball, field hockey, gymnastics, lacrosse, softball, swimming, tennis, track and field, and volleyball.

Housing and Student Organizations. Women's and coeducational dormitories offer a choice of limited or unrestricted visiting hours for the opposite sex. Thirteen percent of undergraduate women live in residence halls. Awareness-training on sexism, sex education, birth control, sexual harassment, alcoholism, crisis management, and suicide prevention is offered to residence-hall staff.

Three percent of women students join social sororities. Forty-two minority women belong to all-minority sororities.

Special Services and Programs for Women. *Health and Counseling.* The health service is staffed by 2 male physicians and 7 other health-care providers, 6 of them women. It provides gynecological services, birth control, and limited assistance for rape and assault victims. The counseling center employs 3 men and 6 women, one a minority woman. Counselors are offered training on sex-role stereotyping, racial bias, sexual harassment, rape prevention, returning students, sexuality, women and careers, and women and depression— all as part of an ongoing program. Counseling services specific to women include assistance with gynecological problems, birth control, abortion, and rape and assault.

Safety and Security. Measures consist of campus, municipal, and state police, night-time escorts for women students, night-time campus-wide bus service to residences, emergency telephone and alarm systems, self-defense courses, programs on campus safety and crime prevention, and a rape crisis center. No rapes and 21 assaults were reported for 1980–81.

Career. Services include workshops, nonsexist/nonracist printed materials, job discrimination information on nontraditional occupations, and lectures and panels by women employed in nontraditional fields.

Other. Student Services operates the Women's Center, founded in 1972, which serves 850 women annually—25 percent of them black women—under the direction of a full-time, salaried student director and a budget of $17,000.

Institutional Self-Description. "Towson State is a place where women can study, find support and encouragement, and reach their full potential. One of the five goals of the university ensures this: 'The University shall provide equal educational opportunity for the population it serves.' "

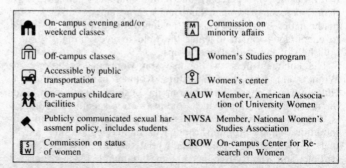

🏛 On-campus evening and/or weekend classes	🄼🄰 Commission on minority affairs
🏛 Off-campus classes	📖 Women's Studies program
🚌 Accessible by public transportation	👤 Women's center
👫 On-campus childcare facilities	AAUW Member, American Association of University Women
🔨 Publicly communicated sexual harassment policy, includes students	NWSA Member, National Women's Studies Association
🅂🅆 Commission on status of women	CROW On-campus Center for Research on Women

University of Maryland, Baltimore County

5401 Wilkens Avenue
Catonsville, MD 21228
Telephone: (301) 455-1000

4,641 undergraduates

	Amer. Ind.	Asian Amer.	Blacks	Hispanics	Whites
F	8	24	611	13	1,735
M	6	21	291	18	1,735
%	0.3	1.0	20.2	0.7	77.8

 AAUW

Founded in 1966 to provide a public liberal arts campus for the Baltimore area, UMBC is the newest center in Maryland's university system. Of the 5,396 students, 4,641 are undergraduates. Fifty-four percent of undergraduates are women, of whom 8 percent attend part-time. In addition to on-campus day and evening classes, a summer session and self-paced/contract learning are available. UMBC has no formal continuing education program, although it sponsors a non-credit workshop for community women who want to return to college. Three-quarters of students commute to the campus, which is accessible by public transportation. On-campus parking is available at a fee.

Private childcare may be arranged near campus.

Policies to Ensure Fairness to Women. The Director of Human Relations has part-time responsibility for policy and practices relating to equal-employment-opportunity and sex-equity legislation. A formal policy prohibiting sexual harassment of students, faculty, and staff has been communicated in writing to faculty and staff. Complaints of sexual harassment are resolved informally and confidentially or through a formal grievance procedure. The Commission on the Status of Women reports directly to the Chancellor. This active body, which includes voting student members, meets regularly, prepares a public report on the status of women, and takes public stands on issues of concern to students. The Commission on Minority Affairs addresses the concerns of minority women.

Women in Leadership Positions. *Students.* Opportunities for women to exercise campus-wide leadership are limited. Of 21 campus-wide positions available to students during a recent three year period, four were held by women: student senate president, manager of the radio station, president of the residence-hall council, and president of the senior class. Of six honorary societies, one has a woman president.

Faculty. Twenty-two percent of the full-time faculty are women, including 5 black and 2 Asian American women. There are 3 female faculty for every 100 female students and 10 male faculty for every 100 male students.

Administrators. Except for the chief business officer and the chief planning officer, all top administrators are male. Women chair two of 26 departments (English and dance) and direct two of the eight academic units (the Learning Resource Center and Special Sessions). Three of 15 regents are women.

Women and the Curriculum. Most women earn degrees in social sciences (37 percent) and psychology (25 percent). Three percent major in the nontraditional fields of mathematics and physical sciences. Half of those enrolled in experiential learning programs are women.

Seven courses on women are taught in six departments. Recent offerings include Sex Roles and Inequality, Sociology of Women, and Perspectives on Women in Literature. Courses offered by the schools of education and social work provide some instruction on matters specific to women. A Women's Studies Program is in formation.

Minority Women. Twenty-five percent of female undergraduates are black women, 1 percent are Asian American, and 1 percent are American Indian and Hispanic. One of the female regents is a black woman, as is 1 of the 5 women on the faculty senate. Residence-hall staff and counselors are offered awareness-training on racial bias. Eighty-five of the 120 women who join sororities are members of all-minority sororities.

Women and Athletics. Almost one-third of intercollegiate athletes are women, who receive 30 percent of athletic scholarships. Four intramural sports are offered. Of seven paid coaches for intercollegiate sports, six are women. Women's intercollegiate sports are basketball, cross-country, field hockey, gymnastics, lacrosse, tennis, track, and volleyball.

Housing and Student Organizations. Twenty-four percent of undergraduates live in single-sex and coeducational dormitories, all with restricted hours for visitors of the opposite sex. Residence-hall staff are offered workshops on sexism, racism, sex education, and crisis intervention. Five percent of undergraduate women belong to social sororities.

Special Services and Programs for Women. *Health and Counseling.* The student health service staff includes several male physicians and four female health-care providers, who offer birth control and gynecological treatment. The counseling center also offers services in these areas, in addition to counseling on abortion, rape and assault, nutrition, smoking, and exercise. The center employs two female and three male counselors.

Safety and Security. Measures consist of campus police patrol, night-time escort service, self-defense courses for women, information courses on safety and assault prevention, and a rape crisis center. For 1980–81, 29 assaults (ten on women) and no rapes were reported.

Career. The college offers career workshops, nonsexist/nonracist printed material, information on job discrimination, and programs to establish contacts between alumnae and female students.

Other. The Women's Union, a student advocacy group, provides services for women students. The Women's Center is headed by a part-time, salaried director who is a black woman. The Women's Commission sponsors a battered women's program, an annual women's week, and theater and other women's art programs. The Student Service Committee on Women sponsors a lecture series.

Institutional Self-Description. None provided.

University of Maryland, College Park

College Park, MD 20742
Telephone: (301) 454-4796

★★★ Women and the Curriculum

★★ Women and Athletics

27,871 undergraduates

	Amer. Ind.	Asian Amer.	Blacks	Hispanics	Whites
F	45	181	1,302	146	10,838
M	59	248	877	154	12,694
%	0.4	1.6	8.2	1.1	88.6

 AAUW NWSA

Founded in 1856 as Maryland Agricultural College, and a state-supported university since 1920, the University of Maryland at College Park is located outside Washington, D.C. It attracts over 36,900 students to a wide variety of undergraduate, graduate, and professional studies. University College serves the adult student; scheduling includes weekend classes. On-campus evening classes and a summer session are available.

Women are 47 percent of the 27,871 undergraduates; 15 percent of the women attend part-time. The average age of undergraduates is 22. For the 70 percent of undergraduates who live off campus or commute, the university is accessible by public transportation. There is on-campus parking, with free transportation from distant parking lots.

Private childcare arrangements may be made nearby.

Policies to Ensure Fairness to Women. A full-time equal opportunity officer is responsible for policy and practices related to employment and sex equity for students. The assistant to the Chancellor for legal affairs oversees compliance with handicapped accessibility. A campus policy prohibits sexual harassment. Complaints are handled informally and confidentially or through a formal grievance procedure. The Chancellor's Commission on Women sponsors seminars for faculty women and a yearly recognition of outstanding women on campus. The Committee on Minority Affairs addresses the concerns of minority women.

Women in Leadership Positions. *Students.* Opportunities for women students to exercise all-campus leadership are below average for public research universities in this guide. In recent years, women have presided over the student court twice and have managed the campus radio station once.

Faculty. Women are 22 percent of a full-time faculty of 1,395. According to a recent report, 22 black, 10 Asian American, and 6 Hispanic women are on the full-time faculty. There are 3 female faculty for every 100 female students and 9 male faculty for every 100 male students.

Administrators. The head librarian and director of institutional research are women. Women head seven of 54 departments including English; French and Italian; Hebrew and East Asian; textiles and consumer economics; and physical education. The Dean of Graduate Studies is female.

Women and the Curriculum. A majority of the women earn bachelor's degrees in education (14 percent), business and management (12 percent), social sciences (12 percent), home economics (10 percent), and fine arts and communications (7 percent each). Eleven percent major in such nontraditional areas as agriculture, architecture, computer science, engineering, mathematics, and the physical sciences. One-tenth of the engineering students are female; the proportion of women taking degrees in agriculture is above the national average. An innovative program encourages women to prepare for careers in engineering. Forty-three percent of the students in cooperative education programs are women.

The Women's Studies Program offers a 21-credit undergraduate certificate and a major through Individual Studies. The history department offers an M.A. in Women's History; the American Studies Program offers an M.A. in Women's Culture. Over 40 courses a semester are available through Women's Studies and cooperating departments. Recent offerings include Women and Contemporary Society, Theories of Feminism, Women and Urban Ethnicity, Women and Religion, Economic Problems of Women, Women Novelists, Sex Roles, American Women and Sport, and History of American Feminism. An official committee advocates and monitors the inclusion of women's materials and perspectives across the curriculum.

Such issues as mathematics confidence among females, sex-fair curricula, and coeducational physical education classes are part of the preparation of future teachers. Affirmative action and equal opportunity are topics of faculty workshops.

The National Women's Studies Association and the scholarly periodical *Feminist Studies* are housed at the university.

Minority Women. Approximately 13 percent of undergraduate women are members of minority groups, mostly black women. Fifty-one minority women are in all-minority, 16 in integrated, sororities.

Courses, services, and organizations address the interests of minority women. Black Women in America, Black Women Writers of the Harlem Renaissance, Women in African History, and Racism and Intergroup Conflict are among recent course offerings. Three minority women are on the professional residence-hall staff; one full-time and two part-time staff in the counseling center are minority women. Residence-hall staff are offered awareness-training on inter-cultural differences. OMSE, Nyumburu, Alpha Queens, and the Archonian Club meet on campus.

Women and Athletics. Excellent intramural and intercollegiate programs offer a high number and variety of individual and team sports. Club and coeducational sports are also available. The university reports special facilities for racquetball, squash, and roller-skating. Fifteen percent of intramural and 51 percent of intercollegiate athletes are women. Women receive one-fifth of the athletic scholarships awarded. There are ten women varsity coaches. Women's intercollegiate sports offered are basketball, cross-country, field hockey (two teams), gymnastics, lacrosse (two teams), swimming, tennis, track and field, and volleyball.

Housing and Student Organizations. For the 30 percent of undergraduates who live on campus, single-sex and coeducational dormitories and housing for married students and single parents with children are available. A married woman student whose spouse is not enrolled may live in married students' housing. Dormitories have some restrictive hours for visitors of the opposite sex.

Twelve percent of the full-time undergraduate women belong to social sororities. Sororities and fraternities provide housing for their members. A number of student organizations serve as advocates for women, including the Maryland Women's Rugby Club, the Gay Student Alliance, and Feminist Exchange.

Special Services and Programs for Women. *Health and Counseling.* The student health service provides medical attention specific to women, including gynecological, birth control, abortion, and rape and assault treatment. Eight of 14 full-time physicians are female. The regular student health insurance covers abortion at no extra cost. In the counseling service, staffed by 18 professionals (two-thirds women), students have access to counseling of particular concern to women.

Safety and Security. Measures include campus police with arrest authority, night-time escorts for women, night-time campus-wide bus service, high-intensity lighting, emergency alarm and telephone systems, self-defense courses for women, information sessions on safety and crime prevention, and a rape crisis center. A total of 133 assaults and 3 rapes (plus 6 attempted rapes) were reported for 1980–81.

Career. Workshops, lectures, and printed materials concentrated on women in nontraditional careers and fields of study, as well as other kinds of career counseling, are available.

Other. The student government funds a Women's Center, staffed by a part-time, student volunteer. Lecture series, theater and other arts programs, a women's crisis hotline, and an annual women's week are sponsored events and services on campus.

Institutional Self-Description. None provided.

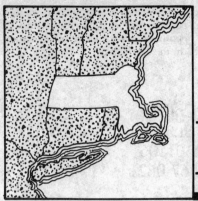

MASSACHUSETS

Anna Maria College

Sunset Lane, Paxton, MA 01612

Telephone: (617) 757-4586

Women in Leadership
- ★★ students
- ★★ faculty
- ★★★ administrators

498 undergraduates

	Amer. Ind.	Asian Amer.	Blacks	Hispanics	Whites
F	5	2	2	6	428
M	0	0	0	0	46
%	1.0	0.4	0.4	1.2	96.9

 AAUW

Some 1,178 students attend this liberal arts college operated by the Roman Catholic Sisters of St. Anne. Founded in 1946 as a college "for women of modest means," Anna Maria College became coeducational in 1973, and women still account for almost 90 percent of the 498 undergraduates. Twenty-five percent of all women attend part-time, and 25 percent of women are between the ages of 25 and 40.

Anna Maria College offers associate, bachelor's, and master's degrees in a variety of fields. An adult continuing education program, available through the division of continuing education, currently enrolls 139 reentry women. Evening classes are available both on and off campus, and there is a summer session. Located near Worcester, the campus is accessible by public transportation. On-campus parking is also available for the 59 percent of students who commute.

Policies to Ensure Fairness to Women. An equal-opportunity officer is responsible part-time for policy relating to matters of equal employment opportunity, handicapped accessibility, and sex equity. A written campus policy prohibiting sexual harassment of students, faculty, and staff has been communicated in writing to the campus community.

Women in Leadership Positions. *Students.* Women have held nearly all the student leadership posts during a recent three-year period.

Faculty. Of the total full-time faculty of 29, 45 percent are women. There are 4 female faculty for every 100 female students.

Administrators. Seventy-five percent of the chief administrators, including the President, are women. Of the 15 department chairs, 5 are women: biology/health studies, languages/literature/liberal studies, nursing, education, and biological studies. Half the members of the faculty senate and Board of Trustees are women. In a recent year, the commencement speaker was a black woman, as was 1 of the 3 recipients of honorary degrees.

Women and the Curriculum. Thirty-three percent of the women who earn bachelor's degrees major in the health professions, and over 19 percent major in education; 12 percent earn degrees in biology. Half of the women who earn two-year degrees major in the arts and sciences, and half major in health technologies.

The department of social work offers instruction on services for battered women, displaced homemakers, and childcare. There are no courses on women.

Women and Athletics. Opportunities for participation in intramural and intercollegiate sports are adequate for a college of this size. Seventy-four percent of the intramural and 70 percent of the intercollegiate athletes are women. Intercollegiate sports are basketball, field hockey, and softball.

Housing and Student Organizations. Forty-one percent of the undergraduates live on-campus in coeducational dormitories with restrictive hours for visitors of the opposite sex. The seven female and one male residence-hall directors receive awareness-training on sexism and sex education.

Special Services and Programs for Women. *Health and Counseling.* The student health service employs one male physician and four female health-care providers. The counseling center has one male counselor. Counseling, but not medical treatment, is provided for medical concerns specific to women. The student health insurance policy at Anna Maria covers maternity and abortion at no extra charge.

Safety and Security. Measures consist of local police, campus police without arrest authority, and an emergency alarm system in isolated locations. No rapes or assaults were reported on campus for 1980–81.

Career. Career placement services provide printed materials and job discrimination information on nontraditional careers for women and maintain programs to establish contacts between alumnae and female students.

Institutional Self-Description. "Anna Maria College provides a liberal arts education with career options, within a coeducational context, within Christian traditions. The college has a long tradition of nurturing educational opportunity for women, for the first in families to attend college, or for those experiencing career change. Dormitory life, excluding 'open housing,' preserves the student's freedom from conformist pressures."

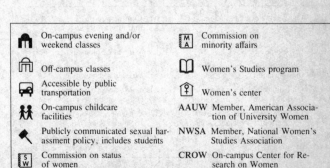

🏠 On-campus evening and/or weekend classes	MA Commission on minority affairs
🏛 Off-campus classes	📖 Women's Studies program
🚐 Accessible by public transportation	👤 Women's center
👫 On-campus childcare facilities	AAUW Member, American Association of University Women
↖ Publicly communicated sexual harassment policy, includes students	NWSA Member, National Women's Studies Association
SW Commission on status of women	CROW On-campus Center for Research on Women

Aquinas Junior College
15 Walnut Park, Newton, MA 02158
Telephone: (617) 244-8134

Women in Leadership
★★★ students
★★★ faculty
★★★ administrators

320 undergraduates

	Amer. Ind.	Asian Amer.	Blacks	Hispanics	Whites
F	0	0	2	0	318
M	0	0	0	0	0
%	0.0	0.0	0.6	0.0	99.4

A Roman Catholic institution, Aquinas is a two-year college for women. Its suburban campus, located near Boston, attracts 320 students. The median age of students is 20.

The college offers associate degree programs in business, health, and early childhood education. A summer session is available. A Continuing Education Program includes some evening classes. Public transportation and on-campus parking for a nominal yearly fee are available.

Private childcare facilities are located near the campus.

Women in Leadership Positions. *Students.* Women hold all student leadership positions.

Faculty. All 24 of the full-time faculty are women.

Administrators. Women are four of the five major administrators, including President, vice-president, chief student life officer, and head librarian. Women chair the four academic departments—secretarial, humanities/science, medical, and early childhood. The Coordinator of Academic Programs is a woman, as are all nine trustees.

Women and the Curriculum. Women earn two-year degrees in business (61 percent), health (22 percent), and early childhood education (17 percent). An innovative program encourages women to pursue careers in accounting. The school of business provides instruction on matters of job discrimination.

The human sciences department offers a course on Women in American Society and the Continuing Education Program offers Women in Middle Management.

Women and Athletics. There is no sports program.

Special Services and Programs for Women. *Health and Counseling.* There is no student health service. The student counseling center is staffed by one woman; no services specific to women are available.

Safety and Security. The college relies upon the services of the local town police. No rapes or assaults were reported for 1980–81.

Career. Lectures and panels on women's employment in non-traditional fields are available.

Institutional Self-Description. "Aquinas Junior College, an independent, two-year Catholic college, has as its primary aim

learning at the post-secondary level and the promotion of the growth and development of persons responsible to God and society. Aquinas provides the opportunity for career preparation and the acquisition of knowledge in the humanities."

Bay Path Junior College
588 Longmeadow St.
Longmeadow, MA 01106
Telephone: (413) 567-0621

Women in Leadership
★★★ students
★★★ faculty

637 undergraduates

	Amer. Ind.	Asian Amer.	Blacks	Hispanics	Whites
F	0	1	8	2	624
M	0	0	0	0	0
%	0.0	0.2	1.3	0.3	98.3

A private, non-sectarian two-year college for women, Bay Path was founded in 1897. All but two of its 635 undergraduates attend full-time. The median age of students is 19. The college offers a range of associate degree programs, including liberal arts, business, public service, and health. A program in Continuing Education for Women is available. The suburban campus, near Springfield, is accessible by public transportation for the 24 percent of students who commute. On-campus parking is provided.

Policies to Ensure Fairness to Women. Two administrators are responsible part-time for reviewing policies and monitoring compliance with equal-employment-opportunity, sex-equity, and handicapped-access legislation. A formal policy on sexual harassment has been communicated in writing to students, faculty, and staff; complaints are resolved through a formal grievance procedure.

Women in Leadership Positions. *Students.* Women hold all student leadership positions.

Faculty. Half of the 22 full-time faculty are women. There are 2 female faculty for every 100 female students.

Administrators. The President of the college is a woman, as is the Academic Dean. Of six departments, women chair business law and English. Ten of 24 trustees are women.

Women and the Curriculum. Nearly 80 percent of two-year degrees and certificates earned by women are in business programs. The school of business provides information on job discrimination.

The English and behavioral sciences departments offer two courses on women: Women in Literature and Sociology of Women.

Women and Athletics. Students participate in intramural softball and tennis.

Housing and Student Organizations. Two dormitories that have restrictive hours for male visitors house the 76 percent of students who live on campus. Four of the six residence-hall directors are women; directors are offered awareness-training on birth control and rape.

Special Services and Programs for Women. *Health and Counseling.* A student health service staffed by three women health-care providers and a student counseling center staffed by two women provide counseling and medical treatment for gynecological problems and rape and assault.

Safety and Security. Measures include campus police, night-time escort service, a campus-wide emergency telephone system,

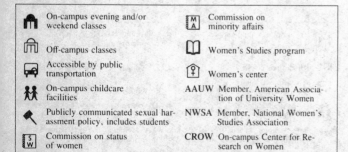

🏛	On-campus evening and/or weekend classes	Ⓜ Ⓐ	Commission on minority affairs
🏚	Off-campus classes	📖	Women's Studies program
🚌	Accessible by public transportation	🚺	Women's center
👥	On-campus childcare facilities	AAUW	Member, American Association of University Women
🔨	Publicly communicated sexual harassment policy, includes students	NWSA	Member, National Women's Studies Association
�SW⌐	Commission on status of women	CROW	On-campus Center for Research on Women

an emergency-alarm system, self defense courses and information sessions on campus safety. No rapes or assaults on women were reported for 1980–81

Career. Services include nonsexist/nonracist printed information on nontraditional fields of study and networking between students and alumnae.

Institutional Self-Description. ''Bay Path Junior College exists solely to provide superior education for women. It provides for the variety of roles now available to women, including preparation for a career, for continuing study, for civic and professional participation, and for women's distinctive role in society.''

Berkshire Community College
Pittsfield, MA 01201
Telephone: (413) 499-4660

Women in Leadership
  ★★ **faculty**
  ★★ **administrators**

2,064 undergraduates

	Amer. Ind.	Asian Amer.	Blacks	Hispanics	Whites
F	0	1	30	9	1,010
M	0	8	29	5	966
%	0.0	0.4	2.9	0.7	96.0

A public, two-year college, Berkshire offers comprehensive educational services to 3,211 students, 2,064 of whom are enrolled in degree programs. Half of the undergraduates are women; 38 percent of women attend part-time. About one-fourth of the student body is over age 25.

The college offers programs in liberal arts and pre-professional training, including business, engineering, computer science, environmental studies, visual and graphic arts, physical education, human services, and nursing. Evening classes, both on and off campus, and self-paced/contract learning are available, as well as a summer session. The division of continuing education enrolls 2,000 reentry women. Ten percent of these women are from minority groups, with black women the largest group. A nonresidential institution, Berkshire is accessible by public transportation, and free on-campus parking is provided.

On-campus childcare facilities can accommodate 27 percent of all students' requests. Private childcare facilities are available near the campus.

Policies to Ensure Fairness to Women. The affirmative action officer serves part time as a voting member of policymaking councils concerned with equal-opportunity legislation. An informal and confidential mechanism resolves complaints of sexual harassment. The Committee on Minority Affairs addresses the concerns of minority women.

Women in Leadership Positions. *Students.* Women have limited opportunities to exercise leadership on campus. In recent years, women have served once as editor-in-chief of the campus newspaper and head of the sophomore class, and twice as head of the entering class.

Faculty. Women are 41 percent of the full-time faculty of 70, a proportion above average for public two-year colleges in this guide. The college reports that 2 of the 28 full-time female faculty are black women. The ratio of female faculty to female students is 4 to 100; the ratio for males is 6 to 100.

Administrators. Three of the 8 chief administrators are women: chief student-life officer, chief development officer, and director of institutional research. Of the nine departments, three are chaired by women: business, English, and secretarial arts. The chair of

the nursing division is a woman. One of the 2 college trustees is female, as are 2 of the 15 regents.

Women and the Curriculum. Most women graduate in the arts and sciences, with smaller numbers receiving degrees and certificates in business, and commercial and health technologies. Women students are encouraged to prepare for nontraditional careers through programs for women in science, engineering, accounting, computer science, and electronics. The mathematics department offers a special program to build mathematics confidence. Women account for 70 percent of those enrolled in the cooperative education program, and 82 percent of those enrolled in internships and practicums. They also account for one-third of the participants in science field service, and just over half of participants in the experiential learning program.

The physical education department provides instruction on how to teach coeducational classes. There are no courses on women.

Women and Athletics. Over half of intramural and club athletes are women. Women participate in a wide range of individual and team intramurals, including basketball, soccer, water polo, tennis, badminton, volleyball, golf, gymnastics, softball, and skiing. Of the 140 intercollegiate athletes, 43 percent are women. Two of the paid varsity coaches are also women. Intercollegiate sports offered include basketball, soccer, and softball.

Special Services and Programs for Women. *Health and Counseling.* The student health service is staffed by 1 male physician and 1 female health-care provider. The student counseling center, which employs 3 women and 1 man, offers a number of services specific to women, including birth control, abortion, and rape and assault counseling. Family counseling and referral are also provided.

Safety and Security. Measures consist of campus police with no arrest authority, and a rape crisis center. For 1980–81, no rapes or assaults were reported on campus.

Career. Berkshire provides career information on nontraditional fields of study, as well as information on job discrimination.

Other. The college co-sponsors and is the site of the ''Focus on Women Conference,'' held annually in Berkshire County, Massachusetts. The three-day series of workshops, lectures, and exhibits is designed to help women become more active in economic, political, educational, and social life.

Institutional Self-Description. ''The academic and social climate at Berkshire Community College, as fostered by faculty, administrators, and student-service personnel, is one of equal opportunity for women and men. Women seeking careers in fields which have historically been male-dominated, such as engineering and business data processing, are actively encouraged and counseled in their pursuits.''

Bradford College
320 S. Main St., Bradford, MA 01830
Telephone: (617) 372-7161

Women in Leadership
  ★★★ **faculty**
  ★ **administrators**

280 undergraduates

	Amer. Ind.	Asian Amer.	Blacks	Hispanics	Whites
F	1	0	2	6	171
M	0	0	2	3	73
%	0.4	0.0	1.6	3.5	94.6

 AAUW

Bradford College, a private liberal arts college, was founded in 1803 as a country academy for local boys and girls. In 1836 it became an all-female institution; in 1932, a junior college for women; and in 1970 a coeducational four-year college. Bradford enrolls 314 students, 280 of whom are undergraduates. Sixty-eight percent of the students are women and 15 percent of the women attend part-time. The median age of all undergraduates is 20.

Bradford offers a range of undergraduate programs in the liberal arts and sciences, education, and pre-professional studies. Classes are offered in the evening. Twenty-eight percent of the undergraduates commute to campus; public transportation and on-campus parking are available.

Private childcare facilities are available near campus.

Policies to Ensure Fairness to Women. No policy on sexual harassment exists; an informal and confidential campus mechanism resolves complaints.

Women in Leadership Positions. *Students.* There are no campus-wide student leadership positions at Bradford.

Faculty. Fourteen of the 27 full-time faculty are women. There are 9 female faculty for every 100 female students and 17 male faculty for every 100 male students.

Administrators. The chief executive officer and chief development officer are women; the five other top-level administrators are men. Of five department heads, the chair of the humanities department is a woman. Fifty-two percent of the trustees and two of the three members of the faculty senate are women. One of the two recent commencement speakers was a woman.

Women and the Curriculum. Among the 18 women who earned bachelor's degrees in a recent year, 9 majored in interdisciplinary studies and 7 in fine arts. All two-year degrees are awarded in arts and science.

Two courses on women are offered through the literature/communications and sociology departments: The Creative Woman, and Women in Society.

Women and Athletics. For a college of its size, Bradford offers women adequate opportunities to participate in intercollegiate and intramural sports. Intramural sports include lacrosse, archery, and swimming. No information was provided on the number of female athletes, but one of the two paid intercollegiate coaches is a woman. The intercollegiate sports offered are basketball and volleyball.

Housing and Student Organizations. Seventy-two percent of the undergradutes reside on campus in coeducational dormitories with no restrictive hours for visitors of the opposite sex. The three female and three male residence-hall directors receive awareness-training on sexism, sex education, racism, and birth control

Special Services and Programs for Women. *Health and Counseling.* The student health service employs two male physicians and one female health-care provider. There are no health services specific to women. The counseling service has two women counselors. Counseling on birth control, abortion, and rape and assault is available.

Safety and Security. Measures consist of campus police with weapons training and arrest authority, high-intensity lighting, an emergency alarm system at isolated locations, information sessions on campus safety, and a rape crisis center. No information was provided on the incidence of rapes or assaults on campus for 1980–81.

Career. Services include career workshops and job discrimination information on nontraditional occupations for women. Updated files of alumnae by specific careers are maintained.

Institutional Self-Description. "Bradford College is an independent, New England college with 400 men and women. It offers A.A. degree and B.A. programs in humanities, the arts, social sciences, and administration and management, and has a 178-year history of quality education in liberal arts. Bradford's overall purpose is to assist persons to think clearly, communicate effectively, and become more capable of moral, rational, and humane choices."

Clark University
950 Main Street, Worcester, MA 01610
Telephone: (617) 793-7711

★ **Women and the Curriculum**

★★ **Women and Athletics**

2,189 undergraduates

	Amer. Ind.	Asian Amer.	Blacks	Hispanics	Whites
F	2	4	41	11	993
M	0	7	15	14	1,058
%	0.1	0.5	2.6	1.2	95.6

NWSA

A private, liberal arts university founded in 1887, Clark enrolls 3,106 students. The campus is located about one hour from Boston. Women are 49 percent of the 2,189 undergraduates; 44 percent of the women attend part-time. The median age of all undergraduates is 20.

Clark offers bachelor's, master's, and doctoral programs. Schedules include off-campus day and evening classes, as well as on-campus evening classes, and a summer session. There is also a continuing education division. Sixty-five percent of the undergraduates commute to campus; public transportation and on-campus parking are available.

Childcare facilities, open on campus between 9 a.m. and 3 p.m., accommodate 30 children, and give priority to full-time students and faculty. The facility is run as a cooperative with a fixed fee. Private facilities are available nearby.

Policies to Ensure Fairness to Women. The Affirmative Action Officer and the Personnel Director oversee equal-opportunity, sex-equity and handicapped-access policy and compliance. A written policy prohibiting sexual harassment of students, faculty, and staff has been communicated to the campus community. Complaints are resolved through a formal campus grievance procedure.

Women in Leadership Positions. *Students.* There are two campus-wide leadership positions at Clark, and both have been held by men during recent years.

Faculty. Women are 18 percent of the full-time faculty of 141. There are 3 female faculty for every 100 female students and 12 male faculty for every 100 male students.

Administrators. The chief administrators are men, except the director of women's athletics. Two of the 16 departments are chaired by women: education; and government/international relations. The Dean of Students is a black woman; 4 other deans are men.

Women and the Curriculum. Most bachelor's degrees awarded to women are in the social sciences (33 percent) and psychology (25 percent). Seven percent are in the nontraditional fields of mathematics and physical sciences; women are 65 percent of those who receive degrees in mathematics. Fifty-three percent of students in cooperative education and 49 percent of students in internships are women.

The Women's Studies Program offers an undergraduate concentration and courses through several departments. Recent course offerings include Introduction to Women's Studies; The Family; Women and Politics; and Images of Women in Film. An official committee is responsible for the continuing development of the Women's Studies Program, and for courses on women in traditional departments.

The physical education department provides instruction on teaching coeducational classes, and the division of business offers instruction on the problems of job discrimination, sexual harassment in the workplace, and women in management. Faculty are offered workshops on women in leadership and equal opportunity.

Women and Athletics. The women's sports program offers excellent opportunities for participation in intramural, intercollegiate, and club sports. Forty-two percent of the participants in intercollegiate sports are women; 12 of the 25 paid intercollegiate coaches are women. Intercollegiate sports are basketball, crew, cross-country, field hockey, softball, swimming, tennis, track, and volleyball.

Housing and Student Organizations. Sixty-five percent of the undergraduates reside on campus in single-sex and coeducational dormitories that have no restrictive hours for visitors of the opposite sex. Housing for married students and single parents is available. A married woman whose husband is not enrolled may not live in married students' housing. The five male and two female residence-hall directors (one a minority woman) are offered awareness-training on sex education, racism, and affirmative action. Forty-nine undergraduates, including 16 women, belong to fraternities and sororities.

Special Services and Programs for Women. *Health and Counseling.* The student health service employs one male physician and five female health-care providers. The counseling center has a staff of two male supervisors and advanced graduate students. Medical treatment is available for gynecological problems and birth control. The regular student health insurance covers abortion at no extra charge. The counseling center offers such services specific to women as abortion and rape and assault counseling. Counselor/therapists receive in-service training on avoiding sex-role stereotyping and racial bias.

Safety and Security. Measures include campus police, a nighttime escort service for women, high-intensity lighting, a campus-wide emergency telephone system, an emergency alarm system in isolated locations, self-defense courses for women, information sessions on safety and rape and assault prevention, and a rape crisis center. No rapes and 14 assaults (one on a woman) were reported for 1980–81.

Career. Services include printed materials on nontraditional fields of study and careers for women, updated files of alumnae by specific careers and networking between alumnae and female students.

Other. The campus Women's Center, with an annual budget of $3,000, provides services, referrals, and information to women at Clark. The center's library serves as a meeting place for women. Theater and other women's arts programs are sponsored by the department of visual and performing arts.

Returning Women Students. There are 630 women between the ages of 26 and 40 enrolled as part-time undergraduates. In addition, 175 reentry women are enrolled in continuing education classes, 10 percent of them are minority women, largely Hispanics.

Institutional Self-Description. "Clark University began admitting women graduate students in 1900 and women undergraduates in 1942. Enrollment currently stands at 1,900 undergraduates and 300 graduate students. The student-body size and the small urban campus combine to offer an unusual and intimate setting for learning."

College of The Holy Cross
Worcester, MA 01610
Telephone: (617) 793-2222

2,569 undergraduates

	Amer. Ind.	Asian Amer.	Blacks	Hispanics	Whites
F	0	5	37	7	1,040
M	0	7	58	14	1,396
%	0.0	0.5	3.7	0.8	95.0

 AAUW

Founded in 1843, Holy Cross is a four-year, Roman Catholic college operated by the Jesuits. It offers bachelor's programs in the liberal arts, sciences, and business. The 2,569 undergraduates, 42 percent of them women, all attend full-time. The median age of undergraduates is 20. Fifteen percent of the undergraduates commute to the campus, located near downtown Worcester. Public transportation and on-campus parking are available.

Women in Leadership Positions. *Students.* No information was supplied.

Faculty. Sixteen percent of the 163 full-time faculty members are women, a proportion that is below the national average. There are 2 female faculty for every 100 female students and 9 male faculty for every 100 male students. Women head the departments of political science, psychology, and music.

Administrators. No information was supplied.

Women and the Curriculum. Thirty-nine percent of the degrees granted to women are in the social sciences, 20 percent are in letters, and 9 percent are in the nontraditional fields of mathematics and physical sciences.

Several courses on women are offered through the departments of sociology, theater arts, English, and philosophy: Sociology of Gender, Women and their Stages, American Women Writers, and Philosophers on Women. Workshops on racism and the curriculum are provided for the faculty.

Women and Athletics. There are limited opportunities for women to participate in intramural, intercollegiate, and club sports. Approximately 600 women participate in intramural sports and 270 in intercollegiate sports. Less than 10 percent of athletic scholarships are awarded to women. The intercollegiate sports offered are basketball, crew, field hockey, and lacrosse.

Housing and Student Organizations. Eighty-five percent of the undergraduates live on campus in coeducational dormitories with no restrictive hours for visitors of the opposite sex. Residence-hall directors receive awareness-training on sexism and racism. The Women's Organization, with 30 members, serves as an advocate for women on campus.

Special Services and Programs for Women. *Health and Counseling.* The college health service employs one female physician. It provides gynecological services and treatment for rape and assault victims. The counseling center has two male and one female counselors, who offer gynecological, birth control, and rape and assault counseling. Counselors are given in-service training on sex-role stereotyping and racism.

Safety and Security. Measures include a campus police force, a night-time escort service for women, high-intensity lighting, information sessions on campus safety, and a rape crisis center. One rape was reported on campus for 1980–81.

Career. Services include lectures for students by women employed in nontraditional occupations, and programs to establish contacts between alumnae and female students.

Institutional Self-Description. None provided.

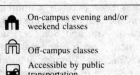

🏛 On-campus evening and/or weekend classes	Ⓜ️Ⓐ	Commission on minority affairs
🏚 Off-campus classes	📖	Women's Studies program
🚌 Accessible by public transportation	🏠	Women's center
👫 On-campus childcare facilities	AAUW	Member, American Association of University Women
✎ Publicly communicated sexual harassment policy, includes students	NWSA	Member, National Women's Studies Association
Ⓢ︎Ⓦ Commission on status of women	CROW	On-campus Center for Research on Women

Emmanuel College

400 The Fenway, Boston, MA 02115
Telephone: (617) 277-9340

Women in Leadership
★★★ students
★★★ faculty
★★★ administrators

522 undergraduates

	Amer. Ind.	Asian Amer.	Blacks	Hispanics	Whites
F	0	0	21	15	476
M	0	0	0	0	0
%	0.0	0.0	4.1	2.9	93.0

 AAUW

Founded in 1919, Emmanuel is a Roman Catholic college for women that enrolls 1,056 students. Its urban campus attracts 522 matriculated students, virtually all of whom attend full-time. The median age of all undergraduates is 20. Recent information indicates that 38 percent of the students are over age 25.

A variety of undergraduate degree programs is available, in addition to a continuing education program that serves 400 students. Classes are held in the evening, on and off campus, as well as during the day and in the summer. One-third of undergraduates live on campus in dormitories that have restrictive visiting hours for men. The campus is accessible by public transportation, and on-campus parking is provided for a fee.

Policies to Ensure Fairness to Women. A part-time equal-employment-opportunity officer handles matters related to affirmative-action laws. Complaints of sexual harassment are resolved through a formal grievance procedure.

Women in Leadership Positions. *Students.* Women hold all student leadership positions. Students are represented on all college committees and on the College Council.

Faculty. Sixty-one percent of the 61 full-time faculty are female. There are 7 female faculty for every 100 female students.

Administrators. Women hold all top positions, which is unusual even among other women's colleges in this guide. Eleven of the 19 departments are chaired by women, including sociology, chemistry, and mathematics.

Women and the Curriculum. Nearly half of the degrees awarded are in psychology; less than 3 percent are in mathematics or physical sciences.

There are no courses on women. The departments of education, business, and mathematics offer some instruction on matters specific to women.

Minority Women. Minority women are 7 percent of the undergraduate population. The student counseling staff receives awareness-training on racism. One of the three female counselors is a minority woman. A black woman was the sole recipient of an honorary degree in 1981; a black woman sits on the Board of Trustees. Black women have their own advocacy and support group, the Black Student Union, with 25 active members and a black student advisor.

Women and Athletics. The limited athletic program offers two intramural sports—swimming and volleyball. The four intercollegiate teams—basketball, cross-country, softball, and tennis—draw 57 participants. Two of the four paid varsity coaches are women.

Special Services and Programs for Women. *Health and Counseling.* The student health service employs 1 male and 2 female physicians, as well as 1 female health-care provider. The student counseling center is staffed by 1 male and 3 female counselors. Medical services specific to women consist of gynecological and rape and assault counseling.

Safety and Security. Measures consist of campus police protection, high-intensity lighting, an emergency telephone system, and instruction on self-defense and campus safety. No rapes and five assaults on women were reported for 1980-81.

Career. Emmanuel sponsors career workshops and lectures on nontraditional occupations, and fosters networking with alumnae. Students may consult files on alumnae career histories for job leads and contacts.

Other. Among the special programs for women are a women's lecture series, theater and creative-arts performances, and assertiveness-training sessions. The Office of Continuing Education serves older women.

Institutional Self-Description. "Emmanuel College is committed to education of the whole woman—in the classroom, in individual counseling, in informal interaction with faculty, and in involvement in policy-shaping bodies of the college. In addition, the mutual exchange between younger and older women students provides insights and understanding which are both enriching and challenging."

Harvard University

Cambridge, MA 02138
Telephone: (617) 495-5000

Women in Leadership
★★★ students

★★ Women and the Curriculum

★ Women and Athletics

6,498 undergraduates

	Amer. Ind.	Asian Amer.	Blacks	Hispanics	Whites
F	11	98	219	65	1,720
M	10	141	243	112	3,569
%	0.3	3.9	7.5	2.9	85.5

AAUW CROW

Harvard University enrolls over 15,000 students in a comprehensive range of undergraduate, graduate, and professional studies. Harvard College and Radcliffe College are the two undergraduate liberal arts divisions. All classes are coeducational; women graduates receive Harvard degrees. A summer session is available.

Women are 33 percent of the 6,498 undergraduates; all women attend full-time. The average age of undergraduates is 20. One percent of women are over age 24. For the commuting student, the campus is accessible by public transportation. There is no parking on campus; free transportation from distant parking lots is provided.

Facilities for childcare include six centers which serve 300 children. Two of the centers assess fees on a sliding scale. The Child Care Advisor's Office provides detailed information on both university and nearby private facilities.

Policies to Ensure Fairness to Women. Equal employment opportunity, sex equity for students, and handicapped access are the responsibility of a member of the administration and a consultant. Complaints of sexual harassment are handled through a formal grievance procedure which has been publicly communicated to students. The Committee on the Status of Women, appointed by the Dean of the Faculty of Arts and Sciences, addresses the concerns of minority women, among other matters.

Women in Leadership Positions. *Students.* Women, who are one-third of the students, also held one-third of the campus-wide offices in a recent three-year period. Women were president of the student assembly, editor-in-chief of the newspaper, and manager of the radio station.

Faculty. According to recent information from Harvard, women are 13 percent of a full-time faculty of 691, a proportion below the national average. There are 4 female faculty for every 100 female students and 13 male faculty for every 100 male students.

Administrators. The president of Radcliffe College is also Vice-President of Harvard University. The head of the Schlesinger Library, the head of the Bunting Institute, and the in-coming head of the Harvard School of Education are women.

Women and the Curriculum. The most popular fields for women are social sciences (33 percent), interdisciplinary studies (14 percent), biology (14 percent), and letters (13 percent). Seven percent of women major in such nontraditional fields as engineering, the physical sciences, and mathematics. Radcliffe reports special programs which encourage women to prepare for careers in science and engineering.

There is no Women's Studies Program. In one recent year, nine undergraduate courses on women were offered through the departments of anthropology, biology, comparative literature, English, government, humanities, social sciences, and the core curriculum. Titles include Women in Chinese Society; The Women's Tradition in Literature; and Women, Society, and Culture. An official committee works to include new scholarship on women in the curriculum.

The Harvard Divinity School has a Women's Studies in Religion Program which supports research and teaching related to the history and function of gender in religious traditions and communities.

The Mary Ingraham Bunting Institute sponsors independent research, writing, and other creative work. The Henry A. Murray Research Center houses an extensive collection of social science information on the changing lives of American women. The Arthur and Elizabeth Schlesinger Library on the History of Women in America is an outstanding resource.

Minority Women. Of the 2,198 undergraduate women, 18 percent are minority-group members. In a recent year, the Harvard Divinity School offered two courses on minority women: Women and the Black Church and Images of Community in Black/White Feminist Literature. The Black Women's Oral History Project is housed at Radcliffe. The Association of Black Radcliffe Women and the Radcliffe Asian Women's Group meet on campus.

Women and Athletics. The intramural and intercollegiate programs are good. Eighteen individual and team sports are available in the intramural program. Special facilities accommodate a large crew program and ice hockey competition. Club sports are also available. One-third of the intercollegiate athletes are women. Intercollegiate sports offered are basketball, crew (lightweight and heavyweight), cross-country, fencing, field hockey, ice hockey, lacrosse, sailing, skiing, soccer, softball, squash, swimming, tennis, and track (indoor and outdoor).

Housing and Student Organizations. Ninety-one percent of the undergraduates live on campus in coeducational dormitories. Residence halls do not restrict hours for visitors of the opposite sex. Staff are offered awareness-training on sex education, birth control, and the avoidance of sexism and racism.

The Radcliffe Union of Students, Radcliffe Lesbians Association, and the Feminist Alliance are groups that serve as advocates for women.

Special Services and Programs for Women. *Health and Counseling.* The student health center provides some medical attention specific to women. Nine of the 31 primary-care physicians are women. Student health insurance covers abortion and maternity at no extra cost. The student counseling center, staffed by 15 women and 13 men, offers gynecological, birth control, abortion, and rape and assault counseling. Staff receive in-service training on the avoidance of sex-role stereotyping and racial bias.

Safety and Security. Measures consist of campus police protection, night-time escort service for women, night-time bus service to residence areas, high-intensity lighting, emergency telephones, and information on safety and crime prevention. Four rapes and 31 assaults were reported for 1980-81.

Career. Career services offered include printed information, speakers, and workshops on women in nontraditional occupations and fields of study, as well as updated files on alumnae by specific careers.

Other. There is a Women's Center. The Associate Dean's Office sponsors a women's lecture series. Education for Action is a resource center which provides information, counseling, and funds for undergraduates interested in social action and social change.

Special Features. Radcliffe's Summer Program in Science allows female high-school students to develop science and mathematics skills while exploring these fields as possible careers.

Institutional Self-Description. "By virtue of their enrollment in Radcliffe College, Radcliffe students are also enrolled in Harvard College and have access not only to all the resources of a major research university but also to all the undergraduate and scholarly programs of a college devoted to women's higher education."

Massachusetts Institute of Technology
77 Massachusetts Avenue
Cambridge, MA 02139
Telephone: (617) 253-1000

| Women in Leadership | ★ Women and the |
| ★★★ students | Curriculum |

4,538 undergraduates

	Amer. Ind.	Asian Amer.	Blacks	Hispanics	Whites
F	0	44	67	6	613
M	8	140	145	88	3,060
%	0.2	4.4	5.1	2.3	88.1

🚐 👫 ⚓ ⬛ ⬛ 📖 ⬛ AAUW

Founded in 1865 as a private technical university, MIT offers comprehensive educational and research programs focused on science and engineering for undergraduate and graduate students. Degrees are available in such areas as engineering, natural science, architecture, urban planning, the humanities, and the social sciences. Summer session classes are available.

Of the more than 8,800 students who attend MIT, 4,538 are undergraduates. Seventeen percent of the undergraduates are women, 2 percent of whom attend part-time. The median age of undergraduates is 20.

Situated on the banks of the Charles River, two miles from downtown Boston, the campus is easily accessible by public transportation. On-campus parking at a fee is available for the 13 percent of students who commute.

University-operated childcare facilities can accommodate 93 children, with faculty and staff making wide use of the service. Up to 50 percent of students' requests for childcare can be met. Charges are based on a fixed hourly fee. Additional private childcare facilities are located near the campus.

Policies to Ensure Fairness to Women. One administrator has full-time responsibility for policy relating to equal-employment-opportunity, educational-sex-equity, and handicapped-access legislation, while another college official serves part-time as a compliance administrator. A written policy prohibiting the sexual harassment of students, faculty, and staff has been publicly communicated to these groups; complaints are resolved either informally and confidentially or through a formal campus grievance procedure. In addition, the Special Assistant to the President is accessible to students who have complaints, grievances, or suggestions.

The 25-member Women's Advisory Group, a presidential committee formed of representatives nominated from various campus women's groups, takes stands on issues of importance to students, faculty, and staff.

Women in Leadership Positions. *Students.* Women have outstanding opportunities to gain leadership experience. They are 17 percent of students and hold one-third of the leadership positions. In a recent three-year period, women served twice as president of the student union board, manager of the campus radio station, and presidents of the senior and junior classes. Women also served one-year terms as editor-in-chief of the campus newspaper and president of the sophomore class. One of four honorary societies is headed by a woman.

Faculty. Ten percent of the 990 full-time faculty are women, a proportion considerably below the average for private research universities in this guide. There are 13 female faculty for every 100 female students and 24 male faculty for every 100 male students.

Administrators. Except for the Dean of Student Affairs, all top administrative positions are held by men. Women chair the department of economics, the Center for Material Science and Engineering, and the Center for Materials Research in Archeology and Ethnology. The institute has seven female trustees.

Women and the Curriculum. Sixty-three percent of women graduate in such nontraditional fields as architecture, computer science, engineering, mathematics, and physical sciences, a proportion significantly above the national average. The most popular fields for women graduates are engineering (41 percent), biology (23 percent), the physical sciences (10 percent), and business (8 percent). Programs to encourage women to prepare for careers in architecture and computer science are available.

The new Women's Studies Program, directed part-time by a permanent faculty member, offers an undergraduate minor. Twenty female and two male faculty will teach courses on women. An official committee supervises the development of the program and reports on the inclusion of scholarship on women across the curriculum. Courses in the business school provide instruction on some matters specific to women. Faculty workshops are held on sexism in the curriculum and on nontraditional occupations for women and men.

Minority Women. Sixteen percent of full-time, female undergraduates are minority women, of whom 9 percent are black, 6 percent are Asian American, and about 1 percent are Hispanic. According to a recent report, the full-time faculty includes two black and two Asian American women. The Dean of Student Affairs is a black woman.

Both the Women's Advisory Group and the Committee on Minority Affairs address the concerns of minority women. The Minority Women's Group and the Minority Interest Group serve as advocates for minority women students. The counseling center employs one minority woman and both counseling and residence-hall staff are offered awareness-training on the avoidance of racial bias. The Office for Minority Education sponsors a program to build confidence in mathematics. Among the hundreds of women served by the Women's Center, 10 percent are minority women, predominantly black and Asian American woman.

Women and Athletics. MIT offers some opportunities for women to participate in organized, competitive sports. Though the institution did not provide information on the women's intramural and club sports programs, it did report that 27 percent of the 856 intercollegiate athletes are women. Among the 41 paid coaches for intercollegiate sports, 9 are women. The intercollegiate sports offered are basketball, crew, fencing, field hockey, gymnastics, softball, swimming, tennis, and volleyball.

Housing and Student Organizations. A variety of housing options is available for the 87 percent of students who live on campus, including single-sex and coeducational dormitories without restrictive hours for visitors of the opposite sex. Independent living groups and housing for married students with or without children, as well as for single parents, are available. A married student whose husband is not enrolled is permitted to live in married students' housing. All residence-hall staff receive awareness-training on sex education and birth control, and on the avoidance of sexism and racism.

Thirty percent of undergraduate students belong to social fraternities or sororities, both of which provide housing for members.

The major campus advocacy group for female students is the Advisory Committee for Women's Students' Interests, a presidential committee which addresses such issues as housing options, support services, and sexual harassment problems. The Association of Women Students, composed primarily of undergraduates, sponsors a variety of activities, including newsletters, potluck suppers with women faculty, and programs for women. There are also lesbian groups, several women's religious groups, and women's groups composed of graduate and postdoctoral students.

Special Services and Programs for Women. *Health and Counseling.* The student health service is staffed by 11 female and 43 male physicians, along with 30 health-care providers, 20 of them women. Among the 23 therapists employed by the counseling center, 10 are women. Medical treatment and counseling are available for gynecological problems, birth control, abortion, and rape and assault. The counseling staff receive in-service training on the avoidance of sex-role stereotyping. Abortion and maternity expenses are covered by the regular student health insurance.

Safety and Security. Measures consist of campus police with weapons training and arrest authority, night-time escort for women students, a campus-wide emergency telephone system, emergency alarm system at isolated locations, self-defense courses for women, information sessions on campus safety and crime prevention, and rape crisis center. One rape and 19 assaults were reported for 1980–81.

Career. Workshops, lectures, printed material, and job discrimination information on nontraditional occupations for women are available, as well as programs to establish networks between female students and alumnae. The university also maintains updated files on alumnae by specific career. The Society of Women Engineers (SWE), an active campus group, holds regular meetings, and sponsors an annual career fair.

Other. The Margaret Cheney Room, a suite of rooms set aside for exclusive use by women students, serves as MIT's Women's Center. The rooms are used for meetings and programs, as well as for relaxation.

Institutional Self-Description. ''Women undergraduate and graduate students are admitted on an equal basis with men, and they participate fully in the five Schools (Architecture, Engineering, Humanities and Social Science, Science, and Sloan). MIT women perform in all areas on a level equal to that of their male peers. The high number of women students in engineering and science reflects the general emphasis of MIT's educational mission. Nevertheless, undergraduates gain breadth in their studies through the curriculum which offers opportunities comparable to that of a first-rate liberal arts institution. Upon graduation, the vast majority of MIT women enter nontraditional fields in science and engineering and are accorded recognition for the rigor of their training at MIT. Women participate fully in extra-curricular activities, athletics, and campus governance. Many leadership positions on campus are held by women.''

Five Colleges:
see Amherst College; Mount Holyoke College; Smith College; University of Massachusetts, Amherst.

Mount Holyoke College

South Hadley, MA 01075
Telephone: (413) 538-2000

Women in Leadership
  ★★★ students
  ★★★ faculty
  ★★★ administrators

★ **Women and the Curriculum**

1,914 undergraduates

	Amer. Ind.	Asian Amer.	Blacks	Hispanics	Whites
F	0	44	86	40	1,689
M	0	0	0	0	1
%	0.0	2.4	4.6	2.2	90.9

🚌 Ⓜ 📖 ⌂ **AAUW**

Founded as a seminary in 1837, Mount Holyoke is the oldest continuing college for women in the nation. A private, non-sectarian institution, the college enrolls 1,914 undergraduates. All students attend full-time. The median age of undergraduates is 20; fewer than 1 percent are over age 25.

Mount Holyoke is a member of the Five Colleges, Inc., a consortium that includes Amherst, Hampshire, and Smith Colleges, as well as the University of Massachusetts in Amherst. Consortium members share academic offerings, along with social and cultural events. Mount Holyoke offers bachelor's degrees in a range of liberal arts and sciences, as well as master's degrees and a cooperative Ph.D. available through the consortium. Adult continuing education is offered through Mount Holyoke's Francis Perkins Program. Five percent of students commute to the campus, which is located in the Connecticut Valley of western Massachusetts. Free bus transportation is available to the Five-Colleges area. On-campus parking is available.

Private childcare facilities are located near the campus.

Policies to Ensure Fairness to Women. The Assistant to the President has part-time responsibility for policy relating to equal employment opportunity, educational sex equity, and handicapped access. A written campus policy on sexual harassment is in preparation; complaints are currently handled informally and confidentially. A Committee on the Multi-Racial Community addresses the concerns of minority women.

Women in Leadership Positions. *Students.* Women hold all leadership posts.

Faculty. Fifty-two percent of the 182 full-time faculty are women. There are 5 female faculty for every 100 students.

Administrators. Seven of the 9 major administrators, including the President, are women. Two of the 4 deans are women. Women chair 13 of 33 departments, including biological science, politics, classics, and interdisciplinary programs in biochemistry, Latin American studies, and Romance languages and literature. Sixteen of 24 trustees are female.

Women and the Curriculum. Most women earn degrees in social sciences (31 percent), letters (15 percent), biological sciences (11 percent), and in fine arts, psychology, and foreign languages (9 percent each). Seven percent major in such nontraditional fields as mathematics and the physical sciences. Eighteen percent of the students earn degrees in science fields. Mount Holyoke offers programs that encourage students to prepare for careers in science, engineering, computer science, and organizational management.

More than 15 courses on women are offered through the relevant departments: The Woman in History, Women Writers, Women and Religion, Women and Work, Feminist Theory, and Women and Law. In 1981–82, more than 100 undergraduates designed a special major in Women's Studies. Beginning in the fall of 1982, a Women's Studies Program, administered by a permanent faculty member, will offer a bachelor's degree. An official committee will supervise the development of the program

and encourage the inclusion of scholarship on women in the curriculum.

The departments of education, physical education, sociology, and psychology include instruction on several matters specific to women. Faculty workshops are offered on sexism and racism in the curriculum, the relationships among sex, race, and selection of major field, and affirmative action and equal opportunity.

Minority Women. Five percent of students are black, 2 percent are Hispanic, and 2 percent are Asian American. Advocacy groups for minority students include the Association of Pan-African Unity, the Asian Student Association, and La Unidad. The department of sociology/anthropology offers The Black Woman in the U.S. One of the 2 female deans is a black woman, as is 1 of the 16 female trustees. The 1981 commencement speaker was a black woman, as were 2 of the 7 honorary degree recipients. Among the 24 lecturers in a recent campus-wide series, 3 were black women, 2 Hispanic women, and 4 were Asian American women. One member of the counseling staff and 3 of the residence-hall directors are minority women. Awareness-training on the avoidance of racial bias is offered to counseling and residence-hall staff.

Women and Athletics. The college offers mixed opportunities for women to participate in a variety of organized intercollegiate athletics. Forty women participate in club sports, while 769 women participate in four intramural team sports. Some 270 women compete in an excellent range of intercollegiate sports; all varsity teams participate in tournament competitions. Seven of the nine paid varsity coaches are women. The intercollegiate sports offered are basketball, crew, field hockey, golf, lacrosse, riding, soccer, softball, swimming, tennis, and volleyball.

Housing and Student Organizations. Ninety-five percent of students live on campus in dormitories without restrictive hours for male visitors. While there is no married students' housing, married women are permitted to live in dormitories without their husbands. Eighteen of the 24 residence-hall directors are women; awareness-training on the avoidance of sexism is offered to all residence-hall staff.

In addition to the minority groups mentioned above, among the student advocacy groups on campus are the Student Government Association, the 40-member Women's Center Groups, a Lesbian Support Group, and Women Against Sexual Harassment (WASH).

Special Services and Programs for Women. *Health and Counseling.* The student health center employs 2 female and 3 male physicians, along with 3 female health-care providers. The counseling center is staffed by 3 women and 1 man, who are offered training on avoidance of sex-role stereotyping. Available services specific to women include medical treatment and counseling on gynecological matters, birth control, abortion, and rape and assault. The regular student health insurance covers abortion and maternity expenses.

Safety and Security. Measures consist of local police, campus police with weapons training and arrest authority, night-time escort for women students, night-time campus-wide van service to residence areas, high-intensity lighting, a campus-wide emergency alarm system, self-defense courses, and information sessions on campus safety and crime prevention. No rapes and seven assaults, four on women, were reported for 1980–81.

Career. Workshops, printed materials, and job discrimination information on nontraditional occupations for women are available, as well as updated files of alumnae careers and programs to establish networks between alumnae and students.

Other. The Dean of Students' Office operates the campus Women's Center on a budget of approximately $4,000. Under the part-time direction of a student volunteer, the center sponsors an annual women's week, a women's lecture series, and in conjunction with the theater arts department, concerts, performances, and other women's art programs. The center also sponsors an annual Women's Weekend which includes workshops, discussion groups, women peformers, and brings to the campus outstanding speakers on women's issues.

Returning Women Students. The Francis Perkins Program provides continuing education for women. Its Center, directed part-time by a permanent faculty member, enrolls 30 reentry women.

Special Features. The history of women's education in the U.S. is the focus of a series of symposia and lectures to be held at Mount Holyoke over the next five years, culminating in the celebration of the college's sesquicentennial in 1987. The College History Collection in the Williston Memorial Library is a valuable resource for research on the history of women's education.

Institutional Self-Description. "Mount Holyoke's liberal tradition is strengthened by its special commitment to women. Each student's thinking is refined as she is introduced to problems in science and in the humanities. Acquisition and development of the crucial qualities of clear thought, generous judgment, and tenacious purpose are the aim of a Mount Holyoke education."

North Adams State College
Church St., North Adams, MA 01247
Telephone: (413) 664-4511

2,256 undergraduates

	Amer. Ind.	Asian Amer.	Blacks	Hispanics	Whites
F	6	8	14	8	1,121
M	2	11	12	6	1,051
%	0.4	0.9	1.2	0.6	97.0

 AAUW

This four-year, state-supported college, located in the Berkshires, enrolls some 2,900 students. Established as a women's college and teacher-training school in 1894, North Adams State is now coeducational. It offers bachelor's programs in the liberal arts, sciences, business, and education. A summer session and evening classes are available, as well as an adult continuing education program.

Fifty-two percent of the 2,256 undergraduates are women; the majority of women are under age 25. Seven percent of women attend part-time. For the 21 percent of undergraduates who commute, the campus is accessible by public transportation. On-campus parking is available.

College-operated childcare facilities can accommodate 85 percent of requests for service. Payment is based on a fixed daily fee, and non-credit students receive a special rate.

Policies to Ensure Fairness to Women. The Director of Special Services and Affirmative Action and two additional staff members have part-time responsibility for reviewing policy and practices relating to equal employment opportunity, handicapped accessiblilty, and sex equity for students. A formal campus grievance procedure is currently being revised to include sexual harassment. A self-designated Committee on the Status of Women reports to the Vice-President of Student Affairs. The Committee on Minority Affairs addresses the concerns of minority women.

Women in Leadership Positions. *Students.* There are ten available campus-wide leadership positions. In a recent three-year period, women held five of these posts for one year each. A woman heads the sole honorary society.

Faculty. Fifteen percent of the 99 full-time faculty are women, a proportion below average for comparable four-year colleges. There is 1 female faculty for every 100 female students; for males, the ratio is 8 to 100. The college reports that 3 members of the full-time faculty are Asian American women.

Administrators. Of the eight top administrators, the director of institutional research is female. Women chair two of the 14 departments: English and music. The Dean of Graduate and Continuing Studies is a woman. One of the 8 trustees is female. The 15 regents include 1 black woman and 1 white woman.

Women and the Curriculum. Twenty-five percent of women earn degrees in education, 25 percent in business, and 13 percent in social sciences. Two percent of women earn degrees in such nontraditional fields as mathematics and physical sciences. Women are 50 percent of students in the cooperative education and internship programs. There are no courses on women.

Women and Athletics. The women's athletic program includes an adequate range of team and individual sports. Intramural sports include water polo, floor hockey, and pool. Women also participate in the alpine racing and ski clubs. Thirty-seven percent of intramural athletes and 61 percent of intercollegiate athletes are female; one of the seven paid coaches is a woman. Intercollegiate sports offered are basketball, cross-country, field hockey, softball, tennis, and volleyball.

Housing and Student Organizations. Women's and coeducational dormitories, housing the 79 percent of undergraduates who reside on campus, do not have restrictive hours for visitors of the opposite sex. On-campus townhouse apartments accommodate both men and women. Two of the three residence-hall directors are women; staff are offered awareness-training on sexism and racism, sex education, and birth control.

Peers for Responsible Student Sexuality functions as a student advocacy group for women, as does the Women's Forum.

Special Services and Programs for Women. *Health and Counseling.* The student health service employs 2 male physicians and 3 female health-care providers. No information was provided on health services specific to women. The counseling center, staffed by 2 women and 2 men, offers counseling for gynecological problems, birth control, abortion, and rape and assault. The regular student health insurance covers abortion and maternity expenses at no extra charge.

Safety and Security. Measures consist of campus police with arrest authority, information sessions for women on campus safety and crime prevention, and a rape crisis center. No rapes were reported for 1980–81; no information is available on the incidence of assaults.

Career. Services include workshops, printed materials, and information on job discrimination in both traditional and nontraditional occupations. A special resource section for women provides information on careers and financial aid. The college maintains updated files of alumnae by specific careers and encourages networking between alumnae and female students.

Other. The Women's Forum sponsors the recently opened Women's Center. The 120-square-foot facility is run on a part-time basis by a student volunteer.

Institutional Self-Description. "North Adams State provides heavy emphasis on general education and liberal arts, with emphasis on professional preparation in areas of business, computer science, medical technology, teacher education, and human services. The mission also includes access for disadvantaged, transfer, and nontraditional students. A developing Women's Center offers services to women. The college provides a special atmosphere for students through its beautiful, safe, rural location, fine academic programs, and personal interest of diverse faculty."

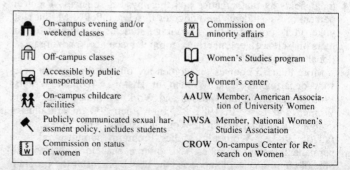

On-campus evening and/or weekend classes	Commission on minority affairs
Off-campus classes	Women's Studies program
Accessible by public transportation	Women's center
On-campus childcare facilities	AAUW Member, American Association of University Women
Publicly communicated sexual harassment policy, includes students	NWSA Member, National Women's Studies Association
Commission on status of women	CROW On-campus Center for Research on Women

Pine Manor College

400 Heath Street,
Chestnut Hill, MA 02167
Telephone: (671) 731-7000

Women in Leadership
★★★ students
★★★ faculty
★★★ adminstrators

615 undergraduates

	Amer. Ind.	Asian Amer.	Blacks	Hispanics	Whites
F	0	11	8	57	464
M	0	0	0	0	50
%	0.0	1.9	1.4	9.7	87.1

Founded in 1911 as a junior college for women, Pine Manor is now a four-year, liberal arts institution for women, although a few men attend part-time. Its suburban campus, just outside of Boston, attracts 615 students, 30 percent of whom attend part-time. The median age of all students is 19.

A limited range of associate and bachelor's degree programs is available, in addition to a continuing education program. Students can cross-register at Boston College and Babson College. Evening classes and a summer session are available. All but 5 percent of students live on campus in dormitories. The college is accessible by public transportation, and there is parking on campus.

Private childcare facilities are available off campus.

Policies to Ensure Fairness to Women. The Director of Career Services assumes part-time responsibility for monitoring compliance with sex-equity laws. A written policy on sexual harassment covers all members of the school community.

Women in Leadership Positions. *Students.* Women hold all campus-wide student offices.

Faculty. Fifteen of the 28 full-time faculty are women. There are 4 female faculty for every 100 female students.

Administrators. All but two of the top-ranking administrators are women. The executive vice president and chief business officer are men. Women head three of the four departments—fine and performing arts, natural and behavioral sciences, and social sciences. About half of the members of an important faculty committee are women; women are also about half the members of the Board of Trustees and of the faculty senate. The 1981 commencement speaker was a black woman.

Women and the Curriculum. All of the associate degrees earned by women are in arts and sciences. A few women take bachelor's degrees—all in fields traditional for women. Special programs in accounting, science, and computer science (''Beyond Computer Literacy'') encourage women to prepare for nontraditional occupations.

Four courses on women are offered by the departments of English, history, humanities, and Spanish: Images of Women in Drama, Women in European History, Women and Work, and Spanish Literature of the 19th Century—Focus on Women. Workshops for faculty examine the relationship of gender to the selection of major field.

Women and Athletics. For a school of its size, Pine Manor offers excellent opportunities to compete in individual and team sports. The intramural sports program includes canoeing, cross-country skiing, and platform tennis, as well as six popular team sports. Two of the four paid intercollegiate coaches are women. Intercollegiate sports offered are basketball, field hockey, lacrosse, softball, and tennis.

Special Services and Programs for Women. *Health and Counseling.* The student health service employs 2 male physicians and 3 female health-care providers. The student counseling center is staffed by 1 male and 1 female counselor. Counseling and treatment for birth control and gynecological problems are available, in addition to abortion and rape and assault counseling. Student health insurance covers maternity expenses.

Safety and Security. Measures consist of campus police with authority to make arrests, high-intensity lighting in all areas, and information on campus safety. No rapes or assaults on women were reported for 1980–81.

Career. The college promotes networking between students and alumnae, encourages the use of files on alumnae careers, and offers information, career workshops, and lectures on nontraditional occupations.

Other. Theater and other women's arts programs are sponsored by the division of fine and performing arts. Assertiveness-training sessions are available. UMOJA is an advocacy group for minority students.

Returning Women Students. Open College, which conducts the adult education program, operates a Continuing Education for Women Center that attracts 60 reentry women. Another 200 women are enrolled in continuing education courses.

Institutional Self-Description. None provided.

Radcliffe College: See Harvard University

Smith College

Northampton, MA 01063
Telephone: (413) 584-2700

Women in Leadership
★★★ students
★★ faculty
★★★ administrators

★ **Women and the Curriculum**

★★★ **Women and Athletics**

2,550 undergraduates

	Amer. Ind.	Asian Amer.	Blacks	Hispanics	Whites
F	4	79	142	25	2,231
M	0	0	0	0	11
%	0.2	3.2	5.7	1.0	90.0

AAUW

Founded in 1871, and the largest of the original Seven Sisters colleges, Smith is a liberal arts college for women that attracts 2,850 students to its campus in the small town of Northampton. There are 2,550 undergraduates, virtually all of whom attend full-time. Membership in the Five College Cooperative Program with Mount Holyoke, University of Massachusetts, Hampshire, and Amherst gives Smith students the opportunity to take a wide variety of courses on these other campuses. Nearly all students live on campus.

Private childcare facilities are available off campus.

Policies to Ensure Fairness to Women. Matters pertaining to sex-fair-employment laws are administered on a part-time basis by the Dean of Faculty, the Personnel Director, and the Secretary of the College. Of the three, the Dean of the Faculty has the authority to make policy in this area. Sex-equity issues are the part-time responsibility of the Assistant to the President, who can also make policy. Handicapped-access policies and practices fall within the jurisdiction of the Assistant to the President for Campus Planning, who assumes the part-time responsibility for overseeing implementation of laws and can make policy.

Staff and faculty, but not students, are protected by a formal policy prohibiting sexual harassment. Complaints are resolved through a campus grievance procedure.

Women in Leadership Positions. *Students.* Women hold all campus-wide student leadership positions.

Faculty. Women are 39 percent of the 262 full-time faculty. There are 4 female faculty for every 100 female students.

Administrators. Women occupy the positions of President, chief student-life officer, head librarian, director of institutional research, and director of athletics. Thirty percent of the 27 departments are chaired by women. The Dean of the Division of Social Sciences and History is a woman.

Women and the Curriculum. Most degrees are awarded in social sciences (35 percent), fine arts (16 percent), letters (13 percent), and biology (11 percent). Seven percent of the women graduate in mathematics or physical sciences. A Dual Degree Program in Engineering is available.

While there is no Women's Studies Program, a faculty project called Women and Social Change has encouraged the development of courses on women and the inclusion of women in such courses as Religious Expression in the Renaissance, Criminology, and Philosophy of Science. Ten courses on women are offered, including The Psychology of Sex Roles, Women and Philosophy, and Women in American Theatre.

Minority Women. Minority women are 10 percent of the student body; advocacy groups include the Black Students Association, the Asian Students Association, and a student chapter of the NAACP.

The Afro-American studies department is chaired by a black woman. A black woman is chief student-life officer. Two black women serve on the Board of Trustees. The student counseling center employs 1 minority woman counselor, and 3 of the 36 residence-hall directors are members of minority groups. Staff are offered training in avoiding racial bias.

Women and Athletics. The athletic program offers an outstanding program as well as unusual facilities for crew and squash. Thirteen intercollegiate sports draw 260 women athletes. Intramural sports include basketball, paddle tennis, soccer, softball, swimming, and table tennis. Seven of the eleven paid varsity coaches are women. All intercollegiate teams play in tournaments. Intercollegiate sports offered are basketball, cross-country, field hockey, gymnastics, lacrosse, riding, soccer, softball, squash, swimming and diving, tennis, track and field, and volleyball.

Housing and Student Organizations. In addition to dormitories, there are two cooperative houses and one apartment cluster. Visiting hours for men are not restricted.

Special Services and Programs for Women. *Health and Counseling.* The student health service is staffed by 2 full-time, female physicians, 1 part-time, female physician, and 5 female health-care providers. The student counseling center employs 3 female and 2 male counselors. Counseling and medical treatment for gynecological problems, birth control, and rape and assault are offered, in addition to abortion counseling. Student health insurance covers abortion expenses.

Safety and Security. Measures consist of campus police protection, night-time campus bus service to residence areas, high-intensity lighting, emergency telephone and alarm systems, and information on campus safety. No information was provided on the incidence of rapes and assaults.

Career. The college promotes networking between students and alumnae, encourages students to consult files on alumnae careers, and offers lectures, career workshops, and information on non-traditional occupations.

Other. A Women's Center, budgeted at $4,215, operates under the supervision of the Student Affairs Office. Coordinated part-time by a student volunteer, the center serves 1,500 women annually, mainly undergraduates, one-quarter of them black women. The center sponsors an annual women's week and women's theater and art shows. The Service Organization of Smith (S O S) sponsors a battered women's program. The Lesbian Alliance is a campus advocacy organization.

Special Features. The Sophia Smith Collection, one of the richest archives in the U.S., contains original papers, reports, publications, and other significant documents relevant to the lives of women both in the U.S. and internationally. Strong collections include those on Margaret Sanger, women and peace, women and the Civil War, the women's suffrage movement, and the performing arts.

Institutional Self-Description. "The College takes its mission to be the provision of the best possible liberal arts education for women of all ages and the provision of the counseling and networks which will enable women to move with the greatest ease into the careers and occupations of their choice on graduation. The college bases the highest premium on intellectual achievement and on the development of leadership in women."

Southeastern Massachusetts University
Old Westport Road
North Dartmouth, MA 02747
Telephone: (617) 999-8000

★ **Women and the Curriculum**

4,825 undergraduates

	Amer. Ind.	Asian Amer.	Blacks	Hispanics	Whites
F	4	13	65	14	1,683
M	10	16	65	11	2,853
%	0.3	0.6	2.8	0.5	95.8

 AAUW

Southeastern Massachusetts University was founded in 1895 as a comprehensive college. It is located in North Dartmouth, a community which contains substantial numbers of black and Portuguese residents. The 7,387 students include 4,825 undergraduates, 37 percent of whom are women. Six percent of students attend part-time. The median age of undergraduates is 20.

The university offers bachelor's degrees in a range of fields, including business, engineering, social sciences, psychology, health professions, and liberal arts. It provides evening classes on and off campus, a summer session, and self-paced/contract learning. Nine hundred women participate in continuing education, administered by Continuing Studies and Special Programs. Seventy-two percent of students commute, using free on-campus parking or public transportation.

Private childcare is available near campus.

Policies to Ensure Fairness to Women. A full-time Affirmative Action Officer reviews policies and advises the President on matters concerning equal employment opportunity, sex equity for students, and handicapped accessibility. A policy on sexual harassment is being formulated. The Comission on the Status of Women, which meets regularly and takes public stands on issues, is appointed by the President and reports to the trustees. An Affirmative Action Office and Committee address the concerns of minority women.

Women in Leadership Positions. *Students.* Women have limited opportunities to exercise campus-wide leadership. In recent years, a woman has held one of the 19 leadership positions available—president of the student union board—for two years.

Faculty. The full-time faculty of 301 includes 65 women. The ratio of female faculty to female students is 4 to 100; for males, it is 8 to 100.

Administrators. All top-level administrative positions are held by men. The Dean of Arts and Sciences and the Dean of the College of Nursing are women. Of 27 departments, eight (history, economics, education, design, music, and three in health professions) are chaired by women. Two of 8 trustees and 2 of 15 regents are women. In one recent year, the commencement speaker was a woman, as was a recipient of an honorary degree.

Women and the Curriculum. Most women earn degrees in health professions (20 percent), business (16 percent), and psychology (16 percent). Four percent major in engineering, mathematics, or physical sciences.

A permanently appointed full-time faculty member is responsible for the Women's Studies Program, which offers an 18-credit undergraduate minor and the B.A. through Interdisciplinary Studies. Recent courses include Women Writers, Women in Contemporary Society, and Philosophy of Feminism. Courses in the departments of education and business and the College of Nursing address some issues specific to women.

Women and Athletics. Forty-one percent of intercollegiate athletes and 30 percent of intramural athletes are women. Intramural sports are coeducational. Three of the 20 paid coaches for intercollegiate sports are women. Intercollegiate sports are basketball, cross-country, fencing, field hockey, softball, swimming and diving, track, and volleyball.

Housing and Student Organizations. Single-sex suites in coeducational buildings, with unrestricted visitation, house the 28 percent of students who live on campus. Residence-hall staff are offered awareness-training on sexism, sex education, racism, birth control, and rape. Advocacy groups for women include a chapter of NOW, the Women's Center, and the Black Student Union.

Special Services and Programs for Women. *Health and Counseling.* Three male physicians and 4 female health-care providers staff the student health center and provide gynecological and birth control treatment. The counseling center employs 2 men, 1 white woman and 1 minority woman, who receive in-service training in the avoidance of sex-role stereotyping and stress. Counseling on gynecological problems, birth control, abortion, and rape and assault is available. The counseling center also sponsors assertiveness training and a women's week.

Safety and Security. Measures consist of campus police, nighttime escort for women students, high-intensity lighting, emergency telephones, self-defense and safety information courses, and a rape crisis center. For 1980–81, one rape was reported.

Career. The university provides career workshops on nontraditional occupations, programs by women in nontraditional professions, nonsexist/nonracist printed material on nontraditional fields of study, and information on job discrimination. Each year the Placement Office sponsors a program on women and employment. SMU has a student chapter of the Society for Women Engineers.

Other. Women's Center serves 500 students, community members, and university staff each year. One of the center's salaried co-directors is always a student. The center sponsors the battered women's and displaced homemakers' programs, and organizes theater and other women's arts programs.

Institutional Self-Description. ''SMU has a well-established Women's Center, an active Women's Studies Program, and a women's literary magazine. We encourage women science and technology majors. There are many feminist women (and men) administrators at high levels. A woman who attends SMU can find ample support. And she can help us do more!''

Suffolk University
41 Temple Street, Boston, MA 02114
Telephone: (617) 723-4700

3,058 undergraduates

	Amer. Ind.	Asian Amer.	Blacks	Hispanics	Whites
F	0	7	70	2	1,238
M	5	16	51	3	1,577
%	0.2	0.8	4.1	0.2	94.8

An independent, non-residential institution founded in 1906, Suffolk University enrolls over 6,000 students. Forty-four percent of

the approximately 3,000 undergraduates are women. About 22 percent of the women attend part-time. The median age of all undergraduate students is 21.

Bachelor's and master's programs are offered in the liberal arts and sciences, management, and law. Two-year degree programs are also available. Part-time programs are available on both the graduate and undergraduate levels, and there are weekend and summer session classes, as well as on- and off-campus evening classes. No on-campus parking is available; the campus is served by public transportation.

Childcare facilities are available near the campus.

Policies to Ensure Fairness to Women. An equal opportunity officer serves part-time to review policies and practices relating to equal-employment-opportunity, sex-equity, and handicapped-access legislation. A written policy prohibits the sexual harassment of faculty and staff, but not of students. Complaints are resolved through a formal campus grievance procedure. A Committee on Minority Affairs addresses the concerns of minority women.

Women in Leadership Positions. *Students.* Women have some opportunities to exercise campus-wide leadership. In recent years, 26 percent of the student leadership positions have been held by women, including presiding officer of the student senate, editor-in-chief of the campus newspaper and, for two years, manager of the campus radio station. Three of the eleven presidents of honorary societies are women.

Faculty. The 185-member full-time faculty is 22 percent female, a proportion somewhat below the national average. There are 4 female faculty for every 100 female students and 10 male faculty for every 100 male students.

Administrators. All top-level administrative positions are held by men, as are the three deanships. Women chair two of the 17 departments: chemistry, and government and economics. Two of 6 recent honorary degree recipients were women, as were 12 of the 30 speakers in major lecture series, including 3 Hispanic women and a black woman.

Women and the Curriculum. Most bachelor's degrees awarded to women are in social sciences (37 percent) and business (20 percent); 3 percent are in the nontraditional fields of mathematics and the physical sciences. The college sponsors programs to encourage women to prepare for careers in accounting, computer science, and law enforcement. Eighty percent of the students in cooperative education and 65 percent of those in science field-service programs are women.

There are no courses on women. An official committee is responsible for collecting curricular materials on women. The department of business offers instruction on the problems of job discrimination, sexual harassment in the workplace, and women in management.

Women and Athletics. There are limited opportunities for participation in competitive individual and team sports. Fourteen percent of the 430 intramural athletes and 19 percent of the 135 intercollegiate athletes are women. One of the 7 paid coaches is a woman. The intercollegiate sports offered are basketball, cross-country, and tennis.

Special Services and Programs for Women. *Health and Counseling.* The student health service employs 1 female physician and 2 female health-care providers, and refers students to Massachusetts General Hospital for medical treatment. The counseling center, staffed by 5 female and 3 male counselors, offers rape and assault counseling.

Safety and Security. Measures consist of a campus police force with weapons training and arrest authority, high-intensity lighting, a general alarm system, self-defense courses for women, and information sessions on campus safety. No rapes and two assaults on women were reported on campus for 1980–81.

Career. Career planning services include information on nontraditional fields of study for women, and on job discrimination, updated files of alumnae by specific careers, and programs to establish contacts between alumnae and female students.

Other. The Women's Program Center, operated by the Director of Student Activity, has an annual budget of $3,035 and serves as the major on-campus advocacy group for women.

Returning Women Students. The adult continuing education program enrolls 1,002 reentry women, 50 percent of whom are members of minority groups. A reentry workshop for women is offered to undergraduates.

Institutional Self-Description. "The Women's Program Center of Suffolk acts as an organizational body for the efforts of individuals concerned with the welfare of Suffolk women and women in general. Recognizing the current debate concerning issues related to women, the center endeavors to provide a forum for women at Suffolk to enter into this debate, to understand the issues, and to fully discuss their ramifications as they relate to individuals and to society as a whole."

Swain School of Design
19 Hawthorn St.
New Bedford, MA 02740
Telephone: (617) 997-7831

Women in Leadership
★★★ students
★ faculty
★★★ administrators

193 undergraduates

	Amer. Ind.	Asian Amer.	Blacks	Hispanics	Whites
F	1	0	6	11	87
M	1	0	2	5	78
%	1.1	0.0	4.2	8.4	86.4

Founded in 1881, the Swain School of Design is a private, four-year college of art and design. Fifty-four percent of the 193 undergraduates are women; 6 percent of women attend part-time. The median age of all students is 20. Students may earn a bachelor of fine arts degree with majors in design, printmaking, painting, and sculpture. Liberal arts and photography courses are also available. Adult students are served by a continuing education program. All students live off campus or commute. The campus is accessible by public transportation; on-campus parking is available.

The college childcare facility can accommodate six children or 10 percent of students' requests. Although the service is free, it is not available on a daily basis. Additional, private childcare facilities are located near the campus.

Policies to Ensure Fairness to Women. The Dean of the College has part-time responsibility for policy on equal employment opportunity and handicapped access. The Title IX Coordinator is responsible, on a part-time basis, for sex equity for students.

Women in Leadership Positions. *Students.* Women held the single campus-wide leadership post, president of the student body, twice during a recent three-year period.

Faculty. Twenty-five percent of a full-time faculty of 12 are women. There are 3 female faculty for every 100 female students and 10 male faculty for every 100 male students.

Administrators. Women hold the posts of chief business officer and head librarian; the chief executive officer and the chief academic officer are men. One woman serves on the 6-member faculty personnel committee. Six of the 16 college trustees are women.

Women and the Curriculum. All bachelor's degrees awarded on this campus are fine arts; 49 percent are earned by women. Half of the student internships go to women. The college does not offer courses on women.

Women and Athletics. Information was not provided.

Special Services and Programs for Women. *Health and Counseling.* The college does not have student health or counseling services.

Safety and Security. Measures consist of local police whose jurisdiction includes the campus. No rapes or assaults on women were reported for 1980-81.

Institutional Self-Description. "The Swain School of Design is a small professional school of art and design with 170 students and 15 faculty members. Every student is well-known by faculty and by other students. As a result, needs of students are handled on an individual basis through the natural relationships that exist on a small campus. Women students, as well as others, find this a congenial, supporting atmosphere."

University of Lowell
University Avenue, Lowell, MA 01854
Telephone: (617) 452-5000

Women in Leadership
★ students

★ Women and the Curriculum

9,036 undergraduates

	Amer. Ind.	Asian Amer.	Blacks	Hispanics	Whites
F	0	10	29	23	2,904
M	0	51	57	23	5,721
%	0.0	0.7	1.0	0.5	97.8

 NWSA

The University of Lowell is a public, four-year institution created in 1976 by the merger of a teachers' preparatory college and a textile institute. Now a comprehensive university emphasizing business, engineering, and the sciences, Lowell enrolls 11,964 students. Of the 9,036 undergraduates, 33 percent are women; 21 percent of women attend part-time. The median age of undergraduate students is 20. Alternative scheduling includes on-campus evening classes and a summer session. The division of continuing education administers adult education. Seventy-five percent of students commute to campus by public transportation or car. On-campus parking is provided, with free transportation from distant lots.

Private childcare is available near campus.

Policies to Ensure Fairness to Women. The full-time Affirmative Action Officer and part-time Title IX Officer—both voting members of policymaking bodies—are responsible for equal educational and employment opportunity and for accessibility for the handicapped. A sexual harassment policy which incorporates a formal campus grievance procedure to resolve complaints has been communicated to faculty, staff, and students.

Women in Leadership Positions. *Students.* Women held nearly one-quarter of the student leadership positions available during recent years: president of the student court, editor of the newspaper (twice), manager of the radio station, residence-hall council president (three times), and sophomore class president. Three of 12 honorary societies have women presidents.

Faculty. Of 414 full-time faculty, 21 percent are women. There are 4 female faculty for every 100 female students and 8 male faculty for every 100 male students.

Administrators. Of nine top-level campus-wide administrators, the chief student-life officer and the director of institutional research are women. Three of seven deans (College of Liberal Arts, College of Health Professions, and College of Education) are women. Women chair four of 30 departments: economics, sociology, nursing, and academic studies.

Women and the Curriculum. Most women major in education (22 percent), health professions (20 percent), and business (19 percent). Five percent of women study engineering. In all, 10 percent of women graduate in nontraditional areas. Lowell offers a Women in Science Program to encourage women to prepare for careers in science.

The Women's Studies Program, which awards an undergraduate minor, offers 20 courses through the departments of English, history, political science, psychology, sociology, language, economics, and biology. The program is directed by a full-time faculty member, and a university committee is responsible for its development.

Women and Athletics. Women participate in club and intercollegiate sports. Twenty-five percent of intercollegiate athletes are women; they receive 20 percent of athletic scholarships. Twelve of 21 paid varsity coaches are women. The intercollegiate sport in which women participate is tennis.

Housing and Student Organizations. Twenty-five percent of students live on campus in single-sex and coeducational dormitories, all without visitation restrictions, and in students family housing. Two white women and one minority woman are among the seven residence-hall directors.

Social fraternities and sororities provide housing; 3 percent of undergraduate women join sororities. The Women's Studies Center and the Society for Women Engineers (with 40 members) serve as advocates for women.

Special Services and Programs for Women. *Health and Counseling.* The health service consists of 2 male physicians, and 3 female and 2 male staff members. Regular student health insurance provides both abortion and maternity benefits. The counseling center is staffed by 2 white women, 1 minority woman, and 1 man. They provide counseling on gynecological problems, birth control, abortion, and rape and assault. The counselors are trained on avoidance of sex-role stereotyping and racial bias, and on providing assistance to displaced homemakers.

Safety and Security. Measures include campus police with arrest authority, night-time campus-wide bus service, high-intensity lighting, self-defense courses, information on safety and rape and assault prevention, and a rape crisis center. No rapes or assaults were reported for 1980–81.

Other. A Women's Center, run by volunteers, serves undergraduate women. The Women's Studies Program sponsors theater and other women's arts programs; the counseling center provides assertiveness training.

Institutional Self-Description. "There is a variety of academic, social, and administrative support groups, which enthusiastically and purposefully respond to women's needs on campus. As a newly formed university through a merger of two older institutions, we have by necessity adopted a flexible and responsible approach to our new status and the new opportunities before us."

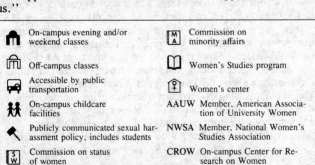

On-campus evening and/or weekend classes		Commission on minority affairs	
Off-campus classes		Women's Studies program	
Accessible by public transportation		Women's center	
On-campus childcare facilities	AAUW	Member, American Association of University Women	
Publicly communicated sexual harassment policy, includes students	NWSA	Member, National Women's Studies Association	
Commission on status of women	CROW	On-campus Center for Research on Women	

University of Massachusetts, Amherst
Amherst, MA 01003
Telephone: (413) 545-0111

★ ★ ★ **Women and the Curriculum**

18,842 undergraduates

	Amer. Ind.	Asian Amer.	Blacks	Hispanics	Whites
F	23	97	332	120	7,791
M	21	141	377	185	9,490
%	0.2	1.3	3.8	1.6	93.0

 **AAUW NWSA**

Established in 1863 under the Morrill Act to meet the Commonwealth's need for an agricultural college, the University of Massachusetts at Amherst attracts over 24,000 students to its undergraduate, graduate, and professional programs. The university is part of the five-college consortium which also includes Amherst College, Mount Holyoke College, Hampshire College, and Smith College. Continuing education classes serve the adult student. Alternative schedules, which include evening classes and a summer session, and instruction at off-campus locations, are available.

Women are 45 percent of the 18,842 undergraduates. The median age of undergraduates is 19. For the 55 percent of students who live off campus or commute, the university is accessible by public transportation. On-campus parking is available for a fee, with free transportation from distant parking lots.

The University Child Care System accommodates 122 children; fees are on a sliding scale. Private childcare arrangements may be made close to campus.

Policies to Ensure Fairness to Women. Three full-time Affirmative Action Coordinators are responsible for policy or monitor compliance in matters of equal employment opportunity, sex equity for students, and access for the handicapped. Complaints of sexual harassment are currently handled informally and confidentially; a formal grievance procedure is being developed. The Committee on the Status of Women meets often; it reports to the faculty senate and publicly addresses the concerns of women students, including minority women. There is also a Committee on Minority Affairs, which addresses the concerns of minority women.

Women in Leadership Positions. *Students.* Women hold less than a third of the student leadership positions. In recent years, women have presided over the student senate and the student court (two times), served as editor-in-chief of the newspaper, and managed the campus radio station.

Faculty. Women make up 16 percent of a full-time faculty of 1,204. According to a recent report, 9 black, 1 American Indian, 4 Asian American, and 7 Hispanic women are on the faculty. The ratio of female faculty to female students is 2 to 100. The ratio of male faculty to male students is 10 to 100.

Administrators. The chief planning and budget officer is a black woman. All other top administrative posts are filled by men. Women chair seven of 90 departments. The Director of Continuing Education is female.

Women and the Curriculum. The most popular majors for undergraduate women are education (14 percent), business and administration (11 percent), home economics (10 percent), social sciences (10 percent), and agriculture (9 percent). Twelve percent of women graduate with bachelor's degrees in nontraditional areas. One-tenth of the engineering students are female; the proportion of degrees in agriculture awarded to women is above the national average. All women graduating with two-year degrees major in natural sciences.

The Women's Studies Program offers an undergraduate major and a certificate minor. Students interested in Women's Studies may choose from 100 or more courses available each year on campus and also through the Five Colleges consortium, in such areas as psychology, law, politics, history, literature, health care, and African-American studies. Among the more than 30 courses offered on the Amherst campus are Introduction to Women's Studies: Issues for Women of the '80s; Foundations of Feminism; The Confessional Novel; Contemporary Women's Fiction; Women and the Health Care System; and Feminist Theory.

Instruction on the teaching of coeducational sports is part of the physical education curriculum. The school of business covers such issues as discrimination in the workplace and women in management. Sexism and the curriculum is a topic addressed by educational programs for the faculty.

Minority Women. Although the representation of minority women is not large, many courses, services, and organizations serve minority students. Six of the residence-hall staff are minority women, as are two of the professional staff in the counseling service. Residence and counseling staffs are offered awareness-training in the avoidance of racial bias. Fifteen percent of the users of Everywoman's Center are from minority groups. The Third World Women's Task Force is an advocacy group located in the Third World Women's Center.

Women and Athletics. No information was provided on intramural or club sports. Intercollegiate sports available to women are basketball, field hockey, gymnastics, lacrosse, skiing, soccer, swimming and diving, tennis, track and field, and volleyball. Approximately 15 percent of athletic scholarships go to women.

Housing and Student Organizations. For on-campus residents, single-sex and coeducational dormitories and housing for married students and single parents with children are available. A married woman student whose spouse is not enrolled may live in married students' housing. Dormitories do not restrict hours for visitors of the opposite sex. Residence-hall staff are offered awareness-training on sexism, sex education, racism, birth control, and sexual assault.

Approximately 4 percent of the undergraduate women belong to social sororities. Sororities and fraternities provide housing for their members. Among the campus organizations that serve as advocates for women are the Women's Media Project, the People's Gay Alliance, Women and Life on Earth, the Poor Women's Task Force, the Lesbian Union and The Third World Women's Task Force.

Special Services and Programs for Women. *Health and Counseling.* The student health service provides medical attention specific to women, including gynecological, birth control, abortion, and rape and assault treatment. Six of 18 physicians are female. The regular student health insurance covers abortion and maternity services at no extra cost. The counseling center, staffed by 7 women and 10 men, provides counseling of particular concern to women. Staff receive in-service training on sex-role stereotyping, racial bias, and handicapped awareness.

Safety and Security. Measures include campus police with arrest authority, high-intensity lighting, emergency telephones, self-defense courses for women, information sessions on safety and crime prevention, and a rape line, investigative unit, and crisis center. A total of 43 assaults and one rape were reported for 1980–81.

Career. Nontraditional career workshops, role-model panels, and printed materials, as well as a job-bank resource library are available.

Other. The Everywoman's Center funded at $91,795 annually, sponsors a number of activities and programs, including services for battered women and displaced homemakers, guest speakers, an annual women's week, cultural events, a program to build confidence in mathematics, and a telephone line of information, referral, and support.

Institutional Self-Description. "The women's community at UMass/Amherst and in the surrounding communities is well organized, diverse, and highly vocal on issues affecting women on campus and in the community, as well as on issues of national and international significance. There is a strong and growing sense of solidarity around women's issues, as evidenced by the strength of campus and community groups.''

University of Massachusetts, Boston
Harbor Campus, Boston, MA 02125
Telephone: (617) 287-1900

Women in Leadership ★ faculty	★★ Women and the Curriculum

6,837 undergraduates

	Amer. Ind.	Asian Amer.	Blacks	Hispanics	Whites
F	8	39	337	84	2,974
M	6	42	205	109	2,910
%	0.2	1.2	8.1	2.9	87.6

🏠 🏛 🚐 👫 🅼🅰 📖 ⚕ AAUW

The University of Massachusetts at Boston is a public, coeducational, urban university founded in 1965. Its 7,947 students include 6,837 undergraduates. Fifty-one percent of undergraduates are women; 9 percent of women attend part-time. The median age of undergraduates is 26; 9 percent of the undergraduate women are over age 40.

The university offers bachelor's and master's degrees in a range of liberal arts fields. Evening and summer session classes are available. All students commute and the campus is accessible by public transportation. On-campus parking is available at a fee; there is free transportation from distant parking lots.

Campus childcare facilities give priority to low-income students who are single parents. Facilities accommodate 53 percent of students' requests. Fees are assessed on a sliding scale.

Policies to Ensure Fairness to Women. The Director of Affirmative Action monitors compliance with equal employment opportunity, sex equity for students, and accessibility for the handicapped. A formal policy on sexual harassment is being developed; complaints are handled through a formal grievance procedure. The Commission on Minority Affairs addresses the concerns of minority women.

Women in Leadership Positions. *Students.* Of four campus-wide student positions, women edited the newspaper once and managed the radio station twice in a recent three-year period.

Faculty. Of 366 full-time faculty members, 29 percent are women, including 5 black, 2 Asian American, and 3 Hispanic women. There are 3 female faculty for every 100 female students and 8 male faculty for every 100 male students.

Administrators. All top administrators are men. Women chair five of 32 departments: psychology, Spanish/Portuguese, community planning, human services, and applied language and mathematics.

Women and the Curriculum. Most women earn degrees in social sciences (27 percent), letters (13 percent), psychology (13 percent), foreign languages (10 percent), and business (9 percent). Three percent of women graduate in mathematics and physical sciences. Academic Support sponsors a program to build skills in mathematics. UMB offers a competency-based program in public and community service; 73 percent of the participants are women.

The Women's Studies Program offers an undergraduate minor and the B.A. as an individual major. More than thirty courses are offered through the program and 13 departments. Recent titles include Women and Society, Women in Third World Countries, Afro-American Women Writers, Social History of Women, Philosophy and Feminism, and Images of Women in Literature. Field work in Women's Studies is also available. The School of Nursing provides instruction about midwifery, home delivery, and reproductive choice.

Women and Athletics. Twelve percent of intramural and 39 percent of intercollegiate athletes are women, as are two of six paid intercollegiate coaches. The intramural program includes co-educational floor hockey, basketball, softball, and volleyball. The intercollegiate sports offered are basketball, soccer, softball, and volleyball.

Special Services and Programs for Women. *Health and Counseling.* The health service, staffed by 3 female and 5 male physicians, provides gynecological treatment and birth control. The counseling center employs 4 men and 1 woman, and provides counseling in gynecology, birth control, abortion, and rape and assault.

Safety and Security. Measures consist of campus police and high-intensity lighting. For 1980-81, no rapes and 29 assaults (13 on women) were reported.

Career. UMB provides workshops and speakers on nontraditional occupations.

Other. The Women's Center, sponsored by the Student Government, operates on a budget of $954 and serves some 200 students. The center functions as an advocacy group for women students. There is a women's self-defense group.

Institutional Self-Description. "Quality programs for low tuition, an option for a competency-based program in public and community service, flexibility in scheduling, the presence of an older student body, and ease of access by either public or private transportation make UMass/Boston an attractive place for women, particularly those within commuting distance."

Wellesley College
Wellesley, MA 02181
Telephone: (617) 235-0320

Women in Leadership
★★★ students
★★★ faculty
★★★ administrators

★★★ **Women and the Curriculum**

★★ **Women and Athletics**

1,939 undergraduates

	Amer. Ind.	Asian Amer.	Blacks	Hispanics	Whites
F	2	85	152	39	1,567
M	0	0	0	0	0
%	0.1	4.6	8.2	2.1	85.0

AAUW NWSA CROW

Wellesley is one of the original Seven Sisters and remains an independent liberal arts college for women. Located in the Boston suburb of Wellesley, the school attracts 2,115 students to its campus. Virtually all of the 1,939 undergraduates attend full-time. The median age of all students is 21.

A variety of undergraduate degree programs is offered, in addition to a continuing education program. All classes meet on campus during the day. Eighty-seven percent of undergraduates live on campus, in dormitories or cooperative housing units. Wellesley is accessible by public transportation, and parking is available on campus.

Private childcare facilities are located on and off campus. The campus facility, which serves 50 pre-school-aged children of students, faculty, and staff, on a first-come, first-served basis, is able to meet most requests. Fees are based on ability to pay.

Policies to Ensure Fairness to Women. A staff member has the part-time responsibility for monitoring compliance with laws regulating handicapped access, sex equity, and sex-fair employment. A written policy prohibits sexual harassment of all members of the college community; it will be communicated to all concerned when a formal grievance procedure, now being discussed, has been formulated.

Women in Leadership Positions. *Students.* Women hold all student leadership positions.

Faculty. Fifty-five percent of the 193 full-time faculty members are women. There are 6 female faculty for every 100 female students.

Administrators. Three-fourths of the key administrators are women, the exceptions being the chief business officer and chief development officer. Women chair two-thirds of 29 departments, including economics, chemistry, mathematics, and physics. All six deans are women. About two-thirds of the Board of Trustees are female. The Academic Council has a majority of female faculty.

Women and the Curriculum. A third of women major in the social sciences. Other popular majors include letters (18 percent), psychology (11 percent), biology (10 percent), and fine arts (10 percent). Six percent of students earn degrees in the nontraditional fields of architecture, mathematics, and physical sciences. Special programs encourage women to study and prepare for careers in science, engineering, and computer science. The mathematics department sponsors a program to build confidence in mathematics.

A Women's Studies Program offers a major through more than 40 courses on women, including Sex Roles in Cross-Cultural Perspective, Sociology of the Black Family, Women in Antiquity, and Women and Women Writers in the Two Germanies Since 1945. An official committee works to expand Women's Studies as well as to collect and develop new curricular materials on women.

Faculty are offered workshops on sexism and the curriculum. The Center for Research on Women, founded in 1974, is unique on a college campus. It houses 30 social scientists who conduct research on such issues as employment policies, aging, and sex-role socialization. One of its programs awards fellowships to faculty engaged in Women's Studies. Wellesley students may work at the Center as research interns or work-study students, and may attend the lunch-seminars.

Minority Women. Fifteen percent of the undergraduates are minority women; a Committee on Minority Affairs addresses their concerns. Minority women have organized several advocacy groups: Ethos has 110 black members; Alianza has 10 Hispanic members; and the Asian Association has about 45 members. Two courses on black women are offered by Women's Studies.

Minority women hold a number of key administrative posts: the chief-student life officer is black; two departments are chaired, respectively, by an Asian American and an Hispanic; 2 of 6 deans are black, as are 2 members of the Board of Trustees; and the members of the Academic Council include 4 black and 4 Asian American women. One staff member of the student counseling center is a minority woman, as is one of the residence-hall directors. Counselors and residence-hall staff receive awareness training on racism.

Women and Athletics. The athletic program is excellent. The intercollegiate sports program draws 150 participants to a variety of individual and team sports, including some less common teams such as squash, crew, and fencing. One hundred women participate in intramural sports, which consist of crew—for which the school has special facilities (but not of competitive standards)—and soccer. Club sports attract 450 students. Of the 10 paid coaches for intercollegiate sports, 8 are women. Intercollegiate sports offered are basketball, crew, fencing, field hockey, lacrosse, soccer, squash, swimming and diving, tennis, and volleyball.

Special Services and Programs for Women. *Health and Counseling.* The student health service employs 5 female physicians, 18 female health-care providers, and 1 male physician. The student counseling center is staffed by five female counselors. Counseling and treatment are provided for gynecological problems, birth control, and venereal disease; counseling (but not treatment) for abortion and rape and assault. Student health insurance covers maternity and abortion expenses.

Safety and Security. Measures consist of campus and local police protection, night-time escort service, an emergency telephone system within the dormitories, emergency alarms in buildings, and instruction on self-defense and campus safety. A rape crisis center is available. One rape and four assaults on women were reported for 1980-81.

Career. The Office for Careers provides information, workshops, and panel discussions on nontraditional careers, as well as access to networks with alumnae.

Other. The college sponsors a federally funded displaced homemaker program that is operated by the Center for Research on Women. Other programs include a women's lecture series and women's arts and theater productions. The Office of Continuing Education administers Continuing Education for Women. Headed by a full-time administrator, and operating out of its own center, the program attracts 218 reentry women.

In addition to minority women's groups, there are four support and advocacy organizations: Committee for Women's Concerns, Women's Alliance, Wellesley Lesbians and Friends, and Slater International Association (for foreign students).

Residence-hall staff receive awareness training on issues of homosexuality, anorexia nervosa, and sexism.

Institutional Self-Description. "Wellesley College is dedicated to the education of women. Its founder, Henry Fowle Durant, saw education as the way women could prepare themselves for 'great conflicts' and 'vast reforms in social life.' Throughout the years, Wellesley has encouraged women to make unconventional choices. Many graduates enter careers in business, law, and medicine—fields long dominated by men."

Wheaton College
Norton, MA 02766
Telephone: (617) 285-7722

Women in Leadership	Women and the
★★★ students	★ Curriculum
★★ faculty	
★★★ administrators	

1,336 undergraduates

	Amer. Ind.	Asian Amer.	Blacks	Hispanics	Whites
F	3	16	24	14	1,267
M	0	0	0	0	0
%	0.2	1.2	1.8	1.1	95.7

🚐 📖 ⚐ **AAUW**

Founded in 1834 as a female seminary, Wheaton has evolved into an independent, four-year, liberal arts college for women. Its rural campus, south of Boston, attracts 1,336 undergraduates. Less than 2 percent of the students attend part-time. The median age of all students is 20.

A range of undergraduate degree programs is available, in addition to a continuing education program. All classes are held on campus, during the day. Public transportation and on-campus parking at a fee are available to the few students who commute. Private childcare facilities are located off campus.

Policies to Ensure Fairness to Women. The Director of Personnel also serves as the affirmative action officer and is responsible full-time for monitoring compliance with laws regarding handicapped access, sex equity for students, and sex-fair employment. Complaints of sexual harassment are handled through a formal campus grievance procedure.

Women in Leadership Positions. *Students.* Women hold all student leadership positions.

Faculty. Forty-six percent of the 82 full-time faculty members are women. There are 3 women faculty for every 100 students.

Administrators. All key administrators, except the chief business officer, are women. Nearly half of the departments are chaired by women, including chemistry and mathematics. Women are well represented on the faculty senate (46 percent) and the Board of Trustees (50 percent). At a recent commencement, women received three of four honorary degrees.

Women and the Curriculum. Most degrees are awarded in the social sciences (35 percent), letters (16 percent), and biology (11 percent). Five percent are awarded in mathematics or physical sciences. The college offers programs for women seeking to prepare for nontraditional careers in science, engineering (dual degree with Georgia Institute of Technology), architecture, computer science, and electronics. A four-week January field experience in Tropical Ecology is also available.

The Women's Studies Program offers a five-course minor. Courses include Economics of Work and Family; Women, Sex, and Love in Greece and Rome; Women in Western Civilization; Women in Asia; and Social History of American Women.

In 1980-81, Wheaton was awarded a three-year grant from the federal government to integrate the new scholarship on women into the curriculum and, specifically, into the introductory courses in all departments. The grant will also underwrite the salaries of two visiting Women's Studies scholars for the 1982-83 school year. Faculty will participate in workshops about new scholarship on women. An official advisory committee of faculty and students is responsible for gathering curricular materials on women and for coordinating administration of the grant.

Minority Women. Six percent of undergraduate women are members of minority groups. The Black Students Society and the Intercultural Awareness Committee have been organized by minority women students. Among the academic department heads are 1 Asian American and 1 Hispanic woman. One black, 1 Asian American, and 1 Hispanic woman sit on the faculty senate. The Board of Trustees includes 1 black woman.

Women and Athletics. One hundred women participate in nine intercollegiate sports. A combination of individual and team sports attracts 300 women to intramural activities. Club sports draw 100 students. Six of 9 paid varsity coaches are women. Intercollegiate sports offered are cross-country, field hockey, lacrosse, sailing, soccer, softball, synchronized swimming, tennis, and volleyball.

Housing and Student Organizations. Virtually all students reside in campus dormitories that have restrictive hours for male visitors. Residence-hall staff receive awareness-training on sexism, sex education, racism, and birth control.

Women's Voice, the Intercultural Awareness Committee, and Women's Action, a lesbian group, are advocacy groups, in addition to the previously mentioned minority student organizations.

Special Services and Programs for Women. *Health and Counseling.* The student health service is staffed by a female and a male physician, as well as three female health-care providers; there is one female counselor on staff. Counseling and treatment are available for gynecological problems, birth control, abortion, and rape and assault. Student health insurance provides partial coverage for abortion and maternity expenses.

Safety and Security. Measures consist of campus and local police, night-time escort, high-intensity lighting, and instruction on self-defense and campus safety. No rapes were reported for 1980-81; information on assaults was not provided.

Career. The Career Planning Office offers mentor and internship programs for juniors. Other services include workshops on assertiveness, communication, and leadership; a summer job bank; panels, information, and career workshops on nontraditional occupations; and networking with alumnae.

Other. An annual women's week is sponsored by the Student Life Office; a women's lecture series by the office of the Provost; theater programs by the drama department.

Institutional Self-Description. "Wheaton, the oldest women's college in New England, offers an historic commitment to quality liberal arts training and a supportive environment for personal and intellectual growth. 'Education for independence' is Wheaton's contemporary mission, with the liberal arts update via computer literacy, writing skills, and career exploration programs."

Wheelock College
200 The Riverway, Boston, MA 02215
Telephone: (617) 734-5200

Women in Leadership
★★★ students
★★★ faculty
★★★ administrators

624 undergraduates

	Amer. Ind.	Asian Amer.	Blacks	Hispanics	Whites
F	0	7	40	3	552
M	0	0	2	1	11
%	0.0	1.1	6.8	0.7	91.4

Established in 1888, Wheelock is an independent, private college that enrolls 986 students. Ninety-eight percent of the 624 undergraduates are women. Bachelor's degrees are awarded only in education; graduate and continuing education degree programs are also available. Graduate classes meet during the evening on and off campus, and during the summer.

For the 40 percent of undergraduates who commute or live off campus, the school is easily reached by public transportation; there are no on-campus parking facilities.

Private childcare is available off campus.

Policies to Ensure Fairness to Women. The Director of Personnel has the part-time responsibility for examining policies and monitoring compliance with equal-employment-opportunity laws. The Director of Student Affairs and the Vice President for Administration have similar responsibilities regarding handicapped-access legislation.

Women in Leadership Positions. *Students.* Women hold all student leadership posts.

Faculty. Sixty-eight percent of the 44 full-time faculty are women. According to a recent report, 3 black women are among the full-time faculty. There are 5 female faculty for every 100 female students.

Administrators. Women hold most of the top administrative posts, although the President and Vice President are men. The Academic Dean, the Graduate Dean, and the Undergraduate Dean are women. Women chair two of nine departments: early childhood, and psychology/sociology. Half of the Board of Trustees are female. The 1981 commencement speaker was a woman.

Women and the Curriculum. All bachelor's degrees awarded are in education; a handful of two-year degrees are awarded in public services.

The English department offers two courses on women writers. An official committee promotes the development of courses on women.

Women and Athletics. The organized athletic program for women is limited. Five intramural teams attract 120 women; club sports are also available. One of the two paid coaches for varsity sports is a woman. The intercollegiate sports offered are field hockey and tennis.

Housing and Student Organizations. There are several housing arrangements for the 60 percent of undergraduates who live on campus: a cooperative house, coeducational dormitories, and women's dormitories. None have restrictions on visiting hours for members of the opposite sex. Residence-hall staff are offered awareness-training on birth control, sex education, and alcoholism. Black women have their own support and advocacy group, NIA.

Special Services and Programs for Women. *Health and Counseling.* The student health center is staffed by 17 women: 3 physicians and 14 health-care providers. Two female counselors staff the counseling center. Counseling and treatment are provided for gynecological problems and birth control, counseling for abortion and rape and assault.

Safety and Security. Measures include campus police, nighttime escort, high-intensity lighting, instruction on self-defense and campus safety, and a rape crisis center. No rapes and one assault on a woman were reported for 1980–81.

Other. The Women's Club functions as a Women's Center, with its own designated space and a budget of $800. Programs such as a women's week, a women's lecture series, and theater and art shows draw about 150 undergraduates and staff annually. The Returning Scholars Program assists reentry women; the Student Affairs Office conducts assertiveness-training workshops for women.

Institutional Self-Description. None provided.

Worcester State College
486 Chandler Street
Worcester, MA 01602
Telephone: (617) 752-7700

Women in Leadership
★ students
★ faculty

3,055 undergraduates

	Amer. Ind.	Asian Amer.	Blacks	Hispanics	Whites
F	1	1	21	8	1,738
M	1	2	22	14	1,194
%	0.1	0.1	1.4	0.7	97.7

 AAUW

This four-year, state-supported college, located near downtown Worcester, enrolls 5,581 students. Founded as a teachers' preparatory school in 1874, Worcester State now offers the bachelor's degree in liberal arts and sciences, as well as master's degrees. Adult education is available through the Program of Graduate and Continuing Education. The college also offers evening classes, both on and off campus, and a summer session.

The median age of undergraduates is 22. Fifty-nine percent of the 3,055 undergraduates are women, 12 percent of whom attend part-time. Eighty-five percent of undergraduates commute. Public transportaion is easily accessible and on-campus parking is available at a fee.

On-campus childcare facilities are available to students, faculty, and staff on a first-come, first-served basis. There are two three-hour sessions, plus lunch, and rates are based on a fixed fee per session. Most students' requests for this service can be accommodated.

Policies to Ensure Fairness to Women. A minority woman serves as Director of Affirmative Action and has full-time responsibility for review of policies and practices related to legislation on equal employment opportunity, accessibility for the handicapped, and sex equity.

Women in Leadership Positions. *Students.* Women students have good opportunities to exercise campus-wide leadership. There are ten elected positions available; in a recent three-year period, women held 47 percent of these student leadership posts, including presiding officer of the student body (two years), presiding officer of the student senate (one year), presiding officer of the student union board (one year), and senior class president (three years). Women also head two of the six honorary societies.

Faculty. Women constitute 30 percent of the 178 full-time faculty. There are 3 female faculty for every 100 female students and 11 male faculty for every 100 male students. The college reports that 2 full-time faculty members are Asian American women.

Administrators. A woman serves as Vice President for Academic Affairs; all other key administrators are men. Women chair six of the 24 departments: art, communication disorders, geography, nursing, elementary and early childhood education, and physical education for women. One of the 15 regents is a white woman, one a black woman.

Women and the Curriculum. Most women earn their degrees in education (30 percent), health professions (18 percent), psychology (14 percent), and social sciences (11 percent). Four percent of women major in such nontraditional fields as mathematics. There are no courses on women.

Women and Athletics. The intramural program offers only team sports to women, supplemented by club sports. Women have good opportunities to participate in both team and individual sports through the intercollegiate program. Sixty-seven percent of the 150 intercollegiate athletes are women, as are seven of the 22 paid intercollegiate coaches. The intercollegiate sports offered are basketball, cross-country, field hockey, softball, tennis, track and field, and volleyball.

Housing and Student Organizations. Single-sex dormitories house the 15 percent of undergraduates who reside on campus. The residence halls do not restrict hours for visitors of the opposite sex. Two of the four residence-hall directors are women, one of whom is a minority woman. Residence-hall staff are offered awareness training on sex education and birth control. Housing for married students is available and is open to spouses who are not enrolled in the college.

Special Services and Programs for Women. *Health and Counseling.* One male physician staffs the student health service on a part-time basis. The student counseling center has a staff of two women and one man; it offers counseling on birth control and abortion. The counseling center and Student Services sponsor assertiveness/leadership training. The regular student health insurance covers abortion and maternity expenses at no extra charge.

Safety and Security. Measures include campus police with arrest authority, information sessions on safety and rape and assault prevention for women, and a rape crisis center. Six assaults, none on women, were reported for 1980–81.

Career. Nonsexist/nonracist printed materials and job discrimination information on nontraditional occupations for women are available. The college also sponsors lectures and panels by women employed in nontraditional fields.

Institutional Self-Description. "Worcester State College offers a specialized undergraduate program in audiology and speech pathology in which 95 percent of the students are women. The campus is located in an urban area, with 300,000 people living within 20 miles of the college."

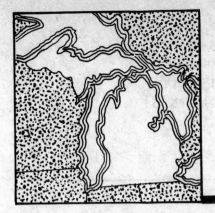

Albion College
Albion, MI 49224
Telephone: (517) 629-5511

Women in Leadership   ★ **Women and Athletics**
    ★ **students**

1,769 undergraduates

	Amer. Ind.	Asian Amer.	Blacks	Hispanics	Whites
F	0	0	17	5	776
M	0	0	16	9	930
%	0.0	0.0	1.9	8	97.3

AAUW NWSA

Founded in 1843, Albion is a private, four-year college affiliated with the Methodist Church. The college enrolls 1,784 students, 1,769 of them undergraduates. Women are 45 percent of the undergraduate population; just 1 percent of the women attend part-time. The median age of undergraduates is 20. Albion offers a range of liberal arts and science programs leading to the bachelor's degree. Summer session classes are available.

Free on-campus parking is available to the 2 percent of undergraduates who commute.

Private childcare facilities are located near the campus.

Policies to Ensure Fairness to Women. The Assistant to the Vice President for Student Life monitors compliance in matters relating to sex equity for students. The college has a Committee on Minority Affairs.

Women in Leadership Positions. *Students.* Women students have good opportunities to gain leadership experience. About one-third of the campus-wide student leadership positions have been held by women in recent years, including presiding officer of the student governing body and the student union board, and editor-in-chief of the campus newspaper. Six of the 15 presidents of honorary societies are women.

Faculty. Twenty-three percent of the 113 full-time faculty are women, a proportion slightly below the national average. There are 3 female faculty for every 100 female students and 9 male faculty for every 100 male students.

Administrators. All the chief administrators are men. Of the 23 departments women chair home economics, theater and speech, and physical education. One woman sits on the 7-member campus-wide tenure and promotions committee. Of a 4 recent recipients of alumni awards, 1 was a woman, as was 1 of the 6 speakers in a recent campus-wide lecture series.

Women and the Curriculum. The majority of degrees earned by women are in social sciences (26 percent), fine arts (10 percent), and letters (17 percent). Six percent of women earn degrees in mathematics or physical sciences. Fifty percent of students participating in college internship programs are women. No courses on women are offered.

Women and Athletics. Opportunities for women to participate in competitive individual and team sports are good. Albion offers a wide array of intramural and intercollegiate sports. Five of the nine paid intercollegiate coaches are women. The intercollegiate sports offered are archery, basketball, cross-country, field hockey, softball, swimming, tennis, track, and volleyball.

Housing and Student Organizations. Single-sex dormitories are available for the approximately 18 percent of students who live on campus; all dormitories have restricted hours for visitors of the opposite sex. Married-student and single-parent housing is also available. The four female and three male residence-hall directors receive awareness-training on racism and birth control.

Fifty-eight percent of the full-time undergraduate women belong to sororities. Two of the 463 women members of sororities are minority women. A Commission on the Status of Women functions as a student advocacy group for women.

Special Services and Programs for Women. *Health and Counseling.* The student health service employs one male physician and one female health-care provider. The counseling center's single counselor is male. Gynecological and rape and assault medical treatment are offered by the health service; the counseling center offers birth control, abortion, and rape and assault counseling. Counselors are offered in-service training on the avoidance of sex-role stereotyping.

Safety and Security. Measures consist of a campus police force without arrest authority, local police, night-time escort service for women, self-defense and campus safety courses for women, high-intensity lighting, and a rape crisis center. Two rapes and four assaults (two of them on women) were reported for 1980–81.

Institutional Self-Description. "Albion emphasizes career-related components in its liberal arts programs, opportunities for practicums and internships, and successful alumnae as role models."

Alpena Community College
Alpena, MI 49707
Telephone: (517) 356-9021

★ **Women and the Curriculum**

1,752 undergraduates

	Amer. Ind.	Asian Amer.	Blacks	Hispanics	Whites
F	3	6	18	0	716
M	7	14	29	2	949
%	0.6	1.2	2.7	0.1	95.5

This public, two-year college serves 1,752 students, 42 percent of whom are women. Sixty-two percent of the women attend part-time. Recent figures from the college indicate an increasing enrollment of women students, with 30 percent of the female population being over 40 years of age. The median age of all undergraduate students is 24.

Alpena offers a university-parallel curriculum and occupational training in business, technical, and vocational areas. The college also operates an adult Continuing Education Program. Evening classes, both on and off campus, and self-paced/contract learning are available.

Eighty-six percent of students commute to the campus, which is not accessible by public transportation. On-campus parking is available. Students who reside on campus live in coeducational dormitories with restrictive hours for visitors of the opposite sex. Private childcare facilities are available nearby.

Policies to Ensure Fairness to Women. The Director of Community Services serves as a part-time equal-employment-opportunity and educational-sex-equity officer, attending policy-making councils and committees as a voting member and reviewing policies and practices generated by these councils. Sexual harassment is prohibited by a written campus policy that has been publicly communicated to students, faculty, and staff. A formal grievance procedure is used in the resolution of complaints.

Women in Leadership Positions. *Students.* Women students have limited opportunities to exercise campus-wide leadership. In a recent three-year period, the editor-in-chief of the campus newspaper was a woman.

Faculty. Of 46 full-time faculty, 17 percent are women, a proportion below average for two-year, public colleges in this guide. There are 2 female faculty for every 100 female students; the ratio for males is 9 to 100.

Administrators. Of the nine top-level administrators, the Dean of Liberal Arts is a woman. A woman chairs one of six departments—business.

Women and the Curriculum. Two-thirds of degrees are earned by women in arts and sciences; 30 percent in business, with small numbers in public service, science, and engineering technologies. Women hold 69 percent of available student internships.

The Women's Studies Porgram, which grants a certificate, offers courses through the departments of English, sociology, business, health, and physical education. Recent titles include Women and Health, Sex Roles, Women in Management, Women in Literature, and Self Defense for Women.

Education courses include information on the development and use of sex-fair curricula; and business courses, on job discrimination, sexual harassment, and women in management. Faculty seminars are provided on sexism and the curriculum, the relationships among sex, race, and the selection of amjor field, and nontraditional occupations for women and men.

Women and Athletics. Of the 39 students participating in intercollegiate sports, three-fourths are women. Fifty percent of all athletic scholarship aid is awarded to womn. The intercollegiate program has two paid coaches, one male and one female. Women's teams participate in post-season tournaments. Women's intercollegiate sports are basketball, bowling, and softball.

Special Services and Programs for Women. *Health and Counseling.* There is no student health service or student counseling center. A local clinic provides health services for the college community; women students who need personal health counseling are referred to local human-services agencies.

Safety and Security. The campus is patrolled by local police. For 1980–81, no rapes or assaults were reported on campus.

Career. Printed information on nontraditional fields of study for women is available.

Institutional Self-Description. ''Alpena Community College is a comprehensive community college, the only post-secondary institution in northeast lower Michigan. The enrollment of women students increases gradually each year and each year many women successfully complete their college programs.''

Aquinas College
1607 Robinson Road. S.E.
Grand Rapids, MI 49506
Telephone: (616) 459-8281

Women in Leadership
★★ students
★ administrators

1,476 undergraduates

	Amer. Ind.	Asian Amer.	Blacks	Hispanics	Whites
F	3	2	36	3	748
M	0	3	9	6	631
%	0.2	0.3	3.1	0.6	95.7

 AAUW

Aquinas College is a coeducational, four-year college operated by the Roman Catholic Dominican Sisters of Grand Rapids. Founded in 1887 as a teachers' college for women, it became a coeducational junior college in 1931, and a four-year liberal arts college in 1942. Aquinas awards associate, bachelor's, and master's degrees. The total enrollment of 1,914 includes 1,476 undergraduates, 54 percent of whom are women. Twenty-nine percent of the women attend part-time. Schedules include on-campus evening and Saturday classes, self-paced/contract learning, external degree programs, and a summer session. Fifty-nine percent of the undergraduates commute to the campus; public transportation and free on-campus parking is available.

Policies to Ensure Fairness to Women. The Personnel Director, the Athletic Director, and the Director of Student Life oversee compliance with laws concerning equal employment opportunity, sex equity for students, and handicapped accessibility.

Women in Leadership Positions. *Students.* Women have excellent opportunities for student leadership. Four of 9 positions have been held by women in recent years. Women head two of the four honorary societies.

Faculty. Twenty-one percent of the 56 full-time faculty members are female, a proportion below the national average. There are 2 female faculty members for every 100 female students and 10 male faculty members for every 100 male students.

Administrators. Two of the eight key administrators are women—the chief academic officer and the director of institutional research. Of the 16 departments, women chair three: history; health, recreation and physical education; and languages.

Women and the Curriculum. Most bachelor's degrees awarded to women are in the social sciences (22 percent), business (21 percent), and education (15 percent); less than 2 percent are in mathematics, the only nontraditional field with recent graduates. Women hold 70 percent of the student internships.

Through Continuing Education for Women, Aquinas offers four courses on women: Philosophy and Feminism, Contemporary Women's Lives, Career Strategies for Women, and Women in Management. Courses in the departments of business, education, and physical education provide some instruction on matters specific to women.

Women and Athletics. For a college of its size, Aquinas offers good opportunities for women to participate in intercollegiate and intramural sports. Forty-three percent of intramural and 31 percent of intercollegiate athletes are women; five of the 15 paid varsity coaches are women. Intercollegiate sports offered are basketball, softball, tennis, track and field, and volleyball.

Housing and Student Organizations. Forty-one percent of the undergraduates reside on campus in coeducational dormitories with restrictive hours for visitors of the opposite sex. The one female and one male residence-hall directors are offered awareness-training on sexism, sex education, racism, birth control, and cultural differences.

MICHIGAN 187

Special Services and Programs for Women. Health and Counseling. The student health service employs 1 male physician; the counseling service has 4 female (1 from a minority group) and 8 male counselors. No services specific to women are offered.

Safety and Security. Measures include a campus police force, night-time escort service for women, high-intensity lights, an emergency alarm system in isolated locations, and information sessions on campus safety. A rape crisis center is available. No rapes and two assaults on women were reported for 1980–81.

Career. A wide variety of career planning services and programs is offered, including workshops and lectures focusing on nontraditional careers for women, job discrimination information, networking between female students and alumnae, and assertiveness training.

Other. Community groups offer programs for battered housewives and displaced homemakers.

Institutional Self-Description. "Women attend Aquinas College because of its academic reputation, individualized financial aids, academic advising, and career placement. Programs include external degree programs, flexibly scheduled; graduate/undergraduate religious studies offerings; master's of management degree program; computer science major; and comprehensive women's athletics. Diversified activities and dormitory arrangements enable undergraduates to meet socially."

Bay de Noc Community College
Escanaba, MI 49829
Telephone: (906) 786-5802

1,191 undergraduates

	Amer. Ind.	Asian Amer.	Blacks	Hispanics	Whites
F	13	0	0	0	585
M	7	0	0	0	584
%	1.7	0.0	0.0	0.0	98.3

This public, two-year college offers comprehensive educational services to 1,191 students, half of whom are women; 37 percent of women attend part-time. The median age of all undergraduates is 24. The college offers two-year degree programs in liberal arts and applied science and one-year certificate programs in a variety of occupational areas. Through its division of community services, the college also operates a Continuing Education for Women Program.

Seven percent of the students reside on campus. No public transportation is available for commuting students; free on-campus parking is provided.

Women in Leadership Positions. Students. Information provided on student leadership is incomplete. In recent years, women have served as president of the student body and presiding officer of the student union board.

Faculty. Of the 41 full-time faculty, 22 percent are female. There are 2 female faculty for every 100 female students and 9 male faculty for every 100 male students.

Administrators. All five of the chief administrative positions are held by men. The business division is chaired by a woman, and women serve as Dean of Science and Health, and Director of Special Needs. The Director of Financial Aid is also a woman.

Women and the Curriculum. All women graduate in the arts and sciences. Women are encouraged to enter programs in such nontraditional career areas as science, engineering, accounting, computer science, law enforcement/corrections, and electronics. Women account for three-fourths of those participating in college internships and practicums.

Several courses on women are offered, through social science and community services. These include Assertiveness Training and Financial Management for Women. Faculty workshops address such issues as sexism and the curriculum, nontraditional careers for women and men, the needs of reentry women, and affirmative action and equal opportunity. Courses in the departments of physical education, nursing, social work, and business provide some instruction on matters specific to women.

Women and Athletics. Over a third of the 200 students who participate in intramural sports are women. The intramural program includes a wide range of both individual and team sports. There is no intercollegiate sports program.

Housing and Student Organizations. Apartments are available on campus for both single and married students. A married woman student whose husband is not enrolled is permitted to live in married students' housing.

Special Services and Programs for Women. Health and counseling. There is no student health service. The student counseling center, staffed by two male counselors, provides services specific to women, including abortion and rape and assault counseling. The college provides in-service training for counselors on the avoidance of sex-role stereotyping.

Safety and Security. The campus is patrolled by local police. Other measures consist of high-intensity lighting in all areas, self-defense courses for women, and a rape crisis center. There was one assault on a woman reported for 1980–81

Career. Career-related materials and activities available on campus include workshops focused on nontraditional occupations and printed information on nontraditional fields of study for women.

Other. The division of social science sponsors an annual women's day and a battered women's program. The Continuing Education for Women Program, operated by Community Services, serves approximately 75 reentry women.

Institutional Self-Description. None provided.

General Motors Institute
1700 W. Third Ave., Flint, MI 48502
Telephone: (313) 762-9873

Women in Leadership   ★ Women and the
★★★ students   Curriculum
★★ faculty

2,179 undergraduates

	Amer. Ind.	Asian Amer.	Blacks	Hispanics	Whites
F	4	27	61	9	541
M	8	79	150	30	1,137
%	0.6	5.2	10.3	1.9	82.0

General Motors Institute is an independent college designed to prepare men and women students for engineering and administrative positions with General Motors Corporation. The college offers degrees only in mechanical, industrial, and electrical engineering, and in industrial administration. On a cooperative education model, students alternately work and study for six-week periods as part of their five-year bachelor's degree program. Of the 2,248 students enrolled, 2,179 are undergraduates. Women are 30 percent of the undergraduates; all students attend full-time.

Forty-five percent of the undergraduates live on campus in coeducational dormitories that have no restrictions on visiting hours for members of the opposite sex. Forty percent of the women belong to sororities, some of which provide housing for members. The campus is accessible through public transportation for the 10 percent of students who commute; parking is available on campus.

Policies to Ensure Fairness to Women. The salaried Personnel Representative reviews policies part-time on matters regarding equal opportunity for employees, students, and handicapped workers and students. A published sexual harassment policy protects students, faculty, and staff. Complaints are resolved through a formal campus grievance procedure.

Women in Leadership Positions. *Students.* Women students have many opportunities to acquire leadership experience. Although they are a minority, women have held most of the leading campus offices in recent years, including student body president, two years, and campus newspaper editor, three years..

Faculty. Forty-seven percent of the 45 full-time faculty are women, well above the average for private coeducational colleges in this guide. There are 3 female faculty for every 100 female students and 2 male faculty for every 100 male students.

Administrators. Men hold all administrative posts, including heads of departments and deanships. Among the 65 regents, there are two women.

Women and the Curriculum. Half of degrees earned by women are in engineering and half are in business. Fourteen percent of the engineering graduates are women. Fifty-three percent of students in experiential learning programs in industrial administration are women, as are 28 percent of students in similar programs in engineering. There are no courses on women.

Women and Athletics. Women have limited opportunities to engage in organized competitive team sports. There are no intercollegiate sports for women. Twenty-four percent of the participants in intramural sports are women. None of the eight intramural activities are team sports.

Special Services and Programs for Women. *Health and Counseling.* The student health center is staffed by one male physician and one female health-care provider. Medical treatment is available for gynecological problems. Counseling on birth control, abortion, and rape and assault is available. Student health insurance covers maternity expenses.

Safety and Security. Measures consist of campus police protection and night-time escorts for women. No rapes or assaults on women were reported for 1980–81.

Institutional Self-Description. None provided.

Grand Valley State Colleges
Allendale, MI 49401
Telephone: (616) 895-6611

6,199 undergraduates

★ **Women and the Curriculum**

	Amer. Ind.	Asian Amer.	Blacks	Hispanics	Whites
F	18	16	133	27	2,863
M	12	20	146	31	2,910
%	0.5	0.6	4.5	0.9	93.5

AAUW

Grand Valley State Colleges, a four-year public institution founded in 1960, occupies a rural campus near Grand Rapids. Some 7,000 students enroll. Forty-nine percent of the 6,199 undergraduates are women; 31 percent of the women attend part-time. The median age of all students is 25. A wide range of alternative full-time and part-time scheduling, including off-campus day and evening courses, a summer session, a weekend college, contract learning, and telecourses, is available. For the 83 percent of students who commute, there is public transportation and free on-campus parking.

College-operated childcare facilities can accommodate 36 children and are open to both students and members of the community. Charges are based on a fixed daily fee; 97 percent of students' requests can be met.

Policies to Ensure Fairness to Women. An Affirmative Action Officer on part-time assignment reviews policies and practices related to equal employment opportunity, sex equity, and handicapped accessibility. Complaints of sexual harassment are handled informally and confidentially. A Commission on Minority Affairs addresses the concerns of minority women.

Women in Leadership Positions. *Students.* Five campus-wide leadership positions are available to students. In a recent three-year period, women have served once each as president of the student body, president of the student senate, president of the student court, and editor-in-chief of the campus newspaper.

Faculty. Women are 24 percent of a full-time faculty of 213, a proportion slightly below the national average. There are 2 female faculty for every 100 female students and 8 male faculty for every 100 male students.

Administrators. The chief student-life officer is a black woman. The rest of the top administrative positions are held by men. Women chair four of 35 departments.

Women and the Curriculum. Most women earn degrees in social sciences (17 percent), education (11 percent), health (12 percent), and fine arts (9 percent). Five percent major in such nontraditional fields as computer science, mathematics, physical sciences, and architecture. The college offers a program to encourage women to prepare for careers in management. Fifty-five percent of student internships and 31 percent of science field-service assignments are awarded to women.

A newly formed Women's Studies Program at William James College offers a bachelor's degree and an undergraduate minor. Recent courses on women include Women in Transition, Feminist View of Culture, Women in History, Women's Movement, Topics in Women's Studies, and Women in Literature. The departments of education, nursing, social work, and business provide instruction on some matters specific to women.

Women and Athletics. One-third of the intercollegiate athletes are women, as are seven of eight paid intercollegiate coaches. Women receive 20 percent of athletic scholarships. Extensive athletic facilities include racquetball, tennis and basketball courts, football and field hockey fields, a ski hill, and a swimming pool (completion expected in 1982). Intercollegiate sports for women are basketball, crew, field hockey, softball, tennis, track, and volleyball.

Housing and Student Organizations. For the 17 percent of undergraduates who live on campus, coeducational dormitories and on-campus apartments are available. Two of the three residence-hall directors are women; staff are offered awareness-training on sexism, racism, sex education, and birth control.

The college has social sororities and fraternities, which do not provide housing for members. The Women's Information Bureau serves as an advocate for women on campus.

Special Services and Programs for Women. *Health and Counseling.* The student health service is staffed by 1 male physician and 2 female health-care providers. The student counseling center employs 3 men and 2 women, including 1 minority woman. Staff receive in-service training on awareness of sex-role stereotyping and racial bias. Counseling and treatment for gynecological matters, birth control, and rape and assault are available.

Safety and Security. Measures consist of campus police with weapons training and arrest authority, and high-intensity lighting. Two rapes and eight assaults, five on women, were reported for 1980–81.

Career. The college offers career workshops, printed information on nontraditional occupations, updated files on alumnae careers, and programs to establish networks between alumnae and women students.

Other. The Women's Center serves both undergraduate and community women. The counseling center, in conjunction with the Women's Resource Center, offers assertiveness-training programs. The Women's Resource Center offers a displaced homemakers' program and sponsors an annual women's week and a women's lecture series.

Returning Women Students. The division of adult continuing education enrolls some 1,300 reentry women, 7 percent of whom are minority women. A special orientation is held for reentry women, as well as a class for credit to assist returning women in their adjustment to college.

Institutional Self-Description. ''Grand Valley State Colleges' commitment to women students is evident in the many support/ academic services provided, including a variety of Women's Studies courses, a women's information bureau, a childcare center, financial aid for part-time students, non-biased counseling and testing services, an extensive career-resource library, CLEP testing, TV telecourses, and off-campus and evening courses.''

Hope College
Holland, MI 49423
Telephone: (616) 392-5111

Women in Leadership
★★★ **students**   ★ **Women and Athletics**

2,085 undergraduates

	Amer. Ind.	Asian Amer.	Blacks	Hispanics	Whites
F	0	6	12	8	934
M	1	7	19	16	1,033
%	0.1	0.6	1.5	1.2	96.6

🏛 ⬛ AAUW

Hope is a coeducational liberal arts college affiliated with the Reformed Church in America. Located on the shores of Lake Michigan, the campus attracts 2,371 students, of whom 2,085 are degree students. Women make up 47 percent of the student body, and all women attend full-time.

The college offers bachelor's degrees in a variety of liberal arts and pre-professional areas. Classes meet on campus during the day and evening. A summer session is available. For the 30 percent of undergraduates who commute or live off campus, public transportation is available as well as on-campus parking for a fee.

Private childcare facilities are available off campus.

Policies to Ensure Fairness to Women. The Registrar is responsible for policy regarding handicapped accessibility. The Director of Athletics handles policy on sex equity. The Provost is responsible for policy pertaining to equal-employment-opportunity laws. A Commission on the Status of Women, appointed by the Provost, includes student members with voting rights and addresses concerns of minority women.

Women in Leadership Positions. *Students.* Women have excellent opportunities to participate in campus leadership. During three recent years, half the student leadership positions—as residence-hall council president and campus newspaper editor—have been held by women. Women preside over four of 18 honorary societies.

Faculty. Thirteen percent of the 134 full-time faculty are women, a proportion below average for similar colleges in this guide. There are 2 female faculty for every 100 female students and 11 male faculty for every 100 male students.

Administrators. Men hold the major administrative positions. Women chair three of 23 departments: dance, nursing, and foreign languages and literature. The 27-member Board of Trustees includes four women.

Women and the Curriculum. Most degrees awarded to women are in business (14 percent), education (14 percent), social sci-

ences (13 percent), and biology (11 percent). Nine percent are in such nontraditional fields as engineering, computer science, mathematics, and physical sciences, a figure above the average for comparable institutions in this guide. Women students receive half of the student internships.

Two courses on women are available through the departments of psychology and physical education: Psychology of Women, and Coaching Women. Although there is no formal Women's Studies Program, students may earn a bachelor's degree in Women's Studies through a composite major or a contract curriculum. The departments of business, education, and social work provide some instruction on matters specific to women. An official committee promotes the further integration of women into the curriculum and collects and develops new teaching materials on women. Faculty workshops are available on teaching reentry women and on affirmative action and equal opportunity.

Women and Athletics. Women have good opportunities to participate in a variety of individual and team sports through intercollegiate, intramural, and club sports programs. About a third of the intercollegiate athletes are female. Eight of 17 paid coaches are women, and there is a woman athletic director. Intercollegiate sports offered are archery, basketball, cross-country, field hockey, softball, swimming, tennis, track and field, and volleyball.

Housing and Student Organizations. Seventy percent of the students live on campus in single-sex or coeducational dormitories that restrict visiting hours for members of the opposite sex.

Fifteen percent of the undergraduate women, including six minority women, belong to social sororities. Sororities provide housing for members.

Special Services and Programs for Women. *Health and Counseling.* The student health center is staffed by one gynecologist part-time and three male physicians on call, in addition to three female health-care providers. One woman staffs the student counseling center. Counseling and treatment are available for gynecological problems, birth control, abortion, and rape and assault. Training on avoidance of racial bias and sex-role stereotyping is available to counselors.

Safety and Security. Measures consist of campus and local police protection, night-time escort for women, self-defense courses for women, instruction on campus safety and crime prevention, and a rape crisis center. No rapes and ten assaults on women were reported for 1980–81.

Career. Workshops on career opportunities, information on nontraditional occupations, and networking between female students and alumnae are available.

Other. In the local community, the Center for Women in Transition offers a battered women's shelter, displaced homemakers' program, assertiveness training, and a telephone referral and information service.

Institutional Self-Description. ''Hope College has alumnae who have distinguished themselves in practically every field of endeavor. Hope has excelled in its natural science programs and has prepared many young women for medical and dental schools. Hope's business program has graduated women who have secured management positions in business and industry. The college community is open, friendly, conducive to the intellectual and spiritual development of men and women.''

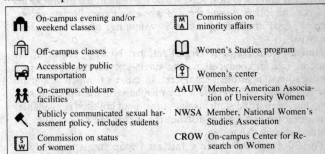

🏛	On-campus evening and/or weekend classes	⬛M A	Commission on minority affairs
🏛	Off-campus classes	📖	Women's Studies program
🚌	Accessible by public transportation	👤	Women's center
👫	On-campus childcare facilities	AAUW	Member, American Association of University Women
🗝	Publicly communicated sexual harassment policy, includes students	NWSA	Member, National Women's Studies Association
⬛S W	Commission on status of women	CROW	On-campus Center for Research on Women

Kalamazoo College
1200 Academy
Kalamazoo, MI 49007
Telephone: (616) 383-8400

1,400 undergraduates

	Amer. Ind.	Asian Amer.	Blacks	Hispanics	Whites
F	0	5	14	5	638
M	1	8	8	5	698
%	0.1	0.9	1.6	0.7	96.7

 AAUW

Kalamazoo, established in 1833, is an independent liberal arts college affiliated with the Baptist Church. Its campus, located midway between Chicago and Detroit, attracts 1,441 students, of whom nearly half are women. The median age of all undergraduates is 19.

The college offers a variety of majors in liberal arts, education, business, and pre-professional areas. The Nontraditional Student Program includes adult continuing education. For the 10 percent of students who commute, the college is within reach of public transportation. Free on-campus parking is available.

Private childcare facilities are close to campus.

Policies to Ensure Fairness to Women. The Vice President makes policy regarding equal employment opportunity, sex equity, and handicapped access regulations. Complaints of sexual harassment are resolved by existing informal and confidential procedures; a specific policy for sexual harassment is being developed.

Women in Leadership Positions. *Students.* Partial data from the college suggest that women students have limited opportunity to gain leadership experience. In recent years, women have served twice as editor-in-chief of the campus newspaper.

Faculty. Seventeen percent of the 82 full-time faculty are women, a proportion below average for similar colleges in this guide. There are 2 female faculty for every 100 female students, and 9 male faculty for every 100 male students.

Administrators. All but two chief administrators are male: the head librarian and the director of institutional research are women. Men chair all departments except sociology/anthropology. Ten of the 50 trustees are women.

Women and the Curriculum. The most popular fields among women are social sciences (30 percent) and fine arts (19 percent). Ten percent of women graduate in such nontraditional areas as mathematics and physical sciences. The college emphasizes experiential learning internships, half of which are awarded to women.

Three courses on women are available: Women's Studies Seminar, Women in Cross-Cultural Perspective, and Literature of Women. Students may arrange independent study in any department, making women the topic of that study. An official committee encourages the further integration of scholarship on women into the academic program and reports on new Women's Studies teaching materials.

Women and Athletics. Kalamazoo has a small intramural sports program, and offers a wide array of women's intercollegiate sports: archery, basketball, field hockey, swimming, tennis, track, and volleyball.

Housing and Student Organizations. Ninety percent of the students live in coeducational or single-sex dormitories or in a coeducational apartment complex, in none of which are there restrictions on visiting hours for members of the opposite sex. Housing for married students with or without children is available. A married woman whose husband is not enrolled may qualify for married students' housing.

The 30-member Women's Interest Group meets regularly to address all women's issues. The Black Student Organization also addresses concerns of women.

Special Services and Programs for Women. *Health and Counseling.* The student health center employs 1 female physician and 2 female health-care providers. One of the 2 professionals at the student counseling service is a woman. Gynecological counseling and treatment, and counseling on birth control, abortion, and rape and assault are provided. Awareness-training is available on sex-role stereotyping and racism.

Safety and Security. Measures consist of campus and local police protection, night-time esocrts for women, high-intensity lighting, informtion on self-defense and campus safety, and a rape crisis center. No rapes or assaults on women were reported for 1980–81.

Career. Services include workshops, panels, and printed materials on nontraditional occupations, job discrimination information, and programs to establish contacts between alumnae and students, including the maintenance of updated files on alumnae careers. Workshops on career advising for women are provided for the faculty.

Other. The Women's Center, coordinated by Student Life, serves as a resource for students, faculty, and staff.

Institutional Self-Description. "A woman would choose Kalamazoo College because of its academic excellence and unusual blend of off-campus experiences with a traditional liberal arts program. A number of avenues allow the exploration of women's issues and concerns in the context of a liberal arts education."

Kendall School of Design
1110 College N.E.
Grand Rapids, MI 49503
Telephone: (616) 451-2787

Women in Leadership
★★ students
★ faculty
★★★ administrators

Enrollment data unavailable.

Located in Grand Rapids, this private, two-year commuter college was founded to educate women and men for professional careers in the visual arts. There are 294 female students, of whom 18 percent attend part-time. The median age of all students is 22. The college runs a continuing education program called PACE and a summer session.

All students commute. Free parking and public transportation are available.

Policies to Ensure Fairness to Women. On a part-time basis, an equal-opportunity officer with policymaking responsibility monitors compliance with equal-employment-opportunity and equal-education-opportunity regulations. A written policy, communicated to the staff, prohibits sexual harassment of students, staff, and faculty. There is a formal grievance procedure to resolve complaints of sexual harassment.

Women in Leadership Positions. *Students.* The single campus leadership position, president of the student body, has been held by women for the past two years.

Faculty. Of 21 full-time faculty, 6 are women. There are 3 female faculty for every 100 female students. A comparable figure is not available for men.

Administrators. The President of the college is a woman, as are the Academic Dean, the chief business officer, and the head librarian. A woman also chairs the interior design department. Of 17 trustees, seven are women.

Women and the Curriculum. Information was not provided.

Women and Athletics. There is no opportunity for organized, competitive sports.

Special Services and Programs for Women. *Health and Counseling.* The college has a counseling center. No other information was provided.

Safety and Security. There were no rapes or assaults reported for 1980-81.

Institutional Self-Description. "The job market for which we educate students is conducive to hiring women."

Madonna College
36600 Schoolcraft Rd., Livonia, MI 48150
Telephone: (313) 591-5000

Women in Leadership
- ★★★ students
- ★★★ faculty
- ★★★ administrators

2,528 undergraduates

	Amer. Ind.	Asian Amer.	Blacks	Hispanics	Whites
F	3	7	210	4	1,582
M	2	2	74	4	640
%	0.4	0.2	11.2	0.3	87.9

Madonna was founded in 1947 as a Roman Catholic women's college. It is still operated by the Felician Sisters but, since 1972, has become a coeducational institution. Located in the Detroit suburb of Livonia, its total enrollment is 2,964 students. Seventy-one percent of the 2,528 undergraduates are women; 56 percent of women attend part-time. The median age of undergraduates is 27—nearly one-fifth of the students are over age 40. Madonna offers a variety of undergraduate degrees, as well as adult continuing education courses. Classes meet day and evening. A summer session is available. For the majority of students who commute, public transportation and on-campus parking are available.

Private childcare facilties are nearby.

Policies to Ensure Fairness to Women. The President assumes part-time responsibility for examing practices and making policy regarding educational sex equity, and handicapped accessibility.

Women in Leadership Positions. *Students.* Women students have excellent opportunities to gain leadership experience. In recent years, women have held most of the three campus-wide offices and presided over the two honorary societies.

Faculty. Seventy percent of the 77 full-time faculty are women. There are 7 female faculty for every 100 female students and 11 male faculty for every 100 male students.

Administrators. The majority of top administrators are women. Women chair 21 of the 32 departments. A woman also directs the division of nursing and emergency medical technology.

Women and the Curriculum. Half of women graduates earn bachelor's degrees in health professions. One woman graduated in mathematics during one recent year.

The departments of business management, English, and sociology offer three courses on women: Women in Management, Women in Literature, and Sociology of Sex Roles.

Minority Women. Twelve percent of female students are minority group women, largely black women. Among the administration and staff, 1 American Indian woman chairs a department, 2 black and 2 Hispanic women are members of the faculty senate,

and 1 of 3 residence-hall directors is a minority woman. Residence-hall staff are offered awareness training on the avoidance of racism. Faculty are offered workshops on racism in the curriculum.

Women and Athletics. The organized athletic program for women is limited to one intercollegiate team, three intramural activities team sports, and club sports. Half the intercollegiate athletes are women, and their paid coach is a woman. The intercollegiate sport is basketball.

Housing and Student Organizations. Coeducational dormitories, which house 6 percent of undergraduates, restrict visiting hours for members of the opposite sex. The three residence-hall directors are women.

Special Services and Programs for Women. *Health and Counseling.* The college has no health service. Two of the four counselors at the student counseling center are female. No medical treatment or counseling specific to women is available.

Safety and Security. Measures consist of campus and local police protection, high-intensity lighting, and instruction on self-defense. No rapes or assaults on women were reported for 1980-81.

Career. The Career Resource Center provides workshops, lectures, and information on nontraditional occupations. Workshops on nontraditional occupations for women and men, the needs of reentry women, and affirmative action and equal opportunity are available to faculty.

Institutional Self-Description. "Madonna College is a four-year, liberal arts college offering more than 50 majors including business administration, criminal justice, gerontology, computer science, nursing and teacher education. Special services are available to the handicapped, especially hearing-impaired persons."

Michigan Technological University
Houghton, MI 49931
Telephone: (906) 487-1885

★ **Women and the Curriculum**

6,687 undergraduates

	Amer. Ind.	Asian Amer.	Blacks	Hispanics	Whites
F	4	3	10	4	1440
M	20	21	19	14	5023
%	0.4	0.4	0.4	0.3	98.6

 AAUW

Founded in 1885, this state-supported institution offers associate, bachelor's, master's, and doctoral programs in engineering and science. The bachelor's degree is available in liberal arts; business; education; and in life, social, and physical sciences. The Division of Education and Public Services sponsors an adult-continuing education program. Some evening classes are available. The university has 7,000 students, 6,687 of whom are undergraduates. Twenty-two percent of undergraduates are women; 7 percent of women attend part-time.

Sixty-five percent of undergraduates commute to the campus, located in Michigan's upper peninsula. Public transportation is accessible and on-campus parking is available for a fee.

University-sponsored childcare facilities accommodate applicants on a first-come, first-served basis. There is a waiting list for this service. Private childcare facilities are available near the campus.

Policies to Ensure Fairness to Women. The Director of Employee Relations serves as the equal opportunity officer. Complaints of sexual harassment are resolved informally and confidentially on a case-by-case basis.

Women in Leadership Positions. *Students.* Women have limited opportunities to exercise campus-wide leadership. In recent years, the one student campus post held by a woman has been editor-in-chief of the campus newspaper. Women also head five of the 16 campus honorary societies.

Faculty. Women are 13 percent of the 350 full-time faculty. There are 3 female faculty for every 100 female students and 6 male faculty for every 100 male students.

Administrators. Men hold all top-level administrative positions. No departments are chaired by women. Of eight university trustees, one is a white woman, one is a black woman.

Women and the Curriculum. Forty-eight percent of women earn degrees in such nontraditional fields as agriculture, engineering, and mathematical and physical sciences. The university sponsors week-long ''Women in Engineering'' sessions throughout the summer for highly qualified female high school students; the program explores careers in engineering, forestry, geology, and management. Women earn one-third of the two-year degrees and certificates awarded: 71 percent in health, 23 percent in science and engineering technologies, and 6 percent in arts and sciences. Approximately 25 percent of students participating in cooperative education programs are women.

There are no courses on women.

Women and Athletics. Women have opportunities to participate in a variety of team and individual sports through the intramural program. The intercollegiate program places more emphasis on individual sports. The university has an ice arena and special facilities for indoor track. Twenty-two percent of the 252 intercollegiate athletes are women, as are five of the 20 paid intercollegiate sports coaches. Women receive 10 percent of athletic scholarship aid. The intercollegiate sports offered are basketball, cross-country, swimming, tennis, track, and volleyball.

Housing and Student Organizations. Coeducational dormitories house the 35 percent of undergraduates who reside on campus. Residence halls do not restrict hours for visitors of the opposite sex. Housing for married students with and without children and for single parents with children is also available. A married women student whose husband is not enrolled may live in married students' housing. Awareness training on birth control and alcohol abuse is offered to residence-hall staff, all of whom are male.

Some of the social sororities and fraternities on campus provide housing for members. Eight percent of female undergraduates belong to sororities. There are three minority women in racially integrated sororities.

Special Services and Programs for Women. *Health and Counseling.* The student health service, which employs 2 physicians (1 male, 1 female), 2 physician's assistants (1 male, 1 female), and 9 other health-care providers provides treatment for gynecological problems, birth control, and rape and assault. The counseling center, staffed by 2 female and 3 male counselors, offers counseling of particular concern to women. The counseling staff offer assertiveness training to male and female students. Counselors recieve in-service training on treatment of rape victims and on depression.

Safety and Security. Measures consist of local police, campus police with weapons training and arrest authority, a rape crisis center, and DIAL HELP, a crisis phone line. One rape and seven assaults (four on women) were reported for 1980–81.

Career. Nonsexist/nonracist printed material on nontraditional occupations for women is available, as well as panels and lectures for students by women employed in these fields.

Other. The faculty and staff of the university, along with a group of community women, recently sponsored Copper Country Women's Heritage Week, during which the accomplishments of local women were highlighted through oral history, taped interviews, and slide shows. Part of this program also focused on minority women.

Institutional Self-Description. ''Michigan Technological University provides outstanding scientific and technological training (engineering, bioscience, computer and mathematical sciences, foresty, and more), with special emphasis on hands-on learning. These areas have been considered nontraditional careers, and are highly marketable at this point.''

Monroe County Community College
Monroe, MI 48161
Telephone: (313) 242-7300

Women in Leadership
★★★ students

2,019 undergraduates

	Amer. Ind.	Asian Amer.	Blacks	Hispanics	Whites
F	3	0	1	1	1,052
M	2	0	1	3	956
%	0.3	0.0	0.1	0.2	99.5

A public, two-year college located near the Michigan-Ohio border, Monroe County serves 2,019 students, 52 percent of whom are female. Two-thirds of the women attend part-time. The median age of all undergraduates is 28.

The college awards associate degrees for university transfer, one- and two-year certificates in occupational areas, and offers a continuing education/community services program. There are day and evening classes both on and off campus, a weekend college program, and self-paced/contract learning. Public transportation is available for students, all of whom commute to the suburban campus. On-campus parking is also available.

On-campus childcare facilities can accommodate 19 children and charge at a fixed daily fee.

Women in Leadership Positions. *Students.* Female students hold positions of campus leadership nearly as often as males. Of the two campus leadership positions—president of the student body and editor-in-chief of the newspaper—the former was held by a woman once in three recent years, and the latter was held twice.

Faculty. The full-time faculty of 48 is 19 percent female, a lower than average proportion for public two-year colleges. There are 2 female faculty for every 100 female students and 13 male faculty for every 100 male students.

Administrators. Of the five chief administrators, the head librarian is a woman. Women chair three of seven units: health sciences, learning resources center, and continuing education. Two of the seven trustees are women.

Women and the Curriculum. Most two-year degrees earned by women are in the arts and sciences, with a smaller number in health technologies and business and commerce. There are no courses on women.

Women and Athletics. No intramural, intercollegiate, or club sports are offered.

Special Services and Programs for Women. *Health and Counseling.* There is no student health service. The student counseling center has a staff of three, two of whom are women. No counseling services specific to women are available.

Safety and Security. The campus is patrolled by local police. Additional safety measures include high-intensity lighting in all areas. For 1980–81, no rapes or assaults were reported.

Other. A Women's Center is operated by the division of continuing education. Approximately 50 women, a combination of community women and undergraduates over 25, use the center, which is staffed part-time by a salaried administrator. The continuing education division also offers a displaced homemakers' program and assertiveness/leadership training.

Institutional Self-Description. ''Equal opportunity for all services and courses offered.''

St. Mary's College
Orchard Lake, MI 48033
Telephone: (313) 682-1885

Women in Leadership
★ **administrators**

141 undergraduates

	Amer. Ind.	Asian Amer.	Blacks	Hispanics	Whites
F	0	1	2	2	58
M	1	2	7	0	65
%	0.7	2.2	6.5	1.5	89.1

St. Mary's College began in 1885 as part of a six-year seminary for the education of Roman Catholic priests. In 1927 it became a private, liberal arts college for men. The college began admitting women in 1972, and attracts 192 students to its two- and four-year programs. Of the 141 students enrolled in degree programs, 45 percent are women.

The 120-acre suburban campus, located in an integrated community near Detroit, offers evening classes and continuing education. On-campus parking is available for the 40 percent of students who commute.

Women in Leadership Positions. *Students.* Opportunities for women to exercise campus-wide leadership are below average for similar institutions in this guide. During recent years women have presided over the student body and sophomore and junior classes, each for one year.

Faculty. Of five full-time faculty members, one is a woman. More recent information from the college indicates that of 10 full-time faculty, 3 are women, and of 32 part-time faculty, 8 are women.

Administrators. The chief development officer and the director of institutional research are women. Men hold the other six top administrative positions. Women chair three of eight departments: natural science and mathematics, English, and religious education. Two of the 17 trustees and two of the 67-member Board of Regents are women. At the 1981 commencement, one of the three speakers was a woman.

Women and the Curriculum. In a recent year, women received 5 of the 17 four-year degrees: 2 in theology, 2 in interdisciplinary studies, and 1 in letters. Of the four two-year degrees and awards granted in a recent year, all were in arts and sciences, and all were awarded to women. Twenty-five percent of students in internship programs are women. No courses on women are offered.

Women and Athletics. The college offers no intercollegiate, intramural, or club sports.

Housing and Student Organizations. The 60 percent of students who reside on campus live in single sex dormitories with restrictive hours for visitors of the opposite sex. One woman and one man are residence-hall directors. Fraternities and sororities do not provide housing for their members.

Special Services and Programs for Women. *Health and Counseling.* Two male physicians and two male health-care providers staff the health center. No medical services specific to women are available. There is no counseling service. Student health insurance does not cover maternity or abortion.

Safety and Security. Local police patrol the campus. For 1980–81, there were no rapes or assaults reported on campus.

Career. Workshops which focus on nontraditional occupations are available.

Institutional Self-Description. "St. Mary's has a small community atmosphere where students preparing for professions, career and graduate school find acceptance regardless of sex, socio-economic or ethnic backgrounds. Personal interest and the small college setting enrich learning and living opportunities for men and women who might not otherwise figure in leadership roles at larger universities.''

Schoolcraft College
18600 Haggerty Road, Livonia, MI 48152
Telephone: (313) 591-6400

Women in Leadership
★ **faculty**

7,894 undergraduates

	Amer. Ind.	Asian Amer.	Blacks	Hispanics	Whites
F	12	18	32	34	3,889
M	25	19	43	32	3,770
%	0.5	0.5	1.0	0.8	97.3

Schoolcraft, a public two-year college located near Detroit, offers comprehensive educational programs to 9,410 students, of whom 7,894 are registered in degree programs. Half of the degree students are women; 77 percent of women attend part-time.

The college offers two-year liberal arts and pre-professional studies, as well as a wide range of terminal career programs. Adult Continuing Education is offered. Day and evening classes, both on and off campus, a summer session, and self-paced/contract learning are available. All students commute to the rural campus, which is accessible by public transportation. Free on-campus parking is provided.

A college-run childcare facility can accommodate 23 children each hour. Available from 7:30 a.m. to 2 p.m., the facility charges at a fixed hourly rate. Private childcare facilities are also available near the campus.

Policies to Ensure Fairness to Women. Three administrators share part-time responsibility for overseeing policies on equal employment opportunity, sex equity for students, and handicapped accessibility. A Committee on the Status of Women reports to the Dean of Continuing Education and Community Services.

Women in Leadership Positions. *Students.* No information was provided regarding women in campus-wide leadership positions. The sole campus honorary society is headed by a woman.

Faculty. Twenty-eight percent of the 141 full-time faculty are women, a proportion below average for public, two-year colleges, but above average for all institutions nationwide. There are 4 female faculty for every 100 female students and 9 male faculty for every 100 male students.

Administrators. Of the six top administrators, the chief academic officer is a woman. Four of 12 deans of academic units and two of seven trustees are women.

Women and the Curriculum. Most of the degrees and certificates awarded to women are in arts and sciences (45 percent), health technologies (28 percent), and business and commerce (20 percent). Four-fifths of students in cooperative education programs are women.

There are no courses on women. The division of business provides instruction on job discrimination, sexual harassment in the workplace, and women in management. Faculty are offered workshops on the needs of reentry women.

Women and Athletics. Schoolcraft offers limited opportunities for women to participate in intramural or intercollegiate sports. Twenty-eight percent of intercollegiate and 43 percent of intramural athletes are women, as are two of eleven paid intercollegiate coaches. The college offers athletic scholarships. The three women's intercollegiate teams—basketball, cross-country, and volleyball—played in recent tournaments.

Special Services and Programs for Women. *Health and Counseling.* The student health service is staffed by two registered nurses. The 12-member staff of the student counseling center includes four women. No services specific to women are provided.

Safety and Security. Measures consist of local police, and campus police who do not have arrest authority. No information was provided on the incidence of rapes and assaults.

Other. The Office of Instruction operates the Women's Resource Center, budgeted annually at $52,323. Under the direction of a full-time, salaried administrator, the center serves some 4,500 visitors annually, primarily older women students and community women. The center's program includes a women's lecture series, speakers' bureau, assertiveness/leadership training, workshops to build mathematics confidence, library, and counseling. The college sponsors WISER (Widowed in Service), an educational support group for widows, and a volunteer recruitment, training, and retention program.

Institutional Self-Description. "The Women's Resource Center provides a nationally recognized program of information, referrals, and counseling to women in transition, i.e., widowed, divorced, displaced, or those who are reentering education or employment. Low-cost workshops, courses, and conferences, focusing on women's concerns, are offered. Employed women are assisted in upgrading skills or changing careers."

Siena Heights College
1247 E. Siena Heights Dr.
Adrian, MI 49221
Telephone: (517) 263-0731

Women in Leadership
★★ faculty

988 undergraduates

	Amer. Ind.	Asian Amer.	Blacks	Hispanics	Whites
F	1	5	47	15	528
M	1	0	44	9	320
%	0.2	0.5	9.1	2.4	87.8

This private, coeducational, Roman Catholic college, founded as a women's college in 1919, occupies a suburban campus southwest of Ann Arbor. Women are 61 percent of the 988 undergraduates; half of women students attend part-time. The median age of all students is 26.

In addition to master's degree programs, Siena Heights offers bachelor's degrees in business, health professions, public affairs, education, fine arts, engineering, and physical sciences. Alternative scheduling includes off-campus evening classes, a summer session, a weekend college, and self-paced/contract learning. Public transportation and on-campus parking are available for the 65 percent of students who commute.

Private childcare facilities are available nearby.

Policies to Ensure Fairness to Women. An informal campus mechanism resolves complaints of sexual harassment.

Women in Leadership Positions. *Students.* Of six campus-wide leadership posts available during a recent three-year period, women held slightly more than one-third, though they are 61 percent of the student body. Women have served two years each as president of the student court, president of the student union board, and presiding officer of the residence halls. A woman also served a one-year term as editor-in-chief of the campus newspaper. One of three campus honorary societies is headed by a woman.

Faculty. Women are 40 percent of the 40 full-time faculty, a proportion considerably above average for private four-year colleges. There are 4 female faculty for every 100 female students and 11 male faculty for every 100 male students.

Administrators. Women hold 2 of 9 administrative positions: chief student-life officer and chief development officer. Four of 8 departments are chaired by women, including natural science, art, communication arts and education, and management. Thirteen of 35 trustees are women. The 1981 commencement speaker was a woman, as were 2 of 3 honorary degree recipients. Two of 3 speakers in a recent campus-wide lecture series were women.

Women and the Curriculum. Most bachelor's degrees awarded to women are in health professions and public affairs. Women are half of the students in internship and cooperative education programs.

Two courses on women are offered through the departments of religious studies and English/literature: Women and Violence and Women in Literature. The departments of education, physical education, and social work offer instruction on some matters specific to women. Faculty workshops on sexism and racism in the curriculum and on the needs of reentry women are available.

Women and Athletics. Siena Heights offers a good variety of team and individual intramural sports. Intercollegiate sports for women are basketball, track, softball, tennis, and volleyball.

Housing and Student Organizations. Single-sex and coeducational dormitories with restrictive hours for visitors of the opposite sex are available for the 35 percent of students who reside on campus. A married student whose husband is not enrolled is permitted to live in married students' housing. The female residence-hall director is offered awareness-training on sexism and sex education.

Special Services and Programs for Women. *Health and Counseling.* There is no student health service. The student counseling center is staffed by one woman, who has received awareness-training on the avoidance of sex-role stereotyping and racial bias. Counseling for gynecological matters, birth control, abortion, and assault is available.

Safety and Security. Measures consist of campus police, high-intensity lighting, an emergency alarm system, information sessions on campus safety, and a rape crisis center. No information was provided on the incidence of rape and assault.

Career. Workshops, lectures, and printed information on non-traditional occupations and fields of study for women are provided, as well as updated files on alumnae by career choices.

Institutional Self-Description. "Siena Heights College believes that individual educational goals should grow out of an encounter with the values which are part of the Adrian Dominican tradition. Specifically, these are the values of the reflective life, the free exploration of ultimate questions, the imperative to witness one's values to the world, the concern for justice in human relationships, and participation in communal celebration. The college is also committed to the idea that goals must develop in light of career possibilities and the realities of society."

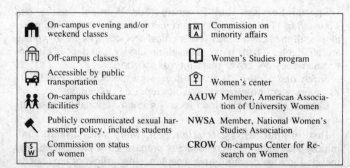

⌂ On-campus evening and/or weekend classes	**MA** Commission on minority affairs
🏛 Off-campus classes	**📖** Women's Studies program
🚌 Accessible by public transportation	**📱** Women's center
👥 On-campus childcare facilities	**AAUW** Member, American Association of University Women
✎ Publicly communicated sexual harassment policy, includes students	**NWSA** Member, National Women's Studies Association
SW Commission on status of women	**CROW** On-campus Center for Research on Women

University of Michigan, Ann Arbor
Ann Arbor, MI 48109
Telephone: (313) 764-1817

★★★ **Women and the Curriculum**

★ **Women and Athletics**

22,324 undergraduates

	Amer. Ind.	Asian Amer.	Blacks	Hispanics	Whites
F	41	157	827	128	8,591
M	45	217	555	125	10,833
%	0.3	1.7	6.4	1.2	90.4

🏠 🚐 👫 🔨 ⑤ⓦ Ⓜ︎Ⓐ 📖 ⑦ **AAUW CROW**

Established in 1817, the University of Michigan is a state-supported institution that attracts some 36,700 students to a comprehensive range of undergraduate, graduate, and professional degree programs. The Extension Service houses a non-credit adult education program. Alternative class schedules include on campus evening classes and a summer session.

Women are 45 percent of the 22,324 undergraduates; 11 percent of women attend part-time. The median age of undergraduates is 19. For the 57 percent of the undergraduates who live off campus or commute, the university is accessible by public transportation. On-campus parking is available for a fee, with free transportation provided from distant parking lots.

University-sponsored childcare accommodates 25 children. Private arrangements for childcare may be made close to campus.

Policies to Ensure Fairness to Women. An Affirmative Action Officer on part-time assignment is responsible for policy related to equal employment opportunities, accessibility of programs and facilities to students, and handicapped access. A campus policy prohibits sexual harassment. Complaints are handled both informally and by a formal grievance procedure. The Committee on the Status of Women, which includes students as voting members, takes stands on issues of concern to students. The Committee on Minority Affairs addresses the concerns of minority women.

Women in Leadership Positions. *Students.* Opportunities for women students to exercise campus leadership are considerably below average for public research universities in this guide. In recent years no woman has held a student office. Women head two of the four honorary societies.

Faculty. Women are 23 percent of a full-time faculty of 1,776. According to recent report, 36 black, 1 American Indian, 23 Asian-American, and 5 Hispanic women are on the full-time faculty. The ratio of female faculty to female students is 4 to 100; the ratio of male faculty to male students is 13 to 100.

Administrators. Men occupy all higher administrative positions. Women chair 18 of 175 departments. The deans of the School of Nursing and the School of Education are female.

Women and the Curriculum. A majority of women earning bachelor's degrees major in the health professions (17 percent), social science (14 percent), psychology (9 percent), education (8 percent), and interdisciplinary studies (8 percent). Eleven percent major in such nontraditional areas as agriculture, architecture, computer science, engineering, mathematics, and the physical sciences. Women are 12 percent of the graduates in engineering. Innovative programs encourage women to prepare for careers in science and engineering.

The Women's Studies Program, under the direction of a permanent faculty member, offers the bachelor's degree in Women's Studies. More than 25 courses are available through Women's Studies and through the departments of economics, English, history, political science, psychology, sociology, anthropology, communication, public health, and the School of Social Work.

Graduate work is also available. Recent offerings include Economic Status of Women, Women and Art in the Middle Ages and Renaissance, Women and Power, Sex and Gender in Health, Medical Anthropology of Women, Introduction to Women's Studies, and Theories of Feminism.

Such current issues as health-care information important to minority women, services for abused spouses, and discrimination in the workplace are included in the curricula of the schools of nursing, social work, and business.

The Center for Continuing Education for Women, which has since 1964 offered a wide range of direct and indirect services to women, is also a center for research on women. Currently its research program is focused on the transition to work, the balancing of work and family commitments, and the center's own impact on the more than 1,000 women who used its services in its first decade. The center has an excellent library, and holds conferences and workshops in issues related to women's education and work.

The Bentley Historical Library houses archival material of interest to women. On campus also is The Institute of Labor and Industrial Relations with a Program on Women and Work, a Union Minorities/Women Leadership Training Program, and the Trade Union Women's Oral History Project.

Minority Women. Of 9,756 undergraduate women, 8 percent are black, 2 percent Asian American, 1 percent Hispanic, and less than 1 percent American Indian. Courses of interest to minority group women include Chicano Experience and Image of Women in Latin American Literature. Two minority women are on the staff of the counseling service; one is a residence-hall director. A black woman is on the Board of Regents. Eighty women are in all-minority sororities; five minority women are in integrated sororities.

Women and Athletics. Intramural and intercollegiate programs offer good opportunities for individual and team sports. Club sports are also available. Sixteen percent of intramural and 27 percent of varsity athletes are women; women receive 20 percent of athletic grants-in-aid. Five of 43 paid varsity coaches are female. Intercollegiate sports offered are basketball, cross-country, field hockey, golf, gymnastics, softball, swimming and diving, synchronized swimming, tennis, track and field, and volleyball.

Housing and Student Organizations. For the 43 percent of the undergraduates who live on campus, residential accommodations include single-sex and coeducational dormitories, cooperative housing, and housing for married students and single parents with children. A married woman student whose spouse is not enrolled may live in married students' housing. Women's and coeducational dormitories may have restricted hours for visitors of the opposite sex. Half of the residence hall directors are women; staff are offered awareness-training on sexism, sex education, birth control, minority relations, women's safety and security, and gay awareness.

Nine percent of the full-time undergraduate women belong to social sororities; sororities and fraternities provide housing for their members. Among organizations which serve as advocates for women are the Undergraduate Women's Association, Minority Women's Workshop, Feminist Legal Services, PIRGIM (Women's Safety Task Force) and Lesbian Advocate.

Special Services and Programs for Women. *Health and Counseling.* The student health service provides some medical attention specific to women: gynecological, birth control, and rape and assault treatment is available. Six of the 17 physicians are female. The regular student health insurance covers maternity at no extra cost. The counseling service, staffed by 15 women and 11 men, provides counseling relevant to women. Staff receive in-service training on sex-role stereotyping, racial bias, sexuality, and sexual preference. Assertiveness training is also offered.

Safety and Security. Measures consist of campus and local police, night-time escorts for women students, bus service to residential areas, and a rape crisis center. A total of 160 assaults (92 on women) and 15 instances of criminal sexual conduct were reported for 1980–81.

Career. Workshops, speakers, and nonsexist/nonracist printed information on nontraditional careers and fields of study for women, as well as an annual career fair and help from the minority coordinator are available.

Other. The Center for Continuing Education for Women functions as a Women's Center providing a variety of services. Among sponsored events on campus are theater and other women's arts programs. Programs to build confidence in mathematics, to assist displaced homemakers, and to provide a telephone line of information, referral, and support are also available.

Institutional Self-Description. "The University of Michigan has a major institutional commitment to affirmative action. Students will find many women's organizations from which to choose, and a high level of concern about equity for women students and staff. Ann Arbor has a history of social activism and offers many supportive services for women."

University of Michigan, Dearborn
4901 Evergreen Rd., Dearborn, MI 48128
Telephone: (313) 593-5000

★ **Women and the Curriculum**

4,708 undergraduates

	Amer. Ind.	Asian Amer.	Blacks	Hispanics	Whites
F	15	15	171	10	1,750
M	17	17	89	19	2,503
%	0.7	0.7	5.6	0.6	92.3

Founded in 1959 as a two-year college of engineering, business, and liberal arts, this state-supported university now offers its 5,957 students a full range of bachelor's and master's level programs. An adult continuing education program is available through the Extension Service. The university offers a variety of alternative schedules, including evening classes both on and off campus, weekend and summer session classes, and opportunities for self-paced/contract learning.

Women are 42 percent of the 4,708 undergraduates. Thirty-three percent of women attend part-time; about 10 percent of women are over age 40. The median age of undergraduates is 22. Ninety-seven percent of undergraduates commute to the suburban campus, located near Detroit. The university is accessible by public transportation and on-campus parking is available at a fee.

University-sponsored childcare facilities can accommodate 60 children with students receiving priority for the service. Fees are based on a fixed daily rate. Private childcare facilities are available near the campus.

Policies to Ensure Fairness to Women. Review of policies and practices related to equal-employment-opportunity, handicapped-accessibility, and sex-equity legislation is the part-time responsibility of the Affirmative Action Coordinator. A campus policy prohibits sexual harassment; complaints are resolved either informally and confidentially or through a formal grievance procedure. Policy and procedures have been publicly communicated in writing to students, faculty, and staff.

The Committee on the Status of Women, elected by faculty and staff members, meets regularly to review campus policy and sponsor programs for women. Both this committee and the Committee on Minority Affairs address the concerns of minority women.

Women in Leadership Positions. *Students.* In recent years, women have held 11 percent of the leadership positions, a proportion significantly below average for four-year public colleges in this guide. The positions held by women were presiding officer of the student governing body and editor-in-chief of the campus newspaper.

Faculty. Twenty-four percent of the 189 faculty members are women. There are 3 female faculty for every 100 female students and 8 male faculty for every 100 male students.

Administrators. Of the nine top administrators, the chief development officer is a woman. A woman chairs one of five departments, behavioral science. One of the the 7-member executive committee of the faculty senate is female, as are 2 of the 8 regents.

Women and the Curriculum. Most women who graduate with bachelor's degrees major in business (25 percent), psychology (22 percent), and social sciences (16 percent). Eleven percent of women major in such nontraditional fields as engineering, computer science, mathematics, and physical sciences, a proportion above average for four-year public universities in this guide. The university sponsors a program encouraging women students to prepare for a career in engineering. Women account for 40 percent of the students in cooperative education programs, which include engineering and management.

The Women's Studies Program offers an undergraduate minor. Such departments as history, political science, psychology, and English offer courses on women. Recent titles include Women in America; Development of Sex Roles, and Women, Politics, and the Law. An official committee reports on the inclusion of women in the curriculum.

Women and Athletics. Opportunities to compete in organized individual and team sports are limited. Women participate in three intramural sports: volleyball, basketball, and fencing. Club sports are also available. Sixteen percent of intramural and 19 percent of intercollegiate athletes are women, and women receive 20 percent of athletic scholarship aid. One of the four paid intercollegiate coaches is a woman. The intercollegiate sports offered are basketball and fencing.

Housing and Student Organizations. Six one-bedroom and 24 two-bedroom apartments are available for the 1 percent of students who reside on campus. Organizations that serve as advocacy groups for women students include the National Organization for Women, the Society of Women Engineers, and the Women of Michigan Advancement Network.

Special Services and Programs for Women. *Health and Counseling.* The student health service provides medical treatment specific to women, including gynecological, birth control, and abortion services. A full clinic staff is available, on a contractual basis, for outpatient care. The regular student health insurance covers abortion and maternity expenses at no extra cost. The student counseling center, staffed by one man and three women (including one minority woman), offers counseling services of special concern to women. Assertiveness/leadership training is available.

Safety and Security. Measures consist of local police, campus police without arrest authority, night-time escort for women students, a campus-wide emergency telephone system, and a rape crisis center. One assault was reported for 1980–81.

Career. The university sponsors career workshops and provides printed material and job discrimination information on nontraditional occupations for women. Women employed in nontraditional fields give lectures and panels for students. Updated files of alumnae by specific career are maintained and there is networking between alumnae and female students.

Other. The Campus Women's Center, sponsored by the Office of Student Affairs, serves about 2,000 women, 10 percent of whom are minority women. Under the direction of its part-time, salaried administrator, the center offers a variety of programs and services for women, including a theater-arts program, a drop-in center, and a telephone service for information, referrals, and support.

The Commission on Women sponsors the Women's Festival, while other campus units sponsor such events as Career Day, the

Health Awareness Fair, and the Susan B. Anthony Award. The university also runs a Women in Film series and sponsors discussion groups on women's issues among students, faculty, and staff.

Institutional Self-Description. ''As part of the University of Michigan system, UM-Dearborn enjoys the resources of a large university and the advantages of moderate size. Students receive personalized instruction from professors rather than teaching assistants. Faculty are sensitive to the diverse opportunities available to today's women and encourage participation in nontraditional studies.''

Univeristy of Michigan, Flint
Flint, MI 48503
Telephone: (313) 762-3322

3,374 undergraduates

	Amer. Ind.	Asian Amer.	Blacks	Hispanics	Whites
F	2	9	252	24	1,475
M	6	6	150	19	1,421
%	0.2	0.5	12.0	1.3	86.1

 AAUW

Established in 1956, this state-supported, urban university offers its 3,921 students a range of bachelor's degree programs in liberal arts and sciences and a selected range of master's programs. Adult continuing education, on-campus evening, and summer session classes are also available. Fifty-two percent of the 3,374 undergraduates in degree programs are women; 43 percent of women attend part-time. With a median age of 25, undergraduate students are slightly older than those at comparable universities; 7 percent of undergraduate women are over age 40. All students commute. Public transportation and on-campus parking at a fee are available.

Private childcare facilities are available near the campus.

Policies to Ensure Fairness to Women. The Affirmative Action Coordinator has part-time responsibility for policy relating to equal-employment-opportunity, handicapped–access, and sex-equity matters. A published campus policy prohibits sexual harassment of students, faculty, and staff; complaints are resolved through a formal grievance procedure. A self-designated Committee on the Status of Women reports to the Affirmative Action Coordinator and takes public stands on issues of concern to students. The committee, which includes student members with voting rights, also addresses the concerns of minority women.

Women in Leadership Positions. *Students.* Women students have few opportunities to exercise campus-wide leadership. In recent years, women have served one term each as presiding officer of the student governing body and editor-in-chief of the campus newspaper. A woman also serves as president of the single campus honorary society.

Faculty. Twenty-three percent of the 123 full-time faculty are women, a proportion slightly below the national average. There are 3 female faculty for every 100 female students and 11 male faculty for every 100 male students.

Administrators. With the exception of the chief academic officer, all top administrators are men. Women chair three of the 22 departments: health care, psychology, and education. One of the three members of the faculty senate and two of the eight regents are women.

Women and the Curriculum. Most bachelor's degrees awarded to women are in education (25 percent), social science (19 percent), business (19 percent), and health professions (11 percent); 2 percent are in such nontraditional areas as computer sicence and physical science, a below-average proportion for

public, four-year institutions in this guide. Fifty-two percent of students in cooperative education programs are female, as are 28 percent of student interns.

Three courses on women are available through the departments of comparative literature, history, and psychology: Women in Contemporary World Literature, History of American Women, and Psychology of Women. Instruction on the development and use of sex-fair curricula is provided by the division of education, and the division of social work offers instruction on services for women with special needs.

Minority Women. Minority women constitute 16 percent of female undergraduates, with black women the largest group. The university reports that one Hispanic and three black women serve on the full-time faculty. One of the university regents is a black woman. Four of nine members of the counseling staff are minority women, and all counselors receive in-service training on avoiding racism.

Women and Athletics. There are no opportunities for women in organized competitive sports.

Special Services and Programs for Women. *Health and Counseling.* The student health service employs one female health-care provider. No medical services specific to women are available. The student counseling center, staffed by seven women and two men, offers birth control and abortion counseling. Counselors receive in-service training on avoiding sex-role stereotyping.

Safety and Security. Measures consist of campus police with arrest authority, night-time escort for women students, high-intensity lighting, a campus-wide, emergency telephone system, self-defense courses for women, information sessions on safety and crime prevention, and a rape crisis center. No information was provided on the incidence of rapes and assaults.

Career. Career workshops and job discrimination information on nontraditional occupations for women are provided, along with lectures and panels by women employed in these fields.

Institutional Self-Description. ''The academic program of the University of Michigan-Flint is centered in the traditional disciplines of the liberal arts and sciences, with which specific career and professional programs are closely articulated. Both the urban setting of the campus and the need for competently trained professionals in education, government, business, and the health and human services fields have led the UM-Flint faculty to develop programs in business and management, urban education, health care, public administration, and a variety of social professional areas.''

Western Michigan University
Kalamazoo, MI 49008
Telephone: (616) 383-1600

★ Women and the Curriculum
★ Women and Athletics

16,864 undergraduates

	Amer. Ind.	Asian Amer.	Blacks	Hispanics	Whites
F	33	23	548	45	7,427
M	23	15	488	57	7,681
%	0.3	0.2	6.1	0.6	90.0

 AAUW

Founded in 1903 as a preparatory school for teachers, Western Michigan is now a state-supported institution with eleven schools and colleges on two campuses, one-half mile apart. Located 140 miles from Detroit in the city of Kalamazoo, it offers its 22,447 students a comprehensive range of undergraduate, graduate, and professional degree programs, in addition to continuing education courses.

Women are nearly half of the 16,864 undergraduates, and 19 percent attend part-time. A quarter of the undergraduate women are over age 25; the median age of all undergraduates is 21. Classes meet on and off campus during the day and evening. On-campus parking at a fee and public transportation are available for the 61 percent of undergraduates who commute.

University-sponsored childcare facilities, open evenings and days, can accommodate about 80 children, primarily of undergraduates, at $1.10 per hour. Additional, private childcare facilities are located off campus.

Policies to Ensure Fairness to Women. A full-time Affirmative Action Officer examines practices and makes policy regarding equal-employment-opportunity, handicapped-access, and sex-equity requirements. A publicized, written sexual harassment policy protects all members of the Western Michigan community; complaints are resolved through formal means. An independent, self-designated Commission on the Status of Women, which includes students as voting members, meets regularly and publishes its findings on issues of concern to women. The commission also sponsors speakers, awards, and programs. The Commission on Minority Affairs is responsive to the concerns of minority women.

Women in Leadership Positions. *Students.* Women students have had some opportunities to exercise leadership experience. In recent years, women have been elected to the offices of student body president, student senate president, student union board president, and residence-hall council president. Women preside over five of eleven honorary societies.

Faculty. Twenty-one percent of the 840 full-time faculty are women, a figure slightly below average for similar schools in this guide. There are 3 female faculty for every 100 female students and 9 male faculty for every 100 male students.

Administrators. Men hold most top administrative positions. The Dean of the School of Leadership, the Director of the Counseling Center, and the Dean of the Graduate College are women. Women chair seven of 49 departments, including dance, home economics, English, blind rehabilitation and mobility, and occupational therapy; a woman heads the social sciences division of General Studies. Two of the nine trustees are women.

Women and the Curriculum. The most popular fields for women graduates are education (23 percent), business (17 percent), and health professions (11 percent). The proportion of women earning public affairs degrees is above the national average. A large engineering program enrolls a small proportion of women. Less than 4 percent of women pursue such nontraditional fields as agriculture, computer science, mathematics, and physical sciences.

A Women's Studies Program offers a 20-credit interdisciplinary minor and a selection of 14 courses on women, including Women's Religious Lives, East and West; Psychology and Woman; and The Role of Women in Ancient Greece and Rome. Over 180 students have taken this minor in recent years. An official committee oversees the program.

The management department offers a course on Women and Management. The departments of business, education, and physical education offer some instruction on matters specific to women.

Women and Athletics. The large organized sports program for women consists of nine intercollegiate teams and at least ten intramural activities. One-third of the intercollegiate athletes are women; women receive 30 percent of the athletic scholarship assistance. Seven of the 33 paid varsity coaches are women. Intercollegiate sports offered are basketball, cross-country, field hockey, gymnastics, softball, swimming and diving, tennis, track and field, and volleyball.

Housing and Student Organizations. Thirty-nine percent of the undergraduates live on campus in single-sex or coeducational dormitories. Housing is available for married students with or without children and for single parents.

Social sororities and fraternities have 1,000 members, nearly half belonging to sororities. All-minority sororities have 75 members. Advocacy groups include Women in Business and Associated Women Students.

Special Services and Programs for Women. *Health and Counseling.* The student health center employs 5 physicians, 1 of whom is female, and 4 health-care providers, 2 of whom are female. The student counseling center's staff consists of 8 women and 10 men. Counseling and treatment are provided for gynecological problems, birth control, abortion, and for rape and assault.

Safety and Security. Measures consist of campus police protection, night-time escort for women, emergency alarms, a brochure on campus safety, and a rape crisis center. Two rapes and 61 assaults on both women and men were reported in 1980–81.

Career. The university offers career workshops, lectures, and information for women interested in nontraditional occupations. Faculty are offered workshops on nontraditional careers for women and men.

Other. The very active Center for Women's Servies, operating under a full-time director, serves about 2,300 persons, primarily community women and undergraduates. It serves displaced homemakers and sponsors internships and opportunities for field placement and independent study.

Handicapped Student Services assists the 100 handicapped students, 50 of whom are women. Half the campus is barrier-free.

Institutional Self-Description. "Western's Center for Women's Services provides support, counseling, academic help, programs and workshops, as well as internships, field placement and independent study opportunities. On-campus housing is readily available and campus police strive to provide a safe environment. Women's Studies courses and courses in many other curricula deal with issues of racism and sexism."

MINNESOTA

Bemidji State University
Bemidji, MN 56601
Telephone: (218) 755-2000

Women in Leadership
★★ administrators ★ **Women and Athletics**

4,165 undergraduates

	Amer. Ind.	Asian Amer.	Blacks	Hispanics	Whites
F	88	6	3	4	1,862
M	65	7	28	4	2,020
%	3.7	0.3	0.8	0.2	95.0

 AAUW

Bemidji State University was founded as a teacher-training school in 1919 and now has some 5,300 students. Forty-eight percent of the 4,165 undergraduates are women, 10 percent of whom attend part-time. Six hundred women participate in continuing education programs. The median age of undergraduates is 21.

Although Bemidji is still primarily a teachers' college, students also earn bachelor's degrees in business, arts and sciences, and social sciences. The college has a master's degree program and also awards some associate degrees. On-and off-campus evening classes and summer sessions are available. The campus is accessible by public transportation. On-campus parking for a fee is also available for the estimated 20 percent of students who commute.

Private childcare is available near the campus.

Policies to Ensure Fairness to Women. The Affirmative Action officer serves part-time as compliance administrator for equal employment opportunity, sex equity for students, and handicapped access. A sexual harassment policy that will establish a formal grievance procedure is now being developed.

Women in Leadership Positions. *Students.* Of five student leadership positions available, the student union board presidency was held by a woman for one of three recent years.

Faculty. Fifteen percent of the full-time faculty are women, a proportion below the average for similar colleges in this guide. There are 2 female faculty for every 100 female students and 7 male faculty for every 100 male students. The college reports that the full-time female faculty includes 1 American Indian and 1 Asian American woman.

Administrators. Three of seven top administrators are white women: president, head librarian, and director of institutional research. Two departments, art and English, are chaired by women. Two of 12 alumni awards were given to women in 1980–81.

Women and the Curriculum. Most four-year degrees awarded to women are in education (45 percent), public affairs (16 percent), business (8 percent), letters (6 percent), and social sciences (6 percent). Four percent of women graduate in mathematics and physical sciences. Women earn three-fourths of two-year degrees

awarded, 57 percent of them in arts and sciences. About 60 percent of student internships and 20 percent of science field-service appointments are held by women.

The department of sociology offers the one course on women, Women in Society. The departments of physical education and social work provide instruction on some matters specific to women. Faculty workshops are held on affirmative action and equal opportunity.

Women and Athletics. Bemidji offers good opportunities for women to participate in organized competitive sports. The intramural program includes a variety of coeducational and all-women's team and individual sports. Women constitute 28 percent of intercollegiate athletes but receive 40 percent of athletic scholarship aid. The intercollegiate sports in which women participate are basketball, field hockey, gymnastics, swimming, tennis, track and field, and volleyball.

Housing and Student Organizations. Fifty-one percent of students live on campus in coeducational dormitories with no restrictions on visiting hours. Five of the six residence-hall directors are women and all residence-hall staff receive awareness training on sexism and racism, sex education, and assertiveness.

Two percent of undergraduate women belong to social sororities. Neither sororities nor fraternities provide housing for members.

Special Services and Programs for Women. *Health and Counseling.* The student health service, which provides gynecological and birth control treatment, is staffed by 1 male physician and 4 female nurses. The 1 female and 4 male counselors offer abortion and rape and assault counseling. The counseling center also offers assertiveness training.

Safety and Security. Measures consist of local police, campus police without arrest authority, self-defense courses for women, and information on safety and rape and assault prevention. For 1980–81, two rapes and nine assaults on women were reported.

Career. Workshops on nontraditional occupations, programs by women employed in nontraditional fields, and job discrimination information are provided.

Institutional Self-Description. None provided.

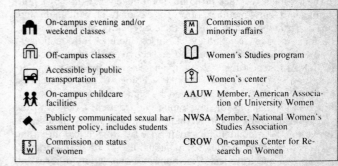

🏛	On-campus evening and/or weekend classes	ⓂⒶ	Commission on minority affairs
🏛	Off-campus classes	📖	Women's Studies program
🚌	Accessible by public transportation	🏠	Women's center
👥	On-campus childcare facilities	AAUW	Member, American Association of University Women
✎	Publicly communicated sexual harassment policy, includes students	NWSA	Member, National Women's Studies Association
ⓈⓌ	Commission on status of women	CROW	On-campus Center for Research on Women

Carleton College
Northfield, MN 55057
Telephone: (507) 663-4000

★ Women and the Curriculum

★ Women and Athletics

1,807 undergraduates

	Amer. Ind.	Asian Amer.	Blacks	Hispanics	Whites
F	2	17	34	11	807
M	3	24	27	15	866
%	0.3	2.3	3.4	1.4	92.6

Carleton College is a four-year, liberal arts college located in a small town an hour from Minneapolis-St. Paul. Incorporated in 1867 by the Congregatinal Church, the college today is a private, non-sectarian institution enrolling 871 full-time women and 936 full-time men. An additional 18 students attend part time. The median age of undergraduates is 20. Virtually all of the students live on campus; there is on-campus parking for the 2 percent who commute.

Private, off-campus childcare facilities are available.

Policies to Ensure Fairness to Women. Carleton's affirmative action office has no specific enforcement responsibilities. Complaints of sexual harassment are handled informally and confidentially. An active Committee on the Status of Women, appointed by the president, includes student members with voting rights. It takes public stands on issues of concern to all women students and makes recommendations to the president. A Committee on Minority Affairs addresses the concerns of minority women.

Women in Leadership Positions. *Students.* Women students have limited opportunities to exercise campus-wide leadership. One campus-wide office was held by a woman in a recent three year period—president of the junior class. Men preside over the three honorary societies.

Faculty. The proportion of full-time faculty members who are women—22 percent—is below the national average. There are 3 female faculty for every 100 female students and 11 male faculty for every 100 male students.

Administrators. Men hold all key administrative positions. Of the 31 departments, women chair six, including Asian studies, Latin American studies, and classical languages.

Women and the Curriculum. Most bachelor's degrees granted to women are in the social sciences (30 percent) and letters (25 percent). Fourteen percent are in the nontraditional areas of mathematics and physical sciences, an unusually high proportion for private colleges in this guide. The 13 percent of women who earn degrees in physical sciences constitute almost half of the degree recipients in that field. Another 11 percent of women earn degrees in biology.

The Women's Studies Program, coordinated part-time by a non-permanent faculty member, offers three courses on women through the departments of English, sociology/anthropology, history, theater arts and psychology. Courses include Introduction to Women's Studies; Comparative Perspective on Women; Race and Sex in America; Men, Women, and Society in America; Perspectives on Women in the Arts; Psychology of Sex Differences. A special major can be arranged by students. An official committee is responsible for developing the program. Courses in the education department for secondary school teachers include information about mathematics avoidance by women and girls, and also instruction on the development and use of sex-fair curricula.

Women and Athletics. The abundance and variety of team and individual sports for women and the high level of participation by women in club, intramural, and intercollegiate sports makes the women's sports program unique among the colleges and universities in this guide. Facilities include arboretum trails, 40 acres of playing fields, two indoor swimming pools, two gymnasiums, and 16 tennis courts. Eleven intercollegiate sports are offered, including basketball, cross-country, field hockey, skiing, softball, swimming, and tennis.

Housing and Student Organizations. Single-sex and coeducational residence halls do not restrict hours for visitors of the opposite sex. The Women's Caucus, the gay community, and Los Amigos are among the student groups that meet on campus.

Special Services and Programs for Women. *Health and Counseling.* Along with the student health service, Carleton has a counseling center, staffed by three female counselors. The center offers services specific to women including birth control, rape and assault, and abortion counseling.

Safety and Security. Measures consist of a night-time escort service for women, information on campus safety, and self-defense courses for women. No rapes or assaults were reported for 1980–81.

Career. The college provides materials and information on nontraditional careers for women, maintains updated files of alumnae by specific careers, and sponsors networking between alumnae and female students.

Other. Carleton women edit and publish a feminist journal, *Breaking Ground.*

Institutional Self-Description. ''Carleton's first graduates were a man and a woman who followed nearly identical programs. Succeeding generations of students have enjoyed the same demanding and egalitarian curriculum and the valuable lessons provided by living in residence. Male and female, they have established themselves as leaders-on campus and in their careers.''

College of St. Benedict
St. Joseph, MN 56374
Telephone: (612) 363-5308

Women in Leadership
★★★ students;
★★★ faculty
★★★ administrators

1,610 undergraduates

	Amer. Ind.	Asian Amer.	Blacks	Hispanics	Whites
F	3	5	5	4	1,573
M	0	0	0	0	0
%	0.2	0.3	0.3	0.3	98.9

 AAUW

Founded in 1913 and operated by the Sisters of the Order of St. Benedict, the College of St. Benedict is a Roman Catholic, liberal arts institution for women. The women's branch of St. John's University for men, the college still maintains a separate administration and Board of Trustees. Its rural campus, northwest of Minneapolis, attracts 1,921 students; virtually all 1,610 undergraduates attend full-time. The median age of all undergraduates is 19.

A wide range of undergraduate degrees is available, in addition to a continuing education program and two-year degrees. Evening classes and opportunities for self-paced/contract learning are also available. Free on-campus parking is provided for the 5 percent of students who commute.

Private childcare facilities are available close to the campus.

Policies to Ensure Fairness to Women. The Director of Personnel assumes the part-time responsibility for monitoring compliance with laws concerning sex equity, equal employment opportunity, and handicapped access. A sexual harassment policy that protects students has been publicized, but not in writing.

Women in Leadership Positions. *Students.* Women hold all student leadership positions.

Faculty. Sixty percent of the 98 full-time faculty are women. There are 4 female faculty for every 100 female students.

Administrators. Women hold most top positions, including President, vice president for academic affairs, chief business officer, chief planning officer, and director of athletics. Women chair six of 19 departments, including biology, education, theology, modern languages, nursing, and psychology. A woman was the sole commencement speaker in 1981.

Women and the Curriculum. Most bachelor's degrees awarded are in education (26 percent), health professions (15 percent), fine arts (10 percent), home economics (10 percent), and business (7 percent). Two percent of degrees awarded are in the nontraditional areas of mathematics and physical sciences. All two-year degrees are in arts and sciences. The mathematics department has a program for building confidence in mathematics.

Five courses focusing on women are offered by the departments of economics/business and administration, history, English, and philosophy. Business students can take a course on Women and Management. Prospective social workers receive instruction on services for battered spouses, displaced homemakers, and childcare. An official committee monitors the inclusion of women in the curriculum and develops curricular materials on women. Faculty are offered workshops on sexism in the curriculum and on the needs of reentry women.

Women and Athletics. The athletics program, good for a college of this size, attracts 80 women to intercollegiate, 250 to intramural, and 50 to club, sports. Five intercollegiate sports and three intramural team sports are offered. All intercollegiate teams play in tournament competition. Three of the five paid intercollegiate coaches are female. Intercollegiate sports offered are basketball, softball, swimming, tennis, and volleyball.

Housing and Student Organizations. Ninety-five percent of all undergraduate women live on campus in dormitories that have restrictive hours for male visitors. Residence-hall staff are offered awareness-training on sexism.

A women's advocacy group, Women for Equality, has 50 active members.

Special Services and Programs for Women. *Health and Counseling.* There is no student health service. A student counseling center, employing one female and one male, provides counseling for victims of rape and assault. Staff are offered training on sex-role stereotyping and racial bias.

Safety and Security. Measures include campus and local police protection, night-time escort, high-intensity lighting, an emergency telephone system, and instruction on self-defense and campus safety for women. A rape crisis center is available. Two assaults on women and no rapes were reported for 1980-81.

Career. The college offers credit courses on job-acquisition skills and career planning, provides workshops and discussions on nontraditional occupations, and encourages networking between students and alumnae.

Other. The office of the Dean of Students, in cooperation with the student government, sponsors an annual women's week. The counseling department works with the Dean of Students to conduct assertiveness-training sessions.

Returning Women Students. Continuing Education for Women, a program that has its own center, enrolls 163 reentry women. Directed by a full-time, female administrator, the program reports to the Office of Academic Affairs.

Institutional Self-Description. "The College of St. Benedict is an academic community for undergraduate women. It maintains close cooperation with St. John's University, a college for men. We are committed to providing an educational content and process in an environment that fosters liberal, Christian, Catholic education in a Benedictine setting."

College of St. Catherine
2004 Randolph, St. Paul, MN 55105
Telephone: (612) 690-6000

Women in Leadership
★★★ Faculty
★★★ Administrators

1,979 undergraduates

	Amer. Ind.	Asian Amer.	Blacks	Hispanics	Whites
F	14	15	10	16	1,903
M	0	0	0	0	0
%	0.7	0.8	0.5	0.8	97.2

AAUW

The College of St. Catherine, founded in 1905, is a Roman Catholic, liberal arts institution for women, under the direction of the Sisters of St. Joseph Carondelet. Located midway between St. Paul and Minneapolis, St. Catherine serves 2,201 students. Only 1 percent of the 1,979 undergraduates attend part-time. The median age of all undergraduates is 23.

A range of undergraduate degree programs is supplemented by an exchange program with the College of St. Thomas, Augsburg College, Hamline University, and Macalester College. A continuing education program, a weekend college, evening classes, and a summer session are available. The campus is easily reached by public transportation, and on-campus parking is available for a fee.

A Montessori school situated on campus serves primarily the children of continuing education students. The school accommodates 20 children and charges a fee of $1 per hour. Private childcare facilities are available off campus.

Policies to Ensure Fairness to Women. The Assistant to the President has the part-time responsibility for monitoring compliance with affirmative-action laws. A written policy on sexual harassment is being developed.

Women in Leadership Positions. *Students.* No information was provided.

Faculty. Sixty-five percent of the 127 full-time faculty are women. There are 4 female faculty for every 100 female students.

Administrators. Women hold all top positions except chief business officer. A black woman is chief development officer. Women chair about half of the 25 departments, including chemistry. A little more than half of the members of the Board of Trustees are women.

Women and the Curriculum. One-third of degrees are awarded in health professions, and another third in education, business, and fine arts. Three percent of women graduate in mathematics and physical sciences. Programs are available to encourage women to prepare for careers in science, engineering (joint program with Washington University in St. Louis), accounting, and computer science.

Five courses on women are offered by the departments of history, theology, sociology, and communications/theater. An official committee works to expand course offerings on women; there is also a task force on the college's commitment to women. Courses in the departments of physical education, social work, and business address some issues specific to women.

Women and Athletics. Six intercollegiate teams attract 122 athletes. Eight intramural teams draw 740 participants to a variety of individual and team activities, including powderpuff football, turkey trot, tennis, golf, broomball, basketball, volleyball, and softball. Fifty-five women belong to sports clubs. Seven of 9 paid coaches for intercollegiate sports are female. Intercollegiate sports offered are basketball, gymnastics, swimming, tennis, track and field, and volleyball.

Housing and Student Organizations. On-campus housing consists of dormitories and apartments that have restrictive hours for male visitors. Residence-hall staff are offered awareness-training on racism and sexism.

The sole women's advocacy group is the Intercultural Student Organization.

Special Services and Programs for Women. *Health and Counseling.* The student health service employs one female physician. The student counseling center is staffed by three female counselors. Counseling for gynecological problems, birth control, abortion, and rape and assault, as well as treatment for gynecological disorders, are available.

Safety and Security. Measures consist of campus police, night-time escort, and instruction on self-defense and campus safety. There is a rape crisis center. One assault against a woman was reported for 1980-81.

Career. The college offers information, lectures, and career workshops on nontraditional occupations, promotes networking with alumnae, and encourages students to consult files on the careers of alumnae.

Returning Women Students. The reentry Adult Program sponsors a Continuing Education for Women Program and Center that enrolls 300 to 450 students in the weekend college. An additional 1,200 reentry women attend other continuing education courses. Faculty are offered special workshops on the needs of returning women students.

Special Features. The library has an extensive women's collection.

Institutional Self-Description. "The College of St. Catherine, a Catholic liberal arts institution, is committed to the education of women of all ages. Our programs are geared to both traditional and nontraditional careers. Our goals are to provide quality education and to help women develop their self-confidence and discover the many choices open to them today."

College of St. Scholastica
1200 Kenwood Ave., Duluth, MN 55811
Telephone: (218) 723-6000

Women in Leadership
★★ students
★★ faculty
★★ administrators

1,121 undergraduates

	Amer. Ind.	Asian Amer.	Blacks	Hispanics	Whites
F	23	0	6	0	879
M	7	0	1	0	190
%	2.7	0.0	0.6	0.0	96.7

 AAUW

St. Scholastica is a four-year, Roman Catholic college operated by the Sisters of St. Benedict. Originally a two-year and then a four-year women's college, it became coeducational in 1967. It serves a student body of 909 women and 212 men. The median age of undergraduates is 20. On-campus parking is available to the 52 percent of students who commute. A summer session is offered.

Private childcare is available off campus, for children aged three to six only.

Policies to Ensure Fairness to Women. The college reports it is now developing a written policy on sexual harassment; complaints are resolved informally and confidentially or through a formal grievance procedure.

Women in Leadership Positions. *Students.* During a recent three-year period, women have held most of the campus-wide leadership positions, including president of the student body, editor of the campus newspaper, and presiding officer of the residence-hall council.

Faculty. Almost half of the 51 full-time faculty are women, and women hold 46 percent of the permanent positions. The ratio of female faculty to female students is 3 to 100, and of male faculty to male students, 13 to 100.

Administrators. Women hold 3 of the 8 top administrative positions, and chair 13 of the 21 academic departments.

Women and the Curriculum. Degrees are awarded to women in health professions (66 percent), home economics (8 percent), and education (6 percent). Three percent of women take degrees in theology. One percent of women major in physical sciences.

Several courses on women are offered through various departments, including The Psychology of Women; Women and the Law; and Contemporary Issues: Women. The departments of business, nursing, and social work provide instruction on some matters specific to women.

Women and Athletics. Four intercollegiate and six intramural sports are offered. Two of the nine paid varsity coaches are women. Intercollegiate sports are basketball, cross-country, tennis, and volleyball.

Housing and Student Organizations. Single-sex dormitories and four-student, single-sex apartments are available. Both men's and women's residences have restrictive hours for visitors of the opposite sex. The residence-hall directors (one male, one female) receive awareness training on sexism, sex education, racism, and birth control.

Special Services and Programs for Women. *Health and Counseling.* The student health service employs 1 woman among its physicians, and 3 registered nurses. The counseling center has 4 women counselors, including 1 minority woman. Gynecological treatment and birth control, abortion, and rape and assault counseling are provided. The student health insurance policy covers maternity care at no extra charge.

Safety and Security. Measures consist of a night-time escort service, self-defense and campus safety information, and a rape crisis center. No rapes or assaults were reported on campus for 1980-81.

Career. The career placement service offers materials and programs on nontraditional occupations for women.

Other. The Student Union offers theater and other women's arts programs.

Institutional Self-Description. "St. Scholastica is owned by a group of religious women. Fifty percent of its Board of Trustees are women. The environment of the college offers to women opportunities to interact extensively with other women, and provides role models for those women who have high career aspirations."

College of St. Teresa
Winona, MN 55987
Telephone: (507) 454-2930

Women in Leadership
★★★ faculty
★★★ administrators

838 undergraduates

	Amer. Ind.	Asian Amer.	Blacks	Hispanics	Whites
F	2	2	5	23	767
M	0	0	0	0	17
%	0.3	0.3	0.6	2.8	96.1

 AAUW

Originally a high school academy, the College of St. Teresa has been a Roman Catholic women's college since 1909. Located two hours from Minneapolis-St. Paul, the college attracts 865 students. The 838 matriculated students attend full-time. The median age of all students is 20.

The college offers a variety of liberal arts and professional degree programs, as well as continuing education courses available through the Women's Institute for Lifelong Learning. Day and evening classes are held both on and off campus. The campus is accessible by public transportation, and on-campus parking is available for the 3 percent of students who commute.

A privately sponsored childcare center operates on campus. Additional private childcare facilities are located off campus.

Policies to Ensure Fairness to Women. An equal-opportunity officer has part-time responsibility for equal employment opportunity, educational sex equity, and handicapped access.

Women in Leadership Positions. *Students.* No information was provided about all-campus leadership. Women head the seven honorary societies.

Faculty. Women are half of the 48 full-time faculty and hold 5 of 19 permanent appointments. There are 3 female faculty for every 100 female students.

Administrators. Women hold 5 of 8 top administrative posts. Women chair five of nine departments, including nursing, education, and fine and performing arts. Half of the members of the faculty senate and ten of the trustees are women.

Women and the Curriculum. Sixty percent of women earn degrees in health professions; education is the second most popular field (13 percent). Less than 3 percent of the women specialize in the nontraditional majors of mathematics and physical sciences. Several departments, e.g. business, social work education, nursing, and physical education, pay some attention to women's issues in their instruction. There are no courses on women.

Women and Athletics. The athletic program is well-balanced for a college of its size, and offers students opportunities to participate in organized competitive individual and team sports. Intramural sports draw 441 women to six activities, including tennis, cross-country, basketball, softball, flag football, and volleyball. The campus has an outdoor ice-skating rink. Club sports attract 15 athletes. Forty-five women participate in four intercollegiate sports—basketball, softball, tennis, and volleyball. Two of the 4 paid intercollegiate coaches are women.

Housing and Student Organizations. Ninety-seven percent of all undergraduate women live in dormitories, which have restrictive hours for male visitors. The all-female residence-hall staff is offered awareness training on racism, sexism, and sex education.

Special Services and Programs for Women. *Health and Counseling.* The student health service employs 1 male physician and 2 female health-care providers. Students are referred to a local clinic and hospital for medical treatment. The student counseling center, staffed by 1 man and 2 women, offers counseling on birth control, abortion, and rape and assault.

Safety and Security. Measures consist of local and campus police, and instruction on self-defense and campus safety. Two assaults on women were reported for 1980–81.

Career. St. Teresa offers its students career workshops, information, and lectures on nontraditional occupations, and maintains files on the careers of its alumnae. There are also programs to encourage women to prepare for careers in engineering, computer science, and law enforcement.

Other. The residence-hall staff and the office of Dean of Students sponsor assertiveness/leadership training sessions.

Institutional Self-Description. "We aim to help women secure an education in the liberal arts and professions, to assist them in developing a sense of responsibility and self-direction, to facilitate their personal growth, and to encourage them in the pursuit of truth and the commitment to Judaeo-Christian moral values."

Gustavus Adolphus College
St. Peter, MN 56082
Telephone: (507) 931-8000

★ **Women and Athletics**

2,199 undergraduates

	Amer. Ind.	Asian Amer.	Blacks	Hispanics	Whites
F	0	0	9	0	1,246
M	0	0	11	0	921
%	0.0	0.0	0.9	0.0	99.1

AAUW

Gustavus Adolphus is a coeducational, liberal arts college affiliated with the Lutheran Church. The campus is located in a town of 9,000 residents, near Minneapolis-St. Paul. Originally designed to provide pastors and teachers for Swedish immigrants to Minnesota, the college's present mission is to create a dialogue between academic disciplines and the Christian heritage.

The college enrolls 2,199 undergraduates, 57 percent of whom are women. The median age of undergraduates is 20. Ninety percent of the students live on campus, 7 percent commute, and the remaining 3 percent are in off-campus programs. There is free on-campus parking.

Private childcare facilities are available off campus.

Policies to Ensure Fairness to Women. The Academic Vice President and the Operations Vice President are responsible for reviewing policies and practices relating to equal employment opportunity, sex equity for students, and handicapped accessibility. The concerns of minority women are addressed by the Committee on Minority Affairs.

Women in Leadership Positions. *Students.* One woman held a campus-wide student leadership position in recent years (manager of the campus radio station).

Faculty. The full-time faculty of 144 is 22 percent female, with women holding 13 percent of the permanent appointments. There are 2 female faculty for every 100 female students and 12 male faculty for every 100 male students.

Administrators. All the chief administrative officers, with the exception of the student-life officer, are men. Of the 23 departments, nursing is chaired by a woman. One woman sits on the 12-member faculty governing body and 1 on an important 9-member faculty committee. Six of the 31 trustees are women. In a recent year, half of the six alumni awards went to women.

Women and the Curriculum. Most women earn degrees in education (17 percent), business (17 percent), the social sciences (15 percent), and biology (13 percent). Eight percent of women graduate with majors in such nontraditional fields as mathematics and physical sciences. The college has received its third National Science Foundation grant for its Women in Science Program. Fifty-five percent of the students participating in experiential learning programs are women.

Two courses on women, Women in Society and Women in the Humanities, are available. An official committee is responsible for developing a Women's Studies Program, and the college has received a $100,000 endowment for library acquisitions relating to women. Courses in the departments of education, physical education, and nursing provide some instruction on matters specific to women.

Women and Athletics. Gustavus Adolphus has a good intramural and intercollegiate sports program for women. Thirty-seven percent of intramural athletes and 31 percent of intercollegiate athletes are women; eleven of the 26 paid coaches are women. Women participate in nine intramural (including coeducational volleyball) and nine intercollegiate sports. Intercollegiate sports are basketball, cross-country, golf, gymnastics, softball, swimming, tennis, track and field, and volleyball.

Housing and Student Organizations. Single-sex and coeducational dormitories are available, all with restrictive hours for visitors of the opposite sex. The residence-hall directors, seven women and eight men, are offered awareness-training on sexism, sex education, and birth control.

Twenty percent of undergraduate women, including 3 minority women, belong to social sororities. Twenty-four women and one man belong to the Women's Awareness Center, an advocacy group for women students.

Special Services and Programs for Women. *Health and Counseling.* The student health service and counseling center provide a number of services specific to women, including gynecological treatment and abortion counseling. The health service employs 5 male physicians and 2 female health-care providers. The counseling service has 1 female and 1 male counselor.

Safety and Security. Measures consist of high-intensity lights and a campus police force without arrest authority. No rapes or assaults on women (but two assaults on men) were reported for 1980-81.

Career. A range of career materials and activities is available, including workshops about nontraditional occupations, updated files of alumnae by specific fields, and programs to establish contacts between alumnae and female students.

Other. The Women's Center, run by a part-time student volunteer, offers a variety of programs and services for students and staff, including an annual women's week, theater and other women's arts programs, and a telephone information and referral service. Approximately 600 women are served by the center's programs each year.

Institutional Self-Description. "Gustavus Adolphus College draws women students to a strong variety of traditional and nontraditional programs. The nontraditional aspects include a Women's Referral Service and the increasingly popular women's athletics program; the traditional aspects include a strong nursing department and a full education curriculum. Other women students are attracted by the general atmosphere of the campus, or the college's ties with the Lutheran Church."

Macalaster College
1600 Grand Avenue, St. Paul, MN 55015
Telephone: (612) 696-6139

Women in Leadership
★ administrators

1,705 undergraduates

	Amer. Ind.	Asian Amer.	Blacks	Hispanics	Whites
F	13	8	37	16	747
M	10	7	29	17	676
%	1.5	1.0	4.2	2.1	91.2

Macalaster is a private, four-year college affiliated with the United Presbyterian Church. The campus draws 1,766 students. Women are 50 percent of the 1,705 students enrolled in degree programs, and virtually all the women attend full-time. Nine percent of undergraduate women are over 25 years of age. Seventy percent of the students live in on-campus residences, 8 percent commute, and the rest live in private housing near campus. On-campus parking is available for commuters.

Private childcare facilities are available off campus.

Policies to Ensure Fairness to Women. Three administrative officers share responsibility for the enforcement of equal-employment-opportunity, sex-equity, and handicapped-access laws. A written campus policy prohibiting sexual harassment of staff and students has been communicated in writing to students, faculty, and staff, and both an informal and confidential and a formal grievance procedure resolve complaints. An educational program on sexual harassment is provided for the faculty.

The Committee on the Status of Women, which reports to the President, has both elected and appointed members, and includes students with voting rights. It takes stands on public issues of concern to students and prepares reports which are distributed to the campus community. The concerns of minority women are addressed by the Committee on Minority Affairs.

Women in Leadership Positions. *Students.* Men have held all campus-wide student leadership positions in a recent three-year period.

Faculty. The proportion of full-time faculty who are women (16 percent) is well below the national average. The ratio of female faculty to female students is 2 to 100; of male faculty to male students, 12 to 100.

Administrators. Two of the 8 major administrative positions are held by women, the student-life officer and head librarian. Women head 2 academic departments, English and French.

Women and the Curriculum. Most women major in the social sciences and humanities. About 5 percent take degrees in mathematics and the physical sciences.

A course called French Women Writers is offered by the French department. The curriculum of the school of education includes instruction on the use of sex-fair curricula and on teaching coeducational classes in physical education.

Women and Athletics. Macalaster provides women with opportunities for four intramural team sports. There are seven intercollegiate sports: basketball, cross-country, softball, swimming, tennis, track and field, and volleyball.

Housing and Student Organizations. Students live in coeducational residences with all-male and all-female floors. The three female residence-hall directors are offered awareness-training on sexism, sex education, racism, and birth control.

Women's advocacy groups include Mac Feminists and the Gay Lesbian Coalition.

Special Services and Programs for Women. *Health and Counseling.* The student health service employs 3 part-time physicians—2 females and 1 male. The 3-member counseling center staff includes 2 females. The health service provides treatment for gynecological matters; the counseling center provides counseling on birth control, abortion, and rape and assault. Counselors receive awareness-training on sex-role stereotyping and racial bias.

Safety and Security. Measures consist of campus police, high-intensity lighting, a night-time escort service, emergency telephone and alarm systems, self-defense courses, safety and assault prevention instruction, and a rape crisis center. One rape and three assaults on women were reported for 1980-81.

Career. The career placement office provides a variety of services and information on nontraditional careers for women and maintains files of alumnae by specific careers. A mentor program for women students is sponsored by alumnae.

Institutional Self-Description. "Macalester offers a strong, supportive environment for women, with many choosing nontraditional majors; opportunities for internships in St. Paul-Minneapolis with organizations working for women's rights (e.g., Minnesota Council on the Economic Status of Women); exciting women faculty spread through most departments; and a good library collection on women's concerns."

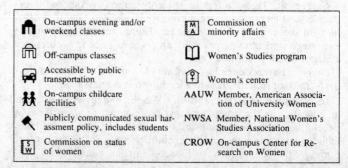

On-campus evening and/or weekend classes	**MA** Commission on minority affairs
Off-campus classes	Women's Studies program
Accessible by public transportation	Women's center
On-campus childcare facilities	AAUW Member, American Association of University Women
Publicly communicated sexual harassment policy, includes students	NWSA Member, National Women's Studies Association
SW Commission on status of women	CROW On-campus Center for Research on Women

Mankato State University
South Road and Ellis Avenue
Mankato, MN 56001
Telephone: (507) 389-2463

| Women in Leadership | ★★ Women and the |
| ★ faculty | Curriculum |

★★ Women and Athletics

8,405 undergraduates

	Amer. Ind.	Asian Amer.	Blacks	Hispanics	Whites
F	7	13	37	12	4,216
M	11	13	37	10	3,858
%	0.2	0.3	0.9	0.3	98.3

🏠 🏛 🚗 👫 🔨 Ⓜ 📖 ⚕ AAUW NWSA

Established in 1867 for the preparation of teachers, Mankato State now offers seven undergraduate and seven graduate degree programs. The student body totals 11,413, of whom 8,405 are undergraduates. Women account for just over half of the undergraduate enrollment; 14 percent of the women attend part-time. Most women are under age 25; those older account for about 13 percent of undergraduates (this figure does not include women in the Friday College, which operates through the Women's Center and attracts 400 reentry women).

In addition to the Friday College, the university offers a variety of schedules, including day and evening classes both on and off campus, weekend courses, and contract learning. On-campus parking is available for the 12 percent of students who commute.

The on-campus daycare center can accommodate 90 children, with students receiving preference. About 80 percent of the requests for this service are met. Private childcare facilities are available near the campus.

Policies to Ensure Fairness to Women. The Vice President for Academic Affairs and Equal Educational Opportunity devotes part-time attention to matters of equal employment opportunity, sex equity and access for the handicapped. A campus policy prohibits sexual harassment of faculty, staff, and students, and has been communicated in writing to all three groups; a formal grievance procedure resolves complaints. A Committee on Minority Affairs attends to the concerns of minority women.

Women in Leadership Positions. *Students.* Although women account for 51 percent of full-time undergraduates, they have held 25 percent of student leadership positions: manager of the campus radio station for one year, and editor of the newspaper, for two. Women head three of the eight honorary societies.

Faculty. Women are 25 percent of the full-time faculty. There are 3 female faculty for every 100 female students and 10 male faculty for every 100 male students.

Administrators. A white woman is the university's chief executive officer. All other top-level administrative positions are held by men. Women chair 6 of the 49 departments, including Scandinavian studies, home economics, medical technology, and emergency care and rescue. A woman serves as Dean of the Arts and Humanities Division.

Women and the Curriculum. Most four-year degrees awarded to women are in education (32 percent), public affairs (15 percent), business (14 percent), and health professions (10 percent). Almost 3 percent of women major in such nontraditional areas as engineering and mathematics. Most two-year degrees awarded to women are in arts and sciences (46 percent), health technologies (29 percent), and business (25 percent).

The Women's Studies Program offers the bachelor's degree, an undergraduate minor, a master's degree with a concentration on women (in Continuing Studies), and a two-year degree in Open Studies. During the past five years, 30 undergraduates have graduated as majors in Women's Studies and 50 as minors. Thirty courses on women are offered through the Women's Studies Program and the departments of minority studies, political science, psychology, sociology, art, history, English, music, social work, speech, education, health science, and library media. Courses offered through departments include Perspectives on Women and Change, a Seminar on Ideology and Feminist Thought, Sexism and Racism, and Women at Mid-Life. Courses offered through Women's Studies include Feminist Scholarship, Ethical Issues in Feminism, and Feminist Pedagogy.

The departments of education, nursing, social work, physical education, and business provide some instruction on matters specific to women. The library's media section offers a course entitled Materials Related to the Women's Movement. An official committee is responsible for developing courses about women in traditional departments and for collecting curricular materials on women. Workshops for the faculty address such topics as sexism and racism in the curriculum, affirmative action and equal opportunity, the needs of reentry women, and nontraditional occupations for both women and men.

Minority Women. Although the percentage of minority women on this campus is very small, attention to their concerns is considerable. At least one course, available through the department of minority studies, focuses on both sexism and racism. This department also sponsors a program to build confidence in mathematics and runs a series of breakfasts for minority women. Faculty are offered workshops on racism in the curriculum, and both residence counselors and residents are offered awareness-training on the avoidance of racism. Student organizations for minorities include the Black Women's Support group, the Black Student Union, and student associations for American Indians, Asian Americans, and Mexican Americans. The personnel of the Minority Group Studies Center also serve minority students.

Women and Athletics. Women receive 30 percent of the athletic scholarships and account for 57 percent of the intercollegiate athletes. While the intramural program does not offer as rich a selection of sports as the intercollegiate, some 2,000 women (33 percent of all intramural athletes) participate in both coeducational and all-women's teams in broomball, bowling, softball, swimming, and volleyball. Nine of the 15 paid intercollegiate coaches are women. The college has extensive facilities for intramural sports. Intercollegiate sports offered are basketball, cross-country, golf, gymnastics, softball, swimming, tennis, track, and volleyball.

Housing and Student Organizations. Coeducational dormitories house the 32 percent of undergraduates who live on campus. Most of the black and foreign women live in dormitories. Two of the three residence-hall directors are women, and all have received awareness-training on sexism, sex education, racism, and birth control (this training is available to students, as well).

Special Services and Programs for Women. *Health and Counseling.* Three male physicians and 9 health-care providers (8 of whom are women) staff a student health service that offers medical treatment for gynecological problems and birth control. The counseling center, 2 of whose 7 members are women, offers abortion and rape and assault counseling. Both maternity and abortion expenses are covered by the student health insurance policy.

Safety and Security. Measures consist of local police, campus police without arrest authority, night-time escort for women students, night-time, campus-wide bus service, self-defense courses for women, information sessions for women on safety and crime prevention, residence halls locked after midnight, and a rape crisis center. Ten assaults (two on women) were reported for 1980–81.

Career. Working closely with the Women's Center, the Career Placement Office offers workshops and nonsexist/nonracist printed information on nontraditional occupations for women, as well as information on job discrimination.

Other. The Women's Center, with a budget of $45,000, serves several thousand women. In addition to operating a warmline, this center, often in conjunction with the Women's Studies Program, sponsors an annual women's week, a women's lecture series, theater and arts programs, a forum for farm women, and provides services for older women and others. The staff of the center and The Women's Studies Program also publish a newsletter six times a year. Just Women, and Forward are student organizations.

Institutional Self-Description. "The atmosphere at Mankato State is pleasant and conducive to learning. An asset is that Mankato is a medium-sized institution with an open environment, where issues can easily be addressed. The Women's Center and Women's Studies Program provide strong leadership in advocating a comfortable environment for women."

Metropolitan State University
121 Metro Square, St. Paul, MN 55101
Telephone: (612) 296-3875

Women in Leadership
- ★ students
- ★★ faculty
- ★ administrators

1,695 undergraduates
Complete enrollment information not available.

Metropolitan State University is an alternative, upper division public institution which serves some 1,659 adult students. All programs are student-designed; there are no major requirements. Three-quarters of the classes meet in the evening; the university is in session year-round. Metropolitan State reports that women are half of the student body. Seventy-two percent of all students attend part-time. The median age of students is 34. All students commute. Public transportation is available.

Policies to Ensure Fairness to Women. Two members of the administration are responsible for policy and practices related to equal employment opportunity and sex equity for students. The Director of Facilities monitors compliance with access for the handicapped. A campus policy prohibiting sexual harassment is currently under review. The Advisory Committee on Women, which includes students as voting members, addresses the concerns of women, including minority women.

Women in Leadership Positions. *Students.* The only campus-wide student office is head of the student senate, which was held by a woman once in a recent three-year period.

Faculty. Women are 44 percent of a full-time faculty of 18, a proportion which is above average for comparable institutions in this guide.

Administrators. The President of the university is a black woman and the chief academic officer a white woman. The other six top administrators are men. Women direct three of four academic centers: arts and sciences, communications, and business/public administration. Two of ten members of the Board of Directors are women.

Women and the Curriculum. All degrees are earned in interdisciplinary studies. Credit is awarded for experiential learning.

Metropolitan offers ten courses on women through Arts and Sciences and Human Services. Recent titles include Survey of Women in Minnesota Life, Twentieth-Century Black Women Novelists, Working Women in the United States, and Career/Life Planning for Women. Human Services provides instruction on

social services of concern to women. A faculty committee reports on curricular developments that include women. Racism and the curriculum is a topic of faculty workshops.

Women and Athletics. No information was provided.

Special Services and Programs for Women. *Health and Counseling.* There is no student health or counseling service. Regular student health insurance covers abortion at no extra cost.

Safety and Security. No information was provided on security measures and on the incidence of rapes and assaults on women.

Career. Services include information on nontraditional occupations for women, career/life planning workshops for women, and programs to establish contacts between alumnae and female students.

Other. The Human Services Center sponsors workshops for battered women. The Advisory Committee on Women's Services offers a women's lecture series. Individualized Educational Planning (IEP) is a ten-week course which includes career, educational, and life planning.

Institutional Self-Description. "Metropolitan State University serves the adult student who has work and/or family responsibilities in a flexible, individualized, fully accredited degree program. Experiential learning is evaluated for credit. Mature women constitute 50 percent of the student body. Individualized advising services are available from a permanent faculty, half of whom are female."

Minneapolis College of Art and Design
133 E. 25 Street, Minneapolis, MN 55404
Telephone: (612) 870-3346

Women in Leadership
- ★ students
- ★ administrators

680 undergraduates

	Amer. Ind.	Asian Amer.	Blacks	Hispanics	Whites
F	6	1	11	2	340
M	8	2	13	2	286
%	2.1	0.5	3.6	0.6	93.3

 AAUW

The Minneapolis College of Art and Design is an independent, four-year, professional college of visual arts. The college offers its 767 students an interdisciplinary program of liberal and studio arts, leading to the bachelor of fine arts degree. Fifty-three percent of the 680 undergraduates are women, 6 percent of whom attend part time. The median age of all undergraduates is 23. Twenty percent of the students reside on campus in college-owned apartments. Free on-campus parking is available for the 80 percent of students who commute.

Private childcare facilities are available near the campus.

Policies to Ensure Fairness to Women. The Administrative Officer of the college is responsible for adherence to equal-employment-opportunity, sex-equity, and handicapped-accessibility laws. The college reports that a sexual harassment policy is being developed.

Women in Leadership Positions. *Students.* Women are more than half of the student body and hold 39 percent of the campus-wide leadership positions. Women have served as president and vice president of the student body, presiding officer of the student court, and presiding officer of the residence-hall council.

Faculty. The proportion of women among the 40 full-time faculty (20 percent) is below the national average. There are 2 female faculty for every 100 female students and 11 male faculty for every 100 male students.

Administrators. Two of the six chief administrative officers are women—the chief student-life officer and the chief development officer. Women chair the departments of development, publications and publicity, and extension programs. About one-third of the trustees are women.

Women and the Curriculum. All students major in art and design. A course on Women in Art is given through the division of liberal arts.

Women and Athletics. There is no opportunity for organized competitive athletics.

Special Services and Programs for Women. *Health and Counseling.* The student health service is staffed by one female health-care provider; no health services specific to women are provided. The student counseling center provides services specific to women, including birth control, abortion, and rape and assault counseling. The counseling center employs one woman.

Safety and Security. Measures consist of a campus police force, high-intensity lighting, a night-time escort service, information sessions on safety and crime prevention, and a rape crisis center. Three assaults were reported for 1980–81.

Career. The college provides information and workshops on nontraditional careers for women and maintains files of alumnae by specific careers.

Institutional Self-Description. "The college's principal purpose is to provide a high-quality educational program which integrates past and present accomplishments in visual-arts education with society's future needs. It stimulates and nurtures a creative state of mind. It prepares students to exert the continuously revitalizing influence of art and design in the solution of visual problems within our society."

Moorhead State University
Moorhead, MN 56560
Telephone: (218) 236-2011

Women in Leadership	Women and the
★★★ students	Curriculum
★ faculty	
	★★★ Women and Athletics

5,381 undergraduates

	Amer. Ind.	Asian Amer.	Blacks	Hispanics	Whites
F	1	11	4	7	2810
M	4	6	16	5	2410
%	0.1	0.3	0.4	0.2	99.0

Founded in 1867 as a teacher-training school, Moorhead State is a four-year, public institution that offers its 6,045 students a wide range of bachelor's and master's programs in liberal arts, sciences, and education, as well as adult continuing education. Alternative scheduling includes evening classes, both on and off campus, a summer session, a weekend college, and self-paced/contract learning.

Women are 53 percent of the 5,381 undergraduates, whose median age is 20. Seven percent of women attend part-time. For the 68 percent of student who commute, the university is accessible by public transportation. On-campus parking is available for a fee.

University-run childcare facilities can accommodate 100 children and meet 80 percent of students' requests for service. Charges are based on a sliding scale according to income. Private childcare facilities are available near the campus.

Policies to Ensure Fairness to Women. Four administrators share part-time responsibility for policy and compliance with legislation on equal employment opportunity, access for the handicapped, and sex equity for students. Campus policy prohibiting

sexual harassment has been publicly communicated in writing to students, faculty, and staff; complaints are resolved through a formal grievance procedure.

A Committee on the Status of Women, appointed by the President and including student members with voting rights, recommends action to the campus Affirmative Action Committee. Both this committee and the Committee on Minority Affairs address the concerns of minority women.

Women in Leadership Positions. *Students.* In three recent years, women held almost all of the five available campus-wide posts at least once. Women served three times as president of the student union board and editor-in-chief of the campus newspaper, and one-year terms as president of the student court and manager of the campus radio station. Women preside over three honorary societies.

Faculty. Twenty-eight percent of the 272 full-time faculty are women. There are 3 female faculty for every 100 female students and 8 male faculty for every 100 male students.

Administrators. With the exception of the chief business officer and one of the athletic directors, all top administrative positions are held by men. Of the 30 departments, women chair English, nursing, social work, mass communication, and sociology and anthropology. The Dean of Natural and Behavioral Science is a women. Three of the 10 regents on the State University Board are women.

Women and the Curriculum. Most women earn four year degrees in the fields of education (32 percent), public affairs (12 percent), business (11 percent), and health professions (10 percent). Almost 3 percent major in such nontraditional fields as engineering, physical sciences, and mathematics. Most of the women graduating with two-year degrees major in business and fine arts.

The Women's Studies Program, headed by a full-time, permanent faculty member, offers a bachelor's degree and an undergraduate minor. Fifteen courses on women are offered through such departments as humanities, history, English, sociology, anthropology, and political science. Recent offerings include Women and History, Images of Women in Literature, Women and Health, Women and Anthropology, Sociology of Sex Roles, Women and Mental Health, and Women and the Law. In addition, a 16-hour Topical Term on Women and Men, An American Dilemma is offered through the departments of chemistry, sociology, and humanities.

An official committee is assigned to develop the Women's Studies Program, to monitor courses which include new scholarship on women, and to develop curricular materials on women. Faculty are offered workshops on sexism and racism in the curriculum and on affirmative action and equal opportunity.

Women and Athletics. Moorhead has an outstanding women's sports program. It offers ten sports in the intramural program. Thirty-eight percent of intramural athletes and 38 percent of intercollegiate athletes are women; women receive 40 percent of athletic scholarships. Three of 12 paid intercollegiate coaches are women. The intercollegiate sports offered are basketball, cross-country, field hockey, golf, gymnastics, softball, tennis, track, and volleyball.

Housing and Student Organizations. Single-sex and coeducational dormitories with restrictive hours for visitors of the opposite sex are available for the 32 percent of undergraduates who live on campus. Three of seven residence-hall directors are women; staff is offered awareness-training on birth control.

Three percent of full-time undergraduate women belong to social sororities. Campus fraternities and sororities provide housing for members. Advocacy groups for women students are: Gay Lesbian Support Groups, Feminist Collective, SPURS, Delta Pi Delta for returning women, and Recipients Alliance.

Special Services and Programs for Women. *Health and Counseling.* The student health service provides some medical attention specific to women, including gynecological care and rape and assault treatment. The staff consists of 5 male physicians and 3 female health-care providers. The regular student health insurance covers abortion and maternity at no extra cost. The student counseling center, staffed by 2 women and 3 men, offers counseling of particular concern to women.

Safety and Security. Measures consist of campus police without arrest authority, self-defense courses for women, information sessions on safety and crime prevention, and a rape crisis center. One rape was reported for 1980-81. The university did not provide information on the incidence of assaults on women.

Career. Services include printed materials and job discrimination information on nontraditional occupations for women. The university also maintains updated alumnae files by specific careers.

Other. The counseling center office offers assertiveness training; there are weekly brown-bag luncheons with speakers, films, and discussions on women's issues. During each academic quarter, the Tri-College Women's Bureau sponsors a speaker or workshop related to women's issues.

Institutional Self-Description. "Moorhead State University recognizes the educational and social value of serving students with diverse ethnic and cultural backgrounds and considers such service to a broader constituency a necessary supplement to its regional educational mission. The university also recognizes the presence of various forms of invidious discrimination in our society and its responsibility to take affirmative action to counteract the effects of this discrimination."

St. Cloud State University

St. Cloud, MN 56301
Telephone: (612) 255-2122

Women in Leadership	★ Women and the
★★ students	Curriculum
★ administrators	★★★ Women and Athletics

9,159 undergraduates

	Amer. Ind.	Asian Amer.	Blacks	Hispanics	Whites
F	7	7	19	11	4,612
M	9	15	19	4	4,338
%	0.2	0.2	0.4	0.2	99.0

🏠 🏛 🚐 👫 ⬋ Ⓜ 📖 AAUW

Some 11,800 students attend this comprehensive public university founded as a teacher training school in 1869. St. Cloud State University now offers bachelor's and master's programs in the liberal arts, sciences, education, and pre-professional fields. Some associate degrees are also available. Flexible scheduling includes evening classes on and off campus, a summer session, and independent study options. Adult students are served by the division of continuing studies.

Fifty-one percent of the 9,159 undergraduates are women; 6 percent of women attend part-time. The median age of undergraduates is 21 years, with 11 percent of women students over 25, and 2 percent over 40. Eighteen percent of students commute to the campus, which is accessible by public transportation. Free, on-campus parking is available.

University-operated childcare facilities can accommodate 40 children, with charges based on a fixed, hourly rate. Full-time students receive first priority, and 95 percent of students' requests for the service can be met. Additional, private childcare facilities are located near the campus.

Policies to Ensure Fairness to Women. Three administrators have responsibility part-time for policy and compliance with legislation regarding equal employment opportunity, sex equity for students, and handicapped access. A written campus policy on sexual harassment of students, faculty, and staff has been communicated in writing to these three groups; complaints are resolved through a formal campus grievance procedure. A Committee on Minority Affairs addresses the concerns of minority women. Faculty are offered workshops on affirmative action and equal opportunity.

Women in Leadership Positions. *Students.* St. Cloud offers excellent opportunities for women to gain leadership experience. In recent years, women have served three times as editor-in-chief of the campus newspaper, twice as president of the student union board, and once as president of the student body, president of the student court, and president of the residence-hall council. A woman presides over one of eight campus honorary societies.

Faculty. Twenty percent of the 431 full-time faculty are women, a proportion below average for public, four-year institutions in this guide. There are 2 female faculty for every 100 female students and 8 male faculty for every 100 male students. According to a recent report, the full-time female faculty includes 3 Asian American women.

Administrators. With the exception of the director of institutional research and the director of women's athletics, all top administrators are men. The Dean of the College of Liberal Arts and Sciences is a woman. Of the 33 academic departments, business education and office administration is chaired by women. Fifteen of the 60 members of the faculty's executive committee are women, as are 2 of 10 members of the State University Board.

Women and the Curriculum. Most women earn bachelor's degrees in education (43 percent) and business (11 percent), with significant numbers in public affairs (8 percent) and fine arts (7 percent). Two percent major in such nontraditional fields as computer science, engineering, mathematics, and physical sciences. Fifty-seven percent of the two-year degrees are awarded to women, all in arts and sciences. Thirty percent of students participating in science field service and 62 percent of student interns are women.

The Women's Studies Program, which awards an undergraduate minor, offers some 19 courses on women through Women's Studies and such departments as English, history, and American studies. Recent offerings include Senior Seminar in Women's Studies, American Women's Culture, Women in Literature, English Novels by Women, and Women in History. The Women's Studies Committee is responsible for the continued development of the program. Education, social work, and physical education offer instruction on some matters specific to women.

The Women's Studies Resource Center makes available materials on topics relating to women. The center also maintains a warmline telephone service for information, referrals, and support.

Women and Athletics. St. Cloud offers outstanding opportunities for women to participate in organized, competitive, team and individual sports. A wide variety of intramural sports are available, including coeducational volleyball, broomball, and floor hockey. The university has a new multipurpose sports facility for indoor track, recreation, and intramural sports. Thirty-two percent of intramural and 43 percent of intercollegiate athletes are women, who receive 30 percent of athletic scholarship aid. Five of 15 paid intercollegiate coaches are women. Intercollegiate sports offered are basketball, cross-country, golf, gymnastics, softball, swimming, tennis, track and field, and volleyball.

Housing and Student Organizations. Thirty percent of undergraduates reside on campus in single-sex or coeducational dormitories with no restrictive hours for visitors of the opposite sex. Three of the seven residence-hall directors are women. All residence-hall staff are offered awareness-training on sex education and birth control, and on the avoidance of sexism and racism.

One percent of undergraduate women belong to sororities that provide housing for members. The Women's Equality Group serves as an advocacy group for women students.

Special Services and Programs for Women. *Health and*

Counseling. Two male physicians and 9 other health-care providers, 8 of them women, staff the student health center. Four men and 2 women staff the counseling center. Services include medical treatment and counseling for gynecological problems, birth control, and rape and assault. Abortion counseling is also available. Counselors are offered training in the avoidance of racial bias and sex-role stereotyping.

Safety and Security. Measures consist of local police, campus police without arrest authority, night-time escorts, self-defense courses, information sessions on campus safety and crime prevention, and a rape crisis center. One rape was reported for 1980–81. No information on the incidence of assaults was provided.

Career. Lectures, workshops, and job discrimination information on nontraditional careers for women are available, along with programs to establish networks between alumnae and female students. Other career services include seminars on such topics as resumes, job interviews, and careers for women; weekly job opportunity bulletins; and vocational counseling.

Other. The division of continuing education offers assertiveness/leadership training, sponsors a women's day, and provides support for older women. The Minority Culture Center is available to minority women. The community-based St. Cloud Area Women's Center operates a Women's House for battered women, a rape crisis center, and a telephone referral service.

Institutional Self-Description. "St. Cloud University is a comprehensive, accredited institution providing undergraduate and graduate programs in business, education, fine arts, industry, and liberal arts and sciences. The university offers a wide range of academic and student services, along with providing opportunities for internships, research, and low-cost overseas study center. A wide variety of social and organizational activities are available, including intramural and intercollegiate sports."

St. Olaf College
Northfield, MN 55057
Telephone: (507) 663-2222

Women in Leadership	★ Women and the
★ faculty	Curriculum
	★ Women and Athletics

2,876 undergraduates

	Amer. Ind.	Asian Amer.	Blacks	Hispanics	Whites
F	4	8	14	0	1,429
M	0	7	10	2	1,384
%	0.1	0.5	0.8	0.1	98.4

[S/W] [M/A] 📖 AAUW NWSA

A coeducational, liberal arts college affiliated with the Lutheran Church, St. Olaf enrolls 2,957 students of whom 2,876 are undergraduates. Slightly more than half the undergraduates are women. The median age of all undergraduates is 20. Ninety percent of the undergraduates live on campus; there is on-campus parking at a fee for those who commute.

Private childcare facilities are available near campus.

Policies to Ensure Fairness to Women. A full-time Coordinator oversees compliance with laws concerning sex equity for students and handicapped accessibility. Two officers, on a part-time basis, review policies and practices relating to equal employment opportunity laws. No formal policy on sexual harassment exists, but a formal grievance procedure resolves complaints. The Committee on the Status of Women is appointed by the President of the college and reports to him. It includes student

members with voting rights; takes stands on issues of concern to women students, faculty, and staff; works with affirmative action officers; and serves as part of a Network for Women with other colleges and the local community. The Committee on Minority Affairs does not address the concerns of minority women.

Women in Leadership Positions. *Students.* Women have held 24 percent of the campus-wide leadership positions during three recent years fewer than at most other coeducational colleges in this guide.

Faculty. Women are 25 percent of the 197 full-time faculty and 13 percent of the permanently appointed faculty. There are 3 female faculty for every 100 female students, and 10 male faculty for every 100 male students.

Administrators. All chief administrators are men, as are the two deans. Women chair two of 26 departments—dance and nursing. The commencement speaker in 1981 was a woman, as was one of the two honorary degree recipients. Women receive a third of alumni awards and are 40 percent of speakers in campus-wide lectures.

Women and the Curriculum. About a quarter of degrees awarded to women are in the health professions and biology. Nearly 6 percent of women take degrees in the nontraditional fields of mathematics and physical sciences.

The Women's Studies Program, headed by a full-time, permanently appointed faculty member, offers an undergraduate concentration in Women§ Studies. A committee is responsible for developing the Women's Studies Program and encouraging the teaching of courses on women. The departments of education and nursing offer some instruction on matters specific to women.

Women and Athletics. A varied program offers women a good choice among eight intramural and nine intercollegiate sports. Intercollegiate sports are basketball, cross-country, golf, skiing, softball, swimming, tennis, track, and volleyball. Women are five of the 18 paid varsity coaches.

Housing and Student Organizations. All-women and coeducational residences are available. Eighty-eight percent of the white women and all the minority women live in campus housing. The four male and seven white female residence-hall directors receive awareness training on sexism, racism, sex education, and birth control.

The Associated Women Students and the Feminine Awareness Caucus, each with about 40 members, serve as advocates for women on campus and sponsor women's lectures. There is also a Senior Women's Honor Society.

Special Services and Programs for Women. *Health and Counseling.* The health service has one male physician and two female health-care providers; the counseling center has a female and a male counselor/therapist. Gynecological, birth control, and rape and assault medical treatment and counseling, and abortion counseling, are available.

Safety and Security. Measures consist of high-intensity lighting in all areas, and campus and local police. No rapes or assaults on women were reported for 1980–81.

Career. The placement office provides a variety of services and information on nontraditonal occupations for women, including support groups for women in medicine, science, and mathematics. There is also an alumnae-parent career advising network.

Other. The Counseling Office and the Dean of Students' Office sponsor assertiveness training. The Academic Support Center and the mathematics department offers a program to build confidence in mathematics.

Institutional Self-Description. "Reasons why a woman might choose St. Olaf College: 1) St. Olaf is a liberal arts college of the American Lutheran Church; 2) strong academic program; 3) offers wide range of off-campus programs including foreign study, urban studies, and numerous special programs; 4) excellent counseling services (career, personal, health care); 5) provides a well-developed and effective academic support center; 6) provides women's support groups."

Southwest State University

Marshall, MN 56258
Telephone: (507) 532-6261

1,759 undergraduates

	Amer. Ind.	Asian Amer.	Blacks	Hispanics	Whites
F	3	6	2	3	750
M	3	9	11	4	968
%	0.3	0.9	0.7	0.4	97.7

Southwest State University is a technical and liberal arts university serving almost 2,000 students, 1,759 of whom are undergraduates. Founded in 1963, Southwest State offers a range of bachelor's programs, including pre-professional degrees in dentistry, fishery and wildlife management, and medicine. Two-year degree programs are also available. An Adult and Continuing Education program attracts about 200 reentry women. Alternative schedules include day and evening classes held both on and off campus, a summer session, and self-paced/contract learning. The university also co-sponsors a cooperative program with Worthington Community College.

Women account for about 43 percent of the undergraduate student body, whose median age is 19. Twelve percent of the women attend part-time. On-campus parking is available at a fee for the 48 percent of students who commute.

Private childcare facilities are available off campus.

Policies to Ensure Fairness to Women. Two women are assigned part-time to review policies and practices relating to laws concerning equal employment opportunity, sex equity, and handicapped access. A policy prohibiting sexual harassment of students, faculty, and staff has been communicated in writing to all three groups.

Women in Leadership Positions. *Students.* Women have limited opportunities to exercise campus-wide leadership. In recent years, women have held one-year appointments as presiding officer of the student court and of the residence-hall council, and editor-in-chief of the campus newspaper.

Faculty. Women are 15 percent of the full-time faculty of 95, a proportion considerably below average for comparable institutions. There are 2 female faculty for every 100 female students and 9 male faculty for every 100 male students.

Administrators. The executive vice president of the university is a woman, but all other top-level positions are filled by men. Women are not represented among the two deans or 15 department heads.

Women and the Curriculum. Among the women who earn bachelor's degrees, 41 percent major in education, 16 percent in business, and 14 percent in letters. One percent major in mathematics. A Women in Science program seeks to encourage women to enter this field. Fifty-seven percent of students in internship programs are women. All women who earn two-year degrees major in business communications.

The university does not offer courses on women. The departments of education, physical education, and business offer some instruction specific to women in their courses. Faculty workshops address the issues of sexism in the curriculum and the needs of reentry women.

Women and Athletics. Opportunities for women to participate in competitive team and individual sports are good for an institution of this size. Club sports are also available. Twenty-eight percent of the 1,600 intramural athletes are women, as are 52 percent of the 164 intercollegiate athletes. Six of 23 paid intercollegiate coaches are women. The intercollegiate sports offered are basketball, softball, swimming, tennis, track and field, and volleyball.

Housing and Student Organizations. Single-sex and coedu-cation dormitories house the 52 percent of students who reside on campus. There are no restrictive hours for visitors of the opposite sex. Residence-hall directors receive awareness-training on sexism, sex education, racism, and birth control.

Special Services and Programs for Women. *Health and Counseling.* Two health-care providers, both women, constitute the staff of the student health service, where birth control is available. The counseling center, staffed by one man and one woman, offers counseling on birth control, abortion, and rape and assault. Abortion and maternity expenses are covered by the regular student health insurance.

Safety and Security. Measures consist of local police, self-defense courses for women, information sessions on safety and crime prevention, and a rape crisis center. One rape was reported for 1980–81, and eight assaults (four against women).

Other. The Women's Resource Center, run under the auspices of Academic Affairs and the Division of Continuing Education, occupies 700 square feet of space. Some 500 women are served through the center, which is headed by a part-time director. Arts and mathematics confidence programs offered through academic affairs are co-sponsored by the Women's Center.

Institutional Self-Description. ''Southwest State University has long recognized the need to offer special assistance to women, and has consequently established the following on-going programs: intramural and intercollegiate women's athletics; Women's Resource Center; scholarships for nontraditional women students; a flexible admission policy for older students; and institutional policies and procedures for affirmative action.''

University of Minnesota, Duluth

2400 Oakland Ave., Duluth, MN 55812
Telephone: (218) 726-8000

7,810 undergraduates

	Amer. Ind.	Asian Amer.	Blacks	Hispanics	Whites
F	35	31	20	4	3,460
M	28	40	30	22	4,034
%	0.8	0.9	0.7	0.3	97.3

AAUW NWSA

The University of Minnesota at Duluth enrolls 8,693 students. Women are 46 percent of the 7,810 undergraduates; 29 percent of women attend part-time. The university offers bachelor's degrees in liberal arts and sciences and in business. There is a small master's degree program, as well as two-year degree programs in some fields. Continuing Education and Extension provides courses for adults. Some evening classes and a summer session are offered. For the students who commute, public transportation is available, as is on-campus parking for a fee.

The university-operated childcare center, which gives priority to students, accommodates 36 children. Daily fees range from $6.80 to $8.20, depending upon whether parents volunteer their time. Additional, private childcare facilities are available nearby.

Policies to Ensure Fairness to Women. The Assistant Provost monitors compliance with equal-employment-opportunity regulations. A published sexual harassment policy protects students, faculty, and staff.

A self-designated Commission on the Status of Women reports to the Provost on issues of concern to women, including minority women.

Women in Leadership Positions. *Students.* In recent years, men have held all of the major campus-wide offices.

Faculty. Twenty percent of the 333 full-time faculty are women, a proportion below the national average. There are 3 female faculty for every 100 female students and 9 male faculty for every 100 male students.

Administrators. All chief administrators, including the eleven deans, are men. Of 37 departments, a woman chairs home economics. Two of twelve regents are women.

Women and the Curriculum. Most women receive bachelor's degrees in education (50 percent). Thirteen percent major in social sciences and 12 percent in business; about 2 percent specialize in nontraditional fields such as physical sciences and mathematics. In a recent year, all but four of the 46 associate degrees—awarded only in arts and sciences and health technologies—went to women.

A new undergraduate minor in Women's Studies will offer 17 courses on women.

Women and Athletics. No information was supplied.

Housing and Student Organizations. Coeducational dormitories that have no restrictions on visiting hours for members of the opposite sex are provided, as well as university-owned apartments. One of three residence-hall directors is a woman; staff are offered awareness-training on human sexuality and birth control.

Students for Women's Progress and WING (Women in New Goals) are advocacy groups for women.

Special Services and Programs for Women. *Health and Counseling.* The student health service employs 2 male physicians and 2 female health-care providers. Two of 3 professionals in the student counseling center are women. Counseling and treatment are available for gynecological problems, birth control, abortion, and rape and assault.

Safety and Security. Measures include campus police with arrest authority, information on crime prevention for women, and a rape crisis center. No rapes or assaults on women were reported for 1980–81.

Career. The career Development and Placement office provides lectures and other forms of information on nontraditional occupations for women, in addition to career-development workshops.

Other. The Women's Coordinating Committee sponsors a women's lecture series. Student Activities runs an information and referral service for women.

Institutional Self-Description. None provided.

University of Minnesota, Morris
Morris, MN 56267
Telephone: (612) 589-2211

Women in Leadership
★★★ students
★ administrators

★ **Women and the Curriculum**

1,580 undergraduates

	Amer. Ind.	Asian Amer.	Blacks	Hispanics	Whites
F	28	1	22	1	684
M	26	4	33	1	750
%	3.5	0.3	3.6	0.1	92.5

AAUW

The University of Minnesota at Morris, a four-year, liberal arts college founded in 1959, has an enrollment of 1,663 students. Of the 1,580 students registered in degree programs, 47 percent are women; 22 percent of the women attend part-time. The median age of students is 20. Alternative schedules include evening classes, both on and off campus, a summer session, and self-paced/contract learning. Bachelor's degrees are offered in the arts and sciences. Adult education is available through the division of continuing education and Regional Programs and Summer Session. The campus is accessible by public transportation. On-campus parking at a fee is available for the 41 percent of students who commute.

Private childcare facilities are located near the campus.

Policies to Ensure Fairness to Women. Three administrators share responsibility, on a part-time basis, for policy relating to equal-employment-opportunity, educational-sex-equity, and handicapped-access legislation. A campus policy prohibiting sexual harassment of students, faculty, and staff has been publicly communicated in writing to faculty and staff, but not to students. A formal campus grievance procedure to resolve complaints is under development. A Committee on Minority Affairs addresses the concerns of minority women.

Women in Leadership Positions. *Students.* Women have exceptionally good opportunities to gain leadership experience. In three recent years, women served once each as president of the student body and editor-in-chief of the campus newspaper, twice as president of the student senate, and three times each as president of the student union board and president of the residence-hall council.

Faculty. Twenty percent of the 91 full-time faculty are women. There are 3 female faculty for every 100 female students and 10 male faculty for every 100 male students.

Administrators. Two of the 7 administrators are women: the academic dean and the chief student-life officer. All four departments are chaired by men. Twenty-six percent of the faculty senate are women, as are 2 of the 12 regents.

Women and the Curriculum. Most women earn degrees in education (30 percent), social sciences (17 percent), and letters (16 percent). Five percent of women graduates major in the nontraditional fields of mathematics and physical sciences. Eighty percent of student interns are women, as are 30 percent of the students in science field-service programs.

A Women's Studies Program offers an undergraduate minor. Courses on women include Women in Literature and Women in Social Science. An official committee is responsible for the development of the program; the part-time coordinator is a permanent faculty member. The division of education provides instruction on the development and use of sex-fair curricula.

Women and Athletics. The college offers limited opportunities for women to participate in organized team and individual sports. Nineteen percent of intramural and 28 percent of intercollegiate athletes are women, as are two of the eight paid coaches for intercollegiate sports. Club sports are also available. The intercollegiate sports offered are basketball, tennis, track and field, and volleyball.

Housing and Student Organizations. Coeducational dormitories with no restrictive hours for visitors of the opposite sex are provided for the 59 percent of students who reside on campus. Housing for married students with or without children is also available. Two of the five residence hall directors are women. All residence-hall staff receive awareness-training on racism and sexism, sex education, and birth control.

The university has three fraternities on campus, but no sororities.

Special Services and Programs for Women. *Health and Counseling.* The student health service is staffed by a male physician and a female health-care provider, while the counseling center employs one woman and one man. Services specific to women include medical treatment and counseling for rape and assault, as well as gynecological and birth control treatment. Abortion counseling and referral are also available. The regular student health insurance covers abortion expenses at no extra cost. Counselors receive awareness-training on avoidance of racial bias.

Safety and Security. Measures consist of campus police with arrest authority and information sessions on campus safety and crime prevention. No rapes, but one assault on a man, were reported for 1980–81.

Other. Student Affairs operates the campus Women's Center, which has 20 active participants and serves 100 women annually. Directed by a student on a part-time basis, the center serves as the major advocacy group for women students. It also contains an updated selection of books in Women's Studies. An annual women's week is sponsored by Student Activities. The division of sciences and mathematics offers a program to build confidence in mathematics.

Minority women receive support from the Minority Student Union, and from a group called Women of Color whose 25 active participants are black women.

Returning Women Students. A Continuing Education for Women Program is sponsored by the Continuing Education Regional Program. Some minority women are enrolled in these courses, most of them American Indian women. The program has a full-time, white, female administrator. The division of continuing education sponsors a program for displaced homemakers, a women's lecture series, and assertiveness training.

Special Features. The university library maintains an updated selection of Women's Studies materials. The art history collection includes 700 slides of women artists and their work. The university gallery regularly schedules one-woman shows.

Institutional Self-Description. "We are a small liberal arts institution. Those involved in women's issues are involved in all aspects of campus life, thereby contributing to an atmosphere in which women are encouraged to express themselves. Women here have a tradition of being quite active in the student newspaper and as leaders in campus governance. The extremely low crime rate of both the campus and the town contribute to an environment in which women experience freedom to move about day and night."

Univeristy of Minnesota, Minneapolis
Minneapolis, MN 55455
Telephone: (612) 373-2851

| Women in Leadership | ★★★ Women and the |
| ★ administrators | Curriculum |

★ Women and Athletics

44,582 undergraduates

	Amer. Ind.	Asian Amer.	Blacks	Hispanics	Whites
F	107	290	372	126	20,732
M	102	406	404	141	21,182
%	0.5	1.6	1.8	0.6	95.6

🏠 🚐 👫 ⚓ S/W M/A 📖 ⚲ **AAUW NWSA**

Founded in 1851, the University of Minnesota, a land-grant institution, enrolls some 63,000 students on the Minneapolis and St. Paul campuses in a comprehensive range of undergraduate, graduate, and professional programs. The division of continuing education and extension includes among its offerings Continuing Education for Women. Evening classes and a summer session are available.

Women are 49 percent of the 44,582 undergraduates; 45 percent of women attend part-time. The median age of undergraduates is 22. For the 78 percent of undergraduates who live off campus or commute, the university is accessible by public transportation. On-campus parking is provided at a fee, with free transportation from distant parking lots.

University-sponsored childcare facilities charge on a sliding scale. An estimated 15 percent of students' requests can be accommodated. Arrangements for private childcare can be made close to campus.

Policies to Ensure Fairness to Women. A full-time equal-opportunity officer is responsible for policy on employment, sex equity for women students, and handicapped accessibility. A published policy prohibits sexual harassment. Complaints are resolved through a formal grievance procedure. One of two committees concerned with the status of women in the university includes students as voting members and takes public stands on issues important to students. The Committee on Minority Affairs addresses the concerns of minority women, among other matters.

Women in Leadership Positions. *Students.* Opportunities for women students to assume campus leadership are below the average for public research universities in this guide. In recent years, women have been student body president once and presiding officer of the student senate twice. They head two of 19 honorary societies.

Faculty. Women make up 18 percent of a full-time faculty of 1,881. There are 3 female faculty for every 100 female students and 11 male faculty for every 100 male students.

Administrators. The chief development officer, the director of institutional research, and the director of women's athletics are women; men hold the other six top positions. Women chair eight of 175 departments. Fourteen of 66 other academic units are headed by women.

Women and the Curriculum. The majority of women graduating with bachelor's degrees major in education (13 percent), health professions (13 percent), interdisciplinary studies (10 percent), social sciences (9 percent), and business and management (8 percent). Ten percent of the women major in nontraditional fields, the highest number being in agriculture, architecture, and engineering. Women earn two-thirds of all two-year degrees awarded, most of them in health technologies (53 percent) and arts and sciences (42 percent). The university reports innovative programs to encourage women to prepare for careers in science and medicine. At least half of the students in programs of cooperative education, internship, and science field-service experiential learning are female. Forty-five percent of the agriculture field-service positions go to women.

The Women's Studies Program offers the B.A. degree, an undergraduate minor, and graduate electives. The program provides 20 courses of its own and coordinates 23 courses on women, including minority women, available through the departments of Afro-American studies, anthropology, Chicano studies, English, social science, history, philosophy, political science, speech, and Scandinavian studies. In addition, Continuing Education for Women offers approximately 20 Women's Studies courses. The Women's Studies Program promotes and reports on the development of courses about women across the curriculum. Such topics as teaching coeducational physical education classes, innovative health-care delivery, health-care information important to minority women, and services for battered spouses are part of the preparation of future teachers, health-care workers, and social workers.

Minority Women. Among 21,627 undergraduate women, less than 2 percent are black, around 1 percent Asian American, and less than 1 percent each Hispanic and American Indian. Fifty women are in all-minority sororities. Four minority women are on the professional staff of the counseling center; one residence-hall director is a minority woman. Counseling and residence-hall staff are offered awareness-training on avoiding racial bias. Such minority student organizations as University Black Women Scholars Together and the Third World Caucus of the Law School serve minority women on campus. An estimated 2 percent of the users of the Women's Center are black women. An Office of Minority and Special Student Affairs is also available. A black woman sits on the Board of Trustees. The Women's Center, in operation since 1960, has one of the best Women's Studies libraries in the country.

Women and Athletics. Intramural and intercollegiate programs offer good opportunities for organized, competitive, individual and team sports. Club sports are also available. Twenty percent of intramural and 30 percent of intercollegiate athletes are women. Women receive 30 percent of athletic scholarships. Twelve of 40 paid varsity coaches are female. All women's intercollegiate teams played in tournaments during 1980. The intercollegiate sports offered are basketball, cross-country, field hockey, golf, gymnastics, softball, swimming and diving, tennis, track and field, and volleyball.

Housing and Student Organizations. Twenty-two percent of undergraduates live on campus. Single-sex and coeducational dormitories and housing for married students and single parents with children are available. A married woman student whose spouse is not enrolled may live in married students' housing. Residence halls may choose to restrict visiting hours for members of the opposite sex. Half of the residence-hall directors are women. Staff are offered awareness-training on sexism, sex education, racism, and birth control.

Seven percent of full-time undergraduate women belong to social sororities. Sororities and fraternities provide housing for their members. The Law School Women's Caucus, University Community Feminists, University Black Women Scholars Together, Students Older Than Average, Unicorn, University Gay/Lesbian Community, and the Women's Auxiliary serve as advocates for women on campus.

Special Services and Programs for Women. *Health and Counseling.* The student health service provides some medical attention specific to women, including gynecological, birth control, and rape and assault treatment. The regular student health insurance covers maternity and abortion at no extra charge. Twenty-three of 36 professional staff in the counseling service are female. Students have access to abortion and rape and assault counseling. Staff receive in-service training on sex-role stereotyping, racial bias, and sexual harassment.

Safety and Security. Measures consist of campus and local police, night-time escort service for women students, high-intensity lighting, emergency alarm and telephone systems, self-defense courses for women, information sessions on safety and crime prevention, and a rape crisis center. Forty-seven assaults (total) and one rape were reported for 1980-81.

Career. Information and activities concentrating on women in nontraditional careers and fields of study are available through various units of the university and through faculty workshops.

Other. The Women's Center, funded annually at $64,996, includes among its activities a women's lecture series and a telephone service of information, referral, and support. The Women's Studies Program sponsors theater and other women's arts programs. Assertiveness training is available through Student Services.

Returning Women Students. The division of continuing education and extension houses a Continuing Education for Women Program, under a full-time director. In addition to a roster of Women's Studies courses, its services include a program for displaced homemakers and one to build confidence in mathematics.

Institutional Self-Description. "The University of Minnesota provides access for students to a wide range of disciplines on both undergraduate and graduate levels, and continually strives to provide educational programs and support for nontraditional students. Scholarly work and service carried on by the university community have gained regional, national, and international distinction. An active feminist scholars' network and numerous support groups for women offered by various departments and through the Minnesota Women's Center and Student Counseling Bureau are special strengths of the university."

Worthington Community College
1450 College Way, Worthington,
MN 56187
Telephone: (507) 372-2107

Women in Leadership
★ administrators
★ students

530 undergraduates

	Amer. Ind.	Asian Amer.	Blacks	Hispanics	Whites
F	3	0	0	0	281
M	0	0	2	0	240
%	0.6	0.0	0.4	0.0	99.1

This public, two-year community college serves 550 students, all of whom commute. Fifty-four percent of students are women, and just over half of the women attend part-time. The median age of all undergraduates is 21. Worthington offers two-year liberal arts and pre-professional programs and a range of occupational programs, including business, secretarial-clerical studies, practical nursing, and agriculture. The adult continuing education program includes a newly opened Adult Center. The college offers evening classes both on and off campus, a weekend college, and a summer session. On-campus parking is free.

Policies to Ensure Fairness to Women. The President of the college and the Dean of Students assume part-time responsibility as equal opportunity officers. Sexual harassment of students, faculty, and staff is prohibited by a written campus policy that has been publicly communicated to students; a formal grievance procedure resolves complaints.

Women in Leadership Positions. *Students.* Women students have good opportunities to exercise leadership on campus. The two campus leadership positions—president of the student body, and editor-in-chief of the campus newspaper—have each been held by a woman once in three recent years.

Faculty. The full-time faculty of 26 is 23 percent female, a proportion below the average for public two-year colleges nationwide. There are 4 female faculty for every 100 female students and 11 male faculty for every 100 male students. The college reports one Hispanic woman on the full-time faculty.

Administrators. Of the six key administrators, the chief academic officer is a black woman and the head librarian is a white woman.

Women and the Curriculum. Most of the degrees and certificates awarded to women are in the arts and sciences and business and commerce. Virtually all students enrolled in internships/practicums are women. The college reports it is "moving in the direction of" creating a Women's Studies Program. Three courses on women are offered by the psychology, history, and health departments.

Women and Athletics. Women participate in intramural sports and account for one-fourth of intercollegiate athletes. Thirty percent of all athletic scholarship aid is awarded to women. The intramural sports program offers a combination of individual and team sports. The intercollegiate sports, all team sports, include basketball, softball, and volleyball.

Special Services and Programs for Women. *Health and Counseling.* There is no student health service. The student counseling center has a staff of two, one of whom is a woman. No information was provided on counseling services.

Safety and Security. Measures consist of local police who patrol the campus, and high-intensity lighting in all areas. No assaults or rapes were reported on campus for 1980-81.

On-campus evening and/or weekend classes	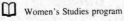 M A Commission on minority affairs	
Off-campus classes	Women's Studies program	
Accessible by public transportation	Women's center	
On-campus childcare facilities	AAUW Member, American Association of University Women	
Publicly communicated sexual harassment policy, includes students	NWSA Member, National Women's Studies Association	
S W Commission on status of women	CROW On-campus Center for Research on Women	

Career. The college provides workshops on nontraditional occupations.

Other. Female staff from the college, working closely with a community group called Women's Awareness, co-sponsor a women's lecture series.

Institutional Self-Description. "A small, rural, community college with a genuine concern for its student body, Worthington particularly encourages adults who are considering returning to school, by providing an adult assessment center designed to assist adults in obtaining needed educational skills and in planning a one or two-year program."

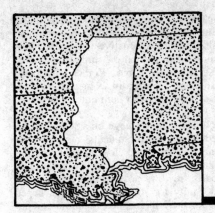

MISSISSIPPI

Millsaps College
Jackson, MS 39210
Telephone: (601) 354-5201

853 undergraduates

	Amer. Ind.	Asian Amer.	Blacks	Hispanics	Whites
F	0	1	18	1	358
M	0	2	24	0	445
%	0.0	0.4	4.9	0.1	94.6

Founded by the Methodist Church as a men's college in 1890, Millsaps College became coeducational a few years later. Of the 972 students, 853 are undergraduates, of whom 44 percent are women. All undergraduates attend full-time. In addition to a liberal arts program the college offers professional and pre-professional studies. The Office of Continuing Education serves the adult student. For the 40 percent of students who commute, public transportation and on-campus parking are available.

Childcare facilities are located both on campus and nearby.

Women in Leadership Positions. *Students.* During recent years, one of the nine available leadership positions was held by a woman—that of president of the student body. Women head three of the 12 honorary societies.

Faculty. Eighteen percent of full-time faculty are women, a proportion considerably below the national average. There are 3 female faculty for every 100 female students and 10 male faculty for every 100 male students.

Administrators. All of the chief administrators are men. Of 20 academic departments, sociology is chaired by a woman.

Women and the Curriculum. Most bachelor's degrees awarded to women are in business (22 percent), social sciences (16 percent), and biological science (15 percent). Approximately 6 percent of women major in the nontraditional fields of mathematics and physical sciences. Half of the students holding internships and practicums are women. There are no courses on women.

Minority Women. Five percent of undergraduate women are members of minority groups. Among 35 trustees, 1 of the 3 women is a black woman. Seven black women belong to an all-minority sorority. Millsaps has a Commission on Minority Affairs that attends to the concerns of minority women.

Women and Athletics. The intramural and intercollegiate sports programs for women are adequate in number and variety for a school of this size. Half the participants in intramural sports are women; the institution supplied no information on the proportion of women intercollegiate athletes. One of the five paid varsity coaches is a woman. Intercollegiate sports for women are basketball, softball, and tennis.

Housing and Student Organizations. Sixty percent of students live on campus in single-sex dormitories or in fraternity houses. College housing is available for single students with children and

for married students with or without children. Women direct four of the five dormitories. Dormitory staff receive awareness-training on sexism and birth control.

About 55 percent of female undergraduates join sororities.

Special Services and Programs for Women. *Health and Counseling.* The student health service is staffed by one nurse. The institution provided no information on the range of health and counseling services available.

Safety and Security. Measures include campus police without arrest authority, a campus-wide emergency telephone system, and self-defense courses. One rape and two assaults on women were reported for 1980–81.

Other. The Office of Continuing Education maintains the Gateway Program to provide academic, personal, and career counseling, childcare, and orientation programs for adult students. This program is used by more women than men.

Institutional Self-Description. "Millsaps College has an exceptional record of preparing young men and women for graduate and professional school. A recently instituted MBA program serves women and men in approximately equal number. The college has expanded its childcare facilities and is developing a more flexible adult degree program, especially for returning women."

Mississippi State University
Mississippi State, MS 39762
Telephone: (601) 325-2224

9,909 undergraduates

	Amer. Ind.	Asian Amer.	Blacks	Hispanics	Whites
F	34	9	397	3	3,373
M	14	14	353	8	5,618
%	0.5	0.2	7.6	0.1	91.5

AAUW

Founded in 1878 as a land-grant institution, Mississippi State University enrolls 12,500 students in a variety of undergraduate and graduate programs. Evening classes and a summer session, as well as off-campus class locations, are available. Women are 39 percent of the 9,909 undergraduates; 13 percent of women attend part-time. For the students who commute or live off campus, parking is available.

University-sponsored childcare facilities accommodate 30 children. Private childcare arrangements may be made close to campus.

Policies to Ensure Fairness to Women. A vice president of the university is responsible for equal-employment policy. An active Committee on the Status of Women includes students as voting members and takes public stands on issues of concern to students. The Committee on Minority Affairs addresses the concerns of minority women.

Women in Leadership Positions. *Students.* Opportunities for women students to exercise all-campus leadership are considerably below the average for public research institutions in this guide. In recent years, no woman has held a student office.

Faculty. Women are 15 percent of a full-time faculty of 754. The ratio of female faculty to female students is 3 to 100; the ratio of male faculty to male students is 12 to 100.

Administrators. Men occupy all key administrative positions. Women chair two of 61 departments: home economics and accounting.

Women and the Curriculum. A majority of women graduate with bachelor's degrees in education, and business and management. The proportion of women majoring in public affairs is above the national average. Eleven percent of women major in nontraditional areas, including agriculture, architecture, computer science, engineering, mathematics, and the physical sciences. No information on the curriculum was supplied.

Minority Women. According to recent information, 16 percent of undergraduate women are from minority groups, black women being the largest number. Thirty women are in all-minority sororities, 3 in integrated sororities. Three of the 20 residence-hall directors are minority women.

Women and Athletics. Opportunities for women to participate in organized competitive sports are limited. The intercollegiate sport offered is basketball.

Housing and Student Organizations. Over 5,000 students live on campus. Single-sex dormitories and housing for married students and single parents with children are available. A married woman student whose spouse is not enrolled may live in married students' housing. Dormitories restrict hours for visitors of the opposite sex. Eleven of 20 residence-hall directors are women. Staff are offered awareness training on sex education, birth control, and alcohol-abuse education.

Twenty-nine percent of full-time undergraduate women belong to social sororities. Sororities and fraternities provide housing for their members.

Special Services and Programs for Women. *Health and Counseling.* The student health service does not provide medical attention specific to women. The health service physician is female. Three of five professional staff in the counseling service are women. Gynecological, birth control, abortion, and rape and assault counseling is available.

Safety and Security. Measures consist of campus police who have weapons training and arrest authority, self-defense courses for women, and information sessions on safety and crime prevention. No information was provided on the incidence of rapes and assaults on women.

Career. The university provides activities and materials on women in nontraditional occupations and fields of study.

Institutional Self-Description. None provided.

University of Mississippi
University, MS 38677
Telephone: (601) 232-7111

7,671 undergraduates

	Amer. Ind.	Asian Amer.	Blacks	Hispanics	Whites
F	2	17	304	4	3,127
M	7	15	237	6	3,690
%	0.1	0.4	7.3	0.1	92.0

 AAUW

Chartered in 1844 to offer instruction in the liberal arts to men, the University of Mississippi began admitting women in 1882.

At the main campus, near Oxford, some 9,600 students enroll in undergraduate and graduate studies. The division of continuing education serves the adult student. Alternative class schedules, including self-paced learning contracts and off-campus locations, are available. A summer session is available. Women are 45 percent of the 7,671 undergraduates; 4 percent of women attend part-time. For the 37 percent of students who commute, parking on campus is free.

University childcare facilities, which charge on a sliding scale, accommodate an estimated 40 percent of students' requests. Private childcare arrangements may be made close to campus.

Policies to Ensure Fairness to Women. An equal-opportunity director, on a part-time basis, reviews policies and practices related to employment, sex equity for students, and handicapped accessibility. A counselor for the handicapped monitors compliance. Complaints of sexual harassment are handled informally and confidentially. The active Committee on the Status of Women includes students as voting members and takes public stands on issues of concern to students. There is a Committee on Minority Affairs, which addresses the concerns of minority women.

Women in Leadership Positions. *Students.* In recent years, women have twice presided over the student senate and the student court, once headed the residence-hall council, and twice been the editor-in-chief of the student newspaper.

Faculty. Women are 19 percent of a full-time faculty of 420. There are 2 female faculty for every 100 female students and 8 male faculty for every 100 male students.

Administrators. All higher administrative positions are filled by men. Women chair two of 52 departments: home economics and art. The director of the Sarah Isom Center for Women's Studies and the Director of Museums are women.

Women and the Curriculum. Half of the bachelor's degrees earned by women are in the fields of education, and business and management. Three percent of women major in nontraditional areas, the largest number being in architecture. Over a quarter of the positions in cooperative education programs that combine academic with related work experience go to women.

Seven undergraduate and graduate courses on women are available in the departments of English, history, political science, law, and education—including Women in Literature, Women in the South, Sex-Based Discrimination, and Women and the Educational Process. As of 1981-82, the Sarah Isom Center for Women's Studies has a full-time director. An official committee is at work to develop a Women's Studies Program and to promote and monitor the integration of women's materials and perspectives across the curriculum.

The department of physical education provides instruction on the teaching of coeducational physical education classes. Services for battered spouses, displaced homemakers, and childcare are among current issues discussed in the preparation of future social workers. Faculty are offered workshops on sexism and racism in the curriculum, nontraditional occupations for women and men, affirmative action, and the needs of reentry women students.

Women and Athletics. The intramural program provides good opportunities for organized, competitive, individual and team sports; the women's intercollegiate program offers fewer sports. Club sports are also available. The university reports a new sports complex under construction. Eighteen percent of intramural and 17 percent of intercollegiate athletes are women. Women receive 20 percent of athletic scholarships. Seven of the 31 paid varsity coaches are women. All teams played in tournaments in 1980. The intercollegiate sports offered are basketball, softball, tennis, and volleyball.

Housing and Student Organizations. Sixty-three percent of undergraduates live on campus. Single-sex and coeducational dormitories and housing for married students and single parents with children are available. A married woman student whose spouse is not enrolled may live in married students' housing. Residence halls restrict hours for visitors of the opposite sex. Ten of 19 residence-hall directors are female.

Forty-six percent of full-time undergraduate women belong to social sororities. There are 50 women in all-minority sororities. Sororities and fraternities provide housing for their members. Organizations on campus which serve as advocates for women, including minority women, are the Association for Women Students, Women in Communications, and Women in Law.

Special Services and Programs for Women. *Health and Counseling.* The student health service provides some medical attention specific to women. The 3 health service physicians are male; 10 other health-care providers are female. The regular student health insurance carries a maternity option. One of 4 professional staff in the counseling service is female. Students have access to birth control, abortion, and rape and assault counseling.

Safety and Security. Measures consist of campus police with arrest authority, night-time escort service for women, high-intensity lighting in most areas, an emergency telephone system, self-defense courses for women, information sessions on safety and campus security, and a rape crisis center. The university reports that there is individual security for each dormitory. Ten assaults (one on a woman) and no rapes were reported for 1980-81.

Career. The university provides materials and activities about women in nontraditional careers.

Other. A program to build confidence in mathematics is a part of the Learning Development Center. Assertiveness training is available through the guidance division. The Association for Women Students sponsors women's lecture series. A telephone line of information, referral, and support is provided by the Associated Student Body.

Special Features. A series of brown bag luncheon programs, scheduled twice a month and sponsored alternately by the Center for Women's Studies and the Commission on the Status of Women, offers women of the university and surrounding areas opportunities to discuss various topics of particular interest and concern to women.

Institutional Self-Description. ''The University of Mississippi offers a variety of intellectual and personal opportunities for all students, with attention to special needs of individuals. The Commission on the Status of Women, Sarah Isom Center for Women's Studies, and the University Child Care and Enrichment Center all provide programs and services of particular relevance to women.''

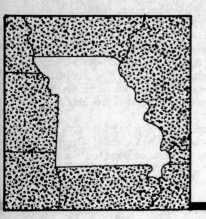

MISSOURI

Central Christian College of the Bible
P.O. Box 70, Moberly, MO 65270
Telephone: (816) 263-3900

120 undergraduates
Complete enrollment data not available.

Central Christian College of the Bible, founded in 1957, is a four-year institution affiliated with the Church of Christ. It prepares students for leadership positions in the church. The approximately 120 undergraduates include 51 women, all of them white. The median age of undergraduates is 20. About 80 percent of the undergraduates live on campus in single-sex dormitories that have restrictions on visiting hours for members of the opposite sex. For commuting students, on-campus parking is available for a fee.

Private childcare facilities are located close to the campus.

Policies to Ensure Fairness to Women. Two administrative officers share the responsibility for making policy regarding laws on equal employment opportunity, sex equity for students, and handicapped access. Complaints of sexual harassment are handled informally and confidentially.

Women in Leadership Positions. *Students.* In recent years, women have served terms as student body president and senior class president.

Faculty. The eight full-time faculty are men. Two of the three part-time faculty are women.

Administrators. Men hold all key positions and constitute the Board of Trustees.

Women and the Curriculum. Information on degrees awarded is not available. Women students hold 40 percent of the internships.

There are no courses on women. However, an official committee is developing a Women's Studies Program.

Women and Athletics. The organized athletic program for women consists of intercollegiate volleyball and three intramural sports. Twelve of the 32 intercollegiate athletes are women; both of the paid varsity coaches are men.

Special Services and Programs for Women. *Health and Counseling.* There is no student health service. The student counseling center has one male professional on staff. No information was provided on counseling services. Student health insurance covers maternity expenses.

Safety and Security. Measures consist of local police protection and high-intensity lighting. No rapes or assaults on women were reported for 1980–81.

Institutional Self-Description. None provided.

Cottey College
1000 West Austin, Nevada, MO 64772
Telephone: (417) 667-8181

Women in Leadership
★★★ students
★★ faculty
★★★ administrators

339 undergraduates

	Amer. Ind.	Asian Amer.	Blacks	Hispanics	Whites
F	4	2	0	4	318
M	0	0	0	0	0
%	1.2	0.6	0.0	1.2	97.0

Cottey College was established in 1884 to provide an educational program for women comparable in quality to ones available to men. A two-year women's college, Cottey serves 346 students, 99 percent of whom attend full-time. The median age of all students is 19. The college offers the first two years of liberal arts. Cottey is primarily a residential college, with 96 percent of the student body living on campus in dormitories that have restricted hours for male visitors. Parking is provided for commuters.

Policies to Ensure Fairness to Women. An Equal Opportunity Officer has part-time responsibility for reviewing policies and practices relating to laws mandating equal employment opportunity, sex equity for students, and access for the handicapped.

Women in Leadership Positions. *Students.* Women hold all student leadership positions.

Faculty. The full-time faculty of 26 is 46 percent female. There are 4 female faculty for every 100 female students.

Administrators. Women hold four of the six chief administrative positions: president of the college, chief student life officer, chief development officer, and head librarian. Three of the seven trustees are women.

Women and the Curriculum. All of the degrees awarded by the college are in the arts and sciences. Women are encouraged to prepare for nontraditional careers in such areas as science, engineering, accounting, and computer science. No courses on women are offered.

Women and Athletics. Women have some opportunities to participate in organized competitive sports, particularly through the intramural program, which offers a variety of team and individual sports. Both of the women coaches for varsity sports are salaried. Athletic scholarships are awarded; the intercollegiate sports are swimming and volleyball.

Special Services and Programs for Women. *Health and Counseling.* The student health service is staffed by one female physician and two female health-care providers; the student counseling center is staffed by three female counselors. Medical treatment and counseling are available for gynecological matters, birth control, and rape and assault. Abortion counseling is also available. In-service training on sex-role stereotyping is provided for the counselors.

Safety and Security. Measures consist of campus police with no arrest authority, local police, information sessions on campus safety, rape and assault prevention, and a rape crisis center. No assaults or rapes were reported on campus for 1980–81.

Career. Services include lectures and panels for students by women employed in nontraditional occupations, updated files of alumnae organized according to specific careers, and programs to establish contacts between alumnae and students.

Other. Special seminars, called breakaways, are offered on alcohol, drugs, abortion, sexuality, hygiene, rape, marriage, assertiveness, self-awareness, study skills, and career options.

Institutional Self-Description. "Cottey College provides an excellent academic program, highly qualified faculty, good instructional equipment, small classes, individual attention, cosmopolitan student body, and opportunities for students to develop leadership skills, confidence, and self-reliance, and to know the risks they are comfortable in assuming."

Kansas City Art Institute
4415 Warwick Blvd.
Kansas City, MO 64111
Telephone: (816) 561-4852

Women in Leadership
★★★ **administrators**

588 undergraduates

	Amer. Ind.	Asian Amer.	Blacks	Hispanics	Whites
F	1	3	6	2	259
M	6	2	22	6	279
%	1.2	0.9	4.8	1.4	91.8

 AAUW

The Kansas City Art Institute, founded in 1885, is an independent, accredited college offering a professional education in art and design. Its urban campus draws 613 students; 588 are enrolled in degree programs. Women are 46 percent of the undergraduates, and 6 percent of women attend part-time. The median age of students is 21. One-fifth of the women students are over age 25. A summer session is available.

The institution grants the bachelor of fine arts degree in a variety of fields: sculpture, painting/printmaking, design, ceramics, fiber, and photography. Almost one-third of the students live in coeducational dormitories that have no restrictions on visiting hours for members of the opposite sex. Public transportation and campus parking are available for commuters.

Policies to Ensure Fairness to Women. The Vice President for Finance is responsible for policy regarding sex equity, equal employment opportunity, and access for the handicapped.

Women in Leadership Positions. *Students.* No campus-wide leadership posts are available.

Faculty. Twenty-three percent of the 44 full-time faculty are women. There are 4 female faculty for every 100 female students, and 11 male faculty for every 100 male students.

Administrators. Women hold three of six administrative posts: chief business officer, chief development officer, and head librarian. One of two academic deans is female.

Women and the Curriculum. All students earn bachelor's degrees in fine arts. Women are half of the student interns. The liberal arts division offers one course specifically on women, Women Artists.

Women and Athletics. There is no opportunity for organized competitive sports.

Special Services and Programs for Women. *Health and Counseling.* The college does not have a health service or a counseling center, but some counseling is available on issues of special concern to women: gynecological problems, birth control, abortion, and rape and assault.

Safety and Security. Measures include campus police without arrest authority, high-intensity lighting, and information on campus safety for women. No rapes or assaults on women were reported for 1980–81.

Career. Workshops, lectures, and information on nontraditional occupations are available, as well as files on careers of alumnae and networking between students and alumnae.

Institutional Self-Description. "Kansas City Art Institute offers the opportunity to explore and develop individually in an environment that fosters professionalism and quality."

Maryville College–St. Louis
13550 Conway Rd., St. Louis, MO 63141
Telephone: (314) 576-9300

Women in Leadership
★ **students**
★★★ **faculty**
★ **Women and the Curriculum**

1,125 undergraduates

	Amer. Ind.	Asian Amer.	Blacks	Hispanics	Whites
F	0	4	107	2	734
M	1	0	36	3	229
%	0.1	0.4	12.8	0.5	86.3

Established by the Religious Order of the Sacred Heart, Maryville is a coeducational, liberal arts college now governed by an independent Board of Trustees. It has a total enrollment of 1,391 students; of these, 1,125 are undergraduates. Three-fourths of the undergraduates are women and over a third of the women attend part-time. The median age of the undergraduates is 25.

Maryville offers associate, bachelor's, and master's degrees in liberal arts. A continuing education program is also available. Alternative scheduling includes evening, weekend, and summer session classes. Off-campus evening classes are also offered.

The suburban campus is not accessible by public transportation. About one-fifth of the undergraduates live in coeducational dormitories that have restrictive hours for visitors of the opposite sex. For those who commute, on-campus parking is available at a fee.

A college-administered childcare center serves 20 children at one time. Eighty percent of students' requests for this service can be met. Charges are based on a fixed hourly rate. Additional, private childcare facilities are located near the campus.

Policies to Ensure Fairness to Women. The Affirmative Action Officer makes policy regarding handicapped-accessibility, sex-equity, and equal-employment-opportunity practices. A written sexual harassment policy protects students, faculty, and staff, but has been officially communicated only to staff and faculty; complaints are resolved through informal and confidential means.

Women in Leadership Positions. *Students.* Women have good opportunities for leadership experience. In three recent years, women have continuously been student union president, and women have held the posts of student body president and student senate president for two successive terms.

Faculty. Fifty-six percent of the 59 full-time faculty are women.

There are 6 female faculty for every 100 female students and 14 male faculty for every 100 male students.

Administrators. With the exception of head librarian, all top administrators are men. Six of eight department directors and ten of 25 trustees are women.

Women and the Curriculum. Twenty-one percent of women specialize in health professions, 14 percent in business, and 17 percent in such nontraditional areas as architecture, computer science, mathematics and physical sciences. The proportion of female majors in nontraditional fields is exceptionally high for comparable institutions. About three-fourths of the participants in cooperative education and internship programs are women. Workshops on sexism and the curriculum and equal opportunity/affirmative action are available to the faculty.

There are no courses on women.

Women and Athletics. The organized sports program for women consists of a variety of intercollegiate teams. Forty-eight percent of the athletes are female, as is one of the six paid varsity coaches. Intercollegiate sports offered are: basketball, soccer, softball, tennis, and volleyball.

Special Services and Programs for Women. *Health and Counseling.* The student health center employs 2 health-care providers, 1 male and 1 female. Three counselors, including 1 woman, staff the student counseling center. The available services specific to women include counseling in birth control, abortion, and rape and assault.

Safety and Security. Measures consist of campus police protection, high-intensity lighting, an emergency alarm system, information on campus safety for women, and a rape crisis center. No rapes and one assault on a woman were reported for 1980–81.

Career. The Career Planning office sponsors a weekly women's forum for discussion of career issues. It also provides workshops, printed materials, job discrimination information, and lectures on nontraditional occupations.

Other. The Dean of Student Affairs and the counseling office sponsor assertiveness training sessions. The Campus Ministry and the Dean of Student Affairs' office conduct a telephone information and referral service for women.

Institutional Self-Description. "Maryville College-St. Louis is an independent, community-focused college committed to the Judeo-Christian tradition, and is dedicated to excellence in assisting students from diverse educational, demographic, and socioeconomic backgrounds reach their maximum intellectual and spiritual potential. It is a small, innovative, private institution responsive to changing individual and societal needs while remaining true to the values and traditions of the past."

Metropolitan Community Colleges
560 Westport Rd.
Kansas City, MO 64111
Telephone: (816) 756-0220

Women in Leadership
★★ faculty
★★★ administrators

Complete enrollment information not available.

The four branches of Metropolitan Community Colleges, Longview, Maple Woods, Penn Valley, and Pioneer, occupy campuses in or near Kansas City. The student population includes 5,717 women, 71 percent of whom attend part-time. The median age of all students is 25. The college offers a comprehensive range of liberal arts and vocational programs. Reentry programs, as well as off-campus day and evening classes, summer sessions, and weekend colleges are available. All students commute; there is both public transportation and on-campus parking.

College-operated childcare facilities can accommodate 60 percent of students' requests; priority is given to full and part-time students. Private childcare arrangements may be made nearby.

Policies to Ensure Fairness to Women. Five administrators monitor compliance with equal-employment-opportunity, sex-equity and handicapped-access legislation. A formal campus grievance procedure which resolves complaints of sexual harassment has been communicated to students, faculty, and staff.

Women in Leadership Positions. *Students.* In a recent three-year period, women held one-third of the campus-wide student leadership positions, serving as president of the student body, president of the student senate, and editor-in-chief of the newspaper. Two of three college honorary societies are headed by women.

Faculty. The college reports that 41 percent of the 243 full-time faculty are women, a proportion above the average for public two-year colleges in this guide.

Administrators. Women hold 4 of 8 major administrative positions, including chief academic officer, chief of student-life programs, head librarian, and director of institutional research. Seven of 19 departments on the three campuses are chaired by women. Two of the department chairs are black women. The Dean of Instructional Services at Penn Valley is a woman, as is 1 of 6 college trustees.

Women and the Curriculum. Information on degrees is not available. Two-thirds of internships and all cooperative education positions go to women.

One course on women, Women in Literature and Life, is offered through the department of English. The departments of physical education and business include instruction on some matters specific to women. The needs of reentry women and equal educational opportunity are topics offered in faculty workshops.

Women and Athletics. One-third of students participating in intercollegiate sports are women, as are two of four paid coaches. Women receive 33 percent of the athletic scholarships. Team sports predominate in the intramural program. Intercollegiate sports offered are softball and volleyball.

Special Services and Programs for Women. *Health and Counseling.* There is no student health service. A student counseling center, staffed by three women and eleven men, provides personal counseling. No medical services or counseling specific to women.

Safety and Security. Measures consist of local police, campus police without arrest authority, high-intensity lighting, self-defense courses for women, information sessions on campus safety, and a rape crisis center. No rapes or assaults were reported for 1980–81.

Career. Services include workshops on nontraditional occupations and information on job discrimination. "Career Crosswords," a nontraditional career fair, is held on the Pioneer Campus.

Other. The Reentry Program sponsors Women's Centers on the various campuses. Services for displaced homemakers, assertiveness training, and a program to build confidence in mathematics are available. Student groups which serve as advocates for women include the Parenting Club and WINGS.

Institutional Self-Description. "The mission of the Metropolitan Community Colleges of Kansas City is to serve its community, and this community is primarily adult. Those facing lifestyle or career change are actively recruited, and their transition to education is eased by the Reentry Programs, available at each of the four neighborhood campuses."

Missouri Southern State College
Newman and Duquesne Roads
Joplin, MO 64801
Telephone: (417) 624-8100

Women in Leadership
★ students
★ administrators

3,900 undergraduates

	Amer. Ind.	Asian Amer.	Blacks	Hispanics	Whites
F	12	7	24	8	1,852
M	35	12	46	9	1,889
%	1.2	0.5	1.8	0.4	96.1

Missouri Southern State enrolls some 3,900 students, all of whom are undergraduates. About half of the students are women; 36 percent of women attend part-time. The median age of students is 23.

The college offers a range of degree programs including general studies. A Return to Learn workshop for reentry women is available through the regularly scheduled summer session. Day and evening classes are available both on and off campus. There is a division of continuing education. Free on-campus parking is available for the 89 percent of students who commute.

Policies to Ensure Fairness to Women. Compliance with sex-equity and access-for-the-handicapped legislation is monitored by the Assistant to the President, who works (part time) on equal employment opportunity issues and is a voting member of policy-making bodies. Sexual harassment of faculty is prohibited by a written policy, which has been communicated to the faculty; complaints are resolved through a formal campus grievance procedure.

Women in Leadership Positions. *Students.* Opportunities for women to exercise campus-wide leadership are good. In recent years, women have held three of nine possible positions, including presiding officer of the student court and editor-in-chief of the campus newspaper. Women also head four of five campus honorary societies.

Faculty. Women are 24 percent of the full-time faculty of 154, a proportion just below the national average. There are 3 female faculty for every 100 female students and 9 male faculty for every 100 male students.

Administrators. Of the seven top-level administrators, women serve as chief development officer and one of the two athletic directors. Of ten academic departments, a woman chairs the department of social science.

Women and the Curriculum. Sixty-one percent of women earn bachelor's degrees in education; 12 percent in business. Forty-four percent of the women awarded two-year degrees major in health technologies, 25 percent major in business and commercial technologies, and 6 percent major in the nontraditional field of mechanical/engineering technologies.

The college does not offer courses on women.

Women and Athletics. The college offers several competitive team and individual sports for women. Twenty-one percent of intramural athletes are women, who participate in badminton, basketball, and coeducational volleyball. Women receive 50 percent of athletic scholarhip aid; three of the ten paid intercollegiate coaches are women. Forty-three percent of the 200 intercollegiate athletes are women, who participate in basketball, softball, tennis, track, and volleyball.

Housing and Student Organizations. Eleven percent of undergraduates live on campus in single-sex and coeducational dormitories. Single-sex dormitories impose restrictive hours on visitors of the opposite sex. Eighty undergraduates, including 52 women, belong to sororities or fraternities.

Special Services and Programs for Women. *Health and Counseling.* Both counseling and medical treatment in areas specific to women, such as gynecological care, birth control, abortion, and rape and assault, are available. The health center is staffed by one male physician and a female health-care provider. No information was provided on the counselng staff.

Safety and Security. Measures consist of campus police without arrest authority, and high-intensity lighting throughout the campus. No rapes or assaults were reported for 1980–81.

Other. A program to build mathematics confidence is directed by the Office of Academic Development. Minority women are served by the campus-based Afro-American Society. SAGE (Students Achieving Greater Education) is an organization for nontraditional students who, in the words of the college, are "primarily women."

Institutional Self-Description. "MSSC is a small liberal arts college located in the southwest corner of the state bordering the Ozarks. The classes are small, allowing for greater individuality among the students. Counselors and instructors encourage both men and women to explore and strive for excellence in the field of their choice. MSSC offers a full program of women's and men's intercollegiate athletics."

Missouri Western State College
4525 Downs Dr., St. Joseph, MO 64507
Telephone: (816) 271-4200

| Women in Leadership | | | ★ Women and the |
| ★ faculty | | | Curriculum |

3,352 undergraduates

	Amer. Ind.	Asian Amer.	Blacks	Hispanics	Whites
F	4	4	38	11	1,528
M	0	5	73	12	1,669
%	0.1	0.3	3.3	0.7	95.6

Some 3,700 students attend this public, four-year college, located in metropolitan St. Joseph. Established in 1915, the university serves 3,352 undergraduates through several degree programs. A Continuing Education for Women Program serves both degree candidates and reentry women. Forty-seven percent of the undergraduates are women. 25 percent of whom attend part-time. The median age of undergraduates is 25. Public transportation and free on-campus parking are available.

Private childcare facilities are available near the campus.

Policies to Ensure Fairness to Women. Policy relating to sex equity, equal employment opportunity, and access for the handicapped is implemented under the direction of a part-time Equal Opportunity Officer.

Women in Leadership Positions. *Students.* Opportunities for women to exercise campus-wide leadership are limited. In three recent years, women have held two of five possible positions for one year each: presiding officer of the student governing body and editor-in-chief of the campus newspaper.

Faculty. Women hold 25 percent of the 138 full-time positions. There are 3 female faculty for every 100 female students and 8 male faculty for every 100 male students.

Administrators. Men hold all top-level administrative positions, except head librarian. Women chair the departments of business/economics and nursing.

Women and the Curriculum. Most women earn bachelor's degrees in education (41 percent) and business (19 percent). Six percent major in the nontraditional fields of agriculture, computer science, and physical sciences. Of the 79 women earning two-year degrees in a recent year, 35 majored in business, 21 in health technologies, and 18 in public services.

The Women's Studies Program offers courses on women through various departments. Recent offerings include: Images of Women in Art, Psychology of Women, and Human Sexuality. In conjunction with other divisions, the program sponsors various activities, including the Continuing Education for Women Program. Further development of the Women's Studies Program and of courses on women in traditional departments is assigned to an official committee.

Faculty workshops have considered the topics of affirmative action and equal opportunity, the needs of reentry women, and the relationships among sex, race, and the selection of a major field.

Women and Athletics. Ten intramural sports, including miniature golf and badminton, are available to the 31 percent of intramural athletes who are female. The intramural program offers mostly team sports; there are facilities for raquetball and beach volleyball. Forty percent of the athletic scholarships were awarded to women, who constitute 34 percent of the intercollegiate athletes. Three of the 12 paid coaches are assigned to women's intercollegiate sports. Women compete in intercollegiate basketball, softball, tennis, and volleyball.

Housing and Student Organizations. About 16 percent of all undergraduates live on campus in single-sex or coeducational dormitories, all of which have restrictive hours for visitors of the opposite sex. There is one male residence-hall director.

Special Services and Programs for Women. *Health and Counseling.* Eight male physicians and 4 female health-care providers staff the health center, which offers treatment for gynecological problems, birth control services, and rape and assault counseling. The student counseling center has a staff of 2 men and 1 woman who provide vocational counseling, but no services specific to women.

Safety and Security. Measures consist of campus police and local police, a fraternity-run, night-time escort service for women, information courses on safety and rape and assault prevention, and a rape crisis center. One rape and one assault on a women were reported for 1980–81.

Career. Information on nontraditional employment is provided through workshops, printed matter, and lectures by women employed in nontraditional occupations.

Returning Women Students. The Continuing Education for Women Program, under the joint auspices of the division of liberal arts and the Women's Studies Program, is headed by a part-time female administrator with a budget drawn from Women's Studies. Almost 200 women take advantage of self-enrichment courses, seminars, and other programs.

Special Features. A research project entitled Women Writers Along the Rivers is designed to locate, catalog, and prepare an annotated bibliography of the writings of women who lived in Missouri and Kansas from 1850–1950.

Institutional Self-Description. "Free seminars every two weeks, as well as continuing education classes, are planned to bring more information and understanding to the campus about women's issues by dealing with traditional disciplines from a woman's perspective, encouraging introspection or assisting her with skill development. Reentry programs ease the transition from the homemaker role."

Rockhurst College
5225 Troost, Kansas City, MO 64110
Telephone: (816) 926-4000

Women in Leadership
★★★ students

1,197 undergraduates

	Amer. Ind.	Asian Amer.	Blacks	Hispanics	Whites
F	0	1	70	10	398
M	0	4	58	15	628
%	0.0	0.4	10.8	2.1	86.7

Formerly a Jesuit College for men, Rockhurst is a private, liberal arts institution still affiliated with the Roman Catholic Church. Some 3,400 students attend, of whom 1,197 are registered in degree programs. Rockhurst has been coeducational since 1969, and women currently make up 40 percent of degree students; 8 percent of the women attend part-time. The median age of all students is 20. Nine percent of the female students are older than 25.

Rockhurst offers bachelor's programs in liberal arts and sciences, business, and education. The evening division is responsible for adult continuing education. A summer session is available. One-third of the undergraduates live oncampus in single-sex dormitories with restrictive hours for visitors of the opposite sex. The campus is accessible by public transportation. On-campus parking is available at a fee.

Private childcare facilities are located near the campus.

Policies to Ensure Fairness to Women. The Vice President is responsible for policy regarding equal opportunity in employment and education and for handicapped access. A presidential Committee on the Status of Women reports to the Academic Dean on issues of concern to women.

Women in Leadership Positions. *Students.* Women students have outstanding opportunity to gain leadership experience. In recent years, women have held all four major campus offices for at least one year. They also head the two campus honorary societies.

Faculty. Twenty-four percent of the 62 full-time faculty are women. There are 3 female faculty for every 100 female students, and 7 male faculty for every 100 male students.

Administrators. All top administrative officers are male. Women chair six of 21 departments: accounting, biology, communications, foreign languages, chemistry, and sociology. The Director of the Evening Division is a woman. Seventeen percent of the faculty senate, 14 percent of the regents, and 7 percent of the trustees are women.

Women and the Curriculum. Half of the women graduates earn bachelor's degrees in business, and about 10 percent each in education, social sciences, biology, and health. Five percent earn degrees in such nontraditional fields as mathematics, physical sciences, and computer science. Women receive 43 percent of co-operative education appointments. Two-thirds of students in internship programs are women. There are no courses on women.

Women and Athletics. Rockhurst offers some opportunities for women to participate in organized sports. Forty-two percent of intercollegiate and 56 percent of intramural athletes are women, as are half of the members of sports clubs; women receive 20 percent of athletic scholarship aid. Three of the four paid varsity coaches are women. All three varsity teams participated in recent tournament competition. The intercollegiate sports offered are basketball, bowling, and volleyball.

Special Services and Programs for Women. *Health and Counseling.* The student health service employs one female health-care provider. One male professional staffs the student counseling center. The college refers women to community agencies for counseling and treatment of problems specific to women, excluding abortion.

Safety and Security. Measures consist of campus and local police protection, night-time escort for women, and high-intensity lighting. No rapes or assaults on women were reported in 1980–81.

Career. The Career Center offers workshops, information, and panels on nontraditional occupations; maintains files on alumnae's careers for students' use; and encourages networking between alumnae and students.

Institutional Self-Description. "The goal of Rockhurst College is the full development of human potential in a Catholic, Jesuit, solidly established urban liberal arts college. Among the many services available to its students are an active Career Center with a history of successful placement in cooperative education arrangements during the Junior/Senior years and in promising careers upon graduation; a Counseling and Learning Center; and an academic advising system which is geared to offering attention to individual needs."

St. Louis Community College, Meramec
11333 Big Bend Boulevard,
St. Louis, MO 63122
Telephone: (314) 966-7500

Women in Leadership
★★★ students
★★ faculty

5,739 undergraduates

	Amer. Ind.	Asian Amer.	Blacks	Hispanics	Whites
F	3	17	111	19	2,645
M	6	8	113	18	2,796
%	0.2	0.4	3.9	0.7	94.9

One of three colleges in the St. Louis Community College system, this public institution offers comprehensive educational services to 10,005 students, of whom 5,739 are degree students. Forty-nine percent of the degree students are women, 47 percent of whom attend part-time. Nearly one-third of students are over age 25, with 10 percent over age 40.

The college offers a two-year college transfer program in liberal arts and pre-professional areas, and one- and two-year career programs in a wide range of occupational fields. Women returning to college are offered special support and services through the Institute for Continuing Education, which operates a Continuing Education for Women Program. Evening classes, both on and off campus, Saturday morning classes, a summer session, and self-paced, contract learning allow flexible scheduling. All students commute to the campus, located in the suburbs of St. Louis; public transportation and on-campus parking are available.

Private childcare facilities are available near the campus.

Policies to Ensure Fairness to Women. The Director of Business Services has part-time responsibility for making policy on equal employment opportunity. Sex equity and handicapped accessibility for students are handled, on a part-time basis, by the Associate Dean of Instruction. A written campus policy on sexual harassment of students, faculty, and staff is currently under development. Complaints of sexual harassment are resolved through a formal campus grievance procedure.

Women in Leadership Positions. *Students.* There is one campus leadership position, editor-in-chief of the newspaper, which has been held by women during a recent three-year period. A woman presides over the single campus honorary society.

Faculty. Thirty-seven percent of the 161 full-time faculty are women, a proportion above average for similar colleges in this guide. The full-time faculty includes 10 black women. There are 4 female faculty for every 100 female students and 6 male faculty for every 100 male students.

Administrators. The ten chief administrative positions are held by men. Women chair four of 13 departments: biology, business education, business administration and economics, and nursing.

Women and the Curriculum. Most two-year degrees and certificates awarded to women are in the arts and sciences (41 percent), health technologies (19 percent), and business and commerce (21 percent). Smaller numbers of women major in public service, data processing, natural science, and mechanical and engineering technologies. The division of instruction sponsors a program to build confidence in mathematics. Half of the students in internship and science field-service programs are women.

The English department offers a course on Women in Literature, and the history/political science department offers a course on Twentieth-Century Women. Faculty workshops are available on such topics as sexism and the curriculum, nontraditional occupations for women and men, the needs of reentry women, and affirmative action and equal opportunity.

Women and Athletics. Athletic scholarships (one per sport) are available for women. Two of the three paid intercollegiate coaches are women, and all women's intercollegiate teams compete in tournaments. The intercollegiate sports offered are basketball, softball, swimming, tennis, and volleyball.

Special Services and Programs for Women. *Health and Counseling.* The student health service is staffed by one female health-care provider. The counseling center employs four women and one man. No information was provided on services specific to women. Counselors are provided with in-service training on sex-role stereotyping and racial bias.

Safety and Security. Measures consist of campus police with arrest authority, a night-time escort for women students, and high-intensity lighting in all areas. There were no assaults or rapes reported on campus for 1980–81.

Career. Printed information and workshops on nontraditional occupations, along with lectures by women employed in these fields, are available. Updated files of alumnae by specific careers are maintained.

Other. The Institute for Continuing Education provides special services and support for reentry women, including assertiveness training and career exploration. The college also sponsors special seminars on such topics as Women and Power and Women in Business.

Institutional Self-Description. "St. Louis Community College at Meramec is a particularly congenial institution for the woman returning to school. She will find a supportive atmosphere, special programs, and many other students like herself."

Saint Louis University
221 North Grand Blvd.
St. Louis, MO 63103
Telephone: (314) 658-2222

Women in Leadership
★ faculty

5,235 undergraduates

	Amer. Ind.	Asian Amer.	Blacks	Hispanics	Whites
F	3	18	397	8	2,412
M	3	45	191	18	2,063
%	0.1	1.2	11.4	0.5	86.8

Founded as a Catholic Academy in 1818, Saint Louis University, a Jesuit institution of some 10,000 students, serves a large urban area with a variety of undergraduate, graduate, and professional programs. Alternative schedules, including self-paced learning contracts, summer session, off-campus locations, and continuing adult education are offered through Metro College.

Women are 55 percent of the 5,235 undergraduates; 38 percent of the women attend part-time. For the 86 percent of undergraduates who commute, there is on-campus parking, with free transportation from distant parking lots.

Private childcare arrangements may be made close to campus.

Policies to Ensure Fairness to Women. An affirmative action officer on a part-time basis and a full-time assistant monitor compliance with equal-employment-opportunity, sex-equity, and handicapped-access legislation. A campus policy prohibits sexual harassment of students, faculty, and staff. Complaints are handled informally and confidentially. The Committee on the Status of Women, which includes students as voting members, addresses the concerns of minority women and sponsors workshops and campus speakers.

Women in Leadership Positions. *Students.* Information on opportunities for women students to exercise campus-wide leadership was not provided by the institution.

Faculty. Of a total full-time faculty of 401, 34 percent are female, which is above the national average. There are 8 female faculty for every 100 female students and 17 male faculty for every 100 male students.

Administrators. Two of 9 top administrators are women: the chief student-life officer is a white woman, and the director of institutional research is a black woman. Women chair the departments of African-American studies, American studies, art and art history, and philosophy.

Women and the Curriculum. Over half of degrees awarded to women are in the health professions, over one-tenth in business and management. Three percent of women major in the nontraditional areas of mathematics and physical sciences.

Individual courses on women are offered in the departments of modern languages, English, philosophy, psychology, and theology, and in the School of Social Work. The availability of a course on Women in Theological Perspectives is particularly significant in an institution that requires coursework in theology. The School of Education reports some attention to mathematics confidence among females and the use of sex-fair materials in the preparation of future teachers. The School of Nursing provides training in midwifery. An unofficial, ad hoc committee is working to develop a Women's Studies Program and to promote the inclusion of scholarship on women in the curriculum.

Women and Athletics. Women participate in both intramural and intercollegiate sports. In the intramural program, team sports predominate. A new recreational complex for intramural sports, due for completion by the end of 1982, will be headed by a woman. The intercollegiate sports offered are basketball, field hockey, softball, swimming, tennis, and volleyball.

Housing and Student Organizations. Fourteen percent of the undergraduates live on campus. Single-sex and coeducational dormitories, housing for married students, single parents, and students with religious vocation are available. A married woman student whose husband is not enrolled may live in married students' housing. Residence halls do not restrict hours for visitors of the opposite sex.

Special Services and Programs for Women. *Health and Counseling.* The student health service is staffed by one female health-care provider. Over half of the 60 counselors in the student counseling service are women, including 2 minority women. No information was provided on health and counseling services.

Safety and Security. Measures include campus and city police, night-time escort service for women, high-ihtensity lighting, an emergency telephone system, and a rape crisis center. No assaults on women or rapes were reported for 1980–81.

Career. A career center offers workshops on nontraditional occupations and a network for contacts between alumnae and female students.

Administrators. The university sponsors a women's lecture series, assertiveness training for women, a program to build confidence in mathematics, and a theater and arts program specially directed to minority women.

Institutional Self-Description. "Saint Louis University is a solidly Jesuit institution which teaches traditional Catholic values while encouraging free intellectual inquiry. Women who choose to work within this framework will find encouragement, particularly from women religious, and opportunities for scholarship."

School of the Ozarks
Point Lookout, MO 65726
Telephone: (417) 334-6411

Women in Leadership
★ faculty

1,368 undergraduates

	Amer. Ind.	Asian Amer.	Blacks	Hispanics	Whites
F	0	0	0	0	729
M	0	1	12	0	603
%	0.0	0.1	0.9	0.0	99.0

 AAUW

The School of the Ozarks, founded in 1906 as a high school, has evolved into an independent Christian college that primarily serves students who are unable to afford the expense of attending other colleges. The rural campus attracts 1,423 students: of those, 1,368 are enrolled in degree programs. Women make up 54 percent of the student body, and 12 percent attend part-time. Fifteen percent of the women students are over age 25. The college offers a variety of liberal arts, business, and pre-professional degrees. Evening classes and a summer session are available.

Four-fifths of the undergraduates live in single-sex dormitories that have restrictions on visiting hours for members of the opposite sex. On-campus parking is available for commuters.

A college-operated childcare center, accommodating all students' requests, serves 20 children at a time for a fixed daily fee.

Policies to Ensure Fairness to Women. The Vice President for Academic Affairs is responsible for examining policies and practices pertaining to sex equity for students, equal employment opportunity, and accessibility for the handicapped.

Women in Leadership Positions. *Students.* Incomplete information on student leadership suggests that women have some opportunity to exercise student leadership. In recent years, women have been elected for one term each to head the student body and the junior and senior classes.

Faculty. Twenty-six percent of the 66 full-time faculty are women, a proportion average for comparable institutions in this guide. There are 3 female faculty for every 100 female students, and 9 male faculty for every 100 male students.

Administrators. All top-ranking administrators are men. Women chair three of 20 departments: education, foreign languages, and home economics. Three of the 21 members of the Board of Trustees are women.

Women and the Curriculum. Most degrees awarded to women are in education (25 percent) and business (16 percent); 14 percent are in such nontraditional areas as engineering, mathematics, and physical sciences. There are no courses on women.

Women and Athletics. The limited organized athletic program for women is very popular. Half of the intercollegiate and intramural athletes are women; female varsity athletes receive 10 percent of the athletic scholarship assistance. Intercollegiate sports offered are basketball, swimming, track, and volleyball.

Special Services and Programs for Women. *Health and Counseling.* The student health service is staffed by one male physician and four health-care providers, three of whom are women. No information was provided on health services specific to women. One of the three professionals at the student counseling service is a woman. Counseling is provided for gynecological problems, birth control, abortion, and rape and assault.

Safety and Security. Measures include campus police with arrest authority and an emergency alarm system. No rapes or other assaults on women were reported for 1980–81.

Institutional Self-Description. "The School of the Ozarks is a small Christian school in a small community. The atmosphere is friendly and informal."

Stephens College
Columbia, MO 65215
Telephone: (314) 442-2211

Women in Leadership	★★ Women and the
★★★ students	Curriculum
★★ faculty	
★ administrators	

1,630 undergraduates

	Amer. Ind.	Asian Amer.	Blacks	Hispanics	Whites
F	1	4	72	2	1,499
M	0	0	1	0	37
%	0.1	0.3	4.6	0.1	95.1

 AAUW NWSA

Founded in 1833, Stephens is a private, independent college primarily for women. Located in a suburban setting in the small city of Columbia, the college attracts 1,630 undergraduates, including 38 men. Eleven percent of the women attend part-time. The median age of all students is 19.

Degrees in a wide range of liberal arts, pre-professional, and professional programs are available, in addition to continuing education and an external degree program (Stephens College Without Walls). The college also offers two-year programs. Classes meet in the evening as well as during the day; there is a summer session. Ninety-two percent of all students live on campus in dormitories that have restrictive hours for male visitors. Sororities, which have 205 members, do not provide housing. Free parking is provided on campus for the 5 percent of students who commute. The school can also be reached by public transportation.

Childcare facilities are available off campus.

Policies to Ensure Fairness to Women. The Executive Vice President, a woman, has the part-time responsibility for examining policies and practices pertaining to equal-employment-opportunity and handicapped-access laws, and can make policy in these areas. Complaints about sexual harassment are handled informally.

Women in Leadership Positions. *Students.* Women hold all student leadership positions and head the eleven honorary societies.

Faculty. Forty-eight percent of the 124 full-time faculty are women, a figure considerably above the national average for all institutions but slightly below the average for women's colleges in this guide. There are 4 female faculty for every 100 female students.

Administrators. Women hold 2 of 7 top positions, executive vice president and chief student-life officer. Of the 22 academic departments, women chair 8, including communications, dance, fashion, music, secondary education, equestrian science, American studies, and physical education. Half the college trustees are women. In 1980-81 the commencement speaker and all speakers in major campus-wide lecture series were women.

Women and the Curriculum. Most four-year degrees to women are in business (22 percent), fine arts (21 percent), and health professions (16 percent). About 4 percent of women major in the nontraditional areas of architecture, mathematics, and physical sciences. All two-year degrees are in the arts and sciences.

Stephens is one of a few colleges in the U.S. that require a Women's Studies course of all students earning the bachelor's degree.

A Women's Studies Program offers a major consisting of 12 Women's Studies courses supplemented by six departmental courses that focus on women. Among the courses offered are Development of Feminist Thought, Women in American Cultures, Women in European History, The Comic/Tragic Spirit of Women in the Performing Arts, Women's Spirituality, and Reproductive Rights and Freedoms. An official Women's Studies Committee oversees the development of the program and sponsors a variety of co-curricular activities. Faculty also participate in workshops on the use of new scholarship on women.

Minority Women. About 5 percent of all undergraduates are minority women, mostly black women. Two courses—Black Women in the U.S. and Women in African Cultures—are offered by Women's Studies. Residence-hall staff receive awareness-training on racism. Faculty are instructed on the relationships among sex, race, and the choice of major field. A black woman sits on the Board of Trustees.

Women and Athletics. Five intercollegiate and three intramural sports are available for women athletes, in addition to stables, a riding arena, and a golf course. All four paid intercollegiate coaches are women. Athletic scholarships are available. Intercollegiate sports offered are golf, softball, swimming, tennis, and volleyball.

Special Services and Programs for Women. *Health and Counseling.* The student health service employs one male physician and one female health-care provider. The student counseling staff of a man and two women are trained to avoid sex-role stereotyping. Counseling and treatment are available for gynecological problems and birth control; counseling only for abortion and rape and assault.

Safety and Security. Measures taken consist of campus and local police, night-time escort for women, high-intensity lighting, instruction on self-defense and campus safety for women, and a rape crisis center. One assault on a woman and no rapes were reported for 1980-81.

Career. The college offers information, lectures, and career workshops on nontraditional occupations. The counseling service runs leadership training sessions.

Other. Women's Studies organizes an annual women's week, women's lecture series, and a speakers bureau on the status of women. A Continuing Education for Women Program serves 650 reentry students, 6 percent of whom are minority women. Special workshops familiarize faculty with the needs of reentry women.

Institutional Self-Description. "Stephens College, an undergraduate women's college, is dedicated to the dignity and equality of women and to an educational program that embodies this dedication. To address the changing needs, roles, and aspirations of women, the college is committed to rigorous examination of its existing programs and experimentation with new ones."

University of Missouri, Columbia

Columbia, MO 65211
Telephone: (314) 882-3387

| Women in Leadership | ★★ Women and the |
| ★ admininstrators | Curriculum |

★ Women and Athletics

17,146 undergraduates

	Amer. Ind.	Asian Amer.	Blacks	Hispanics	Whites
F	14	47	336	19	7,604
M	22	74	236	36	8,577
%	0.2	0.7	3.4	0.3	95.4

AAUW

Established in 1839, the University of Missouri at Columbia is a land-grant state institution which offers a comprehensive range of undergraduate, graduate, and professional programs to some 23,400 students. A summer session and self-paced learning formats are available. The university extension division provides continuing adult education.

Women are 47 percent of the 17,146 undergraduates; 7 percent of women attend part-time. The median age of undergraduates is 19. For the 45 percent of undergraduates who commute, public transportation is available within Columbia only. On-campus parking is provided at a fee, with free transportation from distant parking lots.

Low-cost, university-sponsored childcare programs accommodate an estimated one-quarter of students' requests. Private child-care arrangements can be made close to campus.

Policies to Ensure Fairness to Women. A full-time Director of Equal Opportunity is responsible for policy on employment, sex equity for students, and handicapped accessibility. A published campus policy prohibits sexual harassment; complaints are handled through a formal grievance procedure. The Committee on the Status of Women, which includes students as voting members, works on issues of concern to student, staff, and faculty women. The Committee on Minority Affairs addresses the concerns of minority women.

Women in Leadership Positions. *Students.* Opportunities for women students to exercise all-campus leadership are below average for public research universities in this guide. In recent years, women have presided over the Missouri Students Association, the student senate, and the student union board.

Faculty. Women are 18 percent of a full-time faculty of 986. According to recent information, 12 black, 1 American Indian, 3 Asian American, and 3 Hispanic women are on the faculty. The ratio of female faculty to female students is 2 to 100; the ratio of male faculty to male students is 9 to 100.

Administrators. The Chancellor of the university and the chief business officer are women, which makes Missouri unusual among public research institutions in this guide. The Dean of the College of Home Economics is female. Of 87 departments, women chair four: advertising, child and family development, clothing and textiles, and housing and interior design.

Women and the Curriculum. The majority of women graduating with bachelor's degrees major in education (20 percent), home economics (12 percent), business and management (11 percent), health professions (10 percent), and communications (10 percent). Ten percent of women major in nontraditional fields, with the largest number in agriculture.

The Women's Studies Program offers the B.A. through Interdisciplinary Studies. Approximately 20 courses are available each year through General Studies and such departments as French, history, library science, and anthropology. Recent offerings include Male and Female, Women and the Military, Women in American History, and The Psychobiology of Women. An official committee promotes Women's Studies and monitors its development across the curriculum.

Such current issues as sex-role stereotyping in sports and curriculum, mathematics confidence among females, innovative health-care delivery, and health information important to minority women, services for abused spouses, and workplace discrimination are part of the instruction offered in the preparation of teachers, health-care workers, social workers, and business students.

Minority Women. Of 8,052 undergraduate women, 4 percent are black, less than 1 percent each American Indian, Asian American, and Hispanic. One member of the Board of Regents is a black woman. Two minority women are in integrated, 30 in all-minority, sororities.

Such student organizations as the Legion of Black Collegians, the Black Journalism Student Association, the Black Law Student Association, and Minority Women in Health Careers meet on campus. The Office of Minority Programs and the Women's Center are active on behalf of minority women. Awareness-training on the avoidance of racism and racial bias is offered to residence-hall staff and the staff of the counseling center.

Women and Athletics. Intramural and intercollegiate programs offer good opportunities for organized, competitive, individual and team sports. Club sports are also available. Twenty-six percent of intramural and 23 percent of intercollegiate athletes are women; women receive 34 percent of athletic scholarships. The intercollegiate sports offered are softball, swimming and diving, tennis, and volleyball.

Housing and Student Organizations. Fifty-five percent of undergraduates live on campus. University-owned or sponsored accommodations include single-sex and coeducational dormitories, and housing for married students and single parents with children. A married woman student whose spouse is not enrolled may live in married students' housing. Dormitories restrict hours for visitors of the opposite sex. Ten of 15 residence-hall directors are female. Awareness-training on sexism, birth control, and alcoholism, among other issues, is offered residence-hall staff.

Twenty percent of all full-time undergraduates belong to sororities and fraternities. Among groups that serve as advocates for women are the Association of Women Students and the Professional Women's Caucus in addition to the minority women's groups named above.

Special Services and Programs for Women. *Health and Counseling.* The student health service provides some medical attention specific to women, including gynecological, birth control, and rape and assault treatment. Four of the 8 physicians are female, as are 6 other health-care providers. A voluntary insurance option covers maternity. Nine of a professional staff of 29 in the counseling service are women. Students have access to gynecological, birth control, abortion, and rape and assault counseling. Staff receive in-service training on sex-role stereotyping.

Safety and Security. Measures include armed police, night-time bus service to residence areas, high-intensity lighting, an emergency phone/alarm system, information sessions on safety and crime prevention, and self-defense and firearms-use seminars for women. An Assault, Abuse, and Rape Crisis Center is open in the community. One rape and 50 assaults (about five on women) were reported for 1980-81.

Career. Information and activities about nontraditional careers for women are available.

Other. There is a Women's Center on campus; lecture series, assertiveness training, and a telephone service of information, referral, and support are among its activities.

Institutional Self-Description. "The University of Missouri-Columbia offers a comprehensive range of academic programs, including interdisciplinary studies, which reflect society's changing needs. The university is committed to providing a quality education through a stimulating learning and living environment. Support services, including student activities, workshops, and seminars, enhance opportunities for women."

University of Missouri, Rolla
Rolla, MO 65401
Telephone: (314) 341-4095

| Women in Leadership | ★ Women and the |
| ★★★ students | Curriculum |

4,860 undergraduates

	Amer. Ind.	Asian Amer.	Blacks	Hispanics	Whites
F	2	5	45	3	752
M	12	31	139	10	3,588
%	0.3	0.8	4.0	0.3	94.6

🏠 🏛 👫 🔦 Ⓜ

Established in 1870 as the University of Missouri School of Mines and Metallurgy, the Rolla campus is one of four branches of the University of Missouri. It began awarding degrees in humanities and social sciences in 1967, although its major mission continues to be education in engineering and physical sciences. Located in the Ozarks, two hours from St. Louis, the campus attracts 5,735 students, of whom 4,860 are undergraduates. Eighteen percent of the undergraduates are women; 18 percent of women attend part-time. The median age of undergraduates is 20. Six percent of women are over age 25. On- and off-campus evening classes and a summer session are available. For the three-fourths of the undergraduates who commute, on-campus parking is available at a fee.

University-sponsored childcare facilities accommodate 22 children, at a fee of $6.40 per day. Additional, private childcare centers are located near the campus.

Policies to Ensure Fairness to Women. Sex equity for students, equal opportunity in employment, and access for the handicapped are the joint responsibility of the Director of Affirmative Action, the Provost, the Director of Personnel, and the Dean of Students. A published policy on sexual harassment protects students, faculty, and staff; complaints are handled through a formal grievance procedure. The establishment of a Committee on the Status of Women is under consideration. The Committee on Minority Affairs addresses the concerns of minority women.

Women in Leadership Positions. *Students.* Women make up 18 percent of the students and, in recent years, have held 20 percent of student leadership posts: one-year terms as president of the student union board, editor of the campus newspaper and president of the residence-hall council. Women preside over three of 16 honorary societies.

Faculty. Five percent of the 299 full-time faculty are women. There are 2 female faculty for every 100 female students, and 8 male faculty for every 100 male students.

Administrators. Men hold all key positions. A black woman sits on the nine-member Board of Trustees.

Women and the Curriculum. Three-quarters of the women earn bachelor's degrees in the nontraditional fields of computer science, engineering, mathematics, and the physical sciences. Fifty-one percent of the degrees in engineering go to women; 85 percent of all students graduate in engineering. The Women in Engineering Program, begun in 1975, offers counseling and scholarships. Additional support comes from the Society of Women Engineers. Women hold 25 percent of the computer science internships, 30 percent of the geology field-service assignments, and 12 percent of cooperative education appointments.

There are no courses on women.

Women and Athletics. A large and varied intramural program, clubs sports, and three intercollegiate teams are available. One-fifth of the intramural and one-ninth of the intercollegiate athletes are women. Women receive 15 percent of the athletic scholarships. Two of the ten paid varsity coaches are women. Intercollegiate sports offered are basketball, softball, and tennis.

Housing and Student Organizations. One-fourth of the un-

dergraduates live on campus in single-sex or coeducational dormitories. Dormitories restrict hours for visitors of the opposite sex. Married students with or without children, and single parents, may reside in campus housing. One of two residence-hall directors is a woman; staff are offered awareness-training on birth control, sex education, rape, sexism, and racism.

Twenty-eight percent of undergraduate women belong to social sororities. There is an all-minority sorority. Fraternities and sororities provide housing for their members. The Association of Women Students is an advocacy group for all women. The Association of Black Students is an advocacy group for black women.

Special Services and Programs for Women. *Health and Counseling.* The student health center is staffed by 4 male physicians and 5 female health-care providers. The student counseling center is staffed by 2 women and 2 men. Counseling and medical treatment are provided for rape and assault; treatment is available for gynecological problems. Student health insurance covers maternity expenses at no extra charge; abortion is covered only if pregnancy is involuntary or threatens the woman's health.

Safety and Security. Measures include local and campus police, both with arrest authority, and information sessions on campus safety for women. A total of three assaults (none on women) and no rapes were reported for 1980–81.

Career. Career workshops, panel discussions on nontraditional occupations, and files on alumnae careers for students' use are available.

Other. The extension division sponsors a woman's lecture series. The Counseling and Testing Center runs a five-week orientation program for reentry women.

Institutional Self-Description. ''The University of Missouri at Rolla is primarily an engineering and science institution. The campus has responded to the increased interest of women in the field of engineering and science. Females comprise over one-sixth of the student body. There are scholarship opportunities for both undergraduate and graduate study.''

University of Missouri, St. Louis
8001 Natural Bridge Road
St. Louis, MO 63121
Telephone: (314) 553-0111

| ★ Women and the |
| Curriculum |

| ★ Women and Athletics |

9,474 undergraduates

	Amer. Ind.	Asian Amer.	Blacks	Hispanics	Whites
F	15	35	715	34	3,358
M	29	30	459	30	4,745
%	0.5	0.7	12.4	0.7	85.8

🏠 🏛 🚌 👫 🔦 Ⓢ Ⓜ 📖 ⚲ AAUW

The newest of the four universities in the Missouri system, the St. Louis campus was established in 1963 and now enrolls some 11,271 students. A little over one-third of the 9,474 undergraduates attend part-time. Women account for about 44 percent of all undergraduates, and 40 percent of women attend part-time. The median age of undergraduates is 24. Evening and off-campus classes and various continuing/extension education programs are available. All students commute to the campus, which is accessible by public transportation. On-campus parking is available at a fee.

On-campus childcare services are available in the mornings and can accommodate about 70 children. The facilities serve students and staff, as well as members of the nearby community. Private childcare facilities are available near the campus.

Policies to Ensure Fairness to Women. Matters concerning equal-employment-opportunity, sex-equity, and access-for-the-handicapped legislation are handled full-time by the Director of Affirmative Action, who has voting status on policymaking councils. A written policy prohibiting the sexual harassment of students, faculty, and staff has been communicated to faculty and staff. The university's Affirmative Action Committee recommends policy regarding the status of women and also attends to the concerns of minority women. Members of this committee are appointed by the Chancellor.

Women in Leadership Positions. *Students.* In recent years, men have held all student leadership positions. Women head four of the ten honorary societies.

Faculty. Of the 340 full-time faculty, 23 percent are women, a proportion slightly below the national average. There are 3 female faculty for every 100 female students and 8 male faculty for every 100 male students. Recent information indicates that among the full-time faculty are 7 black, 2 Asian American, and 2 Hispanic women.

Administrators. Men hold all top-level positions and chair the academic departments. The Dean of the School of Nursing is female. In a recent year, two of the three honorary degree recipients were female.

Women and the Curriculum. Most of the bachelor's degrees awarded to women are in education (31 percent) and business (29 percent). About 1 percent are in the nontraditional fields of mathematics and physical sciences. Other fields of study for women include public affairs (12 percent), social sciences (7 percent), and letters (7 percent).

Students may earn an 18-credit certificate/minor through the Women's Studies Program. In addition to two interdisciplinary courses on women, the departments of art, English, history, philosophy, political science, and pyschology offer ten courses. Recent offerings include Women in Visual Arts; History of Feminism in Western Society; Philosophy and Current Issues: Feminism; Women and the Law; and Psychology of Women. The university offers additional courses on women which emphasize career, life-planning, and management topics. These include Widow and Widower: Coping with New Changes; Mid-Life Career Planning for Men and Women; and For Single Mothers. An official committee develops the Women's Studies Program, including the addition of courses on women to departments.

Women and Athletics. There are good opportunities for women to participate in a wide range of individual and team sports. Thirty-one percent of the 2,438 intramural athletes and 45 percent of the 155 intercollegiate athletes are women; women receive 30 percent of the athletic scholarships awarded. Five of the 16 paid intercollegiate coaches are women. Intercollegiate sports in which women participate are basketball, cross-country, field hockey, softball, swimming, tennis, and volleyball.

Housing and Student Organizations. The only housing on campus is provided by sororities and fraternities, whose membership totals 325 (125 women). Twenty percent of women belong to all-minority sororities. The Student Organization for Sisterhood Functions as a major on-campus advocacy group for women.

Special Services and Programs for Women. *Health and Counseling.* The male physician and 3 health-care providers (2 of them women) who staff the student health center offer treatment on matters of gynecology and birth control. A 4-member staff (including 1 woman) offers counseling to victims of rape and assault.

Safety and Security. Measures consist of local police and a campus-wide emergency telephone system. Eight assaults, one against a woman, were reported for 1980–81.

Other. Operating on an annual budget of $17,000, the Women's Center serves about 2,500 women each year, most of them stu-

dents. About 5 percent of those served are black women. The center sponsors an annual women's week.

Returning Women Students. Continuing Education-Extension sponsors a Continuing Education for Women Program that enrolls more than 150 women. Headed full-time by a woman whose duties are divided between faculty and administrative responsibilities, the program has an annual budget of $45,000.

Older or reentry women are also served through the Older Adult Program and the Center for Academic Development/ Returning Students. Continuing Education-Extension offers a mathematics confidence program and training in assertiveness/ leadership.

Institutional Self-Description. "A Women's Studies certificate program and the services of a Women's Center are offered to enhance the educational experience of women students at UMSL. The faculty and students who participate in the Women's Studies Program strive to reinterpret existing knowledge, to discover new concepts, and to develop approaches to the study of women. The Women's Center offers programs, support groups, and referral and advocacy services to women students."

Washington University
Skinker and Lindell Boulevards
St. Louis, MO 63130
Telephone: (314) 889-5199

★★ **Women and the Curriculum**

6,661 undergraduates

	Amer. Ind.	Asian Amer.	Blacks	Hispanics	Whites
F	1	70	257	27	2,310
M	7	112	190	49	3,523
%	0.1	2.8	6.8	1.2	89.1

🏠 🚐 👫 📖 🏠 **AAUW NWSA**

Washington University in St. Louis, a private, non-sectarian university, was established in 1853 as Eliot Seminary. Some 11,000 students enroll in a comprehensive range of undergraduate, graduate, and professional studies. University College is responsible for adult continuing education. Evening classes and a summer session are available.

Women are 41 percent of the 6,661 undergraduates; 35 percent of women attend part-time. The median age of undergraduates is 20. For the one-quarter of the undergraduates who commute, the university is accessible by public transportation. On-campus parking is provided at a fee, with free transportation from distant parking lots.

University childcare facilities accommodate 60 children per half-day session. Private childcare arrangements can be made close to campus.

Policies to Ensure Fairness to Women. The Associate Vice Chancellor for Personnel and Affirmative Action is responsible for policy on equal employment opportunity, accessibility of curriculum and activities to students, and handicapped access. Complaints of sexual harassment are handled informally and confidentially or through a formal grievance procedure. The Affirmative Action Committee includes the status of women and minority women among its concerns.

Women in Leadership Positions. *Students.* Opportunities for women to assume campus-wide leadership are below the average for private research institutions in this guide. In recent years, women have been presiding officer of the student senate, editor-in-chief of the campus newspaper, and president of the senior class. Women head two of the six honorary societies.

Faculty. Women are 15 percent of a full-time faculty of 555.

According to a recent report, 3 black and 13 Asian American women are on the faculty. The ratio of female faculty to female students is 5 to 100; the ratio of male faculty to male students is 19 to 100.

Administrators. All higher administrative positions are occupied by men. An estimated one-half of department chairs are female. A woman is Dean of the College of Arts and Sciences.

Women and the Curriculum. Significant numbers of women earn bachelor's degrees in arts, humanities, and social sciences. The majority graduate from career-oriented programs such as business, the health professions, engineering, education, and architecture. Thirteen percent of women major in nontraditional fields, which is a higher proportion than for most private research institutions in this guide. Washington University offers a special FOCUS program on women for first year students. One or two courses each semester on such subjects as the psychology of women and women and the arts are part of the program. In the core course, students and their advisor analyze the status of women and strategies for change.

The Women's Studies Program offers an undergraduate minor and a bachelor's degree in Women's Studies. Recent courses include The Body Politic: Issues in Women's Health Care; Anthropology of Sex Roles; and Black Women in America. During the past five years, 30 students have graduated with majors in Women's Studies. Courses in the schools of social work, education, and business provide some instruction on matters specific to women.

Minority Women. Of 2,665 undergraduate women, 10 percent are black, less than 1 percent American Indian, 3 percent Asian American, and 1 percent Hispanic. Nineteen women are reported in all-minority sororities. Residence-hall staff are offered awareness-training on racism. The director of the Women's Resource Center is a minority woman. The Association of Black Students, the Women's Resource Center, and the Women's Studies Program are resources for minority women.

Women and Athletics. Intramural and intercollegiate programs offer opportunities for organized, competitive, individual and team sports. There is more variety in the intramural than in the intercollegiate program. Club sports are also available. Twenty-one percent of intramural and 43 percent of intercollegiate athletes are women. Three of the 16 paid varsity coaches are women. All teams played in tournaments in 1980. The intercollegiate sports offered are basketball, cross-country, swimming and diving, tennis, track and field, and volleyball.

Housing and Student Organizations. Twenty-one percent of undergraduates live on campus. Residential accommodations include coeducational dormitories, with one women's floor. There are no restricted hours for visitors of the opposite sex. Four of six residence directors are female. Awareness-training on sexism, sex education, racism, and birth control is offered residence-hall staff.

Eleven percent of the full-time undergraduate women belong to social sororities. Sororities do not provide housing for their members. Among groups on campus which serve as advocates for women are the Women's Programming Board, Women's Resource Project, Society of Women Engineers, Women's Law Caucus, and School of Social Work Women's Caucus.

Special Services and Programs for Women. *Health and Counseling.* The student health service provides medical attention specific to women, including gynecological and birth control services and follow-up treatment for abortion and rape and assault. Four of 17 physicians are female, as are 11 other health-care providers. Four of 7 professional staff in the counseling service are women. Students have access to counseling specific to women. The counseling service offers its staff in-service training on male/female relationships.

Safety and Security. Measures consist of campus and city police, night-time escort service for women students, night-time bus service to residential areas, emergency alarm and telephone systems, information sessions on safety and crime prevention (part of an ongoing program), and a rape crisis center. Ten assaults (total) and two rapes were reported for 1980-81.

Career. The university provides materials and activities about women in nontraditional careers and fields of study.

Other. The Women's Resource Center, under a full-time administrator, sponsors a telephone service for information, referral, and support. Theater and other women's arts programs are presented under the auspices of the Women's Programming Board. A lecture series is part of the programming of Women's Studies.

Special Features. The Olin Fellowships for Women support graduate students. The Olin Conference for Women brings a major speaker on women's issues to campus each year.

Institutional Self-Description. "In addition to its internationally known faculty, small classes, and attractive and central location, WU offers women students an environment in which there is genuine commitment to the well-being of women and to equal access for all women to the opportunities available on campus and in the wider community."

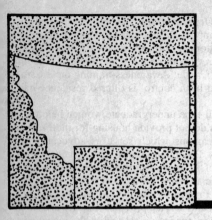

MONTANA

Eastern Montana College
1500 North 30th Street
Billings, MT 59101
Telephone: (406) 657-2011

★ **Women and the Curriculum**

3,047 undergraduates

	Amer. Ind.	Asian Amer.	Blacks	Hispanics	Whites
F	31	0	1	1	1,801
M	24	3	2	5	1,175
%	1.8	0.1	0.1	0.2	97.8

Established in 1927 as a school to train teachers, Eastern Montana College, a member of the Montana State University system, was authorized to grant liberal arts degrees in 1966. Located in Montana's largest city, the college enrolls some 3,400 students, of whom 3,047 are undergraduates. Sixty percent of the undergraduates are women; of these, 20 percent attend part-time. The median age of all students is 24.

Eastern Montana awards undergraduate and master's degrees in a variety of liberal arts and pre-professional fields. Adult continuing education is available through the School of Extended Studies and Community Service. A Continuing Education for Women Program is included in the Women's Studies and Service Center. Flexibility in scheduling is available through evening and summer session classes, independent study, and educational telecommunications systems. Public transportation and on-campus parking are available for the 80 percent of students who commute.

A college-run childcare facility can accommodate 30 children. It charges fees on a fixed hourly rate. Private childcare facilities are located near campus.

Policies to Ensure Fairness to Women. The Personnel Director serves as a part-time equal opportunity officer responsible for equal employment opportunity, sex equity for students, and access for the handicapped. A published policy prohibits sexual harassment of students, faculty, and staff. Complaints are resolved informally and confidentially or through a formal grievance procedure.

Women in Leadership Positions. *Students.* Opportunities for women to exert leadership on campus are limited in relation to their representation in the student body: the seven campus-wide student offices are held by men nearly two-thirds of the time. Women head all of the four honorary societies.

Faculty. Twenty-three percent of the 127 full-time faculty are women. There are 2 female faculty for every 100 female students and 9 male faculty for every 100 male students.

Administrators. Except for the director of institutional research, the chief administrators are men. Women chair the departments of accounting and communications arts.

Women and the Curriculum. Fifty-six percent of women graduate in education and 17 percent in business. About 1 percent of women earn degrees in such nontraditional fields as mathematics. Women earn over half of the two-year degrees.

The Women's Studies Program, under the part-time direction of a permanently appointed faculty member, offers 15 courses through several departments. Recent offerings include Women and the Frontier Experience, Plays By and About Women, and Women and Philosophy. A committee is assigned to develop courses on women within departments as well as within the Women's Studies Program.

Women and Athletics. Seventy women athletes participate in the intercollegiate sports program. Two of the four paid coaches are women. The intercollegiate sports offered are basketball, cross-country, golf, gymnastics, tennis, and track.

Housing and Student Organizations. Coeducational dormitories, without restrictive hours for visitors of the opposite sex, are available for the 19 percent of students who live on campus. Three of the four dormitory directors are women. Dormitory staff receive awareness-training on sexism, racism, birth control, and leadership/assertiveness.

There is one residential fraternity on campus, but no sororities.

Special Services and Programs for Women. *Health and Counseling.* The student health center has one female physician and five female nurses. One of the two-member staff of the student counseling center is a woman. Medical treatment is provided for gynecological problems, birth control, and rape and assault, along with birth control counseling. Counselors receive in-service training on sex-role stereotyping and racial bias.

Safety and Security. Measures consist of local police, campus police with weapons training, night-time escort service on request, self-defense and campus safety courses, and a rape crisis center. No rapes or assaults on women were reported for 1980–81.

Career. Services include workshops and printed material on nontraditional occupations, job discrimination information, and lectures by women employed in nontraditional areas. The Women's Studies and Service Center provides career planning.

Other. The Women's Studies and Service Center is composed of the Women's Center and the Women's Studies Program, and is sponsored by the School of Liberal Arts. The center provides academic and financial counseling. It serves over 300 women annually, 2 percent of whom are minority women, predominantly black women. Under the part-time direction of a female faculty member, the center sponsors annual conferences and weekly lunchtime programs on topics of interest to women and is the site of an annual Women's Equality Day event, co-sponsored by the Federal Women's Program. The center maintains a lending library of current materials of particular interest to women.

The local YWCA provides services for battered women and

displaced homemakers. The School of Extended Studies provides assertiveness training and the office of student services sponsors a mathematics confidence program. The college also has a club for divorced and separated students.

Institutional Self-Description. "A warm welcome to the campus is extended by the staff of the Women's Studies office, which offers assistance with scheduling, planning, decision-making, people to listen and help, and strong support from the 1,000-plus women over 25 currently studying at EMC."

Montana College of Mineral Science and Technology
Butte, MT, 59701
Telephone: (401) 496-4101

★ **Women and the Curriculum**

1,198 undergraduates

	Amer. Ind.	Asian Amer.	Blacks	Hispanics	Whites
F	2	1	2	4	408
M	3	2	2	8	720
%	0.4	0.3	0.4	1.0	97.9

 AAUW

Montana College of Mineral Science and Technology is a state-supported institution in the mining town of Butte, one hour from Helena. Its programs in mineral and engineering science enroll 1,310 students. Women are 35 percent of the 1,198 undergraduates; 38 percent of women attend part-time. The median age of undergraduates is 21.

The college offers an associate degree in arts and sciences, and bachelor's and master's degrees in a variety of fields. Classes meet day and evening; there is a summer session. For the 80 percent of students who commute, public transportation is available, as is on-campus parking for a fee.

Policies to Ensure Fairness to Women. The Dean of Fiscal Affairs is responsible for sex equity for students and equal employment opportunity. A policy on sexual harassment is being developed.

Women in Leadership Positions. *Students.* In a recent three-year period, men held all major campus offices.

Faculty. Six percent of the 63 full-time faculty are women, a proportion below the national average. There are 2 female faculty for every 100 female students and 9 male faculty for every 100 male students.

Administrators. The head librarian is a woman. The other top administrators are men. Women direct the Cooperative Education and Internship program and the department of health, physical education, and recreation. Three of seven regents are women.

Women and the Curriculum. Sixty-one percent of the bachelor's degrees earned by women are in such nontraditional fields as engineering, mathematics, and the physical sciences. Two-thirds of the participants in the Cooperative Education and Internship program are women. Women receive half the two-year degrees awarded, all in arts and sciences.

There are no courses on women.

Women and Athletics. The intramural program offers ten sports, six of which are coeducational. Club sports are also available. Women are 25 percent of intramural and 17 percent of the varsity athletes. Athletic scholarships are available. One of six paid varsity coaches is a woman. The intercollegiate sports offered are basketball and volleyball.

Housing and Student Organizations. One-fifth of the undergraduates live in coeducational dormitories that restrict visiting

hours for members of the opposite sex. Housing is also available for married students with and without children.

SPURS, Society of Women Engineers, and Associated Women of Montana Tech are advocacy groups for women.

Special Services and Programs for Women. *Health and Counseling.* The student health service employs one male physician and four health-care providers, three of whom are female. There is no treatment specific to women. There is no counseling center, but the community health agency provides some counseling and medical treatment specific to women. The student health insurance policy covers maternity expenses at no extra charge.

Safety and Security. Measures consist of campus and local police, both with arrest authority. No rapes or assaults on women were reported for 1980–81.

Career. Services include lectures and information on nontraditional occupations for women, and files on alumnae careers for use by students.

Other. The Society of Women Engineers organizes a women's lecture series. Other women's programs—a battered women's shelter and leadership-training workshops—are available in the community.

Institutional Self-Description. "Montana Tech is a small, growing college with an admirable past and a dynamic present. Engineering degrees, along with the college's reputable placement services, provide excellent career opportunities for women seeking the most value for their investment of money, time, and energy."

Montana State University
Bozeman, MT 59717
Telephone: (406) 994-2341

★ **Women and the Curriculum**

9,084 undergraduates

	Amer. Ind.	Asian Amer.	Blacks	Hispanics	Whites
F	39	3	4	5	3,977
M	35	13	3	5	4,959
%	0.8	0.2	0.1	0.1	98.8

Established in 1893 as a land-grant institution, Montana State University in Bozeman provides undergraduate and graduate programs for some 9,800 students. The division of continuing education serves the adult student. Alternative class schedules, including self-paced learning contracts and off-campus locations, are available.

Women are 45 percent of the 9,084 undergraduates; 8 percent of women attend part-time. The median age of undergraduates is 22. For the 60 percent of undergraduates who live off campus or commute, on-campus parking is available at a fee.

University-sponsored childcare charges fees on a sliding scale. Facilities can accommodate approximately half of students' requests. Private childcare arrangements may be made close to campus.

Policies to Ensure Fairness to Women. A full-time equal-opportunity officer reviews and monitors policies on employment, accessibility of programs and activities to students, and handicapped access. A published policy prohibits sexual harassment of students. Complaints are handled both informally and confidentially and through a formal grievance procedure.

Women in Leadership Positions. *Students.* In recent years, women have been president of the student body, and twice editor-in-chief of the newspaper and manager of the campus radio station.

Faculty. Women constitute 19 percent of a full-time faculty of 540. According to a recent report, 1 black and 2 Hispanic women are on the full-time faculty. The ratio of female faculty to female students is 3 to 100; the ratio for males is 9 to 100.

Administrators. The Head Librarian and the Director of Women's Athletics are women. No women currently chair departments. The Dean of Home Economics, the Director of General Studies, and Dean of the School of Nursing are women.

Women and the Curriculum. More women graduating with bachelor's degrees major in the health professions and education than in other fields. The percentage of women majoring in business is above the national average. Twelve percent earn degrees in nontraditional fields, the largest number being in agriculture and engineering. The university reports an innovative program to encourage women to prepare for careers in engineering. Over 60 percent of the students in cooperative education and internship programs are female. Student Affairs and Services sponsors a program to increase mathematics confidence among women.

Although Montana State will not have a formal Women's Studies Program until fall 1982, a funded project has effectively integrated the study of women into 21 undergraduate courses, and created six new courses on women. Departments with integrated and/or Women's Studies courses are history and philosophy, speech, English, mathematics, Native American studies, film and television, business management, home economics, physical education, agriculture and industrial education, business education, psychology, political science, and the School of Nursing.

Such current issues as mathematics confidence among females, sex-fair curricula, and coeducational physical education classes are part of the preparation of future teachers. The department of business includes discussion of employment discrimination in its curriculum.

Minority Women. Of 4,040 undergraduate women, about 1 percent are members of minority groups, American Indian women constituting the largest group. There are 13 minority women in integrated sororities. The Advance By Choice/Indian Club serves American Indian women.

Women and Athletics. Intramurals offer a good number and variety of individual and team sports. The intercollegiate program is more limited. The university reports that its new Physical Education Complex supports a wide variety of sports. Nineteen percent of intramural and 44 percent of intercollegiate athletes are women. Women receive 20 percent of athletic scholarships. Nine of 27 paid varsity coaches are female. Most women's intercollegiate teams played in tournaments in 1980. The intercollegiate sports offered are basketball, cross-country, gymnastics, skiing, tennis, track and field, and volleyball.

Housing and Student Organizations. Forty percent of the undergraduates live on campus. Single-sex and coeducational dormitories, apartments for single students, and housing for married students and single parents with children are available. A married woman student whose spouse is not enrolled may live in married students' housing. Residence halls determine their own visitation policy. Two of nine residence-hall directors are women. Staff are offered awareness-training on sexism, among other issues.

Twelve percent of undergraduate women belong to social sororities. Sororities and fraternities provide housing for their members. Women's International, Lambda Gay Alliance, and Single Parents/On Campus Living serve as advocacy groups for women on campus.

Special Services and Programs for Women. *Health and Counseling.* The student health service provides some medical attention specific to women, including gynecological, birth control, and rape and assault treatment. One of 7 physicians is female, as are 6 other health-care providers. Two of 8 professional staff in the counseling center are women. Students have access to treatment for gynecological problems, birth control, abortion, and rape and assault, as well as venereal disease counseling. Staff receive in-service training on the avoidance of sex-role stereotyping. Counseling Services sponsors assertiveness training and a telephone service of information, referral, and support.

Safety and Security. Measures consist of campus and city police, high-intensity lighting, self-defense courses for women, and a rape crisis center. No assaults or rapes were reported for 1980-81.

Career. The university provides career workshops and printed matter about women in nontraditional occupations and fields of study and encourages contacts between alumnae and students.

Other. Services for battered women and displaced homemakers, an annual women's week, lecture series, and theater and other arts programs are among activities sponsored by campus or community groups. There is a Women's Community Center in Bozeman. Radio station ASMSU sponsors a Montana Women's Radio Show.

Special Features. The Next Move Program, a support and professional development network of 40 women administrators, faculty, and staff, is preparing a Women's Resource Directory to assist in the process of ''mentoring'' women students. Women students may join the Affiliated Professional Women of MSU as associate members.

Institutional Self-Description. ''The university is taking great strides in strengthening and developing opportunities and programs for women. A widely diversified curriculum leads to bachelor's degrees in 42 fields, master's in 37 areas, and doctor's in 16. The campus is located in a city of 29,000, situated in a scenic and recreational area.''

University of Montana
Missoula, MT 59812
Telephone: (406) 243-0211

Women in Leadership
★ students

6,835 undergraduates

	Amer. Ind.	Asian Amer.	Blacks	Hispanics	Whites
F	114	14	11	13	2,973
M	85	18	21	13	3,499
%	2.9	0.5	0.5	0.4	95.7

A state-supported institution, the University of Montana has two campuses in the town of Missoula. It offers its 8,338 students a wide range of undergraduate, graduate, and pre-professional degrees. The Continuing Education and Summer Programs department is responsible for adult continuing education.

Fifty-six percent of the 6,835 undergraduates are women, and 12 percent of the women attend part-time. Classes meet on campus both day and evening; there is also a summer session. For students who commute, public transportation and on-campus parking for a fee are available.

The campus childcare facility, which accommodates most students', requests charges fees on a sliding scale. Additional, private childcare centers are nearby.

Policies to Ensure Fairness to Women. The Director of Equal Opportunity and Personnel Services has full-time responsibility for monitoring compliance with equal-employment-opportunity, sex-equity, and handicapped-access laws. A written and publicized sexual harassment policy protects all members of the university community; complaints are handled through a formal campus grievance procedure.

Women in Leadership Positions. *Students.* During three recent years, women have held the position of editor-in-chief of the campus newspaper; men have held the other two offices, student body president and student union board president.

Faculty. Fourteen percent of the 388 full-time faculty are women. There are 2 female faculty for every 100 female students, and 10 male faculty for every 100 male students.

Administrators. Except for the chief business officer, the top-level administrators are men. Women chair three of 39 departments: home economics, management, and Native American studies. The Dean of Fine Arts and the Director of Continuing Education and Summer Programs are women, as are three of the seven regents.

Women and the Curriculum. The most popular fields among women graduates are education (20 percent), business (15 percent), and social sciences (11 percent). Nine percent of women pursue nontraditional fields such as agriculture, mathematics, and physical sciences. Approximately half of the students in cooperative work/study programs are women.

No courses on women are offered. The establishment of a Women's Studies Program is under consideration.

Women and Athletics. No information was supplied on the number of women participating in the three intramural sports. Thirty-two percent of the intercollegiate athletes are women and women receive 30 percent of the athletic scholarship aid. One of the 21 paid varsity coaches is a woman. Intercollegiate sports offered are basketball, cross-country, gymnastics, swimming, tennis, track and field, and volleyball.

Housing and Student Organizations. One-fourth of the undergraduates live in either single-sex or coeducational dormitories or in fraternity or sorority housing. The university provides housing for married students with or without children and single parents. Restrictions on visiting hours for members of the opposite sex vary from dormitory to dormitory. Residence-hall staff are offered awareness-training on matters of birth control, sex education, and sexism.

Eight percent of the undergraduate women belong to sororities.

Special Services and Programs for Women. *Health and Counseling.* The student health center is staffed by 4 male physicians and 5 female health-care providers. One of the 6 counselors employed by the student counseling center is a woman. Counseling is provided for gynecological problems, birth control, abortion, and rape and assault; medical treatment is provided for all of these except abortion.

Safety and Security. Measures include campus police with arrest authority, night-time escort for women, emergency telephone and alarm systems, information on campus safety for women, and a rape crisis center. No information was provided concerning the incidence of rapes and assaults.

Career. The university provides career workshops and nonsexist/nonracist printed information on nontraditional fields of study and work for women; panels and lectures by women employed in such areas; and information on job discrimination against women.

Other. A well-funded ($40,000 annually) and student-directed Women's Center serves 7,500, predominantly undergraduate and community, women. The center sponsors brown-bag lunches, assertiveness-training workshops, and theater and other arts programs for women.

Institutional Self-Description. None provided.

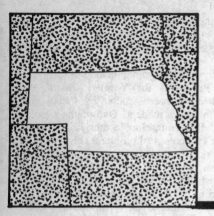

NEBRASKA

Chadron State College
10th and Main St., Chadron, NE 69337
Telephone: (308) 432-4451

1,491 undergraduates

	Amer. Ind.	Asian Amer.	Blacks	Hispanics	Whites
F	7	6	4	6	836
M	6	9	12	3	587
%	0.9	1.0	1.1	0.6	96.4

Situated in a rural area of northwestern Nebraska, Chadron State College enrolls some 1,900 students. Fifty-eight percent of the 1,491 undergraduates are women, 36 percent of whom attend part-time. The median age of undergraduates is 19; about one-fourth of female students are over age 25.

Chadron State offers bachelor's degrees in liberal arts, education, allied health, and pre-professional programs, as well as master's and specialist-in-education degrees. Two-year degrees in several vocational fields were recently introduced. An Adult and Continuing Education Program is also available. Scheduling alternatives include evening and summer session classes, a weekend college, and off-campus classes.

The campus is not accessible by public transportation. Free on-campus parking is available for the 20 percent of students who commute.

College-operated childcare facilities can accommodate all students' requests. Charges are based on a fixed, daily rate. Private facilities are also available near campus.

Policies to Ensure Fairness to Women. Although there is no policy on sexual harassment, a formal campus grievance procedure handles complaints. The Dean for Administrative Services, a voting member of policymaking councils, is assigned on a part-time basis to oversee matters related to equal employment opportunity, sex equity in education, and handicapped accessibility.

Women in Leadership Positions. *Students.* Opportunities for women students to gain leadership experience are limited. In three recent years, women served as presiding officer of the residence hall council. Women head three of the 15 campus honorary societies.

Faculty. Sixteen percent of the 83 full-time faculty are women. There are 2 female faculty for every 100 female students, and 14 male faculty for every 100 male students.

Administrators. Of the eight major administrative positions, one (chief student life officer) is held by a woman. There are no women department chairs or deans. Three of the eleven trustees are women.

Women and the Curriculum. Most bachelor's degrees awarded to women are in education (39 percent), business (16 percent), and fine arts, public affairs, and social sciences (each 8 percent). Three percent are in such nontraditional fields as math-

ematics or physical sciences. Of the 80 percent of two-year degrees awarded to women, most are in business and commercial technologies or data processing. Sixty percent of students participating in cooperative education and internship programs are women.

No courses on women are offered. Courses in the departments of education, physical education, social work, and business provide some instruction on matters specific to women.

Women and Athletics. Women have limited opportunities to participate in organized competitive sports. One-fourth of intramural and 29 percent of intercollegiate athletes are women, who receive 10 percent of athletic scholarship aid. Three of nine paid intercollegiate coaches are women. The intercollegiate sports offered are basketball, softball, track, and volleyball.

Housing and Student Organizations. Single-sex and coeducational dormitories are available for the 40 percent of students who live on campus; housing for married students and single parents is also available. Black, Hispanic, American Indian, and Asian American women account for 4 percent of the female dormitory residents. All nine residence-hall directors are women; they are offered awareness-training on sex education and birth control.

Two percent of women belong to social sororities. Neither sororities nor fraternities provide housing for members.

Special Services and Programs for Women. *Health and Counseling.* The student health service employs one female health-care provider and offers no medical treatment specific to women. One woman staffs the counseling center, which counsels on birth control, abortion, and rape and assault.

Safety and Security. Measures consist of local police, campus police without arrest authority, and high-intensity lighting. No rapes and two assaults, one on a woman, were reported for 1980–81.

Other. The Business Division sponsors assertiveness training.

Institutional Self-Description. ''Chadron has an open campus offering baccalaureate, master's, and education-specialist degrees with no discrimination of sex, race, or age. The campus has the environment of a small rural town with a very low crime rate, offering a good family environment.''

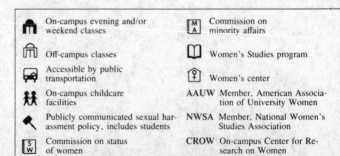

🛏 On-campus evening and/or weekend classes	Ⓜ Commission on minority affairs	
🏛 Off-campus classes	📖 Women's Studies program	
🚌 Accessible by public transportation	🚻 Women's center	
🚻 On-campus childcare facilities	AAUW Member, American Association of University Women	
✎ Publicly communicated sexual harassment policy, includes students	NWSA Member, National Women's Studies Association	
Ⓢⓦ Commission on status of women	CROW On-campus Center for Research on Women	

Creighton University
2500 California St., Omaha, NE 68178
Telephone: (402) 449-2701

Women in Leadership
★ **faculty**

3,226 undergraduates

	Amer. Ind.	Asian Amer.	Blacks	Hispanics	Whites
F	3	36	64	14	1,355
M	3	58	47	19	1,598
%	0.2	2.9	3.5	1.0	92.4

 AAUW

Founded in 1878 as a Jesuit school for men, Creighton University in Omaha has accepted women since 1923; it is still affiliated with the Roman Catholic Church. Some 5,000 students are enrolled in undergraduate, graduate, and professional studies. The Lifelong Learning Center serves the adult student; 176 reentry women enroll in its courses. Evening classes and a summer session are available.

Women constitute 46 percent of the 3,226 undergraduates; 6 percent of the women attend part-time. The median age of undergraduates is 20. For the 62 percent who commute, the university is accessible by public transportation. On-campus parking is available for a fee, with free transportation from distant parking lots.

Policies to Ensure Fairness to Women. On a part-time basis, the Director of Affirmative Action monitors compliance with equal-employment-opportunity and handicapped-accessibility legislation. A campus policy prohibiting sexual harassment is in the process of approval; in the meantime, complaints of sexual harassment are handled informally and confidentially. An active Committee on the Status of Women includes students as voting members and reports to the President. A Committee on Minority Affairs addresses the concerns of minority women.

Women in Leadership Positions. *Students.* In recent years, women have served as chief justice of the student court and twice been editor-in-chief of the campus newspaper. Two of the eleven honorary societies are headed by women.

Faculty. Women are 26 percent of a full-time faculty of 282. Eight black, 1 Hispanic, and 22 Asian American women are on the full-time faculty, according to a recent report. The ratio of female faculty to female students is 5 to 100. The ratio of male faculty to male students is 12 to 100.

Administrators. A woman directs one of three university libraries. All other higher administrative positions are held by men. Women chair the departments of classics, philosophy, nursing, and nurse anesthesiology. Of nine other divisions, women head the School of Nursing, and Summer Session and Lifelong Learning.

Women and the Curriculum. Almost half of the bachelor's degrees earned by women are in the health professions; less than 3 percent are in the nontraditional fields of mathematics and the physical sciences. Individual courses on women, available in the departments of psychology, history, and classics and modern languages, include The American Woman: Her History; and Modern French Women Authors.

Minority Women. Eight percent of the undergraduate women are members of minority groups. Over 2 percent of women in residence halls are black women, 3 percent Asian American, 1 percent Hispanic, and less than 1 percent American Indian. Residence-hall staff are offered awareness-training on racism; counseling staff, in-service training on avoiding racial bias. Eight percent of the Women's Center users are minority women.

Women and Athletics. Intramural and intercollegiate programs offer opportunities for organized, competitive individual and team sports. Some of the intramural sports are coeducational. The uni-

versity reports special facilities for water polo. Club sports are also available. Forty percent of intramural and intercollegiate athletes are women; women receive 30 percent of athletic scholarships. Four of ten paid coaches of varsity sports are female. The intercollegiate sports offered are basketball, softball, tennis, and volleyball.

Housing and Student Organizations. Thirty-eight percent of undergraduates live on campus in single-sex and coeducational dormitories. Residence halls restrict hours for visitors of the opposite sex. Two of three residence-hall directors are female. Staff are offered awareness-training on sex education and on sexism and racism.

Creighton has social sororities and fraternities; they do not provide housing for members.

Special Services and Programs for Women. *Health and Counseling.* The student health service provides some medical attention specific to women, including gynecological and rape and assault treatment. Four male physicians work part-time; three other health-care providers are women. One of four professional staff in the counseling service is female. Students have access to some counseling specific to women. Staff receive in-service training on avoidance of sex-role stereotyping.

Safety and Security. Measures include campus police with arrest authority, night-time escort service for women, night-time bus service to residence areas, high-intensity lighting, an emergency alarm system, self-defense courses for women, information sessions on safety and crime prevention, and a rape crisis center. One rape and three assaults (two on women) were reported for 1980–81.

Institutional Self-Description. "Creighton University's primary mission is to provide quality, value-oriented education in metropolitan Omaha. It is an independent Catholic, Jesuit, and urban institution. It is to share in the explicit and implicit advantages of these characteristics that women enroll in its curriculum, which includes arts and sciences, business administration, and the major health sciences."

Mid-Plains Community College
I-80 and Hwy. 83, North Platte, NE 69101
Telephone: (308) 532-8740

Women in Leadership
★ **students**
★ **faculty**

1,710 undergraduates

	Amer. Ind.	Asian Amer.	Blacks	Hispanics	Whites
F	7	3	4	28	768
M	6	5	2	18	869
%	0.8	0.5	0.4	2.7	95.7

Mid-Plains is a public, two-year college that offers educational programs to 1,710 students. Forty-seven percent of students are women and 72 percent of women attend part-time. The median age of all students is 29.

Mid-Plains offers two-year liberal arts and pre-professional programs, as well as a variety of vocational programs in the areas of trade and technical skills, health occupations, and secretarial skills and business. Evening classes both on and off campus, as well as a summer session are available. Most students commute. Free on-campus parking is available. Single-sex housing, provided for the 5 percent of students who live on campus, has no restrictive hours for visitors of the opposite sex.

Private childcare facilities can be found near campus.

Policies to Ensure Fairness to Women. A written campus policy prohibits sexual harassment of students, faculty, and staff. Complaints are resolved informally and confidentially or through a formal grievance procedure.

Women in Leadership Positions. *Students.* The only campus leadership position, president of the student body, has been held by a woman once in a recent three-year period. The single campus honorary society is headed by a woman.

Faculty. The full-time faculty of 53 is 34 percent female, an average proportion for public, two-year colleges nationwide. There are 8 female faculty for every 100 female students and 12 male faculty for every 100 male students.

Administrators. All five of the chief administrative positions are held by men. Women chair two of of the eight major divisions; health occupations, and secretarial and business. One of the eleven trustees is a woman.

Women and the Curriculum. Most of the degrees and certificates awarded to women are in the arts and sciences and in health technologies. There are no courses on women.

Women and Athletics. Women participate in intercollegiate and intramural basketball and volleyball. One of the two paid varsity coaches is a woman; women receive over 50 percent of the athletic scholarship awards.

Special Services and Programs for Women. *Health and Counseling.* The college does not have a student health service or a student counseling center.

Safety and Security. Measures consist of local police who patrol the campus and high-intensity lighting in all areas. No assaults or rapes were reported for 1980–81.

Career. Services include workshops and lectures on nontraditional occupations and printed information on nontraditional fields of study for women.

Other. The Division of Community Services sponsors a women's lecture series, assertiveness/leadership training, and a program for displaced homemakers.

Institutional Self-Description. "Mid-Plains has a wide range of pre-professional and occupational programs, many of which are traditionally oriented to women in the health and business fields. The college also has encouraged and has a small but substantial enrollment of women in the nontraditional trade and technical fields. Job placement for women in both traditional and nontraditional fields is relatively good."

Nebraska Wesleyan University
50th and St. Paul, Lincoln, NE 68504
Telephone: (402) 466-2371

Women in Leadership
★ students

1,043 undergraduates

	Amer. Ind.	Asian Amer.	Blacks	Hispanics	Whites
F	1	5	12	3	494
M	2	7	11	1	463
%	0.3	1.2	2.3	0.4	95.8

 AAUW

Nebraska Wesleyan is an independent, coeducational institution affiliated with the United Methodist Church. Its campus, near downtown Lincoln, attracts 1,160 students, and of those, 1,043 are enrolled in degree programs. Half of the students are women and 6 percent of the women attend part-time. The median age of students is 20.

The university offers a bachelor's degree in liberal arts, business, and science, as well as associate degrees in some fields.

The Wesleyan Institute for Lifelong Learning is responsible for adult continuing education. Day, evening, and summer session classes are available. On-campus parking is available for the 50 percent of students who commute.

Women in Leadership Positions. *Students.* Women students have good opportunities to exercise campus leadership. In recent years, women have held three of five major campus posts, each for two terms; women also preside over eight of 18 honorary societies.

Faculty. Twenty-four percent of the 74 full-time faculty are women, a proportion which is average for similar colleges in this guide. There are 4 female faculty for every 100 female students, and 11 male faculty for every 100 male students.

Administrators. Except for the head librarian, all chief administrators are men. Women chair three of 20 departments: library science, art, and medical technology. One-fourth of the trustees are women.

Women and the Curriculum. Most women earn bachelor's degrees in education (25 percent), biology (18 percent), and psychology (12 percent). Three percent specialize in such nontraditional areas as mathematics and physical sciences. A few women earn two-year degrees in health technologies and public service. Half of the student internships go to women.

The university offers three courses on women: Women in Management, Philosophy of Women, and Women in European Culture. Prospective social workers receive instruction on services for battered spouses, displaced homemakers, and childcare.

Minority Women. Minority women constitute 2 percent of the undergraduates. Among the 20 full-time female faculty is an Asian American woman, who also sits on the faculty senate. Among the five residence-hall directors is one minority woman. The International Club serves minority women.

Women and Athletics. For a campus of its size, Nebraska Wesleyan has a good organized athletic program for women, especially in intercollegiate sports. Fifty-one percent of the intercollegiate athletes are women, as are five of the ten paid varsity coaches. Women receive half of the athletic scholarship aid. Twenty-two percent of the intramural athletes are women, who participate in six individual and team activities. Intercollegiate sports offered are basketball, cross-country, golf, softball, tennis, track (indoor and outdoor), and volleyball.

Housing and Student Organizations. Single-sex and coeducational dormitories, having no restrictions on hours for visitors of the opposite sex, are available for the 50 percent of undergraduates who live on campus. Three of the five residence-hall directors are women, including one minority woman. Residence-hall staff receive awareness-training on sexism, sex education, and birth control.

Forty-nine percent of undergraduate women belong to social sororities. Some sororities and fraternities provide housing for members.

Special Services and Programs for Women. *Health and Counseling.* The student health service employs one male physician and three health-care providers, two of whom are women. One of four professionals at the student counseling center is a woman. Counseling and treatment are available for gynecological problems, birth control, and rape and assault, in addition to abortion counseling.

Safety and Security. Measures consist of local and campus police protection, night-time escort for women, high-intensity lighting, instruction and information on self-defense and campus safety, and a rape crisis center. No rapes or assaults on women were reported for 1980–81.

Career. Career placement services include workshops and information on nontraditional occupations for women.

Institutional Self-Description. "Nebraska Wesleyan University has an excellent academic reputation, particularly in pre-professional areas. Women with professional ambitions frequently choose Nebraska Wesleyan because of this reputation."

University of Nebraska, Lincoln
Lincoln, NE 68588
Telephone: (402) 472-3417

★★ **Women and the Curriculum**

17,657 undergraduates

	Amer. Ind.	Asian Amer.	Blacks	Hispanics	Whites
F	31	20	98	46	7,508
M	34	35	122	72	9,277
%	0.4	0.3	1.3	0.7	97.3

A public land-grant institution established in 1869, the University of Nebraska, located in the small city of Lincoln, attracts some 22,500 students to a comprehensive range of undergraduate, graduate, and professional studies. Continuing Education provides programs for the adult student. Alternative class schedules, including a summer session and off-campus locations, are available.

Women are 44 percent of the 17,657 undergraduates; 17 percent of women attend part-time. For the 60 percent of the undergraduates who commute, the university is accessible by public transportation. On-campus parking is provided at a fee.

Two childcare facilities are available—one operated by the university, the other in cooperation with the university. Both facilities give priority to low-income students. Private arrangements for childcare may be made close to campus.

Policies to Ensure Fairness to Women. The full-time Affirmative Action officer reviews policies and monitors compliance with equal-employment-opportunity, educational-sex-equity and handicapped-access legislation. A campus policy prohibits sexual harassment; complaints are resolved through a formal grievance procedure. The Chancellor's Commission on the Status of Women, which includes students as voting members, takes public stands on issues and sponsors a women's lecture series.

Women in Leadership Positions. *Students.* In recent years women have been president of the student body, editor-in-chief of the newspaper (three times), and head of the residence-hall council.

Faculty. Women make up 16 percent of a full-time faculty of 1,071. According to a recent report, 1 black, 4 American Indian, 2 Asian American, and 1 Hispanic women are on the full-time faculty. The ratio of female faculty to female students is 3 to 100; the ratio of male faculty to male students is 10 to 100.

Administrators. All of the higher administrative posts are occupied by men. Women chair the departments of political science, publication services, telecommunications, and three departments in home economics—education and family resources; human nutrition and foodservice management; and textiles, clothing, and design. The Dean of the College of Home Economics is female.

Women and the Curriculum. Most bachelor's degrees awarded to women are in education (34 percent), business and management (14 percent), fine arts (8 percent), home economics (7 percent), and the social sciences (7 percent). Eight percent of the undergraduate women major in such nontraditional areas as agriculture, architecture, computer science, engineering, mathematics, and the physical sciences. Most of the two-year degrees earned by women are in business, health technologies, and natural science.

The Women's Studies Program offers a minor and a bachelor's degree. More than 33 courses on women are available through Women's Studies and the departments of English, political science, sociology, anthropology, history, ethnic studies, psychology, speech communication, philosophy, human development, and health and physical education. Recent offerings include Regional Women's Literature, History of Feminist Literature, Women in Politics, Women and Work, Women in Cross-Cultural Perspective, Psychology of Women, Sex Role Development, and Twentieth Century Lesbian Novels. An official committee supports the development of the Women's Studies Program and advocates and monitors the teaching of the new scholarship on women across the curriculum.

Minority Women. Of 7,703 undergraduate women, 1 percent each are black and Hispanic, less than 1 percent each American Indian and Asian American. Courses offered or under development include Native American Women: Heritage and Identity; Black Women Writers; History of Mexican Women; and La Mujer. Residence-hall and counseling staff are offered awareness-traning on racism. Minority women can find support from Multicultural Affairs.

Women and Athletics. Intramural and intercollegiate programs offer a mix of individual and team competition, with intramural sports providing the greater variety. Twelve percent of the intramural and 40 percent of the varsity athletes are women. Athletic scholarships are awarded; 17 of the 45 paid varsity coaches are women. The intercollegiate sports offered are basketball, cross-country, golf, gymnastics, softball/baseball, swimming, tennis, and track.

Housing and Student Organizations. For the 40 percent of the undergraduates who live on campus, single-sex and coeducational dormitories and housing for married students and single parents with children are available. A married woman student whose spouse is not enrolled may live in married students' housing. Men's and women's dormitories restrict hours for visitors of the opposite sex. Five of eleven residence-hall directors are female. Awareness-training on sexism, sex education, racism, and birth control is offered residence staff.

Twenty-one percent of undergraduate women belong to social sororities. Sororities and fraternities provide housing for members. Among groups which serve as advocates for women on campus are the Women's Resource Center, YWCA, and Students for Reproductive Freedom.

Special Services and Programs for Women. *Health and Counseling.* The student health service provides some medical attention specific to women, including gynecological, birth control, and rape and assault treatment. One of 6 physicians is female, as are 20 other health-care providers. The regular student health insurance covers maternity expenses at no extra cost. In the counseling service, staffed by 3 women and 4 men, counseling of particular concern to women is available.

Safety and Security. Campus police have arrest authority. There are night-time escorts for women students to dormitories, bus service at night from the library to dormitories during finals, high-intensity lighting, emergency telephones, information sessions on safety and crime prevention, and a rape crisis center. Twenty-six assaults (14 on women) and three rapes were reported for 1980–81.

Career. Career workshops, speakers, and nonsexist/nonracist printed materials on women in nontraditional occupations and fields of study, as well as a network of contacts between alumnae and students are provided.

Other. The Women's Resource Center, under a full-time director, offers drop-in peer counseling and sponsors groups ranging from self-help and assertiveness to a weekly lesbian rap session. The Studies Skills Center offers a program to build mathematics confidence.

Institutional Self-Description. "The University of Nebraska's Women's Studies faculty has wide-ranging expertise that is reflected in the diversity and attractiveness of our courses. We offer coursework in areas traditionally not represented in the university curriculum, including courses on American Indian, black, lesbian, and Hispanic women's experiences, as well as a full range of courses across the humanities and social sciences. The Women's Resource Center organizes scholastic, political, social, and cultural activities both on campus and in the community, including an annual women's week."

University of Nebraska, Omaha
60th and Dodge Streets
Omaha, NE 68182,
Telephone: (402) 554-2200

Women in Leadership
★★★ students

11,479 undergraduates

	Amer. Ind.	Asian Amer.	Blacks	Hispanics	Whites
F	19	28	386	83	4,749
M	14	37	327	84	5,599
%	0.3	0.6	6.3	1.5	91.4

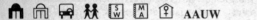 AAUW

Founded in 1908 as a municipal university, Nebraska at Omaha joined the state university system and was renamed in 1968. A total of 14,665 students pursue undergraduate and graduate studies. Women are 46 percent of the 11,479 undergraduates, and 49 percent of women attend part-time.

Alternative schedules include evening classes on and off campus, off-campus day classes, and a summer session. All students commute. Students who drive to the campus must pay for off-campus parking, but transportation from these lots to classroom buildings is provided at no charge. Public transportation is also available.

Childcare facilities are available both on and off campus.

Policies to Ensure Fairness to Women. One full-time and two part-time staff are responsible for matters related to equal employment opportunity, sex equity, and access for the handicapped. The Committee on the Status of Women includes students with voting rights. This committee, which reports to the Chancellor of the university, takes public stands on matters of concern to students and addresses the concerns of minority women. The Committee on Minority Affairs also addresses the concerns of minority women. A written policy prohibits sexual harassment of students, faculty, and staff; formal grievance procedures are being developed.

Women in Leadership Positions. *Students.* The campus has one student leadership position: recently, women have been president of the student body for two consecutive years. Women head five of eleven honorary societies.

Faculty. Women are 20 percent of the 387 full-time faculty. According to recent information, there are 8 black, 1 American Indian, and 4 Hispanic women among the 90 full-time faculty women. There are 3 female faculty for every 100 female students and 9 male faculty for every 100 male students.

Administrators. Men hold all top positions. A black woman chairs one of the 42 academic departments; two of the eight deans are women.

Women and the Curriculum. Most four-year degrees awarded to women are in education (37 percent), business (17 percent), and public affairs (13 percent). About 2 percent of the degrees are in the nontraditional fields of computer sciences, mathematics, and physical sciences. Most two-year degrees awarded to women are in the arts and sciences and public services. The departments of education, physical education, and business provide instruction on some matters specific to women.

Seven courses on women, taught in seven departments, include The Black Woman, Modern French Women Authors, Sociology of Feminism, and History of Women. Faculty workshops address issues of sexism and racism in the curriculum.

Women and Athletics. No information was provided.

Special Services and Programs for Women. *Health and Counseling.* The health service, staffed by a male physician on a part-time basis, and five health-care providers (most of them female), offers no treatment specific to women. The seven-member staff of the counseling center, which includes one white woman and a minority woman, provides counseling on gynecological matters. Counselors receive in-service awareness-training on sex-role stereotyping and racial bias.

Safety and Security. Measures consist of campus police without arrest authority but with weapons training, night-time escort for women students, information sessions on campus safety, and a rape crisis center. No rapes and five assaults (one on a woman) were reported for 1980–81.

Career. The university offers lectures by women employed in nontraditional careers and provides printed information on nontraditional fields of study and careers for women.

Other. The Women's Resource Center, operated by Student Government on a $7,000 annual budget, serves an estimated 9,200 women each year, 15 percent of them minority women. The center's most frequent users are undergraduates over age 25, undergraduates under age 25, and community women, in that order. The center, which is directed by a part-time, salaried student administrator, offers assertiveness training and a telephone warmline (co-sponsored with Women's Services). Women's Networks, a group of faculty and staff women, sponsors professional-growth seminars and a program for battered women. The Gay Action Coalition meets on campus. Non-residential social sororities attract 7 percent of full-time undergraduate women.

The YWCA and Nebraska Coalition for Women sponsor an annual women's week, a women's lecture series, and theater and arts programs.

Institutional Self-Description. "The University of Nebraska at Omaha is an urban commuter campus. Courses are offered from 7:30 a.m. until 10 p.m. In some fields there are also weekend classes. The student population is diverse—over half the students are employed, and the average student age is 26."

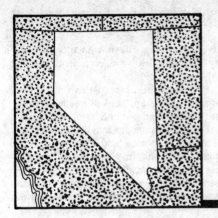

NEVADA

University of Nevada, Las Vegas
4505 Maryland Parkway
Las Vegas, NV 89154
Telephone: (702) 739-3011

★ Women and the
Curriculum

6,067 undergraduates

	Amer. Ind.	Asian Amer.	Blacks	Hispanics	Whites
F	17	49	170	78	2,433
M	10	73	171	104	2,852
%	0.5	2.1	5.7	3.1	88.7

Founded in 1955, the Las Vegas branch of the University of Nevada offers bachelor's degrees in liberal arts and sciences, business, education, nursing, and engineering. Master's and doctoral programs are also offered, along with some two-year degrees. An adult continuing education program is available. Alternative scheduling includes evening classes, a summer session, and self-paced/contract learning. Off-campus locations are available for day and evening classes.

Some 8,500 students attend the Las Vegas campus, 6,067 of them undergraduates. Forty-six percent of the undergraduates are women, 44 percent of whom attend part-time. The median age of all undergraduates is 25.

Ninety-six percent of the undergraduates commute to this suburban campus which is accessible by public transportation. Free, on-campus parking is also provided.

University-run childcare facilities can accommodate 110 children, 40 at a time. Charges are based on a sliding scale, with students receiving the largest discount. Seventy-four percent of students' requests for this service can be met. Additional private childcare facilities are located near the campus.

Policies to Ensure Fairness to Women. A full-time Affirmative Action Officer is responsible for review of policies and practices related to equal-employment-opportunity, educational-sex-equity, and handicapped-access legislation. A written campus policy prohibits sexual harassment of students, faculty, and staff and has been publicly communicated to these groups. A Committee on Minority Affairs addresses the concerns of minority women.

Women in Leadership Positions. *Students.* Women have some opportunity to gain leadership experience. In three recent years, women have served once as president of the student senate and twice as editor-in-chief of the campus newspaper. A woman presides over one of the four campus honorary societies.

Faculty. Twenty-three percent of the 329 full-time faculty are women, a proportion slightly below the average for public, four-year colleges in this guide. There are 5 female faculty for every 100 female students; and 12 male faculty for every 100 male

students. The university reports that the full-time faculty includes 1 Hispanic, 2 Asian American, and 3 black women.

Administrators. With the exception of the director of institutional research, all top-level administrators are male. Three of 37 departments are chaired by women: anthropology, nursing, and radiologic technology. The Dean of the College of Allied Health Professions is a woman. Four of the 9 university regents are women, 1 of them a black woman and 1 an Asian American woman.

Women and the Curriculum. Most women earn bachelor's degrees in business (21 percent), education (21 percent), and health professions (13 percent). Three percent of the women earn degrees in the nontraditional fields of mathematics and physical sciences. All two-year degrees are granted in health technologies; 90 percent are earned by women.

Students may earn a bachelor's degree or an undergraduate minor through the Women's Studies Program. Fourteen undergraduate courses on women are offered through various departments. Recent offerings include Women and Crime, Women in Cross-Cultural Perspectives, Gender and Social Interaction, and Sexual Politics: The Case of Prostitution. An official committee supervises the program and encourages the development of courses on women in traditional departments, collects and develops curricular materials on women, and organizes the Women's Center.

The departments of education and nursing and the division of social work offer some instruction on matters specific to women. Faculty are offered workshops on the needs of reentry women, on sexual harassment, and on women and the medical profession.

Women and Athletics. The university has a good program of intercollegiate sports for women. Twenty-six percent of the intercollegiate athletes are women, who receive 20 percent of athletic scholarship aid. Eight of the 33 paid coaches for intercollegiate sports are women. The college did not provide information on the intramural sports program. The intercollegiate sports offered are basketball, cross-country, softball, swimming, tennis, track and field, and volleyball.

Housing and Student Organizations. Coeducational dormitories with restrictive hours for visitors of the opposite sex are available for the 4 percent of students who reside on campus. The sole residence-hall director is male.

Four percent of full-time undergraduate women belong to social sororities, 30 of them in racially-integrated sororities and 20 in all-minority sororities. Fraternities provide housing for members; sororities do not.

Special Services and Programs for Women. *Health and Counseling.* The student health service employs 1 male physician and 1 female health-care provider. The counseling center is staffed by 3 men and 2 women, 1 a minority woman. Available services specific to women include medical treatment and counseling for gynecological problems and birth control, as well as counseling on abortion and on rape and assault. Counselors are offered training in the avoidance of sex-role stereotyping and racial bias.

Safety and Security. Measures consist of campus police with

arrest authority, night-time escort for women students, high-intensity lighting, information sessions on campus safety and crime prevention, and a rape crisis center. Two rapes and 30 assaults, 10 on women, were reported for 1980–81.

Career. The university maintains updated files of alumnae by career and sponsors programs to establish contacts between alumnae and female students. A career library includes nonsexist/nonracist information on nontraditional fields of study for women.

Other. The Psychological Counseling and Evaluation Center sponsors assertiveness training, a program to build confidence in mathematics, a telephone service of information, referrals, and support, and workshops on step-parenting and couple's communication.

Returning Women Students. The division of adult continuing education offers a number of courses geared to women, among them Self-Defense for Women, Financial Planning and Legal Rights, Body Mechanics for Women, and a coeducational Career Planning Workshop. Half of the women enrolled in adult continuing education courses are minority women.

Institutional Self-Description. ''The University of Nevada, Las Vegas is unique in that, though a relatively young campus, having been granted autonomy in 1968, there exists a core of women scholars on campus (1) who have done extensive work related to women in their respective disciplines, and are most eager to share their experiences and knowledge; (2) who are open to new ideas and programs; (3) who are actively involved in the organization of our first Women's Center.''

University of Nevada, Reno
Reno, NV 89957
Telephone: (702) 784-8000

★ **Women and the Curriculum**

5,446 undergraduates

	Amer. Ind.	Asian Amer.	Blacks	Hispanics	Whites
F	38	38	29	38	2,347
M	24	51	60	46	2,596
%	1.2	1.7	1.7	1.6	93.9

🏠 🏛 🚌 👫 ⚒ 🖼 📖 ⚕ **AAUW**

Founded in 1864, the University of Nevada at Reno is a land-grant institution set in the hills above the city. Undergraduate, graduate, and professional programs enroll some 7,900 students. Extended and continuing education are available. Alternative class schedules, including weekend college, self-paced learning contracts, a summer session, and off-campus locations are offered.

Women are 46 percent of the 5,446 undergraduates; 34 percent of women attend part-time. The median age of undergraduates is 22. For the 86 percent of undergraduates who live off campus or commute, there is limited public transportation. On-campus parking is free.

On-campus childcare facilities accommodate an estimated one-half of students' requests. Fees are on a sliding scale. Private childcare arrangements may be made nearby.

Policies to Ensure Fairness to Women. The Affirmative Action Officer on part-time assignment reviews policy on equal-employment opportunity, sex equity for students, and handicapped accessibility. A published policy prohibits sexual harassment. Complaints are handled through a formal grievance procedure. The Committee on Minority Affairs addresses the concerns of minority women.

Women in Leadership Positions. *Students.* In recent years, women have served as student body president and editor-in-chief of the campus newspaper. Women head six of the seven honorary societies.

Faculty. Women are 20 percent of a full-time faculty of 334. There are 4 female faculty for every 100 female students and 13 male faculty for every 100 male students.

Administrators. The chief student-life officer is a woman. The rest of the higher administrative posts are held by men. Women chair four of 50 departments. The Dean of the School of Nursing and the Dean of the School of Economics are female. The 8 state regents include 1 black, 1 Asian American, and 2 white women.

Women and the Curriculum. A majority of women graduating with bachelor's degrees major in education, the health professions, and business and management. Seven percent major in such nontraditional subjects as agriculture, engineering, mathematics, and the physical sciences. One-third of the science field-service positions go to women.

The Women's Studies Program, under a director who holds a full-time faculty appointment, offers an 18-credit minor. Such courses as Introduction to Women's Studies, Women and Literature, Latin American Women Writers, History of Women, Social Health Roles of Women, and Women and Politics are available through Women's Studies/Interdisciplinary Programs and the departments of English, Spanish, history, sociology and health resources, and political science. The Women's Studies Board promotes the development of women's courses across the curriculum.

Such current issues as sex-fair curricula and coeducational physical education classes, health-care information important to minority women, and services for abused spouses are part of the instruction of future teachers, health-care workers, and social workers.

Minority Women. About 6 percent of undergraduate women are from minority groups, mainly American Indian, Asian American, and Hispanic. Two minority women are residence-hall directors and two are on the professional staff of the counseling service. Counseling staff receive training on the avoidance of racial bias. The Women's Center and Hispanic student groups serve minority women.

Women and Athletics. The intercollegiate program provides some opportunities for organized, competitive, individual and team sports. Forty-four percent of intercollegiate athletes are women; women receive 16 percent of athletic scholarships. Four of six paid varsity coaches are female. Women's teams played in tournaments in 1980. The intercollegiate sports offered are basketball, cross-country, softball, swimming and diving, tennis, and volleyball.

Housing and Student Organizations. Twelve percent of undergraduates live on campus. Single-sex and coeducational dormitories and some housing for married students are available. A married woman student whose spouse is not enrolled may live in married students' housing. Dormitories do not restrict hours for visitors of the opposite sex. All residence-hall directors are female. Staff are offered awareness-training on sex education and birth control.

Seventeen percent of undergraduate women belong to social sororities. Sororities and fraternities provide some housing for their members. Associated Women Students serves as an advocate for women on campus.

Special Services and Programs for Women. *Health and Counseling.* The student health service provides some medical attention specific to women, including gynecological, birth control, and rape and assault treatment. The 2 health service physicians are male. Three of 4 other health-care providers are female. The regular student health insurance covers maternity at no extra charge. Eight of 15 professional staff in the counseling service are female. Staff receive in-service training on avoiding sex-role stereotyping and racial bias. Students have access to gynecological, birth control, and rape and assault counseling.

Safety and Security. Measures consist of campus police with arrest authority and weapons training, and information sessions on safety and crime prevention. Fifty assaults (20 on women) and no rapes were reported for 1980-81.

Career. The university offers workshops, lectures, and printed materials about women in nontraditional occupations and fields of study.

Other. The recently opened Women's Center is supported solely by volunteer efforts. The center co-sponsors with the Women's Studies Program an annual women's week, assertiveness training, and a program to build confidence in mathematics.

Additional services include a telephone line of information, referral, and support, operated under the auspices of the American Association of University Women, and programs for abused women and displaced homemakers at the YWCA. The university cooperates with community groups for services to women and cultural activities.

Institutional Self-Description. "UNR is newly conscious of women's needs, and new residents are bringing a conservative community up to date. There are excellent opportunities for the part-time student with respect to flexible jobs. Women can help shape a growing school to maturity."

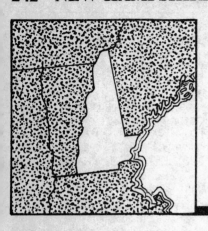

NEW HAMPSHIRE

Castle Junior College
Searles Road, Windham, NH 03087
Telephone: (603) 893-6111

Women in Leadership
★★★ students
★★★ faculty
★★★ administrators

98 undergraduates

	Amer. Ind.	Asian Amer.	Blacks	Hispanics	Whites
F	0	0	0	0	96
M	0	0	0	0	0
%	0.0	0.0	0.0	0.0	100.0

Owned and operated by the Roman Catholic Sisters of Mercy, this private, two-year college has a student body of 103 women, all but five of whom attend full-time. Their median age is 19. The college offers an associate degree in business science and a diploma for completing a one-year course. Once a secretarial school for young women, the college reports that "male members would be admitted if they applied." All students commute to campus, and free parking is available.

Women in Leadership Positions. *Students.* Women hold all leadership positions.

Faculty. The five full-time faculty are women.

Administrators. Women hold the four chief administrative positions.

Women and the Curriculum. All students graduate in business and commerce.

Women and Athletics. No information was provided.

Special Services and Programs for Women. No information was provided.

Institutional Self-Description. None provided.

Dartmouth College
Hanover, New Hampshire 03755
Telephone: (603) 646-2243

★ **Women and the Curriculum**

★★★ **Women and Athletics**

3,435 undergraduates

	Amer. Ind.	Asian Amer.	Blacks	Hispanics	Whites
F	18	13	88	6	830
M	14	24	171	12	2167
%	1.0	1.1	7.7	0.5	89.7

 NWSA

Chartered in 1769 as a private, nonsectarian, liberal arts college for men, Dartmouth now enrolls some 4,000 students. Coeducational since 1972, the college has a 3,435-member undergraduate student body that is 28 percent female. The median age of undergraduates is 20.

Dartmouth offers a wide range of bachelor's programs, as well as graduate programs in arts and sciences, business administration, engineering, and medicine. Classes are scheduled year-round and all undergraduates attend full-time. Between 10 and 15 percent of undergraduates commute to the 175-acre campus which is accessible by public transportation. On-campus parking is available at a fee.

Private childcare facilities are available near the campus.

Policies to Ensure Fairness to Women. A full-time Affirmative Action officer and a part-time assistant are responsible for policies and practices relating to equal-employment opportunity and sex-equity legislation. A written, publicly communicated campus policy prohibits sexual harassment of students, faculty, and staff; complaints are resolved through a formal campus grievance procedure.

Women in Leadership Positions. *Students.* Opportunities for women to exercise campus-wide leadership are limited. In recent years, women have been elected to two campus leadership posts for one year each: editor-in-chief of the campus newspaper and president of the senior class.

Faculty. Twenty percent of the 349 full-time faculty are women. There are 7 female faculty for every 100 female students and 11 male faculty for every 100 male students.

Administrators. Of the ten top-level administrators, the head librarian is female. Women chair 7 of the 17 departments: education, French and Italian, sociology, Spanish and Portuguese, speech, and urban studies. The Dean of Freshmen is a woman. Seven of the 30-member faculty senate are female, as is 1 of the 16 trustees. One of the 6 recent recipients of honorary degrees was also a woman.

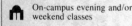
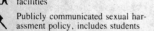

Women and the Curriculum. Most degrees earned by women are in social sciences (35 percent), letters (21 percent), foreign languages (12 percent), and fine arts (7 percent). Nine percent of women earn degrees in the nontraditional fields of agriculture, engineering, mathematics, and physical sciences. One-third of the students participating in internship programs are women.

The Women's Studies Program offers an undergraduate minor and a certificate (comparable to a major). Women's Studies offer 21 courses through departments. Recent offerings include History and Theory of Feminism; Women, Society and Change; Educated Women; and Women in Cross-Cultural Perspective. The University Seminar for Feminist Inquiry—a formal faculty workshop—has served since 1977 as a center for academic scholarship on women.

Minority Women. Thirteen percent of the 972 undergraduate women are minority females, with black women the predominant group. The college reports 1 black, 2 American Indian, 1 Asian American and 2 Hispanic women on the full-time faculty. One of the 8 female department chairs is an Hispanic woman. Topics in Afro-American Women's History and Introduction to Native American Studies are two courses offered. One of 2 two female counselors is a minority woman.

Women and Athletics. Dartmouth offers outstanding opportunities for women to participate in competitive individual and team sports. More than 388 women participate in a wide array of intramural sports, including soccer, and racquetball. There are special facilities for intramural cross-country and alpine skiing, squash, snow sculpture, rock climbing, figure skating, kayacking, and horseback riding. Forty-five percent of the 924 intercollegiate athletes are women, as are 26 of the 57 paid intercollegiate coaches. The intercollegiate sports offered are basketball, crew, cross-country, field hockey, gymnastics, ice hockey, lacrosse, sailing, skiing, soccer, squash, swimming, tennis, and track and field.

Housing and Student Organizations. Single-sex and coeducational dormitories house the approximately 85 percent of undergraduates who reside on campus. None of the residence halls restrict hours for visitors of the opposite sex. Off-campus housing is available for single parents and married students with and without children, and is open to married women whose husbands are not enrolled. There is one female residence-hall director.

Twenty-seven percent of undergraduate women belong to social sororities. A number of fraternities and one of the sororities provide housing for members. There are also a number of cooperative houses on campus.

The Dartmouth Women's Alliance serves as the major advocacy group for women students. Among its activities is an Annual Women's Week, co-sponsored with the Women's Studies program.

Special Services and Programs for Women. *Health and Counseling.* The student health service employs 5 physicians (1 female and 4 male) and 29 other health-care providers, 19 of them women. The student health insurance policy covers some abortion and maternity expenses at no extra charge. The counseling center has a staff of 2 women and 3 men. Health and counseling services specific to women are not provided.

Safety and Security. Measures consist of local police, campus police without arrest authority, night-time escort for women students, high-intensity lighting, emergency telephone system, self-defense courses for women, and information sessions on safety and crime prevention for women. Eleven assaults (two on women) and no rapes were reported for 1980–81.

Career. Placement services include workshops and job discrimination information on nontraditional occupations for women, as well as lectures and panels by women employed in these fields.

Other. The Women's Studies program sponsors such extracurricular activities as a women's lecture series and theater and other women's arts programs.

Institutional Self-Description. "As a small undergraduate college in a rural setting, Dartmouth has preserved a close relationship between faculty and students. Over the years, since the institution of coeducation in 1972, the college has made a commitment to women's education by hiring and tenuring women faculty and supporting a strong Women's Studies Program. Since 1978 women have been admitted on an equal basis with men and the ratio of women to men has been steadily improving."

Rivier College
420 Main St., Nashua, NH 03060
Telephone: (603) 888-1311

Women in Leadership
★★★ **students**
★★★ **faculty**
★★★ **administrators**

893 undergraduates

	Amer. Ind.	Asian Amer.	Blacks	Hispanics	Whites
F	0	1	1	1	752
M	0	8	0	0	133
%	0.0	0.5	0.1	0.1	99.3

Rivier is operated by the Sisters of the Presentation of Mary as a private, Roman Catholic college primarily for women. The campus, located in the city of Nashua, one hour from Boston, attracts 1,711 students, 893 of them undergraduates. Eighty-five percent of the undergraduates are women, and about one-third of the women attend part-time. The median age of all undergraduates is 32, significantly higher than in most colleges.

A variety of two- and four-year degree programs is available, in addition to a master's degree. Continuing education programs, evening and weekend classes, and a summer session are available. Forty-three percent of the undergraduates live on campus; dormitories, available only to women students, prohibit male visitors. For the undergraduates who commute, parking is provided on campus.

Private childcare facilities are available near campus.

Policies to Ensure Fairness to Women. The Personnel Director assumes part-time responsibility for monitoring compliance with laws on educational sex equity, equal employment opportunity, and handicapped access. A sexual harassment policy is being developed.

Women in Leadership Positions. *Students.* Women hold all campus-wide leadership positions.

Faculty. Sixty nine percent of the 36 full-time faculty are women. There are 5 female faculty for every 100 female students.

Administrators. Women hold all top postions. They chair nearly three-fourths of the departments, including chemistry, computer science, mathematics, business, and sociology.

Women and the Curriculum. Most four-year degrees awarded to women are in education (28 percent), home economics (15 percent), and business (12 percent). Most two-year degrees to women are in business programs (44 percent), public service (25 percent), and health technologies (22 percent). Special programs encourage women to prepare for careers in science.

The English and sociology departments offer two courses on women. The business faculty provide instruction about the problems of women in the workplace.

Women and Athletics. Opportunities to participate in organized competitive sports are limited. Thirty-two students play in intercollegiate sports, while 105 students participate in intramural and club sports. There are two paid female varsity sports coaches. Intercollegiate sports offered are basketball and field hockey.

Special Services and Programs for Women. *Health and*

Counseling. The student health service is staffed by one female health-care provider. The student counseling center employs one female counselor. No information was supplied on the availability of medical and counseling services specific to women.

Career. Information about nontraditional careers is available, as is networking with alumnae. A workshop about management development for women is held twice a year. Higher Education Information Day, held yearly, is aimed at women interested in returning to school.

Institutional Self-Description. ''The day division is specifically for undergraduate women. Extracurricular activities are geared for and run by women. Women faculty and administrators are important role models for our students. Also, our counseling program, residential services, and athletic programs are designed for women. Leadership training for women is considered important.''

Safety and Security. Measures consist of campus police protection, night-time escort service and high-intensity lighting. No rapes or assaults on women were reported for 1980-81.

University of New Hampshire
Durham, NH 03824
Telephone: (603) 862-1234

★ **Women and the Curriculum**

★ **Women and Athletics**

9,519 undergraduates

	Amer. Ind.	Asian Amer.	Blacks	Hispanics	Whites
F	7	11	5	12	4,846
M	14	16	20	16	4,495
%	0.2	0.3	0.3	0.3	98.9

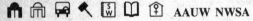 **AAUW NWSA**

Established in 1866, the University of New Hampshire, a land-grant institution located in the small town of Durham, attracts some 12,000 students to a variety of undergraduate, graduate, and professional programs. The division of continuing education serves the adult student. Alternative class schedules, including a weekend college, off-campus locations, evening classes, and a summer session, are available.

Women are 51 percent of 9,519 undergraduates; 7 percent of the women attend part-time. Nine percent of women students are over age 25. For the 49 percent of undergraduates who commute, the university is accessible by public transportation. Parking is available on campus for a fee.

Private childcare arrangements may be made near the university.

Policies to Ensure Fairness to Women. The Director of Affirmative Action is responsible full-time for policy and reviews practices related to equal employment opportunity and sex equity for students. The Coordinator of Handicapped Student Services monitors compliance with handicapped-access legislation. A published policy prohibits sexual harassment of students, faculty, and staff. Complaints are handled either informally and confidentially or through a formal grievance procedure. The active Committee on the Status of Women, which includes students as voting members, reports to the President and takes public stands on issues of concern to students.

Women in Leadership Positions. *Students.* Opportunities for women students to exercise campus-wide leadership are limited. In recent years, women have been president of the student body, presiding officer of the residence-hall council (twice), and editor-in-chief of the student newspaper. Women head the five honorary societies.

Faculty. Women make up 20 percent of a full-time faculty of 514. There are 2 female faculty for every 100 female students and 9 male faculty for every 100 male students.

Administrators. Of eight top-level administrators, the President of the university is female. The Director of Women's Athletics is a woman. Women chair seven of 43 departments: English, French, humanities, nursing, social services, medical technology, and occupational therapy. Eight of 26 trustees are women and, in one recent year, four of eight alumni awards were presented to women.

Women and the Curriculum. A majority of women graduating with bachelor's degrees major in the health professions, public affairs, and business and management. The proportion of women in public affairs is above the national average. Thirteen percent of women graduates major in such nontraditional fields as mathematics, agriculture, architecture, computer science, engineering, and the physical sciences. The percentage of women in agriculture is above the national average. An innovative program encourages women to prepare for careers in engineering. The mathematics department offers a program to build mathematics confidence.

The Women's Studies Program, under a director who holds a full-time faculty appointment, offers a 21-credit undergraduate minor and the B.A. Fifteen undergraduate and graduate courses are available through Women's Studies and seven departments. Recent titles include Introduction to Women's Studies, Colloquium, Women's Literary Traditions, Sex Role Learning and School Achievement, Images of Women in Media, Psychology of Sex Roles, Women and Aging, and Women in Management. The departments of education offer instruction on some matters specific to women. The school of business includes the problem of workplace discrimination in its curriculum.

Women and Athletics. Intramural and intercollegiate programs offer good opportunities for organized, competitive individual and team sports. Club sports are available, and over half the participants are women. The co-recreational intramural program has over 800 women participants. Forty-two percent of intercollegiate athletes are women; women receive 20 percent of athletic scholarships. Thirteen of 32 paid varsity coaches are female. Most women's intercollegiate teams played in tournaments in 1980. The intercollegiate sports offered are basketball, cross-country, field hockey, gymnastics, ice hockey, lacrosse, softball, skiing, swimming, tennis, track, and volleyball.

Housing and Student Organizations. Fifty-one percent of undergraduates live on campus. Residential accommodations include single-sex and coeducational dormitories and housing for married students and single parents with children. A married woman student whose spouse is not enrolled may live in married students' housing. Eleven of 23 residence-hall directors are female. Awareness-training on sexism, sex education, racism, and birth control is offered to the staff.

Seven percent of the undergraduate women belong to social sororities. Sororities and fraternities provide housing for their members. NARAL serves as an advocacy group for women on campus.

Special Services and Programs for Women. *Health and Counseling.* The student health service provides some medical attention specific to women, including gynecological, birth control, and rape and assault treatment. The regular student health insurance policy covers maternity and abortion expenses at no extra charge. One of 6 physicians is female, as are 36 other health-care providers. Five of 8 professional staff in the counseling service are women. Students have access to gynecological, abortion, birth control, and rape and assault counseling.

Safety and Security. Measures include campus police with arrest authority, night-time escort service for women students, a campus-wide night-time bus service, high-intensity lighting, an emergency alarm system, information sessions on safety and crime-prevention, and a rape crisis center. One rape and 35 assaults (11 against women) were reported for 1980–81.

Career. Activities, information, and support for women interested in nontraditional careers and fields of study are available.

Other. The small Women's Center is staffed by a student volunteer. The division of continuing education and the department of sociology sponsor a program for battered women. A women's lecture series and assertiveness training are also available. The counseling service provides a telephone line of information, referral, and support.

Institutional Self-Description. "The most outstanding feature for women is the separate athletic department, with an undefeated women's ice hockey team. There is also an emerging women's community that is receiving university administrative support."

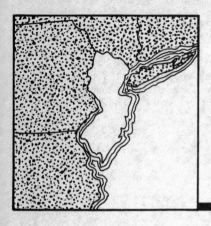

NEW JERSEY

Bloomfield College
Bloomfield, NJ 07003
Telephone: (201) 748-9000

Women in Leadership
★ faculty

1,992 undergraduates

	Amer. Ind.	Asian Amer.	Blacks	Hispanics	Whites
F	0	7	344	10	618
M	0	3	364	9	637
%	0.0	0.5	35.5	1.0	63.0

Established in 1868 as a theological seminary, Bloomfield College is now a coeducational liberal arts institution affiliated with the Presbyterian Church. Located in a racially mixed suburban community, near New York City, the campus attracts 2,420 students, including 1,992 degree students. Forty-nine percent of the students are women; 40 percent of women attend part-time. The median age of all undergraduates is 24. A range of undergraduate degree programs is available, as well as a continuing education program. Alternative schedules include evening and weekend classes, a summer session, and self-paced/contract learning. Eighty-six percent of the students commute to the campus, which is accessible by public transportation. On-campus parking is provided at a fee.

A campus childcare facility serves students' children free of charge and can accommodate 20 children. Private childcare facilities are available off campus.

Policies to Ensure Fairness to Women. An Affirmative Action Officer has the part-time responsibility for handling matters pertaining to the legal requirements for sex-fair employment and sex equity for students. Complaints of sexual harassment are resolved by informal and formal means.

Women in Leadership Positions. *Students.* Insufficient information was provided. One woman held the post of student body president in recent years. A woman heads one of the two honorary societies.

Faculty. Twenty-eight percent of the 51 full-time faculty are women. There are 2 female faculty for every 100 female students, and 5 male faculty for every 100 male students.

Administrators. Of the nine key administrative posts, the chief development officer is a woman. The nursing department is chaired by a woman, the remaining four departments by men.

Women and the Curriculum. Most women major in business and health professions. Women earned more than half the degrees in biology. Bloomfield offers Programs to prepare women for nontraditional careers in accounting, computer science, and law enforcement/corrections.

The humanities department teach courses that focus on women—Women in the West, and Philosophical Perspectives on Women. The departments of social work and nursing provide some instruction on matters specific to women.

Women and Athletics. The women's athletic program consists of intercollegiate basketball.

Housing and Student Organizations. Fourteen percent of the undergraduates live on campus in single-sex dormitories. Ten percent of full-time undergraduate women belong to sororities, which provide housing for members. Fifty minority women belong to racially integrated sororities.

Special Services and Programs for Women. *Health and Counseling.* The student health service employs one female healthcare provider. The student counseling center is staffed by 2 counselors, 1 female and 1 male. No information was provided regarding medical services or counseling specific to women.

Safety and Security. Measures consist of campus police protection. There were no rapes or assaults on women reported for 1980–81.

Career. The college provides career workshops and panel discussions on nontraditional occupations.

Other. A small Women's Center, directed by a full-time, salaried administrator, serves 1,000 undergraduates annually.

Institutional Self-Description. None provided.

Brookdale Community College
Newman Springs Road
Lincroft, NJ 07738
Telephone: (201) 842-1900

Women in Leadership
★★ students
★★ faculty

7,938 undergraduates

	Amer. Ind.	Asian Amer.	Blacks	Hispanics	Whites
F	9	44	302	65	3,774
M	1	33	287	59	3,364
%	0.1	1.0	7.4	1.6	89.9

This public, two-year commuter college enrolls 9,330 students, 7,938 in degree programs. Women are 53 percent of the degree students, and 68 percent of women attend part-time. The median age of all students is 25.

Brookdale offers a wide range of programs in the liberal arts, business, communications/media, health, public service, agriculture, and engineering/technology. Alternative full-time and part-time schedules include evening classes, summer and weekend sessions, and contract learning. Public transportation as well as on-campus parking at a fee are available.

Free childcare facilities, accommodating 50 children of students and members of the community, are available on campus daily from 7:30 a.m. to 5:30 p.m. Private facilities are available nearby.

Policies to Ensure Fairness to Women. The Affirmative Action Officer is responsible part-time for reviewing policies and practices relating to equal-opportunity laws. A Commission on the Status of Women prepares an annual report which is distributed to the campus community.

Women in Leadership Positions. *Students.* During three recent years women have often held the four leadership positions available on campus. They have been editor-in-chief of the campus newspaper for three years, president of the student body for one year, and engineer of the campus radio station for two years.

Faculty. Women are 35 percent of the 147 full-time faculty, a proportion slightly above the average for public two-year colleges in this guide. There are 4 female faculty for every 100 female students and 6 male faculty for every 100 male students.

Administrators. Of nine chief administrators, the head librarian is a woman. Women chair a number of departments, including writing, modern languages, nursing and allied health, sociology, and paralegal studies. The Dean of Applied Humanities is a woman. Half of the faculty senate is composed of women, including 2 black women. Five of the 12 trustees are women.

Women and the Curriculum. Most women take their degrees in arts and sciences (43 percent), health technologies (22 percent), and business programs (22 percent). The college is developing a Women's Studies Program and collecting curricular materials on women. Workshops on nontraditional occupations for women and men, the needs of reentry women, and affirmative action and equal opportunity are offered to faculty. The School of Nursing provides training on health-care information important to minority women.

Women and Athletics. One-fourth of the intercollegiate athletes are women. In the intramural program, women participate in softball, swimming, tennis, and volleyball. Three of the nine paid coaches for intercollegiate athletics are women. Intercollegiate sports for women include cross-country, softball, and tennis.

Special Services and Programs for Women. *Health and Counseling.* The student health service is staffed by 1 male physician. The counseling center has a staff of 18, of whom 3 are white women and 4 are minority women. There are no health or counseling services specific to women.

Safety and Security. Measures include campus police, high-intensity lighting, an emergency alarm system at isolated locations, and special training for students in self-defense. Two assaults on campus, one against a woman, were reported for 1980-81.

Career. The college provides a variety of support services for reentry women and workshops for women interested in entering nontraditional fields of employment.

Other. A Women's Center, administered by a full-time staff member, sponsors assertiveness/leadership training and other programs and services. The most frequent users of the center are community women; about 5 percent of the students who use the center each year are black women. The Brookdale Community College Women's Club, the Student Nurses Organization, and the Office Systems Club serve as advocates for women.

Institutional Self-Description. "Brookdale's commitment to life-long learning, open admission, mastery learning, and individualized instruction, as well as the open-space environment and effective use of student development specialists (counselors) make it attractive to women of all ages."

Cook College: see Rutgers, The State University of New Jersey, New Brunswick.

Cumberland County College
P.O. Box 517, Vineland, NJ 08360
Telephone: (609) 691-8600

Women in Leadership
* ★ faculty
* ★ administrators

1,956 undergraduates

	Amer. Ind.	Asian Amer.	Blacks	Hispanics	Whites
F	13	9	186	83	888
M	7	8	89	62	611
%	1.0	0.9	14.1	7.4	76.6

Established in 1966, this public two-year college provides comprehensive educational services to 1,956 undergraduates, 60 percent of whom are women. Fifty-four percent of the women attend part-time. The median age of all students is 27.

Cumberland offers liberal arts, pre-professional transfer, and a variety of career programs. There is also an adult continuing education program. The college holds evening classes both on and off campus and a summer session. All students commute to the rural campus located near Philadelphia. The college is not accessible by public transportation, but on-campus parking is provided.

Private childcare facilities are located near the campus.

Policies to Ensure Fairness to Women. The Affirmative Action Officer serves part-time as a voting member of policymaking committees, and is responsible for equal employment opportunity, sex equity for students, and handicapped accessibility. A written campus policy prohibits sexual harassment of students, faculty, and staff, and has been publicly communicated in writing to those groups. Complaints of sexual harassment are resolved through a formal campus grievance procedure.

Women in Leadership Positions. *Students.* No information was provided.

Faculty. Women account for 27 percent of the full-time faculty of 51, a proportion which is above average for all institutions nationwide. There is 1 black woman on the full-time faculty. There are 3 female faculty for every 100 female students and 9 male faculty for every 100 male students.

Administrators. Two of the 8 chief administrators are women: the chief student-life officer and the director of institutional research. One of four divisions—nursing/allied health—is headed by a woman. The Dean of Student Development is a woman. Twenty-seven percent of the faculty senate are women, including 1 black woman. Three of 11 trustees are women, 1 of them a black woman.

Women and the Curriculum. Most two-year degrees awarded to women are in the arts and sciences (35 percent), public service (24 percent), business (20 percent), and health technologies (17 percent). Four percent of women earn degrees in natural sciences. Three-fourths of students in cooperative education programs are women. The mathematics department offers mathematics anxiety workshops. Courses in the departments of business, nursing, physical education, and social work provide instruction on some matters specific to women. Faculty workshops are offered on the topics of sexism and the curriculum, racism and the curriculum, nontraditional occupations for women and men, the needs of reentry women, and affirmative action and equal opportunity. No courses on women are offered.

Women and Athletics. Women have some opportunities to participate in a range of club, intramural, and intercollegiate sports. Women are 54 percent of the participants in intercollegiate sports; one of the nine paid intercollegiate coaches is a woman. Intramural sports include individual sports such as archery, tennis, and fencing, and team sports such as softball, basketball, and volleyball. The intercollegiate program offers post-season tournament competition. Intercollegiate sports offered are archery, basketball, fencing, softball, tennis, and volleyball.

Special Services and Programs for Women. *Health and Counseling.* There is no student health service. The student counseling center has a staff of four, including one white woman and one minority woman. Women are referred to local health agencies for treatment and counseling on health problems specific to women.

Safety and Security. Measures consist of campus police, local police, and high-intensity lighting in all areas. No assaults or rapes were reported for 1980–81.

Career. Career services on campus include workshops, lectures, and job discrimination information on nontraditional occupations, and printed information on nontraditional fields of study for women.

Other. Cumberland County College was awarded external funding for a program to assist reentry women. The Transitions Program sponsors a women's lecture series and a telephone service for information, referrals, and support. The continuing education division sponsors assertiveness/leadership training.

Institutional Self-Description. None provided.

Douglass College: see Rutgers, The State University of New Jersey, New Brunswick.

Georgian Court College
Lakewood, NJ 08701
Telephone: (201) 364-2200

Women in Leadership	★ Women and the
★★★ students	Curriculum
★★★ faculty	
★★★ administrators	

562 undergraduates

	Amer. Ind.	Asian Amer.	Blacks	Hispanics	Whites
F	4	7	37	17	489
M	0	0	0	0	0
%	0.7	1.3	6.7	3.1	88.3

 AAUW

Founded in 1908, Georgian Court is a Roman Catholic college for women, notwithstanding the admission of men in recent years to the graduate and evening programs. Situated in a racially mixed community near Trenton, the college attracts 1,072 students, and of those 562 are full-time undergraduate women. According to a recent report, 28 percent of undergraduate women attend part-time and 80 percent of these are older than 25. The median age of all undergraduates is 23.

The bachelor's degree is awarded in liberal arts and sciences, in addition to a master's degree program in education. Continuing education courses meet evenings. One-fourth of the undergraduate women live in dormitories on campus that have restrictive hours for male visitors. The college can be reached by public transportation. On-campus parking is available at a fee for the three-fourths of undergradutes who commute.

Private childcare facilities are available near campus.

Women in Leadership Positions. *Students.* Women hold all nine campus-wide student leadership positions and preside over the eight honorary societies.

Faculty. Sixty-three percent of the 35 full-time faculty are women, a proportion above average for similar colleges in this guide. Fourteen percent of the women have permanent appointments, compared with 46 percent of the men. Among the faculty are two Asian American women and one black woman. There are 4 female faculty for every 100 female students.

Administrators. All the key administrators are women, except for the chief development officer. Women head ten of the 13 departments, including chemistry, mathematics, and physics. Women constitute the overwhelming majority of deans, trustees, and members of the faculty senate. A woman was the main speaker at the 1981 commencement.

Women and the Curriculum. Half of the bachelor's degrees awarded to women are in education; about 5 percent are in mathematics and physical sciences. The college offers several experiential learning programs, including cooperative education, internships, science field service, and outdoor education.

The Women's Studies Program offers a 12-credit minor. Courses are offered through the departments of English, history, philosophy, psychology, religious studies, sociology, and languages. They include Women in America, Philosophy of Feminism, and Religion: Impact on Women. The departments of education, physical education, business, and social work offer instruction on some aspects of women's issues in their classes.

Women and Athletics. The college provides limited opportunities for students to participate in organized team sports. All paid and volunteer coaches are women. Only volleyball is available on an intramural basis; intercollegiate sports include basketball, softball, and volleyball.

Special Services and Programs for Women. *Health and Counseling.* The student health service employs 2 female healthcare providers. Students who seek treatment for medical problems specific to women are referred to private physicians. The student counseling center, staffed by 1 male and 5 female counselors, 1 of whom is a black woman, provides support for victims of rape and assault.

Safety and Security. Measures consist of campus and local police protection, high-intensity lighting, and information sessions on campus safety. No rapes or assaults on women were reported for 1980–81.

Career. Lectures and information on nontraditional occupations are available, as well as networking with alumnae.

Other. The Dean of Students office plans theater and other women's art programs. The counseling center runs leadership training workshops for students.

Institutional Self-Description. "Founded as a women's college over 70 years ago, Georgian Court College provides women with successful role models among its faculty, administrators, and alumnae. Women assume leadership positions in student government, co-and extra-curricular clubs, and athletics. They experience encouragement through the college's academic, personal, and career counseling centers."

Middlesex Community College
Edison, NJ 08818
Telephone: (201) 548-6000

Women in Leadership	★ Women and the
★ students	Curriculum
★★ faculty	
★ administrators	

5,993 undergraduates

	Amer. Ind.	Asian Amer.	Blacks	Hispanics	Whites
F	2	33	186	117	2,962
M	6	32	112	81	2,429
%	0.1	1.1	5.0	3.3	90.5

This public, two-year commuter college was founded in 1964. A total of 10,894 students attend the 260-acre suburban campus located near New Brunswick. Women are 55 percent of the 5,993

undergraduates; 38 percent of women attend part-time. The median age of full-time students is 19, and of part-time students, 27.

The college offers a wide range of programs in arts and sciences, and vocational fields. Alternative scheduling includes off-campus day and evening classes, a spring mini-session, summer sessions, a weekend college, contract learning, and telecourses. Public transportation and on-campus parking at a fee are available.

Childcare facilities for 60 children are available on campus daily from 7:30 a.m. to 5 p.m. An estimated one-third of requests by students are accommodated. Private childcare is available near the campus.

Policies to Ensure Fairness to Women. An Affirmative Action and Compliance Officer is responsible part-time for monitoring compliance with legislation concerning sex equity for students, handicapped access, and equal employment opportunity. A formal campus grievance procedure resolves complaints. Faculty are offered workshops about sexual harassment. A Commission on Minority Affairs addresses the concerns of minority women.

Women in Leadership Positions. Women students have occupied each of the two leadership positions once in three recent years, including editor-in-chief of the campus newspaper and president of the student union board.

Faculty. Women make up 43 percent of the 240 full-time faculty, a proportion above average for public, two-year colleges and considerably above the national average. There are 5 female faculty for every 100 women students and 8 male faculty for every 100 male students.

Administrators. Women hold 2 of 8 major administrative positions, including chief executive officer and chief student-life officer. Eleven of 32 departments are chaired by women, including radiologic technology, chemistry, medical laboratory technology, nurse education, biology, modern languages, and social sciences. Of 8 deans, 3 are women, including those responsible for health technologies, student services, and community education. Women are 42 percent of the faculty senate and 40 percent of the trustees.

Women and the Curriculum. Most two-year degrees and certificates awarded to women are in business (41 percent), health technologies (25 percent), arts and sciences (17 percent), and public service technologies (10 percent). Seven percent of associate degrees are in science and engineering technologies, a high proportion for two-year colleges. Seventy percent of students participating in cooperative education programs are women.

The Women's Studies Program offers an undergraduate minor. Courses include The History of Women, Women in Literature, and Psychology of Women.

Minority Women. A black woman and an Hispanic woman chair departments; one of three female deans is a minority woman; an Hispanic woman sits on the Board of Trustees. The 1981 commencement speaker was an Hispanic woman. A minority woman works at the student counseling center.

Women and Athletics. For a college of its size, Middlesex has a good organized athletics program. Thirty-eight percent of the intercollegiate and 20 percent of intramural athletes are women; four of the 13 paid intercollegiate coaches are women. Athletic scholarships are available. Intercollegiate sports offered are basketball, cross-country, snow skiing, softball, tennis, track and field, and volleyball.

Special Services and Programs for Women. *Health and Counseling.* The student health service is staffed by 1 female health-care provider. No information was provided on medical treatment specific to women. Nine professionals, including 5 women, staff the student counseling center. They provide counseling on gynecological problems, birth control, abortion, and rape and assault. A counselor for the handicapped serves 50 students, 28 of whom are women. Counselors receive training on disability awareness.

Safety and Security. Measures consist of campus police protection and an emergency telephone system. No rapes or assaults on women were reported for 1980–81.

Career. Services include lectures by women in nontraditional occupations, the availability of printed materials on employment and discrimination, and maintaining updated files on the careers of alumnae.

Other. A Women's Center, administered under the auspices of the community education division by a salaried, full-time staff person, annually serves approximately 2,000 women, 10 percent of whom are black women. The division of continuing education enrolls approximately 3,000 reentry women students each year.

An organization of women students and faculty sponsors an annual women's week on campus. The Middlesex Community College Women's Organization is an advocacy group.

Institutional Self-Description. "The college's comprehensive offerings in both transfer and career programs, available full- and part-time, provide access for women in the community and the county to higher education. In addition, support services such as counseling, financial aid, and tutoring are available to assist both traditional and nontraditional (older) students."

New Jersey Institute of Technology
323 High Street, Newark, NJ 07102
Telephone: (201) 645-5321

Women in Leadership
★★★ **students**

3,968 undergraduates

	Amer. Ind.	Asian Amer.	Blacks	Hispanics	Whites
F	0	9	61	19	208
M	0	95	155	163	3,150
%	0.0	2.7	5.6	4.7	87.0

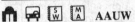 AAUW

Formerly Newark College of Engineering, New Jersey Institute of Technology is a city- and state-supported institution in downtown Newark, a short distance from Manhattan. Its campus, set in an ethnically diverse community, draws 5,669 students including 3,968 undergraduates. Women are 8 percent of the undergraduates and 27 percent of women attend part-time. The median age of undergraduates is 21.

The institute offers associate, bachelor's, master's, and doctor's degrees in the sciences and in technical fields. Continuing education programs for professionals are also provided. Classes meet day and evening, and there is a summer session. For the 90 percent of undergraduates who commute, public transportation is available, in addition to on-campus parking at a fee.

Limited private childcare facilities are located near campus.

Policies to Ensure Fairness to Women. The Director of Affirmative Action has full-time responsibility for making policy regarding equal employment opportunity and handicapped access. The Dean of Student Affairs makes policy regarding sex equity for students. A published policy on sexual harassment protects students, faculty, and staff; complaints are resolved through a formal grievance procedure. A Committee on Minority Affairs, which reports directly to the President, addresses the concerns of minority women.

Women in Leadership Positions. *Students.* In spite of their very small presence on campus, women have held the positions of student body president and student union board president once each in a recent three-year period.

Faculty. Six percent of the 247 full-time faculty are women. There are 7 female faculty for every 100 female students, and 9 male faculty for every 100 male students.

Administrators. Two of the top administrators are women: the Dean of Student Affairs and the chief development officer.

Women and the Curriculum. Women are 6 percent of those earning bachelor's degrees. Sixty-nine percent of women major in such nontraditional fields as architecture, computer science, and engineering. All other bachelor's degrees earned by women are in business and management. Nine percent of the participants in cooperative education programs are women. Women constitute 5 percent of the students in the Air Force ROTC Program, which grants financial assistance and future employment to participants.

Women and Athletics. The limited organized athletic program for women offers four coeducational intramural sports and four intercollegiate sports. One-fifth of the intramural athletes are women, a high proportion considering that only 8 percent of students are female. Two percent of the intercollegiate athletes are women; the 15 paid varsity coaches are men. Intercollegiate sports in which women participate are fencing, riflery, swimming, and tennis.

Housing and Student Organizations. Ten percent of the undergraduates live in coeducational dormitories that do not restrict visiting hours for members of the opposite sex. A male residence-hall director is assisted by two female student assistants. Staff are offered awareness-training on women's health issues, sex education, and on the avoidance of sexism and racism.

Women's Outreach, an advocacy group, has 50 active members, including black women.

Special Services and Programs for Women. *Health and Counseling.* The student health service has 1 male physician and 1 female health-care provider. Three of the 6 professionals at the student counseling center are women. Counseling is available on gynecological problems, birth control, abortion, and rape and assault. No medical treatment specific to women is available.

Safety and Security. Measures include campus police with arrest authority, night-time escorts, and bus service to residence areas. High-intensity lighting is under construction. No rapes and 25 assaults (three on women) were reported for 1980–81.

Career. Services include career workshops and information on nontraditional occupations for women. A pre-college summer program called FEMME introduces female ninth-graders to science- and technology-related careers. Other similar programs are co-educational and focus on careers in urban engineering, computer programming, and science. About half of the 800 participants in these programs are women in junior high school.

Institutional Self-Description. "The university specializes in fields in which career opportunities abound. These are fields in which women are grossly under-represented and in which corporate demand is extraordinary today and will likely expand even further in the decades ahead. The attractive campus of NJIT offers convenient transportation and residential opportunities."

Princeton University

Princeton, NJ 08544
Telephone: (609) 452-3000

★★ **Women and the Curriculum**

4,422 undergraduates

	Amer. Ind.	Asian Amer.	Blacks	Hispanics	Whites
F	4	53	165	59	1,181
M	10	82	157	117	2,384
%	0.3	3.2	7.6	4.2	84.6

♠ ⬛ 📖 ⌂ **AAUW NWSA**

Founded in 1746 as the College of New Jersey, for men, and coeducational since 1969, Princeton University is a privately endowed and predominantly residential institution that attracts some

6,000 students to its undergraduate and graduate programs. Women make up 35 percent of the 4,422 undergraduates. All students attend full-time; their median age is 20. The Center in Continuing Education provides opportunity for local residents to enroll in college courses.

Policies to Ensure Fairness to Women. The Provost and Associate Provost are responsible full-time for reviewing practices and compliance concerning equal employment opportunity, as well as matters of sex equity for students and handicapped accessibility. A published campus policy prohibits sexual harassment. Complaints are handled through a formal grievance procedure. There is a Committee on Minority Affairs which addresses the concerns of minority women.

Women in Leadership Positions. *Students.* Opportunities for women students to assume campus-wide leadership are below the average for private research institutions in this guide. In recent years women have presided over the Honors Committee, been editor-in-chief of the newspaper, and been president of the senior and junior classes.

Faculty. Women are 12 percent of a full-time faculty of 628. There are 5 female faculty for every 100 female students and 19 male faculty for every 100 male students.

Administrators. Information provided on the number of women in administrative positions was not complete.

Women and the Curriculum. A majority of the women graduating with bachelor's degrees major in general letters and social sciences. Fifteen percent major in such nontraditional areas as architecture, engineering, mathematics, and the physical sciences.

The Women's Studies Program, under a director who holds a full-time faculty appointment, offers an undergraduate certificate. In addition to Introduction Women's Studies, courses on women are available through the departments of Latin American studies, sociology, anthropology, psychology, humanistic studies, Afro-American studies, history, politics, American studies, English, and religion. Recent offerings include Anthropology of Gender; Sociology of the Family; Women Writers; Sex Roles and Behavior; Victorian Children's Literature; Gender, Family and Society in American History; and American Women Religious Leaders. The Women's Studies Program committee advocates and monitors the inclusion of scholarship on women throughout the curriculum.

Minority Women. Of the 1,530 full-time undergraduate women, 11 percent are black, 1 percent American Indian, 4 percent Asian American, and 4 percent Hispanic. Courses on minority women include the Black Woman in Society, and Afro-American Women Writers. The Third World Women's Alliance and Latina Women's Group meet on campus.

Women and Athletics. A good number and variety of individual and team sports are available in the intercollegiate program. Some club and intramural sports are also offered. Twenty-eight percent of the intercollegiate athletes are female. All women's varsity teams played in tournaments in 1980. The intercollegiate sports offered are basketball, crew, cross-country, field hockey, track and field, ice hockey, lacrosse, soccer, softball (as of 1981–82), squash, swimming, tennis, and volleyball.

Housing and Student Organizations. Ninety-eight percent of the undergraduates live on campus. Single-sex and coeducational dormitories and housing for married students without children are available. A married woman student whose spouse is not enrolled may live in married students' housing. Dormitories do not restrict hours for visitors of the opposite sex. Among organizations that serve as advocates for women on campus, in addition to those organized by minority women, are the Women's Center, and the Society of Women Engineers, and Gay Alliance.

Special Services and Programs for Women. *Health and Counseling.* The student health service provides medical attention specific to women, including gynecological, birth control, abortion, and rape and assault treatment. One of five physicians is female, as is one health educator. The regular student health insurance policy covers abortion and maternity at no extra cost. One-third of the professional staff in the counseling service are women. Students have access to counseling of particular concern to women.

Safety and Security. Measures consist of campus and local police, night-time escorts for women students, high-intensity lighting, emergency telephones, self-defense courses for women, and information sessions on safety and crime prevention. Fourteen assaults (six on women) and no rapes were reported for 1980–81.

Career. Services of interest to women include workshops and nonsexist/nonracist printed materials concentrated on women in nontraditional occupations and fields of study, alumnae files updated by career, and a special resource section in the Career Services library.

Other. A small Women's Center is staffed by a part-time director and workstudy students.

Special Features. The Miriam Young Holden Collection of 19th-and 20th-century books, most of them focused on American women, ranks as one of the best of its kind in the country.

Institutional Self-Description. "Princeton provides the opportunity to receive a liberal arts education in a coeducational setting in which a wide range of curricular and extra-curricular offerings are available in full measure to men and to women."

Rutgers University, The State University of New Jersey, New Brunswick
New Brunswick, NJ 08903
Telephone: (301) 932-1766

| Women in Leadership | ★★★ Women and the |
| ★ faculty | Curriculum |

20,718 undergraduates

	Amer. Ind.	Asian Amer.	Blacks	Hispanics	Whites
F	14	195	1,090	315	8,632
M	9	169	784	302	9.084
%	0.1	2.0	11.0	3.0	84.0

🏠 🏛 🚐 👫 🔨 📖 ⚕ **AAUW CROW**

Founded in 1766 as Queens College for men, Rutgers became the land-grant institution of New Jersey in 1864, and in 1924 became Rutgers University. In 1945, it became the State University of New Jersey, with the main campus at New Brunswick. Today, the main campus houses four coordinate undergraduate colleges, Rutgers, Cook, Livingston—all coeducational—and the women's college, Douglass. At the New Brunswick campus, over 34,200 students enroll in undergraduate, graduate, and professional programs. University College, the evening division, serves the part-time student. There is a division of continuing education. Alternative class schedules include evening classes, weekend college, and a summer session; off-campus class locations are available.

Women are half of the 20,718 undergraduates; 3 percent of the women attend part-time. The median age of undergraduates is 20. For the commuting student, the New Brunswick campus is accessible by public transportation. There is on-campus parking, with free transportation from distant parking lots.

Three university-sponsored childcare facilities are in operation; fees and capacity vary. Private childcare arrangements can be made near campus.

Policies to Ensure Fairness to Women. The Director of Affirmative Action and Employment Research recommends policy and monitors compliance with equal-employment and handicapped-access legislation. The Director of Student Rights Compliance has policy responsibility for equal access of programs and facilities to all students, including the handicapped. A campus policy prohibits sexual harassment. Complaints are handled

through a written grievance procedure which includes both informal and formal stages.

Women in Leadership Positions. *Students.* Information on opportunities for women students to exercise campus-wide leadership was not provided by the institution.

Faculty. Women are 26 percent of 1,460 full-time faculty, if one considers the Rutgers campus as a whole. Most women faculty hold appointments at Douglass College. Taking the university as a whole, there are 4 female faculty for every 100 female students and 11 male faculty for every 100 male students.

Administrators. All top administrative posts are held by men. The deans of Douglass College, the College of Nursing, the Graduate School of Education, and University College/New Brunswick are female. Women chair 2 departments at Livingston (psychology; Women's Studies); 3 at Rutgers (English; Spanish and Portuguese; sociology and anthropology); 3 at Cook College (home economics; health and physical education; human ecology and social science); and 11 at Douglass (including mathematics; political science; psychology; and Women's Studies).

Women and the Curriculum. A majority of the women who graduate with bachelor's degrees major in social sciences (18 percent), biological sciences (9 percent), general letters (9 percent), psychology (8 percent), and business and management (7 percent). Fifteen percent major in such nontraditional areas as agriculture, architecture, computer science, engineering, mathematics, and the physical sciences. Innovative programs encourage women to prepare for careers in science, engineering, and politics and public leadership. Douglass College sponsors programs to build mathematics confidence. A variety of experiential learning opportunities is available, including field service in pharmacy, science management, speech pathology, and medical technology.

Douglass, Rutgers, and Livingston College each offers a Women's Studies Program, and there is a fourth program at University College, the evening division for the university. In each case, students may earn a certificate (or minor) through taking six courses; students on each campus may also organize an individualized major in Women's Studies. Each college offers from eleven to 34 Women's Studies courses; students may choose from these or may, with permission, substitute courses from other colleges. At Rutgers University as a whole, there are more than 70 Women's Studies courses from which to choose. They include: from Douglass—Women in Antiquity, Women and the Economy, Education and the American Woman, Women in Politics, Woman as Religious Symbol. From Livingston—Women in Anthropological Perspective, Aspects of Human Sexuality, Sexism in Institutions I and II, Radical and Conservative Feminism since 1872. From Rutgers—Family in History, Psychobiology of Sex Differences in Behavior, Women in the Non-Western World. From University College—Psychology of Women, Witchcraft and Magic, Working Women in American Society. In the last five years, 15 to 20 students have majored in Women's Studies, and 200 have minored.

Such current topics as mathematics confidence among females, sex-fair curricula, innovative health-care delivery, health-care information important to minority women, services for abused spouses, and discrimination in the workplace are part of the preparation of future teachers, health-care workers, social workers, and business students.

There are two centers for research on women on the campus in New Brunswick. The Women's Studies Institute runs lecture series, encourages faculty research on women, and supports Women's Studies Programs at the various colleges. The Center for the American Woman and Politics at the Eagleton Institute of Politics focuses its research on women's political participation, especially in electoral politics.

Minority Women. Approximately 16 percent of the undergraduate women are from minority groups, black women being the largest group. Such courses as Black Women Writers (Douglass College), Perspectives on Women in Hispanic Literature

(Livingston College), and the Black Woman (Rutgers College) are offered. Seven residence-hall staff are minority women. Staff in residence halls and the counseling service are offered awareness-training in avoiding racial bias. Ninety-seven women are in all-minority, 74 in integrated, sororities. Among groups that support and advocate the interests of minority women are the Women's Centers of the colleges, Douglass Black Student Congress, Douglass Puerto Rican Students, and the Douglass College Equal Opportunity Board.

Women and Athletics. The intercollegiate program offers a high number and variety of individual and team sports. Information on intramural and club sports is not available. Thirty-two percent of the intercollegiate athletes are women; women receive one-fifth of the athletic scholarships. Twenty-four of 75 paid varsity coaches are female. The intercollegiate sports offered are basketball, crew, fencing, field hockey, golf, gymnastics, track and field, lacrosse, softball, swimming, tennis, and volleyball.

Housing and Student Organizations. For the 57 percent of undergraduates who live on campus, single-sex and coeducational dormitories, single-student apartments, and housing for married students and single parents with children are available. A married woman student whose spouse is not enrolled may live in married students' housing. Men's and coeducational residences do not restrict hours for visitors of the opposite sex; women's dormitories have some restrictions. Residence-hall staff are offered awareness-training on sexism, sex education, racism, and birth control.

Three percent of the undergraduate women belong to social sororities; sororities and fraternities provide housing for their members. A wide spectrum of groups serves as advocates for women. They include the Women's Forum and the Peer Counseling Group (both at University College; the Society of Women Engineers (the School of Engineering); Women's Crisis Center (at Rutgers College); the Douglass College Feminist Collective, the Douglass College Government Association, and the Douglass College Equal Opportunity Board (in which more than half of the participants are black and Puerto Rican women); the Women's Collective and the Lesbian Feminist Coalition (both at Livingston College).

Special Services and Programs for Women. *Health and Counseling.* The student health service provides some medical attention specific to women, including gynecological, birth control, rape and assault, and follow-up abortion treatment. Half of the 18 physicians are female, as are 40 other health-care providers. The regular student health insurance covers abortion and maternity at no extra cost. Students have access to counseling of particular concern to women through the health service and the New Brunswick campus counseling center. Staff receive in-service training on the avoidance of sex-role stereotyping and racial bias.

Safety and Security. Measures include campus police with arrest authority, night-time escorts for women, night-time bus service to residential areas, high-intensity lighting, emergency telephone and alarm system, self-defense courses for women, information sessions on safety and crime prevention, and a rape crisis center. One hundred assaults (18 on women) and five rapes were reported for 1980–81.

Career. The university provides workshops, lectures, and non-sexist/nonracist printed materials on nontraditional occupations and fields of study for women.

Other. Douglass, Rutgers, and Livingston Colleges have active Women's Centers. A variety of programs and services includes help for displaced homemakers, assertiveness training, educational, career, and financial counseling, and a telephone line of information, referral, and support. Lectures and women's arts events are presented under the auspices of Women's Studies.

Institutional Self-Description. "Women's Studies at Rutgers University provides a multi-dimensional view of women and their position in past and present society. This focus introduces new perspectives to vitalize traditional scholarship and also to reinter-pret current academic approaches to the study of women. At each of the colleges the programs are interdisciplinary. The goals of the Women's Studies Programs are to accelerate the growth of feminist consciousness; to serve the needs of women of diverse races, classes, ages, and sexual orientations; to provide the opportunity to develop analytical, verbal, and organizational skills necessary for social change and survival."

Rutgers, The State University of New Jersey, Newark
Newark, NJ 07102
Telephone: (201) 648-5541

Women in Leadership ★ faculty			★ Women and the Curriculum	

3,806 undergraduates

	Amer. Ind.	Asian Amer.	Blacks	Hispanics	Whites
F	2	31	354	187	1,180
M	1	18	168	128	1,706
%	0.1	1.3	13.8	8.3	76.5

The Newark branch of Rutgers, The State University of New Jersey, was founded in 1910 as a private, liberal arts institute. Since 1956, it has been a public commuter university serving the students of northern New Jersey. Some 3,806 of its 10,200 students are undergraduates; 46 percent of undergraduates are women, and 7 percent of the women attend part-time. The median age of undergraduates is 28.

Business, social sciences, health professions, and biology are among the degree programs offered. On-campus evening classes, a summer session, weekend college, and self-paced/contract learning are available. About 1,500 women, of whom 60 percent are minority women, participate in adult education. All undergraduates commute to the campus, which is accessible by public transportation. On-campus parking is available and there is free transportation from fringe parking. Twenty-five students (fewer than 1 percent) join non-residential social sororities and fraternities.

Childcare is available both on and off campus. On-campus facilities accommodate all students' requests and charge fees on a sliding scale. The children of staff and full-time students receive priority.

Policies to Ensure Fairness to Women. A full-time Director of Affirmative Action reviews campus policies and practices regarding equal educational opportunity, affirmative action, and handicapped access. A policy forbidding sexual harassment of students, faculty, and staff has been conveyed in writing to all members of the campus community. A formal grievance procedure resolves complaints. Faculty are offered workshops on affirmative action and equal opportunity.

Women in Leadership Positions. *Students.* Information on opportunities for student leadership was not provided. Two of five honor societies are chaired by women.

Faculty. The 408-member faculty is 31 percent female. There are 8 female faculty per 100 female students and 15 male faculty per 100 male students.

Administrators. Except for the chief planning officer, all administrators are men. Women chair 9 academic departments: Puerto Rican studies, acute illness, chronic illness, health, art, English, finance, foreign languages, and psychology. An unusually high percentage of trustees (60 percent) are women, five of them black women. In addition, two of three commencement speakers in a recent year were women.

Women and the Curriculum. Most women graduating with bachelor's degrees major in health professions (30 percent), business (20 percent), social sciences (16 percent), and biology (11 percent). Just over 1 percent of women study physical sciences and mathematics. Newark encourages women to enter nontraditional careers through programs for women in science, engineering, accounting, and computer science. Internships, science field service, law clinics, and nursing clinics offer opportunities for experiential education.

The Women's Studies Program, directed by a full-time faculty member, offers a 21-credit undergraduate minor. Recent courses include Women in Politics, Women in History, Women Writers, and Women's Rights. Official committees are responsible for developing the Women's Studies Program and collecting and developing curricular materials on women. Courses in the college of nursing, the division of social work, and the School of Business provide some instruction on matters specific to women.

Women and Athletics. Rutgers, Newark has a relatively small women's sports program. Among the intramural sports offered are soccer, basketball, and fencing. Fifty-two percent of the intercollegiate athletes are women, as are two of the five paid intercollegiate coaches. The intercollegiate sports offered are basketball, fencing, softball, tennis, and volleyball.

Special Services and Programs for Women. *Health and Counseling.* Four physicians (3 women and 1 man) and 11 other health-care providers (10 women and 1 man) offer treatment on gynecological problems, birth control, and rape and assault. Counseling is available on gynecological problems, birth control, abortion and rape and assault. The regular student insurance covers maternity and abortion expenses at no extra cost.

Safety and Security. Measures consist of campus police, nighttime escort for women, high-intensity lighting, emergency telephones, emergency alarms, self-defense courses, information on campus safety and rape and assault prevention, and a rape crisis center. For 1980–81, 68 assaults, 20 on women, and no rapes were reported.

Career. Services include workshops, lectures and panels, and printed information on nontraditional occupations for women. The personnel division provides assertiveness training.

Other. Advocacy groups include Women in Transition, Gay Students Organization, Black Students Organization, Women's Organizational Network, and the Organization of Registered Nurses, Women's Caucus, Gay Rights, Women Law Students, and College of Nursing Student Organization serve as advocates for women on campus.

Institutional Self-Description. "The School of Law is now 53 percent female. The Graduate School of Management is 30 percent female and has special programs for women in business. The degree-granting evening college is 55 percent female. The College of Nursing has both graduate and undergraduate programs."

Somerset County College
P.O. Box 3300, Somerville, NJ 08876
Telephone: (201) 526-1200

Women in Leadership
  ★ students
  ★★★ faculty

2,354 undergraduates

	Amer. Ind.	Asian Amer.	Blacks	Hispanics	Whites
F	4	24	94	25	1,105
M	6	14	57	19	1,006
%	0.4	1.6	6.4	1.9	89.7

This public, two-year commuter college serves over 4,000 students in liberal arts and such technical fields as data processing and mechanical engineering. Fifty-three percent of the 2,354 undergraduates are women. Alternative schedules include evening classes on and off campus. All students commute to the campus, where parking is available for a fee.

An on-campus childcare facility, open from 8 a.m. to 5 p.m., can accommodate 65 children, or 85 percent of student, faculty, and staff needs, with students receiving priority.

Policies to Ensure Fairness to Women. A full-time Director of Educational Services administers, but does not set policy for, equal-employment-opportunity regulations. A policy prohibiting sexual harassment of students has been communicated in writing to students.

Women in Leadership Positions. *Students.* There are three campus-wide positions available. In two years of a recent three-year period, women presided over the student government and edited the school newspaper. Women head the sole honorary society.

Faculty. Women are 54 percent of the 86 full-time faculty. There are 7 female faculty to every 100 female students and 6 male faculty to every 100 male students.

Administrators. A woman heads the library; men hold all other top administrative positions. Women chair the departments of nursing, English, social science, and business and public services; a woman is Dean of Community Education. A woman also directs the Learning Resources Center.

Women and the Curriculum. Forty percent of degrees awarded to women are in arts and sciences; 25 percent are in health professions, and 25 percent in business and commerce. No courses on women are offered.

Women and Athletics. Although all intramural sports are offered on a coeducational basis, women do not participate. Women do participate in intercollegiate basketball and tennis. Two of the paid intercollegiate coaches are women.

Special Services and Programs for Women. *Health and Counseling.* The health service is staffed by 2 female health-care providers. Gynecological, birth control, abortion, and rape and assault counseling are available at the counseling center, staffed by 3 men, 1 minority woman, and 2 white women.

Safety and Security. Measures consist of campus police without arrest authority. No rapes or assaults were reported for 1980–81.

Career. Somerset provides career workshops focused on nontraditional occupations, nonsexist/nonracist printed information on such fields, and lectures or panels for students by women employed in nontraditional occupations.

Institutional Self-Description. "Somerset County College initiated the Comeback Program in 1972 to assist individuals who wanted to resume their college education or to begin working toward a college degree. The program is also intended for adults who find themselves in changing roles and would like to enter college either for personal involvement or to enhance job opportunities. Comeback recognizes these concerns and provides necessary information to effectively deal with them."

🏠	On-campus evening and/or weekend classes	[M/A]	Commission on minority affairs
🏛	Off-campus classes	📖	Women's Studies program
🚌	Accessible by public transportation	🚹	Women's center
👫	On-campus childcare facilities	AAUW	Member, American Association of University Women
✎	Publicly communicated sexual harassment policy, includes students	NWSA	Member, National Women's Studies Association
[S/W]	Commission on status of women	CROW	On-campus Center for Research on Women

Stevens Institute of Technology
Castle Point, Hoboken, NJ 07030
Telephone: (201) 420-5105

Women in Leadership
★★★ students

1,408 undergraduates

	Amer. Ind.	Asian Amer.	Blacks	Hispanics	Whites
F	0	6	14	13	137
M	0	48	26	60	1,046
%	0.0	4.0	3.0	5.4	87.6

Stevens Institute of Technology, established in 1870 as an engineering college for men, is now a private, coeducational institution that trains students for careers in science and business, as well as in engineering. Located in the city of Hoboken, overlooking the Hudson River, Stevens attracts 2,472 students, 1,408 of them undergraduates. Twelve percent of the undergraduates are women, almost all of whom attend full-time. The median age of all undergraduates is 20. The college offers an independent studies program and a summer session. The one-fifth of students who commute or live off campus can take advantage of public transportation and on-campus parking.

Stevens Affiliates, a parents' cooperative, operates a pre-school and elementary school program on campus for 85 children. The program is open to all members of the Stevens community and to local residents. Additional, private childcare facilities are available near campus.

Policies to Ensure Fairness to Women. The university Treasurer has the part-time responsibility for handling matters pertaining to equal-employment laws. The Assistant to the Provost attends part-time to matters relating to sex-equity laws. The Dean of Student Affairs is involved, on a part-time basis, with issues regarding handicapped-access legal requirements. All three officers have policymaking power. Complaints of sexual harassment are resolved informally. A Committee on Minority Affairs, addresses the concerns of minority women.

Women in Leadership Positions. *Students.* Although women represent a very small minority of the undergraduates, they have had some opportunity to gain leadership experience. In three recent years, women have served one-year terms as student-body president and student-judiciary president. One of the five campus honorary societies is headed by a woman.

Faculty. Five percent of the 129 full-time faculty are women, a proportion far below the national average. There are 4 female faculty for every 100 female students, compared to 10 male faculty for every 100 male students.

Administrators. Men hold all top positions and deanships, chair all departments, and constitute the entire membership of the tenure, reappointment, and promotions committee. The 42-member Board of Trustees has 2 female representatives. In a recent year, 1 woman and 3 men received honorary degrees.

Women and the Curriculum. Half of the women earn degrees in interdisciplinary studies and half in engineering, a nontraditional field for women. Fifteen percent of students in internship programs are women. There are no courses on women.

Women and Athletics. Women participate in intercollegiate and intramural sports, as well as sports clubs. Several intramural activities draw 100 women, including basketball, volleyball, badminton, and platform tennis (for which the institute has special facilities). Of the 15 paid intercollegiate coaches, 2 are women. The intercollegiate sport offered is fencing.

Housing and Student Organizations. Eighty percent of the undergraduates live on campus in single-sex dormitories. Housing for married students with or without children is also available. A married woman whose husband is not enrolled is permitted to live in married students' housing.

Seven percent of the full-time undergraduate women, including one minority woman, belong to sororities, which provide housing for members. A women's advocacy organization, the Society of Women Engineers, has 40 active members, including several minority women.

Special Services and Programs for Women. *Health and Counseling.* The student health service employs one part-time male physician and one full-time female health-care provider. The student counseling center is staffed by one female counselor. Counseling and treatment for medical problems specific to women are provided by a local clinic.

Safety and Security. Measures consist of campus and local police protection, high intensity lighting, emergency telephone and alarm systems, and information on campus safety for women. No rapes or assaults on women were reported for 1980–81.

Career. Stevens offers career workshops and lectures and distributes information on nontraditional occupations. It also fosters networking with alumnae and promotes the use of files on the careers of alumnae. The Career Resource Center conducts an outreach program designed to encourage high school students to consider opportunities for women in engineering and science. The center was in cooperation with high school guidance counselors.

Institutional Self-Description. "Stevens attracts dedicated students devoted to study in engineering, science and management. Although women comprise only 15 percent of the student body, the are extremely active in extra-curricular activities. There is a great deal of interaction between students, faculty, and administration and a strong sense of comaraderie among all students."

Trenton State College
Hillwood Lakes CN 550
Trenton, NJ 08625
Telephone: (609) 771-1855

Women in Leadership		**★ Women and the**
★★ students		**Curriculum**
★ faculty		**★★★ Women and Athletics**

8,695 undergraduates

	Amer. Ind.	Asian Amer.	Blacks	Hispanics	Whites
F	7	23	375	34	4,697
M	6	21	244	39	3,249
%	0.2	0.5	7.1	0.8	91.4

Founded in 1855 to train teachers, Trenton State is now a multipurpose public college with schools of arts and sciences, business, nursing, education, and industrial technologies. Its 11,000 students include 8,695 undergraduates. Fifty-nine percent of the undergraduates are women, 36 percent of whom attend part-time. Twenty-nine percent of the female undergraduates are age 25 or over; the median age of all undergraduates is 21. Scheduling is facilitated by on-and off-campus evening classes, a summer session, and self-paced/contract learning. A special office administers continuing education programs. Seventy percent of students commute to the campus, which is accessible by public transportation. On-campus parking is available at a fee.

Daytime childcare facilities, available on campus for a fixed fee, can accommodate 15 children. Private childcare facilities are also available near campus.

Policies to Ensure Fairness to Women. One of the duties of the Assistant Vice President for Adminstrative Services is to vote on committees making policies regarding equal employment opportunity, sex equity for students, and handicapped access. A policy forbidding sexual harassment of students, faculty, and staff has been conveyed to all members of the campus community. Complaints are resolved through either an informal campus mechanism or a formal grievance procedure.

Women in Leadership Positions. *Students.* Of 27 leadership positions available in three recent years, women have held ten. They have twice been president of the student union, head of student government, and editor-in-chief of the student newspaper; three times presided over the residence-hall council; and once been head of the senior class. Women chair 3 of the 9 honorary societies and 2 of the 4 professional societies.

Faculty. Of 375 faculty members, 29 percent are women; 64 percent of women hold permanent appointments. The ratio of female faculty to female students is 3 to 100, of male faculty to male students, 12 to 100.

Administrators. Men hold all top positions. The Director of Nursing is a woman and women chair eight of 21 departments: biology, criminal justice, psychology, speech communication/theater, health, physical education and recreation, special education, elementary education and early childhood, and business. A woman received the sole alumni award given in 1980–81; two of the nine trustees are women.

Women and the Curriculum. Most women earn degrees in education (44 percent), health professions (14 percent), business (8 percent), and fine arts (7 percent). Three percent major in fields that are nontraditional for women—mathematics, physical sciences, and engineering. Women faculty have formed two professional societies for students—Women in Engineering and Women in Law Enforcement/Corrections.

The Women's Studies Program, directed by a permanent faculty member, offers an undergraduate minor. In addition to an introductory course in Women's Studies, courses on women are offered through the English and history departments, including Women in Western Civilization, Women in Contemporary literature, Images of Women in American Literature, Images of Women in British Fiction, and Women Writers. The departments of business, education, nursing, and physical education provide some instruction on matters specific to women.

Minority Women. Seven percent of women students are black women. Residence-hall staff are offered workshops on racism. Twenty-two minority women belong to all-minority sororities. Twenty percent of women who use the Women's Center are black women. Of the 16 women on the faculty senate, 1 is black and 1 Hispanic.

Women and Athletics. Outstanding intercollegiate, intramural, and club sport programs have a high proportion of female athletes. Intramural sports include women's and coeducational sports. Thirty-five percent of the 34 paid intercollegiate coaches are women. The intercollegiate sports offered are archery, basketball, cross-country, gymnastics, hockey, lacrosse, softball, swimming, tennis, track (indoor and outdoor), and volleyball.

Housing and Student Organizations. Single-sex and coeducational dormitories house the 30 percent of students who live on campus. Workshops on sexism and racism are available for the one female and two male residence-hall directors.

Four percent of full-time students join non-residential sororities and fraternities. The Women's Center Programming Committee serves as an advocate for women on campus.

Special Services and Programs for Women. *Health and Counseling.* Two part-time, male physicians and 7 female health-care providers offer gynecological and birth control treatment. The 7 counselors, including 4 women, offer counseling on gynecological problems, birth control, abortion, and rape and assault. Counselors are offered training on sex-role stereotyping, racial bias, suicide prevention, sexuality, and crisis management. The counseling center also sponsors a telephone service for information, referrals, and support. Regular student insurance covers abortion but not maternity expenses.

Safety and Security. Measures consist of campus and municipal police, night-time escorts for women, high-intensity lighting, self-defense courses, information sessions on safety and rape and assault prevention, and a rape crisis center. For 1980–81, 15 assaults, including 3 on women, were reported.

Career. Career Placement offers programs on nontraditional careers, maintains files of alumnae by occupation, and sponsors programs to establish contacts between alumnae and female students.

Other. A small Women's Center, on a budget of $1,000, is headed by the Director of the Office for Women and run cooperatively by faculty and students, for 200 women participants each year. The Office for Women also sponsors a Lawyer Referral Service and Rape Victim Support Team.

Group Student Development, a project of the Women's Programming Committee, aids battered women, sponsors an annual women's week, and provides assertiveness training. The Gay Union of Trenton State is an advocacy group for lesbians.

Institutional Self-Description. "As a comprehensive regional college, Trenton State is committed to providing quality academic programs and student-life service. This commitment, coupled with the fact that TSC is recognized as the most selective college in New Jersey, creates an academic and social atmosphere extremely conducive to gaining the skills necessary for professional and personal advancement after graduation."

Union College
1033 Springfield Ave.
Cranford, NJ 07016
Telephone: (201) 276-2600

Women in Leadership
★★ faculty

2,633 undergraduates

	Amer. Ind.	Asian Amer.	Blacks	Hispanics	Whites
F	7	9	183	67	1,085
M	4	11	116	66	1,075
%	0.3	0.8	11.4	5.1	82.4

Established in 1933, this private, two-year community college serves 5,346 students. Just over half of the 2,633 degree students are women, and 40 percent of women attend part-time. Fifty-six percent of the women are over age 25; the median age of all students is 28.

Union offers college transfer and terminal programs in liberal arts, education, biology, engineering, physical sciences, law enforcement, and nursing. Evening classes both on and off campus, a weekend college, and a summer session are available. The suburban campus, near Elizabeth, is accessible by public transportation. Students who drive can make use of free on-campus parking is available.

Women in Leadership Positions. *Students.* The participation of women in campus-wide leadership positions is limited. In a recent three year period, women have served once as president of the student body, presiding officer of the student court, editor-in-chief of the newspaper, and manager of the campus radio station.

Faculty. Forty percent of the full-time faculty of 98 are women.

The full-time faculty includes 1 black woman. There are 5 female faculty for every 100 female students and 7 male faculty for every 100 male students.

Administrators. Of ten chief administrators, two are women—the chief development officer and the director of institutional research. Two departments are chaired by women—chemistry and modern languages. The 23 trustees include a white woman and a black woman.

Women and the Curriculum. All of the women graduating from Union College receive their degrees or certificates in the arts and sciences or in health technologies. There are no courses on women.

Women and Athletics. The intramural program draws approximately 2,000 students, and women account for nearly a third of the athletes in both the individual and team sports. The intercollegiate program, which is more limited, draws 100 athletes, 20 of whom are women. One of the nine paid coaches for intercollegiate sports is a woman. Forty percent of athletic scholarship aid goes to women. The two intercollegiate sports available are basketball and tennis.

Special Services and Programs for Women. *Health and Counseling.* The student health service is staffed by one male physician and one female health-care provider. There is also a student counseling center. Services specific to women are not available.

Safety and Security. Measures consist of campus police with no arrest authority and high-intensity lighting in all areas. No rapes or assaults were reported on campus for 1980–81.

Institutional Self-Description. None provided.

Upsala College
Prospect Street, East Orange, NJ 07019
Telephone: (201) 226-7000

Women in Leadership
★ students

1,149 undergraduates

	Amer. Ind.	Asian Amer.	Blacks	Hispanics	Whites
F	1	6	103	12	373
M	2	5	95	24	517
%	0.3	1.0	17.4	3.2	78.2

Upsala College, established in 1893 primarily to educate Swedish Lutheran students for the clergy, remains church affiliated; it provides liberal arts and career-oriented programs. The suburban campus in East Orange has an enrollment of 1,674 students, including 1,149 undergraduates. Women are 44 percent of the undergraduates, and 9 percent of the women attend part-time. The median age of all undergraduates is 18.

Upsala offers a range of undergraduate and master's degree programs, in addition to continuing education courses. Classes, which meet at two different locations during the day, are supplemented by evening classes, a weekend college, and a summer session. About one-third of the undergraduates commute to the campus, which is accessible by public transportation. Commuters can also park on campus.

A campus childcare facility is open to all members of the Upsala community, as well as to local residents. The facility can accommodate ten children at one time, and it charges a fixed, daily fee. Additional, private childcare facilities are available near campus.

Policies to Ensure Fairness to Women. An Equal-Opportunity Officer has the part-time responsibility for making policy and monitoring compliance with laws pertaining to sex equity for stu-

dents. Complaints of sexual harassment are resolved informally. A Liaison Committee, with representatives elected from the faculty, students, trustees, and administration, reports to the president regarding women's issues.

Women in Leadership Positions. *Students.* Opportunities for women to exercise campus-wide leadership are good. In recent years, women have held a third of the leadership posts, including one-year terms as president of the student judiciary, the student union, the senior, junior, and sophomore and entering classes, as well as, two terms as editor-in-chief of the campus newspaper.

Faculty. One-fifth of the full-time faculty are women. There are 3 female faculty for every 100 female students, compared with 8 male faculty for every 100 male students.

Administrators. Women hold two of the ten major administrative posts—chief student-life officer and chief planning officer. Among the 12 departments, sociology and chemistry are chaired by women.

Women and the Curriculum. The most popular fields for women are business, social sciences, and psychology. Almost half of the students in internship and science field-service programs are women. The learning center helps women to build mathematics confidence.

Two courses on women are offered by the sociology and biology departments.

Women and Athletics. Women's organized athletics includes five intercollegiate and four intramural sports and one sports club. Nineteen percent of intercollegiate athletes and 9 percent of intramural athletes are women. The intramural program consists mainly of individual sports. Intercollegiate sports offered are basketball, softball, tennis, track and field, and volleyball.

Housing and Student Organizations. Sixty-five percent of the undergraduates live on campus in single-sex or coeducational dormitories. Rules regarding visitors of the opposite sex vary among residence halls. Residence-hall staff are offered awareness-training on racism, sexism, birth control, and sex education.

Nine percent of the undergraduate women belong to sororities, which do not provide on-campus housing. Forty minority women belong to all-minority sororities, and 10 to racially integrated ones. The Black Women's Committee is an advocacy group.

Special Services and Programs for Women. *Health and Counseling.* The student health service employs 4 male physicians and 1 female health-care provider. The student counseling center is staffed by 2 female and 2 male counselors. Counseling and treatment are available for gynecological problems, birth control, abortion, and rape and assault.

Safety and Security. Measures consist of campus police protection, high-intensity lighting, and information sessions on campus safety for women. No rapes were reported for 1980–81.

Career. The Office of Academic and Career Counseling provides career workshops, lectures, and information on nontraditional occupations, encourages networking with alumnae, and compiles files on the careers of alumnae.

Other. The Women's Center, which is associated with the Continuing Education Office, serves about 50 women, most of them undergraduates. Two additional programs for women are leadership training, co-sponsored by Cross-Roads Choices and the Montclair Junior League, and the Woman's Network, sponsored by Upsala-Woman's Network and the N.J. Network.

Returning Women Students. Two hundred reentry women are enrolled in the Continuing Education for Women Program. An additional 600 women take adult education courses. Faculty attend workshops on teaching returning women students.

Institutional Self-Description. "Upsala College offers a quality education, and has highly supportive services for both traditional age and reentry women, including academic, personal, and career counseling, childcare, and job placement. The college has highly visible female administrators and faculty, who serve as role models and advisors to women students."

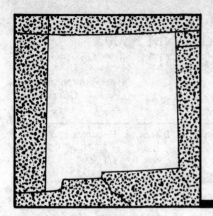

NEW MEXICO

College of Santa Fe
Santa Fe, NM 87501
Telephone: (505) 473-6131

Women in Leadership
★ faculty

1,048 undergraduates

	Amer. Ind.	Asian Amer.	Blacks	Hispanics	Whites
F	65	5	6	210	292
M	22	15	14	192	224
%	8.3	1.9	1.9	38.5	49.4

The College of Santa Fe, founded in 1947 by the Christian Brothers, is a Roman Catholic liberal arts and professional institution. Half of the students are members of minority groups, mainly Chicano and American Indian. The total enrollment is 1,142 students, including 1,048 undergraduates. Women are 55 percent of the undergraduates; 32 percent of the women attend part-time. The median age of all students is 25.

The college offers associate and bachelor's degrees in a variety of fields. An Open Studies Program, evening and summer session classes, and a Center for Continuing Education provide alternatives for scheduling and study. Five percent of the undergraduates live in single-sex dormitories that have no restrictions on visiting hours for members of the opposite sex. Ten percent of women students join social sororities. Free on-campus parking is available for the majority of students who commute.

Private childcare facilities are located near the campus.

Women in Leadership Positions. *Students.* Incomplete information on student leadership indicates that in recent years a woman was elected once as president of the student body.

Faculty. One-third of the 45 full-time faculty are women, a proportion above the average for similar institutions in this guide. There are 4 female faculty for every 100 female students and 8 male faculty for every 100 male students.

Administrators. Women hold two of ten key administrative positions: Dean of Students and Director of Athletics. The Dean of Open Studies and the Coordinator of the Center for Continuing Education are women. Of seven departments, a woman chairs nursing.

Women and the Curriculum. The most popular fields among women graduating with bachelor's degrees are education (27 percent), public affairs (19 percent), and interdisciplinary studies (11 percent). Women earn two-thirds of the two-year degrees granted, mostly in health technologies.

The English department offers a course on women: Special Studies in Women Authors.

Minority Women. Twenty-seven percent of the undergraduates are minority women, 20 percent of these, Chicanas. One of the 15 women on the full-time faculty is Hispanic. A Chicana directs the Center for Continuing Education, and a Chicana was among the four women speakers in a recent campus-wide lecture series. The Women's Center is used primarily by Chicana students. The residence-hall director is a minority woman.

Women and Athletics. The organized athletic program emphasizes team sports. There are six intramural activities and three intercollegiate sports. Women athletes receive 20 percent of the athletic scholarship aid. One of the six paid varsity coaches is a woman. Intercollegiate sports offered are basketball, tennis (co-educational), and volleyball.

Special Services and Programs for Women. *Health and Counseling.* There is no student health service. The student counseling center employs two female professionals. Rape and assault counseling are provided by the campus rape crisis center.

Safety and Security. Measures consist of campus police protection and information on campus safety for women. No rapes or assaults on women were reported for 1980–81.

Career. Career placement services include information on nontraditional occupations for women.

Other. Student Government operates a small Women's Center which is administered by a student volunteer on a part-time basis. The center serves undergraduates, faculty, and staff. A woman heads the Campus Ministry.

Institutional Self-Description. "Co-educational, liberal arts, professional education, 56 percent women attending, non-traditional degree earning work through Open Studies Program, Women's Center available, Rape Center available, Campus Ministry directed by a woman, two female counselors available, and traditional night classes."

New Mexico Institute of Mining and Technology
Campus Station, Socorro, NM 87801
Telephone: (505) 835-5424

Women in Leadership
★ students

★ Women and the Curriculum

814 undergraduates

	Amer. Ind.	Asian Amer.	Blacks	Hispanics	Whites
F	3	3	2	25	168
M	8	12	4	55	503
%	1.4	1.9	0.8	10.2	85.7

 AAUW

Founded in 1889, the New Mexico Institute of Mining and Technology is a state-supported institution whose major emphasis is education and research in science and engineering. Some 1,100 students are enrolled, 814 of them undergraduates; 25 percent are women. The median age of all students is 29.

The institute offers bachelor's degrees in a range of science, engineering, mathematics, liberal arts, and pre-professional fields; masters and doctoral programs are also available. The division of continuing education serves the adult student. Alternative scheduling is available through self-paced study programs, evening classes, and a summer session. The campus is not accessible by public transportation. Free on-campus parking is available for the 51 percent of students who commute.

On-campus daytime childcare facilities accommodate 27 children. Students receive priority and 95 percent of their requests for childcare can be met. Private childcare facilities are located near campus.

Policies to Ensure Fairness to Women. On a part-time basis, the Affirmative Action Officer reviews policies regarding equal employment and educational opportunities. A published policy prohibits sexual harassment of students, faculty, and staff; complaints are resolved through a formal grievance procedure.

Women in Leadership Positions. *Students.* Women are one-fourth of the students and hold one-fifth of the student offices. During three recent years, women served as editor-in-chief of the campus newspaper.

Faculty. Eight percent of the 79 full-time faculty are women, a proportion far below the national average. There are 3 female faculty for every 100 female students and 13 male faculty for every 100 male students.

Administrators. The chief administrators are men, as are the department chairs. Thirteen percent of the faculty senate are women, including three Hispanic women, and one of the five regents is a woman.

Women and the Curriculum. The most popular majors for both men and women students are engineering and physical sciences. Sixty-three percent of women graduates earn degrees in such nontraditional fields as engineering, mathematics, and physical sciences. The institute maintains programs to encourage women to major in nontraditional fields. There are no courses on women.

Women and Athletics. Women have no opportunity for intercollegiate sports. No information was provided for intramural and club sports.

Housing and Student Organizations. Single-sex and coeducational dormitories are available for the 49 percent of undergraduates who live on campus. College housing is available for single students with children and married students with or without children. Three of the nine dormitory directors are women. Dormitory staff are offered awareness-training on racism, sexism, sex education, and birth control. The Association of Women in Science is an advocacy group for women students.

Special Services and Programs for Women. *Health and Counseling.* The institution has neither a student health service nor a student counseling center.

Safety and Security. Measures consist of campus police with weapons training and the authority to make arrests, an emergency alarm system at isolated locations, and information sessions on campus safety and assault prevention. No rapes or assaults on women were reported for 1979, the last year for which figures are available.

Career. Lectures and written material and special programs are available about careers in science, engineering, and computer science. The institute also conducts career conferences for high school and college women in an effort to recruit women students.

Institutional Self-Description. "A new women's dormitory is available, in addition to coeducational dormitories. A female counselor (the Assistant Dean of Students) is available. Part-time job opportunities on the campus are numerous. The job market in the technical fields emphasized at New Mexico Tech is extremely strong."

New Mexico State University
Box 3A, Las Cruces, NM 88003
Telephone: (505) 646-3121

| Women in Leadership ★ students | | | ★ Women and the Curriculum | |

9,659 undergraduates

	Amer. Ind.	Asian Amer.	Blacks	Hispanics	Whites
F	87	13	63	1,201	2,910
M	98	22	99	1,369	3,561
%	2.0	0.4	1.7	27.3	68.7

🏛 ⌂ ⬛ ⬛ ⬛ AAUW

A land-grant institution established in 1888, New Mexico State University, located in a diverse cultural community, provides some 12,400 students with a range of undergraduate and graduate programs. The College of Human and Community Services is responsible for adult continuing education. Evening classes, a summer session, and off-campus class locations are available.

Of the 9,659 undergraduates, 45 percent are women; 19 percent of the women attend part-time. The median age of undergraduates is 22, and 19 percent of women are over age 25. For the 63 percent of students who commute to campus, there is on-campus parking.

Private childcare facilities are available nearby.

Policies to Ensure Fairness to Women. A full-time equal-opportunity officer reviews policy and practices related to employment, accessibility of programs and activities to women students, and handicapped access. Complaints of sexual harassment are handled informally and confidentially. The Committee on the Status of Women addresses the concerns of all women, and the Committee on Minority Affairs also addresses the concerns of minority women.

Women in Leadership Positions. *Students.* Opportunities for women to assume campus leadership are above the average for public research institutions in this guide. In recent years, women have presided over the residence-hall council three times and been editor-in-chief of the campus newspaper once.

Faculty. Women are 16 percent of a full-time faculty of 462. According to a recent report, 4 black, 4 Asian American, and 7 Hispanic women are on the full-time faculty. The ratio of female faculty to female students is 2 to 100. The ratio of male faculty to male students is 8 to 100.

Administrators. The chief student-life officer is a woman. All other chief administrators are men. Women chair seven of 45 departments: art, mathematics, home economics, sociology, educational specialties, and nursing.

Women and the Curriculum. Education and business and management are the most popular majors for women graduating with bachelor's degrees. Over 16 percent major in nontraditional fields. One-tenth of the women graduate with degrees in agriculture. The most popular two-year degree areas for women are health technologies and business. A small proportion (5 percent) major in engineering technologies. Programs encourage women to prepare for careers in science, engineering, and accounting. Thirty-five percent of the positions in cooperative education programs go to women.

Courses on women are offered in the departments of government and history, sociology, and physical education. Recent titles include Born Female in America, Sex Roles, and Team Sports for Women. A Women's Studies Program is being planned. A statewide conference on Women's Studies was held on campus in 1981. An official committee is responsible for collecting curricular materials and developing courses on women in traditional departments. The relationships among sex, race, and choice of major field, the needs of reentry women, and affirmative action are topics considered in faculty workshops.

The physical education department provides instruction on the teaching of coeducational physical education classes. Such current topics as innovative health-care delivery and health-care information important to minority women, services for abused spouses, and workplace discrimination are part of the preparation of health-care providers, social workers, and business students.

Minority Women. Thirty-two percent of female undergraduates are minority women, with Hispanic women the largest group. Thirty-three minority women belong to integrated sororities. A minority woman is a residence-hall director. Residence-hall staff are offered awareness-training in racism. The Coordinator of the Women's Center is an Hispanic woman.

Women and Athletics. Intramural and intercollegiate programs provide adequate opportunities for organized, competitive, individual and team sports. Nineteen percent of intramural and 33 percent of intercollegiate athletes are women. Women receive 30 percent of athletic scholarships. Women's intercollegiate teams played in tournaments in 1980. The intercollegiate sports offered are basketball, softball, swimming, tennis and, volleyball.

Housing and Student Organizations. Thirty-seven percent of the undergraduates live on campus. Residential accommodations include single-sex and coeducational dormitories and housing for married students and single parents with children. A married woman student whose spouse is not enrolled may live in married students' housing. Dormitories restrict hours for visitors of the opposite sex. Half of the residence-hall directors are female. Awareness-training is offered to staff on sexism, sex education, birth control, and depression.

Seven percent of full-time undergraduate women belong to social sororities. Sororities and fraternities provide some housing for their members. The Association for Women Students and the Returning Students' Organization serve as advocates for women on campus, along with MUJER, BASHA, and The Returning Students Organization.

Special Services and Programs for Women. *Health and Counseling.* The student health service provides some medical attention specific to women, including gynecological and birth control counseling. One of 6 physicians is female, as are 3 other health-care providers. Two of 5 professional staff in the counseling service are women. Students have access to gynecological, birth control, and abortion counseling. Staff are offered in-service training in the avoidance of sex-role stereotyping.

Safety and Security. Measures consist of campus police with state certification who provide 24-hour protection, night-time escorts for women students, high-intensity lighting, self-defense courses for women, information sessions on safety and crime prevention, and a rape crisis center. No assaults on women and three rapes were reported for 1980–81.

Career. Workshops and printed materials concentrated on women in nontraditional occupations and fields of study are available.

Other. A Women's Center is operated under the auspices of Student Affairs. Among the activities it co-sponsors with Counseling and Student Development are assertiveness training, holistic health services, sack-lunch seminars, and a telephone service of information, referral, and support. The Association for Women Students sponsors a women's week.

Institutional Self-Description. "New Mexico State University is focusing on the changing needs of women in terms of their self concept, values, and attitudes. The goal of the majority of women's programs at NMSU is to assist women in meeting their needs for information, skill development, life planning, personal growth, and cultural enrichment."

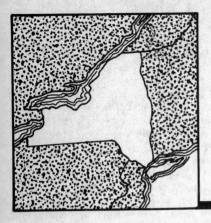

NEW YORK

Adirondack Community College
Bay Road, Glens Falls, NY 12801
Telephone: (518) 793-4491

2,212 undergraduates

	Amer. Ind.	Asian Amer.	Blacks	Hispanics	Whites
F	0	2	7	4	1,242
M	2	2	15	3	932
%	0.1	0.2	1.0	0.3	98.4

This public, two-year commuter college, founded in 1961, is located on a rural campus in northeastern New York. Women make up 57 percent of a student population of 2,212, and almost 60 percent of women attend part-time. The median age of all students is 26; 29 percent of women are over age 25.

Adirondack offers a range of two-year programs in such fields as liberal arts, public service, engineering/technology, and communications/media. A summer session and evening classes on and off campus are offered. Free on-campus parking is available.

Policies to Ensure Fairness to Women. An equal-opportunity officer, on a part-time basis, monitors compliance with sex-equity and handicapped-access legislation.

Women in Leadership Positions. *Students.* According to the incomplete information provided, men have been president of the student body for three recent years.

Faculty. Women are 23 percent of the 65 full-time faculty, a proportion lower than average for two-year colleges. There are 3 female faculty for every 100 female students and 10 male faculty for every 100 male students.

Administrators. Of eight major administrative positions, the director of institutional research is a woman. Women chair three of eight departments: nursing, English, and occupational education. One of the four college deans is a woman, as is one of the ten college trustees.

Women and the Curriculum. Most two-year degrees awarded to women are in liberal arts (40 percent), health technologies (34 percent), and business and commerce (20 percent). The nursing division offers training on home delivery and reproductive choice as well as health-care information important to minority women. There are no courses on women.

Women and Athletics. Information was not provided.

Special Services and Programs for Women. *Health and Counseling.* There is no student health service or counseling center.

Safety and Security. Town police provide the sole security. No assaults on women were reported for 1980–81.

Career. Printed information on nontraditional fields of study for women and on job discrimination is available, as well as counseling for returning women.

Other. The Adult Returning Student Organization is an advocacy group for older women.

Institutional Self-Description. None provided.

Alfred University
Alfred, NY 14802
Telephone: (607) 871-2111

1,814 undergraduates

	Amer. Ind.	Asian Amer.	Blacks	Hispanics	Whites
F	0	1	3	2	870
M	2	1	4	3	918
%	0.1	0.1	0.4	0.3	99.1

Alfred University, established in 1836, is a private coeducational institution that provides a liberal arts and professional education. One division, the College of Ceramics, is state-supported and noted as a center of ceramics engineering. The rural campus, located 70 miles south of Rochester, attracts 2,065 students. Forty-nine percent of the 1,814 undergraduates are women, and 8 percent of the women attend part-time. The median age of all undergraduates is 20.

Alfred offers undergraduate and graduate degrees in a variety of fields. Continuing education courses are offered. All classes, including those of the summer session, meet during the day. Parking is provided on campus for students who commute.

Policies to Ensure Fairness to Women. The Dean of the Graduate School and Special Programs has the part-time responsibility for examining policies and practices pertaining to handicapped-access, affirmative-action, and sex-equity laws. A sexual harassment policy protects all members of the Alfred community.

Women in Leadership Positions. *Students.* Women have limited opportunites to gain campus-wide leadership experience. In three consecutive years, women served three times as editor-in-chief of the campus newspaper, while all other campus leadership positions were held by men. Four of seven honorary societies are led by women.

Faculty. Seventeen percent of the 136 full-time faculty are women. There are 3 female faculty for every 100 female students and 12 male faculty for every 100 male students.

Administrators. All key adminstrators are male, except the head librarian. The Dean of the College of Nursing is a woman. Four of the 18-member faculty senate are female, which is average for comparable institutions in this guide; female representation on the board of trustees is below the average. In one recent year, 11 of the 24 recipients of alumni awards and 1 of the 3 recipients of honorary degrees were female.

Women and the Curriculum. Women earn more than half of the degrees in health professions. Three percent of women major in mathematics and physical sciences. Special programs encourage women to enter the fields of science, engineering, accounting, computer science, and law enforcement/corrections. Almost half the students in experiential learning programs are women.

Two courses on women are offered through the departments of history and literature: American History—History or Herstory and Women in Literature.

Women and Athletics. For a small institution, the organized competitive sports program for women is good. About 25 percent of the intercollegiate and 17 percent of the intramural athletes are women. Two of the ten paid coaches for intercollegiate sports are women. Six individual and team sports are available in the intramural program, including water polo, volleyball, softball, racquetball, badminton, and table tennis. There are also club sports. Intercollegiate sports offered are basketball, soccer, swimming, tennis, track and field, and volleyball.

Housing and Student Organizations. Sixty-five percent of the undergraduates live on campus in coeducational dormitories that have no restrictions on visiting hours for members of the opposite sex. Housing is available for married students with or without children, as well as for single parents with children. Residence-hall staff are offered awareness-training on racism, sexism, sex education, and birth control. Six of the 12 residence-hall staff are women, including one minority woman.

Eighteen percent of the full-time undergraduate women belong to sororities. Five minority women belong to racially integrated sororities. Housing on campus is provided for sorority and fraternity members. The Women's Lyceum, the only women's advocacy group, serves all women, including minority women.

Special Services and Programs for Women. *Health and Counseling.* The student health service is staffed by two male physicians. The student counseling center has a staff of two male counselors. Counseling and treatment are available for gynecological problems, birth control, and rape and assault, in addition to abortion counseling.

Safety and Security. Measures consist of campus and local police protection and a rape crisis center. There were no rapes or assaults on women reported for 1980–81.

Career. The college distributes information on nontraditional occupations, compiles files on the careers of alumnae, and encourages networking with alumnae.

Other. The student affairs office provides a telephone service for information, referrals, and support and sponsors leadership training sessions.

Institutional Self-Description. None provided.

Barnard College

606 W. 120th Street
New York, NY 10027
Telephone: (212) 280-5262

Women in Leadership	Women and the
★★★ students	★★ Curriculum
★★★ faculty	
★★★ administrators	

2,265 undergraduates

	Amer. Ind.	Asian Amer.	Blacks	Hispanics	Whites
F	0	163	105	86	1,839
M	0	0	0	0	0
%	0.0	7.4	4.8	3.9	83.9

 AAUW

Barnard College, founded in 1889, is an independent, liberal arts college for women. Although it is part of Columbia University, it retains its own faculty, administration, curricula—and identity. Barnard women may register in Columbia College courses, and use all libraries. Located on the Upper West Side of Manhattan, Barnard attracts 2,274 students; virtually all attend full-time. The median age of students is 20.

Barnard offers the bachelor's degree in a wide variety of fields. The Office of Resumed Education is responsible for adult continuing education. For the nearly one-half of undergraduates who commute, the campus can be reached by bus and subway.

The psychology department runs a toddler program for 24 children two mornings a week. Additional, private childcare facilities are available off campus.

Policies to Ensure Fairness to Women. The Personnel Officer has the part-time responsibility for policy pertaining to equal employment opportunity and handicapped accessibility. The Dean of Disabled Students is a voting member on policymaking committees. A publicized written sexual harassment policy exists only for the staff. Student complaints of sexual harassment are resolved through informal means.

Women in Leadership Positions. *Students.* Women hold all campus-wide student leadership positions.

Faculty. Fifty-eight percent of the 144 full-time faculty are women, a figure which is high even for women's colleges in this guide. There are 4 female faculty for every 100 female students.

Administrators. Most top-ranking administrators and department heads are women. Women hold the posts of President, chief student-life officer, chief development officer, head librarian, and director of athletics. Women chair 18 of 31 departments, including mathematics and chemistry. Half of the Board of Trustees is female. In a recent year, all four commencement speakers and recipients of honorary degrees were women; five of seven speakers at major campus-wide series were women.

Women and the Curriculum. Most bachelor's degrees awarded to women are in social sciences (32 percent), letters (17 percent), biology (14 percent), and psychology (13 percent); 4 percent are in such nontraditional fields as architecture, physical sciences, and mathematics.

The Women's Studies Program, begun in 1970 and directed by a woman who holds a full-time faculty appointment, has since 1979 offered an undergraduate major. It coordinates about 30 courses, through many different departments, including History of Women's Works; Women Writers of Spain: The Challenge of Change; Studies in Female Selfhood; Literature and Psychology; History of Women in the High Middle Ages; Women in the Third World; and Sex Roles in Cross-Cultural Perspectives. An official Women's Studies Committee works with the director of the program to expand the number of offerings on women and to collect and create new teaching materials on women. The education department provides some instruction specific to women.

The Barnard Women's Center, under the direction of a full-time administrator, and with a budget of $90,000, functions as a resource for Women's Studies, and provides a variety of services for undergraduates, for faculty, and for the New York community of feminists. The Women's Center staffs an excellent resource library, and organizes approximately 25 workshops, seminars, and conferences a year, in addition to the Feminist Scholars annual conference, which draws at least 1,000 participants.

Minority Women. Sixteen percent of the undergraduates are members of minority groups. One of three residence-hall directors is a minority woman, as is a staff member of the student counseling center. Residence-hall advisors are offered awareness-training on avoiding racism. Advocacy groups for minority women include the Barnard Organization of Black Women, the Caribbean Students Association, the Asian Students Association, and the Spanish-American Barnard Association.

Women and Athletics. The organized sports program offers intramural basketball and volleyball; sports clubs are available. The eight full-time and four part-time instructors are women. Intercollegiate sports offered are archery, basketball, cross-country, fencing, swimming and diving, tennis, track and field, and volleyball.

Housing and Student Organizations. Three women's dormitories on campus and additional coeducational dormitories in the neighborhood provide housing for 52 percent of students. There are no restrictions on visiting hours for members of the opposite sex.

In addition to the groups organized by minority women, women's advocacy groups include the Barnard Abortion and Reproductive Rights Network, the Flame (a Jewish club), the Jewish Association for College Youths, the Greek-American Organization, and Lesbians at Barnard.

Special Services and Programs for Women. *Health and Counseling.* The student health center is staffed by 6 physicians, of whom 4 are female, and 5 female health-care providers. The 5 members of the student counseling center staff are women. Counseling and treatment are available for gynecological problems, birth control, abortion, and rape and assault. Student health insurance covers abortion expenses.

Safety and Security. Measures consist of campus police without arrest authority, night-time escort and bus service to residence areas, emergency telephone and alarm system, instruction on self-defense and campus safety, and a campus rape crisis center. One rape and three assaults on women were reported for 1980–81.

Career. The career placement office provides workshops, lectures, and information on nontraditional occupations. It maintains files on alumnae careers for students' use and fosters networking between alumnae and students.

Special Features. The Barnard Library houses the 3,300-volume Overbury Collection of books and manuscripts by and about American women authors. The Women's Counseling Project, located on campus, is an independent referral and peer-counseling service specializing in health care, therapy, sexuality, and legal services for women in the New York metropolitan area. Barnard provides free space and office services, and the project has a close affiliation with the Women's Center.

Institutional Self-Description. "Attracting women students of demonstrated achievement and high promise, Barnard offers them a genuine climate of support; its administrative head has traditionally been a woman; faculty and administration are over 50 percent female; the college is committed to undergraduate teaching. Also, due to cross-registration with Columbia University, Barnard becomes an advocate for women in the surrounding academic community."

City University of New York, Brooklyn College

Brooklyn, NY 11210
Telephone: (212) 780-5671

| Women in Leadership | ★ Women and the |
| ★ faculty | Curriculum |

14,892 undergraduates

	Amer. Ind.	Asian Amer.	Blacks	Hispanics	Whites
F	122	277	1,813	599	5,290
M	61	333	1,162	629	4,471
%	1.3	4.2	20.3	8.5	66.7

 **AAUW NWSA**

Located in the heart of Brooklyn, this public, four-year college was established in 1930 as a branch of the City University of New York. It offers a diverse range of programs in such areas as education, humanities, science, performing arts, and contemporary studies, to the almost 20,000 students currently enrolled. Women are 55 percent of the undergraduate population of 14,892; 22 percent of women attend part-time. More than a third of undergraduate women are members of minority groups.

The college runs an evening session administered through the School of General Studies, as well as a weekend college, off-campus classes, and a summer session. An adult education program is also available. Sororities and fraternities are permitted on a limited basis. There is easy access to public transportation for students, all of whom commute, but the very limited on-campus parking facilities are available only to disabled students.

A small childcare facility, sponsored by the Agency for Child Development, is available to students enrolled in the two-year vocational training program.

Women in Leadership Positions. *Students.* In three recent years, no woman has held a campus-wide student leadership position.

Faculty. Of the 839 full-time faculty members, 31 percent are women. There are 4 female faculty for every 100 female students and 10 male faculty for every 100 male students.

Administrators. Women hold none of the top-level administrative positions. Of the 44 departments, eight are chaired by white women, one by a black woman and one by an Hispanic women. Women serve as deans of the schools of education and of graduate studies and continuing and higher education. In a recent year, one of three honorary degrees was awarded to a woman.

Women and the Curriculum. Most bachelor's degrees to women are awarded in education (25 percent), social sciences (19 percent), psychology (11 percent), and business (9 percent). About three percent of women students earn degrees in such nontraditional areas as computer science and mathematics.

The Women's Studies Program is one of the oldest in the country. A bachelor's degree may be earned in Women's Studies as part of a dual major. Twenty-two courses are offered through Women's Studies and other departments. Recent offerings include Creative Writing From a Feminist Perspective, Women and Film, The Jewish Woman, and The Black Woman In America. Committees are assigned to report on the inclusion of women in the curriculum and to monitor gender bias in course descriptions.

Women and Athletics. There is a high level of participation in the varied intercollegiate sports programs. All the women's teams were in tournament competition in 1980. Women are 58 percent of the 190 intercollegiate athletes and 30 percent of the 226 intramural athletes. Three of the 22 paid coaches for intercollegiate sports are women. Intercollegiate sports in which women compete are archery, basketball, cross-country, fencing, softball, swimming, tennis, track and field, and volleyball.

Special Services and Programs for Women. *Health and Counseling.* The college does not have a student health service. A counseling center staffed by two women and one man offers counseling in rape and assault, birth control, and abortion.

Safety and Security. Measures consist of campus police without arrest authority, a night-time escort service for women, and a campus-wide emergency telephone system. High-intensity lighting is being installed. Four assaults (one on a woman) and one rape were reported for 1980–81.

Other. A full-time, salaried director supervises the Women's Center, which serves undergraduate students and community women. The center sponsors a peer counseling group.

Institutional Self-Description. None provided.

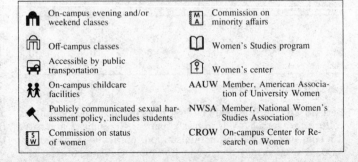

🏛	On-campus evening and/or weekend classes	Ⓜ🄰	Commission on minority affairs
🏛	Off-campus classes	📖	Women's Studies program
🚐	Accessible by public transportation	👤	Women's center
🧑‍🤝‍🧑	On-campus childcare facilities	AAUW	Member, American Association of University Women
✎	Publicly communicated sexual harassment policy, includes students	NWSA	Member, National Women's Studies Association
Ⓢ🅆	Commission on status of women	CROW	On-campus Center for Research on Women

City University of New York, College of Staten Island

130 Stuyvesant Place
Staten Island, NY 10301
Telephone: (212) 390-7733

Women in Leadership   ★ **Women and the Curriculum**
 ★★★ students
    ★ faculty

9,187 undergraduates

	Amer. Ind.	Asian Amer.	Blacks	Hispanics	Whites
F	54	92	872	375	3,028
M	23	254	695	354	3,337
%	0.8	3.8	17.2	8.0	70.1

 NWSA

The College of Staten Island, a public four-year institution, was formed in 1976 with the merger of Staten Island Community College and Richmond College. As part of the City University of New York, the College of Staten Island offers a broad range of two-year, baccalaureate, and master's programs in technology-related and liberal arts fields. Of the more than 9,000 undergraduates, 49 percent are women; 41 percent of women attend part-time. The median age of undergraduates is 24.

The college offers evening and off-campus classes, as well as a weekend program, independent study, and a summer session. Continuing Education serves adult students. All students commute and there is both easy access to public transportation and on-campus parking for a fee.

Daytime childcare is available on campus to both full- and part-time students. Twenty-five percent of all students' requests can be met. Payment is based on a fixed daily fee. Private childcare facilties are available near campus.

Policies to Ensure Fairness to Women. A full-time Affirmative Action Officer is responsible for policy concerning equal employment opportunity, access for the handicapped, and sex equity. A City University-wide policy on sexual harassment of students, faculty, and staff is currently being formulated.

Women in Leadership Positions. *Students.* Opportunities for women students to serve in campus-wide leadership positions are outstanding. In recent years, women have twice been president of the student body, presiding officer of the student governing body, and editor-in-chief of the campus newspaper.

Faculty. Almost 29 percent of full-time faculty are women, a proportion above the national average. Recent information from the campus indicates that there are 2 Hispanic, 4 Asian American, and 10 black women on the full-time faculty. There are 3 female faculty for every 100 female students and 8 male faculty for every 100 male students.

Administrators. Of the eight top-level administrators, the Dean of Students is a woman. Women constitute 30 percent of the faculty senate and 39 percent of the all-college personnel committee. Women chair seven of 17 departments or units: mechanical technology, economics, political science, English, performing and creative arts, philosophy, nursing, and student services.

Women and the Curriculum. Most bachelor's degrees earned by women are in psychology (34 percent), social sciences (18 percent), interdisiciplinary studies (14 percent), and health (13 percent). Four percent earn degrees in such nontraditional fields as engineering and mathematics. Programs encourage women to enter technology-related areas. About 80 percent of all students in internships and cooperative education assignments are women. Most of the two-year degrees earned by women are in health technology (43 percent), arts and science (37 percent), and busi-

ness (16 percent). About 1 percent of these women earn degrees in such nontraditional areas as mechanical engineering and natural science technologies.

The Women's Studies Program, under a full-time, permanent faculty member, offers a B.A. and a minor. Nineteen undergraduate courses, including Sex Roles and Law, Women and Work, and Female Sexuality, are available through the Women's Studies Program and five other departments. Racism and the curriculum is a topic of faculty workshops. The departments of business, education, and nursing provide instruction on some matters specific to women.

Women and Athletics. Opportunities in the intercollegiate program are limited; there are ten sports in the intramural program. Women are 25 percent of the intercollegiate athletes and 25 percent of intramural athletes. Three of eight paid coaches are women. The intercollegiate sports offered are softball, tennis, and volleyball.

Special Services and Programs for Women. *Health and Counseling.* The student health service provides medical treatment for gynecological problems and birth control. The 4 physicians are men; 3 other health-care providers are women. The counseling service, staffed by 17 men and 10 women, offers counseling of particular concern to women. Five of the staff are minority women.

Safety and Security. Measures consist of campus police with no arrest authority, and a mobile patrol in parking areas. No rapes or assault were reported for 1980–81.

Career. Services include speakers and nonracist/nonsexist printed materials on nontraditional occupations and fields of study, as well as contacts between alumnae and female students.

Other. A women's lecture series, co-sponsored by Women's Studies and community organizations, and a project to build mathematics skills are available. *All Ways A Woman,* a student periodical, gives students experience in publishing.

Institutional Self-Description. ''The Women's Studies Program is a well-developed program with many faculty who have achieved national reputations in the field. Women students will find a college community capable of supporting their concerns and interests. A variety of programs and schedules is available to meet a woman's education needs.''

City University of New York, Herbert H. Lehman College

Bedford Park Boulevard West
Bronx, NY 10468
Telephone: (212) 960-8375

Women in Leadership
 ★★ faculty

7,838 undergraduates

	Amer. Ind.	Asian Amer.	Blacks	Hispanics	Whites
F	34	150	1,634	1,327	1,844
M	46	96	775	705	1,134
%	1.0	3.2	31.1	26.2	38.5

 AAUW

Formerly the Bronx campus of Hunter College, this branch of the City University of New York system became coeducational in 1951; it was established as a separate four-year, liberal arts college in 1968. Lehman now offers bachelor's and master's programs in a variety of fields. Adult continuing education courses are offered through the School of General Studies. Alternative scheduling includes evening and summer session classes and a Saturday course. Off-campus class locations are also available.

Some 9,700 students attend this urban college, 7,838 of them undergraduates. Sixty-four percent of the undergraduates are women, 26 percent of whom attend part-time. The median age of all undergraduates is 26, with 31 percent of full-time female undergraduates over age 25 and 5 percent over age 40. All students commute, and the campus is easily accessible by public transportation. On-campus parking is available at a fee.

Private childcare facilities are located near the campus.

Policies to Ensure Fairness to Women. The Director and Assistant Director of Personnel have part-time responsibility for matters relating to equal-employment-opportunity, sex-equity-for-students and handicapped-access legislation. A campus policy prohibiting sexual harassment has been communicated in writing to students, faculty, and staff. A Committee on the Status of Women is appointed by and responsible to the university Chancellor. The Committee prepares an annual report which is distributed to the campus community and which includes the concerns of minority women.

Women in Leadership Positions. *Students.* There are five campus-wide student leadership positions. In recent years, women have served twice as president of the student court and once as editor-in-chief of the campus newspaper. Women also head eleven of the 19 campus honorary societies.

Faculty. Forty-one percent of the 392 full-time faculty are women, a proportion well above average for public four-year colleges in this guide. There are 4 female faculty for every 100 female students and 10 male faculty for every 100 male students.

Administrators. Except for the head librarian, the top-level positions are held by men. Women chair ten of 28 departments, including physics and astronomy, anthropology, sociology, psychology, and political science. A woman also serves as Dean of Humanities. Thirty-seven percent of the faculty senate, 33 percent of the tenure and promotions committee, and 25 percent of the trustees are women.

Women and the Curriculum. Most women earn degrees in health professions (20 percent), social sciences (20 percent), psychology (14 percent), and education (12 percent). Three percent of women graduate in the nontraditional areas of mathematics or physical sciences; in physical sciences, women graduates outnumber the men. In experiential learning programs—internships, cooperative education, and science field service—women are 60 percent of the students.

Seven courses on women are available through such departments as sociology, classics, English, and history. Recent offerings include Women in Antiquity, Women and Health, The Politics of Women's Liberation in the U.S. and Abroad, Cross-Cultural Perspectives on Sex Roles in Society, Human Sexuality, and Sex Roles and Attitudes in Secondary Education. The departments of education, nursing, and social work offer instruction on some matters specific to women.

Minority Women. Sixty-three percent of female undergraduates are members of minority groups, mainly black and Hispanic. Two advocacy organizations for minority women are the Black Women's Club and the Organizacion Mujeres Hispanas. Two black women chair academic departments and six black and five Hispanic women are members of the faculty senate.

Women and Athletics. Opportunites for women to participate in organized team and individual sports are somewhat limited. Sixteen percent of the intramural athletes and half of the 200 intercollegiate athletes are women, as are five of the eleven paid coaches for intercollegiate sports. Most women's varsity teams participated in recent tournament competitions. The intercollegiate sports offered are basketball, cross-country, softball, swimming, tennis, track and field, and volleyball.

Special Services and Programs for Women. *Health and Counseling.* There is no student health service; a student counseling center is staffed by four women and one man. No information was provided on counseling services specific to women.

Safety and Security. Measures consist of campus police without arrest authority, high-intensity lighting, self-defense courses for women, and information sessions on campus safety and crime prevention. No rapes were reported for 1980–81; no information on the incidence of assaults was provided.

Career. Services include workshops and nonsexist/nonracist printed material on nontraditional occupations, as well as lectures and panels by women employed in these areas.

Other. Student Activities operates the campus Women's Center, run by a student volunteer on a part-time basis. Some 300 women are served by the center, most of them undergraduates. Thirty-five percent of its active participants are minority women. Lesbians at Lehman and the Nursing Society are advocacy groups.

Institutional Self-Description. "Since its founding as a women's institution of higher learning in 1931, Lehman College has maintained an educationally stimulating and welcome atmosphere for women. Women students have always excelled in nontraditional as well as traditional career areas."

City University of New York, Hunter College
695 Park Avenue, New York, NY 10021
Telephone: (212) 570-5236

Women in Leadership ★★ faculty	★ Women and the Curriculum

12,121 undergraduates

Complete enrollment information unavailable.

🏠 🚐 📖 AAUW NWSA

Established in 1870 to educate young women who wished to become teachers, Hunter College is a public, coeducational college within the City University of New York system. Some 18,000 students enroll, 12,121 of them undergraduates. Women are 76 percent of the undergraduates; 26 percent of women attend part-time.

Hunter offers bachelor's degrees in the liberal arts, sciences, and pre-professional areas; master's programs are also available. Alternative scheduling includes evening classes, a summer session, and self-paced/contract learning. The Center for Lifelong Learning sponsors continuing education. Located in the heart of Manhattan, Hunter is easily accessible by public transportation. Though almost all students commute, a coeducational residence is available for the 3 percent who live on campus.

Private childcare facilities are located near the college.

Policies to Ensure Fairness to Women. The Provost is responsible for policy on equal employment opportunity, sex equity for students, and handicapped accessibility.

Women in Leadership Positions. *Students.* In recent years, women have held 29 percent of the positions, including one-year terms as president of the student body and presiding officer of the student court, and a three-year term as head of the residence-hall council.

Faculty. Forty-four percent of the 621 full-time faculty are women. There are 4 female faculty for every 100 female students and 16 male faculty for every 100 male students.

Administrators. The President and Dean of Students are women; all other top administrative positions are held by men. The Dean of Nursing is a woman and women chair nine of 30 departments; including biology, classics, history, and nursing.

Women and the Curriculum. Most women earn bachelor's degrees in the health professions (27 percent), social sciences (20 percent), psychology (10 percent), communications (9 percent), fine arts (7 percent), and letters (7 percent). Four percent of women graduates major in such nontraditional areas as mathematics, computer science, and physical sciences. The Office of the Dean of Students sponsors a program to build skills in mathematics. Women are half of the students in cooperative education and internship programs.

The Women's Studies Program, chaired by a full-time, permanent faculty member, offers a minor and the B.A. as a collateral major. Some 15 courses are available through Women's Studies and such departments as anthropology, art, Black and Puerto Rican studies, history, political science, and psychology. Recent offerings include Women in the Developing World; Women, Law, and Poverty; Afro-American Women; and Women in the Arts. Hunter's Women's Studies Program has written the first interdisciplinary textbook for use in introductory courses. *Women's Realities, Women's Choices* was written by nine faculty, representing eight disciplines. A faculty committee oversees the Women's Studies Program and works to develop courses on women in traditional departments. The departments of education, physical education, nursing, and business include instruction on some matters specific to women. Faculty workshops are offered on sexism and the curriculum.

Women and Athletics. Women have limited opportunities to participate in organized competitve sports. There are four sports in the intramural program. Forty percent of intramural and 50 percent of varsity athletes are women, as are half of the 22 paid varsity coaches. Intercollegiate sports offered are basketball, cross-country, fencing, softball, swimming, and track.

Special Services and Programs for Women. *Health and Counseling.* No physicians are retained by the student health service; 1 of 3 other health-care providers is a woman. No medical treatment specific to women is available. The regular student health insurance covers maternity at no extra cost. The counseling center, staffed by 11 women and 6 men, offers birth control, abortion, and rape and assault counseling. Staff receive training in the avoidance of sex-role stereotyping and racial bias.

Safety and Security. Measures consist of campus police without arrest authority, some night-time escorts for women, self-defense courses for women, and a rape crisis center. No information was provided by the college on the incidence of rapes and assaults.

Career. Hunter offers the Tishman Seminars for women college graduates reentering the job market and an evening course for adults on career choice and transition. Students are encouraged to consider nontraditional careers through workshops, guest speakers, and nonsexist/nonracist literature.

Other. A Women's Center is planned. The Office of the Dean of Students sponsors assertiveness training. Lesbians Rising meets on campus. Counseling workshops and evening scheduling of Women's Studies courses assist the returning woman student.

Institutional Self-Description. "Hunter College offers a long tradition of women's higher education in the liberal arts, a concern about and scholarships for reentry women, an active Women's Studies Program, full-scale general and academic advising, a career counseling and placement service, and specific health science, nursing, and social work programs."

Clarkson College of Technology
Potsdam, NY 13676
Telephone: (315) 268-6400

★ **Women and the Curriculum**

3,132 undergraduates

	Amer. Ind.	Asian Amer.	Blacks	Hispanics	Whites
F	1	0	1	2	495
M	8	7	4	9	2,544
%	0.3	0.2	0.2	0.4	99.0

Clarkson College of Technology is a private, non-sectarian institution that prepares 3,420 men and women for careers in engineering, management, and the sciences. Women, first admitted in 1964, now constitute 16 pecent of 3,132 undergraduates, and recent data suggest that their number continues to grow. Virtually all undergraduate women attend full-time. The median age of students is 20. Clarkson College offers undergraduate, professional, and graduate degree programs. Sixteen percent of students commute; on-campus parking is available without charge.

Private childcare facilities are located close to campus.

Policies to Ensure Fairness to Women. The Personnel Director and an assistant have responsibility part-time for monitoring complaince with sex-equity and access-for-the-handicapped laws. Only the Personnel Director has policymaking power. Complaints of sexual harassment are resolved through a formal grievance procedure.

Women in Leadership Positions. *Students.* During a recent three-year period, women occasionally held one of the nine student leadership positions. Women head two of 13 honorary societies.

Faculty. Women are 7 percent of the faculty. The ratio of female faculty to female students is 3 to 100; the ratio of male faculty to male students is 7 to 100.

Administrators. Men hold all the top-level positions except head librarian. All department heads and deans are men, and female representation on the Board of Trustees is minimal.

Women and the Curriculum. Nearly half of the bachelor's degrees awarded to women are in engineering, 31 percent are in business, and 16 percent are in mathematics and physical sciences. There are no courses on women.

Women and Athletics. A good variety of intramural sports is available to women. Twenty-two percent of the intercollegiate athletes are women. The intramural program allows women the opportunity to compete in team sports as water polo and ice hockey. Of four paid varsity coaches, one is a woman. Women's intercollegiate sports are basketball, hockey, lacrosse, tennis, and volleyball.

Housing and Student Organizations. Eighty-four percent of all undergraduates live on campus in either single-sex or coeducational dormitories, in addition to housing provided by sororities and fraternities. Eighteen percent of the undergraduate women, including a few minority women, belong to sororities.

Special Services and Programs for Women. *Health and Counseling.* The student health center is staffed by a male physician, aided by a female health-care provider. The student counseling center employs one female and two male counselors. Services specific to women include treatment and counseling for gynecological problems, birth control, and rape and assault. Student health insurance covers the cost of abortions, and abortion counseling is also available.

Safety and Security. Measures include local police protection, night-time escorts, high-intensity lighting, and self-defense courses. No rapes or assaults were reported for 1980–81.

Other. The Society of Women Engineers is the women's advocacy group on campus; it has a membership of 150. A new

---

🛉	On-campus evening and/or weekend classes	M/A	Commission on minority affairs
🏛	Off-campus classes	📖	Women's Studies program
🚌	Accessible by public transportation	⚲	Women's center
🧑‍🧒	On-campus childcare facilities	AAUW	Member, American Association of University Women
✎	Publicly communicated sexual harassment policy, includes students	NWSA	Member, National Women's Studies Association
S/W	Commission on status of women	CROW	On-campus Center for Research on Women

Women's Student Activities Program gives administrative support to the society's lecture series for women.

Institutional Self-Description. "Women students were first admitted to Clarkson in 1964. In 1980–81, there were approximately 700 women enrolled. Through the years they have consistently performed academically as well as or better than male students in the demanding pre-professional programs. Particularly in engineering, women graduates have frequently been offered slightly higher starting salaries."

College of New Rochelle
Castle Place, New Rochelle, NY 10801
Telephone: (914) 632-5300

Women in Leadership	★ Women and the
★★★ students	Curriculum
★★★ faculty	
★★★ administrators	

3,213 undergraduates

	Amer. Ind.	Asian Amer.	Blacks	Hispanics	Whites
F	0	37	1,066	276	1,301
M	0	1	264	95	147
%	0.0	1.2	41.7	11.6	45.4

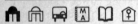

Founded by the Ursuline Order in 1904 as a liberal arts college for women, the College of New Rochelle has become a coeducational, non-denominational institution in the Roman Catholic tradition. The college attracts 4,070 students annually to its main campus in the racially mixed community of New Rochelle. Eighty-four percent of the 3,213 undergraduates are women, and 14 percent of women attend part-time. The median age of students is 35.

The college offers a range of undergraduate, professional, and graduate degree programs. Adult education courses are given by the School of New Resources, with branches in New Rochelle and the Bronx. Alternative schedules include evening classes given on and off campus and self-paced/contract learning. Seventy-three percent of all students commute; dormitories are available only for women enrolled in the School of Arts and Sciences and the School of Nursing. The main campus, located near New York City, is easily reached by public transportation. Parking on campus is free.

Private childcare facilities are available close to campus and accommodate 57 students' children, at a flat rate of $325 per semester. Children of faculty and staff are accepted providing there is room for them.

Policies to Ensure Fairness to Women. The Vice President of Academic Affairs assumes responsibility part-time for reviewing policies and practices regarding sex-equity and handicapped-access legislation, and has policymaking power. Complaints of sexual harassment are handled informally and confidentially.

Women in Leadership Positions. *Students.* Women hold all campus-wide leadership positions and head the sole honorary society.

Faculty. Women are 68 percent of the 80 full-time faculty, a proportion well above the national average. There are 2 female faculty for every 100 female students and 6 male faculty for every 100 male students.

Administrators. Most key administrators are women, with the exception of the chief academic officer, chief business officer, and chief planning officer. Women head 14 of 20 departments, as well as the School of Arts and Sciences, the School of Nursing, and the School of New Resources. Women are 15 of 27 trustees.

Women and the Curriculum. Approximately half the bachelor's degrees awarded to women are in interdisciplinary studies, other popular majors being psychology and fine arts. One percent of women earn degrees in nontraditional fields.

A Women's Studies Program awards the B.A. degree. It offers 12 courses on women, including Theology and Sexuality, Sappho and Lyric Poetry, and Sex Roles in Contemporary Society. A permanent faculty member serves as director of the program. An official committee seeks to expand the number of courses offered on women and encourages the collection of appropriate resource materials.

Minority Women. Minority women make up 43 percent of all students. A Committee on Minority Affairs addresses the concerns of minority women. Two advocacy groups, Amica and Unlimited, each have 30 members, respectively black and Hispanic. Nearly half of the participants in the Women's Center are members of minority groups. Residence-hall staff attend workshops on racism. One department head, 1 trustee, and 3 full-time faculty members are black women.

Women and Athletics. Intercollegiate and intramural sports programs, available for women only, compare favorably to those offered at women's colleges. There are special facilities for water ballet and synchronized swimming. Team and individual intercollegiate sports draw 68 participants; the three paid varsity coaches are women. Intercollegiate sports offered are basketball, softball, swimming, tennis, and volleyball.

Special Services and Programs for Women. *Health and Counseling.* The student health center's staff consists of four female health-care providers. The student counseling center employs four female and two male counselors. Health services specific to women include counseling on gynecological problems, birth control, abortion, and rape and assault. Information on medical treatment specific to women was not provided.

Safety and Security. Measures include local and campus police protection, high-intensity lighting, an emergency telephone system, and a self-defense course for women. Information on the incidence of rapes and assaults was not provided.

Career. The Career Development Center provides assertiveness training for women, lectures by women in nontraditional fields, and networks with alumnae. The Learning Skills Center offers a mathematics skills course. Faculty are offered panels and workshops on the relationships among sex, race, and the choice of careers.

Other. An active Women's Center, administered by a full-time, salaried director, sponsors a women's lecture series. Half of the students in adult education classes are reentry women; faculty are offered programs addressed to the needs of returning women students.

Institutional Self-Description. "Women might choose the College of New Rochelle because of the positive and encouraging atmosphere in which they are urged to develop their full potential, free from the stereotypes of what women can and should do. There are women role models on the faculty and administration and many men with supportive attitudes."

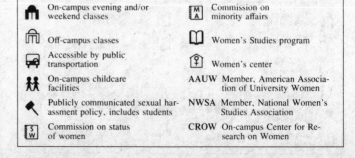

🏠	On-campus evening and/or weekend classes	M/A	Commission on minority affairs
🏛	Off-campus classes	📖	Women's Studies program
🚐	Accessible by public transportation	🏳	Women's center
👫	On-campus childcare facilities	AAUW	Member, American Association of University Women
✒	Publicly communicated sexual harassment policy, includes students	NWSA	Member, National Women's Studies Association
S/W	Commission on status of women	CROW	On-campus Center for Research on Women

College of Saint Rose

432 Western Avenue, Albany, NY 12203
Telephone: (518) 454-5111

Women in Leadership
★★★ faculty
★★★ administrators

1,495 undergraduates

	Amer. Ind.	Asian Amer.	Blacks	Hispanics	Whites
F	0	1	33	5	1,054
M	0	1	14	3	382
%	0.0	0.1	3.2	0.5	96.2

Founded in 1920 as a private liberal arts college for women, the College of Saint Rose is now a coeducational, non-denominational institution with a total enrollment of 2,488 students. Nearly three-fourths of the 1,495 undergraduates are women, and 23 percent of women attend part-time. About 38 percent of all undergraduate women are over age 26.

The institution offers a range of undergraduate, professional, and graduate degree programs, in addition to a substantial continuing education program. Fifty-five percent of the undergraduates commute to the suburban campus; they have access to public transportation and free parking on campus.

Private childcare facilities are located close to campus.

Policies to Ensure Fairness to Women. The Administrative Assistant to the President and the Chairperson of the Affirmative Action Committee have part-time responsibility for supervising policies and practices regarding sex-equity legislation. The Chairperson has additional policymaking responsibilities in dealing with matters of employment. The Director of Academic Counseling has the part-time responsibility for monitoring compliance with laws pertaining to access for the handicapped.

Women in Leadership Positions. *Students.* Though nearly 75 percent of students are women, women have held only one-third of the leadership positions in recent years. The two honorary societies are led by women.

Faculty. Sixty-four percent of the faculty are women, a proportion well above the national average. There are 7 female faculty for every 100 female students and 15 male faculty for every 100 male students.

Administrators. Women hold half of the key administrative positions: chief business officer, head librarian, director of athletics, and chief planning officer. Five of six departments are chaired by women; the two deans are men. Nine of 25 trustees are women.

Women and the Curriculum. Women are awarded three-fourths of the bachelor's degrees; nearly half of these are in education. In a recent year, three women and no men earned mathematics degrees.

The humanities and social sciences departments offer five courses on women, including American Feminism, Spanish Women Writers, and The Legal Status of Women.

Women and Athletics. No information was provided on intramural and club sports. Women make up 56 percent of athletes in the intercollegiate program; one of the two paid varsity coaches is a woman. Intercollegiate sports are basketball, bowling, softball, swimming, tennis, and volleyball.

Housing and Student Organizations. Single-sex and coeducational dormitories house 45 percent of the undergraduates. Restricted hours for visitors of the opposite sex prevail in all the dormitories. Twenty-three of 29 residence-hall staff are white women. Awareness-training on racism, birth control, and sex education is offered to staff.

Special Services and Programs for Women. *Health and Counseling.* The health service is staffed by one male physician and four female health-care providers. The counseling center employs one female counselor. No services specific to women are provided.

Safety and Security. Measures include campus and local police protection, night-time escorts for women, self-defense courses for women, and a rape crisis center. No information was provided on the incidence of rapes and assaults.

Career. Students are offered information on nontraditional careers, lectures by women employed in these fields, and contacts with alumnae.

Institutional Self-Description. "The College of Saint Rose offers special adult student counseling, evening degrees for part-time undergraduate and graduate students, and convenient evening services for adult students. The campus is small and accessible by public transportation. Over 1,500 adult students, 70 percent of whom are women, now attend classes."

Columbia-Greene Community College

P.O. Box 1000, Hudson, NY 12534
Telephone: (518) 828-4181

Women in Leadership
★★ faculty

714 undergraduates

	Amer. Ind.	Asian Amer.	Blacks	Hispanics	Whites
F	0	1	9	1	351
M	1	0	8	1	342
%	0.1	0.1	2.4	0.3	97.1

A public, two-year college, Columbia-Greene occupies a rural campus near Albany. There are 1,214 students. Women are 51 percent of the 714 undergraduates; 27 percent of women attend part-time.

The college offers a range of two-year degree and certificate programs in the liberal arts, business, communications/media, health, public service, and environmental and engineering/technology. Alternative scheduling includes off-campus day and evening classes and five summer sessions. Free on-campus parking is available to students, all of whom commute.

Campus childcare facilities, accommodating 25 children of students, are open daily from 8 a.m. to 5 p.m. There are private childcare facilities near the campus.

Policies to Ensure Fairness to Women. Three administrative officers are assigned part-time to monitor compliance with equal-employment-opportunity and handicapped-access legislation. An informal and confidential campus mechanism resolves complaints of sexual harassment.

Women in Leadership Positions. *Students.* Of three campus-wide student leadership positions, the presidency of the student senate was held by a woman during one of three recent years.

Faculty. Thirty-seven percent of the 35 full-time faculty members are women, a proportion above the average for public two-year colleges. There are 5 female faculty for every 100 female students and 7 male faculty for every 100 male students.

Administrators. Of eight major administrative positions, the chief student-life officer is a woman. A woman chairs the liberal studies division; a woman was one of five speakers in a recent campus-wide lecture series.

Women and the Curriculum. Most women take degrees in liberal arts and sciences (54 percent), with fewer numbers majoring in business/commerical and public services. Women receive 95 percent of internships available in the human services division.

A course on Women in Literature is offered in the liberal studies division. Workshops on the needs of reentry women are offered to faculty.

Women and Athletics. One-third of intercollegiate and intramural athletes are women; three of nine paid intercollegiate coaches are women. Intercollegiate sports include women's basketball, women's softball, coeducational tennis, and women's volleyball.

Special Services and Programs for Women. *Health and Counseling.* There is no student health service; a student counseling center is staffed by two men. No information was provided on the health and counseling services available.

Safety and Security. Measures include campus police, high-intensity lighting, emergency alarms at isolated locations, and non-credit self-defense courses. No rapes or assaults were reported on campus for 1980–81.

Other. The community services division administers the adult education program, which attracts 516 reentry women students. Student Activities sponsors a film series, "The Roles of Men and Women."

Institutional Self-Description. "Campus population is 64 percent female, with a high proportion of reentry women. Daycare services are available, and offices are staffed in the evening. The environment is supportive because of the college's small size, individualized attention, and the services of a Learning Resources Center to assist reentry learners. Reading and study skills courses are available as well."

Cornell University
Ithaca, NY 14853
Telephone: (607) 256-7596

★★★ **Women and the Curriculum**

★★ **Women and Athletics**

7,160 undergraduates

	Amer. Ind.	Asian Amer.	Blacks	Hispanics	Whites
F	3	139	172	68	1,982
M	17	242	209	104	3,966
%	0.3	5.3	5.3	2.4	83.1

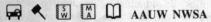 **AAUW NWSA**

Established in 1865 as a combination land-grant and privately-endowed institution, Cornell University, overlooking Cayuga Lake in Ithaca, provides its 10,079 students with a broad array of undergraduate, graduate, and professional programs of study. The Continuing Education Center serves the adult student. A summer session is available.

Of the 7,160 undergraduates in the Endowed College, 34 percent are women, almost all of whom attend full-time. The median age of undergraduates is 21. For the students who live off campus or commute, the university is accessible by public transportation. On-campus parking is available.

Private childcare facilities are available near campus.

Policies to Ensure Fairness to Women. The Provost and Director of Equal Opportunity are responsible for policy on employment, sex equity for students, and handicapped accessibility. Three other full-time officers monitor compliance. A published policy prohibits sexual harassment. Complaints are handled informally and confidentially. The Committee on the Status of Women, which includes students as voting members, reports to the Provost. The Committee on Minority Affairs addresses the concerns of minority women.

Women in Leadership Positions. *Students.* Opportunities for women students to assume campus leadership are considerably below the average for private research institutions in this guide.

In a recent year, a woman was president of the senior class. Women head six of the eleven honorary societies.

Faculty. Women are 13 percent of a full-time faculty of 775. According to a recent report, the full-time faculty includes 1 Asian American, 1 Hispanic, and 3 black women. There are 4 female faculty for every 100 female students and 14 male faculty for every 100 male students.

Administrators. Men occupy all higher administrative positions. Of the 85 departments, a women chairs Asian studies. The Dean of the Graduate School is female. Women make up 20 percent of the Board of Trustees (including two black and two Hispanic women) and 33 percent of the regents (including a black woman).

Women and the Curriculum. Most women who graduate with bachelor's degrees from the Endowed College major in the social sciences, engineering, the biological sciences, and psychology. Twenty-three percent of women major in such nontraditional areas as architecture, engineering, mathematics, and the physical sciences, a proportion making Cornell unique among private research universities in this guide.

The Women's Studies Program, one of the two oldest in the country, offers an undergraduate minor, an individualized major through Arts and Sciences, and an interdisciplinary graduate minor. More than 30 undergraduate and graduate courses originate in Women's Studies or are cross-listed with the program. Recent offerings include Writing as Women, Major Nineteenth-Century Female Novelists, Anthropology of Women, The Biological Basis of Sex Differences, and Women in American Society. An official committee continues to develop the Women's Studies Program. The School of Business provides instruction on the discrimination that women face in the workplace.

Minority Women. Of 2,414 undergraduate women, 7 percent are black, 6 percent Asian American, 3 percent Hispanic, and less than 1 percent American Indian. Two of the 21 residence-hall directors are minority women. Residence-hall staff are offered awareness-training on racism. The university reports COSEP as a group where minority women would find support from other women.

Women and Athletics. Intramural and intercollegiate programs provide excellent opportunities for organized, competitive, individual and team sports. The university reports special facilities for intramural ice hockey, polo, skiing, and fencing. Thirty-seven percent of intercollegiate athletes are women. Twelve of 66 paid intercollegiate coaches are female. The intercollegiate sports offered are basketball, bowling, crew, cross-country, fencing, field hockey, gymnastics, ice hockey, lacrosse, polo, skiing, swimming and diving, tennis, track and field, and volleyball.

Housing and Student Organizations. Forty-one percent of undergraduates live on campus. Women's and coeducational dormitories and housing for married students and single parents with children are available. A married woman student whose spouse is not enrolled may live in married students' housing. Residence halls do not restrict hours for visitors of the opposite sex. Thirteen of 21 residence-hall directors are female. Staff are offered awareness-training on racism and birth control.

Social sororities and fraternities provide housing for their members. Organizations which serve as advocates for women on campus include Society of Women Engineers, Women's Law Coalition, GAYPAC, and Feminist Alliance.

Special Services and Programs for Women. *Health and Counseling.* The student health service provides some medical attention specific to women, including gynecological and birth control treatment. The regular student health insurance covers abortion and maternity at no extra charge. Four of 9 physicians in the health service are female, as are 6 of 9 other health-care providers. Half the counselors in the counseling service are women. Students have access to abortion and rape and assault counseling.

Safety and Security. Campus police have arrest authority. Nighttime bus service to residence areas, high-intensity lighting, emergency telephone system, information sessions on safety and crime prevention, and a rape crisis center are available. Information on the incidence of rapes and assaults on women was not provided.

Career. Career workshops, role model lectures, and printed material about women in nontraditional occupations and fields of study, as well as a program of contacts between alumnae and students are provided by the university.

Other. The Dean of Students' office sponsors a telephone line of information, referral, and support. Women's Studies sponsors women's lecture series. Assertiveness training is available through the personnel department.

Institutional Self-Description. "For over a century, Cornell University's dedication to excellence in teaching and research has been widely recognized. The campus is located in an incredibly beautiful area filled with lakes and waterfalls. Students who enjoy the challenges of learning and a diversity of students, faculty, and programs will succeed at Cornell."

Dutchess Community College
Pendell Road
Poughkeepsie, NY 12601
Telephone: (914) 471-4500

Women in Leadership
★ faculty
★ administrators

3,918 undergraduates

	Amer. Ind.	Asian Amer.	Blacks	Hispanics	Whites
F	3	11	117	33	1,811
M	5	8	266	76	1,556
%	0.2	0.5	9.9	2.8	86.6

Some 5,995 students attend this public, two-year commuter college. Slightly more than half of the 3,918 matriculated students are women, one-third of whom attend part-time. The median age of all students is 25.

Degree programs are available in such fields as arts and sciences, business, public service, health, natural science, and mechanical/engineering technologies. Alternative full-time and part-time schedules include off-campus day and evening classes and a five-week summer session. Public transportation and free on-campus parking are available.

Low-cost daytime childcare facilities can accommodate up to 70 children of students, faculty, and staff. Private childcare facilities are available near the campus.

Policies to Ensure Fairness to Women. The Dean of Planning and Information Services has part-time responsibility for policy relating to equal-employment-opportunity, sex-equity, and handicapped-access legislation. A written campus policy prohibits sexual harassment of students, faculty, and staff; complaints are resolved through a formal campus grievance procedure. An Equal Employment Opportunity Committee, appointed by and responsible to the President, meets regularly and prepares an annual report for distribution to the campus community. This committee addresses the concerns of women, including minority women.

Women in Leadership Positions. *Students.* During a recent three-year period, women held nearly one-fourth of the student leadership positions, including president of the student body, senate, court, and union, editor-in-chief of the campus newspaper, and manager of the campus radio station. Thirteen of 20 student senators are women; in two recent years, women have served as student representatives to the Board of Trustees.

Faculty. One-third of the 132 full-time faculty are women, an average proportion for two-year colleges, but well above average for all colleges nationwide. There are 3 female faculty for every 100 female students and 6 male faculty for every 100 male students. The college reports 1 Asian American woman on the full-time faculty.

Administrators. Of the seven top administrators, the director of institutional research and the chief business officer are women. Women chair three of 13 departments: performing arts and communication, human sciences, and mathematics.

Women and the Curriculum. Most women major in health (46 percent), business (24 percent), arts and sciences (16 percent), and public service technologies (10 percent). Women hold 85 percent of student internships.

Three courses on women are offered by the departments of English and humanities, history/government/economics, and behavioral sciences: Women in 20th-Century American Literature, Psychology of Women, and A Study of the American Woman. The division of social work provides training on services for battered spouses, displaced homemakers, and childcare, while the School of Business offers instruction on problems encountered by women in the workplace.

Women and Athletics. Opportunities for women to participate in competitive sports are limited to four team sports. Thirty-one percent of intercollegiate athletes and 42 percent of intramural athletes are women, as are all the club-sport athletes. Two of the three paid coaches for varsity sports are women, and all women's varsity teams play in tournament competition. Intercollegiate sports for women include basketball, softball, and volleyball.

Special Services and Programs for Women. *Health and Counseling.* The student health service, staffed by 1 male physician and 2 female health-care providers, does not provide medical treatment specific to women. One woman and 1 man staff the student counseling center. Information on couseling services was not provided.

Safety and Security. Measures consist of campus police without arrest authority, and high-intensity lighting in all areas. No rapes or assaults on women were reported for 1980–81.

Career. Services include workshops on nontraditional fields, lectures by women employed in these areas, and a program to establish contacts between alumnae and female students.

Other. The Office of Handicapped and Disabled Services serves the 245 handicapped students. A 12-member women's consciousness-raising group meets on campus.

Institutional Self-Description. None provided.

D'Youville College
320 Porter Ave., Buffalo, NY 14201
Telephone: (716) 886-8100

Women in Leadership
★★ students
★★★ faculty
★★ administrators

1,443 undergraduates

	Amer. Ind.	Asian Amer.	Blacks	Hispanics	Whites
F	12	17	126	34	1,101
M	0	4	8	2	139
%	0.8	1.5	9.3	2.5	85.9

A nonsectarian, independent, liberal arts institution, D'Youville College was founded by the Grey Nuns of the Sacred Heart in 1908. Some 1,500 students are enrolled, of whom 1,443 are registered in degree programs. Coeducational since 1972, the college is still predominantly female, with women constituting 90 percent of degree students. Nineteen percent of the women attend part-time. The median age of all undergraduates is 23.

D'Youville offers bachelor's degrees in a range of liberal arts, professional, and pre-professional fields. Adult education courses are available through the division of continuing studies. Evening and summer session classes are also available. The urban campus is easily accessible by public transportation. On-campus parking for a fee is also available for the three-fourths of students who commute.

Private childcare facilities are located near the campus.

Policies to Ensure Fairness to Women. The Assistant Director of Development has responsibility part-time for monitoring compliance with legislation relating to handicapped access and sex equity for students. While there is no published policy on sexual harassment, complaints are handled through a formal campus grievance procedure.

Women in Leadership Positions. *Students.* Women have excellent opportunities to gain student leadership experience. In a recent three-year period, women held many of the leadership posts, including president of each of the four classes, residence-hall council president, editor-in-chief of the campus newspaper, president of the student judiciary, student senate president, and student body president. One of the two honorary societies is led by a woman.

Faculty. Three-fourths of the 79 full-time faculty are women, a proportion well above average for similar colleges in this guide. There are 6 female faculty for every 100 female students, compared to 16 male faculty for every 100 male students.

Administrators. Four of the nine key administrative posts are held by women, including the chief executive officer, chief student-life officer, head librarian, and director of athletics. Of three departments, nursing is chaired by a woman. Women occupy 10 seats on the 19-member Board of Trustees. In one recent year, the commencement speaker and the 2 recipients of alumni awards were women. The sole honorary degree recipient was a black woman. In addition, 6 of the 8 speakers in a major campus-wide lecture series were women, including 1 Hispanic and 2 black women.

Women and the Curriculum. Three-fourths of the women earn degrees in the health professions. Instruction on some matters specific to women is offered in business, nursing, and social-work courses. A course on Women Writers is offered in the English department.

Women and Athletics. Women are 58 percent of the intercollegiate athletes and receive half of the athletic scholarship aid granted. The most popular intramural sport for women is volleyball. Two of the six paid varsity coaches are women. Intercollegiate sports are basketball, bowling, tennis, and volleyball.

Housing and Student Organizations. One-fourth of the undergraduates live in coeducational or women's dormitories that have restrictions on visiting hours for members of the opposite sex. Awareness-training on sex education, drugs, alcohol abuse, and morals development is available to residence-hall directors—two women. A married woman student whose husband is not enrolled may live in married students' housing.

Special Services and Programs for Women. *Health and Counseling.* The student health service is staffed by two male health-care providers; the counseling center, by one female counselor. Counseling and treatment are available for gynecological problems and for rape and assault. Counseling on birth control and abortion is available. Student health insurance covers maternity expenses at no extra charge.

Safety and Security. Measures consist of campus and local police protection, night-time escorts for women, and information on campus safety for women. One rape and three assaults on women were reported for 1980–81.

Career. Services include workshops, lectures, and information on nontraditional occupations, and files on the careers of alumnae.

In addition, career planning workshops are held for returning students.

Returning Women Students. The division of continuing studies enrolls 75 reentry women, 40 percent of whom are members of minority groups, mainly black.

Special Features. A Center for Women in Management brings 150 women to campus for monthly meetings. Assertiveness training workshops are also conducted for the benefit of the participants.

Institutional Self-Description. "D'Youville College is an urban institution with a student body that is 80 percent female. Its mission is to provide students with career training coupled with a strong background in the liberal arts. The environment encourages and provides the opportunity for students to become responsible members of society."

Erie Community College
Main and Young Roads
Amherst, NY 14221
Telephone: (716) 634-0800

Women in Leadership
- ★ students
- ★ faculty
- ★ ★ ★ administrators

8,954 undergraduates

	Amer. Ind.	Asian Amer.	Blacks	Hispanics	Whites
F	13	17	457	27	3,015
M	8	27	356	14	4,960
%	0.2	0.5	9.1	0.5	89.7

Erie, a public, two-year college, occupies three campuses—North, South, and City—located in and near Buffalo. Women are 40 percent of the 8,954 undergraduates; 30 percent of women attend part-time. The median age of all students is 25.

The college offers a wide range of two-year programs in liberal arts, business, health, public service, mechanical/engineering technologies, and natural science. Alternative full-time and part-time scheduling includes off-campus day and evening classes and summer sessions. Public transportation and on-campus parking are provided.

Private childcare facilities are available near campus.

Policies to Ensure Fairness to Women. One full-time administrator is responsible for policy and compliance regarding equal-employment-opportunity, sex-equity, and handicapped-access legislation. A campus policy prohibiting sexual harassment of students, faculty, and staff has been communicated in writing to members of the college community. A Commission on the Status of Women, appointed by the President of the college, which includes student representatives with voting rights, meets regularly and prepares an annual report. The Committee on the Status of Women as well as the Commission on Minority Affairs address the concerns of minority women.

Women in Leadership Positions. *Students.* Women have good opportunities to excercise campus-wide leadership. While women are 40 percent of students, they held 28 percent of leadership posts in recent years.

Faculty. Women are 29 percent of the 321 full-time faculty. There are 4 female faculty for every 100 female students and 6 male faculty for every 100 male students.

Administrators. On North and City Campuses, seven of nine top administrators are women, including the chief development officer, director of institutional research, and chief planning officer. The head librarians on all three campuses are women. The three campuses have 57 departments; women chair 14, including English, occupational therapy, nursing, secretarial science, business administration, and physics. The Academic Dean on North Campus is female.

Women and the Curriculum. Most women take degrees in health (41 percent) and business (28 percent), with significant numbers in public service and liberal arts, and the remainder in natural science, data processing, and mechanical/engineering technologies.

The departments of English and social science offer a course on Women in Literature. Official committees of the college are responsible for developing a Women's Studies Program, courses on women in departments, and collecting curricular materials on women.

Women and Athletics. Almost half of intercollegiate and almost two-thirds of intramural athletes are women. Intercollegiate sports for women are basketball, bowling, cross-country, soccer, softball, track, and volleyball.

Special Services and Programs for Women. *Health and Counseling.* The North Campus student health service is staffed by 3 male physicians and 3 female health-care providers; the counseling center by 3 women, including 1 minority woman and 3 men. The South Campus student health service is staffed by 1 male physician and 1 female health-care provider; a counseling center by 2 women and 1 man. The City Campus student health service is staffed by 1 male physician and 1 female health-care provider; a student counseling service is staffed by 2 women, 1 a minority woman, and 1 man. On all three campuses counseling but not medical treatment is available for matters concerning gynecology, birth control, abortion, and rape and assault. Counselors receive in-service training on sex-role stereotyping and racial bias.

Safety and Security. Measures on all three campuses consist of campus police, patrol by local police, high-intensity lighting, self-defense courses for women, and information sessions on rape and assault prevention. No rapes and ten assaults (five on women) were reported for 1980–81.

Career. The college provides workshops, lectures, and printed information on nontraditional occupations, as well as information concerning job discrimination in those fields. A new Women's Center, to be opened on the City Campus, with satellite offices on North and South Campuses, will have career and vocational counseling services and testing, a job data bank, and workshops for women.

Other. Assistance in developing mathematics skills is available on all three campuses. Assertiveness training is offered by the counseling service on City and North Campuses. There is a Minority Student Association on North Campus. For older students, the New Majority Club meets on North and City Campuses, the Phoenix Club on South Campus.

Institutional Self-Description. "Erie Community College will provide women with: 1) an opportunity to examine and assess their career development, 2) occupational education programs which prepare them for realistic employment, 3) skills-retraining and pertinent state-of-the-art courses for those who seek promotion and career advancement within business and industry."

Fordham University

Rose Hill Campus: Bronx, NY 10458
Mid-Manhattan Campus: Lincoln Center, NY 10023
Telephone: (212) 933-2233

Women in Leadership
★★★ students
★ faculty

7,791 undergraduates

	Amer. Ind.	Asian Amer.	Blacks	Hispanics	Whites
F	8	47	602	395	2,675
M	10	36	337	286	3,268
%	0.2	1.1	12.3	8.9	77.5

 AAUW

Founded in 1841, Fordham is a university in the Jesuit tradition which offers undergraduate and graduate instruction in the liberal arts and sciences and selected professional areas to some 15,000 students. The two main campuses are located in New York City. Evening classes and a summer session are available.

Women are 49 percent of the 7,791 undergraduates; 31 percent of the women attend part-time. The median age of undergraduates is 21. Both the Rose Hill and the Mid-Manhattan Campuses are accessible by public transportation. Rose Hill Campus has limited parking.

Private childcare arrangements can be made nearby.

Policies to Ensure Fairness to Women. There is an Affirmative Action Coordinator. Fordham reports that its statutes provide equal policy, procedures, and protection to all members of the institution.

Women in Leadership Positions. *Students.* Fordham reports equal representation of male and female students in campus-wide leadership positions in recent years.

Faculty. Women are 26 percent of a full-time faculty of 489. The ratio of female faculty to female students is 5 to 100, of male faculty to male students, 10 to 100.

Administrators. The director of institutional research and the head librarian are women. Women chair ten of 33 departments. The Dean of the Graduate School of Social Service and the Dean of General Studies are women.

Women and the Curriculum. A majority of the degrees awarded undergraduate women are in the social sciences (31 percent), psychology (17 percent), general letters (13 percent), and business and management (10 percent). Fewer than 2 percent are in the nontraditional subjects of mathematics and physical sciences.

There are no courses on women.

Women and Athletics. The university provides "a variety of intramural, recreational and lifetime sports activities."

Special Services and Programs for Women. *Health and Counseling.* Student health services are available only at Rose Hill Campus. No medical attention specific to women is available. The counseling center employs three full-time staff, including one minority and one white woman. No counseling specific to women is available.

Safety and Security. Fordham reports a "full range of security services for all students." Information on the incidence of rapes and assaults was not provided.

Other. Career planning and placement services are available. Each campus has a Students' Center. The EXCEL program, which meets on the Mid-Manhattan Campus, attracts many reentry women. It offers day and evening, full- and part-time programs.

Institutional Self-Description. "Fordham believes it provides education characterized by intellectual quality and attention to

 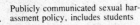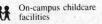

values implemented in terms of the Catholic and Jesuit traditions of the university. Other factors combine in helping to realize this educational objective: a medium-sized university, small classes, proximity of graduate schools on both campuses, substantial ethnic mixture of students, and location in New York City.

Hamilton College
Clinton, NY 13323
Telephone: (315) 859-4011

★ **Women and the Curriculum**

★ **Women and Athletics**

1,571 undergraduates

	Amer. Ind.	Asian Amer.	Blacks	Hispanics	Whites
F	1	5	17	5	521
M	0	10	19	8	956
%	0.1	1.0	2.3	0.8	95.8

Throughout most of its long history (founded in 1793), Hamilton has been a liberal arts college for men. In 1978, the college became coeducational as a result of merging with its coordinate women's college, Kirkland. The campus attracts 1,586 students. Women are 36 percent of the undergraduates and almost all attend full-time. The median age of the undergraduates is 20.

A variety of undergraduate degree programs is offered in addition to an adult education program, Hamilton Horizons. All classes meet on campus during the daytime. Essentially a residential college, only 5 percent of the students live off campus or commute. On-campus parking is available at a fee.

A campus childcare facility is open to all members of the Hamilton community on a first-come, first-served basis. The center accommodates 17 children at one time and can meet most requests by students.

Policies to Ensure Fairness to Women. The Assistant to the President serves as the equal opportunity coordinator and has part-time responsibility for monitoring compliance with sex-equity and affirmative action laws. A formal campus grievance procedure resolves complaints of sexual harassment. The Faculty for Women's Concerns reports informally to the Dean of the College on matters pertaining to the status of women on campus. The group meets regularly, takes public stands on issues of concern to female students, and addresses the concerns of minority women.

Women in Leadership Positions. *Students.* Women have very limited opportunities to gain campus-wide leadership experience. Only once in the last three years has a woman been elected to a term in one of the seven major student leadership posts, president of the student government.

Faculty. Eighteen percent of the 131 full-time faculty are women. There are 4 female faculty for every 100 female students and 11 male faculty for every 100 male students.

Administrators. Nine top-level administrators are men. The director of institutional research is a woman. A woman chairs the comparative literature department, and men chair the other 23 departments.

Women and the Curriculum. Most of the women earn degrees in fine arts, letters, and social sciences. Twelve percent of men and 1 percent of women major in physical sciences or mathematics.

The Women's Studies Program, directed by a full-time, permanently appointed faculty member, grants an interdisciplinary minor. Seventeen courses are offered through the departments of anthropology, comparative literature, English, history, psychology, philosophy, religion, sociology, and German. An official committee is responsible for developing the Women's Studies Program. The mathematics department provides instruction on mathematics confidence.

Women and Athletics. For a small institution, Hamilton has an outstanding women's sports program in terms of the number and variety of teams and the high participation rate among women. There are ten intercollegiate sports, at least ten intramural sports, as well as club sports. About 30 percent of the intercollegiate and 44 percent of the intramural athletes are women. The intramural sports include track and field, lacrosse, skiing, and squash. A women's ice hockey team, a club activity, plays on the campus ice rink. Intercollegiate sports offered are basketball, cross-country, field hockey, lacrosse, soccer, softball, squash, swimming, tennis, and track and field (including winter track).

Housing and Student Organizations. Ninety-five percent of the students live on campus in coeducational dormitories that have no restrictions on visiting hours for members of the opposite sex. The college has fraternities but not sororities.

Special Services and Programs for Women. *Health and Counseling.* The student health service employs 2 male physicians and 1 male and 9 female health-care providers. The student counseling center is staffed by 9 female counselors. Counseling and treatment are available for gynecological problems and birth control, and counseling is available on abortion and rape and assault.

Safety and Security. Measures consist of campus police protection, self-defense courses for women, instruction on crime prevention and campus safety for women, and a rape crisis center. One rape and no assaults on women were reported for 1980–81.

Career. The college offers workshops, lectures, and information on nontraditional occupations, compiles files on the careers of alumnae, and fosters networking between students and alumnae.

Other. A women's lecture series is sponsored by the Women's Studies faculty and committee. Assertiveness training sessions are organized by the Student Affairs Office. The Gay Alliance, the Black and Latin Student Union, and the Women's Center are advocacy groups on campus.

Special Features. The library has an extensive collection of materials, including rare items, on the history of the women's movement.

Institutional Self-Description. ''Because of its location, size, and close student-faculty relations, the college plays a central role in the lives of its students, and best serves those students who want to be actively engaged in the life of the college. Men and women of intellectual promise who share a commitment to the college's educational purposes, are prepared to be active participants in their own education, and desire the intimacy of a small, competitive college in a rural setting will enjoy Hamilton.''

Hartwick College
Oneonta, NY 13820
Telephone: (607) 432-4200

Women in Leadership   ★ **Women and Athletics**

1,392 undergraduates

	Amer. Ind.	Asian Amer.	Blacks	Hispanics	Whites
F	2	1	8	1	772
M	0	7	13	3	585
%	0.1	0.6	1.5	0.3	97.5

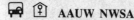 **AAUW NWSA**

A private, four-year, coeducational institution located one hour from Binghamton, Hartwick College was founded in 1928 and now enrolls some 1,400 students. The median age of the 1,392 undergraduates is 19. Fifty-six percent of the undergraduates are women, almost all of whom attend full-time.

Hartwick offers a variety of bachelor's programs in the liberal arts and sciences, as well as a wide range of off-campus, study abroad, and dual degree programs with other colleges. A continuing education program is offered to nursing students. Summer session classes are available. Public transportation and free on campus parking are available to the 30 percent of students who commute.

Private childcare facilities are located near the campus.

Policies to Ensure Fairness to Women. Complaints of sexual harassment are resolved informally and confidentially.

Women in Leadership Positions. *Students.* Opportunities for women to exercise campus-wide leadership are limited. In three recent years, women have held two student campus posts: editor-in-chief of the campus newspaper twice and presiding officer of the student court once. Four of the seven honorary societies are headed by women.

Faculty. Twenty-four percent of the 101 full-time faculty are women, a proportion near the national average. There are 3 female faculty for every 100 female students and 13 male faculty for every 100 male students. The college reports that the full-time faculty includes 1 Asian American woman.

Administrators. Two of the 9 top-level administrators are women: director of institutional research and chief planning officer. Of the 21 departments, women chair 2, art and nursing.

Women and the Curriculum. Most women earn bachelor's degrees in health professions (28 percent), social sciences (20 percent), and fine arts (11 percent). Five percent of the women earn degrees in the nontraditional fields of mathematics and physical sciences.

Several courses on women are offered, including Women in American History, Women and Social Change, Psychology of Women, and Women and Religion. The Women's Center and the departments of sociology and anthropology sponsor student and faculty workshops on racism and sexism in the curriculum.

Women and Athletics. Women have good opportunities to participate in a wide array of competitive team and individual sports. The most popular intramural sports are softball and indoor soccer. Ten club sports are also available. Forty-two percent of the 559 intramural athletes and 55 percent of intercollegiate athletes are women, and women receive 40 percent of athletic scholarships awarded. Three of the eleven paid intercollegiate coaches are women. The intercollegiate sports offered are basketball, cross-country, field hockey, lacrosse, soccer, swimming, tennis, and track.

Housing and Student Organizations. Seventy percent of students reside on campus in single-sex or coeducational dormitories that do not restrict hours for visitors of the opposite sex. Four of the six residence-hall directors are women and all residence-hall staff are offered awareness-training on sexism and sex education.

Thirteen percent of undergraduate women belong to social sororities; sororities and fraternities provide housing for members.

Special Services and Programs for Women. *Health and Counseling.* The student health service offers gynecological services for women. The counseling center, staffed by one male and one female counselor, offers a number of services specific to women, including birth control, abortion, and rape and assault counseling. The regular student health insurance covers abortion expenses at no extra charge.

Safety and Security. Measures consist of local police, campus police without arrest authority, a night-time escort for women students, night-time, campus-wide bus service to residence areas, a campus-wide emergency telephone system, an emergency alarm system at isolated locations, and a rape crisis center. One assault on a woman and no rapes were reported for 1980–81.

Career. Placement services include printed information on nontraditional fields of study for women and lectures and panels by women employed in nontraditional occupations. The college also sponsors programs to establish contacts and networks between alumnae and female students.

Other. The division of educational affairs operates the Women's Center, which has 15 active members. Some 250 undergraduate women are served by the center, which is run on a volunteer basis by a member of the faculty. The Women's Center functions as the major advocacy group for women students and sponsors such programs and activities as a Women's Support Group, a Women's Conference, Annual Women's Week, a women's lecture series, and assertiveness/leadership training programs. Hartwick also has a women-focused campus newspaper.

Institutional Self-Description. "Hartwick offers a high-quality, undergraduate education which is firmly in the liberal arts tradition. Its central commitment is to the intellectual and personal development of each individual student. Women will find a supportive and humane atmosphere in which they are taken seriously as whole persons."

Hilbert College
5200 S. Park Ave., Hamburg, NY 14075
Telephone: (716) 649-7900

Women in Leadership
★★★ **faculty**
★ **administrators**

581 undergraduates

	Amer. Ind.	Asian Amer.	Blacks	Hispanics	Whites
F	1	0	18	7	372
M	1	0	7	5	170
%	0.3	0.0	4.3	2.1	93.3

Founded in 1957 as a junior college for members of the Franciscan Sisters of St. Joseph and other religious orders, Hilbert became a coeducational, two-year college in 1969. Some 581 students are enrolled in this private, non-denominational institution. Sixty-nine percent of these students are women, one-third of whom attend part-time. The median age of all students is 22.

Hilbert offers evening and weekend classes, as well as a summer session. Eight-two percent of students commute to the suburban campus in Buffalo. Free parking is available on the campus, which is accessible by public transportation.

Policies to Ensure Fairness to Women. Two Equal-Opportunity Officers, on a part-time basis, monitor compliance with equal employment-opportunity, sex-equity, and handicapped-access legislation. A published campus policy prohibits sexual harassment of students, faculty, and staff.

Women in Leadership Positions. *Students.* One of the few leadership positions available, the presidency of the student body, was held by a woman in a recent year.

Faculty. Fifty-six percent of the 16 faculty members are women, a proportion higher than the average for private, two-year colleges. There are 3 female faculty for every 100 female students, and 5 male faculty for every 100 male students.

Administrators. The President of the college and the Director of the Library are women. The remaining six major administrative posts are held by men. Women chair the departments of human services, English, secretarial science, mathematics, and science.

Women and the Curriculum. Sixty-two percent of women graduates take two-year degrees in business programs, 22 percent in public service technologies, and 17 percent in arts and letters. The college offers programs to encourage women to prepare for careers in accounting, law enforcement, and legal assistance. The

Admissions Office has a program designed to build confidence in mathematics.

There are no courses on women.

Women and Athletics. Twenty-five of the 56 intramural athletes and 37 of the 70 intercollegiate athletes are women; women receive 40 percent of athletic scholarship aid. Three of the five paid intercollegiate coaches are women; all three women's intercollegiate teams play in post-season tournaments. Women participate in two intramural sports—tennis and volleyball. The intercollegiate sports offered are basketball, softball, and volleyball.

Housing and Student Organizations. Eighteen percent of students live on campus in either coeducational dormitories or in fraternity or sorority houses. Thirteen percent of students residing on campus are black women. Residence halls have restrictive hours for visitors of the opposite sex. The single residence-hall director is a white woman. Fifteen undergraduate women belong to sororities.

Special Services and Programs for Women. *Health and Counseling.* There is no student health service. A student counseling center is staffed by one woman. There are no counseling services on problems specific to women.

Safety and Security. Measures consist of campus police and high-intensity lighting. No assaults on women were reported for 1980–81.

Career. Workshops and materials focusing on nontraditional occupations and job discrimination are available, along with programs to establish contacts between alumnae and female students. The college also maintains updated files of alumnae by specific career.

Other. A full-time Adult Admissions Counselor and a college-readiness program assist older women. The Admissions Office provides assertiveness and leadership training.

Institutional Self-Description. "Hilbert has a small-college setting with the atmosphere of openness, complemented by faculty availability and small classes. Support services for the non-traditional student include a full-time Adult Admissions Counselor, career counseling, adult orientation to college, and a college-readiness program."

Hofstra University

1000 Fulton Ave., Hempstead, NY 11550
Telephone: (516) 560-0500

Women in Leadership   ★ Women and the Curriculum
   ★ faculty

6,540 undergraduates

	Amer. Ind.	Asian Amer.	Blacks	Hispanics	Whites
F	4	22	235	70	2,493
M	6	26	172	70	3,364
%	0.2	0.7	6.3	2.2	90.6

🏠 🏛 🚌 👫 🄼🄰 📖 ⚧ **AAUW**

Hofstra University was established in 1935 as a private, coeducational liberal arts college. Located in the Long Island suburb of Hempstead, 25 miles east of Manhattan, the university enrolls 10,809 students. Of the 6,540 undergraduates, 44 percent are women, and 18 percent of the women attend part-time. The median age of all undergraduates is 21.

The university offers a wide variety of associate and bachelor's degree programs, along with graduate and professional degrees. Continuing education courses are available. Classes at the main, Hempstead campus, which meet during the day and evening, are supplemented by day and evening classes held at branch campuses in Old Westbury and Commack, Long Island. New College, a division of Hofstra, conducts a University Without Walls program

that allows students to work independently. A summer session is also available. Two-thirds of the undergraduates commute or live off campus. The university can be reached by public transportation and provides on-campus parking.

A campus childcare facility, open to all members of the Hofstra community, accommodates all applicants. Fees are based on a sliding scale, according to income. Additional, private childcare facilities are available near campus.

Policies to Ensure Fairness to Women. Two equal opportunity officers are responsible part-time for monitoring compliance with educational-sex-equity, sex-fair-employment, and handicapped-access laws. Procedures for resolving sexual harassment complaints are being developed.

Women in Leadership Positions. *Students.* Opportunities for women students to gain leadership experience are limited. In three recent years, women have held only two of 12 leadership positions: editor-in-chief of the campus newspaper and presiding officer of the student senate. Eight of the 24 honorary societies are led by women.

Faculty. A fourth of the 360 full-time faculty are women. There are 4 female faculty for every 100 female students; the ratio of male faculty to male students is 9 to 100.

Administrators. Of the nine key administrators, two are female: the chief development officer and the director of institutional research. Women chair nine of the 37 departments, and are half of the faculty senate and almost one-fourth of the trustees.

Women and the Curriculum. Women earn nearly half of all bachelor's degrees granted: 30 percent in business, and about 11 percent each in letters and psychology. Five percent of women (and 11 percent of men) major in computer science, mathematics, or physical sciences. Sixty percent of students participating in internship programs are women.

The Women's Program offers an 18-credit minor, the B. A. in Women's Studies, and an M. A. through Interdisciplinary Studies. Twelve courses on women are given by the New College and the departments of history, psychology, sociology, English, and comparative literature. The courses include Psychology of Women, Sociology of Sex Roles, Women in America, and History of Changing Sex Roles. Women's Studies is directed by a full-time, permanently appointed faculty member and developed by an official committee. The departments of education, physical education, and business address some matters relevent to women.

Minority Women. Minority women are nine percent of all undergraduates. The Committee on Minority Affairs addresses the concerns of minority women. The African People's Organization and the Hofstra Organization of Latin Americans are advocacy groups. Twenty-five women belong to an all-minority sorority and 5 are in racially integrated sororities. One black woman and an Hispanic woman chair departments; the faculty senate has 1 black female member; and 1 black woman sits on the Board of Trustees. Three black women, 3 Hispanic women, and 1 Asian American woman serve on the full-time faculty.

Women and Athletics. Hofstra offers good opportunities for women to participate in organized competitive sports through the intercollegiate program; women's intramurals include three team sports. Almost half of the intercollegiate athletes and 6 percent of intramural athletes are women. Forty percent of the paid coaches in intercollegiate sports are women, and women receive 30 percent of athletic scholarships awarded. Club sports are also available. Intercollegiate sports offered are basketball, fencing, field hockey, gymnastics, lacrosse, sofball, tennis, and volleyball.

Housing and Student Organizations. One-third of the undergraduates live on campus in single-sex or coeducational dormitories that have no restrictions on visiting hours for members of the opposite sex. Five of seven residence-hall directors are women; they are offered awareness-training on sexism, sexuality, and racism.

Four percent of the full-time undergraduate women belong to sororities. Neither sororities nor fraternities proved housing for members. The Hofstra Organization for Women functions as an advocacy group for female students.

Special Services and Programs for Women. *Health and Counseling.* The student health service is staffed by 1 male physician and 2 female health-care providers. Information was not provided about medical services specific to women. The student counseling center employs 8 female and 7 male counselors. Counseling is available for gynecological problems, birth control, abortion, and rape and assault.

Safety and Security. Measures consist of campus and local police protection, night-time bus service to dormitories, high-intensity lighting, an emergency alarm system, and instruction on self-defense and campus safety for women. One assault on a woman and no rapes were reported for 1980–81.

Career. The university provides information about nontraditional careers for women.

Other. A small Women's Center, operating on $1,090 annually, attracts primarily undergraduate women. A student volunteer directs the center on a part-time basis. A women's lecture series is co-sponsored by Women's Studies and New College. A telephone warmline is run by the counseling center and the Dean of Students' office.

Institutional Self-Description. "Hofstra University demonstrates its commitment to the education of women through the following: national conferences on women and women writers; a developing Women's Studies Program; active Women's Studies network featuring monthly meetings and newsletter; several eminent Women's Studies women scholars. The proportion of women on the faculty, at all professorial ranks, and tenured, is greater than national norms."

Houghton College
Houghton, NY 14744
Telephone: (716) 567-2211

Women in Leadership
★ Administrators

1,161 undergraduates

	Amer. Ind.	Asian Amer.	Blacks	Hispanics	Whites
F	1	1	6	1	615
M	3	3	9	2	480
%	0.4	0.4	1.3	0.3	97.7

Houghton College, established in 1883 as a seminary, is an evangelical, church-related, liberal arts college for men and women. The campus attracts 1,201 students, and of those; 1,161 are undergraduates. Women are 55 percent of the undergraduates, and all but 2 percent of women attend full-time. The median age of all students is 20. The college offers degrees in a variety of undergraduate fields. Classes meet on campus during the day and at the branch campus in West Seneca. On-campus parking is provided for the 5 percent of students who live off campus or commute.

Private childcare facilities are available off campus.

Women in Leadership Positions. *Students.* In three recent years, women have held two out of eight campus leadership posts: student body president for two years and campus newspaper editor for one year.

Faculty. Fifteen percent of the 72 full-time faculty are women, a proportion that is below the average for similar institutions in this guide. There are 2 female faculty for every 100 female students and 12 male faculty for every 100 male students.

Administrators. Two of the eight top-level administrators—the chief student-life officer and the head librarian—are women.

Women head the division of education and psychology and the division of history and social sciences.

Women and the Curriculum. About one-fourth of bachelor's degrees earned by women are in education and one-fourth in letters. Ten percent of women major in biology and 10 percent in psychology; 4 percent of women graduate in mathematics or physical sciences. A few women earn two-year degrees in public-service technologies. About half of student internships go to women.

There are no courses on women. The physical education department instructs prospective teachers on conducting coeducational physical education classes.

Women and Athletics. The intercollegiate sports program includes two women's teams and two coeducational teams. Intramural team sports such as volleyball, basketball, soccer, and softball are available. There are facilities for skiing and cross-country. Intercollegiate sports are field hockey and volleyball.

Housing and Student Organizations. Ninety-five percent of students live on campus in single-sex dormitories that have restrictions on the visiting hours of members of the opposite sex. Three of five residence-hall directors are women; residence-hall staff receive awareness-training on sex education.

Special Services and Programs for Women. *Health and Counseling.* The student health service is staffed by 1 part-time male physician and three nurse practitioners. The student counseling center employs 1 male and 1 female counselor. Counseling for gynecological problems is available. Information was not provided about medical services specific to women.

Safety and Security. Measures consist of campus police and information on campus safety for women. No rapes or assaults on women were reported in 1980-81.

Career. Houghton provides career workshops for women on nontraditional occupations.

Institutional Self-Description. "Our women graduates have regularly been successful in entering professional schools of medicine, dentistry, nursing, music, education, etc. The Christian position—evangelical and conservative—combined with the somewhat idyllic setting and fine women on the faculty and staff, are all conducive to intellectual, social, and spiritual development."

Hunter College: see City University of New York, Hunter College.

Keuka College
Keuka Park, NY 14478
Telephone: (315) 536-4411

Women in Leadership
★★★ students
★★★ faculty
★★ administrators

521 undergraduates

	Amer. Ind.	Asian Amer.	Blacks	Hispanics	Whites
F	2	3	19	12	481
M	0	0	0	0	4
%	0.4	0.6	3.7	2.3	93.1

Keuka College, established in 1890 as a coeducational preparatory school, has since 1919 been an independent, liberal arts institution for women. Its rural campus, adjacent to Lake Keuka in the Finger Lakes region, has an enrollment of 532 students; all but a few attend full-time. The median age of students is 20. Eight percent of students are over age 25.

The college offers a variety of liberal arts, professional, and pre-professional degrees, in addition to continuing education courses. Classes meet on campus both day and evening. A weekend college and a summer session are available. Thirteen percent of the students commute; free parking is provided.

Private childcare facilities are available close to the campus.

Policies to Ensure Fairness to Women. The Director of Personnel has responsibility for monitoring compliance with laws on equal employment opportunity, sex equity, and access for the handicapped. Complaints of sexual harassment are handled on an informal and confidential basis. A self-designated Committee on the Status of Women meets regularly, includes student members, and states its views on issues of special concern to women.

Women in Leadership Positions. *Students.* Women occupy all of the campus-wide student leadership positions.

Faculty. Fifty-four percent of the 52 full-time faculty are women. There are 5 women faculty for every 100 women students.

Administrators. Women hold 3 of the 8 top positions: President, head librarian, and director of athletics. A woman is Director of Student Affairs. Women chair 2 of 7 departments—nursing and physical education.

Women and the Curriculum. Nearly half of the women graduates specialize in health professions; 14 percent pursue interdisciplinary studies.

Six courses on women are offered in the behavioral and social sciences and the humanities. Recent titles include Women and the West, Psychology of Women, Women's Literature, and Women in Management. Continuing Education gives special instruction to help students build confidence in mathematics. Faculty are offered workshops on nontraditional occupations, advising minority women students, and the needs of reentry women.

Minority Women. Minority women are 7 percent of the student population; they are predominantly black or Hispanic. Both the Committee on the Status of Women and the Committee on Minority Affairs address the concerns of minority women. The Intercultural Society has 25 black or Hispanic members and serves as a support and advocacy group. Residence-hall staff receive awareness-training on racism.

Women and Athletics. For a college of its size, Keuka offers women good opportunities to participate in organized sports, whether club, intramural, or intercollegiate. Of the three paid coaches whose part-time duties include varsity sports, all are women. The varsity sports available for women are basketball, swimming, tennis, and volleyball.

Housing and Student Organizations. Eighty-seven percent of the women live in dormitories on campus that do not restrict visiting hours for men. The residence-hall staff are women, who are offered awareness training on sex education, birth control, and drug education.

Special Services and Programs for Women. *Health and Counseling.* The student health service is staffed by one male physician and two female health-care providers. The staff of the student counseling center consists of one female counselor. Counseling is provided for gynecological problems, birth control, abortion, and rape and assault. No information was provided on health services specific to women.

Safety and Security. Measures include campus and local police protection, an emergency telephone system, high-intensity lighting, and instruction on self-defense and rape and assault prevention. No information was supplied on rapes or assaults for 1980–81.

Career. The college maintains files on alumnae careers and collects information about opportunities for women in nontraditional occupations. All students are required to perform five weeks of field study that allows for experimentation with different careers, including nontraditional careers.

Other. The Management Club and the business administration/management department sponsor a women's lecture series. Leadership Training Workshops are organized by the continuing education department. This department, in cooperation with the Rochester Area Colleges Consortium (of which Keuka is a member), recently ran a conference on "Women and Work."

Institutional Self-Description. "Keuka's students are encouraged to create individualized learning experiences within course structures. The college has a successful, ten-year experience with student-initiated majors. Every student plans and carries out, each year, for credit, a five-week, off-campus field period, testing personal goals and strengthening motivation for self-education."

Marist College
Poughkeepsie, NY 12601
Telephone: (914) 471-3240

Women in Leadership
★ students

1,941 undergraduates

	Amer. Ind.	Asian Amer.	Blacks	Hispanics	Whites
F	1	4	21	15	776
M	1	4	29	22	1,068
%	0.1	0.4	2.6	1.9	95.0

🏠 🚐 👫 👫 AAUW

Established in 1929 by the Marist Brothers as a liberal arts men's college, Marist is now an independent, nondenominational, coeducational institution. The college enrolls 2,302 students. Forty-two percent of the 1,941 undergraduates are women, and 22 percent of the women attend part-time. The median age of all undergraduates is 19.

The college offers associate, bachelor's, and master's degrees in a variety of fields. It also offers adult education courses. Classes are scheduled during the day and evening; there is a summer session. For the 20 percent of undergraduates who commute, the campus is accessible by public transportation. Free on-campus parking is available.

A campus childcare facility gives priority to the children of faculty and staff although three-fourths of students' requests for childcare are honored. Twenty-five children can be accommodated at one time in either the morning or afternoon session.

Policies to Ensure Fairness to Women. On a part-time basis, an affirmative action officer has policymaking power. A campus policy on the sexual harassment of students, faculty, and staff has been communicated in writing to all members of the Marist community.

Women in Leadership Positions. *Students.* Women have opportunities to exercise campus-wide student leadership. In three recent years women held 23 percent of the student leadership posts, serving one-year terms as president of the student union board, editor-in-chief of the campus newspaper, residence-hall council president, and presidents of the senior and sophomore classes. Women have served twice as president of the entering class.

Faculty. Seventeen percent of the 79 full-time faculty are women. There are 2 female faculty for every 100 female students compared to 7 male faculty for every 100 male students.

Administrators. Men hold all top-level administrative positions. The dean and the members of the tenure, reappointment, and promotions committee are also men. Two women, including one black woman, sit on the 28-member Board of Trustees.

Women and the Curriculum. Most of the four-year degrees awarded to women are in psychology and business. Six percent of the women earn degrees in the nontraditional fields of mathematics and physical sciences. Sixty percent of students participating in internship programs are women.

Three courses focusing on women are offered by the history department: Women in Great Books, History of American Feminism, and Emergence of Women in Western Civilization.

Women and Athletics. In the small sports program, about one-fourth of the intercollegiate and 7 percent of the intramural athletes are women. Intramural sports include crew, basketball, volleyball, track, tennis, and swimming. Women receive 30 percent of athletic scholarship aid. Intercollegiate sports offered are basketball, crew, swimming, tennis, and track and field.

Housing and Student Organizations. Eighty percent of the undergraduates live on campus in coeducational dormitories that have no restrictions on visiting hours for members of the opposite sex. Residence-hall staff receive awareness training on racism, sexism, sex education, and birth control. The college has fraternities (30 members), but not sororities.

Special Services and Programs for Women. *Health and Counseling.* The student health service employs 1 female health-care provider. The student counseling center is staffed by 5 men and 7 women, including 2 minority women. Services specific to women include counseling and treatment for birth control, as well as counseling for rape and assault. Student health insurance covers maternity expenses. The counseling staff are provided with workshops on sex-role stereotyping and racism.

Safety and Security. Measures consist of campus and local police protection, night-time escort for women, high-intensity lighting, an emergency telephone system, instruction on self-defense and campus safety for women, and a rape crisis center. No rapes or assaults on women were reported for 1980–81.

Career. Services include access to files on the careers of alumnae, and information on nontraditional occupations and job discrimination.

Institutional Self-Description. "Marist College, as a liberal arts educational institution, may be singled out from other similar establishments by the particulars of its philosophy, people, location, and buildings. Together these elements help to describe a unique academic community. The essence of this community's character springs from the interrelationships which exist among the people of Marist College."

Marymount College
Tarrytown, NY 10591
Telephone: (914) 631-3200

Women in Leadership	★ Women and the
★★★ students	Curriculum
★★★ faculty	
★★★ administrators	

1,075 undergraduates

	Amer. Ind.	Asian Amer.	Blacks	Hispanics	Whites
F	0	5	70	59	846
M	0	2	4	4	44
%	0.0	0.7	7.2	6.1	86.1

🚌 📖 **AAUW NWSA**

Marymount, established in 1919 by the Religious of the Sacred Heart, is a private, Roman Catholic liberal arts college for women. Thirty miles north of New York City, the campus attracts 1,106 students; all but 5 percent are women. Nine percent of the women attend part-time. The median age of undergraduates is 20.

A variety of undergraduate degrees is available, in addition to a coeducational weekend college and a summer session. Three-fourths of the women live in dormitories on campus that have restricted hours for male visitors. The college can be reached by public transportation, for the 25 percent of students who commute; on-campus parking is available at a fee.

Private childcare facilities are located near the college.

Policies to Ensure Fairness to Women. The Vice President of Finance assumes the part-time responsibility for monitoring compliance with laws pertaining to equal employment opportunity, sex equity for students, and access for the handicapped.

Women in Leadership Positions. *Students.* Women hold all student leadership positions.

Faculty. Fifty-two percent of the 62 full-time faculty are women, a proportion which is average for women's colleges in this guide. There are 3 female faculty for every 100 female students.

Administrators. Most key administrators are women, who hold positions as chief executive officer, chief academic officer, chief student-life officer, head librarian, and director of athletics. Women chair nine of 15 departments: art, business/economics, education, home economics, modern languages, physical education, politics, sociology, and natural science. The 1981 commencement speaker and the two honorary degree recipients were women.

Women and the Curriculum. Most women receive their bachelor's degrees in social sciences (29 percent), psychology (15 percent), and home economics (12 percent). Less than 3 percent specialize in mathematics or physical sciences. Academic programs encourage women to prepare for nontraditional careers in science, engineering, accounting, and computer science.

A Women's Studies Program, directed by a full-time faculty member, offers a minor. Twelve courses are offered through the departments of English, modern lanaguages, history, politics, psychology, religious studies, and sociology. Courses include Women Writers; Women, Education, and Society; Women and Politics; and Women in Management.

An official committee encourages the addition of new courses on women. Faculty are offered workshops on sexism in the curriculum, women in nontraditional occupations, and marriage, family, and careers. The departments of business/economics, education, and social work provide some instruction on matters specific to women.

Women and Athletics. There are no organized intramural sports; club sports are available. The 80 female intercollegiate athletes have four paid coaches, three of whom are women. Intercollegiate sports offered are basketball, riding, softball, swimming, tennis, and volleyball.

Special Services and Programs for Women. *Health and Counseling.* The student health service employs 2 male physicians and 9 female health-care providers. The student counseling center is staffed by 2 men and 1 minority woman. Counseling is available for gynecological problems, birth control, abortion, and rape and assault. No medical treatment specific to women is provided.

Safety and Security. Measures consist of campus police without arrest authority. No information was supplied on the incidence of rapes or assaults.

Career. Services include career workshops, lectures and information about nontraditional occupations, files for student reference on alumnae careers, and assistance in networking between students and alumnae.

Institutional Self-Description. None provided.

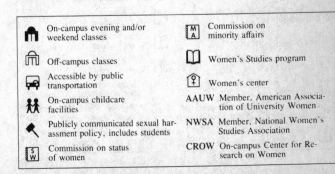

🏠 On-campus evening and/or weekend classes	Ⓜ️Ⓐ Commission on minority affairs
🏛 Off-campus classes	📖 Women's Studies program
🚐 Accessible by public transportation	🚺 Women's center
👫 On-campus childcare facilities	AAUW Member, American Association of University Women
Publicly communicated sexual harassment policy, includes students	NWSA Member, National Women's Studies Association
⑤Ⓦ Commission on status of women	CROW On-campus Center for Research on Women

Mercy College
555 Broadway, Dobbs Ferry, NY 10522
Telephone: (914) 693-4500

Women in Leadership ★★ faculty		★ Women and the Curriculum

4,269 undergraduates

	Amer. Ind.	Asian Amer.	Blacks	Hispanics	Whites
F	34	28	360	321	1,618
M	17	27	292	319	1,253
%	1.2	1.3	15.3	15.0	67.3

 AAUW

Mercy College was established in 1950 by the Sisters of Mercy as a liberal arts college for women. Since 1969, it has been a coeducational, independent, non-sectarian institution. The main campus is located north of New York City. There is a branch campus in Yorktown Heights in addition to extension centers in Peekskill, Yonkers, White Plains, the Bronx, and Miami, Florida. The total enrollment of 8,363 includes 4,269 undergraduates, more than a third of whom are members of minority groups. Women are 55 percent of the undergraduates, and 39 percent of the women attend part-time. The median age of undergraduates is 28. According to a recent report, 11 percent of all women students are over age 40; three-quarters of these women attend part-time.

The college offers bachelor's degrees in a range of fields and an associate degree in arts and sciences. The Center for Lifelong Learning is responsible for adult continuing education. Classes are held during the daytime and evening on the main Dobbs Ferry campus, as well as on the branch campus and extension centers. Other alternative scheduling includes a weekend college and a summer session. The campus of this commuter college can be reached by public transportation, and free on-campus parking is available.

A private childcare facility is located near the campus.

Women in Leadership Positions. *Students.* Women have limited opportunities to exercise student leadership. In recent years, they have held one-year terms as president of the student body, the sophomore, junior, and senior classes, and editor of the campus newspaper. Women head six of the eight honorary societies.

Faculty. Forty-one percent of the 149 full-time faculty are women, a proportion significantly above the average for similar colleges in this guide. There are 4 female faculty for every 100 female students, compared to 7 male faculty for every 100 male students.

Administrators. All key administrative posts are held by men. Women chair six of 14 departments—English, nursing, psychology, speech, philosophy, and mathematics.

Women and the Curriculum. Over two-thirds of bachelor's degrees granted to women are in social sciences (30 percent), psychology (24 percent), and business (18 percent). One percent of women earn degrees in the nontraditional field of mathematics.

A program encourages women to prepare for careers in science. Seventy percent of internships on campus are held by women students.

The Women's Studies Program, directed by a full-time, permanently appointed faculty member, offers the B.A. and B.S. in Interdisciplinary Studies, with Women's Studies as the major concentration. Twenty courses on women, are offered through Women's Studies and ten departments, including an introductory course and a concluding seminar. Recent courses include Sexism in Children's Literature, Italian and Italian-American Women, and Women's Creative Image in the Arts. An official committee oversees the development of the Women's Studies Program and seeks to increase the number of offerings on women.

Faculty workshops are held on topics such as the relationships among sex, race, and choice of major, the needs of reentry women, and nontraditional occupations.

Women and Athletics. A limited program offers three intercollegiate and five intramural sports. Three of ten paid varsity coaches are women; women receive 40 percent of the athletic scholarship aid. Intercollegiate sports offered are basketball, softball, and volleyball.

Special Services and Programs for Women. *Health and Counseling.* The student health service is staffed by one male physician. No medical treatment is available for problems specific to women. The student counseling center employs seven female and three male counselors. Counseling is available for gynecological problems, birth control, abortion, and rape and assault.

Safety and Security. Measures consist of local police protection, night-time escort for women, and high-intensity lighting. No rapes or assaults on women were reported for 1980–82.

Career. Mercy offers information and lectures on nontraditional occupations for women, files on the careers of alumnae for use by students, and programs to promote networking between students and alumnae.

Other. "Forum for Women" is a series of lectures by noted speakers on topics relating to women's personal, political, and professional lives.

Returning Women Students. The Center for Lifelong Learning enrolls 2,618 returning women students, one-third of whom are minority women. Special sessions address the concerns of older women and displaced homemakers.

Institutional Self-Description. "The unique character of the education provided by Mercy College makes it attractive to the adult female. The college makes education easily accessible to the working adult learner by providing nontraditional programs, flexibility in scheduling and location, and making special efforts to provide needed support services to meet the needs of adults returning to education."

Molloy College
1000 Hempstead Avenue
Rockville Centre, NY 11570
Telephone: (516) 678-5000

Women in Leadership ★★★ students ★★★ faculty ★★★ administrators

1,376 undergraduates

	Amer. Ind.	Asian Amer.	Blacks	Hispanics	Whites
F	4	1	62	30	1,255
M	0	0	1	2	19
%	0.3	0.1	4.6	2.3	92.7

 AAUW

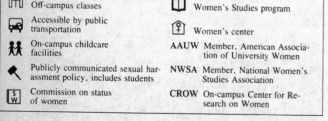

	On-campus evening and/or weekend classes		Commission on minority affairs
	Off-campus classes		Women's Studies program
	Accessible by public transportation		Women's center
	On-campus childcare facilities	AAUW	Member, American Association of University Women
	Publicly communicated sexual harassment policy, includes students	NWSA	Member, National Women's Studies Association
	Commission on status of women	CROW	On-campus Center for Research on Women

Established in 1955 by the Dominican Sisters, Molloy College enrolls some 1,500 students, of whom 1,376 are undergraduates. Although primarily a college for women, men are admitted to the evening, weekend, and nursing programs and make up 2 percent of the student body. Twenty-three percent of the women attend part-time. The median age of all students is 21; about one-third of the women are over age 25 and one-tenth are over age 40.

Molloy offers bachelor's degrees in a variety of liberal arts fields and enrolls a few students in a two-year associate of arts and sciences degree program. Adult continuing education is available. Alternative scheduling includes evening, weekend, and summer session classes. All students commute. Public transportation and on-campus parking are available.

Policies to Ensure Fairness to Women. The Vice President for Business Affairs and Administration assumes full-time responsibility for matters concerning sex equity for students and equal employment opportunities.

Women in Leadership Positions. *Students.* Women hold all campus-wide leadership positions and preside over the nine honorary societies.

Faculty. Eighty-four percent of the 101 full-time faculty are women, a proportion far above average even for women's colleges. There are 8 female faculty for every 100 female students.

Administrators. Women hold all top administrative positions. They chair 13 of 19 departments: mathematics, business management, biology, art, communication arts, education, gerontology, modern languages, nursing, physical education, psychology, religious studies, and sociology/social work. The membership of the faculty senate and the committee on tenure, reappointment, and promotions is overwhelmingly female. On the Board of Trustees, men are in the majority.

Women and the Curriculum. Sixty-seven percent of the women earn bachelor's degrees in health professions, 10 percent in social sciences, and 6 percent in education. The college has special academic programs to encourage women to prepare for careers in science, accounting, computer science, and law enforcement/corrections.

There are four courses on women: Women and Religion, Sociology of Women, Women in Politics, and Exploring Feminism and Spirituality through Movement. Courses in the departments of business, education, social work, and nursing offer some instruction on matters specific to women.

Women and Athletics. The intercollegiate sports program attracts 77 women athletes; two of the three paid coaches are women. No information was provided regarding the intramural activities. Intercollegiate sports offered are basketball, riding, softball, tennis, and volleyball.

Special Services and Programs for Women. *Health and Counseling.* The student health center is staffed by one female health care provider offers emergency care and health education programs, but no medical services specific to women. The staff of the student counseling center consists of five female counselors, one of whom is a minority woman. Counseling is available for birth control and rape and assault. Student health insurance covers maternity expenses at no extra cost.

Safety and Security. Measures consist of campus and local police protection, night-time escort, high intensity lighting, information on campus safety for women, and a rape crisis center. No rapes or assaults on women were reported in 1980–81.

Career. Placement services include distribution of information about opportunities for women in nontraditional occupations, files on alumnae careers, and the promotion of networking with alumnae.

Institutional Self-Description. "Molloy is a small college where students are treated as individuals. Being a women's college, students experience leadership roles, encouraging assertiveness and instilling confidence. A Catholic college with male and female religious and lay faculty Molloy offers students of all denominations an integrated and diverse perspective. Also appealing is Molloy's easy accessibility and campus safety."

Nassau Community College
Garden City, NY 11530
Telephone: (516) 222-7500

Women in Leadership
★★ faculty

14,622 undergraduates

	Amer. Ind.	Asian Amer.	Blacks	Hispanics	Whites
F	89	44	445	151	6,750
M	80	49	211	143	6,648
%	1.2	0.6	4.5	2.0	91.7

Nassau Community is a public, two-year commuter college located on a 225-acre suburban campus near New York City. It enrolls nearly 18,000 students. Slightly more than one-half of the 14,622 matriculated students are women; one-third of women attend part-time. The college offers a range of degree programs in liberal arts, business, health, public services, and engineering/technology. Full-time and part-time schedules as well as a five-week summer session add flexibility to program scheduling. Public transportation and free on-campus parking are available.

Childcare facilities are available on-campus.

Policies to Ensure Fairness to Women. An assistant to the president is responsible for monitoring compliance with laws concerning sex equity, equal employment, and handicapped access. An affirmative action committee which includes student members with voting rights reports annually to the Academic Senate.

Women in Leadership Positions. *Students.* Women have held each of the three major leadership positions—president of the student body, editor-in-chief of the student newspaper, and president of the student union board—once during the past three years.

Faculty. Thirty-seven percent of the 464 full-time faculty members are women, a proportion slightly above average for colleges of this type. There are 3 female faculty for every 100 female students and 6 male faculty for every 100 male students.

Administrators. The president and vice president are men. Information on other administrative positions was not provided.

Women and the Curriculum. Most women earn degrees in arts and science, while a significant proportion also major in health technologies and business and commerce technologies. There are no courses on women.

Women and Athletics. Information was not provided.

Special Services and Programs for Women. *Health and Counseling.* No information was provided on health and counseling services or on safety and security.

Other. A Women's Center, funded by allocations from the student government and advised part-time by a volunteer from the faculty, sponsors an array of lectures and projects, including a women's film festival, women's health week, woman/teacher/artist program, woman composer concert, and lectures and discussion groups on women's labor concerns and on social and political issues for minorities. Five percent of the approximately 450 women served annually by the center are minority women, mostly black women. Six hundred reentry women take courses offered by the continuing education program.

Institutional Self-Description. Information was not provided.

New York City Technical College

300 Jay Street
Brooklyn, NY 11201
Telephone: (212) 643-8595

Women in Leadership
★ faculty
★ administrators

12,241 undergraduates

	Amer. Ind.	Asian Amer.	Blacks	Hispanics	Whites
F	53	223	3,432	1,018	1,102
M	120	411	2,409	1,162	2,182
%	1.4	5.2	48.2	18.0	27.1

A two-year branch of the City University of New York, New York Technical College enrolls 12,241 students in a variety of career-oriented programs. Eighty-one percent of the students are members of minority groups. Forty-eight percent of the students are women; one-third of women attend part-time. The continuing education division serves adults. The median student age is 23 years. There is a summer session. All students commute and use public transportation.

On-campus childcare facilities that can accommodate 55 children charge $7 per day; full-time students, faculty, and staff receive priority for these services. Private, off-campus facilities are also available.

Policies to Ensure Fairness to Women. A Special Assistant to the President has full-time responsibility for equal-employment-opportunity, sex-equity, and handicapped-access laws. A policy forbidding sexual harassment has been drafted and is under consideration by the Board of Trustees. A self-designated Committee on the Status of Women takes public stands on issues of student concern and addresses the concerns of minority women. A Commission on Minority Affairs also addresses the concerns of minority women.

Women in Leadership Positions. *Students.* During a recent three-year period, of the three positions available, women served one year each as president of the student body and editor-in-chief of the campus newspaper.

Faculty. Thirty-one percent of the 398 faculty are women, a proportion above the national average. There are 3 female faculty for every 100 female students and 7 male faculty for every 100 male students.

Administrators. Women serve as President, Dean of Student Affairs, and head librarian; they head the divisions of student affairs, commerce, liberal arts and sciences, and continuing education. Women also chair six of the 30 departments: biological sciences, dental hygiene, nursing, accounting, secretarial science, and Afro-American studies. Women are one-third of the 28-member committee on tenure and promotions.

Women and the Curriculum. The most popular major for women is business and commerce, in which women earn 38 percent of the two-year degrees and certificates awarded. Significant numbers of women also major in health technology, arts and sciences, and public service. Three percent of women major in mechanical and engineering technologies. Programs encourage women to major in the nontraditional fields of science, engineering, architecture, accounting, computer science, and electronics.

Nursing provides health information of special concern to minority women; the department of social work gives instruction on services for battered women, displaced homemakers, and childcare. Nontraditional careers and the needs of reentry women are topics of workshops for faculty. There are no courses on women.

Minority Women. More than eighty percent of women on campus are members of minorty groups, 3,432 of them black women,

1,018 Hispanic women. The Dean of Student Life and one member of the committee on tenure and promotions are black women. In a recent year, 1 of the 2 commencement speakers was a black woman, as was 1 of the 3 speakers in a major campus-wide lecture series. Three of the nine women staff members of the student counseling center are minority women. Eighty percent of reentry students in the Continuing Education for Women program are minority women, predominantly black women.

Women and Athletics. Half of the intercollegiate athletes and one of the ten paid coaches are women. The intramural sports program for women includes three sports. Women's intercollegiate sports are basketball, bowling, softball, track and field, and volleyball.

Special Services and Programs for Women. *Health and Counseling.* There is no student health service. The 25-member staff of the student counseling center includes nine white women and three minority women. The college maintains a special resource library on women and health, and employs a consultant on family planning.

Safety and Security. Measures consist of campus police without arrest authority. Two assaults on women were reported for 1980–81.

Career. The career office schedules lectures on nontraditional careers.

Institutional Self-Description. "NYCTC offers relevant and career-oriented career programs which develop knowledge, skills, and competencies required for initial employment and advancement as technicians or semi-professional workers in industry, business, the professions, and government. These curricula provide women who need retraining with skills and competencies required for entry into new and nontraditional careers."

New York Institute of Technology, Old Westbury Campus

Old Westbury, NY 11568
Telephone: (516) 686-7516

8,330 undergraduates

	Amer. Ind.	Asian Amer.	Blacks	Hispanics	Whites
F	3	8	114	30	2,114
M	6	31	198	76	5,548
%	0.1	0.5	3.8	1.3	94.3

 AAUW

The New York Institute of Technology, a private, four-year college, was founded in 1955 and now enrolls over 9,000 students. It has three campuses—the main campus in Old Westbury, Long Island; a Metropolitan Center in Manhattan; and Commack College Center in Commack, Long Island. Among the student body are 8,330 undergraduates, 28 percent of them women. Almost 55 percent of the women attend part-time. The median age of all undergraduates is 21. Fifty-three percent of women undergraduates are over age 25 and 9 percent are over age 40.

The college offers associate, bachelor's, and master's programs in business, education, science, related technologies, the arts, and pre-professional fields. Alternative schedules and locations include on-campus evening classes, off-campus day and evening classes, a weekend college, self-paced/contract learning, and summer sessions. A continuing education program is offered through the Center for Adult and Professional Education. At the Old Westbury Campus, 18 percent of undergraduates commute. On-campus parking with free transportation from distant parking lots is available.

Women in Leadership Positions. *Students.* In recent years, women have occupied two of the five campus-wide leadership positions for which information was provided. They have served as president of the student body and manager of the campus radio station for one and two years respectively.

Faculty. Women are 18 percent of the 155 full-time faculty, a proportion below the national average. There are 3 female faculty for every 100 female students and 4 male faculty for every 100 male students.

Administrators. Women hold two of nine major administrative positions: chief student-life officer and head librarian. Women also hold the positions of Director of Media and Arts Center, Dean of Admissions, and Registrar. In one recent year, one of the three honorary degree recipients was a woman.

Women and the Curriculum. Most women earn bachelor's degrees in social sciences (57 percent) and business (17 percent). Three percent of women earn degrees in the nontraditional fields of architecture, computer science, and engineering. One-fourth of two-year degrees are awarded to women, all in business and commerce. One-third of available internships are held by women.

There are no courses on women. Faculty workshops are held on the needs of reentry women.

Women and Athletics. Twenty-three percent of intercollegiate athletes and 89 percent of intramural athletes are women, as are 6 of 20 paid varsity coaches. Over 50 percent of athletic scholarships are awarded to women. There are five intramural sports available. Intercollegiate sports offered are basketball, softball, track and volleyball.

Housing and Student Organizations. College-owned off-campus housing, all of it coeducational, is available for resident students. One female and two male residence-hall directors are offered special training on sex education and birth control.

Seventy-two undergraduates, 36 of them women, belong to social fraternities and sororities. The Women's Association serves as an advocacy group for women. The New Black Collegiate Organization meets on campus.

Special Services and Programs for Women. *Health and Counseling.* The college shares a student health service with a neighboring campus. A student counseling center is staffed by four women, including one minority woman, and four men. Services specific to women include counseling and treatment for gynecological matters, as well as birth control, abortion, and rape and assault counseling.

Safety and Security. Measures consist of campus police, high-intensity lighting, and self-defense courses for women. No rapes or assaults were reported for 1980–81.

Career. The college offers career workshops focused on nontraditional careers, lectures for students by women employed in nontraditional occupations, and job discrimination information.

Other. The student services division operates a Women's Center which serves 700 women annually, 5 percent of whom are minority women, largely black or Asian American. Under the direction of a part-time, salaried administrator, the center sponsors a variety of programs and serves both undergraduate and community women. The Women's Career Development Center, in conjunction with the Assistant Dean of Students, sponsors programs in assertiveness training.

Returning Women Students. The Center for Adult and Professional Education operates a continuing education program which attracts approximately 250 reentry women each year. Phase II, a club that focuses on the needs of returning women students, provides support for older women on campus.

Institutional Self-Description. "The mission of our college is to prepare our women students for their future. We prepare them for entry into their careers through majors which are geared to the job market. We give them the latest information available, such as affirmative action, assertiveness, and more. In the large co-curricular life, women gain interpersonal-relation skills, develop leadership skills, gain confidence, and learn to relate to both men and women."

New York School of Interior Design
155 E. 56 St., New York, NY 10022
Telephone: (212) 753-5365

Women in Leadership
★★ faculty
★ administrators

120 undergraduates

	Amer. Ind.	Asian Amer.	Blacks	Hispanics	Whites
F	0	5	3	2	79
M	0	0	1	1	19
%	0.0	4.5	3.6	2.7	89.1

Founded in 1916, the privately supported New York School of Interior Design began granting bachelor of fine arts degrees in 1975. It also offers a three-year diploma and a one-year certificatein professional design. Adult continuing education is offered through the Professional Training Program. Alternative scheduling includes evening classes held both on and off campus, and a summer session.

Among the 886 students who attend, 120 are registered in degree programs. The median age of degree students is 25. The majority (79 percent) of degree students are women; 7 of the women attend part-time. All students commute to the urban campus, which is easily accessible by public transportation.

Women in Leadership Positions. *Students.* There are no student offices.

Faculty. According to recent data, 37 percent of the faculty are women, a proportion considerably above the national average. The faculty includes one Asian American and one Hispanic woman.

Administrators. Of the six chief administrators, 2 are women, the executive vice president and the chief planning officer. Two of the 10 trustees are women, as was the spring 1981 commencement speaker. The recipient of an alumni award in 1980–81 was an Asian American woman. In addition, 2 of the 3 speakers in recent campus-wide lecture series were women.

Women and the Curriculum. Women earn 79 percent of bachelor's degrees, all of which are awarded in interior design. In a recent year, of the 25 students who earned two-year degrees in business, all but 4 were women; among 568 certificates for programs of less than two years, but at least one year, 541 were awarded to women and 27 to men. Women hold 85 percent of the available internships. There are no courses on women.

Women and Athletics. There is no sports program.

Special Services and Programs for Women. *Health and Counseling.* Neither a student health service nor a counseling center is available.

Safety and Security. Measures consist of New York City police and, according to the school, the "usual precautions" for their urban location. No rapes or assaults were reported for 1980–81.

Career. Women students have access to updated files of alumnae by specific career. Approximately 300 reentry women, of whom about 5 percent are minority women, are enrolled in the Professional Training Program.

Institutional Self-Description. "The New York School of Interior Design is located in mid-Manhattan near most of the major showrooms and design firms. Most of our faculty are professionals active in the field. About 90 percent of our students are women and their average age is 30. About half are changing careers, from occupations as diverse as homemaker to investment banking to operating a mobile disco. The appeal of interior design seems to be the chance to combine arts and creativity with a career in a business, with a range of opportunities from freelancing to corporate design firms."

New York University
70 Washington Square South
New York, NY 10012
Telephone: (212) 598-2891

| Women in Leadership ★ faculty | | | ★ Women and the Curriculum | |

9,000 undergraduates

	Amer. Ind.	Asian Amer.	Blacks	Hispanics	Whites
F	12	260	512	301	3,661
M	12	236	287	180	3,208
%	0.3	5.7	9.8	5.5	78.7

  AAUW NWSA

Founded in 1831 as a private institution, New York University occupies a campus around Washington Square in Manhattan. Some 31,600 students are enrolled in a range of undergraduate, graduate, and professional programs. The School of Continuing Education serves the adult student. Evening classes and a summer session are available.

Women make up 54 percent of the 9,000 undergradutes; 21 percent of women attend part-time. For the majority of undergraduates who commute, the university is accessible by public transportation. There is no on-campus parking.

Arrangements for private childcare may be made off campus.

Policies to Ensure Fairness to Women. A full-time affirmative action officer is responsible for policy and compliance with matters of equal employment opportunity, sex equity for students, and handicapped accessibility. A published policy prohibits sexual harassment.

Women in Leadership Positions. *Students.* Information on opportunities for women students to exercise campus-wide leadership was not furnished by the institution.

Faculty. Women are one-quarter of a full-time faculty of 1,187. According to a recent report, 27 black, 18 Asian American, and 17 Hispanic women are on the full-time faculty. The ratio of female faculty to female students is 8 to 100; the ratio of male faculty to male students is 25 to 100.

Administrators. The chief student-life officer and the chief development officer are women. Men hold the other top positions. Women chair 46 of 215 departments and are heads of 18 other academic units.

Women and the Curriculum. A majority of the women who graduate with bachelor's degrees major in fine arts, the health professions, business and management (15 percent each), and social sciences (10 percent). Women earn a higher proportion of degrees in business and public affairs than the average for comparable institutions. Four percent of women major in such nontraditional areas as computer science, mathematics, and the physical sciences. The university reports innovative programs to encourage women to prepare for careers in science, accounting, and computer science. Forty percent of the students in cooperative education programs and internships are female. Women earn two-thirds of the two-year degrees awarded; half of the degrees to women are in arts and sciences and one-fourth are in business.

Thirteen undergraduate and graduate courses on women are offered in the departments of history, psychology, English, sociology, and the University Without Walls. Recent titles include History of Women in Contemporary Society, Women in European History, Women in Revolution, Feminist Theory, The Image of Women in American Literature, and Sociology of Sex Roles. Faculty in the College of Liberal Arts and the School of Education are planning a Women's Studies Program. A committee in the history department collects materials and develops courses on women.

Such current topics as sex-fair curricula, innovative health-care delivery, health-care information important to minority women, services for abused spouses, and discrimination in the workplace are part of the preparation of future teachers, health-care workers, social workers, and business students.

Minority Women. Of 4,746 undergraduate women, 11 percent are black, 6 percent Hispanic, 5 percent Asian American, and less than 1 percent American Indian. The Organization of Black Women serves as a support and advocacy group.

Women and Athletics. Forty-four percent of intercollegiate athletes are women. Intramural and club sports are coeducational. The university reports a new recreational sports center. Four of nine paid varsity coaches are female. Intercollegiate sports offered are basketball, fencing, swimming, and diving, tennis, and volleyball.

Housing and Student Organizations. Thirteen percent of the undergraduates live on campus. Coeducational residence halls are available. A married woman student whose spouse is not enrolled may live in university housing. Dormitories restrict hours for visitors of the opposite sex.

Four percent of undergraduate women belong to social sororities, which do not provide housing for their members. Among groups that serve as advocates for women are the Women's Career Forum, Women in Communications, Gay People's Union, Women's Center, Organization of Black Women, and the Inter-Sorority and Sisterhood Council.

Special Services and Programs for Women. *Health and Counseling.* The student health service provides some medical attention specific to women: gynecological and birth control treatment is available, and abortion by referral. One-third of the physicians are women, as are eight other health-care providers. The regular student health insurance covers maternity at no extra cost. In the counseling center, five of nine professional staff are women. Staff receive in-service training on sex-role stereotyping and racial bias. Students have access to some counseling of particular concern to women.

Safety and Security. Measures include campus and metropolitan police, night-time escorts for all students, high-intensity lighting, emergency alarm and telephone systems, and self-defense courses for women. No information was provided about the incidence of rapes and assaults.

Career. Workshops, panels, and nonsexist/nonracist printed materials on nontraditional careers and fields of study, as well as a network of contacts between alumnae and students are available. The Women's Career Forum sponsors lectures and assertiveness training.

Special Features. WATCH—Women Advancing Through Career Help—focuses on career planning and change; WISDOM—a program designed for older women—provides workshops and other support serves.

Institutional Self-Description. "Not only is NYU located in New York City, it is located in Greenwich Village, a community well known for its high representation by women and women's groups."

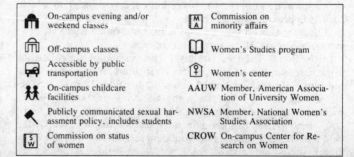

🏛	On-campus evening and/or weekend classes	M A	Commission on minority affairs
🏛	Off-campus classes	📖	Women's Studies program
🚍	Accessible by public transportation	🏠	Women's center
👫	On-campus childcare facilities	AAUW	Member, American Association of University Women
⚒	Publicly communicated sexual harassment policy, includes students	NWSA	Member, National Women's Studies Association
S W	Commission on status of women	CROW	On-campus Center for Research on Women

Niagara University
Niagara University, NY 14109
Telephone: (716) 285-1212

Women in Leadership
★★ faculty

3,204 undergraduates

	Amer. Ind.	Asian Amer.	Blacks	Hispanics	Whites
F	9	5	71	8	1,555
M	8	3	76	16	1,453
%	0.5	0.3	4.6	0.8	93.9

 AAUW

Niagara University, founded in 1856 and operated by the Vincentian Fathers, is an independent, Roman Catholic institution for men and women. Located several miles from Niagara Falls in a Buffalo suburb, it has a total enrollment of 4,478. About half of the 3,204 undergraduates are women, and 7 percent of women attend part-time. The median age of all undergraduates is 27.

The university offers associate, bachelor's, and master's degrees in liberal arts and professional fields. Classes are conducted on and off campus, during the daytime and evening. Opportunities for independent study are available; a summer session is offered. The Office of Special Programs provides adult continuing education. The campus is accessible by public transportation for the 40 percent of undergraduates who commute. On-campus parking is available at a fee.

Policies to Ensure Fairness to Women. The Affirmative Action Officer assumes part-time responsibility for monitoring compliance with laws governing sex equity for students, equal opportunity, and handicapped access. A published campus policy prohibits the sexual harassment of all members of the Niagara community.

Women in Leadership Positions. *Students.* In recent years, women have served twice as president of the student body, the student senate, and the junior class, and once as editor-in-chief of the campus newspaper.

Faculty. Thirty-eight percent of the 165 full-time faculty are women, a proportion above the national average. There are 4 female faculty for every 100 female students and 7 male faculty for every 100 male students.

Administrators. All top-level administrators, except the director of institutional research, are men. Women chair six of 23 departments: history, nursing (introductory, intermediate, and advanced), psychology, and religious studies. The Dean of Women and the Director of Advisement are women. Women have two seats on the 19-member Board of Trustees.

Women and the Curriculum. Over half of the women who earn bachelor's degrees major in health professions; 20 percent of the women graduate in business (as do 60 percent of the men). Two percent of the of the women major in the nontraditional fields of mathematics or physical sciences. Women receive most of the few associate degrees granted, all in business/commerce.

No courses on women are offered. Workshops on affirmative action and equal opportunity are offered to faculty.

Women and Athletics. The limited competitive sports program for women emphasizes team sports. Of the five paid intercollegiate coaches, four are women. The intercollegiate sports offered are basketball, softball, swimming, tennis, and volleyball.

Housing and Student Organizations. Sixty percent of the undergraduates live on campus, in single-sex dormitories that do not permit visits by members of the opposite sex. Residence-hall staff receive awareness-training on sexism, sex education, and racism.

Special Services and Programs for Women. *Health and Counseling.* The student health service employs 3 male physicians and 9 female health-care providers. It does not provide medical services specific to women. One female and 2 male counselors staff the student counseling center. The center offers such services as gynecological and rape and assault counseling. The counselors are offered awareness-training in avoiding sex-role stereotyping and racism.

Safety and Security. Measures consist of campus police protection, high-intensity lighting, and information on campus safety for women. Information on the incidence of rapes and assaults was not reported.

Career. The college provides printed information and nontraditional fields of study for women. The campus ministry organizes leadership training workshops for women.

Institutional Self-Description. None provided.

Pace University, College of White Plains
78 North Broadway, White Plains, NY 10603
Telephone: (914) 682-7000

Women in Leadership
★★ students
★★ faculty
★★★ administrators

582 undergraduates

	Amer. Ind.	Asian Amer.	Blacks	Hispanics	Whites
F	4	6	59	20	285
M	1	7	14	7	179
%	0.9	2.2	12.5	4.6	79.7

Pace University, White Plains, formerly the College of White Plains, was established in 1929 as a Roman Catholic liberal arts college for women. In 1975, it assumed its present identity as one of three Pace campuses. The White Plains campus, an independent college which retains a Catholic tradition, enrolls some 2,000 students, 582 of them undergraduates. Women are 64 percent of all undergraduates, and 21 percent of the women attend part-time. The median age of all undergraduates is 22, although recent data show 42 percent of undergraduate women are over 25.

The college offers a variety of associate, bachelor's, and graduate degree programs, in addition to a continuing education program. Classes which meet during the day and evenings are supplemented by a weekend college and a summer session. Eighty-eight percent of the undergraduates commute to this suburban campus, which is within reach of public transportation. Commuters can park on campus and use free transportation from distant parking lots to classroom buildings.

Private childcare facilities are located near the campus.

Policies to Ensure Fairness to Women. See Pace University, Pace Plaza.

Women in Leadership Positions. *Students.* Opportunities for women to exercise campus-wide leadership are excellent. In the last three years, women have held 56 percent of the campus leadership posts. Women have presided over the student body and junior and sophomore classes for one year, and have served two years as president of the student union board, senior class, and editor-in-chief of the campus newspaper. Women have been president of the entering class for the past three years.

Faculty. Thirty-five percent of the 46 full-time faculty are women, a proportion above the national average. There are 5 female faculty for every 100 students and 16 male faculty for every 100 male students.

Administrators. Three of the five key administrators are women: head librarian, director of institutional research, and chief business officer. Women chair the departments of history/economics/political science, human studies, and arts and letters.

Women and the Curriculum. Half of degrees awarded to women are in interdisciplinary studies.

Four courses on women are taught by faculty from the departments of human studies, arts and letters, and languages. The mathematics department provides instruction on mathematics anxiety.

Women and Athletics. The organized, competitive sports program for women consists of intramural softball and volleyball. About a fourth of the intramural participants are women.

Housing and Student Organizations. Twelve percent of the undergraduates live on campus in coeducational dormitories that have no restrictive hours for visitors of the opposite sex. Three student groups, the Black Student Union, Caribbean Students Association, and Encanto Latino, address the concerns of minority women.

Special Services and Programs for Women. *Health and Counseling.* The student health service is staffed by one female health-care provider. The student counseling center staff consists of one female counselor. No information was provided regarding the availability of services specific to women.

Safety and Security. Measures consist of campus police with no authority to make arrests night-time escort for women students, and high-intensity lighting. No rapes or assaults were reported for 1980–81.

Career. The university offers career workshops and information on nontraditional occupations, along with lectures by women employed in these fields, and encourages the formation of networks with alumnae. The counseling center organizes assertiveness training sessions for women.

Institutional Self-Description. "The good reputation of the Business Program and the liberal arts tradition, as well as the small size of the undergraduate student body are appealing factors in attracting women to this campus."

Pace University, Pace Plaza

Pace Plaza, New York, NY 10038
Telephone: (212) 285-3000

Women in Leadership
★ faculty

5,173 undergraduates

	Amer. Ind.	Asian Amer.	Blacks	Hispanics	Whites
F	10	124	665	273	1,549
M	7	123	345	194	1,769
%	0.3	4.9	20.0	9.2	65.6

Established in 1901, Pace University is a private, non-sectarian, coeducational institution with three campuses, the main one located in downtown New York City. The two suburban campuses are in White Plains and Pleasantville. The Pace Plaza campus attracts 11,496 students, including 5,173 undergraduates. Women are 52 percent of the undergraduates, and 39 percent of women attend part-time. The median age of all undergraduates is 23.

Pace offers associate, bachelor's, and graduate degrees in a wide variety of fields. Classes meet on and off campus during the day and evening. University College is responsible for the various adult continuing education programs. Ninety-eight percent of the undergraduates commute to Pace Plaza, which is accessible by public transportation. Municipal parking is available nearby for a fee.

A campus childcare facility gives priority to the children of faculty and staff, but all students' requests for childcare are met. The center serves 30 children at one time and fees are based on a fixed daily rate. Additional, private childcare facilities are available close to campus.

Policies to Ensure Fairness to Women. An affirmative action officer who is also the University Human Resources Director has the part-time responsibility, for all three campuses, for handling matters relating to sex-fair employment laws. A written, publicized sexual harassment policy protects the staff but not students or faculty. Complaints are resolved through a formal grievance procedure. A Committee on Minority Affairs addresses the concerns of minority women.

Women in Leadership Positions. *Students.* Women have few opportunities to exercise campus-wide leadership. In recent years, women have served once as student-body president and student senate president, and twice as editor-in-chief of the campus newspaper.

Faculty. One-third of the 399 full-time faculty are women. There are 8 female faculty for every 100 female students and 17 male faculty for every 100 male students.

Administrators. Men hold all top positions. Women account for 44 percent of the faculty senate. Four of the 10 members of the faculty tenure committee are women.

Women and the Curriculum. Three-fourths of all women graduating with bachelor's degrees specialize in business. A special program encourages women to prepare for business management careers. Four percent of the women earn degrees in such nontraditional fields as computer science, mathematics, and physical sciences. Most women who earn two-year degrees and certificates major in business/commerce and health technologies. Fifty-six percent of the participants in cooperative education programs are women, as are 88 percent of students in internship programs.

Seven courses on women are offered, including Women and the Law, Women in European Society, and an interdisciplinary course on Women in 19th-Century America. Business students learn about problems confronting women in the workplace. Prospective teachers are shown how to use and create nonsexist teaching materials. Nursing students are informed about issues of concern to minority women.

Minority Women. Forty percent of the female undergraduates are minority women. Recent data report four black and five Asian American women among the full-time faculty. Twenty-five minority women belong to all-minority sororities. Eighty-five percent of reentry women enrolled in adult continuing education courses are minority women, black women mainly.

Women and Athletics. No information was provided on intramural or club sports. Women receive one-fifth of the athletic scholarship aid. The intercollegiate sport offered for women is fencing.

Housing and Student Organizations. Two percent of the undergraduates live on campus in coeducational dormitories with single-sex floors. Residence halls do not restrict visiting hours for members of the opposite sex. Residence-hall staff receive awareness-training on birth control.

Nine percent of the full-time undergraduate women belong to social sororities. Phi Chi Theta, a women's advocacy group, has 25 active members. Graduate women in the School of Business have their own support group.

Special Services and Programs for Women. *Health and Counseling.* The student health center is staffed by two female health-care providers. No medical treatment specific to women is available. Four women and four men staff the student counseling center, which provides referral services on matters specific to women, such as birth control and rape and assault counseling.

Safety and Security. Measures consist of a campus police force. No rapes or assaults on women were reported for 1980–81.

Career. Career placement services include workshops, lectures and information on nontraditional occupations, and programs to foster networking between students and alumnae. Individual interviews for women seeking career information are also available.

Returning Women Students. University College sponsors a variety of continuing education programs for women. The Associate Studies Trimester Evening Program, directed by a minority woman, serves predominantly minority working women who are seeking an associate degree in order to advance to managerial and administrative positions. A Continuing Education for Women program enrolls 470 women. The counseling center organizes assertiveness training workshops for returning women.

Institutional Self-Description. "Well over 200 companies recruit on all the university campuses, and placement regardless of sex is encouraged. A system of alumni networking is being developed and a special career counseling and placement division is in operation. Role models are afforded through faculty appointments and administrators, with several university vice president positions being held by women."

Pace University
Pleasantville-Briarcliff Campus
861 Bedford Road
Pleasantville, NY 10570
Telephone: (914) 769-3200

Women in Leadership
★ **faculty**

3,143 undergraduates

	Amer. Ind.	Asian Amer.	Blacks	Hispanics	Whites
F	7	12	116	29	1,628
M	5	12	35	23	1,253
%	0.4	0.8	4.8	1.7	92.3

Established in 1963, Pace University at Pleasantville-Briarcliff is one of the three campuses of Pace University, a private, coeducational institution of higher learning. At its suburban campus north of New York City, Pace has a total enrollment of 4,743 students, including 3,143 undergraduates. Fifty-seven percent of the undergraduates are women, and 41 percent of women attend part-time. The median age of undergraduates is 22.

Pace offers a variety of associate, bachelor's, and graduate degrees. University College is responsible for adult continuing education. Students may cross-register at any of the three campuses. Classes are scheduled during the day and evening on campus; some courses are offered, evenings, off campus; a weekend college and a summer session are available. For the three-fourths of the undergraduates who commute or live off campus, public transportation is available, as well as on-campus parking.

Policies to Ensure Fairness to Women. See Pace University, Pace Plaza.

Women in Leadership Positions. *Students.* Women students have had little opportunity to exercise campus-wide leadership. In three recent years, a women has been campus newspaper editor; the 5 other major campus leadership positions have been held by men.

Faculty. Thirty-four percent of the 98 full-time faculty are women, a proportion which is above the national average. There are 3 female faculty for every 100 female students, and 6 male faculty for every 100 male students.

Administrators. Men hold all top positions. Women chair eight of 20 departments: computer information science, art, foreign languages, education, secretarial studies, equine studies, A.A.

nursing, and B.S. nursing. On the 30-member Board of Trustees, there are four women.

Women and the Curriculum. Women receive 93 percent of the two-year degrees and certificates, most of which are in areas of health technology. One-half of the women graduating with bachelor's degrees major in health professions and 29 percent specialize in business. Less than 3 percent of the women major in the nontraditional fields of computer science, mathematics, or physical sciences.

The Pleasantville-Briarcliff campus offers three courses on women in the departments of history, literature/composition, and psychology: History of American Women, Images of Women in Literature, and Psychology of Women.

Women and Athletics. The intramural and intercollegiate sports programs provide some opportunities for women. Four of the 21 paid coaches for intercollegiate sports are women. Forty-one percent of the intercollegiate athletes are women, and women receive 30 percent of the available athletic scholarship assistance. Women are 4 percent of participants in the intramural program. Intercollegiate sports offered are basketball, cross-country, fencing, softball, tennis, and volleyball.

Housing and Student Organizations. One-fourth of the undergraduates live on campus in single-sex or coeducational dormitories that have no restrictive hours for members of the opposite sex. The nine women on the 14-member residence-hall staff include one minority woman. Residence-hall staff receive awareness-training on sexism, racism, and counseling about birth control.

Special Services and Programs for Women. *Health and Counseling.* The student health center is staffed by 1 male physician and 3 female health-care providers. The student counseling center employs 3 female and 2 male counselors. Counseling is offered for gynecological problems, birth control, abortion, and rape and assault. No information was provided about medical services specific to women.

Safety and Security. Measures consist of campus police without arrest authority, local police, high-intensity lighting, and an emergency phone system. No information was provided on the incidence of rapes and assaults.

Career. A special program, New Directions for Women, assists women seeking a second career after having been full-time homemakers for a number of years.

Institutional Self-Description. "Well over 200 companies recruit on the three university campuses, and placement regardless of sex is encouraged. A system of alumni networking is being developed and a special career counseling and placement division is in operation. Role models are afforded through faculty appointments and administrators, with several university vice president positions being held by women."

Paul Smith's College
Paul Smiths, NY 12970
Telephone: (518) 327-6211

Women in Leadership
★★★ **students**

1,045 undergraduates

	Amer. Ind.	Asian Amer.	Blacks	Hispanics	Whites
F	0	0	0	0	204
M	0	0	1	1	820
%	0.0	0.0	0.1	0.1	99.8

This private, two-year college is located near Lake Placid in the Adirondacks. Twenty percent of the 1,045 students are women, all of whom attend full-time. The median age of all students is 19. Paul Smith's College offers two-year degree programs in a range of fields, including liberal arts, business, engineering/technology, ecology and environmental technology, forestry, and hotel management. On-campus evening classes, a summer session, contract learning, and transfer programs are available. Two percent of students commute to the campus, which is not accessible by public transportation. Free on-campus parking is available.

Policies to Ensure Fairness to Women. Two administrators have responsibility part-time for policy relating to equal employment opportunity, educational sex equity, and handicapped access. A formal campus grievance procedure which ensures due process resolves complaints of sexual harassment.

Women in Leadership Positions. *Students.* Although women constitute only 20 percent of the students, during a recent three-year period they held half of the available leadership positions, including two-year terms as president of the student body and student senate, editor-in-chief of the campus newspaper, president of the sophomore class, and a one-year term as president of the entering class.

Faculty. Eighteen percent of the 72 full-time faculty are women, a proportion lower than the national average. There are 6 female faculty for every 100 female students and 7 male faculty for every 100 male students.

Administrators. All major administrative positions are held by men. The departments of English, mathematics, and chef training are chaired by women; the division of ecology and environmental technology is also headed by a woman. In one recent year, the commencement speaker was a woman.

Women and the Curriculum. Most women earn two-year degrees in business and commercial technologies (45 percent), public service (29 percent), and natural science (23 percent). The college offers a cooperative education program. There are no courses on women.

Women and Athletics. Team sports predominate in the athletic program for women. Thirty-two percent of intercollegiate athletes are women, who receive 30 percent of the athletic scholarships. Half of the paid coaching staff for intercollegiate sports are women. The college offers intramural basketball, softball, and volleyball, and extensive intramural facilities encourage individual outdoor recreation. Intercollegiate sports offered are basketball, skiing, softball, and volleyball.

Housing and Student Organizations. Eighty-five percent of students live on campus in single-sex or coeducational dormitories that have restrictive hours for visitors of the opposite sex. One-fourth of the 40 residence-hall directors are women.

Special Services and Programs for Women. *Health and Counseling.* A student health service staffed by 3 male physicians and 2 female health-care providers, as well as a student counseling center staffed by 1 woman and 1 man, provide counseling and treatment for birth control and gynecological problems, along with abortion counseling. In addition, prenatal care and treatment for rape and assault are available.

Safety and Security. Measures consist of local police, campus police without arrest authority, and information sessions and lectures on campus safety and rape prevention. No rapes or assaults were reported for 1980–81.

Career. The placement office provides information on job discrimination in nontraditional occupations for women.

Institutional Self-Description. "Paul Smith's College offers an unparalleled natural environment for studying the liberal arts, and a variety of work-oriented curricula giving entry into the rapidly expanding hospitality industry, and into business administration, ecology, forestry, and tourism and travel."

Polytechnic Institute of New York
333 Jay Street, Brooklyn, NY 11201
Telephone: (212) 643-5113

Women in Leadership
★★★ students

2,386 undergraduates

	Amer. Ind.	Asian Amer.	Blacks	Hispanics	Whites
F	3	48	11	8	120
M	7	380	202	158	1,357
%	0.4	18.7	9.3	7.2	64.4

 AAUW

Formed in 1873 by the merger of the New York University School of Engineering with the Polytechnic Institute of Brooklyn, Polytechnic Institute has an urban campus in Brooklyn and a teaching and research center on Long Island. The institute enrolls 6,618 students, including 2,386 undergraduates. Women are 8 percent of the undergraduates; 30 percent of women attend part-time. There is a summer session. The Brooklyn campus is accessible by public transportation; the Long Island campus provides free parking.

Policies to Ensure Fairness to Women. The Affirmative Action Officer, who has policymaking authority, oversees compliance with laws on equal employment opportunity and access for the handicapped. A published policy prohibits sexual harassment of students, faculty, and staff. Complaints are resolved informally and confidentially. A self-designated Committee on the Status of Women publishes a newsletter for the college community.

Women in Leadership Positions. *Students.* The institution reports that women hold three of 14 seats on the student council— the only campus-wide leadership positions.

Faculty. Four percent of the 230 full-time faculty are women, a proportion far below the national average. There are 6 female faculty for every 100 female students and 12 male faculty for every 100 male students.

Administrators. Of the eight top administrators, the director of institutional research is a woman. Of the 15 departments, life science is chaired by a woman. One woman sits on an important seven-member faculty committee.

Women and the Curriculum. Virtually all students major in science or engineering. In one recent year, 91 percent of women graduates earned degrees in the nontraditional fields of computer science, engineering, mathematics, and physical sciences. The institute maintains several programs to encourage minority, reentry, and other women to prepare for nontraditional careers. Nine percent of the students in the cooperative education program are women. Faculty workshops deal with nontraditional occupations and the needs of reentry women.

Women and Athletics. Thirty women participate in intramural sports. The institute has no intercollegiate or club sports for women.

Housing and Student Organizations. Three percent of the students live on campus in coeducational dormitories. The Society of Women Engineers is an advocacy group for women. The National Society of Black Engineers includes black women.

Special Services and Programs for Women. *Health and Counseling.* There are no student health or counseling services.

Safety and Security. Campus guards without arrest authority are supplemented by local police. No rapes or assaults on women were reported for 1980–81.

Other. The Polytechnic Institute is the headquarters of the Women's Reentry Consortium, funded by the National Science Foundation. A small group of faculty and staff, called WISE (Women's Information and Service Exchange), publish a newsletter for the whole campus. With support from the National Science Foundation, Polytechnic has participated in establishing the WIMSE (Women in Math, Science and Engineering) Network.

Institutional Self-Description. "For the woman pursing a non-traditional career, the key to success is the choice of educational institution. Polytechnic is noted for excellence. Polytechnic offers a 'no-frills,' quality education in science and engineering. Ninety-five percent of its graduates are placed in exciting jobs at salaries exceeding national averages."

Russell Sage College
Troy, NY 12180
Telephone: (518) 270-2200

Women in Leadership
★★★ students
★★★ faculty
★ administrators

1,818 undergraduates

	Amer. Ind.	Asian Amer.	Blacks	Hispanics	Whites
F	1	2	33	23	1,602
M	0	0	3	0	146
%	0.1	0.1	2.0	1.3	96.6

Russell Sage, founded in 1916 as a woman's college, focused exclusively on women's education for its first 25 years. Today, the college serves 3,440 students on the Russell Sage campus located near Albany, and in its evening division and Junior College of Albany, where it is coeducational. Ninety-two percent of the undergraduates are women; 17 percent of women students attend part-time.

Undergraduate and graduate degrees are available in a variety of liberal arts and pre-professional fields. The evening division and Junior College offer private education to urban commuting students. Alternative scheduling includes day and evening classes and a weekend college. Three-fourths of the undergraduates live on campus in women's dormitories that have no restrictions on men's visiting hours. The campus is accessible by public transportation, and on-campus parking is available.

A campus childcare facility accommodates 43 children, at a fixed daily fee. All students' requests for this service can be met. Additional, private facilities are located near the campus.

Policies to Ensure Fairness to Women. The Vice President for Student Affairs is responsible for policy relating to handicapped accessibility, equal employment opportunity, and educational sex equity. The Director of Personnel monitors compliance with equal-employment-opportunity laws as they apply to staff. A sexual harassment policy protects students, faculty, and staff; complaints are resolved informally or through a formal grievance procedure.

Women in Leadership Positions. *Students.* Women hold all student leadership positions.

Faculty. Fifty-nine percent of the 135 full-time faculty are women, a proportion which is above average for women's colleges. There are 6 female faculty for every 100 female students.

Administrators. Women hold the positions of chief business officer, chief student-life officer, director of athletics, and academic dean of the Women's College. Women chair nine of 17 departments: biology, education, health education, mathematics, modern languages, nursing, physical therapy, physical education, and sociology.

Women and the Curriculum. Most women earn degrees in health professions (40 percent), education (18 percent), and business (13 percent). Three percent of women major in such nontra-

ditional fields as mathematics or physical sciences. The college offers programs designed to encourage women to prepare for careers in engineering, accounting, computer science, and law enforcement/corrections.

There are no courses on women. The departments of education, physical education, nursing, and business provide instruction on several matters specific to women.

Women and Athletics. The incomplete information provided about the organized sports program indicates that two intramural activities—volleyball and soccer—are available. Intercollegiate sports offered are field hockey and lacrosse.

Special Services and Programs for Women. *Health and Counseling.* The student health center is staffed by two male physicians and six female health-care providers. One female counselor is employed by the student counseling center. Counseling and medical treatment for gynecological problems and birth control are available.

Safety and Security. Measures consist of campus and local police, high-intensity lighting, and instruction on self defense. No rapes or assaults on women were reported for 1980–81.

Career. The Career Development Center offers workshops, lectures, and information on nontraditional occupations, in addition to networking between alumnae and students and files for student use on the careers of alumnae.

Other. A Women's Center attracts 100, primarily older, students each year. Special programs include a mathematics confidence clinic, assertiveness training, and student affairs programs that emphasize self-development. The library has a Women's Studies collection. The Black and Latin Alliance is an advocacy group.

Institutional Self-Description. "A personal approach to your success is the ideal to which Russell Sage College is committed. We direct our programs and services to meet the needs of our women students. Our professional programs, enhanced by the vast liberal arts offering, provide our students with a flexible academic preparation."

St. Bonaventure University
St. Bonaventure, NY 14778;
Telephone: (716) 375-2000

Women in Leadership
★ students

2,139 undergraduates

	Amer. Ind.	Asian Amer.	Blacks	Hispanics	Whites
F	2	0	1	0	995
M	2	2	5	2	1,127
%	0.2	0.1	0.3	0.1	99.3

Founded by the Franciscan Order in 1855, St. Bonaventure is a private coeducational university affiliated with the Roman Catholic Church. It attracts some 2,700 students, including part-time and graduate students, to its campus located southwest of Buffalo. Women represent 47 percent of the 2,139 undergraduates. The median age of undergraduates is 20. Virtually all students attend full-time. For commuting students, on-campus parking is available.

Private childcare is available off campus.

Policies to Ensure Fairness to Women. An equal-opportunity officer, on a part-time basis, monitors compliance with sex-equity and handicapped-access legislation. Complaints of sexual harassment are handled informally and confidentially.

Women in Leadership Positions. *Students.* Three campus leadership positions exist for students. In recent years women served as presiding officer of the student government for two years and editor-in-chief of the campus newspaper for one year.

Faculty. Women account for 13 percent of the 145 full-time faculty and 4 percent of the 80 permanently appointed faculty. There are 2 female faculty for every 100 female students, compared with 11 male faculty for every 100 male students.

Administrators. Men hold all top positions. Two of 30 departments are chaired by women: management, and marketing. Two of the 18 faculty senate members are women; a woman was 1 of the 3 recipients of honorary degrees in spring 1981.

Women and the Curriculum. Most women take degrees in education (22 percent), business (19 percent, versus nearly 52 percent of men), and communications (17 percent); 4 percent take degrees in mathematics and the physical sciences.

Individual courses on women are offered by the departments of sociology, management sciences, classical languages, and theology. The physical education department and the schools of social work and business provide instruction on some matters specific to women.

Women and Athletics. Women participate in both intramural and intercollegiate sports. Forty percent of the athletic scholarships awarded in 1980 went to women. Intercollegiate sports include basketball, field hockey, softball, swimming, tennis, track, and volleyball.

Housing and Student Organizations. Three-quarters of all students reside on-campus in single-sex and coeducational dormitories or apartment complexes. There are restrictive hours for visitors of the opposite sex. Residence-hall staff receive awareness-training on sexism.

The Women's Council serves as an advocate for women on campus.

Special Services and Programs for Women. *Health and Counseling.* The student health service is staffed by 2 male physicians and 7 female health-care providers. It does not provide services specific to women. One of the 6 counselors is a woman. Counseling is available on gynecological problems, birth control, abortion, rape and assault, and alcohol and drug abuse.

Safety and Security. Measures include campus and local police, a night-time escort for women students, and high-intensity lighting. Of the three assaults reported for 1980–81, two were on women.

Other. A woman's lecture series is offered by the School of Business in cooperation with the Olean Zonta Club. In conjunction with the Office of Academic Affairs, the School of Business sponsors assertiveness training.

Institutional Self-Description. "St. Bonaventure University was founded as an institution of higher learning whose goal is to impart to young men and women a liberal education of academic excellence with its principal objective of developing the integrated person. Supported by its special heritage as a university founded in the Franciscan tradition, the institution seeks to communicate knowledge of the values of Western culture and to distill and convey the values of community service in profession and practice as integrating forces in the life of the individual in society."

	On-campus evening and/or weekend classes		Commission on minority affairs
	Off-campus classes		Women's Studies program
	Accessible by public transportation		Women's center
	On-campus childcare facilities	AAUW	Member, American Association of University Women
	Publicly communicated sexual harassment policy, includes students	NWSA	Member, National Women's Studies Association
	Commission on status of women	CROW	On-campus Center for Research on Women

---

St. Lawrence University
Canton, NY 13617
Telephone: (315) 379-5011

★ **Women and the Curriculum**

2,288 undergraduates

	Amer. Ind.	Asian Amer.	Blacks	Hispanics	Whites
F	0	0	18	0	1,052
M	0	0	27	0	1,155
%	0.0	0.0	2.0	0.0	98.0

AAUW

Founded in 1856 as a Universalist theological school, Saint Lawrence University later became the first chartered coeducational institution in New York State. Of the 2,503 students, 2,288 are undergraduates. Forty-seven percent of the undergraduates are women, virtually all of whom attend full-time. The median age of all students is 20 years. St. Lawrence awards bachelor's degrees in a variety of fields. No public transportation is available for the 1 percent of students who commute; on-campus parking is provided without charge.

Private childcare facilities are available nearby.

Policies to Ensure Fairness to Women. The Associate Dean of the College has part-time responsibility for establishing policies relating to equal-employment-opportunity, educational—sex-equity and handicapped-accessibility laws. Complaints of sexual harassment are resolved through a formal grievance procedure. The Committee on the Status of Women, appointed by the President, includes voting student members and prepares an annual report which is distributed to the campus community. The committee also considers issues of concern to minority women

Women in Leadership Positions. *Students.* Women have limited opportunities to exercise leadership on campus. In recent years, women have served one year each as president of the student board, student court, and entering class; women have been editor-in-chief of the campus paper three years in succession. Women head six of the 18 honorary societies.

Faculty. Seventeen percent of the 157 full-time faculty are women. Three women sit on the 11-member faculty senate. There are 3 female faculty for every 100 students and 11 male faculty for every 100 male students.

Administrators. The top administrators are men. Of the 21 departments, psychology is chaired by a woman. Six of the 42 trustees are women.

Women and the Curriculum. A third of the women graduate in social sciences; significant numbers earn degrees in the humanities and in psychology. Twelve percent of women graduates, and 13 percent of men, earn degrees in mathematics or physical sciences. Eleven percent of women graduates major in biology. Women hold 45 percent of the internships and practicums and account for 38 percent of the student participants in science field work.

The Women's Studies Program is coordinated by a committee that also collects curricular materials and develops courses on women in traditional departments. Women's Studies courses may be incorporated into a student's multi-field major. Three courses on women are offered through the departments of English, government, and psychology: Women in Literature, Women in Politics, and Psychology of Women. Faculty workshops cover the topics of affirmative action and equal opportunity, sexism in the curriculum, nontraditional careers for women and men.

Women and Athletics. About 900 women participate in intramural and club sports, including several annual mini-tournaments. There are five intramural sports. The intercollegiate program provides a balance between team and individual sports. Women account for 37 percent of the intercollegiate athletes; four of the 19 paid coaches are women. Intercollegiate sports for women include basketball, field hockey, ice hockey, lacrosse, riding, skiing, soccer, swimming, tennis, and volleyball.

Housing and Student Organizations. Ninety-five percent of students live on campus in single-sex or coeducational dormitories, theme cottages, small apartment-cottages, and fraternity and sorority houses. Two percent of undergraduate women living in dormitories are black women. Two of the seven dormitory directors are women. Dormitory staff are offered awareness-training on sex education, birth control, and sexism.

Half of the 780 members of Greek social organizations are sorority women, five of whom are minority women. Student advocacy groups for women include the Black Student Union, the Native American Organization, and a women's group called Chrysalis.

Special Services and Programs for Women. *Health and Counseling.* The student health service is staffed by 1 full-time physician, assisted part-time by another male physician and full-time by 13 health-care providers, of whom 11 are women. Two of the 13-member staff of the student counseling center are women. Counseling and medical treatment are available for gynecological problems, birth control, and rape and assault; only counseling is available for abortion.

Safety and Security. Measures include campus police without arrest authority, and information about campus safety and assault prevention. No rapes and three assaults (one against a woman) were reported for 1980–81.

Career. Career planning programs offer lectures and literature on nontraditional occupations, job discrimination, and student-alumnae networks.

Other. The Office of Student Affairs maintains a Women's Center with a part-time faculty coordinator. Student Services provides assertiveness training and sponsors an annual women's week. Chrysalis sponsors a women's lecture series.

Institutional Self-Description. "Positive coeducation implies learning and achieving together, without deference to sexual stereotypes, in a setting where equal opportunity exists naturally in every facet of campus life. Men and women must view each other as co-learners experiencing and contributing to the same educational process. The degree to which this equality is made real will determine the level of success of coeducation at St. Lawrence. Properly realized, it becomes a new education for everyone."

Sarah Lawrence College
Bronxville, NY 10708
Telephone: (914) 337-0700

Women in Leadership	★ Women and the
★★ faculty	Curriculum
★★★ administrators	

852 undergraduates

	Amer. Ind.	Asian Amer.	Blacks	Hispanics	Whites
F	0	8	19	4	625
M	0	1	4	2	168
%	0.0	1.1	2.8	0.7	95.4

📖 🏛 **AAUW**

Some 990 students attend Sarah Lawrence, a private, liberal arts college located north of Manhattan. Founded as a college for women in 1928, it has been coeducational since 1968. Seventy-nine percent of the 852 degree students are women, 14 percent of whom attend part-time. The median age of all students is 19.

Bachelor's and master's degrees are offered in a variety of liberal arts and pre-professional fields. The Center for Continuing Education serves adult women. The college also offers self-paced/contract learning opportunities and a summer session. The sub-

urban campus is accessible by public transportation. Free on-campus parking is also available for the 24 percent of students who commute.

Private childcare facilities are available near the campus.

Women in Leadership Positions. *Students.* Information on student leadership positions is not available.

Faculty. Thirty-six percent of the full-time faculty of 61 are women. There are 4 female faculty for every 100 female students, and 2 male faculty for every 100 male students.

Administrators. Women hold four of the seven top-level administrative positions, including chief executive officer, Director of Graduate Studies, chief student-life officer, Dean of Administration and Communications, Dean of Studies, head librarian, and Director of the Center for Continuing Education. Sixteen of the 25 trustees are female.

Women and the Curriculum. Undergraduates do not have majors or minors; all degrees are interdisciplinary. Students concentrate in broad fields of study such as the social sciences, literature and writing, music, languages, sciences and mathematics. The college offers programs to encourage women to prepare for careers in health advocacy and human genetics.

The Women's Studies Program offers an M.A. in Women's History and no undergraduate degree. Courses open to undergraduates and graduate students include Women and American History, Women Writers in the 18th Century, and Women in Anthropology. A committee is responsible for the development of the Women's Studies Program and for encouraging the inclusion of women in other courses. A workshop on the relationships among sex, race, and selecton of a major field is available to the faculty.

Women and Athletics. The small intramural program attracts about 40 women. Both paid varsity coaches are women. The five women's varsity teams competed in recent tournaments. Intercollegiate sports offered are basketball, riding, softball, tennis, and volleyball.

Housing and Student Organizations. Single-sex and coeducational dormitories, housing the 76 percent of undergradutes who live on campus, do not have restrictive hours for visitors of the opposite sex. Awareness-training on sexism, and racism, sex education, and birth control is available to residence-hall staff.

The Feminist Alliance serves as an advocacy group for all women students. The Third World Organization is an advocacy group especially for minority students, including women.

Special Services and Programs for Women. *Health and Counseling.* The student health service has a staff of 1 female and 6 male physicians and 3 female health-care providers. It offers gynecological and birth control treatment. The student counseling center offers services in these areas, as well as abortion and rape and assault counseling. One of the 6 counselors is a woman. The regular student health insurance covers maternity expenses at no extra charge.

Safety and Security. Measures consist of campus and local police, a night-time escort service for women students, high-intensity lighting in all areas, a campus-wide emergency telephone system, courses in self-defense for women, and a rape crisis center. No rapes and one assault on a woman were reported for 1980–81.

Career. The entry of women into nontraditional occupations is encouraged through career workshops, lectures, panels, and printed information on nontraditional fields of study and on job discrimination. The college also supports programs to establish contacts between alumnae and female students, and maintains files on alumnae by specific careers.

Other. The Women's Studies Office serves as an information and planning center for women-related activities and events.The Women's History Program sponsors an annual women's week and publications on women's history sources.

Institutional Self-Description. "Sarah Lawrence College is an independent liberal arts college with a tradition of academic innovation. It pioneered in developing programs for mature women returning to school (Center for Continuing Education, 1962), and in Women's History (1972). It is nationally recognized as a center for research on women and feminist scholarship and has an academic program which includes a strong Women's Studies component. A basic philosophy is its commitment to individualized education.''

Schenectady County Community College
78 Washington Avenue
Schenectady, NY 12305
Telephone: (518) 346-6211

Women in Leadership
★★★ students
★★ faculty
★ administrators

1,299 undergraduates

	Amer. Ind.	Asian Amer.	Blacks	Hispanics	Whites
F	2	4	34	8	555
M	3	2	25	5	656
%	0.4	0.5	4.6	1.0	93.6

Located in the city of Schenectady, this public, two-year commuter college offers a comprehensive range of liberal arts, career, technical, community service, and continuing education programs. The median age of the 2,672 students is 27. Half the students are enrolled in degree programs, and 47 percent of these students are women. Free on-campus parking is provided.

Private childcare facilities are available near campus.

Women in Leadership Positions. *Students.* A woman was president of the student body for three recent years. Women served as editor-in-chief of the campus newspaper and presided over the board of the student union for one of these years.

Faculty. Of the full-time faculty, 14 (36 percent) are women. There are 3 female faculty for every 100 female students and 6 male faculty for every 100 male students.

Administrators. Women hold two of the six top positions: student-life officer and head librarian. None of the 5 department chairs is a woman. One of the 3 members of the faculty senate and 1 of the 10 college trustees are women. There are 4 (of 15) female regents, one of them a black woman.

Women and the Curriculum. About half the degrees to women are awarded in business programs, slightly more than a quarter in public service programs, and most of the rest in arts and sciences. The business department offers instruction on some topics specific to women. There are no courses on women.

Women and Athletics. Opportunities for organized sports are limited. The intramural program consists of indoor soccer and volleyball. Forty percent of intramural athletes and 26 percent of intercollegiate athletes are women, as are three of the seven paid intercollegiate coaches. The intercollegiate teams in which women compete are tennis, track, and volleyball.

Special Services and Programs for Women. *Health and Counseling.* There is no student health service. The counseling center, staffed by three women and two men, provides counseling on such matters as birth control, gynecology, abortion, and rape and assault. An optional student health insurance plan covers both maternity and abortion expenses.

Safety and Security. Measures consist of an evening escort service for women and high-intensity lighting. A rape crisis center is also available. No rapes or assaults on women were reported for 1980–81.

Career. The placement office offers workshops, job discrimination information, and printed materials on nontraditional careers for women, as well as lectures by women employed in these fields. ''Options in a Changing World,'' a special program offered on and off campus, helps students and members of the community to develop skills in choosing careers. The Office of Continuing Education offers assertiveness training and a program for women returning to the workforce.

Other. The Black Student Alliance is available to black women.

Institutional Self-Description. ''This urban campus, easily accessible by major public transportation, demonstrates its responsiveness to females by targeted counseling programs to reentry female adults, willingness to serve nontraditional students, a 53 percent female enrollment, academic programs with special appeal for women, and a student personnel program sensitive to women's needs.''

Siena College
Loudonville, NY 12211
Telephone: (518) 783-2300

2,534 undergraduates

	Amer. Ind.	Asian Amer.	Blacks	Hispanics	Whites
F	0	8	20	10	939
M	0	6	35	16	1,498
%	0.0	0.6	2.2	1.0	96.3

An independent, liberal arts institution, Siena College was founded by the Franciscan Fathers as a Roman Catholic undergraduate college for men; it became coeducational in 1968. Located in a suburban community north of Albany, the college enrolls 2,993 students. Of the 2,534 undergraduates, 39 percent are women; 10 percent of the women attend part-time. The median age of all students is 19.

Siena offers a traditional liberal arts curriculum, as well as programs in accounting, finance, and marketing. There is a summer session. The Office of Summer and Evening Sessions offers evening courses for reentry women on a non-degree basis. On-campus parking and public transportation are available to the 55 percent of students who commute.

Childcare is available near campus.

Policies to Ensure Fairness to Women. The college reports it is developing a committee on affirmative action; at present the Director of Personnel has part-time responsibility for matters involving equal-opportunity laws. There is a Committee on the Status of Women, which reports to, and is appointed by, the Vice President for Academic Affairs. The committee supervises compliance on affirmative action and equal-opportunity policy and addresses the concerns of minority women.

Women in Leadership Positions. *Students.* There are eight student leadership positions. In recent years, women have been president of the student body, presiding officer of the student judiciary, editor-in-chief of the campus newspaper, and president of the junior class—all for one year each. Women head two of six honorary societies.

Faculty. There are 17 women on the full-time faculty of 120; 2 of the women hold permanent appointments. There are 2 female faculty for every 100 female students, and 7 male faculty for every 100 male students.

Administrators. Men hold all top-level administrative positions. There is 1 female department chair (fine arts) out of 23, 1 woman on the 4-member faculty senate, and 3 female trustees out of 27. In one recent year, 1 of the 4 recipients of honorary degrees was a woman.

Women and the Curriculum. Almost half of female graduates earn degrees in business and 25 percent in social sciences. About 3 percent of women earn degrees in the nontraditional fields of mathematics and physical sciences.

Courses entitled Women in Politics and Women in Literature are offered. The college's Jerome Dawson Library houses a collection of books and journals on Women's Studies. Sexism and role expectations are topics covered in faculty workshops.

Women and Athletics. A sizable proportion of women participate in a moderate array of intramural, intercollegiate, and club sports. Three of the 13 paid coaches for intercollegiate sports are women. Women receive 40 percent of athletic scholarship. The intercollegiate sports offered are baseball, basketball, tennis, track, and volleyball.

Housing and Student Organizations. Forty-five percent of all students live on campus in single-sex or coeducational dormitories, or off campus in college-sponsored housing. Twenty women belong to sororities, which do not provide housing for members.

Special Services and Programs for Women. *Health and Counseling.* The student health service offers gynecological treatment and has a staff of 2 male physicians and 6 female health-care providers. Four of the 7 therapists employed by the counseling center are women. All are offered in-service training on the avoidance of sex-role stereotyping.

Safety and Security. Measures consist of local police, campus police without arrest authority, and high-intensity lighting. No rapes and one assault on a woman were reported for 1980-81.

Career. Lectures and panels by women employed in nontraditional occupations are provided along with printed materials and job discrimination information.

Other. A women's lecture series is offered by the office of the Dean of Students, and both an assertiveness/leadership training program and a rape prevention program for ROTC women are offered by the Counseling Center. The Black-Latins Student Union serves minority women.

Institutional Self-Description. "Women are active in campus life and have held top leadership positions in student government, the campus newspaper, and ROTC. The college is well-known for its tradition of community among students, faculty, and staff, and is located on an attractive suburban campus near the state capital."

Skidmore College
Saratoga Springs, NY 12866
Telephone: (518) 584-5000

| Women in Leadership | ★ Women and the Curriculum |
| ★★ faculty | ★ Women and Athletics |

2,284 undergraduates

	Amer. Ind.	Asian Amer.	Blacks	Hispanics	Whites
F	0	2	57	9	1,740
M	0	4	62	9	401
%	0.0	0.3	5.2	0.8	93.7

NWSA AAUW

Founded in 1911 as the Young Women's Industrial Club of Saratoga Springs, Skidmore remained a women's college until 1971, and women still account for almost 80 percent of the 2,284 undergraduates (although the most recent information is that women are now about 70 percent of students). About 7 percent of female students attend part-time. The median age of all students is 20 years. In addition to traditional bachelor's degree programs, the college offers an alternative program, Skidmore University Without Walls, as well as a summer session. The campus is accessible by public transportation, and on-campus parking is provided for the 15 percent of students who commute.

Private childcare facilities are available near the campus.

Policies to Ensure Fairness to Women. The Director of Personnel serves part-time as the affirmative action officer responsible for compliance with sex-equity, equal-employment-opportunity, and handicapped-access legislation. A formal grievance procedure resolves complaints of sexual harassment, and a written policy on sexual harassment is being drafted.

Women in Leadership Positions. *Students.* Women hold about a third of campus leadership positions. In three recent years, women served once as president of the student court, the residence-hall council, and the entering class. For two consecutive years women have been editor-in-chief of the campus newspaper, manager of the radio station, and president of the junior class. Women have presided over the senior class for three consecutive years. Four of seven honorary societies are headed by women.

Faculty. Thirty-five percent of the 150 full-time faculty are women. There are 3 female faculty for every 100 female students and 23 male faculty for every 100 male students.

Administrators. Of the top administrators, the student-life officer is a woman. Women chair 5 of 20 departments (American studies, foreign languages, nursing, music, and business) and hold 2 of 6 seats on the faculty tenure and promotions committee. Two of the 4 honorary degrees awarded in 1981 went to women.

Women and the Curriculum. Most degrees awarded to women are in fine arts (19 percent), social sciences (13 percent), business (12 percent), humanities (12 percent), health professions (12 percent), and education (10 percent). Two percent of women graduate in mathematics and physical sciences. Women are 40 percent of students in the alternative college, Skidmore University Without Walls, and 75 percent of students in internships and practicums.

Skidmore's Women's Studies Program offers a B.A. degree and an undergraduate minor. It includes an interdisciplinary introductory course and 22 courses on women offered by various departments. Courses include Women and the Law, Sociology of Sex Roles, Women Writers, and Women in American Culture. A Women's Studies Committee approves courses and policies for the program, and directs itself to matters of special concern to women. Faculty workshops cover such topics as affirmative action and sexism/racism in the curriculum. In addition, Skidmore is a member of a 16-college consortium devising ways to integrate feminist scholarship into traditional courses. Courses in the departments of business, education, and nursing provide some instruction on matters specific to women.

Women and Athletics. Skidmore provides a good intercollegiate and intramural sports program. Slightly more than half of the intercollegiate athletes are women. Seven of the 20 paid varsity coaches are women. Intercollegiate sports offered are basketball, crew, field hockey, ice hockey, lacrosse, polo, soccer, swimming, tennis, and volleyball.

Housing and Student Organizations. Eighty-five percent of undergraduates live on campus in single-sex or coeducational dormitories. The residence-hall directors—seven white women and two men—are offered awareness-training on sexism, racism, birth control, rape crisis, and alcohol and drug abuse. Student advocacy groups include Network, Student Progressive Network, and the Gay Forum. Network sponsors an annual women's week

Special Services and Programs for Women. *Health and Counseling.* The student health service has 1 male and 1 female physician, and 7 female health-care providers. The student counseling staff, 1 man and 1 woman, offer counseling on gynecology, abortion, birth control, and rape. Medical treatment is provided for all of these except abortion. The regular student health insurance policy covers maternity and abortion at no extra cost.

Safety and Security. Measures include armed campus and local police, night bus service, self-defense courses, and a rape crisis center. One rape and four assaults on women were reported in 1980–81.

Career. The career placement office provides a variety of information, materials, courses, and services to women students. The college reports it has an extensive library on career options for all women, including minority women.

Special Features. The Women's Studies Committee gives an annual Women's Studies award and publishes a newsletter. It works closely with Network.

Institutional Self-Description. "A women's college until 1971, Skidmore maintains a firm commitment to women students. With strong programs in the arts, humanities, sciences and social sciences, and professional areas, Skidmore offers its students small classes and an unusually accessible and professionally active faculty. Co-curricular life includes a rich athletic program with an emphasis on recreational skills and intramural competition, and an opportunity for significant participation in all college governance."

Southampton College of Long Island University
Southampton, NY 11968
Telephone: (516) 283-4000

Women in Leadership
★ administrators

1,427 undergraduates

	Amer. Ind.	Asian Amer.	Blacks	Hispanics	Whites
F	3	0	40	16	598
M	6	9	56	25	674
%	0.6	0.6	6.7	2.9	89.1

Southampton, founded in 1963, is the newest of Long Island University's three campuses; it is situated two hours from New York City in the resort community of Southampton. Nearly half of the 1,427 students are women and 15 percent of the women attend part-time.

The institution offers bachelor's and master's degrees in a variety of fields. There is a continuing education program. Classes met during the day and evening; there is a summer session. Single-sex and coeducational dormitories house half of the undergraduates and have no restrictions on visiting hours for members of the opposite sex. Commuters, who make up about 50 percent of the student body, may park on campus without charge.

Policies to Ensure Fairness to Women. The Dean of Administration reviews and makes policy regarding equal employment practices, sex equity for students, and access for the handicapped. Complaints of sexual harassment are handled informally and confidentially. A Committee on the Status of Women, appointed by and responsible to the Dean for Academic Affairs, meets regularly to review issues of concern to women, especially those from minority groups.

Women in Leadership Positions. *Students.* Women students assume few positions of leadership. In recent years, women have held two of five major all-campus student posts: editor of the campus newspaper and presiding officer of the student union board, each for one year.

Faculty. Twenty-three percent of the 35 full-time faculty are women. There is 1 female faculty for every 100 women students and 4 male faculty for every 100 male students.

Administrators. The chief student-life officer and the director of athletics are women, men hold most of the key administrative positions. A woman chairs the teacher education division; the remaining five divisions are led by men. In a recent year, a woman received the sole honorary degree awarded.

Women and the Curriculum. The most popular fields among women receiving bachelor's degrees are biology (18 percent),

education (17 percent), fine arts (16 percent), and business (14 percent). Sixty-three percent of the students participating in co-operative education are women, as are 20 percent of the student interns. No courses on women are offered.

Women and Athletics. The limited organized athletic program for women offers volleyball as the intramural sport. Women make up 16 percent of intercollegiate athletes and receive 10 percent of athletic scholarships in the varsity sports offered: cross-country, tennis, and volleyball.

Special Services and Programs for Women. *Health and Counseling.* The student health center employs one male physician and five female health-care providers. The student counseling center is staffed by one male counselor. Counseling and treatment are available for gynecological problems and birth control, as well as rape and assault and abortion counseling.

Safety and Security. Measures include campus police without arrest authority, and a campus-wide emergency telephone system. No rapes or assaults on women were reported for 1980–81.

Career. Southampton offers career workshops, panels, and information on nontraditional occupations of special interest to women.

Institutional Self-Description. "Southampton offers a student an opportunity to be exposed to quality academic programs in a setting that is informal and personal. Students attend classes that are generally small, and work very closely with faculty, who make themselves most accessible. The strength of the curriculum, the beauty of the setting, and the caliber of the faculty combine to make Southampton an ideal choice."

State University of New York, Agricultural Technical College at Alfred
Alfred, NY 14802
Telephone: (607) 871-6288

3,980 undergraduates

	Amer. Ind.	Asian Amer.	Blacks	Hispanics	Whites
F	27	1	7	4	1,657
M	23	2	7	3	2,249
%	1.3	0.1	0.4	0.2	98.1

A branch of the State University of New York, this public, two-year technical college is located on a rural campus in the foothills of the Allegheny Mountains. Women are 43 percent of a student population of 3,980, and all but 1 percent of these women attend full-time.

The college offers degrees in a wide range of programs, including liberal arts, business, health, natural science, public service, engineering/technology, and agriculture. Students specializing in agricultural studies may take advantage of opportunities afforded by the working dairy farm located on the campus. On-campus evening classes, a summer session, cooperative education programs, and extension learning under the Empire State College program provide students with opportunities for flexible programming. On-campus parking is available at a fee for the 20 percent of students who commute, and there is free transportation from remote parking lots.

Policies to Ensure Fairness to Women. Two administrators are responsible part-time for policy relating to equal-employment-opportunity and handicapped-access legislation. A written campus policy, prohibiting sexual harassment of students, faculty, and staff, has been publicly communicated to faculty and staff only. Complaints are resolved through a formal campus grievance procedure.

Women in Leadership Positions. *Students.* This campus offers few opportunities for women students to participate in campus leadership. In one recent year a woman served as president of the student senate.

Faculty. Of 212 full-time faculty, 15 percent are women, a lower-than-average proportion for public two-year colleges. There are 2 female faculty for every 100 female students and 8 male faculty for every 100 male students.

Administrators. All chief administrative positions are held by men. One department, secretarial science, is chaired by a woman. Half of the 12-member faculty senate is female. In one recent year, 1 of the 2 commencement speakers was a woman, as were 8 of the 25 speakers in the major campus-wide lecture series.

Women and the Curriculum. Women receive 43 percent of all two-year degrees awarded. Thirty-nine percent of women graduates take degrees in business, 31 percent in health programs, and 14 percent in natural science. Five percent of women earn degrees in engineering technologies. A Women in Engineering program is designed to attract women to this nontraditional field. Ninety percent of students enrolled in cooperative education programs are women. There are no courses on women.

Women and Athletics. Women have some opportunities to participate in both intercollegiate and intramural athletics. Fifty-four percent of the 140 intercollegiate athletes are women, as are six of the seven paid intercollegiate coaches. Team sports predominate in the intramural program. The women's intercollegiate sports program includes basketball, cross-country, riflery, softball, swimming and diving, tennis, and volleyball.

Housing and Student Organizations. Eighty percent of the student population live on-campus in either coeducational dormitories with restrictive hours for visitors of the opposite sex, or in sorority or fraternity houses. Five of twelve residence-hall directors are women. Residence-hall staff receive crisis-intervention training.

Special Services and Programs for Women. *Health and Counseling.* A student health service, staffed by two male physicians, and a student counseling center staffed by one woman and two men, provide counseling and medical treatment specific to women, including birth control and abortion.

Safety and Security. Measures include campus police with authority to make arrests, high-intensity lighting, self-defense courses for women, and information sessions on campus safety and assault prevention. No rapes and three assaults against women were reported on campus for 1980–81.

Career. Lectures on employment opportunities for women in nontraditional occupations and on job discrimination are available through placement services.

Other. The Alfred Community Women's Center is accessible to students.

Institutional Self-Description. "The SUNY A&T College at Alfred has excellent facilities and, particularly in the Engineering School, modern, sophisticated equipment. Job placement for our graduates is outstanding. Approximately 25 percent of our graduates continue on to four-year programs. The faculty is sincere, dedicated, and committed to success for women."

State University of New York, Agricultural & Technical College at Canton

Cornell Drive, Canton, NY 13617
Telephone: (315) 386-7011

Women in Leadership
★ students

2,336 undergraduates

	Amer. Ind.	Asian Amer.	Blacks	Hispanics	Whites
F	12	0	11	13	939
M	4	4	27	12	1,314
%	0.7	0.2	1.6	0.6	96.9

This public, two-year technical college is a branch campus of the State University of New York. Its campus is located near the St. Lawrence River and the Canadian border. Women are 41 percent of the 2,336 degree students; 5 percent of women attend part-time. Seventeen percent of women are over age 25.

Degree programs include the liberal arts, business, health, public service, agriculture, and engineering/technology. The Office of Continuing Education and Community Service serves adult returning students. Alternative full-time and part-time schedules include contract learning, and both on- and off-campus day and evening classes. On-campus parking is available for the 30 percent of students who commute.

Private childcare facilities are available near the campus.

Policies to Ensure Fairness to Women. A written campus policy prohibiting sexual harassment of students, faculty, and staff has been communicated in writing to all members of the college community. A formal campus grievance procedure ensures due process in the resolution of complaints. On a part-time basis, the Director of Personnel and Affirmative Action, assisted by a part-time officer, monitors compliance with equal-employment-opportunity, educational-sex-equity, and handicapped-access legislation.

Women in Leadership Positions. *Students.* Women students have good opportunities for leadership on this campus. In recent years, women have served two years as president of the student senate, two years as editor-in-chief of the campus newspaper, and one year each as president of the student body and of the residence-hall council.

Faculty. Women are 23 percent of the 114 full-time faculty, a proportion below the average for public, two-year colleges. There are 3 female faculty for every 100 female students and 7 male faculty for every 100 male students. The college reports that 1 black and 1 American Indian woman are on the full-time faculty.

Administrators. All major administrative posts are held by men. Women are one-third of the faculty senate, nearly half of the trustees, and a third of the regents.

Women and the Curriculum. Women earn 44 percent of all degrees and certificates awarded. The most popular fields of study among women graduates are business (33 percent), health (23 percent), and public service, natural science, and liberal arts (14 percent each).

The department of nursing provides some instruction on midwifery, home delivery, and reproductive choice. There are no courses on women.

Women and Athletics. There are some opportunities for women to participate in competitive team sports. Twenty-nine percent of intercollegiate, 24 percent of intramural, and 67 percent of club athletes are women. Of the seven paid varsity coaches, four are female. Intercollegiate sports for women include basketball, skiing, softball, and volleyball.

Housing and Student Organizations. Forty-two percent of the

🏛	On-campus evening and/or weekend classes	[M A]	Commission on minority affairs
🏛	Off-campus classes	📖	Women's Studies program
🚌	Accessible by public transportation	⚲	Women's center
👫	On-campus childcare facilities	AAUW	Member, American Association of University Women
✎	Publicly communicated sexual harassment policy, includes students	NWSA	Member, National Women's Studies Association
[S W]	Commission on status of women	CROW	On-campus Center for Research on Women

students reside on campus in either coeducational dormitories or fraternity and sorority houses. The residence-hall staff consists of two women and two men, who are offered awareness-training on sex education, sexism, and birth control.

Special Services and Programs for Women. *Health and Counseling.* The college provides a student health service, staffed by 1 part-time physician and 4 health-care providers, 3 of them women. A student counseling center is staffed by 1 woman and 2 men. No information was provided regarding counseling and medical services specific to women. A student health insurance policy covers maternity expenses at no extra charge.

Safety and Security. Measures consist of night-time escorts for women students, high-intensity lighting, self-defense courses, and information sessions on rape and assault prevention. No information was provided on the incidence of rapes and assaults.

Career. Workshops, lectures, and information on employment for women in nontraditional occupations and problems of job discrimination are available through placement services.

Institutional Self-Description. "Excellence of programs and faculty and a friendly and open small college environment are this college's strong points. Opportunity and services are equally available to every student who seeks or needs them. Women are strongly urged to participate and enter nontraditional programs and activities."

State University of New York, Albany
Albany, NY 12222
Telephone: (518) 457-8590

★★★ **Women and the Curriculum**

★ **Women and Athletics**

9,669 undergraduates

	Amer. Ind.	Asian Amer.	Blacks	Hispanics	Whites
F	12	63	197	103	4,231
M	35	63	170	118	4,631
%	0.5	1.3	3.8	2.3	92.1

🏠 🚐 👪 [S/W] [M/A] 📖 NWSA CROW

Established in 1844 as a school for educating teachers, the State University of New York at Albany has since 1963 provided a full range of undergraduate and graduate programs. The new campus enrolls some 15,200 students. The College of Continuing Studies serves the adult student. Evening classes and a summer session are available.

Women are 48 percent of the 9,669 undergraduates; 4 percent of the women attend part-time. The median age of undergraduates is 20. For the one-third of the students who commute, the university is accessible by public transportation. There is on-campus parking, with an annual registration fee only.

University-sponsored childcare facilities charge on a sliding scale and can accommodate one-quarter of students' requests. Private childcare arrangements may be made close by.

Policies to Ensure Fairness to Women. A full-time Assistant to the President for Affirmative Action is responsible for policy on equal employment opportunities. An associate director reviews policies and practices related to sex equity for students and handicapped accessibility. SUNYA's President has made a policy statement on sexual harassment. Complaints are handled both informally and confidentially and through a formal grievance procedure. The Committee on Women's Concerns, which includes students as voting members, takes public stands on issues of concern to students. The Committee on Minority Affairs addresses the concerns of minority women.

Women in Leadership Positions. *Students.* Opportunities for women students to exercise campus-wide leadership are well below the average for public research institutions in this guide. In recent years, women have been twice elected student body president. A woman heads one of the two honorary societies.

Faculty. Women are 14 percent of a full-time faculty of 684. According to recent report, 7 black, 2 Asian American, and 2 Hispanic women are on the full-time faculty. The ratio of female faculty to female students is 2 to 100. The ratio of male faculty to male students is 12 to 100.

Administrators. Men occupy all higher administrative posts. Women chair three of 35 departments. The Dean for Undergraduate Education is a woman.

Women and the Curriculum. The majority of women graduating with bachelor's degrees major in social sciences (20 percent), general letters (14 percent), business and management (13 percent), and psychology (12 percent). The proportion of women earning degrees in public affairs is above the national average. Less than 4 percent earn degrees in mathematics and the physical sciences. Just under half of the science field-service positions go to women.

The Women's Studies Program, under the direction of a full-time faculty member, offers an 18-credit minor and a B.A. through interdisciplinary studies. Thirty-four courses are available through Women's Studies and cooperating departments. Recent women's studies courses include Introduction to Feminism; Classism, Racism, and Sexism; Sociology of Sex Roles; and Women in the Political Economy. Individual courses on women are given in the departments of history, anthropology, Hispanic and Italian studies, Puerto Rican studies, English, classics, Afro-American studies, physical education, social welfare, criminal justice, and the School of Education. The Women's Studies Advisory Committee supports the program and promotes development of courses on women in traditional departments. The Center for Women in Government, affiliated with the Graduate School of Public Affairs, operates as a research, training, and information clearing house to eliminate sex discrimination faced by women working in the public sector.

Minority Women. Of 4,626 undergraduate women, 4 percent are black, 2 percent Hispanic, 1 percent Asian American, and less than 1 percent American Indian. A minority woman is director of a residence hall. Awareness-training on racism is optional for residence-hall staff. Counselors in the counseling center are offered in-service training in the avoidance of racial bias. Eight women are in all-minority sororities. Groups on campus supportive of minority women include the Albany State University Black Alliance, the African Students Association, the Chinese Student Association, Fuerza Latina, Rights for American Indians, and the Pan Caribbean Association. The Student Association Central Council has a task force on minority affairs.

Women and Athletics. Intramural and intercollegiate programs provide good opportunities for organized, competitive sports. The intramural program consists largely of team sports. Sixteen percent of intramural and 36 percent of intercollegiate athletes are women. No athletic scholarships are awarded. Of the 36 paid coaches for intercollegiate sports, 16 are women. The intercollegiate sports offered are: basketball, cross-country, gymnastics, soccer, softball, swimming, synchronized swimming, tennis, track and field, and volleyball.

Housing and Student Organizations. For the two-thirds of the undergraduates who live on campus, coeducational dormitories are available. Residence halls do not restrict hours for visitors of the opposite sex. Eight of 12 full-time residence-hall directors are female. Staff are offered awareness-training on sex education, racism, and birth control.

Less than one percent of the undergraduate women belong to social sororities. Sororities and fraternities do not provide housing for their members. Among groups that serve as advocates for women on campus are the Feminist Alliance, SUNYA Gay and Lesbian Association, the International Student Association, the

Jewish Student Coalition, WIRA, Returning Women Students, and Middle Earth.

Special Services and Programs for Women. *Health and Counseling.* The student health service provides some medical attention specific to women, including gynecological, birth control, and rape and assault treatment. Half of the eight health-service physicians are female as are 18 of the 20 health-care providers. The regular student health insurance covers abortion at no extra charge and maternity up to $150. Half of the counselors in the counseling service are women. Students have access to gynecological, birth control, abortion, rape and assault, and crisis intervention counseling. Professional staff are offered in-service training in avoiding sex-role stereotyping and racial bias.

Safety and Security. Measures consist of campus police with weapons training and arrest authority, night-time escorts for women, night-time bus service to residence areas, high-intensity lighting, emergency alarm and telephone systems, self-defense courses for women, information sessions on safety and crime prevention, and a rape crisis center. Twenty-two assaults (four on women) and no rapes were reported for 1980–81.

Career. Workshops, lectures, printed materials, and other information focused on women in nontraditional occupations and fields of study, as well as a program of contacts between alumnae and female students are available.

Other. An annual women's week is sponsored by the Albany State University Black Alliance and a women's lecture series by Women's Studies. There is a university warmline of information, referral, and support. The counseling center houses a women's resource library.

Special Features. The activities of the President's task force on women's safety have heightened awareness of women's safety issues and resulted in increased security measures.

Institutional Self-Description. "SUNYA offers a varied and rigorous academic environment within which women students are becoming increasingly self-aware. The Women's Studies Program and the Affirmative Action Office provide support, as the dozen or so groups of women students, faculty, and staff accomplish a great deal with volunteer labor and low budgets."

State University of New York, Binghamton

Binghamton, NY 13901
Telephone: (607) 798-2000

★★ **Women and the Curriculum**

7,318 undergraduates

	Amer. Ind.	Asian Amer.	Blacks	Hispanics	Whites
F	9	20	140	73	3,563
M	3	33	100	53	3,258
%	0.1	0.7	3.3	1.7	94.1

🏠 🏛 🚐 👫 ⚲ 📖 📖 ⚱ **AAUW NWSA**

The Undergraduate and Graduate University Center of the State University of New York at Binghamton was formed in 1965 around Harpur College (1946), which still serves as the undergraduate liberal arts unit of the university. Undergraduate programs are also available in the schools of nursing, management and general studies. The more than 10,000 students include 7,318 undergraduates. Women are 52 percent of the undergraduates, and almost 7 percent of women attend part-time. The median age of all undergraduates is 20. There are evening classes both on and off campus; an adult continuing education program is available through the School of General Studies and Professional Education. Fifty-three percent of undergraduates commute; they have access to public transportation and free on-campus parking.

An on-campus, daytime childcare service can accommodate 120 children and is available to both full- and part-time students. Eighty percent of all student requests for this service can be met.

Policies to Ensure Fairness to Women. Equal employment opportunity, access for the handicapped, and sex equity issues are the responsibility, on a full-time basis, of the Assistant to the President for Affirmative Action. A published campus policy prohibits sexual harassment of students, faculty, and staff; complaints are handled through a formal grievance procedure. The Affirmative Action office meets with department chairs and directors to review required responsibilities.

Women in Leadership Positions. *Students.* The incomplete information provided by the institution suggests that women may have held none of the campus-wide leadership positions in recent years. A woman heads one of the two campus honorary societies.

Faculty. Eighteen percent of a full-time faculty of 463 are women, a proportion below the national norm. There are 2 female faculty for every 100 female students and 12 male faculty for every 100 male students.

Administrators. The top administrators are men, except the head librarian and the director of athletics. Of the 22 departments, music is chaired by a woman. The Dean of Nursing is a woman. Women are 18 percent of the faculty senate and 23 percent of an important faculty committee. In addition, 43 percent of trustees and 33 percent of college regents are women, and 35 of 55 recent alumni awards went to women.

Women and the Curriculum. Most degrees awarded to women are in social sciences (27 percent), psychology (13 percent), biology (11 percent), and business (8 percent). Over 9 percent of women graduates major in such nontraditional fields as mathematics and physical sciences. Half the architecture degrees are earned by women. An innovative program encourages women students to prepare for careers in science.

The Women's Studies Program offers an undergraduate certificate; students may create an undergraduate major in Women's Studies through the Innovative Projects program. More than 30 undergraduate and graduate courses available through Women's Studies and various departments include: Economics of Female Employment, History of American Womanhood, Social Organization and Feminism, and Women and Health Care. A course entitled Human Services in Broome County: Women, is offered off campus.

Minority Women. Four percent of undergraduate women are black women, 2 percent Hispanic, and less than 1 percent Asian American or American Indian. Three percent of women students in continuing education courses are black women. Recent data show that among the 69 full-time faculty are a black, an Asian American, and an Hispanic woman. Both the head librarian and the director of athletics are black women. Courses on minority women include Minority Voices in American Literature, as well as Black Women's Consciousness, a course jointly sponsored by the department of sociology and the Afro-American studies program.

A Commission on Minority Affairs addresses the concerns of minority women. Other advocates for minority women are the Black, Latin American, Caribbean, and African Student Unions. Programs especially geared to minority women include a lecture series jointly sponsored by the Pluralistic Women's Coalition of the Afro-American Studies program and the YWCA.

Women and Athletics. A sizable women's and coeducational intramural sports program offers mostly team sports; there is a smaller intercollegiate progam. Club sports are also available. Three of the 14 paid varsity coaches are women. Intercollegiate sports offered are basketball, cross-country, softball, swimming and diving, tennis, track and field, and volleyball.

Housing and Student Organizations. Coeducational dormitories, some with single-sex areas, house the 47 percent of undergraduates who live on campus. There are no restrictive hours for visitors of the opposite sex. A married student whose husband is not enrolled is permitted to live in married students' housing. Fourteen of the 26 residence-hall directors are women; awareness-training on sexism, listening skills, and drug and alcohol use is available.

Two percent of undergraduate woemn belong to sororities, which provide housing for members.

Special Services and Programs for Women. *Health and Counseling.* The student health service provides medical treatment for gynecological problems, birth control, and rape and assault. The 4 staff physicians are male, while 11 health-care providers are female. Regular student health insurance covers abortion and maternity expenses at no extra cost. Counseling and referral services on gynecology, birth control, abortion, and rape and assault are available at the student counseling center. The counseling staff of 3 men and 1 woman are offered in-service training on sex-role stereotyping and racial bias.

Safety and Security. Measures consist of campus police with arrest authority, night-time escort for women students, high-intensity lighting, self-defense courses for women, information sessions on safety and crime prevention, and a rape crisis center. Five assaults, one on a woman, were reported for 1980–81.

Other. The Student Association is responsible for the campus Women's Center, which is run as a collective without a permanent, designated director. The Center has 50 active participants, serves about 300 women, and functions as the main support group for women on campus. Handicapped women may find additional support services from the Program for Students with Disabilities and the Association for Disabled Individuals.

Returning Women Students. A Continuing Education for Women Program, headed by a woman administrator on a part-time basis, enrolls 81 returning women. An additional 190 reentry women, five of them black women, are enrolled in other adult continuing education programs. A Center for Continuing Education for Women is operated by the School of General Studies.

Institutional Self-Description. "Students find that the values of a liberal arts education are central to their SUNY-Binghamton experience. An outstanding liberal arts program is combined with excellent programs of applied and career related studies; nearly two-thirds of undergraduates plan to pursue graduate and professional school. The Woman's Studies Program is part of the university commitment to excellence."

State University of New York, Buffalo
Amherst Campus, NY 14260
Telephone: (716) 636-2000

★★★ **Women and the Curriculum**

14,406 undergraduates

	Amer. Ind.	Asian Amer.	Blacks	Hispanics	Whites
F	24	74	550	64	4,817
M	24	172	491	93	7,699
%	0.3	1.8	7.4	1.1	89.3

 AAUW

Founded in 1846 as a medical school, the State University of New York at Buffalo, with its main campus in suburban Amherst, has evolved into a broad-based university center that provides a range of undergraduate, graduate, and professional programs for some 21,600 students. Both the summer session and Millard Fillmore College (the evening college) offer programs. There is a division of continuing education.

Women are 39 percent of the 14,406 undergraduates; 17 percent of undergraduate women attend part-time. The median age of undergraduates is 25. Seventy percent of the undergraduates live off campus or commute. The university is accessible by public transportation. On-campus parking is free, with free transportation from distant parking lots.

Private child-care facilities are available off campus.

Policies to Ensure Fairness to Women. A full-time Affirmative Action Officer reviews policies and monitors compliance with equal-employment-opportunity, sex-equity-for-students, and handicapped-access legislation. There is also an Office of Service for the Handicapped, with a full-time director and staff. A published policy prohibits sexual harassment; complaints are handled through a formal grievance procedure.

Women in Leadership Positions. *Students.* Opportunities for women students to assume campus leadership positions are far below the average for public research institutions in this guide. In three recent years, a woman has served a one-year term as editor-in-chief of the campus newspaper.

Faculty. Women are 14 percent of a full-time faculty of 840. The ratio of female faculty to female students is 3 to 100. The ratio of male faculty to male students is 10 to 100.

Administrators. Men occupy all higher administrative posts. Women chair six of 89 departments. The Dean of the School of Social Work and the Dean of the School of Nursing are women.

Women and the Curriculum. A majority of the women earning bachelor's degrees major in the social sciences (19 percent), business and management (15 percent), general letters (14 percent), and psychology (12 percent). Nine percent major in such nontraditional areas as architecture, computer science, engineering, mathematics, and the physical sciences. Programs encourage women to prepare for careers in law enforcement, management, and pharmacy. Women account for 40 percent of the science field-service positions.

The Women's Studies Program, one of the oldest and largest in the U.S., was for its first ten years located both in the residential Women's Studies College and in the American studies departments, jointly administered largely through faculty-student committees. Since 1981, the program has become an administrative unit with its own faculty-director. Women's Studies now offers an undergraduate minor, the B.A. in Women's Studies, and an M.A. through a Women's Studies concentration in American studies. During the past five years, approximately 20 students have taken a minor, 50 the B.A., and 20 the M.A. More than 50 courses are available in Women's studies, and another 25 courses on women through American studies and such other departments as sociology, psychology, nursing, anthropology, and classics. Courses include Women in the Health Care System, Reproductive Anthropology, Women as Rebels in World Literature, Minority Women in the U.S., Introduction to Mothers and Daughters, Women in Film, Women in the Middle East, and Theories of Feminism. The program's introductory course, Women in Contemporary Society, has involved team-teaching by undergraduate students in a unique form nationally recognized.

Minority Women. Of the 5,640 undergraduate women, 10 percent are black, 1 percent Asian American, 1 percent Hispanic, and less than 1 percent American Indian. Two residence-hall directors and one of the professional staff in the counseling service are minority women. Approximately 15 women are in all-minority sororities. More than a dozen Women's Studies courses explore the cultures and experiences of minority women in the U.S. and third-world women abroad. The Third World Student Association and the Black Student Union meet on campus.

Women and Athletics. Intramural and intercollegiate programs offer limited opportunities for organized, competitive, individual and team sports. Club sports are also available. Six percent of intramural and 30 percent of intercollegiate athletes are women. Of the 31 paid coaches for intercollegiate sports, one-third are women. The intercollegiate sports offered are basketball, bowling, field hockey, softball, tennis, track and field, and volleyball.

Housing and Student Organizations. Thirty percent of the undergraduates live on campus. Coeducational dormitories are available, with women's floors if requested. Hours for visitors of the opposite sex are not restricted. Twelve of 21 residence-hall directors are female. Awareness-training on racism and sexism is offered staff.

Two percent of undergraduate women belong to social sororities. Sororities and fraternities provide some housing for their members. Among groups which serve as advocates for women, including minority women, are the Society of Women Engineers, Women in Management, Anti-Rape Task Force, Women's Caucus, and Women's Scholars Group.

Special Services and Programs for Women. *Health and Counseling.* The student health service provides some medical attention specific to women, including gynecological, birth control, and rape and assault treatment. Five of the 15 physicians are female, as are 24 other health-care providers. The regular student health insurance covers abortion and maternity at no extra charge. Three of 4 professional staff in the counseling service are women. Students have access to gynecological, birth control, abortion, and rape and assault counseling. Staff are offered in-service training in the avoidance of sex-role stereotyping and racial bias.

Safety and Security. Measures consist of campus police with weapons training and arrest authority, night-time escorts for women students, night-time bus service to residence areas, high-intensity lighting, emergency telephone and alarm systems, self-defense courses for women, information sessions on safety and crime prevention, and a rape crisis center. Twenty-two assaults (seven on women) and two rapes were reported for 1980–81.

Career. Career workshops and nonsexist/nonracist printed information on nontraditional occupations, lectures by women employed in these fields, and a program to establish contacts between alumnae and students are provided.

Other. Women's theater and other arts programs are sponsored by Shakespeare's Sisters and the departments of theater and dance. Assertiveness training and a telephone service of information, referral, and support are provided by Student Affairs.

Returning Women Students. The Access Center and Adult Advisement programs provide special services for women returning to school or changing careers. Some 1,475 women, 13 percent from minority groups, enrolled in continuing education classes in 1980–81. The division of undergraduate education operates project Quarter Plus; special advising services are available.

Institutional Self-Description. "SUNY at Buffalo provides a wide array of courses and services to women students. Over 75 undergraduate programs are offered in Arts and Science areas plus professional programs in Engineering, Management, Nursing, Pharmacy, and Health Related Professions. Individualized academic and career advisement is available to help students make full use of the university's immense resources."

State University of New York, College at Buffalo

1300 Elmwood Avenue,
Buffalo, NY 14222
Telephone: (716) 878-4000

Women in Leadership	Women and the
★ faculty	Curriculum
★ administrators	

8,715 undergraduates

	Amer. Ind.	Asian Amer.	Blacks	Hispanics	Whites
F	28	9	546	49	4,122
M	10	20	278	44	3,514
%	0.4	0.3	9.6	1.1	88.6

🏠 🏛 🚌 👫 Ⓜ️ 📖 AAUW NWSA

Founded in 1871 as a school for the education of teachers, the College at Buffalo joined the State University of New York system in 1948. It now offers a broad range of bachelor's and master's programs in arts and sciences to over 10,000 students. Women are 55 percent of the 8,715 undergraduates; 9 percent of women attend part-time. The median age of undergraduates is 20. Fifteen percent of women students are over age 25. Off-campus day classes, a weekend college, a summer session, independent study, and evening classes both on and off campus are available. The Office of Life-Long Learning offers adult continuing education. For the 80 percent of undergraduates who commute, the campus is accessible by public transportation. There is on-campus parking.

College childcare facilities can accommodate 50 children; a fixed daily fee is assessed. Private arrangements may be made nearby.

Policies to Ensure Fairness to Women. The full-time Human Development/Affirmative Action officer is responsible for monitoring equal-employment-opportunity, access-for-the-handicapped, and sex-equity policies and practices. A published policy prohibits sexual harassment. Complaints are handled through a formal grievance procedure. The Committee on Minority Affairs addresses the concerns of minority women, among other matters.

Women in Leadership Positions. *Students.* In a recent three-year period, women served once as president of the student body and editor-in-chief of the campus newspaper and twice as manager of the campus radio station. In addition, women preside over half of the campus honorary societies.

Faculty. Women are 26 percent of the 531 full-time faculty, just above average for similar four-year colleges in this guide. The ratio of female faculty to female students is 3 to 100 and the ratio of male faculty to male students is 12 to 100.

Administrators. Women hold two of the eight top administrative positions: vice president for academic affairs and head librarian. Women chair some academic units, including consumer studies and home economics; design; health, physical education and recreation; mathematics; and interdisciplinary studies. Thirty-seven percent of the Board of Trustees are female.

Women and the Curriculum. Most women earn degrees in education (44 percent), public affairs (10 percent), and home economics (9 percent). Four percent major in such nontraditional areas as computer science, engineering, and mathematics.

The Women's Studies Program, under a part-time, permanent faculty member, offers nine courses. Recent titles include Introduction to Women's Studies, Folklore of Women, Psychology of Women, and Women in History. A committee oversees the Women's Studies Program and reports on curricular developments that include women. Such current issues as sex-fair curricula, coeducational physical education classes, and services for battered spouses are part of the preparation of future teachers and social workers. A program to build skills in mathematics is available through the mathematics department.

Minority Women. Among the almost 9,000 women, 11 percent are black, 1 percent are Hispanic, and less than 1 percent are Asian American or American Indian. Two minority women serve as residence-hall directors. Staff are offered training on avoiding racism. A minority woman serves on the staff of the counseling center. Such groups as Adelante Estudiantes Latinos and the Afro-American Student Organization meet on campus.

Women and Athletics. The college has a small women's sports program. Twenty-three percent of the intramural and 36 percent of the intercollegiate athletes are women. Club sports are also available. The intercollegiate sports are basketball, bowling, cross-country, field hockey, softball, swimming and diving, tennis, track and field, and volleyball.

Housing and Student Organizations. Coeducational dormitories, some with single-sex floors, house the 20 percent of undergraduates who live on campus. Dormitories do not restrict hours for visitors of the opposite sex. Seven of the eleven residence-hall directors are women; staff are offered awareness-training on sex education and birth control and on the avoidance of sexism and racism.

One percent of women students belong to social sororities. Sororities do not provide housing. Womanspace is the major student advocacy group for women. It sponsors consciousness-raising groups, as well as social and educational activities.

Special Services and Programs for Women. *Health and Counseling.* The student health service provides some medical attention specific to women and abortion by referral. One of 4 physicians is female, as are 4 other health-care providers. The regular student health insurance covers prenatal maternity expenses at no extra charge. The counseling center, staffed by 2 women and 3 men, provides counseling of particular concern to women. Staff receive training on sexuality and the avoidance of sex-role stereotyping.

Safety and Security. Measures include campus police with arrest authority, night-time escort for women students, emergency telephones, building check-in service, a rape crisis center, and information on campus safety and crime prevention. There were 22 assaults (one on a woman) reported for 1980-81.

Career. Workshops, speakers, and printed materials on nontraditional occupations and fields of study, as well as updated files on alumnae by specific careers are available.

Other. Project EVE of Everywoman's Opportunity sponsors services for women. The Women's Studies Academy offers courses in arts, humanities, natural and social and sciences, as well as women's lecture series, theater and arts programs and serves as an umbrella organization for Women's Studies activities and as a link between the college and the community. The college hosted the Fourth Annual Conference of the New York Women's Studies Association.

Institutional Self-Description. ''At SUNY/College at Buffalo, the services offered to women are adequate: Womanspace, the Women's Studies Academy, and Project EVE provide an environment receptive to women's concerns. The structures to foment a feminist education are in place, and a considerable part of the college community is committed to making them work.''

State University of New York, College at Cortland

P.O. Box 2000
Cortland, NY 13045
Telephone: (607) 753-2011

Women in Leadership   ★ **Women and Athletics**
  ★ **faculty**

5,077 undergraduates

	Amer. Ind.	Asian Amer.	Blacks	Hispanics	Whites
F	6	14	51	19	2,965
M	1	14	39	21	1,932
%	0.1	0.6	1.8	0.8	96.7

Established as a teacher-training school, and transformed in 1963 into a four-year College of Arts and Sciences, the State University of New York, College at Cortland is located about 30 miles south of Syracuse. Almost 6,000 students are enrolled in a variety of bachelor's and master's programs. Alternative scheduling includes self-paced/contract learning, as well as evening classes both on and off campus, and a summer session. An adult education division is also available.

Women are 60 percent of the 5,077 undergraduates; 3 percent of women attend part-time. The median age of all students is 20.

There is no public transportation for the 46 percent of students who commute. Free on-campus parking is available, as well as free transportation from remote parking lots.

Private childcare facilities are available nearby.

Policies to Ensure Fairness to Women. A full-time Affirmative Action Officer reviews policies and practices relating to equal-employment-opportunity, access-for-the-handicapped, and sex-equity legislation. A formal campus grievance procedure handles complaints of sexual harassment, but no policy prohibiting much harassment has been publicly communicated to students.

Women in Leadership Positions. *Students.* While most student campus leaders are male, women have served in recent years as editor-in-chief of the campus newspaper and presiding officer of the residence-hall council.

Faculty. Women are 27 percent of the 287 full-time faculty, slightly above average for public four-year institutions. There are 3 female faculty for every 100 female students and 11 male faculty for every 100 male students.

Administrators. Most of the top administrators are men. The director of women's athletics is a woman. Two of 27 departments are chaired by women: international communications and culture, and women's physical education.

Women and the Curriculum. Over half of women graduate in education, 12 percent in social sciences, and 9 percent in public affairs; 4 percent earn degrees in mathematics and physical sciences. Women's Academic and Career Choices encourages women to choose nontraditional areas of study.

Four courses on women are offered by the departments of English, history, sociology, and economics: Women in Literature, History of Women in the U.S., Sex Roles, and Women in Economics. A committee is responsible for encouraging the development of other courses on women. The physical education department provides instruction on the teaching of coeducational classes.

Women and Athletics. The College at Cortland has a good women's sports program. Forty percent of the 3,000 intramural athletes are women, who participate in such sports as ice hockey and water polo, and in coeducational team sports. Eighteen of the 20 paid varsity coaches for women's sports are women. Almost half of the 400 intercollegiate athletes are women and most of the women's varsity teams play in tournament competition. The intercollegiate sports in which women compete are basketball, cross-country, field hockey, golf, gymnastics, ice hockey, lacrosse, soccer, softball, and track (indoor).

Housing and Student Organizations. Coeducational dormitories with no restrictive hours for visitors of the opposite sex are available for the 54 percent of undergraduates who live on campus. The 14 residence-hall directors, eight of whom are women, are offered awareness-training on sexism, racism, birth control, and sex education.

About 3 percent of full-time undergraduate women belong to sororities. Both fraternities and sororities provide housing for members. An advocacy group for women is Aware.

Special Services and Programs for Women. *Health and Counseling.* The student health service provides medical treatment and counseling for gynecological problems, birth control, and rape and assault. The staff consists of 1 male physician and 4 other health-care providers, 3 of whom are male. Student health insurance covers abortion and maternity expenses at no extra cost.

Safety and Security. Measures consist of local police who include the campus in their jurisdiction, night-time escort service, high-intensity lighting, emergency alarm systems in isolated locations, and information sessions on campus safety and crime prevention. Six assaults, including four sexual assaults on women, were reported for 1980–81.

Career. Services include workshops, printed materials, and job discrimination information on nontraditional fields for women, as well as lectures and panels by women employed in these areas.

Institutional Self-Description. ''The College at Cortland is a public, coeducational, residential campus of the State University of New York, offering programs in the liberal arts and sciences and professional studies. Cortland offers extensive foreign-language and study-abroad programs and comprehensive extracurricular programs, including 14 intercollegiate varsity teams for women.''

State University of New York, College at Geneseo

Geneseo, NY 14454
Telephone: (716) 245-5617

Women in Leadership ★ **Women and the Curriculum**
  ★ faculty
  ★ **Women and Athletics**

4,565 undergraduates

	Amer. Ind.	Asian Amer.	Blacks	Hispanics	Whites
F	1	3	32	17	2,928
M	0	4	22	12	1,534
%	0.1	0.2	1.2	0.6	98.0

The State University of New York's College at Geneseo offers bachelor's degrees in liberal arts, sciences, and teacher education to some 5,300 students. Master's degrees are also awarded in some fields. There are 4,565 undergraduates, whose median age is 19. Sixty-five percent of the undergraduates are women, 3 percent of whom attend part-time. Alternative scheduling includes evening and summer session classes.

Forty-five percent of students commute to the campus, located one hour from Rochester. On-campus parking is available for commuting students.

Private childcare facilities are located near the campus.

Policies to Ensure Fairness to Women. A full-time Affirmative Action Officer reviews policies and practices related to equal employment opportunity, sex equity for students, and handicapped access. A published campus policy prohibits sexual harassment of students, faculty, and staff; complaints are resolved either informally and confidentially or through a formal campus grievance procedure.

An Affirmative Action Advisory Committee, appointed by the President, addresses the concerns of women, including minority women. The committee, which includes student members with voting rights, meets regularly and takes public stands on issues important to students.

Women in Leadership Positions. *Students.* Women have limited opportunities to exercise campus-wide leadership. In recent years, a woman served once as president of the student body, while the other two available student leadership posts were held by men. Two of the five honorary societies are headed by women.

Faculty. Twenty-seven percent of the 285 full-time faculty are women, an average proportion for public four-year colleges in this guide. There are 3 female faculty for every 100 female students, compared to 14 male faculty for every 100 male students. The college reports 1 Hispanic, 2 black, and 4 Asian American women on the full-time faculty.

Administrators. The major administrative positions are held by men. Women chair two of 26 departments, including the department of learning skills. Twenty-five percent of the faculty senate are women, as are 2 of the 5 members of the tenure and promotions committee.

Women and the Curriculum. Most women earn degrees in education (38 percent), health professions (13 percent), psychology (10 percent), and social sciences (9 percent). Three percent of women graduates major in the nontraditional fields of mathematics and physical sciences. The college has a program designed to encourage women to prepare for management careers. Sixty-nine percent of students in the college's internship program are women.

Undergraduate students may earn a minor through the Women's Studies Program. More than 20 courses are available through the Women's Studies Program and through such departments as English, management science, history, sociology, and psychology. Recent offerings include Issues in Feminism; Equal Opportunity Employment; Women in Western Society; and Women, Men, and Culture. An official committee is assigned to develop additional courses on women in departments. The Director of Women's Studies holds a full-time, permanent faculty position. Workshops on nontraditional occupations, the needs of reentry women, and affirmative action and equal opportunity are available to faculty. The division of business provides instruction on job discrimination, sexual harassment in the workplace, and women in management.

Women and Athletics. The college offers good opportunities for women to participate in organized team and individual sports. Forty-four percent of intramural athletes and 38 percent of intercollegiate athletes are women; one of the two paid coaches for intercollegiate sports is female. The intercollegiate sports offered are basketball, cross-country, softball, swimming, synchronized swimming, track, and volleyball.

Housing and Student Organizations. Women's and coeducational dormitories are available for the 55 percent of undergraduates who live on campus. There are no restrictive hours for visitors of the opposite sex. Housing for married students is open to the husbands of married women students. Ten of the 15 residence-hall directors are women. All residence-hall staff are offered awareness-training on birth control, sexism, racism, and self-defense.

Sororities and fraternities provide housing for members. The major advocacy group for women students is Women Together. Two percent of its 250 active members are minority women, predominantly black women. Black women are members of the Minority Student Union

Special Services and Programs for Women. *Health and Counseling.* Three male physicians, 1 female physician's assistant, and 16 other health-care providers (13 of them women) staff the student health service. Medical services specific to women include birth control and gynecological treatment. The counseling center, staffed by 3 men and 1 woman, offers gynecological, birth control, abortion, and rape and assault counseling. The regular student health insurance covers maternity and abortion expenses at no extra cost.

Safety and Security. Measures consist of local police, campus police with weapons training and arrest authority, night-time escort for women students, a campus-wide emergency telephone system, self-defense courses for women, and information on safety and crime prevention. Two rapes and 14 assaults, four on women, were reported for 1980–81.

Career. The college offers workshops and printed information on nontraditional occupations for women, as well as panels and lectures by women employed in these fields. Job discrimination information is available from the Affirmative Action Office, while other career services and programs are offered by the Women's Center.

Other. The Affirmative Action Office operates the Women's Center on a budget of approximately $750. The Center serves some 250 women. It sponsors the student-based Women Together, which maintains close ties to faculty and staff members and organizes a variety of events, including an annual women's week. The Student Association sponsors women's arts programs, while Adult Education offers assertiveness training.

Institutional Self-Description. ''Geneseo boasts a Women's Studies Program and an enthusiastic student organization called Women Together. Enormous inroads have been made in affirmative action for women, particularly in the area of academic affairs, where 67 percent of new full-time faculty hired this year are women; where 50 percent of all promotions have been for women; and where women earn 99 percent of what men earn on tenure-track positions at all levels—possibly setting national records.''

State University of New York, College at New Paltz
New Paltz, NY 12562
Telephone: (914) 257-2121

| Women in Leadership | ★★ Women and the |
| ★ administrators | Curriculum |

4,048 undergraduates

	Amer. Ind.	Asian Amer.	Blacks	Hispanics	Whites
F	98	52	217	64	1,721
M	86	39	151	56	1,300
%	4.9	2.4	9.7	3.2	79.8

🏠 🏛 🚐 👫 [S/W] [M/A] 📖 ♀ NWSA

The State University of New York at New Paltz is a four-year college of arts and sciences that enrolls nearly 7,000 students. Fifty-six percent of the 4,048 undergraduates are women; 8 percent of women attend part-time. The college offers a diverse range of bachelor's and master's programs. Evening classes are available both on and off campus, as are weekend college and a summer session. Public transportation and on-campus parking are available for commuting students.

On-campus daytime childcare facilities are available to full- and part-time students. Fees are based on a sliding scale according to income. Private childcare services are also available at nearby, off-campus locations.

Policies to Ensure Fairness to Women. Equal-opportunity matters are the part-time responsibility of the Affirmative Action Officer. There is no formal campus policy on sexual harassment; complaints are handled informally and confidentially. A Committee on the Status of Women, whose members are elected by the faculty, includes students as voting members. There is also a Committee on Minority Affairs.

Women in Leadership Positions. *Students.* Information was not supplied.

Faculty. Twenty-four percent of a full-time faculty of 334 are women, a proportion slightly below the national average. There are 4 female faculty for every 100 female students and 15 male faculty for every 100 male students.

Administrators. The chief executive officer is a woman. Of the eight other top-level administrative positions, women serve as chief development officer and director of athletics. Women also chair the departments of physical education, art history, and art education.

Women and the Curriculum. Most women earning bachelor's degrees major in education (25 percent), the social sciences (23 percent), and fine arts (14 percent). Two percent earn degrees in such nontraditional fields as mathematics and physical sciences.

The Women's Studies Program awards the bachelor's degree in Women's Studies and an undergraduate minor. Students may also earn a master's of professional studies degree in humanistic education by specializing in women's services or Women's Studies. Thirty-six undergraduate and graduate courses are offered through the program and in conjunction with various other departments. Among recent courses are Women and Violence in America; Lesbianism: History and Culture; Women in Sports; Feminism: Theory and Practice; Black Woman; and Issues of Racism and Sexism in the Helping Professions. The School of

Education provides instruction in the development and use of sexfair curricula.

Women and Athletics. No information was provided.

Housing and Student Organizations. Both single-sex and coeducational dormitories are provided for undergraduate students. Women's advocacy groups include the Women's Crisis Center, Women's Caucus, and CASA (sexuality and reproductive rights).

Special Services and Programs for Women. *Health and Counseling.* The student health service provides medical treatment for gynecological and birth control needs. There is also a student-run birth control clinic on campus. A student counseling center, staffed by one woman and three men, offers advice and referrals on gynecology, birth control, abortion, and rape and assault.

Safety and Security. Measures include night-time, campus-wide bus service to residence areas, information sessions on safety and crime prevention, and a rape crisis center. Information on rapes or other reported assaults was not provided.

Other. Reentry women are served by a Returning Women's Program sponsored by Women's Studies, the Women's Center, and Continuing Education. The Women's Studies Program sponsors a variety of cultural and educational activities, many geared to minority women, including a women's lecture series, theater and other women's arts programs, an annual women's week, and the Women's Studies Annual Conference. There is also an Office of Women's Programs run by the student services division. The Women's Center sponsors assertiveness training and a telephone warmline.

Special Features. Students interested in scholarship on women have access to the Alice Fix Memorial Library on Women. There is also a monthly Women's Studies newsletter and a Women's Studies film series.

Institutional Self-Description. ''SUNY at New Paltz offers stimulating academic programs and varied supportive services for women. A strong Women's Studies program grants a B.A. and an emphasis in the master's of professionl studies degree. The projects of the Women's Center, the Returning Women's Program, Office of Women's Programs, and student-run Women's Crisis Center and Birth Control Clinic add to the overall integration of personal and social change in an educational experience for women.''

State University of New York, College at Old Westbury
Old Westbury, NY 11568
Telephone: (516) 876-3185

Women in Leadership	★ Women and the
★★ faculty	Curriculum
★ administrators	

2,259 undergraduates

	Amer. Ind.	Asian Amer.	Blacks	Hispanics	Whites
F	3	3	516	162	690
M	1	13	335	106	407
%	0.2	0.7	38.1	12.0	49.1

 🏠 🚐 👫 ⚲ 📖 ♀ AAUW

Founded in 1966 and opened in 1971 as a branch of the State University of New York, the College at Old Westbury offers bachelor's degrees in liberal arts, sciences, and professional studies, mainly through interdisciplinary programs. In addition to regular class schedules, there are evening and summer session classes, along with some opportunities for self-paced/contract learning. Sixty-one percent of the 2,259 students are women, 32 percent of whom attend part-time. The median age of students is 23. Half of women students are over age 25; one-fifth are over age 40.

Located on Long Island, 22 miles from Manhattan, the campus is, to some degree, accessible by public transportation. Seventy-nine percent of the students commute by car, and free on-campus parking is available.

College-run childcare facilities can accommodate 60 children. Students receive priority for this service and fees are based on a fixed daily rate. Private childcare facilities are available near the campus.

Policies to Ensure Fairness to Women. The Affirmative Action Officer has full-time responsibility for policy relating to equal-employment-opportunity, handicapped-accessibility, and sex-equity legislation. A published campus policy prohibits sexual harassment of students, faculty, and staff; complaints are resolved through a formal campus grievance procedure.

Women in Leadership Positions. *Students.* Women have few opportunities to exercise campus-wide leadership. Of the two student campus leadership positions, one (editor-in-chief of the campus newspaper) was held by a woman for one of three recent years.

Faculty. The proportion of female faculty members is well above average for public four-year colleges: women are 44 percent of the 82 full-time faculty. There are 4 female faculty for every 100 female students and 7 male faculty for every 100 male students.

Administrators. Three of the ten top-level administrators are women: chief academic officer, chief student-life officer, and director of institutional research. Of the 17 departments, women chair American studies, biological sciences, bilingual/bicultural studies, early and elementary childhood education, and sociology. Women have been recent recipients of alumni awards and honorary degrees.

Women and the Curriculum. Women earn bachelor's degrees in education and in business (18 percent in each), social sciences (17 percent), interdisciplinary studies (14 percent), and biological sciences (11 percent).

The Women's Studies Program offers an undergraduate concentration for students who major in American studies. A Women's Studies internship is also available. The American studies program offers 21 Women's Studies courses, including Women and Work; Women Across Culture; Marxism and Feminism; and Women, State and Class. Additional courses on women are available in the departments of biological sciences, bilingual/bicultural studies, business and management, and others. The American studies program oversees the continued development of the Women's Studies Program. Faculty seminars address such issues as sexism and racism in the curriculum; the relationships among sex, race, and selection of major field; and nontraditional occupations for women and men.

Minority Women. Fifty percent of the undergraduate women are minority women, most of whom are black. There are 10 black, 3 Asian American, and 4 Hispanic women on the full-time faculty. The chief student-life officer, 1 of the 5 female department chairs, and the recipients of recent honorary degrees and alumni awards are black women. Seventy-five percent of undergraduate women living in residence halls are black women and 14 percent are Hispanic. Awareness-training on racism is available to residence-hall directors. Two members of the student counseling center staff are minority women.

Women's Studies and other programs offer a number of courses on black and third-world women. Recent offerings include The Literature of Black Women, Women in the Black Community, El Machismo y La Mujer, and Black Women and Liberation. Minority women may find support at the Women's Center, which is run on a part-time, volunteer basis by an Hispanic woman, and from the Women's Caucus. Such groups as International and Alianza Latina address the concerns of minority women.

Women and Athletics. No information was provided.

Housing and Student Organizations. Single-sex and coedu-

cational dormitories house the 21 percent of students residing on campus; visiting hours for members of the opposite sex are restricted. On-campus housing is available for married students with and without children. Two of the four residence-hall directors are women; they are offered awareness-training on sexism, sex education, and birth control.

Four percent of undergraduate women belong to social sororities and 7 percent of men belong to fraternities; none of these groups provides housing for members. All sororities and fraternities are racially integrated.

Special Services and Programs for Women. *Health and Counseling.* The student health service provides general medical treatment, as well as gynecological and birth control services. Three of the 7 staff physicians are women, as are 9 of the 10 otherhealth-care providers. The counseling center, staffed by 4 women and 3 men, offers special services for women, including abortion, and rape and assault counseling.

Safety and Security. Measures consist of local police, campus police with arrest authority, and a night-time campus-wide bus service. One assault on a woman was reported for 1980–81.

Career. Workshops on nontraditional occupations, including lectures by women employed in those fields, are available.

Institutional Self-Description. ''Our special mission—to serve those historically bypassed by traditional higher educational opportunities—created a special place for women of all ages, ethnic, and social-class backgrounds. A very feminist feeling pervades Old Westbury due to the presence of so many women fulfilling their dreams as students, faculty, and administrators.''

State University of New York, College at Oneonta
Oneonta, NY 13820
Telephone: (607) 431-3500

★ **Women and the Curriculum**

5,541 undergraduates

	Amer. Ind.	Asian Amer.	Blacks	Hispanics	Whites
F	2	3	128	26	3,159
M	2	6	132	28	2,027
%	0.1	0.2	4.7	1.0	94.1

The State University of New York, College at Oneonta offers a full range of bachelor's and master's level programs in liberal arts and professional studies to some 6,000 students. An adult continuing education program is also available. Sixty percent of the 5,541 undergraduates are women; almost 3 percent of women attend part-time. Evening classes are available both on and off campus. There is a summer session. For the 33 percent of undergraduates who commute, the campus is accessible by public transportation. Free on-campus parking is also available.

Private childcare facilities are available near the campus.

Policies to Ensure Fairness to Women. The Affirmative Action Officer is responsible part-time for policy on equal employment opportunity, sex equity, and access for the handicapped. A published campus policy prohibits sexual harassment; a formal campus grievance procedure resolves complaints. The Committee on the Status of Women provides support for the student Women's Alliance and advice on issues of concern to women. It reports directly to the President of the college. Committee members, including students with voting rights, are nominated by various constituencies and appointed by the President. Both this committee and the Committee on Minority Affairs address the concerns of minority women.

Women in Leadership Positions. *Students.* In three recent years, women have served once as president of the student body, once as presiding officer of the student senate, and three years each as president of the student union board and editor-in-chief of the campus newspaper. Women head two of the five honorary societies.

Faculty. Women are 23 percent of a full-time faculty of 341, a proportion slightly below average for public four-year colleges. There are 2 female faculty for every 100 female students and 23 male faculty for every 100 male students.

Administrators. A woman serves as director of athletics; but the other top-level administrative positions are held by men. Women chair six of 27 departments: geography, health and physical education, political science, home economics, sociology, and conservation of historic and artistic works. The Dean of Professional Studies is female.

Women and the Curriculum. Most degrees earned by women are in the fields of education (27 percent), home economics (18 percent), and social sciences (16 percent). Over 5 percent are in such nontraditional areas as mathematics and physical sciences.

The Women's Studies Program, directed by a full-time, permanent faculty member, offers an undergraduate minor. Twenty five courses on women are available through Women's Studies and 12 departments. Courses include Images of Women in Western Art, Women in Politics, and Psychology of Sexism in School and Society.

The schools of business and education provide instruction on some matter specific to women.

Minority Women. Almost 4 percent of undergraduate women are members of minority groups. The English department offers a course on Black Women as Literary Artists, and the School of Nursing provides instruction on health-care information of special interest to minority women. A minority woman serves as a residence-hall director. Awareness-training on racial bias is offered to residence-hall and counseling staffs.

Women and Athletics. Intramural and intercollegiate programs offer adequate opportunities to participate in organized team and individual sports. Club sports are also available. Almost 20 percent of intramural and 43 percent of intercollegiate athletes are women. Five of the 15 salaried intercollegiate coaches are women. Intercollegiate sports offered are basketball, cross-country, field hockey, lacrosse, softball, swimming, tennis and volleyball.

Housing and Student Organizations. Coeducational dormitories house the 66 percent of undergraduates who live on campus. Some have quiet sections available on request; none restrict hours for visitors of the opposite sex. Six of the 15 residence-hall directors are female. Staff are offered awareness-training on sex education and birth control.

Approximately 50 undergraduate women belong to sororities, which provide off-campus housing for members. The student Women's Alliance serves as an advocacy group for women students.

Special Services and Programs for Women. *Health and Counseling.* The student health service provides medical treatment for gynecology, abortion, and rape and assault. The 2 physicians and 1 physician's assistant are men; 11 other health-care providers are women. A counseling center, staffed by 2 women and 1 man, provides gynecological, birth control, abortion, and rape and assault counseling. Staff are offered in-service training on sex-role stereotyping.

Safety and Security. Along with local police, who include the campus in their jurisdiction, there are campus police with weapons training and arrest authority. Other measures consist of nighttime, campus-wide bus service, self-defense courses for women, information sessions on safety and crime prevention, and a rape crisis center. One rape and five assaults were reported for 1980–81.

Institutional Self-Description. None provided.

State University of New York, College at Oswego

Oswego, NY 13216
Telephone: (315) 341-2500

Women in Leadership ★★★ administrators	★ Women and the Curriculum
	★★ Women and Athletics

6,684 undergraduates

	Amer. Ind.	Asian Amer.	Blacks	Hispanics	Whites
F	5	9	80	14	2,917
M	1	21	77	34	3,476
%	0.1	0.5	2.4	0.7	96.4

Located on the shore of Lake Ontario, the College at Oswego was founded in 1861 and joined the State University of New York in 1948. A four-year college of arts and sciences, it now offers its 7,767 students a full range of bachelor's and master's level programs, as well as adult continuing education. Women are 45 percent of the 6,684 undergraduates; almost 4 percent of the women attend part-time. The median age of undergraduates is 20. For the 42 percent of undergraduates who commute, the campus is accessible by public transportation. Free on-campus parking and transportation from remote parking lots are available.

Private childcare facilities are available near the campus.

Policies to Ensure Fairness to Women. The Affirmative Action Officer on part-time assignment is responsible for policy-review and compliance concerning equal employment opportunity, sex equity for students, and handicapped accessibility. A formal policy on sexual harassment has been communicated to students, faculty, and staff. Complaints are resolved either informally and confidentially or through a formal grievance procedure.

Women in Leadership Positions. *Students.* Although almost half of all undergraduates are women, they hold few student leadership positions. During a recent three-year period, women served one-year terms as president of the student senate, editor-in-chief of the campus newspaper, and manager of the campus radio station.

Faculty. Eighteen percent of the full-time faculty of 391 are women, a proportion below the national average. The college reports that 3 minority women (1 Asian American and 2 American Indian) serve on the full-time faculty. There are 2 female faculty for every 100 female students and 9 male faculty for every 100 male students.

Administrators. The President, the Dean of Professional Studies, the director of institutional research, and the head librarian are women. One of the two directors of athletics is a woman. Women chair three of the 32 departments: communication studies, women's health and physical education; and music. In one recent year, half the alumni awards went to women.

Women and the Curriculum. Twenty-three percent of undergraduate women earn degrees in education. Women also take degrees in social sciences (13 percent), psychology (12 percent), fine arts (10 percent), and business (7 percent). Almost 7 percent major in such nontraditional fields as mathematics, computer science, and physical sciences. Women constitute 47 percent of students in cooperative education programs.

The Women's Studies Program, administered by a full-time director, offers a 21-credit minor. Nineteen undergraduate courses on women are available through communication studies, history, anthropology/sociology, English, biology, American studies, Russian, Spanish, and business administration. Recent offerings include Sociology of Sex Roles, Women in History, Women in 20th-Century British Fiction, and Women Writers of Spain and

Spanish America. The divisions of education and business offer some instruction on matters of concern to women. The faculty is offered workshops on sexism and racism in the curriculum and on nontraditional occupations for women and men.

Women and Athletics. Strong intramural and intercollegiate programs offer women excellent opportunities to participate in a range of individual and team sports. Club sports are also available. The college reports special facilities for intramural ice hockey, racquetball, fencing, and water polo. Nine paid varsity coaches are women. The intercollegiate sports in which women compete are basketball, bowling, cross-country, field hockey, ice hockey, softball, swimming, tennis, and volleyball.

Housing and Student Organizations. Single-sex and coeducational dormitories house the 58 percent of the undergraduates who live on campus. The residence halls do not restrict hours for visitors of the opposite sex. Seven of the eleven residence-hall directors are women. Staff are offered awareness-training on sex education, birth control, and alcohol and drug abuse.

Seven percent of undergraduate women belong to social sororities. Six minority women belong to racially integrated sororities. Both sororities and fraternities provide housing for members.

Special Services and Programs for Women. *Health and Counseling.* The student health service provides birth control and treatment for gynecological problems. One of the three staff physicians is female, as are ten other health-care providers. The regular student health insurance covers maternity at no extra cost. Half of the counseling center staff are female. Counseling for rape and assault victims as well as assertiveness/leadership training are available.

Safety and Security. In addition to local police whose jurisdiction includes the campus, measures consist of campus police with weapons training and arrest authority, night-time escort for women students, high-intensity lighting, self-defense courses for women, information sessions on safety and crime prevention, and a campus-based rape crisis center. Thirteen assaults (five on women) and two rapes were reported for 1980–81.

Career. Nonsexist/nonracist printed information on nontraditional fields of study for women and on job discrimination in nontraditional occupations is available. The college maintains a file on alumnae by specific careers.

Other. The Student Association runs the campus Women's Center, staffed by a student volunteer on a part-time basis. Two percent of women who use the center are minority women. The center has a library of periodicals and other reference materials.

Institutional Self-Description. "Oswego offers industrial-arts teacher education (nationally and internationally known), which would welcome an increase in the rather small number of women and minority students. We are intent on providing quality education for students and believe we have a significant number of female role models among our faculty and staff."

State University of New York, College at Plattsburgh
Plattsburgh, NY 12901
Telephone: (518) 564-2000

Women in Leadership
★★ students

★ **Women and the**
Curriculum

5,183 undergraduates

	Amer. Ind.	Asian Amer.	Blacks	Hispanics	Whites
F	22	12	32	24	2,847
M	15	10	43	18	2,088
%	0.7	0.4	1.5	0.8	96.6

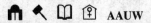 AAUW

More than 6,000 students are enrolled in this public, four-year institution located on the shores of Lake Champlain. Established in 1889 as a teacher-training school, the College at Plattsburgh now offers a broad range of four-year programs in liberal arts, pre-professional areas, health science, education, and business. Fifty-seven percent of the over 5,000 undergraduates are women; 3 percent of women attend part-time.

There is a division of continuing education. Evening classes are available both on and off campus, and there is a summer session. The median age of all undergraduates is 20. Free on-campus parking is available to the 17 percent of students who commute; there is no public transportation.

Private facilities for childcare are available nearby.

Policies to Ensure Fairness to Women. The Director of Personnel and Affirmative Action is responsible part-time for monitoring compliance with and reviewing policies about equal employment opportunity, handicapped accessibility, and sex equity for students. An Affirmative Action Committee which lists women and minorities among its concerns and a committee which addresses the needs of the handicapped serve the President in an advisory capacity. A published campus policy prohibits sexual harassment of students, faculty, and staff, and there is a formal grievance procedure to resolve complaints.

Women in Leadership Positions. *Students.* Opportunities for women to exercise campus-wide student leadership are excellent. In recent years, women have held four of the six campus-wide leadership positions, serving as president of the student body, presiding officer of the student senate, head of the union board (for two years), and head of the student union (for three years). Women head three of the eight honorary societies.

Faculty. Women constitute 24 percent of the 312 full-time faculty, a proportion slightly below the national average. There are 3 female faculty for every 100 female students and 11 male faculty for every 100 male students.

Administrators. Seven of the 8 top-level administrative positions are held by men; a woman is director of institutional research. Women make up 33 percent of the faculty senate. Four of the 35 departments are chaired by women: anthropology, sociology, home economics, and nursing.

Women and the Curriculum. Most degrees awarded to women are in education (33 percent), health services (12 percent), social sciences (11 percent), and home economics (11 percent). Three percent of women undergraduates earn degrees in nontraditional majors—mathematics or the physical sciences.

Undergraduates may minor in the recently established Women's Studies Program. In addition to Introduction to Women's Studies offered by the program, eight other courses on women—including Women in Art, and Perspectives on Women's Health—are offered in the departments of behavioral science, art, anthropology, English, nursing, psychology, history, economics, and sociology.

Instruction in the development and use of sex-fair curricula is available in the division of education; the nursing division provides training in home delivery, reproductive choice, and health-care information important to minority women.

Women and Athletics. Women are 30 percent of the athletes in the intramural program, which offers only team sports, and 44 percent of the 284 intercollegiate athletes. Five of the 12 paid varsity coaches are women. Although the college does not offer athletic scholarships, financial support is available through the Booster Club, and women have received approximately 30 percent of this assistance. Intercollegiate sports in which women compete are basketball, cross-country, field hockey, soccer, swimming, tennis, track and field, and volleyball.

Housing and Student Organizations. Coeducational dormitories house the 49 percent of undergraduates who live on campus; there are no restrictive hours for visitors of the opposite sex. The 12 residence-hall directors, four of whom are women, receive awareness-training on sexism, racism, human sexuality, and birth control.

Two of the four sororities on campus provide housing for members. The Center for Women's Concerns functions as the primary advocacy group for women students.

Special Services and Programs for Women. *Health and Counseling.* The student health service, staffed by 1 physician and 10 female health-care providers, offers limited gynecological treatment. For birth control, abortion, and treatment for rape and assault, the service refers students to appropriate community-based agencies. Regular student health insurance covers some of the expenses for abortion and maternity care. A counseling center, staffed by 2 male counselors and 1 male consulting psychologist, offers counseling in gynecology, abortion, rape, and assault.

Safety and Security. Measures consist of an unarmed campus patrol with arrest authority, night-time escort service for women students, high-intensity lighting, information sessions for women on safety and rape assault prevention, and a rape crisis center. Self-defense courses for women, run independently of the campus security office, are also available. Two sexual assaults on women were reported for 1980-81.

Career. A Career/Life Planning and Placement office is available to all students.

Other. A small Women's Center, run on a part-time basis by a volunteer student coordinator, is located in the division of behavioral sciences. There is an off-campus battered women's program sponsored by Women, Inc.

Special Features. The College at Plattsburgh recently hosted the first annual Weekend Women's Festival, which featured workshops, films, speakers, and music.

Institutional Self-Description. None provided.

State University of New York, College at Purchase

Purchase, NY 10577
Telephone: (914) 253-5000

| Women in Leadership | ★ Women and the |
| ★ faculty | Curriculum |

1,847 undergraduates

	Amer. Ind.	Asian Amer.	Blacks	Hispanics	Whites
F	0	1	123	12	930
M	0	0	60	10	676
%	0.0	0.1	10.1	1.2	88.6

🏠 🚐 🧑‍🤝‍🧑 🔨 📖 ⚕

Established in 1971, Purchase, located north of New York City, is a four-year arts and science college in the SUNY system, with special emphasis on the fine and performing arts. Over 3000 students enroll. In addition to the bachelor's programs, adult continuing education is available. Evening classes and a summer session are offered.

Women are 50 percent of the 1847 undergraduates; 1 percent of women attend part-time. The median undergraduate age is 20. For the 29 percent of students who commute, the college is accessible by public transportation. Parking on campus is free.

The Children's Center provides up to 40 hours a week of childcare; fees are on a sliding scale. The facility can accommodate 35 children. Private arrangements may be made close to campus.

Policies to Ensure Fairness to Women. The Executive Assistant to the President serves part-time as an affirmative action officer, shares policymaking responsibility with a committee, and monitors compliance with equal employment opportunity, sex equity, and handicapped accessibility. A published policy prohibits sexual harassment; complaints are handled both informally and through a formal grievance procedure.

Women in Leadership Positions. *Students.* In recent years, women have been editor-in-chief of the campus newspaper once and presided over the residence-hall council.

Faculty. Women are 28 percent of a full-time faculty of 130. According to a recent report, 2 black and 2 Asian American women are on the faculty. There are 3 female faculty for every 100 female students and 12 male faculty for every 100 male students.

Administrators. All key administrative posts are filled by men. Women chair one-quarter of the departments, including philosophy, biology, psychology, printmaking. The Dean of the Dance Division, and the Dean for Continuing Education are female.

Women and the Curriculum. The majority of women major in fine arts (38 percent), social sciences (23 percent), letters (12 percent), biological science (10 percent), and interdisciplinary studies (8 percent). Three percent major in mathematics and physical sciences. Women hold 60 percent of the internships in experiential learning programs.

The Women's Studies Program offers a concentration in Women's Studies. Eight courses are available in the natural and social sciences, the humanities, and the arts. Thirteen faculty provide individual tutorials in Women's Studies. Recent course offerings include introduction to Women's Studies I and II; Fiction of American Women; Women: A Cross-Cultural View; French Women Writers; Psychology of Women; and Women as Artists and Subjects. A committee oversees the Women's Studies Program and collects curricular materials for the development of new courses on women. Such issues as nontraditional fields of study, the needs of reentry women, and educational equity are topics of faculty workshops.

Minority Women. Among 1,812 undergraduate women, 7 percent are black, 1 percent Hispanic, and less than 1 percent Asian American. A black woman is on the Board of Trustees. A minority woman is a residence-hall director. Awareness-training on avoiding racism is offered residence staff. Twenty percent of the users of the Women's Center are members of minority groups. The Black Students Association and Latinos Unidos are active on campus.

Women and Athletics. Opportunities for women students to participate in intramual and intercollegiate sports are limited. There are six sports in the intramural program. Club sports are also available. Fourteen percent of the intramural and 28 percent of the intercollegiate athletes are women. All varsity teams played in tournaments in 1980. The intercollegiate sports are basketball, fencing, frisbee, and tennis.

Housing and Student Organizations. For the 71 percent of the undergraduates who live on campus, coeducational dormitories and apartments are available. Residence halls do not restrict hours for visitors of the opposite sex. Three of five residence-hall directors are women; staff are offered awareness-training on racism and birth control.

Gay and Lesbian Union, Women's Union, and the International Students Organization serve as advocates for women on campus.

Special Services and Programs for Women. *Health and Counseling.* The student health service provides medical treatment for gynecological problems and birth control. The student-run and funded Alternative Clinic works with the Health Service to augment gynecological and birth control treatment and deal with other women's health matters. One of the two Health Service physicians is female. The regular student health insurance covers abortion and maternity at no extra cost. The counseling service staff offer counseling on gynecological matters, birth control, and assault.

Safety and Security. Measures include campus and local police, occasional student-run night-time escorts for women, high-intensity lighting in some areas, emergency telephones, information on safety and crime prevention, and a rape crisis center. Two assaults and one rape were reported for 1980-81.

Other. The Women's Center, sponsored and coordinated by the faculty of Women's Studies and the counseling service, serves as an umbrella organization for activities such as the Alternative Clinic, support groups and workshops for above-traditional-age women, the Women's Union, guest speakers, cultural events, and "drop-in" service. The center also has a library. Assertiveness training and a telephone line of information, referral, and support are sponsored by counseling center staff, a program to build confidence in mathematics by the division of educational opportunity.

Institutional Self-Description. "The college offers an interdisciplinary Women's Studies concentration, with an outstanding faculty. Many support offices are directed by women who are particularly sensitive to the concerns and aspirations of women students. All general academic programs are challenging and rigorous, and training in the arts is outstanding. Location in Westchester County provides access to a creative and stimulating intellectual, social, and cultural environment."

State University of New York, College of Technology at Utica/Rome
811 Court Street, Utica, NY 13502
Telephone: (315) 792-3302

1,912 undergraduates

	Amer. Ind.	Asian Amer.	Blacks	Hispanics	Whites
F	0	1	14	5	1,066
M	1	1	18	3	803
%	0.5	0.1	1.7	0.4	97.8

A branch campus of the State University of New York system, this public, urban commuter college is located near Albany. SUNY Utica/Rome is an upper division technology college for two-year transfer students from community colleges, agricultural and technical colleges, and junior colleges. Some 3,000 students are enrolled, 1,912 of them undergraduates. Fifty-seven percent of the undergraduates are women, and 56 percent of the women attend part-time. The median age of all students is 27. Approximately one-fifth of women undergraduates are over age 25.

The college offers a range of programs including business/public management, nursing, human services, criminal justice, natural science, industrial technology, computer and informational science, and medical record technology. Alternative programming includes evening classes held both on and off campus and a summer session. Continuing education courses are available through the division of graduate studies and continuing education. All students commute; the campus is accessible by public transportation. On-campus parking is also available.

Policies to Ensure Fairness to Women. Information was not provided.

Women in Leadership Positions. *Students.* Women students have some opportunities to exercise campus-wide leadership. During three recent years, women have held two of five leadership positions: president of the student union board for three years and editor-in-chief of the campus newspaper for two years.

Faculty. Of 63 full-time faculty members, 24 percent are women. There are 3 female faculty for every 100 female students, and 9 male faculty for every 100 male students.

Administrators. No information was provided.

Women and the Curriculum. Fifty-seven percent of the women earn degrees in the health professions, 19 percent in public affairs, 11 percent in business, 6 percent in social sciences, and 4 percent in education. The college offers a program designed to

encourage women to prepare for careers in technology. Half of the students with internships and 10 percent in cooperative education programs are women. There are no courses on women.

Women and Athletics. No information was provided.

Special Services and Programs for Women. *Health and Counseling.* The student health service, staffed by 3 male physicians and 6 female health-care providers, provides treatment for gynecological problems and birth control. A student counseling center, staffed by 3 women, including 1 minority woman, and 1 man provides gynecological, birth control, abortion, rape and assault counseling. Counselors are offered awareness-training on sex-role stereotyping and racial bias.

Safety and Security. Measures consist of campus police with no arrest authority, night-time escort for women students, high-intensity lighting, a campus-wide emergency telephone system, an emergency alarm system, a rape crisis center, and a security paging system. Information was not provided on the incidence of rapes and assaults.

Career. Career-placement information concerning job discrimination and nontraditional fields of study is available, including nonsexist audio-visual materials on programs of study.

Other. Assertiveness and leadership training are available for women through the continuing education division. Project MOVE (Maximizing Opportunities in Vocational Education), a program for developing curriculum and training to eliminate sex bias in elementary and secondary education, is located on campus.

Institutional Self-Description. "[A student at SUNY-Utica/Rome may take advantage of] professional programs that offer maximum opportunities for career development, e.g., business, computer and information science, and engineering technologies."

State University of New York, Regents External Degree
Cultural Education Center, Albany, NY 12230
Telephone: (518) 474-3703

Enrollment Data Not Available

The Regents External Degree program is designed "to provide a flexible, evaluative college program which removes many of the obstacles traditionally preventing adults from earning degrees." It awards both associate and bachelor's degrees, without requiring classroom attendance or residence. The program has no campus and provides no instruction, but rather assesses the academic accomplishments of students who have studied independently and at their own pace. Degree requirements may be met through many alternative means, including courses studied independently and at an individual's pace, courses studied at regionally accredited colleges, proficiency examinations, courses in military-service schools, or examination by the Regents.

Women in Leadership Positions. *Students.* There are no student leadership positions.

Faculty. Not applicable.

Administrators. Men hold both top-level administrative positions. Four of 8 institutional directors are women, including the Coordinator of Test Administration and Head of the Office of Programs Development.

Women and the Curriculum. Women receive 21 percent of bachelor's degrees; three-fourths of the degrees earned by women are in interdisciplinary studies, and most of the remaining are in health professions. Women receive 21 percent of associate degrees awarded, divided almost equally between health technologies and arts and sciences.

Women and Athletics. There is no organized athletic program.

Special Services and Programs for Women. There are no health or counseling services and no security measures.

Institutional Self-Description. "Regents External Degrees provide flexible alternatives for all adults who cannot pursue college degrees through the traditional routes. Since women have tended to suffer those limitations more than men, this program may be especially important to them."

Syracuse University
Syracuse, NY 13210
Telephone: (315) 423-1870

★ **Women and the Curriculum**

11,931 undergraduates

	Amer. Ind.	Asian Amer.	Blacks	Hispanics	Whites
F	21	44	415	49	4,807
M	16	50	369	88	5,562
%	0.3	0.8	6.9	1.2	90.8

🏠 🚐 👫 📖 ⌂ NWSA

Founded in 1870, Syracuse University, a private non-sectarian institution, serves some 20,000 students with a range of undergraduate, graduate, and professional programs. Alternative schedules include evening classes and self-paced learning contracts. University College, with a downtown location, is responsible for adult continuing education.

Women are 46 percent of the 11,931 undergraduates; 7 percent of the women attend part-time. The median age of undergraduates is 21. For the 45 percent of undergraduates who live off campus or commute, the university is accessible by public transportation. On-campus parking is available at a fee, with free transportation from distant parking lots.

University childcare facilities charge on a sliding scale according to income. An estimated 90 percent of students' requests can be accommodated. Private childcare arrangements may be made close to campus.

Policies to Ensure Fairness to Women. The Special Assistant to the Chancellor for Affirmative Action is responsible for policy on equal employment opportunities, sex equity for students, and handicapped access. A formal grievance procedure handles complaints of sexual harassment.

Women in Leadership Positions. *Students.* Opportunities for women students to assume campus-wide leadership are below average for private research institutions in this guide. In recent years women have been president of the student body, presiding officer of the student senate, presiding officer of the student court, and editor-in-chief of the campus newspaper.

Faculty. Women are 19 percent of a full-time faculty of 899. One American Indian, 1 Asian American, and 2 black women are on the full-time faculty. The ratio of female faculty to female students is 3 to 100. The ratio of male faculty to male students is 12 to 100.

Administrators. The co-director of athletics is a woman. Other higher administrative posts are held by men. Women (including one black woman) chair six of 48 departments. The directors or deans of nine other academic units are female, including the Dean of the School of Nursing, the Dean of the College For Human Development, the Dean of the School of Information Studies, and the Dean of the School of Music.

Women and the Curriculum. Half of the women graduating with bachelor's degrees major in fine arts (17 percent), communications (12 percent), business and management (12 percent), and the health professions (10 percent). The number of women graduating with degrees in public affairs is above the national average. Five percent of women major in such nontraditional areas as architecture, computer science, engineering, mathematics, and the physical sciences.

The College of Arts and Sciences houses a Women's Studies Program. Twenty undergraduate and graduate courses on women are available in ten departments. Recent offerings include Women in American History; Food, Family, and Fertility; Power, Conflict, and Violence in the Family; Recent Women Poets; Women in Art; Greek Goddesses; and Women in Economic Development.

Minority Women. Of the 5,443 undergraduate women, 8 percent are black and less than 1 percent each are Hispanic, Asian American, and American Indian. Sixty-five minority women are in integrated, 70 in all-minority, sororities. Awareness-training on racism is offered to residence-hall staff and students. The Afro-American Society meets on campus.

Women and Athletics. Intramural and intercollegiate programs provide adequate opportunities for organized, competitive individual and team sports. Club sports are also available. The university reports special facilities for track and field. Nine percent of intramural and 30 percent of intercollegiate athletes are women; women receive 20 percent of athletic scholarships. Seven of 39 paid coaches for intercollegiate sports are women. The intercollegiate sports offered are basketball, crew, field hockey, swimming and diving, tennis and volleyball.

Housing and Student Organizations. Fifty-five percent of the undergraduates live on campus. Single-sex and coeducational dormitories, apartments for single graduate students, and housing for married students and single parents with children are available. A married woman student whose spouse is not enrolled may live in married students' housing. Residence halls do not restrict hours for visitors of the opposite sex. One-third of the residence-hall directors are female. Staff are offered awareness-training on sexism, sex education, birth control, racism, and other issues.

Eight percent of undergraduate women belong to social sororities. Sororities and fraternities provide housing for their members. Among organizations which serve as advocates for women on campus are the Women's Center and the Gay Students' Association.

Special Services and Programs for Women. *Health and Counseling.* The student health service provides some medical attention specific to women, including gynecological and birth control treatment. Three of the six physicians are female. The regular student health insurance covers abortion and maternity at no extra charge. One of four full-time professional staff in the counseling center is a woman. Students have access to gynecological, birth control, and abortion counseling. Counselors receive in-service training in marriage and family counseling.

Safety and Security. Measures consist of campus police with arrest authority, night-time bus service to residence areas, emergency telephone system, information sessions on safety and crime prevention, posters and leaflets on safety and security, and a rape crisis center. Twenty-nine assaults (six on women) and two rapes were reported for 1980–81.

Career. Workshops and printed information on women in nontraditional careers, lectures by women employed in these fields and a program of contacts between alumnae and female students are provided by career placement or some other unit.

Other. An active Women's Center is funded by student fees and staffed by a student volunteer. The Women's Studies Program sponsors a women's lecture series and theater and other women's arts programs. A program to build confidence in mathematics is available through the Academic Support Center.

Special Features. An informal group of women deans, vice presidents, and directors meets periodically with women who hold positions which involve daily interaction with students to define ways to improve the self-image and broaden the career horizons of female students.

Institutional Self-Description. "Women have played an important role in the Syracuse University community throughout the history of the institution. Syracuse was founded as a coeducational institution and has a long list of distinguished female graduates dating back to the 19th century. Today women holding positions at all faculty ranks and administrative levels serve as role models for our female undergraduate and graduate students.''

Utica College, Syracuse University
Burrstone Road, Utica, NY 13502
Telephone: (315) 792-3111

Women in Leadership
★ faculty

1,563 undergraduates

	Amer. Ind.	Asian Amer.	Blacks	Hispanics	Whites
F	3	3	62	15	732
M	1	2	49	8	684
%	0.3	0.3	7.1	1.5	90.8

Founded in 1946, Utica College, a coeducational, privately controlled liberal arts college, enrolls a total of 2,004 students. One of the 20 colleges of Syracuse University, it maintains a separate campus. Four-year degrees in a wide variety of undergraduate programs, including arts-engineering, fine arts, computer science, construction management, and occupational therapy are offered. Alternative schedules include evening classes and a summer session. There is continuing adult education.

Women are 52 percent of the 1,563 students registered in degree programs; 16 percent of women attend part-time. Twenty-three percent of women are over age 25, and the median age of all students is 20. Public transportation and on-campus parking are available to the 50 percent of students who commute.

Private childcare facilities are available near campus.

Policies to Ensure Fairness to Women. Two equal-opportunity officers, on a part-time basis, share policy-making responsibility for equal opportunity in employment and sex equity for students.

Women in Leadership Positions. *Students.* Women constitute more than half of the students and hold less than a third of campus leadership positions. In recent years, women have presided over the student union board, managed the campus radio station, and have twice been editor-in-chief of the newspaper.

Faculty. Women are 27 percent of the 89 full-time faculty and 12 percent of the permanently appointed faculty. There are 11 male faculty for every 100 male students and 3 female faculty for every 100 female students.

Administrators. Men hold all key positions. Four of the 22 academic deans are women, one of whom is a black woman. Women are 35 percent of the 157 members of the faculty senate, a statistic that includes 1 Asian American woman and 21 black women.

Women and the Curriculum. One-third of female graduates earn degrees in the health professions. Public affairs and communications are also most popular fields for women. Three percent of women major in mathematics or physical sciences; they are half the students graduating in those fields. A program encourages women to enter careers in computer sciences.

One course on women—The Women's Movement—is offered by the history department. An official committee is responsible for developing a women's lecture series; a seminar series on the new scholarship on women is offered by the faculty. The departments of education, social work, and business provide some instruction on matters specific to women.

Women and Athletics. Women participate in intercollegiate, coeducational intramural, and club sports. About 30 percent of

athletic scholarships go to women. Special features include an Olympic-sized swimming pool, a sauna, and an exercise room. The intercollegiate sports offered are basketball and swimming.

Housing and Student Organizations. Fifty percent of the students live on campus in single-sex and coeducational dormitories with no restrictions on visitors of the opposite sex. Twenty-five percent of all full-time undergraduates belong to sororities and fraternities. There are 25 women in all-minority sororities.

Special Services and Programs for Women. *Health and Counseling.* The health service staff consists of one male physician and a female health-care provider. No medical treatment specific to women is provided. Two therapists, one a woman, provide rape and assault counseling.

Safety and Security. Measures include campus police, high-intensity lighting, self-defense courses for women, information on rape and assault prevention, and a rape crisis center. Information on the incidence of rapes and assaults was not provided.

Career. Lectures and printed information on women employed in nontraditional occupations and job discrimination information are available.

Institutional Self-Description. ''Utica College is a private, coeducational, four-year career and liberal arts college awarding the Syracuse University degree. Our 2,200 students are primarily from New York and the Northeastern states. A modern, suburban campus enhances an informal atmosphere where a diverse student body enjoys a close, personal relationship with faculty and staff.''

Vassar College
Poughkeepsie, NY 12601
Telephone: (914) 452-7000

Women in Leadership
  ★★ faculty
  ★★★ administrators
★ Women and the Curriculum

2,310 undergraduates

	Amer. Ind.	Asian Amer.	Blacks	Hispanics	Whites
F	3	43	118	19	1,189
M	1	15	25	11	814
%	0.5	1.7	2.9	1.3	93.7

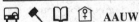 AAUW

Founded in 1861, Vassar is one of the Seven Sister Colleges and a pioneer in women's higher education. Coeducational since 1969, it offers to 2,387 students bachelor's programs in a variety of liberal arts fields. Sixty-one percent of the 2,310 degree students are women, almost all of whom attend full-time. The median age of undergraduates is 20. About 100 students are considered ''older,'' and 80 percent of these are women.

Three percent of students commute to the campus, located north of New York City. The college is accessible by public transportation, and on-campus parking is available at a fee.

Private childcare facilities are located near the campus.

Policies to Ensure Fairness to Women. The Vice President for Administration and Student Services has part-time responsibility for policy regarding equal employment opportunity, sex equity for students, and handicapped access. A written, published sexual harassment policy protects students, faculty, and staff; complaints are resolved through a formal grievance procedure.

Women in Leadership Positions. *Students.* Although women students are in the majority, men hold most of the campus leadership posts. During three recent years, women twice held the important positions of student body president and editor-in-chief of the campus newspaper. Women preside over two of the four honorary societies.

Faculty. Forty percent of the 187 full-time faculty are women, a proportion well above average for private coeducational institutions in this guide. There are 5 female faculty for every 100 female students, and 13 male faculty for every 100 male students.

Administrators. Women hold 4 of the 7 top administrative positions, including president, chief student-life officer, chief development officer, and director of athletics. Women chair 11 of 31 departments. Among the departments chaired by women are geology/geography, economics, and computer science. Women also constitute two-thirds of the Board of Trustees.

Women and the Curriculum. Twenty-seven percent of women at Vassar graduate in social sciences, 20 percent in psychology, 17 percent in letters, and 12 percent in fine arts. Four percent major in such nontraditional fields as mathematics and physical sciences.

The Women's Studies Program, directed by a permanent faculty member, offers the B.A. degree. Some 20 courses a year are offered, including Introduction to Women's Studies, Male and Female in Anthropological Perspective, History of European Women from 1750 to the Present, Sex and Power in American Politics, Biological Determinants of Human Sexuality, Feminism and Legal Reform in the U.S. and England, and two unusual courses: Eleanor Roosevelt (offered by the American Culture program) and Hannah Arendt (offered by the philosophy department). The department of education offers a reading course called Sexism, Ageism in the Curriculum; it also provides instruction on the development and use of sex-fair curricula.

Minority Women. Minority women are 13 percent of the undergraduate student body; most are black women. An administrator for minority affairs addresses the concerns of minority women. One black and one Hispanic woman chair departments. Two minority women serve as residence-hall directors.

Women and Athletics. Students may participate in organized competitive sports through a coeducational program that offers a good variety of individual and team sports. The intercollegiate sport in which women participate is field hockey.

Housing and Student Organizations. Ninety-seven percent of the students live on campus in women's dormitories, coeducational dormitories, or townhouse apartments. Most students live in coeducational housing. Restrictions on visiting hours for members of the opposite sex vary from dormitory to dormitory. Student housing also accommodates married students with and without children and single parents. Half of the 14 residence-hall directors are female.

Feminist Union serves as an advocacy group for women students.

Special Services and Programs for Women. *Health and Counseling.* The student health center employs 2 physicians, 1 of whom is female, and 18 health-care providers, 17 of them women. Three of the 6 members of the student counseling staff are women. Counseling and medical treatment are available for gynecological problems and birth control. Counseling for abortion and rape and assault is also available. Student health insurance covers abortion and maternity expenses.

Safety and Security. Measures consist of campus and local police protection, night-time escort for women, emergency telephone system, instruction on self-defense and campus safety, and a rape crisis center. No rapes or assaults were reported for 1980–81.

Career. Vassar offers career workshops, panels, and information on nontraditional occupations. The college also promotes networking between alumnae and women students and encourages students to consult files on the careers of alumnae.

Other. The Women's Studies Program sponsors the Women's Center, which is administered by a faculty member.

Special Features. Vassar's library houses the private papers of over 60 prominent 19th- and 20th-century women leaders in such areas as higher education, politics, women's rights, the arts, and science.

Institutional Self-Description. "Vassar has admitted and graduated strong, independent, creative, intelligent, caring women for over 100 years. Now we admit and graduate men who have those same characteristics. Small classes, a rich liberal arts curriculum, and a residential environment create a healthy, stimulating community where for four years students can share the luxury of liberal learning."

Wells College
Aurora, NY 13026
Telephone: (315) 364-3265

Women in Leadership	★ Women and the
★★★ students	Curriculum
★★ faculty	
★★★ administrators	

494 undergraduates

	Amer. Ind.	Asian Amer.	Blacks	Hispanics	Whites
F	2	3	18	8	457
M	2	3	0	0	0
%	0.4	0.6	3.7	1.6	93.7

AAUW

Wells is an independent, liberal arts college for women. Its campus, located near Ithaca, attracts 494 students, virtually all of whom attend full-time. The median age of all students is 21. Wells offers bachelor's programs in a variety of liberal arts fields, as well as a limited continuing education program. All but 4 percent of the students live in dormitories on campus; for those who commute, on-campus parking is available.

A campus childcare facility accommodates 15 children. All student requests for this service can be met, and charges are based on a fixed, daily rate.

Policies to Ensure Fairness to Women. The Director of Personnel has part-time responsibility for examining policies and practices pertaining to equal-employment opportunity and sex-equity laws. The Superintendent of Buildings and Grounds reviews policies and practices relating to handicapped accessibility.

Women in Leadership Positions. *Students.* Women hold all leadership positions.

Faculty. Forty-four percent of the 57 full-time faculty are women, a proportion which is below average for women's colleges in this guide, but much higher than the national average. There are 5 female faculty for every 100 female students.

Administrators. Except for the chief business officer, most top-level administrators are women. About half of the trustees are female.

Women and the Curriculum. Half of women graduates earn degrees in letters or social sciences. Four percent graduate in such nontraditional fields as mathematics or physical sciences.

A new Women's Studies Program offers a minor; its courses include Ethics and Feminism, The Family and Changing Sex Roles, Socialism and Feminism in 19th- and 20th-Century Europe, and Women from Romanticism to Realism. An official committee reports on and collects new teaching materials on women.

Women and Athletics. The organized athletic program is popular and varied. Six intercollegiate teams engage 166 women; eight intramural activities, such as canoeing, platform tennis, sailing, cross-country skiing, tennis, and basketball attract 320 participants; 80 women belong to sports clubs. Intercollegiate sports offered are bowling, field hockey, lacrosse, soccer, swimming, and tennis.

Special Services and Programs for Women. *Health and Counseling.* The student health center employs two male physicians and three female health-care providers. Counseling and treatment are provided for gynecological problems, birth control, and rape and assault. Abortion counseling is also available. Health insurance covers maternity expenses at no extra cost.

Safety and Security. Measures consist of campus police protection, night-time escort, emergency telephone system, and information on campus safety. Information was not provided on the incidence of rapes and assaults for 1980–81.

Career. The Career Service Office conducts assertiveness training sessions, a mathematics confidence clinic, and workshops and panels on nontraditional occupations. It also encourages networking between students and alumnae, and maintains files on alumnae careers.

Other. The Women's Resource Center, sponsored by student government, operates on an annual budget of $750 and plans such activities as the annual women's week. The Women's Studies Program organizes a women's lecture series.

Institutional Self-Description. "Wells College values individuality. There is a close relationship between faculty and students, a strong student government, and a great diversity in the student body. The Wells environment provides for serious study, development of the talents of women, and personal fulfillment of each unique individual."

Westchester Community College
75 Grasslands Road, Valhalla, NY 10595
Telephone: (914) 347-6979

Women in Leadership
★ faculty

5,422 undergraduates

	Amer. Ind.	Asian Amer.	Blacks	Hispanics	Whites
F	10	69	230	39	1,818
M	20	78	335	63	2,666
%	0.6	2.8	10.6	1.9	84.2

A public, two-year, commuter college founded in 1946, Westchester enrolls some 7,884 students, of whom 5,422 are registered in degree programs. Forty percent of the degree students are women and slightly more than one-third of women attend part-time. Thirty-one percent of women students are between 26 and 39 years of age, and 12 percent are over 40. The median age of all students is 25.

The college offers a comprehensive range of two-year programs, including liberal arts transfer, certificate, and degree programs in such areas as business, health, public service, and engineering/technology. Continuing education courses, available through the department for community services, enroll approximately 3,000 women, 12 percent of them minority women, largely blacks.

Alternative scheduling includes on- and off-campus evening classes, two five-week summer sessions, and a weekend college. The college is accessible by public transportation, and free on-campus parking is available.

Private childcare facilities are available within driving distance.

Policies to Ensure Fairness to Women. A publicized, written campus policy prohibits the sexual harassment of faculty and staff. A formal grievance procedure resolves complaints. A Commission on the Status of Women, constituted by the President of the college but otherwise autonomous, meets regularly to monitor the progress of women's rights on campus. The commission addresses the concerns of minority women. One administrator is assigned part-time to monitor legislation concerning employment opportunity, sex equity for students, and handicapped access.

Women in Leadership Positions. *Students.* Opportunities for women to exercise campus-wide leadership are limited. In one recent three year period, women held the positions of president of the student body and editor-in-chief of the newspaper, for one year each.

Faculty. Of 173 full-time faculty, one-third are women, an average proportion for public two-year colleges in this guide, but above the national average. There are 4 female faculty for every 100 female students and 5 male faculty for every 100 male students. Recent data show that there are 4 black, 5 Asian American, and 1 Hispanic woman among the full-time faculty.

Administrators. Men hold all key administrative positions. Women chair six of 22 departments: modern languages, developmental center, nursing, English, food services, and human services. Two of 10 trustees are women, including 1 black woman. Fifteen of 51 representatives to the faculty senate are women, including 1 Asian American woman.

Women and the Curriculum. Most women earn degrees in liberal arts (45 percent), business (29 percent), and public services (13 percent). Courses on Women in Literature and Women in Myth and Legend are offered in the department of English.

Women and Athletics. Among two-year colleges, Westchester offers a good sports program. Thirty-one percent of the intercollegiate and 28 percent of the intramural athletes are women, as are three of the 23 paid varsity coaches. Intercollegiate sports are basketball, bowling, softball, tennis, and volleyball.

Special Services and Programs for Women. *Health and Counseling.* The student health service is staffed by 4 health-care providers, 2 of whom are women. Nine of 22 counselors in the student counseling center are women, including 1 minority woman. Counseling but not treatment is available for birth control, abortion, gynecological problems, and rape and assault. Counselors are offered awareness-training on issues relating to sex-role stereotyping and racial bias.

Safety and Security. Measures consist of campus police with authority to make arrests, local town police with campus jurisdiction, and high-intensity lighting. No assaults on women were reported for 1980–81.

Other. A Women's Forum, administered under the division of student personnel services by a salaried, full-time counselor, is used by approximately 400 women students, community women, and faculty members each year, one-fourth of whom are black women. The programs, include a women's lecture series, workshops and seminars on topics of special concern to older women, and a telephone referral service, as well as special support for displaced homemakers, older women, and rape/assault victims.

Institutional Self-Description. None provided.

William Smith College
Geneva, NY 14456
Telephone: (315) 789-5500

Women in Leadership
★★★ students
★ administrators

★ **Women and the Curriculum**

1,795 undergraduates

	Amer. Ind.	Asian Amer.	Blacks	Hispanics	Whites
F	0	1	24	5	666
M	0	0	37	16	1,038
%	0.0	0.1	3.4	1.2	95.4

Founded in 1908 as an independent, liberal arts college for women, William Smith College is now a coordinate institution with Hobart College for men. The two colleges share a campus; students attend the same classes and are served by the same faculty, library, and laboratory facilities. Each college has its own Dean, admissions office, residential areas, and student government. Hobart has 1,096 students; William Smith has 699. All William Smith students are undergraduates and all but 8 are full-time students. The median age of all students is 20.

Bachelor's degrees are awarded in arts and sciences and fine and applied arts. The continuing education division serves a small number of reentry students. Ninety-nine percent of the students live on campus or nearby. No public transportation is available for the small number of commuters. On-campus parking is provided.

Private childcare facilities are available near campus.

Policies to Ensure Fairness to Women. Two administrative officers share responsibility for developing and reviewing policies concerning equal-opportunity legislation. A published policy prohibits sexual harassment of students; complaints are resolved through a formal grievance procedure. A recently formed Commission on the Status of Women is a self-designated group of faculty members drawn from the Women's Studies Committee. A Commission on Minority Affairs takes up matters of concern to minority women students.

Women in Leadership Positions. *Students.* Since William Smith has its own student government, these offices are always held by women. Top positions at the campus newspaper and radio station, open to both men and women, usually go to men.

Faculty. Twenty-four percent of the 117 full-time faculty of the coordinate colleges are women, just below the national average. There are 4 female faculty for every 100 female students and 8 male faculty for every 100 male students.

Administrators. Two of the top administrators, the Director of Athletics and the Dean of Student Life, are women. Women form one-third of the 33-member Board of Trustees. Two members of an important 6-member committee of the faculty are women. A woman chairs one academic department—history.

Women and the Curriculum. All degrees are awarded jointly by the coordinate colleges. The most popular majors for women are social sciences, psychology, and literature. Six percent of women graduates earn degrees in the nontraditional fields of mathematics and physical sciences. The college offers a mathematics confidence program. Since the experiential learning program of each college is separate, William Smith's externs and cooperative-education students are women.

The Women's Studies Program offers both a major and a minor. Five interdisciplinary courses are listed as Women's Studies courses and eight other courses on women, in several departments, are cross-listed with Women's Studies. Courses include Female Experience, Mythologies, Feminism in America and Feminist Theory. The English and philosophy departments coordinate the Women's Studies Program, which a 14-member interdepartmental committee advises. Faculty are offered workshops on sexism in the curriculum.

Women and Athletics. Because William Smith has its own athletic program, all 175 intercollegiate and 200 intramural and club athletes are women. The nine paid coaches are women. A strong intercollegiate program offers basketball, field hockey, lacrosse, soccer, swimming, and tennis.

Housing and Student Organizations. Ninety percent of William Smith students live on campus in women's or coeducational dormitories or cooperatives. The Women's Coalition is an advocacy group for women. The Third World Coalition is an advocacy group for black women, the Latin American Association for Hispanic women.

Special Services and Programs for Women. *Health and Counseling.* The student health service has 1 male physician and 4 female nurses. One of the 4-member student counseling staff is a woman. Staff are offered in-service training in the avoidane of sex-role stereotyping and racism. Counseling and medical treatment are available for gynecological problems, birth control, and rape; only counseling is provided for abortion.

Safety and Security. Measures include campus police without arrest authority, supplemented by the local police force, nighttime escort service, high-intensity lighting, self-defense courses, and a rape crisis center. No rapes were reported for 1980–81.

Career. The college career office offers lectures and literature on nontraditional careers and student-alumnae networks.

Other. The college sponsors an annual women's lecture series.

Institutional Self-Description. ''William Smith is a liberal arts college which tries to foster a desire to learn, the ability and habit of careful analysis, a devotion to hard work, and confidence in tackling problems. Our innovative interdisciplinary curriculum includes special programs including Women's Studies, urban studies, and American studies. Women of William Smith are expected to direct their own lives, to be visible.''

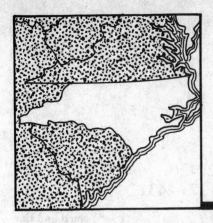

NORTH CAROLINA

Appalachian State University
Boone, NC 28608
Telephone: (704) 262-3177

8,094 undergraduates

	Amer. Ind.	Asian Amer.	Blacks	Hispanics	Whites
F	6	5	77	6	4,142
M	5	7	118	8	3,702
%	0.1	0.2	2.4	0.2	97.1

Almost 10,000 students attend Appalachian State, a comprehensive public university founded in 1903 as the Appalachian Training School for Teachers. Women are 52 percent of the 8,094 undergraduates; 8 percent of women attend part-time. Degrees in education and business predominate, though social sciences, public affairs, architecture, and arts and sciences are offered. There is a College of Continuing Education. For the 55 percent of students who commute, there is public transportation, on-campus parking at a fee, and free transportation from remote parking lots.

University-run childcare facilities accommodate all students' requests, at an hourly fee. Private childcare facilities are available near the campus.

Policies to Ensure Fairness to Women. A full-time Director of Equal Opportunity and four part-time staff vote on policymaking committees, review campus policies, and monitor compliance with laws concerning equal employment opportunity, sex equity for students, and handicapped accessibility. A public campus policy prohibits sexual harassment of students, faculty, and staff. A formal grievance procedure resolves complaints. The Commission on Minority Awareness addresses the concerns of minority women.

Women in Leadership Positions. *Students.* Opportunities for women to gain leadership experience are limited. In three recent years, women held two of the five campus-wide student positions available: editor of the campus newspaper and manager of the radio station, each for one year. Women chair eleven of 13 honor societies.

Faculty. Twenty-four percent of the 508 full-time faculty are women. Recent data show that 1 Asian American woman, 1 Hispanic woman, and 3 black women are among the 135 full-time, female faculty. The ratio of female faculty to students is 3 to 100; for males, the ratio is 11 to 100.

Administrators. Most top administrators are men. The chief planning officer, The Dean of the Graduate School, and the Director of the Center for Appalachian Studies are women, as are five department chairs—psychology, foreign languages, home economics, educational media, and reading education. Of 32 members of the Board of Governors, 5 are women, including 1 black woman; 2 of 13 trustees are women.

Women and the Curriculum. Over half of the degrees awarded to women are in education (51 percent). The next most popular areas of study are business (9 percent) and social sciences (9 percent). Three percent of women major in the nontraditional fields of mathematics, computer science, and physical sciences.

The Women's Studies Program, directed by a full-time faculty member, awards an undergraduate minor. Among courses that are offered by Women's Studies and through other departments are Introduction to Women's Studies, Women and Film, and Sex Roles in Contemporary Society. An ad hoc committee is developing the Women's Studies Program.

Women and Athletics. The participation of women in intercollegiate and intramural sports is high, and there is a wide variety of team and individual sports in the intramural program. Other information on intercollegiate sports was not provided.

Housing and Student Organizations. Appalachian State offers single-sex dormitories with visitation policies that vary. Coeducational housing has no visitation restrictions; there are also apartments for married students with and without children and single parents with children.

Nine percent of the full-time women undergraduates belong to sororities, which have special floors in dormitories. The Association for Women Students and The Black Student Alliance are advocacy groups.

Special Services and Programs for Women. *Health and Counseling.* Two male physicians and 12 other health-care providers (11 women) offer such services specific to women as gynecological, birth control, and rape and assault treatment, and abortion referrals. Twelve counselors (5 women) are offered awareness-training on sex-role stereotyping, racial bias, and consciousness-raising. They provide counseling on problems specific to women. Regular student insurance covers both maternity and abortion.

Safety and Security. Measures consist of campus, local, and state police; campus-wide bus service to residence areas until 11:30 p.m.; high-intensity lighting; and information courses on campus safety and rape and assault prevention. Information was not provided about the incidence of rapes and assaults.

Career. Appalachian State provides occasional career workshops on nontraditional occupations, programs by women employed in nontraditional careers, especially as part of courses, and job discrimination information on nontraditional professions.

Other. OASIS sponsors a battered women's program. An ad hoc committee sponsors an annual Women and the Arts Festival. The theater department sponsors theater and other arts programs for women. Psychological Services and the mathematics department offer a mathematics confidence program; Psychological Services also provides assertiveness training.

Special Features. Women's issues are addressed by a faculty-based group, Faculty Concerned with the Status of Women, and by The Center for Instructional Development which funded a workshop to evaluate the Women's Studies Program.

Institutional Self-Description. "There are a number of women faculty who take seriously their importance as role models for female students, and there is a core of genuine concern for the special needs of women students, including reentry women, lesbians, battered women, and those interested in the academic study of women. Unfortunately, the number of such faculty and staff is low in camparison to the need, so that there are always more demands on the time of those persons than it is possible to fill.''

Atlantic Christian College
Wilson, NC 27893
Telephone: (919) 237-3161

Women in Leadership
★★ faculty

1,564 undergraduates

	Amer. Ind.	Asian Amer.	Blacks	Hispanics	Whites
F	4	1	90	3	868
M	0	2	47	1	538
%	0.3	0.2	8.8	0.3	90.5

Atlantic Christian College is a church-related, liberal arts college founded in 1902 by the Disciples of Christ. It serves 1,591 students at its campus located near Raleigh. Women are 62 percent of the 1,564 degree students, and approximately 8 percent of the women attend part-time. The median age of all students is 21. For the 45 percent of undergraduates who commute, there is public transportation and on-campus parking.

Private childcare facilities are available near the campus.

Women in Leadership Positions. *Students.* Few opportunities for student leadership exist. In one recent year, a woman served as president of the student body.

Faculty. Of a total full-time faculty of 86, 33 are women (2 of the women have permanent appointments, compared with 32 of the men). There are 4 female faculty for every 100 female students and 10 male faculty for every 100 male students.

Administrators. All top-level administrative positions are held by men. Of the 12 departments, a woman chairs nursing.

Women and the Curriculum. Forty percent of the women graduate in education, and 20 percent in health professions. The 3 percent of women who earn degrees in mathematics and physical sciences represent the majority of the college's graduates in those fields. There are no courses on women.

Women and Athletics. A variety of individual and team sports is available, and the level of female participation in both intramural and intercollegiate programs is high. The intercollegiate sports offered are basketball, softball, tennis, track, and volleyball.

Housing and Student Organizations. For the 55 percent of students who live on campus, single-sex dormitories with restrictive hours for visitors of the opposite sex are available.

Seventeen percent of the full-time undergraduate women belong to sororities. Thirty-two women belong to all-minority sororities.

Special Services and Programs for Women. *Health and Counseling.* The college has a student health service staffed by four female health-care providers. No services specific to women are provided. There is no counseling center.

Safety and Security. Measures include campus police with no authority to make arrests and a night-time escort for women students. No information was provided on the incidence of rapes or assaults.

Career. Services include workshops focused on nontraditional

occupations, and printed informaton on nontraditional fields of study.

Other. There is an Over 30s Support Group for older women students, and a Women's Interdormitory Association.

Institutional Self-Description. None provided.

Bennett College
Washington Street
Greensboro, NC 27420
Telephone: (919) 273-4431

Women in Leadership	★ Women and the
★★★ students	Curriculum
★★★ faculty	
★ administrators	

608 undergraduates

	Amer. Ind.	Asian Amer.	Blacks	Hispanics	Whites
F	0	1	606	1	0
M	0	0	0	0	0
%	0.0	0.2	99.7	0.2	0.0

NWSA

Bennett was established in 1873 as a coeducational school for the preparation of black teachers. Now a private women's college affiliated with the United Methodist Church, it still serves a predominantly black student body. Its 614 students attend full-time. The median age of students is 19.

The college offers undergraduate degrees in a variety of fields. Classes meet during the day on and off campus. Ninety-five percent of the students live in dormitories that restrict hours for male visitors. For commuters, public transportation is available, and students may park on campus for a fee.

A college-operated childcare center is open to the public, as well as to students. Additional, private childcare facilities are near campus.

Women in Leadership Positions. *Students.* Women hold all student leadership positions.

Faculty. Seventy-one percent of the 52 full-time faculty are women, a proportion which is higher than that for most women's colleges in this guide. Three Hispanic and 9 white women serve on the predominantly black faculty. There are 6 female faculty for every 100 female students.

Administrators. Three of 9 top administrators—the chief student-life officer, the director of athletics, and the head librarian—are black women. Women direct the divisions of social sciences and humanities. Five black and 3 white women chair eight of 12 departments, including communications, visual arts and humane studies, home economics, business and economics, and social and behaviorial sciences. Almost all of the campus speakers in recent lecture series have been black women.

Women and the Curriculum. The most popular fields for women graduates are education (34 percent) and interdisciplinary studies (21 percent). Approximately 4 percent of women graduate in the nontraditional areas of mathematics or physical sciences. Special programs encourage women to prepare for careers in engineering, science, and accounting.

The Women's Studies Program, under the direction of a faculty member, offers a minor. Introduction to Women's Studies and Seminar on Women are offered by the program itself; courses are offered through the departments of English, philosophy, African American studies, and sociology. The departments of physical education and sociology provide instruction on some matters specific to women.

Women and Athletics. No information was supplied

Special Services and Programs for Women. *Health and Counseling.* The student health service employs 1 male physician and 1 female health-care provider. One of 2 professionals at the student counseling center is a minority woman. No information was provided on the health and counseling services available.

Safety and Security. No information was supplied.

Career. Services include workshops, lectures, and information on nontraditional occupations, as well as programs to promote networking between alumnae and students.

Special Features. The Thomas F. Holgate Library contains the Afro-American Women's Collection, consisting of more than 300 primary and secondary sources on 19th and 20th century black women.

Institutional Self-Description. None provided.

Caldwell Community College and Technical Institute

1000 Hickory Blvd., Hudson, NC 28638
Telephone: (704) 728-4323

Women in Leadership
- ★★★ students
- ★★ faculty
- ★ administrators

1,221 undergraduates

	Amer. Ind.	Asian Amer.	Blacks	Hispanics	Whites
F	1	0	40	0	564
M	1	1	51	0	554
%	0.2	0.1	7.5	0.0	92.2

On its suburban campus, Caldwell provides some 1,600 students with both technical and vocational training and the first two years of liberal arts education. Of 1,221 degree students, just over half are women; 46 percent of women attend part-time. Alternative schedules include evening classes on and off campus and self-paced/contract learning. There is an adult continuing education program. All students commute to the campus, where free parking is available. The median age of all students is 27.

Women in Leadership Positions. *Students.* In recent years, women held the two available campus-wide posts for two years: president of the student body and presiding officer of the student senate.

Faculty. Women are 39 percent of the 51 full-time faculty. There are 6 female faculty members for every 100 female students and 10 male faculty for every 100 male students.

Administrators. Of the seven key positions, women head the library and the business office. A woman chairs the humanities and social sciences department, and a woman directs the counseling service. Two of the 12 trustees are women.

Women and the Curriculum. Most two-year degrees awarded to women are in health technologies (39 percent), arts and sciences (26 percent), and business and commercial programs (20 percent). The humanities department offers a course entitled Women's Studies.

Women and Athletics. Caldwell offers a variety of team and individual intramural sports. There is a fitness trail. Women compete in intercollegiate basketball and tennis.

Special Services and Programs for Women. *Health and Counseling.* There are no health services, but two women counselors address problems of birth control, abortion, rape and assault. They also provide gynecological and marriage counseling, as well as help for battered women.

Safety and Security. The campus is equipped with high-intensity

lighting, and offers self-defense courses. No rapes or assaults on women were reported for 1980–81.

Other. A community Council on Women sponsors programs for battered women and displaced homemakers. Continuing education provides assertiveness training for women.

Institutional Self-Description. None provided.

Campbell University

Buies Creek, NC 27506
Telephone: (919) 893-4111

Women in Leadership
- ★ faculty

1,792 undergraduates

	Amer. Ind.	Asian Amer.	Blacks	Hispanics	Whites
F	9	2	42	0	755
M	7	13	72	1	864
%	0.9	0.9	6.5	0.1	91.7

A liberal arts college near Raleigh, Campbell University was founded in 1877 by the Southern Baptists and still retains its church ties. Campbell introduced master's and law degree programs in 1979. Day and evening classes are held both on and off campus. A summer session is also available.

The total student population is 2,317. Forty-six percent of the 1,792 undergraduates are women, 10 percent of whom attend part-time. The median age of undergraduates is 24, with 30 percent of the women older than 25 and 5 percent older than 40. On-campus parking is available at a fee for the 20 percent of students who commute.

Private childcare facilities are located near the campus.

Policies to Ensure Fairness to Women. A written campus policy prohibits sexual harassment of students, faculty, and staff. An informal and confidential campus mechanism resolves complaints of sexual harassment.

Women in Leadership Positions. *Students.* Information was not provided on student leadership.

Faculty. Twenty-nine percent of the 104 full-time faculty are women, a proportion above the national average. There are 4 female faculty for every 100 female students, and 8 male faculty for every 100 male students.

Administrators. Among the ten top-level administrators is one woman, the chief business officer. Three academic departments are chaired by women: education, psychology, and home economics.

Women and the Curriculum. Over half of the women who earn bachelor's degrees major in education (39 percent) or home economics (15 percent). Five percent major in the nontraditional fields of mathematics, computer science, and physical sciences. In a recent year, women earned nine of the 14 two-year degrees awarded in arts and science. There are no courses on women.

Women and Athletics. No information was provided.

Housing and Student Organizations. Single-sex dormitories do not allow visitors of the opposite sex. Housing is available to married students with and without children, and to single parents with children. A married woman student whose husband is not enrolled may live in married students' housing. Seven of 14 residence-hall directors are women.

Special Services and Programs for Women. *Health and Counseling.* The student health service employs four female and one male health-care providers and the counseling center has one male counselor. Neither center provides services specific to women.

Safety and Security. Measures include campus police with authority to make arrests, and self-defense courses for women. There were no rapes or assaults reported for 1980–81.

Institutional Self-Description. None provided.

Duke University
Durham, NC 27706
Telephone: (919) 684-8111

★★ **Women and the Curriculum**

5,879 undergraduates

	Amer. Ind.	Asian Amer.	Blacks	Hispanics	Whites
F	1	18	162	10	2,493
M	4	53	123	26	2,862
%	0.1	1.2	5.0	0.6	93.1

 **AAUW CROW**

Established in 1838 as Trinity College for Men, and merged with Woman's College in 1972, Duke University provides a range of undergraduate, graduate, and professional curricula for some 9,700 students. The Office of Continuing Education serves the adult student. Part-time study and a summer session are available.

Women are 47 percent of the 5,879 undergraduates; fewer than 1 percent of women attend part-time. For the 15 percent of undergraduates who commute, the university is accessible by public transportation. There is on-campus parking, with free transportation from remote parking lots.

Private childcare arrangements may be made near the campus.

Policies to Ensure Fairness to Women. The full-time Equal Opportunity Officer is responsible for equal employment opportunity, sex equity for students, and access for the handicapped. A published policy prohibits sexual harassment.

Women in Leadership Positions. *Students.* Although women are 47 percent of the undergraduates, in three recent years they held 20 percent of student leadership positions. They were editor-in-chief of the campus newspaper twice and president of the senior class once.

Faculty. Women are 16 percent of a full-time faculty of 347. According to recent report, 6 black, 1 Hispanic, and 2 Asian American women are on the full-time faculty. The ratio of female faculty to female students is 2 to 100; the ratio of male faculty to male students is 9 to 100.

Administrators. Men hold all the top administrative positions. The head of the history department is a woman, as is the Dean of Trinity College of Arts and Sciences. The proportion of women (28 percent) on the Board of Trustees is high compared to similar institutions in this guide.

Women and the Curriculum. Most bachelor's degrees earned by women are in social sciences (22 percent), the health professions (16 percent), psychology (11 percent), and the biological sciences (9 percent). Twelve percent are in such nontraditional subjects as computer science, engineering, mathematics, and the physical sciences. Women are one-quarter of the engineering students and nearly one-third of the physical sciences students, proportions that are above average for private research institutions. An innovative program encourages women to prepare for careers in engineering.

The Women's Studies Program, instituted in 1981–82 and directed by a permanent faculty member who is male, offers elective courses. Eleven courses on women are available through the departments of anthropology, English, health, history, political sci-

ence, religion, and sociology. Recent titles include Sex Roles, Feminist Novel in England, Women in Sports, The Social History of American Women, and Women in Developing Societies. An official committee works to expand the Women's Studies Program and courses on women in departments. The School of Business addresses issues of discrimination and women in management.

A Center for Research on Women, recently funded by the Ford Foundation, focuses on women in the South. Center resources will be used to fund doctoral research and to foster a network of individuals interested in the study and teaching of materials on women, with special emphasis on traditionally all-female, black, and rural institutions.

Minority Women. Of 2,732 undergraduate women, 6 percent are black, 1 percent Asian American, and less than 1 percent each American Indian and Hispanic. Thirty women are in all-minority sororities. Four of the residence-hall staff are minority women. The Black Student Association, is an advocacy group.

Women and Athletics. Team sports predominate in the intramural program; the intercollegiate program offers competition in individual sports. Club sports are also available. Twenty-three percent of the varsity athletes are women; women receive 20 percent of the athletic scholarships. Most of the women's teams played in tournaments in 1980. Three of the 27 paid varsity coaches are women. The intercollegiate sports available are basketball, fencing, field hockey, golf, gymnastics, swimming, tennis, and volleyball.

Housing and Student Organizations. For the 85 percent of undergraduates who live on campus, single-sex and coeducational dormitories are available. Dormitories do not restrict hours for visitors of the opposite sex.

Twenty-eight percent of full-time undergraduate women belong to social sororities. Sororities do not provide housing for members. The Association of Duke Women serves as an advocate for women on campus.

Special Services and Programs for Women. *Health and Counseling.* The student health service provides some medical attention specific to women, including gynecological and birth control treatment. Three of 10 physicians are female, as is 1 other health-care provider. The counseling service, staffed by 3 women and 5 men, offers abortion and rape and assault counseling.

Safety and Security. Measures include campus police with arrest authority, night-time escorts for women students, information sessions on safety and crime prevention, and a rape crisis center. No information was provided on the incidence of rapes and assaults.

Career. Occupational panels presented by women in nontraditional occupations and nonsexist/nonracist printed career information are available.

Other. The Office of Continuing Education sponsors assertiveness training and a program to build skills in mathematics.

Institutional Self-Description. "Duke men and women are provided the variety and therefore the flexibility which can best prepare students for rich personal lives and for their role as citizens in an uncertain future."

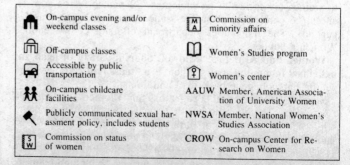

♦ On-campus evening and/or weekend classes		[MA] Commission on minority affairs	
🏛 Off-campus classes		📖 Women's Studies program	
🚌 Accessible by public transportation		⚥ Women's center	
👬 On-campus childcare facilities		AAUW Member, American Association of University Women	
♦ Publicly communicated sexual harassment policy, includes students		NWSA Member, National Women's Studies Association	
[SW] Commission on status of women		CROW On-campus Center for Research on Women	

Durham Technical Institute

1637 Lawson St., Drawer 11307
Durham, NC 27703
Telephone: (919) 596-9311

Women in Leadership
 ★ students
 ★★ faculty
 ★ adminstrators

2,261 undergraduates

	Amer. Ind.	Asian Amer.	Blacks	Hispanics	Whites
F	17	7	608	6	422
M	10	9	548	2	632
%	1.2	0.7	51.1	0.4	46.6

Durham Technical Institute is a public, two-year college offering vocational and technical education to 2,842 students, 2,261 of whom are enrolled as undergraduates. The undergraduate population is 47 percent female; three-fourths of women attend full-time. The median age of undergraduates is 25.

Durham offers associate degrees and certificates in a wide variety of vocational and technical areas. It also offers an adult continuing education program. Evening classes both on and off campus, a weekend college program, self-paced/contract learning, telecourses, and a summer session are available. An urban, commuter college, Durham Technical is accessible by public transportation, and on-campus parking is provided.

Private childcare facilities are located near the campus.

Policies to Ensure Fairness to Women. The Affirmative Action Officer serves part-time as a voting member of committees established to ensure compliance with equal-employment-opportunity and sex-equity legislation. The Director of Counseling Services is responsible part-time for compliance with laws concerning handicapped access. Complaints of sexual harassment are resolved through a formal grievance procedure.

Women in Leadership Positions. *Students.* The only all-campus leadership position, that of president of the student body, was held by a woman once in a recent three-year period.

Faculty. The full-time faculty of 72 is 43 percent female, a proportion above the average for public, two-year colleges. There are 4 female faculty for every 100 female students; the ratio of male faculty to male students is the same.

Administrators. The Executive Vice President of the college is a white woman; the head librarian is a black woman. Men hold the other five chief positions. Of six departments, a woman chairs nursing.

Women and the Curriculum. Most of the women receive their degrees and certificates in business and commerce and in health technologies.

The division of general education offers two courses on women: the History of Women and Feminism, and Career Preparatory Training for Former Homemakers. Courses in the departments of business and nursing provide some instruction on matters specific to women.

Women and Athletics. Approximately 200 women take part in intramural sports. Some 30 women compete in intercollegiate sports; 2 of the 3 paid varsity coaches are women. Intercolligiate sports offered are basketball and softball.

Special Services and Programs for Women. *Health and Counseling.* The student health service has 3 male physicians and 6 female health-care providers. The student counseling center has a staff of 3, including 1 minority woman. Services include counseling and medical treatment for gynecological and birth control needs, and counseling only for abortion or rape and assault. The

college offers counselors in-service training on avoiding sex-role stereotyping and racial bias.

Career. Services include workshops focused on nontraditional occupations, lectures/panels for students by women employed in nontraditional fields, and printed information on nontraditional areas of study for women.

Institutional Self-Description. "Durham Technical Institute provides quality vocational and technical education, which, for many women, can be the key to a higher-paying job. Students can choose from a variety of scheduling options. Not only are day, evening, and weekend courses available, but also televised courses for college credit."

Fayetteville State University

Murchison Road, Fayetteville, NC 28301
Telephone: (919) 486-1111

Women in Leadership
 ★★ faculty

2,012 undergraduates

	Amer. Ind.	Asian Amer.	Blacks	Hispanics	Whites
F	3	2	1,118	4	68
M	0	2	715	3	85
%	0.2	0.2	91.7	0.4	7.7

Fayetteville State University, an historically black teachers college founded in 1867, still serves a predominantly black student body. It has a total enrollment of 2,125 students, including 2,012 undergraduates. Women are 60 percent of the undergraduates; 8 percent of women attend part-time. The median age of the undergraduates is 21; one-third of women students are over age 25.

The university offers bachelor's degrees in the liberal arts, along with some associate degrees. The Center for Continuing Education serves the adult student. Classes meet on and off campus in the day and evening. Weekend and summer session classes are also available. Forty-eight percent of students commute to the campus, which is accessible by public transportation. On-campus parking at a fee is available.

A university-operated childcare center accommodates 105 children and can meet 90 percent of students' requests for this service. Charges are based on a fixed daily rate. Private childcare facilities are located near campus.

Policies to Ensure Fairness to Women. An administrative official, part-time, monitors compliance with equal-employment-opportunity policy. Complaints of sexual harassment are resolved through a formal campus grievance procedure.

Women in Leadership Positions. *Students.* Eight campus-wide leadership posts are available to students. In three recent years, although they are 60 percent of students, women held fewer than 30 percent of the positions. Two of eight honorary societies are headed by women.

Faculty. Thirty-six percent of the 152 full-time faculty are women, a proportion above the average for colleges nationwide. There are 5 female faculty for every 100 female students and 13 male faculty for every 100 male students. The college reports that the predominantly black full-time faculty includes 3 Hispanic and 20 white women.

Administrators. Except for the chief development officer and the chief planning officer, the top-ranking administrators are men. The college reports that the 5 deans are black women. Women chair two of six divisions: business/economics, and physical/life sciences. Thirteen percent of the faculty senate are women, including 5 black and 3 white women. Of the 4 women on the 13-

member Board of Trustees, 2 are white and 2 black. Of the ten alumni awards recently awarded, five were awarded to black women.

Women and the Curriculum. Over half of the women earn bachelor's degrees in education. Other popular fields for women graduates are social sciences (17 percent) and business (15 percent). About 5 percent of women major in mathematics. Women earn approximately 10 percent of the two-year degrees awarded in business and arts and sciences.

The university offers no courses on women. The departments of business, social work, and physical education offer instruction of some matters specific to women. Faculty workshops examine nontraditional occupations for men and women and the needs of reentry women students.

Women and Athletics. The small athletic program for women includes individual and team sport. There are two intercollegiate and four intramural teams. Twenty-seven percent of the varsity and 34 percent of the intramural athletes are women, who receive 10 percent of the athletic scholarships. Two of seven paid varsity coaches are women. Intercollegiate sports offered are basketball and track.

Housing and Student Organizations. Single-sex and coeducational dormitories with restrictive hours for visitors of the opposite sex house the 48 percent of students who live on campus. Eight of the 24 residence hall directors are minority women.

Three percent of women belong to all-minority sororities.

Special Services and Programs for Women. *Health and Counseling.* The student health service employs 1 male physician and 2 female health-care providers. Three of 4 professionals at the student counseling center are minority women. Counseling and treatment for gynecological problems and birth control, and treatment for rape and assault are provided.

Safety and Security. Measures consist of campus and local police protection, night-time escort for women, high-intensity lighting, and a rape crisis center. No information was provided concerning the incidence of rapes or assaults.

Career. Workshops, lectures, and information on nontraditional occupations and files on alumane careers are available.

Institutional Self-Description. None provided.

Gaston College
Dallas, NC 28034
Telephone: (704) 922-3136

Women in Leadership
★ faculty
★ administrators

2,756 undergraduates

	Amer. Ind.	Asian Amer.	Blacks	Hispanics	Whites
F	1	0	161	0	1,198
M	0	0	150	1	1,204
%	0.1	0.0	11.5	0.1	88.5

This public, two-year, commuter college, founded in 1964, the 2,756 matriculated students, half of whom are women. Fifty-one percent of women attend part-time. The median age of all students is 28.

Gaston offers degree programs in liberal arts, an array of vocational fields. It offers a wide range of alternative full-time and part-time schedules, including on-campus evening classes, off-campus day and evening classes, two summer sessions, contract learning, and credit-bearing television and radio courses. On-cam-

pus parking is available; the college is not served by public transportation.

Policies to Ensure Fairness to Women. The duties of one full-time administrator include responsibility for reviewing policies and monitoring compliance concerning equal-opportunity and handicapped-access legislation. A written campus policy prohibits sexual harassment. An informal and confidential mechanism resolves complaints.

Women in Leadership Positions. *Students.* Women have held none of the five major campus leadership positions during three recent years. A woman presides over the campus honorary society.

Faculty. Thirty-one percent of the 85 full-time faculty members are women, above the national average. There are 4 female faculty for every 100 female students and 9 male faculty members for every 100 male students.

Administrators. Of eight major administrators, the Dean of the Academic Division and the head librarian, are women. Four of 27 department chairs are held by women, including those of business, general studies, physical education, and nursing; 1 black and 1 Hispanic woman are among heads of departments. Of 12 college trustees, 1 is a woman.

Women and the Curriculum. Most women students take two-year degrees and certificates in business (39 percent), liberal arts (27 percent), and health technologies (17 percent). Over 70 percent of the students participating in cooperative education programs are women. Innovative programs are offered women in accounting, computer science, law enforcement, and electronics. A program to build confidence in mathematics is offered under the auspices of the Family Life Education Center. There are no courses on women.

Women and Athletics. One-third of the students participating in intramural sports are women. Intramural sports include bowling, pool, softball, tennis, and volleyball. There are no intercollegiate or club sports.

Special Services and Programs for Women. *Health and Counseling.* There is no student health service. A student counseling center is staffed by three women and three men. Counselors, who receive special training on the avoidance of sex-role stereotyping and racial bias, provide counseling for gynecological problems, birth control, abortion, and rape and assault.

Safety and Security. Measures include patrol by campus and local police, high-intensity lighting, and a rape crisis center. No rapes or other assaults were reported for 1980–81.

Career. Students have access to information on careers in nontraditional occupations.

Other. The Family Life Education Center sponsors programs for displaced homemakers, battered women, and training on assertiveness and mathematics confidence.

Institutional Self-Description. "All programs offered at Gaston College are open to women. Over 50 percent of enrollment is female. The opportunities available to women in this geographical area at Gaston College are attractive to all citizens regardless of age, sex, race, or handicap."

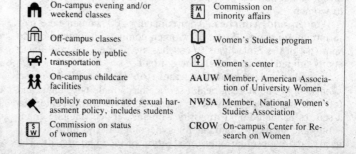

Greensboro College
Greensboro, NC 27420
Telephone: (919) 272-7102

Women in Leadership
★★ faculty

658 undergraduates

	Amer. Ind.	Asian Amer.	Blacks	Hispanics	Whites
F	1	1	89	2	324
M	1	0	39	0	198
%	0.3	0.2	19.5	0.3	79.7

 AAUW

Founded as a United Methodist, liberal arts college for women in 1838, Greensboro has been coeducational since 1954. It offers a range of four-year programs in liberal arts and sciences, as well as a two-year vocational degree in legal administration. Summer session and on-campus evening classes are available. Sixty-four percent of the 658 undergraduates are women; 6 percent of the women attend part-time. The median age of undergraduates is 20.

The campus, is accessible by public transportation. On-campus parking is available for the 20 percent of undergraduates who commute.

Private childcare facilities are available near campus.

Policies to Ensure Fairness to Women. The Business Manager, on a part-time basis, reviews policy regarding equal-employment-opportunity and handicapped-access legislation. The chair of the physical education department acts as a part-time compliance administrator of laws on sex equity for students.

Women in Leadership Positions. *Students.* Though women are 64 percent of the student body, they hold less than one-third of the leadership positions. In recent years women served three times as editor-in-chief of the campus newspaper; twice as presiding officer of the student court and president of the senior class; and once as president of the student union board and president of the junior class. The presidents of the two campus honorary societies are women.

Faculty. Of a total full-time faculty of 38, 37 percent are women, a proportion well above the nationwide average. There are 4 female faculty for every 100 female students and 11 male faculty for every 100 male students.

Administrators. Women are not represented among the college's top-level administrators. Three of the 11 department chairpersons (science and mathematics; behavioral sciences; and foreign languages), are women, as are 5 of 28 trustees.

Women and the Curriculum. Half of the women earn degrees in education, and very small numbers in social sciences, fine arts, and biology. Two thirds of the students in experiential learning programs are women. There are no courses on women. The divisions of education, social work, and business offer some instruction on matters specific to women.

Minority Women. Twenty-one percent of the 419 female undergraduates are black women, with less than 1 percent from other minority groups. Black women also account for 19 percent of the women living in residence halls. The college reports one American Indian woman on the full-time faculty.

Women and Athletics. For a small college, Greensboro offers good opportunities for women's participation in individual and team sports. Forty-three percent of the intercollegiate athletes and 38 percent of the intramural athletes are female, as is one of the seven paid varsity coaches. The intercollegiate sports offered are basketball, swimming and diving, tennis, and volleyball.

Housing and Student Organizations. Single-sex dormitories with restrictive hours for visitors of the opposite sex are available to the 80 percent of students who live on campus. Two of the four residence-hall directors are women; awareness-training on sex education is available.

Special Services and Programs for Women. *Health and Counseling.* The student health service has a staff of 1 female physician and 2 female health-care providers. It does not provide services specific to women. The counseling center, staffed by 1 female and 2 male counselors, provides such services for women as birth control, abortion, and rape and assault counseling.

Safety and Security. Measures include campus police, nighttime escort for women students, information sessions on rape and assault prevention, and a rape crisis center. No rapes and one assault on a woman were reported for 1980–81.

Career. Workshops and printed information on nontraditional occupations are available to students. The college reports an emphasis on individualized attention to students, on experiential learning, and on career-placement services.

Institutional Self-Description. "The college was founded in 1838 as a college for women and accomplished that exclusive mission for more than a century, until it became coeducational. The students are still predominantly women (2 to 1). The facilities and curricular programs are still oriented toward their needs, in a very personal environment."

Mayland Technical College
P.O. Box 547, Spruce Pine, NC 28777
Telephone: (704) 765-7351

Women in Leadership
★★★ students
★★ faculty
★ administrators

522 undergraduates

	Amer. Ind.	Asian Amer.	Blacks	Hispanics	Whites
F	0	0	1	0	228
M	0	0	10	0	283
%	0.0	0.0	2.1	0.0	97.9

Established in 1971, this public, two-year college serves 522 students, 44 percent of whom are women; 38 percent of women attend part-time. The median age of students is 28.

Mayland offers associate degrees, as well as certificates in a number of occupational areas. An adult continuing education program is operated by the department of continuing education. A summer session is available, as are evening classes, both on and off campus. All students commute to the rural campus, near Asheville; free on-campus parking is available.

Private childcare facilities are available near campus.

Policies to Ensure Fairness to Women. The Affirmative Action Officer and the Administrative Assistant have part-time responsibility for reviewing policies concerning and administering compliance with the laws on equal employment opportunity, sex equity for students, and accessibility for the handicapped.

Women in Leadership Positions. *Students.* Women held the position of president of the student body during all of a recent three-year period, and the position of editor-in-chief of the newspaper for two of those three years.

Faculty. The full-time faculty of 25 is 36 percent female, just above the average for similar colleges in this guide. There are 6 female faculty for every 100 female students, and 8 male faculty for every 100 male students.

Administrators. Of six chief administrators, the chief development officer and the head librarian are women. Four of eleven departments are chaired by women: nursing, general education, cosmetology, and early childhood.

Women and the Curriculum. Only a few women earn two-year degrees at Mayland; 90 percent of these are in the field of business. The business and nursing curricula provide some instruction on matters specific to women. There are no courses on women.

Women and Athletics. There are no intercollege or intramural sports. A few women participate in club sports.

Special Services and Programs for Women. *Health and Counseling.* There is no student health service. The student counseling center is staffed by three men and two women; no counseling services specific to women are available.

Safety and Security. The campus is patrolled by local police. Additional safety measures include high-intensity lighting in all areas and an emergency alarm system at isolated locations. No rapes or assaults on women were reported for 1980–81.

Career. Services include workshops on nontraditional occupations, printed information on nontraditional fields of study for women, and job discrimination information on nontraditional occupations for women.

Institutional Self-Description. "Mayland Technical College provides the opportunity for continuing education for all who seek it. Believing that the greatest resource of any area is its people, we seek the optimum development of that resource by helping those who come to develop saleable skills, to upgrade job performance, and to realize the satisfaction of increased personal, social, and cultural growth."

North Carolina Agricultural and Technical State University
312 North Dudley Street
Greensboro, NC 27411
Telephone: (919) 379-5000

Women in Leadership
★★ faculty

4,577 undergraduates

	Amer. Ind.	Asian Amer.	Blacks	Hispanics	Whites
F	0	1	2,040	1	43
M	0	1	2,207	3	99
%	0.0	0.1	96.6	0.1	3.2

Established in 1891 as a college for black women and men, North Carolina Agricultural and Technical State University offers liberal arts, professional, and technical education to a predominantly black student body. Its campus has a total enrollment of 5,385 students, including 4,577 undergraduates. Women are 46 percent of the undergraduates; 6 percent of women attend part-time.

The university offers associate, bachelor's, and graduate degrees. Adult education is provided by the Center for Continuing Education. Alternative scheduling includes evening classes held on and off campus, a summer session, and independent study. Forty-nine percent of students commute to the campus, which is accessible by public transportation. On-campus parking is available at a fee.

A university-operated childcare center accommodates 44 children and charges at a fixed daily fee. Additional, private childcare facilities are located close to the campus.

Policies to Ensure Fairness to Women. While there is no formal policy on sexual harassment, a campus grievance procedure resolves complaints. A Committee on the Status of Women, appointed by and responsible to the Chancellor, takes public stands on issues of importance to students. A Committee on Minority Affairs addresses the concerns of minority women.

Women in Leadership Positions. *Students.* Women have limited opportunities to gain leadership experience. In a recent three-year period, women held five of the ten campus-wide leadership positions for one year each: student body president, student senate president, student court president, senior class president, and campus newspaper editor. Women also preside over four of ten honorary societies.

Faculty. Thirty-seven percent of the 327 full-time faculty are women, a proportion significantly above the national average. There are 6 female faculty for every 100 female students and 9 male faculty for every 100 male students. The college reports that the predominantly black faculty includes 1 Hispanic, 2 Asian American, and 3 white women.

Administrators. All but one of the chief administrators are male; the head librarian is a black woman. The Dean of the School of Nursing is a woman. Women chair seven of 41 departments: foreign languages, speech communication and theater arts, sociology and social service, business education and administrative services, elementary education and reading, media education, and secondary education and curriculum. The Dean of the School of Nursing is a woman. The 13-member Board of Trustees includes 2 black women and 2 white woman. Forty-two percent of the faculty senate are women, 3 of them white women.

Women and the Curriculum. Most bachelor's degrees awarded to women are in education (27 percent), business (17 percent), and health professions (14 percent). Three percent of women earn degrees in the nontraditional fields of agriculture, engineering, and mathematics. Twenty-three percent of students in cooperative education are women. Women earn 90 percent of the two-year degrees awarded, all in health technologies.

There are no courses on women. The departments of physical education, nursing, and business offer some instruction on matters specific to women.

Women and Athletics. One-fourth of the varsity athletes and 16 percent of the intramural athletes are women. Athletic scholarships are granted. Two of the nine paid varsity coaches are women. Intercollegiate sports include softball, tennis, track, and volleyball.

Housing and Student Organizations. Single-sex dormitories with restrictive hours for visitors of the opposite sex house the 51 percent of students who live on campus. Six of eleven residence-hall directors are minority women. Residence-hall staff are offered awareness-training on sex education.

Four percent of women belong to racially integrated sororities. Neither sororities nor fraternities provide housing. The Women's Council serves as an advocacy group for women students.

Special Services and Programs for Women. *Health and Counseling.* The student health service has a staff of 3 male physicians and 9 health-care providers, 8 of them women. The student counseling center employs 5 female professionals, including 1 white woman. Such services specific to women as counseling and medical treatment for gynecological problems, birth control, and rape and assault are available, along with abortion counseling. Counseling staff are offered workshops on sex-role stereotyping and racial bias.

Safety and Security. Measures consist of campus and local police protection, night-time escorts for women, and information on campus safety. Two rapes and 30 assaults on women were reported for 1980–81.

Career. Services include workshops, lectures, and information on nontraditional occupations for women, as well as a newsletter.

Other. The Residence Hall Councils and the Dean of Women co-sponsor a battered women's program, a women's lecture series, assertiveness training, and a telephone information and referral service.

Institutional Self-Description. "The purpose of the university is to provide an intellectual setting where students in higher education may find a sense of identification, belonging, responsibility, and achievement that will prepare them for roles of leadership and service in the communities where they will live and work. In this sense, the university serves as a laboratory for the development of excellence in teaching, research, and public service. The program of the university focuses on the broad fields of agriculture, engineering, technology, business, education, nursing, the liberal arts, and science.''

Queens College
1900 Selwyn Ave., Charlotte, NC 28274
Telephone: (704) 332-7121

Women in Leadership
★★★ students
★★ faculty
★★★ administrators

478 undergraduates

	Amer. Ind.	Asian Amer.	Blacks	Hispanics	Whites
F	1	2	20	1	446
M	0	0	0	0	7
%	0.2	0.4	4.2	0.2	95.0

Queens, founded in 1857, is a Presbyterian college for women. It offers 523 students a variety of undergraduate degrees as well as an evening MBA program. Men and women can also enroll in New College, an undergraduate evening program. Independent study and a summer session are other options.

All but 1 percent of the 478 undergraduates are women, and one-third attend part-time. Thirty-eight percent of the undergraduates live on campus in dormitories that have restrictive hours for male visitors. Half of the full-time female students belong to social sororities. The suburban campus is accessible by public transportation; on-campus parking is available.

Private childcare facilities are located near the campus.

Policies to Ensure Fairness to Women. Complaints regarding sexual harassment are resolved informally and confidentially.

Women in Leadership Positions. *Students.* Women hold all student leadership positions.

Faculty. Forty-two percent of the 43 full-time faculty are women. There are 6 female faculty for every 100 female students.

Administrators. Half of the top administrators are women, including the Vice President, chief student-life officer, and director of athletics. The Deans of New College and of the Graduate School are also women. Women chair the departments of physical education, psychology, foreign languages, and nursing. In a recent year, all recipients of honorary degrees and alumni awards were women.

Women and the Curriculum. About half of the degrees awarded to women are in education, social sciences, or letters.

Three courses on women are taught through the history, sociology, and English departments: Women in Society; American Women: Leaders, Movements; and Women in Literature. Courses in the departments of social work and business provide some instruction on matters specific to women. An official committee reports on new approaches to teaching Women's Studies. Faculty are offered workshops on the needs of reentry women and affirmative action.

Women and Athletics. No information was provided on intramural or club sports. Intercollegiate sports offered are tennis and voleyball. The four paid intercollegiate coaches are women.

Special Services and Programs for Women. *Health and Counseling.* The student health center is staffed by one male physician and four female health-care providers. The counseling center employs two women. Counseling and treatment for birth con-

trol and gynecological problems, as well as counseling on abortion and rape and assault are available.

Safety and Security. Measures consist of campus police with arrest authority, night-time escorts, high-intensity lighting, instruction on self-defense and crime prevention, and a community rape crisis center. Three assaults on women were reported for 1980–81, and no rapes.

Career. The Career Center and Office of Academic Affairs co-sponsor leadership training sessions and theater programs for women. The Career Center also offers workshops and information on nontraditional occupations, in addition to encouraging networking between alumnae and students and maintaining files on alumnae careers for students' use. Through its New Dimensions program, the center provides support for older women and displaced homemakers.

Other. A Women's Center, directed by a faculty member with a budget of $28,000, attracts 700 women annually, predominantly undergraduates and community women.

Institutional Self-Description. None provided.

Salem College
Academy and Church Sts.
Winston-Salem, NC 27108
Telephone: (919) 721-2605

Women in Leadership
★★★ students
★★ faculty
★★★ administrators

567 undergraduates

	Amer. Ind.	Asian Amer.	Blacks	Hispanics	Whites
F	0	0	5	4	553
M	0	0	0	0	1
%	0.0	0.0	0.9	0.7	98.4

AAUW

Founded by Moravian settlers in 1772 and still church-affiliated, Salem College is a small liberal arts institution for women. Some 659 students are enrolled, 567 registered in degree programs. Three percent of the degree students attend part-time. The median age of students is 21; 14 percent are over age 25.

In addition to a variety of bachelor's programs, Salem awards certificates in education. Students may cross-register at Wake Forest University and the North Carolina School of the Arts. Classes meet during the day and evening on campus, supplemented by off-campus day classes. Three-fourths of the undergraduates live on campus in dormitories that restrict men's visiting hours. Commuters can reach the campus by public transportation. Free on-campus parking is available.

Private childcare facilities are available near the college.

Policies to Ensure Fairness to Women. The Assistant to the President has part-time responsibility for examining practices and making policy regarding equal employment opportunity and sex equity for students. The Academic Dean shares policymaking in these two areas. A sexual harassment policy protects students, faculty, and staff; complaints are resolved through a formal grievance procedure.

Women in Leadership Positions. *Students.* Women hold all leadership positions.

Faculty. Forty-four percent of the 55 full-time faculty are women. One Hispanic woman serves on the permanent faculty. There are 4 female faculty for every 100 women students.

Administrators. Though the President and the chief academic officer are male, five of the remaining seven major administrative posts are held by women. Women direct the continuing education and teacher education programs, and chair 4 of 15 departments: English, home economics, physical education, and psychology.

Women and the Curriculum. Two-thirds of women graduates specialize in fine arts, social sciences, psychology, or letters. Three percent pursue such nontraditional fields as mathematics or physical sciences.

Two courses on women are offered through the departments of language and literature, and history: Feminine Perspectives, and American and British Women. Prospective teachers receive instruction on sexism in the curriculum and how to teach coeducational physical education classes. An official committee seeks to expand the number of offerings on women and further the integration of women into the curriculum.

Women and Athletics. The organized sports program consists of one intercollegiate team and three intramural activities—basketball, softball, and volleyball. The intercollegiate sport offered is tennis.

Special Services and Programs for Women. *Health and Counseling.* The student health center is staffed part-time by 3 male physicians, and full-time by 4 female health-care providers, and 1 female physician's assistant. Two women work at the student counseling center. Students in need of medical treatment specific to women are referred to specialists. Counseling is available for gynecological problems, birth control, abortion, and rape and assault. Counselors are offered training in the avoidance of sex-role stereotyping and racial bias.

Safety and Security. Measures consist of campus police, night-time escort, high-intensity lighting, instruction on self-defense and campus safety, and a rape crisis center. No rapes or assaults on women were reported for 1980–81.

Career. Lifespan, a personal and life/career counseling center, runs assertiveness training sessions, career workshops, and panels on nontraditional occupations, promotes networking with alumnae, and maintains files on alumnae careers for students' use.

Other. A Women's Center reaches 560, predominantly undergraduate and community, women. The English department organizes theater performances by and for women. Minority women have organized ONUA. Winston-Salem has a battered women's shelter and a displaced homemaker program.

Returning Women Students. A Continuing Education for Women Program, under a full-time female administrator, draws 180 students. The program sponsors a mathematics confidence clinic and serves older women, displaced homemakers, and minority women. Faculty are offered workshops on the needs of reentry women.

Institutional Self-Description. "Women in the Winston-Salem community are encouraged to continue their education at Salem College as continuing education students. These persons are welcomed to the classroom, for the college believes that lifelong education can provide information about current knowledge, sharpen perceptions of the world, and help each individual develop a more interested and interesting view."

Southeastern Community College
P.O. Box 151, Whiteville, NC 28472
Telephone: (919) 642-7141

Women in Leadership
★ students
★★ faculty

1,853 undergraduates

	Amer. Ind.	Asian Amer.	Blacks	Hispanics	Whites
F	29	0	279	0	654
M	27	0	257	0	604
%	3.0	0.0	29.0	0.0	68.0

A public, two-year commuter college founded in 1965, Southeastern occupies a rural campus near Wilmington, North Carolina. Slightly more than half of the 1,853 undergraduates are women; 48 percent of women attend part-time. Two-fifths of all women students are over age 25 and one-tenth are over 40. The median age of all students is 27.

The college offers a comprehensive range of certificate and degree programs in the liberal arts, business, communications/media, health, public service, agriculture, engineering/technology, and environmental studies. Alternative full-time and part-time scheduling, including off-campus day and evening classes, an eleven-week summer session, and contract learning are available. Some public transportation is available, and on-campus parking is provided.

Limited daytime childcare facilities, with priority given to children of faculty and staff, are available on campus. Private childcare facilities are located nearby.

Policies to Ensure Fairness to Women. A written policy prohibits the sexual harassment of students. Complaints are resolved through a formal campus grievance procedure. Two administrators are assigned part-time to affirmative action and sex equity for students.

Women in Leadership Positions. *Students.* A woman has held the only student leadership position, president of the student body, once in a recent three-year period. A woman also serves as president of the campus honorary society.

Faculty. Women are 49 percent of the 63 full-time faculty. There are 6 female faculty for every 100 female students and 7 male faculty for every 100 male students.

Administrators. Men hold most of the top-level administrative positions, though one of the two academic officers is female. The Dean of College Transfer Programs and the Director of Resources for Student Learning are women, as are the chairs of the departments of English, child development, social sciences, and nursing. Four of 15 college trustees are women.

Women and the Curriculum. Women earn two-thirds of the degrees awarded. Most women take their degrees in liberal arts (40 percent), public service technologies (21 percent), health (19 percent), and business (18 percent). A program to encourage women to prepare for a career in welding is offered. One-half of students participating in cooperative education programs are women. The adult education division offers courses entitled Women and the Law and Displaced Homemakers.

Minority Women. Thirty-two percent of female students are minority women, either black or American Indian. One black woman is on the full-time faculty; the staff of the counseling center includes one minority woman. Approximately one-half of the women served by the Women's Center are black.

Women and Athletics. Slightly less than half of the intercollegiate athletes are women. One of the two coaches for women's sports is female; both coaches serve on a voluntary basis. Women receive 40 percent of athletic scholarships. The intercollegiate sports for women are basketball and softball.

Special Services and Programs for Women. *Health and Counseling.* There is no student health service. The student counseling center staff of five women and one man are offered training on matters concerning sex-role stereotyping and crisis counseling. The staff provides gynecological, birth control, abortion, and rape and assault counseling.

Safety and Security. Measures consist of campus police with weapons training and authority to make arrests, as well as local police. Self-defense courses for women and short courses on campus safety are offered. No rapes or assaults on women were reported for 1980–81.

Career. Career workshops, lectures, and information on nontraditional fields of study for women are available.

Other. A Women's Center, operating under the student development division and administered by a full-time salaried staff member, is used by approximately 1,200 women each year. Programs for battered women and displaced homemakers are offered by the Continuing Education office in conjunction with the Columbus County Council on the Status of Women.

Institutional Self-Description. "A policy of open admissions, a Women's Center, and women currently enrolled in nontraditional occupational programs testify to Southeastern Community College's institutional mission and environment."

University of North Carolina, Chapel Hill
Chapel Hill, NC 27514
Telephone: (919) 962-2211

Women in Leadership	★ Women and the
★ students	Curriculum
	★ Women and Athletics

13,311 undergraduates

	Amer. Ind.	Asian Amer.	Blacks	Hispanics	Whites
F	18	29	557	38	6,448
M	32	31	354	32	5,740
%	0.4	0.5	6.9	0.5	91.8

 **AAUW NWSA**

Opened in 1795 as a college for men, the University of North Carolina at Chapel Hill began admitting some women in 1897. It has been fully coeducational since 1972. Currently, over 20,200 students enroll in a wide range of undergraduate, graduate, and professional studies. The division of extension and continuing education provides programs for the adult student. Alternative class schedules, including a summer session, evening classes, and instruction at off-campus locations, are available.

Women are 53 percent of the 13,311 undergraduates; 2 percent of women attend part-time. The median age of undergraduates is 20. Recent data from the university indicate that 8 percent of women students are over age 25. For the commuting student, the university is accessible by public transportation. Parking on campus is available for a fee, with free transportation from distant parking lots.

Private arrangements for childcare may be made close to campus.

Policies to Ensure Fairness to Women. An Affirmative Action Officer and two assistants to the Chancellor are responsible for policy on equal employment opportunity, sex equity for students, and access for the handicapped. A written campus policy prohibits sexual harassment. Complaints are handled through a formal grievance procedure. The faculty Committee on the Status of Women takes stands on issues of concern to students. The Com-

mitteee on Minority Affairs addresses the concerns of minority women.

Women in Leadership Positions. *Students.* Opportunities for women to exercise campus leadership are above average for public research universities in this guide. In recent years, women have twice presided over the student senate, and once presided over the student court, the student union board, and the residence-hall council. For three consecutive years, women served as president of the senior class. Women head ten of the 19 honorary societies.

Faculty. Women are 21 percent of a full-time faculty of 1,297. According to a recent report, 25 black, 1 American Indian, 5 Asian American, and 3 Hispanic women are on the full-time faculty. The ratio of female faculty to female students is 4 to 100. The ratio of male faculty to male students is 17 to 100.

Administrators. The director of institutional research is a woman. All other higher administrative posts are held by men. Women chair 10 of 136 departments and direct 4 of 50 other academic units. The Dean of the School of Nursing is female.

Women and the Curriculum. The most popular majors for undergraduate women are the health professions (20 percent), business and administration (15 percent), social sciences (12 percent), and education (10 percent). Four percent of women earn degrees in nontraditional fields.

The Women's Studies Program, directed by a permanent faculty member, offers the B.A. Twenty courses on women are available through Women's Studies and the departments of Romance languages, speech communication, African studies, comparative literature, and economics. Recent titles include: Twentieth-Century Women Artists; Sex Roles: Cross-Cultural Perspectives; Minorities and Women in the Media; and Women's Autobiography. The Advisory Board of Women's Studies works to develop the program. Instruction in the teaching of coeducational physical education classes, innovative health-care delivery, and services for battered spouses are among the offerings provided in the physical education department, and by the nursing and social work schools.

Minority Women. Approximately one-tenth of the female undergraduates are from minority groups, with black women forming the largest group. In addition to the presence of black and other minority women on the faculty, one dean and one member of the Board of Governors are black women. Fifty-seven women are in all-minority sororities. One residence-hall director is a minority woman. Residence-hall staff are offered awareness-training on racism. The Black Student Movement meets on campus.

Women and Athletics. Intramural and intercollegiate programs offer good opportunities for participation in individual and team sports, with a large number and variety of each. The university reports Wimbleton volleyball on outside grass courts and special intramural facilities for tin-can floor hockey, water basketball, and frisbee golf. Twenty-three percent of intercollegiate athletes are women; women receive between 20 and 30 percent of the athletic scholarships. All women's varsity teams played in tournaments in 1980. Six of 30 paid coaches for intercollegiate teams are women. The intercollegiate sports offered are basketball, cross-country, fencing, field hockey, golf, gymnastics, soccer, softball, swimming and diving, tennis, track and field, and volleyball.

Housing and Student Organizations. For the 54 percent of the undergraduates who live on campus, single-sex and coeducational dormitories, and housing for married students and single parents with children, are available. A married woman student whose spouse is not enrolled may live in married students' housing. Dormitories restrict hours for visitors of the opposite sex. Five of 12 residence-hall directors are female. Staff are offered awareness-training on sexism and racism.

One-fifth of the undergraduate women belong to social sororities. Sororities and fraternities provide housing for their members. The Associated Women Students, Society of Hellenas, Organization for Women in Business, the Carolina Gay Alliance, and Women in Law serve as advocates for women on campus.

Special Services and Programs for Women. *Health and Counseling.* The student health and counseling services provide some attention of particular concern to women, including gynecological, birth control, and rape and assault treatment and counseling.

Safety and Security. Measures consist of campus and local police with arrest authority, night-time escorts for women students, night-time bus service to residence areas, high-intensity lighting, emergency alarm and telephone systems, self-defense courses for women, information sessions on safety and crime prevention, and a rape crisis center. Six assaults (four on women) were reported for 1980–81.

Career. Nonsexist/nonracist printed materials on women in nontraditional occupations and fields of study are available.

Other. The Association for Faculty Women is organized for mutual support and to address women's issues throughout the university.

Institutional Self-Description. "This university is a large, major research university with a long history of academic excellence. It has made commitments to a growing Women's Studies Program and to an outstanding women's athletic program. It offers opportunities for a good education with choices in programs, activities, and people."

University of North Carolina, Charlotte
UNCC Station, Charlotte, NC 28223
Telephone: (704) 597-2000

Women in Leadership
★ faculty

6,934 undergraduates

	Amer. Ind.	Asian Amer.	Blacks	Hispanics	Whites
F	4	12	277	11	2,750
M	4	14	195	28	3,496
%	0.1	0.4	7.0	0.6	92.0

 NWSA

North Carolina founded the Charlotte Center of the state university in 1946 to serve returning veterans. In 1965, it became a comprehensive four-year institution in the University of North Carolina system. Of the 8,800 students, 6,934 are undergraduates, 44 percent of whom are women; 20 percent of women attend part-time. The median age of undergraduates is 21. One-fifth of women students are over age 25.

UNCC offers a variety of bachelor's, pre-professional, and master's degrees. A summer session, on- and off-campus evening classes, and off-campus day classes are available. Continuing Education administers adult education. Two-thirds of undergraduates live off campus, commuting by public transportation or parking in on-campus facilities that are available for a fee.

Private childcare is available near campus.

Policies to Ensure Fairness to Women. The Director of Personnel is responsible for equal employment and educational opportunity; the Safety Coordinator attends to accessibility for the handicapped. Both are voting members of policymaking councils and are empowered to review campus regulations in their areas of concern. A public policy prohibits sexual harassment; complaints are resolved through a formal grievance procedure A Commission on Minority Affairs addresses the concerns of minority women.

Women in Leadership Positions. *Students.* In three recent years women students have occupied one-fourth of the campus-wide leadership positions. Women preside over four of the nine honorary societies.

Faculty. Of 410 full-time faculty, 26 percent are women. Among the 31 percent of faculty women who hold permanent appointments are 6 black, 2 Asian American, and 1 Hispanic woman. There are 4 female faculty for every 100 female students and 10 male faculty for every 100 male students.

Administrators. A woman is director of institutional research, men hold the other top positions. The Dean of the College of Nursing is female, as are the chairs of two of 25 departments—foreign languages and Afro-American and African studies. Three of the 12 trustees are white women.

Women and the Curriculum. Most women earn their bachelor's degrees in the health professions (21 percent), psychology (11 percent), social sciences (11 percent), and public affairs (9 percent). Three percent of women study architecture, engineering, mathematics, and physical sciences. Faculty committees are developing a Women's Studies Program, reporting on curricular developments that include women, and developing or collecting curricular materials that include women.

Two courses on women—Surviving Female, and Counseling Needs of Women—are offered. The departments of business and physical education and the School of Nursing provide some instruction on matters specific to women.

Women and Athletics. Twenty-nine percent of intercollegiate and 34 percent of intramural athletes are women; women receive 38 percent of athletic scholarship aid. Three of the eleven paid intercollegiate coaches are women. There is a wide choice of team and individual intramural sports. Intercollegiate sports in which women participate are basketball, softball, tennis, and volleyball.

Housing and Student Organizations. UNCC provides a choice of men's dormitories with limited visitation, coeducational dormitories in which students vote each year on visitation, and private apartments. There are five residence-hall directors—two men and three women; they receive training on a wide variety of topics, including sex education, birth control, racism, and sexism.

Eight percent of women join social sororities; 52 minority women are in all-minority sororities. Women in Engineering, Women in Architecture, and the Student Nurses Association serve as advocates for women on campus.

Special Services and Programs for Women. *Health and Counseling.* The health center—staffed by 1 female and 4 male physicians part-time, 6 female nurses, and 1 female nurse-practitioner—provides gynecological, birth control, and rape and assault treatment and abortion referrals. The health center counsels women about birth control and abortion. The counseling center staff (2 men and 3 white women) aids rape and assault victims. Abortion is covered by student medical insurance.

Safety and Security. Measures include campus and county police, both with arrest authority, night-time escorts for women, high-intensity lighting, occasional self-defense courses for women, and information sessions on campus safety and assault prevention. A rape crisis center is available in the community. For 1980–81, 26 assaults (three against women) and one rape were reported on campus.

Career. UNCC provides talks and discussions about nontraditional occupations; job discrimination information on nontraditional occupations; and programs to establish links between students and alumnae.

Other. The Mental Health Center administers a battered women's program. Women's Studies sponsors an annual women's week and theater and other women's arts programs. The Counseling Center and County Women's Commission provide assertiveness training. Peer counselors aid displaced homemakers.

Institutional Self-Description. None provided.

University of North Carolina, Greensboro

1000 Spring Garden St.,
Greensboro, NC 27412
Telephone: (919) 379-5000

Women in Leadership ★ **Women and the Curriculum**
★★ **faculty**

6,563 undergraduates

	Amer. Ind.	Asian Amer.	Blacks	Hispanics	Whites
F	8	14	530	7	4,218
M	1	3	110	3	1,647
%	0.1	0.3	9.8	0.2	89.7

 AAUW

The University of North Carolina at Greensboro was founded in 1892 as the State Normal and Industrial College for Women. Master's degree programs were added later, and in 1963 UNCG established doctoral programs and became a coeducational state university. Of the 10,000 students, 6,500 are undergraduates, 73 percent of them women; 8 percent of women attend part-time. The median age of full-time undergraduates is 20; of part-time undergraduates, 28. Evening classes, summer sessions, tutorials and independent studies, and some off-campus day and evening classes are available. The Office of Continuing Education aids returning students. Forty-seven percent of students live off-campus, commuting by car or public transportation. On-campus parking at a fee and free transportation from fringe parking areas are provided.

Both on-campus and private, off-campus childcare are available. On-campus daycare costs $40.00 per week.

Policies to Ensure Fairness to Women. The Assistant to the Chancellor and the Director of Personnel assume part-time responsibility for laws pertaining to equal employment opportunity, sex equity for students, and handicapped accessibility. As compliance officers, they are also charged with reviewing university policies and practices. A policy that prohibits sexual harassment of students, faculty, and staff has been communicated in writing to the entire campus community.

The Commission on the Status of Women is appointed by the Chancellor and Vice Chancellor and reports to the Academic Cabinet. The commission, which meets regularly, includes student members with voting rights.

Women in Leadership Positions. *Students.* Although women constitute 73 percent of students, they have held less than one-third of the campus-wide leadership positions. In three recent years, women have served three times as president of the student union board, once as editor-in-chief of the campus newspaper, and once as manager of the campus radio station. Women head seven of the 12 honorary societies.

Faculty. Of 533 faculty, 36 percent are women. Recent data show that 7 full-time faculty are black women. The female faculty to female student ratio is 4 to 100; for males it is 23 to 100.

Administrators. All top administrators are male. The deans of two traditionally female schools—home economics and nursing—are women. Women chair seven departments: anthropology, art, classical civilization and history, clothing and textiles, foods-nutrition, food service management, and home economics education. Women are well represented on the faculty senate (41 percent), campus-wide tenure committee (57 percent), and Board of Trustees (50 percent). In a recent year, the commencement speaker was a woman; women constituted five of the seven recipients of alumni awards and a third of all speakers in major lecture series.

Women and the Curriculum. Most degrees awarded to women are in education (23 percent), home economics (18 percent), health professions (14 percent), and business (9 percent). Four percent of women graduate in mathematics and physical sciences.

The Women's Studies Program, which offers an undergraduate minor, is chaired by a full-time, permanently appointed faculty member and coordinated part-time by a graduate student. Women's Studies offers two interdisciplinary courses and coordinates eleven courses on women in other departments. A committee continues to develop the Women's Studies Program and courses on women in departments. The school of education provides some instruction on matters specific to women.

Minority Women. A full-time female Director of Minority Affairs is charged with addressing the concerns of minority women. Three of the 7 women who spoke on campus in one recent year and 8 of the 276 women in the faculty senate are black women, as is 1 of the 6 female trustees. Fifty-nine percent of undergraduate black women live in residence halls. Five of the 12 female residence-hall directors are minority women, and all residence-hall staff are offered awareness-training on racism. Fifty-one women belong to all-minority sororities.

Women and Athletics. Fifty-one percent of intercollegiate, 45 percent of intramural, and 33 percent of club athletes are women. Of five paid intercollegiate coaches, two are women. Intramurals offer a wide variety of team and individual sports, including a coeducational sports day. UNCG has an on-campus golf course. Intercollegiate sports are basketball, softball, swimming, tennis, and volleyball.

Housing and Student Organizations. Single-sex and coeducational dormitories, with restrictive hours for visitors of the opposite sex, house the 53 percent of undergraduates who live on campus. Residence-hall staff are offered awareness-training on the avoidance of sexism, and racism, and on suicide prevention.

Four percent of women join non-residential social sororities. The Gay Student Union is a student advocacy group.

Special Services and Programs for Women. *Health and Counseling.* The health service, is staffed by 3 female and 2 male physicians and 17 female and 2 male health-care providers. Medical treatment is available for gynecological problems, birth control, and rape and assault. The 1 female and 2 male counselors address matters relating to abortion, birth control, marital problems, and special needs of older women and welfare recipients.

Safety and Security. Measures consist of campus police, nighttime escorts for women, an emergency telephone system, self-defense courses, information sessions on campus safety, and a rape crisis center. One rape and 29 assaults (22 on women) were reported for 1980-81.

Career. Workshops on nontraditional occupations, programs by women in nontraditional careers, printed materials on nontraditional fields, job discrimination information, and programs to establish contacts between alumnae and female students are provided.

Other. The Family Research Center manages a battered women's program. Women's Studies organizes a women's lecture series and theater and other women's arts programs. The Adult Students Office serves displaced homemakers and older women; The Chancellor's Office sponsors a Task Force for the Promotion and Study of Women's Leadership Skills.

Institutional Self-Description. "This institution, founded for the purpose of educating women and once called Women's College of Greensboro, has supplied the state with a high caliber of woman leaders through this century. Present efforts of the Task Force for Promotion and Study of Women's Leadership Skills may enable the university again to address the specific, unique needs of women students. This institution is especially open to women returning for education later in their lives."

Wake Forest University

P.O. Box 7613, Reynolda Station,
Winston-Salem, NC 27109
Telephone: (919) 761-5766

3,055 undergraduates

	Amer. Ind.	Asian Amer.	Blacks	Hispanics	Whites
F	1	7	47	5	1,075
M	3	6	88	10	1,805
%	0.1	0.4	4.4	0.5	94.5

 AAUW

Founded in 1834 as a manual labor institution, Wake Forest became a liberal arts college in 1838. A university since 1967, the institution prepares some 4,700 students for a variety of undergraduate, graduate, and professional degrees. A summer session is available.

Women are 37 percent of the 3,055 undergraduates; 2 percent of the women attend part-time. For the 15 percent of undergraduates who commute, the university is accessible by public transportation. On-campus parking is available at a fee.

Private childcare facilities are available close to campus.

Policies to Ensure Fairness to Women. A full-time Equal-Opportunity Director is responsible for policy on employment, accessibility of activities and programs to students, and handicapped access. No policy exists on sexual harassment of students. There is a Director of Minority Affairs.

Women in Leadership Positions. *Students.* Opportunities for women students to assume campus leadership positions are below the average for private research institutions in this guide. In recent years women have been presiding officer of the student court and editor-in-chief of the campus newspaper.

Faculty. Women are 17 percent of a full-time faculty of 242. One Hispanic, 1 Asian American, and 2 black women are on the full-time faculty, according to a recent report. The ratio of female faculty to female students is 4 to 100. The ratio of male faculty to male students is 11 to 100.

Administrators. Men fill all higher administrative posts. Women chair two of 22 departments: art and romance languages. One of eight deans or directors of academic units is female.

Women and the Curriculum. The majority of women graduating with bachelor's degrees major in the social sciences (19 percent), general letters (17 percent), and business and management (14 percent). Seven percent major in the nontraditional fields of mathematics and the physical sciences.

Individual courses on women are offered through the departments of history, psychology, sociology, and speech communication and theater arts. Recent offerings include the Rhetoric of the Women's Movement and Women in American History. Affirmative action and equal opportunity are topics covered in faculty workshops.

Women and Athletics. Intramural and intercollegiate programs offer a wide variety of individual and team sports. Twenty-six percent of intercollegiate athletes are women, as are 7 of 28 paid intercollegiate coaches. The intercollegiate sports offered are basketball, cross-country, field hockey, golf, tennis, track, and volleyball.

Housing and Student Organizations. Eighty-five percent of undergraduates live on campus in single-sex and coeducational dormitories. Housing for married students and single parents with children is also available. A married woman student whose spouse is not enrolled may live in married students' housing. Men's and women's dormitories restrict hours for visitors of the opposite sex. Four of eight residence-hall directors are women.

Approximately 27 percent of undergraduate women belong to social organizations. Student groups which serve as advocates for women on campus include the Women's Residence Council and Women in Law.

Special Services and Programs for Women. *Health and Counseling.* The student health service, staffed by two female physicians, does not provide medical attention specific to women. Two of three counselors in the student counseling service are women. Students have access to counseling on birth control, abortion, and rape and assault. The counseling center provides in-service training for personnel on the avoidance of sex-role stereotyping and racial bias.

Safety and Security. Measures consist of campus and city police, night-time escort service for women, an emergency alarm system, self-defense courses for women, information sessions on safety and crime prevention, and a rape crisis center. Ten assaults (three on women) and one rape were reported for 1980–81.

Career. Workshops, lectures, and printed materials concentrated on women in nontraditional careers and fields of study are available.

Institutional Self-Description. "Wake Forest University consists of medical, law, graduate, and graduate management schools, as well as undergraduate schools of arts and sciences and business and accountancy. Although Wake Forest is a major university, enrollment is purposefully small. This smallness allows for a meaningful and close contact between students and faculty."

Western Piedmont Community College

Morganton, NC 28655
Telephone: (704) 437-8688

Women in Leadership
★★ faculty
★★ administrators

1,159 undergraduates

	Amer. Ind.	Asian Amer.	Blacks	Hispanics	Whites
F	0	0	39	1	531
M	5	1	49	3	529
%	0.4	0.1	7.6	0.4	91.5

Located at the foot of the Blue Ridge Mountains, this public, two-year college offers liberal arts transfer programs, associate degrees, and one-year vocational programs in such areas as nursing, business, waste-water treatment, engineering technology, and medical assistance. Of the 1,499 students, 1,159 are registered for degree programs. Forty-nine percent of the degree students are women; 28 percent of the women attend part-time. The median age of degree students is 26. All students commute to this rural campus. Public transportation is not available, but free, on-campus parking is provided.

Private childcare facilities are available near campus.

Policies to Ensure Fairness to Women. The Coordinator of Personnel Services has part-time responsibility for policy regarding matters of equal employment opportunity, handicapped access, and sex equity. A written campus policy on sexual harassment has been publicly communicated to students, faculty, and staff. Complaints are resolved through a formal campus grievance procedure.

Women in Leadership Positions. *Students.* In recent years, women have served once as president of the student body and twice as editor-in-chief of the campus newspaper. A woman also heads Phi Theta Kappa, the campus honorary society.

Faculty. Of 55 full-time faculty, nearly half are women, an above-average proportion for public, community colleges in this guide. There are 6 female faculty for every 100 female students; the ratio for males is 12 to 100.

Administrators. Of seven top leadership positions, women hold three: development officer, head librarian, and student-life officer. Women chair the departments of nursing, dental assisting, and medical office assisting. A woman also heads the division of health services.

Women and the Curriculum. Most two-year degrees earned by women are in health technologies (64 percent). No courses on women are offered.

Women and Athletics. Opportunities are limited for women in intercollegiate and intramural sports. Women participate in in-tramural softball and volleyball, and in intercollegiate basketball and tennis.

Special Services and Programs for Women. *Health and Counseling.* Three women, including one minority woman and two men, staff the student counseling center. No services specific to women are available. There is no student health service on campus.

Safety and Security. Measures consist of local police who patrol the campus. No rapes or assaults were reported for 1980–81.

Institutional Self-Description. None provided.

NORTH DAKOTA

Mayville State College
Mayville, ND 58257
Telephone: (701) 786-2301

777 undergraduates

	Amer. Ind.	Asian Amer.	Blacks	Hispanics	Whites
F	65	0	2	1	418
M	28	0	4	0	259
%	12.0	0.0	0.8	0.1	87.1

🏠 👫 AAUW

Mayville State is a public, four-year college located north of Fargo. Of 811 students, 777 are undergraduates. Sixty-three percent of undergraduates are women, 18 percent of whom attend part-time. The median age of students is 20. About 12 percent of women students are over age 25.

Founded in 1925 as a teacher-training school, Mayville awards three-quarters of its degrees in education. The college offers both associate and bachelor's degrees. Evening and summer classes are available. Seventy-five percent of students live in single-sex and coeducational dormitories that restrict hours for visitors of the opposite sex, or in family housing. Parking on campus is available to the 23 percent of students who commute.

On-campus childcare at $6.50 per day accommodates 90 percent of student requests.

Policies to Ensure Fairness to Women. A part-time compliance administrator with no policymaking responsibilities manages equal educational and employment opportunity, and handicapped access.

Women in Leadership Positions. *Students.* In recent years women held about a third of the campus-wide student leadership positions: editor of the campus newspaper one year, president of the senior class two years, the junior class two years, the sophomore class three years, and the freshman class two years.

Faculty. Ten of 44 faculty members are female. One woman and ten men hold permanent appointments. There are 3 female faculty for every 100 female students and 12 male faculty for every 100 male students.

Administrators. All top-level administrators are men. The art department is chaired by a woman. In 1980–81, half the recipients of alumni awards and half the speakers in campus-wide lecture series were women.

Women and the Curriculum. Of four-year degrees awarded to women, 83 percent are in education, the rest in business (11 percent), letters, social sciences, and biology. Women receive over 90 percent of all two-year degrees, about equally divided between business and public services programs. Women receive 80 percent of cooperative education and 50 percent of internship assignments.

There are no courses on women. The development and use of sex-fair curricula, methods of teaching coeducatonal physical ed-

ucation classes, and issues for women in the workplace are addressed in the appropriate courses. Faculty are offered workshops on career selection and nontraditional occupations for women and men.

Women and Athletics. Women students have some opportunity to participate in organized, competitive athletics. Intramural sports are all team sports. Twenty-seven percent of intercollegiate and 37 percent of intramural athletes are women. Intercollegiate women athletes receive 20 percent of athletic scholarships. Three of the seven paid intercollegiate coaches are women. Intercollegiate sports offered are basketball, gymnastics, softball, track, and volleyball.

Special Services and Programs for Women. *Health and Counseling.* The health service is staffed by a male physician and a woman health-care provider. Counseling by a white woman is available on birth control and abortion. Regular medical insurance includes maternity expenses.

Safety and Security. Measures consist of municipal police and high-intensity lighting. No assaults or rapes were reported for 1980–81.

Institutional Self-Description. "Mayville State College is a small state institution where the slogan 'school of personal service' is truly put into action. The faculty/student ratio is low, and students' academic and personal needs can be met on an individualized basis."

University of North Dakota
University Station
Grand Forks, ND 58201
Telephone: (701) 777-2011

Women in Leadership   ★★ **Women and Athletics**
★ **administrators**

7,552 undergraduates

	Amer. Ind.	Asian Amer.	Blacks	Hispanics	Whites
F	94	11	17	12	3,511
M	51	21	19	5	3,752
%	1.9	0.4	0.5	0.2	96.9

🏠 🏛 🚐 👫 ⚒ 🆂🆆 🏚 AAUW

Established in 1883 as a university for the Dakota Territory, the University of North Dakota enrolls 9,500 students in a range of undergraduate and graduate programs. Adult continuing education is available. Evening classes, a summer session, and off-campus locations for classes are offered.

Women are 49 percent of the 7,552 undergraduates; 8 percent of women attend part-time. The median age of all students is 22. For the 54 percent of undergraduates who commute or live off campus, the university is accessible by public transportation. On-campus parking is available at a fee.

Low cost university childcare is available on a first-come, first-served basis. Facilities can accommodate 56 children. Arrangements for private childcare may be made near the campus.

Policies to Ensure Fairness to Women. The full-time Affirmative Action Officer reviews policies and practices related to equal-employment opportunites, sex equity for students, and handicapped accessibility. A published policy prohibits sexual harassment; complaints are handled through a formal grievance procedure. An active Committee on the Status of Women takes public stands on issues important to students and addresses the concerns of minority women.

Women in Leadership Positions. *Students.* Opportunities for women students to assume campus-wide leadership are considerably below the average for public research institutions in this guide. In recent years no woman has held student office.

Faculty. Women are 24 percent of a full-time faculty of 400. There are 3 female faculty for every 100 female students and 8 male faculty for every 100 male students.

Administrators. Two of eight top administrators are women: the Vice-President for Academic Affairs and the head librarian. Seven of 48 departments are chaired by women. The Dean of the College of Nursing is female.

Women and the Curriculum. Most bachelor's degrees awarded to women are in health professions and education; 3 percent are in such nontraditional fields as science and engineering.

No courses on women are offered. Official committees are responsible for developing courses on women in departments; they also collect curricular materials on women. Faculty are offered workshops on the new scholarship about women. Instruction on such topics as sex-fair curricula, reproductive choice, health-care information important to minority women, services for battered spouses, and discrimination in the workplace is part of the preparation of future teachers, health-care workers, social workers, and business students.

Women and Athletics. Intramural and intercollegiate programs provide excellent opportunities for organized competitive individual and team sports. Forty-three percent of intercollegiate athletes are women; women receive 20 percent of athletic scholarships. Six of 22 paid varsity coaches are female. All women's intercollegiate teams played in tournaments during 1980. The intercollegiate sports offered are basketball, cross-country, field hockey, golf, gymnastics, softball, swimming, tennis, and volleyball.

Housing and Student Organizations. Forty-six percent of the undergraduates live on campus. Single-sex and coeducational dormitories and housing for married students and single parents with children are available. A married woman student whose spouse is not enrolled may live in married students' housing. Men's and women's dormitories may restrict hours for visitors of the opposite sex. Five of 12 residence hall directors are female. Staff are offered awareness-training on sexism, birth control, and handicapped awareness.

Ten percent of full-time undergraduate women belong to social sororities. Sororities and fraternities provide housing for their members. The Associated Women Students serves as an advocate for women on campus.

Special Services and Programs for Women. *Health and Counseling.* The student health service provides some medical attention specific to women, including gynecological and birth control treatment. One of three physicians is female, as are nine other health-care providers. The regular student health insurance covers maternity at no extra charge. Half of the professional staff members in the counseling service are women. Some counseling specific to women is available. Staff are offered in-service training on sex-role stereotyping and racial bias.

Safety and Security. Measures consist of campus police with arrest authority, self-defense courses for women, information sessions on safety and crime prevention, and a rape crisis center. Five assaults on women and no rapes were reported for 1980–81.

Other. A campus Women's Center, under the direction of a full-time administrator offers a lecture series, assertiveness training, and a mathematics confidence program.

Institutional Self-Description. None provided.

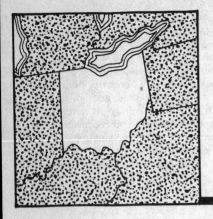

OHIO

Antioch College
Yellow Springs, OH 45387
Telephone: (513) 767-7331

Women in Leadership ★ **Women and the Curriculum**
★★★ students
★★ faculty

2,282 undergraduates

	Amer. Ind.	Asian Amer.	Blacks	Hispanics	Whites
F	36	15	418	97	778
M	23	6	223	50	606
%	2.6	0.9	28.5	6.5	61.5

🏠 ⚔ 📖 ⚕ **AAUW**

Founded in 1852 as a non-sectarian, coeducational liberal arts institution, Antioch College has nine branch campuses in the U.S. and abroad, with the main one in the small town of Yellow Springs, outside of Dayton. Antioch has a total enrollment of 4,730 students, 2,282 of them undergraduates. Fifty-nine percent of the undergraduates are women; 5 percent of women attend part-time. The median age of all students is 21.

A variety of liberal arts and pre-professional degree programs is offered, with graduate programs available at the branch campuses. Cooperative education is central to Antioch's philosophy; hence, all students alternately work full-time and study full-time. Half of the undergraduate students are in residence at any one time. A weekend college and a continuing education program attract 75 women. Five percent of the undergraduates commute. Free on-campus parking is available.

Private childcare facilities are located near the campus.

Policies to Ensure Fairness to Women. The Affirmative Action Officer, on a part-time basis, and the Dean of Administration are jointly responsible for overseeing practices and policies regarding sex equity and handicapped access. A sexual harassment policy is incorporated in the general Community Standards Code that governs the college, and a Community Standards Board is authorized to conduct formal hearings if complaints arise.

Women in Leadership Positions. *Students.* Women have outstanding opportunities to exercise campus leadership: they have occupied the positions of residence-hall council president, editor-in-chief of the campus newspaper, and student judiciary president for three recent years. The student body president and the student government president have been women for two recent years.

Faculty. Thirty-five percent of the 195 full-time faculty are women. There are 5 female faculty for every 100 female students, compared to 15 male faculty for every 100 male students.

Administrators. Among the key administrators, the Academic Dean is a woman. No departments are chaired by women. Five of the 21 trustees are women.

Women and the Curriculum. The major field of study for women is interdisciplinary studies, with public affairs the next most popular major. Two percent of females major in the nontraditional areas of architecture and physical sciences.

Women's Studies is an area of concentration within the program for interdisciplinary majors. Eight courses on women are available through Humanities, Human Services, and Social Theory. Courses include Women in American Society, Literature by Women in Southern Ohio, Sexual Politics, and Psychology of Women, as well as Introduction to Women's Studies. The program is coordinated by a part-time, temporary faculty member. Recently, Antioch has had a federal grant from the National Endowment for the Humanities to support a two-year Women's Studies Visiting Scholar. Antioch also reports publishing a Women's Studies Resource Kit and strengthening Women's Studies materials in the library.

Minority Women. Forty-two percent of the female undergraduates are minority women. Minority women are represented on the staff of the residence halls, the faculty, the Board of Trustees, and the committee on tenure, reappointments, and promotions. Fifteen percent of reentry women are minority women.

Women and Athletics. There is no intercollegiate sports program, but a good intramural sports program exists. Thirty percent of the 135 intramural athletes are women. The most popular intramural sports for women are badminton, basketball, football, handball, soccer, softball, swimming, tennis, and volleyball.

Housing and Student Organizations. Ninety-five percent of undergraduates live on campus in coeducational dormitories; housing is also available for married students with or without children and for single parents.

Special Services and Programs for Women. *Health and Counseling.* An infirmary is staffed by five female health-care providers. Three male physicians in the community are available for treatment specific to women, such as birth control, abortion, rape and assault, and gynecological emergencies. The student counseling center has one counselor, who is female. The counseling center and the Women's Center provide rape and assault counseling.

Safety and Security. Measures consist of armed campus police, night-time escort for women, high-intensity lighting, an emergency telephone system, and a self-defense course for women. No rapes or assaults on women were reported for 1980–81.

Other. A Women's Center, budgeted annually at $2,200, is staffed part-time by a salaried student coordinator. With a core of 60 active participants, and serving 500 women a year, the center sponsors an annual women's week, a women's lecture series, theater and other arts activities, and assertiveness-training workshops.

Institutional Self-Description. "Today, more than ever before, the founding principles of coeducation and equality are being fulfilled. Female students are active participants and leaders in class, interest groups, and governance. Our curriculum reflects a commitment to women and their contributions. Our cooperative education opportunities include jobs of particular interest to women. And finally, the college provides support groups and outstanding role models for our female students."

Art Academy of Cincinnati
Eden Park, Cincinnati, OH 45202
Telephone: (513) 721-5205

Women in Leadership
★ faculty
★★ administrators

155 undergraduates

	Amer. Ind.	Asian Amer.	Blacks	Hispanics	Whites
F	0	0	2	1	88
M	0	0	4	0	60
%	0.0	0.0	3.9	0.7	95.5

Founded in 1869 as part of the Cincinnati Museum Association, the Art Academy of Cincinnati began awarding bachelor's of fine arts degrees in 1979. There are 195 students, 155 of them enrolled in the bachelor's degree program; 59 percent of the degree students are women. Twenty-five percent of women attend part-time. According to recent information about 23 percent of women students are over age 40, and the median age of all students is 25. Alternative schedules include on-campus evening classes and a summer session. All students commute. The campus can be reached by public transportation, and free on-campus parking is provided.

Private childcare is available near campus.

Women in Leadership Positions. In three recent years, a woman held a one-year term as president of the senior class—the sole leadership position.

Faculty. Four of the 11 full-time faculty are women.

Administrators. Women hold three of five top positions—executive vice president and head librarian, and chief student-life officer. Department chairs are rotated annually; the institution reports that in one recent year women chaired three of the seven departments. Three of the seven members of the Board of Trustees are women.

Women and the Curriculum. Information on degrees earned by women is not available. Women hold 60 percent of the internships and practicums. There are no courses on women. Curricular materials on women are being collected by an official committee.

Women and Athletics. The academy has no sports program.

Special Services and Programs for Women. *Health and Counseling.* There is no student health service. Academy students may use the services at the University of Cincinnati.

Safety and Security. Measures include campus and municipal police, campus-wide bus service to residential areas, high-intensity lighting, and a rape crisis center. Two assaults on women and no rapes were reported for 1980–81.

Institutional Self-Description. "The academy provides strong role models among administrators and faculty."

Baldwin-Wallace College
275 Eastland Road, Berea, OH 44017
Telephone: (216) 826-2900

2,389 undergraduates

	Amer. Ind.	Asian Amer.	Blacks	Hispanics	Whites
F	0	4	99	17	1,022
M	3	7	81	14	1,135
%	0.1	0.5	7.6	1.3	90.6

 AAUW

Baldwin-Wallace College, located in a suburban community near Cleveland, was founded in 1845 as a United Methodist, liberal arts college. Some 3,244 students are enrolled, 2,389 of them undergraduates. Forty-eight percent of the undergraduates are women; a quarter of the women attend part-time. The median age of all undergraduates is 20. For the 35 percent of the students who commute, there is free on-campus parking and public transportation. Alternative schedules include evening, weekend, and summer session classes.

Private childcare facilities are located off campus.

Policies to Ensure Fairness to Women. The Assistant to the President acts in a full-time capacity to develop policy on equal-employment-opportunity, sex-equity, and handicapped-access legislation. A formal campus grievance procedure ensures due process in the resolution of sexual harassment complaints. A Commission on Minority Affairs addresses the concerns of minority women.

Women in Leadership Positions. *Students.* Opportunities for women to exercise campus-wide leadership are somewhat limited. In recent years women have served once as presiding officer of the student senate, presiding officer of the student union board, editor-in-chief of the campus newspaper, and president of the junior class.

Faculty. Women are 21 percent of the 131 full-time faculty. There are 3 female faculty for every 100 female students and 10 male faculty for every 100 male students.

Administrators. Men hold all key positions. Women chair five of the 29 departments: foreign languages and literature, political science, home economics, music theory, and women's health and physical education. Women head the division of health and physical education and the Reimenschneider Bach Institute. In a recent year, one of four honorary degrees was awarded to a woman.

Women and the Curriculum. Most bachelor's degrees awarded to women are in business (28 percent), education (18 percent), psychology (11 percent), social sciences (11 percent), and fine arts (9 percent). Two percent of the women major in mathematics or physical sciences. A Women in Business program encourages women to prepare for nontraditional careers.

Individual courses on women are offered by the theater, home economics, history, and English departments. One such course is Black Culture in America. The physical education department and the division of business offer instruction on some matters specific to women.

Women and Athletics. Twenty-three percent of the intercollegiate athletes are women, as are five of the 20 paid intercollegiate coaches. No information was provided on the intramural sports program. Intercollegiate sports offered include basketball, cross-country, softball, tennis, track, and volleyball.

Housing and Student Organizations. Sixty-five percent of the students live on-campus in single-sex or coeducational dormitories that have restrictive hours for visitors of the opposite sex. The five women among the 15 residence-hall staff include two minority women. Staff are offered awareness-training on racism and birth control.

Twenty-four percent of the full-time female undergraduates be-

---

long to sororities. There are three minority women in racially integrated sororities and 20 in all-minority sororities.

Special Services and Programs for Women. *Health and Counseling.* The student health service employs three male physicians and six female health-care providers. Some medical attention specific to women is provided, including gynecological and birth control treatment. The counseling center, staffed by one male and three female counselors, offers counseling on matters of birth control, gynecology, abortion, and rape and assault.

Safety and Security. Measures include campus and local police, night-time escort for women students, and high-intensity lighting. One rape was reported for 1980–81; no information on assaults was provided.

Career. Printed information on nontraditional fields of study and job discrimination is available to students. Files of alumnae by specific careers are kept current.

Other. An annual women's week is sponsored by the Associate Vice President of Student Affairs and ACES, and a women's lecture series is sponsored by Baldwin-Wallace Professional Women. Assertiveness/leadership training is offered by Developmental Services.

Institutional Self-Description. "Baldwin-Wallace attempts to maintain a diverse student body in order to share, understand, and respect differing ideas and heritages in order to create an environment that provides the student with maximum opportunity for self-development."

Bowling Green State University
Bowling Green, OH 43403
Telephone: (419) 372-2531

★ **Women and the Curriculum**

13,646 undergraduates

	Amer. Ind.	Asian Amer.	Blacks	Hispanics	Whites
F	0	13	453	57	7,351
M	3	10	248	35	5,380
%	0.1	0.2	5.2	0.7	94.0

⌂ 🏛 ▥ 📖 ☖ **AAUW NWSA**

Bowling Green State University, established in 1910 as a school for the training of teachers, and as a university since 1935, is located in a small community in northwestern Ohio. Some 17,000 students enroll in a variety of undergraduate and graduate programs. Continuing education, summer, and regional programs are available, along with alternative class schedules, including self-paced learning contracts and off-campus locations.

Women are 58 percent of the 13,646 undergraduates; 4 percent of women attend part-time. The median age of undergraduates is 20. For the 45 percent of undergraduates who commute, there is on-campus parking.

Private childcare facilities are available near the campus.

Policies to Ensure Fairness to Women. An equal-opportunity officer initiates affirmative action policies for approval by the administration and monitors practices related to employment and sex equity for students. The officer for handicapped services monitors compliance with policy on handicapped accessibility. A policy prohibiting sexual harassment is pending faculty approval. Currently complaints are handled through the university's equal-opportunity office. The Office of Educational Development addresses a broad range of minority concerns, including those of minority women.

Women in Leadership Positions. *Students.* There are some opportunities for women in student leadership. In recent years women have been president of the student body, presiding officer of the student union board, editor-in-chief of the newspaper (two times), and manager of the campus radio station. Women head nine of the 20 honorary societies.

Faculty. Women are 23 percent of a full-time faculty of 737. There are 2 female faculty for every 100 female students and 10 male faculty for every 100 male students.

Administrators. Men occupy all key administrative positions. Women chair six of 52 departments. The head of the School of Health, Physical Education and Recreation, the head of the School of Nursing, and the Dean of Firelands College (a branch campus) are women.

Women and the Curriculum. The majority of women earning bachelor's degrees major in education (37 percent), business and management (12 percent), and home economics (8 percent). Two percent major in such nontraditional areas as computer science, engineering, mathematics, and the physical sciences. Thirty-one percent of the students in cooperative education programs are female. All women graduating with two-year degrees major in business and commercial technologies.

The Women's Studies Program, under a full-time director, offers a 30-quarter-hour undergraduate minor and a B.A. In addition to such Women's Studies courses as Introduction to Women's Studies and Women and Religion, more than 20 courses on women are available in the departments of philosophy, psychology, English, history, sociology, theater, popular culture, ethnic studies, and health and physical education. An official committee promotes and monitors the teaching of new courses on women.

Such current issues as mathematics confidence among females, sex-fair curricula, coeducational physical education classes, health-care information important to minority women, services for battered spouses, and discrimination in the workplace are part of the preparation of future teachers, health-care providers, social workers, and business students. Sexism and racism in the curriculum and affirmative action are topics for faculty workshops.

Women and Athletics. Intramural and intercollegiate programs provide opportunities for organized, competitive, individual and team sports. The university reports special facilities for ice hockey. Forty percent of intercollegiate athletes are women; women receive 30 percent of athletic scholarships. Seven of 31 paid varsity coaches are female. The intercollegiate sports offered are basketball, cross-country, field hockey, golf, gymnastics, softball, swimming and diving, track and field, tennis, and volleyball.

Housing and Student Organizations. Fifty-five percent of undergraduates live on campus in single-sex and coeducational dormitories. Ten of 17 residence hall directors are female. Staff are offered awareness-training on sex education and human relations.

Thirteen percent of the full-time undergraduate women belong to social sororities. Sororities and fraternities provide housing for their members. Among groups which serve as advocates for women on campus are the Commuter Off-Campus Organization, Gay Union, Graduate Student Senate, Black Student Union, Women in Business, Women in Communication, United Christian Fellowship, and Destiny.

Special Services and Programs for Women. *Health and Counseling.* The student health service provides some medical attention specific to women, including gynecological, birth control, and rape and assault treatment. One of 4 physicians is female, as are 6 of 8 other health-care providers. The regular student health insurance covers abortion and maternity at no extra charge. Four of 7 professional staff in the counseling service are women. Students have access to gynecological, birth control, abortion, and rape and assault counseling.

Safety and Security. Measures consist of campus and local police, a volunteer-run night-time escort service for women students, self-defense courses for women, information sessions on safety and crime prevention, and a rape crisis center. Two rapes and a total of 18 assaults were reported for 1980-81.

Other. The campus Women's Center, Women for Women, under the auspices of Student Affairs, is staffed by a part-time student. The center operates a telephone service of information, referral, and support. Women's Studies sponsors a women's lectures series and cultural programs.

Returning Women Students. The Center for Continued Learning, under a full-time director, is responsible for continuing education for women. Approximately 2 percent of the 275 women enrolled in courses are black and Hispanic women. Among the services available for reentry women is assertiveness training.

Special Features. Bowling Green is developing an extensive collection of archival materials about the history of women in northwest Ohio, including oral histories and literary materials. A Women's Studies archivist has been appointed and a recent federal grant will increase acquisition opportunities.

Institutional Self-Description. ''Women faculty and staff are highly visible and respected members of the university community. They provide excellent role models and serve as valuable resources for students and colleagues. The many academic programs available are considered to be competitive with those of comparable institutions and are open to qualified students whether or not the program has traditionally enrolled primarily men or women students. A major in Women's Studies is available.''

Capital University
2199 East Main Street
Columbus, OH 43209
Telephone: (614) 236-6011

Women in Leadership
★★★ students
★★ faculty

1,608 undergraduates

	Amer. Ind.	Asian Amer.	Blacks	Hispanics	Whites
F	1	5	133	2	802
M	2	3	68	3	582
%	0.2	0.5	12.6	0.3	86.5

Capital University was founded by the American Lutheran Church in 1850, and now enrolls some 2,600 students. Fifty-nine percent of the 1,608 undergraduates are women, 8 percent of whom attend part-time. Capital offers bachelor's degrees in arts and sciences, nursing and music; master's degree programs are also available. A University Without Walls program offers the opportunity for self-paced learning and credit for prior learning experience. Summer sessions and evening classes are available. The median age of all undergraduate students is 21. Public transportation is accessible for the 40 percent of undergraduates who commute. On-campus parking is available at a fee.

Private childcare facilites are located near campus.

Policies to Ensure Fairness to Women. The Affirmative Action Officer, on a part-time basis, monitors compliance with equal-employment-opportunity legislation. A campus policy prohibits sexual harassment of students, faculty, and staff; and a formal campus grievance procedure resolves complaints. A Committee on Minority Affairs addresses the concerns of minority women.

Women in Leadership Positions. *Students.* Opportunities for women to exercise campus-wide leadership are outstanding. During a recent three-year period, the presiding officer of the student court, the presiding officer of the student union, and the editor-in-chief of the campus newspaper were women. In one of those years, women served as president of the residence-hall council and headed one of the four honorary societies.

Faculty. Of a total full-time faculty of 118, 36 percent are female. There are 5 female faculty for every 100 female students and 12 male faculty for every 100 male students.

Administrators. Of the 8 top-level administrators, the Director of Athletics is a woman. One of the 19 departmental chairpersons is a woman (Physical Education), and 2 of the 6 deans are women (Dean of the School of Nursing, and Director of the University Without Walls). Four of the 29 regents are women.

Women and the Curriculum. The most popular majors for women are education (21 percent) and the health professions (31 percent). The division of nursing provides instruction on midwifery, home delivery, and reproductive choice. There are no courses on women.

Women and Athletics. Information on the participation of women in intramural sports is not available. Capital does have a good program of individual and team intercollegiate sports for women. One-fifth of 344 varsity athletes are female, as is one of the six paid coaches. The intercollegiate sports offered are basketball, cross-country, softball, tennis, track, and volleyball.

Housing and Student Organizations. Men's and women's dormitories, available for the 60 percent of students who live on campus, have restrictive hours for visitors of the opposite sex. Three of the four residence-hall directors are women, and all residence-hall staff are offered awareness training on sexism, sex education, and birth control.

Approximately one-fourth of the women students are sorority members. Thirty minority women are members of all-minority sororities and 12 belong to racially integrated sororities. Neither sororities or fraternities provide housing for members.

Special Services and Programs for Women. *Health and Counseling.* One male physician and two female health-care providers staff the student health center and provide such services specific to women as gynecological treatment and birth control. The counseling center employs one male and one female counselor. It provides gynecological, birth control, and rape and assault counseling.

Safety and Security. Measures consist of campus police without arrest authority, night-time escorts for women, high-intensity lighting, self-defense courses for women, short courses on rape and assault prevention, and a rape crisis center. Information was not provided on the incidence of rapes and assaults for 1980-81.

Career. Career placement services include career workshops, printed materials, and job discrimination information on nontraditional occupations, along with lectures and panels by women employed in these fields.

Institutional Self-Description. ''The University Without Walls program provides the opportunity for women to earn a college degree in a program of independent study. A strong career planning and placement service is of special benefit to students.''

Chatfield College
St. Martin, OH 45118
Telephone: (513) 875-5511

Women in Leadership
★★★ administrators

38 undergraduates

	Amer. Ind.	Asian Amer.	Blacks	Hispanics	Whites
F	0	0	1	0	28
M	0	0	0	0	9
%	0.0	0.0	2.6	0.0	97.4

Established in 1958 as a teacher's college, this two-year Roman Catholic college now offers a liberal arts program leading to an associate degree. Of 38 matriculated students, three-quarters are women. More than half of the women attend part-time. More recent data from the college indicate an expanded enrollment, with 88 female students. The median age of the student body is 31.

Evening classes both on and off campus are available, as is a summer session. Free on-campus parking is available. There is no public transportation.

Women in Leadership Positions. *Students.* There are no campus leadership positions for students.

Faculty. No data was supplied on full-time faculty. The college indicates that of 28 part-time faculty members, half are women.

Administrators. Women hold five of seven chief administrative positions: chief executive officer, chief academic officer, chief business officer, chief student-life officer and head librarian.

Women and the Curriculum. All of the two-year degrees awarded are in the arts and sciences. There are no courses on women.

Women and Athletics. There are no sports programs.

Special Services and Programs for Women. *Health and Counseling.* There is no student health service; there are no counseling services.

Safety and Security. The college is patrolled by local police. No rapes or assaults were reported on campus for 1980–81.

Institutional Self-Description. "Chatfield College maintains a non-discriminatory, open admissions policy for all persons regardless of race, color, creed, sex, national origin, or handicap. With a small student body, the college is able to be flexible in meeting the needs of women by way of nontraditional class scheduling and offerings."

Cincinnati Technical College
3520 Central Parkway,
Cincinnati, OH 45223
Telephone: (513) 559-1520

1,808 undergraduates

	Amer. Ind.	Asian Amer.	Blacks	Hispanics	Whites
F	1	3	140	3	537
M	2	14	142	1	957
%	0.2	0.9	15.7	0.2	83.0

A public, two-year technical college, Cincinnati serves 3,264 students. Of the 1,808 matriculated students, 38 percent are women. Eighteen percent of women attend part-time, and 32 percent of women are over age 25. The college offers a range of one- and two-year programs in allied health technologies, business, engineering, mathematics, and physical sciences. The extended services division offers adult continuing education. Evening classes, both on and off campus, weekend college, and self-paced/contract learning are available.

The campus, located on an urban campus in Cincinnati, is accessible by public transportation; on-campus parking is available for a fee. All students commute.

Women in Leadership Positions. *Students.* Information was not provided on student leadership.

Faculty. Woman make up 19 percent of the 107 full-time faculty. There are 4 female faculty for every 100 female students and 9 male faculty for every 100 male students.

Administrators. Of eight top administrators, the chief student life officer is the only woman. The Dean of Health Technologies is a woman. Three of the ten trustees are women, including two black women.

Women and the Curriculum. Most of the degrees and certif-

icates awarded to women are in business, commerce, and health technologies.

There are no courses on women. An official committee has responsibility for collecting and developing curricular materials on women. Workshops provided for faculty include affirmative action and equal opportunity, and the needs of reentry women.

Women and Athletics. No information was provided.

Special Services and Programs for Women. *Health and Counseling.* There is no student health service. The student counseling center has a staff of three, one of whom is a white woman, one a minority woman. Counseling services specific to women are not available. The regular student health insurance policy covers maternity at no extra charge.

Safety and Security. Measures include campus and city police, self-defense courses for women, and a rape crisis center. No information was provided on the incidence of rapes and assaults.

Career. Activities include workshops focused on nontraditional occupations and lectures/panels for students by women employed in nontraditional occupations.

Institutional Self-Description. None provided.

Cleveland Institute of Art
11141 East Boulevard
Cleveland, OH 44106
Telephone: (216) 421-4322

Women in Leadership
★★★ **students**
★ **faculty**
★ **administrators**

532 undergraduates

	Amer. Ind.	Asian Amer.	Blacks	Hispanics	Whites
F	0	3	8	2	288
M	0	1	23	4	200
%	0.0	0.8	5.9	1.1	92.3

 AAUW

Cleveland Institute of Art, founded in 1882, is a private art school. It offers a five-year undergraduate degree in 14 professional fields and, in cooperation with Case Western Reserve, a four-year program in art education. Located in the center of Cleveland's University Circle, the institute shares its campus as well as its dining and housing facilities, and extra-curricular activities, with Case Western Reserve University. Of the 832 students enrolled, 532 are undergraduates. Fifty-seven percent of the undergraduates are women; 7 percent of the women attend part-time. The median age of undergraduates is 21.

One-fourth of undergraduates live in single-sex and coeducational dormitories that have no restrictions on visiting hours for members of the opposite sex. For commuting students, campus parking for a fee and public transportation are available.

Private childcare facilities are located off campus.

Policies to Ensure Fairness to Women. An administrator makes policy, monitors compliance, and examines practices pertaining to equal-employment-opportunity regulations. A sexual harassment policy that protects students, faculty, and staff has been communicated in writing to all but students; complaints are resolved through a formal grievance procedure.

Women in Leadership Positions. *Students.* In three recent years, women have served twice as president of the student body—the only student leadership position.

Faculty. Thirty-one percent of the 35 full-time faculty are women. There are 4 female faculty for every 100 female students and 11 male faculty for every 100 male students.

Administrators. Women hold posts as Dean of Students and head librarian; the other four chief administrators are men. Women chair four of 15 departments: liberal arts, ceramics, enamelling, and fibers.

Women and the Curriculum. All degrees are in fine arts. The sole course on women is Women in Literature.

Women and Athletics. There are no organized competitive sports.

Special Services and Programs for Women. *Health and Counseling.* Students may use the Case Western Reserve health service, where medical is treatment is available for gynecological problems, birth control, abortion, and rape and assault. One of two professionals at the student counseling center is a woman. Counseling for gynecological problems, birth control, abortion, and rape and assault is available.

Safety and Security. Measures consist of campus police protection, night-time escorts for women, high-intensity lighting, an emergency alarm system, instruction on self-defense and campus safety, and a community rape crisis center. No information was provided on the incidence of rape and assault for 1980–81.

Career. Services include workshops, information, and panels on nontraditional occupations and on job discrimination, files on alumnae careers for use by students, and programs to promote networking between alumnae and students.

Institutional Self-Description. "We admit students of measurable talent, with interest in what they are doing, who are dedicated to the prospect of becoming professional artists or designers; people with inquiring minds who can simultaneously develop individuality while functioning in a community. We continually put quality ahead of quantity."

College of Wooster
Wooster, OH 44691
Telephone: (216) 264-1234

★ **Women and the Curriculum**

★★★ **Women and Athletics**

1,824 undergraduates

	Amer. Ind.	Asian Amer.	Blacks	Hispanics	Whites
F	0	6	37	4	821
M	0	4	49	2	901
%	0.0	0.6	4.7	0.3	94.4

Founded in 1866 to prepare Presbyterian men and women for the service professions, the College of Wooster, though no longer a denominational college, still maintains a voluntary relationship with the United Presbyterian Church. Its total enrollment of 1,960 includes 1,824 students registered in degree programs, all of whom attend full-time. Women are 48 percent of the students. The median age of all students is 20. A summer session is offered. The campus is accessible by public transportation for the 4 percent of students who commute.

Private childcare is available near campus.

Policies to Ensure Fairness to Women. A part-time Affirmative Action Officer with a voice in policymaking oversees compliance with equal-employment, sex-equity, and handicapped-access laws. A Committee on the Status of Women, which includes student members, takes public stands on issues of concern to students. The Office of Black Student Affairs and the Black Stud-

ies Committee address the concerns of minority women. A policy on sexual harassment is under development.

Women in Leadership Positions. *Students.* Women students have limited opportunities to exercise campus leadership. In recent years, women have been editor-in-chief of the newspaper once and president of the student body twice.

Faculty. Women are 20 percent of the 127 full-time faculty. There are 3 female faculty for every 100 female students and 11 male faculty for every 100 male students.

Administrators. Men hold all top positions except one—the Dean of Faculty. Of 24 academic departments, one is chaired by a black woman—Black Studies. Eight of the 37 trustees are women, a proportion above average for similar institutions in this guide. A woman was one of three recipients of honorary degrees in 1980-81.

Women and the Curriculum. Over half of women graduates receive degrees in the humanities or social sciences. Ten percent of women earn degrees in mathematics or physical sciences.

A Women's Studies Program, directed by a woman who holds a full-time faculty position, offers an undergraduate minor. Fourteen courses are offered through several departments, including Women in the Economy, Feminist Perspectives on Sociology and Society, and Fiction by Women. A Women's Studies Committee develops new courses on women. The Educational Policy Committee is considering a proposal to require students to take at least one course which examines discrimination against women or minorities.

Women and Athletics. For a private, coeducational college, Wooster's outstanding athletic program offers women an unusually wide variety of intercollegiate and intramural team and individual sports. Women are 34 percent of intercollegiate and 44 percent of intramural athletes. Six of 19 paid varsity coaches are women. The intercollegiate sports are basketball, cross-country, field hockey, lacrosse, softball, swimming, tennis, track and field, and volleyball.

Housing and Student Organizations. Ninety-six percent of students live on campus in single-sex and coeducational dormitories. The 13 residence-hall directors, seven of whom are women, are offered awareness-training on sexism, sex education, and racism.

The Women's Resource Center, the Black Women's Association, and the Pro-Choice Group are advocates for women on campus.

Special Services and Programs for Women. *Health and Counseling.* The staff of the student health service consists of one male physician and nine health-care providers. Treatment is available for gynecological problems and birth control. One man and one woman staff the student counseling center; they provide counseling on birth control, abortion, and rape.

Safety and Security. Measures consist of campus police with authority to make arrests, local police, night-time escorts for women, workshops on self-defense, and a rape crisis center. No rapes or assaults on women were reported for 1980-81.

Other. A small Women's Center, with a part-time student coordinator, organizes lectures, workshops, and other special events on campus.

Career. The college provides career workshops on nontraditional occupations, lectures by women employed in these occupations, and files on alumnae by specific careers.

Institutional Self-Description. "Commitment to the education of women was one of the principles upon which the College of Wooster was founded in 1866, and throughout its history the college has opened its entire curriculum and its co-curricular program to women. Women are visible in leadership roles at all levels, both on campus and in the college's national volunteer network; and distinguished alumni frequently return to the campus to participate in women's affairs. Wooster's goal for its adventure in education is coeducation in the fullest sense of the term."

Cuyahoga Community College District
700 Carnegie Avenue,
Cleveland, OH 44115
Telephone: (216) 241-5966

Women in Leadership
★★ faculty

28,100 undergraduates

Enrollment data not available.

Cuyahoga Community College District, a public, two-year institution, consists of three main campuses: the main Metropolitan Campus in downtown Cleveland, the Eastern Campus in Warrensville, and the Western Campus in the Cleveland suburb of Parma. The total enrollment for the three campuses is 28,100 students, half of them women. According to recent information provided by the college, 72 percent of the more than 14,000 female students are enrolled part-time. The median age of all undergraduates is 25; 17 percent of women are over age 40.

Cuyahoga offers two-year degrees in a variety of career and technical programs. Classes are held both on and off campus, day and evening. Weekend and summer session classes are also available. Adult education is provided by the Lifelong Learning Center. The campuses can be reached by public transportation, and students may park on campus for a fee.

The college operates two childcare centers. The Metropolitan Campus childcare facility accommodates 1 percent of students' requests and gives priority to children of full-time students. The Western Campus facility serves 90 percent of students' requests. Additional, private childcare facilities are located near each campus.

Policies to Ensure Fairness to Women. The Executive Vice Chancellor, Director of Human Resources, and the three campus Presidents share responsibility for policy regarding sex-equity, equal-employment-opportunity, and handicapped-access practices. The Coordinator of Human Resources monitors compliance with sex-equity and equal-employment-opportunity regulations. Complaints of sexual harassment are handled by a college-wide grievance procedure.

Women in Leadership Positions. *Students.* Women have some opportunity to exercise student leadership. In a recent three-year period, women were student body president and editor-in-chief of the campus newspaper for one year. A woman presides over the single honorary society.

Faculty. Thirty-eight percent of the 381 full-time faculty are women, a proportion well above average for colleges nationwide. There are 4 female faculty for every 100 female students. The ratio of male faculty to male students is not available.

Administrators. The chief academic officer is a black woman; the other five top administrators are men. Women chair 20 of 49 departments.

Women and the Curriculum. Women earn 57 percent of the two-year degrees awarded: 54 percent in health technologies, 26 percent in business, 17 percent in public service, and 3 percent in data processing. One-half of the students in cooperative education and internship programs are women.

One course on women—Introduction to Social Science: Women in America—is available through the social science department on the Metropolitan Campus. The departments of nursing, business, and social work offer instruction on some matters specific to woman.

Minority Women. One-third of undergraduate women are members of minority groups. The Commission on Minority Affairs addresses the concerns of minority women. The chief academic officer and the chairs of five departments are black women. Thirty-three black women and 2 Asian American women are

among the full-time faculty. One of the 2 female trustees is a black woman. Six professionals at the student counseling center are minority women. Twenty-three percent of returning female students in continuing education are minority women, largely black women.

Women and Athletics. Cuyahoga provides some opportunities for women to participate in organized competitive sports. The Metropolitan Campus offers seven intercollegiate and ten intramural sports, as well as sports clubs. The intramural program stresses individual sports. Women receive one-fifth of the athletic scholarships awarded; five of the 21 paid intercollegiate coaches are women. Intercollegiate sports offered are basketball, bowling, golf, soccer, tennis, and volleyball.

Special Services and Programs for Women. *Health and Counseling.* The student health service employs 2 male physicians and 9 health-care providers, 8 of them female. The student counseling center's staff of 32 professionals includes 12 women. Gynecological and birth control counseling and treatment, as well as abortion and rape and assault counseling, are provided.

Safety and Security. Measures consist of campus and local police protection, night-time escort for women, emergency telephone system, instruction on self-defense for women, and a rape crisis center. No rapes and four assaults on women were reported for 1980–81.

Career. The Career Planning Office offers workshops, printed materials, and job discrimination information on nontraditional occupations for women, along with lectures by women employed in these fields.

Other. Each campus has its own Women's Center; jointly the centers serve over 1,500 women annually. The centers are operated by the Lifelong Learning Center with financial support from the college and from a federal grant for serving displaced homemakers. In cooperation with a Lifelong Learning Center program called "Women Focus," the Women's Centers sponsor a lecture series, assertiveness training, and a program to build skills in mathematics.

Institutional Self-Description. "The college mission is to provide low-cost, quality, lifelong educational opportunities accessible to all. The college is committed to educational, cultural, and occupational offerings which meet the continuing and community educational needs of Cuyahoga County residents, with special informational and guidance programs designed for women interested in personal growth, career exploration and upgrading, and consumer survival. Career and technical occupational programs are offered in more than 50 fields."

Defiance College
701 North Clinton Street
Defiance, OH 43512
Telephone: (419) 784-4010

Women in Leadership
★ students

767 undergraduates

	Amer. Ind.	Asian Amer.	Blacks	Hispanics	Whites
F	0	0	16	4	346
M	0	0	21	14	348
%	0.0	0.0	4.9	2.4	92.7

 AAUW

Founded in 1850 as Defiance Female Seminary, this four-year institution, affiliated with the United Church of Christ, became coeducational in 1903. The college offers courses leading to B.A. and B.S. degrees. A summer session is offered. Of the 767 undergraduates, 48 percent are women, and 20 percent of the women attend part-time. Twenty-one percent of women are age 25 or older, and the median age of all students is 21. Free on-campus parking is available to the 30 percent of students who commute.

Women in Leadership Positions. *Students.* Opportunities for women to exercise campus-wide student leadership are good. Women have been president of the student body, student union board, and junior class, for one year each; editor-in-chief of the campus newspaper and president of the first-year, sophomore, and senior classes, for two years each. Women head three of five honorary societies.

Faculty. Women are 22 percent of the 51 full-time faculty, a proportion slightly lower than the national average. There are 4 female faculty for every 100 female students and 12 male faculty for every 100 male students.

Administrators. Men hold all top administrative positions. A woman chairs the department of physical education.

Women and the Curriculum. More than a third of women take degrees in education, and about 2 percent in the physical sciences. The appropriate academic departments provide information on sex-fair curricula, battered spouses, and job discrimination. There are no courses on women.

Women and Athletics. For a college of its size, Defiance has a good intramural and intercollegiate athletic program for women. About one-third of the intercollegiate and half the intramural athletes are women. Two of the six paid varsity coaches are women. Intercollegiate sports are basketball, softball, track, and volleyball.

Housing and Student Organizations. Seventy percent of the students live on campus in single-sex dormitories or in fraternity or sorority houses. Twenty-eight percent of full-time undergraduate women belong to sororities, and six minority women belong to racially-integrated sororities.

Special Services and Programs for Women. *Health and Counseling.* The student health center is staffed by a female health-care provider; there is no student counseling center. No medical services specific to women are provided.

Safety and Security. Town police provide security. One rape and four assaults (one on a woman) were reported for 1980–81.

Career. The college offers information on nontraditional occupations, job discrimination, and the careers of alumnae.

Institutional Self-Description. "The Defiance College has a small campus in a rural community with a near-equal split between male and female students. The flexibility of the curriculum enhances student opportunities for creative work. There are young, energetic women on the Defiance College faculty who maintain excellent student-faculty relationships."

Denison University
P.O. Box B Granville, OH 43023
Telephone: (614) 587-0810

Women in Leadership	★★ Women and the
★ students	Curriculum
★ faculty	
★ administrators	

2,035 undergraduates

	Amer. Ind.	Asian Amer.	Blacks	Hispanics	Whites
F	0	4	32	2	937
M	0	2	34	1	1,000
%	0.0	0.3	3.3	0.2	96.3

✦ ⌨ 📖 ⚱ **AAUW NWSA**

Denison University, a non-denominational, liberal arts college, was founded in 1832 by American Baptists. Separate men's and women's institutes became coordinate colleges and formally merged in 1927. Virtually all of the 2,044 students attend full-time; 48 percent are women. The median age of all students is 20. Free on-campus parking is provided for the 5 percent of students who commute; the campus is not accessible by public transportation.

Private childcare facilities are available near campus.

Policies to Ensure Fairness to Women. On a part-time basis, an affirmative action officer, with a voice in policymaking, monitors compliance with equal-employment-opportunity, educational-sex-equity, and handicapped-accessibility laws. Complaints of sexual harassment are resolved through a formal grievance procedure. The college has an active Commission on the Status of Women, with a self-designated membership that reviews salaries, prepares reports on women's concerns, and takes stands on issues of concern to students.

Women in Leadership Positions. *Students.* Women have good opportunities to exercise student leadership. In recent years, women have held one-third of the campus positions. Women head eight of the 17 honor societies.

Faculty. Of 149 full-time faculty, 25 percent are women, a proportion that is the national average. There are 4 female faculty for every 100 female students and 11 male faculty for every 100 male students.

Administrators. Among the 8 top administrators, the development officer and the Director of Women's Athletics are women. Women chair 3 of 21 academic departments: philosophy, physical education, and dance. Six of 32 trustees are women, one of whom is a black woman.

Women and the Curriculum. About half the degrees awarded to women are in the social sciences and psychology. Six percent of women earn degrees in mathematics and physical sciences. Denison has established several programs, one with foundation support, to encourage women to enter nontraditional careers. Half the students assigned to internships and science field-service projects are women The mathematics department has a program to help students gain confidence in the use of mathematics.

A full-time faculty member coordinates the Women's Studies Program, which offers a minor and a B.A. in Women's Studies. Twenty-one courses on women are offered by 12 departments; two of the courses focus on minority women. A Committee on Women's Studies encourages the development of courses on women as well as the integration of feminist scholarship into traditional courses. Faculty workshops on nontraditional occupations, sexism and racism in the curriculum, and affirmative action are part of an ongoing faculty seminar on minorities and Women's Studies.

Denison requires that every undergraduate take a course that examines discrimination against women and/or members of minority groups.

Minority Women. The Committee on Women addresses the concerns of minority women. The Black Students' Union, with 73 members, 40 percent of them black women, is concerned with issues affecting minority women. Four of 25 residence-hall directors are minority women. Residence-hall and counseling staff are offered awareness-training on racial bias. Eight minority women serve on the full-time faculty: 3 black women, 3 Asian Americans, and 2 Hispanic women. Three of 19 speakers in a recent campus-wide lecture series were black women.

Women and Athletics. Women are 10 percent of intramural and 42 percent of the intercollegiate athletes. Five of the 16 paid varsity coaches are women. Most teams enter post-season competition. Intercollegiate sports for women are basketball, bowling cross-country, field hockey, lacrosse, soccer, swimming, tennis, track and field, and volleyball.

Housing and Student Organizations. Ninety-five percent of the students live on campus in single-sex or coeducational dormitories or in fraternity houses. Women students have the option of living in dormitories with or without restrictive visiting hours. Nine of the 25 dormitory counselors are women, and four of them are members of minority groups. Dormitory counselors are offered awareness-training on sexism, sex education, birth control, and homophobia.

Sororities do not provide housing.

Special Services and Programs for Women. *Health and Counseling.* The student health service staff of 1 male physician and 8 female health-care providers offer treatment for gynecological problems, birth control, and rape and assault. One of the 2 counselors in the counseling center is a woman. Counselors, who are offered training on the avoidance of sex-role stereotyping and racial bias, provide counseling to women for gynecological problems and for birth control, abortion, and rape and assault.

Safety and Security. Measures include campus and town police, night-time escort service, self-defense and rape-prevention courses, and a rape crisis center. Six assaults and no rapes on women were reported for 1980–81.

Career. The college provides workshops and information on nontraditional careers, job discrimination, and alumnae networking.

Other. The Women's Center, whose part-time coordinator is a faculty member, publishes a newsletter that goes to all students. Its programs include a telephone service for information and referrals.

Institutional Self-Description. "Denison has long demonstrated a commitment to women students—many feminist faculty, women and men; a large number and variety of courses, Women's Studies and transformed; a general education requirement in minority and Women's Studies; services such as planned parenthood, a woman psychologist, workshops, the Women's Resource Center; close faculty-student relationships and extraordinary leadership opportunities; an emphasis on career, consortial activities, convocations, internships, Women's Emphasis, and a grant from the Mellon Foundation on nontraditional careers for women."

Dyke College
1375 East Sixth Street
Cleveland, OH 44114
Telephone: (216) 696-9000

Women in Leadership
★★ faculty

1,077 undergraduates

	Amer. Ind.	Asian Amer.	Blacks	Hispanics	Whites
F	1	2	430	6	238
M	0	2	136	4	249
%	0.1	0.4	53.0	0.9	45.6

Dyke College is an independent, coeducational, business-oriented institution. It offers bachelor's and associate degrees and emphasizes continuing education. Self-paced learning, a summer session, and on-site training programs are provided. Dyke has 1,446 students in all, 1,077 of whom are enrolled in degree programs. Women are 63 percent of the degree students; 30 percent of women attend part-time. Black women are 41 percent of the students. The median age of all undergraduates is 29. Four percent of the full-time female undergraduates belong to sororities. All students commute to the campus, which is accessible by public transportation. There is no on-campus parking available.

Policies to Ensure Fairness to Women. The Deans of Administration and of Student Affairs, and the Director of Student Life, each have responsibility part-time for enforcing compliance with equal-opportunity laws.

Women in Leadership Positions. *Students.* Opportunities for women to hold campus leadership positions are poor. In recent years, women have been president of the student body and of the senior class for one year each. The one honorary society on campus is headed by a woman.

Faculty. Women are 10 of 26 full-time faculty. According to recent information, 14 of 49 part-time faculty members are women, including 6 black and 4 Asian American women; 5 black women are on the full-time faculty. There are 2 female faculty for every 100 female students and 9 male faculty for every 100 male students.

Administrators. Men hold all top positions. Three of the eight directors of academic units are women.

Women and the Curriculum. Women are 61 percent of the full-time students and earn 35 percent of degrees. Almost all degrees earned by women are in business and commerce technologies. There are no courses on women.

Women and Athletics. The competitive organized sport available for women is intramural basketball.

Special Services and Programs for Women. *Health and Counseling.* There is no student health service. Counseling is provided by a staff of nine, including three minority women and five white women. Counseling on issues specific to women is not available.

Safety and Security. Measures include a night-time escort service, emergency alarm system, courses on assault prevention, and a rape crisis center. The campus is under the jurisdiction of the municipal police force. No rapes or assaults on women were reported for 1980-81.

Career. Workshops on women employed in nontraditional occupations and information on discrimination in employment opportunities are available.

Institutional Self-Description. "Dyke College is a business-oriented institution providing serious career education to men and women. The college has an outstanding reputation for placement in business and business-related fields, which makes it especially attractive to women seeking careers in business."

Kent State University, Tuscarawas
University Drive, N.E.
New Philadelphia, OH 44663
Telephone: (216) 339-3391

Women in Leadership
★ faculty

817 undergraduates

	Amer. Ind.	Asian Amer.	Blacks	Hispanics	Whites
F	0	1	2	0	459
M	0	0	3	0	352
%	0.0	0.1	0.6	0.0	99.3

A branch campus of Kent State University, this public, two-year commuter college, founded in 1962, is located near Akron, Ohio. The total enrollment is 858. Of the 817 students enrolled in degree programs, 57 percent are women; slightly over half of women attend part-time. The median age of all students is 22. Recent data show that 43 percent of women are over age 24.

Transfer and degree programs include liberal arts, business, health, and engineering/technology. Alternative full-time and part-time scheduling, including on-campus and off-campus evening classes, two summer sessions, and contract learning are available. Free parking is provided.

Private childcare facilities are available near campus.

Policies to Ensure Fairness to Women. A written policy prohibits the sexual harassment of students, faculty, and staff; a formal campus procedure resolves complaints. Institutional compliance with equal-opportunity and affirmative-action legislation is monitored at the main campus of Kent State University.

Women in Leadership Positions. *Students.* The only student leadership position on this campus, president of the student body, has been held by men for three recent years.

Faculty. Thirty-one percent of the 32 full-time faculty members are women. There are 5 female faculty for every 100 female students and 13 male faculty for every 100 male students.

Administrators. Of five chief administrators, one, the Assistant to the Dean of the College, is a woman. One of the six trustees is a woman.

Women and the Curriculum. Most women take their two-year degrees and certificates in liberal arts (36 percent), health (28 percent), business (20 percent), and public service (10 percent). Workshops on the needs of reentry women are provided for the faculty. There are no courses on women.

Women and Athletics. The opportunity for organized, competitive sports is limited. The 26 women athletes in the intercollegiate program participate in basketball, tennis, and volleyball. Sixteen women participate in the intramural teams. All seven paid coaches for intercollegiate sports are men. Intercollegiate sports offered are basketball, tennis, and volleyball.

Special Services and Programs for Women. *Health and Counseling.* There is no student health service and no student counseling center. Most requests for informal counseling are referred to local agencies.

Safety and Security. Measures include patrol by the local town police, high-intensity lighting, and informal sessions on campus safety. No assaults on women were reported for 1980–81.

Career. The college provides career workshops, lectures/panels by women employed in nontraditional occupations, and printed information on nontraditional occupations for women.

Institutional Self-Description. "Our campus is small, offering a woman the opportunity to become comfortable early in her academic career. Faculty members, staff members, and other students care about each student becoming successful. Programs are structured to meet community needs."

Kenyon College
Gambier, OH 43022
Telephone: (614) 427-2244

★ **Women and Athletics**

1,461 undergraduates

	Amer. Ind.	Asian Amer.	Blacks	Hispanics	Whites
F	0	4	6	1	598
M	0	6	7	3	820
%	0.0	0.1	0.1	0.1	99.7

[S/W] [♀] **AAUW**

Founded in 1824 as a liberal arts, Episcopal college for men, Kenyon offers bachelor's degrees in arts and sciences. Women have been admitted since 1969 and now constitute 42 percent of the 1,473 students; virtually all students attend full-time. The median age of students is 21. All undergraduates live on campus.

Private childcare facilities are located near the college.

Policies to Ensure Fairness to Women. The Equal Opportu-

nity Coordinator, on a part-time basis, oversees compliance with equal-opportunity legislation. A formal grievance procedure for resolving sexual harassment complaints is in the final stages of development. The Committee on the Status of Women, which includes voting student members, takes public stands on student concerns and also addresses the concerns of minority women.

Women in Leadership Positions. *Students.* The few student offices available are held by men most of the time. In recent years, women have served one-year terms as president of the student body, editor-in-chief of the campus newspaper, and manager of the campus radio station.

Faculty. Eighteen percent of the 105 full-time faculty are women, a proportion below the national average. There are 3 female faculty for every 100 female students and 10 male faculty for every 100 male students.

Administrators. All of the chief administrators are men. One of 18 departments, drama, is chaired by a woman.

Women and the Curriculum. Two percent of women major in physical sciences. The most popular majors for women are literature and social sciences.

Several courses on women are offered by the departments of anthropology, history, modern foreign languages, and philosophy: Sex Roles in Cross-Cultural Perspective; History of the Ideas of Female and Male, Image of Women, European Cross-Currents, and Philosophical Issues in Feminism. A committee responsible for monitoring the status of women in the curriculum is developing a Women's Studies Program. The topic of sexism in the curriculum is addressed in faculty workshops.

Women and Athletics. Kenyon's intramural and intercollegiate athletic programs for women are good. The number and variety of sports offered and the proportion of women who participate are high. Women account for 43 percent of the intercollegiate athletes. Two of the eight paid coaches for intercollegiate sports are women. Intercollegiate sports for women include basketball, cross-country, field hockey, lacrosse, swimming, tennis, track and field, and volleyball.

Housing and Student Organizations. All students live on campus in single-sex or coeducational dormitories with no restrictions on hours for visitors of the opposite sex. Counseling staff, called student resident assistants, are present only in first-year dormitories. Staff are offered awareness-training on sex education and birth control.

There are no sororities on campus, but 20 women along with 530 men belong to fraternities. The Black Students Union is an advocacy group.

Special Services and Programs for Women. *Health and Counseling.* The student health service is staffed by two male physicians and four health-care providers, three of whom are women. Both staff members of the student counseling center are men. Counseling and medical treatment are provided for gynecological problems, birth control, abortion, and rape.

Safety and Security. Measures consist of campus security officers who cooperate with local law enforcement agencies, nighttime escort service, and a rape crisis center. No rapes or assaults on women or men were reported for 1980–81.

Career. Female students have access to lectures and printed information about nontraditional careers, job discrimination, and student-alumnae networks.

Other. The student activities office maintains a Women's Center, with a part-time student coordinator, that serves about 100 women a year. The history department sponsors a women's lecture series.

Institutional Self-Description. "Kenyon seeks to develop those capacities, skills, and talents which are essential to women today. These include the abilities to speak and write clearly so as to advance thoughts and arguments cogently; to discriminate between the essential and the trivial; to work independently and with others; to comprehend our culture as well as other cultures."

Marietta College
Marietta, OH 45750
Telephone: (614) 373-4643

Women in Leadership
★★ students

1,395 undergraduates

	Amer. Ind.	Asian Amer.	Blacks	Hispanics	Whites
F	0	0	9	1	499
M	0	2	12	2	856
%	0.0	0.1	1.5	0.2	98.1

 AAUW

Founded by Congregationalists in 1797, Marietta College is an independent, non-denominational, coeducational liberal arts institution. It offers its 1,575 students evening classes, self-paced learning, and a range of degree programs. Women are 37 percent of the 1,395 students enrolled in degree programs; 6 percent of women attend part-time. The median age of all students is 21. On-campus parking is available at no charge for the 13 percent of students who commute, and the college is accessible by public transportation.

Private childcare facilities are available near campus.

Policies to Ensure Fairness to Women. The Associate Dean of Students, on a part-time basis, reviews policies and practices concerning sex-equity laws for students. The Director of Personnel, also on a part-time basis, monitors compliance with other equal-opportunity laws. A written statement on sexual harassment of students, faculty, and staff has been communicated to these groups; complaints are resolved informally or through formal grievance procedures.

Women in Leadership Positions. *Students.* Women students exercise leadership nearly in proportion to their numbers. In recent years, they have presided over the student court once, over the residence-hall council three times, and have been editor-in-chief of the student newspaper twice. Women head all four honorary societies.

Faculty. Women make up 13 percent of the full-time faculty. There are 2 female faculty for every 100 female students and 9 male faculty for every 100 male students.

Administrators. Men hold all top positions. A woman chairs one of the 22 academic departments. One of the two speakers at the 1981 commencement was a woman.

Women and the Curriculum. Nearly a quarter of women who graduate take degrees in business programs; other popular fields for women are education (17 percent) and arts and letters (14 percent). Four percent of women major in mathematics and physical sciences.

Four courses on women are offered, including Women in Families, Philosophy of Feminism, and Psychology of Women. The appropriate departments provide information on teaching sex-fair curricula and on job discrimination and sexual harassment in the workplace.

Women and Athletics. Women are 40 percent of intramural athletes and 15 percent of intercollegiate athletes. Club sports are available. Intercollegiate sports in which women participate are basketball, crew, field hockey, softball, tennis, and volleyball.

Housing and Student Organizations. Seventy-eight percent of students live on campus, in single-sex or coeducational dormitories, or in sorority or fraternity houses. Thirty-seven percent of all undergraduates belong to sororities and fraternities. Three minority women belong to racially integrated sororities.

Special Services and Programs for Women. *Health and Counseling.* The student health service is staffed by 1 male physician and 2 health-care providers (1 of whom is a woman.) The counseling staff of 5 includes 2 women. Medical treatment is provided for gynecological problems, and counseling is available

on birth control, abortion, and rape and assault. Counselors are offered awareness-training on the avoidance of sex-role stereotyping.

Safety and Security. Measures include a night-time escort service for women, high-intensity lighting, self-defense courses, and a rape crisis center. The campus is patrolled by college police with the power to make arrests. No rapes or assaults on women were reported for 1980–81.

Career. The college offers workshops and information on nontraditional careers and job discrimination, and provides networking between students and alumnae.

Other. A women's lecture series is sponsored by the Co-Curricular Committee.

Institutional Self-Description. "Women will find academic programs that interest them—everything from art to accounting to teaching to petroleum engineering—and an active women's intercollegiate sports program. They will also find a healthy social scene with five national sororities and an active women's organization."

Mount St. Joseph on the Ohio
Mount St. Joseph, OH 45051
Telephone: (513) 244-4200

Women in Leadership
★★★ students
★★★ faculty
★★ administrators

★ **Women and the Curriculum**

1,080 undergraduates

	Amer. Ind.	Asian Amer.	Blacks	Hispanics	Whites
F	1	2	38	7	945
M	0	0	4	0	74
%	0.1	0.2	3.9	0.7	95.1

Founded in 1920 by the Sisters of Charity, Mount St. Joseph on the Ohio is a Roman Catholic, women's college that stresses career preparation with a liberal arts foundation. Its suburban campus, just outside of Cincinnati, draws 1,355 students, most of them women, including 1,080 undergraduates. About one-fourth of the undergraduate women attend part-time. The median age of undergraduates is 28.

The college offers degrees in a variety of four-year and two-year programs, in addition to a master's in education. There is also a continuing education program. Classes meet during the evening as well as the day, and are supplemented by a weekend college and a summer session. Women live on campus in dormitories that restrict hours for male visitors. Public transportation and campus parking are available.

A campus childcare facility accommodates about 60 children of students for a fee of $.70 per hour. Additional, private childcare facilities are available near the campus.

Policies to Ensure Fairness to Women. The Executive Assistant to the President has part-time responsibility for policy regarding equal-employment-opportunity, sex-equity, and handicapped-accessibility laws. A formal sexual harassment policy protects students, faculty, and administrators; complaints are resolved informally and confidentially.

Women in Leadership Positions. *Students.* Women hold all campus-wide leadership positions.

Faculty. Seventy-nine percent of the 61 full-time faculty are women. One black woman is on the full-time faculty. There are 6 female faculty for every 100 female students.

Administrators. Women hold four of nine top administrative positions: chief executive officer, chief student-life officer, head librarian, and director of athletics. Women chair 9 of the 14 departments, including biology, business, mathematics, music, and sociology. Half of the Board of Trustees are female. In a recent year, the commencement speaker was a woman, as were the three recipients of honorary degrees.

Women and the Curriculum. Most women graduating with bachelor's degrees major in the health professions (41 percent) and education (20 percent); 1 percent major in such nontraditional fields, as mathematics. Most women who earn two-year degrees specialize in business/commerce and health technologies.

The Women's Studies Program offers an undergraduate minor and a certificate. Courses on women are taught through the departments of art, biology, English, and continuing education. Courses offered recently were Women in Art; Reproduction and Development; Mothers and Daughters; and Women: Fact, Fiction and Future. An official committee from the Greater Cincinnati Consortium develops the program and reports on new developments in the teaching of Women's Studies. Students training for careers in teaching, business, and social work receive some instruction on matters specific to women.

Women and Athletics. For a college of its size Mount St. Joseph has a good women's athletics program. It offers a large intramural program, four intercollegiate teams, and athletic scholarships. There are four paid women coaches for the varsity sports offered: basketball, tennis, track, and volleyball.

Special Services and Programs for Women. *Health and Counseling.* Three women counselors work at the counseling center; there is no student health center. Counseling services specific to women are not available.

Safety and Security. Measures include instruction on self-defense and a community rape crisis center. No rapes or assaults on women were reported for 1980–81.

Career. The college provides career workshops, panels, and information on nontraditonal occupations, as well as files on alumnae careers for students' use.

Other. A Women's Center, run under the auspices of the continuing education department, is used primarily by older undergraduates and community women. In addition to informal peer counseling, the center offers a women's lecture series.

Returning Women Students. Forty-seven percent of all undergraduate women are over age 25. A Continuing Education for Women Program is operated through the Women's Center and the continuing education department. Among the programs geared to reentry women are assertiveness training and a mathematics confidence clinic. The office of Dean of Students sponsors a program for displaced homemakers. A monthly "brown bag break" brings older women together for informal lunch discussions. Faculty are offered workshops on the needs of returning women students.

Institutional Self-Description. "Because the Mount is a small college, a student is more than a number. The size of the student body allows and fosters an opportunity to know administrators and faculty personally and to form close student relationships. But most of all, being a student at the Mount means being a part of a college community where women are valued, and where the main objective is the education of women."

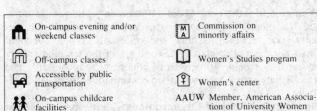

	On-campus evening and/or weekend classes		Commission on minority affairs
	Off-campus classes		Women's Studies program
	Accessible by public transportation		Women's center
	On-campus childcare facilities	AAUW	Member, American Association of University Women
	Publicly communicated sexual harassment policy, includes students	NWSA	Member, National Women's Studies Association
	Commission on status of women	CROW	On-campus Center for Research on Women

Oberlin College and Conservatory of Music
Oberlin, OH 44074
Telephone: (216) 775-8121

★ **Women and the Curriculum**

2,725 undergraduates

	Amer. Ind.	Asian Amer.	Blacks	Hispanics	Whites
F	2	44	138	15	1,161
M	2	24	133	16	1,148
%	0.2	2.5	10.1	1.2	86.1

 AAUW NWSA

Founded by Congregationalists in 1833 as the first coeducational college, and the first college that black people could attend, Oberlin is an independent, nondenominational liberal arts institution and conservatory of music. Ninety-six percent of the 2,779 students attend full-time, and half of them are women. The median age of all students is 20. Alternative schedules include on-campus evening classes and, for the conservatory only, a summer session. On-campus parking is provided for the 20 percent of students who commute; the college cannot be reached by public transportation.

Private childcare facilities are available nearby.

Policies to Ensure Fairness to Women. The Director of Personnel and the Provost, each on part-time assignment, oversee compliance with sex-equity, equal-employment-opportunity, and handicapped-access laws. A written policy on sexual harassment, which will be publicly communicated, is being formulated. A Committee on the Status of Women, appointed by the faculty, takes public stands on issues of concern to women and prepares reports for appropriate groups in the college. Issues of special interest to minority women are addressed by the Committee on Special Education Opportunities.

Women in Leadership Positions. *Students.* Opportunities for women to exercise student leadership are limited. Of the positions described by the college, women have been presiding officer of the student senate twice and head of the student court once, during three recent years.

Faculty. Women are 18 percent of the 207 full-time faculty, a proportion below the national average. There are 3 female faculty for every 100 female students and 13 male faculty for every 100 male students.

Administrators. Men hold all top positions, except for the director of women's athletics. Women chair three of 28 academic departments: biology, history, and East Asian studies. Two women sit on the 10-member committee on tenure, reappointment, and promotions; 8 women are on the 28-member Board of Trustees.

Women and the Curriculum. Most degrees awarded to women are in fine arts (22 percent), letters (21 percent), social sciences (18 percent), and biological sciences (10 percent). The nontraditional fields of mathematics and physical sciences account for 6 percent of degrees to women. "Women in Work" workshops are offered to encourage women to prepare for nontraditional careers.

The Women's Studies Committee coordinates a Women's Studies Program. Thirteen students have graduated with individualized majors in Women's Studies during the past few years. More than a dozen courses on women, including an Introduction to Women's Studies, are offered through Women's Studies and seven departments. They include Male and Female in American Fiction, Nature and Status of Women, Images of Women in Chinese and Japanese Art, and Women in Sports. In addition, faculty workshops in Women's Studies have encouraged 26 faculty (13 women, 13 men) to reconstruct traditional courses so as to focus on women and men.

Minority Women. More than 7 percent of the students are minority women. An Asian American woman chairs an academic department. Black women are a majority of the students in three coeducational advocacy organizations: Abusua, Oberlin Law Society, and National Black Science Student Organization. La-Union, a coeducational Latino group, serves Hispanic women, and Asian American Alliance serves Asian American women. All these student groups are chaired or co-chaired by women.

Women and Athletics. The athletic program offers a range of intercollegiate and intramural team and individual sports. Women are an estimated 10 percent of intramural and 38 percent of intercollegiate athletes. Five of the ten paid varsity coaches are women. Intercollegiate sports for women include basketball, cross-country, field hockey, lacrosse, swimming, tennis, track and field, and volleyball.

Housing and Student Organizations. Eighty percent of students live on campus in single-sex or coeducational dormitories that have no restrictive hours for visitors of the opposite sex. Three dormitories—Asia House, African Heritage, and Third World House—offer residential programs around issues of interest to minority students. and Thurston Hall functions similarly as a women's collective. Ten of the 21 dormitory counselors are women, and four of these are members of minority groups. Staff are offered awareness-training on stress, depression, values clarification, and sexuality.

Student advocacy groups include Pro-Choice, Gay Union, and the minority organizations listed above—all of which are coeducational.

Special Services and Programs for Women. *Health and Counseling.* The college health service has a woman physician and 18 other health-care providers of whom 3 are women. Two of the 5 counselors in the student counseling office are women. Counseling is provided for gynecological problems, birth control, abortion and rape, and medical treatment for all the above except abortion.

Safety and Security. Measures include campus and town police, night-time escort service, self-defense courses, and a rape crisis center. Four assaults on women were reported in 1980–81.

Career. The college offers lectures and workshops about non-traditional occupations, maintains updated files of alumnae by specific career, and encourages contacts between alumnae and students.

Other. The Women's Center, operated under the auspices of the Associate Dean of the College of Arts and Sciences, has a part-time, volunteer, student director. On a budget of $2,000, it serves about 400 women annually, 6 percent of whom are minority women. The Experimental College provides a battered women's program. Women's Studies holds an afternoon lecture series—well-attended by students—called Sandwich Seminar. Black studies offers theater and other women's arts programs. A program to build mathematics confidence is co-sponsored by Developmental Services and the mathematics department, and assertiveness training is offered by the Human Development Program. A telephone warmline, COPE, is sponsored by the Lorain County Mental Health Agency. The Sexual Information Center provides support to rape and assault victims. A feminist literary magazine is headquartered on campus.

Institutional Self-Description. "As the first college in the United States to grant degrees to women and blacks, Oberlin strives to maintain its commitment to individual liberties. Women's concerns are currently alive and well on campus, in the form of both abundant feminist and women-related student activities, and a healthy component of Women's Studies courses."

Ohio Dominican College
1216 Sunbury Road, Columbus, OH 43219
Telephone: (614) 253-2741

Women in Leadership
★★★ **faculty**
★★★ **administrators**

685 undergraduates

	Amer. Ind.	Asian Amer.	Blacks	Hispanics	Whites
F	1	4	95	4	316
M	0	1	35	4	179
%	0.2	0.8	20.3	1.3	77.5

 AAUW

Founded in 1911 as a Roman Catholic, liberal arts institution for women, Ohio Dominican College became coeducational in 1964. Of its 860 students, 685 are undergraduates. Sixty percent of the undergraduates are women, one-sixth of whom attend part-time. Sixty-seven women students are over age 40, and 156 are between ages 25 and 40; the median age of all students is 21 years.

In addition to the bachelor's degree in arts, science, and science education, Ohio Dominican offers two-year associate degrees in several fields. Evening classes and a weekend college are available. The division of continuing education serves the adult student. Public transportation and on-campus parking for a fee are available to the 70 percent of students who commute.

Policies to Ensure Fairness to Women. The Director of Institutional Research is responsible part-time as a voting member of policymaking councils for equal employment opportunity, educational sex equity, and handicapped access.

Women in Leadership Positions. *Students.* Opportunities for women to exercise leadership are limited in relation to their representation in the student body. During three recent years, men have held the top campus-wide student offices almost three-fourths of the time. Women head two of the three honorary societies.

Faculty. Sixty-one percent of the 44 full-time faculty are women, a proportion far above the national average. There are 7 female faculty for every 100 female students and 8 male faculty for every 100 male students.

Administrators. More than half of the chief administrators are women, including the President and the chief academic officer. Women chair 13 of the 18 departments, including health and physical education, history, mathematics, philosophy, political science and criminal justice, psychology, religious studies, and sociology.

Women and the Curriculum. The most popular majors for women are education (23 percent) and public affairs (20 percent). Three percent of women earn degrees in mathematics or the physical sciences. Programs encourage women to prepare for nontraditional careers in science, accounting, law enforcement, social welfare, and criminal justice. Women hold half the available college internships and practicums.

Three departments offer courses on women: Women and Sports, Women in the Criminal Justice System, and Women: Literature and Psychology.

Women and Athletics. About 140 women participate in intramural basketball, indoor soccer (for which the college has unusually good facilities), tennis, and volleyball. Women account for half the intercollegiate athletes and six of the ten paid varsity coaches; they receive 40 percent of athletic scholarship aid. The intercollegiate sports for women are basketball, softball, and volleyball.

Housing and Student Organizations. Thirty-four percent of students live on campus in women's or coeducational dormitories, which restrict hours for visitors of the opposite sex. Of the 202 undergraduate women living in residence halls, 82 percent are white, 10 percent black, 2 percent Hispanic, 2 percent Asian American, and 9 percent international. One of the three dormitory directors is a woman. Residence-hall directors are offered awareness-training on sex education, alcoholism, and drugs.

Special Services and Programs for Women. *Health and Counseling.* The student health service has a part-time, male physician and a full-time, female nurse. One of the two-member student counseling staff is a woman. Counseling is available for gynecological problems, birth control, abortion, and rape and assault. No medical services specific to women are available.

Safety and Security. Measures consist of campus police without arrest authority, night escort service, high-intensity lighting in all areas, campus-wide emergency telephone system, and information on safety and assault prevention. Two rapes and two assaults on women were reported for 1980–81.

Career. The career office offers lectures on nontraditional occupations and information on student-alumnae networks.

Other. The student counseling center provides assertiveness training, and the mathematics department, a mathematics confidence program.

Institutional Self-Description. "Ohio Dominican College is sponsored by the Dominican Sisters of St. Mary of the Springs. Its trustees, administration, and faculty exemplify a cooperative and balanced working relationship between men and women."

Ohio State University
Columbus, OH 43210
Telephone: (614) 422-1021

Women in Leadership ★★★ students	★★★ Women and the Curriculum
	★★ Women and Athletics

36,455 undergraduates

	Amer. Ind.	Asian Amer.	Blacks	Hispanics	Whites
F	23	106	1,214	59	15,216
M	15	120	847	92	18,490
%	0.1	0.6	5.7	0.4	93.2

🏠 🏛 👫 ⬛ ⬛ 📖 ⚲ **AAUW NWSA**

The Ohio State University at Columbus, a land-grant institution established in 1870, provides undergraduate, graduate, and professional curriculum for over 51,400 students. The Office of Continuing Education offers the adult student both credit and non-credit programs. Alternative class schedules, including weekend college a summer session, self-paced learning contracts, evening and off-campus classes are available.

Women are 46 percent of the 36,455 undergraduates; 6 percent of the women attend part-time. The median age of full-time undergraduate women is 20, of part-time undergraduate women, 28. For the students who commute or live off campus, the university is accessible by public transportation. On-campus parking is available at a fee, with free transportation from distant parking lots.

University-sponsored childcare facilities charge on a sliding scale. One hundred and thirty-eight children, infants, and pre-schoolers can be accommodated. Private childcare arrangements may be made close to campus.

Policies to Ensure Fairness to Women. A full-time Director and an Associate Director of Affirmative Action review policies and practices related to equal employment opportunity, accessibility of all activities and programs to women and men students,

and handicapped access. The policy on sexual harassment is currently being revised. Complaints are handled informally and confidentially, or through a formal grievance procedure. Policy and procedures have been communicated in writing to faculty and staff. The active Committee on the Status of Women, which includes students as voting members, takes public stands on issues of concern to students. It addresses the concerns of minority women, as does the Committee on Minority Affairs.

Women in Leadership Positions. *Students.* Opportunities for women students to exercise all-campus leadership are considerably above the average for public research universities in this guide. In recent years, women have presided over the student court, student union board, residence-hall council, and senior class. Women have also served for three years as editor-in-chief of the newspaper and managed the campus radio station for two years. Women head 13 of the 38 honorary societies.

Faculty. Sixteen percent of the 1,855 full-time faculty are women. According to a recent report, 4 percent of the full-time female faculty are black, 4 percent Asian American, and 1 percent Hispanic. There are 2 female faculty for every 100 female students and 8 male faculty for every 100 students.

Administrators. A woman is chief academic officer of the university; men hold the other top-level positions. Women chair 14 of 140 departments. The head of the School of Home Economics and the head of the School of Nursing are female.

Women and the Curriculum. Most bachelor's degrees awarded to women are in education (17 percent), health professions (16 percent), agriculture (9 percent), and business and management (9 percent). Thirteen percent of women take degrees in nontraditional areas, including agriculture, computer science, engineering, mathematics, and physical sciences. Programs encourage women to prepare for careers in agriculture and engineering. The Task Force on Academic Excellence for Women investigates opportunities and problems for women in nontraditional careers. The two-year degrees awarded to women are in health technologies and natural science.

The Women's Studies Program, which operates out of a Center for Women's Studies administered by a full-time director, offers a 23-quarter-hour undergraduate minor, and the B.A. in Women's Studies, as well as the individually designed M.A. and Ph.D. More than 34 undergraduate and graduate courses are offered, eleven in Women's Studies, and the rest through anthropology, black studies, comparative literature, classics, education, and other departments. Courses include Senior and Honors Seminars, as well as Anthropology of Women, Women and Film, Women and Theology, and The Black Woman. Recently, 20 students have earned the B.A. in Women's Studies, and 20 others have been minors. An official committee promotes the development of courses on women in disciplinary departments.

The Center for Women's Studies publishes a monthly newsletter (circulation approximately 4,000), containing editorials, feature stories, reports on research, and other information of interest to women; it also publishes a bimonthly review of current books on women in all areas of academic and intellectual inquiry. The Women's Studies Library is one of the largest of its kind in the country and is rapidly acquiring important research materials, especially in Women's History.

Minority Women. Eight percent of female undergraduates are minority women, black women being the largest group. Sixty-seven black women are in all-minority sororities. Four minority women are on the staff of the counseling service. Counseling staff and residence hall staff are offered awareness-training in the avoidance of racial bias. The university reports that minority women would find other supportive women in the Office of Minority Affairs, the Hispanic Student Programs, and the Women's Center.

Women and Athletics. Intercollegiate and intramural programs provide excellent opportunities for organized, competitive, individual and team sports. Club sports are also available. The university reports that 18 different facilities are used in recreational and intramural programming. Women receive 33 percent of athletic scholarships. Eleven of 29 head coaches are female. The intercollegiate sports offered are basketball, cross-country, fencing, field hockey, golf, gymnastics, softball, swimming and diving, synchronized swimming, tennis, track, and volleyball.

Housing and Student Organizations. One quarter of the undergraduates live on campus. Residential accommodations include single-sex and coeducational dormitories, as well as housing for married students, single parents with children, and graduate students. A married woman student whose spouse is not enrolled may live in married students' housing. Single-sex residence halls restrict hours for visitors of the opposite sex. Residence-hall staff are offered awareness-training on sexism, sex education, racism, and birth control.

Twelve percent of full-time undergraduate women belong to social sororities. Sororities and fraternities provide housing for their members. Among groups which serve as advocates for women on campus are Association of Women Students, Gay Women's Support, Students for a Free Choice, and Women's Programming Advisory Committee.

Special Services and Programs for Women. *Health and Counseling.* The student health service provides some medical attention specific to women, including gynecological, birth control, and rape and assault treatment. Half of the physicians are female, as are 26 of 31 other health-care providers. The regular student health insurance covers abortion and maternity at no extra charge. Sixteen of 30 professional staff in the counseling center are women. Gynecological, birth control, abortion, and rape and assault counseling may be obtained.

Safety and Security. Measures consist of campus police with arrest authority, night-time bus service to residence areas, high-intensity lighting, emergency alarm and telephone system, self-defense courses for women, information sessions on safety and crime prevention, a rape crisis center, and the OSU Emergency Squad. For 1980–81, four rapes and 14 assaults on women were reported.

Career. The university offers career workshops, nonsexist/nonracist printed matter on women in nontraditional occupations, lectures and panels by women employed in these fields, and a program of contacts between students and alumnae. Faculty workshops discuss nontraditional careers for men and women.

Other. The Office of Student life is responsible for the Women's Center, which is headed by a full-time faculty director. Older students, university staff, and community women are the principal users of the center. Activities include a women's lecture series, theater and other arts programs, and assertiveness training.

Several community groups provide services for women, including Choices for Victims of Domestic Violence, a committee against sexual harassment, and information and referral on a variety of issues. Handicapped women on campus would find special support from the Office for the Physically Impaired.

Returning Women Students. Fifty-six percent of students enrolled in Continuing Education programs are women. The Office of Continuing Education sponsors an annual women's day.

Special Features. In 1983 OSU will host the Sixth Annual Convention of the National Women's Studies Association.

Institutional Self-Description. "The Ohio State University Women's Studies support-faculty numbers 125 persons in academic areas from anthropology to zoology. The close cooperation between Women's Studies and Women's Services ensures continuous academic and non-academic programming for women; and the Task Force on Academic Excellence for Women works to enlarge possibilities for all women, especially those in nontraditional fields."

Ohio University
Athens, OH 45701
Telephone: (614) 594-5174

★ **Women and the Curriculum**

11,592 undergraduates

	Amer. Ind.	Asian Amer.	Blacks	Hispanics	Whites
F	15	14	387	9	4,867
M	18	10	312	12	5,513
%	0.3	0.2	6.3	0.2	93.0

 AAUW

Established in 1804 in the Northwest Territory, Ohio University is a public institution that enrolls some 13,700 students in a variety of undergraduate and graduate programs. The Office of Continuing Education serves the adult student. Evening classes, a summer session, and off-campus class locations are available.

Women are 46 percent of the 11,592 undergraduates; 12 percent of the women attend part-time. The median age of undergraduates is 20. The university reports that about one-fourth of undergraduate women are older than 25 and that 60 percent of these attend part-time. For the 2 percent of undergraduates who commute, the university is accessible by public transportation. On-campus parking is available at a fee.

University childcare facilities charge on a sliding scale and are available to full-time and part-time students. Three-quarters of students' requests can be accommodated. Private childcare arrangements may be made near the campus.

Policies to Ensure Fairness to Women. The Executive Assistant to the President is responsible for policy on equal employment opportunity, accessibility of all curriculum and activities to both male and female students, and handicapped access. Three other officers review policies and practices and monitor compliance. A policy prohibiting sexual harassment of students, staff, and faculty has been communicated in writing to faculty.

Women in Leadership Positions. *Students.* Opportunities for women students to assume positions of campus leadership are considerably below the average for public research institutions in this guide. In recent years, women have served one-year terms as president of the residence-hall council and president of the senior class. Women also preside over half of the 14 honorary societies.

Faculty. Women are 18 percent of a full-time faculty of 664. One American Indian, 1 Hispanic, 3 Asian American, and 3 black women are on the full-time faculty, according to recent report. The ratio of female faculty to female students is 3 to 100. The ratio of male faculty to male students is 10 to 100.

Administrators. The chief student-life officer is a woman. Other higher administrative positions are held by men. Women head four of 48 schools and departments. The Dean of the College of Health and Human Services is a black woman.

Women and the Curriculum. The majority of women graduating with bachelors degrees major in education (31 percent), the health professions (10 percent), the fine arts (9 percent), and communications (9 percent). The proportion of women majoring in public affairs is above the national average. Two percent of the undergraduate women major in nontraditional areas. A few students earn two-year degrees in arts and sciences and health technologies, 40 percent of them women.

The Women's Studies Program offers a new 30-credit certificate. Recent undergraduate courses on women are available in the department of English and the School of Art. An official committee collects curricular materials on women and is developing the Women's Studies Program. The College of Business, the department of social work, and the Schools of Physical Education and Nursing provide some instruction on matters specific to women. Faculty workshops are offered on affirmative action and nontraditional occupations for women and men.

Minority Women. Of 5,292 undergraduate women, 7 percent are black and less than 1 percent each American Indian, Asian American, and Hispanic. Forty women are in all-minority sororities. Staff in residence halls and the counseling center are offered awareness-training in the avoidance of racial bias. There is a local chapter of the NAACP on campus.

Women and Athletics. The intercollegiate program provides good opportunities for organized, competitive individual and team sports. Information about intramural and club sports was not provided by the institution. Thirty-seven percent of intercollegiate athletes are women. Women receive 30 percent of athletic scholarships. Five of 22 paid intercollegiate coaches are women. All teams played in tournaments in 1980. The intercollegiate sports offered are: basketball, cross-country, field hockey, lacrosse, softball, swimming, tennis, track (indoor and outdoor), and volleyball.

Housing and Student Organizations. Single-sex and coeducational dormitories and housing for married students and single parents with children are available for students who live on campus. A married woman whose spouse is not enrolled may live in married students' housing. Both restricted and nonrestricted hours for visitors of the opposite sex obtain in the residence halls. Six of 22 residence-hall directors are female. Staff are offered awareness-training on such issues as sexism, sex education, racism, birth control, and cross-cultural awareness.

Seven percent of the undergraduate women belong to social sororities. Sororities and fraternities provide housing for their members. Organizations which serve as advocates for women include Athens Women's Collective, Friends of My Sister's Place, and NARAL/Athens Abortion Rights.

Special Services and Programs for Women. *Health and Counseling.* The student health service provides some medical attention specific to women, including gynecological, birth control, and rape and assault treatment. The four health service physicians are male. Twenty of 23 health-care providers are female. One-third of the professional staff in the counseling service are women. Students have access to gynecological, birth control, abortion, and rape and assault counseling. Staff receive in-service training on sex-role stereotyping and racial bias.

Safety and Security. Measures consist of campus police with weapons training and arrest authority, night-time escorts for women, self-defense courses for women, information sessions on safety and crime prevention, and a rape crisis center. Information on the incidence of rapes and assaults was not provided.

Career. Workshops and printed materials concentrated on women in nontraditional careers are provided along with lectures by women employed in these fields. Students are sent free of cost to events like the Ohio Women's Career Convention.

Other. Such community organizations as My Sister's Place and the Tri-County Community Action Agency sponsor services for women, including a telephone line of information, referral, and support. Assertiveness training is available under the auspices of the Dean of Students' office. The Athens Women's Collective sponsors theater and other women's art events.

Institutional Self-Description. "Ohio University has: created a Women's Studies Program; established a women's programming internship; increased safety and security measures in residence halls; increased budget and support staff for women's athletics; hired more women faculty and staff; and actively recruited women for historically male-dominated academic programs."

Ohio Wesleyan University
Delaware, OH 43015
Telephone: (614) 369-4431

Women in Leadership	★ Women and the
★ students	Curriculum
★ faculty	
	★ Women and Athletics

2,286 undergraduates

	Amer. Ind.	Asian Amer.	Blacks	Hispanics	Whites
F	0	3	53	3	1,037
M	0	2	59	7	1,021
%	0.0	0.2	5.1	0.5	94.2

 AAUW

Founded in 1842, Ohio Wesleyan University is a private, four-year liberal arts institution. Although affiliated with the United Methodist Church, the university is accessible to students of all religious denominations. Bachelor's degrees are offered in a range of liberal arts and pre-professional areas. Alternative schedules include on-campus evening classes, off-campus day classes, self-paced/contract learning, and a summer session. Forty-nine percent of the 2,286 undergraduates are women, and virtually all students attend full-time. The median age of all students is 19. Free parking is provided on campus for the 15 percent of students who commute or live near campus.

Private childcare facilities are available nearby.

Policies to Ensure Fairness to Women. A full-time affirmative action officer with a voice in policy oversees compliance with sex-equity, equal-employment-opportunity, and handicapped-access laws. A written policy on sexual harassment of students, faculty, and staff has been publicly communicated to the campus community; complaints are resolved through a formal grievance procedure. The Committee on the Status of Women, a standing committee of the faculty, includes elected student representatives with voting rights and administrators appointed by the President. The committee takes public stands on women's issues and the concerns of minority women, and circulates its reports to the entire university community.

Women in Leadership Positions. *Students.* In recent years, women have been president of the student body, head of the student senate, and editor-in-chief of the campus newspaper, each for two years. Women head three of 13 honorary societies.

Faculty. Women are 25 percent of the 153 full-time faculty. There are 4 female faculty for every 100 female students and 10 male faculty for every 100 male students.

Administrators. Men hold all top positions except chief student-life officer. Of 28 academic departments women chair four: community studies, politics and government, Romance languages, and speech-communications. A woman is Dean of the Riverside School of Nursing. Women constitute 26 percent of the faculty senate.

Women and the Curriculum. Most degrees awarded to women are in social sciences (14 percent), letters (13 percent), fine arts (11 percent), education (11 percent), and home economics (10 percent). Five percent of women take degrees in the nontraditional fields of mathematics or physical sciences. Women are 50 percent of participants in internships and practicums.

The Women's Studies Program, directed part-time by a permanent faculty member, awards the B.A. in Women's Studies. The program offers an introductory course called Woman in Contemporary Society, an advanced Seminar, an Independent Study Project, and a Directed Reading Project in Women's Studies. Majors must take additional courses on women through departmental offerings which currently include Women in American

History, Sociology of Women, Literary Perspectives on Women, and Women and Sport. An official committee supervises the program. Faculty workshops are available on racism and sexism in the curriculum and on affirmative action. The appropriate departments provide information on sex-fair curricula, mathematics avoidance, midwifery, and reproductive choice.

Women and Athletics. The athletic program for women offers a good variety of intercollegiate and intramural individual and team sports. Women are 38 percent of intercollegiate athletes. Six of the 14 paid varsity coaches are women. Intercollegiate sports include basketball, cross-country, field hockey, lacrosse, softball, swimming, tennis, track and field, and volleyball.

Housing and Student Organizations. Single-sex and coeducational dormitories are available to the 85 percent of students who live on campus. Students vote on restrictions of visiting hours in single-sex dormitories; coeducational dormitories generally allow unrestricted visiting hours. The five residence-hall directors, including two women, are offered awareness-training on sexism, sex education, racism, and birth control. A small residential unit, the Women's House, provides housing for women involved in women-centered programming for the whole campus.

Forty percent of the full-time undergraduate women belong to sororities, which do not provide housing for members. Among groups that function as advocates for women are: Women's Task Force, SUBA, Sisters United, Horizons International, Women's Resource Center, and Student Y. Half of the 60 members of Student Y are women.

Special Services and Programs for Women. *Health and Counseling.* The student health service is staffed by 1 male and 1 female physician and 2 female health-care providers. One of the 2 counselors in the student counseling center is a woman. Counseling is available on gynecological problems, birth control, abortion, and rape. Medical treatment is available for all of the above except abortion. Counselors receive awareness-training on sex-role stereotyping, racial bias, and rape counseling.

Safety and Security. Measures include both campus and local police, night-time bus service to residential areas, high-intensity lighting, self-defense courses, information sessions on campus safety, and a rape crisis center. Two rapes and seven assaults (three on women) were reported for 1980–81.

Career. Services include workshops focused on nontraditional careers, lectures and panels for students by women employed in nontraditional occupations, and programs to establish networks between alumnae and female students.

Other. The Ohio Wesleyan Women's Resource Center has a budget of $2,000 that is supplemented by institutional funds from the Women's Task Force and the Women's Studies Program. An administrator with part-time responsibility for the center organizes a biweekly seminar series.

Special Features. Ohio Wesleyan is a participant in the Great Lakes Colleges Association, which has an active Women's Studies Program that sponsors several workshops each year for faculty and students, as well as an annual conference and summer institute for faculty.

Institutional Self-Description. "Ohio Wesleyan is a liberal arts college which combines small classes and close personal contact with its excellent faculty with a rich diversity of programs. Its fine academic programs have produced graduates who have won national honors and been accepted into prestigious graduate and professional schools in all parts of the curriculum. It serves its students with a nationally recognized career planning and placement service."

Sinclair Community College
444 West Third Street, Dayton, OH 45402
Telephone: (513) 226-2500

Women in Leadership
★★★ students
★★ faculty
★ administrators

13,958 undergraduates

	Amer. Ind.	Asian Amer.	Blacks	Hispanics	Whites
F	19	49	1,649	38	6,320
M	21	33	826	26	4,480
%	0.3	0.6	18.4	0.5	80.2

A public, two-year commuter college, Sinclair enrolls 13,958 students. Sixty percent of the students are women, three-fourths of whom attend part-time. Two-thirds of all women are over age 23; the median age of all students is 30.

Sinclair offers two-year degrees and certificates in a range of liberal arts, science, business, and pre-professional fields. Evening classes, weekend college, and a ten-week summer session are available. The division of continuing education is responsible for adult programs. The college is accessible by public transportation, and on-campus parking is provided.

Childcare facilities accommodating 50 children are available on campus. Students, faculty, and staff may take advantage of the services from 7 a.m. to 5:30 p.m. for a daily fee of $7 full-time and $4 part-time. The college reports that three-fourths of child-care requests are accommodated each year, on a first-come, first-served basis.

Policies to Ensure Fairness to Women. A policy prohibiting the sexual harassment of students, faculty, and staff is in the process of being communicated in writing to these groups. Complaints are resolved informally and confidentially or through as formal grievance procedure. Two administrators are assigned part-time to monitor compliance with legislation concerning equal employment opportunity, sex equity, and handicapped access. Commission on the Status of Women, with members appointed by the President of the college, is being formed.

Women in Leadership Positions. *Students.* There are two student leadership positions available. During a recent three-year period, women served three times as president of the student senate and twice as editor-in-chief of the campus newspaper. A woman heads the one campus honorary society.

Faculty. Forty-three percent of the 226 full-time faculty are women, a proportion above the average for public two-year colleges in this guide. Recent information indicates that the 96 full-time faculty women include 14 black, 1 Asian American, and 2 Hispanic women. There are 5 female faculty for every 100 female students and 9 male faculty for every 100 male students.

Administrators. Of 8 top-level administrators, the chief development officer and the head librarian are women. The Dean of the Public Services Division is a woman. Fourteen of 37 departments are chaired by women, including 3 black women and 1 Asian American woman. Departments chaired by women include

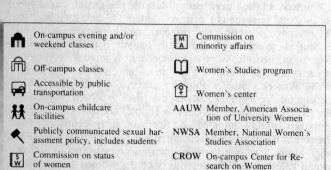

On-campus evening and/or weekend classes	Commission on minority affairs [M A]
Off-campus classes	Women's Studies program
Accessible by public transportation	Women's center
On-campus childcare facilities	AAUW Member, American Association of University Women
Publicly communicated sexual harassment policy, includes students	NWSA Member, National Women's Studies Association
Commission on status of women [S W]	CROW On-campus Center for Research on Women

physical science, health technologies, secretarial, English, psychology, sociology, and early-childhood education. Four of 9 trustees are women, including 2 black women.

Women and the Curriculum. Most women take two-year degrees and certificates in the fields of health (41 percent), business (32 percent), public service (13 percent), and liberal arts (10 percent). Sixty percent of students participating in cooperative education and internship programs are women, as are more than 80 percent of the students in the credit-bearing programs, Lifelong Learning and the College Without Walls.

Two courses on women—Images of Women and Self-Defense for Women—are offered by the division of general studies and the division of public services.

Women and Athletics. The athletic program offers a variety of intercollegiate and intramural team and individual sports. Women are 29 percent of intramural and 67 percent of intercollegiate athletes. Four of the six paid varsity coaches are women. Intercollegiate sports for women include basketball, softball, tennis, and volleyball.

Special Services and Programs for Women. *Health and Counseling.* There is no student health service. Three of four staff members in the student counseling center are women, including one minority women. No information was provided on counseling services specific to women.

Safety and Security. Measures include campus police with weapons training and authority to make arrests, night-time escort service for women students, high-intensity lighting, emergency alarm system at isolated locations, and a credit-bearing self-defense course. Twelve assaults on women were reported for 1980–81.

Career. Lectures by women employed in nontraditional occupations are available, along with printed information on nontraditional fields of study and careers for women. Project Focus, a voluntary association of Sinclair faculty and staff, is responsible, in conjunction with the Dean of Students and Student Government, for a Women's Awareness Week that focuses on career and leadership issues. Project Focus also sponsors a Women's Re-Entry Program, a Women Alone Workshop series, and other lecture series.

Other. A displaced homemakers' program is administered through the Office of the Dean of Students, in cooperation with the Montgomery County CETA program.

Institutional Self-Description. "Women are choosing to study here because faculty and staff provide a supportive environment. A reentry program offers a seven-credit program emphasizing career planning, study skills, and personal growth. Low tuition and accessibility encourage women to attend."

Union for Experimenting Colleges and Universities
Provident Bank Building
P.O. Box 85315, Cincinnati, OH 45201
Telephone: (513) 621-6444.

Women in Leadership
★★★ **administrators**

725 undergraduates

	Amer. Ind.	Asian Amer.	Blacks	Hispanics	Whites
F	245	0	107	26	131
M	40	0	92	10	71
%	39.5	0.0	27.6	5.0	28.0

The Union for Experimenting Colleges and Universities is a nationwide, degree-granting consortium offering the B.A., B.S., and Ph.D. degrees. The Union's undergraduate degree program,

the University Without Walls, maintains offices in Cincinnati, New Orleans, and San Francisco. It offers adult students an opportunity to earn a degree while meeting work and childcare responsibilities. The Union offers non-campus, individually designed programs of study based upon independent study, directed readings, internships, on-the-job education, tutorials, classroom instruction, and other strategies for learning. Women make up 70 percent of the 725 undergraduates. The median age of all undergraduates is 36.

Women in Leadership Positions. *Students.* There are no student leadership positions.

Faculty. The core faculty are described by the institution as "learning facilitators and evaluators . . . the principal representatives of the institution with whom each [student] works throughout the program."

Administrators. Women hold 3 of 6 administrative positions: chief business officer, director of institutional research, and chief planning officer. A black woman and 2 white women are among the 5 directors of Units of the Union: Dean of the Union East, Dean of the Union Midwest, and the Director of the University without Walls, New Orleans. Four of 13 members of the governing body are women, including 1 American Indian woman and 2 black women. Three women sit on the 15-member Board of Regents.

Women and the Curriculum. Most degrees granted to women are in public affairs (29 percent), psychology (20 percent), business (16 percent), and the social sciences (16 percent). The Union does not offer prescribed curricula; students working with core faculty design their own curricula. Graduate students may earn a Ph.D. in Women's Studies.

Women and Athletics. No athletic program is available.

Special Services and Programs for Women. *Health and Counseling.* There are no health and counseling services.

Institutional Self-Description. "In the Union's learning process, faculty assist learners in discovering their learning needs; in developing workable educational plans; in using the best available resources; and in achieving excellence in their fields. Common elements of Union programs are: individually tailored programs; academic recognition for demonstrated prior learning; use of various learning methodologies such as independent study, tutorials, internships; integration of theory and practice; use of community resources; and interdisciplinary study."

University of Akron
302 East Buchtel Ave., Akron, OH 44325
Telephone: (216) 375-7281

Women in Leadership	**★ Women and the**
★ faculty	**Curriculum**

18,039 undergraduates

	Amer. Ind.	Asian Amer.	Blacks	Hispanics	Whites
F	31	29	1,067	34	7,768
M	40	49	574	21	8,287
%	0.4	0.4	9.2	0.3	89.7

 AAUW

The University of Akron, established as a church-related institution, was for many years a city university. Since 1967 it has been part of the state system. It serves some 22,600 students with a variety of undergraduate, graduate, and professional programs. The Adult Resource Center is responsible for continuing adult education. Alternative class schedules, including weekend college, summer session, and off-campus locations, are available.

Women are half of the 18,039 undergraduates; 40 percent of

the women attend part-time. The median age of undergraduates is 25. For the 90 percent of the undergraduates who commute, the university is accessible by public transportation. On-campus parking is provided at a fee.

Childcare facilities operated by the university are open until 10:00 p.m. (hot meals served), which is rare among public research universities in this guide. The university estimates that the facility can accommodate 85 percent of students' requests. Private childcare arrangements may be made close to campus.

Policies to Ensure Fairness to Women. One full-time and two part-time officers review policy and monitor compliance concerning equal employment opportunity, sex equity for students, and handicapped accessibility. Complaints of sexual harassment are handled informally and confidentially.

Women in Leadership Positions. *Students.* Opportunities for women students to exercise all-campus leadership are about average for public research institutions in this guide. In recent years, women have presided over the student senate, the student court, and three times over the residence-hall council. Women head 13 of 23 honorary societies.

Faculty. Women are one-quarter of a full-time faculty of 645. Recent data show that 1 Asian American, 3 black, and 1 Hispanic woman are among the full-time faculty. The ratio of female faculty to female students is 3 to 100; of male faculty to male students, 9 to 100.

Administrators. The head librarian is a woman; men hold all other top administrative posts. Women chair two of 40 departments—home economics, and classics. The Dean of the College of Nursing is a woman.

Women and the Curriculum. Most women graduating with bachelor's degrees major in education, the health professions, and business. Under 2 percent major in engineering, mathematics, and the physical sciences. Most women (61 percent) graduating with two-year degrees major in business and commercial programs.

The Women's Studies Program, called Gender Identity and Roles, offers a certificate (comparable to a major). Some 20 courses on women are offered through the departments of biology, economics, English, history, sociology, education, speech, social work, home economics, and the Institutes of Life-Span Development and Peace Studies. Recent offerings include Hormones and Behavior, Women in the Labor Force, Women Writers, Soviet and U.S. Women, and Sociology of Sex Roles. An official committee promotes and monitors the development of courses on gender identity and roles.

Such current issues as mathematics confidence among females, coeducational physical education classes, sex-fair curricula, services for abused spouses, and discrimination in the workplace are included in the instruction of future teachers, social workers, and business students. The relationships among sex, race, and career preparation, as well as nontraditional occupations for men and women, the needs of reentry women, and affirmative action, are topics in faculty workshops.

Minority Women. Thirteen percent of undergraduate women are members of minority groups. Minority women belong to both integrated and all-minority sororities. Residence-hall staff and staff in the counseling center are offered awareness-training on avoiding racial bias. The Black Cultural Center and Black United Students are advocacy groups.

Women and Athletics. Intramural and intercollegiate programs provide limited opportunities for organized, competitive sports. Thirteen percent of intramural and 23 percent of intercollegiate athletes are women; women receive 15 percent of athletic scholarships. About a third of the 19 paid coaches for intercollegiate teams are women. The intercollegiate sports offered are basketball, softball, tennis, and volleyball.

Housing and Student Organizations. One-tenth of the undergraduates live on campus in single-sex dormitories and apartments. Residence halls restrict hours for visitors of the opposite sex. Seven of the nine residence-hall directors are female. Staff are offered awareness-training on sex education, racism, and birth control.

Seven percent of full-time undergraduate women belong to social sororities, which provide housing for their members. Among student organizations which serve as advocates for women are the Association for Women Students, Aware, Law Association for Women's Rights, Psychology Club, and Social Work League.

Special Services and Programs for Women. *Health and Counseling.* The student health service, staffed by 1 male physician, does not provide medical attention specific to women. Six women provide additional health-care services. Two of the 6-member counseling staff are women. They receive in-service training on sex-role stereotyping and racial bias.

Safety and Security. Measures include campus and city police, night-time escorts for women students, high-intensity lighting, emergency alarm and telephone systems, self-defense courses for women, information sessions on safety and crime prevention, and a rape crisis center. Information was not provided on the incidence of rapes and assaults.

Career. Workshops, lectures, and printed materials concerning women in nontraditional occupations and fields of study, as well as a program of contacts between alumnae and students, are available.

Other. The Institute of Life-Span Development sponsors an annual women's week; the Office of Student Development holds a women's film festival. Assertiveness training and a program to build confidence in mathematics are offered through Team Leadership and the education and psychology departments.

Returning Women Students. The Adult Resource Center is responsible for programming for women and men. It serves about 2,500 reentry women annually, 20 percent of whom are mainly black women. Services include a program for displaced homemakers.

Institutional Self-Description. "The University of Akron is the third largest state university in Ohio. As an urban university, there is greater opportunity for liaisons with community and women's groups for experiential learning. The student body is diverse in background and broad in age range."

University of Cincinnati
Cincinnati, OH 45221
Telephone: (513) 475-8000

★★★ **Women and the Curriculum**

★ **Women and Athletics**

19,910 undergraduates

	Amer. Ind.	Asian Amer.	Blacks	Hispanics	Whites
F	10	45	1,523	20	6,732
M	16	46	936	32	10,470
%	0.1	0.5	12.4	0.3	86.8

 AAUW NWSA

Established in 1819, the University of Cincinnati is an urban, state-supported institution that provides a range of undergraduate, graduate, and professional studies for some 33,200 students. A division of continuing education serves the adult student. Alternative class schedules include a weekend college, off-campus day and evening classes, independent study, and a summer session.

Forty-two percent of the 19,910 undergraduates are women; 21 percent of women attend part-time. The median age of all undergraduates is 23. The university reports that 12 percent of female undergraduates are older than 35. For the estimated 91 percent of undergraduates who live off campus or commute, the university is accessible by public transportation. On-campus parking is available at a fee.

University childcare facilities charge fees on a sliding scale. An estimated 60 percent of students' requests can be accommodated.

Policies to Ensure Fairness to Women. A full-time Equal Opportunity Officer is responsible for policy and review of practices related to employment, sex-equity for students, and handicapped accessibility. A published policy prohibits sexual harassment; complaints are handled both informally and confidentially and through a formal grievance procedure. The active Committee on the Status of Women takes public stands on issues of importance to students and addresses the concerns of minority women.

Women in Leadership Positions. *Students.* Opportunities for women students to assume campus leadership are limited. Of eight positions in a recent three-year period, women served one-year terms as president of the student body, presiding officer of the student union board, editor-in-chief of the campus newspaper, and presiding officer of the residence-hall council.

Faculty. Women are 24 percent of a full-time faculty of 1,054, a proportion slightly below the national norm. Twenty-two black women, 2 American Indian, 5 Asian American, and 2 Hispanic women are on the full-time faculty, according to a recent report. The ratio of female faculty to female students is 4 to 100; the ratio of male faculty to male students is 9 to 100.

Administrators. All top administrative posts are held by men. Women chair 13 of 86 departments. The Dean of the College of Nursing is female.

Women and the Curriculum. A majority of the women earn bachelor's degrees in education, the health professions, and business and management. Eight percent major in such nontraditional fields as architecture, computer science, engineering, mathematics, and the physical sciences, with the largest number in architecture. Women earn about half of the two-year degrees awarded; one-third of these are in arts and sciences, one-third in business, and one-fourth in health technologies.

The Center for Women's Studies, under a director who holds a permanent faculty appointment, offers a 30-credit certificate, a B.A. through Interdisciplinary Studies, a graduate minor, and the M.A. through Education. Some 75 courses on women are offered through Women's Studies and such departments as English, history, sociology, anthropology, and psychology. Recent offerings include Women in Culture and Society, African-American Women in U.S. Society, The Contemporary Black Woman, Women in Asia, Feminist Political Philosophy, Women in Politics, The British Woman Writer, and Human Sexuality.

An official committee encourages the development of new courses incorporating scholarship on women. Sexism, nontraditional occupations for men and women, and the needs of reentry women are topics of faculty workshops. Sex-fair curricula, the teaching of coeducational physical education classes, health-care information important to minority women, services for abused spouses, and workplace discrimination are current issues covered in the preparation of future teachers, health-care providers, social workers, and business students.

Minority Women. Of 8,330 undergraduate women, 18 percent are black women and less than 1 percent each American Indian, Asian American, and Hispanic. Sixty-three women are in all-minority sororities. Residence-hall counselors are offered awareness-training on racism. The United Black Association and the Black Program Board are advocacy groups. One member of the faculty senate and 1 of 2 female trustees are black women.

Women and Athletics. An excellent intramural and a good intercollegiate program provide opportunities for organized, competitive, individual and team sports. Forty-two percent of intramural and 25 percent of intercollegiate athletes are women; women receive 20 percent of athletic scholarships. Six of 26 paid intercollegiate coaches are female. Women's intercollegiate teams played in tournaments during 1980. The intercollegiate sports offered are basketball, golf, soccer, swimming and diving, tennis, track, and volleyball.

Housing and Student Organizations. For the estimated 9 percent of undergraduates who live on campus, single-sex and co-educational dormitories and apartments open to married or single students are available. Residence halls do not restrict hours for visitors of the opposite sex. Three of eight residence-hall counselors are female. Staff are offered awareness-training on sexism, sex education, racism, and birth control.

An estimated 9 percent of the full-time undergraduate women belong to social sororities. Sororities and fraternities provide housing for their members. The Women's Center and Lesbian/Gay Alliance are advocacy groups.

Special Services and Programs for Women. *Health and Counseling.* The student health service provides some medical attention specific to women, including treatment for gynecological problems and birth control. Half of the full-time physicians are female, as are 27 other health-care providers. Twelve of 18 counselors in the counseling service are women. Gynecological, birth control, and rape and assault counseling are available.

Safety and Security. Measures consist of campus police with weapons training and arrest authority, night-time escorts, high-intensity lighting, an emergency telephone system, information sessions on safety and crime prevention, and a rape crisis center. Three assaults on women and two attempted rapes were reported for 1980–81.

Career. Career workshops on women in nontraditional occupations and job discrimination information are available.

Other. The Office of Women's Programs and Services sponsors an annual women's week, a women's lecture series, assertiveness training, and theater and other arts programs for women.

Institutional Self-Description. "An urban university on the fringes of the inner city, the University of Cincinnati has a culturally diverse student population and affords many opportunities for community involvement. The President has an Advisory Committee on Women's Issues. The Office of Women's Programs and Services, with its programming to present positive role models and outreach activities, and the Center for Women's Studies are strong advocates for women."

University of Dayton
300 College Park, Dayton, OH 45469
Telephone: (513) 229-0123

★ **Women and the Curriculum**

6,631 undergraduates

	Amer. Ind.	Asian Amer.	Blacks	Hispanics	Whites
F	2	9	182	17	2,411
M	4	16	155	44	3,612
%	0.1	0.4	5.2	1.0	93.4

🏠 🏛 🚌 ⬚ ⬚ 📖 AAUW NWSA

Founded in 1850 by the Society of Mary as a boarding school for boys, this private, Roman Catholic university now enrolls some 9,900 students, of whom 6,631 are undergraduates. Women were admitted in 1935 and today constitute 40 percent of the undergraduates; 8 percent of women attend part-time. The median age of undergraduates is 19.

In addition to the College of Arts and Sciences, there are schools of business adminstration, engineering, and education. Alternative schedules include evening classes, a summer session, and self-paced/contract learning. Off-campus class locations are also available. The campus is accessible by public transportation. For the 19 percent of students who commute, on-campus parking is available for a fee.

Private childcare facilities are available near campus.

Policies to Ensure Fairness to Women. A full-time affirmative action officer monitors compliance with equal-employment opportunity, sex-equity, and handicapped-access legislation. Sexual harassment complaints are handled through a formal campus grievance procedure. A Committee on the Status of Women, appointed by the President, prepares an annual report which is distributed to the campus community. Both this committee and the Committee on Minority Affairs address the concerns of minority women.

Women in Leadership Positions. *Students.* No information was provided on campus-wide student offices. Women head 21 of the 40 honorary societies.

Faculty. Sixteen percent of the full-time faculty of 355 are women, a proportion considerably below the national average. There are 2 female faculty for every 100 female students and 8 male faculty for every 100 male students.

Administrators. Two of the 9 top administrators are women: chief student-life officer and director of institutional research. Women chair 5 of the 45 departments: secretarial studies, home economics, physical education, philosophy, and social work. In a recent year, 1 of 2 honorary degree recipients was a woman; 2 of 12 alumni award recipients were also women.

Women and the Curriculum. Most women earn bachelor's degrees in education (22 percent), business (16 percent), public affairs (10 percent), and communications (9 percent). Ten percent of women earn degrees in the nontraditional fields of engineering, computer science, mathematics, and physical sciences. Among the women who earn two-year degrees, 71 percent major in business and commerce and the others in mechanical/engineering technologies. Special programs encourage women (including reentry women) to prepare for nontraditional careers in science and engineering. Women constitute 28 percent of students in cooperative education programs, 40 percent of student interns, and 50 percent of those in science field service. In addition, 53 percent of students involved in self-directed learning programs are women.

The Women's Studies Program offers an undergraduate minor. Twelve courses are offered through Women's Studies and ten departments. They include Women in Art, Women in Management, Women Aging, and Anglo-American Feminism. An official committee on Women's Studies develops courses, collects curricular materials, and holds workshops, open to the general public, with nationally recognized speakers on women's issues. Workshops on nontraditional careers, the needs of reentry women, and affirmative action are provided for faculty. Appropriate departments provide information on sex-fair curricula, services for battered spouses and displaced homemakers, and job discrimination and sexual harassment in the workplace.

Women and Athletics. The university has a varied intramural sports program for women. Thirty-two percent of the intramural athletes and 23 percent of the intercollegiate athletes are women, and women receive 30 percent of athletic scholarships. Three of the ten paid intercollegiate coaches are women. Intercollegiate sports for women include basketball, field hockey, softball, tennis, and volleyball.

Housing and Student Organizations. Forty-three percent of the students live on campus in single-sex dormitories with restrictive hours for visitors of the opposite sex, or in fraternity or sorority houses. Half of the residence-hall counselors are female, including one minority woman. Residence-hall staff are offered awareness-training on sexism and racism, stress management, and rape counseling.

Twelve percent of the full-time undergraduate women belong to sororities.

Special Services and Programs for Women. *Health and Counseling.* The student health service employs 1 male physician. The six-member staff of the student counseling center includes 2 women, 1 of whom is black. Counseling and medical treatment for gynecological problems and rape and assault are available.

Counseling staff receive training on the avoidance of sexism and racism and on rape counseling.

Safety and Security. Measures consist of campus police with authority to make arrests, night-time escort service for women, high-intensity lighting, self-defense courses for women, and information sessions on safety and crime prevention. Two rapes and three assaults (none on women) were reported for 1980–81.

The Women's Interest Group has offered mini-courses on rape and has organized a campus-wide escort service for women students. The group has also instituted Help Houses in off-campus areas to assist those students who fear or are victims of assault.

Career. Services include career workshops and printed information on nontraditional occupations, along with lectures and panels by women employed in nontraditional fields.

Other. A Women's Center, with a part-time, student-volunteer coordinator, serves about 1,500 women a year, 3 percent of whom are members of minority groups, largely black. There is a Center for Afro-American Affairs. The Women's Studies Program sponsors a women's lecture series. The Women's Interest Group sponsors an annual women's week.

Returning Women Students. The continuing education program, called the Metro Center for Adults, serves approximately 300 reentry women. The Fast Track Reentry Program for Women in Engineering, sponsored by the School of Engineering and the National Science Foundation, is nationally regarded as a model reentry strategy for training women who have backgrounds in mathematics, chemistry, or physics, and who are seeking greater job challenges. The university reports that graduates of the program have been sought by many industries, including some among the Fortune 500. The university has also pioneered a series of non-academic programs to recruit women and minorities into such nontraditional fields as mathematics, science, and engineering.

Institutional Self-Description. "The qualities attributed to the University of Dayton are those which would benefit equally men and women who choose to study here. Chief among those qualities is the continuing discussion of values that happens in classes of varied disciplines, and the growing inquiry about women in the arts, in society, in philosophy, in business, in communications, and in politics."

Wilmington College
Wilmington, OH 45177
Telephone: (513) 382-6661

★ **Women and the Curriculum**

825 undergraduates

	Amer. Ind.	Asian Amer.	Blacks	Hispanics	Whites
F	0	0	19	7	194
M	0	1	137	3	429
%	0.0	0.1	19.8	1.3	78.9

 AAUW

Wilmington College, a church-related liberal arts institution, was founded in 1863 by the Society of Friends. Virtually all of the 838 students attend full-time; 28 percent are women. The median age of students is 20 years. The college offers bachelor's degrees in a variety of fields, as well as two-year associate of arts degrees. All students are required to devote one term to study, work, or service in an off-campus location. Alternative schedules include evening and summer session classes. Off-campus class locations are also available. Free on-campus parking is provided for the 39 percent of students who commute. The college cannot be reached by public transportation.

Private childcare is available off campus.

Policies to Ensure Fairness to Women. The Secretary of the

College serves as a part-time equal-opportunity officer and is responsible for the development of policy relating to equal employment opportunities, sex equity for students, and access for the handicapped. A written policy and procedures on sexual harassment are being formulated

Women in Leadership Positions. *Students.* Opportunities for women students to gain leadership experience are extremely limited. The institution reports only three campus-wide student offices. In three recent years, a woman served once as president of the student union board. One of the two campus honorary societies is headed by a woman.

Faculty. Eighteen percent of the full-time faculty are women, a proportion below the national average. There are 4 female faculty for every 100 female students and 6 male faculty for every 100 male students.

Administrators. All chief administrative officers and all department chairs are men. Five of the 22 trustees are women. In 1980–81 the commencement speaker was a woman, and women received two of four honorary degrees.

Women and the Curriculum. The most popular majors for women graduates are education (47 percent), letters (10 percent), and social science (10 percent). About 40 percent of participants in student internship and cooperative education programs are women.

A new Women's Studies Program, whose coordinator holds a full-time faculty position, offers an undergraduate minor. Recent courses available through the departments of literature and history include: Introduction to Women's Studies, Women in Literature, and History of Women in Europe.

Women and Athletics. For its size, Wilmington has a good intramural and intercollegiate sports program for women, providing opportunities to compete in organized team and individual sports. Forty-two percent of intramural athletes and 24 percent of intercollegiate athletes are women, as are two of the seven intercollegiate coaches. Intercollegiate sports for women include basketball, softball, tennis, track and field, and volleyball.

Housing and Student Organizations. Sixty-one percent of students live on campus in single-sex or coeducational dormitories. Of the women living in dormitories, 11 percent are black and 2 percent are Hispanic. Three of the seven residence-hall directors are women. Residence-hall staff are offered awareness training on birth control and alcohol abuse.

Thirteen percent of female students belong to sororities. Sororities and fraternities do not provide housing for members.

Special Services and Programs for Women. *Health and Counseling.* The student health service has one male physician and a female nurse. The staff of the student counseling center, one man and one woman, are offered training on the avoidance of sexism and racism. Available services specific to women include gynecological, birth control, abortion, and rape counseling, and medical treatment for all of the above except abortion.

Safety and Security. Measures consist of campus police without arrest authority, nighttime escort service for women, high-intensity lighting, self-defense courses, and information sessions on rape and assault prevention. No rapes or assaults on women were reported for 1980–81.

Career. Services include workshops and other information on nontraditional occupations for women and a program to build networks between alumnae and female students.

Other. The Office of Student Services sponsors an annual women's week, and the psychology department provides assertiveness and leadership training.

Institutional Self-Description. ''Wilmington is a Christian college (sponsored by the Society of Friends) dedicated to the intellectual development of any person seeking self-improvement. The educational mission is to provide career preparation with a liberal arts foundation. This rural campus provides the proper atmosphere for students to live and learn. Special programs for women are offered to aid in their career preparation.''

Wittenberg University
Springfield, OH 45501
Telephone: (513) 327-7323

2,253 undergraduates

	Amer. Ind.	Asian Amer.	Blacks	Hispanics	Whites
F	0	2	58	1	1,101
M	0	2	61	1	1,008
%	0.0	0.2	5.3	0.1	94.4

Founded in 1845, Wittenberg University is an independent liberal arts institution that is supported by the Lutheran Church; it includes schools of music and of community education. Of the 2,546 students, 2,253 are undergraduates. Women are 52 percent of the undergraduates. The median age of all students is 20. Wittenberg offers bachelor's degrees in a variety of fields, as well as a master's degree in sacred music. Combined programs with other institutions are offered in engineering, forestry, and nursing. Evening classes, a summer session, and a continuing education program also are available. For the 25 percent of students who commute, the campus is accessible by public transportation, and parking is provided on campus for a fee.

Private childcare is available nearby.

Policies to Ensure Fairness to Women. The Associate Director of Business is responsible for policies on equal employment opportunity. A sexual harassment policy and a procedure for dealing with complaints are being formulated. A Committee on the Status of Women, which includes student members, reports to the Coordinator of the Women's Program. The committee takes public stands on issues concerning women students and deals with matters of particular interest to minority women students. A Committee on Minority Affairs addresses concerns of minority women.

Women in Leadership Positions. *Students.* Women have not been prominent in campus-wide leadership positions. In three recent years, period women held three of eight positions: campus newspaper editor for two years; senior class president for two years; and president of the residence-hall council for one year.

Faculty. Eighteen percent of the full-time faculty are women, a figure well below the national average. There are 2 female faculty for every 100 female students, compared with 11 male faculty for every 100 male students.

Administrators. All of the top-level administrators are men. Of 23 academic departments, only business administration is chaired by a woman.

Women and the Curriculum. The most popular majors among women are education (18 percent), fine arts (17 percent), and interdisciplinary studies (14 percent). Four percent of female graduates take degrees in mathematics or physical sciences.

The college offers six courses on women, taught in the departments of business, English, history, political science, and sociology. Courses include Women in Management, Sexual Warfare in Fiction, Women in History and Politics, and Marriage and the Family.

Minority Women. Six percent of undergraduate women are members of minority groups. One full-time faculty member is a black woman. Fifteen minority women are members of an all-minority sorority. Residence-hall advisors are offered awareness-training on sexism. Concerned Black Students is an advocacy organization that serves black women.

Women and Athletics. For college of its size, Wittenberg offers good opportunities for women to participate in organized, competitive sports, particularly in intercollegiate sports. Seven of 15 paid varsity coaches are women. Three of six intramural sports are coeducational and three are for women. The intercollegiate sports are basketball, bowling, field hockey, lacrosse, softball, swimming, tennis, track, and volleyball.

Housing and Student Organizations. Fifty-seven percent of women undergraduates live in single-sex or coeducational dormitories and 21 percent live in sorority houses. Six of the nine directors of residence halls are female; staff are offered awareness-training on sexism, racism, birth control, rape, and alcohol.

Fifty-two percent of women belong to sororities. The Women's Group functions as an advocate for female students.

Special Services and Programs for Women. *Health and Counseling.* The college health service has a male physician and two female and one male health-care providers. The student counseling service has one male counselor. Counseling is available for gynecological problems, birth control, abortion, and rape. Medical treatment for gynecological problems is provided.

Safety and Security. Measures include college and local police, night-time escort service for women, information sessions on campus safety, and a rape crisis center. Two rapes and two assaults on women were reported for 1980–81.

Career. Services include lectures, workshops, and printed information on nontraditional occupations and on job discrimination.

Other. Wittenberg has a Women's Center, with a coordinator who is employed part-time; it serves about 300 women annually. An annual women's week and a women's lecture series are sponsored by the Women's Program. The Project Women organization provides a program on battered women and maintains a telephone service for information, referrals, and support.

Institutional Self-Description. "With a primary commitment to students' intellectual development, Wittenberg also seeks to foster a strong sense of community and to maintain an environment where students can gain self-understanding, fulfill their potentials, accept their limitations, and learn to understand and care about people whose backgrounds and cultures differ from their own."

Wright State University
Dayton, OH 45435
Telephone: (513) 873-2310

9,645 undergraduates

	Amer. Ind.	Asian Amer.	Blacks	Hispanics	Whites
F	8	37	374	40	4,311
M	5	29	281	47	4,431
%	0.1	0.7	6.9	0.9	91.4

 AAUW

Wright State, a public university founded in 1946, enrolls some 13,500 students, of whom 9,645 are undergraduates. Half of the undergraduates are women; 36 percent of these women attend part-time. The median age of all undergraduates is 23, with 31 percent of women students over 25 years and 6 percent over 40.

The university offers bachelor's degrees in a wide range of liberal arts, technical, and pre-professional fields, with some graduate degrees also offered at the main campus in Dayton. Undergraduate and graduate courses in business and education are available at the university's Western Ohio Branch Campus. Graduate and advanced undergraduate courses in business and education are also offered at the Piqua Residence Credit Center. Adult education is available. Alternative scheduling includes evening, weekend, and summer session classes. Off-campus class locations are also available.

Ninety-five percent of students commute to the main campus, accessible by public transportation. The university provides on-campus parking for students, some of which is available at a fee.

Private childcare facilities are located near the campus.

Policies to Ensure Fairness to Women. A full-time Director of Affirmative Action Programs is responsible for policies, practices, and compliance in matters relating to equal-employment opportunity, sex-equity for students, and handicapped-access legislation. A policy prohibiting the sexual harassment of students, faculty, and staff is currently being drafted.

Women in Leadership Positions. *Students.* Women have limited opportunities to gain leadership experience. In three recent years, of the four available campus-wide student posts, a woman served one year as president of the student body.

Faculty. Twenty-four percent of the 438 full-time faculty are women, a proportion just below the natural average. There are 3 female faculty for every 100 female students and 10 male faculty for every 100 male students.

Administrators. With the exception of the chief student life officer, all top administrative positions are held by men. Women head the divisions of modern languages, microbiology and immunology, and nursing. Seven of the 36-member Academic Council are female, as are 2 of the 18 members of an important faculty committee, 1 of 12 regents, and 1 of 11 trustees.

Women and the Curriculum. Most women earn degrees in education (37 percent), health professions (18 percent), business (10 percent), and social science (10 percent). Three percent of women graduate in such nontraditional fields as engineering, mathematics, and physical sciences. Thirteen percent of graduates in the university's small engineering program are women. A program encourages women to prepare for a career in weather broadcasting. Three-fourths of the student interns and 39 percent of students in cooperative education programs are women.

Though Wright State does not have a formal Women's Studies Program, it offers a "selective" in Women's Studies through the College of Liberal Arts and awards a certificate in this field. Courses on women are available through the departments of English, psychology, sociology, history, and geography. They include Sex Roles Studies, Sociology of Women, and History of Women. The university reports that the English department may soon develop a Master's "track" in Women's Literary Studies. The divisions of education and nursing include instruction on some issues specific to women.

Minority Women. Of the 4,789 women undergraduates, 10 percent are minority women, with black women predominant. The seven women on the Academic Council include one black and one Hispanic woman. Twelve percent of the undergraduate women who reside in dormitories are black and 1 percent each are Hispanic and Asian American women.

Women and Athletics. Wright State offers a good intercollegiate and an excellent intramural sports program for an institution of its size, with a wide range of coeducational teams in the intramural program. Twenty-six percent of intramural and 33 percent of intercollegiate athletes are women; women receive 30 percent of athletic scholarships. Two of the nine paid intercollegiate coaches are women. The intercollegiate sports offered are basketball, softball, swimming, tennis, and volleyball.

Housing and Student Organizations. Coeducational dormitories are available for the 4 percent of undergraduates who live on campus. None of the dormitories restrict hours for visitors of the opposite sex. One of the two residence-hall directors is a woman. Awareness-training is available to residence-hall staff on sexism and assertiveness.

Four percent of full-time undergraduate women belong to social sororities. While fraternities on campus provide housing for members, sororities do not.

Special Services and Programs for Women. *Health and Counseling.* Six physicians, 3 of them women, and 4 female health-care providers staff the student health center, which provides gynecological treatment. The counseling center employs 3 men and 1 woman and provides counseling on such matters specific to women as gynecological problems, abortion, and rape and assault.

Safety and Security. Measures consist of campus police with

arrest authority, night-time escort for women students, night-time, campus-wide bus service to residence areas, and a rape crisis center. No rapes or assaults on women were reported for 1980–81.

Career. Workshops, printed materials, and job discrimination information on nontraditional occupations for women are available, along with lectures and panels by women employed in these fields, and programs to establish contacts between alumnae and female students.

Returning Women Students. Wright State's Expanded Horizons for Women program enrolls over 200 returning women students in its courses, approximately 13 percent of whom are minority women, mainly black women. The program offers leadership training and workshops to build confidence in mathematics. It provides support to displaced homemakers, welfare women, and single mothers, as well as to older women.

Institutional Self-Description. None provided.

Youngstown State University
410 Wick Avenue,
Youngstown, OH 44555
Telephone: (216) 742-3000

13,501 undergraduates

	Amer. Ind.	Asian Amer.	Blacks	Hispanics	Whites
F	8	10	758	38	5,347
M	4	7	460	24	6,585
%	0.1	0.1	9.2	0.5	90.0

 AAUW

Youngstown is a state-supported university that offers a comprehensive range of associate, bachelor's and master's degree programs. Of the 15,652 students enrolled, 13,501 are undergraduates. Women constitute 46 percent of the undergraduates; 29 percent of women attend part-time. The median age of undergraduates is 21. Classes meet in the evening and on weekends as well as during the day; some also meet off-campus in the evening. A continuing education program is available. For the 99 percent of students who commute, the university can be reached by public transportation; on-campus parking is provided at a fee.

Private childcare facilities are located near the campus.

Policies to Ensure Fairness to Women. The Equal Opportunity Office employs a Director and Assistant Director, who are responsible full-time for making policy and examining policies and practices concerning educational sex-equity, equal-employment opportunity, and handicapped-access laws. The published code of student rights and responsibilities prohibits sexual harassment; complaints are resolved through a formal campus grievance procedure. A Commission on the Status of Women, reporting to the President, meets at least six times a year.

Women in Leadership Positions. *Students.* Women students have limited opportunities to exercise leadership. In a recent three-year period, women held two of five campus-wide offices: student union board president (one year) and campus newspaper editor (two years).

Faculty. Twenty-four percent of the 421 full-time faculty are women, a proportion slightly below the national average. There

are 2 female faculty for every 100 female students and 6 male faculty for every 100 male students.

Administrators. The chief administrators are men, including all seven deans. Women chair seven of 38 departments: business technology, economics, elementary education, English, foreign languages, home economics, and nursing. One woman sits on the nine-member Board of Trustees; one of ten regents is a woman.

Women and the Curriculum. The most popular majors for women who earn bachelor's degrees are education (33 percent), business (15 percent), and public affairs (9 percent). Five percent of women major in the nontraditional areas of engineering, mathematics, and computer science. Women receive 62 percent of the associate degrees granted. Fifty-five percent of women's two-year degrees are earned in health technologies, 28 percent are in business, and 5 percent each in public service and data processing.

Five departments, including black studies, offer courses on women. Courses include Women in Literature; History of Women in the U.S.; and Women: A Philosophical Study. Faculty are offered workshops on sexism and racism in the curriculum.

Minority Women. Six percent of undergraduate women are members of minority groups. Their concerns are addressed by the Committee on Minority Affairs, the office of Minority Student Services, and two advocacy groups —Black United Students and the NAACP student chapter. All-minority sororities have 45 members. Residence-hall staff are offered awareness-training on racism.

Women and Athletics. The organized athletic program for women is large and varied, through female participation is low for a university of this size. The intramural sports program has a good mix of individual and team sports; one-fifth of the participants are women. Women receive one-fourth of the athletic scholarships, and are one-fourth of intercollegiate athletes. The intercollegiate sports offered are basketball, field hockey, gymnastics, softball, swimming and diving, and volleyball.

Housing and Student Organizations. One percent of the undergraduates, all male, live in dormitories on campus. Coeducational housing is under construction.

About 3 percent of the undergraduate women belong to social sororities, which provide some housing for members. The 30-member Organization for Women's Liberation (OWL) is an advocacy group for all women.

Special Services and Programs for Women. *Health and Counseling.* The student health service offers no services specific to women. The student counseling center employs two women and three men. No information was provided on counseling services specific to women.

Safety and Security. Measures include campus police protection, night-time escort for women, an emergency alarm system, self-defense courses for women, and a rape crisis center. No rapes were reported for 1980–81; ten assaults were reported, five of them against women.

Career. Career Services maintains information on nontraditional occupations and files on alumnae careers for students' use.

Other. The student counseling center offers a mathematics confidence program and assertiveness/leadership training.

Institutional Self-Description. "Women living in northeastern Ohio and the adjacent counties of western Pennsylvania who wish to pursue higher education, whether they matriculate or not, can find quality courses, programs, and services at YSU. Many staff and faculty are genuinely concerned with meeting women's needs."

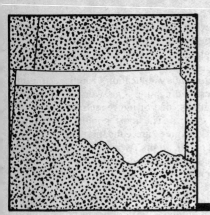

OKLAHOMA

Flaming Rainbow University
419 N. 2nd Street, Stilwell, OK 74960
Telephone: (918) 696-3644

Women in Leadership
★★★ administrators

Enrollment Information Not Available.

Controlled by American Indians, Flaming Rainbow University is a four-year college that serves low-income adult students who live in rural areas. There are extension centers in Tahlequah and Oaks. Eighty-five percent of the students are American Indian, primarily Cherokee. Approximately three-fourths of the students are women. Of the 240 women enrolled, 58 percent are between the ages of 26 and 40; 21 percent are over age 40. The median age of all students is 30.

Flexible scheduling includes evening and off-campus classes, intensive short-term courses, extended semester time frames, and self-paced learning. All students commute. Free parking is provided on campus. There is no public transportation available.

The institution does not have childcare facilities, many students bring their children to classes and to informally supervised play areas.

Policies to Ensure Fairness to Women. The Academic Dean has part-time responsibility for policy relating to equal employment opportunity, sex equity for students, and handicapped accessibility. Complaints of sexual harassment are resolved informally or through a formal grievance procedure. Because most students are minority women, the college does not have a special commission on minority affairs: the needs of minority women are addressed by all councils as an inherent part of college operations.

Women in Leadership Positions. *Students.* There are no student leadership positions.

Faculty. Two of the 19 full-time faculty are women.

Administrators. Eight of the top administrators are women: 4 of them are of traditional tribal identity and 2, although of American Indian descent, have no tribal identity. White women chair two of six departments: science and art. Three of the 9 trustees are women, all American Indians.

Women and the Curriculum. Four of the five degrees awarded by this college in one recent year were earned by women: two in fine arts and one each in psychology and social sciences. Women hold 80 percent of the available internships and practicums. The Dean of Learning Services sponsors a program to build confidence in mathematics. Appropriate departments provide information on services for battered women and displaced homemakers, childcare, job discrimination, and sexual harassment in the workplace.

All third- and fourth-year students are required to take a seminar that examines discrimination against women and minorities. An official committee reports on curricular developments concerning women. Faculty workshops cover the topics of sexism and racism in the curriculum and the needs of reentry women.

Women and Athletics. The college has no intercollegiate sports for women. Fifty women participate in intramural and club sports.

Special Services and Programs for Women. *Health and Counseling.* The college has no student health service; health care is available through Indian Health Services. All three staff members of the student counseling center are women. No counseling specific to women is available.

Safety and Security. Measures consist of local police, high-intensity lighting, and self-defense courses for women. No rapes or assaults on women were reported for 1980–81.

Career. Women students have access to workshops and literature on nontraditional occupations, job discrimination information, and student-alumnae networks.

Other. The Office of Academic Affairs sponsors a program for displaced homemakers.

Institutional Self-Description. "Flaming Rainbow exists to provide educational access and services to nontraditional students—women, American Indians, low-income, rurally isolated, adult, and new to the world of higher education. The college environment and academic process is designed to build upon the strength of the extended family and to enable students to balance family, job, and community responsibilities with a full-time college career."

Northeastern Oklahoma A & M College
Second and I Streets, N.E.
Miami, OK 74354
Telephone: (918) 542-8441

Women in Leadership
★ students
★ faculty
★ administrators

2,376 undergraduates

	Amer. Ind.	Asian Amer.	Blacks	Hispanics	Whites
F	53	3	38	2	911
M	53	3	80	6	1,074
%	4.8	0.3	5.3	0.4	89.3

Established as a school of mining in 1919, Northeastern Oklahoma A & M is a two-year, agricultural and mechanical college that enrolls some 2,700 students, of whom 2,376 are registered in degree programs. Forty-three percent of the undergraduates are women; 16 percent of women attend part-time. The median age of all students is 19.

The first two years of liberal arts and pre-professional programs in a wide variety of fields, as well as numerous terminal programs in business and technical areas are offered. Adult continuing education is available through the Extended Day Program. Evening classes meet both on and off campus. There is a summer session. Free on-campus parking is available to the 60 percent of students who commute.

Private childcare facilities are located near the campus.

Policies to Ensure Fairness to Women. Three administrative officers on part-time assignment are responsible for equal employment opportunity, sex equity for students, and handicapped accessibility. A formal campus grievance procedure handles complaints of sexual harassment. A Committee on Minority Affairs addresses the concerns of minority women.

Women in Leadership Positions. *Students.* Women have good opportunities to gain leadership experience. The posts of student body president, student senate president, editor-in-chief of the campus newspaper, and entering class president were held by women once during three recent years. Women head the two campus honorary societies.

Faculty. Thirty-one percent of the 95 full-time faculty are women, a proportion which is about average for public two-year colleges in this guide. There are 3 female faculty for every 100 female students and 5 male faculty for every 100 male students.

Administrators. Two of the eight top administrators are women: an American Indian woman is chief development officer and a chief business officer. Women chair the departments of nursing and home economics.

Women and the Curriculum. Most of the two-year degrees and certificates awarded to women are in arts and sciences (57 percent), health technologies (16 percent), and business and commerce (17 percent).

The college does not offer courses on women. The department of physical education provides instruction on teaching coeducational classes. The division of mathematics, engineering, and physical sciences offers a program to build skills in mathematics.

Women and Athletics. Women have some opportunities to participate in both intercollegiate and intramural sports. Women constitute 25 percent of intercollegiate and 40 percent of intramural athletes. One-fifth of athletic scholarships go to women. Of eight paid intercollegiate coaches, two are women. The intercollegiate sports offered are basketball, softball, tennis, and track.

Housing and Student Organizations. For the 40 percent of students who reside on campus, housing includes single-sex dormitories that have restrictive hours for visitors of the opposite sex, and accommodations for married students and single parents with children. A married student whose husband is not enrolled is permitted to live in married students' housing. All seven residence-hall directors are women.

Special Services and Programs for Women. *Health and Counseling.* The student health center employs 1 female healthcare provider; the counseling center is staffed by 3 women (1 white and 2 American Indian) and 3 men. No information was provided on health and counseling services specific to women.

Safety and Security. Measures consist of local police, campus police with arrest authority, high-intensity lighting, self-defense courses for women, and information sessions on campus safety and crime prevention. No rapes or assaults on women were reported for 1980–81.

Career. Students have access to workshops and job discrimination information on nontraditional occupations for women.

Institutional Self-Description. "From the woman chairman of the regents to top elective student offices, a positive image of genuine equal opportunity shines. Scholarships, housing facilities, and activities are equal. Achievement is individual, not by stereotypes."

Oscar Rose Junior College

6420 S.E. 15th Street
Midwest City, OK 73110
Telephone: (405) 733-7311

Women in Leadership
★★★ students
★★ faculty

7,626 undergraduates

	Amer. Ind.	Asian Amer.	Blacks	Hispanics	Whites
F	174	53	685	43	2,674
M	126	73	541	81	2,489
%	4.3	1.8	17.7	1.8	74.4

Oscar Rose, a public, two-year college located near Oklahoma City, enrolls some 8,000 students. Just half of the 7,626 undergraduates are women; 59 percent of women attend part-time. The median age of students is 26. Oscar Rose offers the first two years of liberal arts and pre-professional training, and a range of technical and occupational programs. There is also an adult continuing education program. Evening classes are offered on campus, and a summer session is held. The college is accessible by public transportation. On-campus parking is available.

Private childcare can be arranged near the campus.

Policies to Ensure Fairness to Women. The Director of Personnel Services and the Director of Facilities Planning work part-time to develop policy regarding equal-opportunity laws. Complaints of sexual harassment are handled through a formal campus grievance procedure.

Women in Leadership Positions. *Students.* During recent years, women and men have shared equally the two student leadership positions: presiding officer of the student governing body and editor-in-chief of the campus newspaper.

Faculty. The full-time faculty of 146 is 48 percent female, a proportion higher than average for public two-year colleges. There are 5 female faculty to every 100 female students and 4 male faculty to every 100 male students.

Administrators. Of eight chief administrators, the director of institutional research is an American Indian woman. Two of five divisions are chaired by women: business and humanities. Two of seven regents are women. In a recent year, the commencement speaker was a woman.

Women and the Curriculum. Most of the two-year degrees and certificates awarded to women are in the arts and sciences, health technologies, and business and commerce.

The humanities and social science divisions offer three courses on women: Women in Literature, Women in American History, and Sociology of Sex Roles. The departments of business and physical education provide some instruction on matters specific to women. An official committee encourages and reports on curricular developments that include women. Faculty are offered workshops which address the needs of reentry women and the principles of affirmative action and equal opportunity.

Women and Athletics. The intramural program is good; the intercollegiate program is limited. Women receive one-fifth of the athletic scholarships. One of the five paid coaches for varsity sports is a woman. Intercollegiate sports offered are basketball and tennis.

Special Services and Programs for Women. *Health and Counseling.* The student health service is staffed by 2 female health-care providers. The student counseling service has a staff of 10, including 4 white women and 4 minority women. Counseling, but not treatment, is available for gynecological problems, birth control, abortion, and rape and assault. In-service training on avoiding sex-role stereotyping and racial bias is provided for counselors.

Safety and Security. Security measures include campus police with arrest authority, local police, high-intensity lighting, self-defense courses for women, information sessions on campus safety, and a rape crisis center. No information was provided on the incidence of rapes and assaults on women.

Career. Career activities at the college include workshops focused on nontraditional occupations.

Other. The Women's Program Office, with a full-time director, coordinates services to approximately 500 women annually, 20 percent of whom are black women. The most frequent participants are women over age 25. Special services and programs include theater and other women's arts programs, assertiveness/leadership training, and a telephone service for information, referrals, and support.

Institutional Self-Description. None provided.

Southeastern Oklahoma State University
Durant, OK 74701
Telephone: (405) 924-0121

Women in Leadership
★ faculty

3,963 undergraduates

	Amer. Ind.	Asian Amer.	Blacks	Hispanics	Whites
F	142	6	69	7	1,549
M	104	8	89	8	1,606
%	6.9	0.4	4.4	0.4	87.9

Established in 1909 as a school to train teachers, this state-supported college of liberal arts and teacher education attained university status in 1975. Some 4,400 students attend Southeastern, 3,963 of whom are undergraduates. Forty-six percent of the undergraduates are women; 38 percent of the women attend part-time. The median age of all students is 28.

Bachelor's and master's degrees are offered in a range of fields, including liberal arts, sciences, business, education, and preprofessional fields. Evening classes are available both on and off campus. The university also has a summer session. Fifty-four percent of students commute to the campus, which is not accessible by public transportation; free on-campus parking is available.

Policies to Ensure Fairness to Women. *Students.* No information was provided.

Faculty. Twenty-six percent of the 141 full-time faculty are women. There are 3 female faculty for every 100 female students and 7 male faculty for every 100 male students.

Administrators. No information was provided.

Women in Leadership Positions. Information was not provided by the university.

Women and the Curriculum. Most women earn bachelor's degrees in education (68 percent); a few major in business. Six percent of women earn degrees in the nontraditional fields of agriculture, engineering, mathematics, and physical science.

There are no courses on women. The division of physical education offers instruction on how to teach coeducational classes.

Women and Athletics. The institution supplied no information on intramural or club sports. Forty-five women participate in two intercollegiate sports: basketball and volleyball.

Housing and Student Organizations. Single-sex and coeducational dormitories are available for the 33 percent of students who reside on campus; none restrict hours for visitors of the opposite sex. A married student whose husband is not enrolled is

permitted to live in married students' housing. Two women, one a minority woman, are among the five dormitory directors.

Eight percent of undergraduate women join sororities. Ten minority women are members of all-minority sororities.

Special Services and Programs for Women. *Health and Counseling.* The student health service has 1 male health-care provider. It provides general medical treatment but no services specific to women. Two white women and 2 minority women are on the 8-member staff of the student counseling center. No information was provided on counseling services specific to women.

Safety and Security. Measures consist of campus police with arrest authority, local police, and high-intensity lighting. One rape was reported for 1980–81; no information on the incidence of assaults was provided.

Career. Women students have access to updated files of alumnae by specific careers.

Institutional Self-Description. None provided.

University of Oklahoma
660 Parrington Oval, Norman, OK 73019
Telephone: (405) 325-0311

Women in Leadership	★★ **Women and the**
★★ students	Curriculum

★ **Women and Athletics**

15,205 undergraduates

	Amer. Ind.	Asian Amer.	Blacks	Hispanics	Whites
F	212	38	255	43	5,617
M	234	65	267	53	7,705
%	3.1	0.7	3.6	0.7	92.0

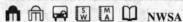 NWSA

Established in 1890 "to provide the means of acquiring a thorough knowledge of the various branches of learning connected with scientific, industrial, and professional pursuits," the University of Oklahoma at Norman now enrolls some 20,700 students in diverse programs of study. The Oklahoma Center for Continuing Education serves the adult student. Alternative class schedules, including self-paced learning contracts, off-campus locations, and a summer session, are available.

Women are 41 percent of the 15,205 undergraduates; 16 percent of women attend part-time. The median age of undergraduates is 20. For the one-fifth of the undergraduates who commute to campus, the university is accessible by public transportation. On-campus parking is available, with free transportation from distant parking lots.

Private arrangements for childcare may be made near the campus.

Policies to Ensure Fairness to Women. A full-time Affirmative Action Officer is responsible for policy on equal employment opportunities, accessibility of curriculum and activities to students, and handicapped access. A written policy on sexual harassment is being developed. Complaints of sexual harassment are handled informally and confidentially. The Committee on the Status of Women, which includes students as voting members, makes recommendations to the Equal Opportunity Committee on issues of concern to women. The Committee on Minority Affairs addresses the concerns of minority women.

Women in Leadership Positions. *Students.* Opportunities for women students to assume campus-wide leadership are well above the average for public research institutions in this guide. In recent years women have been editor-in-chief of the newspaper three times and presided over the student senate, the student union board (two times), and the residence-hall council.

Faculty. Women are 16 percent of a full-time faculty of 753. The ratio of female faculty to female students is 2 to 100; the ratio for males is 8 to 100.

Administrators. The director of institutional research is an American Indian woman. The other higher administrative positions are held by men. Women chair one of 40 departments; seven of 49 other heads of academic units are female.

Women and the Curriculum. A majority of the women who graduate with bachelor's degrees major in education (22 percent), business and management (18 percent), and communications (13 percent). Seven percent major in such nontraditional fields as architecture, engineering, mathematics, and the physical sciences, with the largest number in engineering. The university reports innovative programs to encourage women to prepare for careers in science, engineering, and physics.

The Women's Studies Program offers an 18-credit minor and the master's degree through an individually planned program. Thirty-six courses on women or courses in which the new scholarship on women has been combined with traditional scholarship are available through Women Studies and 15 departments. Offerings include Women in Contemporary Art, Roman Women, Women and Madness, Philosophy and Sex, American Family History, Women and Communication, Sociology of Women, Marxism and Feminism, and European Witchcraft. An official committee promotes the development of courses on women in traditional departments and reports on curricular development. The department of physical education and the School of Social Work offer instruction on some matters specific to women.

Minority Women. Of 6,299 undergraduate women, 4 percent are black, 3 percent American Indian, and less than 1 percent each Asian American and Hispanic. Approximately 110 minority women are in integrated, 60 in predominantly minority, sororities. A minority woman directs a residence hall and one of the professional staff in the counseling center is a minority woman. Residence-hall and counseling staff are offered awareness-training on avoiding racial bias.

Women and Athletics. Intramural and intercollegiate programs offer good opportunities for organized, competitive, individual and team sports. The university reports special facilities for a wide range of recreational and sporting activities. Thirty-nine percent of intramural and 29 percent of intercollegiate athletes are women. Women receive 39 percent of athletic scholarships. Seven of 22 paid varsity coaches are female. Most women's intercollegiate teams played in tournaments in 1980. The intercollegiate sports offered are basketball, golf, gymnastics, softball, swimming and diving, tennis, track and field, and volleyball.

Housing and Student Organizations. One-fifth of the undergraduates live on campus. Single-sex and coeducational dormitories and housing for married students and single parents with children are available. A married woman student whose husband is not enrolled may live in married students' housing. Dormitories have restricted hours for visitors of the opposite sex. Half of the residence-hall directors are female. Residence-hall staff are offered awareness-training on sexism, sex education, racism, and birth control.

Twenty-seven percent of full-time undergraduate women belong to social sororities. Sororities and fraternities provide housing for their members. Among groups which serve as advocates for women on campus are the Women's Studies Student Association, Samothrace, Pre-med Student Association, Women Returning to College, Panhellenic Association, Organization for the Advancement of Women in Law, Women in Architecture, Women in Communications, and Ladies of Exodus.

Special Services and Programs for Women. *Health and Counseling.* The student health service provides some medical attention specific to women, including gynecological and birth control treatment. One-fourth of the physicians are female, as are 84 other health-care providers. Four of 6 professional staff in the counseling service are women. Students have access to gyneco-

logical, birth control, abortion, and rape and assault counseling. Staff are offered in-service training in the avoidance of sex-role stereotyping and racial bias.

Safety and Security. Measures consist of campus and city police, night-time escorts for women students, night-time bus service to residence areas, high-intensity lighting in some areas, emergency telephone and alarm systems, self-defense courses for women, information sessions on safety and crime prevention, and a rape crisis center. A total of 63 assaults (on both men and women), 32 sex offenses, and one rape were reported for 1980–81.

Career. The university provides lectures about women in nontraditional occupations and nonsexist/nonracist printed matter on nontraditional fields of study.

Other. The city of Norman has a Women's Center which campus women may use. Among its activities are services for battered women and rape victims and, in conjunction with the university counseling center, assertiveness training and a telephone line of information, referral, and support. The Women's Studies Program sponsors a lecture series, the Panhellenic Association an annual women's week.

Special Features. A women's bibliography project and a group for women in transition are innovations on campus.

Institutional Self-Description. "The academic atmosphere of the university is serious and forward, with an increasing understanding on the part of students, faculty members, and citizens of the critical role the university will play in the expanding horizon of the state. The social atmosphere is open and friendly, reflecting the southwestern locale of the university."

University of Science and Arts of Oklahoma
17th and Grand, Chickasha, OK 73018
Telephone: (405) 224-3140

Women in Leadership
- ★★ students
- ★★ faculty

920 undergraduates

	Amer. Ind.	Asian Amer.	Blacks	Hispanics	Whites
F	64	6	35	4	386
M	43	8	42	4	244
%	12.8	1.7	9.2	1.0	75.4

 AAUW

Founded in 1908 as a women's college, the University of Science and Arts of Oklahoma became coeducational in 1965 and now enrolls 1,352 students. Of the 920 undergraduates, 515 are women; 31 percent of the women attend part-time. Black and American Indian students represent about a fifth of the enrollment. The median age of undergraduate students is 22.

Alternative scheduling includes off-campus and evening classes, a summer session, and an adult continuing education program. An accelerated three-year degree program is also available in which credit is granted through examination. Free parking near the campus is provided for the 81 percent of undergraduate students who commute.

Private childcare facilities are available near the campus.

Policies to Ensure Fairness to Women. The Vice President of the University Community works part-time as the equal-opportunity officer. The university has a formal grievance procedure to resolve complaints of sexual harassment. Faculty have been offered workshops on affirmative action and equal opportunity.

Women in Leadership Positions. *Students.* Women account for about 54 percent of all full-time undergraduates, and are slightly less than proportionally represented in the student leadership positions on campus. During a recent three-year period, they held all available positions at least once, except president of the student body, and in some years headed both the student union board and the campus newspaper.

Faculty. Women are 35 percent of the full-time faculty, a proportion higher than the national average. There are 5 female faculty for every 100 female students and 12 male faculty for every 100 male students.

Administrators. Women chair 4 of the 9 academic departments (including the combined math-science department). A woman was the speaker at the 1981 commencement, at which women received 5 of 7 alumni awards.

Women and the Curriculum. Forty-one percent of women graduate in education, and 2 percent in nontraditional fields. Most other degrees to women are in home economics, letters, and the social sciences.

Three courses on women are offered through the departments of English, sociology, and psychology: Women in Literature, Sociology of Women, and Psychology of Women.

Women and Athletics. Few women participate in the two intercollegiate sports offered, basketball and tennis. Four intramural sports are offered.

Housing and Student Organizations. Single-sex dormitories are available for the 19 percent of students who live on campus. In the women's dormitories, 40 percent of the residents are black women and 10 percent are members of other minority groups. One of the four residence-hall directors is a woman.

The Afro-American Student Union and the Intertribal Council are student advisory groups.

Special Services and Programs for Women. *Health and Counseling.* The student health service is staffed by one female health-care provider. No information was provided on medical services specific to women. The counseling center, through its staff of three men and one woman, offers counseling on rape and assault, abortion, birth control, and gynecological matters.

Safety and Security. Campus police, with the authority to make arrests, are assisted upon request by local police. There is an emergency alarm system at isolated locations, a rape crisis center, and seminars in rape and assault prevention. No rapes or assaults were reported for 1980–81.

Other. A vocational rehabilitation program is available to the 30 handicapped students on campus, 20 of whom are women.

Institutional Self-Description. "USAO offers degree programs with a strong emphasis in the liberal arts, opportunity for acceleration through its trimester system and credit by examination, and third-trimester tuition-waiver scholarships for Oklahoma students who begin as freshmen and maintain a continuous student status. The small size (1,300 students) provides opportunity for early involvement in university activities, and easy access to professors, who teach freshmen-level as well as senior-level courses."

The University of Tulsa
600 South College, Tulsa, OK 74104
Telephone: (918) 592-6000

4,206 undergraduates

	Amer. Ind.	Asian Amer.	Blacks	Hispanics	Whites
F	31	8	47	7	1,806
M	33	6	84	11	1,819
%	1.7	0.4	3.4	0.5	94.1

 AAUW

Established as a school for the education of American Indian girls and continued as a coeducational college, the University of Tulsa is a private nondenominational institution. Its two campuses enroll some 6,200 students in a range of undergraduate, graduate, and professional studies. The division of continuing education serves the adult student. Evening classes and a summer session are available.

Women are 47 percent of the 4,206 undergraduates; 24 percent of the women attend part-time. The median age of undergraduates is 20. Over three-quarters of the undergraduates live off campus or commute. The university is accessible by public transportation. On-campus parking is available at a fee.

Private arrangements for childcare may be made close to campus.

Policies to Ensure Fairness to Women. An Assistant to the President is assigned part-time to equal employment opportunity and sex equity for students. The campus policy on sexual harassment has been communicated in writing to staff and faculty. The Committee on the Status of Women includes students with voting rights. The Committee on Minority Affairs addresses the concerns of minority women.

Women in Leadership Positions. *Students.* Opportunities for women students to assume campus leadership are below the average for private research universities in this guide. In recent years women have served one term each as presiding officer of the student senate and editor-in-chief of the newspaper. Women head seven of eleven honorary societies.

Faculty. Women are 20 percent of a full-time faculty of 274. One Hispanic, 2 black, and 3 American Indian women are on the full-time faculty, according to recent report. The ratio of female faculty to female students is 4 to 100; the ratio for males is 12 to 100.

Administrators. Men hold all higher positions. Women chair four of 22 departments. The Dean of the College of Nursing is a black woman.

Women and the Curriculum. The majority of women earning bachelor's degrees major in education, the health professions, and business and management. The percentage of women earning degrees in the health professions is above the national average. Five percent of women major in such nontraditional areas as computer science, engineering, mathematics, and the physical sciences.

There are no undergraduate courses on women. Tulsa's Center for the Study of Women's Literature offers a master's degree through the Graduate Faculty of Letters.

Women and Athletics. The intercollegiate program provides opportunities for organized, competitive individual and team sports. Two of the eleven paid intercollegiate coaches are women. The intercollegiate sports offered are basketball, cross-country, golf, swimming and diving, tennis, track and field, and volleyball.

Housing and Student Organizations. Twenty-two percent of the undergraduates live on campus in single-sex and coeducational dormitories that restrict hours for visitors of the opposite sex. One of three residence-hall directors is a woman.

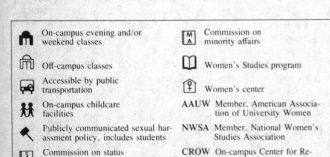

Symbol	Description	Symbol	Description
	On-campus evening and/or weekend classes	M/A	Commission on minority affairs
	Off-campus classes		Women's Studies program
	Accessible by public transportation		Women's center
	On-campus childcare facilities	AAUW	Member, American Association of University Women
	Publicly communicated sexual harassment policy, includes students	NWSA	Member, National Women's Studies Association
S/W	Commission on status of women	CROW	On-campus Center for Research on Women

Twenty-one percent of full-time undergraduate women belong to social sororities, which provide housing for their members.

Special Services and Programs for Women. *Health and Counseling*. The student health service provides some medical attention specific to women, including gynecological and rape and assault treatment. The health service physician is male; three other health-care providers are female. The all-male professional staff in the counseling center are offered in-service training on racial bias. Students have access to gynecological, birth control, and rape and assault counseling.

Safety and Security. Measures consist of campus police who do not have authority to make arrests, night-time escorts for women students, high-intensity lighting, an emergency alarm system, and information sessions on safety and crime prevention. No assaults or rapes were reported for 1980–81.

Institutional Self-Description. "The University of Tulsa has an established policy of equal employment opportunity, of non-discrimination, and of affirmative action. In this respect, the university has made a special effort to hire women who have the qualifications necessary for advancement."

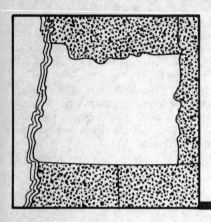

OREGON

Central Oregon Community College
Bend, OR 97701
Telephone: (503) 382-6112

1,699 undergraduates

	Amer. Ind.	Asian Amer.	Blacks	Hispanics	Whites
F	23	4	1	4	904
M	4	0	4	8	744
%	1.6	0.2	0.3	0.7	97.2

Established in 1949, this public two-year college offers comprehensive educational services to 1,867 students, 1,699 of whom are registered in degree programs. Fifty-five percent of the degree students are women, nearly two-thirds of whom attend part-time. Half of the women are 25 and older; 12 percent are older than 40.

The college offers the first two years of liberal arts and preprofessional curricula, and a variety of terminal vocational programs. The Community Education Department offers an adult continuing education program. A summer session, evening classes, and self-paced/contract learning are available. Classes are also held off campus. Approximately 84 percent of the students commute to the campus, which is not accessible by public transportation. Free, on-campus parking is available.

A childcare cooperative for students is operated by Student Services. Private facilities are available near the campus.

Policies to Ensure Fairness to Women. An assistant to the President has part-time responsibility for reviewing compliance with laws on equal employment opportunity, sex equity for students, and handicapped access.

Women in Leadership Positions. *Students.* Opportunities for women to exercise campus-wide leadership are very limited. During three recent years, a woman served once as editor-in-chief of the campus newspaper. All other campus-wide student posts were held by men.

Faculty. The full-time faculty of 67 is 21 percent female. There are 4 female faculty for every 100 female students, compared to 14 male faculty for every 100 male students.

Administrators. Of the nine chief administrators, the head librarian is a woman. No women serve as deans or department chairs. One of the seven college directors is a woman.

Women and the Curriculum. Most of the degrees and certificates awarded to women are in health technologies (44 percent), or arts and sciences (28 percent).

Two courses on women—Women in the Arts and Introduction to Women Writers—are offered by the departments of art and humanities/social science.

Women and Athletics. Women are 46 percent of intercolle-giate and 41 percent of intramural athletes. Club sports are also available. There is one paid female coach. The college provides talent grants for athletes, 40 percent of which go to women. Intercollegiate sports in which women participate are basketball, cross-country, and track and field.

Housing and Student Organizations. Coeducational dormitories, which restrict hours for visitors of the opposite sex, are provided for the 16 percent of students who live on campus. The sole residence hall director is a man.

Special Services and Programs for Women. *Health and Counseling.* The student health service is staffed by one woman health-care provider. There is a student counseling center with one female and two male counselors. Medical treatment and counseling for gynecological matters, birth control, and rape and assault, as well as abortion counseling are available.

Safety and Security. Measures consist of campus police and local police whose jurisdiction includes the campus, and a rape crisis center. No report on the incidence of rapes and assaults was provided by the college.

Career. The college offers workshops, nonsexist/nonracist printed materials, and job discrimination information on nontraditional occupations for women.

Other. A program for displaced homemakers and a women's arts week are sponsored by Student Services. A course on Life Planning for Women is co-sponsored by Student Services and the counseling center. The community education department offers assertiveness/leadership training. The Single Heads of Household Program, a federally supported program in existence since 1979, provides community and campus resources, support classes, workshops, counseling, and career advising to women seeking to return to college.

Institutional Self-Description. None provided.

Lane Community College
4000 E. 30th Avenue
Eugene, OR, 97405
Telephone: (503) 747-4501

Women in Leadership	★ Women and the
★★ students	Curriculum
★★ faculty	

6,984 undergraduates

	Amer. Ind.	Asian Amer.	Blacks	Hispanics	Whites
F	47	31	27	43	3,462
M	56	29	32	34	3,143
%	1.5	0.9	0.9	1.1	95.7

 NWSA

Lane Community College is a public, two-year college that provides comprehensive educational and training opportunities to 6,984 students. Fifty-two percent of the students are women; half attend part-time. The college offers programs in liberal arts and sciences, a wide range of occupational fields, and adult continuing education. Off-campus day and evening classes, a summer session, and self-paced/contract learning are available. All students commute to the campus, which is accessible by public transportation; on-campus parking is free.

Campus facilities accommodate 80 percent of students' requests for childcare. Fees are assessed at a fixed hourly rate.

Women in Leadership Positions. *Students.* Opportunities for women students are excellent. There are three campus-wide student leadership positions: in a recent three year period, women were editor-in-chief of the newspaper for three consecutive years and president of the student body for one year.

Faculty. Women are 43 percent of the 250 full-time faculty, a proportion above the average for public two-year colleges in this guide. There are 6 female faculty for every 100 female students and 7 male faculty for every 100 male students.

Administrators. Men hold the top positions. Women chair two of the 17 departments: home economics and study skills.

Women and the Curriculum. Most women earn degrees in health technologies (27 percent), business and commerce (19 percent), arts and sciences (17 percent), and public service (14 percent). Ten percent of women graduate in the nontraditional fields of mechanical/engineering technologies and data processing.

The Women's Program coordinates several women's educational programs across the college. The Industrial Orientation program offers eight different modules of hands-on experience in such trades as welding, construction, and electronics and machine shop. The Math Renewal Program provides mathematics skill development. Courses on women are available through the department of sociology and other units. Recent titles include American Working Women; Our Bodies, Ourselves; Trends in Women's Studies; and Coping With Stress and Depression. Such issues as sexism and the curriculum, nontraditional occupations, the needs of returning women students, and educational equity are topics of faculty workshops.

Women and Athletics. No information was provided.

Special Services and Programs for Women. *Health and Counseling.* The Student Health Service provides some medical treatment specific to women. There are 3 male physicians employed part-time and 5 female health-care providers. The regular student health insurance covers maternity and abortion at no extra cost. The counseling service, staffed by 8 women and 11 men, offers gynecological, birth control, abortion, and rape and assault counseling.

Safety and Security. Measures include campus police with arrest authority, night-time escorts in emergencies, self-defense courses for women, and a rape crisis center. A total of two assaults (none on women) and no rapes were reported for 1980–81.

Career. The Women's Program offers week-long workshops which give reentry women the opportunity for self- and career assessment.

Other. The Women's Awareness Center, with a budget of $74,600, offers a trained staff to help with information about the college, the community, and issues of concern to women. The center, which serves some 2,500 women annually, includes a resource area, library, and lounge. The Women's Program sponsors a program for displaced homemakers and a series of guest speakers.

Institutional Self-Description. "We have a strong and active Women's Program whose goal is to identify what women students need and see that the college meets those needs. The environment is a supportive one. Programs and people are available to help women reach their academic, career, and personal goals."

Lewis and Clark College
0615 S.W. Palatine Hill Rd.,
Portland, OR 97219
Telephone: (503) 244-6161

Women in Leadership   **★ Women and the Curriculum**
★★ administrators

1,778 undergraduates

	Amer. Ind.	Asian Amer.	Blacks	Hispanics	Whites
F	10	42	8	9	883
M	5	32	7	8	706
%	0.9	4.3	0.9	1.0	92.9

 AAUW

Founded in 1867 by Presbyterian pioneers, Lewis and Clark is an independent, church-related liberal arts institution offering professional training in a variety of fields. There are 3,030 students enrolled, of whom 1,778 are undergraduates. Women are 56 percent of the undergraduates, and 4 percent of the women attend part-time. The median age of all undergraduates is 21. The college offers a continuing education program as well as graduate and professional studies in education, law, music, counseling, public administration, and the training of teachers for the deaf. Alternative schedules consist of on-campus evening classes and a summer session.

The college is located within the metropolitan area of Portland and may be reached by public transportation. Free on-campus parking is provided for the 40 percent of students who commute.

Private childcare facilities are available nearby.

Policies to Ensure Fairness to Women. The Assistant to the President, on a part-time basis, reviews policies and monitors compliance with equal-employment-opportunity, sex-equity, and handicapped-access laws. No written policy on sexual harassment exists; complaints are dealt with informally.

Women in Leadership Positions. *Students.* Women hold few of the seven campus-wide student leadership positions. In recent years they have served one year each as presiding officer of the student court and manager of the campus radio station, and two years as head of the residence-hall council. Women head two of the five honorary societies.

Faculty. Seventeen percent of the 142 full-time faculty are women, a figure considerably below the national average. There are 3 female faculty for every 100 female students and 16 male faculty for every 100 male students.

Administrators. The directors of women's athletics, the library, and institutional research are women; other chief administrators are men. A woman chairs the communications department. Five of 37 trustees are female.

Women and the Curriculum. The most popular major for women is social sciences (18 percent), with fewer numbers in psychology (11 percent), and fine arts (11 percent).

College committees are discussing a Women's Studies Program. Nineteen courses on women are offered in six different departments, and they are coordinated so that a student may design a major in Women's Studies. A required freshman course in Society and Culture reflects feminist scholarship. An official committee collects curricular materials and monitors curricular developments that include material on women. The departments of education and physical education offer instruction on some matters specific to women.

The college has had a federal grant to support a three-week faculty summer workshop on Women's Studies.

Women and Athletics. All but one of the intramural sports in which women participate are coeducational team sports. Women are 35 percent of intercollegiate athletes. Five of the 18 paid varsity coaches and assistant coaches are women. The intercollegiate program for women offers a wide variety of sports, including basketball, cross-country, soccer, softball, swimming, tennis, track and field, and volleyball.

Housing and Student Organizations. Sixty percent of undergraduates live on campus in women's or coeducational dormitories that have no restrictive hours for visitors of the opposite sex. Five of the six residence-hall directors are female, one a minority woman.

Special Services and Programs for Women. *Health and Counseling.* The student health service has a female physician and two female health-care providers. Three of four members of the student counseling staff are women. Counseling is available for gynecological problems, birth control, abortion and rape, and medical treatment for all but abortion. Counselors are offered in-service training in the avoidance of sex-role stereotyping and on sexual preference.

Safety and Security. Measures include campus police with no arrest authority, short courses on self-defense, and a rape crisis center. Two assaults on women and no rapes were reported for 1980–81.

Career. Services include information on nontraditional careers.

Other. A Women's Center with a part-time student coordinator is maintained by the Students' Association. The center sponsors an annual women's week and a women's lecture series. The college provides assertiveness training.

Institutional Self-Description. "Throughout its 114 years the college has been fully coeducational. Faculty and administration share a commitment to a healthy and modern learning environment for women, which is reflected in hiring women faculty, provision of career counseling for women, and transformation of courses to incorporate materials by and about women."

Linfield College
McMinnville, OR 97128
Telephone: (503) 472-4121

1,049 undergraduates

	Amer. Ind.	Asian Amer.	Blacks	Hispanics	Whites
F	3	24	6	5	465
M	6	33	24	5	461
%	0.9	5.5	2.9	1.0	89.7

🏛 👬 🏠 AAUW

Founded in 1849, Linfield College is an independent, liberal arts institution affiliated with the American Baptist Church. The college has 1,101 students, of whom 1,049 are registered in degree programs. Women are 49 percent of degree students, and 22 percent of women attend part-time. An off-campus evening and weekend program is offered, in addition to a summer session and continuing education. Full-time students may elect to alternate 12 months of continuous enrollment with six months of off-campus work. Free on-campus parking is available for the 19 percent of students who commute.

Childcare is available on campus for children of faculty, students, and staff. Private facilities are available off campus.

Women in Leadership Positions. *Students.* No information on campus-wide student leadership positions was supplied.

Faculty. Twenty percent of the 71 full-time faculty are women, a proportion below the national average. There are 3 female faculty for every 100 female students and 11 male faculty for every 100 male students.

Administrators. Men hold all top positions and chair 14 of the 16 departments. Women chair home economics and psychology.

Women and the Curriculum. Most degrees awarded to women are in interdisciplinary studies (36 percent), education (14 per-

cent), and psychology (9 percent). Three percent of the degrees awarded to women are in mathematics or physical sciences. Half of the students in experiential learning programs are women.

The off-campus program offers two courses on women: Sociology of Women and Women in Literature. Courses in the divisions of business, education, and physical education provide some instruction on matters specific to women.

Women and Athletics. No information was provided.

Housing and Student Organizations. Eighty-one percent of the students live on campus in single-sex or coeducational dormitories. On-campus housing is available for married students, with or without children. A married woman student whose husband is not enrolled is permitted to live in married students' housing. Thirteen percent of female dormitory residents are minority women, mostly Asian American and Hawaiian. Dormitory staff are offered awareness-training on racism, birth control, and rape prevention.

One-quarter of full-time undergraduate women belong to sororities; about 20 women are in racially integrated sororities.

Special Services and Programs for Women. *Health and Counseling.* Linfield has no health service. The student counseling center, staffed by one woman, provides counseling on gynecological matters, birth control, abortion, and rape.

Safety and Security. Measures include both campus and local police, courses on campus safety and on self-defense, and a rape crisis center. No rapes or assaults on women were reported for 1980–81.

Career. Information on nontraditional careers, job discrimination, and alumnae networking is available to women students. The Continuing Education Program includes courses on career redirection for women.

Other. A Women's Center is staffed by a part-time salaried student. About 90 reentry women take courses in the Continuing Education and Off-Campus Program.

Institutional Self-Description. "Linfield's off-campus B.A. program, popular with working women, features evening and weekend courses, credit for prior learning, and some independent study. It serves most of Oregon."

Oregon State University
Corvallis, OR 97331
Telephone: (503) 754-0123

★★ Women and the Curriculum

13,691 undergraduates

	Amer. Ind.	Asian Amer.	Blacks	Hispanics	Whites
F	93	166	23	30	5,285
M	149	232	68	48	7,359
%	1.8	3.0	0.7	0.6	94.0

 AAUW

Founded as the State Agricultural College in 1868, Oregon State University now provides a wide range of instruction, research, and public services. Over 16,600 students enroll. The division of continuing education is responsible for programs for the adult student. Evening classes, a summer session, and a limited number of off-campus day and evening classes are available.

Women are 41 percent of the 13,691 undergraduates; 5 percent of women attend part-time. For the majority of the undergraduates who live off campus or commute, OSU is accessible by public transportation. On-campus parking is not available to commuting students.

The university-sponsored childcare facility is two miles from campus. An estimated 40 percent of student requests can be accommodated. Private childcare arrangements may be made close to campus.

Policies to Ensure Fairness to Women. A full-time Affirmative-Action Officer is responsible for policy on equal employment opportunity, accessibility of activities and programs to all students, and handicapped access. A published policy prohibits sexual harassment of students, faculty, and staff. Complaints are handled informally and confidentially or through a formal grievance procedure. The Committee on the Status of Women, which includes students as voting members, addresses the concerns of minority women, as does the Committee on Minority Affairs.

Women in Leadership Positions. *Students.* Opportunities for women students to exercise leadership are average for the public research institutions in this guide. In recent years, women have been president of the student body, presiding officer of the student union board (two times), presiding officer of the residence council, and president of the senior class.

Faculty. Women are 15 percent of a full-time faculty of 708. There are 2 female faculty for every 100 female students and 8 male faculty for every 100 male students.

Administrators. Men hold all key administrative posts, except for a Director of Women's Athletics. Women chair 18 of 151 departments. The Dean of the School of Education, the Dean of Undergraduate Studies, and the Dean of the School of Economics are female. On the Oregon State Board of Higher Education, 3 of 11 members are female, including an Asian American woman.

Women and the Curriculum. Almost half of the women who graduate with bachelor's degrees major in education, home economics, and business and management. Over 13 percent major in such nontraditional areas as agriculture, computer science, engineering, mathematics, and the physical sciences, with the larger numbers in agriculture and engineering. Innovative programs encourage women to prepare for careers in science, engineering, and agriculture. A majority of the positions in cooperative education programs which combine academic with related work experience go to women. Forty percent of the science field-service students are female.

The Women's Studies Program, under a director who holds a full-time faculty appointment, offers a 39-credit certificate (comparable to a major). Twenty-seven courses are available through Women's Studies and such departments as anthropology, business, education, English, history, music, political science, psychology, religion, sociology, and speech. Recent offerings include Writers as Social Critics, Women in Western Music, Women and Law, Psychology of Women, Women Working in America, and Women in Art. An official committee works to augment the Women's Studies Program, collects curricular materials, and promotes the development of courses on women in traditional departments.

Such current issues as mathematics confidence among females, sex-fair curricula, coeducational physical education classes, and discrimination in the workplace are part of the preparation of future teachers and business students.

Minority Women. Minorities constitute 6 percent of the undergraduate women, with Asian American and American Indian women the larger groups. In the residence halls, 4 percent of the women are Asian American, 1 percent black, 1 percent Hispanic, and less than 1 percent American Indian. Twenty women are in integrated, 10 in currently inactive all-minority, sororities. One full-time and 3 part-time staff in the counseling service are minority women. Counseling and residence-hall staff are offered awareness-training on the avoidance of racial bias.

Women and Athletics. The intercollegiate sports program provides some opportunities for organized, competitive sports. Thirty-eight percent of intercollegiate athletes are women; women receive 20 percent of athletic scholarships. Of the 17 paid coaches for women's intercollegiate sports, 6 are women. Five team sports are offered in the intramural program, 78 percent of whose participants are women. Intercollegiate sports are basketball, crew, cross-country, golf, gymnastics, softball, swimming and diving, tennis, track and field, and volleyball.

Housing and Student Organizations. Forty-two percent of the undergraduates live on campus. Single-sex and coeducational dormitories, cooperative housing, and housing for married students and single parents with children are available. A married woman student whose spouse is not enrolled may live in married students' housing. Residence halls place some restrictions on hours for visitors of the opposite sex. Nine of 13 residence-hall directors are female. Awareness-training in sexism, sex education, racism, and birth control, among other issues, is offered the residence-hall staff.

Twenty percent of the full-time undergraduate women belong to social sororities which provide housing for their members. Students for the Advancement of Women and the Campus Task Force of the National Organization of Women serve as advocates for women on campus.

Special Services and Programs for Women. *Health and Counseling.* The student health service provides some medical attention specific to women including gynecological and birth control treatment. Two of 9 physicians are female, as are 43 other health-care providers. One of 4 practitioners in the Mental Health Clinic is a woman. Half of the full-time professional staff in the counseling center are female. Students have access to gynecological, birth control, abortion, and rape and assault counseling. Assertiveness training is available.

Safety and Security. Measures include campus police with arrest authority, night-time escorts for women students, emergency alarm and telephone systems, self-defense courses for women, information sessions on campus safety and crime prevention, and a rape crisis center. Six assaults (five on women) and no rapes were reported for 1980–81.

Career. The university sponsors lectures by women employed in nontraditional occupations and nonsexist/nonracist printed information on nontraditional careers and fields of study.

Other. Undergraduate Studies administers a small Women's Center, staffed by a part-time graduate student who is an Asian American. Among center activities are women's art shows and a telephone line of information, referral, and support. The Women's Studies Program sponsors an annual women's symposium. A program to build confidence in mathematics is sponsored by the Math Learning Center.

Institutional Self-Description. "Opportunity to prepare for professional careers in nontraditional fields; to assume leadership and participate in campus governance; to find numerous living options; and to pursue advanced degrees are among the attractive features of the campus."

Portland Community College
12000 SW 49th Avenue,
Portland, OR 97219
Telephone: (503) 244-6111

Women in Leadership	★ Women and the
★ students	Curriculum
★★ faculty	

17,266 undergraduates

	Amer. Ind.	Asian Amer.	Blacks	Hispanics	Whites
F	113	242	190	173	7,614
M	112	241	190	172	7,580
%	1.4	2.9	2.3	2.1	91.4

Portland Community College has been offering two-year programs of comprehensive educational services since 1961. A public institution, Portland enrolls 17,266 students, half of whom are women. Seventy percent of women attend part-time. The median age of all students is 31.

Portland Community has a college transfer program and offers career education courses in a wide variety of occupational areas. The college also offers an adult continuing education program. Operating out of six educational centers and various locations throughout the community, the college offers day and evening classes both on and off campus, a weekend college, a summer session, and independent study programs. Portland is accessible by public transportation; on-campus parking is available.

College-run childcare facilities, charging fees on a sliding scale, can meet 75 percent of all students' requests. Private childcare facilities are located near the campus.

Policies to Ensure Fairness to Women. The Director of Human Resources serves as a full-time equal opportunity officer responsible for review of policies and practices related to equal-employment-opportunity, sex-equity-for-students, and handicapped-access legislation. Sexual harassment of students, faculty, and staff is prohibited by a written campus policy that has been publicly communicated to all three groups; complaints are resolved through a formal campus grievance procedure.

Women in Leadership Positions. *Students.* Opportunities for women to exercise leadership on campus are good. In a recent three-year period, women served one-year terms as president of the student body, editor-in-chief of the newspaper, and manager of the campus radio station.

Faculty. The full-time faculty of 325 is 38 percent female, a proportion which is above average for public two-year colleges in this guide. There are 5 female faculty for every 100 female students and 6 male faculty for every 100 male students.

Administrators. Eight of nine top-level administrators are men; the Director of Institutional Research is a woman. Women chair five of the 18 departments: language arts, developmental education, nursing, health records, and home economics. Three of the seven trustees are women.

Women and the Curriculum. Most of the two-year degrees and certificates awarded to women are in health technologies (47 percent), arts and sciences (18 percent), business and commerce (17 percent), and public service (10 percent). Seven percent of women graduate in such nontraditional fields as mechanical arts/engineering and natural science.

The Women's Studies Program, under the direction of a part-time administrator, offers seven courses in conjunction with the social science division. Recent Women's Studies courses include Women in Transition; Women of Color in the U.S.; Women in Psychology, Sociology, and Literature; and Female Sexuality. Seven courses on women are also available through the departments of history, phsyical education, anthropology, psychology, and English. Faculty workshops offer training on the needs of reentry women and affirmative action and equal opportunity.

Women and Athletics. For a college of its size, Portland Community offers women good opportunities to participate in organized competitive sports, with wide array of intramural team and individual sports. Forty percent of participants in intercollegiate and intramural sports are female. One of the five paid intercollegiate coaches is a woman. Tournament competition is available for intercollegiate sports, which include bowling, fencing, swimming, and volleyball.

Special Services and Programs for Women. *Health and Counseling.* The student health service is staffed by one physician and one health-care provider, both women. No treatment for problems specific to women is provided. The student counseling center does not provide counseling on matters specific to women.

Safety and Security. Measures consist of campus police, city police, night-time escort service for women (on request), night-time campus-wide bus service, high-intensity lighting in all areas, campus-wide emergency phone system, emergency alarm, at isolated locations, self-defense courses for women, information sessions on campus safety and rape and assault prevention, and a community-based rape crisis center. In 1980–81, 1 rape and 22 assaults (12 physical and 10 verbal) were reported on campus. Of the physical assaults, 6 involved women.

Career. Materials and activities available on campus include workshops and job discrimination information focused on nontraditional occupations, lectures for students by women employed in these fields, and printed information on nontraditional fields of study for women

Other. Student Support Services offers a displaced homemakers' program, assertiveness leadership training, and a program to build confidence in mathematics.

Institutional Self-Description. None provided.

Portland State University
Box 751, Portland OR 97207
Telephone: (503) 229-4422

★★ **Women and the Curriculum**

9,552 undergraduates

	Amer. Ind.	Asian Amer.	Blacks	Hispanics	Whites
F	44	175	133	57	4,020
M	54	215	120	47	4,296
%	1.1	4.3	2.8	1.1	90.8

🏠 🏛 🚌 👫 ⚓ 📖 ⚷ AAUW NWSA

Established in 1946 as Vanport Extension Center, and a university in the Oregon State system since 1969, Portland State University is located in an urban area equidistant from the Pacific Ocean and the Cascades. Some 16,000 students enroll in undergraduate and graduate programs. There is a division of continuing education. Alternative schedules, including evening classes and a summer session, and off-campus locations are available.

Women are 47 percent of the 9,552 undergraduates; one-third of the women attend part-time. The median age of all undergraduates is 24. For the majority of students who commute, the university is accessible by public transportation. There is a fee for parking on campus.

The Helen Gordon Center accommodates half of students' requests for childcare. The fee is $5.75 per day. Private arrangements may be made close to campus.

Policies to Ensure Fairness to Women. Representatives of the Affirmative Action Office, which is responsible for equal employment opportunity, sex equity for students, and access for the handicapped, vote on policymaking committees. A written policy prohibits sexual harassment; complaints are handled through a formal grievance procedure.

Women in Leadership Positions. *Students.* Women hold few campus-wide leadership positions. In recent years, women have been student body president, presiding officer of the student senate, and head of the student union board.

Faculty. Women are 17 percent of a full-time faculty of 491, low for four year institutions in this guide. Thirteen percent of the women hold permanent positions. One full-time faculty member is a black woman. The ratio of female faculty to female students is 3 to 100; for males, the ratio is 12 to 100.

Administrators. The Vice-President for Student Affairs is a Hispanic woman; all other administrative posts are held by men. Women chair three of 46 academic units: Public Health, Middle East Studies Center, and Special Programs.

Women and the Curriculum. Half of the women graduate with degrees in education (18 percent), business (17 percent), and social sciences (15 percent), with significant numbers in interdisciplinary studies, psychology, and arts and humanities. Four percent receive degrees in engineering, physical sciences, and mathematics. Experiential learning options are available in a number of majors.

The Women's Studies Program, one of the oldest in the country, awards a 42-credit certificate, comparable to a major. Over 30 courses are available annually through Women's Studies and the departments of sociology, psychology, economics, history, English, health and physical education, business, and social work. Recent titles include Sociology of Women, Psychology of Women, Women in the U.S. Economy, Women in Early Modern Europe, Women in Nontraditional Literature, 19th-Century British Women Writers, Personal Defense, and Women in Management. Such current issues as sex-fair curricula and coeducational physical education classes are part of the preparation of future teachers. Information on women in the workforce is given in business courses.

Women and Athletics. Thirty-four percent of intercollegiate, 33 percent of intramural, and 43 percent of club athletes are female. Intramurals include a variety of individual and team sports, among them the decathlon and water polo. Of eleven paid coaches, four are women. Women receive 30 percent of the athletic scholarships. Intercollegiate sports offered are basketball, fencing, gymnastics, softball, swimming, tennis, and volleyball.

Housing and Student Organizations. University housing is operated by the nonprofit Portland Student Services for the 5 percent of students who live on campus. Sleeping rooms and apartments are available; married students and single parents with children may live in student housing.

One percent of the undergraduates belong to social sororities and fraternities, which provide housing for their members. The Women's Union, Students for Lesbian and Gay Rights, the Black Cultural Affairs Board, United Indian Students in Higher Education, and the Hispanic Student Union are active groups on campus.

Special Services and Programs for Women. *Health and Counseling.* The Student Health Service provides medical attention specific to women, including gynecological, birth control, abortion, and rape and assault treatment. Two of 6 physicians are female, as are 5 other health-care providers. The counseling service, staffed by 4 women and 4 men, offers counseling of particular concern to women. Staff receive in-service training on avoiding sex-role stereotyping and racial bias. Assertiveness-training is available.

Safety and Security. Campus police have weapons training but no arrest authority. Safety provisions include occasional nighttime escorts for women, bus service to residence areas, high-intensity lighting, emergency telephones, self-defense courses, information on campus safety and crime prevention, and a rape crisis center. Seven assaults on women were reported for 1980–81.

Career. Workshops focused on nontraditional careers, panels, nonsexist/nonracist printed information on nontraditional fields of study, and files on alumnae organized by specific careers are available.

Other. The small student-run Women's Union sponsors an annual women's week and guest speakers. The Women's Studies Program and the Women's Union work closely with community women's groups and provide support for cultural and educational events.

Returning Women Students. The Office of Educational Activities, with assistance from Women's Studies, holds an annual orientation for returning women students. The Women's Studies Program offers a 3-credit course designed to acquaint reentry women with the university.

Institutional Self-Description. "As an urban university aware of diverse student needs, Portland State provides a flexible learning environment particularly attractive to part-time and older women. A variety of classes is offered in the late afternoon and evening, allowing women students with family responsibilities and jobs to attend classes at convenient times. Furthermore, the Women's Studies Program and the Women's Union encourage such activites as brown-bag lunches and ongoing support groups for returning women."

University of Oregon
Eugene, OR 97403
Telephone: (503) 686-3036

| Women in Leadership | ★ Women and the |
| ★ students | Curriculum |

★ Women and Athletics

11,488 undergraduates

	Amer. Ind.	Asian Amer.	Blacks	Hispanics	Whites
F	47	171	47	38	5,110
M	53	169	88	67	5,385
%	0.9	3.0	1.2	0.9	93.9

 AAUW NWSA

Established in the 1870s, the University of Oregon in Eugene provides some 16,600 students with a range of undergraduate, graduate, and professional studies. Continuing education and lifelong learning programs are offered for the adult student. Alternative class schedules include a weekend college, evening classes, and a summer session. Off-campus class locations are available.

Women are 48 percent of the 11,488 undergraduates; 10 percent of the women attend part-time. The median age of all students is 24. For the 65 percent of undergraduates who live off campus or commute, the university is accessible by public transportation and bicycle. On-campus parking is available at a fee.

University childcare facilities accommodate virtually all students' requests. Private arrangements for childcare may be made close to campus.

Policies to Ensure Fairness to Women. A full-time Affirmative Action Officer is responsible for policy and reviews practices related to equal employment opportunity, sex equity for students, and handicapped accessibility. A published policy prohibits sexual harassment. Complaints are handled both informally and confidentially and through a formal grievance procedure. The Committee on the Status of Women, which includes students as voting members, proposes policy, takes public stands on issues of concern to students, and sponsors women's and university-wide events. The Council for Minority Education addresses the concerns of minority women.

Women in Leadership Positions. *Students.* Opportunities for women to assume campus leadership positions are above the average for public research universities in this guide. In recent years women have presided over the student senate, the student court, the student union board (two times), and the residence-hall council, and been editor-in-chief of the campus newspaper. Women head seven of 17 honorary societies.

Faculty. Women are 19 percent of a full-time faculty of 690. According to a recent report, 5 black, 1 American Indian, 8 Asian American, and 6 Hispanic women are on the full-time faculty. The ratio of female faculty to female students is 3 to 100; the ratio for male faculty to male students is 10 to 100.

Administrators. Men occupy all key positions. Women chair seven of 48 departments: art education, art history, dance, linguistics, Romance languages, recreation and park management, and gerontology. The Dean of Health, Physical Education and Recreation is female.

Women and the Curriculum. A majority of the women who graduate with bachelor's degrees major in education, the social sciences, public affairs, and business and management. Seven percent major in such nontraditional areas as architecture, computer science, mathematics, and the physical sciences. The proportion of women in architecture is above the national average. A four-year-old support and information program encourages women to consider careers in science.

The Women's Studies Program, under a director who holds a full-time faculty position, offers a 21-credit certificate. Recent course offerings include Men and Women: Love and Violence (sociology); Perspectives on Third World Women (ethnic studies); Minorities and Health-Care Issues (health education); and Women in U.S. History (history). An official committee provides guidance to the Women's Studies Program and promotes and monitors the teaching of women's courses across the curriculum.

Mathematics confidence among females, sex-fair classroom materials, and the teaching of coeducational physical education classes are issues covered in the preparation of teachers. The School of Business provides instruction on discrimination faced by women in the workplace.

Minority Women. Of 5,413 undergraduate women, 3 percent are Asian American and less than 1 percent each American Indian, black, and Hispanic. A minority woman is on the staff of the counseling service. The Black Student Union, the Asian American Student Union, the Chinese Student Union, MECHA, and the Native American Student Union meet on campus. Additional support for minority women may be found through the Minority Women's Alliance and Racial Justice Committee of the university YWCA chapter. Twenty-one minority women belong to racially integrated sororities.

Women and Athletics. Intramural and intercollegiate programs provide good opportunities for organized, competitive, individual and team sports. Club sports are also available. Twenty percent of the intramural and 35 percent of the intercollegiate athletes are women; women receive 20 percent of athletic scholarships. There are 17 paid coaches for women's teams. The intercollegiate sports offered are basketball, cross-country, golf, gymnastics, soccer, softball, swimming and diving, tennis, track and field, and volleyball.

Housing and Student Organizations. Thirty-five percent of the undergraduates live on campus. Residential accommodations include single-sex and coeducational dormitories and housing for married students and single parents with children. A married woman student whose spouse is not enrolled may live in married students' housing. Residence halls restrict hours for visitors of the opposite sex. Two of three residence-hall directors are female. Awareness-training on sex education and rape prevention is offered residence-hall staff.

Fifteen percent of the full-time undergraduate women belong to social sororities. Sororities and fraternities provide housing for their members. Among groups on campus which serve as advocates for women are Women in Communication, Women in Science, Women in Transition, Women's Law Forum, and Gay Students Alliance.

Special Services and Programs for Women. *Health and Counseling.* The student health service provides some medical attention specific to women, including gynecological, birth control, and rape and assault treatment. Twenty-four-hour emergency infirmary service is available. One of 16 physicians on call is female, as are the 30 nurses. Fourteen of 23 professional staff in the counseling service are women. Students have access to gynecological, birth control, abortion, rape and assault, and 24-hour emergency counseling. Staff are offered in-service training on avoidance of sex-role stereotyping.

Safety and Security. Campus police do not have arrest authority, but city police jurisdiction includes the university. Night-time escorts for women students on request, emergency alarm and telephone systems, self-defense courses for women, information sessions on safety and crime prevention, a rape crisis and assistance program, nightly dormitory patrols, and active neighborhood associations are available. Nine assaults (three on women) and two rapes were reported for 1980-81.

Career. Workshops, role model lectures, and printed information on women in nontraditional occupations and fields of study are available to students.

Other. Various student groups sponsor such activities as an annual women's week and assertiveness training. Women in Science sponsors a lecture series and the College of Education a program to build confidence in mathematics. Services for battered women and a telephone line of information, referral, and support are provided by women's community organizations. The department of gerontology has a program for displaced homemakers. The Physically Handicapped Union of Students meets on campus.

Special Features. Among special features of the university are the Center for the Sociological Study of Women; various professional associations of women, including Women in Administration; and the Northwest Women in Educational Administration program, funded by the Ford Foundation.

Institutional Self-Description. ''Commitment to academic and intellectual freedom in a stimulating and supportive environment; many excellent academic programs; attractive campus and locale; high level of campus and community awareness of women's issues; active women's committees and groups; and strong affirmative action involvement in employment and education characterize the university.''

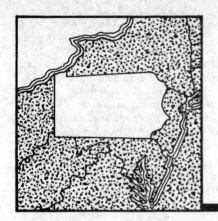

Albright College
13th and Exeter Streets
Reading, PA 19603
Telephone: (215) 921-2381

Women in Leadership
★ faculty

1,267 undergraduates

	Amer. Ind.	Asian Amer.	Blacks	Hispanics	Whites
F	0	5	4	0	644
M	0	10	7	2	581
%	0.0	1.2	0.9	0.2	97.8

 AAUW

Founded in 1856, Albright College is a liberal arts institution affiliated with the United Methodist Church. Total enrollment is 1,614, of whom 1,267 are undergraduates. Fifty-two percent of undergraduates are women, virtually all of whom attend full time. Three percent of women undergraduates are between ages 25 and 40.

In addition to arts and sciences, the college offers programs in home economics, medical technology, and nursing. For the 33 percent of students who commute, the college is accessible by public transportation. There is no parking on campus.

A private childcare center is located on campus.

Policies to Ensure Fairness to Women. Two administrators review policies and practices related to equal employment opportunity, educational sex equity, and handicapped access. The Committee on the Status of Women, which reports to the Dean of Students, includes students as voting members.

Women in Leadership Positions. *Students.* Women have limited opportunities to exercise campus-wide student leadership. In a recent three-year period, women presided over the student union board twice, the campus newspaper once, and the residence-hall council twice. Women head all three campus honorary societies.

Faculty. A third of the full-time faculty are women, a proportion well above the national average. There are 5 female faculty for every 100 female students and 9 male faculty for every 100 male students.

Administrators. Of the nine top administrative officers, the head librarian is a woman. Women chair six of the 21 departments, including English, home economics, modern languages, nursing, and psychology. Seven of 40 trustees are women; one is a black woman.

Women and the Curriculum. Most degrees awarded to women are in biology (16 percent), health professions (16 percent), home economics (13 percent), business (9 percent), and the social sciences (9 percent). Four percent of women graduate in mathematics and physical sciences. There are no courses on women.

Women and Athletics. Intercollegiate and intramural programs offer both individual and team sports. Thirty-eight percent of the intramural and 40 percent of the intercollegiate athletes are women; women are nine of the 24 paid varsity coaches. Intercollegiate sports for women include badminton, basketball, field hockey, softball, tennis, track and field, and volleyball.

Housing and Student Organizations. Two-thirds of the undergraduates live on campus in single-sex or coeducational dormitories, or in fraternity or sorority houses. Half the residence-hall directors are women.

Special Services and Programs for Women. *Health and Counseling.* The student health service has a staff of 1 male physician and 3 female health-care providers. No information was provided on health services specific to women. The student counseling staff consists of 1 man and 1 woman. Counseling is available for gynecological problems, birth control, abortion, and rape and assault.

Safety and Security. Measures include campus police with authority to make arrests, night escort service for women, high-intensity lighting, and information on campus safety and security. No rapes or assaults on women were reported for 1980–81.

Career. Services include contacts between alumnae and female students. A women's week is sponsored annually by the Dean of Students and assertiveness training is offered by the student counseling center.

Institutional Self-Description. None provided.

Allegheny College
North Main Street, Meadville, PA 16335
Telephone: (814) 724-3100

★ **Women and the
Curriculum**

★ **Women and Athletics**

1,854 undergraduates

	Amer. Ind.	Asian Amer.	Blacks	Hispanics	Whites
F	2	2	30	2	833
M	1	5	25	4	948
%	0.2	0.4	3.0	0.3	96.2

 AAUW

Founded in 1815 to provide a liberal arts education for men, Allegheny College is affiliated with the United Methodist Church. The college has been coeducational since 1870; 47 percent of the undergraduates are women. It has a total enrollment of 1,887 students, of whom 1,854 are registered in degree programs. The median age of all students is 20.

Allegheny offers bachelor's programs in liberal arts and pre-professional areas. A summer session is available. Twenty-seven percent of students commute. The campus is not accessible by public transportation; free on-campus parking is provided.

Private childcare facilities are available nearby.

Policies to Ensure Fairness to Women. On a part-time basis, two administrators monitor compliance with equal-employment-opportunity and sex-equity laws. A written, publicly communicated policy prohibits sexual harassment of students; complaints are handled through a formal grievance procedure. A Commission on the Status of Women deals primarily with the concerns of female faculty but also takes public stands on issues of concern to students.

Women in Leadership Positions. *Students.* Opportunities for women students to exercise leadership are limited. During three recent years, women presided over the student senate once and served twice as president of the student union and editor-in-chief of the campus newspaper. One of the five honorary societies is headed by a woman.

Faculty. Women are 19 percent of the full-time faculty, a proportion below the national average. Of the 24 full-time faculty women, 5 are black and 1 is Asian American. There are 3 female faculty for every 100 female students and 11 male faculty for every 100 male students.

Administrators. Of the eight top administrative officers, the head librarian is a woman. Of 21 departments, physics is chaired by a woman. Eight of the 43 trustees are women. Four of the 12 alumni awards given in a recent year went to women.

Women and the Curriculum. Humanities and the social sciences account for over half the degrees conferred on women. Fourteen percent of women major in biology and 8 percent major in mathematics and physical sciences. The mathematics department offers a course to help women gain skills in mathematics. The college reports programs to encourage women to prepare for careers in science and engineering.

A new Women's Studies Program will offer an undergraduate minor beginning in the fall of 1982. Courses on women are offered through the departments of art, English, history, philosophy, political science, psychology, and sociology. Independent study in Women's Studies is available through departments. Course titles include Contemporary American Literature By and About Women, Ida Tarbell and Her World, Sexism and Racism, Women and Violence, and Women and Society.

Women and Athletics. Allegheny has a full and varied intramural and intercollegiate sports program for women. Almost a quarter of the 410 intercollegiate athletes and four of the seven paid coaches are women. Intercollegiate sports for women include basketball, cross-country, softball, swimming, tennis, track and field, and volleyball.

Housing and Student Organizations. Seventy-three percent of the students live on campus in single-sex or coeducational dormitories, or in fraternity houses. Seven percent of the female dormitory residents are minority women. Five of the eight dormitory directors are women. Dormitory staff are offered awareness-training on birth control, loneliness, and alcohol abuse.

Twenty-one percent of full-time undergraduates women belong to sororities. The local chapter of NOW meets on the campus. The Association of Black Collegians is an advocacy group.

Special Services and Programs for Women. *Health and Counseling.* The student health service, staffed by a male physician and four female health-care providers, offers no services specific to women. The student counseling center, staffed by one male and one female counselor, provides assertiveness training, as well as counseling for gynecological problems, birth control, abortion, and rape and assault.

Safety and Security. Measures consist of campus police with arrest authority, high-intensity lighting, self-defense information, and a rape crisis center. Four assaults on women and no rapes were reported for 1980–81.

Career. Services include programs and information about non-traditional occupations, job discrimination, and alumnae networking. A career library has a special section on women's issues.

Special Features. The library contains the collected papers and personal library of author and muckraker IDa M. Tarbell.

Institutional Self-Description. "Compact, personal campus; located in small city; large degree of curricular flexibility, i.e., independent study, study-abroad, individualized majors; noted as pre-professional school (medical, education, dental, law, business, engineering); highly personal career and academic advising; emphasis on unity of undergraduate experience; extensive extra-curricular opportunities; diverse and capable student body."

Allegheny Community College, South Campus

1750 Clairton Road, Rt. 885
West Mifflin, PA 15122
Telephone: (412) 469-1100

Women in Leadership
★ students
★★ faculty
★★★ administrators

3,205 undergraduates

	Amer. Ind.	Asian Amer.	Blacks	Hispanics	Whites
F	3	5	91	2	1,883
M	3	2	47	5	1,214
%	0.2	0.2	4.3	0.2	95.0

One of four campuses of the Community College of Allegheny County, this commuter college provides the first two years of a college transfer program, as well as vocational, career, technical, and community programs. Of 3,205 students, 60 percent are women; 60 percent of women attend part-time. The median age of all students is 27. Public transportation and free on-campus parking are available.

Childcare facilities are available both on and off campus.

Policies to Ensure Fairness to Women. A formal policy prohibits sexual harassment of students, faculty, and staff, but has not been publicly communicated to students. Complaints are resolved through a formal grievance procedure. The Affirmative Action Officer is responsible part-time for implementation of laws concerning equal employment, sex equity, and handicapped access.

Women in Leadership Positions. *Students.* In a recent three-year period, women twice presided over the student government and the student union.

Faculty. Women are 46 percent of the 79 full-time faculty. There are 4 female faculty for every 100 female students and 9 male faculty for every 100 male students.

Administrators. South Campus is one of three public community colleges in this guide headed by a woman. Women in other top leadership positions include the acting chief business officer, the chief development officer, and the head librarian. The chairs of mathematics and nursing are women. Women also direct the Learning Assistance Center and the Allied Health Program.

Women and the Curriculum. Of degrees awarded to women, 35 percent are in health fields, 34 percent in business programs, 20 percent in arts and sciences, and 3 percent in mechanical and engineering technologies.

Two courses on women are offered in behavioral sciences: History of Women and Psychology of Women.

Women and Athletics. Women participate in intramural billiards, coeducational softball, table tennis, and volleyball. One of the six paid varsity coaches is a woman. Women compete on the intercollegiate softball and tennis teams.

Special Services and Programs for Women. *Health and Counseling.* The health service, staffed by a consulting, male physician and a female health-care provider, provides no medical treatment specific to women. The counseling center provides counseling on birth control, gynecology, abortion, and rape and assault.

Safety and Security. Measures consist of local and campus police, high-intensity lighting, self-defense courses, sessions on rape and assault prevention, and a rape crisis center. Information was not provided on the incidence of rapes and assaults.

Other. The Women's Center houses a Women's Studies library and sponsors a lecture series, theater and arts program, and an information and referral clearinghouse. Community Services offers assertiveness training and a program for battered women. The Learning Assistance Center offers mathematics confidence workshops. The Society For Reentry students meets on campus.

Institutional Self-Description. ''The support, dedication, and friendliness of the total staff, the high quality of education available at a low cost, the availability of convenient locations and convenient class-time schedules, the availability of learning-support centers and developmental classes, all lend themselves to assisting women with successful, rewarding experiences.''

Bryn Mawr College
Bryn Mawr, PA 19010
Telephone: (215) 645-5000

Women in Leadership   ★ **Women and the Curriculum**
  ★★★ **students**
  ★★ **faculty**
  ★★★ **administrators**

957 undergraduates

	Amer. Ind.	Asian Amer.	Blacks	Hispanics	Whites
F	0	21	39	16	829
M	0	0	0	0	0
%	0.0	2.3	4.3	1.8	91.6

🚍 [S/W] [M/A] AAUW

Some 1,600 students are enrolled in this private, non-sectarian women's college, founded by Quakers in 1885. As the first college for women to grant bachelor's, master's and Ph.D. degrees, Bryn Mawr has long been a leader in the advancement of higher education for women. Located in a Philadelphia suburb, the college maintains close academic and social ties with a former men's college, Haverford, now coeducational. Much of the student housing and many of the extra-curricular activities and classes are coeducational. Swarthmore College and the University of Pennsylvania also have cooperative programs with Bryn Mawr.

The college offers undergraduate and graduate degrees in a variety of fields. The Office of Special Academic Programs is responsible for adult continuing education. Both the continuing education and graduate degree programs admit men. Almost all of the 957 undergraduates attend full-time; their median age is 20. Eighty-six percent of undergraduates live on campus in women's or coeducational dormitories that have no restrictions on visiting hours for members of the opposite sex. Commuters can reach the campus by public transportation. On-campus parking is available.

An affiliated childcare center, located off campus, can accommodate 25 children, 10 percent of students' requests. Fees are based on the child's age and length of stay.

Policies to Ensure Fairness to Women. The Equal Opportunity Officer has part-time responsibility for policy pertaining to sex equity and handicapped access for students. Complaints of sexual harassment are handled through a formal campus grievance procedure, and students, faculty, and staff have been notified of

this in writing. A Commission on the Status of Women, appointed by the President, recommends programs and policies. A Commission on Minority Affairs addresses the concerns of minority women.

Women in Leadership Positions. *Students.* Women hold all student leadership positions.

Faculty. Forty-three percent of the 138 full-time faculty are women, a proportion slightly below average for women's colleges but higher than for most other colleges in this guide. There are 6 female faculty for every 100 female students.

Administrators. Five of the seven top administrators are women, including the chief executive officer, chief business officer, and development officer. The Deans of the Undergraduate College and the Graduate School of Arts and Sciences are women. Nine of 26 departments are chaired by women: archeology, English, French, Greek, growth and structure of cities, history of art, music, Spanish, and education. More than half of the Board of Trustees are women.

Women and the Curriculum. Forty percent of the women earn bachelor's degrees in the social sciences, and another 40 percent in the arts and humanities. Eleven percent specialize in such non-traditional fields as physical sciences or mathematics. Bryn Mawr offers programs which encourage women to prepare for careers in science and engineering, as well as a program, sponsored by the mathematics department, to help women strengthen their mathematics skills.

Nine courses on women, including Women in the Middle Ages; Women Writing in America; and Sex, Culture and Society, are offered through the departments of anthropology, English, French, history, sociology, and interdepartmental studies. In addition, four graduate courses focus on women and are open to qualified undergraduates. Seventeen other courses pay substantial attention to women and sex roles, including an education course that examines sexism in textbooks. An official committee works to expand the number of offerings on women and to develop and collect new curricula on Women's Studies.

Women and Athletics. For a college of its size, Bryn Mawr offers good opportunities for students to participate in team and individual intercollegiate athletics. There are five paid, female varsity coaches, and some 230 athletes who compete in eight intercollegiate sports: badminton, basketball, field hockey, gymnastics, lacrosse, swimming, tennis, and volleyball.

Special Services and Programs for Women. *Health and Counseling.* The student health center's staff is exclusively female and includes 1 physician and 3 health-care providers. Four of 5 counselors at the student counseling center are women. Medical treatment is available for birth control and gynecological problems; the counseling center provides birth control, abortion, and rape and assault counseling.

Safety and Security. Measures consist of campus police protection, night-time escort, night-time bus service to residence areas, high-intensity lighting, an emergency alarm system, and instruction on self-defense and campus safety. No rapes or assaults on women were reported for 1980–81.

Career. The Career Planning Office organizes leadership training sessions, workshops on balancing the demands of professional and private life, panels and career workshops on nontraditional occupations, and programs to foster networking between alumnae and students. It also maintains files on the careers of alumnae.

Other. The Women's Alliance, an advocacy group, sponsors, among other activities, a women's lecture series. The Office of Special Academic Programs has a reentry program for men and women.

Institutional Self-Description. ''A women's college for its near 100-year history, Bryn Mawr College had the first student government in the country. Students participate in management throughout the college, providing a power base for women. Half the faculty is female, as is most of the administration. Bryn Mawr has a long history of support for women.''

Bucks County Community College
Newtown, PA 18940
Telephone: (215) 968-8182

Women in Leadership
★★ faculty

8,177 undergaduates

	Amer. Ind.	Asian Amer.	Blacks	Hispanics	Whites
F	3	2	23	10	4,496
M	4	6	18	9	3,606
%	0.1	0.1	0.5	0.2	99.1

Bucks County Community College, a public, two-year college located near Philadelphia, offers educational services to 8,177 students, 56 percent of whom are women; 63 percent of women attend part-time. The median age of all students is 29.

The college offers transfer and career programs in the liberal arts and pre-professions and in a variety of occupational areas. Continuing Education for Mature Students (CEMS), the college's continuing education for women program, serves approximately 1,000 reentry women. Alternative scheduling includes evening classes held both on and off campus, a summer session, self-paced/contract learning, and contract classes with business and industry. All students commute; the campus is not accessible by public transportation, but free on-campus parking is available.

College-operated childcare facilities can accommodate 60 percent of all students' requests for service. Services are available from 7:30 a.m. to 5:30 p.m., at a fixed hourly rate. Additional private childcare facilities are located near the campus.

Policies to Ensure Fairness to Women. A written campus policy prohibiting sexual harassment of students, faculty, and staff, has been communicated to faculty and staff only. Complaints of sexual harassment are resolved through a formal campus grievance procedure.

Women in Leadership Positions. *Students.* Information provided on student leadership was incomplete. The college reports that in recent years women served once as president of the student body, twice as editor-in-chief of the campus newspaper, and three times as manager of the campus radio station. The one campus honorary society is headed by a woman.

Faculty. Of the 186 full-time faculty, 35 percent are women. There are 4 female faculty for every 100 female students and 7 male faculty for every 100 male students.

Administrators. All 7 chief administrators are male. The department of nursing is among 12 chaired by a woman.

Women and the Curriculum. Most of the degrees and certificates awarded to women are in the arts and sciences and in business and commerce. Fifty-three percent of students in cooperative education programs and 60 percent of student interns are women.

The department of sociology offers one course on women: Women in Contemporary Society. Faculty workshops are available on nontraditional occupations for women and men, the needs of reentry women, and affirmative action and equal opportunity.

Women and Athletics. Forty-four percent of participants in both intramural and intercollegiate sports are women, as are three of the six paid intercollegiate coaches. Intercollegiate sports offered are basketball, cross-country, field hockey, golf, softball, and tennis.

Special Services and Programs for Women. *Health and Counseling.* The limited health services are provided by one female nurse. The student counseling center has a staff of seven, four of whom are women. No health care specific to women is available. The regular student health insurance policy covers abortion at no extra charge.

Safety and Security. Measures consist of campus police without arrest authority, high-intensity lighting, campus-wide emergency telephone system, information sessions on campus safety and rape and assault prevention, and a rape crisis center. During 1980–81, two assaults on women were reported on campus.

Career. The college provides workshops, lectures, printed materials, and job discrimination information on nontraditional occupations for women. It also encourages networking between alumnae and female students.

Other. The Human Rights Club sponsors an annual women's week. Under the direction of a full-time female administrator, and with a budget of $85,000, CEMS sponsors a displaced homemakers' program, assertiveness and leadership training, a program to build confidence in mathematics, and a telephone service for information, referrals, and support. The Gay Rights Club meets on campus.

Institutional Self-Description. None provided.

Carlow College
3333 Fifth Avenue, Pittsburgh, PA 15213
Telephone: (412) 578-6000

Women in Leadership   ★ **Women and the**
★★★ students   **Curriculum**
★★★ faculty
★★★ administrators

792 undergraduates

	Amer. Ind.	Asian Amer.	Blacks	Hispanics	Whites
F	2	10	93	6	659
M	0	0	2	0	20
%	0.3	1.3	12.0	0.8	85.7

AAUW

Established in 1929, Carlow, formerly Mount Mercy College, is a Roman Catholic women's college. The campus is located near downtown Pittsburgh. Of the 921 students enrolled, 792 are undergraduates (3 percent are men). Fourteen percent of the undergraduate women attend part-time. The median age of students is 21.

The college offers undergraduate degrees in a range of fields. A weekend college program and continuing education courses are available. Juniors and seniors can cross-register at five other Pittsburgh-area colleges. Forty-three percent of the women live on-campus in dormitories that restrict male visitors' hours. Commuters can reach the college by public transportation; on-campus parking is available for a fee.

A campus childcare facility, accommodating all requests by students, charges a daily fee of $5. Carlow also operates an elementary school.

Policies to Ensure Fairness to Women. An equal-opportunity officer has part-time responsibility for examining policies and practices pertaining to equal-employment-opportunity, sex-equity, and handicapped-access laws.

Women in Leadership Positions. *Students.* Women hold all student leadership positions.

Faculty. Sixty-three percent of the 41 full-time faculty are women, a proportion above average for similar colleges in this guide. There are 4 female faculty for every 100 female students.

Administrators. Most of the top administrators are women, including the President, chief academic officer, and chief student-life officer. Women chair 20 of the 21 academic and non-academic departments. More than half of the Board of Trustees are female. In a recent year, all 16 alumni awards went to women; 23 speakers in campus-wide lectures series were women.

Women and the Curriculum. The most popular fields among women graduates are health professions (20 percent), psychology

(19 percent), social sciences (13 percent), and business (12 percent).

A Women's Studies Program grants a 15-credit certificate and offers such courses as Women and Work, Images of Women in Children's Literature, and Women in Nazi Germany.

Minority Women. Fourteen percent of the students are members of minority groups, mainly black. The Office of Minority Affairs is headed by a full-time director. One department head is a black woman, as is a counselor; 1 trustee is a black woman. In recent years, 4 black women were among the 23 female campus speakers. Faculty and residence-hall staff are offered workshops on racism.

United Black Students organizes an annual Black Week. Twelve percent of those enrolled in Continuing Education for Women are minority women, most of them black women.

Women and Athletics. The limited organized sports program provides three intramural sports, predominantly team activities, attracting 210 women, in addition to a sports club and two intercollegiate teams. Two of the five paid varsity coaches are women. The intercollegiate sports are basketball and volleyball.

Special Services and Programs for Women. *Health and Counseling.* The student health center is staffed by 1 male physician and 9 health-care providers, 5 of whom are female. The 4 professionals at the student counseling service are women. Gynecological and rape and assault counseling and treatment as well as abortion and birth control counseling are available.

Safety and Security. Measures include campus police with arrest authority, night-time escorts for women, high-intensity lighting, an emergency telephone system, instruction on self-defense and campus safety, an emergency medical services unit, and a rape crisis center. One rape and five assaults on women were reported for 1980–81.

Career. Among the career placement services available are panels on nontraditional occupations, career workshops, and files on alumnae careers.

Other. The Continuing Education for Women Program and Women's Studies sponsor a well-attended women's lecture series in which nationally known women participate, and workshops on the Emerging Woman Poet, which attract eminent female poets. The Dean of Students' office organizes leadership training sessions.

Returning Women Students. The Continuing Education for Women Program, under a full-time female director, has its own center and attracts more than 100 returning women to its credit courses. The center and the Continuing Education Liaison Committee provide support for older women and displaced homemakers; they also offer assertiveness-training workshops.

Institutional Self-Description. "Carlow College is seriously committed to the education of women of all ages. Academically, Carlow recognizes a Women's Studies department which challenges within the curriculum the cultural stereotypes of women, while simultaneously reinforcing the value of women's history and artistic expression. The Center for Continuing Education and weekend college are also visible testimonies to Carlow's commitment to women."

Carnegie-Mellon University
Pittsburgh, PA 15213
Telephone: (412) 578-2000

Women in Leadership	★ Women and the
★★★ students	Curriculum

3,987 undergraduates

	Amer. Ind.	Asian Amer.	Blacks	Hispanics	Whites
F	4	22	81	3	1,119
M	8	34	117	14	2,525
%	0.3	1.4	5.0	0.4	92.8

 AAUW

Established with the merger of Carnegie Institute of Technology and the Mellon Institute for Research, Carnegie-Mellon University, a private nondenominational institution located in Pittsburgh, now provides a variety of undergraduate, graduate, and professional programs for some 5,550 students. A limited number of evening classes and a summer session are available.

Women are 31 percent of the 3,987 undergraduates; 3 percent of the women attend part-time. The estimated median age of undergraduates is 20. For the one-fifth of the undergraduates who commute, the campus is accessible by public transportation. On-campus parking is available for a fee.

University-sponsored childcare facilities accommodate 85 children—100 percent of requests by students. Private childcare arrangements may be made nearby.

Policies to Ensure Fairness to Women. One full-time and three part-time equal-opportunity officers recommend and/or monitor policy on employment, sex equity, and handicapped access. A policy on sexual harassment, now being developed, will be communicated to students. Complaints are handled through a formal grievance procedure. A voluntary Committee on the Status of Women includes students as voting members and advises the President on issues of concern to women. The Committee on Minority Affairs addresses the concerns of minority women.

Women in Leadership Positions. *Students.* Opportunities for women to assume campus-wide leadership are outstanding. In recent years, women have twice presided over the student senate, twice been editor-in-chief of the newspaper, and once presided over the residence-hall council.

Faculty. Women constitute 14 percent of a full-time faculty of 412. According to recent report, 1 American Indian, 2 Asian American, 1 black, and 2 Hispanic women are on the full-time faculty. The ratio of female faculty to female students is 5 to 100; of male faculty to male students, 13 to 100.

Administrators. Men fill all higher administrative positions and head all academic units.

Women and the Curriculum. Over 40 percent of undergraduate degrees awarded to women are in the fine arts. Thirty-two percent are in nontraditional fields, a proportion which makes Carnegie-Mellon exceptional. The proportion of degrees to women in engineering (21 percent) is above the national average. Women constitute 35 percent of the students in cooperative education programs that combine academic with related work experience. The university reports innovative programs to encourage women to prepare for careers in science, engineering, and computer science, as well as the Women in Science and Engineering program for high school students.

There are no courses on women.

Minority Women. Nine percent of the undergraduate women are members of minority groups; more than half are black women. Awareness-training on the avoidance of racial bias is offered residence-hall and counseling staffs.

Women and Athletics. Forty percent of intramural and 23 percent of intercollegiate athletes are women. Of 19 paid coaches

---

🏠	On-campus evening and/or weekend classes	[M A]	Commission on minority affairs
🏫	Off-campus classes	📖	Women's Studies program
🚌	Accessible by public transportation	🏠	Women's center
👫	On-campus childcare facilities	AAUW	Member, American Association of University Women
✎	Publicly communicated sexual harassment policy, includes students	NWSA	Member, National Women's Studies Association
[S W]	Commission on status of women	CROW	On-campus Center for Research on Women

for intercollegiate sports, five are female. The institution did not provide information on intramural and intercollegiate sports.

Housing and Student Organizations. Eighty percent of the undergraduates live on campus in single-sex and coeducational dormitories. Residence halls do not restrict visiting hours for members of the opposite sex. One of the three residence-hall directors is female. Staff are offered awareness-training on sexism, sex education, racism, and birth control.

Seventeen percent of undergraduate women belong to social sororities, which provide housing for their members. The Society of Women Engineers serves as an advocacy group for women, including minority women.

Special Services and Programs for Women. *Health and Counseling.* The student health service provides some medical attention specific to women, including gynecological and birth control treatment, and abortion and rape and assault treatment by referral. The regular student health insurance covers abortion and maternity at no extra charge. Of three physicians in the health service, one is female, as are two other health-care providers. Half of the professional staff in the counseling service are female. Gynecological and birth control counseling are available. Staff are offered in-service training on the avoidance of sex-role stereotyping and racial bias.

Safety and Security. Measures include campus and city police, night-time escorts for female and male students, night-time bus service to residence areas, high-intensity lighting, emergency alarm and telephone systems, self-defense courses for women, information sessions on safety and crime prevention, and a rape crisis center. No rapes were reported for 1980-81. Information on assaults was not provided.

Career. Career workshops, role model lectures, and printed information which concentrate on women in nontraditional careers, as well as a program of contacts between alumnae and students, are available.

Institutional Self-Description. "Always coeducational, CMU is a campus 'sex blind' in every sense except social."

Cedar Crest College
Allentown, PA 18104
Telephone: (215) 437-4471
Women in Leadership
  ★★★ students
  ★★ faculty
  ★★ administrators
797 undergraduates

	Amer. Ind.	Asian Amer.	Blacks	Hispanics	Whites
F	1	3	20	9	747
M	0	0	0	0	12
%	0.1	0.4	2.5	1.1	95.8

🏠 🚌 👫 ⛺ AAUW

Established in 1867, Cedar Crest is a non-sectarian college for women that is affiliated with the United Church of Christ. Its campus attracts 931 students. One percent of the 797 undergraduates are men; 16 percent of the undergraduates attend part-time. The median age of all students is 25.

The college offers a variety of liberal arts and professional degrees, as well as a weekend college, independent study and a summer session. Students can cross-register at any of the other Lehigh Valley Colleges: Lehigh, Lafayette, Moravian, Muhlenberg, and Allentown College of St. Francis de Sales. The Center for Continuing Education is responsible for adult education. Classes meet both day and evening. For the 41 percent of undergraduates who commute, public transportation and on-campus parking are available.

A campus childcare center, which gives priority to students'

requests, accommodates 15 children at a fee of $1.25 per hour. Additional, private childcare facilities are available near the campus.

Policies to Ensure Fairness to Women. The Director of Operations has the part-time responsibility for policy regarding equal-employment-opportunity, sex-equity-for-students, and handicapped-accessibility laws. Complaints of sexual harassment are resolved through a formal campus grievance procedure.

Women in Leadership Positions. *Students.* Women hold all student leadership positions.

Faculty. Forty-seven percent of the 51 full-time faculty are women, a proportion close to the average for women's colleges in this guide. There are 4 female faculty for every 100 female students.

Administrators. Women hold 3 of 7 important administrative posts: chief student-life officer, head librarian, and director of athletics; the president and chief academic officer are men. Women chair 4 of 19 departments, including drama, biology, management studies, and physical education. Over a third of the Board of Trustees are female.

Women and the Curriculum. About one-third of bachelor's degrees awarded to women are in the health professions; 6 percent are in such nontraditional fields as mathematics and physical sciences. The college encourages women to prepare for engineering careers. There are no courses on women.

Women and Athletics. No information was provided on intramural and club sports. The intercollegiate program offers a modest variety of individual and team sports. Five of the six paid varsity coaches are women. Intercollegiate sports offered are badminton, basketball, field hockey, lacrosse, tennis, and volleyball.

Housing and Student Organizations. Fifty-nine percent of the women students live on campus in dormitories that, with one exception, have restrictions on men's visiting hours. Residence-hall staff are offered awareness-training on sex education, birth control and sexism.

Two advocacy groups meet on campus: the Women's Concerns Forum and the Afro-American Society.

Special Services and Programs for Women. *Health and Counseling.* The student health center's all-female staff consists of two physicians and four health-care providers. The college employs one male counselor. Counseling and medical treatment are provided for gynecological problems, birth control, abortion, and rape and assault. Student health insurance covers maternity expenses.

Safety and Security. Measures include campus and local police with arrest authority, night-time escorts for women, and instruction on self-defense and campus safety. No rapes or assaults on women were reported for 1980–81.

Career. Cedar Crest offers career workshops, lectures, and information on nontraditional occupations; maintains files on alumnae careers for students' use; and promotes networking between alumnae and students.

Other. A full-time director is in charge of the large Women's Center, which is run by the Center for Continuing Education. One thousand women, predominantly community women and older undergraduates, use its services, such as a program for displaced homemakers, assertiveness training sessions, and a mathematics confidence clinic.

Returning Women Students. PORTAL, the Program of Return to Advanced Learning, runs a Continuing Education for Women Program for 254 reentry women. An additional 170 women attend other adult continuing education programs.

Institutional Self-Description. "Cedar Crest understands the changing and complex life patterns of women, encourages them to pursue the academic and occupational goals of their choice, and provides innumerable leadership roles in a supportive environment. Through teaching and counseling women only, the college instills a sense of self-identity and self-reliance which has won battles for them in a male dominated world."

Chatham College
Woodland Rd, Pittsburgh, PA 15232
Telephone: (412) 441-8200

Women in Leadership
★★★ students
★★ faculty
★★★ administrators

★ **Women and the Curriculum**

529 undergraduates

	Amer. Ind.	Asian Amer.	Blacks	Hispanics	Whites
F	0	1	80	0	443
M	0	0	0	0	0
%	0.0	0.2	15.3	0.0	84.5

🏠 🚐 👫 **AAUW NWSA**

An independent, non-sectarian, liberal arts college for women, Chatham was founded in 1869. The campus enrolls 684 students; virtually all of the 529 undergraduates attend full-time. Chatham offers the bachelor's degree in a variety of liberal arts and pre-professional fields, and students may cross-register at nine other institutions in the Pittsburgh area. Evening and summer session classes are available. The Gateway Program is responsible for adult continuing education. Public transportation and free parking on campus are available to the 20 percent of students who commute.

A campus childcare facility accommodates 20 children—15 percent of student's requests. Additional, private childcare facilities are available near the campus.

Policies to Ensure Fairness to Women. The Treasurer and Business Manager is responsible for policy regarding equal employment opportunity, sex equity, and handicapped accessibility.

Women in Leadership Positions. *Students.* Women hold all campus leadership positions.

Faculty. Forty-three percent of the 51 full-time faculty are women, a proportion somewhat below average for women's colleges in this guide, but much higher than the national average. There are 4 female faculty for every 100 female students.

Administrators. Women hold 5 of 7 major administrative posts, including those of President, chief development officer, and chief student-life officer. Women chair 6 of 18 departments: art, education, physical education, political science, administration/management, and communications. One-half of the 26 trustees are female.

Women and the Curriculum. Approximately one-fourth of Chatham's graduates major in social sciences and about 12 percent each in fine arts, letters, business, and communications. Less than 4 percent specialize in such nontraditional fields as mathematics and physical sciences. Chatham offers programs designed to encourage women to prepare for careers in science, management, and computer science. The mathematics department and Community Services sponsor a clinic to build confidence in mathematics.

Twelve courses on women are available through black studies, history, modern languages, philosophy, political science, and sociology/anthropology. Recent offerings include Sex Discrimination and the Law, Philosophy and Feminism, and Images of Women in French Literature. Students may major in Women's Studies through an individualized degree program. An official committee is responsible for developing additional courses on women and for reporting on the inclusion of women in the curriculum.

Minority Women. Minority women constitute 15 percent of the student body. The chief student-life officer is a black woman. The Black Student Union is a student advocacy group. Black Studies offers two courses on women: Black Women in American

Society, and Female Writers of the African Diaspora. Two minority women serve as residence-hall directors. Fourteen percent of the students in the Continuing Education for Women Program are minority women, mostly black women.

Women and Athletics. The organized sports program, good for a college of this size, offers women five intercollegiate teams and ten individual and team intramural activities. Special facilities for intramural sports include two lighted platform-tennis courts, a weightlifting room, and a dance studio. Two of five paid coaches in varsity sports are women. Intercollegiate sports offered are basketball, field hockey, softball, tennis, and volleyball.

Housing and Student Organizations. Seventy-nine percent of students live on campus in dormitories that have restrictive hours for male visitors. The Chatham Feminists and the Student Council of Executive and Professional Women are advocates for women, as is the Black Student Union.

Special Services and Programs for Women. *Health and Counseling.* The student health center is staffed by two female physicians and one female health-care provider. The student counseling center employs one female counselor. Counseling for gynecological problems, birth control, abortion, and rape and assaults is available, as is treatment for gynecological disorders.

Safety and Security. Measures consist of campus police, nighttime escort, emergency alarm system, and instruction on self-defense and campus safety. No rapes or assaults on women were reported for 1980–81.

Career. Lectures and information on nontraditional occupations are available, along with student internships in a variety of work settings, and programs to foster networking between alumnae and students.

Institutional Self-Description. "In recent years, Chatham College has restated its commitment to the education and advancement of women as its primary mission. All of the college's academic and special programs, its counseling and advising systems, and its career preparation programs reflect special appreciation for the status of women and for their opportunities in a changing society. The college's commitment to women is realized within a diversified liberal arts curriculum and enhanced by internships and career-planning programs."

Chestnut Hill College
Germantown and Northwestern Avenues
Philadelphia, PA 19118
Telephone: (215) 248-7000

Women in Leadership
★★★ students
★★★ faculty
★★★ administrators

729 undergraduates

	Amer. Ind.	Asian Amer.	Blacks	Hispanics	Whites
F	0	0	39	42	631
M	0	0	0	0	6
%	0.0	0.0	5.4	5.9	88.7

🏠 🚐 👫 **AAUW**

Chestnut Hill, founded in 1871, is a Roman Catholic liberal arts college for women. Of the 888 students enrolled, 729 are undergraduates; virtually all attend full-time. The median age of undergraduates is 31. Chestnut Hill offers undergraduate degrees in a variety of fields, a limited graduate program, and a large adult education program. Students can cross-register at La Salle College. Classes meet day and evening, as well as during the summer.

Seventy percent of the undergraduate women live on campus in dormitories that prohibit male visitors. The campus is accessible by public transportation; on-campus parking is available for a fee.

A college childcare center accommodates all students' requests, serving 12 children at a time at a fee of $1 per hour. Private childcare facilities are available nearby.

Policies to Ensure Fairness to Women. The Academic Dean, who has part-time responsibility for reviewing policy and practices pertaining to sex-equity, equal-employment-opportunity and handicapped-access laws, is a voting member of policymaking councils. The chair of the Health Committee supervises compliance with handicapped-accessibility requirements. Complaints of sexual harassment are handled informally and confidentially.

Women in Leadership Positions. *Students.* Women hold all student leadership positions.

Faculty. Ten of the nineteen faculty are women. There are 2 female faculty for every 100 female students.

Administrators. Women hold every major administrative position, including the offices of President, Academic Dean, and Dean of the Graduate Division. Women chair all but two of the 18 departments, including physics, mathematics, and chemistry. Women are the majority on the Board of Trustees.

Women and the Curriculum. The most popular fields for women graduates are education (32 percent), social sciences (16 percent), and psychology (13 percent). Eight percent of women pursue such nontraditional fields as mathematics and the physical sciences. Special programs encourage women to prepare for careers in science and in management.

The history and English departments offer two courses on women: Women's History and Women Writers. The education department introduces prospective teachers to nonsexist classroom materials.

Women and Athletics. For a college of its size, Chestnut Hill has a good intercollegiate program, though it offers only one intramural activity. The seven paid varsity coaches are women. Intercollegiate sports offered are badminton, basketball, field hockey, lacrosse, softball, tennis, and volleyball.

Special Services and Programs for Women. *Health and Counseling.* The student health center employs four female healthcare providers. All but one of the five professionals at the student counseling services are women. Pro-life and gynecological counseling are available.

Safety and Security. Measures include campus and local police protection, high-intensity lighting, an emergency alarm system, and instruction on campus safety. No rapes or assaults on women were reported for 1980–81.

Career. The college informs students about opportunities in nontraditional occupations, fosters networking with alumnae, and maintains files on alumnae by careers.

Returning Women Students. The continuing education division, under a female full-time director, enrolls 189 women; 12 percent of the women are members of minority groups, mainly black women. Continuing Education also provides assertiveness

training and a telephone information and referral service especially for older women, including displaced homemakers.

Institutional Self-Description. ''Chestnut Hill College was founded by women as a college for women. It takes women seriously, respecting their academic excellence and the special sensitivities that characterize them. Never needing to prove herself, a woman is free to accept challenges, develop talents, and become the uniquely special person she was born to be.''

Cheyney State College
Cheyney, PA 19319
Telephone: (215) 758-2296

Women in Leadership
★★ faculty

2,378 undergraduates

	Amer. Ind.	Asian Amer.	Blacks	Hispanics	Whites
F	10	2	1,177	4	27
M	9	4	1,090	5	50
%	0.8	0.3	95.3	0.4	3.2

 AAUW

Founded as an agricultural college in 1837, Cheyney State is the oldest historically black college in the United States. The college remains predominantly black, with a total enrollment of 2,637 students, of whom 2,378 are undergraduates. Women constitute 51 percent of the undergraduates; 12 percent of the women attend part-time. The median age of undergraduates is 22.

The college offers bachelor's degrees in liberal arts, sciences, engineering, and education; master's degree programs are also available. The division of adult continuing education sponsors a Continuing Education for Women Program. Alternative scheduling includes day and evening classes held both on and off campus, a summer session, weekend classes, and self-paced/contract learning.

The campus is accessible by public transportation. Free on-campus parking is available for the 42 percent of students who commute.

The college-operated childcare center accommodates 20 children, and can meet virtually all students' requests for this service. Additional, private childcare facilities are available close to campus.

Policies to Ensure Fairness to Women. An affirmative action officer on part-time assignment is responsible for policy on sex equity for students and equal employment opportunity. Complaints of sexual harassment are handled informally and confidentially.

Women in Leadership Positions. *Students.* In a recent three-year period, all campus-wide offices were held by men. Three honorary societies are headed by women.

Faculty. Thirty-eight percent of the 181 full-time faculty are women, a proportion significantly above the national average. There are 6 female faculty for every 100 female-students and 11 male faculty for every 100 male students.

Administrators. Men hold all top positions. One Asian American woman and 4 black women chair 5 of 14 departments: English, life science, educational administration and foundations, education, and home economics. Three of 9 trustees are black women. Two of the 5 members of the faculty senate are white women.

Women and the Curriculum. Most women major in education (40 percent), social sciences (16 percent), and business (16 percent). Less than 1 percent major in the nontraditional field of physical sciences. One-half of the undergraduates in cooperative education and 35 percent of student interns are women.

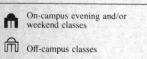

No courses on women are offered.

Women and Athletics. Cheyney State offers a generous athletic program for women, for a college of its size. Twenty-seven percent of the intramural athletes and one-fourth of the intercollegiate athletes are women, as are five of 20 paid coaches. Intercollegiate sports offered are badminton, basketball, cross-country, soccer, tennis, track, and volleyball.

Housing and Student Organizations. Fifty-eight percent of undergraduates live on campus in single-sex dormitories that restrict hours for visitors of the opposite sex. Residence-hall staff are offered awareness training on sex education and birth control.

About 3 percent of women join social sororities. Sororities and fraternities do not provide housing for their members.

Special Services and Programs for Women. *Health and Counseling.* The student health service employs 1 male physician and six female health-care providers. The college has a student counseling center. Gynecological and birth control counseling and treatment are provided, in addition to abortion counseling.

Safety and Security. Measures consist of campus police protection. Information on the incidence of rapes and assaults was not reported by the college.

Institutional Self-Description. "To provide for its undergraduates, in addition to the foundation of liberal arts, a number of career-oriented degree programs which prepare students for employment in business, industry, public administration, and the professions. To develop in students a sense of belonging, creative potential, personal worth, and social responsibility."

Dickinson College
Carlisle, PA 17013
Telephone: (717) 243-5121

1,660 undergraduates

	Amer. Ind.	Asian Amer.	Blacks	Hispanics	Whites
F	1	2	18	12	812
M	0	5	13	6	785
%	0.1	0.4	1.9	1.1	96.6

AAUW

Dickinson College, founded as a classical academy in 1773, is a private, four-year liberal arts institution that enrolls 1,727 students. Of the 1,660 students enrolled in degree programs, 51 percent are women; less than 1 percent of women attend part-time. The median age of all students is 19.

The college offers bachelor's degrees in liberal arts and sciences, education, and professional fields. The continuing education division offers courses for the adult student. Off-campus study programs are available. There are some evening classes and a summer session. The campus is not accessible by public transportation. Free on-campus parking is provided for the 10 percent of students who commute.

Private childcare facilities are available near the campus.

Policies to Ensure Fairness to Women. The Director of Personnel is responsible for monitoring compliance with equal-employment-opportunity, sex-equity-for-students, and handicapped-access legislation. The Affirmative Action Officer reviews policy. A published policy prohibits sexual harassment; complaints are resolved informally and confidentially or through a formal grievance procedure.

A Commission on the Status of Women, appointed by the President, which includes students as voting members, prepares an annual report. The Committee on Minority Affairs addresses the concerns of minority women.

Women in Leadership Positions. *Students.* Women have some opportunities to exercise campus-wide leadership. In a recent three-year period, women served one-year terms as president of the student body, president of the student senate, manager of the campus radio station, and senior class president. The college estimates that seven of the 14 honorary societies are headed by women.

Faculty. Eighteen percent of the 113 full-time faculty are women, a proportion below the national average. Recent data show that an Asian American and an Hispanic woman are on the female faculty. There are 2 female faculty for every 100 female students and 12 male faculty for every 100 male students.

Administrators. The head librarian is the only woman among the 8 top administrators. Women chair 5 of the 25 academic departments: anthropology, American studies, English, French, and fine arts. Three of the 48 trustees are women; 1 of 3 recent honorary degree recipients was a woman, as was 1 of 3 recent recipients of alumni awards.

Women and the Curriculum. The most popular majors for women graduates are social sciences (32 percent) and letters (20 percent). Four percent of women earn degrees in mathematics and physical sciences. Sixty-five percent of student interns are women.

Nine courses on women are offered through the departments of French, sociology, religion, history, philosophy, English, and German. Recent offerings include Relations Between Men and Women, Women in the Middle Ages, Philosophy of Feminism, and Literary Images of Women. Such issues as mathematic skills for women, sex-fair curricula, and coeducational physical education classes are part of the preparation of future teachers.

Women and Athletics. Dickinson offers opportunities for women to participate in a wide variety of organized, competitive, individual and team sports. Forty percent of the intercollegiate athletes, 41 percent of the intramural athletes, and 40 percent of club athletes are women, as are nine of the 30 paid varsity coaches. Intercollegiate sports offered are basketball, cross-country, field hockey, lacrosse, softball, swimming, tennis, and volleyball.

Housing and Student Organizations. Single-sex and coeducational dormitories which do not restrict hours for visitors of the opposite sex are available for the 90 percent of students who live on campus. One of the two dormitory directors is a minority woman. Staff are offered awareness-training on sexism, sex education, racism, and birth control.

Approximately half of the full-time women students belong to sororities. Sororities do not provide housing for their members. The Panhellenic Council serves as an advocacy group for sorority women. The Congress of African Students meets on campus.

Special Services and Programs for Women. *Health and Counseling.* The college health service has 2 part-time, male physicians and 5 female nurses. Two of the 3 members of the student counseling staff are women, including a minority woman. Medical treatment and counseling for gynecological problems and rape and assault and counseling for birth control and abortion are available. The regular student health insurance covers maternity expenses at no extra cost.

Safety and Security. Measures consist of local police, campus police with weapons training and arrest authority, night escort service for women, information sessions on campus safety and crime prevention, and a rape crisis center. Five assaults on women and no rapes were reported for 1980–81.

Career. The college offers workshops, speakers, and printed information on nontraditional occupations for women.

Other. The division of education services operates a small Women's Resource Center, staffed by a student volunteer. Assertiveness training is provided by the Personnel Office. The counseling center sponsors a stress-reduction program and offers support to a variety of women with special needs.

Institutional Self-Description. "Dickinson women have full access to all academic programs. Women are encouraged to participate in programs of international study, internships, and leadership activities designed to develop personal capacities for leadership in their professional lives and in their roles as citizens. Friendship and self-knowledge are important values to Dickinson women and men."

Edinboro State College
Edinboro, PA 16444
Telephone: (814) 732-2720

4,774 undergraduates

	Amer. Ind.	Asian Amer.	Blacks	Hispanics	Whites
F	1	10	70	2	2,387
M	3	7	82	2	1,974
%	0.1	0.4	3.4	0.1	96.1

🏠 🏛 🚐 👫 👶 **AAUW**

Founded in 1857 as a teachers' preparatory school, Edinboro State is now a multi-purpose institution offering associate, bachelor's, and master's degrees in the arts and sciences and education. It also offers continuing education. Of the 5,713 students, 4,774 are undergraduates. Fifty-four percent of undergraduates are women; 8 percent of women attend part-time. The median age of all undergraduates is 20. On and off campus evening classes and a summer session are available. Ten percent of students commute to campus which is accessible by public transportation. Free on-campus parking is available.

On-campus childcare is offered to students, faculty, and staff at $1.20 per hour. Private childcare facilities are available nearby.

Policies to Ensure Fairness to Women. The Affirmative Action Officer, Human Relations/Desegregation Coordinator, and Director of Equal Opportunity in Sports are responsible for campus policy on equal employment opportunity, sex equity for students, and handicapped access. Complaints of sexual harassment are handled informally and confidentially.

Women in Leadership Positions. *Students.* In three recent years, women's participation in the seven campus-wide leadership posts was limited to editing the campus newspaper (once) and presiding over the residence hall council (3 times). Women chair eight of 16 honorary societies.

Faculty. Fifteen percent of the 344 full-time faculty are women. According to recent information, there are 2 black women and 1 Asian American woman among the full-time faculty. There are 2 female faculty for every 100 female students and 15 male faculty for every 100 male students.

Administrators. All top administrators are white men. Of the 28 departments, library science and health and physical education are chaired by women. The Dean of the School of Nursing is a woman. Two white women and one black woman are among the nine trustees. In a recent year, both the commencement speaker and the honorary degree recipient were women.

Women and the Curriculum. Most bachelor's degrees awarded to women are in education (42 percent), public affairs (11 percent), health professions (9 percent), and arts and letters (13 percent). Sixty percent of associate degrees are awarded to women, who major in data processing and health technologies. About 2 percent of women major in the nontraditional fields of mathematics and physical sciences.

Four courses on women are offered by three departments: Images of Women in Literature, Philosophy of Women, Sex/Race Images in Language and Literature, and Sexism in the Classroom. Courses in the departments of physical education and social work provide instruction on some matters specific to women. Faculty committees report on developments that include women in the curriculum, and collect curricular materials on women.

Faculty are offered workshops on sexism and racism in the curriculum; the relationships among sex, race, and major field; nontraditional occupations for men and women; the needs of reentry women and affirmative action and equal opportunity.

Women and Athletics. Women students have good opportunities to participate in organized competitive sports. Women's intramurals include a variety of individual and team sports. Two of the 17 paid varsity coaches are women. Thirty-six percent of the 242 intercollegiate athletes are women, who compete in basketball, cross-country, gymnastics, softball, tennis, track and field, and volleyball.

Housing and Student Organizations. Single-sex dormitories and housing for married students without children are available for the 45 percent of students who reside on campus. Single-sex dormitories restrict visiting hours during the week, but not on weekends. A staff of five white women and two men direct the residence halls.

Social sororities and fraternities are nonresidential. The Women's Center and Commonwealth Association of Students (including black women members) serve as advocates for women on campus.

Special Services and Programs for Women. *Health and Counseling.* One male physician and six female aides provide treatment for gynecological problems and birth control; counseling for rape and assault victims is available.

Safety and Security. Measures consist of campus police and information sessions on campus safety. No rapes and 20 assaults were reported for 1980–81.

Career. Services include workshops on nontraditional occupations, nonsexist/nonracist literature on nontraditional fields of study, job discrimination information, and updated files of alumnae by specific careers.

Other. A faculty volunteer administers the Women's Center on a part-time basis. The personnel deans offer a telephone line of information, referral, and support.

Institutional Self-Description. "Edinboro State College should particularly appeal to women because of the low cost and variety and quality of its academic offerings. The cultural and recreational facilities are the best in northwestern Pennsylvania. Only one case of sex discrimination has ever been submitted to the Equal Opportunity Employment Commission, and there has never been an official sexual harassment complaint submitted at the college, making it the best record in the Pennsylvania State College and University system."

Gettysburg College
Gettysburg, PA 17325
Telephone: (717) 334-3131

Women in Leadership
★★ **students**

1,954 undergraduates

	Amer. Ind.	Asian Amer.	Blacks	Hispanics	Whites
F	1	1	7	6	932
M	0	2	10	2	992
%	0.1	0.2	0.9	0.4	98.5

Founded in 1832 as a men's college and coeducational since 1888, Gettysburg College is an independent, liberal arts institution affiliated with the Lutheran Church. The college enrolls 1,969 students, including 1,954 undergraduates. Women are 49 percent of undergraduates, and almost all women attend full-time. The median age of students is 20 years.

Gettysburg offers bachelor's degrees in liberal arts, mathematics and science, education, and business. Pre-professional degree programs include dentistry, medicine, law, and engineering. Adult continuing education is also available. The campus is not accessible by public transportation. Free on-campus parking is available for the small percentage of students who commute.

Private childcare facilities are available nearby.

Policies to Ensure Fairness to Women. Monitoring compliance with equal-employment-opportunity, sex-equity-for-students, and handicapped-accessibility laws is the responsibility part-time of the Associate Dean of the College. A written policy against sexual harassment of students, faculty, and staff has been communicated throughout the college; complaints are resolved through a formal grievance procedure. A Committee on Minority Affairs addresses the concerns of minority women.

Women in Leadership Positions. *Students.* Women have excellent opportunities for student leadership. In a recent three-year period, 43 percent of the student offices were held by women, including editor-in-chief of the student newspaper for one year and president of the senior class for three years. Women head three of 12 honorary societies.

Faculty. Sixteen percent of 129 full-time faculty are women, a proportion which is below the national average. There are 2 female faculty for every 100 female students and 11 male faculty for every 100 male students.

Administrators. Men hold all chief administrative positions. A woman chairs the department of classics. Eleven percent of the trustees are women.

Women and the Curriculum. Most degrees awarded to women are in the social sciences (27 percent), with significant numbers in business (15 percent), psychology (14 percent), and letters (12 percent). Ten percent of women graduate in biology. Seven percent of women earn degrees in mathematics or physical sciences. Women students hold half of internship and science field-service assignments.

The departments of English and interdisciplinary studies offer two courses on women: Contemporary Southern Women Writers and Women in the Ancient World. The departments of education, business, and physical education offer instruction on some matters relevant to women. Workshops on affirmative action and equal opportunity are offered to faculty.

Women and Athletics. A well-rounded program of individual and team sports offers women both intramural and intercollegiate opportunities. About one-third of the intercollegiate athletes are women, who participate in basketball, cross-country, field hockey, lacrosse, softball, swimming, tennis, and volleyball.

Housing and Student Organizations. Eighty-five percent of undergraduates live on campus in single-sex and coeducational dormitories, as well as in common-interest-group and fraternity houses. All dormitories have restricted hours for visitors of the opposite sex. Ten of the 13 dormitory directors are women. Residence staff are offered awareness-training on the avoidance of sexism and racism, and on sex education and birth control.

About 42 percent of full-time student women belong to sororities, which do not provide housing for members. Advocacy groups include the Black Students Union and Campus Action Group. The latter, although open to both men and women, is primarily concerned with women's issues and works closely with the local chapter of NOW.

Special Services and Programs for Women. *Health and Counseling.* The college health service has 1 male physician and 7 other health-care providers, of whom 6 are women. Two of the 4 members of the counseling staff are women. Counseling and treatment for gynecological problems and rape and assault are provided, along with birth control and abortion counseling. In-service training for counselors is available on assertiveness, and in the avoidance of sex-role stereotyping and sex bias.

Safety and Security. Measures consist of local police, campus police with weapons training, night escort service, easily located emergency telephones, an emergency alarm system, and self-defense courses. No rapes and two assaults on women were reported for 1980–81.

Career. The college offers information on discrimination in interviewing practices and workshops on the "dual-career couple."

Special Features. In conjunction with other institutions of the Central Pennsylvania Consortium, Gettysburg sponsors an annual Women's Studies Conference.

Institutional Self-Description. "Gettysburg College, which

became coeducational in 1888, recognizes women as scholars and is appealing to all students who desire a quality, comprehensive educational experience in the liberal arts. While the academic program is primary, it is supplemented and enhanced by co-curricular programs in areas such as the arts, athletics, and government, which allow students to develop along many dimensions."

Harcum Junior College
Bryn Mawr, PA 19010
Telephone: (215) 525-4100

Women in Leadership
★★★ students
★★★ faculty
★★★ administrators

824 undergraduates

	Amer. Ind.	Asian Amer.	Blacks	Hispanics	Whites
F	2	0	68	4	741
M	0	0	0	0	0
%	0.3	0.0	8.3	0.5	90.9

Founded in 1915, Harcum Junior College is a private, two-year women's college which serves 955 students, including 824 undergraduates. All undergraduates attend full-time. The median age of students is 19 years; 8 percent of women are over age 25. The college offers associate degrees in arts and science. Adult continuing education, evening classes, and a summer session are available.

Sixty-three percent of the students live on campus. Commuting students can use public transportation. On-campus parking is available for a fee.

Private childcare facilities are available nearby.

Policies to Ensure Fairness to Women. The student handbook includes a written campus policy prohibiting sexual harassment of students.

Women in Leadership Positions. *Students.* Women hold all student leadership positions.

Faculty. The full-time faculty of 30 is 70 percent female. There are 3 female faculty for every 100 female students.

Administrators. Of the six key administrators, the chief student-life officer, the head librarian, and the director of athletics are women. Of the four departments, behavioral science is chaired by a woman. One-third of the 18 trustees are women.

Women and the Curriculum. Most of the two-year degrees and certificates awarded are in business and commerce (39 percent) and health technologies (37 percent).

The college offers a course on Women in Literature. An official committee has the responsibility of developing courses on women within departments.

Women and Athletics. Intramural, club, and intercollegiate sports are offered. Thirty women participate in club sports, 64 take part in the intramural program, and 82 compete at the intercollegiate level. Two of the three paid varsity coaches are women. Intercollegiate sports include badminton, basketball, field hockey, softball, tennis, and volleyball.

Housing and Student Organizations. Sixty-three percent of the students on campus live in dormitories that have restricted hours for male visitors. Of the undergraduates residing on campus, 8 percent are black and 1 percent are Hispanic. The 12 residence-hall directors are white women. Awareness-training is offered to residence-hall staff on sex education, birth control, sexism, and racism. Advocacy groups include the Organization of Black Students and the International Club.

Special Services and Programs for Women. *Health and Counseling.* The student health service is staffed by one male physician and three female health-care providers. Medical treatment for matters specific to women is not provided. The student counseling center provides counseling on gynecological matters, birth control, abortion, rape and assault, and sexually-transmitted diseases. Counselors are offered in-service training in the avoidance of sex-role stereotyping and racial bias.

Safety and Security. Security measures include campus police and information sessions on campus safety and rape and assault prevention. One assault and no rapes were reported for 1980–81.

Career. Services include lectures for students by women employed in nontraditional occupations, printed information on nontraditional fields of study for women, updated files of alumnae by specific careers, programs to establish contacts between alumnae and students, career-planning workshops, on-campus recruitment, job placement, and visits by representatives of four-year colleges.

Other. The counseling center offers assertiveness and leadership training, a program to build mathematics confidence, and a telephone service for information, referrals and support. The Dean of Students sponsors a theater/arts program, a women's lecture series, and special assistance for battered women.

Institutional Self-Description. "The college offers some 20 programs which prepare young women for professional and semi-professional occupations. Moreover, many of these programs prepare the associate-degree recipient to transfer to four-year programs, which are an extension of their Harcum experience. Harcum's location on Philadelphia's Main Line offers the student many advantages not available elsewhere."

King's College

133 N. River St., Wilkes-Barre, PA 18711
Telephone: (717) 826-5900

1,813 undergraduates

	Amer. Ind.	Asian Amer.	Blacks	Hispanics	Whites
F	0	3	4	3	687
M	0	8	4	6	1,091
%	0.0	0.6	0.4	0.5	98.5

 AAUW

Some 2,100 students attend King's College, a Roman Catholic, liberal arts institution founded in 1946. Initially established to educate the sons of miners, the college became coeducational in 1970. Women now constitute 38 percent of the 1,813 students registered in degree programs; 11 percent of women attend part-time.

The college offers bachelor's degrees in such fields as liberal arts and sciences, business, and pre-professional areas. It also has a three-year degree program and adult continuing education. Alternative schedules include evening classes, a summer session, and independent-study opportunities. For the 55 percent of students who commute, the campus is accessible by public transportation. Parking on campus is available for a fee.

Private childcare facilities are available near the campus.

Policies to Ensure Fairness to Women. The Director of Administrative Planning, a voting member of policymaking councils, has part-time responsibility for equal employment opportunity, sex equity for students, and handicapped accessibility. Complaints of sexual harassment are resolved informally and confidentially. The Committee on the Status of Women, appointed by the President, prepares an annual report which is distributed to the campus community.

Women in Leadership Positions. *Students.* Women have few opportunities for leadership. In three recent years, women presided over the student body twice and over the sophomore class once. Three of the nine honorary societies are headed by women.

Faculty. Women are 12 percent of the 91 full-time faculty, a proportion far below the national average. There are 2 female faculty for every 100 female students and 8 male faculty for every 100 male students.

Administrators. All chief administrators are men. Of 27 departments, women chair four: accounting, languages, physician's assistant, and developmental learning. A woman is chair of the humanities division. One woman sits on the 8-member faculty council.

Women and the Curriculum. The most popular majors for women are business (26 percent) and public affairs (20 percent). Five percent of women earn degrees in mathematics and physical sciences. The mathematics department conducts mathematics confidence courses. Forty percent of student interns are women.

The college offers four courses on women: Women's Issues in Social Work, Women in Management, Women in Literature, and The American Woman. The departments of education, social work, and business include some issues specific to women in their curricula.

Women and Athletics. King's College offers limited opportunities for women to participate in organized competitive sports. A small intramural program for women offers three sports, while the intercollegiate program is more varied. Thirty-five percent of intramural and 45 percent of intercollegiate athletes are women, as are four of 15 paid coaches. The intercollegiate sports offerd are basketball, cross-country, riflery, softball, swimming, tennis, and volleyball.

Housing and Student Organizations. Forty-five percent of the students live on campus in single-sex dormitories which restrict hours for visitors of the opposite sex. Forty percent of undergraduate women live in dormitories. One of two residence-hall directors is female.

Special Services and Programs for Women. *Health and Counseling.* The student health service employs one male physician. The regular student health insurance covers maternity at no extra cost. The student counseling service has a staff of three, including one woman. Counseling for gynecological problems and rape and assault is available. College counselors are offered awareness-training on sexism and racism, as well as on equal rights for all students.

Safety and Security. Measures consist of campus police without arrest authority, high-intensity lighting, self-defense courses for women, and a rape crisis center. No rapes or assaults on women were reported for 1980–81.

Career. The college provides lectures and information on nontraditional occupations for women and contacts between alumnae and female students.

Other. The office of the Dean of Students maintains a telephone service for referrals and support. The psychology department offers an assertiveness training workshop.

Institutional Self-Description. "King's College offers its students preparation for a purposeful life, not only through intellectual training, but by also offering opportunities for development of religious, social, and personal values. The college's small size allows for a sincere concern with the individual's overall development."

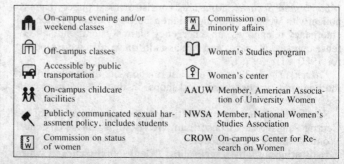

Lafayette College

Easton, PA 18042
Telephone: (215) 250-5000

Women in Leadership
★ students

★ Women and the
Curriculum

★ Women and Athletics

2,229 undergraduates

	Amer. Ind.	Asian Amer.	Blacks	Hispanics	Whites
F	0	1	14	5	738
M	0	1	41	10	1,395
%	0.0	0.1	2.5	0.7	96.7

 AAUW

Lafayette College, a private, four-year institution affiliated with the United Presbyterian Church, was founded in 1826 and became coeducational in 1970. Of the 2,373 students who attend, 2,229 are registered in degree programs. Thirty-five percent of the degree students are women; 2 percent of women attend part-time. The median age of all students is 20 years, with 8 percent of the women over 25 and 2 percent over 40.

The college offers bachelor's degrees in liberal arts and sciences, as well as in engineering. Adult education is offered through the Office of Special Programs. Flexible scheduling is facilitated by evening and summer session classes. For the 7 percent of students who commute, the college is accessible by public transportation. Free on-campus parking is available.

Private childcare facilities are located near the campus.

Policies to Ensure Fairness to Women. The Director of Personnel and the Dean of Students are responsible, on a part-time basis, for monitoring compliance with equal-employment-opportunity and educational-sex-equity legislation. The college is planning to draft a policy on sexual harassment; currently, complaints are resolved through informal, confidential means. The Committee on the Status of Women, which includes student representatives with voting rights, takes public stands on issues of concern to students, faculty, and staff.

Women in Leadership Positions. *Students.* Opportunities for leadership experience are good. In a recent three-year period, women served twice as president of the student union board and once as editor-in-chief of the campus newspaper. One of the eight campus honorary societies is headed by a woman.

Faculty. Thirteen percent of the 156 full-time faculty are women, a proportion considerably below the national average. There are 3 female faculty for every 100 female students and 10 male faculty for every 100 male students. The college reports that the full-time faculty includes 2 Asian American women.

Administrators. Of the 8 chief administrators, only the head librarian is a woman. The department of education is chaired by a woman. Three of 35 trustees are women, as was a recent commencement speaker and 1 of 5 recent honorary degree recipients.

Women and the Curriculum. Most women earn degrees in social science (37 percent) and biology (16 percent). Twenty-two percent of women major in such nontraditional fields as mathematics, engineering, or physical sciences. Departmental workshops and individual counseling are offered to encourage women to enter nontraditional occupations. Over half the students in cooperative education and internship programs are women, as are one-third of students in science field service.

Five courses on women are offered through five departments: Introduction to Women's Studies, Literary Women, Psychology of Sex Roles, Sex and Gender: A Cross-Cultural Development, and Women in European and American History. The department of education provides instruction on the development and use of sex-fair curricula. Faculty workshops are offered on nontraditional

occupations for women and men and on the needs of reentry women.

Women and Athletics. Lafayette offers good opportunities for women to participate in organized, competitive sports, with an unusually wide variety of intramural and intercollegiate sports. Twenty-eight percent of intramural athletes, 35 percent of club athletes, and 26 percent of intercollegiate athletes are women. Of the 28 paid coaches, eight are women. Intercollegiate sports for women include basketball, cross-country, fencing, field hockey, lacrosse, softball, swimming, tennis, track and field, and volleyball.

Housing and Student Organizations. Single-sex and coeducational dormitories without restrictive hours for visitors of the opposite sex are provided for the 93 percent of students who live on campus, along with college-owned apartments, a scholars' house, and social dormitories. Dormitory staff are offered awareness training on the avoidance of sexism and on sex education.

Forty-three percent of female students belong to social sororities, including two minority women in racially integrated sororities. Both sororities and fraternities provide housing for members. Student advocacy groups for women include the Association of Lafayette Women, the Society of Women Engineers, and the Association of Black Collegians, which has a majority of women members.

Special Services and Programs for Women. *Health and Counseling.* The student health center employs 1 male physician and 6 female health care providers, while the student counseling center employs 2 women and 2 men. Available services specific to women include counseling and medical treatment for birth control, abortion, and rape and assault, as well as counseling for gynecological problems. The regular student health insurance covers maternity and abortion expenses at no extra cost.

Safety and Security. Measures consist of local police, campus police with no arrest authority, night escort service for women, and a rape crisis center. No rapes and four assaults on women were reported for 1980–81.

Career. Workshops, lectures, printed materials, and job discrimination information on nontraditional occupations for women are available, as are files on alumnae careers, and programs to establish networks between alumnae and female students.

Career. The counseling center conducts assertiveness training and sponsors a program to build confidence in mathematics.

Institutional Self-Description. "Independent, coeducational, and residential, Lafayette is a college in the truest sense of the word. It is exclusively undergraduate with all programs and departments united. It was the first college to incorporate engineering into an existing humanities, social science, and natural science curriculum, and the combination of these disciplines distinguishes Lafayette from other small undergraduate colleges. Classes are small, housing for all four years is guaranteed, and the women's athletic program offers depth and strength, and in fact the lacrosse team won the Division II national championship in 1980."

La Roche College

900 Babcock Blvd., Pittsburgh, PA 15237
Telephone: (412) 367-9300

Women in Leadership
★★★ faculty
★★★ administrators

1,052 undergraduates

	Amer. Ind.	Asian Amer.	Blacks	Hispanics	Whites
F	0	3	13	0	637
M	0	3	31	0	353
%	0.0	0.6	4.2	0.0	95.2

 AAUW

Founded in 1963 as a Roman Catholic liberal arts college for prospective women teachers, La Roche College is now a coeducational, church-related institution that prepares 1,260 students for a variety of careers. The student body consists of 1,052 undergraduates, 62 percent of whom are women; 51 percent of all women attend part-time. The median age of all students is 28.

A range of undergraduate, pre-professional, and professional degree programs is offered. In addition to a continuing education program, classes are held off campus, on weekends, and during the evening.

The college is accessible by public transportation. For the 82 percent of students who commute, on-campus parking at a fee is available. Coeducational dormitories are available for students who live on campus.

Private childcare facilities are located near campus.

Policies to Ensure Fairness to Women. The Director of Personnel has the part-time responsibility for monitoring compliance with sex-equity legislation. A formal, well-publicized sexual harassment policy protects all members of the college community. Complaints are handled informally or through a formal grievance procedure.

Women in Leadership Positions. *Students.* Information about students in leadership positions is available solely for the offices of student body president and student senate president, positions to which only men have been elected in recent years.

Faculty. Fifty-five percent of the faculty are female, a proportion above the national average. There are 5 female faculty for every 100 female students; for males, the ratio is the same.

Administrators. Women hold most key posts, except chief student-life officer, chief development officer, and director of athletics. Twelve of the 19 department heads are women.

Women and the Curriculum. Most women take degrees in business and psychology. Eleven percent of women take degrees in mathematics and architecture. The Women in Graphics program encourages women to take advantage of the printing-plant and graphic-arts studios on campus. Workshops to help women develop confidence in mathematics are run by the Learning Center and continuing education department.

Six courses on women are offered through the departments of history, religious studies, English, and psychology, including Women in U.S. History, Women in the World of Work, Women and Religion, Women in Literature.

Women and Athletics. There is no information on the intercollegiate sports program, but intramural activities attract a small number of women participants to such sports as basketball, softball, and volleyball.

Special Services and Programs for Women. *Health and Counseling.* There is no student health service or student counseling center. Residence-hall staff are offered in-service training on sex education, birth control, and racism.

Safety and Security. Measures include campus and local police protection, and a rape crisis center. No rapes or assaults on women were reported for 1980–81.

Career. The Career Center sponsors a variety of activities, including workshops on nontraditional occupations, network formation between students and alumnae, and the formation of sup-

port groups. The Learning Center provides assertiveness-training sessions for women.

Other. There is a Women's Center in the community.

Institutional Self-Description. ''An unusually high proportion of women administrators committed to serving the needs of women in a coed environment makes La Roche an especially attractive place for women. A small college, La Roche offers students individual attention, a flexible schedule, and a variety of role models.''

Lehigh University
Bethlehem, PA 18015
Telephone: (215) 861-3000

★★ **Women and the Curriculum**

4,389 undergraduates

	Amer. Ind.	Asian Amer.	Blacks	Hispanics	Whites
F	0	1	55	3	1,008
M	1	1	55	13	3,203
%	0.1	0.1	1.8	0.4	97.8

AAUW

Founded in 1865 as an independent, liberal arts institution for men, Lehigh University began admitting women in 1971. Over 6,370 students are enrolled. Women are 24 percent of the 4,389 undergraduates; 1 percent of women attend part-time. The median age of all students is 20 years.

Approximately half of the students enroll in the well-known College of Engineering. Lehigh also offers bachelor's, master's, and doctoral degrees in other fields. Summer session classes are available. Five percent of students commute to the campus. Public transportation is accessible and free on-campus parking is provided.

A university-operated childcare facility can accommodate most students' requests. Charges are based on a fixed rate. Additional private facilities are located near the campus.

Policies to Ensure Fairness to Women. The Provost and the Vice President for Administration and Planning are responsible for policy concerning equal employment opportunity, sex equity for students, and handicapped access. Complaints of sexual harassment are handled through a formal campus grievance procedure. An Equal Opportunity Advisory Committee, which includes students as voting members, reports to the President on concerns of women and minorities.

Women in Leadership Positions. *Students.* Lehigh offers limited opportunities for women to gain leadership experience. In a recent three-year period, women held two of the seven available student posts, serving once as president of the Student Activities Council and once as president of the residence-hall council. Two of 14 honorary societies are headed by women. The All-University Forum is also chaired by a woman student.

Faculty. Eight percent of the 326 full-time faculty are women, a proportion well below average for private four-year institutions in this guide. There are 2 female faculty for every 100 female students and 9 male faculty for every 100 male students.

Administrators. Of the eight chief administrators, the head librarian is a woman. Of the 80 departments, a woman chairs one— the department of classics. One of six recent honorary degree recipients was a woman.

Women and the Curriculum. Approximately one-quarter of women graduates earn degrees in business. Twenty-six percent of women major in such nontraditional fields as engineering, mathematics, architecture, and physical sciences, with 25 percent in engineering alone. Another 11 percent earn degrees in biology.

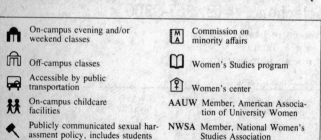

	On-campus evening and/or weekend classes		Commission on minority affairs
	Off-campus classes		Women's Studies program
	Accessible by public transportation		Women's center
	On-campus childcare facilities	AAUW	Member, American Association of University Women
	Publicly communicated sexual harassment policy, includes students	NWSA	Member, National Women's Studies Association
	Commission on status of women	CROW	On-campus Center for Research on Women

The college has several support groups to encourage women to prepare for careers in science, engineering, and business.

Lehigh's Women's Studies Program, under a full-time, permanent faculty member, offers an undergraduate minor. Courses on women are available through the departments of philosophy, religion, classics, history, government, and the College of Arts and Sciences. Recent titles include Philosophy of Women, Women and Religion, and Politics of Women. A committee oversees the Women's Studies Program and reports on curricular developments that include women.

Women and Athletics. No information on intercollegiate or intramural sports was provided.

Housing and Student Organizations. Single-sex and coeducational dormitories, which do not restrict hours for visitors of the opposite sex, are available for the three-fourths of students who reside on campus. Housing for married students and single students with children is also provided. A married woman student whose spouse is not enrolled may live in married students' housing. Two of the three dormitory directors are women. Staff are offered awareness-training on sex education, birth control, self-defense, rape prevention, and assertiveness.

Twenty percent of full-time undergraduate women join social sororities. Both sororities and fraternities provide housing for members. Women Organized to Meet Essential Needs (WOMEN) serves as an advocacy group for all women students.

Special Services and Programs for Women. *Health and Counseling.* The student health service has three male physicians and four female health-care providers. The staff of the student counseling service consists of three men. Counseling and treatment for rape and assault and birth control, medical treatment for gynecological matters, and abortion referral are the available services specific to women. Regular student health insurance covers maternity and some abortion expenses at no extra cost.

Safety and Security. Measures consist of campus police with weapons training and arrest authority, a dormitory security patrol, a campus-wide, emergency telephone system, self-defense courses for women, and a rape crisis center. One rape and 22 assaults (three on women) were reported for 1980–81.

Career. Placement and career-related activities are conducted in conjunction with such campus women's groups as Women in Business. Activities and services include lectures, workshops, and printed materials on nontraditional careers, as well as programs to establish networks between alumnae and female students.

Other. Under the joint sponsorhsip of the Dean of Students, WOMEN, and Women's Studies, an annual women's week and a women's lecture series are held. The Dean of Students and the counseling center sponsor assertiveness training and a telephone service for information, referral and support. Theater and other women's arts programs are sponsored by various academic departments.

Institutional Self-Description. "Our goal is to produce good people who are also good *at* something—young men and women who learn to think to the point where thinking is a habit, who learn to live by a set of values, who learn to develop methods for the intelligent application of knowledge and the will to work as a self-discipline."

⌂ On-campus evening and/or weekend classes	[MA] Commission on minority affairs
⌂ Off-campus classes	📖 Women's Studies program
🚌 Accessible by public transportation	🏠 Women's center
👫 On-campus childcare facilities	AAUW Member, American Association of University Women
📢 Publicly communicated sexual harassment policy, includes students	NWSA Member, National Women's Studies Association
[SW] Commission on status of women	CROW On-campus Center for Research on Women

Lincoln University
Lincoln University, PA 19352
Telephone: (215) 932-8300

Women in Leadership
★ faculty

993 undergraduates

	Amer. Ind.	Asian Amer.	Blacks	Hispanics	Whites
F	0	0	449	0	5
M	0	4	483	0	17
%	0.0	0.4	97.3	0.0	2.3

AAUW

Founded in 1854 as a college for black men, Lincoln University is a coeducational, non-sectarian, private institution that serves a predominantly black student body. It offers bachelor's degrees in liberal arts and sciences, as well as master's degree programs. Lincoln's rural campus, located southwest of Philadelphia, has a total enrollment of 1,132 students. Women are 46 percent of the 993 undergraduates, virtually all of whom attend full-time. The median age of undergraduates is 19. Free on-campus parking is available for the 5 percent of students who commute.

Women in Leadership Positions. *Students.* Women have limited opportunity to exercise their leadership potential. In three recent years, women held one-fourth of the campus-wide leadership posts, including student body president, student senate president, campus newspaper editor, junior-class president, and first-year class president.

Faculty. Twenty-nine percent of the 70 full-time faculty are women, a proportion above the average for institutions nationwide. There are 4 female faculty for every 100 female students and 10 male faculty for every 100 male students. According to recent data from the university, the full-time faculty consists mainly of black men and women. One Hispanic and 9 white women also serve on the faculty.

Administrators. All top-level administrators are male. One white woman and 2 black women chair three of 17 departments: English, education, and physical sciences. One of 4 trustees is a black woman.

Women and the Curriculum. Thirty-one percent of the women who earn bachelor's degrees major in social sciences, 20 percent in business, and 14 percent in psychology. Three percent major in such nontraditional fields as mathematics and physical sciences. Forty-two percent of students in cooperative education programs are women.

There are no courses on women. Courses in the departments of social work and physical education address some issues specific to women.

Women and Athletics. Thirty-one percent of the 98 intercollegiate athletes are women; one of the four paid intercollegiate coaches is female. Intercollegiate sports offered are basketball and volleyball.

Housing and Student Organizations. Ninety-five percent of the undergraduates live in single-sex dormitories that have restricted hours for visitors of the opposite sex. Three of the five residence-hall directors are minority women.

Fifteen percent of the undergraduate women belong to social sororities.

Special Services and Programs for Women. *Health and Counseling.* The student health service employs two male physicians and four female health-care providers. The student counseling center's staff includes two black women. Gynecological counseling and treatment are available in addition to birth control counseling.

Safety and Security. Measures consist of campus police protection and high-intensity lighting. No information was provided about the incidence of rapes and assaults.

Career. The university sponsors workshops and distributes information on nontraditional careers for women.

Institutional Self-Description. "Black women attending Lincoln University have an opportunity to seek and expand their identity due to the fact that the environment is basically black. This factor deters anxieties that could be a hindrance in the educational process for black women."

Millersville State College
Millersville, PA 17551
Telephone: (717) 872-3598

★ **Women and Athletics**

4,900 undergraduates

	Amer. Ind.	Asian Amer.	Blacks	Hispanics	Whites
F	3	29	140	29	2,585
M	3	45	130	29	1,879
%	0.1	1.5	5.5	1.2	91.7

 AAUW

Millersville, founded in 1854, is Pennsylvania's oldest state college. Five thousand of its 6,000 students are undergraduates, 57 percent of them women; 14 percent of women attend part-time. Millersville offers four-year degrees in education, liberal arts, health professions, and library science. Evening and summer classes are available. A Continuing Education Office administers adult education. Twenty-one percent of students commute by public transportation or car, using on-campus parking.

On-campus daytime childcare provides for 20 percent of student requests and charges fees on a sliding scale. Private childcare is available off campus.

Policies to Ensure Fairness to Women. While Millersville lacks a formal policy banning sexual harassment, both informal methods and formal grievance procedures are available to resolve complaints. The Commission on Minority Affairs addresses the concerns of minority women.

Women in Leadership Positions. *Students.* Women have some opportunity for participation in leadership. In a recent three-year period, women held five of the 18 campus-wide positions: president of the student court, president of the student union, editor of the newspaper, manager of the radio station, and president of the residence-hall council. Women head two of five honorary societies.

Faculty. Twenty-four percent of the 302 faculty are women, a proportion slightly below the national average. Among the full-time faculty are 2 black, 1 Asian American, and 4 Hispanic women. The ratio of female faculty to female students is 3 to 100; the ratio of male faculty to male students is 12 to 100.

Administrators. All top administrators are men, with the exception of the director of athletics. Of 29 departments, women chair nursing and social work.

Women and the Curriculum. Most women graduate in education (51 percent), with smaller numbers in a wide variety of other fields. Almost 6 percent of women take degrees in mathematics, computer science, and physical sciences. Fifty-five percent of the students in cooperative education programs and internships are women.

Three courses on women are offered through the departments of art, English, and philosophy: Women in Art, Women in Literature, and Philosophical Workshop. Faculty are offered workshops on sexism, racism, and equal-employment laws.

Women and Athletics. Opportunities for experience in organized athletics are good. Thirty-nine percent of intramural athletes are women, who participate in a wide variety of team and individual sports. Forty-five percent of intercollegiate athletes are women, who receive 10 percent of scholarship aid. Thirteen of the 27 paid coaches for intercollegiate sports are women. Varsity sports are archery, basketball, cross-country, field hockey, lacrosse, softball, swimming, and synchronized swimming.

Housing and Student Organizations. Single-sex and coeducational dormitories, with no restrictions on visiting hours for members of the opposite sex, are staffed by 4 white women, 2 minority women, and 4 men. Seven percent of full-time women students join sororities. Ten minority women are members of a minority sorority. The Commonwealth Association of Students serves as an advocate for women on campus.

Special Services and Programs for Women. *Health and Counseling.* One male physician and 6 female aides provide gynecological and birth control services, and treatment for rape and assault. One female and 2 male counselors offer couunseling in the above areas and on abortion. Counseling staff are offered training in the avoidance of sex-role stereotyping and racial bias.

Safety and Security. Measures consist of campus and local police with arrest authority, self-defense courses for women, and information sessions on campus safety and rape/assault prevention. For 1980–81, 12 assaults and no rapes were reported.

Career. Services include programs by women in nontraditional occupations, job discrimination information, nonsexist/nonracist literature on nontraditional fields, updated files of alumnae by careers, and programs to establish contacts between alumnae and students.

Institutional Self-Description. None provided.

Moore College of Art
20th and The Parkway
Philadelphia, PA 19103
Telephone: (215) 568-4515

Women in Leadership
★★★ **students**
★★ **faculty**
★★★ **administrators**

587 undergraduates

	Amer. Ind.	Asian Amer.	Blacks	Hispanics	Whites
F	0	5	38	6	535
M	0	0	0	0	0
%	0.0	0.9	6.5	1.0	91.6

AAUW

A private, non-sectarian institution founded in 1844, Moore is the only art college for women in the country. It offers its 587 students undergraduate degrees in a variety of fine and applied arts, as well as certification in art education. Eighteen percent of students attend part-time, and about 30 percent are over age 25. Moore offers alternative schedules in the form of independent study opportunities, a summer session, and a Continuing Education Program that enrolls more than 100 students. Both day and evening classes are available.

Thirty percent of students live in dormitories with restricted hours for male visitors or in college-owned apartments near the campus. Centrally located in Philadelphia, the campus is accessible by public transportation. On-campus parking is available at a fee.

Private childcare facilities are available near the campus.

Policies to Ensure Fairness to Women. The Vice President has part-time responsibility for policy pertaining to equal employment opportunity and handicapped access. The Registrar/Dean is responsible for policies concerning both handicapped access and sex equity for students. A published campus sexual harassment policy protects students, faculty, and staff; complaints are resolved through a formal grievance procedure.

Women in Leadership Positions. *Students.* Women hold all student leadership positions.

Faculty. Forty-seven percent of the 45 full-time faculty are women, a proportion far above the national average. Women constitute 55 percent of the fine arts faculty, 70 percent of the creative writing faculty, and 100 percent of the dance faculty. There are 4 female faculty for every 100 female students.

Administrators. Five of the seven key administrators are women, although the President and chief academic officer are men. Women chair six of eight departments, including art education, humanities, fabric design, interior design, fashion illustration, and advertising design.

Women and the Curriculum. Ninety-two percent of students earn degrees in fine arts, while the balance major in art education. Cooperative education and internship programs are available. The humanities department offers two courses on women: Women/Arts; Women/Assertion. An official committee is charged with developing additional courses on women.

Minority Women. Eight percent of the students are minority women, largely black women. One department is chaired by a black woman; the faculty senate includes 3 black women, 2 Hispanic women, and 1 Asian American woman; among the 18 female trustees are 1 Hispanic and 2 black women. Recent campus speakers included 1 black and 1 Hispanic woman. Two of the 8 residence-hall directors are minority women. About 8 percent of those enrolled in continuing education courses are minority students, mainly black women.

Women and Athletics. Moore provides no opportunities for organized competitive sports.

Special Services and Programs for Women. *Health and Counseling.* The student health center is staffed by one male physician and one female health-care provider. There is no counseling center. No medical treatment specific to women is available. Gynecological, birth control, abortion, and rape and assault counseling are available through the health center.

Safety and Security. Measures consist of campus police without arrest authority, night-time bus service to residence areas, high-intensity lighting, an emergency alarm system, and instruction on campus safety. No rapes or assaults on women were reported for 1980–81.

Career. Career counseling services include workshops and lectures on nontraditional occupations, programs to create networks between alumnae and students, and updated files on the careers of alumnae.

Institutional Self-Description. "The college was created in 1844, and continues today to provide the finest art education for the serious woman who seeks the highest quality entry-level professional training for art and design."

Neumann College
Aston, PA 19014
Telephone: (215) 459-0905

Women in Leadership
★★★ faculty
★★★ administrators

625 undergraduates

	Amer. Ind.	Asian Amer.	Blacks	Hispanics	Whites
F	0	2	23	0	489
M	0	2	2	0	109
%	0.0	0.3	4.0	0.0	95.7

 AAUW

Neumann College, a Roman Catholic, liberal arts institution, was founded in 1965 as Our Lady of Angels College. It has a total of 675 students, of whom 625 are enrolled in degree programs. The median age of students is 23. Though Neumann has been coeducational since 1980, 82 percent of its undergraduate students are women; 43 percent of the women attend part-time.

Students may earn bachelor's degrees in a variety of liberal arts fields; there is also an adult continuing education program. Both day and evening classes are available, along with opportunities for independent study. All students commute to the suburban campus, located near Philadelphia. The college is accessible by public transportation. Free on-campus parking is also available.

A college-operated childcare facility accommodates 50 children and can meet 70 percent of students' requests. Charges are based on a fixed daily rate.

Policies to Ensure Fairness to Women. An affirmative action officer monitors compliance with regulations for equal employment opportunity.

Women in Leadership Positions. *Students.* Information provided by the college does not permit an assessment of student leadership opportunities for women.

Faculty. Seventy-seven percent of the 35 faculty members are women, a proportion far above the national average. There are 9 female faculty for every 100 female students.

Administrators. Most key administrators are women, including the President, chief academic officer, chief development officer, and chief student-life officer. Women chair all four departments: nursing, natural sciences, humanities, and behavioral sciences. Nine of 15 trustees are women.

Women and the Curriculum. Over one-half of the degrees awarded to women are in the health professions. All the men and one-fourth of the women earn degrees in interdisciplinary studies. All majors offer internships, and 60 percent of the interns are women. There are no courses on women.

Women and Athletics. For a small college, Neumann has a good organized athletic program. Seven intramural activities provide a variety of team and individual sports. Club sports are also available. The three paid varsity coaches are women. Intercollegiate sports offered are basketball, softball, tennis, and volleyball.

Special Services and Programs for Women. *Health and Counseling.* The staff of the student health service consists of one female health-care provider. Two female professionals work at the student counseling center. No information was provided on counseling and medical treatment specific to women.

Safety and Security. Measures consist of campus police protection and self-defense courses for women. No information was provided on the incidence of rapes or assaults.

Career. Placement services include lectures on nontraditional occupations for women.

Other. The counseling office and the Continuing Education for Women Program offer leadership training. The mathematics department sponsors a mathematics confidence clinic.

Institutional Self-Description. "The institution is sponsored and directed by committee women who trace their lineage in the Christian humanist tradition back to St. Francis of Assisi. The unique strength of the institution is this humanistic Christian atmosphere, which allows a woman to grow and change in a supportive environment while meeting her specific academic and career needs."

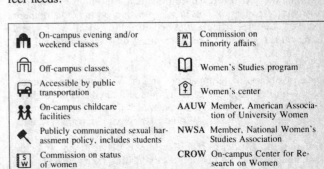

On-campus evening and/or weekend classes

Off-campus classes

Accessible by public transportation

On-campus childcare facilities

Publicly communicated sexual harassment policy, includes students

Commission on status of women

Commission on minority affairs

Women's Studies program

Women's center

AAUW Member, American Association of University Women

NWSA Member, National Women's Studies Association

CROW On-campus Center for Research on Women

Pennsylvania State University Capitol Campus
PSU/Capitol, Middletown, PA 17057
Telephone: (717) 948-6000

1,601 undergraduates

	Amer. Ind.	Asian Amer.	Blacks	Hispanics	Whites
F	0	4	41	1	428
M	1	14	23	5	1,076
%	0.1	1.1	4.0	0.4	94.4

🏠 🏛 🚌 AAUW

The Pennsylvania State University, Capitol Campus, part of a complex of 19 branch campuses, offers the last two years of B.A. programs and some graduate degrees. Its 2,656 students include 1,601 undergraduates. Thirty percent of undergraduates are women, of whom 19 percent attend part-time. The median age of all undergraduates is 26.

Degrees are awarded in business, engineering, the social sciences, interdisciplinary studies, and education. Weekend, on- and off-campus day and evening classes, and a summer session provide alternatives to the regular schedule. A Continuing Education Program serves the campus. Fifty-two percent of students commute, using public transportation or on-campus parking.

Policies to Ensure Fairness to Women. Although no written policy exists concerning sexual harassment, a formal campus grievance procedure resolves complaints. Equal-opportunity officers are located on the main campus of the Pennsylvania State University.

Women in Leadership Positions. *Students.* Of the five student leadership positions available in recent years, women served one-year terms as president of the student body and editor of the campus newspaper.

Faculty. Twelve percent of the 102 faculty members are women, a proportion far below the national average. There are 3 female faculty for every 100 female students and 9 male faculty for every 100 male students.

Administrators. Except for the chief development officer/director of institutional research, all top administrators are men. One of the 7-member faculty senate and 1 of 5 members of the faculty promotion committee are women. In a recent year, 1 of 4 speakers in a campus-wide lecture program was a woman.

Women and the Curriculum. Most women take degrees in business (38 percent), the social sciences (35 percent), education (13 percent), and interdisciplinary studies (11 percent). Forty-four percent of the men and 3 percent of the women receive degrees in engineering. Cooperative educational programs are used mostly by men, but 90 percent of the participants in internships and practicums are women.

Three courses on women are offered, including Feminine/Masculine, Autobiography, and Women in Transition in the Novel. An official committee is responsible for developing courses on women. Programs designed for faculty address the needs of reentry women and discuss equal employment opportunity laws. The department of education provides instruction on the development and use of sex-fair curricula; the department of social work offers training on services for battered spouses, displaced homemakers, and childcare.

Women and Athletics. Women have some opportunity to participate in organized, competitive sports. Women's intramurals include a limited selection of individual and team sports. Eighty-two percent of club athletes are women. Of six paid intercollegiate coaches, one is a woman. Women participate in varsity tennis and volleyball.

Housing and Student Organizations. Coeducational and single-sex housing with no restrictions on visiting hours, and student family housing, are available for the 48 percent of students living on campus. Sixteen percent of white women, 2 percent of black women, and 2 percent of Asian American women live on campus. One woman and one man serve as residence-hall directors; they are offered training on sex education, racism, and birth control.

Student advocacy groups include the Black Student Union and the Graduate Student Organization.

Special Services and Programs for Women. *Health and Counseling.* The health service, staffed by a male physician and two female health-care providers, provides gynecological treatment and birth control. One man and a woman, trained to understand sex-role stereotyping and racial bias, offer counseling on gynecological issues, birth control, abortion, and rape and assault. Counselors are offered training in the avoidance of sex-role stereotyping and racial bias. Regular student health insurance covers maternity.

Safety and Security. Measures include campus and municipal police with arrest authority, information sessions on campus safety, and a rape crisis center. Two assaults, both on men, were reported for 1980–81.

Career. Workshops on nontraditional occupations are available, as are programs by women in nontraditional professions, and information on job discrimination. Programs establish links between alumnae and students.

Other. The counseling office and Women in Crisis aid battered women. The Cultural Arts Series offers theater and other women's art programs. There is a student telephone service for information, referrals, and support. Returning Women serves displaced homemakers, older women, and rape and assault victims. Potential Reentry Opportunities in Business and Education (PROBE) serves women in a three-county area. PROBE offers programs for displaced homemakers, a program to build skills in mathematics, and (with the counseling center) assertiveness-training.

Institutional Self-Description. "As the only upper-division (junior and senior years) and graduate center in Pennsylvania, Capitol Campus makes available innovative, quality programs to traditional and nontraditional students. Programs are available on a full- or part-time basis through day, evening, and weekend courses. Credit for prior experiential learning is available through the CLEP examination."

St. Francis College
Loretto, PA 15940
Telephone: (814) 472-7000

Women in Leadership
★★★ students

1,127 undergraduates

	Amer. Ind.	Asian Amer.	Blacks	Hispanics	Whites
F	0	1	3	1	471
M	0	2	8	9	627
%	0.0	0.3	1.0	0.9	97.9

🏠 🏛 🚌

Founded in 1847 as St. Francis Academy for men, this private Roman Catholic college became coeducational in 1940. Among the 1,654 students enrolled, 1,127 are undergraduates, of whom 42 percent are women. Less than 1 percent of women attend part-time. The median age of undergraduates is 20 years; 5 percent of women are over age 25.

St. Francis offers bachelor's degrees in a range of liberal arts and pre-professional fields; master's degrees are also offered. Adult education is available through the division of community education services. Alternative schedules include on-campus evening and summer session classes, self-paced/contract learning, and off-campus day and evening classes.

The campus is accessible by public transportation. On-campus parking is available for the one-fourth of students who commute.

Policies to Ensure Fairness to Women. One administrator has part-time responsibility for monitoring compliance with legislation regarding sex equity for students. Complaints of sexual harassment are handled informally and confidentially.

Women in Leadership Positions. *Students.* St. Francis offers outstanding opportunities for women to gain leadership experience. In a recent three-year period, women held all seven available campus-wide posts at least once, including one-year terms as president of the student senate and student union board and a two-year term as editor-in-chief of the campus newspaper. Four of eight honorary societies are headed by women.

Faculty. Seventeen percent of the 65 full-time faculty are women, a proportion considerably below the national average. There are 2 female faculty for every 100 female students and 8 male faculty for every 100 male students.

Administrators. Of the eight chief administrators, the head librarian is a woman. Women chair four of the 15 departments: foreign languages, library science, nursing, and religious studies. Two of 15 trustees are female.

Women and the Curriculum. Most women earn degrees in business (21 percent), letters (11 percent), and social sciences (10 percent). One percent of women earn degrees in mathematics or the physical sciences. Forty percent of internships are awarded to women.

The college offers two courses on women through the departments of history/political science and behavioral science: Women in American History and Introduction to Women's Studies. The divisions of nursing and social work include some issues of concern to women in their courses.

Women and Athletics. St. Francis has a full and varied intramural program and an adequate intercollegiate program. Club sports are also available. Thirty-seven percent of intramural and 23 percent of varsity athletes are women, as are three of seven paid varsity coaches. Athletic scholarships for women became available in 1981. Intercollegiate sports for women are basketball, cross-country, tennis, track, and volleyball.

Housing and Student Organizations. Three-fourths of the students live on campus in single-sex dormitories, which restrict hours for visitors of the oppposite sex, or in married students' housing. One of three dormitory directors is a woman; staff are offered awareness-training on avoidance of sexism.

One-fourth of female students belong to social sororities. Sororities and fraternities provide housing for their members.

Special Services and Programs for Women. *Health and Counseling.* The student health service, staffed by 1 male physician and 3 female health-care providers, provides no medical treatment specific to women. The student counseling center employs 2 men and 1 woman; abortion and rape counseling is available.

Safety and Security. Measures consist of campus police without arrest authority, night-time escort service for women, courses on self-defense, information sessions on campus safety and crime prevention, and a rape crisis center. Six assaults (two on women) and no rapes were reported for 1980–81.

Career. The college offers workshops, lectures, and printed materials on nontraditional occupations, as well as a program to establish networks between alumnae and female students and updated files of alumnae by specific career.

Institutional Self-Description. "Caring faculty and staff, close-knit student body, quiet rural campus, increasing number of women in faculty and administration, and developing attention to Women's Studies and to reentry women all contribute to a steadily increasing women's presence at St. Francis College."

Seton Hill College
Greensburg, PA 15601
Telephone: (412) 834-2200

Women in Leadership
★★★ **students**
★★★ **faculty**
★★★ **administrators**

748 undergraduates

	Amer. Ind.	Asian Amer.	Blacks	Hispanics	Whites
F	0	4	34	16	694
M	0	0	0	0	0
%	0.0	0.5	4.6	2.1	92.8

🏠 ⚒ 👫 AAUW

Seton Hill, a Roman Catholic college for women, enrolls 878 students, of whom 748 are registered in degree programs. The median age of students is 20, and all but 4 percent attend full-time. The college offers the bachelor's degree in a variety of liberal arts fields, and maintains an exchange program with St. Vincent College for men. There is a continuing education program. Evening, weekend, and summer session classes are available. Three-fourths of the students live on campus in dormitories that restrict men's visiting hours. On-campus parking is available at a fee.

A college-operated childcare center accommodates all students' requests. Charges are based on a fixed daily rate. Private childcare facilities are located near the campus.

Policies to Ensure Fairness to Women. A sexual harassment policy protects students, faculty, and staff, and has been communicated in writing to students. Complaints are resolved informally and confidentially or through a formal grievance procedure.

Women in Leadership Positions. *Students.* Women hold all campus-wide leadership positions.

Faculty. Sixty-four percent of the 47 full-time faculty are women, a proportion above the average for similar colleges in this guide and far above the national average. There are 4 female faculty for every 100 female students.

Administrators. Women hold 7 of the 9 top-level administrative positions and chair 10 of 18 departments: English, French, Spanish, German, biology, chemistry, history, sociology, religious studies, and home economics. One department chair is an Hispanic woman, who also sits on the faculty senate. Half of the 30 trustees are women.

Women and the Curriculum. The most popular fields for women graduates are home economics (15 percent), psychology (12 percent), and fine arts (11 percent). Three percent of women earn degrees in such nontraditional areas as mathematics and physical sciences.

Four courses on women are offered through the departments of English, history, and sociology: Women in Literature, Women in the Americas, Women in Society, and Minority Experience. Courses in the departments of business and social work include some instruction on matters specific to women.

Women and Athletics. Seton Hill's sports program includes five team or individual intramural sports. One of the two paid coaches for intercollegiate sports is a woman. Intercollegiate sports offered are basketball, softball, tennis, and volleyball.

Special Services and Programs for Women. *Health and Counseling.* The student health center is staffed by 1 male physician and 3 female health-care providers. Three women, including 1 minority woman, staff the counseling center. Gynecological counseling and treatment are offered, along with birth control and rape and assault counseling. Counselors are offered training in the avoidance of sex-role stereotyping and racial bias.

Safety and Security. Measures consist of campus police with

arrest authority, night-time escort service, high-intensity lighting, emergency telephone and alarm systems, and instruction on self-defense and campus safety. No rapes and one assault on a woman were reported for 1980–81.

Career. The Career Services Office offers printed material, panels, and workshops on nontraditional occupations, as well as career services for reentry women. Files on careers of alumnae are available, and networking between alumnae and students is encouraged.

Institutional Self-Description. "Seton Hill, founded in 1883 and rechartered as a college in 1918, has a proud tradition in the education of women. Among the purposes included in its mission statement are the 'opportunity for the student to incorporate in her liberal arts education preparation for graduate study and/or professional work;' and 'the student's discovery of her promise as a woman.' "

Slippery Rock State College
Slippery Rock, PA 16057
Telephone: (412) 794-2510

Women in Leadership	★ Women and the
★ faculty	Curriculum
	★ Women and Athletics

5,021 undergraduates

	Amer. Ind.	Asian Amer.	Blacks	Hispanics	Whites
F	1	3	80	1	2,586
M	4	1	132	7	2,197
%	0.1	0.1	4.2	0.2	95.4

Founded in 1889 as a preparatory college for teachers, Slippery Rock State College now offers bachelor's degrees in education, arts and sciences, business, and health professions, as well as master's degrees. Continuing education courses are available through Graduate and Special Academic Programs. Scheduling alternatives include evening and summer session classes. Off-campus classes are also available. Some 5,000 of the almost 6,000 students are undergraduates, 53 percent of them women; 7 percent of women attend part-time. The median age of undergraduates is 20. Free on-campus parking is available to the 16 percent of students who commute.

A college-run childcare facility can accommodate 33 children. Students receive priority and charges are based on a sliding scale, according to income. Private childcare facilities are located near the campus.

Policies to Ensure Fairness to Women. A full-time Affirmative Action Officer administers compliance with laws concerning equal employment opportunity, sex equity for students, and handicapped access. A written policy forbidding sexual harassment of students, faculty, and staff has been publicly communicated to the campus community. Complaints are resolved through a formal grievance procedure. The Commission on the Status of Women includes student members with voting rights, meets frequently, and prepares a public annual report. Unions, student groups, and the President appoint members of the commission, which reports to the President. Both this commission and the Commission on Minority Affairs address the concerns of minority women.

Women in Leadership Positions. *Students.* Opportunities for women students to gain campus-wide leadership experience are limited. In recent years, women have served twice as editor-in-chief of the campus newspaper; they have also served regularly as presiding officer of the student court, a position rotated among women and men. Women head ten of the 20 campus honorary societies.

Faculty. Twenty-five percent of the 306 faculty are women; 78 percent of women have permanent positions. There are 3 female faculty for every 100 female students and 10 male faculty for every 100 male students.

Administrators. All top administrators are men. Women chair three of 29 departments: physical education, history, and sociology/anthropology. Eleven of the 60 faculty senate members, 2 of 18 members of the tenure, reappointments, and promotions committee, and 1 of the 9 trustees are women. In a recent year, one alumni award was given to a man and one to a woman.

Women and the Curriculum. Most women earn degrees in education (60 percent), public affairs (13 percent), and social sciences (6 percent); fewer than 1 percent are in mathematics and physical sciences. Ten percent of the science field-service assignments and 30 percent of student internships are held by women.

The Women's Studies Program, chaired by a full-time, permanently appointed faculty member, awards certificates. Courses are offered by the program and the departments of history, physical education, psychology, English, sociology/anthropology, French, nursing, and political science. Recent courses include Women in French Literature, Self-Care for Women, Women in Sport, and Women in Society. An official committee develops the Women's Studies Program, reports on women in the curriculum, collects and develops curricular materials on women, and publishes *Focus,* a newsletter on women. Workshops on affirmative action and equal employment opportunity are provided for the faculty. Courses in the departments of business, education, nursing, and social work provide some instruction on matters specific to women.

Women and Athletics. Slippery Rock has a good women's athletic program, with respect to student participation and the wide variety of offerings. Thirty-four percent of 651 varsity athletes, 29 percent of intramural athletes, and 23 percent of club athletes are women; women receive 30 percent of athletic scholarships. Eight of the 28 paid varsity coaches are women. The intercollegiate sports offered are basketball, cross-country, field hockey, gymnastics, lacrosse, softball, swimming, tennis, track, and volleyball.

Housing and Student Organizations. Thirty-nine percent of students live on campus in single-sex or coeducational dormitories and in student family housing. The five female and two male residence-hall directors are offered awareness-training on sex education, racism, and birth control.

Ten percent of full-time female students join social sororities. Ten women belong to an all-minority sorority. Although fraternities provide housing for members, sororities do not. Sisters Incorporated is a black women's advocacy group. The Association for Non-Traditional Students is an advocacy group for older women.

Special Services and Programs for Women. *Health and Counseling.* A health service, staffed by 2 male physicians and 7 female aides, provides gynecological and rape and assault treatment. Two men and 1 minority woman offer counseling in areas of concern to women. Counselors are offered awareness-training on human sexuality and sex-role stereotyping.

Safety and Security. Measures consist of campus police, high-intensity lighting, self-defense courses, information on campus safety, and a rape crisis center. One rape and 29 assaults were reported for 1980–81.

Career. Slippery Rock's Student Development intervention programs provide information on nontraditional occupations for women, as does an undergraduate Career Personalization course.

Institutional Self-Description. "Since the founding of Slippery Rock State College almost 100 years ago, women have been in the majority among the student body. One of the primary missions of the college is to educate the total student (male or female) not just in the classroom, but also in her or his personal growth and development."

Swarthmore College
Swarthmore, PA 19081
Telephone: (215) 447-7000

Women in Leadership
★ students

1,231 undergraduates

	Amer. Ind.	Asian Amer.	Blacks	Hispanics	Whites
F	1	13	43	8	481
M	0	9	37	4	591
%	0.1	1.9	6.7	1.0	90.3

🚐 ⬜ ⬜ ⬜ AAUW

Swarthmore, an independent, non-sectarian college, was founded by the Society of Friends in 1864. It offers its 1,256 students bachelor's degrees in liberal arts and engineering. Most students are registered in degree programs and attend full-time. Forty-six percent of student are women.

The campus is accessible by public transportation. On-campus parking is available to the 5 percent of students who commute.

Private childcare facilities are available near campus.

Policies to Ensure Fairness to Women. A woman administrator is responsible, on a part-time basis, for review of policies on equal employment opportunity, sex equity for students, and handicapped access. The college employs a part-time Equal Opportunity Officer. A Committee on the Status of Women, appointed by the President, includes students with voting rights. The concerns of minority women are addressed by this committee and by the Committee on Minority Affairs.

Women in Leadership Positions. *Students.* Women have good opportunities to exercise leadership on this campus. In recent years, the top student offices were held by women more than one-third of the time.

Faculty. Twenty-one percent of the 133 full-time faculty are women, a proportion slightly below the national average. There are 5 female faculty for every 100 female students and 16 male faculty for every 100 male students.

Administrators. The chief administrators are men. Women chair the division of humanities and the division of natural science and engineering, as well as the departments of classics, education, and sociology/anthropology. In a recent year, a woman was one of four honorary degree recipients and commencement speakers.

Women and the Curriculum. The most popular majors for women are social sciences (26 percent), literature (20 percent), and biological science (17 percent). Seven percent of women earn degrees in engineering, mathematics, and physical sciences.

Three courses on women are offered in the departments of English literature, history, and psychology: Images of Women in the 18th-Century Novel, Women and the Family in American History, and Psychology of Women.

Women and Athletics. For a college of this size, the intercollegiate sports program for women is good. The intramural and club programs offer cross-country, soccer, softball, squash, track, and volleyball. Women account for 46 percent of the intercollegiate athletes and eight of the 26 paid coaches. Intercollegiate sports for women include badminton, basketball, field hockey, gymnastics, lacrosse, softball, swimming, tennis, and volleyball.

Housing and Student Organizations. Ninety percent of the students live on campus in single-sex or coeducational dormitories. Nineteen of the 20 dormitory assistants are women, two of them minority women. Residence-hall staff are offered awareness-training on birth control, sexism, and racism.

About 6 percent of Swarthmore men belong to fraternities; the college has no sororities. The Women's Athletic Association Council, Women against Rape, the Gay-Lesbian Union, the staff of the Women's Center, and the Swarthmore Afro-American Society are campus advocacy groups.

Special Services and Programs for Women. *Health and Counseling.* The student health center has 6 part-time physicians, all men, and 6 health-care providers, all women. Of the 4-member staff of the student counseling center, 1 is a minority woman, 1 a white woman. Services include counseling and medical treatment for gynecological matters and birth control, as well as counseling for abortion and rape and assault.

Safety and Security. Measures consist of night-time escort service for women students, campus-wide night bus service to residential areas, high-intensity lighting, and self-defense courses for women. Information on the incidence of rapes and assaults on women was not provided.

Career. Workshops and literature on nontraditional occupations, job discrimination, and student-alumnae networks are available.

Other. Swarthmore's Alice Paul Women's Center is maintained by the Dean's Office and has a volunteer student director. The Dean's Office also provides assertiveness training.

Special Features. The Friends Historical Library and Peace Collection preserves over 400 letters of Lucretia Mott, the personal papers of Jane Addams, and records of such peace groups as the Women's International League for Peace and Freedom and Women's Strike for Peace.

Institutional Self-Description. "Swarthmore offers: sciences and engineering in the liberal arts context; two modes of study—independence in concentrated seminars for External Examination or diversified-study in-course program; small student body; wide participation in athletics, college committees, and extracurricular activities; continuous coeducational history since 1864; a rolling, wooded campus 30 minutes by train from Philadelphia."

Temple University
Philadelphia, PA 19122
Telephone: (215) 787-7000

★ Women and the Curriculum
★★ Women and Athletics

17,443 undergraduates

	Amer. Ind.	Asian Amer.	Blacks	Hispanics	Whites
F	56	89	2,007	248	6,107
M	44	109	1,118	199	7,527
%	0.6	1.1	17.9	2.6	77.8

 🏠 🏛 🚐 👫 📖

Established in 1884 and dedicated to "higher education for able students of limited means," Temple University, located in north Philadelphia, is a public institution which serves over 33,000 students with diverse undergraduate, graduate, and professional programs. The Adult Program provides continuing education studies. Alternative class schedules, including a summer session, and instruction at off-campus locations, are available.

Women make up 48 percent of the 17,443 undergraduates; one-fifth of the women attend part-time. For the 93 percent of the undergraduates who live off campus or commute, the university is accessible by public transportation. On-campus parking is available for a fee, with free transportation from distant parking lots.

University-sponsored childcare facilities accommodate 120 children on a first-come, first-served basis. Private childcare may be arranged nearby.

Policies to Ensure Fairness to Women. A policy on sexual harassment is currently being developed. A committee of the Faculty Senate is involved with equity issues for faculty women.

Women in Leadership Positions. *Students.* Information was not provided.

Faculty. Women are 24 percent of a full-time faculty of 1,348. According to recent report, 40 black women are among the women on the faculty. The ratio of female faculty to female students is 5 to 100; the ratio of male faculty to male students is 14 to 100.

Administrators. The director of women's athletics is female; other top administrators are male. Women, including one black and one Hispanic woman, chair 16 of 134 departments. The Deans of the School of Allied Health, the School of Social Administration, and the College of Music are women.

Women and the Curriculum. Women earn bachelor's degrees in education (23 percent), business and management (13 percent), the health professions (12 percent), and public affairs (10 percent). Three percent major in nontraditional fields. The most popular areas among women graduating with two-year degrees and certificates are public service and health technologies. The university offers a special program to build mathematical skills.

The Women's Studies Program offers an undergraduate major. Courses are available thorugh the program and a number of cooperating departments. Recent titles include Introduction to Women's Studies, Popular Fiction for Women, Sexism and Ordinary English, Image of Women in American, European, and Japanese Film, Women and the Law, Women's Sexuality, and The Sociology of Sex Roles. The Women's Studies director holds a full-time faculty appointment. An official committee is responsible for developing Women's Studies on campus.

Such current issues as mathematics confidence among females, sex fair curricula, teaching coeducational sports, and discrimination in the workplace are part of the preparation of future teachers and business students.

Women and Athletics. Intramural and intercollegiate programs provide excellent opportunities for individual and team sports. Club sports are also available. The university reports astroturf fields and track facilities. One-fifth of the intramural and one-third of the intercollegiate athletes are women. Most of the women's varsity teams played in tournaments in 1980. The intercollegiate sports offered are badminton, basketball, bowling, cross-country, fencing, field hockey, gymnastics, lacrosse, softball, swimming and diving, tennis, track and field, and volleyball.

Housing and Student Organizations. For the 7 percent of undergraduates who live on campus, residential accommodations include single-sex and coeducational dormitories, apartments, and sororities and fraternities. A married woman student whose spouse is not enrolled may live in university housing. Dormitories do not restrict hours for visitors of the opposite sex. Residence-hall staff are offered awareness-training on the avoidance of sexism and racism.

Special Services and Programs for Women. *Health and Counseling.* The student health service provides some medical attention specific to women including gynecological and birth control treatment. The counseling service, staffed by seven women and eight men, provides some counseling of particular interest to women, including abortion and rape and assault therapy. Staff are offered in-service training on the avoidance of sex-role stereotyping and racial bias.

Safety and Security. Measures include campus and city police, night-time escorts for women students, emergency alarm and telephone systems, self-defense courses for women, and information sessions on safety and crime prevention. No rapes and 85 assaults were reported for 1980–81.

Career. Workshops, lectures, and nonsexist/nonracist printed materials on women in nontraditional careers and fields of study are available, as well as a program of networking between female alumnae and students.

Returning Women Students. Women's Studies houses a Women's Re-Entry Program which offers a series of academic and supportive services.

Institutional Self-Description. "The primary goal of Temple University has historically been to provide education to special student populations. These students include the economically disadvantaged, adults only able to attend college part-time, and returning students. The University offers a wide range of services to meet special needs. Many of these programs and services are directed toward women."

University of Pennsylvania
Philadelphia, PA 19104
Telephone: (215) 243-5000

★ **Women and the Curriculum**

8,604 undergraduates

	Amer. Ind.	Asian Amer.	Blacks	Hispanics	Whites
F	1	115	281	51	2,913
M	9	161	213	69	4,549
%	0.1	3.3	5.9	1.4	89.2

🏠 🚌 👫 ✒ 📖 ⚐ AAUW

Established in 1740 as a men's college and coeducational since 1880, the University of Pennsylvania, a private institution located in a multi-cultural urban setting, provides a comprehensive range of undergraduate, graduate, and professional studies to over 19,800 students. The College of General Studies serves the adult learner. Evening classes and a summer session are available.

Women are 40 percent of the 8,604 undergraduates; 3 percent of women attend part-time. For the commuting student, the university is accessible by public transportation. On-campus parking is available at a fee, with free transportation from distant parking lots.

University-sponsored childcare facilities can accommodate approximately 60 children. Private arrangements for childcare may be made close to campus.

Policies to Ensure Fairness to Women. A full-time affirmative action officer reviews policies and practices and advises the President on matters of equal employment opportunity, sex equity for students, and handicapped accessibility. A campus policy prohibits sexual harassment.

Women in Leadership Positions. *Students.* Opportunities for women students to exercise campus leadership are limited. In a recent three-year period, women presided over the student senate and student union board and served as manager of the campus radio station during one year, while men held all five posts the remainder of the time.

Faculty. Women are 15 percent of a full-time faculty of 992. There are 4 female faculty for every 100 female students and 17 male faculty for every 100 male students.

Administrators. The Provost is a woman. The other higher administrative posts are held by men. The deans of the School of Nursing and the School of Social Work are female.

Women and the Curriculum. The most popular majors for women are social sciences (22 percent), the health professions (19 percent), and business and management (15 percent). Six percent graduate with degrees in such nontraditional areas as architecture, computer science, engineering, mathematics, and the physical sciences. Close to one-fifth of the undergraduate degrees in engineering go to women. Women earn one-third of the two-year degrees awarded, half in arts and sciences and half in business and commerce.

The Women's Studies Program offers an undergraduate minor and an individualized B.A. Courses on women are available through Women's Studies and cooperating departments. Recent offerings include Women and the Law, Concepts of Female Nature, Biology of Women, Women in Philosophy, and Comparative Analysis of Sex Roles. An official committee works to collect curricular materials and to further develop the Women's Studies Program.

Innovative health-care delivery, services for abused spouses, and discrimination in the workplace are part of the instruction provided future health-care workers, social workers, and business students.

Women and Athletics. The intramural program offers individual and team sports. The university reports special facilities for crew, swimming, and squash. Athletic scholarships are not awarded. No information was provided about intercollegiate sports.

Housing and Student Organizations. For the undergraduates who live on campus, coeducational dormitories and housing for married students and single parents with children are available. Dormitories do not restrict hours for visitors of the opposite sex.

Social sororities provide housing for their members. Among organizations that serve as advocates for women are the Penn Women's Alliance, Gays and Lesbians at Penn, and the women's caucuses in the professional schools.

Special Services and Programs for Women. *Health and Counseling.* The student health service provides medical attention specific to women: gynecological, birth control, abortion, and rape and assault treatment is available. The university reports that several physicians are female, several male. The regular student health insurance covers abortion and maternity at no extra cost. Through the counseling service, students have access to counseling of particular concern to women. The university reports one female psychiatrist on staff. There are also some minority women counselors.

Safety and Security. Measures consist of night-time escorts for women students, night-time bus service on and off campus, high-intensity lighting, emergency alarm and telephone systems, self-defense courses for women, information sessions on safety and crime prevention, and a rape crisis center. Information on the incidence of rapes and assaults was not provided by the university.

Career. Workshops, speakers, and printed materials on women in nontraditional careers and fields of study are available, as well as a program of contacts between alumnae and female students.

Other. The Women's Center, under a full-time director, and a recent budget of $110,000, sponsors a range of services and activities, including an annual women's week, lecture series, women's arts events, assertiveness training, a program to build confidence in mathematics, and a telephone line of information referral, and support.

Special Features. APPLE—which provides nonsexist leadership training for undergraduate women and men—is a feature of the Graduate School of Education.

Institutional Self-Description. "Penn is unique among urban universities from the point of view of its environment, safety program, and services that address women's needs. The Women's Studies Program offers a major. The prestige of the Penn degree makes it easier to break into careers in law, medicine, business, and other fields."

	On-campus evening and/or weekend classes		Commission on minority affairs
	Off-campus classes		Women's Studies program
	Accessible by public transportation		Women's center
	On-campus childcare facilities	AAUW	Member, American Association of University Women
	Publicly communicated sexual harassment policy, includes students	NWSA	Member, National Women's Studies Association
	Commission on status of women	CROW	On-campus Center for Research on Women

University of Pittsburgh, Johnstown
Johnstown, PA 15904
Telephone: (814) 266-9661

Women in Leadership
★★★ students

3,072 undergraduates

	Amer. Ind.	Asian Amer.	Blacks	Hispanics	Whites
F	0	2	28	0	1,334
M	0	1	25	0	1,679
%	0.0	0.1	1.7	0.0	98.2

 AAUW

The University of Pittsburgh at Johnstown was established as a junior college branch campus of the University of Pittsburgh, a private university. In 1970 it became a public, four-year branch of the University of Pittsburgh. Its 3,072 students are all undergraduates; their median age is 21. Forty-four percent are women, one-third of whom attend part-time. Degrees are awarded in engineering, business, education, and arts and sciences. On-and off-campus evening classes and summer sessions are available. The Office of Continuing Education administers adult education, in which 450 women participate. One-half of the students commute, using public transportation or on-campus parking available for a fee.

Policies to Ensure Fairness to Women. The Director of Administration and Budget reviews campus policies to ensure compliance with laws pertaining to fair-employment practices, sex equity for students, and access for the handicapped. A sexual harassment policy has been publicly communicated to staff, students, and faculty.

Women in Leadership Positions. *Students.* Opportunities for women to hold leadership positions are outstanding. In recent years, women held each top campus position at least twice. In addition, women chair three of five honorary societies.

Faculty. Nineteen percent of the 113 faculty are women. One of the full-time faculty is a black woman. The ratio of female faculty to female students is 2 to 100; there are 7 male faculty to 100 male students.

Administrators. Except for the director of institutional research, all top administrators are men. Of five major divisions of the college, humanities is chaired by a woman. In a recentyear, three of 18 speakers in a campus-wide lecture series were women.

Women and the Curriculum. Most women graduate in education (24 percent), social sciences (23 percent), business (13 percent), and psychology (13 percent). Four percent major in engineering and 2 percent, mathematics and physical sciences. Half of the students undertaking internships are women.

Three courses on women are available through the departments of history, anthropology, and psychology: History and Social Role of Women, Anthropology of Women, and Psychological Development of Women.

Women and Athletics. There is a good variety of sports in the intramural program, including weightlifting. Twenty-seven percent of intramural athletes are women. One of the seven paid varsity coaches is a woman. A third of the varsity athletes are women, who participate in basketball, golf, gymnastics, and volleyball.

Housing and Student Organizations. Single-sex dormitories, townhouses, and lodges, all with no restrictions on visiting hours, house 45 percent of the undergraduates.

Eleven percent of full-time undergraduates join non-residential sororities and fraternities. In a recent year, two minority women (of 30 on campus) joined sororities. The Black Action Society and Association of Women Students serve as advocates for women on campus.

Special Services and Programs for Women. *Health and Counseling.* Three female health-care providers supply medical treatment for gynecological problems, birth control, abortion, and rape and assault. A man and a woman provide counseling in the same areas.

Safety and Security. Measures include municipal police, night-time escorts for women, emergency telephones, and an alarm system. No rapes, and two assaults—neither of them against women—were reported for 1980–81.

Institutional Self-Description. "A relatively new degree-granting unit of the university, we pursue a fresh, contemporary approach to undergraduate education through diverse program offerings which range from the traditional to the strongly career-oriented. Directed study and extracurricular activities are encouraged for all students, and some organizations and opportunities are especially for women."

University of Pittsburgh, Main Campus
4200 Fifth Avenue, Pittsburgh, PA 15260
Telephone: (412) 624-4141

Women in Leadership ★ faculty			★ Women and the Curriculum	

15,735 undergraduates

	Amer. Ind.	Asian Amer.	Blacks	Hispanics	Whites
F	12	50	940	27	6,369
M	11	97	685	45	7,326
%	0.2	0.9	10.4	0.5	88.0

 AAUW

Established in 1787, the University of Pittsburgh is now an independent, state-related institution which enrolls 28,700 students in a variety of undergraduate, graduate, and professional programs. Alternative class schedules, including evening classes, a weekend college, a summer session, and off-campus locations are available.

Women are 47 percent of the 15,735 undergraduates; 27 percent of women attend part-time. The median age of undergraduates is 21. For the three-quarters of the undergraduates who live off campus or commute, the university is accessible by public transportation. There is on-campus parking for a fee and free transportation from distant lots.

The university childcare facilities charge fees on a sliding scale; the YWCA provides tuition aid.

Policies to Ensure Fairness to Women. An Affirmative Action Officer is responsible part-time for policy on equal employment, sex equity for students, and handicapped accessibility. A full-time assistant monitors compliance. A published policy prohibits sexual harassment; complaints are handled both informally and confidentially and through a formal grievance procedure. The University Affirmative Action Committee, which includes students as voting members, addresses issues of concern to all women, including minority women.

Women in Leadership Positions. *Students.* Opportunities for women students to assume campus leadership are well below average for private research universities in this guide. In recent years, women have served one year as editor-in-chief of the campus newspaper and one year as presiding officer of the residence-hall council.

Faculty. Women are 25 percent of a full-time faculty of 1,307. Among the full-time faculty are 48 black, 22 Asian American, and 3 Hispanic women. There are 6 female faculty for every 100 female students and 16 male faculty for every 100 male students.

Administrators. The head of libraries is a woman; the other top administrative positions are filled by men. Women chair eight of

87 departments. The deans of the School of Nursing, of Health Related Professions, and of Graduate Programs in Arts and Sciences are women.

Women and the Curriculum. The majority of women earning bachelor's degrees major in the health professions (22 percent), social sciences (12 percent), general letters (12 percent), and education (11 percent). Ten percent major in nontraditional areas, in engineering, mathematics, and the physical sciences. All women graduating with two-year degrees major in health technologies.

The Women's Studies Program, under a full-time faculty member who directs the program part-time, offers an 18-credit certificate and the B.A. and M.A. through interdisciplinary studies. Twenty courses originate in Women's Studies or are cross-listed with Women's Studies and eight other departments. Recent offerings include Black Urban Women; Psychology and History of Black Women; Literary and Social Views of Women; European Women; Women, Achievement, and Work; Sociology of the Family; and Women's Studies Field Placement. An official committee promotes and monitors the development of Women's Studies across the curriculum, as well as research focused on women. The Women's Studies Program has close ties with Hillman Library and the Media Resource Center. The program awards three annual prizes for the best graduate and undergraduate research on women and sponsors regular teaching and current "state-of-the-field" seminars for faculty and students. The development and use of sex-fair curricula and the teaching of coeducational physical education classes are part of the instruction provided future teachers.

Women and Athletics. Intramural and intercollegiate programs offer adequate opportunity for organized, competitive, individual and team sports. Forty-five percent of intramural and 33 percent of intercollegiate athletes are women. Women receive 20 percent of athletic scholarships. Fourteen of 50 paid intercollegiate coaches are female. All women's intercollegiate teams played in tournaments in 1980. The intercollegiate sports offered are basketball, field hockey, gymnastics, track, swimming, tennis, and volleyball.

Housing and Student Organizations. One-quarter of undergraduates live on campus in single-sex or coeducational dormitories, where hours for visitors of the opposite sex are restricted. Awareness-training on the avoidance of sexism and racism, and on birth control, sex education, and sexual harassment and rape is offered to staff in residence halls. Four of the seven directors are female.

Nine percent of undergraduate women belong to social sororities. Sororities and fraternities provide housing for their members.

Special Services and Programs for Women. *Health and Counseling.* The student health service provides treatment for gynecological disorders and information about birth control. The three health service physicians are female, as are ten other health-care providers. Half the 14 professional staff in the counseling service are women. Students have access to gynecological, birth control, abortion, and rape and assault counseling.

Safety and Security. Measures include campus and city police, night-time bus service to residence areas, high-intensity lighting, emergency alarm and telephone system, self-defense courses for women, information sessions on safety and crime prevention, and an "alert-a-buddy" system for people working alone. A total of 34 assaults (15 on women) and no rapes were reported for 1980–81.

Career. Workshops, role model lectures, and printed information concentrated on women in nontraditional careers and fields of study, as well as a network of contacts between alumnae and students, are available.

Other. The Women's Center, with a full-time director and a budget of $48,000, sponsors programs for battered women and displaced homemakers; assertiveness-training and a telephone line of referral, information, and support. The Women's Studies Program sponsors a women's lecture series. A program to build skills in mathematics is available through the Learning Skills Center.

Institutional Self-Description. "Core faculty in psychology, literature, history, sociology, and library and information science assist the Women's Studies Program. An additional resource is the faculty in other schools of the university who advise and support the students in a number of areas. Options exist for a self-designed major, supervised field placement, and independent study."

Villa Maria College
2551 West Lake Rd., Erie, PA 16505
Telephone: (814) 838-1966

Women in Leadership
★★★ students
★★★ faculty
★★★ administrators

512 undergraduates

	Amer. Ind.	Asian Amer.	Blacks	Hispanics	Whites
F	0	5	11	2	492
M	0	0	0	0	0
%	0.0	1.0	2.2	0.4	96.5

🏠 🚐 👫 ⚲ AAUW

Villa Maria, established in 1925, is an independent, Roman Catholic college for women operated by the Sisters of St. Joseph. Its suburban campus has a total enrollment of 551 students. Ten percent of the students attend part-time. The median age of students is 20.

The college offers a variety of associate and bachelor's degrees. The Alternative Learning Center is responsible for adult continuing education. Classes meet day and evening; there is also a summer session. Fifty-seven percent of the women live in dormitories on campus that restrict visiting hours for members of the opposite sex. Commuters can reach the college by public transportation; there is free parking on campus.

A campus childcare center serves 22 children at a monthly fee of $200; 30 percent of students' requests for this service are accommodated. Additional, private childcare facilities are available off campus.

Policies to Ensure Fairness to Women. The Vice President for Business Affairs has the part-time responsibility for policy pertaining to equal-employment, sex-equity-for-students, and handicapped-access laws.

Women in Leadership Positions. *Students.* Women hold all student leadership positions.

Faculty. Three-fourths of the 48 full-time faculty are women, a proportion above average for women's colleges in this guide. There are 8 female faculty for every 100 female students.

Administrators. With the exception of the chief development officer, the top administrators are women. Women chair four of seven departments: humanities, business, human ecology, and nursing. The 19-member Board of Trustees includes four women.

Women and the Curriculum. About two-thirds of the women receive bachelor's degrees in health professions; 3 percent, in such nontraditional fields as mathematics and physical sciences. Special programs encourage women to prepare for careers in accounting and science.

Four courses on women are offered through the departments of theology, business, philosophy, and interdisciplinary studies: Women in Christian Tradition, Women in Management, Philosophy of Woman, and Images of Women in Literature and Arts. The departments of education, social work, and nursing provide some instruction on matters specific to women.

Women and Athletics. The small organized sports program offers four intercollegiate and two intramural sports, as well as athletic scholarships. The two paid varsity coaches are women. Intercollegiate sports available are basketball, softball, tennis, and volleyball.

Special Services and Programs for Women. *Health and Counseling.* The staff of the student health center consists of three female health-care providers. Medical treatment for matters specific to women is not available. Two female professionals provide counseling on gynecological problems, birth control, and rape and assault.

Safety and Security. Measures include campus and local police protection, high-intensity lighting, an emergency alarm system, instruction on self-defense and campus safety, and a rape crisis center. No rapes or assaults on women were reported for 1980–81.

Career. The Counseling Center and the Placement Office provide information on traditional and nontraditional occupations.

Other. An active Women's Center, under a full-time director, attracts 500 women annually, predominantly undergraduates and women from the community. The Counseling Center and The Continuing Education for Women Program serve battered women and displaced homemakers; they sponsor various other programs for women, such as an annual women's week, assertiveness training, a telephone information and referral service, and consciousness-raising sessions. Theater and arts productions by and for women and a women's lecture series are also available.

Institutional Self-Description. "Villa Maria College is a community that remains fully committed to the value and dignity of the individual woman. The curriculum in all programs stresses strong career preparation within the broader framework of liberal education. Our flexible schedule of internships and field placements enhances students' opportunities for growth and self-discovery."

West Chester State College
West Chester, PA 19380
Telephone: (215) 436-1000

Women in Leadership
★ faculty

★★ **Women and the Curriculum**

6,417 undergraduates

	Amer. Ind.	Asian Amer.	Blacks	Hispanics	Whites
F	1	11	301	23	3,413
M	2	9	165	15	2,466
%	0.1	0.3	7.3	0.6	91.8

🏠 🏛 🚐 👫 ⚲ 🔲 📖 ⚲ AAUW NWSA

Founded as a teacher-training school in 1812, West Chester State is a four-year, public college that enrolls some 8,400 students. It offers bachelor's degrees in health fields, business, liberal arts and science, as well as education; master's degrees are also available. The graduate and continuing studies division is responsible for adult continuing education. Classes meet on and off campus during the day and evening, and there is a summer session.

Women are 58 percent of the 6,417 undergraduates; 9 percent of women attend part-time. The median age of undergraduates is 20. Recent data from the college indicates that 17 percent of all women undergraduates are over 25 and that two-thirds of these older students attend part-time; there are over 600 returning women students on campus. The campus is accessible by public transportation. For the 57 percent of undergraduates who commute, on-campus parking for a fee is provided.

A college-operated childcare center accommodates 35 children, at no fee, and can meet half of students' requests. Additional, private childcare facilities are located nearby.

Policies to Ensure Fairness to Women. Three administrators are responsible (one on a full-time and two on a part-time basis) for policy and compliance with legislation pertaining to equal employment opportunity, handicapped access, and sex equity for students. A published sexual harassment policy protects students, faculty, and staff; complaints are resolved through a formal campus grievance procedure or, when appropriate, through informal, confidential means.

A self-designated faculty women's coalition, along with the Institute for Women issue reports on matters of concern to women. The institute sponsors the Title IX/Sex Discrimination Board.

Women in Leadership Positions. *Students.* Women have some opportunity to exercise their leadership potential. In three recent years, women held one-third of all campus-wide offices, including one-year terms as president of the student senate, of the student union board, and of the residence-hall council, as well as a three-year term as editor-in-chief of the campus newspaper.

Faculty. Twenty-nine percent of the 477 full-time faculty are women, a proportion above the national average. There are 4 female faculty for every 100 female students and 14 male faculty for every 100 male students. Faculty women participate in Leadership Development for Women Faculty, a program of the Pennsylvania State College and Universities system.

Administrators. All top administrators are men; women serve as the Coordinators of the Faculty of Arts and Sciences and of Health Science. Women chair six of 33 departments: art, psychology, special education, nursing, music education, music, history, and literature. Twenty percent of the faculty senate are women, as are 2 of the 7 trustees.

Women and the Curriculum. Most women earn degrees in education (52 percent), public affairs (11 percent), and health professions (10 percent). Two percent specialize in such nontraditional fields as computer science, mathematics, and physical sciences.

The Women's Studies Program, under the direction of a permanent faculty member, grants an undergraduate minor. Courses on women are offered through Women Studies and the departments of history, psychology, art, humanities, nursing, and French. They include Health Issues for Women, Women in Modern Fiction, Women in America, Women and Men in French Literature, and Women in Contemporary Society. All students are required to take a Human Relations course that examines discrimination against women and male members of minority groups.

Women and Athletics. West Chester State offers a large and varied intercollegiate sports program for women. No information was supplied regarding the intramural program. Two-thirds of the intercollegiate athletes are women, as are eight of the 35 paid intercollegiate coaches. Intercollegiate sports offered are badminton, basketball, cross-country, field hockey, gymnastics, lacrosse, softball, swimming, tennis, track and field, and volleyball.

Housing and Student Organizations. Forty-three percent of the undergraduates live in women's dormitories or coeducational dormitories. The women's dormitories restrict hours for visitors of the opposite sex; coeducational dormitories do not. Five of 12 residence-hall directors are women, and all residence-hall staff are offered awareness-training on homosexuality.

Four percent of women students belong to social sororities, some of which are residential. One all-minority sorority has 20 members. Panhellenic serves as an advocacy group for women students. Over 6 percent of its 147 members are minority women, predominantly black women. There is also a Title IX Advocacy Group on campus.

Special Services and Programs for Women. *Health and Counseling.* The student health service employs 2 male physicians and 4 female health-care providers. Two of the 7 professionals at the student counseling center are women. Abortion counseling is the only service specific to women provided on campus. Students are referred to Planned Parenthood for gynecological matters and birth control.

Safety and Security. Measures consist of campus and local police protection, high-intensity lighting, instruction and information on self-defense and campus safety for women, and a rape crisis center. Five rapes and 27 assaults were reported for 1980–81.

Career. The college offers workshops, lectures, and panels on nontraditional occupations, as well as programs to promote networking between female students and alumnae.

Other. A Women's Center, under the direction of a full-time faculty member, sponsors theater and arts programs for women, assertiveness training, two scholarships, a telephone information and referral service, and a monthly newsletter. In cooperation with the Women's Studies Program, the Center organizes an annual women's week and a women's lecture series.

Special Features. West Chester State is a member of the Pennsylvania State College Consortium, which obtains grants for women's projects. The college grants the Grace Cochran Award for Research on Women.

Institutional Self-Description. "West Chester State College has acknowledged its commitment to the needs of all women students. Services offered by the Women's Center attract, sustain, and encourage students, especially older, returning women. The center provides advisements and referrals regarding personal and academic problems, a free drop-off center, support groups, and a monthly newsletter, *For All Women.* It has an excellent, growing Women's Studies Program, taught by able and enthusiastic teachers/scholars from a wide spectrum of disciplines."

Widener College of Widener University
Chester, PA 19013
Telephone: (215) 499-4000

Women in Leadership
  ★★ faculty

3,126 undergraduates

	Amer. Ind.	Asian Amer.	Blacks	Hispanics	Whites
F	1	5	165	3	1,197
M	2	9	101	6	1,637
%	0.1	0.5	8.5	0.3	90.7

 AAUW

Founded as a military academy in 1821, Widener College became affiliated with Brandywine College in 1976 and acquired university status in 1979. It offers its 3,952 students bachelor's programs in liberal arts and sciences and pre-professional fields, as well as associate, and master's degrees. Widener's evening division, University College, provides adult continuing education. Weekend and summer session classes are available. Forty-four percent of the 3,126 undergraduates are women; 40 percent of women attend part-time.

The campus, located near Philadelphia, is accessible by public transportation. On-campus parking for a fee is available for the 51 percent of students who commute.

College childcare facilities accommodate 40 children; fees are based on a fixed, daily rate. Thirty percent of students' requests can be met. Additional, private childcare facilities are located near the campus.

Policies to Ensure Fairness to Women. Compliance with legislation regarding equal employment opportunity and sex equity for students is monitored on a part-time basis by the Director of

Personnel and the Dean and Assistant Vice President of Student Affairs.

Women in Leadership Positions. *Students.* Widener offers limited opportunities for women to exercise campus-wide leadership. In three recent years, women served once as presidents of the student senate, student union board, senior class, and sophomore class, and as manager of the campus radio station, and twice as freshman class president. Three of the ten honorary societies are headed by women.

Faculty. Women are 37 percent of the 113 full-time faculty, a proportion above the national average. There are 5 female faculty for every 100 female students and 6 male faculty for every 100 male students.

Administrators. Of the 9 chief administrators, two are women; the head librarian and the chief student-life officer. Women chair one of three divisions: social science. The Dean of Nursing is a woman. Two of the 29 trustees are female, 1 of them a black woman.

Women and the Curriculum. Over half (58 percent) of bachelor's degrees earned by women are in health professions, with a significant number in business. Three percent of women students major in mathematics, engineering, and the physical sciences. Business and arts and sciences are the popular fields for women taking two-year degrees. Widener sponsors a program to encourage women to prepare for careers in engineering. Twenty-five percent of the business students and 20 percent of the engineering students in cooperative education programs are women, as are 90 percent of student interns.

Widener offers three courses on women, in the social science and humanities divisions: Sex Roles, Women in American Society, and Issues on the Women's Movement. The departments of nursing and social work include instruction on some matters specific to women.

Women and Athletics. Opportunities for women to participate in intramural sports are limited. The intercollegiate program is good for a college of this size. Thirty percent of the intercollegiate athletes are women. Intercollegiate sports offered are basketball, cross-country, field hockey, golf, lacrosse, softball, swimming, and tennis.

Housing and Student Organizations. Forty-nine percent of the students live on campus in single sex or coeducational dormitories. Some of the women's dormitories restrict hours for visitors of the opposite sex. Dormitory staff are offered awareness-training on sex education, avoidance of sexism and racism, birth-control, and security.

Twenty-four percent of the full-time undergraduate women belong to sororities. Both sororities and fraternities provide housing for members. A small number of minority women belong to racially-integrated sororities. The college reports one women's advocacy group, the Society of Women Engineers.

Special Services and Programs for Women. *Health and Counseling.* The student health service, staffed by one male physician and six female health-care providers, provides medical attention specific to women. Counseling for gynecological problems, birth control, abortion, and rape and assault is offered by two nurse practitioners.

Safety and Security. Measures consist of local police who co-operate with the campus force, a night-time escort service, high-intensity lighting, an emergency alarm system, self-defense and rape prevention information, and a rape crisis center. No rapes and five assaults (none on women) were reported for 1980–81.

Institutional Self-Description. "Widener College is located in a major metropolitan area near Philadelphia, and enjoys the benefits of various cultural, social, and educational opportunities. Widener, although now a multi-component university, engenders a small college atmosphere. Teaching faculty are people-oriented, giving individualized attention to students. A variety of work experience opportunities through internships and coop programs with many placements leading to post-graduate employment."

Williamsport Area Community College
Williamsport, PA 17701
Telephone: (717) 326-3761

Women in Leadership
★★★ students

2,775 undergraduates

	Amer. Ind.	Asian Amer.	Blacks	Hispanics	Whites
F	0	1	13	0	662
M	5	7	70	1	2,016
%	0.2	0.3	3.0	0.1	96.5

Affiliated with the state since 1965 as a public, two-year community college, Williamsport offers comprehensive educational services to 3,288 students, 2,775 of whom are undergraduates. Approximately one-fourth of the undergraduates are women and 86 percent of women attend full-time. Almost half of all students are under age 20; 10 percent of women students are over 40.

The college offers the first two years of liberal arts and sciences and a variety of terminal vocational programs. Adult continuing education is offered through the Center for Lifelong Education. Day and evening classes both on and off campus, self-paced/contract learning, and a summer session are available. The campus is accessible by public transportation, and free on-campus parking is provided.

On-campus childcare facilities, available for students who are parents, are open from 8 a.m. to 10 p.m. and charge a nominal hourly rate; they usually can accommodate all students' requests. Private childcare facilities are available off campus.

Policies to Ensure Fairness to Women. The Personnel Director serves as an equal opportunity officer for the staff, while the Dean of Student Development acts in a similar manner for students. Sexual harassment of students, faculty, and staff is prohibited by a written campus policy that has been publicly communicated to all three groups.

Women in Leadership Positions. *Students.* Though they are a minority, women participate actively in student leadership on campus. In a recent three-year period, women held five of the nine possible posts, including president of the student body twice, presiding officer of the student governing body twice, and editor-in-chief of the campus newspaper once.

Faculty. The full-time faculty of 168 is 14 percent female, considerably below average for public, two-year colleges. There are 4 female faculty for every 100 female students and 7 male faculty for every 100 male students.

Administrators. Of eight chief administrators, seven are men; an Hispanic woman is acting chief academic officer. Men chair all eight departments and direct all five of the major academic units.

Women and the Curriculum. Most of the two-year degrees and certificates are awarded to women in business and commerce (40 percent), health technologies (25 percent), and natural science (19 percent). One-third of the students in experiential learning programs are women.

Women in Literature is offered through the division of communications, humanities, and social science. Faculty educational programs are available on sexism and the curriculum and on non-traditional occupations for women and men.

Women and Athletics. Small numbers of women participate in the intercollegiate and intramural sports programs. There are two paid women coaches on the seven-member varsity staff. Intercollegiate sports for women include basketball, coeducational cross-country, field hockey, and coeducational tennis.

Special Services and Programs for Women. *Health and Counseling.* Limited health services are provided by one female nurse. The student counseling center is staffed by six full-time counselors, two of whom are women. The regular student health insurance policy covers abortion and maternity at no extra charge. Counseling and medical treatment of health problems specific to women are not available.

Safety and Security. The campus is patrolled by campus police who have no arrest authority. For 1980–81, no rapes or assaults were reported on campus.

Career. The Counseling and Career Development Center and the Adult Career and Education Service provide individual counseling to all students. Career materials and activities include workshops focused on nontraditional occupations, lectures by women employed in nontraditional occupations, printed information on nontraditional fields of study for women, and job discrimination information on nontraditional occupations for women. In addition, a Career/Life Planning Workshop for Displaced Homemakers is offered four times a year. Career/Life Planning for Women is offered through the Center for Lifelong Education.

Other. An annual women's week is sponsored by the student activities coordinator.

Institutional Self-Description. "Support services and career development workshops draw women to the campus. Many technical programs are available and are open to both men and women. Many of the programs attract women who wish to get into a nontraditional field."

Wilson College
Chambersburg, PA 17201
Telephone: (717) 264-4141

Women in Leadership	★ Women and the
★★★ students	Curriculum
★★ faculty	
★★★ administrators	

194 undergraduates

	Amer. Ind.	Asian Amer.	Blacks	Hispanics	Whites
F	0	16	7	3	163
M	0	0	0	0	0
%	0.0	8.5	3.7	1.6	86.2

A liberal arts college for women, Wilson is affiliated with the Presbyterian Church. The college has a total enrollment of 217 students, of whom 194 are full-time students registered in degree programs. The median age of students is 19; a few older women are enrolled part-time.

Wilson offers bachelor's degrees in a range of liberal arts and science fields. A small Continuing Education for Women Program is operated by Student Services. Some evening classes are available. About three-fourths of the women live on campus in dormitories, some with restricted hours for visitors of the opposite sex. Free on-campus parking is available for commuters.

Private childcare facilities are located near the campus.

Policies to Ensure Fairness to Women. The Comptroller serves as the affirmative action officer. Complaints of sexual harassment are handled informally and confidentially. A self-designated Commission on the Status of Women includes students as voting members, meets regularly, and reports to the Provost for External Affairs on matters of concern to women.

Women in Leadership Positions. *Students.* Women hold all student leadership positions.

Faculty. Eleven of the 30 full-time faculty are women. There are 6 female faculty for every 100 female students.

Administrators. Women occupy all major administrative positions except that of chief business officer. Three of ten departments are chaired by women: American studies, behavioral studies, and social and political institutions. About half of the trustees are women.

Women and the Curriculum. Approximately one-fourth of women graduates major in social sciences and another fourth in biology. Wilson offers a dual degree program designed to encourage women to prepare for careers in science and management. The college also has an internship program.

The Women's Studies Program offers 15 courses, including Introduction to Women's Studies. Other recent offerings include Women and Religious Traditions, Medieval Women, and French Women Writers. The program does not confer degrees in Women's Studies, but it does attempt to involve all faculty members in the development of a curriculum that reflects scholarship on women. Courses in the departments of business, education, and physical education provide instruction on some matters specific to women.

Minority Women. Minority women are 14 percent of the student body. The Commission on the Status of Women responds to their concerns. A black woman sits on the 23-member Board of Trustees. The sociology department emphasizes the experiences of minority women in a course on American minority groups. The members of the residence-hall staff, who include one minority woman, receive awareness training on racism.

Women and Athletics. Though Wilson does not offer intramural sports, it does have a varied program of intercollegiate and club sports. The six paid intercollegiate coaches are all women. Intercollegiate sports offered are basketball, field hockey, gymnastics, lacrosse, riding, tennis, and volleyball.

Special Services and Programs for Women. *Health and Counseling.* The student health center is staffed by two male physicians and two female health-care providers. One female professional works at the student counseling center. Gynecological counseling and medical treatment, as well as birth control, abortion, and rape and assault counseling are provided.

Safety and Security. Measures consist of campus police protection and information on campus safety. No rapes or assaults were reported for 1980–81.

Career. Services include workshops, lectures, and information on nontraditional occupations, files on alumnae careers for students' use, and programs to promote networking between alumnae and students.

Other. The Women's Studies Program and the Provost's Office sponsor a women's lecture series. The Student Services Office offers leadership training and is the most likely place for women with special needs to find support.

Institutional Self-Description. "Founded as a college for young women, Wilson has been educating women for over a hundred years, and this experience is important in creating 'the edge' that researchers say contributes to the high achievement attained by graduates of women's colleges. Our commitment to women's education of the best academic quality is *not* mandated by law."

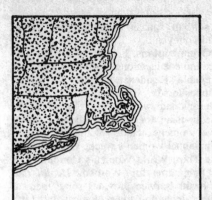

RHODE ISLAND

Barrington College
Middle Highway, Barrington, RI 02806
Telephone: (401) 246-1200

Women in Leadership
* ★ faculty
* ★★ administrators

476 undergraduates

	Amer. Ind.	Asian Amer.	Blacks	Hispanics	Whites
F	0	1	13	4	241
M	0	0	17	2	184
%	0.0	0.2	6.5	1.3	92.0

Founded in 1900, Barrington College is a private, nondenominational institution with a strong evangelical Protestant focus. Of the 516 students, 476 are undergraduates. Fifty-five percent of the degree students are women, 9 percent of whom attend part-time. The median age of all students is 20 years.

Barrington offers bachelor's degrees in liberal arts and sciences, business, education, and pre-professional fields. Evening and summer session classes are available. The suburban campus is accessible by public transportation. On-campus parking is also available to the 31 percent of students who commute.

Policies to Ensure Fairness to Women. Sexual harassment complaints are resolved informally and confidentially. The Commission on Minority Affairs addresses issues of interest to minority women.

Women in Leadership Positions. *Students.* Seven student leadership positions are available each year. In three recent years, women have served as president of the student body and editor-in-chief of the campus newspaper. The sole campus honorary society has a woman president.

Faculty. Thirty-two percent of the 22 full-time faculty are women, a proportion higher than the national average. There are 3 female faculty for every 100 female students and 8 male faculty for every 100 male students.

Administrators. Of the eight top positions, three are held by women, including chief academic officer, head librarian, and director of institutional research. Women chair the departments of education and of social and behavioral sciences.

Women and the Curriculum. The most popular majors for women graduates are education (31 percent), public affairs (14 percent), and letters (10 percent). Programs prepare women for careers in science, engineering, accounting, and computer science. Approximately half of student interns and 40 percent of students in science field-service projects are women.

There are no courses on women. The departments of business and physical education offer instruction on some matters specific to women. Faculty workshops are offered on affirmative action and equal opportunity.

Women and Athletics. For a college of its size, Barrington has a good sports program for women. Half the 105 intercollegiate athletes and three of the eight paid intercollegiate coaches are women. Intercollegiate sports for women are basketball, field hockey, softball, and volleyball.

Housing and Student Organizations. Sixty-nine percent of the students live on campus, in single-sex dormitories with restrictive hours for visitors of the opposite sex. One of the two residence-hall directors is a woman. Dormitory staff are offered awareness-training on the avoidance of sexism and racism, as well as on birth control.

Special Services and Programs for Women. *Health and Counseling.* The student health service has 1 male physician and 1 female health-care provider. The staff of the student counseling center consists of 1 man and 1 woman. Counseling and medical treatment for gynecological problems, birth control, and rape and assault are available, as is abortion counseling.

Safety and Security. Measures consist of campus police without arrest authority, local police, self-defense courses, information sessions on campus safety, and a rape crisis center. No rapes and two assaults, none on women, were reported for 1980–81.

Career. Workshops and other information on nontraditional occupations, job discrimination, student-alumnae networks, and files on alumnae by specific careers are available to women students.

Institutional Self-Description. "Women do very well academically on our campus—are encouraged by male and female faculty. A third of our faculty is female; women are often speakers at convocation—especially academic convocations; many women continue to graduate schools; many women are student leaders; women strongly urged to achieve and actively participate."

Brown University
Providence, RI 02912
Telephone: (401) 863-2386

★★ Women and the
Curriculum

5,307 undergraduates

	Amer. Ind.	Asian Amer.	Blacks	Hispanics	Whites
F	0	83	172	22	2,137
M	1	78	158	41	2,496
%	0.1	3.1	6.4	1.2	89.3

AAUW CROW

Brown University, founded in 1764 to provide "the Community a Succession of Men duly qualified for Discharging the Offices of Life with usefulness and reputation," and Pembroke College, established in 1891 for the education of women, merged in 1971. Some 6,800 students enroll in the undergraduate, graduate, and professional schools of this private, non-sectarian institution. The program for Resumed Undergraduate Education serves the adult student.

Women are 46 percent of the 5,307 undergraduates. For the one-fifth of the undergraduates who live off campus or commute, the university is accessible by public transportation. Parking on campus is available at a fee, with free transportation from distant parking lots.

The Brown-sponsored childcare facilities charge fees on a sliding scale. Seventy-five children may be accommodated. Private arrangements for childcare may be made close to campus.

Policies to Ensure Fairness to Women. The Affirmative Action Officer reviews policies and practices relating to equal employment opportunities, sex equity for students, and handicapped accessibility. A published campus policy prohibits sexual harassment; complaints are handled through a formal grievance procedure. The Committee on the Status of Women, which includes students as voting members, identifies and examines such issues as the status of women students in nontraditional majors. The Committee on Minority Affairs addresses the concerns of minority women, among other matters.

Women in Leadership Positions. *Students.* Opportunities for women to exercise all-campus leadership are near the average for private research universities in this guide. In recent years, women have been president of the student body and presiding officer of the student senate, union board (twice), and residence-hall council (twice).

Faculty. Fourteen percent of a full-time faculty of 459 are female. There are 3 female faculty for every 100 female students and 14 male faculty for every 100 male students.

Administrators. The director of institutional research is female; males hold the other top administrative posts. Women chair 2 of 54 departments: art history and linguistics. The Dean of the College is female; women direct 8 of 31 administrative units. Thirteen of 54 trustees are women.

Women and the Curriculum. A majority of women earn bachelor's degrees in social science (26 percent), letters (23 percent), and the biological sciences (14 percent). Nine percent graduate with degrees in such nontraditional areas as computer science, engineering, mathematics, and the physical sciences. The proportion of degrees earned in engineering by women is above the national average. The university reports that informal organizations and support systems encourage women in science, engineering, computer science, and law enforcement programs.

As of early 1982, a Women's Studies Program offers the B.A. in Women's Studies. Twenty-two undergraduate or graduate courses are offered through 12 departments. Courses include History of American Women; Sisterhood, Brotherhood, and Collectivism; Ideology and Social Bonding in American Life; Theory and Practice of Oral History; Love in the Middle Ages; Feminist Theories of Discourse and Sexuality; The Women's Movement in Russia; and Women and Health Care.

The Pembroke Center for Teaching and Research on Women, which administers the Women's Studies Program, has grants from the Ford Foundation and the National Endowment for the Humanities to focus for three years on a research project called "Cultural Construction of the Female." An official committee works to develop the Women's Studies Program and advocates and monitors the teaching of women's materials and perspectives across the curriculum.

Women and Athletics. Brown offers very good intercollegiate opportunities, both with respect to the number and variety of available individual and team sports. Thirty-six percent of the varsity athletes are female, as are one-fifth of the intramural players. The university reports special facilities for ice hockey and indoor tennis. Information on sports in the intramural program was not provided. Women's varsity teams played tournament competition in 1980. The intercollegiate sports offered are basketball, crew, cross-country, field hockey, gymnastics, ice hockey, lacrosse, soccer, softball, squash, swimming and diving, tennis, track and field, and volleyball.

Housing and Student Organizations. For the 80 percent who live on campus, single-sex and coeducational dormitories and co-operative housing are available. Residence halls do not restrict hours for visitors of the opposite sex.

One percent of the undergraduate women belong to social sororities; sororities provide housing for their members. Campus organizations which serve women include Women of Brown United, which sponsors an annual women's week, Women's Political Task Force, and the Third World Women's Committee.

Special Services and Programs for Women. *Health and Counseling.* The student health service provides some medical attention specific to women, including gynecological and birth control treatment. Two of three physicians are female. The regular student health insurance covers abortion and maternity at no extra cost. In the counseling service, staffed by seven, counseling on gynecological matters, birth control, abortion, and rape and assault is available.

Safety and Security. Information was not provided by the institution.

Career. Workshops, speakers, and nonsexist/nonracist printed materials focused on women in nontraditional occupations and fields of study, as well as a program of contacts between alumnae and students are available.

Other. The Sarah Doyle Women's Center, with a budget of $50,000, under a full-time administrator, sponsors women speakers, theater and other arts programs, assertiveness training, a program to build confidence in mathematics, and a telephone line of information, referral, and support.

Institutional Self-Description. "The Pembroke Center for Teaching and Research on Women and the Sarah Doyle Women's Center provide many and varied programs for women, including a concentration in Women's Studies. Growing numbers of women faculty, numerous university offices sensitive to the interests of women, and an excellent women's athletics program make the atmosphere a positive one."

Providence College
River Ave. and Eaton St.
Providence, RI 02918
Telephone: (401) 865-1000

3,464 undergraduates

	Amer. Ind.	Asian Amer.	Blacks	Hispanics	Whites
F	0	4	17	4	1,510
M	1	2	18	8	1,900
%	0	0.2	1.0	0.4	98.4

 **AAUW**

Founded in 1917, this coeducational, Roman Catholic college, operated by the Dominican Fathers, enrolls some 5,800 students. Women are 44 percent of an undergraduate population of 3,464, all of whom attend full-time. The median age of all students is 19.

The college offers bachelor's degree programs in the liberal arts, business, education, public service, natural science, and physical sciences. Adult students are served by the School of Continuing Education. Evening classes and a summer session are available.

The campus is accessible by public transportation. On-campus parking is also available to the 50 percent of students who commute.

Policies to Ensure Fairness to Women. An Affirmative Action Officer has responsibility part-time for monitoring compliance with equal-employment-opportunity, sex-equity, and handicapped-access legislation. A published sexual harassment policy has been communicated to the campus community; complaints are resolved through a formal campus grievance procedure. A Commission on the Status of Women, which includes student representatives with voting rights, is appointed by and responsible to the President.

Women in Leadership Positions. *Students.* Women occupied three of ten campus-wide leadership positions in recent years. These include one-year terms as president of the student senate and editor-in-chief of the campus newspaper, and two years as entering class president.

Faculty. Women are 19 percent of the 157 full-time faculty, a proportion below the national average. There are 2 female faculty for every 100 female students and 7 male faculty for every 100 male students.

Administrators. All ten major administrative positions are held by men. One of 24 department chairs, biology, is a woman; 2 of 8 division directors are female—the Director of Anthropology and the Director of Sociology. The Director of the Counseling Center is a woman. One of 6 honorary degree recipients in the spring 1981 semester was a woman.

Women and the Curriculum. Most women earn degrees in business (20 percent), interdisciplinary studies (13 percent), public affairs (10 percent), social sciences (10 percent), and liberal arts (10 percent). Two percent of women earn degrees in the nontraditional fields of mathematics and physical sciences. There are no courses on women.

Women and Athletics. Half of the intercollegiate athletes and one-third of the paid intercollegiate coaching staff are women. Women receive 30 percent of athletic scholarships awarded. The college offers both intramural and intercollegiate ice hockey. Intercollegiate sports include basketball, cross-country, field hockey, ice hockey, lacrosse, softball, tennis, track, and volleyball.

Housing and Student Organizations. One-half of the undergraduates live on campus in single-sex dormitories that have restrictive hours for visitors of the opposite sex.

Special Services and Programs for Women. *Health and Counseling.* A student health service is staffed by two male physicians and ten female health-care providers; the student counseling center employs five male counselors. No medical treatment specific to women is available. Counseling for gynecological problems, birth control, abortion, and rape and assault is available.

Safety and Security. Measures consist of campus police without arrest authority. Eleven assaults were reported on campus for 1980–81, five of them against women.

Institutional Self-Description. None provided.

Rhode Island School of Design
2 College Street, Providence, RI 02903
Telephone: (401) 331-3511

| Women in Leadership | ★ Women and the |
| ★★ administrators | Curriculum |

1,331 undergraduates

	Amer. Ind.	Asian Amer.	Blacks	Hispanics	Whites
F	3	12	8	8	708
M	2	12	15	4	483
%	0.4	1.9	1.8	1.0	94.9

This private, coeducational college, founded in 1877, combines professional art and design training with a liberal arts education. Women are 58 percent of a student population of 1,331, all of whom attend full-time.

RISD offers 18 bachelor's degree programs including architecture, design, fine arts, illustration, and photographic studies. Three summer session terms are available for transfer students who have one year of college; six-week workshops for adults and a five-week pre-college term for high school students are offered. The college collects and exhibits works of art in the campus museum. A European Honors program is available in Rome, Italy. Four percent of students commute to the campus, which is accessible by public transportation.

Private childcare facilities are located near the campus .

Policies to Ensure Fairness to Women. One administrator has responsibility part-time for monitoring compliance with equal-employment-opportunity, educational-sex-equity, and handicapped-access legislation. A written policy prohibits sexual harassment of students, faculty, and staff; complaints are resolved through a formal grievance procedure. A Commission on Minority Affairs addresses the concerns of minority women.

Women in Leadership Positions. *Students.* Of the three campus-wide leadership positions available in each of three recent years, women served once as president of the student body and president of the student senate.

Faculty. Twelve of the 82 full-time faculty are women, including 1 Asian American woman. There are 2 female faculty for every 100 female students and 12 male faculty for every 100 male students.

Administrators. Three of 7 major administrative positions are held by women, including President, chief development officer, and chief librarian. Women chair the departments of interior architecture, apparel design, and textile design, and lead the ceramics and printmaking programs.

Women and the Curriculum. Two-thirds of women graduates earn degrees in fine arts and 32 percent in architecture. Two-thirds of internships available are held by women. There are no courses on women.

Women and Athletics. No information was provided.

Housing and Student Organizations. Coeducational dormitories and housing for married students are available for the 28 percent of students who reside on campus. Residence halls do not restrict hours for visitors of the opposite sex.

Special Services and Programs for Women. *Health and Counseling.* A student health service is staffed by 2 female and 3 male physicians, along with 4 women health-care providers. The student counseling center employs 2 women. Available services specific to women include counseling and treatment for gynecological matters, birth control, and rape and assault, as well as abortion counseling.

Safety and Security. Measures consist of campus police with authority to make arrests, night-time escorts, high-intensity lighting, night-time bus service to residence areas, campus-wide emergency telephone system, information on campus safety, and a rape crisis center. Information was not provided on the incidence of rapes and assaults.

Other. A continuing education program serves approximately 720 reentry women each year. The Office of Student Development, in conjunction with the division of student affairs, sponsors an assertiveness-training program.

Institutional Self-Description. "RISD offers excellent programs in art and design. It has its own museum and is located in a city that provides many cultural activities. The college also owns a farm on the water approximately ten miles off-campus where students can enjoy swimming, boating, and other outdoor activities."

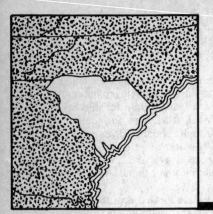

SOUTH CAROLINA

Aiken Technical College
P.O. Drawer 696, Aiken, SC 29801
Telephone: (803) 593-9231

Women in Leadership
★★ faculty
★★ administrators

916 undergraduates

	Amer. Ind.	Asian Amer.	Blacks	Hispanics	Whites
F	2	3	90	0	191
M	1	6	157	0	466
%	0.3	1.0	27.0	0.0	71.7

Aiken Technical College, a public, two-year institution, enrolls 1,093 students, of whom 916 are registered in degree programs. Thirty-one percent of the degree students are women; 37 percent of women attend part-time. The median age of students is 29.

The college offers associate degrees and certificates in a range of business and technical fields, along with a program of adult continuing education. Alternative scheduling includes evening classes, a summer session, and self-paced/contract learning. All students commute to the rural campus.

Policies to Ensure Fairness to Women. The Business Manager is responsible for equal-opportunity programs.

Women in Leadership Positions. *Students.* The single campus-wide leadership position, president of the student body, was held by a man for three recent years.

Faculty. Thirty-eight percent of the 32 full-time faculty are women, a proportion which is above average for public two-year colleges. There are 7 female faculty for every 100 female students and 6 male faculty for every 100 male students.

Administrators. Of the 5 chief administrative positions, 2 are held by women: chief student-life officer (a black woman) and head librarian (a white woman). Three of 6 departments are chaired by women: learning resources, general education, and business.

Women and the Curriculum. Almost all two-year degrees and certificates are awarded to women in business and commerce. The college offers programs to encourage women to prepare for nontraditional careers in engineering and in electronics. There are no courses on women.

Women and Athletics. Aiken offers very limited opportunities for women in sports. Women play intramural and intercollegiate basketball.

Special Services and Programs for Women. *Health and Counseling.* Aiken does not have a student health service. Information was not provided about a student counseling center.

Safety and Security. Measures consist of local police whose jurisdiction includes the campus, and self-defense courses for women. No rapes or assaults on women were reported for 1980–81.

Career. Activities available on campus include workshops on nontraditional occupations for women and lectures for students by women employed in such fields.

Institutional Self-Description. "Classes are small. There is a great deal of support for women who need assistance in all aspects of their life and career."

Benedict College
Harding and Blandon St.
Columbia, SC 29204
Telephone: (803) 256-4220

Women in Leadership
★★ faculty
★ administrators

1,761 undergraduates

	Amer. Ind.	Asian Amer.	Blacks	Hispanics	Whites
F	0	0	1,152	0	0
M	0	0	609	0	0
%	0.0	0.0	100.0	0.0	0.0

Founded in 1870 as a college for black women and men, Benedict is an independent institution that still serves a black student body. Its campus attracts 1,761 students, 65 percent of whom are women. Virtually all the women attend part-time. The median age of students is 20.

The college offers bachelor's degrees in business, education, public affairs, and social and natural science. Classes meet on campus day and evening, and off campus in the evening. An independent study option and summer session are available. Continuing education courses are offered through the evening program. Public transportation and on-campus parking for a fee are available for students who commute or live off campus.

Private childcare facilities are near the campus.

Policies to Ensure Fairness to Women. The Director of Personnel has part-time responsibility for policy on equal employment opportunity. The accountant for payroll monitors compliance with leglislation on sex equity for students. The Director of Student Affairs is in charge of policy on handicapped access. Complaints of sexual harassment are handled informally or through a formal grievance procedure.

Women in Leadership Positions. *Students.* Women have limited opportunity to exercise campus leadership. In recent years, women have presided over the residence-hall council for three consecutive terms and been president of the freshman class.

Faculty. Thirty-six percent of the 98 full-time faculty are women, a proportion above average for institutions nationwide. There are 3 female faculty for every 100 students and 10 male faculty for every 100 male students.

Administrators. The Dean of Academic Affairs, the head librarian, and the director of institutional research are black women. Black women chair two of five divisions: social services, and information and cultural services. Women head the departments of elementary education, biology, English, art, history, social work, business administration, and business education. Two of 8 members of the faculty senate are black women. According to a recent report, 5 white women serve on the predominantly black faculty. Seven women (6 black and 1 white) sit on the 28-member Board of Trustees.

Women and the Curriculum. Most bachelor's degrees awarded to women are in education (38 percent), business (22 percent), and public affairs (17 percent). Two percent of women major in such nontraditional fields as mathematics or physical sciences. Innovative programs encourage women to prepare for careers in science, engineering, accounting, computer science, and law enforcement/corrections. Three-fourths of student internships are awarded to women.

There are no courses on women. The departments of physical education, social work, and business provide some instruction on matters specific to women.

Women and Athletics. The organized athletic program for women is varied and popular. Forty-three percent of intramural and 33 percent of varsity athletes are women; women receive 30 percent of athletic scholarship aid. Intercollegiate sports are basketball, softball, and volleyball.

Housing and Student Organizations. Seventy-seven percent of students live in single-sex dormitories that prohibit visitors of the opposite sex. Four of the seven residence-hall directors are minority women. Sixty women are in sororities.

Special Services and Programs for Women. *Health and Counseling.* The student health service has 1 male physician and 1 female health-care provider. Three of 5 professionals at the student counseling center are women. Birth control, abortion, and rape and assault counseling are available. No information was provided about medical services specific to women.

Safety and Security. Measures consist of campus police protection, night-time escorts for women, high-intensity lighting, information on crime prevention for women, and a rape crisis center. One rape and two assaults on women were reported for 1980–81

Career. Services include workshops, lectures, and information on nontraditional occupations, in addition to files on alumnae careers and programs to promote networking between alumnae and students.

Institutional Self-Description. ''The black society being essentially matriarchal in nature, and Benedict being a college with predominantly black students, women here are normally ascribed a leadership role; they readily find the opportunity to fulfill their particular needs or exercise their special aptitudes, in an atmosphere of operating as equals among equals.''

	On-campus evening and/or weekend classes		Commission on minority affairs
	Off-campus classes		Women's Studies program
	Accessible by public transportation		Women's center
	On-campus childcare facilities	AAUW	Member, American Association of University Women
	Publicly communicated sexual harassment policy, includes students	NWSA	Member, National Women's Studies Association
	Commission on status of women	CROW	On-campus Center for Research on Women

Chesterfield-Marlboro Technical College
Cheraw, SC 29520
Telephone: (803) 537-5286

Women in Leadership
★ students
★★★ faculty
★★ administrators

502 undergraduates

	Amer. Ind.	Asian Amer.	Blacks	Hispanics	Whites
F	0	0	81	1	109
M	1	0	98	1	211
%	0.2	0.0	35.7	0.4	63.8

This public, two-year commuter college serves 502 students, 36 percent of whom are black. Thirty-eight percent of students are women. Chesterfield-Marlboro offers programs in business and commerce, engineering and mechanical technologies, as well as liberal arts. The median age of all students is 26; recent data indicate that 40 percent of the undergraduate women are over age 25. Evening classes, self-paced learning, and work-study arrangements are offered. Free on-campus parking is provided.

Private childcare facilities are available near campus.

Women in Leadership Positions. *Students.* There are three leadership positions. In recent years, women have edited the newspaper three times.

Faculty. The full-time faculty consists of 12 women and 10 men. There are 11 female faculty for every 100 female students and 5 male faculty for every 100 male students.

Administrators. Unusual among community colleges, a woman is chief of academic affairs. Women also head the library, the office of institutional research, and the department of developmental studies.

Women and the Curriculum. Most degrees awarded to women are in business and arts and sciences. There are no courses on women.

Women and Athletics. There is no opportunity for organized competitive sports.

Special Services and Programs for Women. *Health and Counseling.* There are no health or counseling services.

Safety and Security. In addition to patrols by campus police, there are an emergency telephone system and high-intensity lighting. No rapes or assaults on women were reported for 1980–81.

Career. The Career Center provides lectures and workshops on nontraditional careers and job discrimination.

Institutional Self-Description. ''Chesterfield-Marlboro provides a caring environment in which women are encouraged to continue upward mobility. The Career Center is geared to help women find their place in nontraditional careers.''

Coker College
Hartsville, SC 29550
Telephone: (803) 332-1381

Women in Leadership
★ students
★★ faculty

302 undergraduates

	Amer. Ind.	Asian Amer.	Blacks	Hispanics	Whites
F	2	0	31	0	164
M	0	0	21	0	84
%	0.7	0.0	17.2	0.0	82.1

 AAUW

Some 321 students attend Coker College, a private institution founded in 1908. Established as a college for women, it became coeducational in 1970. Sixty-five percent of the 302 students registered in degree programs are women; 14 percent of women attend part-time. The median age of all students is 24, with 16 percent of women students between 26 and 40 and 5 percent over 40.

Coker offers bachelor's degrees in liberal arts and sciences and pre-professional fields. Off-campus locations are available for some day and evening classes and there is a summer session. Forty percent of students commute. The campus is not accessible by public transportation. Free on-campus parking is provided.

Policies to Ensure Fairness to Women. The Dean of Students monitors compliance with legislation on equal employment opportunity, sex equity for students, and access for the handicapped. Complaints of sexual harassment are handled informally and confidentially.

Women in Leadership Positions. *Students.* Opportunities for women to gain leadership experience are good. In a recent three year period, women held half of the campus-wide student posts, including president of the student body, student senate, and student union board, as well as editor-in-chief of the campus newspaper.

Faculty. Women are 36 percent of the 36 full-time faculty, a proportion above average for colleges, nationwide. There are 8 female faculty for every 100 female students and 27 male faculty for every 100 male students.

Administrators. All of the chief administrators are men. Women chair 5 of the 17 departments: business, education, sociology, drama, and dance. Thirty-two percent of the faculty senate and 41 percent of the trustees are women. Both the recent commencement speaker and a recent honorary degree recipient were women.

Women and the Curriculum. Most women earn degrees in psychology and education. Three-fourths of student interns are women.

The college offers two courses on women through the departments of sociology and business administration: Sex Roles, and Women in Management. In addition, the divisions of physical education, social work, and business include instruction on some matters specific to women in the curricula. An official committee develops curricular materials on women. Faculty workshops are held on affirmative action and equal opportunity.

Women and Athletics. Opportunities for women to participate in organized competitive sports are limited. About half of the 80 intramural athletes are women, who participate in four intramural sports. One of the three paid intercollegiate coaches is a woman. Fifty percent of all athletic scholarships are awarded to women. The intercollegiate sports offered are basketball, tennis, and volleyball.

Housing and Student Organizations. Sixty percent of the students live on campus in single-sex or coeducational dormitories that restrict hours for visitors of the opposite sex. Fifteen percent of the female dormitory residents are black women. Dormitory staff (one woman and one man) are offered awareness-training on issues of sexism and sex education.

Special Services and Programs for Women. *Health and Counseling.* The student health service employs one female and three male physicians, as well as one female health-care provider. It provides such services specific to women as gynecological treatment and counseling for birth control, abortion, and rape and assault. There is no student counseling center.

Safety and Security. Measures consist of local police and campus police without arrest authority. Two assaults (one on a woman) were reported for 1980–81.

Career. The college provides workshops and job discrimination information on nontraditional occupations for women.

Institutional Self-Description. ''Coker emphasizes its smallness. Classes are limited to 20 students and many average ten or less. Internships and field service are designed to provide on-the-

job experiences to enhance career decisions and development. Students may determine their own curriculum through independent study or an individualized, interdisciplinary major. The campus is small enough for every student to become involved and to participate as a leader in some aspect of campus life. There is a close, informal relationship between students, faculty, and administration at Coker.''

Converse College
Spartanburg, SC 29301
Telephone: (803) 585-6421
Women in Leadership
★★★ students
★ faculty
726 undergraduates

	Amer. Ind.	Asian Amer.	Blacks	Hispanics	Whites
F	0	3	19	0	704
M	0	0	0	0	0
%	0.0	0.4	2.6	0.0	97.0

 AAUW

Established in 1889, Converse College is an independent women's college. The college offers a bachelor's degree in liberal arts, a master's program, and includes a professional music school that admits male graduate students. Cross registration at Wofford College, a nearby Methodist institution, is an option.

Of the 963 students enrolled, 726 are undergraduates, and all attend full-time. The median age of students is 19. Ninety-three percent of the women live on campus in dormitories that prohibit male visitors. Commuters can park on campus.

Private childcare facilities are available near campus.

Policies to Ensure Fairness to Women. A Coordinator is responsible, on a part-time basis, for compliance with equal-employment-opportunity, sex-equity, and handicapped-access legislation. A policy on sexual harassment is being considered.

Women in Leadership Positions. *Students.* Women occupy all campus-wide positions.

Faculty. Thirty-one percent of the 71 full-time faculty are women, a proportion above average for most colleges, but below average for women's colleges in this guide. One full-time faculty member is a black woman, who also sits on the faculty senate. There are 3 female faculty for every 100 female students.

Administrators. Men hold all top administrative positions. The director of athletics is a woman. Women chair five of 26 departments, including education, humanities, string music, and health, and physical education. Forty percent of the trustees are women.

Women and the Curriculum. Twenty-nine percent of the graduates earn degrees in fine arts, 22 percent in education, and 15 percent in social sciences. Four percent of the women major in such nontraditional fields as mathematics and physical sciences.

Converse offers three courses on women: Women in the Labor Force, Women's Role, and Topics in Women's Studies.

Women and Athletics. The limited organized athletic program combines individual and team sports. There are three intercollegiate teams and four intramural activities. Club sports are also available. One of the two paid varsity coaches is a woman. Intercollegiate sports offered are basketball, field hockey, and tennis.

Special Services and Programs for Women. *Health and Counseling.* The student health center has a staff of two male physicians and four female health-care providers. Gynecological counseling and treatment are available.

Safety and Security. Measures consist of campus police protection and high-intensity lighting. No rapes or assaults on women were reported for 1980–81.

Career. The college offers career workshops, lectures, and information on nontraditional occupations, maintains files on alumnae's careers, and encourages networking between students and alumnae.

Other. A Women's Center, under a full-time administrator, sponsors leadership training sessions. The theater and art departments organize dramatic and creative arts programs by and for women.

Institutional Self-Description. "Converse is an independent, four-year, liberal arts college for women, with a professional school of music. Since its founding in 1889, the college has remained dedicated to the principle that women deserve the best education possible. The goal of a Converse educaton is to shape contributing members of society who are able to make responsible, intelligent decisions."

Lander College
Greenwood, SC 29646
Telephone: (803) 229-8300
Women in Leadership
★★ **faculty**
1,694 undergraduates

	Amer. Ind.	Asian Amer.	Blacks	Hispanics	Whites
F	4	3	184	4	836
M	1	5	96	0	546
%	0.3	0.5	16.7	0.2	82.3

 AAUW

Founded as an institution for women in 1872, Lander College became coeducational in 1943. Of the 1,694 undergraduates enrolled, 61 percent are women; 19 percent of women are members of minority groups. The median age of students is 23. State-supported since 1973, the college offers bachelor's degrees in a variety of liberal arts fields, along with some two-year degrees.

Twenty-three percent of the women attend part-time. Evening and summer session classes are available, as well as some off-campus day classes. The Continuing Education Program administers adult education. Free on-campus parking is available for the 60 percent of students who commute.

Childcare is available near campus.

Policies to Ensure Fairness to Women. The Personnel Director reviews campus policies on equal employment opportunity. Sexual harassment of faculty and staff is prohibited; complaints are resolved through a formal grievance procedure; both policy and procedures have been communicated to staff and faculty.

Women in Leadership Positions. *Students.* In a recent three-year period, a woman served once as editor-in-chief of the campus newspaper, one of four campus-wide student leadership positions. One of three honorary societies is chaired by a woman.

Faculty. Thirty-five percent of the 86 faculty members are women. The ratio of female faculty to female students is 4 to 100; for men, the ratio is 11 to 100.

Administrators. Of eight top-level administrators, the head librarian is a woman. A woman chairs the department of nursing education. Three white women and one black woman are among the 16 trustees.

Women and the Curriculum. Women earn bachelor's degrees in education (48 percent), home economics (12 percent), business (10 percent), and psychology (6 percent); 3 percent of women major in mathematics and physical sciences. About 20 percent of all degrees earned by women are two-year degrees in health technologies. Women hold about two-thirds of the available cooperative education and internship assignments. The physical education department instructs students on how to teach coeducational physical education. There are no courses on women.

Women and Athletics. Women participate in organized competitive sports through intramural and intercollegiate programs.

Twenty-seven percent of intramural and 56 percent of intercollegiate athletes are women. One of the nine paid intercollegiate coaches is a woman; women receive 20 percent of athletic scholarships awarded. The intercollegiate sports offered are basketball, tennis, and volleyball.

Housing and Student Organizations. Forty percent of students live in single-sex or coeducational dormitories, all with restrictive hours for visitors of the opposite sex.

Twelve percent of full-time women students join social sororities. Of the 98 women in sororities, 25 are in all-minority groups.

Special Services and Programs for Women. *Health and Counseling.* Four male physicians and a woman health-care provider staff the student health center. One male and one minority female counselor staff the counseling center; they are offered training on avoidance of sex-role stereotyping. Services specific to women include abortion counseling, as well as medical treatment and counseling for rape and assault victims.

Safety and Security. Measures consist of campus and municipal police, night-time escorts for women, and high-intensity lighting. No rapes were reported for 1980–81.

Career. Career workshops on nontraditional occupations are available, as well as information on job discrimination, and alumnae files organized by career.

Institutional Self-Description. None provided.

Piedmont Technical College
P.O. Drawer 1467, Greenwood, SC 29646
Telephone: (803) 223-8357
Women in Leadership
★★★ **students**
★ **faculty**
1,725 undergraduates

	Amer. Ind.	Asian Amer.	Blacks	Hispanics	Whites
F	3	2	257	0	360
M	1	2	400	0	700
%	0.2	0.2	38.1	0.0	61.5

Founded in 1966, this public, two-year college serves 1,725 students, 36 percent of whom are women. One-third of women attend part-time. The median age of all students is 25, and 13 percent of the women are over age 25.

Piedmont provides one- and two-year diplomas and certificates and two-year associate degree programs in technical fields. Piedmont offers evening classes, both on and off campus, and an adult continuing education program. All students commute. The campus is not accessible by public transportation, but free on-campus parking is provided for students.

Private childcare facilities are available near the campus.

Policies to Ensure Fairness to Women. An assistant to the President serves part-time as an administrator of equal-employment-opportunity legislation. The college does not have a written policy on sexual harassment; a formal campus grievance procedure resolves complaints.

Women in Leadership Positions. *Students.* Although a minority on campus, women have outstanding opportunities to exercise campus-wide leadership. Both of the major leadership positions, president of the student body and editor-in-chief of the newspaper, were held by women for three recent years. A woman serves as president of one of the two campus honorary societies.

Faculty. The 52 full-time faculty are 29 percent female, a proportion below average for public, two-year colleges, but above the national norm. There are 4 female faculty for every 100 female students and 5 male faculty for every 100 male students.

Administrators. The 9 chief administrators are men. Four of 17 departments are chaired by women: allied health, data processing, human services, and secretarial science. Thirty-one percent of the faculty senate is female, including 4 black women. One of the 12 trustees is a woman.

Women and the Curriculum. Most women earn two-year degrees in business and commerce (53 percent), public service (23 percent), and health technologies (19 percent). The college reports an increase in the number of women majoring in such nontraditional fields as engineering and industrial technologies, from 26 students for 1978–79, to 61 students for 1979–80. There is also a special program, Expanding Career Horizons, for female high school students interested in exploring nontraditional careers. Another program encourages women to prepare for a career in electronics. Half of the students in cooperative education are women.

There are no courses on women. The departments of business and social work provide some instruction on matters specific to women.

Women and Athletics. No intercollegiate or club sports are offered. About 75 women participate in the intramural program, which includes softball, volleyball, and tennis.

Special Services and Programs for Women. *Health and Counseling.* There is no student health service. The counseling center has a staff of four women, one of whom is a minority woman. The center offers gynecological, birth control, abortion, and rape and assault counseling.

Safety and Security. No information was provided by the college.

Career. Services include workshops, printed materials, and job discrimination information on nontraditional careers for women, as well as panels by women employed in these fields.

Other. A small Women's Center, with a yearly budget of $2,028, is coordinated by a full-time administrator and serves approximately 100 women a year. Student Services, which is responsible for the Women's Center, offers special support to displaced homemakers. The division of continuing education offers a women's lecture series and assertiveness/leadership training.

Institutional Self-Description. "The provision of high-quality technical education at a reasonable cost, to every resident of the seven-county area served by Piedmont Technical College, continues to be a primary mission. Because training in one- and two-year programs is tied directly to area job-market needs, it reflects the current need for women in high technology careers."

University of South Carolina, Columbia
Columbia, SC 29208
Telephone: (803) 777-4204

★ **Women and the Curriculum**

16,905 undergraduates

	Amer. Ind.	Asian Amer.	Blacks	Hispanics	Whites
F	9	58	1,361	33	6,693
M	13	56	844	52	7,727
%	0.1	0.7	13.9	0.5	84.7

🏠 🏛 👫 ✦ 🄢🅆 🄼🅰 📖 **AAUW NWSA**

Established in 1801 as one of the first publicly-supported universities in the U.S., the University of South Carolina enrolls some 24,800 students in a range of undergraduate, graduate, and professional studies. Alternative class schedules, which include a summer session, weekend college, and classes at off-campus locations, are available.

Women are 48 percent of the 16,905 undergraduates; 18 percent of women attend part-time. On-campus parking is available free and at a fee, with free transportation from distant parking lots.

Childcare facilities are available on campus. Private childcare arrangements may be made nearby.

Policies to Ensure Fairness to Women. A published campus policy prohibits sexual harassment of students, faculty, and staff. The Committee on the Status of Women, appointed by the university President, reports to the Affirmative Action Committee. The Committee on Minority Affairs addresses the concerns of minority women.

Women in Leadership Positions. *Students.* Information on opportunities for women students to exercise leadership was not provided.

Faculty. One-fifth of a full-time faculty of 949 are women. The ratio of female faculty to female students is 3 to 100; the ratio of male faculty to male students is 10 to 100.

Administrators. Men hold all key positions. Information about women in other administrative positions was not provided.

Women and the Curriculum. Most bachelor's degrees earned by women are in education (25 percent), business (15 percent), and communications (11 percent). Three percent of undergraduate women earn degrees in such nontraditional subjects as computer science, engineering, mathematics, and the physical sciences. One-tenth of the students in the engineering program are women. Most two-year degrees awarded to women are in business/commerce technologies.

The Women's Studies Program offers an undergraduate minor and a major through Interdisciplinary Studies. Two introductory courses, Women in Western Culture and Women in Society, are offered in addition to courses through departments. Recent courses include Sociology of Sex Roles, Women Writers, Psychology of Women, and Historical Perspectives on Women in America. The university-appointed Women's Studies Committee administers and coordinates the program, encourages the development of courses on women, and sponsors special community services and public events.

Women and Athletics. Information was not provided.

Housing and Student Organizations. For undergraduates who live on campus, women's and men's dormitories are available. Social sororities and fraternities provide housing for their members.

Special Services and Programs for Women. *Health and Counseling.* The student health service provides some medical attention specific to women, including gynecological and birth control treatment. Students have access to gynecological, birth control, and abortion counseling through the student counseling center. Assertiveness training is also available.

Safety and Security. Measures include campus police with arrest authority and night-time escorts for women students. Information on incidence of rapes and assaults on women was not reported.

Other. The Women's Studies Program offers an on-going series of lectures and discussions on subjects of concern to women. The theater department presents women's theater productions. An annual Women's History Week is held under the auspices of the South Carolina Commission on Women.

Institutional Self-Description. None provided.

University of South Carolina, Salkehatchie
Allendale, SC 29810
Telephone: (803) 584-3446

Women in Leadership
  ★★ **faculty**
   ★ **administrators**

276 undergraduates

	Amer. Ind.	Asian Amer.	Blacks	Hispanics	Whites
F	0	0	52	0	110
M	0	0	14	0	100
%	0.0	0.0	23.9	0.0	76.1

🏠 🏛 ✦

Established as a public, two-year community college in 1965, the Salkehatchie Campus of the University of South Carolina offers liberal arts and sciences to 351 students, 276 of whom are degree candidates. Continuing education is available. Alternative schedules include evening classes on campus, off-campus day and evening classes, and a summer session.

Women are 59 percent of the undergraduates; one-third of women attend part-time. Forty percent of the women are over age 24. The median age of all undergraduates is 22. All students commute. The college is not accessible by public transportation. On-campus parking is available for a fee.

Policies to Ensure Fairness to Women. A written campus policy prohibits sexual harassment; complaints are resolved informally or through a formal grievance procedure. Policy and procedures have been publicly communicated in writing to students, faculty, and staff.

Women in Leadership Positions. *Students.* Women's participation in leadership positions is limited. In a recent three-year period, women were twice presiding officers of the student governing body.

Faculty. Five of the 13 faculty are women.

Administrators. Of the six key administrators, the chief business officer and the head librarian are women. A woman chairs one of the three departments, and one woman sits on the 9-member Board of Trustees.

Women and the Curriculum. All women graduate in the arts and sciences. There are no courses on women.

Women and Athletics. There are no opportunities for women to participate in intercollegiate or intramural sports. A small number of women participate in club sports.

Special Services and Programs for Women. *Health and Counseling.* There is no student health service and no student counseling center.

Safety and Security. Local police patrol the campus. No assaults or rapes were reported for 1980–81.

Institutional Self-Description. None provided.

Voorhees College
Denmark, SC 29042
Telephone: (803) 793-3351

Women in Leadership
★★ faculty
★ administrators

781 undergraduates

	Amer. Ind.	Asian Amer.	Blacks	Hispanics	Whites
F	0	2	474	0	1
M	0	0	301	0	0
%	0.0	0.3	99.6	0.0	0.1

Founded in 1897 as a two-year college for black women and men, Voorhees has evolved into a four-year institution. It is affiliated with the Episcopal Church. Classes meet on campus, both day and evening. There is a summer session and an adult continuing education program. Voorhees awards two-year as well as bachelor's degrees.

Women are 61 percent of the 781 undergraduates; all women attend full-time. The median age of undergraduates is 18. Voorhees can be reached by public transportation; the 10 percent of students who commute can park on campus.

Private childcare services are available near campus.

Policies to Ensure Fairness to Women. The Personnel Officer is responsible full-time for monitoring compliance and examining practices pertaining to sex-equity and equal-employment laws.

Women in Leadership Positions. *Students.* Women have limited opportunities to exercise student leadership. In recent years, women have been campus newspaper editor and residence-hall council president. A woman heads one of the two honorary societies.

Faculty. Forty-two percent of the 43 full-time faculty are women, a proportion significantly above average for colleges nationwide. There are 4 female faculty for every 100 female students, and 8 male faculty for every 100 male students.

Administrators. The chief development officer, head librarian, and director of institutional research are women. Of six divisions, a woman chairs humanities. Three of 6 members of the Committee on Faculty are black women. Ten women, including 5 black women, sit on the 38-member Board of Trustees.

Women and the Curriculum. Most bachelor's degrees earned by women are in education (46 percent), social sciences (28 percent), and business (26 percent). Three-fourths of the student interns are women. No courses on women are offered.

Women and Athletics. For a college of this size, the women's sports program is good. Half of the intercollegiate and 44 percent of the intramural athletes are women. A few women participate in club sports. Two of the seven paid varsity coaches are women. Intercollegiate sports offered are basketball, cross-country, softball, and track and field.

Housing and Student Organizations. Ninety percent of the students live on campus in single-sex dormitories that have restricted hours for visitors of the opposite sex. Two of the four residence-hall staff are minority women.

Eleven percent of women students belong to social sororities.

Special Services and Programs for Women. *Health and Counseling.* There is a student health service, but the college did not provide information on the type of treatment available or on the number of physicians. The student counseling center's three professionals are minority women. Counseling is available for birth control, abortion, and rape and assault.

Safety and Security. Measures consist of local and campus police, both with arrest authority. One assault on a woman and no rapes were reported for 1980-81.

Career. Services include workshops and lectures on nontraditional occupations, files on alumnae careers for the use of students, and programs to foster networking between students and alumnae.

Institutional Self-Description. None provided.

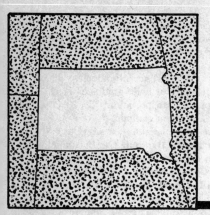

SOUTH DAKOTA

South Dakota State University
Brookings, SD 57007
Telephone: (605) 688-4111

★ **Women and the Curriculum**

5,846 undergraduates

	Amer. Ind.	Asian Amer.	Blacks	Hispanics	Whites
F	10	17	12	1	2,565
M	22	8	13	2	3,086
%	0.6	0.4	0.4	0.1	98.5

 **AAUW**

Founded in 1881 as a land-grant college, South Dakota enrolls 7,194 students, of whom 5,846 are undergraduates. Forty-five percent of the undergraduates are women, 7 percent of whom attend part-time. The median age of all students is 28 years.

South Dakota State offers undergraduate and graduate degrees in a wide range of pre-professional, vocational, and liberal arts programs. Adult students are served by the continuing education program. Evening, summer session, and off-campus classes are available. The campus is not accessible by public transportation. On-campus parking is available for the 40 percent of students who commute.

Private childcare facilities can be found near the campus.

Women in Leadership Positions. *Students.* The top student offices are almost always held by men.

Faculty. Twenty-four percent of the 315 full-time faculty are women, a proportion just below the national norm. There are 3 female faculty for every 100 female students and 8 male faculty for every 100 male students.

Administrators. All of the top administrators are men. Women chair eight of 28 departments: English, speech, textiles and clothing, home economics education, and several nursing departments. The Deans of Nursing, Home Economics, and the Summer School are women.

Women and the Curriculum. The most popular majors for women graduates are health professions (23 percent), social sciences (15 percent), and home economics (15 percent). Nine percent of women earn degrees in the nontraditional fields of agriculture, architecture, engineering, mathematics, and physical sciences. One-third of internship and science field-service assignments are awarded to women.

The Women's Studies Program offers an 18-credit minor. Recent courses on women include Women in American Culture, Biology and Women, Feminism and Theology, Sociology of Sex Roles, and Women in the Labor Force. An official committee is responsible for the continued development of the Women's Studies Program. The Center for Pioneer Women's Studies has the beginnings of a collection of materials and archives.

Women and Athletics. Women have limited opportunities to participate in organized competitive sports, through both intramural and intercollegiate programs. Women receive 20 percent of athletic scholarships; two paid intercollegiate coaches are women. Intercollegiate sports for women include basketball, cross-country, gymnastics, swimming, tennis, and volleyball.

Housing and Student Organizations. Sixty percent of undergraduates live on campus in women's or coeducational dormitories or in fraternity houses. Three of the six dormitory directors are women. University housing is available for single students with children and married students with or without children. A married student whose spouse is not enrolled is permitted to live in married students' housing.

Although fraternities provide housing for members, sororities do not.

Special Services and Programs for Women. *Health and Counseling.* The student health service employs 1 male physician and 2 female health-care providers. No medical treatment specific to women is provided. The counseling center employs 3 women and 2 men and provides counseling for gynecological problems, birth control, abortion, and rape and assault.

Safety and Security. No information was provided.

Other. The Women's Center, sponsored by United Ministries of Higher Education, serves about 200 women a year, particularly older women. The center runs a program for battered women and has a crisis team to assist assault victims.

Institutional Self-Description. "South Dakota State has good programs and some good people. While it is not naturally a strongly chauvinistic university, because of a longstanding commitment to women's professional education, there is not much actual consciousness of women's issues."

National College
P.O. Box 1780, Rapid City, SD 57709
Telephone: (605) 394-4800

Women in Leadership
★★★ **students**
★★★ **faculty**

2,634 undergraduates

	Amer. Ind.	Asian Amer.	Blacks	Hispanics	Whites
F	55	5	13	25	591
M	58	8	140	224	1,497
%	4.3	0.5	5.9	9.5	79.8

National College is a private, non-sectarian, coeducational institution that offers a career-oriented academic program. The main campus, located in Rapid City, a town in western South Dakota, serves 2,634 undergraduates, 26 percent of whom are women.

Virtually all women students attend full-time. The median age of all students is 22.

Associate and bachelor's degrees are granted, in addition to one- and two-year diplomas. All degrees are in business-related and technical fields. Evening classes, on and off campus, supplement daytime scheduling. On-campus parking is available at a fee. Extension campuses are scattered in cities in the Southwest and Midwest.

Childcare facilities are available near campus.

Policies to Ensure Fairness to Women. Implementation of sex-fair employment practices is the part-time responsibility of an equal-opportunity officer, who can also make policy in this regard.

Women in Leadership Positions. *Students.* During three recent years women were president of the residence-hall council and men president of the student body—the only campus-wide student leadership positions.

Faculty. Fifteen of the 26 full-time faculty (63 percent) are women, far above the national average. The ratio of female faculty to female students is 2 to 100; the ratio of male faculty to male students is 1 to 100.

Administrators. Except for the Dean of Students, the top administrative positions are held by men. Women chair the departments of secretarial science, fashion merchandising, and medical administration assisting.

Women and the Curriculum. Women receive 9 percent of bachelor's degrees and 25 percent of two-year degrees and certificates—almost all in business. Several programs encourage women to prepare for careers in electronics, accounting, and computer sciences. No courses on women are offered.

Women and Athletics. Intercollegiate sports attract 45 participants, more than half of them women; women receive 10 percent of athletic scholarships. Club sports draw 678 students, and half are women. There are opportunities for women athletes to compete in rodeo, water skiing, and canoeing, in addition to a variety of other intramural activities. Intercollegiate sports include basketball, rodeo, and volleyball.

Housing and Student Organizations. Single-sex and coeducational dormitories are available. One of the two residence-hall directors is a woman. Sororities and fraternities do not provide housing for their members.

Special Services and Programs for Women. *Health and Counseling.* An outpatient clinic is staffed by one female healthcare provider. The student counseling center's therapists (including a minority woman and three men) provide birth control, abortion and rape and assault counseling.

Safety and Security. Measures include campus police protection, high-intensity lighting, emergency telephone system, and self-defense information sessions for women. No information was provided on the incidence of rapes and assaults on women.

Other. A community Women's Center, unrelated to the college, is situated on campus and readily accessible to women students.

Institutional Self-Description. "In striving to fulfill its mission, National College seeks a balance between stability and flexibility which enables the college to improve ongoing programs and to establish new programs pursuant to the needs and interests of its students and the business community at large."

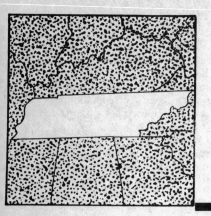

TENNESSEE

Belmont College
1800 Belmont Blvd., Nashville, TN 37203
Telephone: (615) 383-7001

Women in Leadership
★ faculty

1,225 undergraduates

	Amer. Ind.	Asian Amer.	Blacks	Hispanics	Whites
F	0	0	30	0	565
M	0	0	33	0	542
%	0.0	0.0	5.4	0.0	94.6

Founded as Ward-Belmont College for Women, Belmont became a four-year, coeducational college in 1951, maintaining its affiliation with the Baptist Convention. Ninety-three percent of the 1,314 students are registered in degree programs. Half of the degree students are women; 22 percent of the women attend part-time. The median age of all students is 20 years.

Belmont offers bachelor's and associate degrees in the liberal arts, sciences, and pre-professional areas. Alternative schedules include evening, summer session, and weekend classes. The campus is accessible by public transportation. On-campus parking is available for the 60 percent of students who commute.

Private childcare facilities can be found near the campus.

Women in Leadership Positions. *Students.* Opportunities for women to acquire leadership experience are limited. In a recent three-year period, women served consistently as president of the student court, the only one of eight available positions to be held by women. Women preside over two of the eight honorary societies.

Faculty. One-third of the 77 full-time faculty are women, a proportion above the national average. There are 5 female faculty for every 100 female students and 10 male faculty for every 100 male students.

Administrators. All of the chief administrators and three-fourths of the department chairs are men. Women chair the departments of behavioral sciences, communication arts, and nursing. Except for the Dean of Women, all deans are male. One of 33 trustees is a woman.

Women and the Curriculum. Most women earn bachelor's degrees in education (28 percent), business (27 percent), and public affairs (16 percent). Almost all two-year degrees awarded to women are in health technologies.

There are no courses on women. Programs to encourage women to prepare for careers in science, accounting, computer science, and law enforcement are available. Forty percent of students in cooperative education programs and 70 percent of student interns are women.

Women and Athletics. For a college of its size, Belmont offers good opportunities for women to participate in organized, com-petitive sports. The intramural program is extensive; the intercollegiate is smaller. Thirty-one percent of intramural athletes and almost half of intercollegiate athletes are women. One of the five paid intercollegiate coaches is female. Forty percent of the athletic scholarship funds go to women. Intercollegiate sports for women are basketball, tennis, and track.

Housing and Student Organizations. Forty percent of the students live on campus in single-sex dormitories with restrictive hours for visitors of the opposite sex. Two of the four dormitory directors are women.

Eight percent of full-time student women belong to social sororities. Neither sororities or fraternities provide housing for members. Advocacy groups for women include the Women's Student Government Association which has 400 active participants, 20 percent of whom are black women.

Special Services and Programs for Women. *Health and Counseling.* The student health service employs one male physician and one female health-care provider. Counseling and medical treatment are available for gynecological problems; counseling for rape and assault is also available.

Safety and Security. Measures consist of campus police with arrest authority, self-defense courses, and a rape crisis center.

Returning Women Students. While Belmont has no formal adult continuing education program, there are approximately 200 reentry women enrolled, 7 percent of whom are black women. Faculty workshops are available on the needs of reentry women. An advocacy group, Women in Continuing Education, has 30 active participants, of whom ten are black women.

Institutional Self-Description. "Belmont College is a liberal arts-centered, church-related institution dedicated to education as a means of enhancing the student's appreciation of his cultural heritage, of increasing his effectiveness in assimilating and communicating ideas and facts, and of equipping him for citizenship in a free society."

East Tennessee State University
Johnson City, TN 37614
Telephone: (615) 929-4112

Women in Leadership
★ faculty

8,273 undergraduates

	Amer. Ind.	Asian Amer.	Blacks	Hispanics	Whites
F	11	10	131	10	4,182
M	16	17	122	7	3,739
%	0.3	0.3	3.1	0.2	96.1

 AAUW

East Tennessee State University enrolls 9,971 students, including 8,273 undergraduates. Fifty-three percent of undergraduates are

women, and 21 percent of women attend part-time. The median age of undergraduates is 19. Twenty-eight percent of women are over age 25, and half of these older women attend part-time.

The university offers associate, bachelor's, and graduate degrees in a variety of fields. A continuing education program serves adult students. Classes meet on and off campus, day and evening, and there is a summer session. For the 60 percent of undergraduates who live off campus or commute, public transportation and on-campus parking for a fee are available.

Private childcare facilities are available near campus.

Policies to Ensure Fairness to Women. The Affirmative Action Officer/Director of Internal Research is responsible part-time for policy on sex equity for students, equal employment opportunity, and handicapped access. A published sexual harassment policy protects students, faculty, and staff. A formal campus grievance procedure handles complaints.

Women in Leadership Positions. *Students.* Women students have limited leadership opportunities. In recent years, women have held four of six campus-wide offices, in most cases for one year each. Women preside over 30 of 45 honorary societies.

Faculty. Twenty-six percent of the 408 faculty are women, a proportion slightly above average for institutions nationwide. There are 3 female faculty for every 100 female students and 10 male faculty for every 100 male students.

Administrators. Except for Dean of Faculties, men hold all higher administrative posts. Women chair four of 40 departments, including nursing, home economics, and physical education and recreation. The Dean of the School of Nursing and the Director of the Counseling Center are women.

Women and the Curriculum. The most popular fields among women receiving bachelor's degrees are education (35 percent), health professions (18 percent), and public affairs (13 percent). Three percent of women specialize in such nontraditional areas as computer science, mathematics, and physical sciences. A special program encourages women to prepare for science careers.

The English department gives one course on women: Women in Literature. The physical education department provides some instruction on some matters specific to women.

Minority Women. Minority women constitute 4 percent of undergraduate women. One black woman serves on the 17-member Board of Regents. Three minority women direct residence halls and 1 minority woman serves as a professional counselor. Additional sources of support come from the Black Student Affairs Office. Residence-hall staff are offered awareness-training on racism.

Women and Athletics. The women's athletic program offers a good variety of sports for a school of this size. Thirty percent of varsity athletes are women, and women receive 30 percent of the athletic scholarship aid. One-fourth of the intramural players are women. Intercollegiate sports offered are basketball, cross-country, gymnastics, coeducational riflery, tennis, track, and volleyball.

Housing and Student Organizations. Thirty percent of undergraduates live in single-sex dormitories and university-owned apartments. Housing is available for single parents and for married students, with or without children. Dormitories vary in their policies regarding visiting hours for members of the opposite sex.

Seven percent of undergraduate women belong to social sororities, which do not provide housing for members.

Special Services and Programs for Women. *Health and Counseling.* The student health service employs 5 male physicians and 2 female health-care providers. Of the 7 professionals who work at the student counseling center, 5 are women. Birth control and gynecological counseling and treatment are provided, as well as counseling for rape and assault.

Safety and Security. Measures consist of campus and local police protection, night-time escort for women, and information on crime prevention for women. Two rapes and three assaults on women were reported for 1980–81.

Career. Services include workshops on nontraditional occupations and nonsexist/nonracist printed information on nontraditional fields of study for women.

Other. The counseling center runs assertiveness training workshops. The sociology department sponsors a battered women's program. The University Center Program Committee plans theater and other arts shows for women.

Institutional Self-Description. "Location, hands-on environment in computer science, and tuition is below the national average.".

LeMoyne-Owen College
807 Walker Avenue, Memphis, TN 38126
Telephone: (901) 774-9090

Women in Leadership
★★ faculty

978 undergraduates

	Amer. Ind.	Asian Amer.	Blacks	Hispanics	Whites
F	0	0	628	0	1
M	0	4	341	0	1
%	0.0	0.4	99.4	0.0	0.2

LeMoyne-Owen, a private, historically black college affiliated with the United Church of Christ, was founded to educate teachers. It now offers bachelor's degrees in education, business, liberal arts and sciences. Among the 990 students who enroll, almost all of whom are black, 978 are registered in degree programs. Sixty-four percent of the degree students are women; 2 percent of the women attend part-time. The median age of all students is 20.

All students commute to the campus. The college may be reached by public transportation. On-campus parking is free. About 11 percent of the women students belong to social sororities.

Childcare facilities are located close to the campus.

Policies to Ensure Fairness to Women. One administrator has responsibility part-time for monitoring compliance with sex-equity, equal-employment-opportunity, and handicapped-access laws.

Women in Leadership Positions. *Students.* Women have few opportunities to gain leadership experience. In recent years, women have served one-year terms each as president of the sophomore class and the entering class. Women preside over the two campus honorary societies.

Faculty. Forty-seven percent of the 47 full-time faculty are women, a proportion which is above average for colleges nationwide. There are 4 female faculty for every 100 female students and 7 male faculty for every 100 male students.

Administrators. Two of the 9 chief administrative officers are black women: head librarian and chief planning officer. Black women chair two of five divisions: social sciences and professional studies. Forty-one percent of the faculty senate are women (17 black and 4 white). Three of 9 trustees are black women.

Women and the Curriculum. Most women earn bachelor's degrees in education (30 percent), business (19 percent), and public affairs (16 percent). Nearly 8 percent major in such nontraditional areas as mathematics or physical sciences. Three-fourths of the student interns and two-thirds of the cooperative education participants are women.

There are no courses on women. The departments of physical education and social work offer instruction on some issues specific to women.

Women and Athletics. Thirty percent of the intercollegiate athletes are women, who receive 30 percent of athletic scholarships. Both paid coaches are women. The intercollegiate sport offered is basketball.

Special Services and Programs for Women. *Health and Counseling.* The student health service employs one female health-care provider; two minority women staff the student counseling center. Medical treatment specific to women is not available. Abortion, birth control, and rape and assault counseling are available. Counselors are offered awareness-training on the avoidance of sex-role stereotyping.

Safety and Security. There is campus police protection. No rapes and one assault on a woman were reported for 1980–81.

Career. The college provides career workshops, printed information on nontraditional occupations for women, and panels and lectures by women employed in these fields.

Institutional Self-Description. "Every woman is important at LeMoyne-Owen College. The college is sensitive to the challenges imposed upon it by a changing society. In an effort to prepare both men and women to make meaningful contributions to society, the college offers a liberal arts education in 18 degree areas coupled with a cooperative education job experience program. Women comprise 35 percent of the college's distinguished graduates being employed in professions such as law, medicine, engineering, government, and politics."

Memphis State University
Memphis, TN 38152
Telephone: (901) 454-2231

★★ **Women and the Curriculum**

14,915 undergraduates

	Amer. Ind.	Asian Amer.	Blacks	Hispanics	Whites
F	9	22	1,959	3	5,647
M	11	34	1,090	3	5,932
%	0.1	0.4	20.7	0.1	78.8

🏠 🏛 🚐 ⌷ ⌷ 📖 **AAUW CROW**

On its urban campus, Memphis State University serves some 21,000 students, including 14,915 undergraduates. Fifty-two percent of undergraduates are women; 30 percent of women attend part-time. Almost half the undergraduate women are age 25 or older; the median age of all undergraduates is 21. The undergraduate degree programs include business, education, engineering, social sciences, health professions, home economics, and arts and sciences. An Office of Continuing Education administers adult education. Eighty-six percent of undergraduates commute by public transportation or car; on-campus parking is provided at a fee. Private childcare is available near campus.

Policies to Ensure Fairness to Women. The Affirmative Action Officer, on a part-time basis, reviews policy and practices concerning equal employment opportunity, sex equity for students, and handicapped access. The full-time Affirmative Action Administrator oversees compliance with equal-educational-opportunity laws. A formal campus grievance procedure handles complaints of sexual harassment. The Commission on the Status of Women is appointed by and reports directly to the President. It meets regularly, includes students with voting rights, and addresses the concerns of white and minority women.

Women in Leadership Positions. Of 15 leadership positions available in a recent three-year period, women chaired the student union board twice and edited the newspaper once. Women chair 15 of 35 honorary societies.

Faculty. Of 737 faculty members, 23 percent are women. According to a recent report, 14 black women, 1 American Indian woman, and 1 Asian American woman are on the faculty. The

ratio of female faculty to female students is 3 to 100; of male faculty to male students, 11 to 100.

Administrators. Women hold 2 of 9 top positions: chief development officer and director of institutional research. The Dean of the Graduate School is a woman, and women chair 3 of 44 departments: nursing, home economics, and library service. Three of the 16 regents are women.

Women and the Curriculum. Most bachelor's degrees are awarded to women in education (33 percent) and business (21 percent). Three percent of women graduate in the nontraditional fields of engineering, mathematics, and the physical sciences. In a recent year, all women graduating with two-year degrees and certificates majored in health technologies. About 45 percent of students who participate in internships, practicums, and science field service are women.

The Women's Studies Program, directed on a part-time basis by a permanent faculty member, offers a minor and a B.A. Recent courses include Psychology of Women, Women and Work, and History of Women in America—offered through the departments of psychology, economics, and history, respectively. The departments of education, physical education, nursing, social work, and business provide instruction on some matters specific to women. A faculty committee oversees the development of the program and reports on the inclusion of scholarship on women across the curriculum.

In January 1982, the Center for Research on Women was established with a three-year grant from the Ford Foundation, its function to conduct, promote, and advance research on women in the South, and on minority women nationally. The center will publish a newsletter, act as a clearinghouse, organize conferences and help Women's Studies Programs in the south to develop projects addressed to the educational and career goals of working-class and minority women.

Women and Athletics. Five hundred women participate in intramurals. Twenty-six percent of the intercollegiate athletes are women; women receive one-fifth of athletic scholarships. Seven of 26 paid varsity coaches are female. Intercollegiate sports offered are basketball, cross-country, golf, gymnastics, tennis, track, and volleyball.

Housing and Student Organizations. For the 14 percent of undergraduates who live on campus, single-sex dormitories, which limit hours for visitors of the opposite sex, and married students' housing are available. A married woman student whose spouse is not enrolled may live in married students' housing. Eight of 11 residence directors are women; awareness-training on sexism, racism, and birth control is offered staff.

Eight percent of full-time undergraduates join social sororities and fraternities. Sororities are nonresidential. Sixty women belong to all-minority sororities.

Special Services and Programs for Women. *Health and Counseling.* One male physician and 3 female health-care providers offer gynecological, birth control, and rape and assault treatment. The counseling service, staffed by 4 men and 2 white women, provides counseling of concern to women. Staff receive in-service training on avoiding sex-role stereotyping and racial bias.

Safety and Security. Measures consist of campus police with weapons training and authority to make arrests, night-time escorts for women, high-intensity lighting in most areas, emergency alarms, self-defense courses, information sessions on campus safety and assault prevention, and a rape crisis center. No rapes were reported for 1980–81. Information on assaults was not provided.

Career. Services include workshops on nontraditional careers, programs by women in nontraditional occupations, nonracist/nonsexist literature on nontraditional fields, files of alumnae by career, and programs to establish contacts between female students and alumnae. The College of Business and Economics offers four-week sessions on Career Planning for Women, and the campus chapter of NOW sponsors a Career Fair for Women.

Other. The Alumni Association sponsors an Annual Women's Day. The Office of Conferences, Institutes, and Special Programs offers a workshop on Financial Planning for Women. The Office of Continuing Education offers a short course, Changing Role of Women in Religion. Monthly brown-bag lunches host speakers on subjects of interest to women. Mini-College, oriented toward older, reentry students, offers courses at various locations in Memphis. Most of its 400 students are women.

Institutional Self-Description. None provided.

Middle Tennessee State University
Murfreesboro, TN 37132
Telephone: (615) 898-2300

★ **Women and the Curriculum**

8,650 undergraduates

	Amer. Ind.	Asian Amer.	Blacks	Hispanics	Whites
F	3	8	455	6	3,825
M	9	6	320	11	3,879
%	0.1	0.2	9.1	0.2	90.4

 AAUW

Middle Tennessee State is a public university offering two and four-year degrees in arts and sciences, agriculture, education, business, and health professions. It enrolls 10,314 students, including 8,650 undergraduates. Half the undergraduates are women, of whom 12 percent attend part-time. The median age of undergraduates is 21. Summer sessions, on- and off-campus evening classes, and Saturday classes are offered. The Office of Continuing Education serves 300 reentry women, half of them black women. Sixty-nine percent of students commute to campus, parking on-campus for a fee.

The MTSU Home Economics Nursery School gives priority to low-income families in the community. Private childcare facilities are available near campus.

Policies to Ensure Fairness to Women. The Director of Affirmative Action is a full-time compliance administrator for equal-employment-opportunity, sex-equity, and handicapped-access laws. A publicly communicated, written policy prohibits sexual harassment of students, faculty, and staff.

Women in Leadership Positions. *Students.* Of the four positions available during each of three recent years, a woman was editor of the campus newspaper.

Faculty. Twenty-four percent of 400 full-time faculty are women. There are 2 female faculty for every 100 female students and 8 male faculty for every 100 male students.

Administrators. All top administrators are men. Women chair five of 29 departments: nursing, home economics, education and special education, psychology, and foreign languages. Nine of the 47-member faculty senate and 2 of the 5-member tenure and promotions committee are white women. Of 10 speakers in a recent major campus lecture series, 1 was a black woman and 2 were white women.

Women and the Curriculum. Most bachelor's degrees awarded to women are in education (32 percent), business (12 percent), and social sciences (11 percent). The most popular two-year degree is in health technologies. Eight percent of women major in such nontraditional fields as agriculture, mathematics, computer science, physical sciences, engineering, and architecture. Special programs encourage women to take courses in science, agriculture, accounting, computer science, and criminal law. Three-fourths of participants in cooperative education and half the students in science field service are women.

The Women's Studies Program, under a director who holds a full-time faculty appointment, awards an undergraduate minor. Courses are offered through Women's studies and selected departments. Recent offerings include The American Woman, Women in Business, The Political Status of Women, and Women in Literature. An official committee supervises the Women's Studies Program. The departments of education, physical education, nursing, social work, and business provide instruction on some matters specific to women.

Women and Athletics. In the small athletics program, 22 percent of varsity athletes and 30 percent of intramural athletes are women; women receive 16 percent of athletic scholarships. Three of 17 varsity coaches are women. Club sports are also available. Women's intercollegiate sports are basketball, tennis, track, and volleyball.

Housing and Student Organizations. Single-sex dormitories with restricted visitation hours for members of the opposite sex, and student/faculty housing accommodate 31 percent of students. Thirteen white women, two minority women, and nine men, who receive in-service training on personal security, direct residence halls.

Eight percent of full-time undergraduate women join social sororities. Sorority housing consists of suites in dormitories; fraternities have off-campus housing. Forty minority women join all-minority sororities. A campus chapter of the (National Organization of Women) is in formation.

Special Services and Programs for Women. *Health and Counseling.* One male physician and 5 assistants, 4 of whom are female, provide birth control and pap smears. Three men counsel on gynecological matters, abortion, and rape and assault.

Safety and Security. Measures consist of campus police, night-time escorts for women, high-intensity lighting, self-defense courses, and information sessions on campus safety. Four rapes and ten assaults (three on women) were reported for 1980-81.

Career. Nonsexist/nonracist literature on nontraditional fields of study and job discrimination information are available.

Other. The small Women's Center—chaired part-time by a faculty member—serves 500 women a year, and offers a course on mathematics. The Office of Continuing Education and the psychology department sponsor assertiveness/leadership training.

Institutional Self-Description. "MTSU has a strong Women's Group, WISE activities, and a woman recruiter. The university's President has a strong commitment to women's concerns."

Nashville State Technical Institute
120 White Bridge Rd.
Nashville, TN 37209
Telephone: (615) 741-1245

Women in Leadership
★★ **students**
★ **faculty**
★ **administrators**

3,754 undergraduates

	Amer. Ind.	Asian Amer.	Blacks	Hispanics	Whites
F	3	2	359	5	1,410
M	3	8	274	12	1,613
%	0.2	0.3	17.2	0.5	82.0

A public, two-year college, Nashville State offers career training in technical and business fields to 3,754 students, just under half of whom are women. Seventy-two percent of women attend part-time. The median age of all students is 27.

The college offers one and two-year programs to train or retrain adults for employment as technicians. There is an adult continuing education program. Nashville Technical offers day and evening courses both on and off campus, as well as a weekend college and a summer session. All students commute. The suburban campus is accessible by public transportation and offers free on-campus parking.

Private childcare facilities are available close to campus.

Policies to Ensure Fairness to Women. The head of Planning and Development is responsible part-time for compliance with equal-opportunity laws. A formal campus grievance procedure resolves complaints of sexual harassment.

Women in Leadership Positions. *Students.* In recent years, women have held 44 percent of the campus-wide student leadership positions: women have been president of the student body once, of the senior class twice, and of the entering class once. A woman heads the sole honorary society.

Faculty. The faculty of 68 is 32 percent female, above average for institutions nationwide. The part-time faculty is 26 percent female. There are 4 female faculty for every 100 female students and 7 male faculty for every 100 male students.

Administrators. Of seven chief administrators, the chief academic officer and the head librarian are women. Women head the Educational Resource Center and chair nine of 35 departments, including banking and special programs, business data processing, medical lab technology, occupational therapy, and secretarial science.

Women and the Curriculum. Most two-year degrees and certificates earned by women are in data processing and business and commerce. In a recent year, 22 women graduated in mechanical and engineering technologies. Fifteen percent of students participating in cooperative education are women, as are 93 percent of those in internships. The Committee to Recruit Women to Engineering Technology encourages women to enter nontraditional fields and occupations.

There are no courses on women. Workshops on nontraditional occupations for women and men, the needs of reentry women, and equal educational opportunity are provided for faculty.

Women and Athletics. There are no intercollegiate or club sports for women. The intramural program attracts 75 women and consists largely of individual sports.

Special Services and Programs for Women. *Health and Counseling.* There is no student health service. One of the six-member student conseling staff is a woman. Counselors are offered in-service training on the avoidance of sex-role stereotyping.

Safety and Security. Measures include campus police without arrest authority, local police, and high-intensity lighting in all areas. There is a rape crisis center. One attempted assault on a woman was reported for 1980–81.

Career. The college sponsors a "Women Who Work" speakers' bureau, workshops focused on nontraditional occupations, lectures by women employed in nontraditional occupations, and printed information on nontraditional fields of study for women.

Institutional Self-Description. "At Nashville Tech, a woman has the choice of day and evening courses, as well as a weekend college, in scheduling classes to best fit her life circumstances. Co-op education is available which allows her to earn while she learns. Job placement averages 95 percent for the one and two-year programs of study in high-demand, competitive-salary fields. Other features: financial aid, counseling, free parking close to buildings."

Roane State Community College
Harriman, TN 37748
Telephone: (615) 354-3000, ext. 207

Women in Leadership
★★★ students
★★ faculty

2,885 undergraduates

	Amer. Ind.	Asian Amer.	Blacks	Hispanics	Whites
F	3	3	35	3	1,464
M	0	4	58	6	1,308
%	0.1	0.2	3.2	0.3	96.1

Roane State is a public, two-year college. It serves 3,229 students, 2,885 of whom are enrolled in degree or certificate programs. Slightly over half the students are women, and two-thirds of women attend part-time. The median age of students is 29; 46 percent of women students are age 25 or older.

The college offers the first two years of liberal arts and pre-professional programs, and a variety of one- and two-year certificate programs. The college offers day and evening classes, both on and off campus, and self-paced contract learning (in developmental studies). There is an adult continuing education program. All students commute by automobile. On-campus parking for a fee is available.

Women in Leadership Positions. *Students.* Most of the four campus-wide student leadership positions available each year were held by women in recent years.

Faculty. Thirty-nine percent of 76 full-time faculty are women, including 2 Asian American and 2 black women. There are 6 female faculty for every 100 female students and 8 male faculty for every 100 male students.

Administrators. Of 10 chief administrators, the Coordinator of Institutional Research is a woman. Departments chaired by women include allied health and nursing, mathematics/science, and humanities. Two of the 17 trustees are women, including 1 black woman.

Women and the Curriculum. Most of the degrees and certificates awarded to women are in the arts and sciences or business and commerce. Three-fourths of participants in the cooperative education program are women, most of whom are in secretarial fields.

Courses in the departments of education, physical education, and business provide some instruction on matters specific to women. The social science and humanities departments offer two courses on women: Psychology of Women and Women in American Literature.

Women and Athletics. Women have limited opportunities to participate in intramural and intercollegiate athletics. Women play intercollegiate basketball and tennis.

Special Services and Programs for Women. *Health and Counseling.* The student health service is staffed by 2 female health-care providers and 1 male physician who provide treatment by referral. The student counseling center has a staff of 2 women and 1 man. Some treatment and counseling are available for gynecological matters, and rape and assault. Counseling is also available for birth control and abortion. In-service training on avoiding sex-role stereotyping is provided for counselors.

Safety and Security. Measures include campus police with weapons training, night-time escort service for women students, and high-intensity lighting. For 1980–81, one assault on a woman was reported.

Career. Services include workshops focused on nontraditional occupations, printed information on nontraditional fields of study for women, and job discrimination information on nontraditional occupations for women.

Other. Women's Centers are being developed at the main campus and at off-campus locations. The counseling center offers assertiveness/leadership training, a program to build skills in mathematics, and a telephone service for information, referrals, and support.

Institutional Self-Description. "At a low cost, we provide high-quality instruction in small class and/or individualized situations. We build confidence in students, both female and male, who are unfamiliar with traditional four-year institutions, preparing them to continue in a four-year setting."

Shelby State Community College
Box 40568, Memphis, TN 38104
Telephone: (901) 528-6800

Women in Leadership
★★★ faculty

3,926 undergraduates

	Amer. Ind.	Asian Amer.	Blacks	Hispanics	Whites
F	3	5	1,904	3	636
M	2	1	844	3	524
%	0.1	0.2	70.0	0.2	29.6

Founded in 1970 as a two-year, comprehensive community college, Shelby State is affiliated with the State University and Community College system of Tennessee and prepares its students for transfer to four-year institutions. Seventy percent of the undergraduates are black students. The college attracts 4,954 students, of whom 3,926 are enrolled in undergraduate degree programs. Sixty-five percent of undergraduates are women; 40 percent of women attend part-time. The median age of undergraduates is 24, with 10 percent of women over age 40.

There is a continuing education and community services program. On- and off-campus day and evening classes, a summer session, and self-paced/contract learning programs facilitate scheduling. All students commute. Public transportation and parking for a modest fee are available.

On-campus childcare and off-campus private childcare facilities are available.

Policies to Ensure Fairness to Women. The Director of Personnel serves as part-time administrator to monitor compliance with equal-employment-opportunity legislation. There is no written sexual harassment policy; a formal campus grievance procedure resolves complaints. An active Committee on the Status of Women, its members appointed by the President, includes student members with voting rights. A Committee on Minority Affairs, along with the Committee on the Status of Women, address the concerns of minority women.

Women in Leadership Positions. *Students.* Women have little opportunity to exercise campus-wide leadership. Of the two positions available, a woman was presiding officer of the student senate once in a recent three-year period. A woman heads the only honorary society on campus.

Faculty. Women are 51 percent of the full-time faculty, which makes Shelby rare among coeducational colleges. There are 5 female faculty for every 100 female students and 11 male faculty for every 100 male students.

Administrators. Women are 2 of 9 top administrators: chief academic officer and director of institutional research. Women head 6 of 16 departments: speech and theater, secretarial technology, education, consumer and family studies, nursing, and nutrition and dietetics. One of the female department chairs is a black woman; the other 5 are white. The Dean of Instruction and the Chair of Education and Public Services are women. Of 18 regents, 2 are white women and 1 is a black woman.

Women and the Curriculum. Most women earn two-year degrees and certificates in arts and sciences (46 percent), health technologies (22 percent), and business (13 percent). Seventy-eight percent of participants in cooperative education and 81 percent in internships and practicums are women.

There is one course on women: Women's Literature. Faculty are offered workshops on racism and the curriculum, the relationships among sex, race, and the selection of a major field, nontraditional occupations for men and women, and the needs of reentry women.

Women and Athletics. Twenty percent of intramural athletes are women, who participate in racquetball, tennis, and badminton. Twenty-eight percent of intercollegiate athletes are women; women are awarded 30 percent of athletic scholarship aid. One of the four paid coaches for intercollegiate sports is a woman. The intercollegiate sports offered are basketball and tennis.

Special Services and Programs for Women. *Health and Counseling.* Shelby State has no student health service. A student counseling center is staffed by seven counselors, of whom four are minority women. No services specific to women are provided.

Safety and Security. Measures consist of campus police without arrest authority and local police patrol. No information was provided on the incidence of rapes and assaults.

Institutional Self-Description. None provided.

Southwestern at Memphis
200 North Parkway, Memphis, TN 38112
Telephone: (901) 274-1800

Women in Leadership
★★ students

1,008 undergraduates

	Amer. Ind.	Asian Amer.	Blacks	Hispanics	Whites
F	0	2	15	3	471
M	0	1	4	4	496
%	0.0	0.3	1.9	0.7	97.1

 AAUW

A private, four-year institution affiliated with the Presbyterian Church, Southwestern at Memphis was founded in 1848. It offers bachelor's degrees in liberal arts and sciences and pre-professional areas. Adult students are served by the Center for Continuing Education. Of the 1,031 students who attend Southwestern, 1,008 are registered full-time in degree programs. Half the students are women. The median age of all students is 20 years. One-fourth of students commute to the campus, which is accessible by public transportation. On-campus parking is also available.

Private childcare facilities can be found near campus.

Policies to Ensure Fairness to Women. The institution's legal counselor and two administrative officers share responsibility part-time for policy and compliance concerning legislation on equal employment opportunity and sex equity for students. Complaints of sexual harassment are resolved through a formal grievance procedure, which has been communicated to faculty and staff in a handbook.

Women in Leadership Positions. *Students.* Southwestern offers excellent opportunities for women to gain leadership experience. In a recent three-year period, women held the top student offices 44 percent of the time, including president of the student court for two years; president of the student union board and editor-in-chief of the campus newspaper for one year each. Two of nine campus honorary societies have female presidents.

Faculty. Ten percent of the 78 full-time faculty are women, a proportion far below the national average. There are 2 female faculty for every 100 female students and 14 male faculty for every 100 male students.

Administrators. One of the 10 chief administrators, the head librarian, is a woman. Women chair two of the 18 departments: education and communication arts. Four of 36 trustees are female. Two of 6 recent honorary degree recipients were women.

Women and the Curriculum. Most degrees earned by women are in social sciences (37 percent), psychology (16 percent), letters (15 percent), and fine arts (8 percent). Six percent of women major in physical sciences or mathematics.

There are no courses on women.

Women and Athletics. For a college of its size, Southwestern has a good intramural and intercollegiate sports program for women. Twenty-one percent of intercollegiate athletes, 42 percent of intramural athletes, and all club athletes are women. One of the eight paid intercollegiate coaches is a woman. Intercollegiate sports offered are basketball, cross-country, tennis, and volleyball.

Housing and Student Organizations. Three-fourths of the students live on campus in single-sex dormitories. Nine of the 25 dormitory directors are women, including one minority woman. Staff are offered awareness-training on avoidance of racism and sexism, as well as on sex education.

Fifty-five percent of female students belong to social sororities, including 7 minority women in racially integrated groups. Neither fraternities nor sororities provide housing for members. The Women's Undergraduate Board serves as an advocacy group. Five percent of its 500 active participants are minority women, with blacks and Asian Americans predominant. The Black Student Association serves as an advocacy group for minority women; most of its members are women.

Special Services and Programs for Women. *Health and Counseling.* One male and 3 female physicians staff the student health service, along with 2 female health-care providers. Two male professionals staff the student counseling center. Counseling and medical treatment for gynecological problems and rape and assault are available. Counseling on birth control and abortion is available.

Safety and Security. Measures consist of campus police without arrest authority, night escorts for women students, information sessions on campus safety and crime prevention, self-defense courses, and a rape crisis center. One rape and two assaults on women were reported for 1980–81.

Career. Workshops, lectures, job discrimination information, and printed materials on nontraditional occupations for women are available, along with updated alumnae files by specific careers and networking between alumnae and female students.

Other. The Center for Continuing Education sponsors a women's lecture series and the counseling center offers assertiveness training.

Institutional Self-Description. "Southwestern at Memphis' one commitment is to a liberal arts and sciences education of the highest quality because it is the education that gives you the opportunity to develop your mind, to identify and examine the many options open to you, and the freedom to make the best choice to fulfill your own potential."

Tennessee Technological University
Box 5007, Cookeville, TN 38501
Telephone: (615) 528-3241

Women in Leadership
★★ students

6,251 undergraduates

	Amer. Ind.	Asian Amer.	Blacks	Hispanics	Whites
F	5	4	57	0	2,479
M	7	7	90	12	3,292
%	0.2	0.2	2.5	0.2	96.9

Founded in 1915, Tennessee Technological University is a state-supported comprehensive institution, with a commitment to serve the Upper Cumberland region. The large, rural campus, located east of Nashville, serves 7,252 students. Forty-two percent of the 6,251 undergraduates are women; 19 percent of women attend part-time. The median age of undergraduates is 20.

The university offers a variety of associate, bachelor's and graduate degrees. The division of extended sevices is responsible for adult continuing education. Classes meet on and off campus in the day and evening. There is a summer session. For the 59 percent of undergraduates who commute, campus parking for a fee is available.

Two university-operated childcare centers meet 15 percent of students' requests, accommodating up to 20 children at a fee of $.50 an hour. Admission is on a first-come, first-served basis, and the centers remain open until 11:30 p.m. There are additional, private childcare facilities nearby.

Policies to Ensure Fairness to Women. The Executive Assistant to the President/Affirmative Action Officer is responsible for policy, practices, and compliance with sex equity for students, equal employment opportunity, and handicapped access. A published sexual harassment policy protects students, faculty, and staff; complaints are handled through a formal campus grievance procedure.

Women in Leadership Positions. *Students.* Women students have excellent leadership opportunities. In recent years, women have held five of six major campus offices for one term, and been the editor of the campus newspaper for three consecutive terms. Women head eleven of 24 honorary societies.

Faculty. Nineteen percent of the 305 faculty are women, a proportion below the national average. There are 3 female faculty for every 100 female students and 7 male faculty for every 100 male students.

Administrators. The top administrators are men. The Dean of Nursing and the Dean of Home Economics are women. A woman chairs one of 33 departments, that of administration/supervision/curriculum. In a recent year, three of the five recipients of alumni awards were women.

Women and the Curriculum. Most bachelor's degrees earned by women are in education (43 percent), with a significant number in business (15 percent). About 12 percent are in such nontraditional areas as agriculture, computer science, engineering, mathematics, and physical sciences. Special programs encourage women to prepare for engineering and science careers. The elementary education department sponsors a mathematics anxiety clinic. One-half of the students engaged in internships and science field work and 17 percent of those in cooperative education are women.

No courses on women are offered. The departments of education, nursing, and business provide some instruction on matters specific to women.

Women and Athletics. Nine activities offer a balance of individual and team sports. Half the participants in the popular intramural program are women. Fifteen percent of varsity athletes are women, and women receive 20 percent of the athletic scholarships. Three of eleven paid varsity coaches are women. The intercollegiate sports are basketball, riflery, tennis, and volleyball.

Housing and Student Organizations. Forty-one percent of undergraduates live in single-sex dormitories that have restrictive hours for visitors of the opposite sex. The university provides housing for married students with or without children and for single parents.

Eleven percent of full-time undergraduate women belong to sororities, which house their members. An all-minority sorority has 12 members. The Society of Women Engineers serves as an advocacy group.

Special Services and Programs for Women. *Health and Counseling.* The student health service employs 1 part-time male physician and 6 health-care providers, 5 of whom are women. Two of 4 professionals at the student counseling center are women. Counseling and treatment are available for gynecological problems and birth control

Safety and Security. Measures consist of campus police protection, high-intensity lighting, an emergency telephone system, and instruction for women on self-defense, campus safety, and rape and assault. No rapes or assaults on women were reported for 1980–81.

Career. Services include workshops, lectures, and information on nontraditional occupations for women, in addition to a career day.

Other. The counseling center and the educational psychology department sponsor a displaced homemakers' program. The counseling center also organizes a women's lecture series and assertiveness/leadership training.

Institutional Self-Description. "Tennessee Technological University offers an outstanding program in engineering as well as very strong programs in nursing, biological sciences, environmental sciences, business, education, agriculture, and liberal arts. Women interested in enrolling in one of the above fields may be interested in attending Tennessee Technological University."

Vanderbilt University
Nashville, TN 37235
Telephone: (615) 322-7311

★★ **Women and the Curriculum**

4,933 undergraduates

	Amer. Ind.	Asian Amer.	Blacks	Hispanics	Whites
F	0	10	55	2	2,234
M	0	9	40	3	2,533
%	0.0	0.4	1.0	0.1	97.6

 AAUW

Established in 1873, Vanderbilt University, a private nondenominational institution located in Nashville, provides 7,400 students with a range of undergraduate, graduate, and professional studies. Women are 47 percent of the 4,933 undergraduates. The median age of undergraduates is 20. For the 15 percent who commute, the university is accessible by public transportation. On-campus parking is available.

Private childcare facilities are available nearby.

Policies to Ensure Fairness to Women. A full-time Director and Associate Director of Equal Opportunity review policies and practices related to employment, sex equity for students, and handicapped accessibility. A published policy prohibits sexual harassment. Complaints are handled both informally and confidentially or through a formal grievance procedure.

Women in Leadership Positions. *Students.* Opportunities for women students to assume campus leadership are average for private research institutions in this guide. In recent years, women have twice been student body president and presiding officers of the student court and residence-hall council. Women head 14 of 27 honorary societies.

Faculty. Of the 570 faculty members, 22 percent are women, including 2 black women. There are 5 female faculty to every 100 female students and 17 male faculty to every 100 male students.

Administrators. Men occupy all top administrative posts. Of 61 departments, women chair five—all in the School of Nursing. The Dean of the School of Nursing is a woman. One-fifth of the faculty senate are women.

Women and the Curriculum. Most women graduating with bachelor's degrees major in the health professions (23 percent), the social sciences (16 percent), and general letters (12 percent). The proportion of women majoring in business and management and the fine arts is above the national average. Seventeen percent of women major in nontraditional fields. An innovative program encourages women to prepare for careers in engineering. Over half of the positions in experiential learning programs go to women.

The Women's Studies Program offers a range of elective courses through Women's Studies and the departments of history, Spanish, psychology, education, and anthropology. Recent offerings include Women and Public Policy, Women's History, Sex and Gender, and Women Writers of Latin America. An official committee oversees the development of the Women's Studies Program. Such current issues as mathematics confidence among females, sex-fair curricula, coeducational physical education classes, reproductive choice, and health-care information important to minority women are part of the preparation of future teachers and health-care providers.

Women and Athletics. Intramural and intercollegiate programs provide opportunities for organized, competitive individual and team sports. Women receive 20 percent of athletic scholarships awarded. Two of the 27 paid coaches are women. Women's intercollegiate teams played in tournaments in 1980. The intercollegiate sports offered are basketball, cross-country, swimming, tennis, and volleyball.

Housing and Student Organizations. Eighty-five percent of undergraduates live on campus. Single-sex or coeducational dormitories, and housing for married students and single parents with children are available. A married woman student whose spouse is not enrolled may live in married students' housing. Each residence hall sets its policy governing visitors of the opposite sex. Half the residence-hall directors are women. Awareness-training is offered to staff on alcohol, drugs, rape and stress.

Half of the undergraduate women belong to social sororities; twenty-eight women are in all-minority sororities. Sororities and fraternities provide housing for officers only. The Society of Women Engineers, Women Law Students Association, Divinity Women, and American Medical Women's Association serve as advocates for women on campus. The African American Association is supportive of black women.

Special Services and Programs for Women. *Health and Counseling.* The student health service provides some medical attention specific to women, including gynecological and birth control treatment. Three of the 5 physicians are women, as are 16 other health-care providers. Eighteen of 33 staff in the counseling service are women. Students have access to gynecological, birth control, abortion, and rape and assault counseling. Assertiveness training is also available.

Safety and Security. Measures include regular campus police, student trainees, city police, night-time escorts for women students, high-intensity lighting in some areas, an emergency alarm system for fire, emergency telephones, self-defense courses for women, information sessions on safety and crime prevention, and a rape crisis center. Fourteen assaults (12 on women) and no rapes were reported for 1980–81.

Other. A Women's Center is part of the Office of the President. Among activities and services provided are an annual women's week and a telephone line of information, referral, and support.

The YWCA sponsors programs for battered women and dis-placed homemakers. A women's lecture series, theater, and other women's arts programs are sponsored by Women's Studies, ac-ademic departments, and the Episcopal Chaplain's Office.

Institutional Self-Description. "There is an active community of students, faculty, and staff at Vanderbilt which is deeply com-mitted to educational and social equity for all persons, regardless of sex or race. While regional traditions and attitudes also persist, diversity in lifestyle, political, and social participation has grown in recent years."

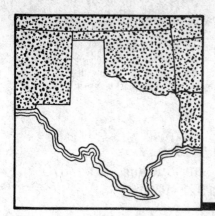

Amarillo College

Box 447, Amarillo, TX 79178
Telephone: (806) 376-5111

Women in Leadership
★★★ students
★★ faculty

4,222 undergraduates

	Amer. Ind.	Asian Amer.	Blacks	Hispanics	Whites
F	13	12	102	111	2,006
M	17	17	168	127	1,708
%	0.7	0.7	4.0	6.0	88.9

Amarillo is a public, two-year college offering educational programs and services to 4,737 students. Of the 4,222 undergraduates, 53 percent are women, two-thirds of whom attend part-time. The median age of undergraduates is 27.

The college offers the first two years of liberal arts and one- and two-year technical, occupational, trade, industrial, and adult continuing education programs. Evening classes both on and off campus, a weekend college, a summer session, and self-paced, contract learning are availble. Amarillo College is accessible by public transportation, and on-campus parking is available. All students commute.

An on-campus childcare facility, available from 7:30 a.m. to 6:00 p.m., serves students, faculty, and staff. Private facilities near campus are also available.

Policies to Ensure Fairness to Women. The Director of Personnel has full-time responsibility for policy and compliance with equal-employment-opportunity legislation. A Committee on the Status of Women, reporting to the Director of Women's Programs, offers "input on plannning." A formal campus-wide grievance procedure resolves complaints of sexual harassment.

Women in Leadership Positions. *Students.* The participation of women in campus-wide leadership is above average for public, two-year colleges. In three recent years, women served twice as presiding officer of the student governing body and three times as editor-in-chief of the campus newspaper. A woman heads one of the two honorary societies.

Faculty. The full-time faculty of 186 is 44 percent female. There are 10 female faculty for every 100 female students and 12 male faculty for every 100 male students.

Administrators. The seven chief administrators are men. Women chair the divisions of access, allied health,, nursing, and counseling, and 12 of the 143 departments. Of the eight regents, two are women.

Women and the Curriculum. Most degrees and awards conferred upon women are in health technologies (45 percent), the arts and sciences (29 percent), and business and commerce (18 percent). No courses on women are offered. Courses in the departments of nursing, social work, and business provide some instruction on matters specific to women.

Women and Athletics. Women have good opportunities in intramural and limited opportunities in intercollegiate sports. Approximately 300 women participate in the intramural program. Intramural sports include flag football, volleyball, slow-pitch, and basketball. Half of athletic scholarship are awarded to women. Women participate in intercollegiate basketball.

Special Services and Programs for Women. *Health and Counseling.* The student health service is staffed by two female health-care providers. Six women staff the student counseling center. No treatment specific to women is available.

Safety and Security. Measures include campus police with arrest authority, high-intensity lighting in all areas, self-defense courses for women, information sessions on campus safety, rape and assault prevention, and a rape crisis center. For 1980-81, there were no rapes or assaults reported on campus.

Career. Support Services for Women is designed to help women enter nontraditional career fields. Counseling, assessment, entry help, and a support group already in the field are available.

Other. The Office of Women's Programs sponsors a displaced homemakers' program and assertiveness/leadership training. Coordinated by a full-time administrator, the Women's Center serves approximately 500 women annually, the most frequent participants being community women and undergraduates over age 25.

Institutional Self-Description. "At Amarillo College the motto is 'The student comes first.' About 34 percent of these students are women over the age of 24 years, and they do come first. Faculty and staff are available to help these women find what they need. Services include personal, vocational, and academic counseling; individual assessment; life skills training; and job placement help."

Henderson County Junior College

Athens, TX 75751
Telephone: (214) 675-6210

Women in Leadership
★ faculty

2,349 undergraduates

	Amer. Ind.	Asian Amer.	Blacks	Hispanics	Whites
F	0	0	135	9	794
M	2	0	333	91	924
%	0.1	0	20.5	4.4	75.1

This public, two-year college offers comprehensive educational services to 2,531 students, 2,349 of whom are enrolled as undergraduates. Women account for 40 percent of the undergraduates; 58 percent of women attend part-time. The median age of undergraduates is 26.

Henderson County offers the first two years of liberal arts and pre-professional training for college transfer, terminal programs in technical and occupational fields, and adult continuing education. Day and evening classes are available both on and off campus, and the college holds a summer session. Ten percent of undergraduates reside on campus. Free on-campus parking is available to commuters.

On-campus childcare is available, as well as private facilities nearby. The on-campus facilities, which can accommodate all requests by students, are open from 7:30 a.m. to 4:30 p.m. and charge $6 a day.

Policies to Ensure Fairness to Women. An administrator has part-time responsibility for monitoring compliance with equal-employment-opportunity and sex-equity legislation. No written campus policy exists on sexual harassment; complaints are handled either informally and confidentially or through a formal grievance procedure that has been communicated in writing to faculty and staff.

Women in Leadership Positions. *Students.* Women enjoy a limited role in student leadership. Out of six possible positions in a recent three-year period, a woman served for one year as president of the student body. A woman heads the only honorary society.

Faculty. The 79-member full-time faculty is 29 percent female, a proportion above the national average. There are 6 female faculty for every 100 female students and 11 male faculty for every 100 male students.

Administrators. All the chief administrators are men. Of six major departments, a woman chairs business administration.

Women and the Curriculum. Most of the two-year degrees and certificates awarded to women are in the arts and sciences. There are no courses on women.

Women and Athletics. Women have limited opportunities to participate in organized sports. A third of the intramural athletes are women; the most popular sports are volleyball and basketball. One of the four paid varsity coaches is a woman; 30 percent of the athletic scholarship aid goes to women. Basketball is the intercollegiate sport in which women participate.

Housing and Student Organizations. The 10 percent of the students who live on campus reside in single-sex dormitories that have restricted hours for visitors of the opposite sex. Of five residence-hall directors, one is a white woman and one a minority woman. Awareness-training on birth control is offered to residence-hall staff.

Special Services and Programs for Women. *Health and Counseling.* There is no student health service. The student counseling center has a staff of three men and three women. No services specific to women were reported.

Safety and Security. Security measures include campus police with arrest authority, and high-intensity lighting in all areas. A total of three assaults were reported on campus for 1980–81, none involving women.

Career. Workshops on nontraditional occupations and job dis-crimination information on nontraditional occupations for women are available.

Institutional Self-Description. "Henderson County Junior College is an equal-opportunity institution which provides educational opportunities on the basis of merit without discrimination because of race, color, religion, sex, age, national origin, or handicap."

Incarnate Word College
4301 Broadway, San Antonio, TX 78209
Telephone: (512) 828-1261

Women in Leadership
★★★ students
★★★ faculty

1,145 undergraduates

	Amer. Ind.	Asian Amer.	Blacks	Hispanics	Whites
F	1	0	94	359	441
M	0	0	24	61	102
%	0.1	0.0	11.0	38.8	50.2

Founded in 1881 by the Roman Catholic Sisters of Charity, Incarnate Word College became coeducational in 1973. Of the 1,355 students who attend, 1,145 are registered in degree programs. Eighty-one percent of degree students are women; 20 percent attend part-time. The median age of all students is 24, with 33 percent of women students between 25 and 40.

The college offers bachelor's degrees in the liberal arts and sciences. Adult students are served by the Adult and Continuing Education Office. Day and evening classes held both on and off campus and a summer session are available. Seventy-seven percent of students commute to the campus, which is accessible by public transportation. On-campus parking is available for a fee.

College-operated childcare facilities accommodate 45 children on a first-come, first-served basis. Charges are based on a fixed daily fee. Most students' requests can be met. Private childcare facilities are located near the campus.

Policies to Ensure Fairness to Women. Two administrators have part-time responsibility for monitoring compliance with equal employment opportunity, sex equity for students, and handicapped accessibility. Complaints of sexual harassment are handled informally and confidentially.

Women in Leadership Positions. *Students.* Opportunities for women to assume leadership are outstanding. In a recent three-year period, women presided over the student body and residence-hall council three times and were editor of the newspaper twice. Both campus honorary societies are headed by women.

Faculty. Women are 65 percent of a full-time faculty of 71, a proportion significantly above the national average. There are 6 female faculty for every 100 female students and 15 male faculty for every 100 male students. According to recent data, 1 American Indian, 1 Asian American, 3 Hispanic, and 3 black women are on the faculty.

Administrators. Two of the 9 top administrative positions are held by women: chief executive officer and chief planning officer. Women chair 2 of 5 academic units: the division of social sciences, business administration, and multidisciplinary studies, and the division of nursing. Thirteen of 20 members of the Board of Trustees are women.

Women and the Curriculum. Almost half (47 percent) of women graduates major in health professions, with a significant number in education. Two percent of women earn degrees in the nontraditional fields of architecture and the physical sciences. The

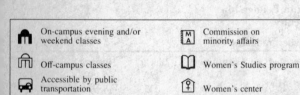

🏠	On-campus evening and/or weekend classes	Ⓜ Ⓐ	Commission on minority affairs
🏛	Off-campus classes	📖	Women's Studies program
🚐	Accessible by public transportation	🎗	Women's center
👫	On-campus childcare facilities	AAUW	Member, American Association of University Women
✎	Publicly communicated sexual harassment policy, includes students	NWSA	Member, National Women's Studies Association
Ⓢ Ⓦ	Commission on status of women	CROW	On-campus Center for Research on Women

college offers a program designed to encourage women to prepare for careers in science. Three-fourths of students in cooperative education programs and 71 percent of student interns are women.

The college offers one course on women: Women in American History. The divisions of education, physical education, and nursing include some issues specific to women in their curricula. Workshops on nontraditional occupations, the needs of reentry women, and affirmative action and equal opportunity are held for the faculty.

Women and Athletics. The intramural program offers a range of individual and team sports. Thirty-five percent of intramural athletes are women. Varsity offerings are limited. Varsity teams participated in recent tournament competition. The intercollegiate sports are basketball, softball, tennis, and volleyball.

Housing and Student Organizations. Single-sex dormitories, which restrict hours for visitors of the opposite sex, house the 23 percent of students who live on campus. Four of the five residence-hall directors are women, three of them minority women. Residence-hall staff are offered awareness-training on avoidance of racism.

Six percent of full-time female students join campus sororities, including 20 minority women who belong to racially-integrated sororities.

Special Services and Programs for Women. *Health and Counseling.* One female health-care provider staffs the student health center and the counseling center employs one male professional. Gynecological counseling is the only service provided specific to women.

Safety and Security. Measures consist of campus police without arrest authority. No rapes or assaults on women were reported for 1980–81.

Career. The college offers workshops and speakers on nontraditional occupations, as well as networks between alumnae and female students.

Other. WENCOE (Women in Education: New Careers, Opportunities, Experiences), a program of continuing education for women, has a $33,500 budget. In a recent year, some 438 reentry women participated; over one-fifth of the women are minority-group members, largely Hispanic.

Institutional Self-Description. "Since its foundation, Incarnate Word College has been committed to the education of women. The curriculum has developed in an attempt to meet the changing roles of women in society, especially in the area of career preparation. Special outreach programs exist for older women returning to college. Outstanding role models are present among faculty and women administrators."

Midwestern State University
3400 Taft Boulevard
Wichita Falls, TX 76308
Telephone: (817) 692-6611

Women in Leadership
★★ students

4,058 undergraduates

	Amer. Ind.	Asian Amer.	Blacks	Hispanics	Whites
F	4	7	110	39	1,904
M	5	15	70	63	1,811
%	0.2	0.6	4.5	2.5	92.2

 AAUW

Founded in 1922 as a two-year college, Midwestern State became a public university in 1961. It offers associate, bachelor's, and master's degrees, as well as adult continuing education. Its campus attracts 4,475 students, including 4,058 undergraduates.

Women are half the undergraduates; 38 percent of women attend part-time. The median age of undergraduates is 21.

Classes meet on and off campus during the day and evening. There is a summer session. For the 89 percent of students who commute, on-campus parking is available for a fee. Private child-care facilities are available near campus.

Policies to Ensure Fairness to Women. The Personnel Director, on a part-time basis, monitors compliance with affirmative-action and handicapped-access regulations. The Vice President of Student Affairs has part-time responsibility for policy regarding sex equity for students. A published sexual harassment policy protects all members of the university community; complaints of sexual harassment are handled through a formal grievance procedure.

Women in Leadership Positions. *Students.* Women students have excellent opportunities to obtain leadership experience. In a recent three-year period, women twice edited the campus newspaper, presided over the residence-hall council three times, and were presidents of the senior, sophomore, and entering classes. Eleven of 19 honorary societies are headed by women.

Faculty. Twenty-three percent of the 139 faculty are women, a proportion slightly below average for similar institutions in this guide. There are 2 female faculty for every 100 female students and 8 male faculty for every 100 male students.

Administrators. Men occupy the top-level administrative posts, except for head librarian. Of 15 departments, a woman chairs nursing. A woman sits on the nine-member Board of Trustees.

Women and the Curriculum. Most bachelor's degrees awarded to women are in education (43 percent) and business (19 percent). One percent are in the nontraditional field of physical sciences. Women receive 72 percent of associate degrees granted, all in health technologies.

No courses on women are offered. The departments of business, social work, and physical education provide some instruction on matters specific to women.

Women and Athletics. The organized athletic program for women is adequate. Women are 22 percent of intercollegiate and 32 percent of intramural athletes; women receive 30 percent of athletic scholarships. Two of the seven paid varsity coaches are women. Intercollegiate sports offered are basketball, tennis, and volleyball.

Housing and Student Organizations. Twelve percent of undergraduates live in coeducational and men's dormitories that restrict hours for visitors of the opposite sex. Both residence-hall directors are women.

Nine percent of undergraduate women belong to social sororities. The University Association for Women, the NAACP student chapter, and the American Indian Association meet on campus.

Special Services and Programs for Women. *Health and Counseling.* The student health service employs two male physicians and one female health-care provider. No information was provided on counseling or health services specific to women.

Safety and Security. Measures consist of campus police with weapons training and arrest authority. No rapes or assaults on women were reported for 1980–81.

Career. Services include printed information on nontraditional fields of study for women and job discrimination information.

Other. The Dean of Students organizes an annual women's week, as well as leadership training sessions. The University Association of Women and Office of Student Affairs sponsor a mathematics anxiety clinic for women. The University Women's Association also assists older, reentry women.

Institutional Self-Description. "Midwestern State University is a public, coeducational institution which espouses a liberal arts philosophy. We seek to develop 'the sound mind in the sound body'; we seek to educate our students as whole persons. Midwestern is a student-oriented university in a thriving, friendly community."

North Texas State University
Denton, TX 76203
Telephone: (817) 788-2122

12,230 undergraduates

	Amer. Ind.	Asian Amer.	Blacks	Hispanics	Whites
F	14	19	709	169	4,994
M	17	13	514	176	5,028
%	0.3	0.3	11.0	3.0	86.0

Chartered in 1890 as Texas Normal College, North Texas State University, located in a small city north and west of Dallas, has been a university since 1961. Some 17,300 students enroll in a variety of undergraduate, graduate, and professional programs. The College of Education is responsible for adult continuing education studies. Alternative class schedules, off-campus locations, and a summer session are available.

Women are one-half of the 12,230 undergraduates; 24 percent of women attend part-time. The median age of all undergraduates is 21. For the three-quarters of the undergraduates who commute or live off campus, on-campus parking is available at a fee.

University childcare facilities can accommodate 30 children. Private childcare arrangements may be made close to campus.

Policies to Ensure Fairness to Women. A full-time equal-opportunity officer and a full-time assistant monitor compliance with equal-employment-opportunity, sex-equity, and handicapped-accessibility legislation and suggest policy for approval by the regents. A written campus policy prohibits sexual harassment; a formal grievance procedure handles complaints; policies and procedures are printed in the student handbook. The Committee on the Status of Women reports to the faculty senate on issues of concern to women, including minority women. The Committee on Minority Affairs addresses the concerns of minority women, among other matters.

Women in Leadership Positions. *Students.* Few opportunities exist for women students to assume campus leadership. In recent years, women have held the campus-wide office of editor of the newspaper for three semesters only. Two of the four honorary societies are headed by women.

Faculty. Women are 19 percent of a full-time faculty of 663. According to recent reports, 5 black, 2 American Indian, and 2 Hispanic women are on the full-time faculty. The ratio of female faculty to female students is 3 to 100; of male faculty to male students, 12 to 100.

Administrators. Men fill all top administrative positions. One of 44 departments (physical education) is headed by a woman. The Director of the School of Home Economics is female.

Women and the Curriculum. A majority of women earn bachelor's degrees in education (41 percent), business and management (16 percent), and the fine arts (15 percent). Less than 2 percent major in nontraditional subjects, with the largest number in computer science.

A small Women's Studies Program offers an undergraduate minor, but has no formal director or committee. Four courses are available through the departments of history, psychology, and sociology: Psychological Dynamics of Women, Sociology of Childhood and Adolescence, The Role of Women in Society, and Women in U.S. History. Affirmative action and equal opportunity are offered in faculty workshops. Such current issues as mathematics confidence among females, sex-fair curricula, coeducational physical education classes, childcare services, and women in management are part of the preparation of future teachers, social workers, and business students.

Women and Athletics. Intramural and intercollegiate programs offer adequate opportunities for organized competitive sports. Team sports predominate in the intramural program, some of which are coeducational. Club sports are also available. Twenty-four percent of intercollegiate athletes are women; women receive 21 percent of athletic scholarships. Five of the 28 paid coaches for intercollegiate teams are women. The intercollegiate sports offered are baseball, cross-country, golf, track, tennis, and volleyball.

Housing and Student Organizations. One-quarter of the undergraduates live on campus. Single-sex and coeducational dormitories and housing for married students are available. Residence halls restrict hours for visitors of the opposite sex. Eight of 15 residence-hall directors are female. Awareness-training on sexism, sex education, racism, and birth control is offered to residence-hall staff.

Eleven percent of undergraduate women belong to social sororities. Fifty-seven minority women are in integrated sororites. Sororities and fraternities provide housing for their members. Groups which serve as advocates for women on campus include the Yes Main Band and Women in Communication.

Special Services and Programs for Women. *Health and Counseling.* The student health service provides some medical attention specific to women: gynecological and birth control treatment are available. The 4 health service physicians are male. Thirteen of 15 other health-care providers are female. One of 3 professional staff in the counseling service is a woman. Students have access to gynecological, birth control, abortion, and rape and assault counseling. In-service training on sex-role stereotyping is available to therapists.

Safety and Security. Measures include campus police with weapons training and arrest authority, night-time escort service, self-defense courses, information sessions on safety and crime prevention, and a community-based rape crisis center. Twenty-eight assaults (14 on women) and two rapes were reported for 1980–81.

Career. Career workshops, lectures, and printed information on women in nontraditional occupations and fields of study are available.

Other. The campus Women's Center, staffed by a faculty member and a student, sponsors an annual women's week, a lecture series, theater and other women's arts programs, and a program to build confidence in mathematics.

Institutional Self-Description. "A mid-sized, moderate-priced state university, NTSU offers a selection of 134 graduate and undergraduate degree fields. A Women's Studies minor is offered. The student body is currently 51 percent female, supported by Services for Women and Returning Students, with programs open to all students and community members."

Paris Junior College
2400 Clarksville, Paris, TX 75460
Telephone: (214) 785-7661

Women in Leadership
★ **students**
★★ **faculty**

1,643 undergraduates

	Amer. Ind.	Asian Amer.	Blacks	Hispanics	Whites
F	6	4	86	4	741
M	9	2	90	3	649
%	0.9	0.4	11.0	0.4	87.2

Paris Junior College, a public, two-year institution, serves some 1,800 students, of whom 1,643 are registered in degree programs. Fifty-two percent of the degree students are women; 55 percent of women attend part-time. The median age of all students is 27.

The college offers two-year degrees and certificates in liberal arts, agriculture, business, health technologies, trade, and technical skills. A continuing education program is available for adult students. Alternative scheduling includes evening classes both on and off campus, a summer session, and independent-study options. Free on-campus parking is available to the 88 percent of students who commute.

Private childcare facilities are located near the campus.

Policies to Ensure Fairness to Women. Policy related to legislation on equal employment opportunity and educational sex equity is the responsibility part-time of the Vice President for Administrative Affairs. A written campus policy prohibiting sexual harassment of students, faculty, and staff has been publicly communicated to these groups; complaints are resolved through a formal campus grievance procedure. The Director of the Center for Women appoints members of a Committee on the Status of Women, which acts in an advisory capacity and reports to the Dean of Instructional Support Services. Both this Committee and the Committee on Minority Affairs address the concerns of minority women. Faculty workshops are held on affirmative action and equal opportunity.

Women in Leadership Positions. *Students.* The participation of women in campus-wide leadership is good. Women have held three of four campus wide posts—editor-in-chief of the campus newspaper and president of the sophomore and entering classes—for two of three recent years. The two campus honorary societies are headed by women.

Faculty. Of the 83 full-time faculty, 41 percent are women. According to recent data, 1 full-time, female faculty member is a black woman. There are 9 female faculty for every 100 female students and 10 male faculty for every 100 male students.

Administrators. All top administrative positions are held by men. Women chair three of ten departments: English, nursing, and communications. The Dean of Instructional Support Services is a woman.

Women and the Curriculum. Most women earn degrees in arts and sciences (50 percent) and health technologies (37 percent). A program encourages women to prepare for careers in business and industry. Thirty percent of student internships are held by women.

There are no courses on women. The departments of business and physical education offer instruction on some matters specific to women. A committee has been assigned to develop a Women's Studies Program.

Women and Athletics. Paris offers both intramural and intercollegiate sports for women. Twenty-five percent of intercollegiate athletes and 31 percent of intramural athletes are women, who receive 30 percent of athletic scholarship aid. One of five paid intercollegiate coaches is a woman. Intercollegiate sports offered are basketball and tennis.

Housing and Student Organizations. Of the 12 percent of students who live on campus, 20 percent are black and 5 percent are Asian American. On-campus housing includes single-sex and-coeducational dormitories without restrictive hours for visitors of the opposite sex, as well as housing for married students and single parents. A married student whose husband is not enrolled is permitted to live in married students' housing. Two of the four residence-hall directors are women.

Special Services and Programs for Women. *Health and Counseling.* There is no student health service on campus. A counseling center, staffed by two women and four men, provides counseling on gynecological problems, birth control, abortion, and rape and assault.

Safety and Security. Measures consist of campus police with weapons training and arrest authority, local police, high-intensity lighting, an emergency alarm system at isolated locations, and information sessions on campus safety and crime prevention. No rapes and one assault on a woman were reported for 1980–81.

Career. Services include workshops and job discrimination information on nontraditional occupations for women, along with lectures for students by women employed in these fields.

Other. The division of instructional support services operates the campus Women's Center with a $20,000 budget. Headed by a full-time faculty member, the center serves about 1,000 women annually, with older women students and community women the primary participants. Ten percent of those served are minority women, predominantly black women. The center sponsors counseling for displaced homemakers, assertiveness-training, and a woman's symposium.

Institutional Self-Description. "As a comprehensive 'open door' community college, Paris Junior College offers programs of individualized instruction and learning support which motivate each student to his/her highest potential of learning experience."

Paul Quinn College
1020 Elm Street, Waco, TX 76704
Telephone: (817) 753-6415

Women in Leadership
★★★ students
★★ faculty
★ administrators

421 undergraduates

	Amer. Ind.	Asian Amer.	Blacks	Hispanics	Whites
F	1	0	186	0	0
M	0	0	210	3	1
%	0.3	0.0	98.8	0.8	0.3

Founded in 1872 as an historic black college, Paul Quinn became a liberal arts institution "for all youth" in 1968. It is affiliated with the African Methodist Church. Forty-six percent of the 421 undergraduates are women; 7 percent of women attend part-time. The median student age is 25.

The college offers undergraduate degrees in a range of fields. The evening division is responsible for adult continuing education. Classes meet day and evening and during the summer. Three-fourths of the students live in single-sex dormitories that restrict visiting hours for members of the opposite sex. Eighty-four percent of women belong to social sororities. For students who commute, public transportation and campus parking for a fee are available.

Policies to Ensure Fairness to Women. No policy exists on sexual harassment; complaints are handled through a formal campus grievance procedure.

Women in Leadership Positions. *Students.* Women have outstanding opportunities for student leadership. In a recent three-year period, women held each of the seven major offices for at least one term and served as residence-hall council president for three consecutive terms.

Faculty. Forty-eight percent of the 25 full-time faculty are women, a proportion well above the national average. According to recent report, 8 black women and 1 American Indian woman are on the full-time faculty. There are 7 female faculty for every 100 female students, and 6 male faculty for every 100 male students.

Administrators. The chief business officer, the head librarian, and the director of institutional research are black women. Other top administrators are men. Women (2 black, 1 American Indian) chair three of ten departments: English, sociology/social work, and physical education. A black woman and a white woman sit on the 23-member Board of Trustees.

Women and the Curriculum. Forty percent of bachelor's degrees awarded to women are in public affairs; the rest are in business and education. There are no courses on women.

Women and Athletics. Forty-one percent of intercollegiate athletes and about half of intramural athletes are women. One of three paid varsity coaches is a woman. Women receive 40 percent of athletic scholarships. Information was not provided on the intercollegiate sports offered.

Special Services and Programs for Women. *Health and Counseling.* The student health service employs 1 male physician and 1 female health-care provider. The student counseling center staff consists of 6 minority women, 1 white woman, and 4 men. Counseling for birth control, gynecological problems, abortion, and rape and assault, as well as birth control treatment, is available. Student health insurance covers maternity expenses.

Safety and Security. Measures consist of campus police protection and high-intensity lighting. No rapes or assaults on women were reported for 1980–81.

Career. The Placement Office sponsors career workshops, provides information on nontraditional occupations, and maintains files on alumnae careers for student use.

Institutional Self-Description. None provided.

Southern Methodist University
Dallas, TX 75275
Telephone: (214) 692-3260

Women in Leadership ★ **Women and the Curriculum**
★ **students**

5,421 undergraduates

	Amer. Ind.	Asian Amer.	Blacks	Hispanics	Whites
F	2	15	76	65	2,487
M	4	8	99	89	2,477
%	0.1	0.4	3.2	2.9	93.3

🏠 🚌 🔨 ⬚ ⬚ 📖 ⚲ **AAUW NWSA**

Founded in 1911, Southern Methodist University is a private, non-sectarian institution affiliated with the Methodist Church. Over 8,600 students enroll in undergraduate, graduate, and professional programs. Continuing Education, evening classes, and a summer session are available.

Women are 49 percent of the 5,421 undergraduates; 7 percent of women attend part-time. The median age of undergraduates is 22. For the 59 percent of students who commute, the university is accessible by public transportation. There is on-campus parking.

Private childcare facilities are available near the campus.

Policies to Ensure Fairness to Women. The Affirmative Action Officer, on full-time assignment, reviews policies and practices related to equal employment opportunity, accessibility of programs and activities to students, and handicapped access. A campus policy prohibits sexual harassment. Complaints are handled through a formal grievance procedure. The Committee on the Status of Women, which includes students as voting members, reports to the President and takes public stands on issues. A Committee on Minority Affairs addresses the concerns of minority women, among other matters.

Women in Leadership Positions. *Students.* Women hold one-third of campus leadership positions. In recent years, women have presided over the student judiciary (three times), and the student union board, and twice served as the editor-in-chief of the campus newspaper. Women chair 12 of 21 honorary societies.

Faculty. Women are 22 percent of a full-time faculty of 433. There are 4 female faculty for every 100 female students and 14 male faculty for every 100 male students.

Administrators. Men hold the top administrative positions. Women chair three of 38 departments: biology, communication disorders, and dance. Fifteen percent of the Board of Trustees are women.

Women and the Curriculum. The majority of women earn bachelor's degrees in business (27 percent), education (13 percent), and communications (13 percent). Seven percent major in such nontraditional areas as engineering, mathematics, computer science, and the physical sciences. Innovative programs encourage women to consider careers in science, engineering, computer science, and electronics. Over one-quarter of the students in cooperative education programs are female.

The Women's Studies Program offers an undergraduate minor. Thirteen courses on women are available through the departments of anthropology, English, history, political science, psychology, sociology, art history, religion, foreign languages, economics, and the division of liberal studies. Recent titles include Portraits of Women in Literature; Women: Images and Perspectives; Women in Politics; Changing Sex Roles; Woman, Myth, and Society; and Labor Economics. An official committee develops the Women's Studies Program and encourages the inclusion in the curriculum of the new scholarship on women. Such issues as mathematics confidence among females, sex-fair curricula, and coeducational physical education classes are part of the preparation of future teachers. Faculty are offered workshops on sexism and the curriculum and on the needs of reentry women.

Women and Athletics. A good intramural program offers individual and team sports. Thirty-one percent of intramural and 20 percent of varsity players are female. Athletic scholarships are awarded, although information about the percentage going to women is not available. The intercollegiate sports offered are basketball, golf, swimming and diving, and tennis.

Housing and Student Organizations. For the 41 percent of the undergraduates who live on campus, accommodations include single-sex and coeducational dormitories and housing for married students and single parents with children. A married woman student whose spouse is not enrolled may live in married students' housing. Men's and women's dormitories may choose to restrict hours for visitors of the opposite sex. Eleven of 16 residence-hall directors are women.

Fifty-six percent of the undergraduate women belong to social sororities. Sororities and fraternities provide housing for their members. Twenty women belong to all-minority sororities. Among organizations which serve as advocates for women are Women in Communications, Inc. and the Women's Interest Coalition.

Special Services and Programs for Women. *Health and Counseling.* The student health service provides some medical attention specific to women, including treatment for gynecological problems and for rape and assault, as well as birth control. Half of physicians are female. Three of 7 therapists in the Mental Health Clinic are women. Counseling specific to women, including counseling about abortion, is available. Professional staff are offered in-service training on the avoidance of sex-role stereotyping and racial bias.

Safety and Security. Measures include campus and city police, high-intensity lighting, emergency telephone and alarm systems, self-defense courses for women, information sessions on safety and crime prevention, and a rape crisis center. Night-time escorts for women are scheduled to begin in 1982. One assault on a woman was reported for 1980–81.

Career. Career services for women include workshops, panel presentations, and printed materials which concentrate on nontraditional occupations and fields of study.

Other. A campus Women's Center, directed by a full-time administrator, sponsors a program for displaced homemakers, an annual women's week, assertiveness training, and a resource library.

Special Features. For the last 17 years, SMU has held a two-day "Symposium on Women" which attracts nationally known speakers and participants from colleges and universities in the region.

Institutional Self-Description. "The university cherishes for all its students and teachers its tradition of freedom of inquiry, thought, and expression. Although SMU contains distinguished graduate and professional programs, it puts special emphasis upon undergraduate education and upon a balance between the general and the special, the liberal and the professional studies."

Texas A&I University
Kingsville, TX 78363
Telephone: (512) 595-3501

5,157 undergraduates

	Amer. Ind.	Asian Amer.	Blacks	Hispanics	Whites
F	5	19	109	1,401	812
M	8	54	139	1,215	1,052
%	0.3	1.5	5.2	54.3	38.7

🏠 🏛 🚐 👫 AAUW

Texas A&I, a public university with branch campuses at Laredo and Corpus Christi, was established as a teacher-training school in 1923. Of its 6,300 students, 5,000 are undergraduates, 46 percent of them women. Twenty-six percent of women students attend part-time. Twenty percent of women students are over 25 years. More than 60 percent of students are members of minority groups.

The university offers undergraduate and some graduate degrees in the liberal arts and sciences and a range of pre-professional fields. Adult students are served by the Center for Continuing Education. Evening and summer session classes are available, as are off-campus class locations. Located 40 miles outside Corpus Christi, the main campus is accessible by public transportation. On-campus parking is available for the one-fourth of students who commute.

An on-campus childcare facility provides daytime care for 36 children aged two through five, charging fees at a fixed hourly rate. All students' requests for childcare are met. Private childcare facilities are located near campus.

Policies to Ensure Fairness to Women. The Administrator of Personnel Services and Affirmative Action Officer has full-time responsibility for compliance with laws on equal opportunity and sex equity for students. The university is in the process of formulating a policy on sexual harassment.

Women in Leadership Positions. *Students.* In a recent three-year period, a woman served one year as manager of the campus radio station; all other campus-wide student positions were held by men. Two of the seven honorary societies have women presidents.

Faculty. Eighteen percent of the 206 full-time faculty are women. There are 2 female faculty for every 100 female students and 7 male faculty for every 100 male students.

Administrators. Men hold all top positions. Of 25 departments, women chair three—English, home economics, and modern languages. Three of the nine regents are women.

Women and the Curriculum. Most women earn degrees in education (56 percent), business (9 percent), social sciences (9 percent), psychology (4 percent), and letters (4 percent). Seven percent of women graduate in such nontraditional fields as agriculture, computer science, engineering, mathematics, and the physical sciences. Women are half of the students in cooperative education, internship, and science field-service programs designed to combine practical work experience with formal study.

Three courses on women are offered through the departments of history, political science, and psychology and sociology: Women in History; Women and Politics; Women, Change and Society. The departments of physical education and business offer instruction on some matters specific to women.

Minority Women. Sixty percent of women students are Hispanic, 5 percent are black, and less than 1 percent are Asian American and American Indian. There is one all-minority sorority on campus; others are racially integrated. Two of the 3 female departments chairs are Hispanic women. In addition, 3 of the 5 residence-hall directors and 2 of 3 female counselors are minority women.

Women and Athletics. Women have some opportunities to participate in organized competitive sports. A good variety of individual and team sports is available in the intramural program; lighted playing fields permit evening participation. Although only one-fourth of the intercollegiate athletes are women, they receive 40 percent of athletic scholarships awarded. Two of the eight paid varsity coaches are women. All women's varsity teams participated in recent tournament competition. Intercollegiate sports include basketball, tennis, track, and volleyball.

Housing and Student Organizations. About 20 percent of undergraduates live on campus in single-sex or coeducational dormitories or in housing for married students and single parents with children. Coeducational dormitories do not restrict hours for visitors of the opposite sex. All five residence-hall directors are women.

Five percent of women belong to social sororities. Neither sororities nor fraternities provide housing for members.

Special Services and Programs for Women. *Health and Counseling.* The student health service employs 1 male physician and 3 female nurses; the counseling center has a staff of 3 women and 4 men. Some counselors are graduate students. No medical treatment specific to women is provided. Student requests regarding birth control and abortion are referred to Planned Parenthood. The counseling center provides instruction on rape and assault prevention.

Safety and Security. Measures consist of campus police with arrest authority, a night-time escort service for women, and information sessions on campus safety and rape and assault prevention. No information was provided about the incidence of rapes and assaults.

Career. The university provides workshops, printed materials, and job discrimination information on nontraditional occupations for women.

Institutional Self-Description. "Texas A&I seeks to 'recognize and provide for individual differences in background, and in interests, needs, and attitudes of its students so that each may achieve his/her highest personal development.' Training in teaching, research, and service constitute the three areas of university endeavor, each area allowing broad scope for the preference and abilities of the prospective student. We are in a growing state and region, and the opportunities that have historically accompanied such a state, allowing men chances and challenges, are now there for women as well."

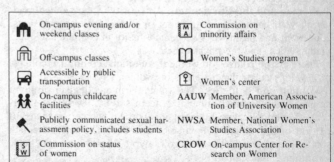

🏛 On-campus evening and/or weekend classes	Ⓜ️Ⓐ	Commission on minority affairs
🏛 Off-campus classes	📖	Women's Studies program
🚐 Accessible by public transportation		Women's center
👫 On-campus childcare facilities	AAUW	Member, American Association of University Women
📢 Publicly communicated sexual harassment policy, includes students	NWSA	Member, National Women's Studies Association
Ⓢ️Ⓦ Commission on status of women	CROW	On-campus Center for Research on Women

Texas Christian University
2800 South University Dr.
Fort Worth, TX 76129
Telephone: (817) 921-7000

Women in Leadership
★ faculty

4,455 undergraduates

	Amer. Ind.	Asian Amer.	Blacks	Hispanics	Whites
F	7	16	120	48	2,373
M	8	3	102	48	1,731
%	0.3	0.4	5.0	2.2	92.1

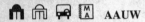 AAUW

Opened in 1873 as AddRann Male and Female College, Texas Christian University was established in 1902 as a private institution under the auspices of the Christian Church. Texas Christian enrolls some 5,900 students in a variety of undergraduate, graduate, and professional programs. The division of continuing education provides adult continuing education. Alternative class schedules include on and off-campus programs during days and evenings, and a summer session.

Fifty-eight percent of the 4,455 undergraduates are women; 14 percent of women attend part-time. Recent information indicates one-fourth of women students are older than 25; 5 percent, older than 40. The median age of all undergraduates is 20. For commuting students, the campus is accessible by public transportation. On-campus parking is available for a fee.

Arrangements for private childcare may be made close to the university.

Policies to Ensure Fairness to Women. An equal opportunity officer on part-time assignment is responsible for policy on employment, accessibility of programs and activities to men and women students, and handicapped access. A campus policy prohibits sexual harassment. Complaints are treated through a formal grievance procedure. The Committee on Minority Affairs addresses the concerns of minority women, among other matters.

Women in Leadership Positions. *Students.* Opportunities for women students to exercise campus leadership are below the average for institutions in this guide. In a recent three-year period, out of eight possible leadership positions, women have been president of the student body and editor-in-chief of the student newspaper for one year each.

Faculty. Women are one-third of a full-time faculty of 298, a proportion which is above the national average. Of these women, according to a recent report, 1 is Asian American and 3 are black. The ratio of female faculty to female students is 4 to 100; the ratio of male faculty to male students is 12 to 100.

Administrators. The chief student-life officer and the director of institutional research are women; men hold all other top positions. Women chair five of 35 departments: home economics, journalism, reading education, nursing, and accounting. The Dean of Harris College of Nursing is female.

Women and the Curriculum. A majority of the women graduating with bachelor's degrees major in the health professions, education, and business. Two percent major in computer science, mathematics, and the physical sciences.

There are no courses on women. An official committee collects or develops curricular materials on women.

Women and Athletics. The women's intercollegiate program emphasizes individual rather than team sports. Twenty-one percent of intercollegiate athletes are women; women receive 10 percent of the athletic scholarships awarded. The intercollegiate sports offered are basketball, golf, gymnastics, track and field, swimming, and tennis.

Housing and Student Organizations. Forty-five percent of the undergraduates live on campus in single-sex and coeducational dormitories. Residence halls restrict hours for visitors of the opposite sex. Eleven of 20 residence-hall directors are female.

Thirty-seven percent of undergraduate women belong to social sororities. Sororities and fraternities provide housing for their members.

Special Services and Programs for Women. *Health and Counseling.* The student health service provides no medical attention specific to women. One of 3 physicians is female, as are 10 of 12 other health-care providers. Four of 6 counselors in the counseling service are women. No counseling specific to women is provided.

Safety and Security. Campus police have arrest authority. A rape crisis center is available. No information was provided about the incidence of rapes and assaults.

Career. Lectures by women in nontraditional careers, and a program of contacts between alumnae and students are available.

Institutional Self-Description. None provided.

Texas State Technical Institute, Harlingen
Box 2628, Harlingen Industrial Airpark
Harlingen, TX 78550
Telephone: (512) 425-4922

1,159 undergraduates

	Amer. Ind.	Asian Amer.	Blacks	Hispanics	Whites
F	0	0	2	262	45
M	0	0	1	728	103
%	0.0	0.0	0.3	86.8	13.0

The Harlingen Campus of Texas State Technical Institute, a public, two-year college, provides occupationally oriented programs to 1,159 students, 87 percent of whom are Hispanic. Twenty-seven percent of the undergraduates are women; 14 percent of women attend part-time. The median age of undergraduates is 20.

Texas State Technical offers certificate and associate degree programs in technical and vocational areas, including field or laboratory work, and related academic, technical, and remedial instruction. Evening classes and an adult continuing education program are offered. Public transportation and on-campus parking are available.

Private childcare facilities are available nearby.

Policies to Ensure Fairness to Women. The Personnel Director has part-time responsibility, as a voting member of policy-making councils, for equal employment opportunity, educational sex equity, and handicapped access. Complaints of sexual harassment are handled through a formal campus grievance procedure. These procedures have been publicly communicated in writing to faculty and staff.

Women in Leadership Positions. *Students.* No woman held the one campus leadership position, president of the student body, during a recent three-year period.

Faculty. The full-time faculty is 19 percent female, a proportion considerably below the average for public, two-year colleges in this guide. There are 6 female faculty for every 100 female students, and 10 male faculty for every 100 male students.

Administrators. The five top-level administrators are men. Three of 19 departments are chaired by women: operating room technician, nurse aide, and medical record clerk/transcriptionist.

Women and the Curriculum. Women earn 12 percent of two-year degrees awarded, graduating in health, mechanical and engineering, and data processing technologies. Innovative programs encourage women to prepare for nontraditional careers in architecture, computer science, and electronics. There are no courses on women.

Women and Athletics. Women participate in intramural tennis and volleyball.

Housing and Student Organizations. The 18 percent of students who reside on campus are housed in single-sex dormitories that have restrictive hours for visitors of the opposite sex. Housing is available for married students with and without children.

Special Services and Programs for Women. *Health and Counseling.* The limited student health service is staffed by one female health-care provider. Three men staff the student counseling center. No information was provided on health and counseling services specific to women. The regular student health insurance policy covers maternity expenses at no extra charge.

Safety and Security. The campus is patrolled by campus police, who have arrest authority. For 1980–81, no rapes or assaults were reported on campus.

Institutional Self-Description. "The campus is located within 30 miles of South Padre Island, where students can enjoy surfing, swimming, fishing, and sailing, and 25 miles from the Mexican border, where they may choose to dine or shop for Mexican curios. The campus has modern, two-bedroom apartments with kitchens, as opposed to the regular dormitories."

University of Texas, Arlington
Arlington, TX 76019
Telephone: (817) 273-2101

Women in Leadership
★ **students**

15,217 undergraduates

	Amer. Ind.	Asian Amer.	Blacks	Hispanics	Whites
F	31	47	510	169	4,944
M	40	102	551	312	7,582
%	0.5	1.0	7.4	3.4	87.7

This large (18,292 students) public university offers a wide range of undergraduate and graduate degree programs. About 38 percent of the 15,217 undergraduates are women. Almost all the students commute, and about one-third of undergraduates attend part-time. Alternative schedules include on-campus evening classes and a summer session.

Private childcare facilities are available near campus.

Policies to Ensure Fairness to Women. A written policy prohibits sexual harassment of students, faculty, and staff; a formal grievance procedure resolves complaints. Both the policy and the procedure for resolving complaints have been publicly communicated to the university community. The Committee on the Status of Women, appointed by the Committee on Committees, reports to the President of the university and advises him on issues important to women. The university has a full-time affirmative action officer.

Women in Leadership Positions. *Students.* During three recent years, women were president of the student body once, editor-in-chief of the campus newspaper twice, and president of the entering class once. Women head 15 of the 27 honorary societies.

Faculty. Of 590 full-time faculty, 20 percent are women, including 4 black, 2 American Indian, 3 Hispanic, and 3 Asian American women. Women hold 12 percent of the 395 permanent faculty positions.

Administrators. Men hold all key positions. The Dean of the School of Nursing is a woman. Nine women sit on the 58-member faculty senate, and 3 women sit on the 9-member Board of Regents.

Women and the Curriculum. Most degrees awarded to women are in business (21 percent), social sciences (14 percent), health professions (14 percent), and letters (8 percent). Seven percent of degrees to women are in the nontraditional fields of architecture, mathematics, and physical sciences. A Science Career Facilitation Project is headed by a woman faculty member from the chemistry department. In connection with this project, a Woman's Fair, held in October 1980, attracted several thousand participants to a round of seminars and demonstrations. Women are 37 percent of the students in cooperative education programs and 93 percent of students in internships.

Four courses on women are offered, including Women in Society and Women in Leadership, by the departments of English, history, sociology, and social work. Courses offered by the departments of education, nursing, and business provide some instruction on issues specific to women.

Women and Athletics. Women receive 20 percent of athletic scholarships. Three of the 23 paid varsity coaches are women. The intercollegiate sports offered are basketball, cross-country, fencing, softball, tennis, track, and volleyball.

Housing and Student Organizations. Eight percent of the undergraduates live on campus. Single-sex and coeducational dormitories are available, as well as housing for married students with and without children and single parents with children.

Sororities, which attract 12 percent of full-time women students, provide housing for their members. Forty-four black women belong to all-minority sororities; there are no racially integrated sororities.

Special Services and Programs for Women. *Health and Counseling.* The student health service, staffed by 1 female and 3 male physicians and 10 female health-care providers, offers treatment for matters related to gynecological problems and birth control. One woman provides counseling services specific to women.

Safety and Security. Measures include campus police with arrest authority, high-intensity lighting in major traffic areas, a crime prevention unit, information sessions on campus safety, and rape and assault prevention for women, and a rape crisis center. No rapes and 22 assaults (9 on women) were reported for 1980–81.

Career. Services include career workshops and panel discussions on nontraditional careers for women.

Other. Student advocacy groups include the Association of Mexican American Students, Professional Black Women's League, and Society of Women Engineers.

Institutional Self-Description. "While UTA is the fifth largest university in Texas, women can expect to experience the benefits of our numerous resources as well as individualization and concern for their present and future plans. UTA is a place where women can earn a good education in a pleasant atmosphere, and where they can grow intellectually, spiritually, and socially."

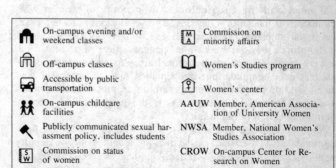

On-campus evening and/or weekend classes

Off-campus classes

Accessible by public transportation

On-campus childcare facilities

Publicly communicated sexual harassment policy, includes students

Commission on status of women

Commission on minority affairs

Women's Studies program

Women's center

AAUW Member, American Association of University Women

NWSA Member, National Women's Studies Association

CROW On-campus Center for Research on Women

University of Texas, Austin
University Station, Austin, TX 78712
Telephone: (512) 471-1849

Women in Leadership ★ students	★ Women and the Curriculum
	★ Women and Athletics

33,669 undergraduates

	Amer. Ind.	Asian Amer.	Blacks	Hispanics	Whites
F	17	136	500	1,119	13,530
M	30	162	372	1,462	15,429
%	0.1	1.0	2.7	7.9	88.4

From its enabling legislation in 1881, the University of Texas at Austin has been thought of as an institution for the "promotion of literature, and the arts and sciences." Currently over 43,000 students enroll in a comprehensive range of undergraduate, graduate, and professional programs. The division of continuing education houses a Continuing Education for Women Program. A limited number of evening classes and a summer session are available.

Women are 46 percent of the 33,669 undergraduates; 13 percent of women attend part-time. The average age of undergraduates is 21. Eighty-five percent of the undergraduates commute to campus. The university is accessible by public transportation. On-campus parking is provided for a fee.

Private childcare facilities are available near the campus.

Policies to Ensure Fairness to Women. A full-time Equal-Opportunity and Affirmative Action Officer is a consultant on policies and practices related to equal employment opportunity and handicapped accessibility. A written policy on sexual harassment is being developed for students. Currently, complaints are handled informally and confidentially through the Dean of Students' Office. Ad hoc Committees on Women and Minority Affairs advise departments and the administration.

Women in Leadership Positions. *Students.* Opportunities for women students to exercise campus leadership are good. In recent years, women have presided over the student union board and residence-hall council, been editor-in-chief of the newspaper, and been elected to the College Council and Senior Cabinet. Women head more than a third of the 45 honorary societies.

Faculty. Women make up 19 percent of a full-time faculty of 1,798. According to a recent report, 1 black, 4 Asian American, and 8 Hispanic women are on the full-time faculty. The ratio of female faculty to female students is 3 to 100; male faculty to male students, 9 to 100.

Administrators. Men hold all top positions, except for a co-director of athletics. Women head five of the 15 academic departments and serve as Deans of the School of Nursing and of the Lyndon Baines Johnson School of Public Affairs.

Women and the Curriculum. The majority of women who graduate with bachelor's degrees major in business (16 percent), the social sciences (11 percent), psychology (10 percent), the health professions (9 percent), and general letters (8 percent). Six percent major in such nontraditional areas as architecture, computer science, engineering, mathematics, and the physical sciences. The proportion of women earning degrees in mathematics is above the national average, as is the proportion of women taking degrees in public affairs.

An undergraduate minor in Women's Studies is pending final approval. Sixteen courses on women are available in the departments of Asian studies, African-American studies, American studies, educational psychology, English, European studies, government, history, cultural foundations of education, Middle Eastern studies, psychology, Persian, sociology, speech communications, and law. Recent offerings include Women in Southeast Asia; Race, Sex, and Social Inequality; Women in the Arts; Women Writers; Women's Roles in French Literature; The Psychology of Sex; Male/Female Roles in the Middle East; and Occupations and Professions. An ad hoc committee is at work to develop Women's Studies offerings.

Minority Women. Of 15,542 undergraduate women, 7 percent are Hispanic, 3 percent black, and less than 1 percent each Asian American and American Indian. The university estimates that 100 women are in all-minority sororities. Four minority women are on the staff of residence halls; one minority woman is on the professional staff in the counseling services. Residence-hall and counseling staff are offered awareness-training on the avoidance of racial bias.

Women and Athletics. Intramural and intercollegiate programs provide good opportunities for organized, competitive individual and team sports. Club sports are also available. The university reports special facilities for swimming and diving. Thirty-seven percent of the intramural and 34 percent of the intercollegiate athletes are women; women receive 30 percent of the athletic scholarships. Women's intercollegiate teams performed well in tournaments in 1980. The intercollegiate sports offered are basketball, cross-country, golf, gymnastics, swimming and diving, tennis, track and field, and volleyball.

Housing and Student Organizations. Fifteen percent of the undergraduates live on campus. Single-sex and coeducational dormitories, housing for married students and single parents with children, and cooperatives are available. A married woman student whose spouse is not enrolled may live in married students' housing. Residence halls restrict hours for visitors of the opposite sex. Residence-hall staff are offered awareness-training on the avoidance of sexism and racism and on sex education, racism, birth control, and handicapped issues.

Nineteen percent of full-time undergraduate women belong to social sororities which provide housing for their members. The university chapter of the National Organization for Women (NOW) serves as an advocate for women, including minority women, on campus.

Special Services and Programs for Women. *Health and Counseling.* The student health service provides some medical attention specific to women including gynecological, birth control, and rape and assault treatment. Five of 21 physicians are female, as are 100 other health-care providers. Twelve of 17 professional staff in counseling/psychological services are women. Staff are trained in the avoidance of sex-role stereotyping and racial bias, and the needs of the handicapped. Students have access to gynecological, birth control, abortion, and rape and assault counseling. Assertiveness training and a telephone line of information, referral, and support are among the services offered.

Safety and Security. Measures include campus police with arrest authority, night-time escorts for women, night-time bus service to residence areas, information and crime prevention sessions and measures, and a rape crisis center. Thirty-two assaults and one rape were reported for 1980-81.

Career. Workshops, lectures, printed materials which focus on women in nontraditional careers and fields of study, and a program of contacts between alumnae and students, as well as job hunting strategies, support groups, and nonsexist individual counseling are among the services available.

Other. Activities and services both on and off campus of interest to women include an annual women's week, women's studies colloquia, theater and other arts events, and programs to build confidence in mathematics and to assist battered women and displaced homemakers. The university reports that older women and handicapped women would find other supportive women at Students Older than Average and Services for the Handicapped.

Returning Women Students. Recent data indicate that 12 percent of the undergraduate women are over age 24. The Dean of Students Office is responsible for Services for Returning Students. In 1980-81, over 5,000 women enrolled in courses for credit, another 4,600 in non-credit courses. Faculty are offered instruction on mid-life transitions and the needs of adult students.

Special Features. The Humanities Research Center holds the world's largest collection of manuscripts and materials of 20th century writers, including those of the poet Anne Sexton. The Hogg Foundation for Mental Health supports projects of concern to women, including seed money for the Austin Center for Battered Women. The Project for Minorities and Women in Research sponsors symposia for doctoral and post-doctoral students.

Institutional Self-Description. "A major research university, the University of Texas at Austin is composed of diverse groups and opportunities, including many top-rate women scholars who are particularly supportive of their women students. The stimulating Austin milieu contains women who are putting Texas on the map in a number of exciting scholarly, artistic, and socially significant ways."

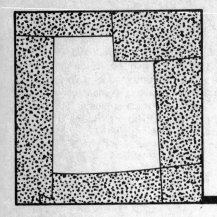

UTAH

Utah State University
Logan, UT 84322
Telephone: (801) 750-1000

★ **Women and the Curriculum**

7,729 undergraduates

	Amer. Ind.	Asian Amer.	Blacks	Hispanics	Whites
F	18	30	16	32	3,147
M	21	29	58	26	3,817
%	0.5	0.8	1.0	0.8	96.8

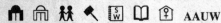 **AAUW**

Established in 1888 as a land-grant college, Utah State University enrolls some 9,200 undergraduate and graduate students. Extension and Continuing Education serve the adult student. Evening classes, a summer session, and off-campus class locations are available.

Women are 44 percent of 7,729 undergraduates; 7 percent of the women attend part-time. Sixteen percent of the undergraduates commute to campus.

University childcare facilities accommodate three-quarters of students' requests; single parents have priority. Arrangements for private childcare may be made close to campus.

Policies to Ensure Fairness to Women. The full-time Affirmative Action Officer is responsible for policy related to equal employment opportunity, educational sex equity, and access for the handicapped. A staff assistant monitors compliance. The institutional policy against sexual harassment has been communicated to students in writing; complaints are resolved either informally and confidentially or through a formal grievance procedure. The Committee on the Status of Women, which includes students as voting members, takes public stands on issues of concern to students and reports its recommendations to the Vice-Provost.

Women in Leadership Positions. *Students.* Opportunities for women students to assume all-campus leadership are below the average. In three recent years, women have been chair of the student union board, editor-in-chief of the newspaper, and presiding officer of the residence-hall council. Women head ten of 29 honorary societies.

Faculty. Women are 16 percent of a full-time faculty of 495. There are 2 female faculty for every 100 female students and 10 male faculty for every 100 male students.

Administrators. Men hold the top-level administrative positions. A woman is Dean of the College of Family Life. Of 40 departments, women chair accounting, and home economics and consumer education. Two women sit on the 11-member Board of Trustees and 1 woman on the 16-member Board of Regents.

Women and the Curriculum. Thirty-nine percent of the women who graduate with bachelor's degrees major in education;

12 percent major in nontraditional subjects. Two-thirds of women majoring in nontraditional fields earn degrees in agriculture, with smaller numbers in engineering, architecture, and computer or physical sciences. Women are more than one-third of the students in cooperative education programs; 45 percent of the students in Forestry Summer Camp are female.

The Women's Studies Program offers a certificate through Interdisciplinary Studies. Recent course offerings available through various departments and cross-listed with Women's Studies include Sex Roles in American Society, Women in Politics, History of Women in America, Women and Health, and Career Exploration. An official committee is responsible for developing the Women's Studies Program, as well as for collecting curricular materials and advocating the teaching of courses on women.

Future health-care providers are given instruction on health-care information important to minority women. Social work students receive instruction on such current issues as services for abused spouses and displaced homemakers.

Women and Athletics. The intercollegiate program offers opportunities for women in team and individual competitive sports. Women receive 20 percent of the athletic scholarships awarded. There are nine paid coaches for women's intercollegiate teams. The intercollegiate sports offered are basketball, cross-country, gymnastics, softball, track and field, and volleyball.

Housing and Student Organizations. For the students who live on campus, single-sex dormitories and housing for married students and single parents with children are available. Men's and women's residence halls restrict hours for visitors of the opposite sex. A married woman student whose spouse is not enrolled may live in married students' housing. All residence-hall directors are female. Staff are offered awareness-training on birth control.

Six percent of the full-time undergraduate women belong to social sororities. Sororities and fraternities provide housing for their members. The Conference on Women's Issues and Concerns and the Women's Center serve as advocates for women on campus.

Special Services and Programs for Women. *Health and Counseling.* The student health service provides medical treatment for gynecological problems. The health service physicians are male; six other health-care providers are female. The regular student health insurance includes maternity coverage at no extra charge. Three of seven professional staff in the counseling service are women. Students have access to birth control, abortion, and rape and assault counseling.

Safety and Security. Measures include city and campus police with arrest authority, and a night-time escort service for women students. No information was provided on the incidence of rapes and assaults on women.

Career. Printed materials on nontraditional occupations and fields of study for women are available.

Other. The Office of Student Services houses a Women's Center, under the direction of a full-time faculty member. A women's lecture series, assertiveness training, and a program to build confidence in mathematics are among the center's activities. Older women students and women from the local community are the primary users of the center. The Women's Center provides 30–40 scholarships a year to returning women students. Scholarships are funded entirely through contributions from the community. The Council on Women's Issues and Concerns sponsors an annual women's week.

USU has a Women and International Development Committee and is a member of the Consortium of Utah Women in Higher Education, a state-wide support system.

Institutional Self-Description. ''USU is a land-grant college in a small rural town. The curriculum is varied and provides opportunities for women in natural resources, landscape architecture, athletics, and other areas. The engineering program has special scholarships for women. Women faculty are active in national professional organizations. There is strong support among women on campus and in the community.''

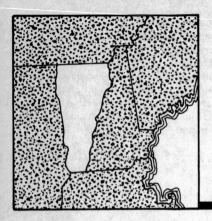

VERMONT

Burlington College
90 Main St., Burlington, VT 05401
Telephone: (802) 862-9616

Women in Leadership
★★★ administrators

81 undergraduates

	Amer. Ind.	Asian Amer.	Blacks	Hispanics	Whites
F	0	0	2	0	50
M	0	0	0	0	27
%	0.0	0.0	2.5	0.0	97.5

Burlington College is a private, four-year college that enrolls ninety-seven students, 81 of them in degree programs. Sixty-four percent of the degree students are women, 19 percent of whom attend part-time. The median age of all students is 30.

A limited range of undergraduate degree programs is available, in addition to a continuing education program. Evening and summer session classes are available. All students commute to the campus which is accessible by public transportation.

Private childcare facilities are located near the campus.

Policies to Ensure Fairness to Women. One administrator is responsible for policy on equal-employment-opportunity and sex-equity legislation. Sexual harassment complaints are handled informally and confidentially. A Committee on Minority Affairs addresses the concerns of minority women.

Women in Leadership Positions. *Students.* In a recent three-year period, the sole campus-wide student post, editor-in-chief of the campus newspaper, was held by a woman for one year.

Faculty. No information is available.

Administrators. Women hold two of the four key administrative posts: chief business officer and chief student-life officer. One division is headed by a woman. Two of the 17 trustees are female.

Women and the Curriculum. In one recent year, 7 of the 5 degrees awarded were earned by women, 4 in psychology and 1 in education. Sixty percent of student interns are women.

In recent years, two students designed a major in Women's Studies. The college offers one course on women, Archetype of the Feminine. The holistic health program allows students to study midwifery, home delivery, and nontraditional health maintenance. An official committee works to enrich curricular materials with the new scholarship on women. Nontraditional occupations for women and men and the needs of reentry women are topics of faculty workshops.

Women and Athletics. There is no opportunity for organized competitive sports.

Special Services and Programs for Women. *Health and Counseling.* There is a student counseling center, staffed by one woman therapist, but no student health center. No counseling specific to women is available.

Safety and Security. Measures consist of local police protection and a rape crisis center. No rapes or assaults on women were reported for 1980–81.

Career. The college provides workshops on nontraditional occupations.

Other. Project Liberation, a program designed to meet the educational needs of low-income, single parents, provides support for displaced homemakers and welfare women.

Institutional Self-Description. "The mission of the college is to address students as individuals and help them increase their awareness, knowledge, and competence. We believe that individuals thus strengthened in personal dignity will improve the quality of their own lives and that of their communities."

College of St. Joseph the Provider
Rutland, VT 05701
Telephone: (802) 775-0806

Women in Leadership
★★★ students
★★★ administrators

187 undergraduates

	Amer. Ind.	Asian Amer.	Blacks	Hispanics	Whites
F	0	0	1	0	145
M	0	0	3	0	38
%	0.0	0.0	2.1	0.0	97.9

 AAUW

Formerly St. Joseph's Teacher's College, the institution was founded as a two-year college to prepare the Roman Catholic Sisters of St. Joseph for teaching careers in parochial schools. In the early sixties St. Joseph's admitted lay students, and in the seventies it became a coeducational liberal arts college. Some associate degrees are still awarded. Evening classes are available both on and off campus and there is a summer session.

Of the 323 students who attend, 187 are registered in degree programs. Seventy-eight percent of the degree students are women, 12 percent of whom attend part-time. The campus, located about 160 miles from Boston, is not accessible by public transportation. Free on-campus parking is available for the 33 percent of full-time students who commute.

Private childcare facilities are available near campus.

Policies to Ensure Fairness to Women. Compliance with legislation regarding equal employment opportunity, sex equity for students, and handicapped accessibility is the part-time responsibility of the college business manager.

Women in Leadership Positions. *Students.* Opportunities for women to acquire leadership experience are outstanding. Women have held the five available positions 87 percent of the time in recent years.

Faculty. One of the 10 full-time faculty is a woman.

Administrators. Five of the nine chief administrators are women. One department, education, is chaired by an Hispanic woman.

Women and the Curriculum. Almost all bachelor's degrees awarded to women are in education. Eighty percent of student interns are women.

Two courses on women—Sociology of Women and Women in Literature—are available. The business department offers instruction on issues specific to women.

Women and Athletics. There is no intramural sports program. Two-thirds of the 30 intercollegiate athletes and one of three paid coaches are female. About 40 percent of athletic scholarship aid is awarded to women. The intercollegiate sports offered are basketball and volleyball

Housing and Student Organizations. Sixty-six percent of full-time students live on campus in single-sex or coeducational dormitories that have restrictive hours for visitors of the opposite sex. One of the two dormitory directors is a woman.

Special Services and Programs for Women. *Health and Counseling.* The institution has no student health service or student counseling center.

Safety and Security. Measures consist of a night-time security guard. No rapes or assaults on women were reported in 1980–81.

Institutional Self-Description. "CSJP is concerned with the development of each individual student, regardless of age or sex. We are much too small to offer many of the organizations and services dealt with by this study, but we do offer a secure and caring environment for learning."

Community College of Vermont
P.O. Box 81, Montpelier, VT 05632
Telephone: (802) 828-2401

Women in Leadership
★★★ administators

1,694 undergraduates

	Amer. Ind.	Asian Amer.	Blacks	Hispanics	Whites
F	0	0	0	0	1,268
M	0	0	0	0	426
%	0.0	0.0	0.0	0.0	100.0

A public, two-year institution, Community College of Vermont has no campus but serves its 1,694 students through four regional directors. Three-fourths of students are women, and 95 percent of women attend part-time. Seventy-six percent of women are over age 25; the median age of all students is 33.

The college offers the first two years of liberal arts, and degrees and certificates in business, health technologies, and public service. It provides individualized programs leading to an associate degree.

Policies to Ensure Fairness to Women. The Director of Administrative Services has part-time responsibility as a voting member of a policymaking council for equal employment opportunity, sex equity, and handicapped accessibility.

Women in Leadership Positions. *Students.* There are no campus leadership positions.

Faculty. There are no full-time faculty. Of the 320 part-time faculty, 65 percent are women, including one black and one Asian American woman.

Administrators. Of the three top-level administrators, the chief executive officer and the chief business officer are women. Three of the four regional directors are also women. Women are 50

percent of the faculty senate and 29 percent of the board of trustees. In one recent year, both commencement speakers were women.

Women and the Curriculum. All two-year degrees and certificates awarded to women are in the arts and sciences. Seventy percent of the students in cooperative education and internships are women. There are no courses on women.

Women and Athletics. There are no athletic programs.

Special Services and Programs for Women. *Health and Counseling.* There is no student health service or student counseling center.

Safety and Security. No rapes or assaults were reported for 1980–81.

Institutional Self-Description. "Community College of Vermont has no campus, but rather is an integral part of the communities of Vermont. Each student has an advisor who provides support and referral services in the area."

Goddard College
Plainfield, VT 05667
Telephone: (802) 454-8311

Women in Leadership	★ Women and the
★★★ faculty	Curriculum
★★★ administrators	

250 undergraduates

Complete enrollment data not available.

Goddard College is a private, four-year institution with a reputation as a leader in educational experimentation. Founded in 1938 and accredited in 1959, the college offers individually planned studies. Enrollment is limited to 250 students, all admitted on a noncompetitive basis. The college offers off-campus, independent-study options. On-campus evening classes and a summer session are also available.

Goddard awards bachelor's and master's degrees in a range of liberal arts and sciences. The campus is not accessible by public transportation. Three percent of students commute; on-campus parking is available.

Private childcare facilities are located near the campus.

Policies to Ensure Fairness to Women. Goddard's president is responsible for policy and compliance regarding equal-employment-opportunity, educational-sex-equity, and handicapped-accessibility legislation. There is an informal, self-designated Committee on the Status of Women. A Committee on Minority Affairs addresses the concerns of minority women.

Women in Leadership Positions. *Students.* Goddard does not have the traditional student leadership posts.

Faculty. According to recent data from the college, five of the seven core faculty are women.

Administrators. Women hold 4 of 7 top administrative positions: chief student-life officer, chief development officer, head librarian, and director of institutional research. Women chair 5 of 7 departments: feminist studies, visual arts, performing arts, social and cultural ecology, human behavior, and teacher education. Three of 17 trustees are female.

Women and the Curriculum. Women earn 70 percent of bachelor's degrees awarded; most major in fine arts (20 percent), education (19 percent), psychology (17 percent), and letters (16 percent). Four percent of women major in such nontraditional fields as agriculture, architecture, and mathematics.

Goddard has an active Feminist Studies Program headed by a member of the core faculty. Both a B.A. and an M.A. in Feminist Studies are available. The program offers independent study, as well as courses on women. Among recent courses are Readings in Radical Feminism, Women's Writing Workshop, Twentieth-Century Women Poets, and Introduction to Feminism. Students in teacher education receive instruction in such matters as sex-fair curricula and coeducational physical education classes. Human behavior and business courses include issues specific to women.

Women and Athletics. Goddard does not have an athletics program.

Housing and Student Organizations. For the 70 percent of students who live on campus, coeducational dormitories without restrictive hours for visitors of the opposite sex and housing for married students are available. A married student whose husband is not enrolled is permitted to live in married students' housing. There is one student residence limited to women, the Dorothy Canfield Fisher House, which also functions as an informal Women's Center.

The Feminist Studies Program serves as the major advocacy group for women students.

Special Services and Programs for Women. *Health and Counseling.* Goddard has a contractual arrangement with the Plainfield Health Center. Three physicians, 2 of them women, and 5 other health-care providers are available. The center provides medical attention specific to women, including gynecological, birth control, abortion, and rape and assault treatment. Two women and 4 men among the core faculty are trained as counselors and can provide a variety of counseling services specific to women. Counselors receive awareness-training on sex-role stereotyping and racial bias.

Safety and Security. Measures consist of local police, campus police without arrest authority, and self-defense courses for women. No rapes or assaults on women were reported for 1980–81.

Other. The Feminist Studies Program sponsors a weekly women's lecture series entitled "Moon Over Vermont." Recent topics included violence against women, single parenting, mother-daughter relationships, racism and feminism, and feminist therapy. The Feminist Studies Program and The Teacher's Center co-sponsor a program to build skills in mathematics.

Institutional Self-Description. "Goddard has undertaken a major new experiment, building its learning community around student-staff collaboration in every aspect of the college's operation. Students and faculty create the curriculum about the needs and issues important to them. Students are encouraged to develop their abilities to learn, think, and act with intelligence and responsibility. At Goddard, growth and development are understood not only as individual matters, but to help students move toward more effective membership in humankind: as cooperator, facilitator, citizen, leader, agent of change."

Southern Vermont College
Monument Road, Bennington, VT 05201
Telephone: (802) 442-5427

Women in Leadership
★ students
★★ faculty

338 undergraduates

	Amer. Ind.	Asian Amer.	Blacks	Hispanics	Whites
F	0	0	4	3	163
M	0	0	5	1	146
%	0.0	0.0	2.8	1.2	96.0

Southern Vermont College, a private, four-year, nondenominational institution, was established in 1926 as a Roman Catholic business school. Some 360 students attend the college, 338 of whom are registered in degree programs. Fifty-three percent of degree students are women; 18 percent of women attend part-time. The median age of all students is 20 years.

The college offers bachelor's and associate degrees in a variety of liberal arts and pre-professional fields. The Evening College administers adult continuing education courses. Alternative scheduling includes evening classes, held on and off campus, a summer session, and a January winter session. Free, on-campus parking is available for the 36 percent of students who commute.

Private childcare facilities are located near the campus.

Policies to Ensure Fairness to Women. Two administrators share part-time responsibility for review of policies and practices related to legislation on access for the handicapped. A policy prohibiting the sexual harassment of staff is currently being formulated; complaints are resolved through informal, confidential means. An ad hoc Committee on the Status of Women, which includes student members, takes public stands on issues of concern to students, including minority women.

Women in Leadership Positions. *Students.* Opportunities for women to acquire leadership experience are good. In a recent three-year period, women served twice as editor-in-chief of the campus newspaper, and once, respectively, as president of the student body, president of the student court, president of the residence hall council, and co-chair of the student union board.

Faculty. Forty-three percent of the 14 full-time faculty are women, a proportion significantly above the average nationwide. There are 4 female faculty for every 100 female students and 6 male faculty for every 100 male students.

Administrators. Except for the head librarian, all chief administrators are male. Thirty-three percent of the faculty senate are female, as are 6 of 21 trustees.

Women and the Curriculum. Women earn 27 percent of the few bachelor's degrees awarded; most women major in public affairs (56 percent). Women earn 58 percent of the two-year degrees awarded. Forty-eight percent major in business, 24 percent in public service, and 16 percent in health technologies. The college sponsors programs to encourage women to prepare for careers in accounting, law enforcement, and management. Sixty percent of student interns are women.

Several courses on women are offered: Career and Life Management for Women, Women in Work, and Women in Literature. The departments of social work and business include instruction on some issues specific to women. Faculty workshops are offered on the needs of reentry women and on affirmative action and equal opportunity.

Women and Athletics. No intramural sports are available to women. Forty percent of the 100 intercollegiate athletes are women; the paid varsity coach is male. The campus has special facilities for skiing. The intercollegiate sports offered are basketball, skiing, soccer, and softball.

Housing and Student Organizations. Forty-five percent of students live on campus in coeducational dormitories without restrictive hours for visitors of the opposite sex. Half of the ten residence-hall directors are women; all residence-hall staff are offered awareness-training on assertiveness and birth control.

Taskforce: Issues on Returning Women serves as an advocacy group for women students.

Special Services and Programs for Women. *Health and Counseling.* The student health service employs three male physicians and one female health-care provider. The counseling center employs one female professional and provides counseling on birth control, abortion, rape and assault, and sexual harassment. The regular student health insurance covers maternity and abortion expenses at no extra cost.

Safety and Security. Measures consist of campus police without arrest authority, night-time bus service to residential areas, self-defense courses, a 24-hour emergency hotline, and a rape crisis center. One rape was reported for 1980–81; no information was provided on the incidence of assaults.

Career. Lectures and printed information on nontraditional occupations for women and job discrimination information are available.

Institutional Self-Description. "SVC is a small career-oriented institution. The curriculum is a blending of the liberal arts, career studies, and management courses, based on the principle that vocational preparation and the liberal arts are mutually supporting parts of a whole education. The individualized attention that a small college can provide—both by faculty and by peers—strengthens the growing process of learning."

Vermont College/Norwich University
Montpelier, VT 05602
Telephone: (802) 229-0522

Women in Leadership
★★★ students

406 undergraduates

	Amer. Ind.	Asian Amer.	Blacks	Hispanics	Whites
F	7	2	4	2	336
M	0	0	1	0	52
%	1.7	0.5	1.2	0.5	96.1

 AAUW

Founded in 1834 as a coeducational Methodist seminary, Vermont College became, in 1972, a branch of Norwich University, a military college. Eighty-seven percent of the 406 undergraduates are women, virtually all of whom attend part-time. Eighty-five women undergraduates are between ages 25 and 40; five are over age 40. The median age of students is 19. Two-year associate degrees are granted in a variety of business, human services, and technical fields. The college has a four-year program in medical technology. Adult students are served by the division of continuing education. There is a summer session. On-campus parking is available for the 40 percent of students who commute.

Private childcare is available near campus.

Policies to Ensure Fairness to Women. The Personnel Director serves part-time to develop policy statements regarding equal-employment-opportunity, sex-equity and handicapped-access-laws. A faculty Committee on the Status of Women, appointed by the President, meets frequently and prepares reports for the Board of Trustees. The committee also addresses the concerns of minority women.

Women in Leadership Positions. *Students.* Opportunities for women to exercise leadership are outstanding. Of the 12 positions available during a three year period, women held all but one.

Faculty. Twenty-three percent of the 31 faculty are women, a proportion slightly below the national average. There are 2 female faculty for every 100 female students.

Administrators. Two of the 9 chief administrators—the student-life officer and the head librarian—are women. Women chair eight of the nine departments. In a recent year, the commencement speaker was a woman, as was 1 of the 2 recipients of honorary degrees.

Women and the Curriculum. The most popular two-year degrees for women are in health technologies, public service, and business. Appropriate departments provide instruction on teaching coeducational physical education classes, services for battered women and displaced homemakers, and information on job discrimination and sexual harassment in the workplace. Women hold almost all of the student internships and practicums. There are no courses on women.

Women and Athletics. There is no intramural sports program for women. The college has good facilities for skiing. Seventeen percent of the intercollegiate athletes and three of the 15 paid coaches are women. Intercollegiate sports for women include basketball, cross-country, field hockey, riflery, softball, swimming, and track.

Housing and Student Organizations. Sixty percent of the students live on campus in women's or coeducational dormitories. Two percent of female residents are black women. The female dormitory directors are offered awareness-training on birth control and alcohol abuse.

Special Services and Programs for Women. *Health and Counseling.* The student health service has 5 physicians, including 1 woman, and 6 female health-care providers. No services specific to women are available. The sole counseling staff member is male. Counseling is available for gynecological problems, birth control, abortion, and rape and assault.

Safety and Security. Measures consist of campus police without arrest authority, night escort service, high-intensity lighting, and information sessions on campus safety and assault prevention. No rapes or assaults on women were reported for 1980–81.

Career. Printed information concerning nontraditional careers for women is available.

Institutional Self-Description. "The grounds are pleasant, the community safe, supportive, and peaceful. The philosophy is focused on educating women to be thoughtful people and competent professionals. The college offers a unique blend of traditional two-year curricula as well as several low-residency programs, both undergraduate and graduate."

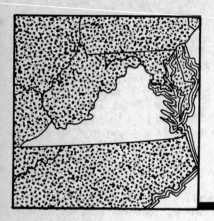

VIRGINIA

Dabney S. Lancaster Community College
Route 60, West Clinton Forge, VA 24422
Telephone: (703) 862-4246

Women in Leadership
★★ faculty

471 undergraduates

	Amer. Ind.	Asian Amer.	Blacks	Hispanics	Whites
F	0	0	12	0	225
M	0	0	9	0	224
%	0.0	0.0	4.5	0.0	95.5

Dabney S. Lancaster Community College is a two-year comprehensive institution that serves 1,186 students. Of 471 undergraduates, 51 percent are women. The median age of students is 28. Thirty-five percent of women are over age 25; 12 percent are over age 40.

The college offers liberal arts programs, as well as two-year degrees and certificates in vocational and technical fields. Evening classes are held both on and off campus. A summer session, self-paced/contract learning and continuing education are available. All students commute. On-campus parking is free. There is no public transportation.

Private childcare facilities are located near the campus.

Policies to Ensure Fairness to Women. One administrator has part-time responsibility for review of policy and compliance with equal-employment-opportunity legislation.

Women in Leadership Positions. *Students.* Opportunities for women in student leadership are limited. In a recent three-year period, the single campus-wide post, president of the student body, was held by a man.

Faculty. Thirty-eight percent of the 34 full-time faculty are women, a proportion above the national average. There are 11 female faculty for every 100 female students and 16 male faculty for every 100 male students. The college reports that the full-time faculty includes 2 black women.

Administrators. With the exception of head librarian, all chief administrative positions are held by men. One of the four academic divisions is chaired by a woman. Three of nine trustees are women.

Women and the Curriculum. Most women earn two-year degrees in health technologies (46 percent) and arts and sciences (27 percent). Sixty percent of students in cooperative education programs are women. A program to develop skills in mathematics is sponsored by Developmental Studies.

There are no courses on women. Faculty workshops are held on the needs of reentry women.

Women and Athletics. There is no intercollegiate program. Ten sports, including canoeing, backpacking and hiking, skiing, and tennis are available in the intramural program.

Special Services and Programs for Women. *Health and Counseling.* There is no student health service. The counseling center, staffed by one man and one minority woman, offers no counseling specific to women.

Safety and Security. Measures consist of local police, and campus police without arrest authority. No rapes or assaults on women were reported for 1980–81.

Other. The Institutional Division offers assertiveness and leadership training. Developmental Studies sponsors a program to build confidence in mathematics. The college also sponsors developmental and remedial instructional programs.

Institutional Self-Description. "Inclusion of forestry and wildlife programs in the curricula, as well as recreational opportunities in the beautiful mountain environment, draw men and women lovers of the outdoors as faculty and students. The small classes and low student-faculty ratio is one important factor among others in students' academic success."
l/l

Ferrum College
Ferrum, VA 24088
Telephone: (703) 365-2121

Women in Leadership
★ faculty

1,469 undergraduates

	Amer. Ind.	Asian Amer.	Blacks	Hispanics	Whites
F	2	5	76	1	471
M	1	9	76	3	820
%	0.2	1.0	10.4	0.3	88.2

Founded in 1913 as a junior college, Ferrum College is now a Methodist-related coeducational institution. It is located southwest of Roanoke in the foothills of the Blue Ridge Mountains. Of the 1,546 students, 1,469 are undergraduates and 38 percent are women. Less than 1 percent of women attend part-time. The median age of all students is 19.

Ferrum offers a broad range of two-year degree programs and a somewhat narrower range of bachelor's degree programs. Students who successfully complete the two-year program may enter the senior division. Classes are given at night as well as during the day. Twelve percent of the students commute to this essentially residential college. On-campus parking is available, as well as free transportation from remote parking lots to campus buildings.

A childcare facility on campus accommodates 18 children and charges a daily fee of $7.

Women in Leadership Positions. *Students.* Incomplete information was supplied. In recent years, men have held the two positions reported—campus newspaper editor and student body president.

Faculty. Thirty percent of the 70 full-time faculty are female, which is above the national average. There are 4 female faculty for every 100 female students and 5 male faculty for every 100 male students.

Administrators. Men hold all key administrative positions except Dean of Student Activities. A woman heads the art department and another heads the business administration and public affairs division.

Women and the Curriculum. Almost half the bachelor's degrees awarded to women are in public affairs. In a recent year, two women (and five men) took degrees in theology.

One course, offered by the psychology department, focuses on women.

Women and Athletics. Of the 224 participants in intercollegiate sports, 24 percent are women. A quarter of the intramural athletes are women, the most popular sports being coeducational volleyball, softball, and woman's softball. Club sports are also available. One of the paid varsity coaches is a woman. Intercollegiate sports offered are basketball, softball, tennis, and volleyball.

Housing and Student Organizations. Eighty-eight percent of all undergraduates live on campus in either single-sex or coeducational dormitories; housing for married students with or without children and for single parents is also available. All dormitories have restrictive visiting hours for members of the opposite sex. Two of the five residence-hall staff are women, and all are offered awareness-training on sex education, birth control, and alcohol abuse.

Social sororities and fraternities do not provide housing for their members. The Black Student Union meets on campus.

Special Services and Programs for Women. *Health and Counseling.* The student health service, staffed by one female physician and three female health-care providers does not provide medical treatment specific to women. The student counseling center has a predominantly female staff which includes a minority woman. Counseling on birth control, abortion, gynecological problems, and rape and assault is available.

Safety and Security. Measures consist of campus police protection and information sessions for women on rape and assault prevention. Information was not provided on the incidence of rapes and assaults.

Career. Services include information about opportunities in nontraditional jobs, panel discussions by women who are employed in nontraditional fields, and career workshops.

Other. The Commission on Minority Affairs addresses the concerns of minority women.

Institutional Self-Description. None provided.

🏛 On-campus evening and/or weekend classes	[M A]	Commission on minority affairs
🏛 Off-campus classes	📖	Women's Studies program
🚐 Accessible by public transportation	👤	Women's center
👥 On-campus childcare facilities	AAUW	Member, American Association of University Women
✎ Publicly communicated sexual harassment policy, includes students	NWSA	Member, National Women's Studies Association
[S W] Commission on status of women	CROW	On-campus Center for Research on Women

Hollins College
Hollins College, VA 24020
Telephone: (703) 362-6000

Women in Leadership
★★★ students
★ faculty
★★★ administrators

919 undergraduates

	Amer. Ind.	Asian Amer.	Blacks	Hispanics	Whites
F	0	2	13	7	880
M	0	0	0	0	0
%	0.0	0.2	1.4	0.8	97.6

🏛 [S W] [M A]

Established as a coeducational institution in 1842, Hollins College has been a liberal arts college for women since 1856. Over 900 students enroll in undergraduate programs. The Adult Studies program serves the older student. Some evening classes are offered. There is a graduate summer session in liberal studies. Four percent of the students attend part-time. The median undergraduate age is 20. For the 9 percent who commute, on-campus parking is available, with free transportation from distant parking lots.

Private childcare arrangements may be made nearby.

Policies to Ensure Fairness to Women. Administrative officers share responsibility for policy and practices relating to equal opportunity. A campus policy on sexual harassment of students is forthcoming. There is a Committee on the Status of Women, which is active and includes students as voting members. The Committee on Minority affairs addresses the concerns of minority women.

Women in Leadership Positions. *Students.* All student leadership positions are held by women.

Faculty. Women are 33 percent of a full-time faculty of 64, below average for women's colleges, but above the national average. The ratio of full-time female faculty to full-time female students is 2 to 100.

Administrators. The President of the college, chief academic officer, chief student-life officer, and director of athletics are women, as are one-fourth of the department heads. Forty-four percent of the 25 trustees are female.

Women and the Curriculum. The most popular majors at Hollins are social sciences (29 percent), fine arts (15 percent), letters (14 percent), and psychology (14 percent). One percent of the women major in mathematics or the physical sciences. The college reports innovative programs to encourage women to prepare for careers in science, accounting, and computer science.

Women, Culture, and Society is offered in the department of sociology. An official committee collects curricular materials for the development of courses on women. Services for abused spouses and discrimination in the workplace are covered in the curricula for future social-service workers and business students. The needs of reentry women is a topic of faculty workshops.

Women and Athletics. Hollins' intercollegiate program provides some variety in individual and team sports. The varsity field hockey and lacrosse teams won championships in recent competition. A program of intramurals was inaugurated in 1981–82; team sports predominate. The intercollegiate sports offered are basketball, fencing, field hockey, lacrosse, riding, soccer, tennis, and volleyball.

Housing and Student Organizations. Ninety-one percent of the undergraduates live in dormitories, some with restricted hours for male visitors. Awareness-training on sexism, sex education, racism, and birth control is offered residence-hall staff.

Special Services and Programs for Women. *Health and Counseling.* The student health service provides some medical attention specific to women, including gynecological and birth control treatment. The health service physician is male; five other health-care providers are female. Students have access to counseling of particular concern to women. The counseling staff consists of one woman therapist.

Safety and Security. Measures include campus police with arrest authority, night-time escorts, campus-wide bus service, an emergency alarm system, and information sessions on safety and crime prevention. One assault and no rapes were reported for 1980–81.

Career. Workshops, lectures, and printed information focused on women in nontraditional occupations and fields of study, as well as a program of contacts between alumnae and students, are provided.

Institutional Self-Description. "Hollins is a selective college, offering a rigorous academic program balanced by a supportive community to help students grow into young women who will face their futures with confidence. Our commitment to the liberal arts provides students with a broadly based perspective as they develop skills in critical thinking, reasoning, and expression. For 140 years Hollins has been an environment supportive of women, and each student is encouraged to develop her potential as an individual to the maximum, to excel and to gain confidence to meet future challenges."

/l

John Tyler Community College
13101 Jefferson Davis Highway
Chester, VA 23831
Telephone: (804) 748-6481

Women in Leadership
★★★ students
★★ faculty

1,082 undergraduates

	Amer. Ind.	Asian Amer.	Blacks	Hispanics	Whites
F	2	1	134	1	386
M	0	3	118	5	432
%	0.2	0.4	23.3	0.6	75.6

Located on a suburban campus south of Richmond, John Tyler is a public, two-year college. Its 3,758 students are offered a comprehensive range of degree and non-degree programs, including liberal arts and vocational fields. There is a continuing education program for adults. Of the 1,082 students enrolled in degree or certificate programs, 48 percent are women; 60 percent of women attend part-time. The median age of students is 27. Classes are offered day and evening, both on and off campus, as well as on Saturday and during the summer. Self-paced learning is available. Free on-campus parking is provided for students, all of whom commute.

Policies to Ensure Fairness to Women. An equal-employment-opportunity officer is responsible part-time for reviewing policies and monitoring compliance with federal and state regulations. There is no written sexual harassment policy; a formal campus grievance procedure resolves complaints.

Women in Leadership Positions. *Students.* Women have outstanding opportunities to gain leadership experience. Women have presided over the student government and the student body for two years of a recent three-year period. During one year, a woman was head of the student court. A woman heads the sole honorary society.

Faculty. Of 72 full-time faculty, 39 percent are women. According to recent information, the full-time faculty includes 1

Hispanic and 3 white women. There are 13 female faculty to every 100 female students and 20 male faculty to every 100 male students.

Administrators. All top administrative positions are held by men. One of 5 directors of divisions is a woman. Women chair the departments of developmental studies, human services, mental health technology, childcare aide, and instructional aide. Among 18 trustees, 4 are women, including 1 black woman.

Women and the Curriculum. Sixty-five percent of two-year degrees awarded to women are in health technologies, 18 percent in business and commerce. The divisions of nursing and social work provide some instruction on matters specific to women. There are no courses on women.

Women and Athletics. There are limited opportunities for women in organized sports. Women play intramural softball and tennis and participate in club sports.

Special Services and Programs for Women. *Health and Counseling.* There is no student health service, but a female physician is on call. The counseling center, staffed by two white women and two minority women, provides counseling on abortion, rape, and assault. The professional staff is offered assertiveness training as well as instruction in the avoidance of race and sex bias.

Safety and Security. Measures include college police without arrest authority, high-intensity lighting, an emergency telephone system, alarms at isolated locations, self-defense courses, and information on rape and assault prevention. There were no rapes or assaults reported for 1980–81.

Career. Services include information on such issues as nontraditional careers and job discrimination, and lectures and panels on nontraditional fields.

Institutional Self-Description. "The college provides a broad range of one-and two-year occupational/technical programs to meet the diversification of employment and personal needs of its students. In addition, the college offers excellence in college transfer programs and adult continuing education programs, to keep pace with a rapidly changing world."

Mary Baldwin College
Staunton, VA 24401
Telephone: (703) 885-0811

Women in Leadership
★★★ students
★★ faculty
★★ administrators

700 undergraduates

	Amer. Ind.	Asian Amer.	Blacks	Hispanics	Whites
F	0	1	15	7	674
M	0	0	0	0	1
%	0.0	0.1	2.2	1.0	96.7

 AAUW

Founded as a female seminary in 1842, Mary Baldwin is a liberal arts college for women affiliated with the Presbyterian Church. Some 719 students enroll, 700 of them registered in bachelor's degree programs. Virtually all students attend full-time. The median age of undergraduates is 18. Adult continuing education is offered.

Small numbers of students commute to the campus, which is accessible by public transportation. On-campus parking is also available. Ninety-five percent of the undergraduate women live on campus in dormitories, some of which have restrictive hours for male visitors.

Private childcare facilities are located nearby.

Policies to Ensure Fairness to Women. An Affirmative Action Officer has part-time responsibility for policies and practices regarding equal-employment-opportunity laws. Complaints of sexual harassment are resolved through a formal grievance procedure. A Commission on the Status of Women, chosen by faculty, meets regularly and takes stands on issues of concern to students, including minority women students.

Women in Leadership Positions. *Students.* Women hold all student leadership positions.

Faculty. Forty-eight percent of the 52 full-time faculty are women, a proportion about average for women's colleges in this guide, but far above the national average. There are 4 female faculty for every 100 female students.

Administrators. Women hold three of eight major administrative positions: chief executive officer, chief student-life officer, and director of athletics. A woman directs the professional training and experimental learning division. Thirteen of 28 trustees are women.

Women and the Curriculum. Most graduates earn degrees in social sciences (23 percent), interdisciplinary studies (16 percent), and fine arts (13 percent). Six percent pursue such nontraditional areas as mathematics and physical sciences. Programs are offered to encourage women to specialize in science and accounting.

Eight courses on women are offered through seven departments. Recent titles include Major Women Artists, Writing by Women, Biology of Women, and Personal Finance. The departments of social work, education, and business include some women's issues in their curricula. An official committee is assigned to develop and collect new curricular materials on women. Workshops for faculty are held on the issues of nontraditional occupations for women and men, the needs of reentry women, and affirmative action and equal opportunity.

Women and Athletics. For a small college, Mary Baldwin has a well-organized athletic program that includes seven intramural sports. There are four paid intercollegiate coaches. Intercollegiate sports offered are basketball, fencing, golf, riding, swimming, and tennis.

Special Services and Programs for Women. *Health and Counseling.* The student health center is staffed by 2 male physicians and 3 female health-care providers. Five of the 6 professionals at the student counseling service are women. The college offers a gynecological, birth control, abortion, and rape and assault counseling. No information was provided on medical services specific to women.

Safety and Security. Measures consist of campus and local police protection, night-time escort service, high-intensity lighting, and information on campus safety. No rapes or assaults on women were reported for 1980–81.

Career. The college offers career workshops, panels, and information on nontraditional occupations, promotes networking between students and alumnae, and maintains files on alumnae careers for students' use.

Other. The theater, art, and music departments sponsor special programs for and about women. The office of the Dean of Students sponsors assertiveness-training workshops, speakers, and other programs. The United Students Association serves as an advocacy group for women, including minority women.

Returning Women Students. The Adult Degree Program provides continuing education for women. The program has its own center, with a budget of $105,676 and a faculty director.

Institutional Self-Description. "Imagine a beautiful hilltop campus. Consider a superior academic program and gifted faculty whose first concern is you, the individual. If you are concerned about realizing your potential, if you value a solid liberal arts education and career options like business or mass communications, you should think of Mary Baldwin College."

Old Dominion University
Hampton Blvd., Norfolk, VA 23508
Telephone: (804) 440-3000

★★ **Women and the Curriculum**

8,921 undergraduates

	Amer. Ind.	Asian Amer.	Blacks	Hispanics	Whites
F	17	42	371	25	3,905
M	14	54	217	40	4,231
%	0.4	1.1	6.6	0.7	91.3

Old Dominion, a public university founded in 1930, enrolls some 14,000 students, of whom 8,900 are undergraduates. Forty-nine percent of the undergraduates are women; 14 percent of women attend part-time. The median age of undergraduates is 26.

The university offers undergraduate and graduate degrees in the biological and physical sciences, business, education, engineering, health professions, the social sciences, and, to a lesser extent, the liberal arts. Alternative scheduling includes evening classes, both on and off campus, and a summer session. The campus is easily accessible by public transportation. On-campus parking is also available for the 54 percent of undergraduates who commute.

Private childcare facilities are available near campus, and the university is investigating the possibility of establishing on-campus facilities.

Policies to Ensure Fairness to Women. The Director of Affirmative Action and the Equal Employment Opportunity Compliance Specialist—both full-time administrators—monitor compliance with laws on equal employment opportunity, sex equity for students, and access for the handicapped. A policy forbidding sexual harassment of students, faculty, and staff has been publicly communicated to faculty and staff only. A formal grievance procedure resolves complaints of sexual harassment.

The Faculty Women's Caucus makes recommendations on women's concerns to the faculty senate. An Affirmative Action Committee includes the concerns of minority women in its deliberations.

Women in Leadership Positions. *Students.* Women have limited opportunities to gain leadership experience. In three recent years, women twice presided over the student court.

Faculty. Women constitute 23 percent of the 591 full-time faculty, a proportion slightly below the national average. Eleven percent of the female faculty hold permanent appointments, a proportion below average for public, four-year institutions in this guide. There are 4 female faculty for every 100 female students and 12 male faculty for every 100 male students.

Administrators. Except for head librarian, men hold the top-level administrative positions. Women chair five of 48 departments: finance, the writing center, curriculum and instruction, nursing, and child study and special education. The Dean of the School of Business Administration is a woman.

Women and the Curriculum. Most women earn degrees in education (28 percent), the health professions (17 percent), business (12 percent), and social sciences (12 percent). Four percent of women earn degrees in engineering, computer science, mathematics, and physical sciences. In one recent year, more women than men earned degrees in mathematics. One-third of students in cooperative education and in internship programs are women.

The Women's Studies Program, directed part-time by a permanent faculty member, awards a 12-credit certificate, the B.A. through Interdisciplinary Studies and the M.A. through the Humanities Institute. The program offers 15 undergraduate and graduate courses under its own aegis, and another 25 courses through the departments of English, criminal justice, sociology, nursing, political science, history, speech, philosophy, psychology, art, French, and others. Courses include Introduction to Women's Studies; Women and Power; Quests for Utopia: Classic to Feminist; Women and the Military; Women in the Developing World; Women's Health and Medical Care; Communication between the Sexes; The Struggle for Equality in Victorian and Edwardian England, 1850–1918; The Role of Women in American Education. An offical committee encourages the development of new courses and the inclusion of scholarship on women in all courses. Faculty workshops are offered on sexism and the curriculum, and on affirmative action and equal opportunity. The leadership of Women's Studies on campus is partly responsible for the changing of the institutional mission; its new language reflects a sensitivity to white women and members of minority groups of both sexes.

Minority Women. Ten percent of female undergraduates are members of minority groups:nearly 9 percent are black women, 1 percent are Asian American, and less than 1 percent are American Indian or Hispanic. Forty women belong to all-minority sororities. Eight black and 2 Asian American women serve on the full-time faculty. The 17-member Board of Visitors (regents) includes 1 black woman. One of 3 residence-hall directors is a minority woman. The Multicultural Center and the Women's Center are available to minority women.

Women and Athletics. Thirty-eight percent of intercollegiate, 80 percent of intramural, and 67 percent of club sports athletes are women; women receive 30 percent of athletic scholarships. Seven of 25 paid intercollegiate coaches are women. All women's varsity teams enter into tournament competition. Intercollegiate sports in which women participate are basketball, field hockey, lacrosse, swimming, tennis, and track.

Housing and Student Organizations. Single-sex dormitories with restricted hours for visitors of the opposite sex, and coeducational dormitories, are available for the 12 percent of undergraduates who live on campus. Residence-hall staff are offered awareness training on sexism, sex education, and birth control.

Seven percent of undergraduate women belong to sororities, which provide housing for members. The ten-member Student Women's Caucus serves as an advocacy group for all women, and includes black women among its active participants.

Special Services and Programs for Women. *Health and Counseling.* The health service staff of three male part-time physicians and seven female health-care providers offers treatment for gynecological problems, birth control, abortion (including follow-up), and rape and assault. Counseling is also available on these items. No information was provided on the size and gender of the counseling staff.

Safety and Security. Measures consist of campus and local police, high-intensity lighting, emergency telephones and alarms, courses on safety, and a rape crisis center. For 1980–81 one rape and 29 assaults (18 on women) were reported.

Other. The division of student affairs operates the campus Women's Center with a budget of $44,000. Under the direction of a full-time faculty member, the center provides counseling and administers a Continuing Education for Women Program, which serves 500 students, 15 percent of them minority women. The center sponsors a warmline for support and referrals, a mathematics confidence program, assertiveness training, and an annual women's week. In conjunction with the Women's Studies Program, it sponsors theater and arts programs.

The Women's Studies Program offers a women's lecture series. The Assistant Dean for Student Development is responsible for assisting handicapped women.

Institutional Self-Description. "The university is receptive to women-oriented programs, and a Women's Center is available for student and community use. Also, the Women's Studies Program promotes cross-disciplinary study to encourage fresh perspectives on women's past and current accomplishments in an effort to create a more egalitarian approach to teaching and learn-

ing. Further, the Women's Studies Program urges the university at large to expand the viewpoint in all courses to meet the same objectives of acknowledging and respecting the full range of women's achievements, past, present, and future.''

Randolph-Macon College
Ashland, VA 23005
Telephone: (804) 798-8372

Women in Leadership
★★ students

928 undergraduates

	Amer. Ind.	Asian Amer.	Blacks	Hispanics	Whites
F	0	4	2	2	359
M	3	5	9	4	533
%	0.3	1.0	1.2	0.7	96.9

Founded as a liberal arts college for men in 1830, Randolph-Macon is a private, four-year institution affiliated with the United Methodist Church. Coeducational since 1971, the college enrolls some 920 students, 40 percent of them women. All women attend full-time. The median age of all students is 19. Bachelor's degrees are offered in a variety of liberal arts and sciences. Evening classes and a summer session are offered. Two percent of students commute to the campus, located near Richmond. While Randolph-Macon is not accessible by public transportation, on-campus parking is available. For the 98 percent of students who live on campus, single-sex dormitories and housing for married students with and without children are provided.

Policies to Ensure Fairness to Women. Implementation of educational-sex-equity and handicapped-access legislation is the part-time responsibility of the Dean of the College, a voting member of policymaking councils. Complaints of sexual harassment are resolved informally and confidentially.

Women in Leadership Positions. *Students.* Opportunities for women to exercise student leadership are excellent. In three recent years, women served twice as president of the student senate and president of the sophomore class, and once as president of the student court, editor-in-chief of the campus newspaper, and presidents of the junior and first-year classes. Two of the six honorary societies are headed by women.

Faculty. Nineteen percent of the 58 full-time faculty are women, a proportion below the national average. There are 3 female faculty for every 100 female students and 8 male faculty for every 100 male students.

Administrators. With the exception of the head librarian, all key administrative posts are occupied by men. Women chair four of 18 departments: sociology, religion, computer science, and education.

Women and the Curriculum. Most women earn degrees in psychology (33 percent) and the social sciences (21 percent). Six percent of women graduates major in such nontraditional fields as mathematics and physical sciences. Forty percent of student interns are women. A Life Roles Awareness Committee offers workshops on nontraditional occupations for women and men.

The departments of English, French, and education each offer one course on women: Special Topics: Women in Literature; Women in French Literature; and The Development of Sex Roles in American Education and Culture. The department of education also provides instruction on the development and use of sex-fair curricula. An ad hoc committee works to expand the number of courses on women and to alert faculty about recent developments in women's scholarship. It is also developing a new Gender Studies Program.

Women and Athletics. Twenty-five percent of intercollegiate athletes and 34 percent of intramural athletes are women. Women receive 20 percent of athletic scholarships awarded. Club sports are also available. Two of seven paid varsity coaches are women. Intercollegiate sports offered are basketball, field hockey, lacrosse, and tennis.

Special Services and Programs for Women. *Health and Counseling.* The student health service is staffed by two male physicians and two female health-care providers. The counseling center employs one male professional. Birth control and abortion counseling are available. No medical treatment specific to women is available.

Safety and Security. Measures consist of local police and campus police with arrest authority. No rapes or assaults on women were reported for 1980–81.

Other. The college reports plans to open a Life Roles Awareness Center that would perform some of the same functions as a Women's Center, and also serve men. The Life Roles Awareness Committee sponsors a lecture series on life roles and directs most of its programs to women's interests.

Institutional Self-Description. "A small liberal arts institution, Randolph-Macon College provides a personalized learning environment which gives students the opportunity to explore points of view, to question, and to discuss ideas and their implications. Within this context, the college offers several Women's Studies courses as well as an extensive series of programs dealing with gender-role issues."

Randolph-Macon Woman's College

2500 Rovermont Avenue
Lynchburg, VA 24503
Telephone: (804) 846-7392

Women in Leadership
★★★ students
★★ faculty
★★★ administrators

680 undergraduates

	Amer. Ind.	Asian Amer.	Blacks	Hispanics	Whites
F	0	0	18	3	640
M	0	0	0	0	2
%	0.0	0.0	2.7	0.5	96.8

🚌 ⬚ **AAUW**

Randolph-Macon Woman's College, established in 1891, is an independent institution, affiliated with the United Methodist Church. It has a total enrollment of 706 students, 680 of whom are undergraduates. The median age of undergraduates is 19. All students attend full-time.

Randolph-Macon offers bachelor's degrees in a variety of fields, as well as an adult continuing education program. For the 3 percent of students who commute, the campus is accessible by public transportation. On-campus parking is available at a fee.

Private childcare facilities are available near the campus.

Policies to Ensure Fairness to Women. The Director of Business Affairs is responsible for policy and practices regarding equal-employment-opportunity, sex-equity, and handicapped-access laws. Complaints of sexual harassment are handled through a formal procedure. A Commission on the Status of Women, appointed by the President, includes students as voting members, meets regularly, and takes public stands on issues of concern to women, including minority women.

Women in Leadership Positions. *Students.* Women hold all campus-wide leadership positions.

Faculty. Forty-three percent of the 65 full-time faculty are women, a proportion far above the national average. There are 4 female faculty for every 100 female students.

Administrators. Women occupy half of the key administrative posts, including those of Dean of the College and chief student-life officer. Women chair nine of 27 departments: American studies, chemistry, communications, dance, German, French, Spanish, Russian, and Latin American studies. Fifty-four percent of the faculty senate are women.

Women and the Curriculum. Forty-four percent of the women earn degrees in the social sciences, 14 percent in letters, and 10 percent in fine arts. Three percent specialize in such nontraditional fields as mathematics and physical sciences. The college reports special programs to encourage women to major in computer science, engineering (a cooperative program with Vanderbilt University), science, and accounting.

The department of sociology offers one course on women, Gender Roles. The physical education department provides some instruction on matters specific to women. An official committee addresses the inclusion of women in the curriculum.

Women and Athletics. For a college of its size, Randolph-Macon has a substantial athletic program. There are eight intercollegiate teams, four intramural activities (mostly team sports), and two sports clubs. The five paid varsity coaches are women. Intercollegiate sports offered are basketball, fencing, field hockey, lacrosse, riding, swimming, tennis, and volleyball.

Housing and Student Organizations. Ninety-seven percent of the women live on campus in dormitories that restrict men's visiting hours. Residence-hall staff are offered awareness training on sexism, sex education, birth control, and crisis intervention. The Women's Caucus and the Black Students Association are advocacy groups.

Special Services and Programs for Women. *Health and Counseling.* The student health service has three male physicians and eight female health-care providers. One female professional works at the student counseling center. Counseling and treatment are available for gynecological problems and birth control; counseling is offered for abortion and rape and assault.

Safety and Security. Measures consist of campus and local police protection, night-time escort service, instruction on self-defense and campus safety, an emergency telephone system, and a rape crisis center. One rape was reported for 1980–81.

Career. The college provides workshops, information, and panels on nontraditional occupations, fosters networking between students and alumnae, and compiles files on alumnae careers.

Other. The office of the Dean of Students organizes an annual women's week, a women's lecture series, theater and arts programs for women, leadership training, and a mathematics confidence clinic.

Special Features. A campus-based Women's Center—independent of the college—runs a displaced homemakers' program which annually serves 200 women from the community.

Institutional Self-Description. "As a woman's college with a long-standing commitment to educational excellence in the liberal arts, we have the additional responsibility of assisting our students in developing a balanced picture of their past, a realistic assessment of their present, and an informed, self-aware approach to the range of alternatives open to them in the future. This responsibility is fundamental to our mission: 'the pursuit of excellence in educating women to live fully in the contemporary world'."

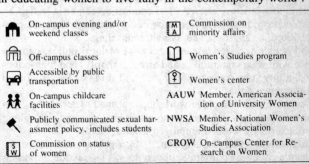

🏛 On-campus evening and/or weekend classes	[M A] Commission on minority affairs
🏛 Off-campus classes	📖 Women's Studies program
🚌 Accessible by public transportation	👤 Women's center
👥 On-campus childcare facilities	**AAUW** Member, American Association of University Women
📣 Publicly communicated sexual harassment policy, includes students	**NWSA** Member, National Women's Studies Association
[S W] Commission on status of women	**CROW** On-campus Center for Research on Women

Southern Seminary Junior College
Buena Vista, VA 24416
Telephone: (703) 261-6181

Women in Leadership
★★★ students
★★★ faculty
★★★ administrators

237 undergraduates

	Amer. Ind.	Asian Amer.	Blacks	Hispanics	Whites
F	0	0	4	0	226
M	0	0	0	0	0
%	0.0	0.0	1.7	0.0	98.3

Established in 1867 as a preparatory school for girls, Southern Seminary Junior College is a private, two-year women's college located in the Blue Ridge Mountains between Charlottesville and Roanoke. Virtually all of the 237 women enrolled attend full-time. The median age of students is 19. Two-year degrees and certificates are awarded in arts and science, as well as in business and commercial fields. Free on-campus parking is available for the 11 percent of students who commute. The campus is not accessible by public transportation.

Policies to Ensure Fairness to Women. The Business Manager has part-time responsibility for monitoring compliance with equal employment opportunity, sex equity for students, and handicapped accessibility.

Women in Leadership Positions. *Students.* Women hold all student leadership positions.

Faculty. Eight of the 14 full-time faculty are women. There are 3 female faculty for every 100 female students.

Administrators. Half of the top administrators are women: the Vice President for Academic and Student Affairs, the head librarian, and the director of athletics. Women chair two of the four academic divisions: humanities and physical education. Five of 20 trustees are women.

Women and the Curriculum. Most women earn degrees in arts and sciences (61 percent), with smaller numbers in business and commerce (30 percent) and the rest in public services (9 percent). There are no courses on women.

Women and Athletics. For a college of its size, Southern Seminary offers a very good athletics program. One hundred and five women participate in six intramural sports, including volleyball, badminton, and swimming. Seventy-four women participate in varsity sports, and three of the four varsity coaches are women. All six intercollegiate teams competed in recent tournaments. The intercollegiate sports offered are basketball, equitation, golf, softball, tennis, and volleyball.

Housing and Student Organizations. Eighty-nine percent of students live in on-campus dormitories; some areas are off-limits to visitors of the opposite sex. The four residence-hall directors receive awareness-training on birth control.

Special Services and Programs for Women. *Health and Counseling.* The student health service employs two male physicians and one female health-care provider. No medical treatment specific to women is offered. The counseling center is staffed by one female professional who provides gynecological, birth control, abortion, and rape and assault counseling.

Safety and Security. Measures consist of local police, campus police with weapons training and arrest authority, and high-intensity lighting. One rape (off-campus) and no assaults on women were reported for 1980–81.

Career. Services include workshops, printed materials, and job discrimination information on nontraditional occupations, along with lectures by women employed in these fields.

Institutional Self-Description. "As a private, non-sectarian, women's college, Southern Seminary has as its mission providing a college for young women who want a high degree of personal attention and personal interaction. Our class-size average is 12; all our faculty and administrators are easily accessible; and our mission is to encourage intellectual and social growth in a traditional setting."

Sweet Briar College
Sweet Briar, VA 24595
Telephone: (804) 381-5500

Women in Leadership
★★★ students
★★ faculty
★ administrators

657 undergraduates

	Amer. Ind.	Asian Amer.	Blacks	Hispanics	Whites
F	0	2	6	2	624
M	0	0	0	0	0
%	0.0	0.3	1.0	0.3	98.0

M/A AAUW

Sweet Briar is a private, liberal arts college for women. Founded in 1901, it now has 669 students, of whom 657 are registered in degree programs. The median age of students is 20 and almost all attend full-time.

Sweet Briar offers the bachelor's degree in a variety of liberal arts fields, as well as a small continuing education program. Cross-registration with Randolph–Macon Woman's College and Lynchburg College is available. Most students reside on the campus, which is not accessible by public transportation. For the 2 percent of students who commute, on-campus parking is available.

Policies to Ensure Fairness to Women. Policy regarding equal-employment-opportunity, sex-equity, and handicapped-access legislation is the part-time responsibility of one administrator.

Women in Leadership Positions. *Students.* Women hold all campus-wide leadership positions.

Faculty. Forty-four percent of the 66 full-time faculty are women, a proportion slightly below average for women's colleges in this guide, but above the national average. There are 4 female faculty for every 100 female students.

Administrators. Women are Dean of the College and director of athletics; all other top administrators are men. Women chair nine of 21 departments, including anthropology/sociology, art history, chemistry, history, mathematics, psychology, and theater arts. Half of the members of the Board of Trustees are women.

Women and the Curriculum. Forty-four percent of degrees are awarded in the social sciences, 17 percent in fine arts, and 14 percent in letters. Eight percent of students earn degrees in mathematics or physical sciences. Special programs encourage students to prepare for careers in such nontraditional areas as engineering. The mathematics department offers instruction in mathematics confidence.

Sweet Briar offers three courses on women through the departments of modern languages and English: Women and Literature, Images of Women in the Italian Renaissance, and Women in the Theatre of Henry de Montherlant. Prospective teachers learn to recognize and treat mathematics avoidance in female students, and to teach coeducational physical education classes.

Minority Women. About 2 percent of the students are minority women. A Commission on Minority Affairs addresses their concerns. The Racial Awareness Movement serves as an advocacy group for black students. Several black women participated in recent campus-wide lecture series. The professional counseling and residence-hall staffs are offered awareness training on racism.

Women and Athletics. For a college of its size, Sweet Briar has a strong intercollegiate program. All varsity teams play in tournament competition; six of the seven paid coaches are women. Intercollegiate sports offered are basketball, golf, field hockey, lacrosse, riding, swimming and diving, tennis, and volleyball.

Housing and Student Organizations. Ninety-eight percent of the students live in dormitories that restrict men's visiting hours. Residence-hall staff are offered awareness training on sexism, sex education, birth control, assertiveness, and racism.

A chapter of the National Organization for Women meets on campus.

Special Services and Programs for Women. *Health and Counseling.* The student health center has two male physicians and five female health-care providers. Counseling and treatment for gynecological problems, birth control, and rape and assault are available, in addition to abortion counseling. The college does not have a student counseling center, but provides professional counseling in various campus offices. The counseling staff are offered awareness training on sexual harassment, sex-role stereotyping, and racial bias.

Safety and Security. Measures consist of campus police protection, night-time escort service, and information sessions on self-defense and campus safety. No rapes or assaults on women were reported for 1980–81.

Career. The Career Planning Office offers workshops, lectures, and information on nontraditional careers, as well as workshops on such job-related skills as problem solving, leadership, assertiveness, time management, job hunting, and resume writing. The Career Connection, an alumnae advisory network, provides students with career information, shadowing experience, and professional contacts. The college also maintains files on alumnae careers for student use.

Institutional Self-Description. "Although alert to and involved in women's issues, Sweet Briar students seem to consider themselves persons of universal interests and abilities, and do not seem totally immersed in special programs or studies devoted to women's issues."

University of Richmond
Richmond, VA 23173
Telephone: (804) 285-6000

★ **Women and the Curriculum**

2,563 undergraduates

	Amer. Ind.	Asian Amer.	Blacks	Hispanics	Whites
F	1	0	7	4	1,028
M	0	3	36	2	1,456
%	0.0	0.1	1.7	0.2	97.9

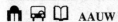 AAUW

Established in 1830 as a college for training Baptist ministers, the University of Richmond remains affiliated with the Baptist Church, and has become a comprehensive, coeducational university. It consists of Westhampton College for women, Richmond College for men, T. C. Williams School of Law, Graduate School, School of Business Administration, and University College. The enrollment of 4,409 students includes 2,563 undergraduates. Women are 41 percent of the undergraduates and virtually all women attend full-time. The median age of undergraduates is 20.

The university offers a variety of liberal arts, pre-professional, and professional degrees, in addition to a continuing education program. Classes meet day and evening. Ninety percent of the undergraduates live in single-sex dormitories that restrict visiting hours for members of the opposite sex. Public transportation and campus parking are available for commuting students.

Policies to Ensure Fairness to Women. The Vice President

for Student Affairs has the part-time responsibility for establishing policy on sex-equity issues

Women in Leadership Positions. *Students.* Women students hold all student leadership posts on the Westhampton College campus, as do men on the Richmond College campus. It is not clear, from information provided by the university, how many competitive posts are held by women and by men.

Faculty. Nineteen percent of the 194 full-time faculty are women, a proportion below the national average. There are 3 female faculty for every 100 female students and 11 male faculty for every 100 male students.

Administrators. Except for the Dean of Westhampton College, the chief university administrators are men. Women chair three of 21 departments: mathematics, modern languages, and psychology. Seven women sit on the 55-member Board of Trustees.

Women and the Curriculum. Twenty-six percent of the women receiving bachelor's degrees major in business, while 20 percent specialize in the social sciences. Seven percent of the women specialize in such nontraditional areas as mathematics and physical sciences. Faculty are offered workshops on nontraditional careers for men and women.

A new Women's Studies Program, directed by a full-time faculty member, offers a major. Courses include Psychology of Women, Women and Creativity, and Sociology of Sex Roles, in addition to Introduction to Women's Studies. An official committee oversees the development of the program. Prospective teachers learn to lead coeducational physical education classes and how to use nonsexist curricula.

Women and Athletics. No information was supplied regarding intramural or club sports. The organized intercollegiate program for women is adequate and varied. About one-third of the varsity athletes are women. The intercollegiate sports offered are basketball, field hockey, lacrosse, soccer, swimming, tennis, and track and field.

Special Services and Programs for Women. *Health and Counseling.* The student health service employs 2 male physicians and 3 female health-care providers. One of 2 professionals at the student counseling center is a woman. Gynecological and birth control counseling and treatment are provided, in addition to abortion and rape and assault counseling.

Safety and Security. Measures include campus police with arrest authority, night-time escorts for women, high-intensity lighting, an emergency telephone system, and instruction and information on self-defense and campus safety for women. No information on the incidence of rapes or assaults was supplied.

Career. Services include workshops, panels, and information on nontraditional occupations, files on alumnae careers, and programs to foster networking between alumnae and students.

Other. A well-funded ($50,000) Women's Center annually attracts 2,000 users, predominantly community women.

Institutional Self-Description. "Westhampton College is one of five coordinate colleges which make up the University of Richmond. Westhampton College is a liberal arts, undergraduate college for women with an enrollment of 950 students. It provides the environment of a small women's college while providing the benefits and services of a university community."

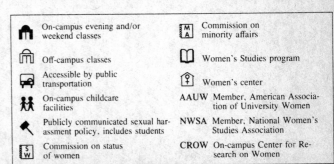

♠ On-campus evening and/or weekend classes	M A Commission on minority affairs
♠ Off-campus classes	📖 Women's Studies program
🚌 Accessible by public transportation	👤 Women's center
👫 On-campus childcare facilities	AAUW Member, American Association of University Women
↯ Publicly communicated sexual harassment policy, includes students	NWSA Member, National Women's Studies Association
S W Commission on status of women	CROW On-campus Center for Research on Women

Virginia Polytechnic Institute and State University

Blacksburg, VA 24061

Telephone: (703) 961-7500

★ **Women and the Curriculum**

17,416 undergraduates

	Amer. Ind.	Asian Amer.	Blacks	Hispanics	Whites
F	9	46	111	19	6,210
M	7	74	198	18	10,504
%	0.1	0.7	2.0	0.2	97.2

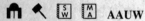 AAUW

Established in 1872 as the Virginia Agriculture and Mechanical College as a result of the Morrill Land-Grant Act, Virginia Polytechnic Institute and State University currently enrolls over 20,000 students in research, instructional, and extension programs. The Donaldson Brown Center for Continuing Education serves the adult student. Evening classes and a summer session are available.

Women are 37 percent of the 17,416 undergraduates; 5 percent of the women attend part-time. Fifty-one percent of the undergraduates commute to campus. On-campus parking is free.

Private arrangements for childcare may be made near the university.

Policies to Ensure Fairness to Women. A full-time equal-opportunity officer reviews policies and practices related to employment, sex equity for students, and handicapped accessibility. Three other full-time officers monitor compliance. A published policy prohibits sexual harassment. Complaints are handled both informally and confidentially or through a formal grievance procedure. The active Committee on the Status of Women, which includes students as voting members, takes public stands on issues of concern to students. The Committee on Minority Affairs addresses the concerns of minority women, among other matters.

Women in Leadership Positions. *Students.* According to the incomplete information provided, in one recent year women have been president of the student body, presiding officer of the student union board, editor-in-chief of the newspaper, and manager of the campus radio station.

Faculty. Women are 14 percent of a full-time faculty of 1,402. According to a recent report, 9 black and 3 Asian American women are on the full-time faculty. The ratio of female faculty to female students is 3 to 100. The ratio of male faculty to male students is 12 to 100.

Administrators. Men fill all high-level administrative posts. Women chair four of 191 departments.

Women and the Curriculum. A majority of women earning bachelor's degrees major in home economics, agriculture, business and management, and education; 24 percent major in nontraditional areas such as agriculture, computer science, mathematics, and the physical sciences. Roughly one-quarter of the students in cooperative education programs and 18 percent in science field-service programs are women. Twelve percent of the ROTC students are women.

Such current issues as the teaching of coeducational sports classes and discrimination in the workplace are part of the instruction received by physical education teachers candidates and business students. There are no courses on women.

Women and Athletics. Intramural and intercollegiate programs provide some opportunity for organized, competitive individual and team sports. The number and variety of offerings in the intramural program are noteworthy. The university reports women's participation in co-recreational sports is very high. Club sports are also available. Women receive 20 percent of the athletic scholarships awarded. Women's intercollegiate teams played in tournaments in 1980. The intercollegiate sports offered are basketball, field hockey, swimming, tennis, and volleyball.

Housing and Student Organizations. Forty-nine percent of undergraduates live on campus. Residential accommodations include men's and women's dormitories. Residence halls restrict hours for visitors of the opposite sex. Eleven of 26 residence-hall directors are female.

Eleven percent of the full-time undergraduate women belong to social sororities. Sororities do not provide housing for their members.

Special Services and Programs for Women. *Health and Counseling.* The student health service provides medical attention specific to women, including gynecological, birth control, abortion, and rape and assault treatment. One of 10 physicians is female, as are 18 of 20 other health-care providers. Five of 12 professional staff in the counseling service are women. Students have access to counseling on gynecological problems, birth control, abortion, and rape and assault.

Safety and Security. Measures include campus police with arrest authority, information sessions on safety and crime prevention, and a rape crisis center. Information was not provided on the incidence of rapes and assaults.

Other. The College of Engineering sponsors a women's lecture series. The Employee Training Office provides assertiveness training and a program to build confidence in mathematics.

Institutional Self-Description. None provided.

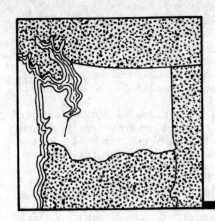

WASHINGTON

Central Washington University
Ellensburg, WA 98926
Telephone: (509) 963-1111

5,479 undergraduates

	Amer. Ind.	Asian Amer.	Blacks	Hispanics	Whites
F	36	43	40	57	2,675
M	72	45	31	37	2,394
%	2.0	1.6	1.3	1.7	93.4

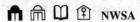 **NWSA**

Central Washington University, a state-supported, liberal arts institution, was founded in 1890 as a school for training teachers. It now offers bachelor's and master's programs in education, business, and pre-professional fields, as well as in the liberal arts and sciences. Flexible scheduling opportunities include day and evening classes held both on and off campus and a summer session. Adult continuing education is available through the division of off-campus programs.

Of the 7,400 students who attend Central Washington, 5,479 are undergraduates. Fifty-two percent of the undergraduates are women, 18 percent of whom attend part-time. The median age of undergraduates is 22 years. More than half the students commute. The campus is not accessible by public transportation. Parking on campus is available for a fee.

Private childcare facilities are located near the campus.

Policies to Ensure Fairness to Women. The Director of Affirmative Action has full-time responsibility for review of policy and compliance concerning educational, sex-equity legislation. A written campus policy prohibits sexual harassment of students, faculty, and staff, and has been publicly communicated to faculty and staff; a formal campus grievance procedure handles complaints.

Women in Leadership Positions. *Students.* The institution did not provide information on campus leadership positions.

Faculty. Of the 297 full-time faculty, 16 percent are women, a proportion well below the national average. There are 2 female faculty for every 100 female students and 11 male faculty for every 100 male students. According to a recent report, the full-time faculty women include 1 black, 1 Asian American, and 1 American Indian woman.

Administrators. All chief administrative positions are held by men; the Director of Summer Session is a woman. Women chair three of 46 departments, including anthropology, and health sciences.

Women and the Curriculum. Most women earn degrees in education (49 percent) and business (16 percent), with significant numbers in public affairs (8 percent) and social sciences (6 per-

cent). Less than 1 percent of women major in the nontraditional field of the physical sciences. Fifty-seven percent of students in cooperative education programs are women.

The newly formed Women's Studies Program, headed part-time by a permanent faculty member, offers an undergraduate minor. A committee oversees the development of the program and reports on the inclusion of the new scholarship on women in the curriculum. The divisions of education, physical education, and business include instruction on some issues specific to women in their curricula. Faculty workshops are held on such topics as sexism and racism in course materials, the needs of reentry women, and affirmative action and equal opportunity.

Women and Athletics. While the university did not provide information on intramural sports, it reported some opportunities for women in the intercollegiate program. Twenty-eight percent of varsity athletes are women, as are eight of the 16 paid intercollegiate coaches. Intercollegiate sports offered are basketball, cross-country, field hockey, swimming, tennis, track and field, and volleyball.

Housing and Student Organizations. Single-sex and coeducational dormitories which do not restrict hours for visitors of the opposite sex are provided for the 35 percent of undergraduates who reside on campus. Housing for married students with or without children and for single parents is also available. A married woman student whose husband is not enrolled may live in married students' housing. Eleven of the residence-hall directors are women, and all residence-hall staff are offered awarenss-training on sex education, birth control, and the avoidance of sexism and racism.

Special Services and Programs for Women. *Health and Counseling.* The student health service employs 1 male physician and 5 female health-care providers: the counseling center is staffed by 5 professionals, 1 of whom is a woman. Available services specific to women include medical treatment and counseling for gynecological matters, birth control, abortion, prenatal care, and rape and assault.

Safety and Security. Measures consist of information sessions on campus safety and crime prevention, and a rape crisis center. Information about the incidence of rapes and assaults on women was not provided.

Career. Students have access to workshops, lectures, and job discrimination information on nontraditional occupations for women.

Other. Undergraduates Studies operates the campus Women's Center, with a budget of $1,500. Five percent of the women who use the center are minority women. The Center for Women's Studies sponsors a women's lecture series. The counseling center offers assertiveness and leadership training.

Institutional Self-Description. None provided.

Clark College
1800 E. McLoughlin Boulevard
Vancouver, WA 98663
Telephone: (206) 694-6521

Women in Leadership ★ **Women and the**
★★ students **Curriculum**
★ faculty
★★ administrators

2,261 undergraduates

	Amer. Ind.	Asian Amer.	Blacks	Hispanics	Whites
F	11	4	4	6	1,058
M	9	12	10	9	1,079
%	0.9	0.7	0.6	0.7	97.1

Clark College is a public institution that provides the first two years of liberal arts education and a wide range of technical and vocational progams. Alternative scheduling includes evening and summer session classes, as well as self-paced/contract learning. Off-campus class locations are also available.

Clark enrolls 8,000 students, of whom 2,261 are registered in degree programs. Forty-nine percent of the degree students are women; 38 percent of women attend part-time. The median age of all student is 28. Seventeen percent of all women enrolled are older than 40. All students commute and free on-campus parking is available. The campus is accessible through a limited range of public transportation.

College-run childcare facilities, open only to the children of students, can meet 95 percent of requests for service. Additional, private childcare facilities are located near the campus.

Policies to Ensure Fairness to Women. One administrator has part-time responsibility for review of policy and compliance regarding legislation on equal employment opportunity, sex equity for students, and handicapped access. A written campus policy prohibits sexual harassment of students, faculty, and staff, and will soon be publicly communicated to those three groups. Complaints of sexual harassment are handled through a formal grievance procedure. The Director of Minority Affairs addresses the concerns of minority women.

Women in Leadership Positions. *Students.* Clark offers excellent opportunities for women to gain leadership experience. In three recent years, women held slightly less than half of the campus-wide posts available each year.

Faculty. Thirty-three percent of the 110 full-time faculty are women, a proportion which is average for public, two-year colleges in this guide, and above the national average for all colleges. There are 5 female faculty for every 100 female students and 9 male faculty for every 100 male students. The college reports 1 black woman among the full-time faculty.

Administrators. Four of the 10 top administrators are women: chief business officer, director of athletics, chief planning officer, and head librarian. The head librarian is a black woman. Three of eight departments are chaired by women. Two of 5 trustees are women. Three of the 7-member faculty senate are female, including 1 black woman.

Women and the Curriculum. Most women major in arts and sciences (43 percent) and health technologies (39 percent). Fifty-five percent of students in cooperative education and 90 percent of student interns are women. Women constitute 9 percent of students in an experiential learning program in land surveying and 20 percent in an engineering-technician program.

The Women's Studies Program offers 16 courses on women through Women's Studies and the departments. Recent offerings include Introduction to Women's Studies; Women in the Middle Years; Women's Awareness; Frontier Women; and Autobiogra-

phial Writing—the Feminine Experience. The departments of education, nursing, and business offer instruction on issues specific to women in their courses. Faculty workshops are available on sexism and racism in the curriculum, the relationships among sex, race, and the selection of major field, nontraditional occupations, the needs of reentry women, and affirmative action and equal opportunity.

Women and Athletics. Thirty percent of intramural athletes and 36 percent of intercollegiate athletes are women, as are four of 12 paid intercollegiate coaches. Women receive 40 percent of athletic scholarships. Intercollegiate sports offered are basketball, cross-country, fencing, tennis, track, and volleyball.

Special Services and Programs for Women. *Health and Counseling.* Student Health employs 2 male physicians and 6 health-care providers, 5 of whom are women. No treatment specific to women is available. The counseling center is staffed by 2 men and 1 woman. Counseling is available on gynecological problems, birth control, abortion, rape and assault, and nutrition. Training in breast and gynecological self-examination is also available, as well as counseling on sexually-transmitted diseases. Counselors receive in-service training on avoiding sex-role stereotyping and racial bias.

Safety and Security. Measures consist of campus police without arrest authority and a rape crisis center. Two rapes and three assaults, one on a woman, were reported for 1980–81.

Career. In addition to printed information on nontraditional occupations for women, services include programs on women in nontraditional careers and a survey of vocational careers for women.

Other. The Office of Instruction operates the campus Women's Center, which serves some 2,700 women each year. Headed by a full-time, salaried administrator, the center sponsors programs for displaced homemakers, assertiveness training, a women's lecture series, as well as a program to build skills in mathematics.

Institutional Self-Description. "Clark College offers a reentry program, such special classes as Survey of Vocational Careers, Women's Studies courses, and job training at a reasonable cost."

Eastern Washington University
Cheney, WA 99004
Telephone: (509) 235-2371

★★ **Women and the**
Curriculum

5,597 undergraduates

	Amer. Ind.	Asian Amer.	Blacks	Hispanics	Whites
F	73	17	24	16	2,809
M	32	23	45	15	2,421
%	1.9	0.7	1.3	0.6	95.5

AAUW NWSA

Eastern Washington is a comprehensive public university. Of 7,000 students, 5,597 are undergraduates, 53 percent of the them women; 12 percent of women attend part-time. The median age of undergraduates is 21. Undergraduate and some graduate programs are available in education, business, social sciences, health professions, and arts and sciences. The Continuing Education program sponsors adult education. Public transportation, free transportation from remote parking lots, and on-campus parking for a fee are available to the 72 percent of students who commute.

Childcare is available near campus.

Policies to Ensure Fairness to Women. The Executive Assistant to the President assumes policymaking responsibilities, on a full-time basis, for equal-employment-opportunity and access-for-the-handicapped laws and regulations. A publicly communicated, written policy prohibits sexual harassment of students, faculty, and staff. A Committee on the Status of Women, which reports to the Provost for Academic Affairs, takes public stands on issues of concern to women students and sponsors workshops on women's issues. A Commission on Minority Affairs addresses the special concerns of minority women. Faculty are offered workshops on affirmative action and equal employment opportunity.

Women in Leadership Positions. *Students.* Of seven campus-wide student leadership positions available annually, the only one held by a woman in a recent three-year period has been the editorship of the newspaper. Women head four of 16 honorary societies.

Faculty. Fifty-five of 290 faculty members are women, almost half of whom hold permanent appointments. Three faculty women are black women and one is an American Indian. The ratio of female faculty to female students is 2 to 100; for males the ratio is 12 to 100.

Administrators. Men hold all top administrative positions, except that of director of athletics. Women chair two of 31 departments—home economics and speech pathology and audiology. Of five trustees, one is a white and one a black woman.

Women and the Curriculum. Most degrees earned by women are in education (33 percent), health professions (14 percent), business (11 percent), and public affairs (8 percent); 2 percent are in architecture, mathematics, and physical sciences.

The Women's Studies Program, which offers an undergraduate minor, is directed by a woman who holds a permanent faculty appointment. Some 25 courses on women are offered through Women's Studies and such departments as English, history, psychology, and sociology. The courses include Racism and Sexism; Coping with Re-Entry; Women in Power; Grandmothers, Mothers, and Daughters; Women, Literature, and Social Change; and Women in History. An official committee supervises the Women's Studies Program and encourages the development of courses on women in traditional departments. The departments of business, education, and social work provide some instruction on matters specific to women.

Eastern Washington is one of the few institutions in the U.S. that requires every undergraduate to take at least one course examining discrimination against women and minorities.

Women and Athletics. No information on intramural or club sports was provided. Twenty-eight percent of intercollegiate athletes are women, who receive 30 percent of athletic scholarships. Five of the 24 paid varsity coaches are women. Varsity sports for women are cross-country, gymnastics, softball, swimming, tennis, track, and volleyball.

Housing and Student Organizations. Single-sex and coeducational dormitories, as well as housing for married students with or without children and single parents with children, are available for the 28 percent of undergraduates who live on campus. A woman student whose husband is not enrolled is permitted to live in married student's housing. The three male and three female residence-hall directors are offered training about sexism and self-assertiveness.

The Women's Student Action Council, an advocacy group, sponsors workshops, speakers, and dormitory programs.

Special Services and Programs for Women. *Health and Counseling.* Health service is provided by contract with a local clinic. One female and three male counselors provide gynecological, birth control, abortion, and rape and assault counseling.

Safety and Security. Measures include night-time escort for women students, night-time, campus-wide bus service to residence areas, information sessions on campus safety and rape and assault prevention, and a rape crisis center. For 1980–81, the three reported assaults were all against men.

Career. Career workshops, programs by women in nontraditional occupations, and alumnae files organized by career are available.

Other. The well-funded Women's Center, operating on a budget of nearly $40,000 annually, serves 1,500 women per year, 25 percent of them from minority groups. The center's salaried coordinator works three-fourths-time. Academic Affairs and the Women's Center provide a battered women's program, displaced homemakers' program, women's lecture series, theater and other women's arts programs, and assertiveness/leadership training. The Center for Psychological Services sponsors a warmline—called Rap-in.

Institutional Self-Description. "Women's programs offer: 1) a Women's Studies minor with many academic classes; 2) a returning women's program; 3) a handsome Women's Center with a quiet, comfortable lounge for meeting friends, studying, holding meetings, a library, referral services, a scholarship file, support groups, stimulating noon programs—coffee, tea, and refrigerator for sack lunches, and career/personal counseling."

Green River Community College
12401 S.E. 320th, Auburn, WA 98002
Telephone: (206) 883-9111

Women in Leadership
- ★ students
- ★ faculty

3,042 undergraduates

	Amer. Ind.	Asian Amer.	Blacks	Hispanics	Whites
F	19	14	19	12	1,248
M	18	25	23	35	1,568
%	1.2	1.3	1.4	1.6	94.5

NWSA

This public, two-year college founded in 1965 serves some 6,300 students, of whom 53 percent are women. Of the 3,042 students registered in degree programs, 44 percent are women; 23 percent of women attend part-time. The median age of students is 27, and recent figures indicate that 19 percent of women students are over age 40.

The college offers liberal arts and engineering transfer programs, as well as a range of vocational and technical programs including electronics, civil engineering technology, air traffic control, court reporting, forestry, and welding technologies. Alternative scheduling includes day and evening classes held both on and off campus, a weekend college, a summer session, and self-paced/contract learning. The Associate Dean of Instruction supervises adult continuing education.

All students commute to the suburban campus which is accessibly by public transportation. There is a fee for parking on campus.

Policies to Ensure Fairness to Women. The Dean of Students has responsibility part-time for policy relating to equal-employment-opportunity, equal-educational-opportunity, and handicapped-access legislation. A written campus policy prohibits sexual harassment of staff; complaints are resolved by a formal grievance procedure. An active Committee on the Status of Women reports to the Coordinator of the Women's Program, includes student members with voting rights, and takes public stands on issues of importance to students. Both this committee and the Committee on Minority Affairs address the concerns of minority women.

Women in Leadership Positions. *Students.* The participation of women in campus-wide leadership is good. Of the seven campus-wide posts available in recent years, women held the presidencies of the sophomore class, the student governing body, and the student union each for two years.

Faculty. Twenty-seven percent of the 99 full-time faculty are women. There are 3 female faculty for every 100 female students and 5 male faculty for every 100 male students.

Administrators. All top administrators are male. Women chair the departments of health and social sciences. Of five trustees, two are women.

Women and the Curriculum. Fifty-eight percent of women earn degrees in arts and sciences, 16 percent in business and commerce, 14 percent in health technologies, and 5 percent in public service. Five percent of women graduate in such nontraditional fields as mechanical and engineering technologies. Programs encourage women to enter such nontraditional careers as science, engineering, architecture, accounting, computer science, law enforcement, and electronics. Twenty percent of students in cooperative education programs and 10 percent of student interns are women.

A Women's Program offers three courses on women: Survival Skills, Black Women Today, and Women and Nontraditional Work. The department of business offers one course on women: Personal Finance—Women. In addition, the departments of physical education, nursing, social work, and business offer instruction on some matters specific to women in their curricula. An official committee is assigned to collect curricular materials on women. Faculty workshops are held on such topics as sexism in the curriculum, affirmative action, nontraditional careers, and the needs of reentry women.

Women and Athletics. Fifty percent of intercollegiate and 32 percent of intramural athletes are women. Half the athletic scholarships go to women. Four of eleven paid varsity coaches are women. The intramural program offers a good number and variety of team sports. Intercollegiate teams include basketball, cross-country, soccer, softball, tennis, track and field, and volleyball.

Special Services and Programs for Women. *Health and Counseling.* The student health service, staffed by one woman health-care provider, makes referrals for medical treatment. The student counseling service has a staff of five, of whom two are women. It offers such services specific to women as gynecological, birth control, abortion,and rape and assault counseling.

Safety and Security. Measures consist of campus police without arrest authority, high-intensity lighting, self-defense courses, and a rape crisis center. Of two assaults reported for 1980–81, one was on a woman.

Career. Career information programs include workshops and lectures on nontraditional careers, nonsexist/nonracist printed information on careers, information on job discrimination, and networking between alumnae and female students.

Other. Continuing Education houses the Women's Center, staffed by a full-time director. Of the 8,000 women served annually by the center, 5 percent are members of minority groups.

Institutional Self-Description. ''GRCC has a personalized advising process whereby each student is assigned a faculty member for guidance in program and class selection. Women's Center-sponsored 'Sampler' gives new entry students that first tour and acquaintance with the system. This sampler gives students the opportunity for support-group formation.''

♠ On-campus evening and/or weekend classes	Ⓜ️Ⓐ Commission on minority affairs
🏛 Off-campus classes	📖 Women's Studies program
🚌 Accessible by public transportation	🏠 Women's center
👫 On-campus childcare facilities	AAUW Member, American Association of University Women
◄ Publicly communicated sexual harassment policy, includes students	NWSA Member, National Women's Studies Association
Ⓢ/Ⓦ Commission on status of women	CROW On-campus Center for Research on Women

Seattle Central Community College
1701 Broadway, Seattle, WA 98122
Telephone: (206) 587-3800

Women in Leadership
★★ **faculty**

3,972 undergraduates

	Amer. Ind.	Asian Amer.	Blacks	Hispanics	Whites
F	70	97	277	27	1,358
M	52	83	267	31	1,185
%	3.5	5.2	15.8	1.7	73.8

Seattle Central, the only urban two-year college in the Washington State Community College system, offers comprehensive educational services to 8,432 students, 3,972 of whom are enrolled in degree programs. Just over half of the degree students are women, two-thirds of whom attend full-time. The median age of all undergraduates is 29.

Seattle Central offers the first two years of liberal arts and preprofessional programs, as well as occupational and vocational programs leading to certificates and associate degrees. It provides on-campus evening classes, a summer session, and offers vocational training at two branch campuses. All students commute. The main campus is accessible by public transportation; students can park on campus for a fee.

On-campus childcare facilities accommodate 70 children at a fixed daily rate. Twenty-one percent of all students' requests for the service can be met. Private childcare facilities are available near the campus.

Policies to Ensure Fairness to Women. The Director of Minority Affairs/Affirmative Action and the Director of Special Programs both serve as full-time equal-opportunity officers, who review policies and practices relating to equal-employment-opportunity, educational-sex-equity, and handicapped-access legislation. A Commission on Minority Affairs addresses the concerns of minority women.

Women in Leadership Positions. *Students.* Women students held 30 percent of the leadership positions on campus in a recent three-year period. Women were president of the student body once and editor-in-chief of the campus newspaper twice.

Faculty. Thirty-nine percent of the 184 full-time faculty are women. According to recent information, the 87 full-time female faculty include 15 black, 13 Asian American, and 2 Hispanic women. There are 5 female faculty for every 100 female students and 7 male faculty for every 100 male students.

Administrators. All chief administrators are male, except for the head librarian. Three of the eight departments are chaired by women: business and commerce, health and human services, and basic studies. One department chair is a black woman and 1 is Asian American. Two of the 5 trustees are women, 1 of whom is Asian American.

Women and the Curriculum. Most women earn degrees in the arts and sciences (31 percent), public service (21 percent), and business/commercial technologies (20 percent). The college sponsors a program designed to prepare women for a career in trades. Sixty percent of the students in cooperative education programs are women.

The department of human development offers several courses on women: Introduction to Women in Trades, Women in Society, and Math Without Fear. Topics for faculty workshops include racism and the curriculum, the relationships among sex, race, and selection of major field, nontraditional occupations for women and men, and the needs of reentry women.

Women and Athletics. The college has no gymnasium and no organized intercollegiate or intramural sports programs. A few women students participate in club sports.

Special Services and Programs for Women. *Health and Counseling.* There is no student health service. No information was provided on student counseling.

Safety and Security. Security measures include campus police, high-intensity lighting in all areas, information sessions on campus safety and crime prevention, and a rape crisis center. During 1980–81, seven assaults were reported on campus, two on women.

Career. Career Center Services of special interest to women include workshops and job discrimination information on nontraditional occupations, lectures by women employed in such occupations, and printed information on nontraditional fields of study for women. There is also a course on career planning.

Other. The campus Women's Center serves approximately 5,000 women annually, 40 percent of whom are black or Asian American women. Operated by Student Services with a budget of $23,500 and directed by a full-time administrator, the center is used primarily by older students, community women, and staff.

The college has an active Women's Program which has recently grown from a half-time, one-person office to a full-time office with three additional part-time staff people. The program's publication, *The Women's Forum Quarterly,* appears three times a year and is distributed statewide. The program sponsors a women's lecture series, a telephone service for information, referrals and support, and programs specifically geared to deaf women and reentry women. The college has one of the largest programs for the deaf on the West Coast, and is the only Women's Program in Washington with a special emphasis on deaf women.

Institutional Self-Description. "Seattle Central offers excellent trade and industrial training in printing, carpentry, marine engineering, welding, and machine shop. The college is sensitive to women in nontraditional trades. Our campus has an excellent developmental program and college transfer program. It is located in an inner city with a diverse cultural mix (45 percent ethnic-minority student body). Technical training is available in high-paying fields: chemical technology, culinary arts, drafting, respiratory therapy, etc."

Spokane Community College
N. 1810 Greene St., Spokane, WA 99207
Telephone: (509) 535-0641

Women in Leadership
★ faculty

4,071 undergraduates

	Amer. Ind.	Asian Amer.	Blacks	Hispanics	Whites
F	35	15	12	14	1,621
M	48	29	26	24	2,216
%	2.1	1.1	0.9	0.9	95.0

Spokane Community is a public, two-year college that provides a variety of full- and part-time day and evening programs to over 9,000 students. Forty-two percent of the 4,071 undergraduates are women, and all but 11 percent of the women attend full-time. The average age of day students is 26; of evening students, 34. Spokane Community offers two-year transfer and vocational programs and adult education. Alternative schedules include evening classes both on and off campus, weekend college, and Tuesday-Thursday College. There is a Continuing Education for Women Program. All students commute by public transportation or car; on-campus parking is provided.

An on-campus daycare facility, limited to 25 children, can accommodate about 30 percent of students' requests. Students have priority at the facility, which charges $75 per month or $1.10 an hour. Private childcare facilities are also available near campus.

Policies to Ensure Fairness to Women. Four administrators are responsible part-time for compliance with legislation concerning equal employment opportunity, sex equity for students, and handicapped access. Two of the administrators have policymaking authority. A written policy on sexual harassment of students, faculty, and staff has been publicly communicated to faculty and staff; complaints are handled informally. The Sex Equity Task Force, appointed by and responsible to the President of the college, meets frequently and makes recommendations on matters of interest to women.

Women in Leadership Positions. *Students.* There are two campus leadership positions. In a recent three year period, a woman was editor of the newspaper for one year.

Faculty. Twenty-eight percent of the 197 full-time faculty are women. There are 4 female faculty for every 100 female students and 6 male faculty for every 100 male students.

Administrators. Men hold the top-level positions, except head of the library. Women chair four of 22 departments: cosmetology, secretarial sciences, allied health, and nursing. Two women sit on the 5-member Board of Trustees. One of the 4 commencement speakers in 1981 was a woman.

Women and the Curriculum. Most two-year degrees awarded to women are in arts and sciences (42 percent), with smaller numbers in business and commercial technologies (25 percent), and health technologies (17 percent).

The liberal arts division offers four courses on women: Growth and Development for Women, Interpersonal Relations, Emerging Women, and Women's Issues. An official committee develops curricular materials on women and encourages the development of Women's Studies courses. Faculty are offered workshops and other educational programs on sexism and racism in the curriculum, and the needs of reentry women.

Women and Athletics. No information was provided.

Special Services and Programs for Women. *Health and Counseling.* There is no student health service. The student counseling center makes referrals only.

Safety and Security. Campus and city police are available. Security measures include high-intensity lighting in all areas, information sessions on rape and assault precautions, self-defense courses for women, and a rape crisis center. There were two assaults on women reported for 1980–81. Information on the incidence of rapes was not provided.

Career. Services include career workshops, lectures by women employed in nontraditional fields, and information on job discrimination. There is also a Non-Traditional Career Club on campus. Faculty are offered workshops on nontraditional careers for women.

Other. The well-funded Women's Center ($40,000 a year) serves 500 women annually. Assertiveness training and a women's lecture series are sponsored by the liberal arts division. The local YWCA sponsors a battered women's program and, in cooperation with the college, a program to build women's skills in mathematics.

Institutional Self-Description. "Spokane Community College strongly supports the increasing numbers of women choosing to attend this campus, and provides an environment in which *every* student may have the opportunity to succeed, regardless of age, income, background or educational experience."

Washington State University

Pullman, WA 99164
Telephone: (509) 335-1794

★ **Women and the Curriculum**

★★ **Women and Athletics**

13,677 undergraduates

	Amer. Ind.	Asian Amer.	Blacks	Hispanics	Whites
F	61	96	95	52	5,701
M	53	128	146	77	6,902
%	0.9	1.7	1.8	1.0	94.7

🏠 🏛 👫 ⚒ [S/W] [M/A] 📖 ⚧ **NWSA**

Established in 1890 as a land-grant institution, Washington State University, located in eastern Washington State, attracts some 16,680 students to a range of undergraduate, graduate, and professional programs. The Office of Continuing University Studies provides adult education and extension services. Alternative class schedules, off-campus locations, and a summer session are available.

Women are 45 percent of the 13,677 undergraduates; 4 percent of the women attend part-time. The median age of undergraduates is 21. For the 38 percent who live off campus or commute, bus service is available in Pullman only. On-campus parking is provided for a fee.

WSU estimates that 40 percent of requests by students for childcare can be accommodated in low-cost campus facilities. There is a long waiting list. Private childcare arrangements may be made near the university.

Policies to Ensure Fairness to Women. The full-time Director of Affirmative Action originates and reviews policies relating to equal employment opportunities, sex equity for students, and handicapped accessibility; full-time assistant and associate directors monitor compliance. A published policy prohibits sexual harassment. Complaints are handled through a formal grievance procedure. An active Committee on the Status of Women, which includes students as voting members, reports to the president. The Committee on Minority Affairs addresses the concerns of minority women.

Women in Leadership Positions. *Students.* Information on opportunities for women students to assume campus-wide leadership was not provided by the institution.

Faculty. Women are 15 percent of a full-time faculty of 783. There are 2 female faculty for every 100 female students and 9 male faculty for every 100 male students.

Administrators. The Director of Libraries and chief development officer are women. Women chair five of 30 departments: electrical engineering, child and family studies, clothing, textiles, and interior design, women's physical education, and nursing. The Colleges of Social Science and Humanities, Home Economics, and Nursing are headed by women.

Women and the Curriculum. Most women graduating with bachelor's degrees major in education (17 percent), health professions (12 percent), home economics (11 percent), and business (11 percent). Ten percent major in nontraditional subjects, mostly agriculture. Women students are encouraged to prepare for nontraditional careers by conferences and through innovative programs in science and engineering. A proposed cooperative education program to combine academic with related work experience will seek the participation of women, ethnic and racial minorities, older students, and the handicapped.

The Women's Studies Program offers an 18-credit minor. Twenty courses on women are available through the departments of sociology, history, psychology, political science, fine arts, English, child and family development, and Women's Studies. Recent courses include Women in the Workplace, Sociology of Professions and Occupations, History of Women in the American West, Psychology of Women, and Women Artists. The Women's Studies Director is responsible for promoting and monitoring the integration of women's materials and perspectives across the curriculum.

Such current issues as sex-role stereotyping in sports and sex-fair curricula are part of the preparation of future teachers. Services for abused spouses and displaced homemakers are topics covered in the School of Social Work.

Minority Women. Twenty-four minority women are in integrated, 32 in all-minority, sororities. A minority woman is a student assistant in the counseling center. Counseling staff receive in-service training on multi-cultural counseling and racial bias. Residence-hall staff are offered awareness-training on racism.

Such organizations as the Council of Ethnic Women, Mujeres Unitas, Native American Women, Black Women's Kaukus, and Asian American Women serve as advocates for minority women. The Council of Ethnic Women sponsors an annual women's week.

Women and Athletics. Intramural, club, and intercollegiate programs offer excellent opportunities for organized, competitive individual and team athletics, with a high number and variety of sports in each program. Forty-eight percent of intramural and 28 percent of intercollegiate athletes are women; women receive 30 percent of athletic scholarships. Almost a third of the 37 paid coaches for intercollegiate sports are women. All women's intercollegiate teams played in tournaments in 1980. The intercollegiate sports offered are basketball, cross-country, field hockey, gymnastics, skiing, swimming and diving, tennis, track and field, and volleyball.

Housing and Student Organizations. Sixty-two percent of undergraduates live on campus. Single-sex and coeducational dormitories, cooperative housing, and housing for married students and single parents with children are available. Dormitories restrict hours for visitors of the opposite sex. Ten of 18 residence-hall directors are women. Staff are offered awareness-training on the avoidance of sexism, and on sex education, birth control, and drugs and alcohol.

Twenty percent of full-time undergraduate women are members of social sororities, which provide housing for their members. Associated Women Students serves as an advocacy group for women on campus.

Special Services and Programs for Women. *Health and Counseling.* The student health service provides some medical attention specific to women, including gynecological, birth control, and rape and assault treatment. One of 8 physicians is female, as are 10 other health-care providers. The regular student health insurance partially covers abortion and maternity expenses. Four of the 10 permanent staff of the counseling service are women. Students have access to birth control, abortion, rape and assault, and eating disorders counseling.

Safety and Security. Measures consist of campus police with arrest authority and a night-time escort service for women students. A rape crisis center is available. Forty-one assaults (15 on women) and five rapes were reported for 1980–81.

Other. A Women's Center has a part-time faculty director. Programming includes alternatives to violence, assertiveness training (in cooperation with the counseling service), and an occasional lecture series. Theater and other arts programs run by the Association for Women Students and a telephone service of information, referral, and support sponsored by the Dean of Students Offices are also available.

Special Features. Regional women's history is stressed at WSU. Special help for returning women, organized by other returning women, is available through the Reentry Advisory Program.

Institutional Self-Description. "Female enrollments in the sciences are rising rapidly, especially in engineering and veterinary medicine. Many groups, among them the Office of Programs for Women and the Women's Studies Program, are actively working to meet the changing needs of women students."

Western Washington University
Bellingham, WA 98225
Telephone: (206) 676-3757

★ **Women and the Curriculum**

8,327 undergraduates

	Amer. Ind.	Asian Amer.	Blacks	Hispanics	Whites
F	39	63	52	19	4,127
M	31	48	42	30	3,806
%	0.8	1.3	1.1	0.6	96.1

🏠 🏛 🚐 👫 🔨 📖 ⚲ **AAUW**

Established as a teachers' preparatory school in 1893, Western Washington University was designated a regional university in 1977. Some 9,800 students are attracted to its undergraduate and master's programs. There is a division of continuing adult education. Alternative schedules include evening classes and a summer session; some classes are located off campus.

Women are 52 percent of the 8,327 undergraduates; 5 percent attend part-time. For the 67 percent who live off campus or commute, the university is accessible by public transportation. There is on-campus parking, with free transportation from distant parking lots.

Childcare facilities are cooperative and charge fees on a sliding scale. Forty-five children can be accommodated. Private arrangements may be made nearby.

Policies to Ensure Fairness to Women. The Director of Affirmative Action is responsible for policy and monitors compliance with equal-employment-opportunity, sex-equity, and handicapped-accessibility legislation. A campus policy prohibits sexual harassment; complaints are handled both informally and confidentially through a formal grievance procedure. There is a Committee on Minority Affairs.

Women in Leadership Positions. *Students.* Opportunities for women students to exercise all-campus leadership are limited. In recent years, a women was president of the student body once.

Faculty. Women are 15 percent of a full-time faculty of 429. There are 2 female faculty for every 100 female students and 10 male faculty for every 100 male students.

Administrators. The Director of Women's Athletics is female. Males hold all other higher administrative positions. Women chair three of 37 departments: home economics, physical education, and nursing. One of six deans or directors of academic units is a woman.

Women and the Curriculum. A majority of undergraduate degrees earned by women are in education (21 percent), business (12 percent), social sciences (12 percent), public affairs (9 percent), and interdisciplinary studies (8 percent). Three percent major in such nontraditional areas as architecture, computer science, engineering, mathematics, and the physical sciences.

The Women's Studies Program, directed part-time by a permanently appointed faculty member, offers an undergraduate minor through liberal studies and the residential college. A recent course in the program is Issues of the Women's Movement. An official committee collects curricular materials and works to develop the Women's Studies offerings.

Such current issues as mathematics confidence among females, sex-fair curricula, coeducational physical education classes, health-care information important to minority women, and workplace discrimination are part of the preparation of future teachers, health-care workers, social workers, and business students, respectively.

Women and Athletics. Small intercollegiate and intramural programs provide limited opportunities for individual and team sports. Coeducational and club sports are also available. Forty-two percent of the varsity and one-third of the intramural athletes are women. Nine of 24 paid coaches are female. The intercollegiate sports offered are: basketball, crew, cross-country, soccer, track and field, and volleyball.

Housing and Student Organizations. Fairhaven is the residential college. For the 33 percent who live on campus, single-sex and coeducational dormitories and housing for married students, single parents with children, and senior citizens are available. A married woman whose spouse is not enrolled may live in married students' housing. Residence halls restrict hours for visitors of the opposite sex. Seven of 15 residence-hall directors are female. Staff are offered awareness-training on sex education and birth control.

Among groups which serve as advocates for women on campus are the Women's Center, Women's Space, and the Union of Sexual Minorities.

Special Services and Programs for Women. *Health and Counseling.* The student health center provides medical treatment for gynecological prolems. Physicians are on contract from the community. There are eight female health-care workers on staff. The counseling center, staffed by six women and four men, offers gynecological, birth control, abortion, and rape and assault counseling. Staff are offered in-service training on the avoidance of sex-role stereotyping and racial bias.

Safety and Security. In addition to campus and city police, a night-time escort service for women, night-time bus service to residence areas, high-intensity lighting, self-defense courses, information sessions on safety and crime prevention, and a rape crisis center are available. No rapes were reported for 1980–81; information on assaults was not provided.

Career. Workshops, speakers, printed materials, and job discrimination information relating to women in nontraditional careers, as well as a program of contacts between alumnae and students are provided by career services or other units.

Other. A Women's Center, under the direction of a salaried student, offers programs throughout the year. Women's Space, a resource center for the exploration of women's issues, includes a library, instruction, and social groups. Chrysallis Art Gallery promotes women's art. STRATA (Students That Return After Time Away) helps older students returning to campus, offers social activities, childcare cooperatives, and support groups.

Institutional Self-Description. "Western Washington University offers a concentration in Women's Studies through the Department of Liberal Studies and Fairhaven College. A variety of on-campus organizations offer unique opportunities for women to gather, learn, and share experiences."

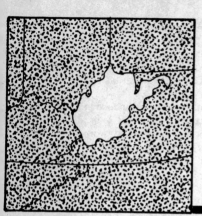

WEST VIRGINIA

Glenville State College
Glenville, WV 26351
Telephone: (304) 462-7361

Women in Leadership
★★★ students
★ faculty

1,319 undergraduates

	Amer. Ind.	Asian Amer.	Blacks	Hispanics	Whites
F	6	1	9	1	643
M	4	2	30	0	594
%	0.8	0.2	3.0	0.1	95.9

A public, four-year college, Glenville State serves 1,700 students, including 1,300 degree students. Half the undergraduates are women; 28 percent of women attend part-time. Both four- and two-year degrees are awarded, most of them in business and education. On- and off-campus evening sessions and summer sessions are available. Twenty percent of students commute; on-campus parking is provided at a fee.

Policies to Ensure Fairness to Women. The part-time Equal Opportunity/Affirmative Action Officer votes on policymaking committees; a part-time Coordinator reviews campus policies concerning the handicapped. A written policy prohibiting sexual harassment of faculty and staff has been communicated to those groups.

Women in Leadership Positions. *Students.* Women held most of the student leadership positions during a recent three-year period, including student body president, editor-in-chief of the newspaper, manager of the radio station, president of the residence-hall council, and head of all four classes.

Faculty. Twenty-nine percent of the 72 faculty members are women. Thirty-eight percent of women (and 53 percent of men) hold permanent faculty appointments. There are 4 female faculty for every 100 female students and 9 male faculty for every 100 male students.

Administrators. All top administrators are men. A woman chairs the language arts department.

Women and the Curriculum. Most four-year degrees awarded to women are in education (54 percent), public affairs (15 percent), and business (10 percent). Two percent are in computer science, the only nontraditional field offered. Women earn 44 percent of two-year degrees awarded, most of them in business and public service programs. Women receive about one-third of student internships and science field-service appointments.

The education department offers pre-service training for teachers on mathematics avoidance and provides instruction on the development and use of sex-fair curricula. There are no courses on women.

Women and Athletics. Women are 20 percent of the 202 intercollegiate and 40 percent of the 250 intramural athletes. The limited intramural program offers women three team sports. Of 15 paid intercollegiate coaches, two are women. The intercollegiate sports in which women compete are basketball, track and field, and volleyball.

Housing and Student Organizations. Single-sex dormitories with restricted hours for visitors of the opposite sex, as well as housing for married students and single parents with children, are provided for the 60 percent of students who live on campus. Campus sororities provide housing for members.

Special Services and Programs for Women. *Health and Counseling.* The health-service, staffed by 1 man and 1 woman, provides treatment for gynecological problems and for rape and assault. One man and 1 woman counsel on gynecological problems, birth control, and abortion.

Safety and Security. Measures consist of campus police and high-intensity lighting. In 1980–81, four assaults, none on women, were reported.

Career. Workshops and job discrimination information on nontraditional occupations, updated files of alumnae by specific careers, and programs to establish contacts between alumnae and female students are available.

Other. The Office of Student Affairs sponsors an annual women's week.

Institutional Self-Description. None provided.

Parkersburg Community College
Route 5, Box 167-A
Parkersburg, WV 26101
Telephone: (304) 424-8000

Women in Leadership
★★★ students
★★ faculty

1,964 undergraduates

	Amer. Ind.	Asian Amer.	Blacks	Hispanics	Whites
F	5	3	7	3	1,033
M	2	4	4	2	919
%	0.4	0.4	0.6	0.3	98.5

A comprehensive, public, two-year college, Parkersburg attracts some 3,000 students, of whom 1,964 are registered in degree programs. Fifty-three percent of degree students are women; 57 percent of women attend part-time. The median age of all students is 26, with 37 percent of the women between 26 and 40, and 12 percent over age 40.

Parkersburg offers associate degrees and certificates in arts and sciences, vocational fields, and pre-professional areas. Adult education is available through the division of continuing education/community services. Alternative scheduling options include evening classes, a summer session, a weekend college, and self-paced/contract learning; off-campus class locations are also available. All students commute to the suburban campus. Free, on-campus parking is available; the campus is not accessible by public transportation.

The college-operated childcare facility can accommodate 18 children on a first-come, first-served basis. Charges for the service, which is available from 7:30 a.m. to 10 p.m., are based on a fixed daily fee. Three-fourths of students' requests for the service can be met.

Policies to Ensure Fairness to Women. Two administrators have full-time responsibility for monitoring compliance with legislation on equal employment opportunity, sex equity for students, and handicapped accessibility. Complaints of sexual harassment are resolved through a formal campus grievance procedure.

Women in Leadership Positions. *Students.* The two campus-wide leadership positions are usually held by women. In a recent three-year period, women served three times as editor-in-chief of the campus newspaper and once as president of the student body. The sole campus honorary society is headed by a woman.

Faculty. Forty-one percent of the 74 full-time faculty are women, a proportion above the average for public two-year colleges in this guide. There are 7 female faculty for every 100 female students and 11 male faculty for every 100 male students.

Administrators. All chief administrative positions are held by men. Women chair two of seven departments: business and humanities. Four of the 11 faculty senate members are women, including 1 Asian American woman. Four women sit on an important 7-member faculty committee. One of 6 trustees is a woman, as is 1 of the 12 regents. In a recent year, the sole commencement speaker was a woman.

Women and the Curriculum. Most women earn two-year degrees in health technologies (61 percent), with smaller numbers in business (13 percent), public affairs (12 percent), and arts and sciences (11 percent). Two percent of women graduate in such nontraditional fields as mechanical arts and engineering.

There are no courses on women. The division of social work includes instruction on some issues specific to women.

Women and Athletics. Parkersburg offers a small intramural program, but there are no intercollegiate sports. Thirty-five percent of the intramural athletes are women, who participate in bowling, coeducational softball, tennis, and volleyball.

Special Services and Programs for Women. *Health and Counseling.* The student health service is staffed by 1 male physician and 1 female health-care provider. The counseling center employs 2 female and 2 male professionals. No medical treatment specific to women is available. Counseling is available for gynecological problems, birth control, abortion, and rape and assault.

Safety and Security. Measures consist of campus police without arrest authority, night-time escorts, and high-intensity lighting. No rapes or assaults on women were reported for 1980–81.

Career. Workshops and nonsexist/nonracist printed information on nontraditional occupations for women are available.

Institutional Self-Description. None provided.

West Virginia State College
Institute, WV 25112
Telephone: (304) 766-3000

Women in Leadership
★ students
★★ faculty

3,127 undergraduates

	Amer. Ind.	Asian Amer.	Blacks	Hispanics	Whites
F	0	13	315	1	1,236
M	0	39	382	0	1,141
%	0.0	1.7	22.3	0.0	76.0

West Virginia State is a public, liberal arts college located in a village just outside Charleston. It enrolls 3,678 students, including 3,127 undergraduates. Half the undergraduates are women; half the women attend part-time. The average age of undergraduates is 26.

The college offers associate and bachelor's degrees in a range of fields, as well as an adult education program and a weekend college. Classes meet on campus day and evening and off campus in the evening. There is a summer session. For the majority of students who live off campus or commute, there is public transportation and campus parking for a fee.

An on-campus childcare center is open to all members of the college community. Additional, private childcare facilities are nearby.

Policies to Ensure Fairness to Women. The Affirmative Action Coordinator is responsible part-time for the implementation of laws pertaining to sex equity, equal employment opportunity, and handicapped access.

Women in Leadership Positions. *Students.* In a recent three-year period, women served one year in each of the two student leadership positions.

Faculty. Forty-one percent of 131 full-time faculty are women, a proportion above the national average. Of the female faculty, 15 are black women. There are 7 female faculty for every 100 female students and the same ratio for male faculty to male students.

Administrators. The top administrators are men, except the Provost for Academic Affairs. Women chair six of 21 departments: English, business administration, biology, economics, modern languages, and consumer resources. Half of the 18-member faculty senate are women.

Women and the Curriculum. Most women graduates earn bachelor's degrees in interdisciplinary studies (24 percent), public affairs (20 percent), and education (15 percent). Five percent major in such nontraditional areas as mathematics or physical sciences. Most women receiving two-year certificates and degrees specialize in business and commerce technologies and public service technologies.

Five courses on women, including Images of the Mountain Woman; Women, Change and Society; and Sexism and the Law are offered by the departments of English, psychology, political science, general studies, and sociology.

Minority Women. Twenty-one percent of undergraduate women are members of minority groups, mainly black. The college Provost is a black woman. Black women chair two departments and hold three seats on the 18-member faculty senate. One of two honorary degree recipients at the 1981 graduation was black woman.

Women and Athletics. Incomplete information on the organized women's sports program indicates three intercollegiate teams, two of which are coeducational. Intercollegiate sports offered are basketball, golf (coeducational), and tennis (coeducational).

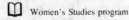

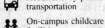
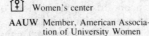
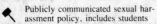

On-campus evening and/or weekend classes

Off-campus classes

Accessible by public transportation

On-campus childcare facilities

Publicly communicated sexual harassment policy, includes students

Commission on status of women

Commission on minority affairs

Women's Studies program

Women's center

AAUW Member, American Association of University Women

NWSA Member, National Women's Studies Association

CROW On-campus Center for Research on Women

Housing and Student Organizations. Eight percent of undergraduates live in single-sex dormitories. A married students' dormitory is available for students with or without children.

Special Services and Programs for Women. *Health and Counseling.* The student health service has one male physician. There is a student counseling center. No information was provided on health and counseling services specific to women.

Safety and Security. No information was supplied.

Other. Assertiveness training workshops are offered.

Institutional Self-Description. "WVSC is a place where women are doing, rather than talking about doing, things for institutional change. Although Women's Studies and programs for women have not yet been developed, the potential exists. Women have recently achieved positions of policy- and decision-making that will soon have effects on curriculum and institutional goals."

West Virginia University
Morgantown, WV 26506
Telephone: (304) 293-3430

★ **Women and the Curriculum**

★★★ **Women and Athletics**

14,356 undergraduates

	Amer. Ind.	Asian Amer.	Blacks	Hispanics	Whites
F	1	5	72	5	6,027
M	6	11	102	9	7,809
%	0.1	0.1	1.2	0.1	98.5

Established in 1867 as a comprehensive land-grant and state institution, West Virginia University attracts some 21,400 students to a variety of undergraduate, graduate, and professional degree programs. There is a Center for Extension and Continuing Education for adult students. Off-campus classes and alternative class schedules, including self-paced learning contracts, weekend courses, evening classes, and a summer session are available.

Women are 43 percent of the 14,356 undergraduates; 9 percent of the women attend part-time. The median age of undergraduates is 20; 7 percent are older than 25. For the student who lives off campus, the university is accessible by public transportation. Campus parking is covered by student fees.

Private arrangements for childcare may be made close to the university.

Policies to Ensure Fairness to Women. A full-time Assistant to the President reviews policies and practices related to equal employment opportunities and the accessibility of all programs and activities to students, including the handicapped. A published policy prohibits sexual harassment. Complaints are handled through a formal grievance procedure. The Council for Women's Concerns, which includes students as voting members, the Affirmative Action Committee, and the Black Community Concerns Committee address issues of concern to women, including minority women.

Women in Leadership Positions. *Students.* Opportunities for women students to assume campus-wide leadership are far below the average for public research institutions in this guide. In recent years, no woman has held a campus-wide student office. Women head three of six honorary societies.

Faculty. Women are 22 percent of a full-time faculty of 964. According to a recent report, 10 black, 2 American Indian, 10 Asian American, and 2 Hispanic women are on the full-time faculty. The ratio of female faculty to female students is 4 to 100. The ratio of male faculty to male students is 10 to 100.

Administrators. Men occupy all higher administrative positions. Women chair 13 of 105 departments; one woman chair is Asian American. The Dean of the School of Nursing and the Director of Gerontology are female.

Women and the Curriculum. Most women earning bachelor's degrees major in the health professions, education, business and management, and home economics. Ten percent major in such nontraditional areas as agriculture, architecture, computer science, engineering, and the physical sciences, with the greater numbers in agriculture and engineering.

The Women's Studies Program offers electives, including a course called Introduction to Women's Studies. Other courses available through the departments of English, history, political science, psychology, and sociology/anthropology, include Human Sexuality, Appalachian Women, Images of Women in Literature, Women and Politics, Policy and Law, and Sociology of Sex Roles. The Women's Studies Program, directed part-time by a permanent, full-time faculty member, works to augment offerings, collects curricular materials on women, and advocates the development of courses on women in traditional departments.

Such current issues as sex-fair curricula, coeducational sports classes, reproductive choice, health-care information important to minority women, services for abused spouses, and discrimination in the workplace are part of the preparation of future teachers, health-care providers, social workers, and business students.

Women and Athletics. Intramural and intercollegiate programs offer outstanding opportunities for organized, competitive, individual and team sports. Club sports are also available. The university reports special facilities for riflery and indoor archery. Twenty percent of intramural, 25 percent of club, and 56 percent of intercollegiate athletes are women. Women receive 30 percent of the athletic scholarships. Fourteen of 27 paid coaches are female. Women's intercollegiate teams played in tournaments in 1980. The intercollegiate sports offered are basketball, cross-country, gymnastics, riflery, softball, swimming, tennis, track and field, and volleyball.

Housing and Student Organizations. Approximately one-quarter of the undergraduates live on campus. Single-sex and coeducational dormitories and housing for married students and single parents with children are available. A married woman student whose spouse is not enrolled may live in married students' housing. Residence-halls restrict hours for visitors of the opposite sex. Half of the residence-hall directors are female. Awareness-training on sexism and racism is offered to the staff.

Fourteen percent of the full-time undergraduate women belong to social sororities; 25 women are in all-minority sororities. Sororities and fraternities provide housing for their members. Among groups which serve as advocates for women on campus is Samothrace.

Special Services and Programs for Women. *Health and Counseling.* The student health service provides some medical attention specific to women, including gynecological, birth control, and rape and assault treatment. Two of 7 physicians are female, as are 6 other health-care providers. Three of 8 professional staff in the counseling service are women. Staff are offered in-service training on sex-role stereotyping, racial bias, and gay rights. Students have access to gynecological, birth control, abortion, and rape and assault counseling. Assertiveness training is available.

Safety and Security. Measures include campus police with arrest authority, bonded deputy sheriffs, night-time bus service to residence areas, information sessions on safety and crime prevention, and a rape crisis center. A total of 35 assaults, two of them sexual, were reported for 1980–81.

Career. Workshops and nonsexist/nonracist printed materials which focus on women in nontraditional careers and fields of study, as well as a career library with sections for displaced homemakers and women in nontraditional occupations are provided.

Other. The Women's Studies Program sponsors a lecture series and an annual women's film festival. There is a woman's theater group. Community organizations sponsor services for battered women and displaced homemakers, as well as a telephone line of information, referral, and support.

Special Features. The Buswell Award recognizes outstanding contributions to women on campus. The Women's Resource Guide, annual women's festival, Women in Law, and feminist audio-visual materials are of particular interest.

Institutional Self-Description. "At West Virginia University, women with goals in nontraditional fields such as business or accounting, mining or engineering would find very strong academic programs. Self-motivated women interested in encouraging nonracist, nonsexist, curricula would find an improving environment in which their contributions could be significant."

Wheeling College
316 Washington Avenue
Wheeling, WV 26003
Telephone: (304) 243-2233

Women in Leadership
★★ administrators

777 undergraduates

	Amer. Ind.	Asian Amer.	Blacks	Hispanics	Whites
F	0	2	5	1	371
M	0	3	18	2	369
%	0.0	0.7	3.0	0.4	96.0

  AAUW

Established by the Jesuits in 1954, Wheeling College is a coeducational, liberal arts institution that remains affiliated with the Roman Catholic Church. Of the 1,144 students who are enrolled, 777 are undergraduates. About half the undergraduates are women, 87 percent of whom attend part-time. A variety of undergraduate, graduate, and professional degree programs is offered, in addition to a Continuing Education Program run by the evening division. For the 30 percent of students who commute, the college is easily reached by public transportation. Parking on campus is available.

Private childcare facilities are located close to campus.

Policies to Ensure Fairness to Women. The Affirmative Action Officer is responsible part-time for monitoring compliance with sex-equity and handicapped-access laws. Complaints of sexual harassment are handled informally.

Women in Leadership Positions. *Students.* Men hold every important student leadership position, including president of the student body and of the student senate; women head the two honorary societies.

Faculty. Women's representation among the 60 full-time faculty is slightly below the national average: 22 percent, including 1 Asian American woman. There are 3 female faculty for every 100 female students, and 12 male faculty for every 100 male students.

Administrators. Women hold nearly half the key positions, including chief academic officer, chief planning officer, director of institutional research, director of the evening division, and head librarian. They chair two of the 15 departments—biology and nursing.

Women and the Curriculum. Women receive 46 percent of degrees awarded, mainly in business and the health professions. A course on British and American fiction treats women writers.

Women and Athletics. The college has a small intramural sports program and a larger intercollegiate program. Of the 60 intercollegiate athletes, nearly half are women; women receive 30 percent of the athletic scholarships. Intercollegiate sports offered include basketball, cross-country, softball, tennis, and volleyball.

Housing and Student Organizations. Seventy percent of undergraduates live on campus in either single-sex or coeducational dormitories, which have restrictive visiting hours for members of the opposite sex. More than half of the residence-hall staff are women, and all staff are offered awareness-training on sex education, racism, birth control, and assertiveness.

Special Services and Programs for Women. *Health and Counseling.* The student health service has 1 male physician and 1 female health-care provider who provide birth control counseling and treatment and gynecological treatment. The student counseling center has 1 female and 1 male counselor.

Safety and Security. Measures include campus police, high-intensity lighting, and an emergency telephone system. No rapes or assaults were reported for 1980–81.

Career. Services for women include career planning workshops on nontraditional occupations, the distribution of information about opportunities in these areas, and networking with alumnae.

Other. The evening division sponsors a program to help women overcome mathematics anxiety.

Returning Women Students. The Continuing Education Program, under the auspices of the evening division, admits 85 reentry women. "Crossroads" is the name of a new support program designed to help women returning to school.

Institutional Self-Description. "Wheeling College's mission statement specifically encourages women students by affirming their right to equality in educational and career opportunities. In addition, special seminars, speakers, and courses are planned for women students, faculty, and staff. Wheeling College is proud to have strong women administrators and faculty."

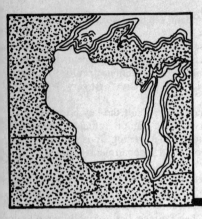

WISCONSIN

Madison Area Technical College
211 North Carroll Street
Madison, WI 53703
Telephone: (608) 266-5100

Women in Leadership
★★★ students
★★ faculty

7,628 undergraduates

	Amer. Ind.	Asian Amer.	Blacks	Hispanics	Whites
F	12	43	51	21	4,165
M	4	25	70	33	3,133
%	0.2	0.9	1.6	0.7	96.6

Founded in 1912 as a school of vocational and adult education, Madison Area Technical College is a public, two-year institution. It serves 7,628 students, 57 percent of whom are women; 53 percent of the women attend part-time. The median age of all students is 20.

Two-year degrees and certificates are offered in such fields as accounting, marketing, dental and medical assistance, civil engineering, and mechanical technologies. Evening, weekend, and summer session classes are available, along with off-campus class locations. All students commute to a centrally located, high-rise building in downtown Madison. Limited public transportation is available.

Policies to Ensure Fairness to Women. A full-time Affirmative Action Officer reviews policies and practices related to legislation on equal employment opportunity, educational sex equity, and handicapped accessibility. A written campus policy, publicly communicated to the college community, prohibits sexual harassment of students, faculty, and staff; complaints are handled through a formal campus grievance procedure.

Women in Leadership Positions. *Students.* During a recent three-year period, women have held five of nine possible student leadership positions.

Faculty. Of 315 full-time faculty, 41 percent are women. According to recent information, the full-time female faculty includes 1 black woman. There are 6 female faculty for every 100 female students and 10 male faculty for every 100 male students.

Administrators. Of 7 top administrators, the chief student-life officer is female. Women chair the departments of general studies, home economics, and practical nursing. Two of the 7 regents are female, one of them a black and the other a white woman. In one recent year, the commencement speaker was a woman.

Women and the Curriculum. The most popular major for both women and men is business and commerce, with women taking 55 percent of the degrees in that field. A third of the women earn degrees in health technologies, with fewer numbers in arts and sciences, data processing, mechanical/engineering technologies, natural science, and public service.

There are no courses on women. The departments of nursing and business provide instruction on some matters specific to women.

Women and Athletics. For a college of its size, Madison Area Tech offers a good program of athletics for women. Forty percent of intercollegiate and intramural athletes are women, as are 52 percent of club athletes. Four of 14 paid intercollegiate coaches are women. Intercollegiate sports offered include basketball, bowling, cross-country, softball, tennis, and volleyball.

Special Services and Programs for Women. *Health and Counseling.* The student health center, staffed by 1 female health-care provider, provides no medical services specific to women. The counseling center employs 4 men and 4 women, including 2 minority women. Counseling is available for gynecological problems, birth control, abortion, and rape and assault. An alcohol and drug abuse program is also available.

Safety and Security. Measures consist of local police, campus police with arrest authority, and a rape crisis center. No rapes and one assault on a man were reported for 1980–81.

Career. Services include nonsexist/nonracist printed information on nontraditional occupations for women, along with panels for students by women employed in nontraditional fields.

Other. The division of student services sponsors a Women's Center which serves 900 women a year, of whom 3 percent are minority (largely black) women. Headed by a full-time director and with a budget of $37,000, the center works directly with undergraduate and community women or refers them to local community agencies.

Institutional Self-Description. "Madison Area Technical College is committed to the policy of both equal education and employment opportunities for women. Our policies include a strong Title IX commitment, sexual harassment statement, and a number of education and support service programs. We are also emphasizing and encouraging minority women to participate in our educational programs."

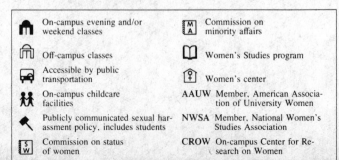

On-campus evening and/or weekend classes

Off-campus classes

Accessible by public transportation

On-campus childcare facilities

Publicly communicated sexual harassment policy, includes students

Commission on status of women

Commission on minority affairs

Women's Studies program

Women's center

AAUW Member, American Association of University Women

NWSA Member, National Women's Studies Association

CROW On-campus Center for Research on Women

Madison Business College
1110 Spring Harbor Dr.
Madison, WI 53705
Telephone: (608) 238-4266

Women in Leadership
★★★ students
★★★ faculty

332 undergraduates

	Amer. Ind.	Asian Amer.	Blacks	Hispanics	Whites
F	0	0	13	0	189
M	0	0	4	1	108
%	0.0	0.0	5.4	0.3	94.3

A private two-year college located in the state capital, Madison Business College serves 332 students. Sixty-five percent of students are women, and 27 percent of women attend part-time. The median age of students is 22. The college offers the associate degree in such fields as legal, court, and conference reporting, general business management, marketing, and accounting. There is a summer session. All students commute; both public transportation and on-campus parking at a fee are available.

Policies to Ensure Fairness to Women. A written campus policy, publicly communicated to students, prohibits sexual harassment of students.

Women in Leadership Positions. *Students.* The single campus-wide student governance position, that of student senate president, was held by women during two of three recent years.

Faculty. Of 7 full-time faculty, 5 are women.

Administrators. Of six top administrators the head librarian is a woman. A woman chairs the department of secretarial science.

Women and the Curriculum. All degrees are awarded in business and commerce. The business curriculum provides instruction about the problems of job discrimination and sexual harassment. There are no courses on women.

Women and Athletics. Thirty-five of 50 intramural athletes are women. No intercollegiate sports are offered.

Special Services and Programs for Women. *Health and Counseling.* There are no health or counseling services.

Safety and Security. Local police patrol the campus, which is equipped with high-intensity lighting. There is a rape crisis center. No rapes or assaults on women were reported for 1980–81.

Institutional Self-Description. None provided.

Marquette University
615 North 11th Street
Milwaukee, WI 53233
Telephone: (414) 224-7700

8,088 undergraduates

	Amer. Ind.	Asian Amer.	Blacks	Hispanics	Whites
F	9	32	240	63	3,184
M	13	52	194	77	4,160
%	0.3	1.1	5.4	1.7	91.5

Established in 1881 as an institution of learning in the Jesuit tradition, Marquette University, located in downtown Milwaukee, serves over 11,000 students with a variety of undergraduate, graduate, and professional programs of study. The division of continuing education offers continuing education credits for the adult student. Evening classes, a summer session, and graduate courses taught in extension centers are available.

Women are 44 percent of the 8,088 undergraduates; 7 percent of the women attend part-time. For the one-third of undergraduates who commute, the university is accessible by public transportation. On-campus parking is available for a fee. Private arrangements for childcare may be made close to the university.

Policies to Ensure Fairness to Women. A full-time Affirmative Action Officer reviews policies and practices which relate to equal employment opportunity and sex equity for students. A full-time Coordinator oversees accessibility for the handicapped. The Title IX grievance procedure which covers discrimination based on sex has been formulated and disseminated on campus. The Equal Opportunity Advisory Council, which includes student members, receives reports from the Task Force on Women's Progress and the Task Force on Minorities' Progress.

Women in Leadership Positions. *Students.* Opportunities for women students to exercise campus leadership are not good. In recent years a woman was presiding officer of the inter-residence hall for one year. Women head 12 of 25 honorary societies.

Faculty. Women are one-fifth of a full-time faculty of 505. According to a recent report, 1 black woman is on the full-time faculty. The ratio of female faculty to female students is 3 to 100. The ratio of male faculty to male students is 10 to 100.

Administrators. Men fill all higher administrative posts. Women chair two of 41 departments. Seventeen of 61 other academic units are headed by women, including the School of Nursing.

Women and the Curriculum. Nearly half of the women graduating with bachelor's degrees major in the health professions. The proportion of women who take degrees in communications is above the national average. Four percent of the women major in such nontraditional areas as engineering, mathematics, and the physical sciences. Over 9 percent of the students in the engineering cooperative education program are women.

Several courses on women are offered by the departments of anthropology/sociology, French, and political science. They include American Women and Men: Changing Cultural Patterns; Feminists and Femmes Fatales in Nineteenth-Century French Literature; Women in the Third World: Life, Struggle and Work; and Women in American Politics.

Such current issues as mathematics confidence among females, sex-fair curricula, innovative health-care delivery, health-care information important to minority women, services for abused spouses, and discrimination in the workplace are part of the preparation of future teachers, health-care providers, social workers, and business students.

Minority Women. Of 3,539 undergraduate women, 7 percent are black, less than 2 percent Hispanic, and less than 1 percent each Asian American and American Indian. An estimated 37 women are in all-minority sororities. A minority woman is director of a residence hall. Residence-hall staff and staff in the counseling service are offered awareness-training on avoiding racial bias. Both female recipients of honorary degrees in the spring of 1981 were black women.

Women and Athletics. Intramural and intercollegiate programs provide adequate opportunities for organized, competitive, individual and team sports. The number of intramural participants and the variety of sports are noteworthy. Soccer is available as a club sport for women. The university reports special indoor tennis courts in Haelfer Center. Sixty percent of intercollegiate athletes are women. Of the 78 women competing in intercollegiate sports, 41 percent receive scholarship support. Women's teams played in tournaments in 1980. The intercollegiate sports offered are basketball, cross-country, track and field, tennis, and volleyball.

Housing and Student Organizations. One-third of the undergraduates live on campus. Single-sex and coeducational dormitories, apartments for singles, and housing for married students and single parents with children are available. A married women student whose spouse is not enrolled may live in married students' housing. Residence halls restrict hours for visitors of the opposite sex. Five of seven residence-hall directors are women. Awareness-training on sexism and racism is offered residence-hall staff.

Two percent of the full-time undergraduate women belong to social sororities. Sororities do not furnish housing for their members. The Women's Advisory Board and the Leaven organization serve as advocates for women, including minority women, on campus.

Special Services and Programs for Women. *Health and Counseling.* The student health service provides some medical attention specific to women, including gynecological and rape and assault treatment. One of 6 physicians is female, as are 6 of 7 other health-care providers. The regular student health insurance covers maternity at no extra cost. Two of 7 professional staff in the counseling service are women. Students have access to some counseling specific to women. Staff receive training on sex-role stereotyping and racial bias.

Safety and Security. Measures include city police and campus police with citizen's arrest authority, night-time escorts for students, a shuttle bus at night to the outlying residence hall, high-intensity lighting, self-defense courses for women, information seminars on safety and crime prevention, a rape crisis center, and the Public Safety Office as a 24-hour "safehouse." No information was provided on the incidence of rapes and assaults.

Career. Services include talks by women employed in nontraditional occupations and printed information on nontraditional careers. The Dean of Students' Office encourages networking between professional women in the community and students.

Other. The Dean of Students sponsors the Women's Center. One-fifth of the approximately 500 users of the center are black women. An annual women's week and a women's lecture series are co-sponsored by various campus groups. Theater and other women's arts programs are provided under the auspices of the theatre and the Committee on Fine Arts. Assertiveness training is available through the counseling center.

Institutional Self-Description. "Marquette University is a Jesuit, Catholic, medium-sized school with a compact campus located in an urban setting rich in ethnic diversity. Marquette is committed to intellectual and moral excellence and offers a variety of academic programs. A majority of our qualified women graduates receive placement in distinguished graduate and professional schools."

Mid-State Technical Institute

500 32nd Street N.
Wisconsin Rapids,
WI 54494
Telephone: (715) 423-5650

Women in Leadership
★★★ students
★★ faculty

1,234 undergraduates

	Amer. Ind.	Asian Amer.	Blacks	Hispanics	Whites
F	5	13	0	10	601
M	5	4	0	5	588
%	0.8	1.4	0.0	1.2	96.6

Part of Wisconsin's multi-campus public technical institute, Mid-State offers a variety of two-year technical programs, including such specialties as civil highway technology, mechanical design technology, and instrumentation. Half of its 1,234 students are

women. Thirty percent of the women attend part-time. All students commute, and parking is free on campus.

Policies to Ensure Fairness to Women. Rare among community colleges, Mid-State has Commissions on the Status of Women and on Minority Affairs. The Commission on Women meets two or three times a year and submits recommendations to the college's administrative council. Two administrators are assigned part-time to the enforcement of federal policies concerning discrimination against faculty, students, and the handicapped.

Women in Leadership Positions. *Students.* During two of three recent years, women have been the editor of the student newspaper and have held the chief office of the student government—the only campus leadership positions available.

Faculty. Forty-three percent of the 73 full-time faculty are women, including, according to recent information, 1 American Indian woman and 1 Asian American woman. There are 7 female faculty for every 100 female students and 13 male faculty for every 100 male students.

Administrators. A woman is director of the library. Men hold all other top administrative positions. Women chair the departments of health and home economics, and the division of community and adult education.

Women and the Curriculum. Virtually all degrees to women are awarded in programs in business and health-care technologies.

The adult continuing education program sponsors two women's studies courses: Choice, Change and Challenges; and Women and the World of Business and Finance. Faculty are offered workshops on topics such as sexism and the curriculum, nontraditional careers for women and men, and affirmative action and equal opportunity.

Women and Athletics. A very limited intramural sports program includes coeducational volleyball and open gym. Intercollegiate sports are bowling and volleyball.

Special Services and Programs for Women. *Health and Counseling.* The student health service is staffed by 1 male consulting physician and 1 female health-care provider. No information was provided on medical treatment specific to women. The school nurse provides counseling on gynecological, birth control, abortion, rape and assault, diet, stress, and other health issues. Additional counseling is available from a staff of seven that includes two white women and a minority woman.

Safety and Security. Local police patrol the campus, which is equipped with high-intensity lighting. A supervisor is on duty in the evenings. No rapes or assaults on women were reported for 1980–81.

Career. The career planning center sponsors workshops and lectures on nontraditional careers.

Other. A newly developed and funded Women's Center, headed by a full-time staff specialist, offers assertiveness training and a program for displaced homemakers..

Institutional Self-Description. "An open-door admissions policy encourages 'open career' attitude-planning to all applicants—men and women. There are programs that are offered only at Mid-State or only at a few other technical institutes within Wisconsin or the Midwest."

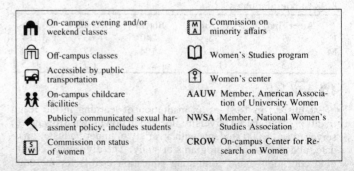

🏠 On-campus evening and/or weekend classes	M A Commission on minority affairs
🏛 Off-campus classes	📖 Women's Studies program
🚌 Accessible by public transportation	🛉 Women's center
👫 On-campus childcare facilities	AAUW Member, American Association of University Women
⚲ Publicly communicated sexual harassment policy, includes students	NWSA Member, National Women's Studies Association
S W Commission on status of women	CROW On-campus Center for Research on Women

Mount Mary College
2900 Menomonee River Pkwy.
Milwaukee, WI 53222
Telephone: (414) 258-4810

Women in Leadership
★★★ students
★★★ faculty
★★★ administrators

1,087 undergraduates

	Amer. Ind.	Asian Amer.	Blacks	Hispanics	Whites
F	5	0	47	4	1,008
M	0	0	0	0	0
%	0.5	0.0	4.4	0.4	94.7

Founded in 1913, Mount Mary is an independent women's college affiliated with the Roman Catholic Church. Its urban campus draws a total of 1,115 students, virtually all of them enrolled in degree programs. About a fourth of undergraduates attend part-time; their median age is 21. The college offers degrees in liberal arts, pre-professional and professional areas. The Encore Program is responsible for adult continuing education. Classes meet both day and evening and during the summer. For the 80 percent of students who commute, public transportation and campus parking are available.

The college-operated childcare facility accommodates an estimated 5 percent of requests by students. Admission is on a first-come, first-served basis. Additional, private childcare facilities are available nearby.

Policies to Ensure Fairness to Women. On a part-time basis, an administrator monitors compliance with sex-equity laws. Sexual harassment complaints are resolved informally and confidentially. There are faculty workshops on equal-employment-opportunity regulations.

Women in Leadership Positions. *Students.* Women hold all student leadership positions.

Faculty. Seventy-seven percent of the 34 full-time faculty are women (including one Hispanic woman), a proportion above average for women's colleges in this guide. There are 3 female faculty for every 100 female students.

Administrators. Women hold all top-level administrative posts. Women chair all but one of 19 departments. The trustees and most of the members of the faculty senate and Board of Regents are women.

Women and the Curriculum. Half of the bachelor's degrees awarded are in health professions, business, or fine arts. In a recent year, 2 percent of degrees were in the physical sciences. Programs and new majors encourage women to prepare for careers in science, telecommunications, and computer science.

Five courses on women are available through the departments of social work, anthropology, behavioral science, music, and English. They include Assertiveness for Women in Health Professions, Cultural Roles of Women, Women's Communication Issues, and Women Writers. An official committee develops and collects new Women's Studies curricula. Faculty workshops examine sexism in the curriculum.

Minority Women. Five percent of the undergraduate women are members of minority groups. The Commission on Minority Affairs responds to their concerns; a female minority counselor and the office of the Dean of Students are additional resources. An Hispanic woman chairs an academic department; one black and one Hispanic were among women who spoke in a recent campus-wide lecture series. Faculty workshops are offered on such topics as racism/sexism in the curriculum and equal-employment-opportutnity regulations.

Two advocacy groups meet on campus: Coretta Scott King Association (20 members); and the Hispanic Student Group (15 members). Minority women are active in the International Relations Club.

Women and Athletics. The athletic program emphasizes team sports. Both paid varsity coaches are women. Intercollegiate sports offered are basketball, softball, and volleyball.

Housing and Student Organizations. One-fifth of the undergraduates live in dormitories that restrict men's visiting hours. The 50-member Student Association and the 24-member International Relations Club meet regularly.

Special Services and Programs for Women. *Health and Counseling.* The student health service has 1 male physician and 1 female health-care provider. Two of the 3 professionals at the student counseling center are women. Rape and assault and gynecological counseling and treatment are available, as well as birth control counseling.

Safety and Security. Measures include campus and local police protection, high-intensity lighting, information on campus safety, and a rape crisis center. No rapes or assaults on women were reported for 1980–81.

Career. Services include workshops, lectures, and information on nontraditional occupations, files on alumnae careers, and programs to promote networking between alumnae and students. Faculty are offered workshops on nontraditional careers for women.

Other. Several departments, including that of social work, administer programs for displaced homemakers and for battered women. The Dean of Students and the Student Affairs office organize a women's lecture series and leadership training sessions. The mathematics department helps women acquire confidence in mathematics.

Peer counselors are sources of support for welfare women, older women, and rape and assault victims. The Abilities Unlimited Program serves handicapped women.

Returning Women Students. Thirty-eight percent of the undergraduate women are over age 25. A Continuing Education for Women Program, under a full-time director, attracts 100 students, including some minority women. An additional 250 returning women students enroll in professional programs.

Institutional Self-Description. "Think about the advantages of a women's college: supportive environment; professional training anchored in the liberal arts; a wide variety of leadership experience; female role models; women's sports teams; career counseling tailored to challenges facing women today. These advantages can be yours at Mount Mary College."

Nicolet College and Technical Institute
P.O. Box 518, Rhinelander, WI 54501
Telephone: (715) 369-4410

Women in Leadership
★★★ students

605 undergraduates

	Amer. Ind.	Asian Amer.	Blacks	Hispanics	Whites
F	19	0	0	0	248
M	27	0	0	0	310
%	7.6	0.0	0.0	0.0	92.4

Founded in 1967 to serve the Rhinelander district in northern Wisconsin, this public two-year community college currently enrolls 950 students. Of the 605 degree and certificate students, 44 percent are women, and 44 percent of women attend part-time. The median age of all students is 28; 10 percent of women are over age 40. Besides liberal arts transfer courses, the college offers vocational and technical training, adult education courses, and community service programs. Classes are available on and off campus, day and evening; there is a summer session. All students commute to campus; parking is free and the college runs a limited bus service.

A college childcare center, open from 7:30 a.m. to 6:00 p.m., five days a week, accommodates 65 percent of requests.

Policies to Ensure Fairness to Women. On a part-time basis, the Affirmative Action Officer, who has policymaking responsibility, monitors compliance with regulations pertaining to sex equity for students, equal employment opportunity, and handicapped access. The college is developing a sexual harassment policy to cover faculty and staff; student complaints are resolved through a formal grievance procedure.

Women in Leadership Positions. *Students.* There are two campus-wide student leadership positions available. During a recent three-year period, women served as student body president once and editor-in-chief of the campus newspaper twice.

Faculty. Of 40 full-time faculty, 6 are women. There are 4 female faculty for every 100 female students and 17 male faculty for every 100 male students.

Administrators. The top administrators as well as the four department heads are men. A woman serves as Coordinator of Community Services Coordinators.

Women and the Curriculum. Women earn 30 percent of two-year degrees and certificates. In one recent year, six women majored in arts and sciences, eight in business and commerce, and one in mechanical and engineering technologies. Nicolet offers three courses on women: Psychology of Women, Women in History, and History of Women in the U.S.

Women and Athletics. Information was not supplied.

Special Services and Programs for Women. *Health and Counseling.* There are no health services. The student counseling center is staffed by one woman and one man. No services specific to women are offered.

Safety and Security. Local police patrol the campus, which is equipped with high-intensity lighting. No rapes or assaults were reported for 1980–81.

Career. The Women's Resource Bureau offers special-interest classes on career development. Career workshops focus on nontraditional occupations, and lectures by women in nontraditional occupations are available.

Other. Over 300 women use the Women's Center, which operates under the auspices of the Women's Resource Bureau and is staffed by a full-time coordinator. The center offers a women's lecture series, theater and arts programs, assertiveness training, career development, an annual "Woman-Imaging" conference and art show, and a national demonstration project for displaced homemakers.

Institutional Self-Description. "Nicolet College provides opportunities for career preparation in 25 occupational fields, including nontraditional areas, and for transfer to baccalaureate degree programs. The college offers counseling services, some of which are especially related to women's special needs. It sponsors a Women's Resource Bureau and a Displaced Homemakers' Program."

Ripon College
Ripon, WI 54971
Telephone: (414) 748-8118

926 undergraduates

	Amer. Ind.	Asian Amer.	Blacks	Hispanics	Whites
F	0	5	10	4	397
M	1	0	9	3	487
%	0.1	0.6	2.1	0.8	96.5

AAUW

Founded in 1850, Ripon is a private, non-denominational, co-educational liberal arts college. Its campus draws 926 undergraduates, 45 percent of whom are women. Virtually all the women attend full-time. The median age of all students is 19. A wide variety of undergraduate programs is available, including programs in engineering, the sciences, and forestry. Six percent of the students commute. Free parking is available on campus.

The nearest childcare facility is a nursery school located off campus.

Policies to Ensure Fairness to Women. An affirmative action officer is responsible part-time for implementing handicapped-access and sex-fair-employment laws. The Committee on Minority Affairs attends to the concerns of minority women. Complaints of sexual harassment are handled informally.

Women in Leadership Positions. *Students.* Men hold all campus-wide student leadership positions.

Faculty. The proportion of full-time faculty who are women is far below the national average: 5 of 67 members, including 1 Hispanic woman. There is 1 female faculty member for every 100 female students, and 12 male faculty members for every 100 male students.

Administrators. Except for the head librarian, all key administrators are male. No information was provided on the gender of the department heads or deans.

Women and the Curriculum. The major fields of study for women are the humanities and the social sciences. Four percent of the degrees granted to women are in the nontraditional areas of mathematics and the physical sciences. No courses on women are offered.

Women and Athletics. Women are 31 percent of intercollegiate and 38 percent of intramural athletes. The intercollegiate sports offered are basketball, softball, swimming, tennis, track and field, and volleyball.

Housing and Student Organizations. Ninety-four percent of the undergraduates live on campus in either coeducational or single-sex dormitories. Sororities attract about 20 percent of women students.

Special Services and Programs for Women. *Health and Counseling.* The student health center is staffed by three physicians, including one woman, in addition to five health-care providers, four of whom are women. Counseling and treatment are offered for gynecological problems, birth control, and rape. Abortion counseling is also available. There is no student counseling center.

Safety and Security. No information was provided, except for a self-defense course for women. No rapes or assaults were reported for 1980–81.

Career. Services include workshops and information on nontraditional careers, and files on the careers of alumnae.

Institutional Self-Description. "Ripon's goal is to provide a responsive and effective educational experience, one which has assimilated the most recent and valuable developments in the various fields of knowledge and has taken into account the evolving nature of our society and the changing needs of individuals within that society."

🏠 On-campus evening and/or weekend classes		Ⓜ︎Ⓐ Commission on minority affairs	
🏛 Off-campus classes		📖 Women's Studies program	
🚌 Accessible by public transportation		⚢ Women's center	
👥 On-campus childcare facilities		AAUW Member, American Association of University Women	
🔻 Publicly communicated sexual harassment policy, includes students		NWSA Member, National Women's Studies Association	
Ⓢ︎Ⓦ Commission on status of women		CROW On-campus Center for Research on Women	

Silver Lake College of the Holy Family

2406 S. Alverno Road
Manitowoc, WI 54220
Telephone: (414) 684-6691

Women in Leadership
★★★ faculty
★★★ administrators

240 undergraduates

	Amer. Ind.	Asian Amer.	Blacks	Hispanics	Whites
F	0	1	1	1	192
M	0	0	0	0	45
%	0.0	0.4	0.4	0.4	98.8

 AAUW

Founded in 1935 as a Roman Catholic liberal arts college for women, Silver Lake College has evolved into a coeducational institution. It remains affiliated with the Roman Catholic Church but is open to students regardless of their religious faith. The college has a total enrollment of 313. The median age of all students is 22. Eighty-one percent of the undergraduates are women; 14 percent of the women attend part-time.

The college offers a variety of four-year degree programs as well as two-year degrees, and a continuing education program that attracts 18 reentry women students. All students commute; free on-campus parking is available.

Private childcare facilities are located near the campus.

Policies to Ensure Fairness to Women. It is the part-time responsibility of a Conciliator to oversee the implementation of sex-equity and handicapped-access legislation. Complaints of sexual harassment are resolved through a formal grievance procedure.

Women in Leadership Positions. *Students.* Women have held half of the student leadership posts, in recent years, including presiding officer of the student judiciary (one year), editor of the campus newspaper (two years), and president of the residence-hall council (three years). A woman heads the only campus honorary society.

Faculty. Of the 32 full-time faculty, 91 percent are women.

Administrators. All key administrators are women, except the chief development officer and the chief business officer. Women head all six academic divisions and chair almost every department, including mathematics, biology, and philosophy and religious studies.

Women and the Curriculum. Women receive about 80 percent of the bachelor's degrees granted, mostly in education (66 percent) and arts and letters (15 percent). In a recent year, women received all seven two-year degrees—in health technologies. The education department instructs students on how to develop nonsexist learning materials. There are no courses on women.

Women and Athletics. The intramural sports program offers a wide range of individual and team sports. The intercollegiate sports program for women consists solely of basketball.

Special Services and Programs for Women. *Health and Counseling.* There is no student health service; a student counseling center is staffed by one woman. No information was provided on counseling services.

Safety and Security. Measures include city police protection and high-intensity lighting. No rapes or assaults were reported for 1980-81.

Career. The College sponsors career workshops on nontraditional occupations for women, provides literature about opportunities in these areas, and maintains files on careers of alumnae.

Institutional Self-Description. "Silver Lake College is operated, to a large degree, by enlightened women who are concerned about women's issues and social justice."

Southwest Wisconsin Vocational-Technical Institute

Bronson Blvd., Fennimore, WI 53809
Telephone: (608) 822-3262

Women in Leadership
★ faculty
★★ administrators

824 undergraduates

	Amer. Ind.	Asian Amer.	Blacks	Hispanics	Whites
F	1	2	0	0	414
M	3	1	0	1	402
%	0.5	0.4	0.0	0.1	99.0

A public, two-year vocational college, Southwest Wisconsin is located in the small town of Fennimore. The 824 students commute to campus; half the students are women. The median age of all students is 20. Courses are offered at a variety of locations and hours. There is an adult continuing education program.

Childcare facilities are available on campus.

Women in Leadership Positions. *Students.* During recent years, women have presided over the student union for three consecutive terms and served single terms as president of the student body and the student senate.

Faculty. Thirty percent of the 77 full-time faculty are women. There are 7 female faculty for every 100 female students and 15 male faculty for every 100 male students.

Administrators. Women hold three of eight key administrative positions, including student-life officer, director of institutional research, and director of athletics. Women also chair the departments of foods, business, health, and student services. Four of 7 members of the faculty senate are women, as well as 2 of the 7-member Board of Trustees.

Women and the Curriculum. All students, male and female, earn their degrees in business. There are no courses on women.

Women and Athletics. No information was provided on the opportunities for intercollegiate and intramural sports.

Special Services and Programs for Women. *Health and Counseling.* The student health service, staffed by 1 woman healthcare provider, offers services related to birth control, gynecology, abortion, rape and assault. A staff of three women and three men counsel students on the above. The student health insurance policy covers maternity expenses.

Safety and Security. Measures include local police and high-intensity lighting. No rapes or assaults were reported for 1980-81.

Career. The placement office provides lectures and panels on nontraditional careers, as well as information on job discrimination. It also maintains updated files of alumnae by specific career.

Institutional Self-Description. None provided.

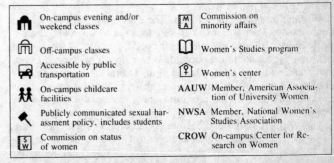

University of Wisconsin, Eau Claire
Eau Claire, Wisconsin 54701
Telephone: (715) 836-2100

Women in Leadership	★ Women and the
★★★ students	Curriculum
★ administrators	
	★ Women and Athletics

9,450 undergraduates

	Amer. Ind.	Asian Amer.	Blacks	Hispanics	Whites
F	24	12	27	6	5,155
M	16	10	45	8	4,071
%	.4	.2	.8	.2	98.4

Founded in 1916 as a preparatory school for teachers, the University of Wisconsin, at Eau Claire is now a public, multi-purpose university and center for continuing education. Of the 10,494 students, 9,450 are undergraduates. Fifty-six percent of the undergraduates are women, of whom 5 percent attend part-time. The median age of students, including graduate students is 22.

On- and off-campus evening classes, a summer session, and an interim semester facilitate scheduling. The Educational Opportunity Office administers continuing education. For the 67 percent of students who commute, the campus is accessible by public transportation; on-campus parking facilities are available for a fee.

Both nearby private childcare and a licensed, on-campus nursery school are available. On-campus daycare, accommodating 40 percent of students' requests, charges fees according to income.

Policies to Ensure Fairness to Women. The Vice Chancellor and two assistants make, review, and enforce policies pertaining to equal-opportunity laws. A written policy that prohibits sexual harassment of students, staff, and faculty has been publicly communicated in writing to all members of the campus community. Complaints are resolved through either an informal mechanism or a formal grievance procedure. The Commission on the Status of Women—which is appointed by and reports to the Chancellor—includes student members with voting rights, meets regularly, takes public stands on issues of concern to students, and addresses the concerns of minority women.

Women in Leadership Positions. *Students.* Women students assume major campus-wide leadership positions. In three recent years, women held every campus-wide position at least once and edited the newspaper each year. A woman chairs one of the four honorary societies.

Faculty. Twenty-one percent of 374 faculty members are women. There are 2 female faculty for every 100 female students and 7 male faculty for every 100 male students.

Administrators. Of the nine top administrative positions, women hold three: Chancellor, head librarian, and director of women's athletics. Of five deans, the Dean of the School of Nursing is a woman; of 35 departments, women chair physical education and six others, all in the health professions. Women make up 28 percent of the faculty senate. One of 16 trustees is a black woman and four are white women.

Women and the Curriculum. The largest number of four-year degrees to women are awarded in education (33 percent), health professions (16 percent), and business (12 percent). Two percent of women graduate in the nontraditional fields of physical sciences and mathematics. The Academic Skills Center offers mathematics confidence training. Women constitute 45 percent of the students in cooperative education programs and 77 percent of the students in internships.

The Women's Studies Program, chaired part-time by a faculty member, offers an undergraduate minor. Courses include: Images of Women in Contemporary Literature, Women and Religion,

Psychology of Women, Women and Politics, and Women and Art. An official committee is charged with developing the Women's Studies Program, encouraging the teaching of courses on women in traditional departments, and collecting curricular materials on women. Faculty are offered workshops on sexism, racism, and the curriculum; sex, race, and the selection of major field; needs of reentry women; affirmative action and equal opportunity; feminist theory; and feminism in the curriculum. The departments of physical education, social work, and business offer instruction on some matters specific to women.

Women and Athletics. The participation of women is high in the intramural program, which includes a good variety of team and individual sports. Seven of 23 paid varsity coaches are female. Of the 671 intercollegiate athletes, 35 percent are women. Intercollegiate sports offered include basketball, cross-country, gymnastics, swimming, tennis, track and field, and volleyball.

Housing and Student Organizations. Single-sex and coeducational dormitories with restricted visiting hours house the 33 percent of students who live on campus. Residence-hall directors (seven men and six white women) are offered training on sexism, sex education, birth control, personality development, assertiveness, and rape prevention.

Two percent of students join residential sororities and fraternities; one minority woman belongs to a sorority. Four organizations, all with women presidents, serve as advocates for women on campus—Ebony Ladies, Sigma Gamma Zeta (for older students), American Indian Student Council, and Black Students.

Special Services and Programs for Women. *Health and Counseling.* One male physician provides gynecological treatment. Four men and three white women are offered training on sex-role stereotyping, legal aspects of counseling, neural-linguistic programming, and chemical abuse. They counsel on gynecological matters, birth control, abortion, and rape and assault. The counseling center offers a battered women's program, a displaced homemakers' program, and assertiveness training.

Safety and Security. Measures consist of campus and municipal police, night-time escorts for women, high-intensity lighting, emergency telephones, information sessions on safety, and a rape crisis center. One rape and seven assaults (three of them against women) were reported for 1980–81.

Career. Services include workshops on nontraditional occupations, programs by women in nontraditional careers, nonsexist/nonracist literature on nontraditional fields of study, job discrimination information, and networking between alumnae and students.

Returning Women Students. The Educational Opportunity Office administers Continuing Education for Women, which is staffed by a full-time director. Sixteen hundred reentry women participate in CEW programs.

Institutional Self-Description. "Women constitute a majority of our student body, hold leadership positions in student government, and are accepted in nontraditional majors in increasing numbers. A female Chancellor, other high-level administrators, and faculty provide significant role models. UW, Eau Claire, is committed to providing full educational opportunity to all its students."

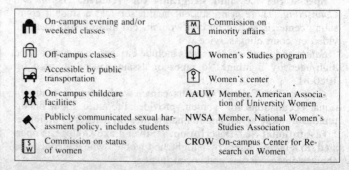

On-campus evening and/or weekend classes		Commission on minority affairs	
Off-campus classes		Women's Studies program	
Accessible by public transportation		Women's center	
On-campus childcare facilities		AAUW Member, American Association of University Women	
Publicly communicated sexual harassment policy, includes students		NWSA Member, National Women's Studies Association	
Commission on status of women		CROW On-campus Center for Research on Women	

University of Wisconsin, Green Bay

Green Bay, WI 54302

Telephone: (414) 465-2111

★ **Women and the Curriculum**

2,665 undergraduates

	Amer. Ind.	Asian Amer.	Blacks	Hispanics	Whites
F	39	6	13	4	1,305
M	14	8	11	4	1,205
%	2.0	0.5	0.9	0.3	96.2

The University of Wisconsin at Green Bay emphasizes "the interdisciplinary, problem-centered study of man in the environment." The university offers two-and four-year undergraduate programs in arts and sciences, business, education, health, and pre-professional fields. Summer session, self-paced/contract learning, an extended degree program, evening classes both on and off campus, and off-campus daytime classes are available.

The university attracts 3,715 students, of whom 2,665 are undergraduates. Fifty-two percent of undergraduates are women; 31 percent of women attend part-time. The median age of all undergraduates is 22. Public transportation and on-campus parking for a fee are available to the 86 percent of students who commute.

An on-campus childcare facility can accommodate all requests for this service, which is available to students, faculty, and staff. The facility is open from 7:30 a.m. to 5:45 p.m. and charges $.95 an hour. Private childcare facilities are available off campus.

Policies to Ensure Fairness to Women. The Affirmative Action Officer advises the Chancellor on policies related to equal employment opportunity, handicapped accessibility, and sex equity for students. A campus policy prohibits sexual harassment; complaints are handled both informally and confidentially and through a formal grievance procedure.

An active Committee on the Status of Women, appointed by the Chancellor, includes students as voting members and addresses concerns of minority women.

Women in Leadership Positions. *Students.* In a recent three year period, women were president of the student body for three consecutive years and editor-in-chief of the campus newspaper for one year.

Faculty. Eighteen percent of the 152 full-time faculty are women, a proportion below the national average. There are 3 female faculty for every 100 female students and 12 male faculty for every 100 male students.

Administrators. Men hold all top administrative positions. Of 37 departments, women chair two: social change and development and sociology. Five of 16 regents are women.

Women and the Curriculum. All four-year degrees awarded are in interdisciplinary studies.

A Women's Studies Program, directed by a full-time faculty member, offers a B.A. and a minor. Among the courses available are Women in the Visual and Performing Arts, Woman as Worker, and Women in Cross-Cultural Perspectives. A committee is responsible for developing Women's Studies and for reporting on curricular material on women. The departments of business, education, and social work provide instruction on some matters specific to women. Faculty workshops address sexism and the curriculum, the needs of reentry women, and affirmative action and equal opportunity.

Women and Athletics. Women participate in intramural volleyball and softball. The three paid varsity coaches are women. The intercollegiate sports offered are basketball, cross-country, field hockey, swimming and diving, and tennis.

Housing and Student Organizations. All resident students live in coeducational student apartments that restrict hours for visitors of the opposite sex. Twenty women and 20 men belong to soror-

ities and fraternities. The Women's Student Union serves as an advocacy group for women.

Special Services and Programs for Women. *Health and Counseling.* The student health service, staffed by two nurses, provides no treatment specific to women. The student medical insurance covers abortion at no extra cost. The counseling center, employing one female and two male counselors, offers birth control, abortion, and rape and assault counseling. Counselors are offered in-service training on sex-role stereotyping.

Safety and Security. Measures consist of campus police with weapons training and authority to make arrests, local police protection, high-intensity lighting in all areas, emergency telephone and alarm systems, self-defense courses for women, information sessions on campus safety, and a rape crisis center. No rapes or assaults were reported on campus for 1980–81.

Career. Services include workshops, nonsexist/nonracist printed materials, and speakers on nontraditional occupations for women, as well as contacts between alumnae and female students.

Other. A small Women's Center, coordinated by a student, operates on an annual budget of $3,000 to serve both campus and community women. An annual women's week, speakers, and other cultural events are sponsored by the Women's Center. The Office of OUTREACH is responsible for a continuing education program and offers assertiveness/leadership training. A telephone hotline is available for referrals and support.

Institutional Self-Description. "Women's Studies and personal programs of study can be developed by the student into a college major. A large proportion of returning adult students are women. The university is small enough to provide individual attention and has a strong interdisciplinary approach to education."

University of Wisconsin, Milwaukee

Box 413, Milwaukee, WI 53201

Telephone: (414) 963-4444

Women in Leadership
★★ **students**

★★ **Women and the Curriculum**

18,325 undergraduates

	Amer. Ind.	Asian Amer.	Blacks	Hispanics	Whites
F	60	75	837	175	7,848
M	38	95	471	175	8,317
%	0.5	0.9	7.2	1.9	89.4

AAUW NWSA

The University of Wisconsin at Milwaukee was founded in 1956 as a public, four-year college. Its 24,818 students include 18,325 undergraduates; 49 percent are women, of whom one-third attend part-time. The median age of undergraduates is 23. Degrees are awarded in arts and sciences, education, architecture, and the health professions. On- and off-campus day and evening classes, a summer session, and a weekend college facilitate scheduling. Urban Outreach, a special downtown campus, provides continuing education programs. Ninety-four percent of students commute to campus, using public transportation or on-campus parking, which is available for a fee.

On-campus childcare facilities accommodate 80 percent of students' requests; the fees charged vary according to the income of the parents. Private childcare is available near the campus.

Policies to Ensure Fairness to Women. The full-time Special Assistant to the Chancellor for Equal Opportunity reviews university policies and monitors compliance concerning laws on equal employment opportunity, sex equity for students, and access for the handicapped. A written campus policy prohibits the sexual harassment of students, faculty, and staff. A formal grievance procedure resolves complaints. The self-designated Committee on the Status of Academic Women—which includes students with voting rights—meets regularly, takes public stands on issues of concern to students, addresses the concerns of minority women, and works to ensure women full representation in university governance.

Women in Leadership Positions. *Students.* In recent years, undergraduate women have held a good number of campus-wide leadership positions, including president of the student court, president of the student union, editor of the campus newspaper, and manager of the campus radio station. Women head nine of 13 honor societies.

Faculty. Twenty-three percent of 761 faculty members are women, including 8 black, 2 Asian American, and 2 Hispanic women. The ratio of female faculty to female students is 3 to 100; for males, the ratio is 9 to 100.

Administrators. Except for the chief development officer, all top administrators are men. The Dean of the School of Nursing is a woman, as are the chairs of linguistics, psychology, and dance. Thirty-seven percent of the faculty senate and 14 percent of the promotions committee are female; 5 of 16 regents are women. The 1981 commencement speaker was a woman.

Women and the Curriculum. Most degrees awarded to women are in education (24 percent), health professions (22 percent), and business (9 percent); there are significant numbers also in fine arts and the social sciences. Programs in science, engineering, and architecture encourage women to prepare for nontraditional careers; 3 percent of women graduate in physical sciences, engineering, architecture, and mathematics.

The Women's Studies Program, which is chaired part-time by a permanently appointed faculty member, offers an 18-credit certificate (minor) and the B.A. through Interdisciplinary Studies. More than 410 courses are offered through 17 different departments, including administrative leadership, Afro-American studies, anthropology, communications, criminal justice, English, history, philosophy, political science, social welfare, sociology, and zoology. Introduction to Women's Studies is offered through the comparative literature department; Women's Studies Seminar through the history department. Other courses include Biology of Women; Women and Law; Issues and Problems in German Literature and Society: Feminism, Sexism, and Fairy Tales; Women Writers of the Short Story; Major Film Directors: Politics and Sexuality; and Masculinity/Femininity: A Social Science Approach to Sex Roles. The departments of education and social work provide some instruction on matters specific to women.

The Resource Center in the Office of Women's Studies houses reference materials including bibliographies, course outlines, files of newpaper clippings, film catalogs, a library of leading journals and publications, and information on financial assistance for undergraduate and graduate female students. The campus library has an extensive Women's Studies collection with major strengths in such areas as women and economics, health care, day care, and sports.

Women and Athletics. Forty-three percent of 230 varsity athletes are women, as are 9 of 24 paid intercollegiate coaches. Thirty-two women participate in four intramural sports. The intercollegiate sports offered are basketball, cross-country, field hockey, gymnastics, swimming and diving, tennis, track, and volleyball.

Housing and Student Organizations. Coeducational dormitories with restrictive hours for visitors of the opposite sex house 6 percent of undergraduates. Ninety percent of women living in residence halls are white, 8 percent are black, and 2 percent Hispanic and Asian American. Residence halls are staffed by 12 men and 18 women.

One percent of full-time undergraduate women belong to non-residential, social sororities, including 15 women in all-minority sororities. Advocates for women on campus are the Women's Caucus and Women in Education (for returning women students).

Special Services and Programs for Women. *Health and Counseling.* The student health service, staffed by 2 female and 2 male physicians, along with 9 health-care providers (7 women and 2 men), offers such services specific to women as birth control, abortion, and rape and assault treatment. Three women and 1 man, with awareness-training on sex-role stereotyping and racial bias, staff the student counseling center. Counseling is available for gynecological problems, birth control, abortion, and for victims of rape and assault. Regular student health insurance covers both abortion and maternity expenses.

Safety and Security. Measures consist of campus police with arrest authority, night-time escorts for women, night-time, campus-wide bus service to residence areas, emergency telephones, self-defense courses for women, information sessions on safety and crime prevention, and a rape crisis center. For 1980-81, 30 assaults and no rapes were reported.

Career. Services include workshops and job discrimination information on nontraditional occupations for women.

Other. Special constituencies are served by a variety of campus agencies: displaced homemakers by the Special Students Office; handicapped women by the Disabled Students Office; lesbians by the Feminist Center and Gay People's Union; older women by the Adult Student Alliance; Center; and minority women by the Spanish Speaking Outreach Institute, the Native American Office, and Afro-American Studies. The Special Students Office sponsors the Women's Support Group for nontraditional students. Other organizations of interest are the UWM Women's League (primarily a social club) and the Student Feminist Center. A literary magazine and an art gallery feature works by women.

Institutional Self-Description. "As a major university in an urban setting, the University of Wisconsin at Milwaukee offers a unique blending of campus and community. Flexible scheduling offers students who have family and/or work responsibilities an opportunity to attend classes in the evening or on Saturday. A variety of courses offered off campus at local libraries and shopping centers offer convenient access to introductory college courses in nontraditional settings. The Women's Studies Program coordinates courses and research on women-related topics, sponsors educational programs, and provides a resource center for women on campus."

University of Wisconsin, Oshkosh,
800 Algoma Blvd., Oshkosh, WI 54901
Telephone: (414) 424-0200

Women in Leadership	★ Women and the
★★ students	Curriculum
★ faculty	

7,458 undergraduates

	Amer. Ind.	Asian Amer.	Blacks	Hispanics	Whites
F	17	10	89	8	3,759
M	12	8	94	15	3,446
%	0.4	0.2	2.5	0.3	96.6

Located on the banks of Lake Winnebago, the University of Wisconsin at Oshkosh, founded in 1871 as a preparatory school for teachers, became a college in 1925, and gained university status in 1964. In 1971 it became a part of the University of Wisconsin system. The university offers bachelor's and graduate degree programs, and has a division of continuing education. Alternative schedules include evening classes and off-campus, weekend classes, self-paced/contract learning, a summer session, and three-, seven-, and 14-week courses. The college attracts 9,823 students.

Women are 52 percent of the 7,458 undergraduates; 13 percent of women attend part-time. The median age of all undergraduates is 19. Public transportation and on-campus parking for a fee are available to the 66 percent of undergraduates who commute.

Childcare facilities are available for students, faculty, and staff, at a fee based on a sliding scale up to $4.50 a day. The campus facility, which accommodates all requests, operates from 7:30 a.m. to 5:00 p.m. Private childcare is available nearby.

Policies to Ensure Fairness to Women. The Assistant to the Chancellor is a permanent, full-time consultant on matters pertaining to sex equity, equal employment opportunity, and handicapped access. Formal grievance procedures with regard to sexual harassment are being devised.

Women in Leadership Positions. *Students.* Women have shared student leadership almost equally with men in recent years. Of the five student leadership positions, women have been student-body president once, presiding officer of student government twice, presiding officer of the student union once, editor-in-chief of the campus newspaper twice, and presiding officer of the residence-hall council once.

Faculty. Women are one-quarter of a full-time faculty of 425. There are 3 female faculty for every 100 female students and 10 male faculty for every 100 male students.

Administrators. Men hold all higher administrative positions, with the exception of head librarian and the director of women's athletics. Women chair four of 31 departments—social work, library science, curriculum, and instruction. Of 5 deans, 2 are female—Dean of the Graduate School and Dean of the College of Nursing. Of 28 members of the faculty senate, 5 are women, including 1 black woman. Two women are on the 9-member campus-wide promotions committee; 5 women are on the 16-member Board of Regents. In 1981, the spring commencement speaker was a woman, and 3 of 6 campus-wide lecturers were women.

Women and the Curriculum. Most women take degrees in education (29 percent), health professions (25 percent), and business (10 percent).

A Women's Studies Program, staffed by eight women and six men, offers an undergraduate minor. Courses include Men and Women in Literature, Twentieth-Century Women Authors, Sex Differences in Society, and Women and Religion. A committee encourages the development of courses on women in departments and maintains the Women's Studies Program. "Faculty College," a workshop, addresses sexism and racism in the curriculum. The departments of business, education, nursing, physical education, and social work provide some instruction on matters specific to women.

Minority Women. Although minority students are less than 3 percent of the student body, the Multicultural Center has its own building, a full-time director, two full-time minority counselors, and a full-time secretary.

Women and Athletics. The athletic program for women offers a variety of intercollegiate sports. The intramural program offers six sports, half of them coeducational. Intercollegiate sports for women include badminton, basketball, field hockey, gymnastics, riflery, skiing, softball, swimming, tennis, track and field, and volleyball.

Housing and Student Organizations. Thirty-four percent of undergraduates live in women's and coeducational dormitories. One women's and one coeducational dormitory have restrictive hours for visitors of the opposite sex. The eleven residence-hall directors, six of whom are women, are offered awareness-training on the avoidance of sexism and racism, and on cultural programming, assertiveness, and communications techniques.

Seventy undergraduate women belong to sororities, which do not provide housing for members.

Special Services and Programs for Women. *Health and Counseling.* A male physician is available for medical treatment, which includes birth control. Abortion costs are covered by the regular student health insurance; maternity benefits can be obtained for an additional annual charge of $145. A counseling center, staffed by one woman and seven men, who are aided by four practicum students, is available for gynecological, birth control, abortion, and rape and assault counseling.

Safety and Security. Measures include campus police with weapons training and the authority to make arrests, assistance from the Oshkosh police when necessary, and a community rape-crisis center. One rape and six assaults (one on a woman) were reported for 1980–81.

Other. The Woman's Center, under the part-time direction of a student, has a budget of $6,000 and annually serves about 400 women, 15 percent of them black women. It sponsors an annual women's week. The Winnebago County Rape Crisis Center sponsors a program for battered women.

Institutional Self-Description. "The university has a specific and published goal (approved by the adminstration, faculty, and student body) supporting affirmative action, particularly the elimination of stereotyping. In addition, the campus provides all students with the opportunity to design Independently Planned Majors suited to career interests and ambitions; this flexibility has been particularly important to returning, nontraditional women students. Experiential learning is recognized and credit is awarded as appropriate."

University of Wisconsin, Parkside
Box 2000, Kenosha, WI 53141
Telephone: (414) 553-2345

Women in Leadership   ★ **Women and the Curriculum**
  ★★★ students
    ★★ administrators

4,106 undergraduates

	Amer. Ind.	Asian Amer.	Blacks	Hispanics	Whites
F	2	9	106	14	1,695
M	8	10	76	28	2,104
%	0.3	0.5	4.5	1.0	93.8

The University of Wisconsin, Parkside is a public, four-year college. Of 5,241 students, 4,106 are undergraduates; 45 percent of the undergraduates are women, of whom 42 percent attend part-time. The median age of undergraduates is 21.

Degrees are awarded in business, the social sciences, engineering, and arts and sciences. Scheduling alternatives include on-and off-campus day and evening classes, summer sessions, self-paced/contract learning, and occasional courses for credit on public television. All students commute by public or private transportation. Parking is available on campus; there is free transportation from distant lots to classroom buildings.

On-campus day and evening childcare accommodates 75 percent of students' requests.

Policies to Ensure Fairness to Women. On a part-time basis, four staff members review policies and monitor practices pertaining to equal-employment-opporutnity, sex-equity-for-students, and handicapped-access laws. The Equal Opportunity Officer and one staff person responsible for handicapped access have policy-making responsibilities. The Affirmative Action Officer is a compliance administrator only. A written campus policy prohibiting sexual harassment has been communicated to faculty and staff; complaints are resolved through the general campus grievance procedure. The Chancellor appoints the Commission on the Status of Women, which includes student members with voting rights, meets regularly, and addresses the concerns of women, including those from minority groups. The Commission on Minority Affairs also attends to the special concerns of minority women.

Women in Leadership Positions. *Students.* Women hold important leadership positions on this campus. In recent years, they served twice as president of the student body, three times as president of the student senate, and once as president of student court, president of student union, and editor of the campus newspaper. A woman heads one of two honorary societies.

Faculty. Eighteen percent of the 161 full-time faculty are women. Among the full-time faculty is one Asian American woman. The ratio of female faculty to female students is 3 to 100; the corresponding ratio for males is 10 to 100.

Administrators. Of seven top administrators, women are chief student-life officer, head librarian, and director of institutional research. Women chair two of eight divisions—fine arts and education. Of 16 regents, one is a black woman and four are white women.

Women and the Curriculum. Most women receive their bachelor's degrees in social sciences (21 percent), business (20 percent), psychology (13 percent), and arts and sciences. Eight percent of women graduate in the nontraditional fields of physical sciences, mathematics, and engineering. The education division and Community Student Services offer mathematics confidence training. The education, nursing, and business programs offer some instruction on matters specific to women.

The Women's Studies Program, which is chaired part-time by a permanently appointed faculty member, offers an undergraduate minor. Courses include Introduction to Women's Studies, Women in Western Civilization, Philosophy and Feminism, Images of Women, and Sex Roles in Cross-Cultural Perspective. An official committee is charged with monitoring the Women's Studies Program, developing courses on women in departments, reporting on curricular developments that include women, and developing curricular material on women. Faculty are offered workshops on nontraditional occupations for women and men, needs of reentry women, and affirmative action and equal opportunity.

Women and Athletics. The intramural sport for women is bowling. Club sports are available. Thirty-two percent of 224 varsity athletes are women; they receive 20 percent of athletic scholarships. Three of twelve paid intercollegiate coaches are women. Intercollegiate sports are basketball, bowling, cross-country, fencing, softball, swimming, tennis, track, and volleyball.

Special Services and Programs for Women. *Health and Counseling.* Medical treatment is provided by contractual agreement with an off-campus physician. Counseling on birth control and other gynecological matters is provided off campus by four men and one white woman.

Safety and Security. Measures consist of campus police with weapons training and arrest authority, high-intensity lighting, and information courses on campus safety. Two assaults on women were reported for 1980–81.

Career. Services include workshops on nontraditional occupations, programs by women in nontraditional careers, job discrimination information, updated files on alumnae by careers, programs to establish contacts between alumnae and women students, and workshops on assertiveness and how to dress for success.

Other. University Extension and community agencies sponsor an annual women's conference. Dramatic Arts organizes theater and other women's arts programs. A peer support program offers to students who have interrupted their educations for five or more years the help of students who have already made successful reentries.

Women in Business, Women's Concourse (half of whose members are black or Hispanic), and Minority Student Union serve as advocates for women on campus. All three groups are chaired by women, and half the members of the Minority Student Union are women.

Special Features. The library learning center has developed an extensive collection of Women's Studies materials, including the complete periodical collection of *Herstory.*

Institutional Self-Description. "Because UW-Parkside serves a large number of nontraditional and part-time students, it offers numerous services and programs to meet special needs of single parents, working women, and housewives. Support groups, evening hours for childcare and counseling services, career-oriented programs, a Women's Studies minor, and a commitment to the hiring of female faculty and staff at both entry and higher level positions, all contribute to a supportive environment for women students of all ages."

University of Wisconsin, Stevens Point
2100 Main St., Stevens Point WI 54481
Telephone: (715) 346-0123

Women in Leadership ★★ students	★ Women and the Curriculum
	★ Women and Athletics

7,918 undergraduates

	Amer. Ind.	Asian Amer.	Blacks	Hispanics	Whites
F	32	7	12	4	3,720
M	31	14	13	7	3,982
%	0.8	0.3	0.3	0.1	98.5

 AAUW

The University of Wisconsin at Stevens Point offers a range of undergraduate as well as associate and master's degrees. Some 8,966 students enroll. Women constitute nearly half the 7,918 graduates; 9 percent of women attend part-time. The median age of undergraduates is 20.

Classes meet evenings on and off campus and during the day on campus. There is a large adult continuing education program. A summer session is available. For the 59 percent of students who commute, public transportation and campus parking for a fee are available.

A university-operated childcare center accommodates 90 percent of requests, at a fee of $.75 per hour or $26 per week. Additional, private childcare facilites are nearby.

Policies to Ensure Fairness to Women. The Assistant to the Chancellor for Equal Opportunity and Affirmative Action has part-time responsibility for policy regarding sex-equity, equal-employment-opportunity, and handicapped-access legislation. The university is in the process of establishing a sexual harassment policy protecting all members of the community. An informal mechanism handles complaints; a formal grievance procedure is being developed. A Commission on the Status of Women, appointed by the Chancellor, includes students as voting members, publicizes its views on issues of concern to women, and takes public stands on issues of concern to students.

Women in Leadership Positions. *Students.* Women students assume important leadership positions. In recent years, women have held almost every major campus office for at least one term, including president of the student body, student senate, student union board, and residence-hall council, and editor of the campus newspaper.

Faculty. Twenty percent of the 390 faculty are women, a proportion below the national average. There are 2 female faculty for every 100 female students and 8 male faculty for every 100 male students.

Administrators. Men occupy the top-level administrative positions and chair all departments except theater arts. Five of the 16 regents are women.

Women and the Curriculum. Most bachelor's degrees earned by women are in education (34 percent), home economics (13 percent), and social sciences (11 percent). Eight percent are in such nontraditional areas as agriculture, mathematics, and physical sciences. An innovative program encourages women to prepare for science careers; a similar program is planned for careers in natural resources. The mathematics department sponsors a mathematics anxiety clinic for women. Forty-five percent of students in cooperative education and 70 percent of those in internship programs are women.

The Women's Studies Program, headed by a part-time director, offers an undergraduate minor. Nine courses are available through Women's Studies and the departments of English, history, political science, psychology, and communications. Recent titles include Introduction to Women's Studies, Women in Literature, Women in Media, and History of European Women. During the past five years, 45 students have minored in the program. The education and physical education departments provide some instruction on matters specific to women. An official committee develops the Women's Studies Program and creates new curricula. Nontraditional occupations for men and women and affirmative action and equal opportunity are topics for faculty workshops.

Minority Women. Two percent of undergraduate women are members of minority groups, mainly American Indian. The Commission on the Status of Women and the Commisssion on Minority Affairs address the concerns of minority women. Professional counselors and residence-hall staff are offered awareness training on avoiding racism. The Black Student Coalition and the American Indian Council are advocates for minority women.

Women and Athletics. The organized athletic program for women is good. Eight intercollegiate teams attract 158 women athletes. At least ten intramural activities, mainly team sports, including coeducational volleyball and football, are offered. Thirty percent of intramural athletes are women. Five paid varsity coaches are women. Intercollegiate sports offered are basketball, cross-country, field hockey, softball, swimming, tennis, track, and volleyball.

Housing and Student Organizations. Forty-one percent of undergraduates live in single-sex and coeducational dormitories that have restricted hours for visitors of the opposite sex.

Less than 1 percent of undergraduate women belong to social sororities; sororities provide housing for their members. Among groups that serve women on campus are NOW (National Organization for Women), Women's Awareness Association, Women's resource Center Committee, The Gay People's Union.

Special Services and Programs for Women. *Health and Counseling.* The student health service has a staff of 3 male physicians and 6 health-care providers, 4 of whom are women. Two of 5 professionals at the student counseling center are women. Counseling and treatment are available for gynecological problems, birth control, and rape and assault. Counselors are offered in-service training on the avoidance of sex-role stereotyping.

Safety and Security. Measures consist of campus and local police protection, night-time escort for women, instruction and information on self-defense and campus safety, and a rape crisis center. No rapes and 7 assaults on women were reported for 1980–81.

Other. A Women's Resource Center sponsors a displaced homemakers' program, assertiveness training, and a telephone information and referral service. Together with the Women's History Week Committee, it sponsors an annual women's week. The Family Crisis Center aids battered women.

Returning Women Students. A Continuing Education for Women Program has its own center and attracts 375 students. An additional 1,200 returning women are enrolled in other continuing education courses. Faculty are offered workshops on the needs of reentry women.

Institutional Self-Description. "Quality undergraduate edu-

cation is at the heart of the university's mission, and the enrollment of women and minorities is increasing. Through a strong affirmative action effort over the past few years, more women and minorities are being considered for faculty and administrative postions, and new programs are being developed not only for the nontraditional student but for women in nontraditional fields as well."

University of Wisconsin, Superior
1800 Grand Ave., Superior, WI 54880
Telephone: (715) 392-8101

| Women in Leadership | ★ Women and the |
| ★ students | Curriculum |

1,741 undergraduates

	Amer. Ind.	Asian Amer.	Blacks	Hispanics	Whites
F	12	2	37	0	712
M	15	1	37	5	875
%	1.6	0.2	2.6	0.3	95.3

Founded in 1893, University of Wisconsin at Superior is a public university with 2,282 students enrolled in bachelor's and master's programs. There are 1,741 undergraduates, whose median age is 22. Forty-three percent of the undergraduates are women, 15 percent of whom attend part-time.

Bachelor's degrees are awarded in education, business, and arts and sciences. The university offers a variety of scheduling alternatives, including on- and off-campus day and evening classes, weekend college, a summer session, and self-paced/contract learning. The Center for Continuing Education administers adult education programs. Seventy-three percent of students commute to campus. Limited public transportation is available, along with on-campus parking at a fee.

On-campus childcare accommodates 95 to 100 percent of students' requests. Charges are based on a fixed hourly rate, with a lower fee for each additional child. Private childcare facilities are also available near campus.

Policies to Ensure Fairness to Women. The Affirmative Action Officer and the Title IX Coordinator, on a part-time basis, review university policies affecting equality for women and minorities and oversee grievance procedures in case of complaints. The draft of a sexual harassment policy has been publicly communicated in writing to students, faculty, and staff. A formal grievance procedure for resolving complaints is being developed. There is a Commission on Minority Affairs.

Women in Leadership Positions. *Students.* Superior has four campus-wide leadership positions. In three recent years, women served once as president of the student union and editor-in-chief of the campus newspaper, and twice as manager of the campus radio station.

Faculty. Nineteen percent of 119 faculty members are women. The ratio of female faculty to female students is 4 to 100; the ratio for men is 11 to 100.

Administrators. All top administrators are male. Of 16 regents, one is a black woman and four are white women. Thirty-one percent of the faculty senate are women. Three of 15 departments—psychology, language and literature, and health and physical education—are chaired by women.

Women and the Curriculum. Most women earn bachelor's degrees in education (28 percent), business (15 percent), and public affairs (10 percent). A few women earn two-year degrees, all in arts and sciences. Four percent of women major in the nontraditional fields of computer science and physical sciences.

The Women's Studies Program, chaired part-time by a permanently appointed faculty member, offers an undergraduate minor. Fifteen Women's Studies courses are offered in nine departments. These include Assertiveness Training, Women and Power, Topics in the History of Human Sexual Attitudes, and courses on women and arts, film, literature, and sports. A university committee is developing courses on women in traditional departments. Curricular innovations in education, physical education, social work, and business address some concerns specific to women.

Women and Athletics. Women have some opportunity to participate in individual and team sports through both intramural and intercollegiate programs. One-third of 300 varsity athletes are women, who participate in basketball, cross-country, gymnastics, track, and volleyball.

Housing and Student Organizations. Single-sex and coeducational dormitories without restrictive hours for visitors house 27 percent of students. Of the women living in residence halls, 95 percent are white, 2 percent black, and 3 percent members of other minority groups. One man and two white women serve as residence-hall directors; they are offered training on the avoidance of racism and on birth control.

Five percent of women students are members of sororities.

Special Services and Programs for Women. *Health and Counseling.* The student health service, staffed by 1 female nurse and 1 part-time male physician, offers birth control and rape and assault treatment. The counseling center employs 1 woman and 3 men and provides some personal counseling on problems specific to women.

Safety and Security. Measures consist of campus and municipal police and high-intensity lighting in all areas. Faculty programs include awareness-training on sexual assault. Six assaults (two on women, including one rape) were reported for 1980–81.

Career. Services include workshops and printed information on nontraditional occupations, programs by women in nontraditional careers, job discrimination information, and updated files of alumnae by occupation.

Other. Women's Studies and Extension operate the small Women's Resource Center. Directed by a part-time, salaried administrator, it serves 400 women each year. Graduate students and older undergraduates use the center more than younger students. The Resource Center and the Center for Continuing Education sponsor a women's lecture series.

Institutional Self-Description. "UW-Superior, located in friendly, predominantly rural Douglas County, Wisconsin, provides the primary university opportunity for women in the area. The university offers not only extensive evening and weekend courses, but also competency-based programs through its Extended Degree Program, providing varied and flexible degree opportunities to women with family and/or vocational responsibilities. Individual counseling and advising are available for all women students."

University of Wisconsin, Whitewater
800 West Main Street
Whitewater, Wisconsin 53190
Telephone: (414) 472-1234

Women in Leadership	★ Women and the
★ students	Curriculum
	★★ Women and Athletics

7,157 undergraduates

	Amer. Ind.	Asian Amer.	Blacks	Hispanics	Whites
F	6	5	110	31	3,371
M	7	7	89	44	3,395
%	0.2	0.2	2.8	1.1	95.8

🏠 🏛 👫 ⬚ 📖 AAUW NWSA

The University of Wisconsin at Whitewater was founded in 1868 as a teacher-training school and became a public university in 1971. Its 9,601 students include 7,157 undergraduates; 50 percent of undergraduates are women, 8 percent of whom attend part-time. The median age of undergraduates is 21. Whitewater awards bachelor's degrees in arts, business, and education. Scheduling alternatives include on- and off-campus evening classes, summer sessions, and intersessions. The continuing education program includes 743 returning women students. Fifty percent of students live off campus and either walk to the campus or park their cars on campus; some space is available free of charge.

Nearby private and on-campus childcare is available. On-campus daycare, which accommodates 90 percent of students' requests, charges $3.50 a day per child.

Policies to Ensure Fairness to Women. Three upper-level administrators, including the Vice Chancellor, are responsible on a part-time basis for university policies and practices relating to equal-employment-opportunity and sex-equity-for-students legislation. The Director of Rehabilitation/Education Services reviews handicapped accessibility policies. A sexual harassment policy that will include a formal grievance procedure and cover students, faculty, and staff is being developed. The Chancellor appoints the Commission on the Status of Women. This commission includes student members with voting rights, meets regularly, prepares a publicly distributed report at least annually, takes public stands on issues of concern to students, and reports to the Regents Task Force on the Status of Women.

Women in Leadership Positions. *Students.* In three recent years, women were president of the student board and editor of the newspaper once, and president of the residence-hall council three times. Women chair nine of 20 honorary societies.

Faculty. Twenty-one percent of the 370 full-time faculty are women; 66 percent of women hold permanent positions. Recent data show that among the 122 full-time female faculty are 2 black, 1 American Indian, and 1 Hispanic women. There are 2 female faculty for every 100 female students and 9 male faculty for every 100 male students.

Administrators. Except for the women's athletic director, the top administrators are men. Of 37 departments, women chair 5, including theater/dance; psychology; business education and office administration; and health, physical education and recreation. One black and four white women are among the 16 regents. In a recent year, the commencement speaker was a woman and 1 of 4 alumni awards was granted to a woman.

Women and the Curriculum. Two-thirds of women earn degrees in education and business. Two percent of women graduate in the nontraditional field of mathematics. Sixty percent of student interns are women.

Under a director who holds a permanent, full-time faculty position, the Women's Studies program awards an undergraduate minor and an individualized undergraduate major. Six courses are offered by Women's Studies and 15 courses in departments. Courses range from an Introduction to Women's Studies through a variety of specialized courses, including Women in Cross-Cultural Perspective, Counseling Women and Girls, Women Writers, Self-Defense, and Women Speakers in America. University committees are developing the Women's Studies Program, devising courses on women in traditional departments, and developing curricular materials on women.

Women and Athletics. Twenty-six percent of varsity, 30 percent of intramural, and 45 percent of club athletes are women. Seven of the eleven paid coaches are female. The active intramural program includes a large selection of women's and coeducational team sports and some individual sports. Intercollegiate sports are basketball, field hockey, golf, gymnastics, softball, swimming, tennis, track, and volleyball.

Housing and Student Organizations. Fifty percent of students live in single-sex and coeducational dormitories which do not restrict visiting hours for members of the opposite sex. Nine white women, two minority women, and six men, who are offered awareness-training on a broad variety of areas, direct residence halls. Five percent of full-time undergraduates join residential sororities and fraternities.

There are 16 minority-group women in integrated sororities and an equal number in all-minority sororities. Associated Women Students serves as an advocate for women on campus and sponsors an annual women's week.

Special Services and Programs for Women. *Health and Counseling.* Two female physicians, assisted by 8 female and 1 male health-care providers, offer gynecological and birth control services, as well as rape and assault treatment. Three men and 1 white woman counsel on gynecological matters, birth control, abortion, and rape and assault.

Safety and Security. Measures include campus and municipal police with arrest authority, high-intensity lighting, emergency telephones and alarms, self-defense courses, and information on campus safety. No rapes or assaults were reported for 1980-81.

Career. Career placement programs include workshops on nontraditional occupations, lectures by women in nontraditional careers, nonsexist/nonracist literature, and job discrimination information.

Other. Student Services and academic departments sponsor assertiveness training. The Alumni Office sponsors a women's day. Older women find support at Older and Wiser Learners (OWLS); handicapped women at Students Accessible Society.

Special Features. Over the past five years, the Andersen Library has built a strong collection of books on women, and this campus has access to the services and publications of the Women's Studies Librarian-at-Large for the University of Wisconsin system. Following a regent-sponsored study of the status of women, the Chancellor has appointed a Committee for Promoting Opportunities for Women to improve conditions for women students, faculty, and employees.

Institutional Self-Description. "Whitewater has a strong, Women's Studies Program with over 20 undergraduate and graduate courses taught by feminist scholars. Women students find support in such active groups as the Association of Women Students and the Returning Student Association. The campus has good childcare facilities and a strong undergraduate women's intercollegiate athletic program."

Viterbo College
815 South 9th Street
La Crosse, WI 54601
Telephone: (608) 784-0040

Women in Leadership
- ★★★ students
- ★★ faculty
- ★★ administrators

944 undergraduates

	Amer. Ind.	Asian Amer.	Blacks	Hispanics	Whites
F	0	3	16	3	740
M	1	3	1	1	155
%	0.1	0.7	1.8	0.4	97.0

 AAUW

Viterbo College is a private, four-year, coeducational college operated under the auspices of the Roman Catholic Church. The total enrollment is 1,012. Women make up 82 percent of the 944 undergraduates; 11 percent of the women attend part-time. The median age of all students is 21.

Viterbo offers a range of professional, pre-professional, and liberal arts degree programs. Most students commute. The campus is accessible by public transportation. On-campus parking is provided.

Private childcare facilities are located close to the campus.

Policies to Ensure Fairness to Women. The Business Manager shares responsibility for policies related to equal-employment-opportunity, sex-equity, and handicapped-access legislation. An assistant monitors compliance. Complaints of sexual harassment are dealt with informally and confidentially.

Women in Leadership Positions. *Students.* Women have outstanding opportunities to exercise campus leadership. During a recent three year period, women held the eight student offices at least once and several of them three times.

Faculty. Forty-seven percent of a full-time faculty of 49 are women. There are 3 female faculty for every 100 female students and 19 male faculty for every 100 male students.

Administrators. Women are chief academic officer, chief student-life officer, and head librarian; men occupy the other four key posts. Women chair ten of the 19 departments, including chemistry, religious studies, and philosophy.

Women and the Curriculum. Women receive 80 percent of the bachelor's degrees awarded; of these, two-thirds are in health professions.

The English department offers Women and Literature.

Women and Athletics. About 4 percent of the female undergraduates participate in intercollegiate sports. Seven sports are offered in the intramural program. One of the two paid varsity coaches is a woman. The intercollegiate sports offered are basketball and volleyball.

Housing and Student Organizations. Twenty-seven percent of undergraduates live on campus in single-sex dormitories and apartments for juniors and seniors. Dormitories restrict visiting hours for visitors of the opposite sex. The residence-hall staff is predominantly female; staff are offered awareness-training on sex education.

Special Services and Programs for Women. *Health and Counseling.* The student health service is staffed by one female health-care provider; there is no resident physician. Students seeking medical treatment or counseling specific to women are referred to local agencies. The student counseling center has four counselors, three of whom are women.

Safety and Security. Town police are responsible for campus security. Other measures include a night-time escort service for women and information sessions on rape and assault prevention. There is a community-based rape crisis center. For 1980–81, no rapes or assaults were reported.

Other. Seventy percent of the more than 200 students in the adult continuing education program are women. Faculty attend workshops on the needs of reentry women. A program which will allow registered nurses to obtain the B.A. at an accelerated pace has been planned.

Institutional Self-Description. "The mission of Viterbo College is to provide a quality liberal arts and a career-oriented professional or pre-professional education which is rooted in the Catholic tradition and experienced within the context of an ecumenical Christian community. Viterbo offers the availability of specialized majors, the opportunity to participate in small classes with individualized instruction, a pleasant and convenient geographic setting, and the availability of a generous scholarship program."

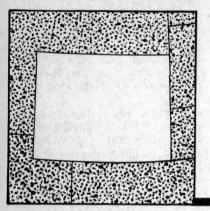

WYOMING

Casper College
125 College Drive, Casper, WY 82601
Telephone: (307) 268-2675
Women in Leadership
★★ students
★ faculty

1,428 undergraduates

	Amer. Ind.	Asian Amer.	Blacks	Hispanics	Whites
F	4	0	1	13	719
M	2	2	10	11	650
%	0.4	0.1	0.8	1.7	97.0

Casper is a public two-year college that serves 3,919 students. Fifty-two percent of the 1,428 undergraduates are women; 14 percent of women attend part-time. The median age of undergraduates is 20. The college offers two-year degrees in liberal arts, and in such vocational fields as agriculture, accounting, computer science, electronics, and mining technologies. Alternative schedules include day and evening classes offered on campus and self-paced/contract learning options. There is a School of Continuing Education. Thirty-six percent of students live on campus. Public transportation is available only to the handicapped; on-campus parking and shuttle service from remote lots are provided free to all commuters.

Policies to Ensure Fairness to Women. A Personnel Officer has responsibility part-time for monitoring compliance with equal-employment-opportunity and sex-equity regulations. The President of the college appoints the members of the Affirmative Action Committee, which promotes educational and employment opportunities for women and members of minority groups. A publicly communicated formal policy prohibits sexual harassment of students, staff, and faculty; complaints are resolved through a formal grievance procedure.

Women in Leadership Positions. *Students.* Of four campus leadership positions, women have held three: student body president for one year and editor of the newspaper and presiding officer of the residence-hall council for two years during a recent three-year period. A woman student presides over the honorary society.

Faculty. Of 121 faculty, 30 percent are women. There are 6 female faculty to every 100 female students and 14 male faculty to every 100 male students.

Administrators. All key administrative positions except head librarian are held by men. Women chair the divisions of business and language and literature, and a woman directs the nursing programs. In a recent year, the commencement speaker was a woman.

Women and the Curriculum. Most two-year degrees awarded to women are in arts and sciences (57 percent), health technolo-

gies (20 percent), and business programs (19 percent). The college reports that some women major in such nontraditional fields as engineering, mining technology, automotive service, and construction. Pamphlets on avoiding sexism in classroom materials are distributed to faculty. Workshops for faculty on equal opportunity and sexual harassment are available. There are no courses on women.

Women and Athletics. Forty percent of athletes in coeducational intramural sports and almost half of athletes in intercollegiate sports are women. Women receive 46 percent of athletic scholarship aid. Three of six paid varsity coaches are women. Intercollegiate sports include golf, gymnastics, rodeo, tennis, trapshooting, and volleyball.

Housing and Student Organizations. Thirty-six percent of students live on campus. Coeducational dormitories and housing for married students and single parents are available. A married student whose spouse is not enrolled may live in married students' housing. Dormitories restrict hours for visitors of the opposite sex. Residence hall-staff are offered awareness-training on sex education and birth control.

Special Services and Programs for Women. *Health and Counseling.* The health service, which provides no medical treatment specific to women, is staffed by a female physician part-time and one female health-care provider. One of four staff in the counseling service is a woman; gynecological and birth control counseling are available.

Safety and Security. Measures consist of campus police with arrest authority. Two assaults (neither on a woman) were reported for 1980–81.

Institutional Self-Description. ''Casper College is committed to maintaining a balance betweeen general and vocational education so that its students achieve both intellectual and vocational maturity. The qualified and dedicated faculty and staff at Casper College provide an educational environment which is personal, cordial, and serious.''

Eastern Wyoming College
3200 West C, Torrington, WY 82240
Telephone: (307) 532-7111
Women in Leadership
★★ students
★ faculty

379 undergraduates

	Amer. Ind.	Asian Amer.	Blacks	Hispanics	Whites
F	1	0	2	6	224
M	1	1	3	8	133
%	0.5	0.3	1.3	3.7	94.2

This two-year college was originally an extension center of the

University of Wyoming. It became a community college, offering transfer and vocational courses, in 1956. Of 645 students, 379 are in degree programs. Of these, 61 percent are women, and 17 percent of the women attend part-time. The median age is 28. The college offers two-year degrees in such fields as business, ecology, health, and liberal arts.

Evening classes are held on and off campus. Workshops, seminars, and minicourses are offered through Community Services. Thirty-five percent of students live on campus. Parking for commuters is free.

Policies to Ensure Fairness to Women. The Secretary to the President serves as part-time equal-employment-opportunity officer with responsibility for monitoring compliance with federal policies. An active Committee on the Status of Women, responsible to the Dean of College Services, reports regularly and publicly to the campus community. Student committee members have voting rights. The Committee on Minority Affairs as well as the Women's Committee address the concerns of minority women. Complaints of sexual harassment are resolved informally or through a formal grievance procedure.

Women in Leadership Positions. *Students.* There are three student leadership positions. During three recent years, women presided over the residence-hall council for three consecutive terms and were editor-in-chief of the campus newspaper for two terms. Women head two of the three honorary societies.

Faculty. Of 28 full-time faculty, 7 are women.

Administrators. An American Indian woman heads the library; the other six top-level positions are held by men. Two of the seven trustees are women.

Women and the Curriculum. Most of the two-year degrees awarded to women are in health technologies (40 percent) and arts and sciences (38 percent). Women are 75 percent of the students in practicums or internships.

There are no courses on women. A committee is planning a Women's Studies Program and collecting curricular materials on women.

Women and Athletics. Women are 33 percent of intramural and 57 percent of intercollegiate athletes; one of the three paid varsity coaches is a woman. Intercollegiate sports offered are basketball, rodeo, tennis, track, and volleyball.

Housing and Student Organizations. Thirty-five percent of students live in single-sex dormitories that have restricted hours for visitors of the opposite sex. Four percent of the undergraduate women living in dormitories are Hispanic women. A married woman whose husband is not enrolled is permitted to live in married students' housing. Three of the four residence-hall directors are women.

Every Woman's Resource Center, functions as an advocacy group for women on campus.

Special Services and Programs for Women. *Health and Counseling.* Student health is staffed part-time by 1 male physician and 1 female health-care provider. The student counseling staff of 3 white women and 2 men provides counseling on gynecological problems, birth control, abortion, and rape and assault. Counselors are offered training on sex-role stereotyping.

Safety and Security. Measures consist of local police, self-defense courses for women, and information on rape and assault prevention. No rapes or assaults on women were reported for 1980–81.

Career. Workshops on nontraditional careers, information on job discrimination, and nonsexist/nonracist printed information on nontraditional careers for women are available to students. Faculty are offered workshops on nontraditional careers for women and men.

Other. College Services operates the Women's Center, which provides leadership/assertiveness training and sponsors a women's lecture series, theater and other women's arts programs, and a program for battered women.

Institutional Self-Description. None provided.

University of Wyoming
Laramie, WY 82071
Telephone: (307) 766-1121

| Women in Leadership | ★ Women and the |
| ★ students | Curriculum |

7,160 undergraduates

	Amer. Ind.	Asian Amer.	Blacks	Hispanics	Whites
F	17	26	30	51	2,917
M	18	18	65	54	3,724
%	0.5	0.6	1.4	1.5	96.0

 AAUW NWSA

Established in 1886 as a land-grant college, the University of Wyoming in Laramie provides a range of undergraduate, graduate, and professional studies to some 8,900 students. Programs emphasize areas of concern to the state and region. Alternative class schedules, including self-paced, learning contracts, evening classes, and off-campus locations and a summer session are available.

Women are 43 percent of the 7,160 undergraduates; one-tenth of the women attend part-time and one-fourth of women students are older than 25. The median age of undergraduates is 22. For the 70 percent of undergraduates who commute or live off campus, on-campus parking is free.

Low-cost university childcare facilities accept children on a first-come, first-served basis. Private arrangements for childcare may also be made near the campus.

Policies to Ensure Fairness to Women. A full-time Employment Practices Officer monitors compliance with legislation on equal employment opportunity, sex equity, and handicapped accessibility. A formal grievance procedure resolves complaints of sexual harassment. The Office of Minority Affairs includes in its charge the concerns of minority women.

Women in Leadership Positions. *Students.* Opportunities for women students to exercise campus leadership are good. In recent years women were president of the student body and three times editor-in-chief of the campus newspaper. Three of the five presidents of honorary societies are women.

Faculty. Women are 17 percent of a full-time faculty of 651. According to a recent report, 3 Asian American women are on the total faculty. The ratio of female faculty to female students is 4 to 100. The ratio of male faculty to male students is 14 to 100.

Administrators. All high-level administrative posts are occupied by men. Women chair eight of 57 departments. The Dean of the College of Arts and Sciences and the Dean of the School of Nursing in the College of Health Sciences are female.

Women and the Curriculum. A majority of women graduating with bachelor's degrees major in education (28 percent), the health professions (13 percent), business and management (10 percent), and public affairs (8 percent). Nine percent major in nontraditional areas, with the largest number in agriculture. A program to encourage females to consider careers in engineering brings ninth-grade girls to campus. One-third of the students doing field work in Wyoming archeology are women. The Math-Science Teaching Center sponsors a program to build confidence in mathematics.

The Women's Studies Program offers an undergraduate "option." Nine courses on women are offered through the departments of sociology, English, art, psychology, and history. Recent titles include Sex Roles and Society, Women Writers and Female Criticism, History of Women in Art, and Sources and Problems in Women's History. An official committee is responsible for developing the Women's Studies offerings and promoting the teaching of new scholarship on women. Such current issues as mathematics confidence among females, sex-fair curricula, coeducational sports classes, reproductive choice, health-care information important to minority women, services for abused spouses, and discrimination in the workplace are part of the preparation of future teachers, health-care workers, social workers, and business students.

Minority Women. Four percent of undergraduate women are from minority groups, the largest of which is Hispanic. A minority woman is director of a residence hall. Residence-hall staff are offered awareness-training on racism. Among student organizations where minority women would find support are the Women's Center, the Black Student Association, Keepers of the Fire, and Chicano Students.

Women and Athletics. Intramural and intercollegiate programs provide opportunities for organized, competitive, individual and team sports. The university reports special facilities for trap shooting and skiing in the area. Thirty percent of athletic scholarships go to women. Four of 23 paid coaches for intercollegiate sports are female. Some women's intercollegiate teams played in tournaments in 1980. The intercollegiate sports offered are basketball, cross-country, skiing, softball, swimming, track and field, and volleyball.

Housing and Student Organizations. Thirty percent of the undergraduates live on campus. Residential accommodations include single-sex and coeducational dormitories and housing for married students and single parents with children. A married woman whose spouse is not enrolled may live in married students' housing. Men's and women's residence halls vary in their restrictions upon visitors of the opposite sex. Half of the residence-hall directors are women. Awareness-training on sexism and racism is offered residence-hall staff.

One-tenth of full-time undergraduate women belong to social sororities. Sororities and fraternities provide housing for their members.

Special Services and Programs for Women. *Health and Counseling.* The student health service provides some medical attention specific to women, including gynecological and birth control treatment. One of four physicians is female; a female psychiatrist is employed part-time. Half of the permanent staff of the counseling center are women. No counseling specific to women is offered, although personal, marriage, and academic counseling are available. The counseling center sponsors assertiveness training.

Safety and Security. Measures include campus police with arrest authority, night-time escorts for women students, an emergency telephone system, self-defense courses for women, information sessions on safety and crime prevention, and a rape crisis center. Seven assaults upon students were reported for 1980–81; one of these was a rape.

Other. A campus Women's Center is staffed by a student with a faculty advisor. Among the center's services and activities are a Sexual Assault and Family Violence Education project, a telephone line of information, referral, and support, theater and other arts programs (with the theater and art departments), and a women's oral history project. Women's Studies sponsors a women's lecture series. The Humanities Resource Center has a women's film collection. Handicapped women would find support from the Walk and Roll Alliance. Gays and Lesbians of Wyoming (GLOW) meet on campus.

Returning Women Students. The Center for Adult Re-Entry sponsors a program for displaced homemakers. Older women would find other supportive women at the Re-Entry Center.

Special Features. The university's archives include the Women's History Collection of materials from the women's movement of the 1960s and 1970s, a unique resource that used to be the "Berkeley Women's History Library."

Institutional Self-Description. "Wyoming, the first state to grant women suffrage, is known as the Equality State. The University of Wyoming, the only four-year institution of higher education in the state, maintains this tradition of remaining in the vanguard of women's rights in its policies and practices."

Western Wyoming Community College

P.O. Box 428
Rock Springs, WY 82901
Telephone: (307) 382-2121

Women in Leadership
★★★ students
★★ faculty

923 undergraduates

	Amer. Ind.	Asian Amer.	Blacks	Hispanics	Whites
F	5	3	3	13	460
M	1	8	19	25	359
%	0.7	1.2	2.5	4.2	91.4

Located in a small city in southwestern Wyoming, this public, two-year college was founded in 1959. Of 1,264 students, 923 are enrolled in degree programs. Fifty-three percent of undergraduates are women, and 64 percent of women attend part-time. The median age of undergraduates is 28. Over one-fourth of women students are over age 40. The college provides both liberal arts transfer programs and a comprehensive range of vocational courses, including secretarial science, data processing, welding, mining technologies, building trades, and medical laboratory technology.

Alternative schedules and locations include evening classes on and off campus, self-paced learning, a summer session, and an adult education program. Seventy percent of students commute; free on-campus parking is available.

Free day and evening childcare facilities accommodate all requests.

Policies to Ensure Fairness to Women. On a part-time basis, a staff officer with policymaking authority is responsible for equal employment, educational sex equity, and accessibility for the handicapped. The faculty are provided with information about affirmative action and equal opportunity.

Women in Leadership Positions. *Students.* The three campus leadership positions, president of the student body, editor of the campus newspaper, and presiding officer of the residence-hall council, were held by women for each of three recent years. A woman presides over the one honorary society.

Faculty. Of 40 faculty, 35 percent are women. According to recent information, 1 female faculty member is a black woman and 1 is Asian American. There are 8 female faculty for every 100 female students and 19 male faculty for every 100 male students.

Administrators. Of eight top administrators, the head librarian is a woman. A black woman and a white woman chair the divisions of business and humanities, respectively. Sixteen of the 39-member faculty senate are women, including 1 black and 1 Asian American woman. Three of the 7 college trustees are women.

Women and the Curriculum. Most degrees awarded to women are in arts and sciences (82 percent), with smaller numbers in data processing and business and commerce. Courses on women include Women in History, Introduction to Women's Studies, Sex-Role Stereotyping, and Women Returning to School.

Women and Athletics. The modest program includes both intramural and intercollegiate sports. Of 36 intercollegiate athletes, 18 are women. Over 50 percent of athletic scholarships go to women, and two of the four paid varsity coaches are women. Intercollegiate sports offered are basketball, tennis, and volleyball.

Housing and Student Organizations. Thirty percent of students live on campus in coeducational dormitories that have no restrictive visiting hours, as well as in housing for married students and single parents. Of four residence-hall directors, one is a minority woman and two are white women. Directors are offered awareness-training on racism and birth control.

Special Services and Programs for Women. *Health and Counseling.* The student health service, staffed by one female health-care provider, does not give treatment specific to women. A staff of one white woman and one man in the student counseling center provides counseling for gynecological problems, birth control, abortion, and rape and assault.

Safety and Security. Measures include local police patrolling the campus, information sessions on rape and assault prevention, and a rape crisis center. For 1980–81, there were no reported rapes and one assault on a woman.

Career. Workshops on nontraditional careers and nonsexist/ nonracist printed information on nontraditional fields of study are available.

Other. The Student Personnel Office sponsors a Women's Center, which serves 100 women a year, 10 percent of whom are minority women. A faculty member directs the center, which provides cultural and support activities for women of varying lifestyles and life circumstances. With supervision from Adult Education, the Women's Center offers assertiveness/leadership training, assault prevention, and a women's lecture series. The local YWCA sponsors a battered women's program and a telephone information and referral service. The Independent Study Laboratory provides reentry women with individualized study assistance and support.

Institutional Self-Description. "Western Wyoming College has been able to reach out to the community through the Women's Center and provide support groups for women returning to school. Special classes designed especially for women, and the children's center, which offers an educational experience to children free of charge, have been very helpful to the women of our community."

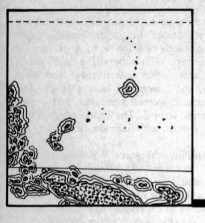

GUAM

University of Guam
University Substation
Mangilao, Guam 96913
Telephone: (671) 734-3434

Women in Leadership
★★ faculty
★ administrators

2,961 undergraduates

	Amer. Ind.	Asian Amer.	Blacks	Hispanics	Whites
F	4	1,146	16	21	239
M	7	996	12	37	271
%	0.4	77.9	1.0	2.1	18.6

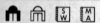

This comprehensive public university serves some 3,000 students, more than 77 percent of whom are Asian American. Founded in 1952 to expand higher education in Micronesia, the university now offers a wide range of undergraduate programs in liberal arts, pre-professional studies, and education. The university offers day and evening classes both on and off campus, as well as a summer session.

Women are 51 percent of the 2,961 undergraduates; 39 percent of the women attend part-time. Over 40 percent of women students are over age 25 and 10 percent are over age 40. On-campus parking is available for the 90 percent of undergraduates who commute.

Private childcare facilities are available nearby.

Policies to Ensure Fairness to Women. Responsibility for compliance with equal employment opportunity is shared by the EEO Coordinator and the Women's Program Coordinator. A written campus policy prohibits sexual harassment of students, faculty and staff; a formal campus grievance procedure resolves complaints. The Coordinator of the Women's Program prepares reports on the status of women for the President of the university and the Civil Service Commission. A Committee on Minority Affairs addresses the concerns of minority women.

Women in Leadership Positions. *Students.* Although women represent more than half of the undergraduate student body, men hold all campus-wide student leadership positions.

Faculty. Women are 37 percent of the full-time faculty of 153, an above average proportion for four-year, public universities. There are 6 female faculty for every 100 female students and 14 male faculty for every 100 male students.

Administrators. Women hold the posts of President and Dean of Library Services. The other five chief administrative positions are held by men. Six of the 20 departments are chaired by women: elementary education, English and applied linguistics, commu-nications, modern languages and literature, nursing, and home economics education. Thirty-three percent of the members of the tenure and reappointments committees, and of the regents, are women.

Women and the Curriculum. One-half of the bachelor's degrees earned by women are in education, while 21 percent are in business. Among the two-year degrees awarded to women, 83 percent are in health technologies.

Thirty percent of students participating in internship programs are women. Courses in the departments of nursing and social work provide some instruction on matters specific to women. There are no courses on women.

Minority Women. Almost three-fourths of the undergraduates are Asian American, and more than 50 percent of these students are women. The President of the university is an Asian American woman. Three Asian American women serve as regents and 14 serve on the full-time faculty, along with 2 black women. Eight percent of undergraduate women living in residence halls are Asian American and 2 percent are black. The 3 female residence-hall directors are minority women.

Women and Athletics. The university does not offer intramural sports, but there is a small intercollegiate sports program. Of the 165 athletes, 27 percent are women, as are seven of the 23 paid varsity coaches. The four women's teams, which have all participated in recent tournament competitions, are basketball, softball, tennis, and volleyball.

Housing and Student Organizations. Ten percent of the undergraduates live on campus in coeducational dormitories that do not restrict hours for visitors of the opposite sex. Three of the eight residence-hall directors are women.

Special Services and Programs for Women. *Health and Counseling.* The student health service, staffed by 1 male physician and 1 female health-care provider, offers medical treatment in gynecology and birth control. The counseling center offers gynecological, birth control, abortion, and rape and assault counseling. The 4-member counseling staff include 2 women, one a minority woman.

Safety and Security. Measures consist of local police, campus police without arrest authority, and high-intensity lighting. Two assaults neither on women, were reported for 1980–81.

Institutional Self-Description. "The mission of the University of Guam, a public land-grant institution, is to provide higher education programs for the people of Guam and the Western Pacific island communities, including undergraduate programs that build upon the Western Pacific's unique and varied cultural traditions and offer career opportunities together with a fundamental liberal arts education; research and graduate programs that are responsive to the specific needs of Guam and other Western Pacific island communities and contribute to their economic growth and stability; and community service programs that promote intercultural interaction, societal development, and personal development."

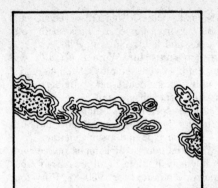

PUERTO RICO

Electronic Data Processing University, College of Puerto Rico, Inc.

555 Muñoz Rivera Ave.
Hato Rey, PR 00918
Telephone: (809) 765-3560

Women in Leadership
★★★ **students**
★ **faculty**
★ **administrators**

1,226 undergraduates

	Amer. Ind.	Asian Amer.	Blacks	Hispanics	Whites
F	0	0	0	267	0
M	0	0	0	959	0
%	0.0	0.0	0.0	100.0	00.0

A private, two-year college, this institution offers instruction only in data processing. It serves an entirely Puerto Rican student body of 1,226, 22 percent of whom are women. Six percent of women attend part-time. According to recent information, 15 percent of women are over age 25; the median age of all students is 19.

All students commute to the campus, on which parking is provided free of charge.

Women in Leadership Positions. *Students.* There are three student leadership positions. In three recent years, women were president of the student body for two consecutive years, and editor-in-chief of the campus newspaper and president of the second-year class for one year each.

Faculty. Eight of the 26 full-time faculty are women. There are 3 female faculty for every 100 students and 2 male faculty for every 100 male students.

Administrators. Three of the nine top-level administrators are women: chief development officer, head librarian, and chief planning officer. Women chair the departments of English and mathematics.

Women and the Curriculum. All two-year degrees and certificates awarded to women are in data processing technologies. There are no courses on women. Faculty are offered workshops on equal-employment-opportunity legislation.

Women and Athletics. Information was not provided.

Special Services and Programs for Women. *Health and Counseling.* Health services are provided by a local hospital. Two men staff the student counseling center. Services specific to women are not available.

Safety and Security. The campus is patrolled by college police who do not have arrest authority. No rapes or assaults on women were reported for 1980–81.

Career. Workshops focused on nontraditional occupations, lectures by women employed in such occupations, and printed in-

formation on such occupations are available to students. The department of mathematics sponsors a program to build mathematics confidence.

Institutional Self-Description. "The institutional philosophy is that technological higher education must be founded on a sound socio-humanistic basis. Our mission is to offer private industry and government agencies the highly qualified personnel (men or women) necessary to fill the needs of the ever growing data processing centers in Puerto Rico."

University of Puerto Rico, Mayaguez Campus

Mayaguez, PR 00708
Telephone: (809) 832-4040

Women in Leadership
★ **faculty**

★ **Women and the Curriculum**

8,435 undergraduates

	Amer. Ind.	Asian Amer.	Blacks	Hispanics	Whites
F	0	0	0	3,259	0
M	0	0	0	5,176	0
%	0.0	0.0	0.0	100.0	0.0

Founded in 1911 as the College of Agriculture, a land-grant institution, the University of Puerto Rico's Mayaguez Campus offers bachelor's degrees in agriculture, business administration, arts and sciences, and engineering. Associate, master's and doctoral degrees are also offered. Evening and summer session classes are available.

Some 8,800 students are enrolled in this four-year, state-supported university, 8,435 of them undergraduates. Thirty-nine percent of the undergraduates are women; 11 percent of women attend part-time. The median age of all students is 19. All students commute to the Mayaguez campus, which is accessible by public transportation. On-campus parking is available. Both sororities and fraternities provide housing for members.

Private childcare facilities are located near the campus.

Policies to Ensure Fairness to Women. An equal-opportunity Officer is assigned to supervise matters relating to sex equity for students. The college did not provide information on the nature or level of this officer's responsibilities. The university does not have a formal policy on sexual harassment. Complaint of sexual harassment are resolved through various campus grievance procedures, depending on the nature and circumstances of the case.

Women in Leadership Positions. *Students.* All student leadership posts are held by men. A woman presides over one of the six campus honorary societies.

Faculty. Thirty-four percent of the 473 full-time faculty are women, a proportion above average for public, four-year institutions in this guide. There are 6 female faculty for every 100 female students and 7 male faculty for every 100 male students. The college reports that all faculty members are Hispanic.

Administrators. Except for the Dean of Academic Affairs, the top administrators are men. Five of 27 departments are chaired by women: social sciences, nursing, humanities, mathematics, and crop protection. Nineteen percent of the 42-member faculty senate are women. One of the 15 speakers in a recent campus-wide lecture series was a woman.

Women and the Curriculum. Most women earn bachelor's degrees in business (21 percent), biology (19 percent), and health professions (10 percent). Eighteen percent of women graduate in the nontraditional fields of agriculture, engineering, mathematics, and physical sciences. Thirty-three percent of the two-year degrees awarded are earned by women, all in health technologies. Six percent of students in cooperative education programs are women.

Faculty workshops are offered on the relationship between sex, race, and selection of major field, nontraditional occupations for women and men, and affirmative action and equal opportunity. There are no courses on women.

Women and Athletics. The Mayaguez campus offers some opportunities for women to participate in organized team and individual sports. Seventeen percent of intramural and 30 percent of intercollegiate athletes are women, who receive 30 percent of athletic scholarship aid. Two of the 17 paid intercollegiate coaches are women. All women's varsity teams competed in recent tournaments. The intercollegiate sports offered are: basketball, softball, swimming, tennis, track and field, and volleyball.

Special Services and Programs for Women. *Health and Counseling.* The student health services employs 1 female and 2 male physicians, along with 7 other health-care providers, 5 of them women. The counseling center has a staff of 15, of whom 5 are women. Available services specific to women include medical treatment and counseling for gynecological problems and birth control, as well as counseling for rape and assault victims.

Safety and Security. Measures consist of campus police with arrest authority and high-intensity lighting in all areas. No rapes and no assaults on women were reported for 1980–81. Fifty-four assaults on men were reported.

Career. Services include workshops on nontraditional occupations, panels by women employed in these fields, and a program to foster networks between alumnae and female students.

Other. General support for women students is provided by the Congreso de Creación Feminina en el Mundo Hispánico. A special committee of the Office of the Dean of Academic Affairs sponsors an annual women's week.

Institutional Self-Description. "In Puerto Rico, traditionally the professions of engineering have been more associated with men. Changes in attitude and new trends related to better job opportunities have increased the enrollment of women in these fields of study. New academic programs preferred by women have been established. In our campus, women get the same treatment and are expected to work as hard as men."

Intercollegiate Sports Chart*

Available Sports

Four-Year Colleges and Universities**

State	College/University	Volleyball	Track and Field	Tennis	Swimming and Diving	Softball	Skiing	Lacrosse	Gymnastics	Golf	Field Hockey	Cross-Country	Basketball	Miscellaneous***
AL	Alabama SU	•	•	•								•	•	
	Huntingdon C	•		•										
	Livingston U	•				•							•	
	Spring Hill C			•									•	
	Tuskegee	•	•	•									•	
	U of Alabama	•	•	•	•	•			•	•		•	•	
	U of North Alabama	•		•									•	
AK	U of Alaska, Fairbanks	•									•		•	RF
AZ	Arizona SU	•	•	•	•	•			•	•	•	•	•	AR, BM
	U of Arizona	•		•	•	•			•	•		•	•	SS
AR	U of Arkansas, Fayetteville												•	
	U of Arkansas, Pine Bluff												•	
CA	Armstrong C	•												
	California S Polytechnic U, Pomona	•	•	•		•			•	•	•	•	•	
	California SU, Chico	•	•			•			•			•	•	
	California SU, Dominguez Hills	•		•	•	•							•	BM
	California SU, Fresno	•		•	•				•				•	BM

	State	Institution		Other
	CA	California SU, Long Beach		AR, BM, FN
		C of Notre Dame		
		Menlo C		
		Mills C		CR
		Pitzer C		
		Pomona C		
		San Diego SU		
		San Francisco SU		BM, SC
		San Jose SU		FN, CR
		Scripps C		
		Sonoma SU		FN
		U of California, Berkeley		
		U of California, Davis		
		U of California, Los Angeles		CR, FN, BM
		U of California, Riverside		
		U of California, Santa Barbara		
		U of Southern California		CR
		Whittier C		
	CO	Colorado SU		
		U of Colorado, Boulder		
		U of Northern Colorado		
	CT	Central Connecticut SC		

*Only those institutions having intercollegiate sports in which women participate are listed.

**A & I Agricultural & Industrial, A & M Agricultural & Mechanical, A & T Agricultural & Technical, C College, CC Community College, JC Junior College, S State, SC State College, S & T Science & Technology, SU State University, U University

***AR Archery, BB Baseball, BL Bowling, BM Badminton, CR Crew, FN Fencing, HR Horseback Riding, IH Ice Hockey, PO Polo, RF Riflery, RO Rodeo, SC Soccer, SK Skiing, SL Sailing, SQ Squash, SS Synchronized Swimming, TS Trap Shooting, XC Cross-Country Skiing

Intercollegiate Sports Chart*

Available Sports

Four-Year Colleges and Universities**	Miscellaneous***	Volleyball	Track and Field	Tennis	Swimming and Diving	Softball	Skiing	Lacrosse	Gymnastics	Golf	Field Hockey	Cross-Country	Basketball
CT													
Connecticut C	CR	•		•	•			•	•		•	•	•
St. Joseph C		•				•							•
Southern Connecticut SC		•	•	•	•	•			•		•	•	•
U of Connecticut	SC	•	•	•	•	•		•	•	•	•	•	•
Yale U	CR, FN, IH, SC		•	•	•	•			•				•
DE													
Delaware SC			•										•
U of Delaware		•		•	•			•			•		•
DC													
American U		•	•	•	•	•					•	•	•
Catholic U of America		•	•	•							•		•
George Washington U	SQ, SC, CR, BM	•	•	•	•	•			•		•	•	•
Mount Vernon C		•								•	•		•
FL													
Florida International U		•		•	•							•	•
Jacksonville U		•		•		•							
U of South Florida	CR	•		•		•							•
U of West Florida		•		•		•					•		•
GA													
Agnes Scott C				•									
Berry C			•	•								•	•

State	Institution													
GA	Emory U		•	•	•								•	•
	Georgia SU			•	•	•							•	•
	Piedmont C	•		•										•
	Spelman C	•	•	•	•	•							•	•
	Wesleyan C	•	•	•	•	•							•	•
HI	U of Hawaii, Manoa	•	•	•	•	•				•			•	•
ID	Boise SU	•	•	•					•		•		•	•
	C of Idaho	•					•							
	Idaho SU	•	•	•	•	•			•		•		•	•
	U of Idaho	•	•	•	•	•			•		•		•	•
IL	Bradley U	•	•	•		•							•	•
	Concordia C	•	•	•	•				•		•			•
	Illinois SU BM	•	•	•	•	•			•	•	•			•
	Loyola U of Chicago	•												•
	Monmouth C	•		•		•								•
	Mundelein C	•		•										•
	National C of Education	•		•										•
	Northeastern Illinois U	•	•	•					•		•	•	•	•
	Northern Illinois U BM	•	•	•	•	•			•	•	•	•	•	•
	Northwestern U	•	•	•	•	•						•	•	•
	Quincy C	•		•		•								•
	Rosary C	•		•		•								•

*Only those institutions having intercollegiate sports in which women participate are listed.

**A & I Agricultural & Industrial, A & M Agricultural & Mechanical, A & T Agricultural & Technical, C College, CC Community College, JC Junior College, S State, SC State College, S & T Science & Technology, SU State University, U University

***AR Archery, BB Baseball, BL Bowling, BM Badminton, CR Crew, FN Fencing, HR Horseback Riding, IH Ice Hockey, PO Polo, RF Riflery, RO Rodeo, SC Soccer, SK Skiing, SL Sailing, SQ Squash, SS Synchronized Swimming, TS Trap Shooting, XC Cross-Country Skiing

Intercollegiate Sports Chart*

Available Sports

Four-Year Colleges and Universities**

Sport	IL: Sangamon SU	SIU, Carbondale	SIU, Edwardsville	U of Illinois, Chicago Circle	IN: Ball SU	Butler U	DePauw U	Goshen C	Indiana SU, Evansville	Indiana SU, Terre Haute	Indiana U, Bloomington	Indiana U, Southeast	Indiana U-Purdue U, Fort Wayne	Indiana U-Purdue U, Indianapolis	Purdue U, Calumet	Purdue U, West Lafayette	St. Mary-of-the-Woods C
Miscellaneous***		BM			BM					AR, BL, BM							
Volleyball	•	•		•	•	•	•	•	•	•	•		•	•	•	•	•
Track and Field		•	•	•				•		•			•			•	
Tennis	•	•	•	•	•	•	•	•	•	•	•		•			•	•
Swimming and Diving		•		•	•		•			•	•					•	•
Softball		•		•	•	•	•		•		•			•			•
Skiing																	
Lacrosse					•												
Gymnastics		•		•	•					•	•						
Golf		•		•			•			•	•					•	
Field Hockey		•	•		•		•	•		•	•					•	
Cross-Country		•	•	•	•					•	•					•	
Basketball	•	•	•	•	•	•	•	•	•	•	•	•	•	•	•	•	•

State	Institution	1	2	3	4	5	6	7	8	9	10	11	12	Notes
IA	Clarke C	•						•				•		
	Drake U	•	•					•		•	•	•		
	Grand View C	•						•				•		
	Iowa SU of S & T	•	•		•	•		•	•	•	•	•		
	Loras C	•	•					•	•	•	•	•		
	U of Dubuque	•						•			•	•		
	U of Iowa	•		•	•	•		•	•	•	•	•		
KS	Bethel C	•	•							•		•		
	Emporia SU	•	•			•		•	•	•	•	•		
	St. Mary's C								•					
	Wichita SU	•	•		•			•			•			
KY	Eastern Kentucky U	•		•		•			•	•	•			RF
	Morehead SU	•	•		•			•	•	•			•	BL, SC
	Northern Kentucky U	•						•		•		•		
	U of Louisville	•	•	•		•		•		•	•	•		
LA	Tulane U	•						•	•					
ME	Unity C											•		
	U of Maine, Orono	•	•	•		•		•	•	•	•	•	•	RF, SL
MD	Bowie SC	•										•		
	Frostburg SC	•		•		•		•	•		•			
	Goucher C	•	•	•		•		•	•	•		•		FN, HR

*Only those institutions having intercollegiate sports in which women participate are listed.

**A & I Agricultural & Industrial, A & M Agricultural & Mechnical, A & T Agricultural & Technical, C College, CC Community College, JC Junior College, S State, SC State College, S & T Science & Technology, SU State University, U University

***AR Archery, BB Baseball, BL Bowling, BM Badminton, CR Crew, FN Fencing, HR Horseback Riding, IH Ice Hockey, PO Polo, RF Riflery, RO Rodeo, SC Soccer, SK Skiing, SL Sailing, SQ Squash, SS Synchronized Swimming, TS Trap Shooting, XC Cross-Country Skiing

Intercollegiate Sports Chart*

Available Sports

Four-Year Colleges and Universities**	Basketball	Cross-Country	Field Hockey	Golf	Gymnastics	Lacrosse	Skiing	Softball	Swimming and Diving	Tennis	Track and Field	Volleyball	Miscellaneous***
MD													
Hood C	•		•			•			•	•		•	BM
Johns Hopkins U	•	•	•			•			•	•			SQ, FN
Loyola C	•		•			•			•	•		•	
St. Mary's C of Maryland	•					•				•		•	SL
Salisbury SC	•		•			•		•	•	•	•	•	
Towson SU	•	•	•		•	•		•	•	•	•	•	
U of Maryland, Baltimore County	•	•	•		•	•		•	•	•		•	
U of Maryland, College Park	•		•		•	•		•	•	•	•	•	
MA													
Anna Maria C	•		•					•		•			
Boston SC	•							•				•	
Bradford C	•			•								•	
Clark U	•	•	•				•	•	•	•	•	•	CR
C of the Holy Cross	•		•			•						•	CR
Emmanuel C	•	•								•			
Harvard U	•	•	•					•	•	•	•	•	CR, FN, IH, SL, SC, SQ
Massachusetts Institute of Technology	•		•				•	•	•	•		•	CR, FN
Mount Holyoke	•		•	•				•	•	•		•	CR, HR, SC

Institution	Sports
North Adams SC	
Pine Manor C	
Smith C	HR, SC, SQ
Southeastern Massachusetts U	FN
Suffolk U	
U of Lowell	BL
U of Massachusetts, Amherst	SC
U of Massachusetts, Boston	SC
Wellesley C	CR, FN, SQ, SC
Wheaton C	SC, SL, SS
Wheelock C	
Worcester SC	
MI	
Albion C	AR
Aquinas C	
Grand Valley SC	CR
Hope C	AR
Kalamazoo C	AR
Madonna C	
Michigan Technical U	
Siena Heights C	SS
U of Michigan, Ann Arbor	
U of Michigan, Dearborn	FN

*Only those institutions having intercollegiate sports in which women participate are listed.

**A & I Agricultural & Industrial, A & M Agricultural & Mechanical, A & T Agricultural & Technical, C College, CC Community College, JC Junior College, S State, SC State College, S & T Science & Technology, SU State University, U University

***AR Archery, BB Baseball, BL Bowling, BM Badminton, CR Crew, FN Fencing, HR Horseback Riding, IH Ice Hockey, PO Polo, RF Riflery, RO Rodeo, SC Soccer, SK Skiing, SL Sailing, SQ Squash, SS Synchronized Swimming, TS Trap Shooting, XC Cross-Country Skiing

480 INTERCOLLEGIATE SPORTS CHARTS

Intercollegiate Sports Chart*

Available Sports

Four-Year Colleges and Universities**	Basketball	Cross-Country	Field Hockey	Golf	Gymnastics	Lacrosse	Skiing	Softball	Swimming and Diving	Tennis	Track and Field	Volleyball	Miscellaneous***
MI													
Western Michigan U	•	•	•		•			•	•	•	•	•	
MN													
Bemidji SU	•		•		•				•	•	•	•	
Carleton C	•	•	•				•		•	•	•	•	SC, XC
C of St. Benedict	•							•	•	•		•	
C of St. Catherine	•				•			•	•	•	•	•	
C of St. Scholastica	•	•								•		•	
C of St. Theresa	•							•		•		•	
Gustavus Adolphus C	•	•		•	•			•	•	•	•	•	
Macalester C	•	•						•	•	•	•	•	
Mankato SC	•	•		•	•			•	•	•	•	•	
Moorhead SU	•			•				•		•	•		
St. Cloud SC	•	•		•	•			•	•	•	•	•	
St. Olaf C	•	•		•			•	•	•	•	•	•	
Southwest SU	•	•		•	•			•	•	•	•	•	
U of Minnesota, Minneapolis	•	•	•					•	•	•	•	•	
U of Minnesota, Morris	•								•		•	•	
MS													
Millsaps C	•							•		•			

	Mississippi SU	•												
	U of Mississippi	•							•		•		•	
MO	Central Christian C of the Bible												•	
	Maryville C	•							•		•		•	SC
	Missouri Southern SC	•							•		•	•	•	
	Missouri Western SC	•							•		•		•	
	Rockhurst C	•											•	BL
	St. Louis U	•		•					•	•	•		•	
	School of the Ozarks	•									•	•	•	
	Stephens C				•				•	•	•		•	
	U of Missouri, Columbia	•	•		•	•			•	•	•	•	•	
	U of Missouri, Rolla	•							•		•			
	U of Missouri, St. Louis	•	•	•					•	•	•		•	
	Washington U	•	•							•	•	•	•	
MT	Eastern Montana C	•	•		•	•					•	•		
	Montana C of Mineral S & T	•											•	
	Montana SU	•	•			•		•			•	•	•	
	U of Montana	•	•			•				•	•	•	•	
NE	Chadron SC	•							•			•	•	
	Creighton U	•							•		•		•	
	Nebraska Wesleyan U	•	•		•				•		•	•	•	
	U of Nebraska, Lincoln	•	•		•	•			•	•	•	•		

*Only those institutions having intercollegiate sports in which women participate are listed.

**A & I Agricultural & Industrial, A & M Agricultural & Mechnical, A & T Agricultural & Technical, C College, CC Community College, JC Junior College, S State, SC State College, S & T Science & Technology, SU State University, U University

***AR Archery, BB Baseball, BL Bowling, BM Badminton, CR Crew, FN Fencing, HR Horseback Riding, IH Ice Hockey, PO Polo, RF Riflery, RO Rodeo, SC Soccer, SK Skiing, SL Sailing, SQ Squash, SS Synchronized Swimming, TS Trap Shooting, XC Cross-Country Skiing

Intercollegiate Sports Chart*

Available Sports

Four-Year Colleges and Universities**

State	College/University	Volleyball	Track and Field	Tennis	Swimming and Diving	Softball	Skiing	Lacrosse	Gymnastics	Golf	Field Hockey	Cross-Country	Basketball	Miscellaneous***
NV	U of Nevada, Las Vegas	•	•	•	•	•						•	•	
	U of Nevada, Reno	•		•	•	•						•	•	
NH	Dartmouth C		•	•		•	•	•	•		•	•	•	IH, CR, SL, SC, SQ
	Rivier C										•		•	
	U of New Hampshire	•	•	•	•	•	•	•	•		•	•	•	IH
NJ	Bloomfield C												•	
	Georgian Court C	•				•							•	
	New Jersey Institute of Technology			•										FN, RF
	Princeton U	•	•	•	•	•		•		•	•	•	•	
	Rutgers, the SU, Newark	•		•		•							•	FN
	Rutgers, the SU, New Brunswick	•	•	•	•	•		•	•		•		•	CR, FN
	Stevens Institute of Technology													FN
	Trenton SC	•	•	•	•	•		•	•		•	•	•	AR
	Union C			•									•	
	Upsala C	•		•									•	
NM	C of Santa Fe	•		•									•	
	New Mexico SU	•		•	•	•							•	

NY	Code												
Alfred U	SC	•		•	•								•
Barnard C	AR, FN	•	•	•	•							•	•
CUNY (City U of New York), Brooklyn C	AR, FN	•	•	•	•							•	•
CUNY, C of Staten Island		•		•	•	•						•	•
CUNY, Herbert H. Lehman C		•	•	•						•		•	•
CUNY, Hunter College	FN	•	•	•							•	•	•
Clarkson C of Technology				•	•	•		•		•	•	•	•
C of New Rochelle		•	•	•	•	•							•
C of St. Rose	BL	•	•	•	•	•						•	•
Cornell U	BL, IH	•	•	•	•	•	•	•	•	•	•	•	•
D'Youville C	BL	•	•	•	•	•		•	•				•
Hamilton C	SQ, SC	•	•	•	•	•				•	•	•	•
Hartwick C	SC	•	•	•	•	•				•	•	•	•
Hofstra U	FN	•	•	•	•	•	•	•		•	•	•	•
Houghton C		•	•	•	•								•
Keuka C		•		•									•
Marist C	CR	•	•	•	•	•					•	•	•
Marymount C	HR	•	•	•	•	•				•	•	•	•
Mercy C		•	•	•	•	•					•	•	•
Molloy C	HR	•	•	•	•							•	•
New York Institute of Technology		•	•	•	•	•					•	•	•
New York U	FN	•	•	•						•	•	•	•

*Only those institutions having intercollegiate sports in which women participate are listed.

**A & I Agricultural & Industrial, A & M Agricultural & Mechanical, A & T Agricultural & Technical, C College, CC Community College, JC Junior College, S State, SC State College, S & T Science & Technology, SU State University, U University

***AR Archery, BB Baseball, BL Bowling, BM Badminton, CR Crew, FN Fencing, HR Horseback Riding, IH Ice Hockey, PO Polo, RF Riflery, RO Rodeo, SC Soccer, SK Skiing, SL Sailing, SQ Squash, SS Synchronized Swimming, TS Trap Shooting, XC Cross-Country Skiing

Intercollegiate Sports Chart*

Available Sports

Four-Year Colleges and Universities**	Basketball	Cross-Country	Field Hockey	Golf	Gymnastics	Lacrosse	Skiing	Softball	Swimming and Diving	Tennis	Track and Field	Volleyball	Miscellaneous***
NY													
Niagara U	•							•	•	•		•	
Pace U, New York City		•											FN
Pace U, Pleasantville-Briarcliff	•		•					•		•		•	FN
Russell Sage C						•							
St. Bonaventure U	•		•					•	•	•	•	•	
St. Lawrence U	•		•			•	•		•	•		•	HR
Sarah Lawrence C	•									•		•	IH, HR, SC
Siena C	•							•		•	•	•	BB
Skidmore C	•		•			•			•	•		•	CR, IH, PO, SC
Southampton C of Long Island U		•								•		•	
SUNY (SU of New York), Albany	•	•			•			•	•	•	•	•	SC, SS
SUNY, Binghamton	•	•						•	•	•	•	•	
SUNY, Buffalo	•	•	•					•		•	•	•	BL
SUNY, C at Buffalo	•	•	•					•	•	•	•	•	BL
SUNY, C at Cortland	•	•		•	•	•		•	•	•	•		IH, SC
SUNY, C at Geneseo	•	•						•			•	•	SS
SUNY, C at Oneonta	•	•	•			•		•	•	•		•	

State	Institution	1	2	3	4	5	6	7	8	9	10	11	Other***
	SUNY, C at Oswego	•		•	•	•				•	•	•	BL, IH
	SUNY, C at Plattsburgh	•	•	•	•	•				•	•	•	SC
	SUNY, C at Purchase				•							•	
	SUNY, C of Technology, Utica/Rome	•		•	•							•	
	Syracuse U	•		•	•	•	•					•	CR
	Utica C of Syracuse U	•		•		•						•	
	Vassar C	•	•	•	•	•				•	•	•	SC, SQ
	Wells C			•	•	•			•				BL, SC
	William Smith C	•	•	•	•	•			•	•		•	SC
NC	Atlantic Christian C	•	•	•								•	
	Duke U	•	•	•	•	•	•	•				•	FN
	Fayetteville SU	•		•									
	Greensboro C	•	•	•				•				•	
	North Carolina A & T SU	•		•									
	Queens C	•	•	•								•	
	Salem C	•		•									
	U of North Carolina, Chapel Hill	•	•	•	•	•	•	•		•	•	•	FN, SC
	U of North Carolina, Charlotte	•	•	•	•	•				•		•	
	U of North Carolina, Greensboro	•	•	•	•	•		•		•		•	
	Wake Forest U	•	•	•	•	•				•		•	
ND	Mayville SC	•	•	•		•		•				•	
	U of North Dakota	•	•	•	•	•		•				•	

*Only those institutions having intercollegiate sports in which women participate are listed.

**A & I Agricultural & Industrial, A & M Agricultural & Mechanical, A & T Agricultural & Technical, C College, CC Community College, JC Junior College, S State, SC State College, S & T Science & Technology, SU State University, U University

***AR Archery, BB Baseball, BL Bowling, BM Badminton, CR Crew, FN Fencing, HR Horseback Riding, IH Ice Hockey, PO Polo, RF Riflery, RO Rodeo, SC Soccer, SK Skiing, SL Sailing, SQ Squash, SS Synchronized Swimming, TS Trap Shooting, XC Cross-Country Skiing

Intercollegiate Sports Chart*

Available Sports

Four-Year Colleges and Universities**

OH

Sport	Baldwin-Wallace C	Bowling Green SU	Capital U	Mt. St. Joseph-on-the-Ohio	C of Wooster	Defiance C	Denison U	Kenyon C	Marietta C	Oberlin C	Ohio Dominican C	Ohio SU	Ohio U	Ohio Wesleyan U	U of Akron	U of Cincinnati	U of Dayton
Miscellaneous***							BL, SC		CR			FN, SS				SC	
Volleyball	•	•	•	•	•	•	•	•	•	•	•	•	•	•	•	•	•
Track and Field	•	•	•	•	•		•	•				•				•	
Tennis	•	•		•	•		•	•	•	•		•	•	•	•	•	•
Swimming and Diving	•	•	•	•	•		•	•		•		•	•	•		•	
Softball		•			•				•		•	•	•	•	•		•
Skiing	•	•	•														
Lacrosse					•		•	•		•		•	•				
Gymnastics		•										•					
Golf		•										•				•	
Field Hockey		•			•		•	•		•							•
Cross-Country	•	•	•		•		•	•		•		•	•				
Basketball	•	•	•	•	•	•	•	•	•	•	•	•	•	•	•	•	•

	Institution												Code
OH	Wilmington C	•				•						•	
	Wittenburg U	•	•			•			•	•		•	BL
	Wright SU	•				•	•					•	
	Youngstown SU	•	•			•		•		•		•	
OK	Southeastern Oklahoma SU	•										•	
	U of Oklahoma	•	•			•		•	•			•	
	U of Science and Arts of Oklahoma	•				•			•			•	
	U of Tulsa			•		•				•		•	
OR	Lewis and Clark C	•	•	•	•	•	•		•	•		•	SC
	Oregon SU	•	•	•	•	•	•	•		•	•	•	CR
	Portland SU	•	•	•		•	•	•		•		•	FN
	U of Oregon	•	•	•	•	•	•	•	•			•	SC
PA	Albright C	•	•	•	•	•	•			•	•	•	BM
	Allegheny C	•	•	•	•	•	•				•	•	
	Bryn Mawr C	•	•	•	•	•		•	•	•	•	•	BM
	Carlow C	•		•	•						•	•	
	Cedar Crest C	•	•			•	•		•		•	•	BM
	Chatham C	•	•	•		•					•	•	
	Chestnut Hill C	•	•	•	•	•	•			•	•	•	BM
	Cheyney SC	•	•	•	•	•	•				•	•	BM, SC
	Dickinson C	•	•	•	•	•		•	•	•	•	•	
	Edinboro SC	•	•	•		•	•	•				•	

*Only those institutions having intercollegiate sports in which women participate are listed.

**A & I Agricultural & Industrial, A & M Agricultural & Mechanical, A & T Agricultural & Technical, C College, CC Community College, JC Junior College, S State, SC State College, S & T Science & Technology, SU State University, U University

***AR Archery, BB Baseball, BL Bowling, BM Badminton, CR Crew, FN Fencing, HR Horseback Riding, IH Ice Hockey, PO Polo, RF Riflery, RO Rodeo, SC Soccer, SK Skiing, SL Sailing, SQ Squash, SS Synchronized Swimming, TS Trap Shooting, XC Cross-Country Skiing

Intercollegiate Sports Chart*

Available Sports

Four-Year Colleges and Universities**

PA

Four-Year College/University	Volleyball	Track and Field	Tennis	Swimming and Diving	Softball	Skiing	Lacrosse	Gymnastics	Golf	Field Hockey	Cross-Country	Basketball	Miscellaneous***
Gettysburg C	•		•	•	•		•			•	•	•	
King's C	•		•	•	•						•	•	RF
Lafayette C	•	•	•	•	•		•			•	•	•	FN
Lincoln U	•											•	
Millersville SC				•			•			•	•	•	AR, SS
Neuman C	•		•		•							•	
Pennsylvania SU, Capital Campus	•		•		•								
St. Francis C	•	•	•		•						•	•	
Seton Hill C	•		•		•						•	•	
Slippery Rock SC	•		•	•			•	•		•	•	•	
Swarthmore C	•	•	•	•			•	•		•		•	BM
Temple U	•	•	•	•			•	•		•	•	•	BL, BM, FN
U of Pittsburgh	•		•					•		•		•	
U of Pittsburgh, Johnstown	•								•			•	
Villa Maria C	•				•							•	
West Chester SC	•	•	•		•		•			•	•	•	BM
Widener C			•	•			•		•	•	•	•	

State	Institution												Other
PA	Wilson C	•		•			•		•	•	•	•	HR
RI	Barrington C	•				•			•			•	
	Brown U	•	•	•	•		•	•		•	•	•	CR, IH, SC, SQ
	Providence C	•	•				•	•		•	•	•	IH
SC	Benedict C	•		•		•						•	
	Coker C	•		•								•	
	Converse C			•					•			•	
	Lander C	•										•	
	Voorhees C		•			•					•	•	
SD	National C	•		•					•			•	RO
	South Dakota SU	•		•				•			•	•	
TN	Belmont C			•							•	•	
	East Tennessee SU	•	•	•				•			•	•	RF
	LeMoyne-Owen C			•								•	
	Memphis SU	•	•	•				•	•			•	
	Middle Tennessee SU	•	•	•							•	•	
	Southwestern, Memphis	•		•							•	•	
	Tennessee Technological U	•		•							•	•	RF
	Vanderbilt U	•		•	•	•					•	•	
TX	Incarnate Word C	•		•								•	
	Midwestern SU	•		•								•	
	North Texas SU	•	•	•					•	•	•	•	

*Only those institutions having intercollegiate sports in which women participate are listed.

**A & I Agricultural & Industrial, A & M Agricultural & Mechanical, A & T Agricultural & Technical, C College, CC Community College, JC Junior College, S State, SC State College, S & T Science & Technology, SU State University, U University

***AR Archery, BB Baseball, BL Bowling, BM Badminton, CR Crew, FN Fencing, HR Horseback Riding, IH Ice Hockey, PO Polo, RF Riflery, RO Rodeo, SC Soccer, SK Skiing, SL Sailing, SQ Squash, SS Synchronized Swimming, TS Trap Shooting, XC Cross-Country Skiing

Intercollegiate Sports Chart*

Available Sports

Four-Year Colleges and Universities

	Four-Year Colleges and Universities**	Basketball	Cross-Country	Field Hockey	Golf	Gymnastics	Lacrosse	Skiing	Softball	Swimming and Diving	Tennis	Track and Field	Volleyball	Miscellaneous***
TX	Southern Methodist U	●			●					●	●			
	Texas A & I U	●									●	●	●	
	Texas Christian U	●	●		●	●				●	●	●		
	U of Texas, Arlington	●	●						●		●	●	●	FN
	U of Texas, Austin	●	●		●	●					●	●	●	
UT	Utah SU	●				●						●	●	
VT	C of St. Joseph the Provider	●												SC
	Southern Vermont C	●						●	●				●	SC
	Vermont C	●	●	●					●	●				RF
VA	Ferrum C	●							●		●	●	●	
	Hollins C	●		●							●		●	FN, HR, SC
	Mary Baldwin C	●			●						●			HR, FN
	Old Dominion U	●		●			●			●	●	●		
	Randolph-Macon C	●		●			●				●			
	Randolph-Macon Woman's C	●		●						●	●		●	FN, HR
	Sweet Briar C	●		●	●		●		●		●		●	HR
	U of Richmond	●		●			●			●	●	●		SC

State	Institution	Additional sports***
VA	Virginia Polytechnic Institute and SU	
WA	Central Washington U	
	Eastern Washington U	
	Washington SU	
	Western Washington U	CR, SC
WV	Glenville SC	
	West Virginia SC	
	West Virginia U	RF
	Wheeling C	
WI	Marquette U	
	Mt. Mary C	
	Ripon C	
	Silver Lake C	
	U of Wisconsin, Eau Claire	
	U of Wisconsin, Green Bay	
	U of Wisconsin, Milwaukee	
	U of Wisconsin, Oshkosh	BM, RF
	U of Wisconsin, Parkside	BL, FN
	U of Wisconsin, Stevens Point	
	U of Wisconsin, Superior	
	U of Wisconsin, Whitewater	
	Viterbo C	

*Only those institutions having intercollegiate sports in which women participate are listed.

**A & I Agricultural & Industrial, A & M Agricultural & Mechanical, A & T Agricultural & Technical, C College, CC Community College, JC Junior College, S State, SC State College, S & T Science & Technology, SU State University, U University

***AR Archery, BB Baseball, BL Bowling, BM Badminton, CR Crew, FN Fencing, HR Horseback Riding, IH Ice Hockey, PO Polo, RF Rifley, RO Rodeo, SC Soccer, SK Skiing, SL Sailing, SQ Squash, SS Synchronized Swimming, TS Trap Shooting, XC Cross-Country Skiing

Intercollegiate Sports Chart*

Available Sports

Four-Year Colleges and Universities**

	College	Miscellaneous***	Volleyball	Track and Field	Tennis	Swimming and Diving	Softball	Skiing	Lacrosse	Gymnastics	Golf	Field Hockey	Cross-Country	Basketball
WY	U of Wyoming		•	•		•	•	•					•	•
GU	U of Guam		•		•		•							•
PR	U of Puerto Rico, Mayaguez		•	•	•	•	•							•

Two-Year Colleges and Universities**

	College	Miscellaneous***	Volleyball	Track and Field	Tennis	Swimming and Diving	Softball	Skiing	Lacrosse	Gymnastics	Golf	Field Hockey	Cross-Country	Basketball
AR	Phillips County CC													•
CA	Columbia C		•	•	•	•	•						•	•
	Cosumnes River C		•	•	•	•	•						•	•
	Diablo Valley C		•	•	•					•			•	•
	East Los Angeles C	BM, AR, SC	•	•	•		•						•	•
	Gavilan C		•	•	•								•	•
	Los Angeles Valley JC		•											•
	Monterey Peninsula C		•			•	•						•	•
	Orange Coast C	BM, SL	•	•	•	•	•	•		•		•	•	•
	Oxnard C		•	•	•	•	•						•	•
	Santa Ana C		•	•	•	•	•						•	•
	Santa Rosa JC		•	•	•	•	•			•			•	•

CA	West Hills CC	•	•	•		•					•	
	West Kern CC District, Taft C	•	•	•		•					•	
	Yuba CC District	•	•	•	•	•			•	•	•	
CT	Norwalk CC	•		•		•					•	
DE	Brandywine C	•	•	•		•			•	•	•	
FL	Broward CC	•	•	•		•			•		•	
	Lake-Sumter CC								•			
IL	City C of Chicago, Wilbur Wright C	•	•	•	•	•		•		•	•	
	Kaskaskia C	•		•	•	•				•	•	
	Rock Valley C	•	•	•	•	•			•	•	•	
	Triton C	•		•	•	•	•				•	
	Hutchinson CC	•	•	•	•	•				•	•	
MD	Anne Arundel CC — BM, SL	•	•	•	•	•	•	•	•	•	•	
	Chesapeake C	•										
KS	Garrett CC	•									•	
MA	Berkshire CC — SC	•				•					•	
MI	Alpena CC — BL	•	•			•					•	
	Schoolcraft C									•	•	
MN	Worthington CC	•	•	•	•							
MO	Cottey C	•	•	•	•	•						
	Metropolitan CC	•	•	•		•						
	St. Louis CC, Meramec	•	•	•	•	•					•	•

*Only those institutions having intercollegiate sports in which women participate are listed.

**A & I Agricultural & Industrial, A & M Agricultural & Mechnical, A & T Agricultural & Technical, C College, CC Community College, JC Junior College, S State, SC State College, S & T Science & Technology, SU State University, U University

***AR Archery, BB Baseball, BL Bowling, BM Badminton, CR Crew, FN Fencing, HR Horseback Riding, IH Ice Hockey, PO Polo, RF Riflery, RO Rodeo, SC Soccer, SK Skiing, SL Sailing, SQ Squash, SS Synchronized Swimming, TS Trap Shooting, XC Cross-Country Skiing

Intercollegiate Sports Chart*

Available Sports

Two-Year Colleges and Universities**	State	Basketball	Cross-Country	Field Hockey	Golf	Gymnastics	Lacrosse	Skiing	Softball	Swimming and Diving	Tennis	Track and Field	Volleyball	Miscellaneous***
Mid Plains CC	NE	•											•	
Brookdale CC	NJ		•						•		•			
Cumberland County C		•							•		•		•	AR, FN
Middlesex County C		•	•						•		•	•	•	SK
Somerset County C		•									•		•	
Union C		•									•			
Columbia-Greene CC	NY	•							•		•		•	
Dutchess CC		•							•				•	
Erie CC, North Campus		•	•						•			•	•	SC, BL
Hilbert C		•							•				•	
New York City Technical C		•							•	•		•	•	BL
Paul Smith's C		•						•	•				•	
Schenectady County Commercial C													•	
SUNY (SU of New York) A & T C, Alfred		•	•					•		•	•	•	•	RF
SUNY A & T, Canton		•									•	•	•	
Westchester CC		•							•		•		•	BL
Caldwell CC	NC	•									•			

State	Institution							
NC	Durham Technical						•	
	Southeastern CC					•	•	
	Western Piedmont CC		•				•	
OH	Cuyahoga CC District (BL, SC)	•	•		•	•	•	•
	Kent State U, Tascarawas	•	•		•		•	
	Sinclair CC	•	•				•	
OK	Northeastern Oklahoma A & M C		•	•	•		•	
	Oscar Rose JC		•				•	
OR	Portland CC (FN, BL)	•	•		•		•	
PA	Allegheny CC, South Campus		•			•	•	
	Bucks County CC		•		•	•	•	
	Harcum JC (BM)	•	•		•	•	•	
	Williamsport Area CC		•			•	•	
SC	Aiken Technical C		•		•		•	
	Roane State CC		•				•	
TN	Shelby State CC		•				•	
TX	Amarillo C		•				•	
	Henderson County JC		•				•	
	Paris JC		•				•	
VA	Southern Seminary JC (HR)	•	•		•	•	•	
WA	Clark C (FN)	•	•	•	•	•	•	
	Green River CC (SC)	•	•		•	•	•	

*Only those institutions having intercollegiate sports in which women participate are listed.

**A & I Agricultural & Industrial, A & M Agricultural & Mechanical, A & T Agricultural & Technical, C College, CC Community College, JC Junior College, S State, SC State College, S & T Science & Technology, SU State University, U University

***AR Archery, BB Baseball, BL Bowling, BM Badminton, CR Crew, FN Fencing, HR Horseback Riding, IH Ice Hockey, PO Polo, RF Riflery, RO Rodeo, SC Soccer, SK Skiing, SL Sailing, SQ Squash, SS Synchronized Swimming, TS Trap Shooting, XC Cross-Country Skiing

Intercollegiate Sports Chart*

Available Sports

	Two-Year Colleges and Universities**	Miscellaneous***	Volleyball	Track and Field	Tennis	Swimming and Diving	Softball	Skiing	Lacrosse	Gymnastics	Golf	Field Hockey	Cross-Country	Basketball
WI	Madison Area Technical C	BL	•		•		•						•	•
	Mid-State Technical I	BL	•											
WY	Casper C	RO, TS	•		•					•	•			•
	Eastern Wyoming C	RO	•	•	•									•
	Western Wyoming CC		•		•									•

*Only those institutions having intercollegiate sports in which women participate are listed.

**A & I Agricultural & Industrial, A & M Agricultural & Mechnical, A & T Agricultural & Technical, C College, CC Community College, JC Junior College, S State, SC State College, S & T Science & Technology, SU State University, U University

***AR Archery, BB Baseball, BL Bowling, BM Badminton, CR Crew, FN Fencing, HR Horseback Riding, IH Ice Hockey, PO Polo, RF Riflery, RO Rodeo, SC Soccer, SK Skiing, SL Sailing, SQ Squash, SS Synchronized Swimming, TS Trap Shooting, XC Cross-Country Skiing

I. INSTITUTIONAL CHARACTERISTICS

1. Name of institution. _____

2. Address of institution. _____

_____ 3. Telephone number. (   ) _____

4. Name(s) and title(s) of respondent(s). _____

_____ 7-8

5. Type of Institution.

   1□ Public   2□ Private, non-denominational   3□ Private, denominational (specify) _____ 9.10

   NOTE: Other identifying information for the institution will be obtained from the National Center for Education Statistics.

6. State the **institutional mission** (founding purpose) at time of establishment (e.g., normal school, women's college, etc.).

   _____

   _____ 11-12

7. If mission has changed, describe and give year. _____ 13-14

   _____ 15-17

8. Check types of **alternative schedules and locations** for undergraduate classes offered by the institution.

   1□ Evening classes   5□ Off-campus daytime classes
   2□ Summer session   6□ Off-campus evening classes
   3□ Weekend college   7□ None
   4□ Self-paced/contract learning □ Other (specify) _____ 18
                                                                        19

9. Please provide the best enrollment figures available for 1980-81 for the following groups of undergraduate women. Estimate if necessary. Please make certain that each value in the TOTAL column is the sum of the values on its left.

Age of Undergraduate Women		Black, non-Hispanic	Native American	Asian-American	Hispanic	White, non-Hispanic	Other	TOTAL
18-25	(full-time)	20-4	25-8	29-33	34-8	39-43	44-7	48-53
	(part-time)	54-8	59-62	63-7	68-72	73-7[1]	7-10	11-16
25-40	(full-time)	17-21	22-5	26-9	30-3	34-8	39-42	43-7
	(part-time)	48-52	53-6	57-60	61-4	65-9	70-3	74-8[2]
Over 40	(full-time)	7-10	11-3	14-7	18-21	22-5	26-8	29-33
	(part-time)	34-7	38-40	41-4	45-8	49-52	53-5	56-60

10. Give the **median age** of all undergraduate students. _____ 61-62

11. Give the percentage of all full-time undergraduate women receiving **student financial aid,** 1980-81. _____ percent 63-64

12. Part-time students (enrolled for less than 12 credit hours) are eligible for student financial aid. 1□ Yes 2□ No 65

13. **Childcare** expenses are considered in the financial needs assessment of students. 1□ Yes 2□ No 66

14. Give the number of **handicapped** students. Total _____ Women _____ 67-69   70-72

15. Please check below the groups residing in significant numbers within 10 miles of the campus (at least 10 percent of the population).

   1□ Black, non-Hispanic   4□ Hispanic
   2□ Native American   5□ White, non-Hispanic
   3□ Asian-American   6-9□ Other ethnic groups (specify) _____ 73

16. Give the percentage of undergraduate students who **reside** on the campus. _____ percent 74-75

17. Give the percentage of undergraduate students who **commute** to the campus. _____ percent 76-77

18. Public transportation is available for commuting students. 1□ Yes 2□ No 78[3]

19. On-campus parking is available to commuting students. 1□ Yes 2□ No 3□ Paid 4□ Free 7

20. Free transportation from remote parking lots to classroom buildings is available. 1□ Yes 2□ No 8

21. **Childcare** facilities are available on campus for students who are parents. 1□ Yes 2□ No 9

22. Private childcare facilities are available nearby, off-campus. 1 ☐ Yes 2 ☐ No   10
Proceed to question 29 if no childcare facilities are available on campus.

23. Rank the groups below eligible for childcare (one is the highest priority).

Full-time students _____   Faculty _____   11, 12

Part-time students _____   Staff _____   13, 14

Non-credit students _____   Other (specify) _____   15, 16

24. Give the number of students' children your childcare facilities can accommodate. ____   17-20

25. Give the percentage of all student requests for childcare which you can accommodate. ____ percent   21-22

26. Charges for childcare are based on a sliding scale according to income. 1 ☐ Yes 2 ☐ No   23

27. State the daily fee for a student's child in childcare on campus. _____   24-26

28. State the hours during which childcare is available on campus daily. From ____ a.m. to ____ p.m.
     27-30   31-4

29. Name the official title of each **equal opportunity officer**. Check the boxes below that apply for each person. If not applicable, explain.

_____   35

Title of Equal Opportunity Officer	Responsibility				Equal Opportunity Assignment		Level of Responsibility (See key below)				
	EEO	Title IX	Sections 503	504	Full-time	Part-time	a	b	c	d	(specify)
	36	37	38	39	40	41	42	43	44	45	
1. _____	1 ☐	☐	☐	☐	☐	☐	☐	☐	☐	☐	_____
2. _____	☐	☐	☐	☐	☐	☐	☐	☐	☐	☐	_____
3. _____	☐	☐	☐	☐	☐	☐	☐	☐	☐	☐	_____
4. _____	☐	☐	☐	☐	☐	☐	☐	☐	☐	☐	_____
5. _____	☐	☐	☐	☐	☐	☐	☐	☐	☐	☐	_____

Key: Level of Responsibility
a Voting member of policy-making councils or committees
b Reviewer of policies and practices generated by councils and committees
c Compliance administrator; no policy-making responsibility
d Other (specify above)

30. Check below all which apply to the institutional policies and procedures on **sexual harassment.**

A written campus policy prohibits sexual harassment of 1 ☐ students 2 ☐ faculty 3 ☐ staff.

4 ☐ No policy exists on sexual harassment.
5 ☐ An informal and confidential campus mechanism resolves complaints of sexual harassment.
6 ☐ A formal campus grievance procedure which ensures due process resolves complaints of sexual harassment.   46
Other (specify) _____   47

31. Campus policy and procedures on sexual harassment have been publicly communicated in writing to
1 ☐ students 2 ☐ faculty 3 ☐ staff.   48

32. This institution has a **Committee/Commission** (or similar body) on the **Status of Women.** 1 ☐ Yes 2 ☐ No   49
If you answered no to question 32, proceed to question 38.

33. This Committee/Commission reports to _____   50
                                      (title of office or position)

34. The members of this Committee/Commission are 1 ☐ elected 2 ☐ self-designated 3 ☐ appointed.   51

35. If appointed/elected, by what person or what body? _____   52
                                        (title of person or body)

36. The Committee/Commission on the Status of Women
1 ☐ includes student members with voting rights.   4 ☐ takes public stands on issues of concern to students.
2 ☐ has met at least 6 times during 1980-81.   5 ☐ does none of the above.
3 ☐ prepares at least annually a report which is distributed   6-9 ☐ Other (specify) _____   53
to the campus community.

37. The Committee on the Status of Women addresses the concerns of minority women. 1 ☐ Yes 2 ☐ No   54

38. This institution has a **Committee/Commission on Minority Affairs.** 1 ☐ Yes 2 ☐ No   55

39. This Committee/Commission on Minority Affairs addresses the concerns of minority women. 1 ☐ Yes 2 ☐ No   56

II. STATUS OF WOMEN

1. Check the appropriate boxes below to indicate the sex of **student campus leaders**, 1978-81.

Campus Leadership Positions	Position Not Applicable	Position Held by a Woman 1978-79 1979-80 1980-81			Position Held by a Man 1978-81		Elected	Appointed	
President, Student Body	0 ☐	1.2.3 ☐	☐	☐	4 ☐	57	1 ☐	2 ☐	5
Presiding Officer, Student Governing Body/Senate	☐	☐	☐	☐	☐	59	☐	☐	6
Presiding Officer, Student Court/Judiciary	☐	☐	☐	☐	☐	61	☐	☐	6
Presiding Officer, Student Union Board	☐	☐	☐	☐	☐	63	☐	☐	6
Editor-in-Chief, Campus Newspaper	☐	☐	☐	☐	☐	65	☐	☐	6
Manager, Campus Radio Station	☐	☐	☐	☐	☐	67	☐	☐	7
Presiding Officer, Residence Hall Council	☐	☐	☐	☐	☐	69	☐	☐	7
President, Senior Class	☐	☐	☐	☐	☐	71	☐	☐	7
President, Junior Class	☐	☐	☐	☐	☐	73	☐	☐	7
President, Sophomore Class	☐	☐	☐	☐	☐	75	☐	☐	7
President, Freshman Class	0 ☐	1.2.3 ☐	☐	☐	4 ☐	77	1 ☐	2 ☐	7 [4

2. For each **administrative position** held during 1980-81, check the appropriate box to indicate sex and race.

Administrative Position	Not Applicable	Position Held by a Man	Position Held by a Woman					
			Black, non-Hispanic	Native American	Asian-American	Hispanic	White, non-Hispanic	Other
Campus Chief Executive Officer (President, Chancellor, etc.)	1 ☐	2 ☐	3 ☐	4 ☐	5 ☐	6 ☐	7 ☐	8 ☐
Executive Vice President (second to the President, Chancellor, etc.)	☐	☐	☐	☐	☐	☐	☐	☐
Chief Academic Officer	☐	☐	☐	☐	☐	☐	☐	☐
Chief Business Officer	☐	☐	☐	☐	☐	☐	☐	☐
Chief Student Life Officer	☐	☐	☐	☐	☐	☐	☐	☐
Chief Development Officer	☐	☐	☐	☐	☐	☐	☐	☐
Head Librarian	☐	☐	☐	☐	☐	☐	☐	☐
Director, Institutional Research	☐	☐	☐	☐	☐	☐	☐	☐
Director, Athletics	☐	☐	☐	☐	☐	☐	☐	☐
Chief Planning Officer	1 ☐	2 ☐	3 ☐	4 ☐	5 ☐	6 ☐	7 ☐	8 ☐

3. Give the number of persons in each category listed below for 1980-81. Please make certain that each value in the column **Total Females** is the sum of the values to its right.

Categories	Total Persons	Total Females	Women By Race					
			Black, non-Hispanic	Native American	Asian-American	Hispanic	White, non-Hispanic	Other
Department/Division Chairpersons	17-9	20-1	22-3	24-5	26-7	28-9	30-1	32-3
Deans/Directors of Academic Units	34-5	36-7	38-9	40-1	42-3	44-5	46-7	48-9
Faculty Senate (or other governing body)	50-2	53-4	55-6	57-8	59-60	61-2	63-4	65-6
Campus-wide Tenure, Reappointment, and Promotions Committee	67-8	69-70	71-2	73-4	75-6	77-8[5]	7-8	9-10
Trustees	11-2	13-4	15-6	17-8	19-20	21-2	23-4	25-6
Regents	27-8	29-30	31-2	33-4	35-6	37-8	39-40	41-2
Commencement Speakers, Spring 1981 ☐ Not applicable	43-4	45-6	47-8	49-50	51-2	53-4	55-6	57-8
Honorary Degree Recipients, Spring 1981 ☐ Not applicable	59-60	61-2	63-4	65-6	67-8	69-70	71-2	73-4
Alumni Awards, 1980-81 ☐ Not applicable	75-6	77-8[6]	7-8	9-10	11-2	13-4	15-6	17-8
Speakers in major campus-wide lecture series ☐ Not applicable	19-20	21-2	23-4	25-6	27-8	29-30	31-2	33-4

500 EVERYWOMEN'S QUESTIONNAIRE

4. List those departments that are chaired by women. _____

_____

_____ 35-36

5. List the exact title of each woman who is Dean/Director of an academic unit larger than a department. _____

_____

_____ 37-38

6. Complete the table below on the number of faculty and administrators by sex and race for 1980-81. To facilitate answering this question, use data from your Higher Education Staff Information categories (EEO-6).

EEO-6 Category	Primary Occupational Activity	Total Persons	Total Females	Black, non-Hispanic	Native American	Asian-American	Hispanic	White, non-Hispanic	Other
	Executive/ Administrative								
IV, 1, p. 6	Part-time								
		39-41	42-4	45-6	47-8	49-50	51-2	53-5	56-7
II, A, 9, p. 2	Full-time								
		58-61	62-4	65-7	68-9	70-1	72-3	74-6	77-8[7]
	Tenured Faculty								
IV, 2, p. 6	Part-time								
		7-9	10-2	13-4	15-6	17-8	19-20	21-3	24-5
III, A, 7, p.5	Full-time								
		26-9	30-2	33-5	36-7	38-9	40-1	42-4	45-6
	All Faculty*								
IV, 2+3+4, p. 6	Part-time								
		47-50	51-3	54-6	57-8	59-60	61-2	63-5	66-7
II, A, 18, p. 2	Full-time								
		68-71	72-4	75-7[8]	7-8	9-10	11-2	13-5	16-7

*Please include full, associate, and assistant professors, instructors, and lecturers. Do not include graduate assistants and research fellows.

III. THE CURRICULUM

NOTE: Information on the major fields of study and degrees granted to women and men will be obtained from the National Center for Education Statistics.

1. Check below the **innovative programs** offered by your institution for encouraging women students to prepare for **nontraditional** careers.

1 ☐ Women in Science
2 ☐ Women in Engineering
3 ☐ Women in Agriculture
4 ☐ Women in Architecture
5 ☐ Women in Accounting

6 ☐ Women in Computer Science
7 ☐ Women in Law Enforcement/Corrections
8 ☐ Women in Electronics
9 ☐ None of the above
☐ Other (specify) _____

18
19

2. Give the percentage of students who are women in each **experiential learning program** offered to undergraduates on your campus.

Programs	Program not Available	Percent of Students Who Are Women
Cooperative Education	☐	20-1
Internships/practicums	☐	22-3
Science field service (e.g., Marine Biology, Archaeology. etc.)	☐	24-5
Other (specify) _____ 26		27-8
Other (specify) _____ 29		30-1

3. In the table below provide the requested information on undergraduate students and faculty in courses in the **creative and performing arts.**

Department/Division	Not applicable	Percent of Students Who Are Women	Percent of Faculty Who Are Women
Art (Painting, Sculpture, etc.)	1 ☐ 32	33-4	35-6
Creative Writing	2 ☐	37-8	39-40
Dance	3 ☐	41-2	43-4
Drama/Theater	4 ☐	45-6	47-8
Music	5 ☐	49-0	51-2

4. Check those **innovations** below now included in the curriculum.

☐ The School (Department, Division) of Education offers preservice training for mathematics and elementary school teachers on math avoidance by women and girls. 53

☐ The School (Department, Division) of Education provides instruction on the development and use of sex-fair curricula. 54

☐ The Physical Education Department provides instruction in how to teach coeducational classes in physical education. 55

☐ The School (Department, Division) of Nursing provides training in midwifery, home delivery, and reproductive choice. 56

☐ The School (Department, Division) of Nursing provides training on health care information important to minority women (e.g., forced sterilization, tuberculosis, sickle-cell anemia). 57

☐ The School (Department, Division) of Social Work provides instruction on services for battered spouses, displaced homemakers, and childcare. 58

☐ The School (Department, Division) of Business provides instruction about the problems of job discrimination, sexual harassment in the workplace, women in management. 59

5. Complete the table below, listing information about the following three types of new courses offered on your campus during 1980-81.

a. **Separate courses, labeled Women's Studies,** offered by, in, or through a Women's Studies Program, including courses on minority women.

b. **Individual courses on women,** including courses on Black, Hispanic, or other minority women, offered by departments.

c. **"Transformed" courses** in which new scholarship about women has been combined with traditional scholarship about men.

☐ Check if none of the three types of courses is taught on your campus, and proceed to question 12. 60

Course Title (If more than six are offered, attach additional page, using this format.)	Type of Course (Check all that apply)			Department/Division/Program Offering Each Course	Course Level (Check one)	
	A Women's Studies Program	**B** Courses on Women	**C** "Transformed" Courses		Under-graduate	Graduate
_____	1 ☐	2 ☐	3 ☐ 61	_____ 62-5	1 ☐	2 ☐ 66
_____	☐	☐	☐ 67	_____ 68-71	☐	☐ 72
_____	☐	☐	☐ 73	_____ 74-7	☐	☐ 78-[9]
_____	☐	☐	☐ 7	_____ 8-11	☐	☐ 12
_____	☐	☐	☐ 13	_____ 14-7	☐	☐ 18
_____	☐	☐	☐ 19	_____ 20-3	☐	☐ 24

6. Give the number of faculty teaching the above courses. Men _____ Women _____
   25-6   27-8

7. This institution has a **Women's Studies Program.** 1 ☐ Yes   2 ☐ No   29

8. Check the degrees and credentials available in Women's Studies.

☐ Undergraduate minor   ☐ Graduate minor (M.A. or Ph.D in another field)   30,31
☐ Certificate   ☐ M.A. degree   32,33
☐ Associate degree (A.A.)   ☐ Ph.D degree   34,35
☐ Bachelor's degree (B.A.)   ☐ Ed.D degree   36,37

9. Give the number of students in the last five years who have combined the above three types of courses to form a major or minor.

☐ None 38

Undergraduate majors _____   Undergraduate minors _____
                     39-41   45-7

Graduate majors _____   Graduate minors _____
                42-4   48-50

10. The Women's Studies Program has a Director or Coordinator. 1 ☐ Yes   2 ☐ No   51

11. Check all that apply to the Director of the Women's Studies Program.

1 ☐ Tenured   1 ☐ Full-time   1 ☐ Black, non-Hispanic   3 ☐ Hispanic   5 ☐ Native American
2 ☐ Not on tenure track 2 ☐ Part-time   2 ☐ White, non-Hispanic   4 ☐ Asian-American   6 ☐ Other   52,53,54

12. All undergraduate students, regardless of major field, are required to take at least one course which examines discrimination against 1 ☐ women and/or 2 ☐ minorities.   55

13. Check the faculty positions presently held by at least one faculty member on your campus.   56

   1 ☐ An historian specializing in the history of women in one specific period or country.
   2 ☐ A literary scholar specializing in women writers of a period or nation.
   3 ☐ A social scientist specializing in women or sex roles.

14. Check those responsibilities assigned to an official committee(s).   57

   1 ☐ Developing a Women's Studies Program
   2 ☐ Developing courses on women in traditional departments
   3 ☐ Monitoring the development of "transformed" courses
   4 ☐ Reporting on curricular development that includes women in the curriculum.
   5 ☐ Collecting/developing curricular materials on women
 6-9 ☐ Other (specify) _____

15. Check the topics for workshops or other educational programs provided through **faculty development.**   58

   1 ☐ Sexism and the curriculum
   2 ☐ Racism and the curriculum
   3 ☐ The relationship between sex, race, and selection of major field
   4 ☐ Nontraditional occupations for women and men
   5 ☐ The needs of reentry women
   6 ☐ Affirmative action and equal opportunity
 7-9 ☐ Other (specify) _____

IV. EXTRACURRICULAR ACTIVITIES

1. Please complete the table below on **sports programs for men and women in 1980.**

Programs	Not Applicable	Number of Athletes		Number of Coaches				Number of Coaches for Women's Sports Programs
		Total	Women	Paid		Volunteer		
				Total	Women	Total	Women	
Intercollegiate	☐	59-62	63-6	67-9	70-2	73-4	75-6	77-8[10]
Intramural	☐	7-11	12-6	17-20	21-4	25-8	29-32	33-6
Club	☐	37-40	41-4	45-6	47-8	49-50	51-2	53-4

2. Please complete the tables below on women's sports programs in 1980.

INTRAMURAL SPORTS			**INTERCOLLEGIATE SPORTS**		
List in any order the 10 Most Popular Women's Sports on Campus	Number of Women Participants		List all Intercollegiate Campus Sports (Attach additional sheet if necessary.)	Number of Women Participants	Check if Women's Team played in 1980 Spring or Fall Tournament Competition
					Spring / Fall
1. _____	55-6	57-61	_____	54-5 / 56-9	☐ ☐ 60
2. _____	62-3	64-8	_____	61-2 / 63-6	☐ ☐ 67
3. _____	69-70	71-5	_____	68-9 / 70-3	☐ ☐ 74
4. _____	76-7[11]	7-11	_____	75-6[12] / 7-10	☐ ☐ 11
5. _____	12-3	14-8	_____	12-3 / 14-7	☐ ☐ 18
6. _____	19-20	21-5	_____	19-20 / 21-4	☐ ☐ 25
7. _____	26-7	28-32	_____	26-7 / 28-31	☐ ☐ 32
8. _____	33-4	35-9	_____	33-4 / 35-8	☐ ☐ 39
9. _____	40-1	42-6	_____	40-1 / 42-5	☐ ☐ 46
10. _____	47-8	49-53	_____	47-8 / 49-52	☐ ☐ 53

3. List intramural sports for which your campus has special or unique facilities. _____

                                                   54-55

4. This institution provides **athletic scholarships.** 1 ☐ Yes 2 ☐ No   56

5. Check the proportion of all athletic scholarship aid awarded to women in 1980.

   1 □ NA   2 □ 10 percent   3 □ 20 percent   4 □ 30 percent   5 □ 40 percent   6 □ 50 percent   7 □ over 50 percent   57

6. Check the types of **housing** available for undergraduate students on campus.

   □ Women's dormitories   □ Married students with and without children   58.59
   □ Men's dormitories   □ Single parents with children   60.61
   □ Coed dormitories   □ Other (specify) _____ 62.63

   If no campus housing is available, proceed to question 12.

7. Check all statements that apply to undergraduate residence halls on the campus.

   Men's Dormitories 64
   1 □ No female visitors
   2 □ Restrictive hours for female visitors
   3 □ No restrictive hours for female visitors

   Women's Dormitories 65
   1 □ No male visitors
   2 □ Restrictive hours for male visitors
   3 □ No restrictive hours for male visitors

   Coed Dormitories 66
   1 □ Restrictive hourse for visitors of the opposite sex
   2 □ No restrictive hours for visitors of the opposite sex

8. Give the percentage of all undergraduate women living in residence halls.

   Black, non-Hispanic _____ percent   Hispanic _____ percent   Native American _____ percent
                        67-8   69-70   71-2
   White, non-Hispanic _____ percent   Asian-American _____ percent   Other _____ percent   [13]
                        73-4   75-6   77-8

9. Give the number of residence hall directors.

   Total men and women _____   White women _____   Minority women _____
                        1-10   11-4   15-7

10. Check the issues on which awareness training is offered to residence hall staff.

    1 □ Sexism   2 □ Sex education   3 □ Racism   4 □ Birth control   □ Other (specify) _____   18.19

11. A married woman student whose husband is not enrolled is permitted to live in married students' housing. 1 □ Yes   2 □ No   20

12. This institution has **social fraternities and sororities.** 1 □ Yes   2 □ No   21
    If no fraternities and sororities, proceed to question 16.

13. Fraternities on this campus provide housing for members. 1 □ Yes   2 □ No   22

14. Sororities on this campus provide housing for members. 1 □ Yes   2 □ No   23

15. Please provide the information below.

    Number of undergraduate members of fraternities and sororities _____   24-28

    Number of undergraduate women who belong to sororities _____   29-33

    Number of minority women in racially-integrated sororities _____   34-37

    Number of minority women in all-minority sororities _____   38-4

16. Give the number of undergraduate **honorary societies.**   42-44

17. Give the number of women president of these honorary societies. _____   45-4

18. List the **student clubs/organizations** which serve as advocates for white women and minority women on campus. If they are advocacy groups, include task forces of state student associations, and campus chapters of such national organizations as the National Women Students Coalition and the National Third World Coalition.

Student Advocacy Groups for Women	Number of Active Participants		Percent of Active Minority Women Participants	Specify Minority Women's Group	Check if President is Female
	Total	Women			
Example: Associated Women Students	150	150	30 percent	Black	☑
_____ 48	49-53	54-8	59-60	61	□ 62
_____ 63	64-8	69-73	74-5	76	□ 77
_____ 78[14]	7-11	12-6	17-8	19	□ 20
_____ 21	22-6	27-31	32-3	34	□ 35
_____ 36	37-41	42-6	47-8	49	□ 50
(If additional space is needed, attach another page)					

V. SPECIAL PROGRAMS AND SERVICES

1. The institution has a student **health** service. 1 ☐ Yes   2 ☐ No.   51

2. Give the number of doctors. Women _____ Men _____   52-3   54-5

3. Give the number of other health care providers. Women _____ Men _____   56-8   59-61

4. The institution has a student counseling center. 1 ☐ Yes   2 ☐ No   62

5. Give the number of counselors/therapists.   Total men and women _____   63-64

   White women   _____   65-66

   Minority women   _____   67-68

6. Check below the type(s) of services available to students.

Service	Counseling	Medical Treatment	
Gynecological	☐	☐	69,70
Birth Control	☐	☐	71,72
Abortion	☐	☐	73,74
Rape and Assault	☐	☐	75,76
Other (specify) _____	☐	☐	77,78
			[15]

7. The regular student health insurance policy covers at no extra charge the following expenses.

   Abortion 1 ☐ Yes   2 ☐ No   Maternity 1 ☐ Yes   2 ☐ No   7,8

8. The institution provides in-service training for professional counselors/therapists in the following areas.

   1 ☐ Sex-role stereotyping   2 ☐ Racial bias   3-9 ☐ Other (specify) _____   9

9. Check below the types of **safety/security** facilities and services available on campus.

   Level of Security
   1 ☐ Campus police, with no authority to make arrests
   2 ☐ Campus police, with weapons training
   3 ☐ Campus police, with authority to make arrests
   4 ☐ Local town or city police, whose jurisdiction includes the campus   10

   Facilities/Services
   ☐ Night-time escort for women students
   1 ☐ Night-time, campus-wide, bus service to residence areas
   2 ☐ High-intensity lighting in all areas
   3 ☐ A highly conspicuous, campus-wide, emergency telephone system
   4 ☐ An emergency alarm system at isolated locations
   5 ☐ A ground maintenance system for reporting untrimmed shrubbery and burned-out lights
   6 ☐ Self-defense courses for women
   7 ☐ Information sessions or short courses on campus safety and rape/assault prevention for women   11
   8 ☐ Campus or community-based rape crisis center
   9 ☐ Other (specify) _____   12

10. Give the number of offenses reported on your campus during 1980-81.

    Rapes _____ Total assaults _____ Assaults on women _____   13-4   15-7   18-20

11. Check those materials and activities available on your campus through a **career placement** office or through some other program.

    1 ☐ Career workshops focused on nontraditional occupations
    2 ☐ Lectures/panels for students by women employed in nontraditional occupations
    3 ☐ Nonsexist/nonracist printed information on nontraditional fields of study for women (industrial trades, engineering programs, etc.)
    4 ☐ Job discrimination information (salaries, work environment, upward mobility, etc.) on nontraditional occupations for women
    5 ☐ Updated files of female alumni by specific careers
    6 ☐ Programs to establish contacts and networks between female alumni and female students
    7-9 ☐ Other (specify) _____   21

12. This campus has a **Women's Center**—a special place designated for women's services. 1 ☐ Yes   2 ☐ No   22

    If no center exists, proceed to question 20.

13. Approximate the square feet of space occupied by the Women's Center. _____   23-27

14. Name the institutional division responsible for the Women's Center _____   28-29

15. Specify the total 1980-81 budget for the Women's Center. $ _____   30-36

16. Estimate the total number of women served during 1980-81, including the program participants and visitors to the Women's Center. _____ 37-41

17. Of the total number in the previous queston, estimate the percentage who are minority women. _____ percent   42-43

    Specify the predominant minority group. _____ 44

18. Please rank from 1 to 7 (one is highest frequency) the groups below according to the frequency of their participation in Women's Center activities. Write in NA if group does not participate.

    Undergraduate students (18-25 years old)   _____   45

    Undergraduate students (over 25)   _____   46

    Graduate students   _____   47

    Faculty   _____   48

    Faculty wives   _____   49

    Staff   _____   50

    Community women   _____   51

19. Check below all items that describe the Director/Coordinator of the Women's Center.

    52   53   54   55
    1 ☐ Administrator   1 ☐ Salaried   1 ☐ Full-time   1 ☐ White, non-Hispanic
    2 ☐ Faculty member   2 ☐ Volunteer   2 ☐ Part-time   2 ☐ Minority (specify) _____
    3 ☐ Student

20. A centralized administrative unit is responsible for operating an **adult continuing education** program.

    1 ☐ Yes 2 ☐ No   This unit is called _____ 56.57

21. This institution has a **Continuing Education for Women Program (CEW).** 1 ☐ Yes 2 ☐ No   58

    If campus has no CEW Program, proceed to question 27.

22. Name the institutional division responsible for Continuing Education for Women (CEW). _____ 59

23. The CEW Program operates a Center, a designated space comparable to a Women's Center. 1 ☐ Yes 2 ☐ No   60

24. Specify the total 1980-81 budget for CEW. $ _____ 61-7

25. Give the number of **reentry or returning women** students in CEW courses in 1980-81. _____ 68-72

26. Give the percentage of minority, reentry women students in CEW courses. _____ percent   73-74

    Specify the predominant minority group. _____ 75[16]

27. Give the number of reentry women students in courses offered by other adult and continuing education program(s). _____ 7-11

28. Give the percentage of minority, reentry women students in courses offered by the program(s) in question 27. _____ percent   12-13

    Specify the predominant minority group _____ 14

29. Check all that apply for the Director/Coordinator of the Continuing Education for Women's Program.

    15   16   17   18   19
    1 ☐ Administrator   1 ☐ Female   1 ☐ Full-time   1 ☐ Nontenured   1 ☐ White, non-Hispanic
    2 ☐ Faculty   2 ☐ Male   2 ☐ Part-time   2 ☐ Tenured   2-6 ☐ Minority (specify) _____

30. Check or name the sponsoring groups for each of those **additional programs and services for women** offered in 1980-81. Check box in appropriate column for each program/service especially geared to minority women's needs.

PROGRAMS/SERVICES	Check if Especially Geared to Minority Women	SPONSORING GROUP					
		(1) Campus Institutional Unit (Give full title)	(2) CEW	(3) Women's Center	(4) Women's Studies	(5) Other, including community (Specify)	
Example: Battered women's program	☑	Office of Dean of Students	☐	☐	☐	☑ Tucson Commission on Women	
Battered women's program	☐ 20	1 ☐ _____	2 ☐	3 ☐	4 ☐	5 ☐ _____	21
Displaced homemaker program	☐ 22	☐ _____	☐	☐	☐	☐ _____	23
Annual Women's Week	☐ 24	☐ _____	☐	☐	☐	☐ _____	25
Women's lecture series	☐ 26	☐ _____	☐	☐	☐	☐ _____	27
Theater and other women's arts programs	☐ 28	☐ _____	☐	☐	☐	☐ _____	29
Assertiveness/leadership training	☐ 30	☐ _____	☐	☐	☐	☐ _____	31
Program to build confidence in mathematics	☐ 32	☐ _____	☐	☐	☐	☐ _____	33
Warmline (a telephone service for information, referrals and support)	☐ 34	☐ _____	☐	☐	☐	☐ _____	35
Other (specify) _____	☐ 36	☐ _____	☐	☐	☐	☐ _____	37
_____	☐ 38	☐ _____	☐	☐	☐	☐ _____	39
_____	☐ 40	☐ _____	☐	☐	☐	☐ _____	41

31. Specify the student organization and/or campus offices where the groups listed below would be most likely to find support from other women on your campus.

Displaced homemakers _____   Older women _____   42,43

Handicapped women _____   Rape/assault victims _____   44,45

Lesbians _____   Welfare women _____   46,47

Minority women _____   Other (specify) _____   48,49

32. Brag briefly about other campus-based facilities, special programs, projects, and resources (e.g., Schlesinger Library, Center for Research on Women, SIGNS, etc.) whose focus is primarily women. _____

_____

_____

_____

_____

_____   50-52

33. In **no more than 50 words,** describe those aspects of the institutional mission and environment which might make a woman choose to study on your campus. [Within the limits of space, and with a minimum of editing, this statement will appear in **Everywoman's Guide.**]

_____

_____

_____

_____

_____

_____

_____

_____   53-55

[17]

INDEX

About the Principal Editors and Writers

SUZANNE HOWARD is a freelance educational consultant in the areas of research, leadership training, and program and materials development. She received her Ph.D. in Comparative Education from the University of Michigan. Formerly Assistant Director of the Program for Education at the American Association of University Women, Howard has numerous publications to her credit, among them *But We Will Persist,* a research report on the status of women in higher education, sponsored by the American Association of University Women.

FLORENCE HOWE is Professor of Humanities at the State University of New York, College at Old Westbury, and director of research and publishing at The Feminist Press. She has published many books and articles on literature, educational history, and women's studies, including *No More Masks!, Women and the Power to Change, Women Working: An Anthology of Stories and Poems,* and *Seven Years Later: Women's Studies Programs in 1976*—a monograph commissioned by the National Advisory Council on Women's Educational Programs, a federal agency.

NANCY PORTER is Associate Professor of English at Portland State University, and the author of various articles and monographs on women's studies. She is co-author of *The Effectiveness of Women's Studies Teaching,* a monograph commissioned by the National Institute of Education.

MARY JO BOEHM STRAUSS is a freelance research consultant in the Washington, D.C., area. Recipient of a Ph.D. in Chemistry and Mathematics from Michigan State University, she has taught courses and developed curricular materials on women in science and mathematics, and participated in numerous studies of women's and girls' education. Strauss is co-author of the monograph, *Women's Studies Graduates* commissioned by the National Institute of Education.

WILLIAM ZEISEL is Co-Director of Editors & Scholars, a non-profit service of The Institute for Research in History. He received his Ph.D. in History from Rutgers, the State University of New Jersey. Zeisel has published scholarly articles, and has edited numerous books and essays. He is currently co-editor of the journal *Trends in History.*

A Note on Language and Race

Half of all members of minority groups are women. When we talk about "women" in this book, we attempt wherever possible to be specific about race. We do so out of respect to the interests of minorities in the United States for their own racial identities. The melting pot is not an appropriate image for a society that still discriminates against people of color; the melting pot may, in fact, be a useless image, if one understands and values specific cultural identities, and if one is not afraid of differences. Thus, we have not used the phrase "women and minorities," for all too often that language means white women and male members of minority groups. Rather, we have said "white women" and "women of color" or "minority women," and, wherever possible, we have named the specific minority group.

About The Feminist Press

THE FEMINIST PRESS offers alternatives in education and in literature. Founded in 1970, this nonprofit, tax-exempt educational and publishing organization works to eliminate sexual stereotypes in books and schools and to provide literature with a broad vision of human potential. The publishing program includes reprints of important works by women, feminist biographies of women, and nonsexist children's books. Curricular materials, bibliographies, directories, and a quarterly journal provide information and support for students and teachers of women's studies. In-service projects help to transform teaching methods and curricula. Through publications and projects, The Feminist Press contributes to the rediscovery of the history of women and the emergence of a more humane society.

Feminist Classics from The Feminist Press

Brown Girl, Brownstones, a novel by Paule Marshall. Afterword by Mary Helen Washington. $6.95 paper.

Call Home the Heart, a novel of the thirties by Fielding Burke. Introduction by Alice Kessler-Harris and Paul Lauter and afterwords by Sylvia Cook and Anna W. Shannon. $8.95 paper.

Cassandra by Florence Nightingale. Introduction by Myra Stark. Epilogue by Cynthia Macdonald. $2.50 paper.

The Convert, a novel by Elizabeth Robins. Introduction by Jane Marcus. $5.95 paper.

Daughter of Earth, a novel by Agnes Smedley. Afterword by Paul Lauter. $10.00 cloth, $5.50 paper.

Guardian Angel and Other Stories by Margery Latimer. Afterwords by Louis Kampf, Meridel Le Sueur, and Nancy Loughridge. $16.95 cloth, $7.95 paper.

I Love Myself When I Am Laughing . . . And Then Again When I Am Looking Mean and Impressive by Zora Neale Hurston. Edited by Alice Walker. Introduction by Mary Helen Washington. $16.95 cloth, $7.95 paper.

Life in the Iron Mills by Rebecca Harding Davis. Biographical interpretation by Tillie Olsen. $4.50 paper.

The Living Is Easy, a novel by Dorothy West. Afterword by Adelaide M. Cromwell. $6.95 paper.

The Maimie Papers. Edited by Ruth Rosen and Sue Davidson. Introduction by Ruth Rosen. $15.95 cloth, $6.95 paper.

Portraits of Chinese Women in Revolution by Agnes Smedley. Edited with an introduction by Jan MacKinnon and Steve MacKinnon. $4.50 paper.

Ripening: Selected Work, 1927–1980 by Meridel LeSueur. Edited with an introduction by Elaine Hedges. $14.95 cloth, $7.95 paper.

The Silent Partner, a novel by Elizabeth Stuart Phelps. Afterword by Mari Jo Buhle and Florence Howe. $6.95 paper.

These Modern Women. Edited with an introduction by Elaine Showalter. $4.95 paper.

Weeds, a novel by Edith Summers Kelley. Afterword by Charlotte Goodman. $6.95 paper.

The Woman and the Myth: Margaret Fuller's Life and Writings by Bell Gale Chevigny. $8.95 paper.

Women Working: An Anthology of Stories and Poems. Edited and with an introduction by Nancy Hoffman and Florence Howe. $6.95 paper.

The Yellow Wallpaper by Charlotte Perkins Gilman. Afterword by Elaine Hedges. $2.25 paper.

Other Titles from The Feminist Press

Antoinette Brown Blackwell. A Biography. Elizabeth Cazden. $7.95 paper.

But Some of Us Are Brave: Black Women's Studies. Edited by Gloria T. Hull, Patricia Bell Scott, and Barbara Smith. $14.95 cloth, $8.95 paper.

Complaints and Disorders: The Sexual Politics of Sickness. Barbara Ehrenreich and Deirdre English. $2.95 paper.

Lesbian Studies: Past and Present. Edited by Margaret Cruikshank. $14.95 cloth, $7.95 paper.

Moving the Mountain: Women Working for Social Change. Ellen Cantarow with Susan Gushee O'Malley and Sharon Hartman Strom. $5.95 paper.

Reconstructing American Literature: Courses, Syllabi, Issues. Edited by Paul Lauter. $8.95 paper.

Witches, Midwives, and Nurses: A History of Women Healers. Barbara Ehrenreich and Deirdre English. $2.95 paper.

Women Have Always Worked: A Historical Overview. Alice Kessler-Harris. $14.95 cloth, $5.95 paper.

Women's Studies in Italy by Laura Balbo and Yasmine Ergas. A Women's Studies International Monograph. $5.95 paper.

When ordering, please include $1.00 for postage and handling for one hardcover or one or two paperback books and 35¢ for each additional book. Order from: The Feminist Press, Box 334, Old Westbury, N.Y. 11568. Telephone (516) 997-7660.